Public Records Online

The National Guide to Private & Government Online Sources of Public Records

©2006 By Facts on Demand Press
PO Box 27869, Tempe, AZ 85285
206 W Julie Dr #2, Tempe, AZ 85283
800.929.3811

www.brbpub.com

Public Records Online

The National Guide to Private & Government Online Sources of Public Records
Sixth Edition

©2006 By Facts on Demand Press
PO Box 27869, Tempe, AZ 85285
206 W Julie Dr #2, Tempe, AZ 85283
800.929.3811

ISBN: 1-889150-48-7
Edited by Michael L. Sankey and Peter J. Weber.
Cover Design by Robin Fox & Associates

Cataloging-in-Publication Data

Public records online : the national guide to private &
   government online sources of public records / [edited by
   Michael L. Sankey and Peter J. Weber].- - 6th ed.
     p. cm.
     ISBN: 1-889150-48-7

     1. Electronic public records–United States--
   Directories. 2. Information services industries--United
   States--Directories.   I. Sankey, Michael L., 1949-
   II. Weber, Peter J. (Peter Julius), 1952-

    JK468.P76P83 2004   352.3'87'0973

Contents

51 STATE CHAPTERS ....

Section III – Vendor Information Index 593

Appendix 609

A SPECIAL THANK YOU!

The goal of *Public Records Online*, now in its sixth edition, is to present a current and comprehensive picture of the regulations and procedures for online access to public records. This cannot be done without the help of certain people.

Therefore, we wish to acknowledge and extend a special thank you to—

- All the government administrators and information systems personnel at the 7,000+ government agencies profiled in the book; and

- The database vendors working in the private sector who compile the extensive databases and gateways listed herein.

Our sincere thanks, from Fact on Demand Press, to all of you for taking the time and having the interest to help us assemble this collection of facts. Your valuable assistance is a direct reflection of the accuracy of this publication.

Thank you!

The Research Staff at Facts on Demand Press

Annette Talley
Peter J. Weber
Mark Sankey
Michael Sankey

Introduction

The Doorway to Online Public Records

Today there are literally thousands of public record and public information sources accessible by anyone with a computer and a modem. However, which sites are useful? For the online researcher, recognizing the advantages of these sources can be challenging. All U.S. public record information is not available online—in fact the majority of records are not! The savvy researcher must strive to ascertain where to access the information and then to determine what information is available online and what information is not.

Public Records Online is your key to opening the door to online public records information. Whether you surf the World Wide Web, connect via modem to a court's computer system or utilize a public record vendor's system, this book will serve as your gateway to the world of online public records research.

If the information you desire out there, you need only find its particular "trail." To that end, this book has been designed to be your tour guide and take you precisely to the location you need. With this book in hand you have made the first step on your trip.

We suggest that you read the **Public Record Primer** to fully prepare you for your journey. Once you are familiar with the cyber scenery, you will need only to scan the chapters and sources to find the right trail to take.

Your Access to Over 11,000 Government Agencies and Private Vendor Sources

Public Records Online is especially useful when federal, state, county, and in certain instances, the city and town records are needed for these applications—

> Background Investigation
>
> Competitive Intelligence
>
> Legal Research
>
> Locating People
>
> Locating Assets
>
> Pre-Employment and Tenant Screening
>
> Process Serving
>
> Skiptracing
>
> Genealogy

How This Book Is Organized

Public Records Online is organized into three Sections plus an Appendix—

> 1. Public Record Primer
> 2. Government Online Sources
> 3. Vendor Information Index

The Public Record Primer

The purpose of the Public Record Primer section is to assist the reader in knowing *where to search for specific categories of records*. The Primer gives useful tips on *how to search*. The Primer is an excellent overall source of information that is especially helpful to those new to searching government records, whether online or not. The Primer is not limited to a discussion of only online records, but to all public records and public information.

An important segment of this section is the discussion of privacy issues including public information vs. personal information and how records enter the public domain.

The **Searching Other Federal Records Online** chapter contains an excellent article contributed by Alan Schlein, author of *Find it Online!* published by Facts on Demand Press. Mr. Schlein presents a unique dissertation about the best federal government Internet sites for finding usual information quickly and efficiently.

Another important chapter is **Tips on Using Public Record Vendors.** This chapter contains a wealth of information about commercial public record vendors, especially those who offer online access to their proprietary database of records.

Government Online Sources

Individual state chapters have been compiled into an easy to use format that details what is available online. Free online access and fee-based systems are denoted, with the type or category of records available. Each state chapter is presented in this order—

> State Public Record Agencies
>
> State Licensing and Regulatory Boards
>
> County Courts
>
> County Recorder Offices
>
> Federal Courts

Be sure to review the Online Access notes found at the beginning of each state's County Courts and County Recorder's Office section. This is a good place to find out about statewide online systems.

Vendor Information Index

This index presents 24 Public Record Information Categories. Vendors who offer online access to their proprietary database or offer a sophisticated gateway are listed alphabetically within each category. Each listing includes the vendor's web page and the geographic coverage area. Please note that usually these vendors offer other services beyond the categories mentioned.

The Appendix

The Appendix consists of these items—

Editors' Choices -- 15 Great Websites – A short list of websites to visit and use.

Trade Associations – A list of trade associations connected to the public information industry and their websites.

Our Goal

Our goal is to provide you with a valuable resource — so you can understand what you need, where it might be, and how to access that information like a pro.

Section I

Public Record Primer

Editor's Note—

The *Public Record Primer* is a valuable and educational chapter concerning public records—online or not. The *Primer* is filled with many useful tips and guidelines associated with practices and procedures regarding the access of specific types and categories of public records and government information

We urge all readers, including those unfamiliar or new to public record access as well as the experienced record searchers, to use the *Primer* as a comprehensive and definitive reference tool.

Guidelines for Searching
Public Records

The strict **definition** of **public records** is—

> *"Those records maintained by government*
> *agencies that are open without restriction to public*
> *inspection, either by statute or by tradition."*

If access to a record held by a government agency is restricted in some way, then it is not a public record.

Accessibility Paradox

Adding to the mystique of government records is the accessibility paradox. For example, in some states a specific category of records is severely restricted, and therefore those records are not "public," while the very same category of records may be 100% open in other states. Among these categories are criminal histories, vital records, and workers' compensation records.

Therefore, some of the records examined in this book have restrictions regarding access.

The text in the box printed below is significant. We are not trying to fill up space. As your public record searching takes you from state-to-state, this is the one important adage to keep in mind.

> "Just because records are maintained in a certain way in
> your state or county, do not assume that any other county or
> state does things the same way."

Public vs. Private vs. Personal

Before reading further, let us define types of records held by government or by private industry. Of course, not all information about a company or individual is public. The boundaries between public and private information are not well understood, and continually undergo intense scrutiny.

The following is an introduction to the subject from a viewpoint of a professional record searcher.

Public Record

Public records are records of **incidents** or **actions** filed or recorded with a government agency for the purpose of notifying others — the "public" — about the matter. The **deed** to your house recorded at the county recorder's office is a public record — it is a legal requirement that you record with the county recorder. Anyone requiring details about your property may review or copy the documents.

Public Information

Your **telephone listing** in the phone book is an example of public information; that is, you freely furnished the information to ease the flow of commercial and private communications.

Personal Information

Any information about a person or business that the person or business might consider private and confidential in nature such as your **Social Security Number, DOB or address**, is personal information. Such information will remain private to a limited extent unless it is disclosed to some outside entity that could make it public. **Personal information may be found in either public records or in public information.**

How Personal Information Enters the Public Domain

Many people confuse the three categories above, lump them into one and wonder how "big brother" accumulated so much information. The reality is that **much of this information is given willingly**.

Actually, there are two ways that personal information can enter the public domain — statutory and voluntary. In a **voluntary** transaction, you **share** personal information of your own free will. In a **statutory** transaction, you **disclose** personal information because the law requires you to.

The confusion of terms used today feeds the increasing conflict between privacy advocates and commercial interests. This, in turn, is driving legislation towards more and more **restrictions** on the **dissemination of personal information** — the same personal information that, in fact, is willingly shared by most people and companies in order to participate in our market economy.

Of course, the increased number of identity theft incidents has precipitated well-deserved scrutiny on the manner in which personal information is maintained by and is accessible from government agencies and information providers in the private sector.

Where Public Records Are Held

There are two places you can find public records—

    1. at a government agency

    2. within the database of a private enterprise

Government agencies maintain records in a variety of ways. While many state agencies and highly populated county agencies are computerized, many others use microfiche, microfilm, and paper to store files and indexes. Agencies that have converted to computer will not necessarily place complete file records on their system; they are more apt to include only an index, pointer or summary data from the files.

Private enterprises develop their databases in one of two ways: they buy the records in bulk from government agencies; or they send personnel to the agencies and compile this information by using a copy machine or keying information into a laptop computer. The database is then available for internal use or for resale purposes. An example of a vendor collecting the data for resale is *Superior Information* (800 848-0489). Superior maintains a very comprehensive database of civil judgments, tax liens, Uniform Commercial Code filings and bankruptcy data gathered from the Mid-Atlantic States.

Detailed information about how public record vendors operate is found later in this *Primer.*

> **Editor's Tip:** Public records purchased and/or compiled by private companies for resale purposes must follow the same access and restriction regulations as the related government jurisdiction.

The Common Methods Used to Access Public Records

The following is a look at the various methods available to access public records.

Visit in Person

This is easy if you live close by. Many courthouses and recorders offices have free access terminals open to the public. Certain records, such as corporate or UCC records generally found at the Secretary of State, can be viewed or pulled for free, but will incur a fee for copies. However, a signed release is a common requirement for accessing other records such as motor vehicle and criminal records at the state level.

Mail, Fax, or Telephone

Although some agencies permit phone or fax requests, the majority of agencies prefer mail requests. Some agencies consider fax requesting to be an expedited service that incurs higher fees. Agencies that permit telephone requests may merely answer "Yes" or "No" to questions such as "Does John Doe have a civil court case in his name?" Most courts will not fax results of search requests, but many will fax specific documents if the case file or docket number is given.

Online

The Internet serves as a free means to access certain agency records, or the Internet may serve as the conduit to a fee-based lookup or subscription service. Also, non-Internet private dial systems still exist for some subscription services. When searching online, there is a significant difference between viewing an image of a record versus looking at an index of available records. Keep in mind that most Internet access sites permit the latter, not the former. Usually the searchable and viewable information is limited to name indexes and summary data rather than document images.

Also, many agencies, such as state motor vehicle agencies (DMVs), only provide access to pre-approved, high-volume, ongoing accounts. Typically, this access involves fees and a specified, minimum amount of usage.

The Internet is a good place to find *general* information about a government agency. Many websites contain detailed descriptions of policies and regulations. If records or indices are not searchable on the web, many sites enable one to download or print record request forms,

Hire Someone Else

As mentioned previously, one method to access public records is through a vendor. These vendors must comply with state and federal laws. Thus, if a government agency will not release a record, chances are a vendor will not either. There are a variety of companies that can be hired to perform record searches. An excellent, quick source to find the right vendor for a particular need (beyond those listed at the back of this book) is the Resource Center at www.brbpub.com.

Bulk or Database Purchases

Many agencies offer programs that permit you to purchase all or parts of their database for statistical or commercial purposes. The amount of restrictions varies widely from state-to-state or county-to-county, even within the same record type or category.

Typically, records are available (to those who qualify) in the following media types; FTP, cartridges, paper printouts, labels, disks, CDs, microfiche and/or microfilm.

The Difference Between a Record Search and a Document Request

There is a significant difference between the acts of a searching to see if a public record exists versus obtaining or viewing documents. Many times the latter cannot be accomplished without first doing the former.

Name Searching

Let's say you wish to find out if an individual has a criminal record or if an individual has collateralized certain assets, such as a real estate holding or equipment used in a business. The best way to perform this research is to do a "name search" of an index at the government agency that holds the records. Some government agencies allow a researcher to view the index, others do not permit the public to research and therefore impose a fee for the government employer to do the name search. Other agencies, such as the county Superior Courts in New York, refuse to allow the public to view an index AND refuse to do a name search.

An index may or may not contain dates, the date of birth, or even a partial Social Security Number. Obviously, having this additional information — often referred to as called "personal identifiers"— can be quite helpful (see below).

Using an Internet site to perform a name search often is merely a supplemental search since many agencies withhold personal identifiers on the web.

Requesting a Specific Document

When you know the "document number" or exact location of a record, it becomes much easier to view or obtain a copy. If you are requesting a specific document in person, by mail, phone or fax, the government personnel are much more apt to help you compared to asking them to do a name search.

Using a government web page to search for a specific document is often easier when you have the document number or an identifier like a "docket number." However, images of all the pages in the file may not be available online. This is especially true when searching court records or real estate recordings.

Using Identifiers

As mentioned, every record source will require certain identifiers to process a search request. For example, an agency may ask for the full name, Social Security Number (SSN), date of birth (DOB) and even the last known address of the person to be checked. These identifiers serve two different, though related purposes. First, these identifiers ensure that the repository will be able to properly conduct a search of their existing records.

Perhaps the records are indexed by the last name and also by either the DOB or part of a SSN. Thus, the office simply may not be able to process a record request if it is not provided with a DOB or SSN.

Second, the identifiers act as an important safeguard for both the requesting party and the subject of the search. There is always the chance that the "Harold Johnson" on whom a given repository has a record is not the same "Harold Johnson" on whom a check has been requested. However, the possibility of a misidentification can be decreased substantially if other identifiers can match the individual to the record.

As a general rule when search records at a government agency, information beyond the minimum should be provided whenever possible. Every available piece of information can aid their search. For example, maiden name, alias or other previous names should be included when possible. Although no repository can be expected to give a 100% positive identification (unless it is a match of fingerprints), the more pointers matched, the smaller the chance of a mistake.

Fees, Charges, and Usage

Public records are not necessarily free of charge, certainly not if they are maintained by a private company. Remember that **public records are records of incidents or transactions**. These incidents can be civil or criminal court actions, recordings, filings or occurrences such as speeding tickets or accidents. **It costs money** (time, salaries, supplies, etc.) **to record and track these events**. Common charges found at the government level include copy fees (to make copies of documents), search fees (for clerical personnel to search for records), and certification fees (to certify documents as being accurate and coming from the particular agency). Fees can vary from $.10 per page for copies to a $52.00 search fee for government personnel to do a name search. Also, higher fees are usually involved if records must be pulled from an archive or off-site storage. Some government agencies, usually county level, will allow you to walk in and view records or a record index at no charge. Fewer will release information over the phone.

If a private enterprise is in the business of maintaining a public records database, it generally does so to offer these records for resale. Typical clients include financial institutions, the legal industry, the insurance industry, and private investigation firms, among others. Usually, records are sold via online access or on CD-ROM.

Also, there are a number of public record vendors (we call them search firms) who will do a name search — for a fee. These companies do not warehouse the records, but know where to search and will search on demand for a specific name.

Private companies usually offer different price levels based on volume of usage, while government agencies have one price per category, regardless of the amount of requests. For more information, see the chapter *Tips on Using Public Record Vendors*.

A Few Myths About Searching Public Records Online

The availability of online public records is not as widespread as one might think. According to our research—

- only 35% of public records can be found online;
- nearly every free government public record website contains no personal identifiers.

The federal, state, and local agencies that maintain public record systems make substantial efforts to limit the disclosure of Social Security Numbers, phone numbers, and addresses. Some even try to limit the use of the dates of birth. The Social Security Number is no longer the key search tool identifier it was in the 1980's and early 1990's. The websites with open record searching available to the public generally require only a name, unless a specific case file or docket number or registration number, etc. can be substituted.

The government agencies that offer online access on a fee or subscription basis generally disclose at least partial personal identifiers. Nowadays very few give Social Security Numbers, and those that do may cloak or mask the first 5 digits. Some cloak the month and day of the birth and only release the year of birth. For example, most U.S. District Court and Bankruptcy Court online systems give no personal identifiers on search results, thus making a reliable "name search" nearly impossible.

The lack of identifiers is a real problem for employers or financial institutions who require a certain amount of due diligence. The existence of any possible adverse information may have to be checked by a hands-on search to insure the proper match of the subject to the adverse record.

Also, many government websites offering online record access include a warning or disclosure stating that the data can have errors and/or should be used for informational purposes only. Such sites should be considered as supplemental or secondary sources only. A criminal record search from such as source usually does not in and by itself comply with Fair Credit Reporting Act regulations involving pre-employment screening.

Sometimes the only way to obtain certain records online is from a vendor. The last section of this book lists over 160 private companies that offer online access to their proprietary databases (or gateways) of public record information. A vendor may provide access to many records that may not be otherwise found online via the government online sources.

Using the Freedom of Information Act

The Federal Freedom of Information Act (FOIA) has no bearing on state, county or local government agencies because these agencies are subject to only that state's individual act. Further, the government agencies profiled in this book generally already have systems in place to release information and the FIOA is not needed. However, if you are trying to obtain records from agencies beyond the scope of this book, there are many useful Internet sites that will give you the information you need to complete such a request. We can recommend these sites—

www.usdoj.gov/04foia/

www.spj.org/foia.asp

Public Record & Public Information Categories

The following descriptions of the record categories fall into our definitions of either "public records" or "public information."

In considering the descriptions and definitions to follow, again, keep in mind:

- Just because your state or county has certain rules, regulations and practices regarding the accessibility and content of public records does not mean that any other state or county follows the same rules.

Business Records

Finding information about a privately held entity not listed with the Federal Securities Exchange Commission (SEC) can be difficult. Fortunately, states maintain basic information about businesses that register with them for the purpose of making their business names public and protecting the uniqueness. Much, but not all, of the information collected by government agencies is open to public inspection. For example, annual reports are not available in some states, yet may be available for a fee in others. Most states offer access to some business records online via the Internet. As in many other categories of public records, private companies purchase and/or compile a database for resale.

Below are summaries of the main types of business records.

Corporation Records (found at the state level)

Many state agencies provide a business name check so that a new entity can make sure the name is not already used by an existing business entity.

Checking to see if a company is incorporated is considered a "**status check**." The information that results from a status check typically includes the date of incorporation, status, type, registered agent and, sometimes, officers or directors. This is a good way to find the start of a paper trail and/or to find affiliates of the subject of your search. Some states permit status checks over the telephone.

If available, articles of incorporation (or amendments to them) as well as copies of annual reports may also provide useful information about a business or business owner. However, corporate records may *not* be a good source for a business address because most states allow corporations to use a registered agent as their address for service of process.

Partnership Records (found at the state level)

Some state statutes require registration of certain kinds of partnerships at the state level. Sometimes, these partner names and addresses may be available from the same office that handles corporation records. Some states have a department created specifically to administer limited partnerships and the records associated with them. These filings provide a wealth of information about other partners. Such information can be used to uncover other businesses that may be registered as well.

Limited Liability Companies (found at state level)

A newer form of business entity, similar to a corporation but with the favorable tax characteristics of a partnership, is known as the Limited Liability Company (LLC). An LLC is legal in most every state. An offspring of this, which many states now permit, is the Limited Liability Partnership (LLP).

In most states searchers will find partnership, LLC and LLP records in the same database source as corporations, but savvy searchers know that some states do segregate these searches.

Trademark, Trade Name, Fictitious Name
(found at federal, state or county levels)

"Trade names" and "trademarks" are relative terms. A trademark may be known as a "service mark." Trade names may be referred to as "fictitious names," "assumed names," or "DBAs." States (or counties) will not let two entities register and use the same or close to the same name or trademark

Typically, the state agency that oversees corporation records usually maintains the files for trademarks and/or trade names. Most states will allow verbal status checks of names or worded marks. Some states will administer "fictitious names" at the state level while county agencies administer "trade names," or vice versa.

Patents & Copyrights (found at federal level)

The federal government controls copyrights and patents. The act of filing for public review of trademarks, patents and proprietary materials is designed to protect these assets from being copied.

While one may search for patents and copyrights at the federal level, it is important to note there are several private companies that maintain online searchable databases of trademarks, service marks, and patents.

Sales Tax Registrations (found at state level)

Any individual or firm that sells applicable goods or services to an end-user, is required to register with the appropriate state agency. Such registration is necessary to collect applicable sales tax on the goods and services, and to ensure remittance of those taxes to the state.

45 states collect some sort of sales tax on a variety of goods and services. Of these, 38 will at the very least confirm that a tax permit exists. Each sales tax registrant is given a special state tax permit number, which may be called by various names, including tax ID number or seller's permit number. These numbers are not to be confused with the federal employer identification number.

SEC and Other Financial Data (found at federal level)

The Federal Securities and Exchange Commission (SEC) is the public repository for information about publicly held companies. These companies are required to share their material facts with existing and prospective stockholders. See page 58 for information about the SEC database EDGAR.

Private companies, on the other hand, are not subject to the same public scrutiny. Their financial information is public information only to the extent that the company itself decides to disclose information.

Lien and Security Interest Records

Liens filed by the government and others against individuals and businesses without their consent. Liens are filed, according to a state's law, either at a state agency or county recorder's office. Some states require filing at both locations.

Mortgages and Uniform Commercial Code (UCC) liens are voluntary liens accepted by a borrower in order to obtain financing. Involuntary liens, on the other hand, arise by action of law against a person or business owing a debt that would otherwise be unsecured. The federal and state governments file tax liens when there is a failure to pay income or withholding taxes. Another example: a contractor can file a mechanic's lien to be first in line to receive payment for materials used on a job.

States that offer online access to corporate records generally make their lien records available online also. While there is less likelihood of finding this information online at the local government level, a limited number of local recorder offices make the information available online.

Editor's Tip: Online access of compiled lien information is a very competitive arena for private companies. There are several nationwide database vendors as well as a number of strong regional companies who offer this information online to their clientele.

Uniform Commercial Code
(found at state and sometimes at county or city levels)

All 50 states and the District of Columbia have passed a version of the model Uniform Commercial Code (UCC). UCC filings are used to record liens in financing transactions such as equipment loans, leases, inventory loans, and accounts receivable financing. The Code allows potential lenders to be notified that certain assets of a debtor are already used to secure a loan or lease. *Therefore, examining UCC filings is an excellent way to find bank accounts, security interests, financiers, and assets.*

Revised Article 9 (see page 50) of the Code made significant changes to the location of filings and records. Prior to July 2001, of the 7.5 million new UCC financing statements filed annually, 2.5 million were filed at the state level; 5 million were filed at the local level. Now, less than 3% of filings are done so at the local level. Although there are significant variations among state statutes, the state level is now the best starting place to uncover liens filed against an individual or business.

Detailed information about searching UCC records and recorded documents is found in the *Searching Recording Office Records* chapter.

Tax Liens (found at state and sometimes at county or city levels)

The federal government and every state have some sort of taxes, such as those associated with sales, income, withholding, unemployment, and/or personal property. When these taxes go unpaid, the appropriate state agency can file a lien on the real or personal property of the subject. *Normally, the state agency that maintains UCC records also maintains tax liens.*

Individuals vs. Businesses

Tax liens filed against individuals are frequently maintained at separate locations from those liens filed against businesses. For example, a large number of states require liens filed against businesses to be filed at a central state location (i.e., Secretary of State's office) and liens against individuals to be filed at the county level (i.e., Recorder, Register of Deeds, Clerk of Court, etc.).

State vs. Federal Liens

Liens on a company may not all be filed in the same location. A federal tax lien will not necessarily be filed (recorded) at the same location/jurisdiction as a lien filed by the state. This holds true for both individual liens and as well as business liens filed against personal property. Typically, state tax liens on personal property will be found where UCCs are filed. *Tax liens on real property will be found where real property deeds are recorded*, with few exceptions. Unsatisfied state and federal tax liens may be renewed if prescribed by individual state statutes. However, once satisfied, the time the record will remain in the repository before removal varies by jurisdiction.

Real Estate and Tax Assessor (found at county and local levels)

Traditionally, real estate records are public so that everyone can know who owns what property. Liens on real estate must be public so a buyer or lender knows all the facts. The county (or parish) recorder's office is the record source. However, many private companies purchase entire county record databases and create their own database for commercial purposes.

This category of public record is perhaps the fastest growing in regards to being freely accessible over the Internet. We have indicated all the recorder offices that offer web **name queries;** many more offer location searches (using maps and parcel numbers to locate an address).

Bankruptcies (found at federal court level)

This entails case information about people and businesses that have filed for protection under the bankruptcy laws of the United States. Only federal courts handle bankruptcy cases. Many types of financial records maintained by government agencies are considered public records; bankruptcy records, unlike some other court records, are in this class of fully open court records. There are several private companies that compile databases with names and dates of these records.

Important Records on Individuals

Criminal Records (found at state level, county courts, and federal courts)

Unless a violation of federal law is involved, the information trail of a criminal records starts at the county, city or parish level courthouse. These records are generally submitted to a central state repository of major misdemeanor, felony arrest records and convictions. In turn, states submit criminal record activity to the FBI's National Crime Information Center (which is not open to the public). But there is a huge difference on the record access procedures between the state and the county levels. ***Not all state criminal record repositories open their criminal records to the public***. Of those states that *will* release records to the public, many require the submission of fingerprints or signed release forms. The information that *could be* disclosed on the report includes the arrest record, criminal charges, fines, sentencing and incarceration information. Adding to the confusion is the fact in many states there is a Court Administration Offices that maintains a centralized repository of records open to the public.

In states where records are not released on a statewide basis, the best places to search for criminal record activity is at the city or county level with the county or district court clerk. Many of these searches can be done with a phone call.

There are two other state resources of criminal records—the state prison system (incarceration records) and the agency that maintains the sexual offender records. Most of these agencies offer online access to portions of their records. The specific web pages are found in *Government Online Sources Section*. Further information regarding the access and use of criminal records is found in the *Searching State Agency Records* chapter.

Records of criminal acts that violate federal law are found at the 290 U.S. District Courts.

Litigation and Civil Judgments (found at county, local, and federal courts)

Actions governed by federal laws are found at U.S. District Courts. Actions governed by state laws are found within the state court system at the county level. Municipalities also have courts. Records of civil litigation case and records about judgments are often collected by commercial database vendors. For detailed information about searching civil actions and judgments, please refer to the *Searching County Court Records* chapter.

Motor Vehicle Records (found at state, county level)

Traffic-related violations are tried in local courts and records of convictions are forwarded to a central state repository. The record retrieval industry often refers to driving records as "MVRs." Typical information on an MVR, besides the traffic infractions, might include full name, address, physical description and date of birth. Also, the license type, restrictions and/or endorsements can provide background data on an individual.

The Federal Driver's Privacy Protection Act (DPPA) regulates the policy of which motor vehicle information is released to the public. States must differentiate between *permissible uses* (14 are designated in DPPA) and *casual requesters* to determine who may receive a record with personal information. For example, if a state DMV chooses to sell a record to a "casual requester," the record can contain personal information (address, etc.), but **only** with the **consent** of the subject.

Refer to Searching State Agency Records chapter for more about this subject. Also, for those interested in extensive, detailed information about either driver or vehicle records, refer to BRB Publications' *The MVR Book*.

Vehicle and Vessel Ownership, Registration, VINs, Titles, and Liens (found at state and, on occasion, at county level)

State repositories of vehicle/vessel registration and ownership records hold a wide range of information. Generally, record requesters submit a name to uncover vehicle(s) owned or submit vehicle information to obtain an owner name and address. However, this category of record information is also subject to the DPPA as described above.

The original language of DPPA required the states to offer an "opt out" option to drivers and vehicle owners, if they (the states) sold marketing lists or individual records to casual requesters (those requesters not specifically mentioned in DPPA). An amendment, known as Public Law 106-69, reversed this. Effective June 1, 2000, states automatically opted out all individuals, unless the individual specifically asked to be included. This essentially did away with the sale of marketing lists and sales of bulk or database formats to information vendors and database compilers.

For detailed information about DPPA, Public Law 106-69, and the difference between agencies that handle vehicle records versus vessel records, see page 31.

An important fact to keep in mind when searching for vehicle-related records is that the same state agency that holds driving records is not necessarily the same agency that holds vehicle records. The two agencies can each be part of entirely different state government departments or divisions.

The same is true with vessel records. In some states, the agency maintaining the vessel records is not connected to the agency holding driving record or vehicle records. In these situations, the agency with the vessel records is typically unaware of DPPA and does not necessarily follow the DPPA mandates.

Accident or Crash Reports (found at state level or local level)

For the purposes of this publication, "accident records" or "crash reports" are designated as those reports prepared by the investigating officer. Copies of a *citizen's* accident report are not usually available to the public and are not reviewed herein. Usually the State Police or Department of Public Safety maintains the accident reports, but sometimes these records are maintained by the same agency that holds driving records. When the accident reports are maintained by state DMVs, the DPPA guidelines are followed with regards to honoring record requests.

Typical information found on a state accident report includes drivers' addresses and license numbers as well as a description of the incident. Accidents investigated by local officials or minor accidents where the damage does not exceed a reporting limit (such as $1,000), are not available from state agencies.

Occupational Licensing and Business Registration (found at state boards)

Occupational licenses and business registrations contain a plethora of information readily available from various state agencies. A common reason to call these agencies is to corroborate professional or industry credentials. Often, a telephone call to the agency may secure an address and phone number. Over ½ of the licensing boards in the U.S. offer a searchable online name index. Some boards even show when discipline actions are taken. Refer to the chapter *Searching State Occupational Licensing Boards* for further information.

GED Records (found at state level)

By contacting the state offices that oversee GED Records, one can verify whether someone truly received a GED certificate for the high school education equivalency. These records are useful for pre-employment screening or background checking purposes. Most state agencies will verify over the phone the existence of a GED certificate or even give a "yes-no" answer by fax. Copies of transcripts or diplomas usually are not free-of-charge. When doing a record search, you must know the name of the student at the time of the test and a general idea of the year and test location. GED Records are *not* useful when trying to locate an individual.

Workers' Compensation Records (found at state level)

Research at state workers' compensation boards is generally limited to determining if an employee has filed a claim and/or obtaining copies of the claim records themselves. With the passage of the Americans with Disabilities Act (ADA) in the early 1990s, using information from workers' compensation boards for pre-employment screening was virtually eliminated. Per the ADA, *a review of workers' compensation histories may only be conducted after a conditional job offer has been made* and when medical information is reviewed. However, the ability of conducting this review is still subject to individual state statutes, which vary widely and be stricter than the ADA.

Voter Registration (found at state and county levels)

Voting registration records are a good source to find addresses and voting history. Every state has a central election agency or commission, and all have a central repository of voter information collected from the county level agencies per the federal mandate HAVA. The degree or level of accessibility to these records varies widely from state to state. Generally, registration data can be viewed in person at the local level. Overall, very little online access is offered.

Over half of the states will sell portions of the registered voter database, but only a handful of states permit individual searching by name through the state office. States will allow access for political purposes such as "Get Out the Vote" campaigns or compilation of campaign contribution lists. Nearly every state and local agency blocks the release of Social Security Numbers and telephone numbers found in these records.

Vital Records: Birth, Death, Marriage, and Divorce Records (found at state and county levels)

Copies of vital record certificates are needed for a variety of reasons — social security, jobs, passports, family history, litigation, lost heir searching, proof of identity, etc. Most states understand the urgency of these requests, and many offer an expedited service. *A number of states will take requests over the phone or by fax if you use a credit card.* Searchers must also be aware that in many instances certain vital records are *not* kept at the state level. The searcher must then turn to city and county record repositories to find the information needed.

Most states offer expedited fax and online ordering by utilizing the services from an outside vendor, either VitalChek or USCerts. These state-endorsed vendors maintain individual fax order telephone lines for each state they service. They require the use of a credit card and with that an extra fee in the range of $5.00 to $10.00. Their websites at www.vitalchek.com and www.uscerts.com are good places to order vital records online from many states. Keep in mind that results usually are still mailed.

Older vital records are usually found in the county office archives or state archives. There is an excellent links list of extensive historical genealogy-related databases at http://ancestry.com/default.aspx. Another source of historical vital record information is the Family History Library of the Church of Jesus Christ of Latter Day Saints, located at 35 North West Temple, Salt Lake City 84150. They have millions of microfilmed records from church and civil registers from all over the world.

Credit Information and Social Security Numbers

Social Security Numbers

The Social Security Number (SSN) is the subject of a persistent struggle between privacy rights groups and legitimate business interests that wish to confirm the identity of an individual. The truth is that many individuals gave up the privacy of their number by writing it on a voter registration form, product registration form, or any of a myriad of other voluntary disclosures made over the years.

Today with the justifiable increased concerns over identity theft, the release of SSNs in records, without consent of the subject, is very uncommon. In the past, a major source of finding a SSN was in the "header" of a credit report. But not any more, see below.

Credit Information

Credit data is derived from financial transactions of people or businesses. **Private companies maintain this information; government only regulates access.** Certain credit information about individuals is restricted by laws, such as the Fair Credit Reporting Act, at the federal level and by even more restrictive laws in many states. Credit information about businesses is not restricted by law and is fully open to anyone who requests (pays for) it.

A credit report essentially has two parts — the credit header and the credit history. A credit header is essentially the upper portion of a credit report containing the Social Security Number, age, phone number, last several addresses, and any AKAs. Recently, access to credit header information (see below) was closed to most business entities.

Credit Header Ban Went Into Effect July 1st, 2001

July 1st, 2001 was an important date for skiptracers, fraud investigators, and other businesses that rely on "credit headers." This information has always been available without the consent of the individual subject. Per a federal court ruling, beginning July 1st 2001, access to credit header information was treated in the same manner as access to credit reports—there has to be permission granted by the individual.

The basis of this ban is traced to the Gramm-Leach-Bliley Act (GLB). Section 502 of this act prohibits a financial institution from disclosing nonpublic personal information about a consumer to non-affiliated third parties unless a consumer has elected not to opt out from disclosure. Trans Union and other members of the Individual References Services Group (IRSG), among others, filed suit in an effort to keep this information open for "appropriate commercial purposes." The ruling, dated April 30th, denied this argument. The sale of credit headers seemed to be on borrowed time anyway—originally, the ban was to begin November 2000. However, due to the lawsuits and action involving the FTC, a provision changed the start of the ban until July 1st, 2001.

Impact of Changes

The impact of the ruling (and an FTC opinion) was far ranging. The ruling restricted credit bureaus from selling the above-mentioned data to information vendors who compile their own proprietary databases. But there are some alternatives to those business entities that rely on this type of public record information. The data is grandfathered. Provider companies that purchased files from the credit bureaus can continue to sell the data to their customers. Although data will never be updated from the credit bureaus, the existing data can still be used without the restrictions imposed by the ruling.

The Gramm-Leach-Bliley Act did not deny access to public record sources or databases that may contain age, SSN, phone, prior addresses, and AKAs. The Act only forbade financial institutions from disclosing this data. Therefore, those businesses shut-off from using credit headers had to investigate alternative sources of public records.

Editor's Tip: Keep in mind that a business' credit information is not restricted by law and is fully open to anyone who requests and pays for it.

Additional Record Sources Worth Reviewing

Aviation Records

Records about pilots and ownership & registration of aircraft are often used by private investigators when doing a background report or looking for assets. Pilots are licensed and aircraft is registered with the Federal Aviation Association (FAA) whose website is www.faa.gov. Go the *Vendor Information Index Section* for a list of private companies offering access to pilot or aircraft records.

Education & Employment

Information about an employee's or prospective employee's schooling, training, education, and jobs is important to any employer. Learning institutions maintain their own records of attendance, completion and degree/certification granted. Also, employers will confirm certain information about former employees. This is an example of private information that becomes public by voluntary disclosure. As part of your credit record, this information would be considered restricted. If, however, you disclose this information to Who's Who, or to a product registration questionnaire, the information becomes public.

Environmental

Information about hazards to the environment is critical. There is little tradition and less law regarding how open or restricted information is at the state and local (recorder's office) levels. Most information on hazardous materials, soil composition, even OSHA inspection reports is public record. But many federal websites have removed information since 9/11.

OSHA stands for Occupational Safety and Health Administration, which is part of the U.S. Department of Labor. Their website is www.osha.gov.

Another federal government source is the U.S. Environmental Protection Agency found at www.epa.gov/records. According to *Find it Online* author Alan Schlein, the EPA "…no longer allows direct access to the Envirofacts databases, which explain what toxic chemicals are found in water, hazardous waste, toxic waste, and Superfund sites, and is broken down by community. The EPA had originally created the database to provide the public with direct access to the wealth of information contained in its databases. The public is no longer able to access the information." The same can be said for the U.S. Geological Survey (www.usgs.gov); this agency has removed a number of its reports on water resources.

State Legislation & Regulations

Most state legislative bodies offer free Internet access to bill text and status, some even offer subject queries. Notwithstanding federal guidelines, the state legislatures and legislators control the policies and provisions for the release of state held information. Every year there is a multitude of bills introduced in state legislatures that would, if passed, create major changes in the access and retrieval of records and personal information.

Tenant History

This, like credit history, is another example of a combination of public and proprietary information collected by private businesses for the purpose of tracking an element of personal life important to an industry—in this case the housing rental industry. Database vendors often collect rental history records from property managers and owners. The records are often shared within the industry on a restricted online basis according to disclosure rules set by the companies themselves. Another important part of a Tenant History is a search for eviction notices (forcible detainers) at the local courts. Again, these court records are entered into a vendor's database for re-sale.

Medical

Medical record Information about an individual's medical status and history are summarized in various repositories that are accessible only to authorized insurance and other private company employees. Medical information is neither public information nor a closed record. Like credit information, it is not meant to be shared with anyone unless you give authorization.

Military

Each branch maintains its own records. Much of this, such as years of service and rank, is open public record. However, some details in the file of an individual may be subject to restrictions on access — approval by the subject may be required.

For more information about military records, turn to page 63.

Searching State Agency Records

The previous chapter includes a wealth of knowledge about the various types of public records found at the state level. This chapter gives a more detailed look obtaining state records, regardless if online, with special emphasis on criminal and motor vehicle records.

The State Quick Links Section

Each state chapter begins with a list of important state offices and other logistics that may be helpful to your record searching needs.

The M*ain State URL* or the *Office of the Governor* is a good place to start if you are looking for an obscure agency, phone number or address. We have found that typically the person who answers the phone will point you in the right direction if he or she cannot answer your question.

The *Attorney General's Office* is another excellent starting point. For example, if you are looking for a non-profit organization, this may help you.

The *State Archives* contain an abundance of historical documents and records, especially useful to those interested in genealogy.

Most *State Legislative* bodies offer free Internet access to bill text and status. Some even offer subject queries. Notwithstanding federal guidelines, the state legislatures and legislators control the policies and provisions for the release of state held information. Every year there is a multitude of bills introduced in state legislatures that would, if passed, create major changes for the access and retrieval of records and personal information.

Also, we included the web page for each state's agency that oversees *Unclaimed Funds* and assets. By checking this site in your state you may find a windfall money owed to you!

State Record Categories

These are the possible state agency record categories found in this book within each state chapter—

Accident Reports

Corporation & Other Business Entities

Criminal Records

Divorce Records

Driver Records

Federal Tax Liens

Fictitious or Assumed Names

GED Records

Incarceration Records

Sales Tax Registrations

Sexual Offender Records

State-Investigated Accident Reports

State Tax Liens

Statewide Court Systems

Trademark, Trade Name

Uniform Commercial Code Filings

Vehicle Records

Vessel Records

Vital Records: Birth, Death, Marriage, Divorce

Voter Registration

Workers' Compensation Records

Certain of these categories are more apt to offer online access, and some rarely do.

> "Just because records are maintained in a certain way in your state,
> do not assume that any other state does things the same way."

Searching State Record Repositories

There are distinct segments that create a total picture of record searching, including access methods and privacy restrictions.

Indexing and Storage

The following questions are important to ask when you are searching records—

- How many years of records are accessible?

- When are new records are available in your system?

- How are records indexed and in what format are they maintained?

Searching Criteria and Requirements

When you know how records are indexed you have a better idea of how to search. For example, do you need a case or file number, or can you search by the name and the date of birth and/or the exact years to search. Sometimes privacy restrictions or additional requirements could be in place. For example, the agency requirements are for doing a search could include a signed release from the subject.

Access Methods

As mentioned previously, the following are the possible access methods—

- Mail
- Phone
- In person
- Fax
- Online

Public Records Online lists all agencies that offer online access, either free or on a pay or subscription basis.

Fee and Payments

Possible fees include search fees, copy fees, certification fees, and expedite fees. Also if credit cards are accepted, additional fees may be necessary. Be aware many agencies do not accept personal checks or even business checks. Call and ask first before you mail a request.

Tips on Searching Criminal Records

All states have a central repository of criminal records of those individuals who have been subject to that state's criminal justice system. The information at the state repository is obtained from local county, parish, and municipal courts as well as from law enforcement. Records include fingerprint files and files containing identification segments, and notations of arrests and dispositions. Although usually housed in the Department of Public Safety, often it is the State Police or other state agency that maintains the central repository.

Most states make this repository available to the public, but there is a high degree of non-uniformity regarding what information is released and to whom. Consider the following—

- 21 states release criminal records to the general public without consent of the subject
- 20 states release criminal records to the general public with signed release from the subject
- 16 states require statutory authority to access their records

For those readers who are quick at math (57 states?), please note that some states have two types of criminal records they release.

By far, the vast majority of criminal records (used outside of law enforcement) are used for employment purposes, generally referred to as pre-employment screening or background checks.

Criminal Records and Pre-Employment Screening

A background screen is not meant to stop an individual who has a criminal record in the past from being hired. The purpose of a background screen is to enable the employers to verify the information presented by the applicants and to determine if the applicants are truthful about the past and really are whom they are (and not someone with a false ID or even a terrorist). Employers encourage and expect applicants to be truthful about past activity and employment.

State and federal laws are very strict about what employers can and cannot ask or use when making hiring decisions. The following statistics pertain to state restrictions on criminal record use by employers—

- 19 states prohibit the use of arrest records (i.e., non-conviction records)

- 5 states prohibit the use of misdemeanor convictions

- 13 states prohibit the use of expunged or sealed records

- 4 states restrict the use of records based on time periods

- 2 states limit the use of first offense records

The Federal regulations concerning the use of criminal records by employers come from the Fair Credit Reporting Act (FCRA). If you are an employer ordering criminal records on potential employees, or a pre-employment screening company, it is imperative to become familiar with this law.

Per Derek Hinton, author of the *Criminal Records Manual*, "...there are three main areas in which the FCRA can affect an employer ordering criminal records—

- Releases—What notifications must be made and permissions granted from the subject of the search.

- Arrest vs. convictions, seven-year rule—What information can appear on the report, and what must be suppressed.

- Aged public record for employment purposes—When the vendor databases records, what additional notifications to the subject must be performed."

For detailed specifics regarding FCRA and criminal records, it is suggested to obtain Derek's book or to obtain *The Safe Hiring Manual* by Les Rosen (both available from Facts on Demand Press and BRB Publications).

The National Criminal Record Search

"Ha ha" you may say. "There is no need to search the state and county agencies. I can find a national criminal record search on the Internet for as little as $15.00."

If you are an employer and rely on such search a search as your sole criminal record check, you could very well be exposing your company to a negligent hiring lawsuit. The reality is that there is no such database available to the public. Period. End of story.

There is an excellent article about this topic found on page 79—*Take Caution When Using Private Databases* by Lester S. Rosen.

Motor Vehicle Record Restrictions

The Driver's Privacy Protection Act Title XXXI — Protection of Privacy of Information in State Motor Vehicle Records — was attached as an amendment to the Violent Crime Control Act of 1994 and was signed by President Clinton late that Summer. The intent of the DPPA is to protect the personal privacy of persons licensed to drive by prohibiting certain disclosures of information maintained by the states.

This federal mandate declared that the federal government had the right to restrict or prohibit the release of personal information of persons licensed to drive or own motor vehicles. DPPA prohibits disclosure of personal information from the driver history, vehicle registration, title files held by state DMVs, except for 14 specific "permissible uses." The Act's definition of Personal Information is…

"..information that identifies an individual, including an individual's photograph, social security number, driver identification number, name, address (but not the 5-digit zip code), telephone number, and medical or disability information, but does not include information on vehicular accidents, driving violations, and driver's status."

The permissible uses do, in general, permit ongoing, legitimate businesses and individuals to obtain full record data, but with added compliance procedures.

The Effect of Public Law 106-69

As explained earlier, the original language of DPPA required the states offer an "opt out" option to drivers and vehicle owners, if they (the states) sell marketing lists or individual records to casual requesters (those requesters not specifically mentioned in DPPA). Public Law 106-69, and amendment to DPPA, reversed this. Effective June 1, 2000, this amendment to DPPA instructed the states to automatically opt out all individuals, unless the individual specifically asks to be included. Since all states now have an "opt in" procedure in place, very few individuals request to be placed on marketing lists.

Therefore, passage of Public Law 106-69 was dramatic since it essentially did away with sales of—

- marketing lists;

- records (with addresses and other personal information) to "casual" requesters;

- record databases to information vendors and database compilers (except for vehicle recall purposes, etc.).

Thus, the states' compliance with Public Law 106-69 essentially did away with the sale of marketing lists and sales of bulk or database formats to information vendors and database compilers.

Also, 106-69 created a new category of personal information called sensitive personal information. This category includes the driver's license photograph, Social Security Number, medical and disability information. Subsection 350(b) restricts the dissemination of sensitive personal information without the express consent of the person to whom the information pertains. However, expressed consent is not required for the dissemination of sensitive personal information if released under the following permissible uses in DPPA 2721(b) —

- (1) For use by any government agency, including any court or law enforcement agency;

- (4) For use in connection with any civil, criminal, administrative, or arbitral proceeding;

- (6) For use by any insurer or insurance support organization;

- (9) For use by an employer or its agent or insurer to obtain or verify information relating to a holder of a commercial driver's license.

Therefore, Public Law 106-69 blocks any of the other 10 permissible users mentioned in DPPA from obtaining the four categories of sensitive personal information. Clear as mud, isn't it?

Unless you have a very good and legitimate reason, do not expect a state motor vehicle departments to release photos, addresses, SSNs or disability information.

Also, unless you qualify, do not expect to go online and obtain motor vehicle record information containing personal data.

State Agency Online Public Record Table

Codes

O	Open to Public – No Charge
$$	Commercial Access – Fees Involved
O-$$	Two Systems (fee & free) *or* Free Index with Fees for Record Copies
S	Severe Access Restrictions (Signed Authorization, etc.)
P	Partial Database Available

Note: If **blank**, then not available online to the public

State	Criminal Records	Prison Records	Sexual Offender	Driver Records	UCC Records	Corp. Records	State Courts
Alabama		O-P	O	$$-S	O	O	
Alaska	O-P		O	$$-S	O	O	O-P
Arizona		O-P	O	$$-S	O	O-$$	O-P
Arkansas		O	O	$$-S	O-$$	O	
California			O	$$-S	O-$$	O	
Colorado	$$		O	$$-S	O	O	O-P
Connecticut		O	O	$$-S	O	O	O-P
Delaware			O	$$-S		O-$$	
Dist. of Columbia			O	$$-S	O-$$		
Florida	$$	O	O	$$-S	O	O	
Georgia		O	O	$$-S	O-$$	O-$$	
Hawaii			O	$$-S	O	O	O
Idaho		O	O	$$-S	O-$$	O	
Illinois	$$	O	O	$$-S		O-$$	
Indiana	$$	O	O	$$-S	O-$$	O-$$	
Iowa		O-P	O	$$-S	O	O	O
Kansas	$$	O	O	$$-S	$$	O-$$	
Kentucky		O	O	$$-S	O	O	O-P
Louisiana		O-P	O	$$-S	$$	O-$$	
Maine	$$		O	$$-S	O-$$	O-$$	
Maryland		O-P	O	$$-S	O	O	O-P
Massachusetts				$$-S	O-$$	O-$$	S-P
Michigan	$$	O	O	$$-S	O-$$	O	
Minnesota	$$	O	O	$$-S	O-$$	O-$$	

State	Criminal Records	Prison Records	Sexual Offender	Driver Records	UCC Records	Corp. Records	State Courts
Mississippi		O	O	$$-S	O-$$	O	
Missouri			O	$$-S	O-$$	O	O-P
Montana		O	O	$$-S	$$	O-$$	
Nebraska		O	O	$$-S	$$	O-$$	$$-P
Nevada		O	O	$$-S	$$	O	
New Hampshire			O	$$-S	$$	O-$$	
New Jersey		O	O	$$-S	O-$$	O-$$	$$
New Mexico	$$	O	O	$$-S	O	O-$$	O-P
New York		O	O	$$-S	O	O-$$	$$-P
North Carolina		O	O	$$-S	O	O	O-$$
North Dakota			O	$$-S	O-$$	O	
Ohio	S-$$	O	O	$$-S	O	O-$$	
Oklahoma		O	O	$$-S	O		O-P
Oregon	$$				O-$$	O-$$	$$
Pennsylvania	$$	O	O	$$-S	O	O	O-P
Rhode Island				$$-S		O	O
South Carolina	$$	O	O	$$-S	O	O	
South Dakota			O	$$-S	$$	O	
Tennessee		O	O	$$-S	O	O	
Texas	$$-P		O	$$-S	O-$$	O-$$	
Utah		O	O	$$-S	O-$$	O-$$	$$
Vermont		O	O	$$-S	O	O	
Virginia	$$-S	O	O	$$-S	O	O	O-P
Washington	$$		O	$$-S	$$	O	$$
West Virginia			O	$$-S		O	
Wisconsin	$$		O	$$-S	O-$$	O	O-P
Wyoming			O	$$-S	$$	O	

Codes

O	Open to Public – No Charge
$$	Commercial Access – Fees Involved
O-$$	Two Systems (fee & free) *or* Free Index with Fees for Record Copies
S	Severe Access Restrictions (Signed Authorization, etc.)
P	Partial Database Available

Note: If **blank,** then not available online to the public

Searching State Occupational Licensing Boards

Over 50% of the 8,000+ regulated occupational licenses in the U.S. can be searched online. This book reports over 4,200 Internet web pages that give you the ability to conduct name searches for occupational licensing boards. This chapter offers helpful information for searching the state boards online as well as by telephone or by mail.

The Privacy Question

While some agencies consider this information private and confidential, most agencies at least freely release some basic data over the phone or by mail.

Our research indicates that many agencies appear to make their own judgments regarding what specifically is private and confidential in their files. For example, approximately 45% of the agencies indicate that they will disclose adverse information about a registrant, and many others will only disclose selected portions of the information or merely verify a credential.

In any event, the basic search criteria to follow when you visit a URL or contact a licensing agency is to determine **the specific kinds of information available.**

What Information May Be Available

An agency may be willing to release part or all of the following, either online or over the telephone—

- Field of Certification
- Status of License/Certificate
- Date License/Certificate Issued

- Date License/Certificate Expires
- Current or Most Recent Employer
- Address of Subject
- Complaints, Violations or Disciplinary Actions

Search Fees

In general, there is no fee when searching online. However, there are several trends we observed when determining applicable fees of the various licensing agencies if contacted by mail or telephone. They are—

1. There is no charge to verify if a particular person is licensed; this can usually be done by phone.

2. The fee for copies or faxes ranges from $.25 to $2.00.

3. A fee of $5 to $20 usually applies to written requests. This is due to the fact that written certifications give more information than verbal inquiries, i.e. disciplinary action, exam scores, specific dates.

4. A fee that is $25 or more is typically for a list of licensed professionals. For example, a hospital might need a roster of registered nurses in a certain geographic area.

Searching Tip — Distinguish the Type of Agency

Within the agency category listings, it is important to note that there are five general types of agencies. When you are verifying credentials, you should be aware of what distinguishes each type, which in turn could alter the questions you ask.

Private Certification

Private Licensing and Certification — requires a proven level of minimum competence before a license is granted. These professional licenses separate the true "professions" from the third category below. In many of these professions, the certification body, such as the American Institute of Certified Public Accountants, is a private association whereas the licensing body, such as the New York State Education Department, is the licensing agency. Also, many professions may provide additional certifications in specialty areas.

State Certification

State Licensing and Certification — requires certification through an *examination* and/or other *requirements supervised* directly *by the state* rather than by a private association.

By Individual

Individual Registration — required if an individual intends to offer specified products or services in the designated area, but does not require certification that the person has met minimum requirements. An everyday example would be registering a handgun in a state that does not require passing a gun safety course.

By Business

Business Registration — required if a business intends to do business or offer specified products or services in a designated area, such as registering a liquor license. Some business license agencies require testing or a background check. Others merely charge a fee after a cursory review of the application.

Special Permits

Permits — give the grantee specific permission to do something, whether it is to sell hotdogs on the corner or to erect a three story high sign. Permits are usually granted at the local level rather than the state level of government.

Other Forms of Licensing and Registration

Although the state level is where much of the licensing and registration occurs, you should be aware of other places you may want to search.

Local Government Agencies

Local government agencies at both the **county** and **municipal levels** require a myriad of business registrations and permits in order to do business (construction, signage, etc.) within their borders. Even where you think a business or person, such as a remodeling contractor, should have local registrations you want to check out, it is still best to start at the state level.

County Recording Office and City Hall

If you decide to check on local registrations and permits, call the offices at both the county — try the **county recording office** — and municipal level — try **city hall** — to find out what type of registrations may be required for the person or business you are checking out.

Like the state level, you should expect that receiving basic information will only involve a phone call and that you will not be charged for obtaining a status summary.

Professional Associations

As mentioned above, many professional licenses are based on completion of the requirements of professional associations. In addition, there are *many professional designations* from such associations that *are not recognized as official licenses by government*. Other designations are basic certifications in fields that are so specialized that they are not of interest to the states, but rather only to the professionals within an industry. For example, if your company needs to hire an investigator to check out a potential fraud against you, you might want to hire a CFE — Certified Fraud Examiner — who has met the minimum requirements for that title from the Association of Certified Fraud Examiners.

Other Media Sources

Mail Lists and Databases

Many agencies make their lists available in reprinted or computer form, and a few maintain online access to their files. If you are interested in the availability of licensing agency information in bulk (e.g. mailing lists, tapes, disks) or online, call the agency and ask about formats that are available.

Vendor Databases

A number of private vendors also compile lists from these agencies and make them available online or on CD-ROM. We do not necessarily suggest using these databases for credential searching because they may not be complete, may not be up-to-date and may not contain all the information you can obtain directly from the licensing agency. However, these databases are extremely valuable as a supplemental source of background information on an individual or company that you wish to do business with.

Searching County Court Records

Some Court Basics

Before searching an online index of court records or trudging into a courthouse and demanding to view a document, you should first be aware of some basic court procedures. Whether the case is filed in a state, municipal, or federal court, each case follows a similar process.

The term "County Courts," as used in this publication, refers to those courts of original jurisdiction (trial courts) within each state's court system that handle...

Felonies	Generally defined as crimes punishable by one year or more of jail time
Civil Actions	For money damages (usually greater than $3,000)
Probate	Estate matters
Misdemeanors	Generally defined as minor infractions with a fine or minimal jail time
Evictions	Landlord/tenant actions
Small Claims	Actions for minor money damages (generally under $3,000)

A *civil case* usually commences when a plaintiff files a complaint with a court against defendants. The defendants respond to the complaint with an answer. After this initial round, there may be literally hundreds of activities before the court issues a judgment. These activities can include revised complaints and their answers, motions of various kinds, discovery proceedings (including depositions) to establish the documentation and facts involved in the case. All of these activities are listed on a **docket sheet**, which may be a piece of paper or a computerized index.

Once the court issues a judgment, either party may appeal the ruling to an appellate division or court. In the case of a money judgment, the winning side can usually file it as a judgment lien with the county recorder. Appellate divisions usually deal only with legal issues and not the facts of the case.

In a *criminal case*, the plaintiff is a government jurisdiction. The Government brings the action against the defendant for violation of one or more of its statutes.

In a *bankruptcy case,* which can be heard only in federal courts, there is neither defendant nor plaintiff. Instead, the debtor files voluntarily for bankruptcy protection against creditors, or the creditors file against the debtor in order to force the debtor into involuntary bankruptcy.

State Court Structure

The secret to determining where a state court case is located is to understand how the court system is structured in that particular state. The overall structure of all state court systems has four parts–

> Appellate courts   Limited jurisdiction trial courts
>
> Intermediate appellate courts   General jurisdiction trial courts

The two highest levels, appellate and intermediate appellate courts, only hear cases on appeal from the trial courts. Opinions of these appellate courts are of interest primarily to attorneys seeking legal precedents for new cases.

General jurisdiction trial courts usually handle a full range of civil and criminal litigation. These courts usually handle felonies and larger civil cases.

Limited jurisdiction trial courts come in two varieties. First, many limited jurisdiction courts handle smaller civil claims (usually $10,000 or less), misdemeanors, and pretrial hearing for felonies. Second, some of these courts, sometimes called special jurisdiction courts, are limited to one type of litigation, for example the Court of Claims in New York, which only handles liability cases against the state.

Some states, for instance Iowa, have consolidated their general and limited jurisdiction court structure into one combined court system. In other states there may be a further distinction between state-supported courts and municipal courts. In New York, for example, nearly 1,300 Justice Courts handle local ordinance and traffic violations, including DWI.

Generalizations should not be made about where specific types of cases are handled in the various states. Misdemeanors, probate, landlord/tenant (eviction), domestic relations, and juvenile cases may be handled in either or both the general and limited jurisdiction courts.

How Courts Maintain Records

Case Numbering

When a case is filed, a case number is assigned. Use of a case number is the primary indexing method in every court. Therefore, to searching specific case records, you will need to know—or find—the applicable case number. If you have the number in good form already, your search should be fast and reasonably inexpensive, otherwise you will need to start with a name search.

You should be aware that case numbering procedures are not consistent throughout a state court system. One district may assign numbers by district while another may assign numbers by location (division) within the district, or by judge. Remember: case numbers appearing in legal text citations may not be adequate for searching unless they appear in the proper form for the particular court in which you are searching.

The Docket Sheet

Information from cover sheets and from documents filed as a case goes forward is recorded on the docket sheet. The docket sheet then contains an outline of the case history from initial filing to its current status. While docket sheets differ somewhat in format, the basic information contained on a docket sheet is consistent from court to court. All docket sheets contain–

- Name of court, including location (division) and the judge assigned;
- Case number and case name;
- Names of all plaintiffs and defendants/debtors;
- Names and addresses of attorneys for the plaintiff or debtor;
- Nature and cause (e.g., statute) of action.

Computerization

Most courts are computerized, which means that the docket sheet data is entered into a computer system. Within a state or judicial district, the courts *may* be linked together via a single computer system.

Docket sheets from cases closed before the advent of computerization may not be in the computer system. For pre-computer cases, most courts keep summary case information on microfilm, microfiche, or index cards.

Case documents are not generally available on computer because courts are still experimenting with and developing electronic filing and imaging of court documents. Generally, documents are only available to be copied by contacting the court where the case records are located.

Searching State Courts Online

Online searching is generally limited to a copy of the courts' docket sheets (see above). Most courts are computerized in-house, which means that the docket sheet data is entered into a computer system of the courthouse itself. Checking a courthouse's computer index is the quickest way to find if case records exist online.

A growing number of state courts provide electronic access to their records, as shown on the Table on pages 33-34 and in the state chapters. For example, where "statewide" online systems are available in Alabama, Maryland, Minnesota, New Mexico, Oregon, Washington, and Wisconsin, you still need to understand (1) the court structure in that state, (2) which particular courts are included in their online system, and (3) what types of cases are included. Many professionals using court records consider these online systems to be supplemental; further searching is needed for true diligence.

Without proper consideration of these variables, these online systems are subject to misuse, which can lead to disastrous consequences like failing to discover that an applicant for a security guard position is a convicted burglar.

If Records Are Not Available Online

If you need copies of case records, court personnel may make copies for you for a fee, or you may be able to make copies yourself if the court allows. Also, court personnel may certify the document for you for a fee. Perhaps due to a shortage of staff or fear of litigation, some courts that previously would conduct searches of records on behalf of the public are no longer making that service available. Typically, these courts do one of two things. In some states, the courts refuse to allow searchers in the courthouse and refer requesters to a state agency that maintains a database combining individual court records (which may or may not be current). In other states, the courts simply refuse to conduct searches, leaving the searcher with no choice but to use a local retrieval firm or other individual to conduct the search on his or her behalf.

Court Record Searching Tips

Learn the Index & Record Systems

Most civil courts index records by both plaintiffs as well as the defendants, but some only index by the defendant name. A plaintiff search is useful, for example, to determine if someone is especially litigious.

During the past decade, thousands of courts have installed computerized indexing systems, but many courts still use index books or cards. Computerized systems are considerably faster and easier to search, allowing for more indexing capability than the microfilm and card indexes that preceded them.

Understand the Search Requirements

There is a strong tendency for courts to overstate their search requirements. For civil cases, the usual reasonable requirement is a defendant (or plaintiff) name—full name if it is a common name—and the time frame to search—e.g., 1993-2002. For criminal cases, the court may require more identification, such as date of birth (DOB), to ascertain the correct individual. Other information "required" by courts— such as Social Security Number (SSN)—is often just "helpful" to narrow the search on a common name.

Be Aware of Restricted Records

Most courts have a number of types of case records, such as juvenile and adoptions, which are not released without a court order.

Other Court Search Tips

- Watch for name variations from state to state. Do not assume that the structure of the court system in another state is anything like your own. In one state, the Circuit Court may be the highest trial court whereas in another it is a limited jurisdiction court. Examples are: (1) New York, where the Supreme Court is not very "supreme," and the downstate court structure varies from upstate; and (2) Tennessee, where circuit courts are in districts.

- In many instances two types of courts within a county (e.g., circuit and district) are combined. When phoning or writing these courts, we recommend that your request specifically state in your request that you want both courts included in the search.

- Be aware that the number of courts that no longer conduct name searches has risen. For these courts, you must hire a local retriever, directly or through a search company, to search for you. It should be noted that usually these courts still take specific document copy requests by mail. Because of long mail turnaround times and court fees, local retrievers are frequently used even when the court will honor a request by mail. Many court offer a public access terminal, free of charge, to view case documents or indexes.

- When searching for case records, keep in mind that many of the higher level courts also handle appeals from lower courts.

- If you send requests by mail, send a self-addressed, stamped envelope (SASE). This may very well insure quicker service.

Searching Recording Office Records

The Lowdown on Recorded Documents

Documents filed and record at local county, parish, city or town offices represent some of the best opportunities to gain access to open public records, especially if you are searching online. If you are lucky enough to live in close proximity, you can visit your local office and, for free, view records. Recorded documents are also one of the most available types of public records that can be viewed or obtained via the Internet.

Real Estate

As mentioned previously, real estate records are public so that everyone can know who owns what property. Liens on real estate must be public so a buyer or lender knows all the facts. The county (or parish or city) recorder's office is the source. Also, access is available from many private companies that purchase entire county record databases and create their own database for commercial purposes.

Uniform Commercial Code (UCC)

UCC filings are to personal property what mortgages are to real estate property. UCCs are in the category of financial records that must be fully open to public scrutiny so that other potential lenders are on notice about which assets of the borrower have been pledged as collateral.

As with tax liens, UCC recordings are filed, according to state law, either at the state or local (county, town, parish) level. Until June 30, 2001, liens on certain types of companies required dual filing (must file at BOTH locations, thus records can be searched at BOTH locations). As of July 1, 2001, (see page 50) in most state UCC filings other than those that go into real estate records are no longer filed at the local filing offices, but older filings can still be located there until 2008. As with real estate records, there are a number of private companies who have created their own databases for commercial resale.

A Great Source of Information

Although recorded documents are a necessity to making an informed business-related decision, they are also a virtual treasure trove of data. UCC filing documents contain the names and addresses of creditors and debtors, describe the asset offered for collateral, the date of the filing, and whether or note the loan has been satisfied. This information contained on the statements can lead an experienced investigator to other roads down the information trail. For example, if the collateral is a plane or a vessel, this will lead to registration records, or if the debtor is a business other names on the filing may lead to other traceable business partners or ventures.

Recording Office Searching Rules

The general rules for background searching of UCC records are as follows–:

- *Except in local filing states, a search at the state level is adequate to locate all UCC records on a subject.*

- *Mortgage record searches will include any real estate related UCC filings.*

See pages 49-50 for discussions of special collateral rules.

Due diligence searching, however, usually demands searching the local records in dual filing states as well.

The County Rule

Where to search for recorded documents usually isn't a difficult problem to overcome in everyday practice. In most states, these transactions are recorded at one designated recording office in the county where the property is located.

We call this the "County Rule." It applies to types of public records such as real estate recordings, tax liens, Uniform Commercial Code (UCC) filings, vital records, and voter registration records. However, as with most government rules, there are a variety of exceptions, which are summarized here.

The Exceptions

The five categories of exceptions to the County Rule (or Parish Rule, if searching in Louisiana) are listed below (the details are listed in the chart to follow)—

- Special Recording Districts (AK, HI)

- Multiple Recording Offices (AL, AR, IA, KY, ME, MA, MS, TN)

- Independent Cities (MD, MO, NV, VA)

- Recording at the Municipal Level (CT, RI, VT)

- Identical Names—Different Place (CT, IL, MA, NE, NH, PA, RI, VT, VA)

The Personal Property Problem and the Fifth Exception

The real estate recording system in the US is self-auditing to the extent that you generally cannot record a document in the wrong recording office. However, many documents are rejected for recording because they are submitted to the wrong recording office. There are a number of reasons why this occurs, one of which is the overlap of filing locations for real estate and UCC.

Finding the right location of a related UCC filing is a different and much more difficult problem from finding a real estate recording. In the majority of states, the usual place to file a UCC financing statement is at the Secretary of States office—these are called central filing states. In the dual and local filing states, the place to file, in addition to the central filing office, is usually at the same office where your real estate documents are recorded. However, where there are identical place names referring to two different places, it becomes quite confusing, so hence, the fifth exemption.

The County Rule—States Exceptions Chart

Each of these five categories of recording exceptions is summarized below by state.

AL	Four counties contain two separate recording offices. They are Barbour, Coffee, Jefferson, and St. Clair.
AK	The 23 Alaskan counties are called boroughs. However, real estate recording is done under a system that was established at the time of the Gold Rush (whenever that was) of **34 Recording Districts**. Some of the Districts are identical in geography to boroughs, such as the Aleutian Islands, but other boroughs and districts overlap. Therefore, you need to know which recording district any given town or city is located in.
AR	Ten counties contain two separate recording offices. They are Arkansas, Carroll, Clay, Craighead, Franklin, Logan, Mississippi, Prairie, Sebastian, and Yell.
CT	There is **no county recording** in this state. All recording is done at the city/town level. Lenders persist in attempting to record or file documents in the counties of Fairfield, Hartford, Litchfield, New Haven, New London, Tolland, and Windham related to property located in other cities/towns because each of these cities/towns bears the same name as a Connecticut county.
HI	All recording is done at one central office.

IL	Cook County has separate offices for real estate recording and UCC filing.
IA	Lee county has two recording offices.
KY	Kenton County has two recording offices. Jefferson County has a separate office for UCC filing.
LA	Louisiana counties are called **Parishes**. One parish, St. Martin, has two non-contiguous segments.
ME	Aroostock and Oxford counties have two separate recording offices.
MD	The City of Baltimore has its own separate recording office.
MA	Berkshire and Bristol counties each has three recording offices. Essex, Middlesex and Worcester counties each has two recording offices. Cities/towns bearing the same name as a county are Barnstable, Essex, Franklin, Hampden, Nantucket, Norfolk, Plymouth, and Worcester. UCC financing statements on personal property collateral are submitted to cities/towns, while real estate recording is handled by the counties.
MS	Ten counties contain two separate recording offices. They are Bolivar, Carroll, Chickasaw, Harrison, Hinds, Jasper, Jones, Panola, Tallahatchie, and Yalobusha.
MO	The City of St. Louis has its own recording office.
NE	Fifteen counties have separate offices for real estate recording and for UCC filing.
NH	Cities/towns bearing the same name as a county are Carroll, Grafton, Hillsborough, Merrimack, Strafford, and Sullivan. UCC financing statements on personal property collateral are submitted to cities/towns, while real estate recording is handled by the counties.
NV	Carson City has its own recording office.
PA	Each county has a separate recording office and prothonotary office. UCC financing statements on personal property are submitted to the prothonotary, and real estate documents are submitted to the recorder.
RI	There is **no county recording** in this state. All recording is done at the city/town level. Lenders persist in attempting to record or file documents in the counties of Bristol, Newport, and Providence related to property located in other cities/ towns because each of these cities/towns bears the same name as a Rhode Island county.
TN	Sullivan County has two separate recording offices.

VT	There is **no county recording** in this state. All recording is done at the city/town level. Lenders persist in attempting to record or file documents in the counties of Addison, Bennington, Chittenden, Essex, Franklin, Grand Isle, Orange, Rutland, Washington, Windham, and Windsor related to property located in other cities/towns because each of these cities/towns bears the same name as a Vermont county. Adding to the confusion, there are four place names in the state that refer to both a city and a town: Barre, Newport, Rutland, and St. Albans.
VA	There are 41 independent cities in Virginia. Twenty-seven have separate recording offices. The following 15 share their filing offices with the surrounding county: *INDEPENDENT CITY* *FILE IN*

INDEPENDENT CITY	FILE IN
Bedford	Bedford County
Covington	Alleghany County
Emporia	Greenville County
Fairfax	Fairfax County
Falls Church	Arlington or Fairfax County
Franklin	Southhampton County
Galax	Carroll County
Harrisonburg	Rockingham County
Lexington	Rockbridge County
Manassas	Prince William County
Manassas Park	Prince William County
Norton	Wise County
Poquoson	York County
South Boston	Halifax County
Williamsburg	James City County

Online Searching For Recording Office Records

The 2,400+ county government jurisdictions providing online access to recorded documents can be found in the state chapters in the *Government Online Sources Section*. Most sites are free if viewing an index, but some will charge a fee to view or print an image or copy of a page within the file.

Keep in mind there are a number of private companies who compile and maintain these records and offer them for resale, and they offer the most comprehensive source. Look for a list of these companies in the *Vendor Information Index*.

Special Categories of Collateral

Real Estate Related UCC Collateral

A specific purpose of lien statutes under both the UCC and real estate laws is to put a buyer or potential secured creditor on notice that someone has a prior security interest in real or personal property. UCC financing statements are to personal property what mortgages or deeds of trust are to real property.

One problem addressed by the UCC is that certain types of property have the characteristics of both real and personal property. In those instances, it is necessary to have a way to provide lien notice to two different categories of interested parties: those who deal with the real estate aspect of the property and those who deal with the "personal" aspect of the property.

In general, our definition of real estate related UCC collateral is any property that in one form is attached to land, but that in another form is not attached. For the sake of simplicity, we can define the characteristics of two broad types of property that meet this definition:

Property that is initially attached to real property, but then is separated.

> Three specific types of collateral have this characteristic: minerals (including oil and gas), timber, and crops. These things are grown on or extracted from land. While they are on or in the ground they are thought of as real property, but once they are harvested or extracted they become personal property. Some states have a separate central filing system for crops.

*Property that is initially personal property, but then is attached to land, generally called **fixtures**.*

> Equipment such as telephone systems or heavy industrial equipment permanently affixed to a building are examples of fixtures. It is important to realize that what is a fixture, like beauty, is in the eye of the beholder, since it is a vague concept at best.

UCC financing statements applicable to real estate related collateral must be filed where the real estate and mortgage records are kept, which is generally at the county level—except in Connecticut, Rhode Island and Vermont, where the Town/City Clerk maintains these records. The chart gives the titles of the local official who maintains these records.

Consumer Goods

Among the state-to-state variations, some states required filing where real estate is filed for certain consumer goods. However, as of July 1, 2001 all non-realty related UCC filings in most states, including consumer goods, now go only to the central filing office in the state.

Equipment Used in Farming Operations

Until recently, 33 states required only local filing for equipment used in farming operations. However as of July 1, 2001, all non-realty-related UCC filing has been centralized.

Searching Note

If you are looking for information on subjects that might have these types of filings against them, a search of county records may still be revealing even if you would normally search only at the state level.

The Importance of Revised Article 9

Revised Article 9

On July 1, 2001, Revised Article 9 became law in 46 states and the District of Columbia, with 4 states adopting the law later; Alabama (January 1, 2002), Connecticut (October 1, 2001), Florida (January 1, 2002) and Mississippi (January 1, 2002).

Under this new law, most UCC filings will go to the state where a business is organized, not where the collateral or chief executive offices are located. Thus, you will find new filings against IBM only in Delaware (IBM and many other public companies are Delaware corporations), and not in New York or in any other states where it has branch offices. Therefore, you will need to know where a company is organized in order to know where to find new UCC filings against it.

The place to file against individuals is the state where the person resides.

However, the new law does not apply to federal tax liens, which are still generally filed where the chief executive office is located. IBM's chief executive offices, for example, may still be in New York State.

As stated above, realty-related UCC filings continue to go to land recording offices where the property is located.

Old Article 9

Under old Article 9, Uniform Commercial Code financing statements and changes to them might be filed at two or three government agencies in each state, depending upon the type of collateral involved in the transaction. Each state's UCC statute contained variations on a nationally recommended Model Act. Each variation is explained below. You will still need to know about where UCC filings are located under old Article 9 because the transition period to Revised Article 9 is five years long. UCC filings on record before July 1, 2001 remain effective until they lapse, which is generally five years from initial filing date.

A lot of UCC filings against IBM, for example, made before July 1, 2001 will still be on record in New York's central filing office, and may also be found in county filing offices since New York was a dual filing state, as explained below.

Under old Article 9, 33 states were central filing states. Central filing states are those where most types of personal property collateral require filing of a UCC financing statement only at a central filing location within that state.

Under old Article 9, five states had statewide UCC database systems. Some of these systems are still in effect under Revised Article 9. Minnesota and **Wisconsin** were central filing states with a difference: UCC financing statements filed at the county level are also entered into a statewide database. In **North Dakota** UCC financing statements may be filed at either the state or county level, and all filings are entered into a statewide database. In **Louisiana**, **Nebraska**, and **Georgia**, UCC financing statements may be filed with **any** county (parish). Under Revised Article 9, Minnesota has established a county/state system like North Dakota in all but six county offices, and Nebraska is now a central filing state. In each of these six states the records are entered into a central, statewide database that is available for searching in each county, as well as at the state agency (no state agency in Louisiana or Georgia).

Under old Article 9, eight states required dual filing of certain types of UCC financing statements. The usual definition of a dual filing state is one in which financing statements containing collateral such as inventory, equipment or receivables *must* be filed in *both* a central filing office, usually with the Secretary of State, and in a local (county) office where the collateral or business is located. The three states below were also dual filing states, with a difference. Under Revised Article 9, no dual filing is required within a state

Under old Article 9, the filing systems in three states, MA, NH, and PA, can be described as triple filing because the real estate portion of the filings goes to an office separate from the UCC filing offices. In Massachusetts and New Hampshire, UCC filings were submitted to the town/city while real estate filings go to the county. In Pennsylvania, county government was separated into the Prothonotary for UCC filings and the Recorder for real estate filings. The local filing offices for non-realty-related UCC filings no longer take filings under Revised Article 9, but they will continue to perform searches of the old records.

Some counties in other states do have separate addresses for real estate recording, but this is usually just a matter of local departmentalization.

Under old Article 9, Kentucky and Wyoming were the only *local filing only* states. In both of these states a few filings were also found at the state level because filings for out of state debtors went to the Secretary of State. And in Wyoming, filings for Wyoming debtor accounts receivable and farm products require dual filing. However, under Revised Article 9, all filings have been centralized.

Searching Federal Court Records

The Federal Court system has evolved during the past decade. One problem searchers encounter is that older records may be in a different form or in a different location from newer records. For example, a searcher can go astray trying to find bankruptcy cases in Ohio unless he or she knows about changes at the Dayton records center.

One development that continues to change the fundamental nature of Federal Courts case record access is, of course, computerization. Now, every Federal Court in the United States has converted to a computerized index and prefers on computerized filing. Courts are increasing computerized and rely less on paper.

As mentioned previously, most federal courts no longer provide the date of birth or the Social Security Number on search results. However, a handful will provide the last four digits of the SSN, or they may provide the month and year of birth, but not the day. But these courts are few and far between.

Federal Court Structure

The Federal Court system includes three levels of courts, plus some special courts —

Supreme Court of the United States

The Supreme Court of the United States is the court of last resort in the United States. It is located in Washington, DC, where it hears appeals from the United States Courts of Appeals and from the highest courts of each state.

United States Court of Appeals

The United States Court of Appeals consists of thirteen appellate courts that hear appeals of verdicts from the courts of general jurisdiction. They are designated as follows:

The Federal Circuit Court of Appeals hears appeals from the U.S. Claims Court and the U.S. Court of International Trade. It is located in Washington, DC.

The District of Columbia Circuit Court of Appeals hears appeals from the district courts in Washington, DC as well as from the Tax Court.

Eleven geographic **Courts of Appeals** — each of these appeal courts covers a designated number of states and territories. The chart on pages 59-61 lists the circuit numbers (1 through 11) and location of the Court of Appeals for each state.

United States District Courts

The United States District Courts are the courts of general jurisdiction, or trial courts, and are subdivided into two categories—

The District Courts are courts of general jurisdiction –or trial courts – for federal matters, excluding bankruptcy. Essentially, they hear cases involving federal law and cases where there is diversity of citizenship. Both **civil** and **criminal** cases come before these courts.

The Bankruptcy Courts generally follow the same geographic boundaries as the U.S. District Courts. There is at least one bankruptcy court for each state; within a state there may be one or more judicial districts and within a judicial district there may be more than one location (division) where the courts hear cases. While civil lawsuits may be filed in either state or federal courts depending upon the applicable law, all bankruptcy actions are filed with the U.S. Bankruptcy Courts.

Special Courts/Separate Courts

The Special Courts/Separate Courts have been created to hear cases or appeals for certain areas of litigation demanding special expertise. Examples include the U.S. Tax Court, the Court of International Trade and the U.S. Claims Court.

How Federal Trial Courts Are Organized

At the federal level, all cases involve federal or U.S. constitutional law or interstate commerce. The task of locating the right court is seemingly simplified by the nature of the federal system—

- All court locations are based upon the plaintiff's county of domicile.

- All civil and criminal cases go to the U.S. District Courts.

- All bankruptcy cases go to the U.S. Bankruptcy Courts.

However, a plaintiff or defendant may have cases in any of the 500 court locations, so it is really not all that simple to find them.

There is at least one District Court and one Bankruptcy Court in each state. In many states there is more than one court, often divided further into judicial districts — e.g., the State of New York consists of four judicial districts: Northern, Southern, Eastern, Western. Further, many judicial districts contain more than one court location, usually called a division.

The Bankruptcy Courts generally use the same hearing locations as the District Courts. If court locations differ, the usual variance is to have fewer Bankruptcy Court locations.

Case Numbering

When a case is filed with a federal court, a case number is assigned. This is the primary indexing method. Therefore, in searching for case records, you will need to know or find the applicable case number. If you have the number in good form already, your search should be fast and inexpensive.

You should be aware that case numbering procedures are not consistent throughout the Federal Court system: one judicial district may assign numbers by district while another may assign numbers by location (division) within the judicial district or by judge. Remember that case numbers appearing in legal text citations may not be adequate for searching unless they appear in the proper form for the particular court.

All the basic civil case information that is entered onto docket sheets, and into computerized systems like PACER and CM/ECF(see below), starts with standard form JS-44, the Civil Cover Sheet, or the equivalent.

Docket Sheet

As in the state court system, information from cover sheets and from documents filed as a case goes forward is recorded on the **docket sheet**, which then contains the case history from initial filing to its current status. While docket sheets differ somewhat in format, the basic information contained on a docket sheet is consistent from court to court.

As noted earlier in the state court section, all docket sheets contain—

- Name of court, including location (division) and the judge assigned;
- Case number and case name;
- Names of all plaintiffs and defendants/debtors;
- Names and addresses of attorneys for the plaintiff or debtor;
- Nature and cause (e.g., U.S. civil statute) of action;
- Listing of documents filed in the case, including docket entry number, the date and a short description (e.g., 12-2-92, #1, Complaint).

Assignment of Cases and Computerization

Traditionally, cases were assigned within a district by county. Although this is still true in most states, the introduction of computer systems to track dockets has led to a more flexible approach to case assignment, as is the case in Minnesota and Connecticut. Rather than blindly assigning all cases from a county to one judge, their districts are using random numbers and other logical methods to balance caseloads among their judges.

This trend may appear to confuse the case search process. Actually, the only problem the searcher may face is to figure out where the case records themselves are located. Finding cases has become significantly easier with the wide availability of PACER and Case Management/Electronic Case Filings at remote access, Internet, and onsite terminals in each court location with the same district-wide information base.

Computerized Indexes are Available

Computerized courts generally index each case record by the names of some or all the parties to the case — the plaintiffs and defendants (debtors and creditors in Bankruptcy Court) as well as by case number. Therefore, when you search by name you will first receive a listing of all cases in which the name appears, both as plaintiff and defendant.

Electronic Access to Federal Courts

Numerous programs have been developed for electronic access to Federal Court records. Over the years the Administrative Office of the United States Courts in Washington, DC has developed three innovative public access programs: VCIS, PACER, and most recently the Case Management/ Electronic Case Files (CM/ECF) project. The most useful program for online searching is now CM/ECF. VCIS access is via telephone is being phased out; PACER via Internet or remote dial-up is being replaced by CM/ECF.

Case Management/Electronic Case Files (CM/ECF)

CM/ECF is the new case management system for the Federal Judiciary for all bankruptcy, district and appellate courts. CM/ECF allows courts to accept filings and provide access to filed documents over the Internet. CM/CDF replaced aging electronic docketing and case management systems in all federal courts in 2005. Nearly every federal court is currently CM/ECF operational as we go to press, and the remaining courts are in the process of implementing CM/ECF. It is important to note that when you search ECF, you may be ONLY searching cases that have been filed electronically. A case may not have been filed electronically through CM/ECF, so you must still conduct a search using PACER (where PACER is still operational) if you want to know if a case exists.

One important feature of this system is their National Locator, known as the United States Party Index. This is a name search, used to locate the specific court where records are available.

To sign-up for CM/ECF access, do so through the court. For further information about CM/ECF visit http://pacer.psc.uscourts.gov/cmecf/index.html. Most courts offer tutorials on how to use CM/ECF.

PACER

PACER, the acronym for **P**ublic **A**ccess to **E**lectronic **C**ourt **R**ecords, provides docket information online for open cases at **all U.S. Bankruptcy courts** and **most U.S. District courts**. Currently most courts are available on the Internet. A few systems can be dialed directly using communication software (such as ProComm Plus, pcAnywhere, or Hyperterminal) and a modem. Cases for the U.S. Court of Federal Claims are also available.

Each court maintains its own databases with case information. Because PACER and CM/ECF database systems are maintained within each court, each jurisdiction will have a different URL or modem number. Accessing and querying information from each service is comparable; however, the format and content of information provided may differ slightly.

Sign-up and technical support is handled at the PACER Service Center in San Antonio, Texas; phone 800-676-6856. You can sign up for all or multiple districts at once. In many judicial districts, when you sign up for PACER access, you will receive a PACER Primer that has been customized for each district. The primer contains a summary of how to access PACER, how to select cases, how to read case numbers and docket sheets, some searching tips, who to call for problem resolution, and district specific program variations.

A problem with PACER is that each court determines when records will be purged and how records will be indexed, leaving you to guess how a name is spelled or abbreviated and how much information about closed cases your search will uncover. A PACER search for anything but open cases **cannot** take the place of a full seven-year search of the federal court records available by written request from the court itself or through a local document retrieval company. Many districts report that they have closed records back a number of years, but at the same time indicate they purge docket items every six months.

As previously mentioned, another problem is the lack of identifiers. Most federal courts do not show the DOB on records available to the public. Thus, if a record searcher has a common name and gets one or more hits, each individual case file may need to be reviewed to determine if the case belongs to the subject in mind.

An excellent FAQ on PACER is found at http://pacer.psc.uscourts.gov/faq.html.

Before Accessing PACER or CM/ECF, Search the "National" U.S. Party/Case Index

The U.S. Party/Case Index is a national index for U.S. District, Bankruptcy, and Appellate courts. A small subset of information from each case will be transferred to the U.S. Party/Case Index each night. The system serves as a locator index for PACER. You may conduct nationwide searches to determine whether or not a party is involved in federal litigation. For detailed information on cases found while searching the U.S. Party/Case Index, you will need to visit the PACER or CM/ECF site for the particular jurisdiction where the case is located. The Case Number field in the output will be a direct link to the full case information on the court's computers, whether the court is running the Internet version of PACER or CM/ECF.

Access the U.S. Party/Case Index by via the Internet at http://pacer.uspci.uscourts.gov.

Miscellaneous Online Systems

Some courts have developed their own online systems. For example, the Southern District Court of New York offers CourtWeb, which provides information to the public on selected recent rulings of those judges who have elected to make information available in electronic form.

VCIS

Another access system is **VCIS** (Voice Case Information System). At one time, nearly all of the U.S. Bankruptcy Court judicial districts provide **VCIS**, a means of accessing information regarding open bankruptcy cases by merely using a touch-tone telephone. The advantage? There is no charge. Individual names are entered last name first with as much of the first name as you wish to include. For example, Carl R. Ernst could be entered as ERNSTC or ERNSTCARL. Do not enter the middle initial. Business names are entered as they are written, without blanks. VCIS, like the RACER System, is being replaced by newer technology.

Federal Courts Searching Hints

- VCIS should *only* be used to locate information about open cases. Do not attempt to use VCIS as a substitute for a PACER search.

- This publication includes the counties of jurisdiction for each court and is a good starting point for determining where case records may be found.

- Searchers need to be sure that the Court's case index includes all cases, open and closed, for that particular period, especially important if using CM/ECF. Be aware that some courts purge older, closed cases after a period of time, making a PACER search incomplete. Purge times vary from court to court and state to state.

- Experience shows that court personnel are typically not aware of — nor concerned about — the types of searches performed by readers of this publication. Court personnel often focus on only open cases, whereas a searcher may want to know as much about closed cases as open ones. Thus, court personnel are sometimes fuzzy in answering questions about how far back case records go on PACER, and whether closed cases have been purged. If you are looking for cases older than a year or two, there is no substitute for a real, onsite search performed by the court itself or by a local search expert (if that court allows full access to its indexes).

- Some courts may be more willing than others to give out information by telephone. This is because most courts have converted from the old card index system to fully computerized indexes that are easily accessible while on the phone.

An Important Issue Regarding Federal Court Records–

As mentioned, the U.S. District Courts are quite cumbersome to search because they do not offer the public the ability to use personal identifier when searching. Thus, if you search for records on a common name like John Smith, you will need to pull and view every file to determine if that particular John Smith is the subject of your search. As a result, many employers do not bother searching federal criminal records because the costs are so high.

The fact that 8% of all criminal records (per the U.S. Department of Justice) are found at the federal court level leaves a gapping hole to those interested in true due diligence as part of their record searching criteria. Interestingly, attempts by professional organizations, such as the National Association of Professional Background Screeners (NAPBS), to communicate to the feds about this oversight have been largely ignored.

Federal Records Centers and The National Archives

After a federal case is closed, the documents are held by Federal Courts themselves for a number of years, then stored at a designated Federal Records Center (FRC). After 20 to 30 years, the records are then transferred from the FRC to the regional archives offices of the National Archives and Records Administration (NARA). The length of time between a case being closed and its being moved to an FRC varies widely by district. Each court has its own transfer cycle and determines access procedures to its case records, even after they have been sent to the FRC.

When case records are sent to an FRC, the boxes of records are assigned accession, location and box numbers. These numbers, which are called case locator information, **must be obtained from the originating court in order to retrieve documents from the FRC.** Some courts will provide such information over the telephone, but others require a written request. This information is now available on PACER in certain judicial districts. The Federal Records Center for each state is listed as follows–

State	Circuit	Appeals Court	Federal Records Center
AK	9	San Francisco, CA	Anchorage (Some records are in temporary storage in Seattle)
AL	11	Atlanta, GA	Atlanta
AR	8	St. Louis, MO	Fort Worth
AZ	9	San Francisco, CA	Los Angeles
CA	9	San Francisco, CA	Los Angeles (Central & Southern CA) San Francisco (Eastern & Northern CA)
CO	10	Denver, CO	Denver
CT	2	New York, NY	Boston
DC		Washington, DC	Washington, DC
DE	3	Philadelphia, PA	Philadelphia
FL	11	Atlanta, GA	Atlanta
GA	11	Atlanta, GA	Atlanta
GU	9	San Francisco, CA	San Francisco
HI	9	San Francisco, CA	San Francisco
IA	8	St. Louis, MO	Kansas City, MO

State	Circuit	Appeals Court	Federal Records Center
ID	9	San Francisco, CA	Seattle
IL	7	Chicago, IL	Chicago
IN	7	Chicago, IL	Chicago
KS	10	Denver, CO	Kansas City, MO
KY	6	Cincinnati, OH	Atlanta
LA	5	New Orleans, LA	Fort Worth
MA	1	Boston, MA	Boston
MD	4	Richmond, VA	Philadelphia
ME	1	Boston, MA	Boston
MI	6	Cincinnati, OH	Chicago
MN	8	St. Louis, MO	Chicago
MO	8	St. Louis, MO	Kansas City, MO
MS	5	New Orleans, LA	Atlanta
MT	9	San Francisco, CA	Denver
NC	4	Richmond, VA	Atlanta
ND	8	St. Louis, MO	Denver
NE	8	St. Louis, MO	Kansas City, MO
NH	1	Boston, MA	Boston
NJ	3	Philadelphia, PA	New York
NM	10	Denver, CO	Denver
NV	9	San Francisco, CA	Los Angeles (Clark County, NV) San Francisco (Other NV counties)
NY	2	New York, NY	New York
OH	6	Cincinnati, OH	Chicago; Dayton has some bankruptcy
OK	10	Denver, CO	Fort Worth
OR	9	San Francisco, CA	Seattle

State	Circuit	Appeals Court	Federal Records Center
PA	3	Philadelphia, PA	Philadelphia
PR	1	Boston, MA	New York
RI	1	Boston, MA	Boston
SC	4	Richmond, VA	Atlanta
SD	8	St. Louis, MO	Denver
TN	6	Cincinnati, OH	Atlanta
TX	5	New Orleans, LA	Fort Worth
UT	10	Denver, CO	Denver
VA	4	Richmond, VA	Philadelphia
VI	3	Philadelphia, PA	New York
VT	2	New York, NY	Boston
WA	9	San Francisco, CA	Seattle
WI	7	Chicago, IL	Chicago
WV	4	Richmond, VA	Philadelphia
WY	10	Denver, CO	Denver

Notes to the Chart

GU is Guam, PR is Puerto Rico, and VI is the Virgin Islands.

According to some odd logic, the following Federal Records Centers are not located in the city named above, but are actually somewhere else. Below are the exceptions:

> Atlanta—in East Point, GA
>
> Boston—in Waltham, MA
>
> Los Angeles—in Laguna Niguel, CA
>
> New York—in Bayonne, NJ
>
> San Francisco—in San Bruno, CA

Searching Other Federal Records Online

EDGAR

EDGAR – the **E**lectronic **D**ata **G**athering **A**nalysis and **R**etrieval system – was established by the U.S. Securities and Exchange Commission (SEC) to allow companies to make required filing to the SEC by direct transmission. As of May 6, 1996, all public domestic companies are required to make their filings on EDGAR, except for filings made to the Commission's regional offices and those filings made on paper due to a hardship exemption.

EDGAR is an extensive repository of U.S. corporation information and it is available online.

What Information is Available on EDGAR?

Companies must file the following reports with the SEC:

- 10-K – an annual financial report that includes audited year-end financial statements.
- 10-Q – a quarterly, un-audited report.
- 8K – a report detailing significant or unscheduled corporate changes or events.
- Securities offering, trading registrations, and the final prospectus.

The list above is not conclusive. There are other miscellaneous reports filed, including those dealing with security holdings by institutions and insiders. Access to these documents provides a wealth of information.

How to Access EDGAR Online

Search EDGAR at www.sec.gov/edgar/searchedgar/webusers.htm. Also, a number of private vendors offer access to EDGAR records. LexisNexis acts as the data wholesaler or distributor on behalf of the government. LexisNexis sells data to information retailers, including its own Nexis service.

Aviation Records

The Federal Aviation Association (FAA) is the U.S. government agency with the responsibility for all matters related to the safety of civil aviation. Among its functions the FAA provides the system that registers aircraft and the documents showing title or interest in aircraft. Their website, at www.faa.gov, is the ultimate source of aviation records, airports and facilities, safety regulations, and civil research and engineering.

The Aircraft Owners and Pilots Association is the largest organization of its kind with 340,000+ members. Their website is www.aopa.org and is an excellent source of information regarding the aviation industry. Another excellent source of aircraft information is *Jane's World Airlines* at www.janes.com.

Military Records

This topic is so broad that there can be a book written about it, and in fact there is! *The Armed Forces Locator Directory* from MIE Publishing (864- 595-0891) is an excellent source. The book, now in its 8th edition, covers every conceivable topic regarding military records. Their website www.militaryusa.com offers free access to some useful databases.

The Privacy Act of 1974 (5 U.S.C. 552a) and Department of Defense directives require a written request, signed and dated, to access military personnel records. For further details, visit the NPRC site listed below.

Military Internet Sources

There are a number of great internet sites that provide valuable information on obtaining military and military personnel records. The National Personnel Records Center (NPRC), maintained by the National Archives & Records Administration, is on the Internet at www.nara.gov/regional/mpr.html. The NPRC site is full of useful information and links. Other excellent sites include:

www.army.mil	The official site of the U.S. Army
www.af.mil	The official site of the U.S. Air Force
www.navy.mil	The official site of the U.S. Navy
www.usmc.mil	The official site of the U.S. Marine Corps
www.arng.army.mil	The official site of the Army National Guard
www.ang.af.mil	The official site of the Air National Guard
www.uscg.mil/USCG.shtm	The official site of the U.S. Coast Guard

Best U.S. Government Gateways...

by Alan Schlein

The remainder of this chapter was written and contributed by online pioneer and award winning journalist Alan M. Schlein, author of Find It Online.

We sincerely thank Alan for permitting the use of his material in Public Records Online. *Alan can be reached at his* www.deadlineonline.com. *Check out his website—it is a great source with lots of useful links!*

In the U.S., almost every federal government agency is online. There is a nationwide network of depository libraries, including the enormous resources of the National Archives (www.archives.gov), the twelve presidential libraries, and four national libraries – the Library of Congress, the National Agricultural Library, the National Library of Education, and the National Library of Medicine. There are almost 5000 government websites from more than forty-two U.S. departments and agencies.

Because there are so many government websites, in order to find the starting point for your research, you may need to turn to specialized, purpose-built websites called ***government gateways***, that organize and link government sites. Some gateways are simply collections of links. Others provide access to bulletin boards of specific government agencies so that you find and contact employees with specific knowledge. This "human guidance" is becoming increasingly important in light of the growing number of reports and publications that are no longer printed but simply posted online.

Best Government Gateways (listed alphabetically)

Documents Center
`www.lib.umich.edu/govdocs/index.html`

Documents Center is a clearinghouse for local, state, federal, foreign, and international government information. It is one of the more comprehensive online searching aids for all kinds of government information on the Internet. It is especially useful as a meta-site of meta-sites.

FedLaw
`www.thecre.com/fedlaw/default.htm`

Containing 1,600+ links to law-related information, FedLaw is an extremely broad resource for federal legal and regulatory research. It has very good topical and title indices that group web links into hundreds of subjects. It is operated by the General Services Administration (GSA).

Fedstats
`www.fedstats.gov`

A terrific collection of statistical sites from the federal government and a good central clearinghouse for other federal statistics sites.

FedWorld Information Network
`www.fedworld.gov`

FedWorld helps you search over thirty million U.S. government pages. It is a massive collection of 15,000 files and databases of government sites, including bulletin boards that can help you identify government employees with expertise in a broad range of subjects. A surprising number of these experts will take the time to discuss questions from the general public.

FirstGov
`www.firstgov.gov`

Responding to the need for a central clearinghouse of U.S. federal government sites, the U.S. government developed FirstGov and linked every federal agency to its site as well as every state government. It has an easy-to-use search tool, allowing you to specify if you want federal or state agencies and to easily locate business regulations and vital records. It also lets you look for federal government phone numbers and email addresses. This is an easy-to-use starting point, powered by the AlltheWeb search engine. Also, check out the FAQs of the U.S. government for questions and answers about the U.S. government (`www.faq.gov`).

Google's Uncle Sam
`www.google.com/unclesam`

Google's Uncle Sam site is a search engine geared to looking at U.S. government sites. It is an easy-to-use tool if you know what you are looking for.

Healthfinder
`www.healthfinder.gov`

This is a great starting point for health-related government information. See the Health and Medicine Information Tools sidebar in Chapter 5, Specialized Tools, for more health sites.

InfoMine: Scholarly Internet Resource Collections

http://infomine.ucr.edu

InfoMine provides collections of scholarly internet resources, best for academics. It is one of the best academic resources anywhere, from the librarians at the University of California Riverside. InfoMine's Government Information section is easily searchable by subject. It has detailed headings and its resource listings are very specific. Since it is run by a university, some of its references are limited to student use only.

SearchGov.com

www.searchgov.com

A private company that has an effective search for U.S. government sites.

Speech & Transcript Center

www.freepint.com/gary/speech.htm

This site links directly to websites containing transcripts of speeches. Pulled together by former George Washington University reference librarian and *Invisible Web* author Gary Price, it encompasses government resources, business leaders, and real audio. A large section is devoted to U.S. and international government speech transcripts including Congressional hearings, experts' testimony, and transcripts.

U.S. Federal Government Agencies Directory

www.lib.lsu.edu/gov/fedgov.html

This directory of federal agencies is maintained by Louisiana State Univ. It links to hundreds of federal government internet sites. It is divided by branch and agency and is very thorough, but focus on your target because it is easy to lose your way or become overwhelmed en route.

Best U.S. Government Websites

by Alan Schlein

U.S. tax dollars are put to good and visible use here. A few of the government's web pages are rated as excellent. Some can be used in lieu of commercial tools but only if you have the time to invest.

A few of the top government sites – the Census and the Securities and Exchange Commission – are models of content and presentation. They are very deep, very thorough, and easy to use. If only the rest of the federal government would follow suit. Unfortunately, the best of the federal government is just that: the best. Not all agencies maintain such detailed and relevant resources.

Following are the crown jewels of the government's collection, in ranked order:

U.S. Census Bureau
`www.census.gov`

Without question, this is the U.S. government's top site. It is saturated with information and census publications – at times overwhelmingly so – but worth every minute of your time. A few hours spent here is a worthwhile investment for almost anyone seeking to background a community, learn about business, or find any kind of demographic information. You can search several ways: alphabetically by subject, by word, by location, and by geographic map. The only problem is the sheer volume of data.

One feature, the Thematic Mapping System, allows users to extract data from Census CD-ROMs and display them in maps by state or county. You can create maps on all kinds of subjects – for examples, tracking violent crime or comparing farm income. The site also features the Statistical Abstract of the U.S. with a searchable index at `www.census.gov/statab/www/stateabs.html`

The potential uses of census data are infinite. Marketers use it to find community information. Reporters search out trends by block, neighborhood or region. Educators conduct research. Businesses evaluate new business prospects. Genealogists trace family trees – though full census data is not available for seventy-two years from the date the census is taken. You can even use it to identify ideal communities in which to raise a family. Jennifer LaFleur, now at *The Dallas Morning News* did a story while at *The San Jose Mercury News* using the census site to find eligible bachelors in specific areas of San Jose.

Additional census resources include—

U.S. Census Data Access Tools

http://www.census.gov/main/www/access.html

This site provides a myriad of detailed census data and software that may be downloaded.

State and County QuickFacts

http://quickfacts.census.gov/qfd/

At all its levels, this site has very easy-to-use census information.

Census FactFinder

http://factfinder.census.gov

An easy way to find quickie facts from within the Census' huge website. This is an excellent and easy to use site. Start here when looking for Census documents, since it has a search capability.

Census Industry Statistics

www.census.gov/main/www/industries.html

Industry-by-industry statistics.

And one other census-related site that is superb is the University of Virginia's Fisher Library's historical census data browser, going all the way back to 1790. It can be found at http://fisher.lib.virginia.edu/collections/stats/histcensus/

U.S. Securities and Exchange Commission (SEC)

www.sec.gov

Only the Census site is better than the SEC site, which is a first-rate, must-stop place for information shopping on U.S. companies. Its EDGAR database search site (www.sec.gov/edaux/searches.htm) is easy to use and provides access to documents that companies and corporations are required to file under regulatory laws.

The SEC site is a great starting point for information about specific companies and industry trends. The SEC requires all publicly-held corporations and some large privately-held corporations to disclose detailed financial information about their activities, plans, holdings, executives' salaries and stakes, legal problems and so forth. For more details, see Chapter 9, Business Tools.

Library of Congress (LOC)

www.loc.gov

This site is an extraordinary collection of documents. Thomas, the Library's Congressional online center site (http://thomas.loc.gov/home/) provides an exhaustive collection of congressional documents, including bill summaries, voting records, and the full Congressional Record, which is the official record of Congressional action. This LOC site also links to many international, federal, state, and local government sites. You can also access the library's more than five million records online, some versions in full-text and some in abstract form. Though the library's entire 121 million item collection is not yet available online, the amount online increases daily. In addition to books and papers, it includes an extensive images collection ranging from Frank Lloyd Wright's designs to the Dead Sea Scrolls to the world's largest online collection of baseball cards. The Library of Congress also has a terrific collection of international data on its website at `www.loc.gov/rr/international/portals.html`

U.S. Government Printing Office Home Page (GPO)
`www.access.gpo.gov/`

The GPO is the federal government's primary information printer and distributor. All federally funded information from every agency is sent here, which makes the GPO's holdings priceless. Luckily, the GPO site is well-constructed and easy to use. For example, it has the full text of the *Federal Register*, which lists all federal regulations and proposals, and full-text access to the *Congressional Record*. The GPO also produces an online version of the *Congressional Directory*, providing details on every congressional district, profiles of members, staff profiles, maps of every district and historical documents about Congress. This site will expand exponentially over the next few years, as an increased number of materials go out of print and online. GPO Access also allows you to electronically retrieve much of the bureaucratic paper in Washington, electronically, from the Government Printing Office including searching more than seventy databases and indices. If you need some help finding things, use the topic-specific finder at this site.

National Technical Information Service (NTIS)
`www.ntis.gov`

The best place to find federal government reports related to technology and science, NTIS is the nation's clearinghouse for unclassified technical reports of government-sponsored research. NTIS collects, indexes, abstracts, and sells U.S. and foreign research – mostly in science, technology, behavioral, and social science data.

IGnet
`www.ignet.gov`

This is a truly marvelous collection of reports and information from the Inspector Generals of about sixty federal agency departments. They find waste and abuse within government agencies. It is well worth checking when starting research on government-related matters.

General Accounting Office GAO Reports
`www.gao.gov/decisions/decision.htm`

The Comptroller General Opinions from the last sixty days are posted on this GAO website. These reports and opinions are excellent references. For historical opinions back to 1995, go online to `www.gpoaccess.gov/gaodecisions/index.html`

DefenseLINK – U.S. Department of Defense (DOD)
www.defenselink.mil

This is the brand-name site for Pentagon-related information. There is a tremendous amount of data here – categorized by branch of service – including U.S. troop deployments worldwide. To the Pentagon's credit, they have made this a very easy site to use.

Defense Technical Information Center (DTIC)
www.dtic.mil

The DTIC site is loaded with links and defense information – everything from contractors to weapon systems. It even includes de-classified information about the Gulf War. It is the best place to start for defense information. You can even find a list of all military-related contracts, including beneficiary communities and the kinds of contracts awarded. The only problem with the site is there is no search engine to make it easy to find information.

Bureau of Transportation Statistics
www.bts.gov

The U.S. Department of Transportation's enormous collection of information about every facet of transportation. There is a lot of valuable material here including the Transportation Statistics Annual Report. It also holds financial data for airlines and searchable databases containing information about fatal accidents and on-time statistics for airlines, which can be narrowed to your local airport.

National Archives and Records Administration
www.archives.gov/index.html

A breathtaking collection of research online, for example the National Archives has descriptions of more than 170,000 documents related to the Kennedy assassination. It also contains a world-class database holding descriptions of more than 95,000 records held by the Still Picture and Motion Picture, Sound and Video Branches. This site also links to the twelve Presidential Archives with their records of every person ever mentioned in Executive Branch correspondence. You can view an image of the original document. The Archives Research Center Online has great collections of family history/genealogy research and veterans' service records.

FedWorld.gov
www.fedworld.gov

This thorough government clearinghouse site, run by the Commerce Department's National Technical Information Service, offers access to FirstGov, the U.S. Government's comprehensive
site, but also allows you to search government publications, U.S. Supreme Court decisions, and helps you find government jobs.

Federal Consumer Information Center National Contact Center

`www.info.gov`

> While this is largely a telephone service that gets more than a million calls a year, this website tries to provide a way through the maze of federal agencies. It includes a clearinghouse of phone numbers for all federal agencies, state, and local government sites.

SciTechResources.gov

`www.scitechresources.gov`

> This is a tremendous directory of about 700 science and technology resources on U.S. government sites from the U.S. Department of Commerce, National Technical Information Service.

Department of Homeland Security

`http://www.whitehouse.gov/infocus/homeland/index.html`

> While the U.S. Government has made the Department of Homeland Security a separate agency, it maintains the website under the White House's auspices. As a result, it has good information, but is, like the White House site, more about public relations for the current president and his staff than it is about information. Nonetheless, you can find useful information about the current threat level and information about what U.S. state and local governments are doing on homeland security.

Bureau of National Affairs, The

`www.bna.com`

> An expensive but useful group of topic-focused newsletters providing details on U.S. government action at different federal agencies. Titles include *The Daily Labor Report, Bankruptcy Law Daily*, and *The Biotech Watch*. This private company has hundreds of newsletters you will not find elsewhere.

Tips on Using Public Record Vendors

Hiring Someone to Obtain the Record

There are five main categories of public record professionals: distributors; gateway; search firms and local document retrievers; investigative firms; and verification-screening firms.

Distributors (Proprietary Database Vendors)

These vendors (also known as Primary Distributors) are automated public record firms who combine public sources of bulk data and/or online access to develop their own database product(s). They collect or buy public record information from government repositories and reformat the information in some useful way. They may also purchase or license records from other information vendors, like the phone companies. In the past they purchased the "credit header" information from the credit bureaus, but this is no longer a standard practice. There are approximately 200 public record vendors in this category that collect and warehouse information (not counting marketing companies). Most of these entities are either vertical (multiple types of info collected on a local or regional basis) or horizontal (one type of info collected on a national basis) in nature. Less than 10% are large entities that are both vertical and horizontal with massive amount of data (like ChoicePoint). When a database vendor sells the data, the **vendor is bound by the same disclosure laws attached to the government repository data.** This can range from zero (recorded documents, level three sexual predators, etc.) to severe (voter registration, criminal court case records, etc.).

Gateways

Gateways are companies that provide automated electronic gateway to Proprietary Database Vendors or to government agencies online systems. Gateways do not warehouse records. Gateways thus provide "one-stop shopping" for multiple geographic areas and/or categories of information. Gateways are the companies that are most evident on the Internet as they advertise access to records for many different purposes.

Companies can be *both* Primary Distributors and Gateways. For example, a number of online database companies are both primary distributors of corporate information and also gateways to real estate information from other Primary Distributors.

Search Firms

Search firms are companies that furnish public record search and document retrieval services using online services and/or through a network of specialists, including their own employees or correspondents (see Retrievers below). Search firms rely on, primary distributors and/or networks of retrievers, or they may go direct to the government agency. They combine online proficiency with document retrieval expertise. Search firms may focus either on one geographic region — like New England — or on one specific type of public record information — like criminal records.

A very common sub-category of search firms is known as **Local Document Retrievers**. Retrievers search specific requested categories of public records usually in order to obtain documentation for legal compliance (e.g., incorporations), for lending, and for litigation. They do not usually review or interpret the results or issue reports in the sense that investigators do, but rather return documents with the results of searches. They tend to be localized, but there are companies that offer a national network of retrievers and/or correspondents. The retriever or his/her personnel goes directly to the agency to look up the information. A retriever may be relied upon for strong knowledge in a local area, whereas a search generalist has a breadth of knowledge and experience in a wider geographic range. There are thousands of entities that can be classified as search firms in the U.S., including approximately 3,000 local document retrievers.

The 775+ members of the **Public Record Retriever Network (PRRN)** can be found, by state and counties served, at www.brbpub.com/PRRN. This organization has set industry standards for the retrieval of public record documents and operates under a Code of Professional Conduct. Using one of these record retrievers is an excellent way to access records in those jurisdictions that do not offer online access.

Verification Firms
(Pre-employment Screeners, Tenant Screeners, MVR Vendors)

Verification firms provide services to employers and businesses when the subject has given consent. In this category are pre-employment screening firms and tenant screening firms (both governed by the Fair Credit Reporting Act - FCRA) and motor vehicle record vendors (governed by the Drivers Privacy Protection Act – DPPA). Since these entities usually only perform their services for clients who have specifically received consent from the subjects, they do not warehouse or collect data to be resold. Many times the service provided by a pre-employment screening company is called a background screen or a background report. Their service should not be confused with an investigation as provided by private investigators (see below) or with search firms with an Internet presences that advertise their services for background checks. There are at least 800 pre-employment screening firms in the U.S., not counting many private investigators that may also offer that service when asked. After the FCRA was passed, many, many PIs ceased doing employment screening.

Private Investigation Firms

Investigators use public records as tools rather than as ends in themselves, in order to create an overall, comprehensive "picture" of an individual or company for a particular purpose. They interpret the information they have gathered in order to identify further investigation tracks. They summarize their results in a report compiled from all the sources used. In addition, an investigator may be licensed and may perform the types of services traditionally thought of as detective work, such as surveillance. In many instances, a private investigator doing an investigation and does not have the consent of the subject.

Many investigators also act as search firms or record retrievers and provide search results to other investigators. Some investigators offer pre-employment screening per the FCRA.

Other Vendors of Note

There are two other types of firm worthy of mention that occasionally utilize public records. The Association of Independent Information Professionals (AIIP), at www.aiip.org, has over 700 experienced professional information specialist members from 21 countries. They refer to themselves as Information Brokers (IBS). They gather information that will help their clients make informed business decisions. Their work is usually done on a custom basis with each project being unique. IBs are extremely knowledgeable in online research of full text databases and most specialize in a particular subject area, such as patent searching or competitive intelligence.

A similar organization is the Society of Competitive Intelligence Professionals (SCIP) whose home page is www.scip.org. Per their web "...SCIP provides education and networking opportunities for business professionals working in the rapidly growing field of competitive intelligence (the legal and ethical collection and analysis of information regarding the capabilities, vulnerabilities, and intentions of business competitors)."

Which Type of Vendor is Right for You?

With all the variations of vendors and the categories of information, the obvious question is; "How do I find the right vendor to go to for the public record information I need?" Before you start calling every interesting online vendor that catches your eye, you need to narrow your search to the **type** of vendor for your needs. To do this, ask yourself the following questions—

What is the Frequency of Usage?

If you have on-going, recurring requests for a particular type of information, it is probably best to choose a different vendor then if you have infrequent requests. Setting up an account with a primary distributor, such as LEXIS or Westlaw will give you an inexpensive per search fee, but the monthly minimum requirements will be prohibitive to the casual requester, who would be better off finding a vendor who accesses or is a gateway to one of these vendors.

What is the Complexity of the Search?

The importance of hiring a vendor who understands and can interpret the information in the final format increases with the complexity of the search. Pulling a corporation record in Maryland is not difficult, but doing an online criminal record search in Maryland, when only a portion of the felony records are online, is not so easy.

Thus, part of the answer to determining which vendor or type of vendor to use is to become conversant with what is (and is not) available from government agencies. Without knowing what is available (and what restrictions apply), you cannot guide the search process effectively. Once you are comfortable knowing the kinds of information available in the public record, you are in a position to find the best method to access needed information.

What are the Geographic Boundaries of the Search?

A search of local records close to you may require little assistance, but a search of records nationally or in a state 2,000 miles away will require seeking a vendor who covers the area you need to search. Many national primary distributors and gateways combine various local and state databases into one large comprehensive system available for searching. However, if your record searching is narrowed by a region or locality, then an online source that specializes in a specific geographic region (like Superior Information Services in NJ) may be an alternative to a national vendor. Keep in mind that many national firms allow you to order a search online, even though results cannot be delivered immediately and some hands-on local searching is required.

Of course, you may want to use the government agency online system, if available, for the kind of information you need.

10 Questions to Ask a Public Records Vendor

(Or a Vendor Who Uses Online Sources)

The following discussion focuses specifically on automated sources of information because many valuable types of public records have been entered into a computer and, therefore, require a computer search to obtain reliable results. The original version of the text to follow was written by **Mr. Leroy Cook.** Mr. Cook is the founder and Director of ION and The Investigators Anywhere Resource Line (800-338-3463, http://ioninc.com). Mr. Cook has graciously allowed us to edit the article and reprint it for our readers.

1. Where does he or she get the information?

You may feel awkward asking a vendor where he or she obtained the information you are purchasing. The fake Rolex watch is a reminder that even buying physical things based on looks alone — without knowing where they come from — is dangerous.

Reliable information vendors *will* provide verification material such as the name of the database or service accessed, when it was last updated, and how complete it is.

It is important that you know the gathering process in order to better judge the reliability of the information being purchased. There *are* certain investigative sources that a vendor will not be willing to disclose to you. However, that type of source should not be confused with the information that is being sold item by item. Information technology has changed so rapidly that some information vendors may still confuse "items of information" with "investigative reports." Items of information sold as units are *not* investigative reports. The professional reputation of an information vendor is a guarantee of sorts. Still, because information as a commodity is so new, there is little in the way of an implied warranty of fitness.

2. How long does it take for the new information or changes to get into the system?

Any answer *except* a clear, concise date and time or the vendor's personal knowledge of an ongoing system's methods of maintaining information currency is a reason to keep probing. In view of the preceding question, this one might seem repetitive, but it *really* is a different issue. Microfiche or a database of records may have been updated last week at a courthouse or a DMV, but the department's computer section may also be working with a three-month backlog. In this case, a critical incident occurring one month ago would *not* show up in the information updated last week. The importance of timeliness is a variable to be determined by you, but to be truly informed you need to know how "fresh" the information is. Ideally, the mechanism by which you purchase items of information *should* include an update or statement of accuracy — as a part of the reply — *without* having to ask.

3. What are the searchable fields? Which fields are mandatory?

If your knowledge of "fields" and "records" is limited to the places where cattle graze and those flat, round things that play music, you *could* have a problem telling a good database from a bad one. An MVR vendor, for example, should be able to tell you that a subject's middle initial is critical when pulling an Arizona driving record. You don't have to become a programmer to use a computer and you needn't know a database management language to benefit from databases, *but* it is very helpful to understand how databases are constructed and (*at the least*) what fields, records, and indexing procedures are used.

As a general rule, the computerized, public-record information world is not standardized from county to county or from state to state; in the same way, there is little standardization within or between information vendors. Look at the system documentation from the vendor. The manual should include this sort of information.

4. How much latitude is there for error in a data request? (misspellings or inappropriate punctuation)

If the vendor's requirements for search data appear to be concise and meticulous, then you're probably on the right track. Some computer systems will tell (or "flag") an operator when they make a mistake such as omitting important punctuation or using an unnecessary comma. Other systems allow you to make inquiries by whatever means or in whatever format you like — and then tell you the requested information has *not* been found. In this instance, the desired information may *actually* be there, but the computer didn't understand the question because of the way in which it was asked. It is easy to misinterpret "no record found" as "there is no record." Please take note that the meanings of these two phrases are quite different.

5. What method is used to place the information in the repository and what error control or edit process is used?

In some databases, information may be scanned in or may be entered by a single operator as it is received and, in others, information may be entered *twice* to allow the computer to catch input errors by searching for non-duplicate entries. You don't have to know *everything* about all the options, but the vendor selling information in quantity *should*.

6. How many different databases or sources does the vendor access and how often?

The chance of obtaining an accurate search of a database increases with the frequency of access and the vendor's/searcher's level of knowledge. If he or she only makes inquiries once a month — and the results are important — you may need to find someone who sells data at higher volume. The point here is that it is better to find someone who specializes in the type of information you are seeking than it is to utilize a vendor who *can* get the information, but actually specializes in another type of data.

7. Does the price include assistance in interpreting the data received?

A report that includes coding and ambiguous abbreviations may look impressive in your file, but may not be too meaningful. For all reports, except those you deal with regularly, interpretation assistance can be *very* important. Some information vendors offer searches for information they really don't know much about through sources that they only use occasionally. Professional pride sometimes prohibits them from disclosing their limitations — until *you* ask the right questions.

8. Do vendors "keep track" of requesters and the information they seek (usage records)?

This may not seem like a serious concern when you are requesting information you're legally entitled to; however, there *is* a possibility that your usage records could be made available to a competitor. Most probably, the information itself is *already* being (or will be) sold to someone else, but you may not necessarily want *everyone* to know what you are requesting and how often. If the vendor keeps records of who-asks-what, the confidentiality of that information should be addressed in your agreement with the vendor.

9. Will the subject of the inquiry be notified of the request?

If your inquiry is sub rosa or if the subject's discovery of the search could lead to embarrassment, double check! There are laws that mandate the notification of subjects when certain types of inquiries are made into their files. If notification is required, the way it is accomplished could be critical.

10. Is the turnaround time and cost of the search made clear at the outset?

You should be crystal clear about what you expect and/or need; the vendor should be succinct when conveying exactly what will be provided and how much it will cost. Failure to address these issues can lead to disputes and hard feelings.

These are excellent questions and concepts to keep in mind when searching for the right public record vendor to meet your needs.

Take Caution When Using Private Databases

by Lester S. Rosen

The following copyrighted text appears in Chapter 12 of The Safe Hiring Manual, *written by Lester R. Rosen and published by Facts On Demand Press (BRB Publications, Inc). We sincerely thank Mr. Rosen for allowing us to reprint in this publication.*

Perhaps the newest tool being touted to employers is a "national database search" of criminal records. There are a number of vendors who advertise they have or have access to a "national database of criminal record information." These services typically talk about having over a 120 million records from 38 or more states. Unfortunately, the form of advertising can create an impression in the minds of employers that they are getting the real thing—a true record of the nation's criminal records. Nothing could be further from the truth.

These databases are compiled from a number of various state and county sources. There are a number of reasons that database information may not be accurate or complete. It is critical to understand that these multi-state database searches represent a research tool only, and under no circumstances are they a substitute for a hands-on search at the county level.

The bottom line is that just because a person's name appears in one of these databases, it does not mean that the subject is a criminal. On the other hand, if a person's name does not appear, this likewise should not be taken as conclusive the person is not a criminal. An employer should not develop a false sense of security because an applicant passed a database search without understanding that there are numerous circumstances as described below that even a person with a serious criminal record may not show up.

Our discussion of these databases will focus on two areas—VALUE and LIMITATIONS.

Value

The value of using these database searches is that they cover a much larger geographical area then traditional county-level searches. By casting a much wider net then a single county level search, a researcher may pick-up information that would be missed. The firms that sell database information can show test names of subjects that were "cleared" by a traditional county search, but where criminal records were found using a search of their database.

In fact, it could be argued that failure to utilize such a database demonstrates a failure to exercise due diligence given the widespread availability and low price.

So overall, the best use of these databases is as secondary research tool, or lead "generator" that tells a researcher where else to look.

Limitations

The data that is complied comes from three sources: court records, correctional records, and from a small number of counties that contribute data. The limitations of searching a private database are the inherent issues revolving about completeness, name variations, timeliness, and legal compliance.

Completeness Issues

The various databases that vendors purchase or collect may not be the equivalent of a true all-encompassing multi-state database. First, the databases purchased for resale or accessed at a gateway may not contain complete records from all jurisdictions. For example, not all unified court systems contain records from all counties. Second, for reporting purposes, the records that are actually reported may be incomplete or lack sufficient detail about the offense or the subject. Third, some databases contain only felonies or contain only offenses where a state corrections unit was involved. Fourth, the database may not carry subsequent information or some other matter that could render the database not reportable under the FCRA, or result in some violation of state law concerning the use of criminal records.

The result is a crazy quilt patchwork of data from various sources, with widely different reliability.

Name Variation Issues

An electronic search of a vendor's database may not be able to recognize variations in a subject name, which a person may potentially notice if manually looking at the index. The applicant may have been arrested under a different first name or some variation of first and middle name. A female applicant may have a record under a previous name. Some database vendors have attempted to resolve this problem with a wild card first name search (i.e. instead of Robert, the search use Rob* so that any variations of ROB will come up). However, there are still too many different first and middle name variations. There is also the chance of name confusion for applicants who have a different naming convention where a combination of mother and father's name is used. In addition, some vendors require the use of date of birth in order to prevent too many records from being returned. If an applicant used a different date of birth with the police or courts, this can also cause errors.

Timeliness Issues

There is also the possibility that the records in a vendor's database are stale to some extent. With very slim exceptions, these records are normally updated monthly, at best. Even after a vendor receives new data, there can be lag time before the new data is downloaded into the vendor database. As a result, generally the most current offenses are the ones less likely to come up in a database search.

Legal Compliance Issues

When there is a hit, an employer must be concerned about legal compliance. If the employer performed the search in-house, an employer must have an understanding of the proper use of criminal records in that state. If the employer acts on the results at face value without any additional research, the employer could potentially be sued by an applicant, if the record was not about that applicant.

If a screening firm locates a criminal hit, the screening firm has an obligation under the FCRA Section 613 (a)(2) to send researchers to the court and to pull the actual court records. This section requires that whenever a background-screening firm reports a matter of public record, then the background firm must—

maintain strict procedures designed to insure that whenever public record information which is likely to have an adverse effect on a consumer's ability to obtain employment is reported it is complete and up to date. For purposes of this paragraph, items of public record relating to arrests, indictments, convictions, suits, tax liens, and outstanding judgments shall be considered up to date if the current public record status of the item at the time of the report is reported.

Additional information about the FCRA and databases is covered in Chapters 6 and 10.

For a detailed discussion about the legal uses of a database, see an article co-authored by the author of this book and Carl Ernst (a national expert on the FCRA) called, "National" Criminal History Databases, at www.brbpub.com/CriminalHistoryDB.pdf.

Conclusion About Private Databases

Criminal record vendors should make clear, and employers need to understand, the exact nature and limitations of the data they are accessing. These private database searches are ancillary and can be very useful, but proceed with caution. In other words, it cannot be assumed that a search of a proprietary criminal database by itself will show that a person either is or is not a criminal, but these databases are outstanding secondary tools to do a much wider search.

Section II

Government Online Sources

Individual state chapters have been compiled into an easy to use format that details what is available online. Free online access and fee-based systems are denoted, with the type or category of records available. Five sub-chapters or sections are presented in this order:

1. State Public Record Agencies

2. State Licensing and Regulatory Boards

3. County Courts

4. County Recorder & Assessor Offices

5. Federal Courts (US District and Bankruptcy)

Be sure to review the introductions and Online Access notes found at the beginning of each state's County Courts and County Recorder's Office sections. This is a good place to find out about statewide online systems.

Editor's Tip: Just because records are maintained in a certain way in your state or county do not assume that any other county or state does things the same way.

Alabama

Capital: Montgomery
           Montgomery County
Time Zone: CST
Population: 4,530,182
# of Counties: 67

Quick Links

Website: www.alabama.gov
Governor: www.governor.state.al.us
Attorney General: www.ago.state.al.us
State Archives: www.archives.state.al.us
State Statutes and Codes: www.legislature.state.al.us/prefiled/prefiled.html
Legislative Bill Search: www.legislature.state.al.us
Unclaimed Funds: www.treasury.state.al.us/new_search.asp

State Level ... Major Agencies

Statewide Court Records

Administrative Office of Courts, 300 Dexter Ave, Montgomery, AL 36104-3741; 334-954-5000, Fax-334-242-2099, 8AM-5PM.
www.alacourt.gov
Online search: In the past, commercial remote access to the State Judicial Information System (SJIS) was offered, but this is no longer available. This agency recommends that searchers contact a commercial vendor at www.alacourt.com. State Supreme Court and Appellate decisions are available at www.alalinc.net and at www.judicial.state.al.us/.

Sexual Offender Registry

Department of Public Safety, Sexual Offender Registry, PO Box 1511, Montgomery, AL 36102-1511 (Courier: 301 S Ripley, Montgomery, AL 36109); 334-353-1172, Fax-334-353-2563, 8AM-5PM.
www.dps.state.al.us
Online search: Sex offender data and a felony fugitives list are available online at www.dps.state.al.us/public/abi/system. Search by name, ZIP Code or geographic area.

Incarceration Records

Alabama Department of Corrections, Central Records Office, PO Box 301501, Montgomery, AL 36130 (Courier: 301 S. Ripley Street, Montgomery, AL 36130); 334-353-9500, 8AM-5PM.
http://doc.state.al.us
Online search: Information on current inmates only is available online. Location, AIS number, physical identifiers, and projected release date are released. The database is updated weekly.

Corporation, Limited Partnership, Limited Liability Company, Limited Liability Partnerships, Trade Names, Trademarks/Servicemarks

Secretary of State, Corporations Division, PO Box 5616, Montgomery, AL 36103-5616 (Courier: 11 S Union St, Ste 207, Montgomery, AL 36104); 334-242-5324, 334-242-5325 (Trademarks), Fax-334-240-3138, 8AM-5PM.

www.sos.state.al.us
Online search: The website has free searches of corporate and UCC records. Search individual files for Active Names at http://arc-sos.state.al.us/CGI/SOSCRP01.MBR/INPUT.

Uniform Commercial Code, Federal Tax Liens, State Tax Liens

UCC Division - SOS, UCC Records, PO Box 5616, Montgomery, AL 36103-5616 (Courier: 11 South Union St, Suite 200, Montgomery, AL 36104); 334-242-5231, Fax-334-353-8269, 8AM-5PM.
www.sos.state.al.us
Online search: The agency has UCC information available to search at the web address, there is no fee. Corporation data is also available. You can search by debtor's name or file number. Collateral information and /or image is not available to view online. **Other options:** Bulk sale by CD for $1,500 plus $300 a week for updates.

Birth Certificates

Center for Health Statistics, Record Services Division, PO Box 5625, Montgomery, AL 36103-5625 (Courier: RSA Tower Suite 1150, 201 Monroe St, Montgomery, AL 36104); 334-206-5418, Fax-334-262-9563, 8AM-5PM.
http://ph.state.al.us/chs/VitalRecords/VRECORDS.html
Online search: Online ordering is available from the webpage through a service provider.

Death Records

Center for Health Statistics, Record Services Division, PO Box 5625, Montgomery, AL 36103-5625 (Courier: RSA Tower Suite 1150, 201 Monroe St, Montgomery, AL 36104); 334-206-5418, Fax-334-262-9563, 8AM-5PM.
http://ph.state.al.us/chs/VitalRecords/VRECORDS.HTMl
Online search: Online ordering is available from the webpage through a service provider. **Other options:** Index to records are available on microfilm for $40.00 per roll. There are 6 rolls of records for 1908 through 1959.

Marriage Certificates

Center for Health Statistics, Record Services Division, PO Box 5625, Montgomery, AL 36103-5625 (Courier: RSA Tower Suite 1150, 201 Monroe St, Montgomery, AL 36104); 334-206-5418, Fax-334-262-9563, 8AM-5PM.
http://ph.state.al.us/chs/VitalRecords/VRECORDS.HTMl
Online search: Online ordering is available from the webpage through a service provider. **Other options:** Microfilm rolls are available for purchase at $40.00 each. There are 11 rolls available which includes index to records for 1936 to 1969.

Divorce Records

Center for Health Statistics, Record Services Division, PO Box 5625, Montgomery, AL 36103-5625 (Courier: RSA Tower Suite 1150, 201 Monroe St, Montgomery, AL 36104); 334-206-5418, Fax-334-206-2659, 8AM-5PM.
http://ph.state.al.us/chs/VitalRecords/VRECORDS.HTMl
Online search: Online ordering is available from the webpage through a service provider. **Other options:** There is one microfilm roll of index for records for 1950-59 available for $40.00.

Driver Records

Department of Public Safety, Driver Records-License Division, PO Box 1471, Montgomery, AL 36102-1471 (Courier: 301 S Ripley Street, Montgomery, AL 36104); 334-242-4400, Fax-334-242-9926, 8AM-5PM.
www.dps.state.al.us
Online search: Alabama Interactive has been designated the state's agent for online access of state driving records. A Subscriber Registration Agreement must be submitted and both Alabama Interactive and the Alabama DPS must approve all customers. There is a $75.00 annual administrative fee for new accounts and the search fee is $7.00 per record. The driver license number is needed to search. The system, open 24 hours daily, is Internet-based. Alabama Interactive can be reached at 2 N. Jackson St, #301, Montgomery AL, 36104, (866) 353-3468, www.alabamainteractive.org.

State Level ... Occupational Licensing

Abortion/Reproductive Health Ctr	www.adph.org/providers/
Ambulatory Surgery Center	www.adph.org/providers/
Anesthesiologist Assistant	www.docboard.org/al/
Architect	www.boa.state.al.us/rostersearch/rostersearch.asp
Assisted Living Facility/Unit	www.adph.org/providers/
Auctioneer	www.auctioneer.state.al.us/roster/roster-search-form.asp
Bank	www.bank.state.al.us/bank_search.aspx
Birthing Center	www.adph.org/providers/
Cerebral Palsy Center	www.adph.org/providers/
Check Casher	www.bank.state.al.us/Search_All_Licences2.asp
Chiropractor	https://www.alabamainteractive.org/asbce/VerificationEntryPoint.do;jsessionid=ap_JoQrUmjsg
Consumer Finance Company	www.bank.state.al.us/Search_All_Licences2.asp
Contractor, General	www.genconbd.state.al.us/DATABASE-LIVE/roster.asp
Electrical Contractor	www.aecb.state.al.us/Search/new_search.asp
Electrician, Journeyman	www.aecb.state.al.us/Search/new_search.asp
Engineer/Engineer in Training	www.bels.alabama.gov
Forester	www.alsbrf.org
Gas Fitter	www.pgfb.state.al.us/inquiries.aspx
Geologist	www.algeobd.state.al.us/roster_search.asp
Heating/Air Conditioning Contractor	www.hvacboard.state.al.us/Lic_Search/searchform.asp
Home Builder	www.hblb.state.al.us/Lic_Search/all-ind.asp
Home Health Agency	www.adph.org/providers/
Home Inspector	www.sos.state.al.us/sosinfo/inquiry.cfm
Hospice	www.adph.org/providers/
Hospital	www.adph.org/providers/
Insurance Adjuster/Agent/Broker/Producer	www.aldoi.org/LicenseeSearch/
Insurance Corp/Co./Partnership	www.aldoi.org/CompanySearch/
Interior Designer	www.idboard.alabama.gov/search/start.aspx
Landscape Architect	www.abela.state.al.us/architects.html
Lender/Loan Source	www.bank.state.al.us/Search_All_Licences2.asp
Marriage/Family Therapist	www.mft.state.al.us/Search/search.asp
Massage Therapist	www.almtbd.state.al.us/roster_search.asp
Medical Doctor	www.docboard.org/al/
Medical Gas Piper	www.pgfb.state.al.us/inquiries.aspx
Mental Health Center	www.adph.org/providers/
Mortgage Broker	www.bank.state.al.us/Search_All_Licences2.asp
Notary Public	www.sos.state.al.us/sosinfo/inquiry.cfm?area=notaries%20public
Nursing Home	www.adph.org/providers/
Nursing Home Administrator	www.alboenha.state.al.us/logon.html
Optometrist	www.al-optometry.org
Osteopathic Physician	www.docboard.org/al/
Pawn Shop	www.bank.state.al.us/Search_All_Licences2.asp
Petroleum Product Seller	www.agi.state.al.us/Bonded.asp
Physical Therapist/Therapist Asst	www.pt.state.al.us/License/searchform.asp
Physician Assistant	www.docboard.org/al/
Physiological Lab, Clinical	www.adph.org/providers/
Plumber	www.pgfb.state.al.us/inquiries.aspx
Podiatrist	www.alabamapodiatryboard.org/pages/licensee.html
Pre-Need Sales Agent	www.aldoi.org/LicenseeSearch/
Public Account.-CPA-Non Licensee	www.asbpa.state.al.us/register/register.asp
Real Estate Agent/Sales	www.arec.state.al.us/search.asp
Real Estate Appraiser	http://reab.state.al.us/appraisers/searchform.asp

Real Estate Broker .... www.arec.state.al.us/search.asp
Rehabilitation Center .... www.adph.org/providers/
Reinsurance Intermediary .... www.aldoi.org/LicenseeSearch/
Renal Disease Terminal Treatment Ctr .... www.adph.org/providers/
Rural Primary Care Hospital....................... www.adph.org/providers/
School Superintendent .... www.alsde.edu/html/super_listing.asp?menu=none&footer=general
Sleep Disorder Center................................ www.adph.org/providers/
Social Worker .... www.abswe.state.al.us/Lic_Search/search.asp
Social Worker, Pvt. Practice .... www.abswe.state.al.us/Lic_Search/searchpip.asp
Sports Agent www.sos.state.al.us/cf/sportsagents/sasrch1.cfm
Surplus Line Broker................................... www.aldoi.org/LicenseeSearch/
Surveyor, Land .... www.bels.alabama.gov
Therapist, Marriage and Family................. www.mft.state.al.us/Search/search.asp
U-Pick Location... www.agi.state.al.us/PDFs/UPick.PDF
X-ray (Portable) Supplier........................... www.adph.org/providers/

County Level ... Courts

Court Administration:
www.alacourt.org

Director of Courts, 300 Dexter Ave, Montgomery, AL, 36104; 334-954-5000;

Court Structure:
Circuit Courts are the courts of general jurisdiction; District Courts have limited jurisdiction in civil matters. These courts are combined in all but eight larger counties. Barbour, Coffee, Jefferson, St. Clair, Talladega, and Tallapoosa Counties have two court locations within the county. Jefferson County (Birmingham), Madison (Huntsville), Marshall, and Tuscaloosa Counties have separate criminal divisions for Circuit Courts and/or District Courts.

Misdemeanors committed with felonies are tried with the felony. The Circuit Courts are appeals courts for misdemeanors. District Courts can receive guilty pleas in felony cases.

Online Access Note:
The state has a remote access program called SJIS, which is only open to government agencies. They recommend new users to contact a designated private vendor. For more information, visit their website at www.alacourt.com. Note that fees are involved.

State Supreme Court and Appellate Court decisions are available online at www.judicial.state.al.us or via www.alalinc.net

Baldwin County
Probate Court – Civil Records
Access to probate property records is free at www.deltacomputersystems.com/al/al05/probatea.html.

Calhoun County
Circuit Court – Civil and Criminal Records
Access at www.alacourt.com subscription service. The County sex offender registry is online at www.calhouncountysheriff.org/html/Framsex.html. From Sept. 1999 forward only.

Mobile County
District Court – Civil and Criminal Records
Access at www.alacourt.com subscription service. Access to the Probate court's recordings database is free at www.mobilecounty.org/probatecourt/recordssearch.htm. A second search is at www.mobilecounty.org/probatecourt/judicial.asp.

Washington County
Circuit & District Court – Civil and Criminal Records
www.millry.net/~spgrimes
Access at www.alacourt.com subscription service. Also, access to probate records is by subscription at www.recordsusa.com/recordsusa/default.asp. Credit card-username-password required; choose monthly or per-use plan. Visit the website or call Lisa at 601-264-7701 for information.

County Level ... Recorders & Assessors

Recording Office Organization: 67 counties, 71 recording offices. The recording officer is the Judge of Probate. Four counties have two recording offices: Barbour, Coffee, Jefferson, and St. Clair. The entire state is in the Central Time Zone (CST). Federal and state tax liens on personal property of businesses are filed with the Secretary of State. Other federal and state tax liens are filed with the county Judge of Probate. Counties do not perform separate tax lien searches although the liens are usually filed in the same index with UCC financing statements.

Online Access Note: There is no statewide system, but a limited number of counties offer free online access to recorded documents.

Autauga County *Property, Assessor, Map Records*
Access to the GIS-property database and Tax Office is free at www.emapsplus.com/ALAutauga/maps/. Click on search by name.

Baldwin County *Property, Deed, Recording, UCC Records*
www.co.baldwin.al.us/PageView.asp?PageType=R&edit_id=1
Access to recordings, deeds, and UCCs is at the website, see the "Recording" box. Also, search property appraiser records at www.deltacomputersystems.com/AL/AL05/pappraisala.html. Also, access to probate's property information is free at www.deltacomputersystems.com/al/al05/probatea.html. Property tax information is at www.deltacomputersystems.com/AL/AL05/plinkquerya.html.

Calhoun County *Property, Assessor, GIS Records*
www.calhouncounty.org
Access to the GIS-property database and Tax Office is free at www.emapsplus.com/ALCalhoun/maps/. Click on search by name.

Chambers County *Real Estate, UCC Records*
Access real estate and UCC data for a $49.95 monthly fee. For information, call 706-643-1010. Records are live and go back 5 years.

Clarke County *Property, Assessor, GIS Records*
Access to the GIS-property database and Tax Office is free at www.emapsplus.com/ALClarke/maps/. Click on search by name.

Coffee County (Elba Division) *Property, Assessor, GIS Records*
Access to the GIS-property database and Tax Office is free at www.emapsplus.com/ALCoffee/maps/. Click on search by name.

Colbert County *Property Tax Records*
Access property tax records free at www.deltacomputersystems.com/search.html.

Cullman County *Property, Assessor, GIS Records*
Access to the GIS-property database and Tax Office is free at www.emapsplus.com/ALCullman/maps/. Click on search by name.

De Kalb County *Property, Assessor, Mapping Records*
Access to the GIS-property database and Tax Office is free at www.emapsplus.com/ALDeKalb/maps/. Click on search by name.

Elmore County *Property, Assessor, GIS Records*
Access to the GIS-property database and Tax Office is free at www.emapsplus.com/ALElmore/maps/. Click on search by name.

Escambia County *Property, Assessor, GIS Records*
www.co.escambia.al.us/probate.htm
Access to the county property appraisal data is free at http://property.co.escambia.al.us/search.php?type=appraisal. Also, access to the GIS-property information database and Tax Office is free at www.emapsplus.com/ALEscambia/maps/. Click on search by name.

Etowah County *Property Appraisal, Property Tax Records*
Access to property data through a private company is free at www.deltacomputersystems.com/AL/AL31/pappraisala.html. Also, tax records are free at www.deltacomputersystems.com/AL/AL31/plinkquerya.html.

Fayette County *Property, Assessor Records*
Access to property data is free at www.fayettealmaps.com; Use password "Ruby." You may have to download the map viewer.

Jefferson County (Bessemer Division) *Real Estate, Deed Records*
Access to land records should be available free online by June, 2006. Call County Judge of Probate for details.

Jefferson County (Birmingham Division) *Property Tax, Unclaimed Property, Inmate Records*
www.jeffcointouch.com
Access to the property tax due inquiry is free at http://tc.jeffcointouch.com/taxcollection/HTML/index.asp. No name searching. Also, access to the unclaimed property list is free at www.jeffcointouch.com/jeffcointouch/ieindex.asp. Click on treasurer. Site may be under re-construction. Also, access the sheriff's most wanted list at www.jeffcosheriff.org/most_wanted.php. Search inmate lists at http://sheriff.jccal.org.

Lamar County *Property, Assessor, GIS Records*
Access to the GIS-property database and Tax Office is to be free at www.emapsplus.com/ALLamar/maps/. Click on search by name.

Lauderdale County *Real Estate, Appraisal, Property Tax Records*
Access to property appraisal data is free at www.deltacomputersystems.com/AL/AL41/pappraisala.html. Also, property tax records are free at www.deltacomputersystems.com/AL/AL41/plinkquerya.html.

Lee County *Real Estate, Appraisal, Property Tax, Sex Offender Records*
Assess to property appraisal records is free at www.deltacomputersystems.com/AL/AL43/pappraisala.html. Also search the sheriff's sex offender list at www.icrimewatch.net/index.php?AgencyID=54018.

Limestone County *Real Estate, Recording, Deed, Lien, Property Tax, Assessor, GIS Records*
www.co.limestone.al.us
Access to recording records requires subscription to the PROMIS system; for info or signup contact Michelle Wooley at Syscon at 205-758-2000 x8112. Charge per images viewed; $.25 to print image. Also, access to the GIS-property information database and Tax Office is free at www.emapsplus.com/ALlimestone/maps/. Click on search by name.

Madison County *Property, Assessor, GIS Records*
www.co.madison.al.us
Access to the GIS-property database and Tax Office is free at www.emapsplus.com/ALMadison/maps/. Click on search by name.

Marion County *Property Tax, Land, Mapping Records*
Access the county GIS-mapping and property information data for free at www.marioncountymaps.com/FrameSet.htm.

Marshall County *Property, GIS Mapping Records*
Access to property data requires free registration and password at www.marshallgis.org.

Mobile County
Deed, UCC, Property, Incs, Marriage, Estate Claim, Mortgage, Real/Personal Property, Voter Registration Records
www.mobile-county.net/probate/
Access to the Probate court's recordings database is free at http://records.mobile-county.net; index and most images back to 1984. Marriages are in a separate index at www.mobilecounty.org/probatecourt/recordssearch.htm Also, search real and personal property at http://apps.siteonestudio.com/siteone/towns/mobilecoproptax/. Search registered voters at www.mobilecounty.org/probatecourt/voters/index.asp. Also, City of Mobile property ownership data is free at http://maps.cityofmobile.org/webmapping.htm. Click on Property ownership information and choose to search by name.

Montgomery County *Property, Assessor, Mapping, Unclaimed Property Records*
Access to the GIS-property information database and Tax Office is free at www.emapsplus.com/ALMontgomery/maps/. Click on search by name. Also, access to Probate Court's unclaimed property list is free at www.mc-ala.org/probate/unclprop/default.asp.

Morgan County *Property, Appraisal, Assessor, Tax Payment Records*
Access to the GIS-property information database and Tax Office is free at www.emapsplus.com/ALMorgan/maps/. Click on search by name. Also, access to property appraiser data is free at www.deltacomputersystems.com/AL/AL52/pappraisala.html. Also, search property assessor data free at www.deltacomputersystems.com/AL/AL52/plinkquerya.html. There is also a property tax payment search at https://secure.termnetinc.com/morgan/paymentType.jsp but no name searching.

Russell County *Property, Assessor, GIS Records*
Access to the GIS-property database and Tax Office is free at www.emapsplus.com/ALRussell/maps/. Click on search by name.

St. Clair County (Northern Congressional District) *Property, Appraisal, Assessor Records*
www.stclairco.com/index.php
Access to the GIS-property information database and Tax Office is free at www.emapsplus.com/ALstclair/maps/. Click on search by name. Also, access to property appraiser data is free at www.deltacomputersystems.com/AL/AL59/pappraisala.html. Also, access to county assessor data is free at www.deltacomputersystems.com/AL/AL59/plinkquerya.html.

St. Clair County (Southern Congressional District) *Property, Appraisal, Assessor Records*
Access to property appraiser data is free at www.deltacomputersystems.com/AL/AL59/pappraisala.html. Also, access to county assessor data is free at www.deltacomputersystems.com/AL/AL59/plinkquerya.html. Access to real estate recording records via a private company subscription service is at www.recordsusa.com/Alabama/StClairCnAl.htm.

Shelby County
Recording, Land, Judgment, Deed, UCC, Notary, Fictitious Name, Marriage, Probate, Property Tax Records
www.shelbycountyalabama.com
Access to the probate court recording data is free at www.shelbycountyalabama.com/probate/. Also, search property tax records free at www.shelbycountyalabama.com/taxc_search.asp.

Tuscaloosa County *Real Estate, Lien, UCC, Grantor/Grantee, Probate, Marriage, Mortgage, Incorporation, Property, Jail, Sex Offender, Most Wanted Records*
www.tuscco.com
Access to the records database is free at www.tuscco.com/OnlineServices.cfm. Also included are searches for mortgages, incorporations, bonds, discharges, exemptions. Also, access to property and assessor data is free at www.emapsplus.com/ALTuscaloosa/maps/. Click on owner search. Also, a search is proposed for probate and judgment records at www.tuscco.com/RecordsRoom_Probate.cfm. Also, search for inmates, most wanted, sex offenders, and missing persons at www.tcsoal.org.

Washington County *Real Estate Records*
Access to real estate recording records via a private company subscription service is at www.recordsusa.com/recordsusa/Alabama/WashingtonCnAl.htm.

Federal Courts in Alabama...

Standards for Federal Courts: The universal PACER sign-up number is 800-676-6856. Find PACER and the Party/Case Index on the Web at http://pacer.psc.uscourts.gov. PACER dial-up access is $.60 per minute. Also, courts offering internet access via PACER, Web-PACER or the new CM-ECF charge $.08 per page fee ($.07 per page if record is pre-2005 or unless noted as free).

US District Court -- Middle District of Alabama
www.almd.uscourts.gov
PACER: Case records are available back to 1994. New records are available online after 1 day. PACER is replaced by CM/ECF **Electronic Filing:** CM/ECF data at https://ecf.almd.uscourts.gov.
Dothan Division counties: Coffee, Dale, Geneva, Henry, Houston.
Montgomery Division counties: Autauga, Barbour, Bullock, Butler, Chilton, Coosa, Covington, Crenshaw, Elmore, Lowndes, Montgomery, Pike.
Opelika Division counties: Chambers, Lee, Macon, Randolph, Russell, Tallapoosa.

US Bankruptcy Court -- Middle District of Alabama
www.almb.uscourts.gov
PACER: Case records are available back to 8/2000. Records are purged every 6 months. New records are available online after 2-3 days. **PACER Online Access:** WebPACER is at https://ecf.almb.uscourts.gov. Document images available. **Electronic Filing:** CM/ECF data at https://ecf.almb.uscourts.gov. **Opinions:** View court opinions at https://ecf.almb.uscourts.gov/cgi-bin/PublicOpinion.pl. **Other Online Access:** Calendars free at www.almb.uscourts.gov/calendar.htm. **Phone access:** Voice Case Information System, call 334-954-3868.
Montgomery Division counties: Autauga, Barbour, Bullock, Butler, Chambers, Chilton, Coffee, Coosa, Covington, Crenshaw, Dale, Elmore, Geneva, Henry, Houston, Lee, Lowndes, Macon, Montgomery, Pike, Randolph, Russell, Tallapoosa.

US District Court -- Northern District of Alabama

www.alnd.uscourts.gov

PACER: Case records are available back to 1994. **Electronic Filing:** CM/ECF data at https://ecf.alnd.uscourts.gov. **Opinions:** View court opinions at www.alnd.uscourts.gov/judge_pages.htm.
Birmingham Division counties: Bibb, Blount, Calhoun, Clay, Cleburne, Greene, Jefferson, Pickens, Shelby, Sumter, Talladega, Tuscaloosa.
Florence Division counties: Colbert, Franklin, Lauderdale. No public access at this court.
Gadsden Division counties: Cherokee, De Kalb, Etowah, Marshall, St. Clair.
Huntsville Division counties: Cullman, Jackson, Lawrence, Limestone, Madison, Morgan.
Jasper Division counties: Fayette, Lamar, Marion, Walker, Winston.

US Bankruptcy Court -- Northern District of Alabama

www.alnb.uscourts.gov

PACER: Case records are available back to 11/1976. **PACER Online Access:** ECF replaces PACER. **Electronic Filing:** CM/ECF data at https://ecf.alnb.uscourts.gov. **Opinions:** View court opinions at www.alnb.uscourts.gov/opinions.htm. **Other Online Access:** Calendars free at http://207.41.17.39/index.cfm?prg=publiccalsearch. **Phone access:** Voice Case Information System, call 877-466-0795, 205-254-7337
Anniston Division counties: Calhoun, Cherokee, Clay, Cleburne, De Kalb, Etowah, Marshall, St. Clair, Talladega.
Birmingham Division counties: Blount, Jefferson, Shelby.
Decatur Division counties: Colbert, Cullman, Franklin, Jackson, Lauderdale, Lawrence, Limestone, Madison, Morgan. The part of Winston County north of Double Springs is handled by this division.
Tuscaloosa Division counties: Bibb, Fayette, Greene, Lamar, Marion, Pickens, Sumter, Tuscaloosa, Walker, Winston. The part of Winston County North of Double Springs is handled by Decatur Division.

US District Court -- Southern District of Alabama

www.als.uscourts.gov

PACER: Case records are available back to 1993. **PACER Online Access:** ECF replaces PACER. **Electronic Filing:** CM/ECF data at https://ecf.almd.uscourts.gov. **Opinions:** View court opinions at www.als.uscourts.gov/page.cfm?page=120.
Mobile Division counties: Baldwin, Choctaw, Clarke, Conecuh, Escambia, Mobile, Monroe, Washington.
Selma Division counties: Dallas, Hale, Marengo, Perry, Wilcox.

US Bankruptcy Court -- Southern District of Alabama

www.alsb.uscourts.gov

PACER: Case records are available back to 1993. New records are available online after 1 day. **PACER Online Access:** ECF replaces PACER. **Electronic Filing:** CM/ECF data at https://ecf.alsb.uscourts.gov. **Opinions:** View court opinions at www.alsb.uscourts.gov/opinions.htm. **Other Online Access:** Dockets free at www.alsb.uscourts.gov/crtcal.htm. **Phone access:** Voice Case Information System, call 251-441-5637.
Mobile Division counties: Baldwin, Choctaw, Clarke, Conecuh, Dallas, Escambia, Hale, Marengo, Mobile, Monroe, Perry, Washington, Wilcox.

Editor's Tip: Just because records are maintained in a certain way in your state or county do not assume that any other county or state does things the same way that you are used to.

Alaska

Capital: Juneau
            Juneau Borough
Time Zone: AK (Alaska Standard Time)
Population: 655,435
# of Boroughs/Divisions: 23

Quick Links

Website: www.state.ak.us
Governor: www.gov.state.ak.us
Attorney General- www.law.state.ak.us
State Archives: www.archives.state.ak.us
State Statutes and Codes: www.legis.state.ak.us/folhome.htm
Legislative Bill Search: www.legis.state.ak.us/basis/start.asp
Bill Monitoring: www.legis.state.ak.us/basis/btmf_login.asp?session=24
Unclaimed Funds: www.revenue.state.ak.us/treasury/UCP/ucpsrch.asp

---

Editor's Tip: Remember, Alaska has its own time zones. Alaska Time is one hour earlier than Pacific Standard Time, and four hours earlier than Eastern Standard. Also, Alaska's Aleutian Islands are in Hawaii Time Zone, one hour earlier than Alaska Time.

State Level ... Major Agencies

Statewide Court Records

Office of the Administrative Director, Alaska Court System, 820 W 4th Ave, Anchorage, AK 99501; 907-264-8232 (Administration), 907-264-0491 (Records), Fax-907-264-8291, 8AM-4:30PM.
http://www.state.ak.us/courts/
Online search: The home web page gives access to Appellate opinions. You may do a name search of a partial statewide Alaska Trial Courts database index at http://www.courtrecords.alaska.gov/. There is an old and a new system. Search results give case number, file date, disposition date, charge, and sentence. The index gives the name used on the first pleading only. The new system has Anchorage, Fairbanks and Palmer and is much more current than the old system. A search of the old system is not FCRA-compliant for employment screening purposes.

Sexual Offender Registry

Department of Public Safety, Statewide Services Div-SOCR Unit, 5700 E Tudor Rd, Anchorage, AK 99507; 907-269-0396, Fax-907-269-0394, 8AM-4:30PM.
http://www.dps.state.ak.us/nSorcr/asp/
Online search: Name searching and geographic searching is available at the website.

Corporation, Trademarks/Servicemarks, Fictitious Name, Assumed Name, Limited Partnership, Limited Liability Company, Limited Liability Partnership Records

Corporation Section, Department of Commerce, Community & Econ Dev, PO Box 110808, Juneau, AK 99811-0808 (Courier: 150 Third Street Rm 217, Juneau, AK 99801); 907-465-2530, Fax-907-465-3257, 8AM-5PM.

http://www.dced.state.ak.us/bsc/corps.htm
Online search: At the website, one can access status information on corps, LLCs, LLP, LP (all both foreign and domestic), registered and reserved names. Search by entity name, registered agent name, or by officer name. There is no fee. **Other options:** Bulk purchase is available to approved entities. Call 907-465-2530 for more information.

Uniform Commercial Code

UCC Central File Systems Office, State Recorder's Office, 550 West 7th Ave #1200A, Anchorage, AK 99501-3564; 907-269-8873, 907-269-8899, Fax-907-269-8945, 8AM-3:30PM.
http://www.dnr.state.ak.us/ssd/ucc/index.cfm
Online search: One can search by granter-grantee name, date, document number or document type at www.dnr.state.ak.us/ssd/ucc/search.cfm. There is no fee. **Other options:** Bulk media of the entire UCC database can be purchased from the State Recorder's Office (907-269-8881).

Birth, Death, Marriage, Divorce Certificates

Department of Health & Social Services, Bureau of Vital Statistics, 5441 Commercial Blvd, Juneau, AK 99801; 907-465-3391, Fax-907-465-3618, 8AM-4:30PM.
http://www.hss.state.ak.us/dph/bvs/
Online search: Records may be ordered online via a state-designated vendor at www.vitalchek.com. There is a $5.50 service fee. Use of credit card required.

Driver Records

Division of Motor Vehicles, Driver's Records, 2760 Sherwood Lane #B, Juneau, AK 99801; 907-465-4361 (Motor Vehicle Reports Desk), 907-465-4363 (Licensing), Fax-907-465-5509, 8AM-5PM.
http://www.state.ak.us/dmv
Online search: Online access costs $5.00 per record. This is for pre-approved, ongoing requesters only. Inquiries may be made at any time, 24 hours a day. Batch inquiries may call back within thirty minutes for responses. Search by the first four letters of driver's name, license number and date of birth. This is not a web-based system.

State Level ... Occupational Licensing

Acupuncturist	www.dced.state.ak.us/occ/search3.htm
Anesthetist, Dental, General/Permit	www.dced.state.ak.us/occ/search3.htm
Architect	www.dced.state.ak.us/occ/search3.htm
Athletic Event Promoter	www.dced.state.ak.us/occ/search3.htm
Athletic Trainer	www.dced.state.ak.us/occ/search3.htm
Attorney	www.alaskabar.org/index.cfm?id=4954
Audiologist/Hearing Aid Dealer	www.dced.state.ak.us/occ/search3.htm
Bail Bondsman	www.commerce.state.ak.us/ins/apps/producersearch/InsLicStart.cfm
Bank	www.dced.state.ak.us/bsc/pub/2003_directory.pdf
Barber	www.dced.state.ak.us/occ/search3.htm
Barber Shop Owner/School/Instr.	www.dced.state.ak.us/occ/search3.htm
BIDCOS/CFAB	www.dced.state.ak.us/bsc/pub/2003_directory.pdf
Big Game Guide/Assistant/Transporter	www.dced.state.ak.us/occ/search3.htm
Boxer	www.dced.state.ak.us/occ/search3.htm
Boxing Physician	www.dced.state.ak.us/occ/search3.htm
Boxing/Wrestling Personnel	www.dced.state.ak.us/occ/search3.htm
Chiropractor	www.dced.state.ak.us/occ/search3.htm
Collection Agency/Operator	www.dced.state.ak.us/occ/search3.htm
Concert Promoter	www.dced.state.ak.us/occ/search3.htm
Construction Contractor	www.dced.state.ak.us/occ/search3.htm
Contractor, Civil/Elec./Mech./Mng/Petrol.	www.dced.state.ak.us/occ/search3.htm
Contractor, Residential	www.dced.state.ak.us/occ/search3.htm
Cosmetologist/Hairdresser	www.dced.state.ak.us/occ/search3.htm
Cosmetology Shop Owner/School/Instr	www.dced.state.ak.us/occ/search3.htm
Counselor, Professional	www.dced.state.ak.us/occ/OccSearch/main.cfm
Credit Union	www.dced.state.ak.us/bsc/pub/2003_directory.pdf

Defibrillator Technician............................. https://www.chems.alaska.gov/emsdata/
Dental Hygienist www.dced.state.ak.us/occ/search3.htm
Dentist/Dental Examiner............................ www.dced.state.ak.us/occ/search3.htm
Dietitian/Nutritionist................................. www.dced.state.ak.us/occ/OccSearch/main.cfm
Drug Distributor/Drug Room...................... www.dced.state.ak.us/occ/search3.htm
Electrical Administrator.............................. www.dced.state.ak.us/occ/search3.htm
Emergency Medical Technician.................. https://www.chems.alaska.gov/emsdata/
Employment Agency Operator www.dced.state.ak.us/occ/search3.htm
Engineer... www.dced.state.ak.us/occ/search3.htm
Esthetician... www.dced.state.ak.us/occ/search3.htm
Funeral Director/Establishment www.dced.state.ak.us/occ/search3.htm
Geologist.. www.dced.state.ak.us/occ/search3.htm
Guide/Outfitter, Hunting............................ www.dced.state.ak.us/occ/search3.htm
Hairdresser/Esthetician www.dced.state.ak.us/occ/search3.htm
Hearing Aid Dealer.................................... www.dced.state.ak.us/occ/search3.htm
Independent Adjuster................................. www.commerce.state.ak.us/ins/apps/producersearch/InsLicStart.cfm
Insurance Agent, Managing General........... www.commerce.state.ak.us/ins/apps/producersearch/InsLicStart.cfm
Insurance Occupation................................. www.commerce.state.ak.us/ins/apps/producersearch/InsLicStart.cfm
Insurance Producer .... www.commerce.state.ak.us/ins/apps/producersearch/InsLicStart.cfm
Landscape Architect................................... www.dced.state.ak.us/occ/search3.htm
Lobbyist/Lobbyist Employer .... www.state.ak.us/local/akpages/ADMIN/apoc/lobcov.htm
Marriage & Family Therapist .... www.dced.state.ak.us/occ/OccSearch/main.cfm
Mechanical Administrator........................... www.dced.state.ak.us/occ/search3.htm
Medical Doctor/Surgeon www.dced.state.ak.us/occ/search3.htm
Midwife .... www.dced.state.ak.us/occ/OccSearch/main.cfm
Mortician/Embalmer.................................. www.dced.state.ak.us/occ/search3.htm
Naturopathic Physician www.dced.state.ak.us/occ/search3.htm
Nurse.. www.dced.state.ak.us/occ/search3.htm
Nurse Anesthetist....................................... www.dced.state.ak.us/occ/search3.htm
Nurse-RN/LPN www.dced.state.ak.us/occ/search3.htm
Nurses' Aide... www.dced.state.ak.us/occ/search3.htm
Nursing Home Administrator...................... www.dced.state.ak.us/occ/search3.htm
Occupational Therapist/Assist www.dced.state.ak.us/occ/search3.htm
Optician, Dispensing.................................. www.dced.state.ak.us/occ/search3.htm
Optometrist www.dced.state.ak.us/occ/search3.htm
Osteopathic Physician................................ www.dced.state.ak.us/occ/search3.htm
Paramedic www.dced.state.ak.us/occ/search3.htm
Parenteral Sedation (Dental) www.dced.state.ak.us/occ/search3.htm
Pesticide Permit .... http://info.dec.state.ak.us/eh/pesticide/permits.htm
Pharmacist/Pharmacist Intern/Pharmacy..... www.dced.state.ak.us/occ/search3.htm
Pharmacy Technician.................................. www.dced.state.ak.us/occ/search3.htm
Physical Therapist/Assistant www.dced.state.ak.us/occ/search3.htm
Physician Assistant www.dced.state.ak.us/occ/search3.htm
Pilot, Marine www.dced.state.ak.us/occ/search3.htm
Podiatrist.. www.dced.state.ak.us/occ/search3.htm
Premium Finance Company........................ www.dced.state.ak.us/bsc/pub/2003_directory.pdf
Process Server.. www.dps.state.ak.us/PermitsLicensing/images/CPSlist.pdf
Psychologist/Psychological Assistant www.dced.state.ak.us/occ/search3.htm
Public Accountant-CPA.............................. www.dced.state.ak.us/occ/OccSearch/main.cfm
Real Estate Agent/Broker/Assoc................. www.dced.state.ak.us/occ/search3.htm
Real Estate Appraiser................................. www.dced.state.ak.us/occ/search3.htm
Referee... www.dced.state.ak.us/occ/OccSearch/main.cfm
Reinsurance Intermediary Broker/Mgr .... www.commerce.state.ak.us/ins/apps/producersearch/InsLicStart.cfm
School Administrator/ Special Service .... www.eed.state.ak.us/TeacherCertification/CertSearchForm.cfm
Small Loan Company .... www.dced.state.ak.us/bsc/pub/2003_directory.pdf
Social Worker.. www.dced.state.ak.us/occ/OccSearch/main.cfm

Speech/Language Pathologist www.dced.state.ak.us/occ/search3.htm
Surplus Line Broker.................................. www.commerce.state.ak.us/ins/apps/producersearch/InsLicStart.cfm
Surveyor, Land www.dced.state.ak.us/occ/search3.htm
Tattoo Artist/Body Piercer........................ www.dced.state.ak.us/occ/search3.htm
Teacher .... www.eed.state.ak.us/TeacherCertification/CertSearchForm.cfm
Thrift... www.dced.state.ak.us/bsc/pub/2003_directory.pdf
Transporter, Game www.dced.state.ak.us/occ/search3.htm
Trust Company .... www.dced.state.ak.us/bsc/pub/2003_directory.pdf
Underground Storage Tank Worker/Contr.. www.dced.state.ak.us/occ/search3.htm
Vessel Agent.. www.dced.state.ak.us/occ/search3.htm
Veterinarian/Veterinary Technician........... www.dced.state.ak.us/occ/search3.htm
Viatical Settlement Broker........................ www.commerce.state.ak.us/ins/apps/producersearch/InsLicStart.cfm
Waste Water System Operator................... http://info.dec.state.ak.us/SPS/Permitall2.asp
Wrestler .... www.dced.state.ak.us/occ/OccSearch/main.cfm

County Level ... Courts

Court Administration: Office of the Administrative Director, 820 W 4th Ave, Anchorage, AK, 99501; 907-264-8232; Records: 907-264-0491; www.state.ak.us/courts/

Court Structure: Alaska is not organized into counties but rather into 15 boroughs (3 unified home rule municipalities that are combination borough and city, and 12 boroughs) and 12 home rule cities, which do not directly coincide with the 4 Judicial Districts into which the judicial system is divided. In other words, judicial boundaries cross borough boundaries. Alaska has a unified, centrally administered, totally state-funded judicial system. Municipal governments do not maintain separate court systems.

The four levels of courts in the Alaska Court System are the Supreme Court, the Court of Appeals, the Superior Court, and the District Court. The Supreme Court and Court of Appeals are appellate courts, while Superior Courts and District Courts are trial courts. Probate is handled by Superior Courts.

The Superior Court is the trial court of general jurisdiction. There are 34 Superior Court judgeships located throughout the state. The District Court is a trial court of limited jurisdiction. District Court currently has 17 judges in the state. The Superior Court serves as an appellate court for appeals from civil and criminal cases which have been tried in District Court.

The 1st District encompasses all of southeast Alaska. Magistrates act as judicial officers. This 1st District has five trial/Superior Courts: Ketchikan, Wrangell, Petersburg, Sitka, and Juneau. District Magistrate Courts are Haines, Skagway, Yakutat, Angoon, Kake, Hoona, Craig.

Online Access Note: You may now search court records free at new CourtView system at www.courtrecords.alaska.gov but only for the jurisdictions of Anchorage, Fairbanks, and Palmer. Otherwise, you may do a name search of the remaining statewide jurisdictions on the Alaska Trial Courts database index at www.state.ak.us/courts/names.htm. Search results give case number, file date, disposition date, charge, and sentence. The index gives the name used on the first pleading only. The index is for only those courts on the new case management system. Until all courts are on, this search is not FCRA-compliant for employment screening purposes. The home web page gives access to Appellate Court opinions.

All Alaska Boroughs and Districts (other than Anchorage, Fairbanks, and Palmer)
Civil and Criminal Records
Search names on the Alaska Trial Courts database at www.state.ak.us/courts/names.htm. Web gives basic info.

Anchorage Borough
Fairbanks North Star Borough
Matanuska-Susitna Borough
Superior & District Court – Civil and Criminal Records
Search court records free at new CourtView system at www.courtrecords.alaska.gov/

County Level ... Recorders & Assessors

Recording Office Organization: The Alaskan counties are called boroughs, however, real estate recording is done under a system of 34 recording districts that was established at the time of the Gold Rush. Some of the Districts are identical in geography to boroughs, such as the Aleutian Islands, but other boroughs and districts overlap. Therefore you need to know which recording district any given town or city is located in. A helpful website is www.dnr.state.ak.us/recorders/findYourDistrict.htm.

The entire state except the Aleutian Islands is in the Alaska Time Zone (AK). All state and federal tax liens are filed with the District Recorder. Districts do not perform separate tax lien searches.

Online Access Note: Online access to the state recorder's office database from the Dept. of Natural Resources is available free at www.dnr.state.ak.us/ssd/recoff/search.cfm. This includes property information, liens, deeds, bankruptcies, and more. Images go back to June, 2001; index to 2000; index goes back to mid-1970's depending on the recording district involved. Also, a DNR "land records" database is searchable at www.dnr.state.ak.us/cgi-bin/lris/landrecords.

Aleutian Islands District *Real Estate, UCC Records*
http://data.visionappraisal.com/newportvt/

Anchorage District *Real Estate, UCC, Property Tax, Most Wanted, Stolen Vehicle Records*
www.akrecorder.info
Access is on the statewide DNR system at www.dnr.state.ak.us/ssd/recoff/search.cfm. UCC records can be accessed by phone at 907-269-8899. Also, access to Anchorage real estate property taxes is free at www.muni.org/services/departments/treasury/property/askViewer.cfm. Also, the sheriff's most wanted and stolen vehicle lists are at www.muni.org/apd1/apd911.cfm.

Bethel District *Real Estate, UCC Records*
Access is on the statewide DNR system at www.dnr.state.ak.us/ssd/recoff/search.cfm or at http://akrecorder.info.

Bristol Bay District *Real Estate, UCC Records*
Access is on the statewide DNR system at www.dnr.state.ak.us/ssd/recoff/search.cfm.

Fairbanks District *Real Estate, UCC, Cemetery Records*
www.co.fairbanks.ak.us
Access to the Fairbanks North Star Borough property database is free online at www.co.fairbanks.ak.us/PropertyDB/default.asp. Also, access is on the statewide DNR system at www.dnr.state.ak.us/ssd/recoff/search.cfm. Also, access to cemetery records for a fee is through a private company at www.ancestry.com/search/db.aspx?dbid=4044

Haines District *Real Estate, UCC Records*
Access is on the statewide DNR system at www.dnr.state.ak.us/ssd/recoff/search.cfm.

Homer District *Real Estate, UCC, Assessor Records*
Access the statewide DNR system at www.dnr.state.ak.us/ssd/recoff/search.cfm. Also, access the borough tax assessor rolls free at www.borough.kenai.ak.us/assessingdept/Parcel_QUERY/SEARCH.HTM.

Juneau District *Real Estate, UCC, Assessor Records*
www.juneau.org/cbj/index.php
Access to City of Juneau Property Records database is free online at www.juneau.org/assessordata/sqlassessor.php. Also includes link access to Juneau rentals data and the Records home page. Access is via the statewide DNR system at www.dnr.state.ak.us/ssd/recoff/search.cfm.

Kenai District *Assessor, Real Estate, UCC Records*
Access to Kenai Peninsula Borough Assessing Dept. Public Information Search Page is free at www.borough.kenai.ak.us/assessingdept/Parcel_QUERY/SEARCH.HTM. Also, access data on the statewide DNR system at www.dnr.state.ak.us/ssd/recoff/search.cfm.

Kodiak District   *Real Estate, UCC, Assessor, Property Records*

Access is on the statewide DNR system at www.dnr.state.ak.us/ssd/recoff/search.cfm. Also, search property assessor real property records free at www.kib.co.kodiak.ak.us. Click on "Real Property Records."

Kuskokwim District   *Real Estate, UCC Records*

Access is on the statewide DNR system at www.dnr.state.ak.us/ssd/recoff/search.cfm.

Seldovia District   *Real Estate, UCC, Assessor Records*

Access is on the statewide DNR system at www.dnr.state.ak.us/ssd/recoff/search.cfm. Also, access the borough tax assessor rolls is free at www.borough.kenai.ak.us/assessingdept/Parcel_QUERY/SEARCH.HTM.

Seward District   *Real Estate, UCC, Assessor Records*

Access is on the statewide DNR system at www.dnr.state.ak.us/ssd/recoff/search.cfm. Also, access the borough tax assessor rolls is free at www.borough.kenai.ak.us/assessingdept/Parcel_QUERY/SEARCH.HTM.

Federal Courts in Alaska...

Standards for Federal Courts: The universal PACER sign-up number is 800-676-6856. Find PACER and the Party/Case Index on the Web at http://pacer.psc.uscourts.gov. PACER dial-up access is $.60 per minute. Also, courts offering internet access via PACER, Web-PACER or the new CM-ECF charge $.08 per page fee ($.07 per page if record is pre-2005 or unless noted as free).

US District Court -- District of Alaska

www.akd.uscourts.gov

PACER: Toll-free access phone: 888-271-6212. Local access phone: 907-677-6178. Case records are available back to 1987. New records are available online after 1 day. **Electronic Filing:** CM/ECF data at (Currently in the process of implementing CM/ECF). **Other Online Access:** Court does not participate in the U.S. party case index. Current and next day calendars at www.akd.uscourts.gov. **Phone access:** Voice Case Information System, call 907-222-6940.
Anchorage Division counties: Aleutian Islands-East, Aleutian Islands-West, Anchorage Borough, Bristol Bay Borough, Dillingham, Kenai Peninsula Borough, Kodiak Island Borough, Lake and Peninsula, Matanuska-Susitna Borough, Valdez-Cordova.
Fairbanks Division counties: Bethel, Denali, Fairbanks North Star Borough, North Slope Borough, Northwest Arctic Borough, Southeast Fairbanks, Wade Hampton, Yukon-Koyukuk.
Juneau Division counties: Haines Borough, Juneau Borough, Prince of Wales-Outer Ketchikan, Sitka Borough, Skagway-Hoonah-Angoon, Wrangell-Petersburg.
Ketchikan Division counties: Ketchikan Gateway Borough.
Nome Division counties: Nome.

US Bankruptcy Court -- District of Alaska

www.akb.uscourts.gov

PACER: Case records are available back to 7/1991. Records are purged 6 months. **PACER Online Access:** ECF replaces PACER. Document images available. **Electronic Filing:** CM/ECF data at https://ecf.akb.uscourts.gov. **Opinions:** View court opinions at www.akb.uscourts.gov/index.htm. **Other Online Access:** The old RACER system has been replaced. Court calendars free at www.akb.uscourts.gov/calendars.htm. **Phone access:** Voice Case Information System, call 888-878-3110, 907-271-2658
Anchorage Division counties: All boroughs and districts in Alaska.

Arizona

Capital: Phoenix
            Maricopa County
Time Zone: MST
Population: 5,743,834
# of Counties: 15

Quick Links

Website: http://az.gov/webapp/portal/
Governor: www.governor.state.az.us
Attorney General: www.azag.gov
State Archives- www.lib.az.us/archives/
State Statutes and Codes: www.azleg.state.az.us/ArizonaRevisedStatutes.asp
Legislative Bill Search: www.azleg.state.az.us/Bills.asp
Bill Monitoring: http://alistrack.azleg.state.az.us/
Unclaimed Funds: www.azunclaimed.gov/

State Level ... Major Agencies

Statewide Court Records

Administrative Offices of the Courts, Arizona Supreme Court Bldg, 1501 W Washington, Phoenix, AZ 85007-3231; 602-542-9310, Fax-602-542-9484, 8AM-5PM.
http://www.supreme.state.az.us
Online search: Visit www.supreme.state.az.us/publicaccess/notification/default.asp The Public Access to Court Case Information is a valuable web service providing a resource for information about court cases from 142 out of 180 courts in Arizona. Courts not covered include certain parts of Pima, Yavapai, Mohave, and Maricopa counties. Access information includes: detailed case information, i.e., case type, charges, filing and disposition dates; the parties in the case, not including victims and witnesses; and the court mailing address & location. Opinions from the AZ Supreme Court and Court of Appeals are available from the website listed above. **Other options:** The Maricopa and Pima county courts maintain their own online access systems, but will also, under current planning, be part of the above system.

Sexual Offender Registry

Department of Public Safety, Sex Offender Compliance, PO Box 6638//Mail Code 9999, Phoenix, AZ 85005-6638 (Courier: 2102 W Encanto, Phoenix, AZ 85009); 602-255-0611, Fax-602-223-2949, 8AM-5PM.
http://az.gov/webapp/offender/main.do
Online search: Searching of Level 2 and Level 3 offenders is available online at the website above. Search for an individual by name, or search by ZIP Code or address for known offenders. The site also lists, with pictures, absconders who are individuals whose whereabouts are unknown. **Other options:** A download is available from the webpage for $25.00.

Incarceration Records

AZ Department of Corrections, Records Dept, 1601 W. Jefferson St., Phoenix, AZ 85007; 602-542-5586, Fax-602-542-1638, 8-5PM.
http://www.adc.state.az.us
Online search: For online search, you must provide last name, first initial or ADC number. Any add'l identifiers are welcomed. Location, ADC number, physical Identifiers and sentencing information are released. Inmates admitted and released from 1972 to 1985 may not be searchable on the web. Also available is ADC Fugitives - an alphabetical Inmate Datasearch listing of Absconders and Escapees from ADC. **Other options:** A private company offers free web access at www.vinelink.com/index.jsp.

Corporation, Limited Liability Company Records

Corporation Commission, Corporation Records, 1300 W Washington, Room 101, Phoenix, AZ 85007; 602-542-3026 (Status), 602-542-3285 (Annual Reports), Fax-602-542-3414, 8AM-5PM.
http://www.cc.state.az.us/corp/index.htm
Online search: The website above provides free access to all corporation information. Also, an online system called STARPAS functions 24 hours a day, 7 days a week. Go to http://starpas.cc.state.az.us/instruct.html. **Other options:** To purchase the database, call 602-364-4433.

Trademarks/Servicemarks, Trade Names, Limited Partnerships, Limited Liability Partnerships, Foreign Limited Partnerships

Secretary of State, Trademarks/Tradenames/Limited Partnership Division, 1700 W Washington, 7th Floor, Phoenix, AZ 85007 (Courier: Customer Service, 14 N 18th Ave, Phoenix, AZ); 602-542-6187, Fax-602-542-7386, 8AM-5PM.
http://www.azsos.gov/business_services/TNT/Default.htm
Online search: The website links to three searchable databases. One searches for Registered Names, Trade Names, and Trademarks. Also available is the full Trade Name and Trademark index in data format. Anther lists the registered names in alpha order and states the type of records available. Another way to obtain this data is from http://starpas.cc.state.az.us/instruct.html. **Other options:** Bulk purchase is available on microfiche.

Uniform Commercial Code, Federal Tax Liens, State Tax Liens

UCC Division, Secretary of State, 1700 W Washington, 7th Floor, Phoenix, AZ 85007 (Courier: Customer Service Center, 14 North 18th Ave, Phoenix, AZ 85007); 602-542-6187, Fax-602-542-7386, 8AM - 5PM.
http://www.azsos.gov/business_services/UCC/
Online search: UCC records can be searched for free at www.azsos.gov/scripts/ucc_search.dll. Searching can be done by debtor, secured party name, or file number. From this site you can also download the full UCC index in data format. Note there are 2 searches - a pre 07/01/01 search of the old database, and a strict Revised Article 9 which is current up within 4 days of present. **Other options:** E-mail requests are accepted. Microfilm of filings is available for purchase.

Birth Certificates

Department of Health Services, Vital Records Section, PO Box 3887, Phoenix, AZ 85030 (Courier: 1818 West Adams, Phoenix, AZ 85007); 602-255-3260, 602-364-1300 (Recording), 888-816-5907 (In-state), Fax-602-249-3040, 8AM-5PM.
http://www.azdhs.gov/vitalrcd/index.htm
Online search: Records may be ordered online via www.vitalchek.com, a state-endorsed vendor. Images of birth certificates from 1887 to 1929 and death certificate images from 1878 to 1953 are available free online at http://genealogy.az.gov.

Driver Records

Motor Vehicle Division, Correspondence Unit, PO Box 2100, Mail Drop 539M, Phoenix, AZ 85001-2100 (Courier: Customer Records Services, 1801 W Jefferson, Lobby, Phoenix, AZ 85007); 602-712-8420, 8AM-5PM.
http://www.azdot.gov/mvd/index.asp
Online search: Arizona's online system is interactive and open 24 hours daily. Fee is $3.25 per record. This system is primarily for those requesters who qualify per DPPA. For more information call 602-712-7235. **Other options:** Overnight cartridge ordering is available. Fee is $2.00 for 39 month record, $3.00 for 5 year record. Call 602-712-7235 for details.

Vehicle Ownership, Vehicle Identification

Motor Vehicle Division - Director's Office, Record Services Section, PO Box 2100, Mail Drop 504M, Phoenix, AZ 85001-2100 (Courier: Customer Records Services, 1801 W Jefferson, Rm 111, Phoenix, AZ 85007); 602-712-8420, 8AM-5PM.
http://www.dot.state.az.us/MVD/mvd.htm
Online search: Online access is offered but only to permissible users. Fee is $3.00 per record. The system is open 24 hours a day, seven days a week. For more information, call 602-712-7235.

Editor's Tip: Arizona, which is on Mountain Standard Time, does not observe Daylight Savings Time rules. Thus, from the first Sunday in April to the last Sunday in October, nearly all Arizona locations will have the same clock time as Pacific Daylight Time, the same time as in California. There are exceptions. Some Arizona Indian Reservation offices may observe Daylight Savings Time. Notable is the Navajo Nation Indian Reservation in northeastern Arizona. The Navajos observe DST. This does not include the Hopiland Indian Reservation, which is surrounded by the Navajos.

State Level ... Occupational Licensing

Acupuncturist.. www.azacuboard.az.gov/ASPSearch.htm
Acupuncturist Chiropractor........................... www.azchiroboard.com/ASPSearch.htm
Advance Fee Loan Broker .... http://azdfi.gov/Lists/Lists.htm
Aerial Applicator, Pesticide .... www.kellysolutions.com/az/Pilots/index.asp
Agricultural Grower/Seller .... www.kellysolutions.com/az/RUPBuyers/index.asp
Agricultural Pest Control Advisor .... www.kellysolutions.com/az/PCA/index.asp
Ambulance Service .... www.azdhs.gov/bems/conmaps.htm
Ambulatory Surgical Center .... http://pub.hs.state.az.us/datasvcs/als2/als_med/search/m_searchform.cfm
Applicator (Pesticide), Private/Commerc'l. www.kellysolutions.com/AZ/Applicators/index.asp
Architect .... www.btr.state.az.us/RegistrantSearch.asp
Assayer .... www.btr.state.az.us/RegistrantSearch.asp
Assisted Living Facility .... http://pub.hs.state.az.us/datasvcs/als2/als_alfac/search/m_searchform.cfm
Attorney.. www.azbar.org/content.cfm?text=/LegalResources/findlawyer
Audiologist .... http://pub.hs.state.az.us/datasvcs/als2/als_splic/search/m_searchform.cfm
Bank.. http://azdfi.gov/Lists/BA_List.HTML
Behavioral Health Emergency/Resi. Svcs... www.azdhs.gov/als/databases/
Behavioral Outpatient Clinic/Rehab .... www.azdhs.gov/als/databases/
Charity .... www.azsos.gov/scripts/Charity_Search.dll
Charter School .... www.ade.state.az.us/CharterSchools/search/
Child Residential Home............................... www.azdhs.gov/als/databases/providers_cc.pdf
Chiropractor.. www.azchiroboard.com/ASPSearch.htm
Clinic, Recovery Care/Rural Health .... http://pub.hs.state.az.us/datasvcs/als2/als_med/search/m_searchform.cfm
Collection Agency .... http://azdfi.gov/Lists/Lists.htm
Consumer Lender... http://azdfi.gov/Lists/Lists.htm
Contractor... www.rc.state.az.us/clsc/AZROCLicenseQuery
Court Reporter www.supreme.state.az.us/cr/pdf/merged%20directory2wpd.pdf
Credit Union (state chartered)..................... http://azdfi.gov/Lists/CU_List.HTML
Day Care Establishment.............................. http://pub.hs.state.az.us/datasvcs/als2/als_cc/search/m_searchform.cfm
Debt Management Company .... http://azdfi.gov/Lists/Lists.htm
Deferred Presentment Company .... http://azdfi.gov/Lists/DPC_List.HTML
Degree Program, Vocational....................... http://azppse.state.az.us/directory.html
Detoxification Service .... www.azdhs.gov/als/databases/
Development Disabled Group Home .... http://pub.hs.state.az.us/datasvcs/als2/als_dd/search/m_searchform.cfm
Dispensing Naturopath................................ www.npbomex.az.gov/directories.html
Dry Well Registration................................. www.azdeq.gov/databases/drywellsearch.html
Embalmer.. www.funeralbd.state.az.us/dir.htm
EMS ALS Base Hospital .... www.azdhs.gov/bems/basehosp.htm
Engineer.. www.btr.state.az.us/RegistrantSearch.asp
Escrow Agent.. http://azdfi.gov/Lists/Lists.htm
Family Day Care Home .... www.azdhs.gov/als/databases/providers_cc.pdf
Feed Dealer... www.kellysolutions.com/az/feeddealers/index.asp
Feed Distribution, Commercial................... www.kellysolutions.com/az/FeedDealers/index.asp
Fertilizer Dealer.. www.kellysolutions.com/az/fertdealers/index.asp
Fertilizer Distribution, Commercial .... www.kellysolutions.com/az/FertDealers/index.asp
Fertilizer Product .... www.kellysolutions.com/AZ/Fertilizer/fertilizerindex.asp
Food Packer/Grower/Shipper, Contract ...... www.kellysolutions.com/az
Fruit/Vegetable Broker/Dealer.................... www.kellysolutions.com/az
Funeral Director.. www.funeralbd.state.az.us/dir.htm
Funeral Pre-Need Trust Company .... http://azdfi.gov/Lists/Lists.htm
Geologist... www.btr.state.az.us/RegistrantSearch.asp
Headstart Facility.. http://pub.hs.state.az.us/datasvcs/als2/als_cc/search/m_searchform.cfm
Health Clinic .... http://pub.hs.state.az.us/datasvcs/als2/als_med/search/m_searchform.cfm
Hearing Aid Dispenser................................ http://pub.hs.state.az.us/datasvcs/als2/als_splic/search/m_searchform.cfm

Home Health Agency	http://pub.hs.state.az.us/datasvcs/als2/als_med/search/m_searchform.cfm
Home Inspector	www.btr.state.az.us/RegistrantSearch.asp
Hospice	http://pub.hs.state.az.us/datasvcs/als2/als_med/search/m_searchform.cfm
Hospital/Infirmary	http://pub.hs.state.az.us/datasvcs/als2/als_med/search/m_searchform.cfm
Insurance Agent	www.id.state.az.us/
Insurance Broker P&C only	www.id.state.az.us/
Juvenile Group Home	http://pub.azdhs.gov/datasvcs/jgh_registry/dsp_searchform.cfm
Landscape Architect	www.btr.state.az.us/RegistrantSearch.asp
Liquor Producer/Whsle	www.azll.com/query.htm
Liquor Retail Co-Operative/Agent/Mgr	www.azll.com/query.htm
Lobbyist	www.azsos.gov/scripts/Lobbyist_Search.dll
Long Term Care Facility	http://pub.hs.state.az.us/datasvcs/als2/als_alfac/search/m_searchform.cfm
Massage Therapy School	http://massagetherapy.az.gov/approvedschools.htm
Medical Doctor, Intern/Resident	www.azmd.gov/profile/getlicense.aspx
Medical Facility	http://pub.hs.state.az.us/datasvcs/als2/als_med/search/m_searchform.cfm
Midwife, Lay	http://pub.hs.state.az.us/datasvcs/als2/als_mid/search/m_searchform.cfm
Money Transmitter	http://azdfi.gov/Lists/Lists.htm
Mortgage Banker, Commercial	http://azdfi.gov/Lists/BK_List.HTML
Mortgage Banker/Broker	http://azdfi.gov/Lists/Lists.htm
Motor Vehicle Dealer/Sales Finance	http://azdfi.gov/Lists/MVD_List.HTML
Naturopathic Medical Asst	www.npbomex.az.gov/directories.html
Naturopathic Physician	www.npbomex.az.gov/directories.html
Naturopathic School	www.npbomex.az.gov/School%20Directory.html
Notary Public	www.azsos.gov/scripts/Notary_Search.dll
Nurse-LPN/RN/Nurses' Aide	www.azbn.org/onlineverificationbatch.asp
Optometrist	www.asbo.state.az.us
Osteopathic Physician	http://docfinder.state.az.us
Outpatient Physical Therapy	http://pub.hs.state.az.us/datasvcs/als2/als_med/search/m_searchform.cfm
Out-Patient Surgical Ctr	http://pub.hs.state.az.us/datasvcs/als2/als_med/search/m_searchform.cfm
P&C Broker	www.id.state.az.us/
P&C Managing Agent, Life/Disability	www.id.state.az.us/
Pesticide Company	www.sb.state.az.us/spccsearch.htm
Pesticide Custom Applicator	www.kellysolutions.com/az/CustomAppl/index.asp
Pesticide Distribution	www.kellysolutions.com/az/Dealers/index.asp
Pesticide Registration	www.kellysolutions.com/az/pesticideindex.htm
Pesticide Seller	www.kellysolutions.com/az/Dealers/index.asp
Physical Therapist/Therapist Assistant	www.ptboard.state.az.us/public/ptays/ptSearch.asp
Physician Assistant	www.azmd.gov/profile/getlicense.aspx
Physiotherapist	www.azchiroboard.com/ASPSearch.htm
Plant Operator	www.azdeq.gov/databases/opcertsearch.html
Podiatrist	www.podiatry.state.az.us/directory.htm
Political Action Committee	www.azsos.gov/scripts/superpac.cgi
Post-Secondary Educ. Institution	http://azppse.state.az.us/directory.html
Post-Secondary Voc. Program, Private	http://azppse.state.az.us/directory.html
Premium Finance Company	http://azdfi.gov/Lists/PF_List.HTML
Preschool	http://pub.hs.state.az.us/datasvcs/als2/als_cc/search/m_searchform.cfm
Property Tax Agent	www.appraisal.state.az.us/Directory/TAXAOUT.TXT
Psychologist	www.psychboard.az.gov/directory.htm
Public Accountant-CPA	www.accountancy.state.az.us/scripts/BOAsearch.exe
Public Accounting Firm-CPA/PA	www.accountancy.state.az.us/scripts/BOAsearch.exe
Real Estate Agent/Broker/Sales/Firm	www.re.state.az.us/search.html
Real Estate Appraiser	www.appraisal.state.az.us/Directory/directory.html
Real Estate School/Course	http://159.87.254.2/publicdatabase/SearchSchools.aspx?mode=3
Recovery Center/Rehabilitation Agency	http://pub.hs.state.az.us/datasvcs/als2/als_med/search/m_searchform.cfm
Renal Disease Facility	http://pub.hs.state.az.us/datasvcs/als2/als_med/search/m_searchform.cfm
Sales Finance Company	http://azdfi.gov/Lists/SF_List.HTML

School Bus Transportation Provider .... www.dps.state.az.us/license/schoolbusdriver/default.asp
Seed Dealer.. www.kellysolutions.com/az/SeedDealers/index.asp
Seed Labeler .... www.kellysolutions.com/az/SeedLabelers/index.asp
Speech Pathology... http://pub.hs.state.az.us/datasvcs/als2/als_med/search/m_searchform.cfm
Speech-Language Pathologist..................... http://pub.hs.state.az.us/datasvcs/als2/als_splic/search/m_searchform.cfm
Subdivision Public Report .... http://159.87.254.2/publicdatabase/SearchDevelopments.aspx?mode=2
Surveyor, Land .... www.btr.state.az.us/RegistrantSearch.asp
Telemarketing Firm .... www.azsos.gov/scripts/TS_Search_engine.cgi
Treatment Clinic .... http://pub.hs.state.az.us/datasvcs/als2/als_med/search/m_searchform.cfm
Trust Company .... http://azdfi.gov/Lists/TC_List.HTML
Trust Div. of Chartered Financial Inst. .... http://azdfi.gov/Lists/Lists.htm
Waste Water Facility Operator .... www.azdeq.gov/databases/opcertsearch.html
Water Distribution System Operator........... www.azdeq.gov/databases/opcertsearch.html
Well Drilling Firm .... www.azwater.gov/dwr/content/Drillers/default.asp
X-ray, Portable... http://pub.hs.state.az.us/datasvcs/als2/als_med/search/m_searchform.cfm

County Level ... Courts

Court Administration: Administrative Office of the Courts, Arizona Supreme Court Bldg, 1501 W Washington, Phoenix, AZ, 85007; 602-542-9310; www.supreme.state.az.us

Court Structure: The Superior Court is the court of general jurisdiction. Justice, and Municipal courts generally have separate jurisdiction over case types as indicated in the text. Most courts will search their records by plaintiff or defendant. Estate cases are handled by Superior Court. Fees are the same as for civil and criminal case searching.

Online Access Note: The Public Access to Court Case Information is a valuable web service providing a resource for information about court cases from 141 out of 180 courts in Arizona. Courts not covered include certain parts of Pima, Yavapai, Mohave, and Maricopa counties. Information includes– detailed case information (i.e., case type, charges, filing and disposition dates), the parties in the case (not including victims and witnesses), and the court mailing address and location. Go to www.supreme.state.az.us/publicaccess/default.htm

Opinions from the Supreme Court and Court of Appeals are available from the website.

Apache County

Superior Court - Justice Courts – Civil and Criminal Records
www.co.apache.az.us/clerk
Access to records from 1995 forward is free at www.supreme.state.az.us/publicaccess/. Also, search these Justice Courts- Chinle, Puerco, Round Valley, St Johns.

Cochise County

Superior Court - Justice Courts – Civil and Criminal Records
www.co.cochise.az.us/Court/
Access to records is free at www.supreme.state.az.us/publicaccess/. Also, search these Justice Courts- Benson, Bisbee, Bowie, Douglas, Sierra Vista, Willcox.

Coconino County

Superior Court - Justice Courts – Civil and Criminal Records
Access to records is free at www.supreme.state.az.us/publicaccess/. Also, search these Justice Courts- Flagstaff, Fredonia, page, Williams.

Gila County

Superior Court - Justice Courts – Civil and Criminal Records
Access to records is free at www.supreme.state.az.us/publicaccess/. Also, search these Justice Courts- Northern Regional (Payson), Southern Regional (Globe), and Winkelman.

Graham County
Superior Court - Justice Courts – Civil and Criminal Records
Access to records is free at www.supreme.state.az.us/publicaccess/. Also, search these Justice Courts- Precinct 1, Pima Precinct 2.

Greenlee County
Superior Court - Justice Courts – Civil and Criminal Records
Access to records is free at www.supreme.state.az.us/publicaccess/. Also, search these Justice Courts- Precinct 1, Precinct 2.

La Paz County
Superior Court - Justice Courts – Civil and Criminal Records
www.co.la-paz.az.us/courts.htm
Access to records is free at www.supreme.state.az.us/publicaccess/. Also, search these Justice Courts- Parker, Quartzsite, Salome.

Maricopa County
Superior Court – Civil and Criminal Records
www.superiorcourt.maricopa.gov
Access to civil case dockets free at www.superiorcourt.maricopa.gov/docket/index.asp. Case file can be printed. Also, access to probate court dockets is at www.superiorcourt.maricopa.gov/docket/probate/index.asp. Family court filings are at www.superiorcourt.maricopa.gov/docket/family/index.asp Access to criminal case dockets is free at www.superiorcourt.maricopa.gov/docket/criminal/index.asp.

Navajo County
Superior Court - Justice Courts – Civil and Criminal Records
Access to records is free at www.supreme.state.az.us/publicaccess/. Also, search these Justice Courts- Holbrook, Kayenta, Pinetop-Lakeside, Show Low, Snowflake, Winslow.

Pima County
Superior Court – Civil and Criminal Records
www.cosc.co.pima.az.us
Access to records is free at www.supreme.state.az.us/publicaccess/. Also, search these Justice Courts- Ajo, Green Valley.

Pima County Consolidated Justice Court – Civil and Criminal Records
www.jp.pima.gov/
Access is free http://jp.co.pima.az.us/casesearch/index.php. You can search docket information for civil, criminal or traffic cases by name, docket or citation number.

Pinal County
Superior Court - Justice Courts – Civil and Criminal Records
www.co.pinal.az.us/clerksc/
Access to records is free at www.supreme.state.az.us/publicaccess/. Also, search these Justice Courts- Apache Junction, Casa Grande, Eloy, Florence, Mammoth, Maricopa, Oracle, Superior/Kearny.

Santa Cruz County
Superior Court – Civil and Criminal Records
http://sccazcourts.org
Access to records is free at www.supreme.state.az.us/publicaccess/. Also, search these Justice Courts- East Santa Cruz, Santa Cruz.

Santa Cruz, East Santa Cruz County Justice Court – Civil and Criminal Records
Access civil records free at www.supreme.state.az.us/publicaccess/notification/default.asp. Also, weekly court calendars are at www.sccazcourts.org/court_calendars.htm.

Yavapai County
Superior Court – Civil and Criminal Records
Access to records is free at www.supreme.state.az.us/publicaccess/. Also, search these Justice Courts- Bagdad, Mayer, Seligman, Verde Valley, Yarnell.

Yuma County
Superior Court – Civil and Criminal Records
Access to records is free at www.supreme.state.az.us/publicaccess/. Also, search these Justice Courts- Somerton, Wellton, Yuma.

County Level ... Recorders & Assessors

Recording Office Organization: 15 counties, 16 recording offices. The Navajo Nation is profiled here. The recording officer is the County Recorder. Recordings are usually placed in a Grantor/Grantee index. The entire state is in the Mountain Time Zone (MST), and does not change to daylight savings time. Note that no less than four new telephone area codes have added in recent years: 480 and 623 for east and west Phoenix Metro area respectively, 520 for south and southeastern state, and 924 for west and north of state. Federal and state tax liens on personal property of businesses are filed with the Secretary of State. Other federal and state tax liens are filed with the County Recorder. Several counties will do a separate tax lien search.

Online Access Note: A number of county assessor offices offer online access. The Secretary of State offers online access to UCC records at www.sosaz.com/scripts/UCC_Search.dll.

Apache County *Real Estate, Recording, Deed, Judgment, Lien Records*
www.co.apache.az.us/Recorder/
Access to the recorder is free at www.thecountyrecorder.com/Search.aspx?CountyKey=5. Index goes back to 1985. Also, search the assessor property tax records free at www.co.mohave.az.us/apache/assessor/assessdatalink.asp.

Cochise County *Treasurer Back Tax, Restaurant Inspection Records*
www.co.cochise.az.us/recorders/Default.htm
Access the treasurer's back tax list free at www.co.cochise.az.us/treasurer/BackTax/backtaxmain.htm. Also, search restaurant inspections results at www.co.cochise.az.us/ccwebsite/SelectDistrict.asp

Coconino County *Recording, Grantor/Grantee, Real Estate Records*
www.coconino.az.gov
Access the recorder system free at http://eaglerecorder.coconino.az.gov/recorder/eagleweb/login.jsp. Documents are $1.00 to print; online records go back to 1983; images back to 3/1999. For official or certified copies or inquiries on documents prior to 1983 please contact office at 928-779-6585 or 1-800-793-6181. Also for property owner site for free go to http://gis-map.coconino.az.gov/website/coconino/getgisdata.asp

Gila County *Recording, Deed, Lien, Grantor/Grantee Records*
www.gilacountyaz.gov
Access to the recorder's index are free at http://63.241.138.77/icris/splash.jsp. Search for free, but official copies are $1.00 per page. Records go back to 1985, images back to 1998. Also, search assessor property data free at www.co.mohave.az.us/gila/assessor/assessdatalink.asp.

Graham County *Assessor, Property, Most Wanted, Recording, Deed, Divorce, Judgment, Lien Records*
www.graham.az.gov
Access the assessor database of property and assessments is free at www.co.mohave.az.us./graham/assessor/assessdatalink.asp. Search the most wanted list at www.eaznet.com/~gcso/wanted.htm. Also access to recorder records is at www.thecountyrecorder.com/Search.aspx?CountyKey=1; index goes back to 1984.

Greenlee County *Real Estate, Deed, Lien, Judgment, Vital Statistic, Recording Records*
www.co.greenlee.az.us/Recorder/RecorderHomePage.aspx
Access to recorder records is free at www.thecountyrecorder.com/Search.aspx?CountyKey=2. Index back to 1/1/1978.

La Paz County *Recorder, Deed, Judgment, Lien Records*
www.co.la-paz.az.us/recorder.htm
Access to the recorder document index only is free at www.thecountyrecorder.com.

Maricopa County *Real Estate, Lien, Property, Assessor Records*
http://recorder.maricopa.gov
Access by direct dial-up or the Internet. Dial-up access requires one-time set-up fee of $300 plus $.06 per minute. Dial-up hours are 8am-10pm M-F, 8-5 S-S. Records date back to 1983. For add'l info, contact Linda Kinchloe, 602-506-3637. Also, access to Recorder's database is at http://recorder.maricopa.gov/recdocdata. Records go back to 1968. Also search data back to 2002 for free at the clerk's office. Also search most wanted list at www.mcso.org/submenu.asp?file=mostwanted. Assessor database is at www.maricopa.gov/assessor. Residential data available. Also, perform tax appeal lookups at SBOE site at www.sboe.state.az.us/cgi-bin/name_lookup.pl. Search inmates at www.mcso.org/submenu.asp?file=MugIndex.

Mohave County *Real Estate, Grantor/Grantee, Lien, Assessor, Most Wanted, Sex Offender Records*
www.co.mohave.az.us
Access to the Recorder's System is free at http://eagleweb.co.mohave.az.us/recorder/eagleweb/. Registration and password is required. Fee is $1.00 to fee view image($1.00). Also, online access to the Assessor's property database is free (no registration) at www.co.mohave.az.us/1moweb/depts_files/assessor.htm. A sales history database is also here. Sex offender list is at www.ctaz.com/~mcso/page19.html. Also, the treasurer's tax sale parcel search is at www.co.mohave.az.us/depts/treas/tax_sale.asp. Also, search health inspection rating for food establishments at www.co.mohave.az.us/webapts/aptsnew.htm

Navajo County
Property, Assessor, Grantor/Grantee, Recording, UCC, Tax Lien, Death, Tax Sale, GIS-mapping Records
www.co.navajo.az.us
Access to the recorder's database of land information, UCCs, Liens, and Grantor/Grantee indices is free at www.thecountyrecorder.com/(yiyd5245hv1giy45ry3oju55)/Search.aspx. Documents go back to 1989; images to 1995. Also, access property assessor database free at www.co.navajo.az.us/theCountyRecorder/DataSearch/Searchhome.aspx. Also, a list of tax Lien Auction list is at www.co.navajo.az.us/Treasurers/Treasurers_Start_Page.aspx. Also, the county GIS-mapping site allows manual parcel searching at http://navcogis.co.navajo.az.us/website/NavajoCountyGIS.htm.

Navajo Nation
Property, Assessor, Grantor/Grantee, Recording, UCC, Tax Lien, Death, Tax Sale, GIS-mapping Records
www.co.navajo.az.us
Access to the recorder's database of land information, UCCs, Liens, and Grantor/Grantee indices is free at www.thecountyrecorder.com/Introduction.aspx?CountyKey=4. Documents go back to 1989; images to 1995. Also, access property assessor database free at www.thecountyrecorder.com/(yiyd5245hv1giy45ry3oju55)/Search.aspx. Site may be temp down. Also, a list of tax Lien Auction list is at www.co.navajo.az.us/Treasurers/Treasurers_Start_Page.aspx. Also, the county GIS-mapping site allows manual parcel searching at http://navcogis.co.navajo.az.us/website/NavajoCountyGIS.htm.

Pima County *Assessor, Real Estate, Lien, Recording, Deed, Property Tax, Tax Sale Records*
www.recorder.co.pima.az.us
Access recorder records free at www.recorder.co.pima.az.us/search/login.htm. Also, records on the Pima County Tax Assessor database are free at www.asr.co.pima.az.us/APIQ/index.aspx. Also, a name/parcel/property tax lookup may be performed free on the SBOE site at www.sboe.state.az.us/cgi-bin/name_lookup.pl. Also, search the property tax inquiry database at www.to.co.pima.az.us/property_search.html. Also, search tax lien sale, bankruptcies, and expiring liens free at www.to.co.pima.az.us/tax_lien_sale.html. There is also a real estate property tax search at www.to.co.pima.az.us/tax_lien_sale.html but no name searching.

Pinal County *Grantor/Grantee, Tax Bill, Tax Lien, Tax Sale, Assessor Records*
http://co.pinal.az.us
Access to the recorder's index is free at http://apps.co.pinal.az.us/Recorder/Search/. Also, access to the county treasurer's database of tax liens, tax bills, and tax sales is free at http://co.pinal.az.us/treasurer. Click on appropriate "Tax Searches" button. Also, search the assessor's property tax database free at http://apps.co.pinal.az.us/Assessor/Search/?T=Pinfo.

Santa Cruz County *Assessor, Property Records*
www.co.santa-cruz.az.us
Access to the County Assessor data is free at www.co.mohave.az.us./santacruz/assessor/assessdatalink.asp.

Yavapai County *Assessor, Real Estate, Recording, Deed, Inmate/Offender Records*
www.co.yavapai.az.us
Access to the recording office iCRIS database is free at http://icris.co.yavapai.az.us/icris/splash.jsp. Records from 1976 to present; images from 1976 to present. Also, assessor and land records on the County Geographic Information Systems (GIS) database are free at http://mapserver.co.yavapai.az.us/interactive/map.asp. Information also at http://mapserver.co.yavapai.az.us/parcelinfo/map.asp. Also, the board of supervisors tax sale list is at www.co.yavapai.az.us/events/TaxSales/BOS/taxsalelist.htm. Search the county offender/inmate list for free at www.vinelink.com/offender/searchNew.jsp?siteID=3007.

Yuma County *Property, Assessor Records*
www.co.yuma.az.us
Access to county property data is free at http://itax.co.yuma.az.us:8080/itax/taxSplash.jsp; registration is required.

Federal Courts in Arizona...

Standards for Federal Courts: The universal PACER sign-up number is 800-676-6856. Find PACER and the Party/Case Index on the Web at http://pacer.psc.uscourts.gov. PACER dial-up access is $.60 per minute. Also, courts offering internet access via PACER, Web-PACER or the new CM-ECF charge $.08 per page fee ($.07 per page if record is pre-2005 or unless noted as free).

US District Court -- District of Arizona

www.azd.uscourts.gov

PACER: Case records are available back to 1992. Records are purged every 12 months. New records are available online after 1 day. **PACER Online Access:** ECF replaces PACER. **Electronic Filing:** CM/ECF data at https://ecf.azd.uscourts.gov. **Opinions:** Click on Cases of Interest to view court opinions at www.azd.uscourts.gov. **Other Online Access:** Access to court calendars can be found at www.azd.uscourts.gov.

Phoenix Division counties: Gila, La Paz, Maricopa, Pinal, Yuma. This office manages the Prescott Division records. Some Yuma cases handled by San Diego Division of the Southern District of California.

Prescott Division counties: Apache, Coconino, Mohave, Navajo, Yavapai. Currently, this is an unmanned office; direct record requests to the Phoenix Division.

Tucson Division counties: Cochise, Graham, Greenlee, Pima, Santa Cruz. The Globe Division was closed effective 1/1994, and all case records for that division are now found here.

US Bankruptcy Court -- District of Arizona

www.azb.uscourts.gov

PACER: Case records are available back to 1986. Records are purged every 6 months. **PACER Online Access:** ECF replaces PACER. **Electronic Filing:** CM/ECF data at https://ecf.azb.uscourts.gov. **Opinions:** View court opinions at www.azb.uscourts.gov/opinions. **Other Online Access:** Judge's court calendars free at www.azb.uscourts.gov. **Phone access:** Voice Case Information System, call 602-682-4001.

Phoenix Division counties: Apache, Coconino, Gila, Maricopa, Navajo, Yavapai.

Tucson Division counties: Cochise, Graham, Greenlee, Pima, Pinal, Santa Cruz.

Yuma Division counties: La Paz, Mohave, Yuma.

Arkansas

Capital: Little Rock
             Pulaski County
Time Zone: CST
Population: 2,752,629
# of Counties: 75

Quick Links

Website: www.state.ar.us

Governor: www.arkansas.gov/governor

Attorney General: www.ag.state.ar.us

State Archives: www.ark-ives.com

State Statutes and Codes:
  www.arkleg.state.ar.us/NXT/gateway.dll?f=templates&fn=default.htm&vid=blr:code

Legislative Bill Search: www.arkleg.state.ar.us

Bill Monitoring: https://www.ark.org/dfa/sr1/

Unclaimed Funds: www.state.ar.us/auditor/unclprop/

State Level ... Major Agencies

Arkansas State Police, Identification Bureau, #1 State Police Plaza Dr, Little Rock, AR 72209; 501-618-8500, Fax-501-618-8404. www.asp.state.ar.us
Online search: Online access available but only to employers and professional licensing boards. Registration is required. Agents or 3rd party vendors representing employers are blocked from access, per the state legislators. There is an additional $2.00 to the standard $20.00 search fee. Searches are conducted by name. Search results includes registered sex offenders. For more info on this service, see https://www.ark.org/criminal/index.php. Accounts must maintain signed release documents in-house for three years.

Statewide Court Records

Administrative Office of Courts, 625 Marshall St, 1100 Justice Bldg, Little Rock, AR 72201-1078; 501-682-9400, Fax-501-682-9410. www.courts.state.ar.us
Online search: The home web page gives online access to Supreme Court Opinions and Appellate Court dockets, or access via http://courts.state.ar.us/online/or.html where you will also find Court of Appeals dockets, corrected opinions, and parallel citations. An Attorney search and court rules and administrative orders are also available.

Sexual Offender Registry

Arkansas Crime Information Center, Sexual Offender Registry, One Capitol Mall, 4D200, Little Rock, AR 72201; 501-682-2222, Fax-501-682-2269.
www.acic.org/Registration/index.htm
Online search: Searching is available at www.acic.org/soff/index.php. Search by name or location (county). Includes Level 3 and Level 4 offenders. Also, registered sex offenders are indicated on the criminal record online system maintained by the State Police; however, this system, is only available to employers and professional licensing boards.

Incarceration Records

Arkansas Department of Corrections, Records Supervisor, PO Box 8707, Pine Bluff, AR 71611-8707; 870-267-6424, 870-267-6999.
www.accessarkansas.org/doc/index.html

Online search: The online access at www.accessarkansas.org/doc/inmate_info/ has many search criteria capabilities. Also, a private company offers free web access at www.vinelink.com/index.jsp, including state, DOC, and many county jail systems. **Other options:** The inmate access web page offers a download of the inmate database. Fee includes an annual INA subscription of $50.00 plus $0.10 per record enhanced access fee.

Corporation, Fictitious Name, Limited Liability Company, Limited Partnerships

Secretary of State, Business & Commercial Service Division, State Capitol Bldg, Little Rock, AR 72201 (Courier: Business & Commercial Service Division, 1401 W Capitol Ave Ste 250, Little Rock, AR 72201); 501-682-3409, 888-233-0325, Fax-501-682-3437, 8AM-5PM (4:30 on F).
www.sos.arkansas.gov/corps/
Online search: The Internet site permits free searching of corporation records. You can search by name, registered agent, or filing number. **Other options:** Bulk release of records is available for $.50 per page. Contact Records Dept. 501-682-3409 or visit website for details.

Trademarks/Servicemarks

Secretary of State, Trademarks Section, State Capitol Bldg, Little Rock, AR 72201 (Courier: Business & Commercial Services Div, 1401 W Capitol Ave #250, Little Rock, AR 72201); 501-682-3409, 888-233-0325, Fax-501-682-3437, 8AM-5PM (4:30PM on F).
www.sos.arkansas.gov/corps/trademk/
Online search: Searching is available at no fee over the Internet site. Search by name, owner, city, or filing number. You can also search via email at corprequest@sosmail.state.ar.us. **Other options:** Records can be provided in bulk for $.50 per page. Call 501-682-3409 or visit website for details.

Uniform Commercial Code, Federal Tax Liens

UCC Division - Commercial Srvs, Secretary of State, State Capitol Bldg, Little Rock, AR 72201 (Courier: Commercial Business & Service Division, 1401 W Capitol Ave Rm 250, Little Rock, AR 72201); 501-682-5078, Fax-501-682-3500, 8AM-5PM.
www.sos.arkansas.gov
Online search: Subscribers of INA (Information Network of Arkansas) can search by file number or charter number; subscription fees and search fees involved. Check website for details. UCC Download is available via the Internet, but only to subscribers. Fee is $2,000.00 per month for weekly, bi-weekly or monthly downloads. Watch notifications are available for a $35.00 monthly fee.

Birth, Death Certificates

Arkansas Department of Health, Division of Vital Records, 4815 W Markham St, Slot 44, Little Rock, AR 72205; 501-661-2174, 501-661-2336 (Message Number), 501-661-2726 (Credit Card Line), 800-637-9314 (Toll Free), Fax-501-663-2832, 8AM-4:30PM.
www.healthyarkansas.com
Online search: Records may requested from www.vitalchek.com, or www.uscerts.com, both are state-endorsed vendors. Expedited service fees apply. **Other options:** Research projects require the approval of the director.

Marriage, Divorce Certificates

Arkansas Department of Health, Division of Vital Records, 4815 W Markham St, Slot 44, Little Rock, AR 72205; 501-661-2174, 501-661-2336 (Message Number), 501-661-2726 (Credit Card Line), Fax-501-663-2832, 8AM-4:30PM.
www.healthyarkansas.com
Online search: Records may requested from www.vitalchek.com, a state-endorsed vendor. Expedited service fees apply.

Workers' Compensation Records

Workers Compensation Commission, Operations/Compliance, 324 Spring Street, PO Box 950, Little Rock, AR 72203-0950; 501-682-3930, 800-622-4472, Fax-501-682-6761, 8AM-4:30PM M-F.
www.awcc.state.ar.us
Online search: To perform an online claim search, one must be a subscriber to the Information Network of Arkansas (INA). Records are from May 1, 1997 forward. There is an annual $50 subscriber fee to INA. Each record request is $3.50; if more than 20 are ordered in one month, the fee is $2.50 each request over 20. For more information, visit www.awcc.state.ar.us/electron.html.

Driver Records

Department of Driver Services, Driving Records Division, PO Box 1272, Room 1130, Little Rock, AR 72203-1272 (Courier: 1900 W 7th, #1130, Little Rock, AR 72201); 501-682-7207, 501-682-7908, Fax-501-682-2075, 8AM-4:30PM.
www.accessarkansas.org/dfa/driverservices/

Online search: Access is available through the Information Network of Arkansas (INA). The system offers both batch and interactive service. The system is only available to INA subscribers who have statutory rights to the data. The record fee is $8.00, or $11.00 for commercial drivers. Visit www.arkansas.gov/sub_services.php.

Vehicle Ownership, Vehicle Identification

Office of Motor Vehicles, MV Title Records, PO Box 1272, Room 1100, Little Rock, AR 72203 (Courier: 7th & Battery Sts, Ragland Bldg, Room 1100, Little Rock, AR 72201); 501-682-4692, 800-662-8247, Fax-501-682-4756, 8AM-4:30PM. www.accessarkansas.org/dfa/

Online search: Approved, DPPA compliant accounts may access records online by VIN, plate, or title number. The fee is $1.50. Name searches and certificated documents may be ordered. For further info, go to www.arkansas.gov/itrl/. **Other options:** The bulk purchase of records, except for recall or statistical purposes, is prohibited.

Accident Reports

Arkansas State Police, Crash Records Section, 1 State Police Plaza Drive, Little Rock, AR 72209; 501-618-8130, Fax-501-618-8131. www.asp.state.ar.us/divisions/rs/rs_crash.html

Online search: Limited information is available from the webpage for no charge (names involved), date, county. A record copy s may be purchased for $10.00 plus an additional $2.00 fee. Search by name, license number and/or date range. Once purchased, reports will be available for 30 days and may be repeatedly accessed with an Order ID. For further information regarding the contents of the report, please contact the Arkansas State Police at 501-618-8130. Credit card is required, unless requester is member of INA. Available records date back to 01/02/00.

State Level ... Occupational Licensing

Aesthetician	www.arkansas.gov/cos/
Agriculture Education	www.as-is.org/directory/search_lic.html
Architect	www.state.ar.us/arch/search.html
Asbestos Related Occupation	www.adeq.state.ar.us/compsvs/webmaster/databases.htm
Athletic Trainer	www.aratb.org/search.php
Attorney	http://courts.state.ar.us/attylist/new/
Bank	www.sos.arkansas.gov/corps/search_all.php
Business Education Teacher	www.as-is.org/directory/search_lic.html
Career Education Coordinator	www.as-is.org/directory/search_lic.html
Career Orientation Teacher	www.as-is.org/directory/search_lic.html
Cemetery, Perpetual Care	www.securities.arkansas.gov/starsqldb/asdcsifs/
Check Seller	www.securities.arkansas.gov/starsqldb/asdcsifs/
Child Care Provider	www.state.ar.us/childcare/search.html
Chiropractor	www.accessarkansas.org/asbce/search.html
Contractor	www.state.ar.us/clb/search.html
Cosmetologist/Cosmetology Instr.	www.arkansas.gov/cos/
Counselor, Professional	www.state.ar.us/abec/search.php
Dentist/Dental Hygienist	www.asbde.org
Electrologist/Electrolysis Instructor	www.arkansas.gov/cos/
Embalmer/Embalmer Apprentice	www.arkansas.gov/fdemb/
Engineer/Engineer in Training	www.accessarkansas.org/pels/search.php
Fire Equipment Inspector/Repairer	www.arfireprotection.org/roster/index.html
Fire Extinguisher Sprinkler Inspector	www.arfireprotection.org/roster/index.html
Funeral Director/Apprentice	www.arkansas.gov/fdemb/
Funeral Home/Crematory	www.arkansas.gov/fdemb/
Geologist	www.state.ar.us/agc/bordir2005.xls
Insurance Agency	www.sos.arkansas.gov/corps/search_all.php
Insurance Agency	http://insurance.arkansas.gov/is/Agency/agency.asp
Insurance Company	http://insurance.arkansas.gov/is/companysearch/cosearch.asp
Insurance Sales Agent	http://insurance.arkansas.gov/is/agentsearch/agent.asp
Investment Advisor	www.securities.arkansas.gov/starsqldb/asdsecifs/
Landscape Architect	www.state.ar.us/arch/search.html
Lobbyist	www.sosweb.state.ar.us/elections/elections_pdfs/lobby_lists/2005/2005list.pdf

Manicurist .... www.arkansas.gov/cos/
Marriage & Family Therapist .... www.state.ar.us/abec/search.php
Medicaid Provider.. www.medicaid.state.ar.us/InternetSolution/Provider/Provider.aspx
Medical Doctor/Surgeon/Corporation......... https://www.armedicalboard.org/licenseverf/default.asp
Midwife Nurse .... www.arsbn.org/registry/index.html
Mortgage Loan Broker/Company .... www.securities.arkansas.gov/starsqldb/asdcsifs/
Motor Vehicle Dealer/Dist/Mfg/Rep, New . www.armvc.com/licensee_search/index.html
Notary Public .... www.sos.arkansas.gov/corps/notary/
Nurse/Nurse LPN/Nurse Anesthetist .... www.arsbn.org/registry/index.html
Nursing Home Facility ... www.medicaid.state.ar.us/InternetSolution/General/units/oltc/findafacility/findafacility.htm
Occupational Therapist/Assistant................ https://www.armedicalboard.org/licenseverf/default.asp
Optician .... www.ark.org/directory/detail2.cgi?ID-1050
Optometrist .... www.arbo.org/index.php?action=findanoptometrist
Osteopathic Physician................................. https://www.armedicalboard.org/licenseverf/default.asp
P & C Company... http://insurance.arkansas.gov/pclh/pcweb.asp
Physical Therapist....................................... www.arptb.org/ptroster/search.php
Physician Assistant .... https://www.armedicalboard.org/licenseverf/default.asp
Political Action Committee ... ... www.sosweb.state.ar.us/elections/elections_pdfs/pac_lists/pac_list_02-03-05.pdf
Public Accountant-CPA............................... www.arkansas.gov/asbpa/
Real Estate Agent/Broker/Sales .... www.accessarkansas.org/arec/db/
Real Estate Appraiser.................................. www.arkansas.gov/alcb/search.php
Respiratory Care Practitioner..................... https://www.armedicalboard.org/licenseverf/default.asp
School Counselor... www.as-is.org/directory/search_lic.html
School Principal/Admin/Super .... www.as-is.org/directory/search_lic.html
Securities Agent/Broker/Dealer .... www.securities.arkansas.gov/starsqldb/asdsecifs/
Securities Exemption .... www.securities.arkansas.gov/starsqldb/asdsecifs/
Security Mutual Fund .... www.securities.arkansas.gov/starsqldb/asdsecifs/
Social Worker .... www.state.ar.us/swlb/search/index.html
Solid Waste Facility Operator..................... www.adeq.state.ar.us/compsvs/webmaster/databases.htm
Surveyor, Land/Surveyor-in-Training......... www.accessarkansas.org/pels/search.php
Teacher .... www.as-is.org/directory/search_lic.html
Waste Water Plant Operator .... www.adeq.state.ar.us/compsvs/webmaster/databases.htm

County Level ... Courts

Court Administration: Administrative Office of Courts, 625 Marshall St, Justice Bldg, Little Rock, AR, 72201; 501-682-9400; www.courts.state.ar.us

Court Structure: Circuit Courts are the courts of general jurisdiction and are arranged in 28 circuits. Circuit Courts consist of five subject matter divisions: criminal, civil, probate, domestic relations, and juvenile. A Circuit Clerk handles the records and recordings, however some counties have a County Clerk that handles probate. District Courts, formerly known as Municipal Courts before passage of Amendment 80 to the Arkansas Constitution, exercise countywide jurisdiction over misdemeanor cases, preliminary felony cases, and civil cases in matters of less than $5,000, including small claims. The City Courts operate in smaller communities where District Courts do not exist and exercise citywide jurisdiction.

Online Access Note: A limited but newly improved online computer system at http://courts.state.ar.us/online/or.html from the Administrative Office of Courts offers access to Supreme Court and Court of Appeals opinions and parallel citations, also Appellate Court and Court of Appeals dockets. There is also an Arkansas licensed attorney search and court rules and administrative orders. However, online access to courts at the county level remains almost non-existant.

4 Arkansas Counties - Boone, Crawford, Phillips, Pope
Circuit Court – Civil and Criminal Records
Access court orders online at www.etitlesearch.com; registration and fees apply.

Benton County

Circuit Court – Civil and Criminal Records

www.co.benton.ar.us

Search civil court docket information free at http://209.183.170.177:5061/. Use "option" 21. Also, access to court dockets is by subscription service at www.recordsusa.com/recordsusa/default.asp. Base fee is $49.95 per month and also includes land imaging and unlimited instrument access.

Miller County

Circuit Court – Civil and Criminal Records

Access to court dockets is by subscription service at www.recordsusa.com/recordsusa/default.asp. Base fee is $49.95 per month and also includes land imaging and unlimited instrument access.

Polk County

Circuit Court – Civil Records

Access to court dockets is by subscription service at www.recordsusa.com/recordsusa/default.asp. Base fee is $49.95 per month and also includes land imaging and unlimited instrument access.

Sharp County

Circuit Court – Civil and Criminal Records

Court has outsourced online access to civil, probate, criminal, and all recordings to www.ecourtstor.com; fees are involved.

Union County

Circuit Court – Civil and Criminal Records

Access to circuit court dockets by subscription through RecordsUSA.com. Credit card, username and password is required; choose either monthly or per-use plan. Visit the website for sign-up or call Lisa at 601-264-7701 for information.

Washington County

Circuit Court – Civil and Criminal Records

www.co.washington.ar.us

Online case index at www.co.washington.ar.us/resolution/. Civil cases indexed from 1992 forward. This is a commercial system, $50.00 per month prepaid. Pre-1973 court indices free at www.co.washington.ar.us/ArchiveSearch/CourtRecordSearch.asp. Online case index at www.co.washington.ar.us/resolution/. Criminal cases indexed from 1992 forward. This is a commercial system, $50.00 per month prepaid.

County Level ... Recorders & Assessors

Recording Office Organization: 75 counties, 85 recording offices. The recording officer is the Clerk of Circuit Court, who is Ex Officio Recorder. Ten counties have two recording offices - Arkansas, Carroll, Clay, Craighead, Franklin, Logan, Mississippi, Prairie, Sebastian, and Yell. The entire state is in the Central Time Zone (CST). Federal tax liens on personal property of businesses are filed with the Secretary of State. Other federal and all state tax liens are filed with the Circuit Clerk. Many counties will perform separate tax lien searches. Search fees are usually $6.00 per name.

Online Access Note: There is no statewide access; however two commercial systems are available that each cover roughly half the state. See below.

35 Arkansas Counties *Assessor, Property Records*

Registration and logon is required to search assessor records at www.arcountydata.com. Signup fee is $200 plus $.10 per minute usage. For signup or information call 479-631-8054 or visit at the web. Several counties are now on the new Citrix system - registration and logon is required to search assessor records on Citrix.

Counties include- Arkansas (Southern District), Baxter, Benton, Boone, Bradley, Carroll, Chicot, Clay (East District), Craighead, Crittenden, Dallas, Desha, Faulkner, Fulton, Grant, Greene, Howard, Izard, Johnson, Lee, Logan, Lonoke, Marion, Newton, Pike, Poinsett, Pope, Pulaski, St Francis, Saline, Sebastian, Sharp, Stone, Van Buren, and White .

32 Arkansas Counties *Assessor, Property Records*

Access property data free at www.actdatascout.com. Subscription for deeper info is $20 per month. 50% discount on add'l counties.

Counties include- Ashley, Carroll, Clark, Cleburne, Conway, Crawford, Cross, Garland, Hempstead, Hot Spring, Independence, Jackson, Jefferson, Lafayette, Lawrence, Lincoln, Little River, Madison, Miller, Monroe, Montgomery, Nevada, Ouachita, Perry, Polk, Prairie, Searcy, Sebastian, Sevier, Union, Washington, and Woodruff.

Arkansas County *Assessor, Property Records*
See www.arcountydata.com note at top of section.

Ashley County *Assessor, Property Records*
See www.actdatascout.com note at top of section.

Baxter County *Assessor, Property, Real Estate Recording, Deed Records*
Registration and logon is required to search assessor records on Citrix system, see www.arcountydata.com note at top of section. Also, access recording office land data at www.etitlesearch.com; registration required, fee based on usage.

Benton County *Real Estate, Deed, Circuit Court, Lien, Plat, Property Tax, Judgment, Medical Lien, Inmate, Personal Property Records*
www.co.benton.ar.us
County Assessor, tax collector, medical liens, plats and circuit court information is free online at http://209.183.170.177:5061/. Land records are at http://etitlesearch.com; call 870-856-3055 for subscription info. Also, see www.arcountydata.com note at top of section. Also, search inmate records free at www.co.benton.ar.us/Sheriff/Inmate.htm. Also, search property and personal property data free at www.countyservice.net/bentax.html. Also access land court records by subscription at www.recordsusa.com/recordsusa/Arkansas/BentonCnAr.htm or phone 888-85-IMAGE. $49.95/$79.90 or monthly.

Boone County *Real Estate Recording, Deed, Assessor, Property Records*
Land records are at http://etitlesearch.com. You can do a name search; choose from $45.00 monthly subscription or per click account. Also, see www.arcountydata.com note at top of section.

Bradley County *Assessor, Property Records*
See www.arcountydata.com note at top of section.

Carroll County *Assessor, Property Records*
Chicot County *Assessor, Property Records*
Registration and logon is required to search assessor records on Citrix system. See www.arcountydata.com note at top of section.

Clark County *Assessor, Property Tax Records*
www.clarkcountyarkansas.com
See www.actdatascout.com note at top of section.

Clay County (Eastern District) *Assessor, Property Records*
Registration and logon is required to search assessor records on Citrix system. See www.arcountydata.com note at top of section.

Cleburne County *Assessor, Property Records*
Conway County *Assessor, Property Records*
See www.actdatascout.com note at top of section.

Craighead County *Real Estate, Recording, Deed, Property, Personal Property, Assessor Records*
www.craigheadcounty.org
Access land records at http://etitlesearch.com. You can do a name search; choose from $100.00 monthly subscription or per click account. Also, search personal property, real estate, and assessor records free at www.cratax.countyservice.net. Also, see www.arcountydata.com note at top of section.

Crawford County *Real Estate Recording, Deed, Assessor, Property Tax Records*
www.etitlesearch.com/UsFlashMap/ar_crawford.html
Land records are at http://etitlesearch.com. You can do a name search; choose from $30.00 monthly subscription or per click account. Also, see www.actdatascout.com note at top of section.

Crittenden County *Assessor, Property Records*
See www.arcountydata.com note at top of section.

Cross County *Assessor, Property Records*
Access property data free at www.actdatascout.com. Subscription for deeper info is $20 per month.

Dallas County *Assessor, Property Records*
Desha County *Assessor, Property Records*
See www.arcountydata.com note at top of section.

Faulkner County *Assessor, Property, Personal Property Records*
www.faulknercc.org
Search property and personal property data free at www.countyservice.net. Also, see www.arcountydata.com note at top of section

Fulton County *Assessor, Property Records*
See www.arcountydata.com note at top of section.

Garland County *Assessor, Property, Sex Offender Records*
Access to the sheriff's sex offender list is free at www.hsnp.com/megan/garland_index.cgi. No recording records are available through Garland County; but searching is reportedly available via a private provider County Professional Solicitations, PO Box 55, Brenton, AR 72015. Also, see www.actdatascout.com note at top of section

Grant County *Assessor, Property Records*
Greene County *Assessor, Property Records*
See www.arcountydata.com note at top of section.

Hempstead County *Assessor, Property Records*
Hot Spring County *Assessor, Property Records*
See www.actdatascout.com note at top of section.

Howard County *Assessor, Property Records*
See www.arcountydata.com note at top of section.

Independence County *Real Estate Recording, Deed, Assessor, Property Tax Records*
Land records are at http://etitlesearch.com. You can do a name search; choose from $200.00 monthly subscription or per click account. Also, see www.actdatascout.com note at top of section.

Izard County *Assessor, Property Records*
See www.arcountydata.com note at top of section.

Jackson County *Assessor, Property Records*
See www.actdatascout.com note at top of section.

Jefferson County *Property, Personal Property, Assessor Records*
Search property and personal property data free at www.countyservice.net. Also, see www.actdatascout.com note at top of section.

Johnson County *Assessor, Property Records*
Registration and logon is required to search on the Citrix system. See www.arcountydata.com note at top of section.

Lafayette County *Property, Assessor Records*
Lawrence County *Assessor, Property Records*
See www.actdatascout.com note at top of section.

Lee County *Assessor, Property Records*
See www.arcountydata.com note at top of section.

Lincoln County *Assessor, Property Records*
Little River County *Assessor, Property Records*
See www.actdatascout.com note at top of section.

Logan County *Assessor, Property Records*
Registration and logon is required to search assessor records on the Citrix system. See www.arcountydata.com note at top of section.

Lonoke County *Assessor, Property Records*
See www.arcountydata.com note at top of section.

Madison County *Assessor, Property Records*
See www.actdatascout.com note at top of section.

Marion County *Assessor, Property Records*
Registration and logon is required to search assessor records on the Citrix system. See www.arcountydata.com note at top of section.

Miller County *Land, Deed, Assessor, Property Tax Records*
Access to recorder land records and images are via a private company at www.recordsusa.com/recordsusa/Arkansas/MillerCnAr.htm. Subscription required; basic monthly package including court dockets is $49.95. Call 888-85-IMAGE or visit the website. Also, see www.actdatascout.com note at top of section.

Monroe County *Property, Assessor Records*
Montgomery County *Assessor, Property Records*
Nevada County *Property, Assessor Records*
See www.actdatascout.com note at top of section.

Newton County *Assessor, Property Records*
See www.arcountydata.com note at top of section.

Ouachita County *Assessor, Property Records*
Perry County *Assessor, Property Records*
See www.actdatascout.com note at top of section.

Phillips County *Real Estate Recording Records*
Access land records at http://etitlesearch.com. Name searching; choose from $25.00 monthly subscription or per-click account.

Pike County *Assessor, Property Records*
Poinsett County *Assessor, Property Records*
See www.arcountydata.com note at top of section.

Polk County *Real Estate, Deed, Circuit Court, Lien, Judgment, Assessor, Property Tax Records*
Access to county land and court records is by subscription; visit www.recordsusa.com/recordsusa/Arkansas/PolkCnAr.htm or phone 800-932-5029 or 888-85-IMAGE. Monthly packages are $49.95 or $79.90. Also, see www.actdatascout.com note at top of section.

Pope County *Assessor, Property, Real Estate, Deed, Personal Property Records*
Free access to assessor data is at www.countyservice.net/poptax.html. Last name and zip code are required. Also, search property and personal property data free at www.countyservice.net. Also, access recording office land data at www.etitlesearch.com; registration required, fee based on usage. Also, see www.arcountydata.com note at top of section.

Prairie County *Real Estate Recording, Deed, Assessor, Property Tax Records*
Access recording office land data at www.etitlesearch.com; registration required, fee based on usage. Also, see www.actdatascout.com note at top of section.

Pulaski County *Assessor, Personal Property, Real Estate Recording s & Deeds, Voter Registration Records*
www.co.pulaski.ar.us

At the web page, Click on Online Services for the free search of voter registration and subscription service for real estate records. Also, registration and logon is required to search assessor records on the Citrix system. See www.arcountydata.com note at top of section. Also, access recording office land data at www.etitlesearch.com; registration required, fee based on usage.

Randolph County   *Property, Personal Property, Assessor, Property Tax Records*
Also, search property and personal property data free at www.countyservice.net. Also, see www.actdatascout.com note at top of section.

St. Francis County   *Assessor, Property Records*
See www.arcountydata.com note at top of section.

Saline County   *Assessor, Property, Real Estate Recording, Personal Property Records*
www.salinecounty.org
Access land records at http://etitlesearch.com. You can do a name search; choose from $25.00 monthly subscription or per-click account. Also, search assessor real estate and personal property records free at www.countyservice.net/saltax.html. Also, see www.arcountydata.com note at top of section.

Searcy County   *Assessor, Property Records*
See www.actdatascout.com note at top of section.

Sebastian County   *Assessor, Property, Personal Property Records*
www.sebastiancountyonline.com
Search property and personal property data free at www.countyservice.net. Also, see www.actdatascout.com note at top of section. Also, see www.arcountydata.com note at top of section.

Sevier County   *Assessor, Property Records*
See www.actdatascout.com note at top of section.

Sharp County   *Assessor, Property, Real Estate Recording, Deed Records*
Access land records at http://etitlesearch.com. You can do a name search; choose from $25.00 monthly subscription or per-click account. Also, see www.arcountydata.com note at top of section.

Stone County   *Assessor, Property Records*
See www.arcountydata.com note at top of section.

Union County   *Real Estate, Deed, Circuit Court, Lien, Judgment, Assessor, Property Tax Records*
Access to county land and court records is by subscription; visit www.recordsusa.com/recordsusa/Arkansas/UnionCnAr.htm or phone 800-932-5029 or 888-85-IMAGE. Monthly packages are $49.95 or $79.90. Also, see www.actdatascout.com note at top of section.

Van Buren County   *Real Estate Recording, Deed, Property, Personal Property, Assessor Records*
Access land records at http://etitlesearch.com. You can do a name search; call 870-856-3055 for subscription information. Also, search property and personal property data free at www.countyservice.net. Also, see www.arcountydata.com note at top of section.

Washington County
Real Estate, Deed, Lien, UCC, Recording, Court, Vital Statistic, Assessor, Property Tax Records
www.co.washington.ar.us
Search Clerk's index of real estate, liens, and UCCs (to '92) at www.co.washington.ar.us/resolution/. Username, password and $50.00 subscription required. Also, search property records for free at www.co.washington.ar.us/PropertySearch/MapSearch.asp. Also, search court record archives at www.co.washington.ar.us/ArchiveSearch/CourtRecordSearch.asp. Also, access land records at http://etitlesearch.com. You can do a name search, fees involved, call 870-856-3055 for info. Also, see www.actdatascout.com note at top of section.

White County   *Assessor, Property Records*
See www.arcountydata.com note at top of section.

Woodruff County   *Real Estate Recording, Deed, Assessor, Property Tax Records*
Access land records at http://etitlesearch.com. You can do a name search; choose from $25.00 monthly subscription or per-click account. Also, see www.actdatascout.com note at top of section.

Federal Courts in Arkansas...

Standards for Federal Courts: The universal PACER sign-up number is 800-676-6856. Find PACER and the Party/Case Index on the Web at http://pacer.psc.uscourts.gov. PACER dial-up access is $.60 per minute. Also, courts offering internet access via PACER, Web-PACER or the new CM-ECF charge $.08 per page fee ($.07 per page if record is pre-2005 or unless noted as free).

US District Court -- Eastern District of Arkansas

www.are.uscourts.gov

PACER: Case records are available back to 1987-89. Records are purged every 5 years. New records are available online after 1 day. **PACER Online Access:** Search records using RACER at https://pacer.login.uscourts.gov/cgi-bin/login.pl?court_id=r_aredc. Fees now apply. Document images available. **Electronic Filing:** CM/ECF data at https://ecf.ared.uscourts.gov.
Helena Division counties: Cross, Lee, Monroe, Phillips, St. Francis, Woodruff.
Pine Bluff Division counties: Arkansas, Chicot, Cleveland, Dallas, Desha, Drew, Grant, Jefferson, Lincoln.

US Bankruptcy Court -- Eastern District of Arkansas

www.areb.uscourts.gov

PACER: Case records are available back to 5/1989. Records are purged every 6 months. New records are available online after 1 day. **PACER Online Access:** ECF replaces PACER. **Electronic Filing:** CM/ECF data at https://ecf.areb.uscourts.gov. **Opinions:** View court opinions at www.arb.uscourts.gov/Orders-Rules-Opinions/opinions/opinions.htm. **Other Online Access:** Search court calendars free at www.arb.uscourts.gov/calendars/calendars.htm. **Phone access:** Voice Case Info System, call 800-891-6741, 501-918-5555
Little Rock Division counties: Same counties as included in Eastern District of Arkansas, plus the counties included in the Western District divisions of El Dorado, Hot Springs and Texarkana. All bankruptcy cases in Arkansas prior to mid-1993 were heard here.

US District Court -- Western District of Arkansas

www.arwd.uscourts.gov

PACER: Sign-up number is 501-783-6833. Case records are available back to 9/1990. Records are purged every 5 years. New records are available online after 1 day. **PACER Online Access:** PACER online at http://pacer.arwd.uscourts.gov. **Electronic Filing:** CM/ECF data at https://ecf.arwd.uscourts.gov. **Opinions:** Selected pleadings only; opinions to be online later in 2006. View court opinions at www.arwd.uscourts.gov/go/online-documents.
El Dorado Division counties: Ashley, Bradley, Calhoun, Columbia, Ouachita, Union.
Fayetteville Division counties: Benton, Madison, Washington.
Fort Smith Division counties: Crawford, Franklin, Johnson, Logan, Polk, Scott, Sebastian.
Hot Springs Division counties: Clark, Garland, Hot Springs, Montgomery, Pike.
Texarkana Division counties: Hempstead, Howard, Lafayette, Little River, Miller, Nevada, Sevier.

US Bankruptcy Court -- Western District of Arkansas

www.arb.uscourts.gov

PACER: Case records are available back to 5/1989. Records are purged every 6 months. New records are available online after 1 day. **PACER Online Access:** ECF replaces PACER. **Electronic Filing:** CM/ECF data at https://ecf.arwb.uscourts.gov. **Opinions:** View court opinions at www.arb.uscourts.gov/Orders-Rules-Opinions/opinions/opinions.htm. **Other Online Access:** Search court calendars free at www.arb.uscourts.gov/calendars/calendars.htm. **Phone access:** Voice Case Information System, call 800-891-6741, 501-918-5555.
Fayetteville Division counties: Same counties as included in US District Court - Western District of Arkansas except that counties included in El Dorado and Texarkana Divisions are heard in Little Rock.

California

Capital: Sacramento
           Sacramento County
Time Zone: PST
Population: 35,893,799
# of Counties: 58

Quick Links

Website: www.state.ca.us/state/portal/myca_homepage.jsp
Governor: www.governor.ca.gov/state/govsite/gov_homepage.jsp
Attorney General: http://caag.state.ca.us
State Archives: www.ss.ca.gov/archives/archives.htm
State Statutes and Codes: www.leginfo.ca.gov/calaw.html
Legislative Bill Search: www.leginfo.ca.gov/bilinfo.html
Bill Monitoring: www.leginfo.ca.gov/cgi-bin/postquery?maison=$prfx&nro=$num&act=10
Unclaimed Funds: https://scoweb.sco.ca.gov

State Level ... Major Agencies

Statewide Court Records

Administration Office of Courts, Office of Communications, 455 Golden Gate Ave, San Francisco, CA 94102-3660; 415-865-4200, Fax-415-865-4205, 8AM-5PM.
www.courtinfo.ca.gov
Online search: There is no statewide online computer access available for county court records. The website offers access to all opinions from the Supreme and Appeals courts from 1850 to present. Opinions not certified for publications are available for last 60 days. The site is an excellent source of information about court procedures.

Sexual Offender Registry

Department of Justice, Sexual Offender Program, PO Box 903387, Sacramento, CA 94203-3870 (Courier: 4949 Broadway, Rm H216, Sacramento, CA 95820); 900-448-3000 (Fee Search), 916-227-4199 (Tracking), Fax-916-227-4345, 8AM-5PM.
www.caag.state.ca.us
Online search: Search at http://meganslaw.ca.gov/index.htm. This site will provide access to information on more than 63,000 persons required to register in California as sex offenders. One may search by a sex offender's specific name or by geographic location including ZIP Code. Specific home addresses are displayed on more than 33,500 offenders.

Corporation, Limited Liability Company, Limited Partnerships, Limited Liability Partnerships

Secretary of State, Information Retrieval/Certification Unit, 1500 11th Street, 3rd Fl, Sacramento, CA 95814; 916-657-5448 x1.
www.ss.ca.gov
Online search: The website at http://kepler.ss.ca.gov/list.html offers access to more than 2 million records including corporation, LLC, LP and LLP. Info available includes status, file number, date of filing and agent for service of process. File is updated weekly.

Uniform Commercial Code, Federal Tax Liens, State Tax Liens

UCC Division, Secretary of State, PO Box 942835, Sacramento, CA 94235 (Courier: 1500 11th St, Room 255, Sacramento, CA 95814); 916-653-3516 x2, 8AM-5PM.
www.ss.ca.gov/business/ucc/ucc.htm
Online search: UCC Connect provides an online service at https://uccconnect.ss.ca.gov/acct/acct-login.asp to conduct a variety of inquiries and place orders for copies and debtor search certificates on records and submit UCC filings. Ongoing requesters can become subscribers. Fees are based on name inquires ($5.00) and images viewed ($1.00). The web page has a complete list of fees and excellent FAQ section. Click on the Help tab.

Sales Tax Registrations

Board of Equalization, Sales and Use Tax Department, PO Box 942879, Sacramento, CA 94279-0001; 916-445-6362, 800-400-7115 (In California Only), 800-735-2922, Fax-916-324-4433, 8AM-5PM.
www.boe.ca.gov
Online search: The Internet site provides a permit verification service. Permit number is needed. System is open 5AM to midnight.
Other options: Lists, available for a fee, are sorted in a number of ways including CA Industry Code. For further information and fees, call the Technical Services Division at 916-445-5848

Birth Certificates

State Department of Health Svcs, Office of Vital Records - MS 5103, PO Box 997410, Sacramento, CA 95899-7410 (Courier: 1501 Capitol Ave, Rm 71-1110, Sacramento, CA 95814); 916-445-2684 (Recording), 8AM-4:30PM.
www.dhs.ca.gov/chs/OVR/default.htm
Online search: Applicant must complete a Sworn Statement and a notarized Certificate of Acknowledgment in the presence of a Notary Public. Records may be ordered from a state-designated vendor - www.vitalchek.com.

Death Records

State Department of Health Svcs, Office of Vital Records - MS 5103, PO Box 997410, Sacramento, CA 95899-7410 (Courier: 1501 Capitol Ave, Rm 71-1110, Sacramento, CA 95814); 916-445-2684, 8AM-4:30PM.
www.dhs.ca.gov/chs/default.htm
Online search: Access death records 1940 thru 1997 at http://vitals.rootsweb.com/ca/death/search.cgi. Also, records are available from a state-designated vendor - www.vitalchek.com.

Driver Records

Department of Motor Vehicles, Information Services Branch, PO Box 944247, Mail Station G199, Sacramento, CA 94244-2470 (Courier: 2415 First Ave, Sacramento, CA 95818); 916-657-8098, 916-657-5564 (Requester Accounts), 8AM-5PM.
www.dmv.ca.gov
Online search: The department offers online access, but a $10,000 one-time setup fee may be required. Entities who order from an online vendor must also be pre-approved. The fee is $2.00 per record. The system is available 24 hours, 7 days a week. For more information call 916-657-5582. **Other options:** Employers may monitor their drivers in the Pull Notice Program. The DMV informs the organization when there is activity on enrolled drivers. Call 916-657-6346 for details.

Vehicle Ownership, Identification; Vessel Ownership, Registration

Department of Motor Vehicle, Office of Information Services, PO Box 944247, MS-G199, Sacramento, CA 94244-2470 (Courier: 2415 First Ave, Sacramento, CA 95818); 916-657-8098, 916-657-5564 (Commercial Accounts), 916-657-6893 (Vessel Registration).
www.dmv.ca.gov
Online search: 24 hour online access is limited to certain Authorized Vendors. Requesters may not use the data for direct marketing, solicitation, nor resell for those purposes. A bond is required and very high fees are involved. For more information, call the Electronic Access Administration Section at 916-657-5582. **Other options:** California offers delivery of registration information on FTP VPN, magnetic tape, disk or paper within special parameters. Release of info is denied for commercial marketing purposes.

State Level ... Occupational Licensing

Acupuncturist.. www.acupuncture.ca.gov
Administrative Service................................ www.ctc.ca.gov/credentials/default.html
Adoption Agency.. www.ccld.ca.gov/docs/ccld_search/ccld_search.aspx
Air Conditioning Contractor .... www2.cslb.ca.gov/CSLB_LIBRARY/Name+Request.asp
Alarm Company/Employee/Mgr................. www.dca.ca.gov/bsis/lookup.htm
Apprentice Program.................................... www.dir.ca.gov/databases/das/aigstart.asp
Architect .... www.cab.ca.gov/querylic.htm
Asbestos Consultant/Surveillance.............. www.dir.ca.gov/databases/doshcaccsst/caccsst_query_1.html
Asbestos Contractor................................... www.dir.ca.gov/databases/doshacru/acrusearch.html
Asbestos Trainer .... www.dir.ca.gov/databases/doshcaccsst/aheratp.asp
Asbestos Worker/Trainee........................... www.dir.ca.gov/DOSH/ACRU/TP_AsbestosTrainingCertificates.html
Attorney .... http://members.calbar.ca.gov/search/member.aspx
Audiologist .... www.slpab.ca.gov/
Automobile Dealer/Repair .... www.smogcheck.ca.gov/stdPage.asp?Body=/Consumer/verify_a_license.htm
Bank.. www.dfi.ca.gov/directry/tl.asp
Bar Association.. http://members.calbar.ca.gov/search/ba_search.aspx
Barber Instructor/School............................ www.barbercosmo.ca.gov/license.htm
Barber Shop/Barber/Barber Apprentice ...... www.barbercosmo.ca.gov/license.htm
Baton Training Facility/Instructor.............. www.dca.ca.gov/bsis/lookup.htm
Brake & Lamp Adjuster. Brake Station ...... www.smogcheck.ca.gov/stdPage.asp?Body=/Consumer/verify_a_license.htm
Building Contr., General-Class B .... www2.cslb.ca.gov/CSLB_LIBRARY/Name+Request.asp
Business/Industrial Dev. Company............. www.dfi.ca.gov/directry/bidco.asp
Cabinet/Millwork Contractor..................... www2.cslb.ca.gov/CSLB_LIBRARY/Name+Request.asp
Care Facility for Children, Transitional ...... www.ccld.ca.gov/docs/ccld_search/ccld_search.aspx
Care Facility for Chronically Ill................. www.ccld.ca.gov/docs/ccld_search/ccld_search.aspx
Cemetery, Cemetery Broker/Seller .... www.cfb.ca.gov/lookup.htm
Child Care Center .... www.ccld.ca.gov/docs/ccld_search/ccld_search.aspx
Chiropractor/Chiropractic Business .... www.chiro.ca.gov/licsearch/
Clinic Pharmaceutical Permit..................... www.pharmacy.ca.gov/verify_lic.htm
Community Treatment Facility .... www.ccld.ca.gov/docs/ccld_search/ccld_search.aspx
Concrete Contractor/Company .... www2.cslb.ca.gov/CSLB_LIBRARY/Name+Request.asp
Conscious Sedation Permit .... www.dbc.ca.gov/license_verification.html
Continuing Education Provider................... www.bbs.ca.gov/weblokup.htm
Contractor, Business/Individual.................. www.cslb.ca.gov
Cosmetician/Cosmetologist .... www.barbercosmo.ca.gov/license.htm
Cosmetology School .... https://app.dca.ca.gov/bppve/school-search/default.htm
Cosmetology/Electrology Business/Instr. ... www.barbercosmo.ca.gov/license.htm
Court Reporter (Shorthand Reporter).......... www.courtreportersboard.ca.gov
CPA/CPA Firm... www.dca.ca.gov/cba/lookup.htm
Crane Operator... www.dir.ca.gov/databases/crane/cranesearch.html
Credit Union .... www.dfi.ca.gov/directry/cu.asp
Crematory/Cremated Remains Disposer..... www.cfb.ca.gov/lookup.htm
Day Care, Adult/Child .... www.ccld.ca.gov/docs/ccld_search/ccld_search.aspx
Dental Anesthesia Permit........................... www.dbc.ca.gov/license_verification.html
Dental Assistant/Hygienist......................... www.comda.ca.gov/licensestatus.html
Dentist/Dental Registered Provider............ www.dbc.ca.gov/license_verification.html
Development Corporation............................ www.dfi.ca.gov/directry/directry.asp
Driving School.. https://eg.dmv.ca.gov/olinq/SvOlDs
Drug Wholesaler/Drug Room .... www.pharmacy.ca.gov/verify_lic.htm
Drywall Contractor .... www2.cslb.ca.gov/CSLB_LIBRARY/Name+Request.asp
Earthwork/Paving Contractor .... www2.cslb.ca.gov/CSLB_LIBRARY/Name+Request.asp
Electrical Contr. & Electric Sign Contr. ..... www2.cslb.ca.gov/CSLB_LIBRARY/Name+Request.asp
Electrologist... www.barbercosmo.ca.gov/license.htm

Electrology School...................................... https://app.dca.ca.gov/bppve/school-search/default.htm
Electronics & Appliance Repair.................. www.bear.ca.gov/look-up.htm
Elevator Installation Contr. .... www2.cslb.ca.gov/CSLB_LIBRARY/Name+Request.asp
Embalmer/Embalmer Apprentice................ www.cfb.ca.gov/lookup.htm
Engineer (various disciplines)..................... www.dca.ca.gov/pels/l_lookup.htm
Esthetician.. www.barbercosmo.ca.gov/license.htm
Family Child Care Home .... www.ccld.ca.gov/docs/ccld_search/ccld_search.aspx
Farm Labor Contractor .... www.dir.ca.gov/databases/dlselr/Farmlic.html
Fencing Contractor .... www2.cslb.ca.gov/CSLB_LIBRARY/Name+Request.asp
Firearm Permit.. www.dca.ca.gov/bsis/lookup.htm
Firearm Training Facility/Instr................... www.dca.ca.gov/bsis/lookup.htm
Flooring/Floor Covering Contr. .... www2.cslb.ca.gov/CSLB_LIBRARY/Name+Request.asp
Foster Family Agency................................ www.ccld.ca.gov/docs/ccld_search/ccld_search.aspx
Fumigation.. www.cdpr.ca.gov/docs/license/currlic.htm
Funeral Director/Establishment .... www.cfb.ca.gov/lookup.htm
Funerary Training Establis't/Apprentice..... www.cfb.ca.gov/lookup.htm
Garment Mfg .... www.dir.ca.gov/databases/dlselr/Garmreg.html
Geologist/Geophysicist.............................. www.geology.ca.gov
Geologist, Engineering .... www.geology.ca.gov
Glazier.. www2.cslb.ca.gov/CSLB_LIBRARY/Name+Request.asp
Group Home .... www.ccld.ca.gov/docs/ccld_search/ccld_search.aspx
Healing Art Supervisor .... www.applications.dhs.ca.gov/rhbxray/
Hearing Aid Dispenser............................... www.dca.ca.gov/hearingaid/
Heating & Warm-Air Vent. Contr. .... www2.cslb.ca.gov/CSLB_LIBRARY/Name+Request.asp
Home Furnishings ... www2.dca.ca.gov/pls/wllpub/wllqryna$lcev2.startup?p_qte_code=LIC&p_qte_pgm_code=5710
Horse Racing Entity................................... www.chrb.ca.gov/license_search.htm
Horse Racing Occupation .... www.chrb.ca.gov/license_search.htm
Hospital Pharmaceutical Exemptee............ www.pharmacy.ca.gov/verify_lic.htm
Hydrogeologist .... www.geology.ca.gov/
Hypodermic Needle & Syringe Dist. .... www.pharmacy.ca.gov/verify_lic.htm
Industrial Loan Company, Premium........... www.dfi.ca.gov/directry/tl.asp
Infant Center.. www.ccld.ca.gov/docs/ccld_search/ccld_search.aspx
Insulation/Acoustical Contr. .... www2.cslb.ca.gov/CSLB_LIBRARY/Name+Request.asp
Insurance Adjuster www.insurance.ca.gov/0200-industry/0200-prod-licensing/0200-current-lic-info/
Insurance Agent/Broker.............................. www.insurance.ca.gov/license-status/index.cfm
Insurance Company ... ...   http://cdinswww.insurance.ca.gov/pls/wu_co_lines/ncdw_alpha_co_line$.startup
Insurance Producer www.insurance.ca.gov/0200-industry/0100-license-status/index.cfm
Landscape Architect................................... www.latc.dca.ca.gov/licenseeinfo/search.htm
Landscaping Contractor.............................. www2.cslb.ca.gov/CSLB_LIBRARY/Name+Request.asp
Legal Specialist.. http://members.calbar.ca.gov/search/ls_search.aspx
Legal Specialization Provider .... http://members.calbar.ca.gov/search/cert.aspx
Lobbyist.. http://cal-access.ss.ca.gov/Lobbying/
Locksmith/Locksmith Company................. www.dca.ca.gov/bsis/lookup.htm
Mammographic Facility.............................. www.applications.dhs.ca.gov/rhbxray/
Manicurist... www.barbercosmo.ca.gov/license.htm
Marriage & Family Therapist .... www.bbs.ca.gov/weblokup.htm
Masonry Contractor .... www2.cslb.ca.gov/CSLB_LIBRARY/Name+Request.asp
Medical Doctor, Enforcement Docum't...... www.medbd.ca.gov/pdl.htm
Medical Doctor/Surgeon
   www2.dca.ca.gov/pls/wllpub/wllqryna$lcev2.startup?p_qte_code=MDX&p_qte_pgm_code=6301
Medical Evaluator...................................... www.dir.ca.gov/databases/imc/imcstartnew.asp
Midwife ... .   www2.dca.ca.gov/pls/wllpub/wllqryna$lcev2.startup?p_qte_code=LM&p_qte_pgm_code=6200
Money Order Issuer .... www.dfi.ca.gov/directry/pi.asp
Nuclear Medicine Technologist.................. www.applications.dhs.ca.gov/rhbxray/
Nurse Registered.. www.rn.ca.gov/online/online.htm
Nurse Temporary or Intern .... https://app.dca.ca.gov/rn/tlverif.htm

Occupational Therapist/Therapist Assistant
  www2.dca.ca.gov/pls/wllpub/wllqryna$lcev2.startup?p_qte_code=OT&p_qte_pgm_code=1475
Optometrist .... www.optometry.ca.gov/search.htm
Optometry Practice/Branch Office.............. www.optometry.ca.gov/search.htm
Ornamental Metal Contractor .... www2.cslb.ca.gov/CSLB_LIBRARY/Name+Request.asp
Osteopath .... www.opsc.org/displaycommon.cfm?an=1&subarticlenbr=9
Painting/Decorating Contractor .... www2.cslb.ca.gov/CSLB_LIBRARY/Name+Request.asp
Parking/Highway Improvement Contr. .... www2.cslb.ca.gov/CSLB_LIBRARY/Name+Request.asp
Patrol Operator, Private .... www.dca.ca.gov/bsis/lookup.htm
Payment Instrument Issuer.......................... www.dfi.ca.gov/directry/directry.asp
Pest Control Field Rep./Operator............... www.cdpr.ca.gov/docs/license/currlic.htm
Pesticide Applicator.................................... www.cdpr.ca.gov/docs/license/currlic.htm
Pharmaceutical Whlse./Dist./Exemptee ...... www.pharmacy.ca.gov/verify_lic.htm
Pharmacist/Pharmacist Intern/Technician... www.pharmacy.ca.gov/verify_lic.htm
Pharmacy .... www.pharmacy.ca.gov/verify_lic.htm
Physical Therapist/Assistant
  www2.dca.ca.gov/pls/wllpub/wllqryna$lcev2.startup?p_qte_code=PT&p_qte_pgm_code=6800
Physician Assistant
  www2.dca.ca.gov/pls/wllpub/wllqryna$lcev2.startup?p_qte_code=PA&p_qte_pgm_code=7000
Plastering Contractor .... www2.cslb.ca.gov/CSLB_LIBRARY/Name+Request.asp
Plumber... www2.cslb.ca.gov/CSLB_LIBRARY/Name+Request.asp
Podiatrist... www.bpm.ca.gov
Premium Finance Company......................... www.dfi.ca.gov/directry/pf.asp
Private Investigator .... www.dca.ca.gov/bsis/lookup.htm
Psychiatric Technician................................ www.bvnpt.ca.gov/licverif.htm
Psychologist/Psychological Assistant .... www.psychboard.ca.gov
Psychologist, Educational .... www.bbs.ca.gov/weblokup.htm
Psychologist, Registered .... www.psychboard.ca.gov/
Public Accountant-CPA............................... www.dca.ca.gov/cba/lookup.htm
Public Works Trainer.................................. www.dir.ca.gov/databases/das/pwaddrstart.asp
Radioactive Material Licensee.................... www.applications.dhs.ca.gov/rhbxray/
Radiologic Technologist .... www.applications.dhs.ca.gov/rhbxray/
Real Estate Agent/Sales/Broker/Corp. .... www.dre.ca.gov/licstats.htm
Refrigeration Contractor .... www2.cslb.ca.gov/CSLB_LIBRARY/Name+Request.asp
Registered Veterinary Technician............... www.vmb.ca.gov/lic1list.htm
Repossessor Agency/Mgr./Employee .... www.dca.ca.gov/bsis/lookup.htm
Residential Care for Elderly/Adult.............. www.ccld.ca.gov/docs/ccld_search/ccld_search.aspx
Respiratory Care Practitioner...................... www.rcb.ca.gov/license_verification_forms_instructions.htm
Roofing Contractor .... www2.cslb.ca.gov/CSLB_LIBRARY/Name+Request.asp
Sanitation System Contractor...................... www2.cslb.ca.gov/CSLB_LIBRARY/Name+Request.asp
Security Guard... www.dca.ca.gov/bsis/lookup.htm
Service Contract Seller (Appliance)............ www.bear.ca.gov/look-up.htm
Sheet Metal Contractor .... www2.cslb.ca.gov/CSLB_LIBRARY/Name+Request.asp
Shelter, Temporary .... www.ccld.ca.gov/docs/ccld_search/ccld_search.aspx
Smog Check Station/Technician .... www.smogcheck.ca.gov/stdPage.asp?Body=/Consumer/verify_a_license.htm
Social Rehabilitation Facility...................... www.ccld.ca.gov/docs/ccld_search/ccld_search.aspx
Social Worker, Clinical............................... www.bbs.ca.gov/weblokup.htm
Solar Energy Contractor .... www2.cslb.ca.gov/CSLB_LIBRARY/Name+Request.asp
Specialty Contractor-Class C .... www2.cslb.ca.gov/CSLB_LIBRARY/Name+Request.asp
Speech Pathologist/Audiologist Aide .... www.slpab.ca.gov/
Steel Contractor .... www2.cslb.ca.gov/CSLB_LIBRARY/Name+Request.asp
Studio Teacher .... www.dir.ca.gov/databases/dlselr/StudTch.html
Support Center, Adult .... www.ccld.ca.gov/docs/ccld_search/ccld_search.aspx
Surgical Clinic Pharm., Nonprofit .... www.pharmacy.ca.gov/verify_lic.htm
Surveyor, Land .... www.dca.ca.gov/pels/l_lookup.htm
Swimming Pool Contractor.......................... www2.cslb.ca.gov/CSLB_LIBRARY/Name+Request.asp

Talent Agency.. www.dir.ca.gov/databases/dlselr/Talag.html
Tax Education Provider .... www.ctec.org/index.asp?pid=10
Tax Preparer.. www.ctec.org/verify.asp
Termite Control .... www.cdpr.ca.gov/docs/license/currlic.htm
Thrift & Loan Company .... www.dfi.ca.gov/directry/directry.asp
Tile Contractor, Ceramic/Mosaic................ www2.cslb.ca.gov/CSLB_LIBRARY/Name+Request.asp
Trainer, Public Works................................. www.dir.ca.gov/databases/das/pwaddrstart.asp
Travelers Checks Issuer .... www.dfi.ca.gov/directry/tc.asp
Trust Company .... www.dfi.ca.gov/directry/trust.asp
Veterinarian www.vmb.ca.gov/lic1list.htm
Veterinary Food/Animal Drug Retailer....... www.pharmacy.ca.gov/verify_lic.htm
Veterinary Premise www.vmb.ca.gov/lic1list.htm
Vocational Nurse .... www.bvnpt.ca.gov/licverif.htm
Water Well Driller .... www2.cslb.ca.gov/CSLB_LIBRARY/Name+Request.asp
X-ray Technician/ achine Registration........ www.applications.dhs.ca.gov/rhbxray/

County Level ... Courts

Court Administration: Administrative Office of Courts, 455 Golden Gate Ave, San Francisco, CA, 94102; 415-865-4200; www.courtinfo.ca.gov

Court Structure: In July, 1998, the judges in individual counties were given the opportunity to vote on unification of Superior Courts and Municipal Courts within their respective counties. By late 2000, all counties had voted to unify these courts. Courts that were formally Municipal Courts are now known as Limited Jurisdiction Superior Courts. In some counties, Superior Courts and Municipal Courts were combined into one Superior Court. Civil under $25,000 is a Limited Civil Court, over $25,000 is an Unlimited Civil Court, and if both are over and under, then the court is a Combined Civil Court.

It is important to note that Limited Courts may try minor felonies not included under our felony definition.

Due to its large number of courts, the Los Angeles County section is arranged uniquely in this book.

Online Access Note: The website at www.courtinfo.ca.gov offers access to all opinions from the Supreme Court and Appeals Courts from 1850 to present. Opinions not certified for publications are available for the last 60 days. This site also contains very useful information about the state court system, including opinions from the Supreme Court and Appeals Courts.

There is no statewide online computer access available. However, a number of counties have developed their own online access sytems and provide internet access at no fee. Los Angeles County has a fee-based online system to obtain criminal records county wide or civil case records for limits exceeding $25,000. There is a free lookup by case number only for probate and civil case summaries when under $25,000. Go to www.lasuperiorcourt.org

A convenient Los Angeles County Court Locator is at www.lasuperiorcourt.org/locations

Alameda County

Superior Court – Civil Records
www.alameda.courts.ca.gov/courts
Access to calendars, limited civil case summaries and complex litigations are free from Register of Actions/Domain Web at the website. Search limited cases by number; litigations by case number. At the website, search "Find Your Court Date" to determine if a name has an upcoming court date.

Amador County

Superior Court – Civil and Criminal Records
www.amadorcourt.org
Court calendars are by date up to 10 days ahead at www.amadorcourt.org/courtcal/courtcal.html. Tentative rulings including previous year are free at www.amadorcourt.org/rulings/rulings.html.

Butte County

Superior Court – Civil and Criminal Records
www.buttecourt.ca.gov
Limited case index searching by name is free at www.buttecourt.ca.gov/online_index/cmssearch.cfm. There is also a calendar lookup at www.buttecourt.ca.gov/calendarlookup/cmscalendarlookup.cfm. Limited case index searching by name is free online at www.buttecourt.ca.gov/online_index/cmssearch.cfm. There is also a calendar lookup, see above.

Contra Costa County

Superior Court Main – Civil Records
www.cc-courts.org
Civil case, Probate, Family and Small Claims information is free at www.cc-courts.org/civilcms.htm. Visitors can view microfiche.

Fresno County

Superior Court– Civil Records
www.fresnosuperiorcourt.org
Access to civil, probate, family, small claims cases is free at www.fresnosuperiorcourt.org/case_info/.

Glenn County

Superior Court – Civil and Criminal Records
www.glenncourt.ca.gov
Search case index at www.glenncourt.ca.gov/online%5Findex/.

Kern County

Superior Court – Civil and Criminal Records
www.co.kern.ca.us/courts
Civil case info and calendars available on special kiosk computers located at every court location; calendars soon to be online at website. Access defendant search database free at www.co.kern.ca.us/courts/crimcal/crim_index_def.asp; old records being added. Current court calendars free at www.co.kern.ca.us/courts/crim_index_case_info_cal.asp. Access defendant hearings schedule at www.co.kern.ca.us/courts/crimcal/crim_hearing_srch.asp. Also, search sheriff inmate list at www.co.kern.ca.us/courts/caseinfo_menu.asp. Click on "inmate search.".

Los Angeles County

Los Angeles Superior Court - Central District - Civil – Civil Records
www.lasuperiorcourt.org
For cases over $25,000 there is a fee-based lookup for case images at https://www.lasuperiorcourt.org/OnlineServices/CivilImages/index.asp. Search fee is $4.75, case document file is $7.50. There is a free case summary lookup for cases under $25,000 at https://www.lasuperiorcourt.org/OnlineServices/CivilImages/index.asp, but the lookup is by case number, not by name. Includes probate from 01/97.

Los Angeles Superior Court - Central District - Felony – Criminal Records

Airport Superior Court - West District – Criminal Records
www.lasuperiorcourt.org
Felony and misdemeanor defendant records are online for a fee at www.lasuperiorcourt.org/OnlineServices/criminalindex/. Search fee is $4 to $4.75.

For the following LA County locations - found via the main website at www.lasuperiorcourt.org - there is a free case summary lookup at https://www.lasuperiorcourt.org/OnlineServices/CivilImages/index.asp, but the lookup is by case number, not by name. Also, there is a fee-based name search for records back to 1991 (if Small Claims 1992) at https://www.lasuperiorcourt.org/OnlineServices/CivilImages/index.asp. Fee is $4.75 per search. Felony and misdemeanor defendant records are online for a fee at www.lasuperiorcourt.org/OnlineServices/criminalindex/. Search fee is $4 to $4.75.

> Alhambra Superior Court - Northeast District – Civil and Criminal Records
> Bellflower Superior Court - Southeast District – Civil and Criminal Records
> Beverly Hills Superior Court - West District – Civil and Criminal Records
> Burbank Superior Court - North Central District – Civil and Criminal Records
> Culver City Superior Court - West District – Civil Records
> Downey Superior Court - Southeast District – Civil and Criminal Records
> East Los Angeles Superior Court - Central District – Criminal Records

Glendale Superior Court - NorthCentral District – Civil and Criminal Records
Hollywood Superior Court - Central District – Criminal Records
Huntington Park Superior Court - Southeast District – Civil and Criminal Records
Inglewood Superior Court - Southwest District – Civil and Criminal Records
Malibu Superior Court - West District – Civil and Criminal Records
Metropolitan Branch Superior Court - Central District – Criminal Records
Norwalk Superior Court - Southeast District – Civil and Criminal Records
Pasadena Superior Court - Northeast District – Civil and Criminal Records
Pomona Superior Court - North – Civil and Criminal Records
San Fernando Superior Court - North Valley District – Civil and Criminal Records
San Pedro Superior Court - South District – Civil Records
Santa Clarita Superior Court - North Valley District – Civil and Criminal Records
Santa Monica Superior Court - West District – Civil and Criminal Records
Van Nuys Superior Court - East - Civil – Civil Records
Van Nuys Superior Court - West - Criminal – Criminal Records
West Covina Superior Court - East District – Civil and Criminal Records
West Los Angeles Superior Court - West District – Civil and Criminal Records
Whittier Superior Court - Southeast District – Civil and Criminal Records

Chatsworth Courthouse – Civil Records
www.lasuperiorcourt.org
A fee-based name search for records back to 1991 (if Small Claims 1992) at
https://www.lasuperiorcourt.org/OnlineServices/CivilImages/index.asp is $4.75 per search.

Compton Superior Court - South Central District – Civil and Criminal Records
www.lasuperiorcourt.org
There is a free case summary lookup at https://www.lasuperiorcourt.org/OnlineServices/CivilImages/index.asp, but the lookup is by
case number, not by name. Includes probate from 09/99. There is a fee-based name search for records back to 1991 (if Small Claims
1992) at https://www.lasuperiorcourt.org/OnlineServices/CivilImages/index.asp. Fee is $4.75 per search. Felony and misdemeanor
defendant records are online for a fee at www.lasuperiorcourt.org/OnlineServices/criminalindex/. Search fee is $4 to $4.75.

El Monte Superior Court - East District – Civil and Criminal Records
www.lasuperiorcourt.org
There is a free case summary lookup at https://www.lasuperiorcourt.org/OnlineServices/CivilImages/index.asp, but the lookup is by
case number, not by name. There is a fee-based name search for records back to 1991 (if Small Claims 1992) at
https://www.lasuperiorcourt.org/OnlineServices/CivilImages/index.asp. Fee is $4.75 per search. Felony and misdemeanor defendant
records are online for a fee at www.lasuperiorcourt.org/OnlineServices/criminalindex/. Search fee is $5.

Lancaster Superior Court - North District – Civil and Criminal Records
www.lasuperiorcourt.org
There is a fee case summary lookup at https://www.lasuperiorcourt.org/OnlineServices/CivilImages/index.asp; the lookup is by case
number, not by name. Also includes probate cases from 06/05. The fee is $4.75 per name. A fee-based docket look-up is at
www.lasuperiorcourt.org/OnlineServices/criminalindex/. Fees range from $4.00 to $4.75 depending on volume.

Long Beach Superior Court - South District – Civil and Criminal Records
www.lasuperiorcourt.org
There is a free case summary lookup at https://www.lasuperiorcourt.org/OnlineServices/CivilImages/index.asp, but the lookup is by
case number, not by name. Includes probate from 01/97. There is a fee-based name search for records back to 1991 (if Small Claims
1992) at https://www.lasuperiorcourt.org/OnlineServices/CivilImages/index.asp. Fee is $4.75 per search. Felony and misdemeanor
defendant records are online for a fee at www.lasuperiorcourt.org/OnlineServices/criminalindex/, search fee on line depends on
volume.

Redondo Beach Superior Court - Southwest District – Civil Records
www.lasuperiorcourt.org
There is a free case summary lookup at https://www.lasuperiorcourt.org/OnlineServices/CivilImages/index.asp, but the lookup is by
case number, not by name. There is a fee-based name search for records back to 1991 (if Small Claims 1992) at
https://www.lasuperiorcourt.org/OnlineServices/CivilImages/index.asp. Fee is $4.75 per search. Felony and misdemeanor defendant
records are online for a fee at www.lasuperiorcourt.org/OnlineServices/criminalindex/. Search fee is $4 to $4.75.

Torrance Superior Court - Southwest District – Civil and Criminal Records
www.lasuperiorcourt.org
There is a free case summary lookup at https://www.lasuperiorcourt.org/OnlineServices/CivilImages/index.asp, but the lookup is by case number, not by name. Also includes probate cases from 02/97. A fee-based name search for records back to 1991 (if Small Claims 1992) at https://www.lasuperiorcourt.org/OnlineServices/CivilImages/index.asp is $4.75 per search. Criminal defendant records are online for a fee at www.lasuperiorcourt.org/OnlineServices/criminalindex/. Search fee is $4 to $4.75.

Santa Anita Superior Court - Northeast District – Civil Records
There is a free case summary lookup at https://www.lasuperiorcourt.org/OnlineServices/CivilImages/index.asp, but the lookup is by case number, not by name. There is a fee-based name search for records back to 1991 (if Small Claims 1992) at https://www.lasuperiorcourt.org/OnlineServices/CivilImages/index.asp. Fee is $4.75 per search.

Marin County

Superior Court – Civil and Criminal Records
www.co.marin.ca.us/courts
Access to the current court calendar is free at www.co.marin.ca.us/depts/MC/main/courtcal/name.cfm.

Mendocino County

Superior Court – Civil and Criminal Records
www.mendocino.courts.ca.gov
Search index at www.mendocino.courts.ca.gov/caseindex.html. Online index may be up to 2 months behind.

Monterey County

Superior Court - Marina Division - Monterey Branch - Salinas Division – Civil Records
www.monterey.courts.ca.gov
Access to calendars is free at www.monterey.courts.ca.gov/webcalendar/default.htm.

Napa County

Superior Court - Criminal Division – Criminal Records
www.napa.courts.ca.gov
Access is at www.napa.courts.ca.gov/. There is no fee to search by case number.

Nevada County

Superior Court – Civil and Criminal Records
http://court.co.nevada.ca.us/services/index.htm
Access to case calendar is free at www.court.co.nevada.ca.us/cgi/dba/casecal/db.cgi.

Orange County

Superior Court - Civil Division – Civil Records
www.occourts.org
Civil and family court calendars are online at www.occourts.org/calendars/. Civil, small claims, probate cases index for the county can be purchased on CD; index goes back to 12/31/01 or can be purchased on monthly basis. See www.occourts.org/caseinfo/ or email tthompson@occourts.org.

Riverside County

Superior Court - Civil Division – Civil Records
www.courts.co.riverside.ca.us
Access to civil records is free at www.courts.co.riverside.ca.us/pubacc.htm. Online records date back to 1991 for Riverside, 1994 for Corona, and 1996 forward for most of the remaining limited court cases. Also, criminal indexes are on CD-Rom, but no DOBs. CD-Rom fee is $25.00 per month per department. Overall index goes back to 6/90 and complete name index history is $300.00 per department. For info, contact S Griffin at 951-955-1431.

Superior Court - Criminal Division – Criminal Records
www.courts.co.riverside.ca.us
For free Internet access to records visit the web page. Includes Desert and Riverside felony, misdemeanor, & traffic; and misdemeanor from Corona, Palm Springs, Indio and Blythe.

Blythe Division - Banning Division - Hemet Division - Indio Division - Southwest Justice Center - Temecula Branch
www.courts.co.riverside.ca.us
See Riverside Division location for online information. Also, see Riverside Civil or Criminal Division for information on name
indexes back to 3/89 on CD-rom.

Sacramento County

Superior Court – Civil and Criminal Records

www.saccourt.com
Access to court records back to 1993 is free at https://services.saccourt.com/indexsearchnew/. Search using the DOB, but results are
not shown with the DOB. Includes civil, probate, small claims, unlawful detainer, family as well as criminal. Access to criminal
records back to 1993 is free at https://services.saccourt.com/indexsearchnew/. Search using the DOB, but results are not shown with
the DOB.

San Bernardino County

Superior Court – Civil and Criminal Records

www.sbcounty.gov/courts
Access to civil cases is free at www.sbcounty.gov/courts/genInfo/openaccess.htm. Includes calendars. Daily calendars also at main
website. Access to criminal cases and traffic is free at www.sbcounty.gov/courts/genInfo/openaccess.htm. Includes calendars. Also,
the daily criminal docket is free at the court main website.

San Diego County

Superior Court — Civil and Criminal Records

www.sdcourt.ca.gov
Online searching for case information and calendars is free at www.sdcourt.ca.gov. Also, there is a free party name case search from
the home page. The county system sells a CD-ROM of criminal records; felonies from 6/1974 to 1999; misdemeanors back 10 years.
Online searching for case information and calendars is free at www.sdcourt.ca.gov.

San Francisco County

Superior Court - Civil Division – Civil Records

http://sfgov.org/site/courts_index.asp
Access to the case management system is free at www.sftc.org but does not include family law or small claims. Also, access probate
case data free at www.sftc.org/browser_pages/Probate/probate_frame.htm. Click on "Probate Case View."

Superior Court - Misdemeanor Division – Criminal Records
www.sfgov.org/site/courts_index.asp
Access to the case management system is free at www.sftc.org.

San Joaquin County

Superior Court – Civil and Criminal Records

www.stocktoncourt.org/courts
Free access to civil case summaries, with name searching, at www.stocktoncourt.org/courts/caseinfo.htm. Also, access court calendars
free at www.stocktoncourt.org/stkcrtwwwV5web/SCCalDayIndex.html. Access criminal case summaries free at
www.stocktoncourt.org/courts/caseinfo.htm. Also, access court calendars free at
www.stocktoncourt.org/stkcrtwwwV5web/SCCalDayIndex.html.

San Mateo County

Superior Court – Civil and Criminal Records

www.sanmateocourt.org
Access is free at www.sanmateocourt.org/director.php?filename=./includes/midx_open_access.html. Search all types of county case
records including criminal for free at www.sanmateocourt.org/midx/searchform4_tim.php. Also, search traffic citations at
https://www.sanmateocourt.org/traffic/.

Santa Barbara County

Superior Court – Civil Records

www.sbcourts.org/index.asp
Search general civil index 1975 to present or limited civil back to 1977 free online at www.sbcourts.org/pubindex/. Daily calendars
free at www.sbcourts.org/pubcal/.

Santa Clara County

Superior Court – Civil Records
http://sccsuperiorcourt.org
Civil, Family, Probate, and Small Claims case records and court calendars are free online at www.sccaseinfo.org. CD-rom is also available, fee-$150.00.

Santa Cruz County

Superior Court – Civil Records
www.santacruzcourt.org
Access civil records free at www.santacruzcourt.org/Case%20Info/index.htm. Access using case number or party name.

Shasta County

Superior Court – Civil and Criminal Records

Burney Branch - Superior Court – Criminal Records
www.shastacourts.com
Access the index free at www.shastacourts.com/indexes.php. Also, access using Integrated Justice System.

Siskiyou County

Superior Court – Civil and Criminal Records
www.siskiyou.courts.ca.gov
Access to county superior court records is free at www.siskiyou.courts.ca.gov/CaseHistory.asp. Includes traffic but not juvenile.

Solano County

Superior Court – Civil and Criminal Records
www.solanocourts.com/
Access to records is free at http://courtconnect.solanocourts.com/pls/bprod_cc/ck_public_qry_main.cp_main_idx. Also, civil tentative rulings and probate notes are free at www.solanocourts.com/civil_tent.htm.

Stanislaus County

Superior Court – Civil and Criminal Records
www.stanct.org/courts/index.html
Access the case indices free at www.stanct.org/case_index/.

Tuolumne County

Superior Court - Civil – Civil Records
www.tuolumne.courts.ca.gov
May have civil cases online in 2006; click on "Civil Division" at website.

Superior Court - Criminal – Criminal Records
www.tuolumne.courts.ca.gov
Access criminal records by case number of DR# at www.tuolumne.courts.ca.gov; click on "Criminal Division."

Ventura County

Ventura Superior Court – Civil and Criminal Records
www.ventura.courts.ca.gov
Access to case information, calendars and dockets is free at www.ventura.courts.ca.gov/vent_frameset_puba.htm. Search by defendant or plaintiff name, case number, or date. Access to civil court records 10/93-present. Search probate at www.cagenweb.com/ventura/Probate.html.

County Level ... Recorders & Assessors

Recording Office Organization: 58 counties, 58 recording offices. The recording officer is the County Recorder. Recordings are usually located in a Grantor/Grantee or General index. The entire state is in the Pacific Time Zone (PST). Federal and state tax liens on personal property of businesses are filed with the Secretary of State. Other federal and state tax liens are filed with the County Recorder. Some counties will perform separate tax lien searches. Fees vary for this type of search.

Online Access Note: A number of counties offer online access to assessor and real estate information. The system in Los Angeles is a commercial subscription system.

Alameda County
Assessor, Recording, Deed, Mortgage, Lien, Fictitious Business Name, Property Tax, Inmates, Offender Records
www.acgov.org
Access the clerk-recorder's official public records and fictitious name databases for free at
http://rechart1.co.alameda.ca.us/localization/menu.asp. Also, access to the Property Assessment database is free online at
www.acgov.org/prop_assessment_app/index.jsp. No name searching. Property tax information is found at
www.acgov.org/jsp_app/treasurer/tax_info/index.jsp. Also, to search offender site go to www.vinelink.com

Alpine County   *Birth Records*
Search births 1905-1995 free at www.mariposaresearch.net/php/.

Amador County   *Recording, Deed, Lien, Judgment, Fictitious name, Tax Sale Records*
www.co.amador.ca.us/depts/recorder/index.htm
Access to the county clerk database is free at www.co.amador.ca.us/depts/recorder/criis.htm or www.criis.com/amador/recorded.htm
Also, tax sale information is at www.co.amador.ca.us/depts/treasurer/index.htm; search by year.

Butte County   *Real Estate, Recording, Fictitious Business Name, Inmate Records*
http://clerk-recorder.buttecounty.net
Access to the recorder's database of official documents is free at http://clerk-recorder.buttecounty.net/Riimsweb/Asp/ORInquiry.asp.
Records go back to 1988. Marriages, births and deaths are no longer available. Also, search fictitious business names free online at
http://clerk-recorder.buttecounty.net/RiimsWeb/ASP/FBNInquiry.asp. Also, search the inmate list free at
www.vinelink.com/offender/searchNew.jsp?siteID=5099.

Calaveras County   *Property, Assessor Records*
Access property data free at www.co.calaveras.ca.us/parcelsearch.asp. No name searching. Also, access the GIS Project of property information free at www.co.calaveras.ca.us/departments/gisproj.asp. Click on "The Parcel Information System." No name search at this site.

Contra Costa County
Recording, Fictitious Business Name, Deed, Lien, Judgment, Real Estate, Most Wanted, Marriage Records
www.co.contra-costa.ca.us/depart/elect/Rindex.html
Recorder office records back to 1992 and marriages are free at www.criis.com/contracosta/official.shtml. By order of governor, vital statistic records have been removed from the internet. Fictitious Business names are at www.criis.com/contracosta/sfictitious.shtml.
Also, search the sheriff's most wanted list at www.cocosheriff.org/wanted/wanted.htm.

El Dorado County
Real Estate, Personal Property, Vital Statistic, Fictitious Name, Restaurant Insp, Inmate Records
www.co.el-dorado.ca.us/countyclerk/
Access to the Recorder's index is free at http://main.co.el-dorado.ca.us/CGI/WWB012/WWM501/R. Records go back to 1949. Search business licenses free at http://main.co.el-dorado.ca.us/CGI/WWB012/WWM200/T?S=A. Search Official Records on the recorder database free at http://main.co.el-dorado.ca.us/CGI/WWB012/WWM501/C. Search by date range, name or document number. Search the sheriff's inmate list at www.vinelink.com/offender/searchNew.jsp?siteID=5099. Search county non-confidential marriages and fictitious names for free at http://main.co.el-dorado.ca.us/CGI/WWB012/WWM500/C. Births and deaths have been removed.

Fresno County   *Recorder, Property, Birth, Death, Marriage, Lien, Deed, Mortgage, Inmate Records*
www.co.fresno.ca.us/0420/recorders_web/index.htm
Access to the recorder database is free at www.criis.com/fresno/srecord.shtml. Marriage records are at
www.criis.com/fresno/smarriage.shtml. County Birth Records and death records have been removed from the internet. Also, search
inmate info at www.fresnosheriff.org/InmateInfoCenter/Main.asp and on private company website at www.vinelink.com/index.jsp.

Humboldt County   *Inmate, Offender Records*
www.co.humboldt.ca.us/recorder/
Access to the county correction facility inmate lists is free at www.vinelink.com/offender/searchNew.jsp?siteID=5099.

Imperial County   *Inmate, Offender, Most Wanted Records*
www.co.imperial.ca.us
Search the county inmate list for free at www.vinelink.com/offender/searchNew.jsp?siteID=5011. View the sheriff office most wanted
list at www.icso.org/most_wanted.htm

Inyo County   *Recording, Fictitious Business Name Records*
www.countyofinyo.org
Access to the county clerk recording database may be available free at www.criis.com/inyo/official.shtml. Search site may include
Fictitious Names.

Kern County   *Assessor, Property Tax, Fictitious Business Name, Vital Statistic, Recording, Real Estate,*
Tax Collector, Unclaimed Property Records
http://recorder.co.kern.ca.us
Assessor database records are free at http://assessor.co.kern.ca.us/kips/property_search.asp. Purchase Birth, Death records from
Vitalchek at www.vitalchek.com. Also, search county clerk's fictitious business name database free at
www.co.kern.ca.us/ctyclerk/dba/default.asp. The recorders database of deeds is free at
http://recorder.co.kern.ca.us/kips/property_search.asp. Search fictitious business names and property tax assessment data at
http://kerndata.com. Search tax collector data at www.kcttc.co.kern.ca.us/payment/mainsearch.aspx. Search unclaimed property at
www.kcttc.co.kern.ca.us/searches/unclaimed_monies.cfm.

Kings County   *Inmate Records*
www.countyofkings.com
Search inmate info on private company website at www.vinelink.com/index.jsp.

Lassen County   *Real Estate, Recording, Deed, Tax Sale Records*
http://clerk.lassencounty.org
Access to the recorder database is free at http://icris.lassencounty.org/icris/splash.jsp. Registration is required. Recorded documents go
back to 7/1985. Also, access to tax sales lists is free through a private company at www.bid4assets.com.

Los Angeles County
Assessor, Fictitious Business Name, Inmate, Property Tax, Sex Offender, Most Wanted Records
http://regrec.co.la.ca.us
For assessments use the PDB Inquiry System dial-up svc. for $100 monthly plus $1.00 per inquiry, also $75 sign-up fee for 3-year
dial-up with usage fee of $6.50 per hr or $.11 per minute. PDB registration data is at:
http://assessor.co.la.ca.us/extranet/outsidesales/online.aspx. Tax info line: 213-974-3838. County most wanted list-
www.lapdonline.org/get_involved/most_wanted/most_wanted_main.htm. Search county inmates at
http://app1.lasd.org/iic/ajis_search.cfm. Also search property/assessor data (no name searching) free at
http://assessormap.co.la.ca.us/mapping/viewer.asp. Search Fictitious Name- http://regrec.co.la.ca.us/CLERK/FBN_Search.cfm. Sex
Offenders- http://gismap.co.la.ca.us/sols/viewer.asp.

Marin County
Real Estate, Property Tax, Grantor/Grantee, Recording, Marriage, Business Name, Booking Log Records
www.co.marin.ca.us/depts/AR/main/index.cfm
Search the county Grantor/Grantee index free at www.co.marin.ca.us/depts/AR/RiiMs/index.asp. Also, search the property tax
database at www.co.marin.ca.us/depts/AR/COMPASS/index.asp but there is no name searching. Also, search the real estate sales lists
by month and year by selecting the year. Also, search the marriage records by document index number at
www.co.marin.ca.us/depts/AR/VitalStatistics/index.asp. Marriage records go back to 1948. Search business names by type at
http://marinfo.marin.org/Bizmo/index.cfm. Search the sheriff's booking log at
www.co.marin.ca.us/depts/SO/bklog/XMLProj/index.asp.

Mariposa County *Birth Records*
Search births 1905-1995 free at www.mariposaresearch.net/php/.

Mendocino County *Inmate, Offender Records*
www.co.mendocino.ca.us
Access to the county inmate list is free at www.vinelink.com/offender/searchNew.jsp?siteID=5009.

Merced County
Recorder, Grantor/Grantee, Deed, Real Estate, Most Wanted, Missing Person, Sex Offender Records
http://web.co.merced.ca.us/recorder/
Access to the recorder official records index PARIS system is free at http://139.151.191.2/cgi-bin/odsmnu1.html/input. Search the county most wanted and missing person sites for free at www.mercedsheriff.com. A short list of high risk sex offenders is at http://web.co.merced.ca.us/da/so_high_risk.htm.

Modoc County *Real Estate, Recording, Deed, Fictitious Business Name Records*
Access to the county clerk recording database soon to be free at www.criis.com/modoc/official.shtml. Fictitious business names may also be found.

Monterey County *Inmate, Offender, Most Wanted, Tax Sale Records*
www.co.monterey.ca.us./recorder/
Access to the county jail inmates list is available free at www.vinelink.com/offender/searchNew.jsp?siteID=5099. The county tax defaulted property list is at www.co.monterey.ca.us/taxcollector/Auction.htm. Search assessor data at www.co.monterey.ca.us/assessor/intro2asmt-query.htm; no name searching.

Napa County *Grantor/Grantee, Property, Recording, Deed, Judgment, Lien, Property Tax, Assessor Records*
www.co.napa.ca.us
Access "Official Records" by subscription; fee- $3600 per year. Index goes back to May, 1986; images back to March, 1999. Also, search Official Records Inquiry site for real estate and Grantor/Grantee index back to 5/1986 free at www.co.napa.ca.us/orpublic/ORInquiry.asp. Also, search for property data by address for free at www.co.napa.ca.us/MyProperty/. Also, search assessor's property tax payments free at www.co.napa.ca.us/commerce/propertypayments/.

Nevada County *Real Estate, Recorder, Deed, Judgment, Fictitious Name, Property Tax, GIS Records*
www.mynevadacounty.com/recorder
Access to the county clerk database of recordings and assumed names is free at www.criis.com/nevada/official.shtml. Also, search property tax payment records at http://treas-tax.co.nevada.ca.us/searchtax.php; no name searching. Also, subscription access to Recorders full database is $200 per month fee. Also, daily/weekly/monthly CD-roms are available. Also, search the GIS mapping site by address for property info for free at http://63.205.214.10:1711.

Orange County *Grantor/Grantee, Deed, Lien, Judgment, Fictitious Business Name, Property Tax, Wanted, Missing Person, Inmate, Arrest Records*
www.ocrecorder.com
Orange County Grantor/Grantee index is free online at http://cr.ocgov.com/grantorgrantee/index.asp. Also, search fictitious business names at http://cr.ocgov.com/fbn/index.asp. Also, search property tax records at http://tax.ocgov.com/tcweb/search_page.asp; no name searching. Search sheriff's wanted, missing persons and blotter lists at www.ocsd.org; click on "Crime Bulletins." For inmates, arrests (search by date only), arrest warrants, click on "e-services." Also, search inmate/offender lists at www.vinelink.com/offender/searchNew.jsp?siteID=5004.

Placer County
Recording, Fictitious Name, Marriage, Most Wanted, Missing Person, Jail, Assessor, Property Tax Records
www.placer.ca.gov/clerk/clerk.htm
Recorder office records are free at the website. County Birth and death records have been removed from the internet. Marriage records are at www.criis.com/placer/smarriage.shtml. Search county Fictitious Business Names at www.criis.com/placer/sfictitious.shtml. Search sheriff's most wanted, missing person, and sex offender map at www.placer.ca.gov/sheriff/aware/. The county in-custody roster is at www.placer.ca.gov/sheriff/jail/icr.htm. The assessor's property assessment data is free at www.placer.ca.gov/assessor/assessment-inquiry.htm, no name searching.

Riverside County *Assessor, Property Tax, Fictitious Name, Grantor/Grantee, Deed, Lien, Judgment, Divorce, Wanted, Missing Person Records*
http://riverside.asrclkrec.com

Property tax information from the County Treasurer database is free from EZproperty.com on the internet at https://riverside.ca.ezgov.com/ezproperty/review_search.jsp. A fee is charged for documents found free on the Grantor/Grantee index and assessor data at www.enetwizard.com/shop/affiliates/11467_01/default.asp. Also, access to county fictitious name database is free at http://riverside.asrclkrec.com/ACR/OSfbn.asp. Also, access sheriff's most wanted, missing person, sex offender map at www.riversidesheriff.org/crime/.

Sacramento County
Real Estate, Grantor/Grantee, Deed, Assessor, Business License, Wanted Suspect, Inmate Records
www.ccr.saccounty.net
Access Clerk-recorder Grantee/Grantor index back to 1965 for free at www.erosi.saccounty.net/Inputs.asp. Also, search restaurant inspections at www.emd.saccounty.net/eh/emdfoodprotect.htm. Also, search fictitious names at www.efbn.saccounty.net. Also search property tax & parcels at www.eproptax.saccounty.net; no name searching. Also, find property data at http://assessorparcelviewer.saccounty.net/website/assessor/pv_blank.aspx?g=; no name searching. Also, search City of West Sacramento business licenses at www.cityofwestsacramento.org/cityhall/departments/finance/buslic/blfind.cfm. Search the county wanted suspect list at www.crimealert.org/wanted.cfm. Inmates at www.vinelink.com/index.jsp.

San Benito County   *Most Wanted Records*
www.san-benito.ca.us
Access the sheriff's most wanted list at www.sbcsheriff.org/wanted.html.

San Bernardino County
Recorder, Assessor, Fictitious Name, Grantor/Grantee, Inmate, Property Tax Records
www.co.san-bernardino.ca.us
Records on the County Assessor database are free at www.sbcounty.gov/ttc/tr/trsearch.asp?scretry1=yes&. No name searching. Also, for automated call distribution, call 909-387-8306; for fictitious names information, call 909-386-8970. Search fictitious business names at http://170.164.50.51/fbn/index.html. Also, Auditor/Controller Grantor/Grantee recording index back to 1980 is free at http://acrparis.co.san-bernardino.ca.us/cgi-bin/odsmnu1.html/input. Property can also be searched on PIMS system, registration required, https://nppublic.co.san-bernardino.ca.us/newpims/PimsInterface.aspx. Also, search the inmates/offender list at www.vinelink.com/offender/searchNew.jsp?siteID=5006.

San Diego County   *Assessor, Fictitious Name, Real Estate, Grantor/Grantee, Inmates, Most Wanted, Warrant, Sex Offender, Pet, Missing Children, Tax Sale Records*
www.co.san-diego.ca.us
Records on the County Assessor/Recorder/County Clerk Online Services site are free at www.sdcounty.ca.gov/arcc/arcc_home.html including fictitious business names, indexes, maps, property information. Grantee/grantor index search by name for individual record data at http://arcc.co.san-diego.ca.us/services/grantorgrantee. Search inmates at www.sdsheriff.net/wij/wij.aspx. Property characteristics at- http://arcc.co.san-diego.ca.us/services/propchar/. Search for property data at www.sdcounty.ca.gov/arcc/services/propsales_search.html; no name searching.

San Francisco County
Recorder, Deed, Real Esate, Lien, Judgment, Assessor, Property, Fictitious Business Name, Birth, Death Records
www.sfgov.org
Also search recorders database free at www.criis.com/sanfrancisco/srecord.shtml. Also, access the City Property Tax database free at https://services.sfgov.org/ptx/intro.asp. Click on begin. No name searching; address or block/lot number is required. Also, sex offenders list is at www.sfgov.org/site/police_index.asp?id=24681. Fictitious business names are also searchable at http://services.sfgov.org/bns/start.asp. Limited vital statistic information is searchable at www.sfgenealogy.com/sf/, a privately operated site.

San Joaquin County   *Property, GIS-mapping Records*
www.co.san-joaquin.ca.us
Access property data on the GIS-mapping site free at www.sjmap.org/mapapps.asp; no name searching.

San Luis Obispo County   *Grantor/Grantee, Deed, Judgment, Lien, Real Estate, Mortgage, Divorce, Fictitious Business Name, Missing Person, Most Wanted Records*
www.sloclerkrecorder.org
Search the recorder database for free at www.sloclerkrecorder.org/recorder/searchform.cfm. Search fictitious names at www.sloclerkrecorder.org/countyclerk/fbnstartpage.htm. Also, search the assessor property tax rolls for free at www.slocoassr.net/#; no name searching. There is also an "unsecured roll" search. Also, search the sheriff's alerts page for missing persons and most wanted at http://slosheriff.org/alerts.php.

San Mateo County   *Real Estate, Grantor/Grantee, Deed, Property Tax, Fictitious Name Records*

www.smcare.org
Access the recorder's grantor/grantee index free at www.smcare.org/records/recording/default.asp. Records on county property tax data site is free at http://smctweb1.co.sanmateo.ca.us/index.html. No name searching. There is also a secured property search, but no name searching, at http://smctweb1.co.sanmateo.ca.us/SMCWPS/pages/secureSearch.jsp. Also, search fictitious business names at www.smcare.org/business/fictitious/default.asp.

Santa Barbara County
Assessor, Recorder, Real Estate, Lien, Deed, Vital Statistic, Judgment, Property Tax, Most Wanted Records
www.sbcrecorder.com
Access to assessor online property info system (OPIS) in free at the website with parcel number. Records go back 10 years. Subscribers may download. Full access requires registration. Contact Larry Herrera at herrera@co.santa-barbara.ca.us. Search the grantor/grantee index at www.sb-democracy.com/opis/. Also, search property tax bills at http://taxes.co.santa-barbara.ca.us/propertytax.asp; click on View/Search Secured Property Tax Bills. No name searching. Search the Sheriff's most wanted list at www.sbsheriff.org/mw/index.html.

Santa Clara County
Recording, Grantor/Grantee, Fictitious Business Name, Assessor, Tax Collector, Birth Records
www.clerkrecordersearch.org
Access to the County Clerk-Recorder database is free at www.clerkrecordersearch.org/cgi-bin/odsmnu1.html/input. Search births 1905-1995 free at www.mariposaresearch.net/php/. Also, search fictitious business names for free at www.clerkrecordersearch.org/cgi-bin/FBNSearch.html/input. Also search the assessment roll free a www.sccgov.org/portal/site/asr/. No name searching. Also, search the tax collector database at http://payments.scctax.org/payment/jsp/startup.jsp. No name searching. Also, search for county sex offenders at www.sjpd.org/SexOffenders.cfm.

Santa Cruz County
Assessor, Property Tax, Fictitious Business Name, Recording, Deed, Judgment, Vital Statistic, Inmate Records
www.co.santa-cruz.ca.us/rcd/
Access to the assessor's parcel information data is free at http://sccounty01.co.santa-cruz.ca.us/ASR/. No name searching. Also, search for property information using the GIS map at http://gis.co.santa-cruz.ca.us. Search fictitious business names at http://sccounty01.co.santa-cruz.ca.us/clerkrecorder/Asp/FBNInquiry.asp. Search city business licenses at www.ci.santa-cruz.ca.us/bldb/index.html. Search inmates- www.vinelink.com/offender/searchNew.jsp?siteID=5099. Also, access to the recorder's official records is free at http://sccounty01.co.santa-cruz.ca.us/clerkrecorder/Asp/ORInquiry.asp. Online indexes go back to 1978. Births, Deaths, and Marriages are also searchable back to 1984.

Shasta County   *Assessor, Recorder, Real Estate, Vital Statistic Records*
www.co.shasta.ca.us
Search assessor and recorded documents at www.co.shasta.ca.us/Departments/AssessorRecorder/PubInqDisclaimer.shtml Also, a private site lists various birth, death, and marriage records of the county and more at http://myclouds.tripod.com/shasta/shastaco.html. Records on the City of Redding Parcel Search By Parcel Number Server are free at http://cor400.ci.redding.ca.us/nd/gow3lkap.ndm/input. CA state law has removed owner names.

Sierra County   *Tax Sale Records*
www.sierracounty.ws
Access to tax sales lists is free through a private company at www.bid4assets.com

Siskiyou County   *Recording, Deed, Lien, Land, Fictitious Business Name, Tax Sale Records*
Access to the Recorder records database is free at www.criis.com/siskiyou/srecord_current.shtml. Also, access to the fictitious names database is at www.criis.com/siskiyou/sfictitious.shtml. Also, access to tax sales lists is free through a private company at www.bid4assets.com.

Solano County   *Property Tax, Recording, Grantor/Grantee, Deed, Judgment, Lien, Death, Inmate Records*
www.solanocounty.com
Access the recorder's and assessor's indexes for free at http://recorderonline.solanocounty.com. Access recorded data free at http://recorderonline.solanocounty.com/cgi-bin/odsmnu1.html/input. Also, search the treasurer/tax collector/county clerk property tax database free at www.solanocounty.com/resources/scips/tax/situssearch.asp?navid=531. No name searching. Also, search the county jail inmate list at www.vinelink.com/offender/searchNew.jsp?siteID=5099.

Sonoma County *Real Estate, Recorder, Deed, Lien, UCC Records*
www.sonoma-county.org/recorder
Access recorder index records free at http://deeds.sonoma-county.org/search.asp?cabinet=opr.

Stanislaus County *Recording, Fictitious Name, Deed, Lien, Land, Most Wanted, Missing Person Records*
www.co.stanislaus.ca.us
Recorder office records index of recent records are free at www.criis.com/stanislaus/srecord_current.shtml. Birth, death and marriage records have been removed from the internet. County Fictitious Business Name records are at www.criis.com/stanislaus/sfictitious.shtml. Also, search sheriff's missing persons and most wanted lists at www.stanislaussheriff.com/crimebulletin/.

Sutter County *Recorder, Grantor/Grantee, Real Estate, Fictitious Name, Inmate, Offender Records*
www.suttercounty.org
Access the recorder database free at www.suttercounty.org/apps/recordsquery/clerk/. Records go back to 12/29/1994. Also, access assessment and property tax records free at www.suttercounty.org/doc/apps/recordsquery/recordsquery. Also, to search offender site go to www.vinelink.com

Tehama County *Property Tax, Inmate Records*
www.co.tehama.ca.us
Search property tax data on the county unsecured tax information lookup at www.co.tehama.ca.us/taxcoll/taxinfo.cfm. Access to the county sheriff inmate list is at www.tehamaso.org/inmates/ICURRENT.HTM.

Trinity County *Fictitious Business Name Records*
www.trinitycounty.org/Departments/assessor-clerk-elect/clerkrecorder.htm
Access to the Recorder's fictitious business names database is free at http://halfile.trinitycounty.org. For user name, enter "fbn"; leave password field empty.

Tulare County *Recording, Deed, Judgment, Lien, Vital Statistic, Fictitious Name, Property Tax Records*
www.co.tulare.ca.us
Search the recorders database including births, marriages, deaths free at http://209.78.90.65/riimsweb/orinquiry.asp. Also, search treasurer/tax collector property data free at www.co.tulare.ca.us/government/treasurertax/mytaxes/default.asp; no name searching.

Tuolumne County *Real Estate, Recorder, Deed, Lien, Judgment Records*
www.tuolumnecounty.ca.gov
Access the recorder grantor/grantee index at http://portal.co.tuolumne.ca.us/psp/ps/TUP_ASSESSOR/ENTP/h/?tab=TUP_RECORDER_TAB. Click on Grantor/Grantee Index; turn off your pop-up blocker. Registration and fees required.

Ventura County
Recording, Deed, Grantor/Grantee, Lien, Judgment, Fictitious Name, Most Wanted, Property Tax Records
http://recorder.countyofventura.org/venclrk.htm
Access the county clerks database free at http://recorder.countyofventura.org/venclrk.htm. Also, search property tax data for free at http://prop-tax.countyofventura.org/pisearch.asp; no name searching. Also, the county most wanted list is at www.vcsd.org/wanted_and_offenders/most_wanted.htm.

Yolo County
Assessor, Birth, Death, Marriage, Fictitious Business Name, Davis Cemetery, Restaurant Insp Records
www.yolocounty.org/org/Recorder
Access to recordings on the county clerk database are free at www.criis.com/yolo/srecord_current.shtml. Marriage records are at www.criis.com/yolo/smarriage.shtml. County Fictitious Business Name records are at www.criis.com/yolo/sfictitious.shtml. County Birth records Death records have been removed from the Internet. Also, City of Davis business licenses are free at www.city.davis.ca.us/ed/business/. Davis Cemetery District search is free at http://www2.dcn.org/orgs/cemetery. Also verify or find addresses free at www.ci.davis.ca.us/gis/choosemap.cfm.

Yuba County *Recording, Deed, Judgment, Lien, Property Records*
www.co.yuba.ca.us/content/departments/clerk/
Access the recorded document index free at www.co.yuba.ca.us/content/departments/clerk/landrecords/. Online record go back to 1989.

Federal Courts in California...

Standards for Federal Courts: The universal PACER sign-up number is 800-676-6856. Find PACER and the Party/Case Index on the Web at http://pacer.psc.uscourts.gov. PACER dial-up access is $.60 per minute. Also, courts offering internet access via PACER, Web-PACER or the new CM-ECF charge $.08 per page fee ($.07 per page if record is pre-2005 or unless noted as free).

US District Court -- Central District of California

www.cacd.uscourts.gov

PACER: Case records are available back to 1993. New records are available online after 1 day. **PACER Online Access:** PACER online at http://pacer.cacd.uscourts.gov. Document images available. **Electronic Filing:** CM/ECF data at https://ecf.cacd.uscourts.gov. **Opinions:** Click on Recent Opinions. View court opinions at www.cacd.uscourts.gov. **Other Online Access:** Limited calendars at website.

Los Angeles (Western) Division counties: Los Angeles, San Luis Obispo, Santa Barbara, Ventura.
Riverside (Eastern) Division counties: Riverside, San Bernardino.
Santa Ana (Southern) Division counties: Orange.

US Bankruptcy Court -- Central District of California

www.cacb.uscourts.gov

PACER: Case records are available back to 1992. Records are purged once a year. New records are available online after 1 day. **PACER Online Access:** PACER online at https://pacer.login.uscourts.gov/cgi-bin/login.pl?court_id=CACBLA. Document images available. **Electronic Filing:** CM/ECF data at https://ecf.cacb.uscourts.gov. **Opinions:** Select written opinions only. View court opinions at www.cacb.uscourts.gov/cacb/Welcome.nsf/NNP-Publications-WrittenOpinions?OpenPage. **Phone access:** Voice Case Information System, call 866-522-6053, 213-894-4111

Los Angeles Division counties: Los Angeles (cases filed in certain northern Los Angeles County ZIP Codes may be shared with the San Fernando Valley Division.) .
Riverside (East) Division counties: Riverside, San Bernardino.
San Fernando Valley Division counties: Los Angeles, Ventura (cases filed in certain northern Los Angeles County ZIP Codes are shared with the Los Angeles Division, and cases filed in certain eastern Ventura County ZIP Codes are shared with the Ventura Division).
Santa Ana Division counties: Orange.
Santa Barbara (Northern) Division counties: San Luis Obispo, Santa Barbara, Ventura. Certain Ventura County ZIP Codes are assigned to the new office in San Fernando Valley.

US District Court -- Eastern District of California

www.caed.uscourts.gov

PACER: Case records are available back to 1990, some earlier. Records are purged at varying intervals. New records are available online after 1 day. **PACER Online Access:** ECF replaces PACER. **Electronic Filing:** CM/ECF data at https://ecf.caed.uscourts.gov. **Opinions:** View court opinions at www.caed.uscourts.gov. **Other Online Access:** Judges calendars free at http://207.41.18.73/caed/staticOther/page_460.htm.

Fresno Division counties: Fresno, Inyo, Kern, Kings, Madera, Mariposa, Merced, Stanislaus, Tulare, Tuolumne.
Sacramento Division counties: Alpine, Amador, Butte, Calaveras, Colusa, El Dorado, Glenn, Lassen, Modoc, Mono, Nevada, Placer, Plumas, Sacramento, San Joaquin, Shasta, Sierra, Siskiyou, Solano, Sutter, Tehama, Trinity, Yolo, Yuba.

US Bankruptcy Court -- Eastern District of California

www.caeb.uscourts.gov

PACER: Case records are available back to 8/1990. Records are purged every 6 months. New records are available online after 1 day. **PACER Online Access:** Document images available. **Electronic Filing:** CM/ECF data at https://ecf.caeb.uscourts.gov. **Opinions:** Opinions after 2/16/2005 at www.caeb.uscourts.gov/search/search.asp. View court opinions at www.caeb.uscourts.gov/cortinfo/opinions.asp. **Other Online Access:** Calendars free at www.caeb.uscourts.gov/calendar/calendar.asp. **Phone access:** Voice Case Information System, call

Fresno Division counties: Fresno, Inyo, Kern, Kings, Madera, Mariposa, Merced, Tulare. Three Kern ZIP Codes - 93243, 93523, 93524 -handled by San Fernando Valley in the Central District.
Modesto Division counties: Calaveras, Stanislaus, Tuolumne. Pre-11/2004 San Joaquin records for these ZIP Codes are here: 95220, 95227, 95234, 95237, 95240-95242, 95253, 95258, 95286. Mariposa and Merced counties were transferred to the Fresno Division as of 1/1995. .
Sacramento Division counties: Alpine, Amador, Butte, Colusa, El Dorado, Glenn, Lassen, Modoc, Mono, Nevada, Placer, Plumas, Sacramento, San Joaquin, Shasta, Sierra, Siskiyou, Solano, Sutter, Tehama, Trinity, Yolo, Yuba. Pre-11/2004 San Joaquin records are at Modesto Division for these ZIP Codes: 95220, 95227, 95234, 95237, 95240-95242, 95253, 95258, 95286. There is a hearing location in Bakersfield at 1300 18th St, but no cases or case records there. .

US District Court -- Northern District of California

www.cand.uscourts.gov

PACER: Case records are available back to 1984. Records are purged every 6 months. New records are available online after 1 day. **PACER Online Access:** ECF replaces PACER. **Electronic Filing:** ECF cases data back to 4/2001. CM/ECF data at https://ecf.cand.uscourts.gov. **Other Online Access:** Access to court calendars can be found at www.cand.uscourts.gov.
Oakland Division counties: Alameda, Contra Costa. (Note: Cases may be filed here or at San Francisco Div.; records available electronically at either; the 1st number of the case number indicates the file location: 3=SF, 4=Oak., 5=SJ. .
San Francisco Division counties: Del Norte, Humboldt, Lake, Marin, Mendocino, Napa, San Francisco, San Mateo, Sonoma. (Note: Cases may be filed here or at Oakland Div; records available electronically at either; the 1st number of the case number indicates the file location: 3=SF, 4=Oak., 5=SJ. .
San Jose Division counties: Monterey, San Benito, Santa Clara, Santa Cruz.

US Bankruptcy Court -- Northern District of California

www.canb.uscourts.gov

PACER: Case records are available back to 1993. Records are purged every 6 months to 1 year. New records are available online after 1 day. **PACER Online Access:** ECF replaces PACER. **Electronic Filing:** CM/ECF data at https://ecf.canb.uscourts.gov. **Opinions:** Click on Judges Decisions. View court opinions at www.canb.uscourts.gov. **Other Online Access:** For calendars, click on Calendars at main website. **Phone access:** Voice Case Information System, call 888-457-0604, 415-705-3160
Oakland Division counties: Alameda, Contra Costa.
San Francisco Division counties: San Francisco, San Mateo.
San Jose Division counties: Monterey, San Benito, Santa Clara, Santa Cruz.
Santa Rosa Division counties: Del Norte, Humboldt, Lake, Marin, Mendocino, Napa, Sonoma.

US District Court -- Southern District of California

www.casd.uscourts.gov

PACER: Case records are available back to 1990. New records are available online after 1 day. **PACER Online Access:** PACER online at http://pacer.casd.uscourts.gov. Document images available. **Electronic Filing:** CM/ECF data at (Currently in the process of implementing CM/ECF). **Other Online Access:** Access a computer bulletin board at 619-557-6779.
San Diego Division counties: Imperial, San Diego. Court also handles some cases from Yuma County, AZ.

US Bankruptcy Court -- Southern District of California

www.casb.uscourts.gov

PACER: Case records are available back to 1989. Records are purged every 6 months. New records are available online after 1 day. **PACER Online Access:** PACER online at http://pacer.casb.uscourts.gov. Document images available. **Electronic Filing:** CM/ECF data at http://ecf.casb.uscourts.gov. **Phone access:** Voice Case Information System, call 619-557-6521.
San Diego Division counties: Imperial, San Diego.

Colorado

Capital: Denver
              Denver County
Time Zone: MST
Population: 4,601,403
# of Counties: 64

Quick Links

Website: www.state.co.us
Governor: www.colorado.gov/governor
Attorney General: www.ago.state.co.us
State Archives: www.colorado.gov/dpa/doit/archives/
State Statutes and Codes:

       http://198.187.128.12/colorado/lpext.dll?f=templates&fn=fs-main.htm&2.0

Legislative Bill Search: www.leg.state.co.us/Clics2005a/csl.nsf/MainBills?openFrameset
Unclaimed Funds: www.treasurer.state.co.us/payback/

State Level ... Major Agencies

Criminal Records

Bureau of Investigation, State Repository, Identification Unit, 690 Kipling St, Suite 3000, Denver, CO 80215; 303-239-4208, Fax-303-239-5858, 8AM-4:30PM.
http://cbi.state.co.us
Online search: There is an Internet access at https://www.cbirecordscheck.com/Index.asp. Requesters must use a credit card, an account does not need to be established. However, account holders may set up a batch system. The fee is $6.85 per record.

Statewide Court Records

State Court Administrator, 1301 Pennsylvania St, Suite 300, Denver, CO 80203-2416; 303-861-1111, 800-888-0001, Fax-303-837-2340, 8AM-5PM.
www.courts.state.co.us
Online search: Search opinions at the website. As a result of an initiative of the Colorado Judicial Branch, all district court and all county court records are available through www.cocourts.com, e-screening.com, cojustice.com and Sol Communications. An index (Register of Actions) is available from the vendors for civil, civil water, small claims, domestic, felony, misdemeanor, and traffic cases. Images or copies of documents are not available from any of the commercial sites and may only be obtained by contacting the individual court where the documents were filed.

Sexual Offender Registry

Colorado Bureau of Investigation, SOR Unit, 690 Kipling St, Suite 3000, Denver, CO 80215; 303-239-4222, Fax-303-239-4661, 8AM-4:30PM.
http://sor.state.co.us
Online search: The website gives access to only certain high-risk registered sex offenders in the following categories: Sexually Violent Predator (SVP), Multiple Offenses, and Failed to Register.

Corporation, Trademarks/Servicemarks, Fictitious Name, Limited Liability Company, Assumed Name, Trade Name

Secretary of State, Business Div, 1700 Broadway, #200, Denver, CO 80290; 303-894-2200 x2 (Business Entities), Fax-303-869-4864. www.sos.state.co.us
Online search: The Sec. of State's Business Record Search page offers free searching of corporate names and associate information at www.sos.state.co.us/pubs/business/main.htm. Effective 07/04, some e-filing documents are available. Click on Business Center. Also, search for charitable nonprofit members of CANPO - Colorado Association of Nonprofit Organizations - at www.coloradononprofits.org/member.cfm. Search trade names at www.businesstax.state.co.us/tradenames/. **Other options:** Various information is available as a one time order or via subscription. Transmittal can be through CDs, tapes or FTP.

Uniform Commercial Code, Federal Tax Liens, State Tax Liens

Secretary of State, UCC Division, 1560 Broadway, Suite 200, Denver, CO 80202; 303-894-2200 x2, Fax-303-869-4864. www.sos.state.co.us
Online search: There is free record searching at this agency's website. More extensive data is also available via subscription for ongoing business requesters. **Other options:** Various information is available as a one time order or via subscription. Transmittal can be through CDs, tapes or FTP.

Sales Tax Registrations

Revenue Department, Taxpayers Services Office, 1375 Sherman St, Denver, CO 80261; 303-238-7378, Fax-303-866-3211. www.revenue.state.co.us/main/home.asp
Online search: You can verify a sales tax license or exemption number at www.taxview.state.co.us.

Birth Certificates, Death Records

Department of Public Health & Environment, Vital Records Section HSVR-A1, 4300 Cherry Creek Dr S, Denver, CO 80246-1530; 303-756-4464 (Recorded Message), 303-692-2224 (Credit Card Ordering), 303-692-2234 (General Information), Fax-800-423-1108. www.cdphe.state.co.us/hs/certs.asp
Online search: Records can be ordered online from state designated vendors. Go to www.vitalchek.com/default.asp or www.uscerts.com/.

Marriage Certificates

Department of Public Health & Environment, Vital Records Section, 4300 Cherry Creek Dr S, Denver, CO 80246-1530; 303-756-4464 (Recorded Message), 303-692-2224 (Credit Card Ordering), 303-692-2234, Fax-800-423-1108, 8:30AM-4:30PM. www.cdphe.state.co.us/hs/certs.asp
Online search: Search marriages from 1975 to present in the state of Colorado at www.sctc.state.co.us/marriages/default.aspx. There is no fee. Records can be ordered online from state designated vendors. Go to www.vitalchek.com/default.asp or www.uscerts.com/.

Divorce Records

Department of Public Health & Environment, Vital Records Section, 4300 Cherry Creek Dr S, Denver, CO 80246-1530; 303-756-4464 (Recorded Message), 303-692-2224 (Credit Card Ordering), 303-692-2234, Fax-800-423-1108, 8:30AM-4:30PM. www.cdphe.state.co.us/hs/certs.asp
Online search: Search all divorces/dissolutions from 1851 to 1939 and 1968 to present at www.sctc.state.co.us/marriages/divorces.aspx. There is no fee.

Driver Records

Motor Vehicle Business Group, Driver Control, Denver, CO 80261-0016 (Courier: 1881 Pierce Street, Lakewood, CO 80214); 303-205-5613, Fax-303-205-5990, 8AM-5PM. www.revenue.state.co.us/mv_dir/home.asp
Online search: Online access is available via a state-designated vendor. The vendors receive nightly updates from the state of the entire DMV record history file, then charge a processing fee per record to users and customers. These vendors provide access online to end users. Call Mary Tuttle at 303-205-5762 for a list of the vendors. **Other options:** Colorado offers FTP retrieval for high volume users, call 303-205-5762.

Voter Registration

Department of State, Elections Department, 1700 Broadway #270, Denver, CO 80290; 303-894-2200 x6307, Fax-303-869-4861. www.elections.colorado.gov
Online search: Search campaign finance information at www.sos.state.co.us/cpf/FcpaHome.do. **Other options:** The entire database is available on tape or CD-ROM. The cost is $500. No customization is available.

State Level ... Occupational Licensing

Accident & Health Insurer	https://www.doradls.state.co.us/alison.php
Acupuncturist	https://www.doradls.state.co.us/alison.php
Addiction Counselor	https://www.doradls.state.co.us/alison.php
Architect/Architectural Firm	https://www.doradls.state.co.us/alison.php
Attorney	www.coloradosupremecourt.com/Search/AttSearch.asp
Audiologist	https://www.doradls.state.co.us/alison.php
Barber	https://www.doradls.state.co.us/alison.php
Bus, Charter/Scenic/Children's	www.dora.state.co.us/pls/real/puc_permit.search_form
Casualty Company	http://cdilookup.asisvcs.com/SetupAction.do?type=agy
Charitable Organization	www.sos.state.co.us/ccsa/CcsaInquiryMain.do
Chiropractor	https://www.doradls.state.co.us/alison.php
Common Carrier/Contract Carrier	www.dora.state.co.us/pls/real/puc_permit.search_form
Contractor Registration	https://www.doradls.state.co.us/alison.php
Cosmetologist	https://www.doradls.state.co.us/alison.php
Counselor, Professional	https://www.doradls.state.co.us/alison.php
Credit Union	www.dora.state.co.us/financial-services/homeregu.html
Dentist/Dental Hygienist	https://www.doradls.state.co.us/alison.php
Electrical Contractor	https://www.doradls.state.co.us/alison.php
Electrician Journeyman/Master	https://www.doradls.state.co.us/alison.php
Engineer/Engineer in Training	https://www.doradls.state.co.us/alison.php
Family Therapist	https://www.doradls.state.co.us/alison.php
Fundraising Consultant	
	www.sos.state.co.us/ccsa/PfcInquiryCriteria.do;jsessionid=0000hyDoDyM46WXOoNDYcFU1Y1a:114gdag7h
HazMat Carrier	www.dora.state.co.us/pls/real/puc_permit.search_form
Hearing Aid Dealer	www.dora.state.co.us/pls/real/ARMS_Search.Set_Up
Household Goods/Property Carrier	www.dora.state.co.us/pls/real/puc_permit.search_form
Insurance Agency/Agent	http://cdilookup.asisvcs.com/SetupAction.do?type=indv
Insurance Company	http://cdilookup.asisvcs.com/SetupAction.do?type=agy
Land Surveyor/Land Surveyor Intern	https://www.doradls.state.co.us/alison.php
Life Care Institution	www.dora.state.co.us/financial-services/homeregu.html#life
Life Insurance Company	http://cdilookup.asisvcs.com/SetupAction.do?type=agy
Limousine	www.dora.state.co.us/pls/real/puc_permit.search_form
Lobbyist	www.elections.colorado.gov/WWW/default/Lobbyists/prof_lobrpt.pdf
Lobbyist Volunteer	www.elections.colorado.gov/WWW/default/Lobbyists/vol%20lobby%202005.pdf
Manufactured Housing Mfg.	www.dola.state.co.us/doh/Documents/parkt.htm
Marriage Therapist	https://www.doradls.state.co.us/alison.php
Medical Doctor	https://www.doradls.state.co.us/alison.php
Midwife	https://www.doradls.state.co.us/alison.php
Nurse	www.dora.state.co.us/pls/real/ARMS_Search.Disclaimer_Page
Nursing Care Facility	https://www.doradls.state.co.us/alison.php
Nursing Home Administrator	https://www.doradls.state.co.us/alison.php
Off-Road Charter	www.dora.state.co.us/pls/real/puc_permit.search_form
Optometrist	https://www.doradls.state.co.us/alison.php
Outfitter	https://www.doradls.state.co.us/alison.php
Pharmacist/Pharmacist Intern	https://www.doradls.state.co.us/alison.php
Pharmacy	https://www.doradls.state.co.us/alison.php
Physical Therapist	https://www.doradls.state.co.us/alison.php
Physician Assistant	https://www.doradls.state.co.us/alison.php
Plumber Journeyman/Master/Residential	https://www.doradls.state.co.us/alison.php
Podiatrist	https://www.doradls.state.co.us/alison.php
Psychologist	https://www.doradls.state.co.us/alison.php
Public Accountant-CPA	https://www.doradls.state.co.us/alison.php
Real Estate Agent/Broker/Sales	www.dora.state.co.us/pls/real/re_estate_home

Real Estate Appraiser.................................. www.dora.state.co.us/pls/real/re_estate_home
Reinsurance Intermediary Manager .... www.dora.state.co.us/pls/real/INS_Search.Disclaimer_Page
Respiratory Therapist................................. https://www.doradls.state.co.us/alison.php
River Outfitter.. https://www.doradls.state.co.us/alison.php
Savings & Loan Association...................... www.dora.state.co.us/financial-services/homeregu.html
Securities Broker/Dealer........................... http://pdpi.nasdr.com/pdpi/
Social Worker .... https://www.doradls.state.co.us/alison.php
Solicitor, Paid .... www.sos.state.co.us/cgi-
   forte/fortecgi?serviceName=ccsaprodaccess&templateName=/sessauto/mainMenu_outer_form.forte&hasr=T&hast=T
Stock Broker .... http://pdpi.nasdr.com/pdpi/
Towing Carrier.. www.dora.state.co.us/pls/real/puc_permit.search_form
Trainer for Childcare Workers
   www.cdhs.state.co.us/childcare/word%20files/DIRECTORY%20OF%20APPROVED%20PRE.doc
Trainer, First Aid/CPR
   www.cdhs.state.co.us/childcare/word%20files/DIRECTORY%20OF%20APPROVED%20FIRST%20AID.doc
Veterinarian/Veterinary Student .... https://www.doradls.state.co.us/alison.php
Wireman, Residential................................. https://www.doradls.state.co.us/alison.php

County Level ... Courts

Court Administration: State Court Administrator, 1301 Pennsylvania St, Suite 300, Denver, CO, 80203; 303-861-1111; www.courts.state.co.us

Court Structure: As of 9/1/2001, the maximum civil claim in County Courts was increased to $15,000. The District and County Courts have overlapping jurisdiction over civil cases involving less than $15,000 ($10,000 prior to 9/1/2001). Fortunately, District and County Courts are combined in most counties.

Municipal courts only have jurisdiction over traffic, parking, and ordinance violations.

Online Access Note: As a result of an initiative of the Colorado Judicial Branch, all District Court and all County Court records are available through www.cocourts.com, e-screening.com, cojustice.com and Sol Communications. An index – Register of Actions – is available from the vendors for civil, civil water, small claims, domestic, felony, misdemeanor, and traffic cases. Images or copies of documents are not available from any of the commercial sites and may only be obtained by contacting the individual court where the documents were filed.

Opinions from the Court of Appeals are available from the website.

Delta County

District & County Courts – Civil and Criminal Records
www.7thjudicialdistrictco.org/delta.html
Civil records access is at www.courtlink.lexisnexis.com/colorado or www.cocourts.com. Also, weekly dockets for the 7th district courts are at www.7thjudicialdistrictco.org/docket.html.

Montrose County

7th District & County Courts – Civil and Criminal Records
www.courts.state.co.us/district/07th/dist07.htm
Records access at www.courtlink.lexisnexis.com/colorado or www.cocourts.com. Also, weekly dockets for the 7th district county courts only are at www.7thjudicialdistrictco.org/docket.html.

Pitkin County

9th District & County Courts – Civil and Criminal Records
www.courts.state.co.us/district/09th/dist09.htm
Civil records access is at www.cocourts.com. Search probate 1881-1953 at
www.colorado.gov/dpa/doit/archives/probate/pitkin_probate.htm.

Editor's Note: See the text above about a private, statewide access system.

County Level ... Recorders & Assessors

Recording Office Organization: 63 counties, 63 recording offices. The recording officer is the County Clerk and Recorder. The entire state is in the Mountain Time Zone (MST).

November 15, 2001, Broomfield City and County came into existence, derived from portions of Adams, Boulder, Jefferson and Weld counties. County offices are located at 1 Descombes Dr, Broomfield, CO 80020; 303-469-3301; hours 8AM-5PM. To determine if an address is in Broomfield, parcel search by address at www.co.broomfield.co.us/centralrecords/assessor.shtml. Federal and some state tax liens on personal property are filed with the Secretary of State. Other federal and state tax liens are filed with the County Clerk and Recorder. Many counties will perform tax lien searches, usually at the same fees as UCC searches. Copies usually cost $1.25 per page.

Online Access Note: To date, over 20 Colorado Counties offer free access to property assessor records. Also, the state archives provides limited inheritance tax records for 14 Colorado Counties at www.colorado.gov/dpa/doit/archives/inh_tax/index.html; generally records extend forward only to the 1940s.

At the state level, the Secretary of State offers web access to UCCs, and the Department of Revenue offers trade name searches. See the State Agencies section for details.

Adams County *Assessor, Property Records*
www.co.adams.co.us
Records from the Adams County Assessor database are free at www.co.adams.co.us/subdivision/.

Arapahoe County
Assessor, Property Tax, Real Estate, Deed, Judgment, Lien, Recording, Personal Property Records
www.co.arapahoe.co.us
Access to the recorders database is free at www.co.arapahoe.co.us/OnlineTools/index.asp.

Archuleta County *Real Estate, Recorder, Deed, Lien, Assessor, Property, Sex Offender Records*
http://archuletacounty.org
Access to record data is by internet subscription, fee is $250 monthly. Call Recording office for further info and sign-up. Search assessment property records at www.qpublic.net/co/archuleta/index.html for a fee for full data; search index data free at http://64.234.218.210/cgi-bin/colorado_links.cgi?county=archuleta. Also, search the sex offender site is free at www.archuletacounty.org/so/offenders/offenders/offender.htm.

Boulder County *Assessor, Property Tax, Voter Registration, Recording, Grantor/Grantee, Deed, Judgment, Lien, Most Wanted Records*
www.co.boulder.co.us/clerk
Search the assessor's property database for free at www.co.boulder.co.us/assessor/disclaimer.htm. No name searching. Also, recorder data is on the iCris system at http://icris.co.boulder.co.us/splash.jsp. To search free, login as public, password public. Also, search property tax records at www.co.boulder.co.us/treas/disclaim.htm. No name searching. Also, the county treasurer offers data electronically and on microfiche. Alpha index by owner name is $25.00 per set. Also, search voter registration at www.co.boulder.co.us/clerk/elections/promptforname.html. Name and DOB required. Search sheriff's most wanted at www.co.boulder.co.us/Sheriff/most_wanted/wanted.htm.

Broomfield County *Real Estate, Assessor, Voter Registration Records*
www.co.broomfield.co.us
Access to the assessor property database is free at www.ci.broomfield.co.us/maps/IMS.shtml. Search by address or parcel ID only. Also, search property and tax assessment data free at https://info.ci.broomfield.co.us/Tax/Default.asp. No name searching. Also search voter registration records at www.ci.broomfield.co.us/election/voter_inquiry/. Also, search tax sales list free at www.ci.broomfield.co.us/centralrecords/TaxSale.shtml.

Costilla County *Assessor, Property Records*
Access to assessor property data is free at http://64.234.218.210/cgi-bin/colorado_links.cgi?county=costilla.

Custer County *Assessor, Property Records*

Access assessor final tax roll data free at www.qpublic.net/co/custer/search.html. Full property data is available by subscription as well.

Delta County

Real Estate, Recorder, Deed, Lien, Judgment, Death, Marriage, DOT Release, Assessor, Property Tax Records
www.deltacounty.com
Access recorder records free at http://clerk.deltacounty.com/Search.aspx. Also, access Assessor data on the GIS site for free at www.southwestdata.org/website/delco/deltacounty/disclaimer.htm

Denver County

Assessor, Real Estate, Property Tax, Personal Property, Contract, Inmate, Solicitation Arrest, Restaurant Records
www.denvergov.org
Records on the Denver City and Denver County Assessor database are free at www.denvergov.org/realproperty.asp. Search business personal property at www.denvergov.org/PersProperty.asp. Also, search real estate property tax data for free at www.denvergov.org/treasurypt/PropertyTax.asp. Address or parcel number required to search. Search restaurant inspections at www.denvergov.org/eh/search.asp. Also, search county contracts at www.denvergov.org/contracts/contrak.asp. Search county inmates list at www.vinelink.com/offender/searchNew.jsp?siteID=6001; Prostitution solicitation arrests are at www.denvergov.org/johnstv/.

Douglas County *Deed, Grantor/Grantee, Judgment, Lien, Mortgage, UCC, Vital Statistic, Assessor, Property, Building Permit, Contractor Records*

www.douglas.co.us
Access to recorders data is free at https://secure.douglas.co.us/NASApp/pubdocaccess/advancedSearchAction.do. There is also searches for Marriages, UCCs, and Plat/Maps. Records on the county assessor database are free at www.douglas.co.us/assessor/. You may also download related list data from the site. Also, use the parcel locator at http://publicstaging.douglas.co.us/website/default.htm. Also, search building permits and contractors at https://secure.douglas.co.us/NASApp/building/permitSearch.do.

Eagle County *Assessor, Property, Grantor/Grantee, Deed, Judgment, Lien, Vital Statistic, Will, UCC, Property Sale, Most Wanted, Pet Records*

www.eaglecounty.us
Search clerk and recorder data free at www.eaglecounty.us/cloe/search.cfm. Also, access the County Assessor-Treasurer databases free at www.eaglecounty.us/patie/index_content.cfm. Search comps sales at www.eaglecounty.us/Assessor/saleslist.cfm. Also, view the sheriff's most wanted list at www.eaglecounty.us/sheriff/mostWanted.cfm. Pet lost and found database at www.eaglecounty.us/doggie/lfpetsform.cfm.

El Paso County *Assessor, Public Trustee Sale, Contractor, Grantor-Grantee Records*

http://car.elpasoco.com/
Records on the county Assessor database are free at http://land.elpasoco.com. Search the grantor/grantee index at http://car2.elpasoco.com/rcdquery.asp. Search the county contractor list at www.pprbd.org/contrnames.html.

Fremont County *Assessor, Property, Property Sale Records*

Access to the assessors database is free at www.qpublic.net/fremont/search1.html.

Garfield County *Assessor, Treasurer Records*

Search the assessor and treasurer at www.mitchandco.com/realEstate/garfield/index.cfm.

Gilpin County *Property, Assessor, Marriage Records*

www.co.gilpin.co.us
Access property records free at www.tylerworksasp.com/itax/taxSearch.jsp. Access to county marriage records from 1864 to 1944 is free at www.colorado.gov/dpa/doit/archives/marriage/gilpin_index.htm.

Grand County *Property, Assessor, Recording, Grantor/Grantee, Deed, Lien Records*

http://co.grand.co.us/Clerk/clerkand.htm
Access to Clerk-Recorder index is free at http://co.grand.co.us/Clerk/lookup/. Also, the assessor database is free at http://co.grand.co.us/Assessor/Download_Page.html.

Jefferson County *Assessor, Property, Grantor/Grantee, Deed, Judgment, Recording Records*
https://cr-web.co.jefferson.co.us/
Records on the county Assessor database are free at http://ww14.co.jefferson.co.us/ats/splash.do. No name searching. Also, search the recorder's Grantor/Grantee index for free at https://cr-web.co.jefferson.co.us. Index goes back to 1963; images to 1994.

Lake County *Assessor, Property Records*
http://qpublic.net/co/lake/index.html
Access county assessor property data free at http://64.234.218.210/cgi-bin/colorado_links.cgi?county=lake.

La Plata County *Property, Sale, Parcel Records*
http://co.laplata.co.us
Records on the county Real Estate Parcel Search Page are free at www.laplatainfo.com/search2.html. This is basic property data but for sales and tax data, there is a subscription service for $20.00 per month, credit cards accepted.

Larimer County *Property Tax, Assessor, Treasurer, UCC, Lien, Deed, Judgment, Recording, Voter Registration, Most Wanted Records*
www.larimer.org
Search the county Public Record Databases for free at www.larimer.org/databases/index.htm. Also, search the sheriff most wanted list at www.co.larimer.co.us/Sheriff/MostWanted/Wanted0.htm.

Logan County *Assessor, Property Records*
www.loganco.gov/departments.htm
Access to assessor property data is free at www.qpublic.net/co/logan/search.html.

Mesa County
Grantor/Grantee, Judgment, Lien, Real Estate, Assessor, Real Estate, Property Tax, Voter Registration Records
www.mesacounty.us
Records on the county Assessor database are free at www.mesacounty.us. Click on Assessor lookup and search by address or parcel number. Search on the GIS-mapping/property page at www.gjcity.org/CityDeptWebPages/AdministrativeServices/InformationSystems/GIS/GIS.htm. Also, search the Grantor/Grantee index, liens, judgments, mortgages, etc. at www.co.mesa.co.us/sireweb/sireweb.asp.

Mineral County *Property, Records*
Access property records free at www.qpublic.net/co/mineral/.

Moffat County *Property, Assessor, Treasurer, Most Wanted Records*
Search the treasurer's tax database free at http://65.77.74.205/MoffatCounty/SearchSelect.aspx. Also, access to the sheriff's most wanted list is at www.moffatcountysheriff.com/mostwanted.htm. Also, access to assessor property data free at http://co.moffat.co.us/assessor/default.htm but may not be available at this time.

Montezuma County *Property Tax, Property Sale Records*
www.co.montezuma.co.us
Access to county property information is free at http://itax.co.montezuma.co.us/itax/taxSplash.jsp and registration is required.

Montrose County *Property, Assessor Records*
Access to Property Information Search System is free at http://itax.co.montrose.co.us/itax/taxSplash.jsp. Free registration is required.

Morgan County *Assessor, Property Records*
www.co.morgan.co.us
Search the assessor database free at www.co.morgan.co.us/itax/TaxLogin.jsp. Username and password are both "Public".

Otero County *Real Estate, Recording, Deed, Lien, Assessor, Property Records*
Access to recorded data is by subscription only. Fee is $250 per month but you may signup for a free 30-day trial. Contact the Clerk/Recorder office for more info and sign-up. Also, access property data free at www.oterocountyassessor.net.

Ouray County *Recorder, Deed, Real Estate, Lien, Judgment, UCC, Marriage, Death Records*
www.ouraycountyco.gov
Access the record data free at http://ouraycountyco.gov/recording/oncoreweb/Search.aspx.

Park County   *Assessor, Property Tax, Divorce Records*
www.parkco.org
Records on the county Assessor database are free at www.parkco.org/Search2.asp? including tax information, owner, address, building characteristics, legal and deed information. Also, county divorce records from 1957 to 1974 are free at www.colorado.gov/dpa/doit/archives/divorce/1park.htm.

Pitkin County   *Grantor/Grantee, Assessor, Inmates, Divorce, Probate, Grantor/Grantee Records*
www.aspenpitkin.com
Records on the county Assessor database are free at www.pitkinassessor.org/Assessor/. Grantor/Grantee reception search is also accessible here. Also, search recorded documents at www.pitkinassessor.org/Clerk/search.asp. Also, the sheriff's current inmate list is free at www.aspenpitkin.com/depts/28/inmates.cfm. Divorce records 1931 to 1964 are at www.colorado.gov/dpa/doit/archives/divorce/1pitkin.htm. Also, probate records from 1881 to 1953 are at www.colorado.gov/dpa/doit/archives/probate/pitkin_probate.htm.

Pueblo County
Assessor, Real Estate, Property Sale, Registered Voter, Grantor/Grantee, Marriage Certificates Records
www.co.pueblo.co.us/clerk/
Access to the county assessor database is free at http://assessor.co.pueblo.co.us. Also, access to voter registration data is free at www.co.pueblo.co.us; click on "Registered Voters" Also, for online index of recorded documents go to iCRIS http://icris.co.pueblo.co.us/icris/Login.jsp. Includes grantor/grantee, marriage certificates, etc.

Rio Blanco County   *Assessor, Property Records*
www.co.rio-blanco.co.us
Access assessor property data free at www.co.rio-blanco.co.us/assessor/.

Rio Grande County   *Property Tax, Assessor, Sale Records*
www.qpublic.net/riogrande/
Access to the property assessor's data is free at www.qpublic.net/riogrande/search1.html. A property sale search is also at the assessor website.

Routt County   *Real Estate, Assessor, Property Tax, Treasurer, Deed, Judgment, Property Sale Records*
www.co.routt.co.us
Records on the county Assessor/Treasurer Property Search database are free at www.co.routt.co.us/assessor.html. Also, search records free on the County Clerk & Recorder Reception Search database at www.co.routt.co.us/clerk.html. Also, a gis-mapping site has property data for free at http://maps.co.routt.co.us/website/parcels/index.asp. Search by name.

Saguache County   *Recording, Real Estate, Deed, Lien, Death, Marriage Records*
www.saguachecounty.net
Access to the Recorder data base is free at www.thecountyrecorder.com/Search.aspx?CountyKey=6. Index goes back to 1994; images back to 1994. Search the Assessor database free at www.qpublic.net/co/saguache/.

San Miguel County   *Inmate Records*
www.sanmiguelcounty.org
Access the sheriff's county inmates list free at www.sanmiguelsheriff.com/index.cfm?fuseaction=standard&categoryId=5&subcategoryId=4

Summit County   *Property, GIS-mapping Records*
www.co.summit.co.us
Access to the GIS-mapping site property data is free at www.co.summit.co.us/scripts/esrimap.dll.

Teller County   *Real Estate, Grantor/Grantee, Assessor, Property Tax Records*
www.co.teller.co.us
Access the county clerk real estate database free at http://data.co.teller.co.us/AsrData/wc.dll?Doc~GrantSearch. Records go back to 1978; fee for documents- $1.25 per page. Also, search the assessor database free at http://data.co.teller.co.us/AsrData/wc.dll?AsrDataProc~OwnerNameSearch.

Weld County *Real Estate, Assessor, Treasurer, Property Tax, Most Wanted, Sex Offender Records*
www.co.weld.co.us
Search property information on the map server database at http://maps.merrick.com/website/weld/ or click on the "Property Information" button then search assessor data by name. Also, search the treasurer's property database for free at www.co.weld.co.us/departments/treasurer/tax/index1.cfm. Also, access the sheriff's most wanted and sex offender pages at www.weldsheriff.com/.

Yuma County *Assessor, Property Records*
www.yumacounty.net/clerkrecorder.html
Access to property data is via subscription at a private site; call Assessor office to details.

Federal Courts in Colorado...

Standards for Federal Courts: The universal PACER sign-up number is 800-676-6856. Find PACER and the Party/Case Index on the Web at http://pacer.psc.uscourts.gov. PACER dial-up access is $.60 per minute. Also, courts offering internet access via PACER, Web-PACER or the new CM-ECF charge $.08 per page fee ($.07 per page if record is pre-2005 or unless noted as free).

US District Court -- District of Colorado

www.co.uscourts.gov

PACER: Case records are available back to 1990. Records are purged schedule varies. New records are available online after 1 day. **PACER Online Access:** ECF replaces PACER. **Electronic Filing:** CM/ECF data at www.co.uscourts.gov/cmecf_frame.htm. **Opinions:** View court opinions at www.co.uscourts.gov/opinions_frame2.htm. **Other Online Access:** Current and next week calendars at www.co.uscourts.gov/calendars_frame.htm.
Denver Division counties: All counties in Colorado.

US Bankruptcy Court -- District of Colorado

www.cob.uscourts.gov

PACER: Case records are available back to 7/ 1981. **PACER Online Access:** ECF replaces PACER. **Electronic Filing:** CM/ECF data at https://ecf.cob.uscourts.gov. **Opinions:** View court opinions at www.cob.uscourts.gov/opinions.asp. **Other Online Access:** Calendars free at www.cob.uscourts.gov/calendar.asp. **Phone access:** Voice Case Information System, call 720-904-7419.
Denver Division counties: All counties in Colorado.

Connecticut

Capital: Hartford
           Hartford County
Time Zone: EST
Population: 3,503,604
# of Counties: 8

Quick Links

Website: www.ct.gov
Governor: www.ct.gov/governorrell/site/default.asp
Attorney General: www.ct.gov/ag/site/default.asp
State Archives: www.cslib.org/archives.htm
State Statutes and Codes: www.cga.ct.gov/asp/menu/Statutes.asp
Legislative Bill Search: www.cga.ct.gov/asp/menu/Search.asp
Unclaimed Funds: www.state.ct.us/ott/ucplisting.htm

State Level ... Major Agencies

Statewide Court Records

Chief Court Administrator, 231 Capitol Ave, Hartford, CT 06106; 860-757-2100, 860-757-2270 (External Affairs), Fax-860-757-2215, 8AM-5PM.
www.jud.state.ct.us
Online search: Online access allows for only civil, housing and family cases www.jud2.state.ct.us/civil_inquiry/ Several inquiry methods are offered. Assignment lists and calendars are also available. Opinions from the Supreme and Appellate courts are available from the general website.

Sexual Offender Registry

Department of Public Safety, Sex Offender Registry Unit, PO Box 2794, Middletown, CT 06757-9294 (Courier: 1111 Country Club Rd, Middleton, CT 06457); 860-685-8060, Fax-860-685-8349, 8:30AM-4:30PM.
www.ct.gov/dps/cwp/view.asp?a=2157&Q=294474&dpsNav=|
Online search: The website has two searches: those convicted of a CT law, and those offenders who violated a law in a different state but are living in CT. Search by name or town, ZIP Code, or entire list.

Incarceration Records

Connecticut Department of Corrections, Public Information Office, 24 Wolcott Hill Rd, Wethersfield, CT 06109; 860-692-7780 (Locater), Fax-860-692-7783, 8:30AM-4:30PM.
www.ct.gov/doc/site/default.asp
Online search: Current inmates may be searched at www.ctinmateinfo.state.ct.us/searchop.asp.

Corporation, Limited Partnership, Trademarks/Servicemarks,
Limited Liability Company, Limited Liability Partnership, Statutory Trust

Secretary of State, Commercial Recording Division, 30 Trinity St, Hartford, CT 06106; 860-509-6003, Fax-860-509-6069.
www.sots.ct.gov

Online search: Click on the CONCORD option at the website for free access to corporation and UCC records. The system is open from 7AM to 11PM. You can search by business name, business ID or by filing number. The website also offers online filing. Go to www.concord.sots.ct.gov/CONCORD/index.jsp.

Uniform Commercial Code, Federal Tax Liens, State Tax Liens

UCC Division, Secretary of State, PO Box 150470, Hartford, CT 06115-0470 (Courier: 30 Trinity St, Hartford, CT 06106); 860-509-6002, Fax-860-509-6069, 8:30AM-4PM.
www.sots.ct.gov/CommercialRecording/Crdindex.html
Online search: Records may be accessed at no charge on the Internet. Click on the Business and UCC Inquiries tab. The system is open 7AM to 11PM. **Other options:** Bulk lists and CDs are available for purchase. Call the Financial Area at 860-509-6165.

Driver Records

Department of Motor Vehicles, Copy Records Unit, 60 State St., Wethersfield, CT 06161-0503; 860-263-5154, 8:30AM-4:30PM T-F.
www.ct.gov/dmv/site/default.asp
Online search: Online access is provided to approved businesses that enter into written contract. The contract requires a prepayment deposit for the first 2,500 records. Fee is $15.00 per record. The address is part of the record. For more information, call 203-805-6093. **Other options:** Batch requests are available for approved users, call 203-805-6093 for details.

Vehicle Ownership, Vehicle Identification

Department of Motor Vehicles, Copy Record Unit, 60 State St,, Wethersfield, CT 06161-1896; 860-263-5154, 8:AM-4:30PM T- F.
www.ct.gov/dmv/site/default.asp
Online search: Vehicle record information is available on a volume basis to approved businesses that enter into a written agreement. The contract requires an annual fee and a surety bond. For more information, call 860-805-6093.

State Level ... Occupational Licensing

Acupuncturist	www.dph.state.ct.us/scripts/hlthprof.asp
Alcohol/Drug Counselor	www.dph.state.ct.us/scripts/hlthprof.asp
Antenna Svcs Dealer/Technician	www.dcpaccess.state.ct.us/DCPPublic/LicenseLookup.asp
Appraiser, MVPD/MVR	www.ct-clic.com
Architect	www.dcpaccess.state.ct.us/DCPPublic/LicenseLookup.asp
Architectural Firm	www.dcpaccess.state.ct.us/DCPPublic/LicenseLookup.asp
Asbestos Abatement Worker/Supr.	www.dph.state.ct.us/scripts/hlthprof.asp
Asbestos Consultant/Contractor	www.dph.state.ct.us/scripts/hlthprof.asp
Athletic Promoter	www.dcpaccess.state.ct.us/DCPPublic/LicenseLookup.asp
Attorney/Attorney Firm	www.jud2.state.ct.us/Civil_Inquiry/GetAtty.asp
Audiologist	www.dph.state.ct.us/scripts/hlthprof.asp
Auto Insurance Adjuster	www.ct-clic.com
Bail Bond Agent	www.ct-clic.com
Bail Enforcement Agent	www.ct.gov/dps/lib/dps/special_licensing_and_firearms/licensed_bea.pdf
Bail Enforcement Firearm Instructor	www.ct.gov/dps/lib/dps/special_licensing_and_firearms/bea_instructors.pdf
Bail Enforcement Instructor	www.ct.gov/dps/lib/dps/special_licensing_and_firearms/bea_instructors.pdf
Bailbondsman	www.ct.gov/dps/lib/dps/special_licensing_and_firearms/licensed_bondsman.pdf
Bakery	www.dcpaccess.state.ct.us/DCPPublic/LicenseLookup.asp
Bank/Trust Company	www.ct.gov/dob/cwp/view.asp?a=2228&q=296954&dobNAV_GID=1660
Bank Branch	www.ct.gov/dob/cwp/view.asp?a=2228&q=296954&dobNAV_GID=1660
Bank CEO	www.ct.gov/dob/cwp/view.asp?a=2228&q=300188&dobNAV_GID=1660
Banking Office, Non-depository	www.ct.gov/dob/cwp/view.asp?a=2228&q=296954&dobNAV_GID=1660
Barber	www.dph.state.ct.us/scripts/hlthprof.asp
Bazaar/Raffle Permit	www.ct-clic.com/
Bedding Mfg/Renovation	www.dcpaccess.state.ct.us/DCPPublic/LicenseLookup.asp
Bedding Supply/Sterilizer	www.dcpaccess.state.ct.us/DCPPublic/LicenseLookup.asp
Beekeeper	www.caes.state.ct.us/InspectandRegandGeneral/inspecti.htm
Beverage/Water Bottler	www.dcpaccess.state.ct.us/DCPPublic/LicenseLookup.asp
Bingo Registration	www.ct-clic.com/

Boxer/Boxing Professional .... www.dcpaccess.state.ct.us/DCPPublic/LicenseLookup.asp
Broker/Dealer Agent................................. http://pdpi.nasdr.com/pdpi/
Building Contractor .... www.dcpaccess.state.ct.us/DCPPublic/LicenseLookup.asp
Casino/Casino Occupation.......................... www.ct-clic.com
Casualty Adjuster...................................... www.ct-clic.com
Check Cashing Service .... www.ct.gov/dob/cwp/view.asp?a=2233&q=297868&dobNAV_GID=1663
Child Caring Agency/Facility .... www.state.ct.us/dcf/Licensed_Facilities/listing_CCF.asp
Child Placing Agency .... www.state.ct.us/dcf/Licensed_Facilities/listing_CPA.asp
Child Psychiatric Clinic .... www.state.ct.us/dcf/Licensed_Facilities/listing_OPCC.asp
Chiropractor... www.dph.state.ct.us/scripts/hlthprof.asp
Coach, High/Grade School .... www.state.ct.us/sde/
Collection Agency .... www.ct.gov/dob/cwp/view.asp?a=2233&q=297872&dobNAV_GID=1663
College/University .... www.ctdhe.org/database/default.htm
Contractor, Mechanical.............................. www.dcpaccess.state.ct.us/DCPPublic/LicenseLookup.asp
Cosmetologist .... www.dph.state.ct.us/scripts/hlthprof.asp
Counselor, Professional .... www.dph.state.ct.us/scripts/hlthprof.asp
Credit Union .... www.ct.gov/dob/cwp/view.asp?a=2237&q=298042&dobNAV_GID=1660
Day Treatment Facility, Extended .... www.state.ct.us/dcf/Licensed_Facilities/listing_EDT.asp
Debt Adjuster... www.ct.gov/dob/cwp/view.asp?a=2233&q=297874&dobNAV_GID=1663
Dental Anes/Conscious Sedation Permittee www.dph.state.ct.us/scripts/hlthprof.asp
Dentist/Dental Hygienist............................ www.dph.state.ct.us/scripts/hlthprof.asp
Dessert Mfg, Frozen .... www.dcpaccess.state.ct.us/DCPPublic/LicenseLookup.asp
Dietician/Nutritionist .... www.dph.state.ct.us/scripts/hlthprof.asp
Dog Racing Owner/Trainer......................... www.ct-clic.com/
Druggist Liquor Permittee .... www.dcpaccess.state.ct.us/DCPPublic/LicenseLookup.asp
Electrical Contr./Inspector .... www.dcpaccess.state.ct.us/DCPPublic/LicenseLookup.asp
Electrical Journeyman/Apprentice .... www.dcpaccess.state.ct.us/DCPPublic/LicenseLookup.asp
Electrical Sign Installer.............................. www.dcpaccess.state.ct.us/DCPPublic/LicenseLookup.asp
Electrician.. www.dcpaccess.state.ct.us/DCPPublic/LicenseLookup.asp
Electrologist/Hypertricologist..................... www.dph.state.ct.us/scripts/hlthprof.asp
Electronics Service Dealer/Tech. .... www.dcpaccess.state.ct.us/DCPPublic/LicenseLookup.asp
Elevator Inspector/Mechanic .... www.dcpaccess.state.ct.us/DCPPublic/LicenseLookup.asp
Embalmer... www.dph.state.ct.us/scripts/hlthprof.asp
Emergency Medical Svc Professional......... www.dph.state.ct.us/scripts/hlthprof.asp
Engineer.. www.dcpaccess.state.ct.us/DCPPublic/LicenseLookup.asp
Family Residence, Permanent..................... www.state.ct.us/dcf/Licensed_Facilities/listing_PFR.asp
Farm Winery.. www.dcpaccess.state.ct.us/DCPPublic/LicenseLookup.asp
Fire Protection Inspector/Contr. .... www.dcpaccess.state.ct.us/DCPPublic/LicenseLookup.asp
Funeral Director/Home .... www.dph.state.ct.us/scripts/hlthprof.asp
Glazier .... www.dcpaccess.state.ct.us/DCPPublic/LicenseLookup.asp
Hairdresser.. www.dph.state.ct.us/scripts/hlthprof.asp
Health Care Ctr. Insurer............................. www.ct-clic.com
Health Club.. www.dcpaccess.state.ct.us/DCPPublic/LicenseLookup.asp
Hearing Instrument Specialist..................... www.dph.state.ct.us/scripts/hlthprof.asp
Heating, Piping, Cooling Cont./Journey'n.. www.dcpaccess.state.ct.us/DCPPublic/LicenseLookup.asp
Homeopathic Physician .... www.dph.state.ct.us/scripts/hlthprof.asp
Honey Bee Registration .... www.caes.state.ct.us/InspectandRegandGeneral/inspecti.htm
Hypertrichologist .... www.dph.state.ct.us/scripts/hlthprof.asp
Insurance Adjuster/Public Adjuster .... www.ct-clic.com
Insurance Agent, Fraternal......................... www.ct-clic.com
Insurance Appraiser .... www.ct-clic.com
Insurance Company/Producer .... www.ct-clic.com
Insurance Consultant.................................. www.ct-clic.com
Interior Designer....................................... www.dcpaccess.state.ct.us/DCPPublic/LicenseLookup.asp
Investment Advisor/Agent .... www.ct.gov/dob/cwp/view.asp?a=2250&q=299166&dobNAV_GID=1662
Juice Producer.. www.dcpaccess.state.ct.us/DCPPublic/LicenseLookup.asp

Land Surveyor Firm	www.dcpaccess.state.ct.us/DCPPublic/LicenseLookup.asp
Landscape Architect	www.dcpaccess.state.ct.us/DCPPublic/LicenseLookup.asp
Lead Abatement Consultant/Contract'r	www.dph.state.ct.us/scripts/hlthprof.asp
Lead Abatement Professional/Supervisor	www.dph.state.ct.us/scripts/hlthprof.asp
Lead Consultant	www.dph.state.ct.us/scripts/hlthprof.asp
Lead Planner/Project Designer	www.dph.state.ct.us/scripts/hlthprof.asp
Legalized Gaming Occupation	www.ct-clic.com/
Liquor License	www.dcpaccess.state.ct.us/DCPPublic/LicenseLookup.asp
Liquor Mfg/Dist/Whlse	www.dcpaccess.state.ct.us/DCPPublic/LicenseLookup.asp
Liquor Store/Broker/Shipper	www.dcpaccess.state.ct.us/DCPPublic/LicenseLookup.asp
Loan Company, Small	www.ct.gov/dob/cwp/view.asp?a=2233&q=297878&dobNAV_GID=1663
Lobbyist	www.lims.state.ct.us/public/reports.asp?ethicsPNavCtr=|#44104
Lottery	www.ct-clic.com/
Lottery Sales Agent	www.ct-clic.com/
Marriage & Family Therapist	www.dph.state.ct.us/scripts/hlthprof.asp
Marshall, State	www.jud.state.ct.us/faq/marshals.htm
Martial Arts Facility	www.dcpaccess.state.ct.us/DCPPublic/LicenseLookup.asp
Massage Therapist	www.dph.state.ct.us/scripts/hlthprof.asp
Mausoleum	www.dph.state.ct.us/scripts/hlthprof.asp
Medical Doctor	www.dph.state.ct.us/scripts/hlthprof.asp
Medical Response Technician	www.dph.state.ct.us/scripts/hlthprof.asp
Midwife	www.dph.state.ct.us/scripts/hlthprof.asp
Mobile Home Park/Seller	www.dcpaccess.state.ct.us/DCPPublic/LicenseLookup.asp
Money Forwarder	www.ct.gov/dob/cwp/view.asp?a=2233&q=297862&dobNAV_GID=1663
Money Order/Travelers Check Issuer	www.ct.gov/dob/cwp/view.asp?a=2233&q=297862&dobNAV_GID=1663
Mortgage (1st) Broker/Lender	www.ct.gov/dob/cwp/view.asp?a=2233&q=297864&dobNAV_GID=1663
Mortgage (2nd) Broker/Lender	www.ct.gov/dob/cwp/view.asp?a=2233&q=297866&dobNAV_GID=1663
Naturopathic Physician	www.dph.state.ct.us/scripts/hlthprof.asp
New Home Construction Contr	www.dcpaccess.state.ct.us/DCPPublic/LicenseLookup.asp
Nurse/Nurse - LPN	www.dph.state.ct.us/scripts/hlthprof.asp
Nurse, Advance Registered Practice	www.dph.state.ct.us/scripts/hlthprof.asp
Nursery Plant Dealer	www.caes.state.ct.us/InspectandRegandGeneral/inspecti.htm
Nursery, Plant	www.caes.state.ct.us/InspectandRegandGeneral/inspecti.htm
Nursing Home Administrator	www.dph.state.ct.us/scripts/hlthprof.asp
Occupational Therapist/Assistant	www.dph.state.ct.us/scripts/hlthprof.asp
Off-Track Betting	www.ct-clic.com/
Optical Shop	www.dph.state.ct.us/scripts/hlthprof.asp
Optician	www.dph.state.ct.us/scripts/hlthprof.asp
Optometrist	www.dph.state.ct.us/scripts/hlthprof.asp
Osteopathic Physician	www.dph.state.ct.us/scripts/hlthprof.asp
Paramedic	www.dph.state.ct.us/scripts/hlthprof.asp
Pesticide Applicator	www.kellysolutions.com/CT/Applicators/index.htm
Pesticide-related Business	www.kellysolutions.com/CT/Business/index.htm
Pharmacist/Pharmacist Intern	www.dcpaccess.state.ct.us/DCPPublic/LicenseLookup.asp
Pharmacy	www.dcpaccess.state.ct.us/DCPPublic/LicenseLookup.asp
Pharmacy Technician	www.dcpaccess.state.ct.us/DCPPublic/LicenseLookup.asp
Physical Therapist/Assistant	www.dph.state.ct.us/scripts/hlthprof.asp
Physician	www.dph.state.ct.us/scripts/hlthprof.asp
Physician Assistant	www.dph.state.ct.us/scripts/hlthprof.asp
Pipefitter	www.dcpaccess.state.ct.us/DCPPublic/LicenseLookup.asp
Plumber	www.dcpaccess.state.ct.us/DCPPublic/LicenseLookup.asp
Podiatrist	www.dph.state.ct.us/scripts/hlthprof.asp
Premium Finance Company	www.ct-clic.com

Private Detective Company /Private Eye
  www.ct.gov/dps/lib/dps/special_licensing_and_firearms/licensed_pi_security_companies.pdf

Private Occupational School	www.ctdhe.org/database/default.htm

Psychologist .... www.dph.state.ct.us/scripts/hlthprof.asp
Public Service Technician .... www.dcpaccess.state.ct.us/DCPPublic/LicenseLookup.asp
Radiographer .... www.dph.state.ct.us/scripts/hlthprof.asp
Real Estate Agent/Broker/Sales .... www.dcpaccess.state.ct.us/DCPPublic/LicenseLookup.asp
Real Estate Appraiser .... www.dcpaccess.state.ct.us/DCPPublic/LicenseLookup.asp
Reinsurance Intermediary .... www.ct-clic.com
Rental Car Company .... www.ct-clic.com
Respiratory Care Practitioner .... www.dph.state.ct.us/scripts/hlthprof.asp
Risk Purchasing/Retention Group .... www.ct-clic.com
Sales Finance Company .... www.ct.gov/dob/cwp/view.asp?a=2233&q=297876&dobNAV_GID=1663
Sanitarian .... www.dph.state.ct.us/scripts/hlthprof.asp
Sanitarian, Registered .... www.dph.state.ct.us/scripts/hlthprof.asp
Savings & Loan Association Bank .... www.ct.gov/dob/cwp/view.asp?a=2228&q=296954&dobNAV_GID=1660
Savings Bank .... www.ct.gov/dob/cwp/view.asp?a=2228&q=296954&dobNAV_GID=1660
School Administrator/Supervisor .... www.state.ct.us/sde/
School Guidance Counselor .... www.state.ct.us/sde/
School Library Media Associate .... www.state.ct.us/sde/
School Principal/Superintendent .... www.state.ct.us/sde/
School Psychologist .... www.state.ct.us/sde/
School Social Worker .... www.state.ct.us/sde/
Securities Agent .... http://pdpi.nasdr.com/pdpi/
Securities Broker/Dealer .... http://pdpi.nasdr.com/pdpi/
Security Company Firearms Instructor
    www.ct.gov/dps/lib/dps/special_licensing_and_firearms/certified_security_officers_firearms_instructors-
    blue_cards.pdf
Security Company, Private
    www.ct.gov/dps/lib/dps/special_licensing_and_firearms/licensed_pi_security_companies.pdf
Security Officer Instructor
    www.ct.gov/dps/lib/dps/special_licensing_and_firearms/approved_cj_security_instructor_(public).pdf
Sheet Metal Cont./Journeyman .... www.dcpaccess.state.ct.us/DCPPublic/LicenseLookup.asp
Shorthand Court Reporter .... www.dcpaccess.state.ct.us/DCPPublic/LicenseLookup.asp
Social Worker .... www.dph.state.ct.us/scripts/hlthprof.asp
Solar Energy Contr./Journeyman .... www.dcpaccess.state.ct.us/DCPPublic/LicenseLookup.asp
Speech Pathologist .... www.dph.state.ct.us/scripts/hlthprof.asp
Speech/Language Pathologist .... www.state.ct.us/sde/
Sprinkler Layout Technician .... www.dcpaccess.state.ct.us/DCPPublic/LicenseLookup.asp
Student Athlete Agent .... www.dcpaccess.state.ct.us/DCPPublic/LicenseLookup.asp
Subsurface Sewage Cleaner/Installer .... www.dph.state.ct.us/scripts/hlthprof.asp
Subsurface Sewer Installer/Cleaner .... www.dph.state.ct.us/scripts/hlthprof.asp
Surplus Line Broker .... www.ct-clic.com
Surveyor, Land .... www.dcpaccess.state.ct.us/DCPPublic/LicenseLookup.asp
Teacher .... www.state.ct.us/sde/
Utilization Review Company .... www.ct-clic.com
Vending Machine Operator .... www.dcpaccess.state.ct.us/DCPPublic/LicenseLookup.asp
Vendor, Itinerant .... www.dcpaccess.state.ct.us/DCPPublic/LicenseLookup.asp
Veterinarian .... www.dph.state.ct.us/scripts/hlthprof.asp
Viatical Settlement Broker/Provider .... www.ct-clic.com
Weigher .... www.dcpaccess.state.ct.us/DCPPublic/LicenseLookup.asp
Weights/Measures Dealer/Repair/Regul'r .. www.dcpaccess.state.ct.us/DCPPublic/LicenseLookup.asp
Well Driller .... www.dcpaccess.state.ct.us/DCPPublic/LicenseLookup.asp
Wrestler/Wrestling Manager .... www.dcpaccess.state.ct.us/DCPPublic/LicenseLookup.asp
Youth Camp .... www.dph.state.ct.us/BRS/Youth_camps/youthcamps.htm

County Level ... Courts

Court Administration: Chief Court Administrator, 231 Capitol Av, Hartford, CT, 06106; 860-757-2100; www.jud.state.ct.us

Court Structure: The Superior Court is the sole court of original jurisdiction for all causes of action, except for matters over which the Probate Courts have jurisdiction as provided by statute. The state is divided into 15 Judicial Districts, 20 Geographic Area Courts, and 14 Juvenile Districts. The Superior Court - comprised primarily of the Judicial District Courts and the Geographical Area Courts - has five divisions: Criminal, Civil, Family, Juvenile, and Administrative Appeals. When not combined, the Judicial District Courts handle felony and civil cases while the Geographic Area Courts handle misdemeanors, and most handle small claims. Divorce records are maintained by the Chief Clerk of the Judicial District Courts.

Online Access Note: The judicial branch provides access to civil, small claims and/or family court records via the internet at www.jud2.state.ct.us. Click on "Party Name Inquiry." The site contains party name search, assignment lists, and calendars. Also, questions about the fuller commercial system available through Judicial Information Systems should be directed to the Connecticut JIS Office at 860-282-6500. There is currently no online access to criminal records, however criminal and motor vehicle data is available for purchase in database format. Opinions from the Supreme Court and Appellate Courts are available from the general website.

County Level ... Recorders & Assessors

Recording Office Organization: 8 counties and 170 towns/cities. There is no county recording in this state. The recording officer is the Town/City Clerk. Be careful not to confuse searching in the following towns/cities as equivalent to a countywide search: Fairfield, Hartford, Litchfield, New Haven, New London, Tolland, and Windham. The entire state is in the Eastern Time Zone (EST). All federal and state tax liens on personal property are filed with the Secretary of State. Federal and state tax liens on real property are filed with the Town/City Clerk. Towns will not perform tax lien searches.

Online Access Note: A number of towns offer free access to assessor information. The State's Municipal Public Access Initiative has produced a website of Town/Municipality information at www.munic.state.ct.us. Also, a private vendor has placed assessor records from a number of towns on the Internet. Visit http://data.visionappraisal.com.

Fairfield County

Brookfield Town *Assessor Records*
www.brookfield.org
Search the town assessor field cards at http://data.visionappraisal.com/BrookfieldCT/. Free registration for full data.

Danbury City *Assessor, Land, Permit, Water Information Records*
www.ci.danbury.ct.us
Search the city assessor database at http://data.visionappraisal.com/DanburyCT/. Free registration for full data. Also, search land, permits, and other records on the city public access at
www.ci.danbury.ct.us/Public_Documents/DanburyCT_WebDocs/publicaccess. Follow prompts and use "public" for username and password. Site may be temporarily down.

Fairfield Town *Assessor Records*
Search the town assessor database at http://data.visionappraisal.com/FairfieldCT/ . Free registration for full data.

Greenwich Town   *Property, Assessor, Personal property, Motor Vehicle, Parking Ticket Records*
www.greenwichct.org
Search current tax records free at www.greenwichct.org/ServicesOnline/services_online.asp#. You may also search real estate, personal property, and motor vehicles at www.munis-online.com/citizens/home/citizen_home.asp. There is also a parking ticket search at www.parkingticketpayment.com/greenwich/ but no searching.

New Canaan Town   *Assessor, Property Records*
www.newcanaan.info
Access to property data is at http://data.visionappraisal.com/NewCanaanCT/. Free registration required.

New Fairfield Town   *Assessor Records*
Access the assessor database go to http://data.visionappraisal.com/NewfairfieldCT/. Does not require a username & password to enter database. Just click on link.

Newtown Town   *Property, Assessor Records*
Access property data free at www.prophecyone.us. No name searching.

Norwalk City   *Property, Assessor Records*
www.norwalkct.org
Access to Norwalk property records is free at www.norwalkct.org/norwalk/pckls.asp.

Stamford City   *Assessor, Real Estate, Personal Property, City Businesses Records*
www.cityofstamford.org/Welcome.htm
Access to the city tax assessor database is free online at www.cityofstamford.org/Tax/default.htm. Also, search the city registry of trade names for free at www.cityofstamford.org/TradeNames/default.htm. Also, access assessor at www.cityofstamford.org/TaxCollectionAssessment/default.htm.

Stratford Town   *Assessor Records*
www.townofstratford.com
Search town assessor database at http://data.visionappraisal.com/StratfordCT/. Free registration for full data.

Trumbull Town   *Assessor, Property Records*
Search the assessor database at http://data.visionappraisal.com/TrumbullCT. Requires registration, but is free.

Weston Town   *Land, Marriage, Death, Trade Name, Grantor/Grantee Records*
www.weston-ct.com
Access the Town Clerk's index records free online at www.weston-ct.com/resolution/. For username and password use cott, cott. Maps and surveys are also available. Search page access at www.weston-ct.com/resolution.

Westport Town   *Vital Records, Trade Names, Land Records Records*
www.westportct.gov
Search a variety or public records at http://publicrecords.westportct.gov. Search the Assessor DB at http://data.visionappraisal.com/WestportCT/search.asp.

Wilton Town   *Assessor Records*
www.wiltonct.org/info.htm
Search the town assessor database at http://data.visionappraisal.com/WiltonCT/. Free registration for full data.

Hartford County

Avon Town   *Property Assessor Records*
Access to property data is free at www.avonassessor.com/index.shtml.

Berlin Town   *Real Estate, Marriage, Recorder, Assessor Records*
www.town.berlin.ct.us
Access the recorders index free at www.town.berlin.ct.us/resolution/. Also, search town assessor database at http://data.visionappraisal.com/BerlinCT/. Free registration for full data.

Bloomfield Town   *Property, Assessor Records*
Access property data free at www.prophecyone.us. No name searching.

Bristol City   *Real Estate, Recording, Deed Records*
www.ci.bristol.ct.us
Access to land indexes are to be available by Summer, 2006.

Burlington Town   *Assessor, Property Records*
Search assessor database at http://data.visionappraisal.com/BurlingtonCT.

Canton Town   *Property Records*
www.townofcantonct.org
For search of property address, search by owner name or search sales go to www.cantonassessor.com.

East Windsor Town   *Assessor, Property Records*
www.eastwindsorct.com/Home/
Access property data free at www.prophecyone.us. No name searching.

Farmington Town   *Assessor, Property Records*
www.farmington-ct.org/TownServices/TownClerk/
Access to the property assessor data is free at www.farmington-ct.org; click on Assessor Property search

Glastonbury Town   *Property, Assessor Records*
www.glasct.org
Search town property information free on the GIS Interactive Mapping site at http://gis.glasct.org/. Click on the binoculars for "Parcels" page where you can name search.

Granby Town   *Assessor Records*
Search the town assessor's database at http://data.visionappraisal.com/GranbyCT. Free registration for full data.

Hartford City   *Assessor, Property Records*
Access Assessor Property data free at http://assessor.hartford.gov.

Manchester Town   *Assessor Records*
www.ci.manchester.ct.us/Town_Clerk/index.htm
Search the town assessor database at http://data.visionappraisal.com/ManchesterCT/. Free registration required for full access.

Marlborough Town   *Assessor, Property Records*
www.marlboroughct.com
Search the assessor database at http://data.visionappraisal.com/MarlboroughCT.

New Britain Town   *Assessor Records*
Search the city assessor database at http://data.visionappraisal.com/NewbritainCT/. Free registration for full data.

Newington Town   *Assessor, Property Tax Records*
www.ci.newington.ct.us
Access to assessor property records is free at http://newington.univers-clt.com.

Plainville Town   *Assessor, Property Records*
www.plainvillect.com
Access town assessor property data free at http://plainville.univers-clt.com.

Rocky Hill Town   *Land, Marriage, Death, Trade Name, Recording Records*
www.ci.rocky-hill.ct.us
Access to the Town Clerk's Index Search is free at www.ci.rocky-hill.ct.us/resolution/. Land records go back to 1973; Marriages/Deaths to 1990; trade names to 1987; maps to 1982.

Simsbury Town   *Property, Assessor, Condominium Records*
www.simsbury-ct.gov/townclerk.htm
Access assessment data free at
http://simsburyct.virtualtownhall.net/Public_Documents/Departments/SimsburyCT_Assessment/Assessment%20Data/Asse
ssment%20Information.

South Windsor Town   *Property Transfer Records*
www.southwindsor.org
Access to town clerk's lists of property transfers by year are free at
www.southwindsor.org/TownHall/Property%20Transfer/property.htm. Search back to 1999. No current info available.

Southington Town   *Most Wanted Records*
www.southington.org
Access to the Town's most wanted list is at www.southingtonpolice.org/warrant.htm.

Suffield Town   *Assessor Records*
www.suffieldtownhall.com
Search the town assessor's database at http://data.visionappraisal.com/SuffieldCT. Free registration required for full access.

West Hartford Town   *Assessor, Property Records*
www.west-hartford.com
Access to the assessor property records requires a $50 annual subscription for one user; $200 for 5 users. Details and sign-up are at www.westhartford.org/whprs/.

Wethersfield Town   *Assessor, Property Records*
http://wethersfieldct.com/govt.htm
Access to property data is at http://data.visionappraisal.com/WethersfieldCT/. Free registration for full data.

Windsor Locks Town   *Assessor Records*
Search the town assessor database at http://data.visionappraisal.com/WINDSORLOCKSCT/. Free registration for full data.

Windsor Town   *Assessor, Real Estate Records*
www.townofwindsorct.com
Search the town clerk's land records index for free at www.townofwindsorct.com/records.htm. Index goes back to 1970.
Also, search the town assessor's Taxpayer Information System database at http://data.visionappraisal.com/WINDSORCT/.
Free registration required for full access. Town services search page at www.townofwindsorct.com.

Litchfield County

Colebrook Town   *Assessor Records*
Assessor records online at http://data.visionappraisal.com/ColebrookCT/.

Goshen Town   *Assessor Records*
Search the town assessor database at http://data.visionappraisal.com/goshenCT/. Free registration for full data.

Kent Town   *Assessor, Property Records*
www.kentct.org
Access to property assessor data is at http://data.visionappraisal.com/KentCT/. Free registration required.

New Hartford Town   *Assessor, Property Records*
www.town.new-hartford.ct.us
Access to property data is at http://data.visionappraisal.com/NewhartfordCT/. Free registration required.

New Milford Town   *Assessor Records*
www.newmilford.org/
Search the town assessor database at http://data.visionappraisal.com/NewMilfordCT/. Free registration required for full access.

Roxbury Town *Assessor, Property Records*
www.roxburyct.com
Access to property data is at www.visionappraisal.com/databases/ct/index.htm. Free registration required. Also, the search town assessor database go to http://data.visionappraisal.com/RoxburyCT/. Free registration for full data.

Sharon Town *Assessor Records*
Access assessor data at http://data.visionappraisal.com/SharonCT/.

Torrington City *Assessor, Property Records*
www.torringtonct.org
Access to property data is at http://data.visionappraisal.com/TorringtonCT/. Free registration required.

Watertown Town *Property, Assessor Records*
www.watertownct.org
Access property data free at http://data.visionappraisal.com/watertownct/. Free registration for full data.

Winchester Town *Property, Assessor Records*
www.townofwinchester.org
Access town property tax data after free registration at http://data.visionappraisal.com/WinchesterCT/.

Middlesex County

Clinton Town *Assessor, Property Records*
Search Assessor records at http://data.visionappraisal.com/ClintonCT/.

Deep River Town *Assessor, Property Records*
Search assessor data online at http://data.visionappraisal.com/DeepRiverCT/.

Durham Town *Assessor, Property, Map Records*
http://townofdurhamct.org
Access the assessor's database at http://durham.univers-clt.com. Also, Assessor Maps access at www.townofdurhamct.org/content/18701/18791/default.aspx.

East Haddam Town *Assessor, Property Records*
http://easthaddam.org
Access property data free at http://easthaddam.org/property_value.htm.

Essex Town *Property, Assessor Records*
www.essexct.gov/departments/townclerk.html
Access to property data is at http://data.visionappraisal.com/EssexCT/.

Middlefield Town *Assessor Records*
www.munic.state.ct.us/MIDDLEFIELD/contents.htm
Search town assessor database at http://data.visionappraisal.com/MiddlefieldCT/. Free registration required for full data.

New Haven County

Branford Town *Assessor Records*
Search the town assessor database at http://data.visionappraisal.com/BranfordCT/. Free registration for full data.

Cheshire Town *Assessor, Property Records*
www.cheshirect.org
Access property data free at www.prophecyone.us. No name searching.

East Haven Town *Assessor, Property Records*
Access property data free at www.prophecyone.us. No name searching.

Hamden Town *Assessor Records*
www.hamden.com
Search the town assessor's database at http://data.visionappraisal.com/hamdenct. Free registration required for full access.

Madison Town *Assessor, Property Records*
www.madisonct.org
Search town assessor database at http://data.visionappraisal.com/MadisonCT/. Free registration required for full access.

Meriden City *Property, Assessor Records*
www.cityofmeriden.org
Search by parcel ID or address for property assessor data at www.meridenrealestate.org/meriden208/LandRover.asp

Milford City *Assessor Records*
www.ci.milford.ct.us
Search the city assessor's database at http://data.visionappraisal.com/milfordct/. Free registration required for full data.

Naugatuck Town *Assessor Records*
Search the town assessor database at http://data.visionappraisal.com/NaugatuckCT/. Free registration required for full data.

New Haven City *Assessor Records*
Search the city assessor database at http://data.visionappraisal.com/NewhavenCT/. Free registration required for full data.

North Branford Town *Assessor, Property Records*
Search assessor records at http://data.visionappraisal.com/NorthBranfordCT.

Oxford Town *Property, Assessor Records*
Access property data free at www.prophecyone.us. No name searching.

Prospect Town *Property, Assessor Records*
Access property data free at www.prophecyone.us. No name searching.

Seymour Town *Assessor, Property Records*
Search the assessor database at http://data.visionappraisal.com/SeymourCT/. Requires registration, which is free.

Waterbury City *Assessor, Property, Real Estate Sale Records*
Access to the assessor property data is free at www.waterburyrealestate.org/Waterbury208/LandRover.asp and at http://data.visionappraisal.com/watertownct/.

West Haven City *Assessor Records*
Search town assessor's database at http://data.visionappraisal.com/Westhavenct/. Free registration required for full access.

Woodbridge Town *Assessor Records*
www.munic.state.ct.us/WOODBRIDGE/woodbridge.htm
Search town assessor's database at http://data.visionappraisal.com/woodbridgeCT. Free registration required for full data.

New London County

City of New London *Assessor Records*
www.ci.new-london.ct.us
Search city assessor's database at http://data.visionappraisal.com//NewLondonCT. Free registration required for full access.

Colchester Town *Assessor Records*
www.colchesterct.net
Search the town assessor database at http://data.visionappraisal.com/ColchesterCT/. Free registration for full data.

East Lyme Town   *Assessor, Property Records*
www.eltownhall.com
Search the town assessor database at http://data.visionappraisal.com/EastLymeCT/. Free registration for full data.

Groton Town   *Property, GIS, Tax Payment Records*
Access property data free at http://grotongis.town.groton.ct.us. Click on Interactive Mapping, then Property Viewer, then owner name. Records back to 1990. Search list of tax payments for 2005 free at www.town.groton.ct.us/taxes/listing.asp.

Ledyard Town   *Assessor, Property Records*
www.town.ledyard.ct.us
Search the assessor database at http://data.visionappraisal.com/LedyardCT.

Lyme Town   *Assessor, Property Records*
Access to property data is at http://data.visionappraisal.com/LymeCT/. Free registration required.

North Stonington Town   *Assessor, Property Records*
www.munic.state.ct.us/N_Stonington/
Search the assessor database at http://data.visionappraisal.com/NorthstoningtonCT/.

Norwich City   *Real Estate, Deed, Assessor, Property Tax Records*
www.norwichct.org
Search the city assessor's database at http://data.visionappraisal.com/NorwichCT. Free registration required for full data. Also, access to the clerk's town land records is online by subscription. Index goes back to 1929 and images to 1997. Fee is $350.00 per year; sign-up online at www.norwichct.org/content/155/43/280/81/249.aspx or call 860-823-3734.

Old Lyme Town   *Assessor Records*
Search town Assessor database at http://data.visionappraisal.com/OLDLYMECT. Free registration required for full access.

Waterford Town   *Assessor, Property Records*
Access property data free at www.prophecyone.us. No name searching.

Tolland County

Andover Town   *Assessor Records*
www.andoverct.org
Search town assessor database at http://data.visionappraisal.com/AndoverCT/. Free registration for full data.

Bolton Town   *Assessor, Property Records*
Access property data free at www.prophecyone.us. No name searching.

Ellington Town   *Assessor, property Records*
www.ellington-ct.gov
Online access to assessor records at http://data.visionappraisal.com/EllingtonCT.

Somers Town   *Property, Assessor Records*
www.somersnow.com
Access property data free at www.prophecyone.us. No name searching.

Stafford Town   *Real Estate, Recorder, Deed, Lien, Property Tax, Assessor Records*
www.staffordct.org
Access assessor records free at http://records.staffordct.org/Resolution/search_menu.asp but free registration is required. Also, access assessor property data free at http://stafford.univers-clt.com.

Tolland Town   *Assessor Records*
www.toland.org
Search town assessor database at http://data.visionappraisal.com/TollandCT/. No username or password required, simply click on link.

Windham County

Killingly Town *Assessor, Street Card, Parcel Map, Real Estate Sale Records*
www.killinglyct.gov
Access assessor records free at www.killinglyct.gov/Pages/KillinglyCT_Assessor/index.

Pomfret Town *Assessor Records*
http://pomfretct.org
Search town assessor database at http://data.visionappraisal.com/PomfretCT/. Free registration for full data. Also, can find subdivisions, wetlands and zoning regulations at http://pomfretct.org.

Putnam Town *Assessor, Property Records*
www.putnamct.us
Access to property data is at http://data.visionappraisal.com/PutnamCT/. Free registration required.

Thompson Town *Assessor Records*
www.thompsonct.org
Search the town assessor database at http://data.visionappraisal.com/ThompsonCT/. Free registration for full data.

Woodstock Town *Assessor, Property Records*
Search the assessor database at http://data.visionappraisal.com/WoodstockCT. Requires registration, but is free.

Federal Courts in Connecticut...

Standards for Federal Courts: The universal PACER sign-up number is 800-676-6856. Find PACER and the Party/Case Index on the Web at http://pacer.psc.uscourts.gov. PACER dial-up access is $.60 per minute. Also, courts offering internet access via PACER, Web-PACER or the new CM-ECF charge $.08 per page fee ($.07 per page if record is pre-2005 or unless noted as free).

US District Court -- District of Connecticut

www.ctd.uscourts.gov
PACER: Case records are available back to 11/1991. New records are available online after 1 day. **PACER Online Access:** ECF replaces PACER. **Electronic Filing:** Copies off the ECF terminal are $.10 per page. CM/ECF data at https://ecf.ctd.uscourts.gov.
Opinions: Selected opinions only. View court opinions at www.ctd.uscourts.gov/Opinions.htm.
Bridgeport Division counties: Litchfield (after 2004), Fairfield (prior to 1993). Since 1/1993, cases from any county may be assigned to any of the divisions in the district.
Hartford Division counties: Hartford, Tolland, Windham (prior to 1993). Since 1993, cases from any county may be assigned to any of the divisions in the district.
New Haven Division counties: Middlesex, New Haven, New London (prior to 1993), Litchfield (prior to 2004). Since 1993, cases from any county may be assigned to any of the divisions in the district.

US Bankruptcy Court -- District of Connecticut

www.ctb.uscourts.gov
PACER: Case records are available back to 1979. Records are purged every 6 months. New records are available online after 1 day.
PACER Online Access: ECF replaces PACER. Document images available. **Electronic Filing:** CM/ECF data at https://ecf.ctb.uscourts.gov. **Opinions:** Click on Opinions. View court opinions at www.ctb.uscourts.gov. **Other Online Access:** Search calendars at https://ecf.ctb.uscourts.gov/cgi-bin/PublicCalendar.pl. **Phone access:** Voice Case Information System, call 800-800-5113, 860-240-3345
Bridgeport Division counties: Fairfield.
Hartford Division counties: Hartford, Tolland, Windham.
New Haven Division counties: Litchfield, Middlesex, New Haven, New London.

Delaware

Capital: Dover
              Kent County
Time Zone: EST
Population: 830,364
# of Counties: 3

Quick Links

Website: http://delware.gov
Governor: www.state.de.us/governor/index.shtml
Attorney General: www.state.de.us/attgen
State Archives: www.state.de.us/sos/dpa
State Statutes and Codes: http://198.187.128.12/delaware/lpext.dll?f=templates&fn=tools-
     contents.htm&cp=Infobase&2.0
Legislative Bill Search: www.legis.state.de.us/Legislature.nsf?Open
Unclaimed Funds: www.state.de.us/revenue/information/alphaescheat.shtml

State Level ... Major Agencies

Statewide Court Records

Administrative Office of the Courts, Supreme Court of Delaware, 500 N King St, #11600, Wilmington, DE 19801; 302-255-0090, Fax-302-255-2217, 8:30AM-5PM.
http://courts.delaware.gov
Online search: Supreme Court Final Orders and Opinions (also lower state court opinions) are available at the webpage. There is no statewide access to trial court data.

Sexual Offender Registry

Delaware State Police, Sex Offender Central Registry, PO Box 430, Dover, DE 19903-0430 (Courier: 1407 N Dupont Highway, Dover, DE 19901); 302-739-5882, Fax-302-739-5888, 8AM-4PM.
www.state.de.us/dsp/sexoff/
Online search: Statewide registry can be searched at the website. The site gives the ability to search by Last Name, Development, and city or Zip Code. Any combination of these fields may be used; however, a search cannot be performed if both a city and Zip Code are entered.

Corporation, General Partnerships, Limited Partnership, Trademarks-Servicemarks, Limited Liability Company, Limited Liability Partnerships

Secretary of State, Corporation Records, PO Box 898, Dover, DE 19903 (Courier: 401 Federal Street #4, Dover, DE 19901); 302-739-3073, Fax-302-739-3812, 8AM-4:30PM.
www.state.de.us/corp
Online search: Information is available at https://sos-res.state.de.us/tin/GINameSearch.jsp. The entity information provided on this website, free of charge, consists of the entity name, file number, incorporation/formation date, registered agent name, address, phone number and residency. Additional, detailed information can be obtained for a fee of $20.00.

Birth Certificates, Death Records, Marriage Certificates

Department of Health, Office of Vital Statistics, PO Box 637, Dover, DE 19903 (Courier: William Penn & Federal Sts, Jesse Cooper Bldg, Dover, DE 19901); 302-744-4549, 877-888-0248 (Order), 8AM-4:30PM (Counter closes at 4:15 PM).
www.dhss.delaware.gov/dhss/dph/ss/vitalstats.html
Online search: Access available at vitalchek.com, a state designated vendor.

Driver Records

Division of Motor Vehicles, Driver's License Unit, PO Box 698, Dover, DE 19903 (Courier: 303 Transportation Circle, Dover, DE 19901); 302-744-2506, Fax-302-739-2602, 8AM-4:30PM (12-8PM W).
www.dmv.de.gov
Online search: Online searching is single inquiry only, no batch request mode is offered. Searching is done by driver's license number or name and DOB. A signed contract application and valid "business license" is required. Access is provided 24 hours daily through a 900 number at a fee of $1.50 per minute, plus the $15.00 per screen/record fee. For more information, call 302-744-2606.
Other options: Tape-to-tape and cartridge is offered for high volume, batch requesters.

Vehicle Ownership, Vehicle Identification

Division of Motor Vehicles, Correspondence Section, PO Box 698, Dover, DE 19903 (Courier: 303 Transportation Circle, Dover, DE 19901); 302-744-2511, 302-744-2538, Fax-302-739-2042, 8AM-4:30PM M-T-TH-F; 12-8PM W.
www.dmv.de.gov/services/vehicle_svcs.shtml
Online search: There is an additional $1.50 per minute fee for using the online "900 number" system. Records are $5.00 each. The system is single inquiry mode and open 24/7. Call 302-744-2606. This program is strictly monitored and not available for non-permissible uses. **Other options:** Bulk information can be obtained on a customized basis in tape, cartridge or paper format. However, the purpose of the request is carefully screened and information cannot be resold.

State Level ... Occupational Licensing

New Attorney	http://courts.delaware.gov/bbe/passnames2005.htm
Counselor, Elem./Second'y School	https://deeds.doe.k12.de.us/public/deeds_pc_findeducator.aspx
Engineer	www.dape.org/App/peRoster.asp
Engineering Firm	www.dape.org/App/peRoster.asp
Insurance Broker/Dealer	www.state.de.us/inscom/berg/authorizedcompanies.htm
Library/Media Specialist	https://deeds.doe.k12.de.us/public/deeds_pc_findeducator.aspx
Optometrist	www.arbo.org/index.php?action=findanoptometrist
Real Estate Appraiser	www.asc.gov/content/category1/appr_by_state.asp
School Admin. Supervisor/Asst.	https://deeds.doe.k12.de.us/public/deeds_pc_findeducator.aspx
School Counselor/Principal/Superintendent	https://deeds.doe.k12.de.us/public/deeds_pc_findeducator.aspx
Teacher	https://deeds.doe.k12.de.us/public/deeds_pc_findeducator.aspx

County Level ... Courts

Court Administration: Administrative Office of the Courts, Supreme Court of Delaware, 500 N King St, #11600, Wilmington, DE, 19801; 302-255-0090; http://courts.delware.gov

Court Structure: The Superior Court – the state's court of general jurisdiction – has original jurisdiction over criminal and civil cases except equity cases. Superior Court has exclusive jurisdiction over felonies and almost all drug offenses. The Court of Common Pleas has jurisdiction in civil cases where the amount in controversy, exclusive of interest, does not exceed $50,000. In criminal cases, the Court of Common Pleas handles all misdemeanors occurring in the state except certain drug-related offenses and traffic offenses. The Court of Chancery has jurisdiction to hear all matters relating to equity – litigation in this tribunal deals largely with corporate issues, trusts, estates, other fiduciary matters, disputes involving the purchase of land, and questions of title to real estate as well as commercial and contractual matters. The Justice of the Peace Court has jurisdiction over civil cases in which the disputed amount is less than $15,000. In criminal cases, the Justice of the Peace Court hears certain misdemeanors and most motor vehicle cases (excluding felonies) and the Justices of the Peace may act as committing magistrates for all crimes.

Online Access Note: Chancery, Superior, Common Pleas, and Supreme Courts opinions
and orders are available free online at http://courts.state.de.us/opinions. Supreme, Superior, and Common
Pleas Courts calendars are available free at http://courts.state.de.us/calendars. Chancery Courts and Supreme
Courts filings are available at www.virtualdocket.com. Registration and fees required. There are no known
courts that independently offer online access to their records.

County Level ... Recorders & Assessors

Recording Office Organization: Delaware has 3 counties and 3 recording offices. The recording
officer is the County Recorder in both jurisdictions. Delaware is in the Eastern Time Zone (EST). Federal tax
liens on personal property of businesses are filed with the Secretary of State. Other federal and all state tax
liens on personal property are filed with the County Recorder. Copy and certification fees vary.

Online Access Note: There is no statewide access to recorder or assessor information.

Kent County   *Most Wanted Records*
www.co.kent.de.us
City of Dover most wanted list is at www.doverpolice.org/wanted.htm.

New Castle County
Real Estate, Property Assessor, Recorder, Deed, Marriage, Incs, Sex Offender, Most Wanted Records
www.ncc-deeds.com/recclkshr/default.asp
Records on the City of New Castle Geographic Information System database are free at www.2isystems.com/newcastle/Search2.CFM.
Property information can also be found at www.co.new-castle.de.us/ParcelView/parcelsearch.asp. No name searching. Also, access to
the Recorder of Deeds database is free at www.ncc-deeds.com/recclkshr/. Also, the sheriff's Most Wanted, sex offender and missing
persons lists are at www.co.new-castle.de.us/publicsafety/home/webpage1.asp, Also, City of New Castle provides an acreage search
for free at www.2isystems.com/newcastle/Search2.CFM.

Sussex County   *Real Estate, Property Tax Records*
www.sussexcounty.net/departments/index.cfm?id=19
Access to the tax information website is free at www.sussexcounty.net/e-gov/propertytaxes/index.cfm. Also, search the GIS-mapping
page for free at www.smartmap.com/sussex/. At the map page, click on "search by" and choose "tax parcel (Name)".

Federal Courts in Delaware...

Standards for Federal Courts: The universal PACER sign-up number is 800-676-6856. Find PACER and the Party/Case Index on
the Web at http://pacer.psc.uscourts.gov. PACER dial-up access is $.60 per minute. Also, courts offering internet access via PACER,
Web-PACER or the new CM-ECF charge $.08 per page fee ($.07 per page if record is pre-2005 or unless noted as free).

US District Court -- District of Delaware
www.ded.uscourts.gov
PACER: Case records are available back to 1/1991. Records are purged every few years. New records are available online after 1 day.
PACER Online Access: ECF replaces PACER. **Electronic Filing:** CM/ECF data at https://ecf.ded.uscourts.gov. **Opinions:** Opinions
are for last 30 days only. View court opinions at www.ded.uscourts.gov/CLKmain.htm. **Other Online Access:** Search recent Standing
Orders at www.ded.uscourts.gov/StandingOrdersMain.htm .
Wilmington Division counties: All counties in Delaware.

US Bankruptcy Court -- District of Delaware
www.deb.uscourts.gov
PACER: Case records are available back to 1991. Records are purged every 4 years. New records are available online after 1 day.
PACER Online Access: ECF replaces PACER. **Electronic Filing:** CM/ECF data at https://ecf.deb.uscourts.gov. **Opinions:** View
court opinions at www.deb.uscourts.gov/Opinions/opinions_cover.htm. **Other Online Access:** Online access to WebPacer is available
is available at www.deb.uscourts.gov and click on "Case Information." Chapter 11 filing monthly lists are free at
www.deb.uscourts.gov/Chapter11/chapter11_filings.htm. **Phone access:** Voice Case Information System, call 302-252-2560.
Wilmington Division counties: All counties in Delaware.

District of Columbia

Time Zone: EST
Population: 553,523
# of Divisions/Counties: 1

Quick Links

Website: www.dc.gov

Governor: http://dc.gov/mayor/index.shtm

State Statutes and Codes:
> http://government.westlaw.com/linkedslice/default.asp?SP=DCC-1000

Legislative Bill Search: www.dccouncil.us/lims/default.asp

Unclaimed Funds:
> http://cfo.washingtondc.gov/cfo/cwp/view,a,1326,q,590719,.asp

State Level ... Major Agencies

Sexual Offender Registry

Metropolitan Police Department, Sex Offender Registry Unit, 300 Indiana Ave NW, Rm 3009, Washington, DC 20001; 202-727-4407, Fax-202-727-9292, 8AM-5PM.
http://mpdc.dc.gov/mpdc/site/default.asp
Online search: Class A & B registered sex offenders is provided at the web. Under "Services" click on Sex Offender Registry.

Uniform Commercial Code, Federal Tax Liens, State Tax Liens

UCC Recorder, District of Columbia Recorder of Deeds, 941 North Capitol Street, NE, Washington, DC 20002;, 202-727-5374, 8:30AM-4:30PM.
http://cfo.dc.gov/otr/site/default.asp
Online search: Search the index by name or document number at www.washington.dc.us.landata.com/. Registration is required. There are two commercial plans to purchase images. Note this for all recorded documents, not just UCC. A Subscriber pays $175 per month for unlimited views of images and $2.00 per document image downloaded. Accounts are also available for larger firms with multiple users. A registered "non-subscriber" pays no fee to view documents and $4.00 per document mage downloaded.

Birth Certificates, Death Records

Department of Health, Vital Records Division, 825 North Capitol St NE, 1st Fl, Washington, DC 20002; 202-442-9009, 877-572-6332 (Order), Fax-202-442-4848, 8:30AM-3:30PM.
http://dchealth.dc.gov/services/vital_records/index.shtm
Online search: Orders may be placed online via a state designated vendor at www.vitalchek.com.

Driver Records

Department of Motor Vehicles, Driver Records Division, 65 K Street NE, Rm 200A, Washington, DC 20002; 202-727-1530, 202-727-5000 (General), 8:15AM-4PM.
www.dmv.dc.gov/main.shtm
Online search: Online requests are taken throughout the day and are available in batch the next morning after 8:15 am. There is no minimum order requirement. Fee is $7.00 per record. Billing is a "bank" system which draws from pre-paid account. Requesters are restricted to high volume, ongoing users. Each requester must be approved and sign a contract. For details, call 202-727-5692.

Voter Registration

DC Board of Elections and Ethics, Voter Registration Records, 441 4th St NW, #250 North, Washington, DC 20001; 202-727-2525, Fax-202-347-2648, 8:30AM-4:45PM.
www.dcboee.org
Online search: One may check voter registration status at www.dcboee.org/voterreg/vic_step1.asp. Name, DOB and ZIP are required.
Other options: Records can be purchased on CD, tape, and printed lists. A variety of data is available from party registration to voter history. Minimum fee is $50 plus $10 for a CD. Call at 202-727-2525 for details.

State Level ... Occupational Licensing

Acupuncturist	http://dchealth.dc.gov/prof_license/services/search_licensing.asp
Addiction Counselor	http://dchealth.dc.gov/prof_license/services/search_licensing.asp
Alcohol Mfg./Vendor/Dist.	http://abra.dc.gov/abra/site/default.asp
Alcohol Servers/Sellers	http://abra.dc.gov/abra/site/default.asp
Alcohol Susp'd/Revoked License	http://abra.dc.gov/abra/site/default.asp
Appraiser, Real Estate	www.asc.gov/content/category1/appr_by_state.asp
Attorney	www.dcbar.org/find_a_member/index.cfm
Bank	http://dbfi.dc.gov/dbfi/cwp/view,a,3,q,585840,dbfiNav,|31299|.asp
Check Casher	http://app.dbfi.dc.gov/ifs/default.asp
Chiropractor	http://dchealth.dc.gov/prof_license/services/search_licensing.asp
Counselor, Professional	http://dchealth.dc.gov/prof_license/services/search_licensing.asp
Dance Therapist	http://dchealth.dc.gov/prof_license/services/search_licensing.asp
Dentist/ ental Hygienist	http://dchealth.dc.gov/prof_license/services/search_licensing.asp
Dietitian/Nutritionist	http://dchealth.dc.gov/prof_license/services/search_licensing.asp
Educational Institution, Higher http://dcra.dc.gov/dcra/cwp/view,a,1342,q,600631,dcraNav_GID,1697,dcraNav,|33466|.asp	
Insurance Broker/Agent	https://sbs-dc-public.naic.org/Lion-Web/jsp/sbsreports/AgentLookup.jsp
Insurance Company	http://disb.dc.gov/disr/cwp/view,a,1300,q,581346,disrnav_gid,1644.asp
Investment Advisor	http://pdpi.nasdr.com/pdpi/
Investment Advisor Rep.	http://pdpi.nasdr.com/pdpi/
Lobbyist	http://ocf.dc.gov/rep/repocf4.shtm
Massage Therapist	http://dchealth.dc.gov/prof_license/services/search_licensing.asp
Medical Doctor	http://dchealth.dc.gov/prof_license/services/search_licensing.asp
Midwife Nurse	http://dchealth.dc.gov/prof_license/services/search_licensing.asp
Money Lender	http://app.dbfi.dc.gov/ifs/default.asp
Money Transmitter	http://app.dbfi.dc.gov/ifs/default.asp
Mortgage Broker/Lender	http://app.dbfi.dc.gov/ifs/default.asp
Naturopath	http://dchealth.dc.gov/prof_license/services/search_licensing.asp
Nurse Anesthetist	http://dchealth.dc.gov/prof_license/services/search_licensing.asp
Nurse-LPN, RN, or Clinical	http://dchealth.dc.gov/prof_license/services/search_licensing.asp
Nursing Home Administrator	http://dchealth.dc.gov/prof_license/services/search_licensing.asp
Occupational Therapist	http://dchealth.dc.gov/prof_license/services/search_licensing.asp
Optometrist	www.arbo.org/index.php?action=findanoptometrist
Osteopath	http://dchealth.dc.gov/prof_license/services/search_licensing.asp
Pharmacist/Pharmacy	http://dchealth.dc.gov/prof_license/services/search_licensing.asp
Physical Therapist	http://dchealth.dc.gov/prof_license/services/search_licensing.asp
Physician Assistant	http://dchealth.dc.gov/prof_license/services/search_licensing.asp
Podiatrist	http://dchealth.dc.gov/prof_license/services/search_licensing.asp
Political Campaign Contributor	http://ocf.dc.gov/dsearch/dsearch.asp
Psychologist	http://dchealth.dc.gov/prof_license/services/search_licensing.asp
Real Estate Appraiser	www.asc.gov/content/category1/appr_by_state.asp
Real Estate School ... ... http://dcra.dc.gov/dcra/cwp/view,a,1342,q,600757,dcraNav_GID,1697,dcraNav,|33466|.asp	
Recreational Therapist	http://dchealth.dc.gov/prof_license/services/search_licensing.asp
Respiratory Care	http://dchealth.dc.gov/prof_license/services/search_licensing.asp
Sales Finance Company	http://app.dbfi.dc.gov/ifs/default.asp

Securities Agent/ Broker/Dealer .... http://pdpi.nasdr.com/pdpi/
Social Worker .... http://dchealth.dc.gov/prof_license/services/search_licensing.asp
Taxi Dispatch/ Fleet/Company .... www.dctaxi.dc.gov/dctaxi/cwp/view.asp?a=1187&q=487917
Taxi Insurer.. www.dctaxi.dc.gov/dctaxi/cwp/view.asp?a=1187&q=487938

County Level ... Courts

Court Administration:
Executive Office, 500 Indiana Av NW, Room 1500, Washington, DC, 20001; 202-879-1700; www.dcsc.gov

Court Structure:
The Superior Court in DC is divided into 17 divisions, 4 of which are shown in this book: Criminal, Civil, Family, and Tax-Probate. The Tax-Probate Division of the Superior Court handles probate. Eviction is part of the court's Landlord and Tenant Branch.

District of Columbia Jurisdiction

Superior Court - Civil Division – Civil Records
www.dcbar.org/dcsc
Attorneys and legal professionals participating in the e-Filing Project must register for the CourtLink eFile service either by logging onto www.courtlink.com or calling 1-888-529-7587. Superior Court and Court of Appeals offer access to opinions at www.dcbar.org.

County Level ... Recorders & Assessors

Recording Office Organization:
District of Columbia is in the Eastern Time Zone (EST). Federal tax liens on personal property of businesses are filed with the Secretary of State. Other federal and all state tax liens on personal property are filed with the Recorder.

District of Columbia

Real Estate, Assessor, Recording, Deed, Judgment, Lien, UCC Records
www.dc.gov
Search the recorders database at www.washington.dc.us.landata.com. Registration is required; search index for free; $4.00 fee to view and copy. Subscribe for $175.00 per month or per use, and get docs for $2.00 per page. Records go back to 1973. Search the DC legislation record at www.dccouncil.washington.dc.us/lims/SearchForm.asp.

Federal Courts in District of Columbia...

Standards for Federal Courts: The universal PACER sign-up number is 800-676-6856. Find PACER and the Party/Case Index on the Web at http://pacer.psc.uscourts.gov. PACER dial-up access is $.60 per minute. Also, courts offering internet access via PACER, Web-PACER or the new CM-ECF charge $.08 per page fee ($.07 per page if record is pre-2005 or unless noted as free).

US District Court -- District of Columbia

www.dcd.uscourts.gov
PACER: PACER Online Access: ECF replaces PACER. **Electronic Filing:** CM/ECF data at https://ecf.dcd.uscourts.gov. **Opinions:** View court opinions at www.dcd.uscourts.gov/court-opinions.html. **Other Online Access:** Weekly court schedules at www.dcd.uscourts.gov/court-schedules.html.

US Bankruptcy Court -- District of Columbia

www.dcb.uscourts.gov
PACER: Case records are available back to 1991. Records are purged every 6 months. **PACER Online Access:** ECF replaces PACER. **Electronic Filing:** CM/ECF data at https://ecf.dcb.uscourts.gov. **Opinions:** View court opinions at www.dcb.uscourts.gov/decisions.htm. **Phone access:** Voice Case Information System, call 202-208-1365.

Florida

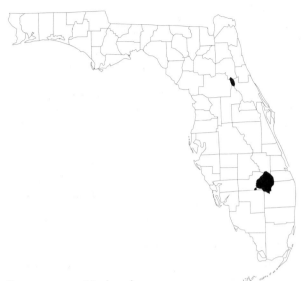

Capital: Tallahassee
            Leon County

Time Zone: EST

Florida's ten western-most counties are CST:
They are: Bay, Calhoun, Escambia, Gulf, Holmes,
Jackson, Okaloosa, Santa Rosa, Walton, Washington.

Population: 17,397,161

# of Counties: 67

Quick Links

Website: www.myflorida.gov

Governor: www.myflorida.com/b_eog/owa/b_eog_www.html.main_page

Attorney General: http://myfloridalegal.com

State Archives: http://dlis.dos.state.fl.us/index.cfm

State Statutes and Codes: www.flsenate.gov/Statutes/index.cfm?submenu=-1&Tab=statutes

Legislative Bill Search: www.flsenate.gov/Welcome/index.cfm

Unclaimed Funds: www.fltreasurehunt.org/ControlServlet?ActionForm=GotoNewPublicSearch

State Level ... Major Agencies

Criminal Records

Florida Department of Law Enforcement, User Services Bureau, PO Box 1489, Tallahassee, FL 32302 (Courier: 2331 Phillip Rd, Tallahassee, FL 32308); 850-410-8109, 850-410-8107, Fax-850-410-8201, 8AM-5PM.
www.fdle.state.fl.us
Online search: Criminal history information from 1967 forward may be ordered over the Department Program Internet site at https://www2.fdle.state.fl.us/cchinet/. The $23.00 fee applies. Juvenile records from 10/1994 forward are also available. Credit card ordering will return records to your screen or via email. Search state's most wanted list at www3.fdle.state.fl.us/fdle/wpersons_search.asp.

Statewide Court Records

State Courts Administrator, 500 S Duval, Supreme Court Bldg, Tallahassee, FL 32399-1900; 850-922-5081, Fax-850-488-0156, 8AM-5PM.
www.flcourts.org
Online search: Many Clerk of Courts/Recorders give access to index data at www.myflorida.com, a government sponsored web site. Supreme Court dockets are available online at http://jweb.flcourts.org/pls/docket/ds_docket_search.

Sexual Offender Registry

Florida Department of Law Enforcement, Sexual Offender/Predator Unit, PO Box 1489, Tallahassee, FL 32302 (Courier: 2331 Phillips Rd, Tallahassee, FL 32308); 888-357-7332, 850-410-8572, Fax-850-410-8599, 8AM-6:30PM.
www3.fdle.state.fl.us/sopu/index.asp?PSessionId=824514917&
Online search: Search the registry from the web page. Searching can be done by name or by geographic area.

Incarceration Records

Florida Department of Corrections, Central Records Office, 2601 Blair Stone Rd, Tallahassee, FL 32399-2500; 850-488-2533, 850-488-1503 (Records), 850-922-0000 (Parole Commission), Fax-850-413-8302, 8AM-5PM.
www.dc.state.fl.us
Online search: Extensive search capabilities are offered from the website. Click on Inmate Population Information Search. Also, a private company offers free web access at www.vinelink.com/index.jsp. Includes state, DOC, and 44 county jail systems. **Other options:** The monthly-updated inmate database is available for $83.00.

Corporation, Limited Partnership, Limited Liability Company, Trademarks/Servicemarks, Fictitious Names, Federal Tax Liens

Division of Corporations, Department of State, PO Box 6327, Tallahassee, FL 32314 (Courier: 409 E Gaines St, Tallahassee, FL 32399); 800-755-5111 (Telephone Inquiries), 850-245-6053 (Copy Requests), 850-245-6056 (Annual Reports), 8AM-5PM.
www.sunbiz.org
Online search: The state's excellent Internet site gives detailed information on all corporate, trademark, limited liability company and limited partnerships; fictitious names; and lien records. Images of filed documents are available from 1996/7 to present. **Other options:** This agency offers record purchases on microfiche sets and on CD disks.

Uniform Commercial Code

UCC Filings, FLORIDAUCC, Inc, 2670 Executive Center Circle West, #100, Tallahassee, FL 32301; 850-222-8526, 8AM-5PM.
www.floridaucc.com
Online search: The Internet site allows access for no charge. Search by name or document number, for records 1997 to present. Images of documents are available from 1997 to present at this site. Tax Liens are not included with UCC filing information. **Other options:** Microfilm reels and CD's of images are available for bulk purchase requesters. Call for more information.

Workers' Compensation Records

Workers Compensation Div, Data Quality & Collector, 200 E Gaines St, Tallahassee, FL 32399; 850-413-1712, Fax-850-414-7341.
www.fldfs.com/wc/
Online search: A myriad of information is available at www.fldfs.com/wc/databases.html.

Driver Records

Division of Drivers Licenses, Bureau of Records, PO Box 5775, Tallahassee, FL 32314-5775 (Courier: 2900 Apalachee Pky, MS90, Neil Kirkman Bldg, Tallahassee, FL 32399); 850-488-0250, 850-922-9000, 8AM-5PM.
www.hsmv.state.fl.us
Online search: Online requests an sold on an interactive basis. The state differentiates between high and low volume users. Requesters with 5,000 or more records per month are considered Network Providers. Call 850-488-6264 to become a Provider. Requesters with less than 5,000 requests per month (called Individual Users) are directed to a Provider. A list of providers is found at the website. Check the status of any Florida Driver License free at https://www6.hsmv.state.fl.us/dlcheck/dlchecking. Simply enter the driver license number. **Other options:** This agency will process magnetic tape requests on a batch basis, for approved users. Call 850-487-4467 for more details.

Vehicle Ownership, Vehicle Identification

Division of Motor Vehicles, Information Research Unit, Neil Kirkman Bldg, A-126, Tallahassee, FL 32399; 850-922-9000, Fax-850-488-8983, 8AM-4:30PM.
www.hsmv.state.fl.us
Online search: Florida has contracted to release vehicle information through approved Network Providers. Accounts must first be approved by the state. For each record accessed, the charge is $.50 plus a transactional fee, and the subscriber fee. Users must work from an estimated 2 1/2 month pre-paid bank. New subscribers must complete an application with the Department 850-488-6710. Also, enter the title # or VIN to check vehicle status at https://www6.hsmv.state.fl.us/rrdmvcheck/mvchecking.

State Level ... Occupational Licensing

Acupuncturist.. http://ww2.doh.state.fl.us/irm00praes/praslist.asp
Air Ambulance.. www.doh.state.fl.us/demo/ems/Providers/Providers.html
Air Conditioning Contractor .... https://www.myfloridalicense.com/licensing/wl11.jsp?SID=
Alcoholic Beverage Permit .... https://www.myfloridalicense.com/licensing/wl11.jsp?SID=
Ambulance Service .... www.doh.state.fl.us/demo/ems/Providers/Providers.html

Architectural Business/Individual .... https://www.myfloridalicense.com/licensing/wl11.jsp?SID=
Asbestos Remover/Contractor/Consultant .. https://www.myfloridalicense.com/licensing/wl11.jsp?SID=
Assisted Living Facility .... www.fdhc.state.fl.us/licensing_cert.shtml
Athletic Agent.. https://www.myfloridalicense.com/licensing/wl11.jsp?SID=
Athletic Trainer.. http://ww2.doh.state.fl.us/irm00praes/praslist.asp
Attorney .... www.floridabar.org/names.nsf/MESearch?OpenForm
Auctioneer/Auction Company .... https://www.myfloridalicense.com/licensing/wl11.jsp?SID=
Audiologist http://ww2.doh.state.fl.us/irm00praes/praslist.asp
Automobile Repossessor............................ http://licgweb.doacs.state.fl.us/access/individual.html
Barber/Barber Assistant/Barber Shop .... https://www.myfloridalicense.com/licensing/wl11.jsp?SID=
Boxer .... https://www.myfloridalicense.com/licensing/wl11.jsp?SID=
Building Code Administrator...................... https://www.myfloridalicense.com/licensing/wl11.jsp?SID=
Building Contractor/Inspector.................... https://www.myfloridalicense.com/licensing/wl11.jsp?SID=
Cemetery.. https://apps.fldfs.com/fclicense/searchpage.aspx
Cemetery Lot Salesperson .... https://apps.fldfs.com/fclicense/searchpage.aspx
Chiropractic-related Occupation http://ww2.doh.state.fl.us/irm00praes/praslist.asp
Clinical Lab Personnel.............................. http://ww2.doh.state.fl.us/irm00praes/praslist.asp
Community Association Manager............... https://www.myfloridalicense.com/licensing/wl11.jsp?SID=
Company in Receivership .... www.fldfs.com/Receiver/receivership_list.asp
Construction Business................................ https://www.myfloridalicense.com/licensing/wl11.jsp?SID=
Continuing Edu. Provider, Medical http://ww2.doh.state.fl.us/irm00praes/praslist.asp
Contractor, General................................... https://www.myfloridalicense.com/licensing/wl11.jsp?SID=
Cosmetologist, Nails/Salon....................... https://www.myfloridalicense.com/licensing/wl11.jsp?SID=
Crematory .... https://apps.fldfs.com/fclicense/searchpage.aspx
Dentist/Dental Assistant............................ http://ww2.doh.state.fl.us/irm00praes/praslist.asp
Dietician/Nutritionist http://ww2.doh.state.fl.us/irm00praes/praslist.asp
Doctor, Limited.. http://ww2.doh.state.fl.us/irm00praes/praslist.asp
Electrical Contractor .... https://www.myfloridalicense.com/licensing/wl11.jsp?SID=
Electrologist/Electrologist Facility.............. http://ww2.doh.state.fl.us/irm00praes/praslist.asp
Elevator Certificates of Operation .... https://www.myfloridalicense.com/licensing/wl11.jsp?SID=
Embalmer... https://apps.fldfs.com/fclicense/searchpage.aspx
Emergency Medical Technician.................. www.doh.state.fl.us/demo/ems/Providers/Providers.html
Employee Leasing Company .... https://www.myfloridalicense.com/licensing/wl11.jsp?SID=
Engineer... www.fbpe.org/pelist/
Engineering Firm .... www.fbpe.org/pelist/
Finance Company, Consumer..................... www.flofr.com/licensing/licensecheck.htm
Firearms Instructor.................................... http://licgweb.doacs.state.fl.us/access/individual.html
Firearms License, Statewide .... http://licgweb.doacs.state.fl.us/access/individual.html
Food Services Establishment .... https://www.myfloridalicense.com/licensing/wl11.jsp?SID=
Funeral Director.. https://apps.fldfs.com/fclicense/searchpage.aspx
Funeral Home .... https://apps.fldfs.com/fclicense/searchpage.aspx
Geologist/Geology Firm .... https://www.myfloridalicense.com/licensing/wl11.jsp?SID=
Hair Braider .... https://www.myfloridalicense.com/licensing/wl11.jsp?SID=
Health Facility .... www.fdhc.state.fl.us/licensing_cert.shtml
Hearing Aid Specialist http://ww2.doh.state.fl.us/irm00praes/praslist.asp
Home Health Care Agency .... www.fdhc.state.fl.us/licensing_cert.shtml
Home Improvement Financer .... www.flofr.com/licensing/licensecheck.htm
Hospital... www.fdhc.state.fl.us/licensing_cert.shtml
Hotel/Restaurant .... https://www.myfloridalicense.com/licensing/wl11.jsp?SID=
Insect Sting Treatment Specialist................ www.doh.state.fl.us/demo/ems/Providers/Providers.html
Installment Seller, Retail........................... www.flofr.com/licensing/licensecheck.htm
Insurance Adjuster/Agent/Title Agent .... www.fldfs.com/data/aar_alis1/
Insurance-related Company .... www.fldfs.com/Data/CompanySearch/index.asp
Interior Design Business/Individual............ https://www.myfloridalicense.com/licensing/wl11.jsp?SID=
Investment Advisor.................................... www.flofr.com/licensing/licensecheck.htm
Kickboxer .... https://www.myfloridalicense.com/licensing/wl11.jsp?SID=

Lab License .... www.fdhc.state.fl.us/licensing_cert.shtml
Landscape Architecture Busin's/Licensee .. https://www.myfloridalicense.com/licensing/wl11.jsp?SID=
Liquor Store .... https://www.myfloridalicense.com/licensing/wl11.jsp?SID=
Lobbyist/Principal
    www.flsenate.gov/lobbyist/index.cfm?requesttimeout=500&mode=list&submenu=2&tab=lobbyist
Lodging Establishment .... https://www.myfloridalicense.com/licensing/wl11.jsp?SID=
Marriage & Family Therapist http://ww2.doh.state.fl.us/irm00praes/praslist.asp
Massage Therapist/School/Facility http://ww2.doh.state.fl.us/irm00praes/praslist.asp
Mechanical Contractor .... https://www.myfloridalicense.com/licensing/wl11.jsp?SID=
Medical Doctor http://ww2.doh.state.fl.us/irm00praes/praslist.asp
Medical Faculty Member http://ww2.doh.state.fl.us/irm00praes/praslist.asp
Mental Health Counselor http://ww2.doh.state.fl.us/irm00praes/praslist.asp
Midwife http://ww2.doh.state.fl.us/irm00praes/praslist.asp
Money Transmitter .... www.flofr.com/licensing/licensecheck.htm
Monument Dealer .... https://apps.fldfs.com/fclicense/searchpage.aspx
Mortgage Broker/Broker Firm .... www.flofr.com/licensing/licensecheck.htm
Mortgage Business School .... www.flofr.com/licensing/licensecheck.htm
Motel/Restaurant .... https://www.myfloridalicense.com/licensing/wl11.jsp?SID=
Nail Specialist .... https://www.myfloridalicense.com/licensing/wl11.jsp?SID=
Naturopath http://ww2.doh.state.fl.us/irm00praes/praslist.asp
Naturopathic Physician http://ww2.doh.state.fl.us/irm00praes/praslist.asp
Notary Public http://notaries.dos.state.fl.us/not001.html
Nuclear Radiology Physicist http://ww2.doh.state.fl.us/irm00praes/praslist.asp
Nurse/Nurse, Practical http://ww2.doh.state.fl.us/irm00praes/praslist.asp
Nursing Assistant http://ww2.doh.state.fl.us/irm00praes/praslist.asp
Nursing Home Administrator http://ww2.doh.state.fl.us/irm00praes/praslist.asp
Nutrition Counselor http://ww2.doh.state.fl.us/irm00praes/praslist.asp
Occupational Therapist http://ww2.doh.state.fl.us/irm00praes/praslist.asp
Optician/Optician Apprentice http://ww2.doh.state.fl.us/irm00praes/praslist.asp
Optometrist http://ww2.doh.state.fl.us/irm00praes/praslist.asp
Orthotist/Prosthetist http://ww2.doh.state.fl.us/irm00praes/praslist.asp
Osteopathic Physician http://ww2.doh.state.fl.us/irm00praes/praslist.asp
Paramedic .... www.doh.state.fl.us/demo/ems/Providers/Providers.html
Pari-Mutuel Wagering .... https://www.myfloridalicense.com/licensing/wl11.jsp?SID=
Pedorthist http://ww2.doh.state.fl.us/irm00praes/praslist.asp
Pest Control Operator .... www.safepesticideuse.com/search/PersonSearch.asp
Pesticide Applicator .... http://licgweb.doacs.state.fl.us/index.html
Pesticide Applicator .... www.safepesticideuse.com/search/PersonSearch.asp
Pesticide Dealer .... http://licgweb.doacs.state.fl.us/index.html
Pharmacist, Consulting http://ww2.doh.state.fl.us/irm00praes/praslist.asp
Pharmacist/Pharmacist Intern http://ww2.doh.state.fl.us/irm00praes/praslist.asp
Physical Therapist/Assistant http://ww2.doh.state.fl.us/irm00praes/praslist.asp
Physician Assistant http://ww2.doh.state.fl.us/irm00praes/praslist.asp
Physicist, Medical http://ww2.doh.state.fl.us/irm00praes/praslist.asp
Pilot, State/Deputy .... https://www.myfloridalicense.com/licensing/wl11.jsp?SID=
Plumbing Contractor .... https://www.myfloridalicense.com/licensing/wl11.jsp?SID=
Polygraph Examiner/Assn Member .... www.floridapolygraph.org/directory/
Preneed Seller, Funeral .... https://apps.fldfs.com/fclicense/searchpage.aspx
Private Investigator/Agency .... http://licgweb.doacs.state.fl.us/access/individual.html
Psychologist/Limited License Psychologist http://ww2.doh.state.fl.us/irm00praes/praslist.asp
Public Accountant-CPA .... https://www.myfloridalicense.com/licensing/wl11.jsp?SID=
Racing, Dog/Horse .... https://www.myfloridalicense.com/licensing/wl11.jsp?SID=
Radiologic Physician, Diagnost'c/Therap'c http://ww2.doh.state.fl.us/irm00praes/praslist.asp
Radiologist http://ww2.doh.state.fl.us/irm00praes/praslist.asp
Real Estate Agent/Broker/Sales .... https://www.myfloridalicense.com/licensing/wl11.jsp?sid=
Real Estate Appraiser .... https://www.myfloridalicense.com/licensing/wl11.jsp?sid=

Recovery Agent School/Instrct./Mgr. .... http://licgweb.doacs.state.fl.us/access/agency.html
Recovery Agent/Agency/Intern .... http://licgweb.doacs.state.fl.us/access/agency.html
Respiratory Care Therapist/Provider........... http://ww2.doh.state.fl.us/irm00praes/praslist.asp
Roofing Contractor .... https://www.myfloridalicense.com/licensing/wl11.jsp?SID=
Sales Finance Company .... www.flofr.com/licensing/licensecheck.htm
School Psychologist................................... http://ww2.doh.state.fl.us/irm00praes/praslist.asp
Securities Broker Dealer/Branch Office ..... www.flofr.com/licensing/licensecheck.htm
Securities Agent/Seller/Associate Person ... www.flofr.com/licensing/licensecheck.htm
Securities Registration .... www.flofr.com/licensing/licensecheck.htm
Security Officer School.............................. http://licgweb.doacs.state.fl.us/access/agency.html
Security Officer/Instructor .... http://licgweb.doacs.state.fl.us/access/individual.html
Social Worker, Clinical/Master.................. http://ww2.doh.state.fl.us/irm00praes/praslist.asp
Solar Energy Contractor .... https://www.myfloridalicense.com/licensing/wl11.jsp?SID=
Speech-Language Pathologist/Audiologist . http://ww2.doh.state.fl.us/irm00praes/praslist.asp
Surveyor, Mapping .... https://www.myfloridalicense.com/licensing/wl11.jsp?SID=
Swimming Pool/Spa Contr. .... https://www.myfloridalicense.com/licensing/wl11.jsp?SID=
Talent Agency... https://www.myfloridalicense.com/licensing/wl11.jsp?SID=
Therapeutic Radiologic Physician.............. http://ww2.doh.state.fl.us/irm00praes/praslist.asp
Tobacco Wholesale.................................... https://www.myfloridalicense.com/licensing/wl11.jsp?SID=
Underground Utility Contractor................. https://www.myfloridalicense.com/licensing/wl11.jsp?SID=
Veterinarian/Veterinary Establishment .... https://www.myfloridalicense.com/licensing/wl11.jsp?SID=
Visiting Mental Health Faculty.................. http://ww2.doh.state.fl.us/irm00praes/praslist.asp
X-ray, Pod, Assistant http://ww2.doh.state.fl.us/irm00praes/praslist.asp
Yacht & Ship Broker/Salesman .... https://www.myfloridalicense.com/licensing/wl11.jsp?SID=

County Level ... Courts

Court Administration: Office of State Courts Administrator, Supreme Court Bldg, 500 S Duval, Tallahassee, FL, 32399-1900; 850-922-5081; www.flcourts.org

Structure: All counties have combined Circuit & County Courts. Circuit Court is the court of general jurisdiction.

Online Access Note: Many Clerks of the Circuit Courts give access to index data at www.myflorida.com, a government sponsored website. Supreme Court dockets are available online at http://jweb.flcourts.org/pls/docket/ds_docket_search. A large number of the courts do offer online access to the public, usually through the Clerk of the Circuit Court. The Florida Legislature mandated that court documents must be imaged and available for inspection over a publicly available website. In response to concerns of identity theft and fraud, the Florida Legislature then passed new laws concerning privacy of public documents on public websites. These laws now make it possible for certain of these documents viewed on the clerk websites to be either redacted of sensitive information or in some cases removed completely. The Clerk of the Circuit Court cannot place an image or copy of the following documents on a publicly available website for general public display – military discharges, death certificates, court files, records or papers relating to Family Law, Juvenile Law, or Probate Law cases.

Alachua County

Circuit & County Courts – Civil Records
www.clerk-alachua-fl.org/Clerk/index.cfm
Civil records can be searched www.clerk-alachua-fl.org/clerk/pubrec.html. Also, access an index of judgments and recorded documents at www.myfloridacounty.com. Fees involved to order copies; save $1.50 per record by becoming a subscriber. Also, search probate and other ancient records free at www.clerk-alachua-fl.org/archive/default.cfm.

Baker County

Circuit & County Courts - Civil – Civil Records
http://bakercountyfl.org/clerk

Access an index of judgments, liens, recorded documents at www.myfloridacounty.com. Fees involved to order copies; save $1.50 per record by becoming a subscriber.

Circuit & County Courts - Criminal – Criminal Records

http://bakercountyfl.org/clerk

Access the circuit-wide criminal quick lookup at http://circuit8.org/golem/gencrim.html. Account and password is required; restricted usage. Call the court for details.

Bay County

Circuit and County Court - Civil – Civil Records

www.baycoclerk.com

Access the clerk's case search database free at www.clerk.co.bay.fl.us/OncoreWeb/. Access an index of judgments, liens, recorded documents at www.myfloridacounty.com. Fees involved to order copies; save $1.50 per record by becoming a subscriber.

Circuit Court - Criminal – Criminal Records

www.baycoclerk.com

Search the clerk's case search database for free at www.clerk.co.bay.fl.us/OncoreWeb/.

Bradford County

Circuit Court – Civil and Criminal Records

http://circuit8.org

Access an index of judgments, liens, recorded documents at www.myfloridacounty.com. Fees involved to order copies; save $1.50 per record by becoming a subscriber. Access to the circuit-wide criminal quick lookup is at http://circuit8.org/golem/gencrim.html. Account and password is required; restricted usage.

Brevard County

Circuit Court – Civil and Criminal Records

www.brevardclerk.us

Access records index free at http://webinfo4.brevardclerk.us/facts/facts_splash.cfm. Online records back to 1988 can be searched by name, case number or citation number.

Broward County

Circuit & County Courts – Civil and Criminal Records

www.browardclerk.org

The county clerk online fee system is being replaced by a web system. Basic information is free at www.browardclerk.org/bccoc2/default.asp. Search by name or case number or case type. The county clerk online fee system is being replaced by a web system. The web allows basic information free at www.browardclerk.org/bccoc2/default.asp Search by name or case number or case type. The "Premium Access" for detailed case information requires a fee, registration and password. Call 954-831-5654 for information or visit the website.

Calhoun County

Circuit & County Court – Civil Records

www.calhounclerk.com

Access an index of judgments, liens, recorded documents at www.myfloridacounty.com. Fees involved to order copies; save $1.50 per record by becoming a subscriber.

Charlotte County

Circuit & County Courts - Civil Division – Civil Records

http://co.charlotte.fl.us/clrkinfo/clerk_default.htm

Access to civil and probate records is by subscription, see the website. Original payment is $186.00 ($150 refundable) plus a usage fee based on number of transactions. Allows printing of copies. For more information, call 941-637-4848. Access an index of judgments, liens, recorded documents at www.myfloridacounty.com. Fees involved to order copies; save $1.50 per record by becoming a subscriber.

Circuit & County Courts - Criminal Division – Criminal Records

http://co.charlotte.fl.us/clrkinfo/clerk_default.htm

Access is free at https://www.co.charlotte.fl.us/scripts/mgrqispi.dll?appname=MPI%20Criminal&prgname=PUBSEARCHF requires that you provide a name and birthdate. Also, full records back to 1990 available by subscription at http://co.charlotte.fl.us/clrkinfo/services/criminalInformation.htm; initial setup cost is $250.00, plus $50.00 monthly payment in advance.

Citrus County

Circuit & County Courts – Civil and Criminal Records
www.clerk.citrus.fl.us/home.jsp
Subscription service to view court record index at www.clerk.citrus.fl.us/home.jsp; fees are involved. Images are not on this system. Also there is an index of judgments, liens, recorded documents at www.myfloridacounty.com. Fees involved to order copies; save $1.50 per record by becoming a subscriber.

Clay County

Circuit & County Courts – Civil and Criminal Records
http://clerk.co.clay.fl.us
Clerk of the circuit court provides free access to records at http://clerk.co.clay.fl.us/asp/pub_pi_queryname.asp. Access an index of judgments, liens, recorded documents at www.myfloridacounty.com. Fees involved to order copies; save $1.50 per record by becoming a subscriber. Access to criminal records is free at http://clerk.co.clay.fl.us/asp/cr_pi_queryname.asp.

Collier County

Circuit Court – Civil and Criminal Records
www.clerk.collier.fl.us
Access is free at www.clerk.collier.fl.us/clerkspublicac/Default.htm. Records include probate, traffic and domestic. Access an index of judgments, liens, recorded documents at www.myfloridacounty.com. Fees involved to order copies; save $1.50 per record by becoming a subscriber. Criminal records access is free at www.clerk.collier.fl.us/clerkspublicac/Default.htm.

County Court – Civil and Criminal Records
www.clerk.collier.fl.us
Access is free at www.clerk.collier.fl.us/clerkspublicac/Default.htm. Records include probate, traffic and domestic. Criminal records access is free at www.clerk.collier.fl.us/clerkspublicac/Default.htm.

Columbia County

Circuit & County Courts – Civil Records
http://www2.myfloridacounty.com/wps/wcm/connect/columbiaclerk
Access an index of judgments, liens, recorded documents at www.myfloridacounty.com. Fees involved to order copies; save $1.50 per record by becoming a subscriber.

Dade County

Circuit & County Courts - Civil – Civil Records
www.miami-dadeclerk.com/dadecoc/
Access a wealth of information through the Clerk of Court's online services website. Choose between Standard (free of charge) and Premier (fee-based) online services. By subscribing to the Premier service, you may access 3 advanced options: Civil/Family/Probate, Public Records, and Traffic. Fees are based on number of units purchased; minimum $5.00, paid in advance. Also, though limited, you may search felony, misdemeanor, civil and county ordinance violations free at www.miami-dadeclerk.com/cjis/search1.asp. Also, search Civil/Family/Probate free at www.miami-dadeclerk.com/default.asp and choose Standard Case Search. Also, now search traffic cases free at www.miami-dadeclerk.com/spirit/publicsearch/defnamesearch.asp.

Circuit & County Courts - Criminal – Criminal Records
www.miami-dadeclerk.com/dadecoc/
The county website offers free and Premier fee-based online services. Though limited, you may search felony, misdemeanor, civil and county ordinance violations free at www.miami-dadeclerk.com/cjis/search1.asp. By subscribing to the Clerk's Premier Services, you will be able to access advanced options in three of the Clerk's internet-based systems: Civil/Family/Probate, Public Records, and Traffic. Fees are $.25 per search, paid in advance. Search traffic cases free at www.miami-dadeclerk.com/spirit/publicsearch/defnamesearch.asp.

De Soto County

Circuit & County Courts – Civil Records
www.desotoclerk.com
Free access to civil, marriage/divorce, small claims, probate, Uresa, traffic/parking, Muni ordinances, domestic relations, name changes, foreclosures at www.desotoclerk.com/dpa/cvweb.asp. Also, access an index of judgments, liens, recorded documents at www.myfloridacounty.com. Fees involved to order copies; save $1.50 per record by becoming a subscriber. Criminal records are soon to be available at the 12th Judicial Circuit website.

Dixie County

Circuit & County Courts – Civil Records
http://www2.myfloridacounty.com/wps/wcm/connect/dixieclerk
Access an index of court judgments at www.myfloridacounty.com. Fees involved to order copies; save $1.50 per record by becoming a subscriber.

Duval County

Circuit & County Courts - Civil Division – Civil Records
www.duvalclerk.com/
Two sources are available. First, online access requires $100.00 setup fee, but no access charges. For more information, call 904-630-1212 x5115. Access an index of judgments, liens, recorded documents at www.myfloridacounty.com. Fees involved to order copies; save $1.50 per record by becoming a subscriber.

Circuit & County Courts - Criminal Division – Criminal Records
Access to criminal records requires $100.00 setup fee, but no access charges. Records go back to 1992. For more information, call Leslie Peterson at 904-630-1212 x5115.

Escambia County

Circuit & County Courts - Civil Division – Civil Records
www.escambiaclerk.com/
Access to county clerk records is free at the web page. Search by name, citation, or case number. Small claims, traffic, and marriage data also available. Access an index of judgments, liens, recorded documents at www.myfloridacounty.com. Fees involved to order copies; save $1.50 per record by becoming a subscriber.

Circuit & County Courts - Criminal Division – Criminal Records
www.escambiaclerk.com/
Access to criminal records is free at web page. Search by name, citation, or case number.

Flagler County and
Franklin County .

Circuit & County Courts – Civil and Criminal Records
www.franklinclerk.com
Access an index of judgments, liens, recorded documents at www.myfloridacounty.com. Fees involved to order copies; save $1.50 per record by becoming a subscriber.

Gadsden County

Circuit & County Courts - Civil Division – Civil Records
www.clerk.co.gadsden.fl.us
Access to the index of civil court judgments, etc. are free from the County Clerk at www.clerk.co.gadsden.fl.us. Also, access an index of judgments, liens, recorded documents at www.myfloridacounty.com. Fees involved to order copies; save $1.50 per record by becoming a subscriber.

Gilchrist County

Circuit & County Courts – Civil Records
http://gilchrist.fl.us/
Search judgments and liens online at http://records.gilchrist.fl.us/oncoreweb/.

Glades County

Circuit & County Courts – Civil Records
Access an index of judgments only available at www.myfloridacounty.com. Fees involved to order copies; save $1.50 per record by becoming a subscriber.

Gulf County
Hamilton County
Hardee County
Hendry County

Circuit & County Courts – Civil Records
Access an index of judgments, liens, recorded documents at www.myfloridacounty.com. Fees involved to order copies; save $1.50 per record by becoming a subscriber.

Hernando County

Circuit & County Courts – Civil and Criminal Records
www.clerk.co.hernando.fl.us
Access to court records is now free at www.clerk.co.hernando.fl.us/SearchType.asp. Online records may go as far back as 1/1983. Your browser must be JavaScript enables (MS Explorer 4.0 or above). Access an index of judgments, liens, recorded documents at www.myfloridacounty.com. Fees involved to order copies; save $1.50 per record by becoming a subscriber.

Highlands County

Circuit & County Courts – Civil Records
www.hcclerk.org
Access to county clerk civil and probate records is free at www.clerk.co.highlands.fl.us/civil/search.masn, from 1991. Also includes small claims, probate, and tax deeds. Access an index of judgments, liens, recorded documents at www.myfloridacounty.com. Fees involved to order copies; save $1.50 per record by becoming a subscriber.

Hillsborough County

Circuit & County Courts – Civil and Criminal Records
www.hillsclerk.com
Access to records at http://207.156.115.73/or_wb1/or_sch_1.asp. Search the Court Progress Dockets free at http://publicrecord.hillsclerk.com/courtdisclaimer.html. A subscription service is also available for records, visit the home page for details and fees. Also, access an index of judgments, liens, recorded documents at www.myfloridacounty.com. Fees involved to order copies; save $1.50 per record by becoming a subscriber.

Holmes County

Circuit & County Courts – Civil Records
Access an index of judgments, liens, recorded documents at www.myfloridacounty.com. Fees involved to order copies; save $1.50 per record by becoming a subscriber.

Indian River County

Circuit & County Courts – Civil and Criminal Records
www.clerk.indian-river.org
Access to county recordings index is free at www.clerk.indian-river.org/recordssearch/ori.asp. Records go back to 1983. Full access to court records is via the clerk's subscription service. Fee is $200.00 per month. For information about free and fee access, call Gary at 772-567-8000 x1216.

Jackson County

Circuit & County Courts – Civil Records
www.jacksonclerk.com
Access an index of judgments, liens, recorded documents at www.myfloridacounty.com. Fees involved to order copies; save $1.50 per record by becoming a subscriber.

Jefferson County

Circuit & County Courts – Civil Records
www.jeffersonclerk.com
Access an index of judgments, liens, recorded documents at www.myfloridacounty.com, for 01/1/73 to current. Fees involved to order copies; save $1.50 per record by becoming a subscriber.

Lafayette County

Circuit & County Courts – Civil Records
Access an index of judgments, liens, recorded documents at www.myfloridacounty.com. Fees involved to order copies; save $1.50 per record by becoming a subscriber.

Lake County

Circuit & County Courts – Civil and Criminal Records
www.lakecountyclerk.org/default1.asp
Access to Clerk of Court records is free at www.lakecountyclerk.org/services.asp?subject=Online_Court_Records. County civil records go back to 1985; Circuit records go back to 9/84. Also, previous 2-weeks civil records and divorces on a private site at http://extra.orlandosentinel.com/publicrecords/search.asp.

Lee County

Circuit & County Courts – Civil and Criminal Records
www.leeclerk.org
Access records free at www.leeclerk.org/court_inquiry_disclaimer.htm. Online records go back to 1988. Includes traffic, felony, misdemeanor, civil, small claims and probate. Access an index of judgments, liens, recorded documents at www.leeclerk.org or www.myfloridacounty.com. Search free but fees involved to order certified copies; save the per-record copy fee by becoming a subscriber; sub fee is $25.00 per month.

Leon County

Circuit & County Courts – Civil Records
www.clerk.leon.fl.us
Also, you may search cases and "High Profile Cases" (re: Election 2000) at www.clerk.leon.fl.us under "Search Court Databases." Registration required. Access an index of judgments, liens, recorded documents at www.myfloridacounty.com. Fees involved to order copies; save $1.50 per record by becoming a subscriber. Access available for high profile cases only.

Levy County
Liberty County
Madison County

Circuit & County Courts – Civil Records
Access an index of judgments, liens, recorded documents at www.myfloridacounty.com. Fees involved to order copies; save $1.50 per record by becoming a subscriber.

Manatee County

Circuit & County Courts – Civil and Criminal Records
www.manateeclerk.com
Online subscription online service is $50 plus $60 per user fee advance; for sign-up information visit the website. Also, court records at Circuit clerk's office are free at www.manateeclerk.com/mpa/cvweb.asp. Access an index of judgments, liens, recorded documents at www.myfloridacounty.com. Fees involved to order copies; save $1.50 per record by becoming a subscriber.

Marion County

Circuit & County Courts – Civil Records
www.marioncountyclerk.org
Access to county clerk civil records is free at www.marioncountyclerk.org/. Click on Case Search found on left side under Courts. Access an index of judgments, liens, recorded documents at www.myfloridacounty.com. Fees involved to order copies; save $1.50 per record by becoming a subscriber.

Martin County

Circuit & County Courts – Civil and Criminal Records
http://clerk-web.martin.fl.us/ClerkWeb
Access to civil case information on the records division database is free at http://clerk-web.martin.fl.us/wb%5For1/. Also includes small claims, recordings, other document types. Criminal and civil records are available through dial in modem for a nominal fee contract with the Clerk. This is the same access mode that government agencies may use free upon request.

Monroe County

Circuit & County Courts – Civil and Criminal Records
www.co.monroe.fl.us
Access to civil cases is free at www.clerk-of-the-court.com/searchCivilCases.asp. Subscription is required for viewing full document library. Access to criminal records is free at www.clerk-of-the-court.com/searchCriminalCases.asp. Includes traffic cases online. Subscription is required for viewing full document library.

Nassau County

Circuit & County Courts – Civil and Criminal Records
www.nassauclerk.com
Access an index of judgments, sentences, county commitments, uniform state commitments, disposition notices and nolle prosequi only at www.myfloridacounty.com. Fees involved to order copies; save $1.50 per record by becoming a subscriber. Limited criminal records online.

Okaloosa County

Circuit & County Courts – Civil and Criminal Records

www.clerkofcourts.cc

3 options available. Access to the full online system (civil, probate, traffic) requires monthly fee of $100.00. For more information, call 850-689-5821. Also, civil records are free at www.clerkofcourts.cc/court/courtsearch.htm. Records go back to 1/86. Search civil index by defendant or plaintiff, date, or file type. Also, access an index of judgments, liens, recorded documents back to 1/1983 at www.myfloridacounty.com. Fees involved to order copies; save $1.50 per record by becoming a subscriber. Both felony and misdemeanor indexes can be searched. Also, the county clerk has placed traffic misdemeanor records free on the Internet at www.clerkofcourts.cc/court/courtsearch.htm.

Okeechobee County

Circuit & County Courts – Civil Records

Index of judgments and recorded documents can be searched at http://204.215.37.218/wb_or1/or_sch_1.asp.

Orange County

Circuit & County Courts – Civil and Criminal Records

http://orangeclerk.ocfl.net

The Teleclerk countywide remote online system has been replaced by the free iclerk system at http://orangeclerk1.onetgov.net/. Set your browser "privacy" to "low." Use "public" as username and password. For more information, call 407-836-2060. Also, previous 2-weeks civil records on a private site at http://extra.orlandosentinel.com/publicrecords/search.asp.

Osceola County

Circuit Court - Civil – Civil Records

www.ninja9.org

Access to court records on the Clerk of Circuit Court database are free at www.osceolaclerkcourt.org/genrlmnu.htm. Also, access an index of judgments, liens, recorded documents at www.myfloridacounty.com. Fees involved to order copies; save $1.50 per record by becoming a subscriber. Also, previous 2-weeks civil records on a private site at http://extra.orlandosentinel.com/publicrecords/search.asp.

Circuit & County Courts - Criminal Division – Criminal Records

www.osceolaclerk.com

Access to criminal records is free at www.osceolaclerkcourt.org/search.htm. Includes party index and case summary searching. Search inmates at www.osceola.org/index.cfm?lsFuses=inmates.

Palm Beach County

Circuit Court – Civil and Probate Records

www.pbcountyclerk.com

Access to the countywide remote online system is free. Civil index goes back to '88. Records also include probate, traffic and domestic. Contact Rowtera Simmons at 561-355-4277 for information. Also, access 15th judicial circuit records at http://web3172.co.palm-beach.fl.us. Registration and password is required. Service may be discontinued. Also, civil records only are free at http://courtcon.co.palm-beach.fl.us/pls/jiwp/ck_public_qry_main.cp_main_idx.

County Court - Civil Division – Civil Records

www.pbcountyclerk.com

Access to the countywide remote online system requires $145 setup and $65 per month fees. Civil index goes back to '88. Records also include probate, traffic and domestic. Contact M. McArthur at 561-355-6846 for information.

Circuit & County Courts - Criminal Division – Criminal Records

www.pbcountyclerk.com

Access to the countywide criminal online system requires $145 setup and $65 per month fee. Records also include probate, traffic and domestic. Contact Mr. McArthur for information. Also, access to 15th judicial circuit records is at http://web3172.co.palm-beach.fl.us. Registration and password required.

Pasco County

Circuit & County Courts - Civil Division – Civil Records

www.pascoclerk.com/

Access to Clerk of Court records via the Internet is a subscription service. Monthly fees are involved. Probate records also available. Call 352-521-4274, ext 4767 for more information. Access an index of judgments, liens, recorded documents at www.myfloridacounty.com. Fees involved to order copies; save $1.50 per record by becoming a subscriber.

Circuit & County Courts - Criminal Division – Criminal Records
www.jud6.org
Access to the countywide criminal online system requires $100 deposit, $50 annual fee and $10 monthly minimum. There is a $.10 per screen charge. The system is open 24 hours daily. Search by name or case number. Call 352-521-4201 for more information about this subscription product.

Pinellas County

Circuit & County Courts – Civil and Criminal Records
www.jud6.org
Access to the countywide online system requires $60 fee plus $5.00 a month and $.05 per screen over 100. Index goes back to 1972. Contact Sue Maskeny at 727-464-3779 for information. Includes probate and traffic records. Also, you can access the clerk's criminal and other data as a free non-subscriber at https://pubtitles.co.pinellas.fl.us/login/loginx.jsp. However, you are on the clock and may be booted if you overuse the system. Also, access an index of judgments, liens, recorded documents at www.myfloridacounty.com. Fees involved to order copies; save $1.50 per record by becoming a subscriber.

Polk County

Circuit Court - Civil Division – Civil Records
www.polkcountyclerk.net/
Free access to ldockets at www.polkcountyclerk.net/RecordsSearch/disclaimer.aspx. A subscription account for complete access to the database requires $150 setup fee, but there is no monthly fees. Call 863-534-7575 for more information.

County Court - Civil Division – Civil Records
www.polkcountyclerk.net
Case index information back to 1983 is free from the County Clerk's website at www.polkcountyclerk.net.

Putnam County

Circuit Court - Civil Division – Civil Records
www.polkcountyclerk.net/
Access to the countywide remote online system requires $400 setup fee and $40. monthly charge plus $.05 per minute over 20 hours. Civil records go back to 1984. System includes criminal and real property records. Criminal records go back to 1972. Contact Putnam County IT Dept to register. Also, access an index of judgments, liens, recorded documents at www.myfloridacounty.com. Fees involved to order copies; save $1.50 per record by becoming a subscriber.

Santa Rosa County

Circuit & County Courts - Civil Division – Civil Records
www.santarosaclerk.com
Access an index of judgments, liens, and court records free at http://oncoreweb.srccol.com/srccol/party5.asp or search at www.myfloridacounty.com where fees involved to order copies; save $1.50 per record by becoming a subscriber.

Circuit & County Courts - Criminal Division – Criminal Records
www.santarosaclerk.com
Access an index of judgments, liens, and court records free at http://oncoreweb.srccol.com/oncoreweb4101/Search.aspx.

Sarasota County

Circuit & County Courts - Civil – Civil Records
www.sarasotaclerk.com
Civil and DV case records from the Clerk of Circuit Court database are free online at www.clerk.co.sarasota.fl.us/srqapp/civilinq.asp. Probate court records are at www.clerk.co.sarasota.fl.us/srqapp/probinq.asp. Also, access an index of judgments, liens, recorded documents at www.myfloridacounty.com. Fees involved to order copies; save $1.50 per record by becoming a subscriber.

Circuit & County Courts - Criminal – Criminal Records
www.sarasotaclerk.com
Criminal and traffic case records from the Clerk of the Circuit Court database are free online at http://clerk.co.sarasota.fl.us/cvdisclaim.htm. Civil, probate and domestic records are also available.

Seminole County
Circuit & County Courts - Civil Division – Civil Records
Access to the County Clerk's online records is free at www.seminoleclerk.org/OfficialRecords. Search by name, clerk's file number, or book & page. Also, previous 2-weeks civil records on a private site at http://extra.orlandosentinel.com/publicrecords/search.asp.

St. Johns County

Circuit & County Courts – Civil and Criminal Records

www.co.st-johns.fl.us

Access to the countywide remote online system requires $200 setup fee plus a monthly fee of $50. Searching is by name or case number. Call Mark Dearing at 904-819-3610 for more information. Also, access the county Clerk of Circuit Court recording database free at http://doris.clk.co.st-johns.fl.us/oncoreweb/Search.aspx. Access an index of judgments, liens, recorded documents at www.myfloridacounty.com. Fees involved to order copies; save $1.50 per record by becoming a subscriber at $25.00 per month.

St. Lucie County

Circuit & County Courts - Civil Division – Civil Records

www.slcclerkofcourt.com/circuitcivil/circuitcivil.htm

Access to civil records at http://public.slcclerkofcourt.com. Case tracking and bond record tracking are available. Access an index of judgments, liens, recorded documents at www.myfloridacounty.com. Fees involved to order copies; save $1.50 per record by becoming a subscriber.

Circuit & County Courts - Criminal Division – Criminal Records

www.slcclerkofcourt.com/felony/felony.htm

Access to bonds, traffic and misdemeanor records is free at http://public.slcclerkofcourt.com. Online records go back to 7/6/1992. Felony records only available to government agencies.

Sumter County

Circuit & County Courts - Civil Division – Civil Records

www.sumterclerk.com/public/

Access an index of judgments, liens, recorded documents at www.myfloridacounty.com. Fees involved to order copies; save $1.50 per record by becoming a subscriber. Faxes accepted if only pre-paid.

Suwannee County

Circuit & County Courts – Civil and Criminal Records

www.suwclerk.org/index2.html

Access to County Clerk of Circuit Court records is at www.suwclerk.org/public.html. Access to County Clerk of Circuit Court records is at www.suwclerk.org/public.html. Criminal records may be temporarily unavailable.

Taylor County

Circuit & County Courts – Civil Records

Access an index of judgments, liens, recorded documents at www.myfloridacounty.com. Fees involved to order copies; save $1.50 per record by becoming a subscriber.

Union County

Circuit & County Courts – Civil and Criminal Records

http://circuit8.org

Access an index of judgments, liens, recorded documents at www.myfloridacounty.com. Fees involved to order copies; save $1.50 per record by becoming a subscriber. Access the circuit-wide criminal quick lookup at http://circuit8.org/golem/gencrim.html. Account and password is required; restricted usage.

Volusia County

Circuit & County Courts - Civil Division – Civil Records

www.clerk.org

Access to the countywide remote online system requires $100 setup fee plus a $25 monthly fee. Windows required. Search by name or case number. Call Thom White 386-822-5004 for more information. Criminal, probate and traffic records are also available. Also, Access an index of judgments, liens, recorded documents at www.myfloridacounty.com. Fees involved to order copies; save $1.50 per record by becoming a subscriber. Also, previous 2-weeks civil records on a private site at http://extra.orlandosentinel.com/publicrecords/search.asp.

Circuit & County Courts - Criminal Division – Criminal Records

www.clerk.org

Two access methods are available. Access to the Clerk of Circuit Courts database of Citation Violations and 24-hour Arrest Reports is free at www.clerk.org/index.html Access to the countywide criminal online system requires $125 setup fee plus a $25 monthly fee. Windows required. Search by name or case number back to 1988. Call 904-822-5710 for more information. Civil, probate and traffic records are also available.

Wakulla County

Circuit & County Courts – Civil Records
www.wakullaclerk.com
Access an index of judgments, liens, recorded documents at www.myfloridacounty.com. Fees involved to order copies; save $1.50 per record by becoming a subscriber. Faxes must be pre-paid. Visitors may review docket books, only court performs name searches. Faxes must be pre-paid.

Walton County

Circuit & County Courts – Civil and Criminal Records
http://clerkofcourts.co.walton.fl.us
Access final judgments or orders on closed cases at http://clerkofcourts.co.walton.fl.us/ORSearch/. Access felony judgments of guilt only at http://clerkofcourts.co.walton.fl.us/ORSearch/.

Washington County

Circuit & County Courts – Civil Records
Access an index of judgments, liens, recorded documents at www.myfloridacounty.com. Fees involved to order copies; save $1.50 per record by becoming a subscriber.

County Level ... Recorders & Assessors

Recording Office Organization: 67 counties, 67 recording offices. The recording officer is the Clerk of the Circuit Court. All transactions are recorded in the "Official Record," a grantor/grantee index. Some counties will search by type of transaction while others will return everything on the index. 57 counties are in the Eastern Time Zone (EST) and 10 are in the Central Time Zone (CST). Federal tax liens on personal property of businesses are filed with the Secretary of State. All other federal and state tax liens on personal property are filed with the county Clerk of Circuit Court. Usually tax liens on personal property are filed in the same index with UCC financing statements and real estate transactions. Most counties will perform a tax lien as part of a UCC search. Copies usually cost $1.00 per page.

Online Access Note: There are numerous county agencies that provide online access to records, but the statewide system MyFlorida.com predominates. My Florida offers free access to the over 60 counties Circuit Clerks of Court recorded document indexes, including real estate records liens, judgments, marriages, and deaths at www.myfloridacounty.com/services/officialrecords_intro.shtml. Fees involved to order copies; save $1.50 per record by becoming a subscriber. Subscription fee is $120.00 per year plus monthly transaction fees for copies.

Any person has the right to request the Clerk/County Recorder to redact/remove his Social Security Number from an image or copy of an Official Record that has been placed on such Clerk/County Recorder's publicly available Internet website.

Alachua County

Property Appraiser, Real Estate, Lien, Judgment, Vital Statistic, Recording, Traffic Citation, Plat Records
www.clerk-alachua-fl.org
Access Clerk's recording database free at www.clerk-alachua-fl.org/Clerk/searchmenu.html. Index goes back to 1971; records to 1990. Also, search County Appraiser's Property page free at www.acpafl.org. Sales search and GIS search also here. Property also at www.emapsplus.com/FLAlachua/maps/. Search ancient records -pre-1940 plats, pre-1970 marriages, deeds, transcriptions, more- free at www.clerk-alachua-fl.org/archive/default.cfm. Search traffic citations at www.co.alachua.fl.us/traffic/. Access an index of recorded documents at www.myfloridacounty.com. Fees involved to order copies; save $1.50 per record by becoming a subscriber. Also, search tax roll data free at www.actcfl.org/collectmax/collect30.asp.

Baker County   *Real Estate, Lien, Recording, Property Records*

Access an index of recorded documents at www.myfloridacounty.com. Fees involved to order copies; save $1.50 per record by becoming a subscriber. Also, search for property data free at www.emapsplus.com/FLBaker/maps/. Choose to search by owner.

Bay County   *Property Tax, Real Estate, Tax Lien, Recording, Appraiser, Property Sale Records*
www.baycoclerk.com
Access to the Clerk of the Circuit Court Recordings database is free at www.baycoclerk.com/index.cfm. Records go back to 1/1987. Search the property appraiser database free at www.qpublic.net/bay/ or at www.qpublic.net/bay/search1.html; search the tax collector data at http://bctc.elementaldata.com/disclaimer.asp. Assessor database is free online at www.qpublic.net/bay/search.html. Access an index of recorded documents at www.myfloridacounty.com. Fees involved to order copies; save $1.50 per record by becoming a subscriber.

Bradford County   *Real Estate, Appraisal, Deed, Judgment, Marriage, Lien, Court, Property Tax Records*
Access to the recorders database is free at www.mybradfordcounty.com. Click on "Official Records." Also, search the property appraiser database at www.bradfordappraiser.com/Search_F.asp. Also, search property data for free at www.emapsplus.com/FLBradford/maps/. Choose to search by owner. Also, an index of recorded documents is at www.myfloridacounty.com. Fees involved to order copies; save $1.50 per record by becoming a subscriber.

Brevard County
Real Estate, Lien, Marriage, Recording, Tax Sale, Property Appraiser, Personal Property, Traffic Records
www.brevardclerk.us
Access clerk's tax lien (1981-95), land records (1995-) & indexed records 1981-9/30/1995 at http://cfweb2.brevardclerk.us/ORM/if_orm_choice.cfm. Registration/password required for full data; application fee- $5.00. Free access to marriage records also. Access index of recorded docs at www.myfloridacounty.com. Fees involved to order copies. Property tax, sales & personal property records at http://brevardpropertyappraiser.com/asp/disclaimer.asp. Property/GIS free at www.emapsplus.com/FLBrevard/maps/. Also, tax deed sale lists free at www.brevardclerk.us/index.cfm?FuseAction=TaxDeedAuctions.Home. Also, the clerk offers a public system at http://webfyi.clerk.co.brevard.fl.us/netfyi/instruct.html that includes plats, traffic, courts and more.

Broward County   *Property, Appraiser, Real Estate, Lien, Recording, Occ. License, Most Wanted, Arrest, Missing, Sex Offender, Vendor Payment Records*
www.broward.org/records
Access to the county records Public Search database 1978-present is free at http://205.166.161.12/oncoreV2/. Also search property/GIS free at www.emapsplus.com/FLBroward/maps/. Also, search the occupational license database at http://bcegov2.broward.org/olsearch/olsearch.asp. Also, search the sheriff's multiple databases at www.sheriff.org. Also, search property tax data for free at http://bcegov.co.broward.fl.us/revenue/nameform.asp. Search appraiser records at www.bcpa.net/index.cfm?page=search. Search vendor payments at www.broward.org/Guests/vendor.htm.

Calhoun County   *Real Estate, Lien, Deed, Judgment, Recording Records*
http://www2.myfloridacounty.com/wps/wcm/connect/calhounclerk
Access an index of recorded documents at www.myfloridacounty.com. Fees involved to order copies; save $1.50 per record by becoming a subscriber.

Charlotte County   *Property Appraiser, Real Estate, Lien, Recording, Marriage, Property Sale, Arrest, Most Wanted, Sex Offender Records*
www.co.charlotte.fl.us
Property records are free at www.ccappraiser.com/record.asp. Sales records are also here and at the tax collector database, free at www.cctaxcol.com/record.asp?. Search recorded data and marriages free at http://208.47.160.77/or/Search.aspx. Bulk database record purchases, by year, are available. Access index of recorded documents at www.myfloridacounty.com. Fees involved to order copies; subscribers save $1.50 per record. Search sheriff data at www.ccso.org/localcrime/crimedatabase.cfm. Also search property/GIS free at www.emapsplus.com/FLCharlotte/maps/ and click on name search.

Citrus County   *Property Appraiser, Real Estate, Lien, Deed, Marriage, Recording, Property Tax, Sex Offender, Personal Property, Probate, Military Discharge, Tax Deed Sale Records*
www.clerk.citrus.fl.us
Access to the Clerk of Circuit Court recording records is free at http://24.129.131.20/search.asp?cabinet=opr. Search property tax records for free at http://citrustaxcollector.governmax.com. Search property appraiser records free at www.pa.citrus.fl.us/ccpaask.html. Also, download land sales data free at www.pa.citrus.fl.us/sales_download.html. Access recorded documents index- www.myfloridacounty.com. Tax deed sales- www.clerk.citrus.fl.us/home.jsp?section=8&item=88. Also, search sheriff sex offender list at www.sheriffcitrus.org/SexOffenders. Search arrests at www.sheriffcitrus.org/ArrestReport/arrests.aspx.

Clay County   *Appraiser, Real Estate, Lien, Recording, Tangible Personal Property, Property Tax, Most Wanted, Sex Offender Records*
www.clayclerk.com
The county clerk of circuit court allows free access to recording records at http://clayclerk.com/oncorewebsearch/. Records go back to 1990. Also, search property/GIS free at www.emapsplus.com/FLClay/maps/. Also, access property appraiser records free at www.ccpao.com/ccpao.asp?page=search; tangible property at www.ccpao.com/tpp/default.htm; account # required. Search treasurer RE & tangible personal property at www.claycountytax.com/Tax_Searchr/porr.html. Also, access an index of recorded documents at www.myfloridacounty.com. Fees involved to order copies; save $1.50 per record by becoming a subscriber. Also, search sex offenders and most wanted at http://claysheriff.com.

Collier County   *Property Appraiser, Real Estate, Lien, UCC, Vital Statistic, Recording, Tax Sale, Wanted, Missing Person, Property Tax, Occupational License Records*
www.clerk.collier.fl.us
Access Property Appraiser database free at www.collierappraiser.com/Search.asp. Also property/GIS free at www.emapsplus.com/FLCollier/maps/. The sheriff's wanted and missing lists are at www.colliersheriff.org. Access court, lien, real estate, UCCs and vital records free at www.clerk.collier.fl.us/clerkspublicac/Default.htm. Lending agency data available. Search property tax roll at www.colliertax.com/search/; Occ License at www.colliertax.com/search/ols.php. Tax deeds sales data is free at www.clerk.collier.fl.us/OfficialRecords/Tax_Deeds/Tax%20Deeds.htm. Also, access recorded document index at www.myfloridacounty.com. Fees involved to order copies; save $1.50 per record by becoming a subscriber.

Columbia County   *Real Estate, Lien, Recording, Probate, Property Tax, Appraiser, GIS, Occ License Records*
http://www2.myfloridacounty.com/wps/wcm/connect/columbiaclerk
Access Clerk of Circuit Courts recording database index free at www.columbiaclerk.com. Click on Order Official Records. Search by name, book/page, file number of document type. This is a www.myfloridacounty.com website; fees are involved to order copies; save $1.50 per record by becoming a subscriber. Search property/GIS free at www.emapsplus.com/FLColumbia/maps/. Also, search property appraiser records free at http://columbia.floridapa.com/GIS/Search_F.asp. Also, search the tax rolls and occupational licenses for free at www.columbiataxcollector.com/collectmax/collect30.asp

Dade County
Real Estate, Recording, Judgment, Lien, Marriage, Tax Deed Sale, Property Appraiser, Property Tax, Plat Records
www.miami-dadeclerk.com/dadecoc/
Record access to 11 databases requires $125 initial setup fee & minimum $52 monthly fee for 208 minutes, $.25 ea. add'l. Records back to 1975. Call 305-596-8148. 2nd service is recorder only at www.miami-dadeclerk.com/dadecoc/Premier_Services.asp; fee is $50 per month. Also, recorder records and plats are free at www.miami-dadeclerk.com/public-records. Property search GIS site free at www.emapsplus.com/FLDade/maps/. Search marriages at www.miami-dadeclerk.com/mlsweb/LicenseSearch.aspx. Tax collector records free at www.co.miami-dade.fl.us/proptax/. Search property at http://gisims2.co.miami-dade.fl.us/MyHome/propmap.asp. Tax deed sales: www.miami-dadeclerk.com/tax-deeds/home.asp.

De Soto County   *Real Estate, Lien, Recording, Property Tax, Wanted Records*
www.co.desoto.fl.us/gen/index2.html
Access an index of recorded documents at www.myfloridacounty.com. Fees involved to order copies; save $1.50 per record by becoming a subscriber. Search property/GIS free at www.emapsplus.com/FLdesoto/maps/. Also, access the property appraiser data free at http://qpublic.net/desoto/search.html. Also, access to the tax collector data is free at www.qpublic.net/dctc/search.html. Search the most wanted list at www.desotosheriff.com/most_wanted.

Dixie County   *Real Estate, Lien, Recording, Assessor, Property Records*
Access an index of recorded documents at www.myfloridacounty.com. Fees involved to order copies; save $1.50 per record by becoming a subscriber. Also, access assessor's property data free at http://dixiefl.patriotproperties.com/default.asp.

Duval County
Property Appraiser, Real Estate, Lien, Recording, Grantor/Grantee, Vital Statistic, Occ. License, Inmate Records
Access Clerk of Circuit Court and City of Jacksonville Official Records grantor/grantee index free at http://205.173.32.5/OnCoreWeb/Search.aspx. Search tax collector real estate data and personal property data free at http://fl-duval-taxcollector.governmax.com/collectmax/collect30.asp. Also, search County Property Appraiser records for Duval County and City of Jacksonville at http://apps2.coj.net/pao. Search occ. licenses for free at http://tc.coj.net/occlicense/. Property/GIS free at www.emapsplus.com/Flduval/maps/. Access an index of recorded documents at www.myfloridacounty.com. Fees involved to order copies. Access inmate information at- www.jaxsheriff.com/inmatesearch/(xhreii55bpunkk3iuhlbth2o)/default.aspx.

Escambia County   *Property Appraiser, Real Estate, Grantor/Grantee, Lien, Recording, Vital Statistic, Property Tax, Tax Sale, Inmate Records*

www.clerk.co.escambia.fl.us
Access to the Clerk of Court Public Records database is free at www.clerk.co.escambia.fl.us/public_records.html. This includes grantor/grantee index and marriage, traffic, court records, tax sales. Also, access the tax collector's Property Tax database is free at http://escambiataxcollector.governmaxa.com/collectmax/collect30.asp. Tax sale info at http://ectc.co.escambia.fl.us/Pageview.asp?edit_id=103 . Also, search the property appraiser records at www.escpa.org/Search.asp. Access an index of recorder documents at www.myfloridacounty.com. Fees involved to order copies; save $1.50 per record by becoming subscriber. Also, Sheriff's office Inmate Lookup is at www.escambiaso.com/jail/main1.htm.

Flagler County   *Property Appraiser, Recording, Real Estate, Lien, Deed, Probate, Judgment, Marriage, Death, Military Discharge, Property Sale Records*

www.flaglerclerk.com
Search recording records free at www.flaglerclerk.com/oncoreweb/Search.aspx. Also, recording index on CD-rom $25 per O.R. book; for info call Vickie Hunter 386-437-7396. Search appraiser property data free at www.qpublic.net/flagler/search.html or http://flaglerpa.com. Check sales at www.qpublic.net/flagler/flaglersearch.html. The state recorders' meta-search site is free at www.myflaglercounty.com. Click on Official Records. Also, search Property/GIS free at www.emapsplus.com/FLflagler/maps/. Access an index of recorded documents at www.myfloridacounty.com. Fees involved to order copies; save $1.50 per record by becoming a subscriber.

Franklin County   *Real Estate, Lien, Recording Records*

http://www2.myfloridacounty.com/wps/wcm/connect/franklinclerk
Access an index of recorded documents at www.myfloridacounty.com. Fees involved to order copies; save $1.50 per record by becoming a subscriber.

Gadsden County   *Real Estate, Recording, Judgment, Deed, Lien, Vital Statistic, Property Appraiser Records*

www.clerk.co.gadsden.fl.us
Access to official records index is free at www.clerk.co.gadsden.fl.us/OfficialRecords/. Index records go back to 1985. Provides index numbers only. Also, access to the property appraiser database is free at www.qpublic.net/gadsden/search.html. Also, search tax collector records at www.gadsdentaxcollector.com/collectmax/collect30.asp. Search property sales at www.qpublic.net/gadsden/gadsdensearch.html. No name searching.

Gilchrist County   *Real Estate, Property Appraiser, Lien, Recording, Deed, Judgment, Marriage, Death Records*

http://gilchrist.fl.us/
Access to the property appraiser database is free at www.qpublic.net/gilchrist/search.html. Also, sales searches are at www.gcpaonline.net; click on Search. Access an index of recorded documents at http://mygilchristcounty.com or www.myfloridacounty.com. Fees involved to order copies; save $1.50 per record by becoming a subscriber. Access is free to recorded documents generally and some courts records at http://records.gilchrist.fl.us/oncoreweb/Search.aspx.

Glades County   *Real Estate, Lien, Recording, Property, GIS Records*

http://www2.myfloridacounty.com/wps/wcm/connect/gladesclerk
Access an index of recorded documents at www.myfloridacounty.com. View docs back to 1/1990 without ordering. Fees involved to order copies; save $1.50 per record by becoming a subscriber. Also, search Property/GIS free at www.emapsplus.com/FLglades/maps/.

Gulf County   *Real Estate, Lien, Deed, Judgment, Marriage, Death, Recording Records*

http://www2.myfloridacounty.com/wps/wcm/connect/gulfclerk
Access an index of recorded documents at www.myfloridacounty.com. Fees involved to order copies; save $1.50 per record by becoming a subscriber.

Hamilton County   *Real Estate, Lien, Recording Records*

Access an index of recorded documents at www.myfloridacounty.com. Fees involved to order copies; save $1.50 per record by becoming a subscriber.

Hardee County
Real Estate, Recording, Lien, Property Appraiser, Most Wanted, Arrest, Inmate, Warrant Records

http://www2.myfloridacounty.com/wps/wcm/connect/hardeeclerk
Access an index of recorded documents at www.myfloridacounty.com. Fees involved to order copies; save $1.50 per record by becoming a subscriber. Also, search property/GIS free at www.emapsplus.com/FLhardee/maps/. Also, online assess to the property

appraiser data is free at www.hardeecounty.net/cfaps/appraiser/propform.cfm. Also, search the sheriff's most wanted, inmate, arrest, warrant and missing person lists at www.hardeeso.com.

Hendry County *Real Estate, Lien, Recording Records*
www.hendryclerk.org
Access an index of recorded documents at www.myfloridacounty.com. Also, search Property/GIS free at www.emapsplus.com/FLhendry/maps/. Also, access the property appraiser database at www.hendryprop.com/GIS/Search_F.asp. Also, Official Records Database found free at http://204.117.204.113/offrec/ormain.htm - Has images from 12/30/1988 -- Book 450 Page 1 to latest available. Web records are updated daily.

Hernando County *Property Appraiser, Real Estate, Lien, Marriage, Recording, Most Wanted, Arrest Records*
www.clerk.co.hernando.fl.us
Access to the clerk's Official Records database is now free at www.clerk.co.hernando.fl.us/disclaimer.asp. Your browser must be Javascript enabled. Includes recordings, marriages, and court records. Also, the county now offers 2 levels of the Public Inquiry System Property Appraiser Real Estate database - Easy Search and Real Time Search - free at www.co.hernando.fl.us/pa/propsearch.htm. Search by owner, address, or parcel key. Also, access recorded document index at www.myfloridacounty.com. Fees involved to order copies. Search sheriff's most wanted and arrests back to 1995 lists at www.hcso.hernando.fl.us.

Highlands County *Property Appraiser, Personal Property, Real Estate,Deed, Lien, Recording, GIS Records*
www.clerk.co.highlands.fl.us
Property appraiser records are free at www.appraiser.co.highlands.fl.us/search.html; tangible personal property records available. Also, online access to the recorders' meta-search site is at www.myflorida.com. Click on Official Records. Free search; fee for documents. Also, online access to deeds, mortgages, judgments from the county recording database are free at www.clerk.co.highlands.fl.us/official/search.html. Records go back to 1983. Also, county tax collector database for personal property and real estate is free at www.collector.co.highlands.fl.us/search/index.html. Search Property/GIS free at www.emapsplus.com/FLhighlands/maps/.

Hillsborough County *Property Appraiser, Personal Property, Real Estate, Lien, Deed, Recording, Warrant, Inmate, Repo/Impound Records*
www.hillsclerk.com
Property appraiser records are free at www.hcpafl.org/www/search/index.shtml. Receive owner data, legal, sales, value summaries. The clerk's recordings index can be searched free at http://publicrecord.hillsclerk.com. Also, access recorded document index at www.myfloridacounty.com; fees involved to order copies; subscribers save $1.50 per record. Call 813-276-8100 x4444 for info. Also, search sheriff's warrants, inmates, repo data free at www.hcso.tampa.fl.us/Page_Headers/online.htm. Images of official records from 1990 to present at www.hillsclerk.com.

Holmes County *Real Estate, Lien, Recording Records*
http://www2.myfloridacounty.com/wps/wcm/connect/holmesclerk
Access an index of recorded documents at www.myfloridacounty.com. Fees involved to order copies; save $1.50 per record by becoming a subscriber.

Indian River County
Property Appraiser, Real Estate, Lien, Vital Statistic, Inmate, Criminal History, GIS Records
www.clerk.indian-river.org
Appraiser information is free, but only some of the recording office information is. Appraiser records are free at www.ircpa.org. Also, search Property/GIS free at www.emapsplus.com/FLindianriver/maps/. Also, access to Clerk of the Circuit Court recording indices are free at www.clerk.indian-river.org/recordssearch/ori.asp. Records go back to 1983. Sheriff's data on inmates and criminal histories at www.ircsheriff.org/programs.cfm. Full real estate, lien and court and vital records from the Clerk of the Circuit Court is at their fee site; subscriptions start $100 per month, increasing with amount of access. For info about free and fee access, call 772-567-8000 x216.

Jackson County *Real Estate, Lien, Recording, Marriage, Probate, Property Tax Records*
http://www2.myfloridacounty.com/wps/wcm/connect/jacksonclerk
Access an index of recorded documents at www.myfloridacounty.com. Fees involved to order copies; save $1.50 per record by becoming a subscriber. Images will go back to 5/1990. Also, search property tax data for free at www.jacksoncountytaxcollector.com/SearchSelect.aspx.

Jefferson County *Property, Real Estate, Lien, Recording Records*
http://co.jefferson.fl.us
Access to the Property Appraiser database is free at http://qpublic.net/jefferson/search.html. Sales searches are also available. Also, online access to the Clerk of Circuit Court recordings database is free at www.myjeffersoncounty.com. Also, search the tax collector database free at www.jeffersoncountytaxcollector.com/SearchSelect.aspx. Access an index of recorded documents at www.myfloridacounty.com. Fees involved to order copies; save $1.50 per record by becoming a subscriber.

Lafayette County *Real Estate, Lien, Recording Records*
http://www2.myfloridacounty.com/wps/wcm/connect/lafayetteclerk
Access an index of recorded documents at www.myfloridacounty.com. Fees involved to order copies; save $1.50 per record by becoming a subscriber.

Lake County *Property Appraiser, Recording, Real Estate, Lien, Marriage, Death, Divorce Records*
www.lakecountyclerk.org
The new county clerk official records database is free online at www.lakecountyclerk.org/services.asp?subject=Online_Official_Records. Records go as far back as 1974. Includes court records. Also, records on the County Property Assessor database are free at www.lakecopropappr.com/property_search.asp. Also, marriage records back to 11/2000 are at www.lakecountyclerk.org/departments.asp?subject=Marriage_Licenses. Also, access to state recorders' meta-search site is free at www.myfloridacounty.com. Click on Official records. Also, private site has previous 2 weeks real estate, marriage, divorce records at http://extra.orlandosentinel.com/publicrecords/search.asp.

Lee County *Property Appraiser, Real Estate, Occ. License, Lien, Recording, Judgment, Business-Personal Tangible Property, Vessel, Vehicle Records*
www.lee-county.com
Access most tax, vehicle, and occupation-related databases free at www.leetc.com/home.asp. Also, search the recorders index free at www.leeclerk.org/OR/Search.aspx or other indexes (subject to change) at www.leeclerk.org/SearchOfficialRecords.htm. But obtain certified copies at the Clerk's office or order certified copies online and search other Florida Counties' Official Records at www.myfloridacounty.com and click on the Order Official Records. Also, search tangible business property at www.leepa.org/Tangible/Business%20Search.htm. The online property info inquiry is at www.leepa.org/Queries/SearchCriteria.htm. Search property/GIS free at www.emapsplus.com/FLlee/maps/.

Leon County
Property Appraiser, Real Estate, Lien, Marriage, Recording, Foreclosure, Contractor, Most Wanted Records
www.clerk.leon.fl.us
Real Estate, lien, and foreclosure records from the County Clerk are free at www.clerk.leon.fl.us. Lending agency information is also available. Also, access to full document images requires user name and password, plus $100 per month. Property Appraiser database records are free at www.co.leon.fl.us/propappr/search.cfm. Access recorded documents index at www.myfloridacounty.com. Fees involved to order copies. Search contractors lists at www.leonpermits.org/contractors/. Also search tax collector rolls at http://dta.co.leon.fl.us/tax/default.asp. Marriages are at http://cvweb.clerk.leon.fl.us/index_marriage.html.

Levy County *Real Estate, Lien, Recording, Property Tax, Property Appraiser, Warrant Records*
www.levyclerk.com
Access the Clerk of Circuit Court recording database free at http://levyclerk.com/scripts/LevyClerk.exe?K. Search by name, book/page, file number or document type. Access an index of recorded documents at www.myfloridacounty.com. Fees involved to order copies; save $1.50 per record by becoming a subscriber. Also, search county warrants list for free at www.levyso.com. Also, access to the property appraiser data is free at www.qpublic.net/levy/search.html. Also, search tax collector data free at www.levytaxcollector.com/collectmax/collect30.asp.

Liberty County *Real Estate, Lien, Recording Records*
http://www2.myfloridacounty.com/wps/wcm/connect/libertyclerk
Access an index of recorded documents at www.myfloridacounty.com. Fees involved to order copies; save $1.50 per record by becoming a subscriber.

Madison County *Real Estate, Lien, Recording, Property, Appraiser, Sale Records*
http://www2.myfloridacounty.com/wps/wcm/connect/madisonclerk
Access an index of recorded documents at www.myfloridacounty.com. Fees involved to order copies; save $1.50 per record by becoming a subscriber. Official Records indexes are for past 10 years. Also, access to the property appraiser's property cards and sale databases is free at www.madisonpa.com/GIS/Search_F.asp.

Manatee County *Property Appraiser, Real Estate, Lien, Recording, Deed, Judgment, Death, Marriage, Condominium, Foreclosure Sale, Tax Deed Sale, Most Wanted Records*
www.manateeclerk.com

Several sources exist. Search and view real estate and recordings records free from the Clerk of Circuit Court and Comptroller's database at www.manateeclerk.com. Also, access an index of recorded documents at www.myfloridacounty.com. Fees involved to order copies. Also, Property Appraiser records are free at www.manateepao.com. Tax deed sales at www.clerkofcourts.com/Sales/TaxDeeds/taxdeed.pdf. Also, property tax records are at www.taxcollector.com/dataaccess/design/1owner.asp. Search foreclosure sales at www.manateeclerk.com. Also, search Property/GIS for free at www.emapsplus.com/FLmanatee/maps/.

Marion County *Property Appraiser, Real Estate, Recording, Tax Collector, Tax Deed Sale, Inmate, Sex Offender, Deed, Lien, Judgment, Death, Marriage Records*
www.marioncountyclerk.org

Property appraiser data at www.propappr.marion.fl.us/MCPASCH.HTML. Tax collector data is at http://mariontaxcollector.governmax.com/collectmax/collect30.asp. Also search recorder records free at http://216.255.240.38/wb_or1/or_sch_1.asp. Access an index of recorded documents at www.myfloridacounty.com. Fees involved to order copies; save $1.50 per record by becoming a subscriber. Also, search sheriff's jail inmate data at http://jail.marionso.com/search.asp. Also, access property data via the GIS mapping site at www.marioncountyfl.org/IS251/GISWEB/gis_home.htm. Click on County Interactive map, then the red ?.

Martin County *Property Appraiser, Real Estate, Lien, Recording, Personal Property, GIS Records*
http://ap3server.martin.fl.us:7778/GOVT/

Access to the clerk of the circuit court recordings database are free at http://clerk-web.martin.fl.us/wb%5For1/or_sch_1.asp. Also, search Property/GIS free at www.emapsplus.com/FLmartin/maps/. Also, records on the county property appraiser database are free at http://paoweb.martin.fl.us. Choose from "Online Property Searches." Personal property searches are also available. County tax collector data files are free at http://taxcol.martin.fl.us/ITM/. Also, online access to the state recorders' meta-search site is free at www.myfloridacounty.com.

Monroe County
Real Estate, Recording, Deed, Lien, Property Tax, Occ. License, Arrest, Inmate, Warrant Records
www.co.monroe.fl.us

Access to the clerk of circuit courts database is free at www.clerk-of-the-court.com/searchOfficialRecords.asp. Also, access to property appraiser data is free at www.mcpafl.org/datacenter/mapdisc.asp? Also, search property tax and occupational licenses free at www.monroetaxcollector.com/collectmax/collect30.asp. Also, search warrant lists at http://www2.keysso.net/WebWarrants/WebWarrantsA.htm; arrests at www.keysso.net.

Nassau County *Real Estate, Lien, Recording, Deed, Property Tax, GIS Records*
www.nassauclerk.com

Access an index of recorded documents at www.myfloridacounty.com. Fees involved to order copies; save $1.50 per record by becoming a subscriber. Also, the recorders database is free at www.nassauclerk.org/OfficialRecords/. Also, search Property/GIS free at www.emapsplus.com/FLnassau/maps/.

Okaloosa County
Property Appraiser, Real Estate, Lien, Recording, Vital Statistic, Property Tax, Occ. License Records
www.clerkofcourts.cc

Several databases are available. Access to Okaloosa County online system requires a monthly usage fee of $100. No addresses listed. Lending agency, traffic and domestic records are. For info, contact Don Howard at 850-689-5821. Access clerk's land and official records for free at http://officialrecords.clerkofcourts.cc/; includes marriage, civil, traffic records. Access tax collector data at http://okaloosa.governmax.com/collectmax/search_collect.asp?. Click on Tax Search. Property Appraiser records free at http://qpublic.net/okaloosa/search1.html; sales & sales lists are at www.okaloosapa.com. Also, online access to the state recorders' meta-search site is free at www.myfloridacounty.com.

Okeechobee County
Property, Recording, Appraiser, GIS, Personal Property, Property Sale, Tax Deed, Judgment Records
www.clerk.co.okeechobee.fl.us

Search the statewide recording database via www.myfloridacounty.com. There is a fee to order. Also, search the Clerk of Courts Tax Deed data free at http://204.215.37.218/wb_or1/or_sch_1.asp. Also, access to the property appraiser database is free at www.okeechobeepa.com/GIS/Search_F.asp. Also search property on GIS site at www.emapsplus.com/FLOkeechobee/maps/; click on name search.

Orange County   *Property Appraiser, Recording, Real Estate, Lien, Vital Statistic, Land Sale, Personal Property, Property Tax, Contractor Records*
www.occompt.com
Real Estate, Lien, and Marriage records on the county Comptroller database are free at
http://officialrecords.occompt.com/wb_or1/or_sch_1.asp. Lending Agency data available. Also, private site has previous 2 weeks real estate, marriage, divorce records at http://extra.orlandosentinel.com/publicrecords/search.asp. Also, appraiser property records are free at www.ocpafl.org/docs/disclaimer.html; click on "Record Searches." Also includes search personal property and residential sales records. Search contractor licenses: www.orangecountyfl.net/ebuilding/ContractorSearch/ContractorSearch.asp. Search property/GIS free at www.emapsplus.com/FLorange/maps/.

Osceola County
Real Estate, Property Tax, Appraiser, Occ. License, Inmate, Appraiser, Recording, Deed, GIS Records
www.osceolaclerk.com
Search recorded documents at www.myfloridacounty.com. Fees involved to order copies; save $1.50 per record by becoming a subscriber. Occupation licenses and tax collector data is free www.osceolataxcollector.com/collectmax/collect30.asp? Property appraiser records are free at www.osceolataxcollector.com/collectmax/collect30.asp?sid=E584F1A07F8540DE97C9BCBC22D10842. To purchase database call 407-343-3700. Data also available on CD-ROM. Fees vary; tax roll data is $75. Also, recording/land records at http://osceolarecorder.governmax.com/recordmax/record40.asp. Search Property/GIS free at www.emapsplus.com/FLosceola/maps/. Search inmate list at www.osceola.org/index.cfm?lsFuses=inmates.

Palm Beach County   *Property Appraiser, Real Estate, Deed, Lien, Judgment, Recording, Vital Statistic, Property Tax, Personal Property, Occ License, Warrant, Sexual Predator, Sheriff Booking Records*
www.pbcountyclerk.com
Access clerk's recording database free at www.pbcountyclerk.com/records_home.html. Records go back to 1968; images back to 1968; includes marriage records 1979 to present. Also, search property/GIS free at www.emapsplus.com/FLpalmbeach/maps/. Also, search real estate, property tax, personal property data at www.co.palm-beach.fl.us/tc_pubaccess/default.asp. Access an index of recorded documents at www.myfloridacounty.com. Fees involved to order copies. Also, property appraiser records are free at www.co.palm-beach.fl.us/papa. Search tax deeds at www.pbcountyclerk.com/dt_web2/or_sch_1.asp. Search occupational licenses at www.co.palm-beach.fl.us/tc_pubaccess/occ/occ_search.asp.

Pasco County   *Property Appraiser, Real Estate, Lien, Vital Statistic, Recording, Occ License, Personal Property, Wanted, Sexual Predator, Contractor/Permit Records*
www.pascoclerk.com
Several sources available. Access to real estate, liens, marriage records requires $25 annual fee plus a $50 deposit. Billing rate is $.05 per minute, $.03 evenings. For information, call 352-521-4529. Also, free access to indexes at www.pascoclerk.com. Click on "records." Access an index of recorded documents at www.myfloridacounty.com. Fees involved to order copies. Search sheriff's wanted and sex predators at http://pascosheriff.com. Also, property appraiser data is free at http://appraiser.pascogov.com w/ sales data & maps. Search tax records and occupational licenses at http://taxcollector.pascogov.com/search/prclsearch.asp. Contractors/permit at http://opal.pascocountyfl.net/.

Pinellas County   *Property Appraiser, Real Estate, Lien, Judgment, Recording, Traffic/Boating Fine, Tax Collector, Personal Property, Tax Deed Sale Records*
http://pinellasclerk.org
Assessor/property records are free at http://pao.co.pinellas.fl.us/search2.html. Also, recording records are no longer at http://clerk.co.pinellas.fl.us. Tax deed sales lists are at http://pubtitlet.co.pinellas.fl.us/servlet/taxdeed.saledates.DM79. Search most wanted at www.co.pinellas.fl.us/sheriff/csprofiles.htm. Also, access recorded document index at www.myfloridacounty.com. Fees involved to order copies. Also, search tax collector data free at www.visualgov.com/pinellascounty.

Polk County   *Property Appraiser, Real Estate, Lien, Vital Statistic, Recording, Personal Property, Occ License Account, Tax Collector, Tax Deed Sale, Warrant, Most Wanted Records*
www.polkcountyclerk.net
Search the county clerk database at www.polkcountyclerk.net/RecordsSearch/disclaimer.aspx for free court records, deeds, mortgages, plats, marriages, resolutions. For copies of documents, call 863-534-4524. Fee is $1.00 per page. Also, appraiser property and personal property records are free at www.polkpa.org/Main/Home.aspx. Also, search occupational license accounts at http://198.31.196.18/occupational_search/.

Putnam County
Real Estate, Lien, Recording, Tax Appraiser, Property, GIS, Occ License, Warrant, Jail Log, Most Wanted Records
www.putnam-fl.com/clk/

Access to the county clerk database requires a $400 setup fee and monthly charge of $40 plus $.05 per minute over 20 hours. Includes civil court records and real property records back to 10/1983. For info, call 904-329-0353. Also, access an index of recorded documents at www.myfloridacounty.com. Fees involved to order copies. The sheriff's warrants, jail, most wanted lists are at www.pcso.us. Also, search property data free on GIS site at www.emapsplus.com/FLPutnam/maps/. Also, search the online tax rolls at www.putnam-fl.com/app/disclaimer.htm. No name searching. Also, search the treasurer's tax rolls and occupational licensing at www.putnam-fl.com/txc/onlineinquiry.htm.

St. Johns County   *Property Appraiser, Real Estate, Lien, Recording, Civil, Probate, UCC, Property Tax, Occ. License, Most Wanted, Sex Offender Records*
www.co.st-johns.fl.us
Access to the county Clerk of Circuit Court recording database is free at http://doris.clk.co.st-johns.fl.us/oncoreweb/Search.aspx. Search by name, parcel ID, instrument type. Includes civil and probate records, UCCs. Access an index of recorded documents at www.myfloridacounty.com. Fees involved to order copies; save $1.50 per record by becoming a subscriber. Also, sheriff sex offender and wanted lists are at www.sjso.org/predator/predator.html. Also, search Property/GIS free at www.emapsplus.com/FLstjohns/maps/. Also, access to county property appraiser database is free at www.sjcpa.us/Disclaimer%20for%20as400.htm.

St. Lucie County
Property Appraiser, Real Estate, Lien, Recording, Marriage, Fictitious Name, Personal Property, GIS Records
www.stlucieco.gov
Access to the clerk of circuit courts database of recordings, deeds, liens, mortgages, marriages, fictitious names is free at http://public.slcclerkofcourt.com. Business searching is also available for a small fee. Access an index of recorded documents at www.myfloridacounty.com. Fees involved to order copies. Also search GIS property data free at www.emapsplus.com/FLStLucie/maps/. Also, property appraiser records are free online at www.paslc.org. Click on "Real estate" or "Personal property" to get search options. Also, search property tax rolls for free at http://216.77.1.194/db/taxsearch.asp.

Santa Rosa County   *Property Appraiser, Real Estate, Lien, Deed, Recording, Marriage, Death, Judgment, Tax Collector, Fugitive Records*
http://www2.myfloridacounty.com/wps/wcm/connect/santarosaclerk
Access to the Clerk's index of recorded documents is at http://oncoreweb.srccol.com/oncoreweb/. Or, go to www.myflorida.com where you may search the index free; fees involved to order copies or view images. Also, access to the appraiser property records is free at www.srcpa.org/property.html or at the main Property Appraiser page at www.srcpa.org click on "Record Search." Search for fugitives at www.santarosasheriff.org/fugitives.shtml. Also, search the real estate tax collector data for free at http://santarosataxcollector.governmax.com/collectmax/collect30.asp; occupational licenses at http://santarosataxcollector.governmax.com/collectmax/search_collect.asp?l_nm=occlic_bus_name&sid.

Sarasota County
Real Estate, Lien, Vital Statistic, Recording, Property Appraiser, Personal Property, GIS Records
www.sarasotaclerk.com
Access Clerk of Circuit Court recordings database free at www.sarasotaclerk.com. Includes civil, criminal, and traffic court indexes. Also search indexes at www.sarasotaclerk.com. Search property/GIS data free at www.emapsplus.com/FLsarasota/maps/. Marriage licenses may be searched; probate also available. Access an index of recorded documents at www.myfloridacounty.com. Fees involved to order copies. Also, search tax collector at http://sarasotataxcollector.governmax.com/collectmax/collect30.asp. Also, property appraiser data is free at www.sarasotaproperty.net/scpa_record_search.asp; includes subdivision/condominium sales. Search sheriff arrests back 30 days at www.sarasotasheriff.org/arrests.asp.

Seminole County   *Property Appraiser, Real Estate, Lien, Recording, Marriage, Divorce, GIS Records*
www.seminoleclerk.org
Access the county clerk of circuit court's recordings database free at http://officialrecords.seminoleclerk.org/. Also, search Property/GIS free at www.emapsplus.com/FLseminole/maps/. Property appraisal records free at www.scpafl.org/pls/web/web_main.main. Also a map search. Also, private site has previous 2 weeks real estate, marriage, divorce records at http://extra.orlandosentinel.com/publicrecords/search.asp. Also, search the tax collector personal property and real estate records for free at www.seminoletax.org/TaxSearch.htm. Also, sheriff's felon, offender, and sex offender lists are at www.seminolesheriff.org.

Sumter County   *Real Estate, Lien, Recording, Property Tax, Occ License Records*
www.sumterclerk.com
Access an index of recorded documents at www.myfloridacounty.com. Fees involved to order copies; save $1.50 per record by becoming a subscriber. Also, search tax collector and occupational licenses for free at http://sumtertaxcollector.governmax.com/collectmax/collect30.asp.

Suwannee County
Real Estate, Lien, Deed, Recording, Property Tax, Marriage, GIS, Inmate, Most Wanted Records
www.suwclerk.org
Access of the county clerk of circuit database index is free at www.suwclerk.org/public.html. This directs you to the statewide database; search index free; subscription required for documents. Also, search the tax collector database free at www.suwanneecountytax.com/collectmax/collect30.asp. Also, search property data on th4e GIS-mapping site at www.emapsplus.com/FLSuwannee/maps/. Also, search sheriff's most wanted and inmate lists at www.suwanneesheriff.com.

Taylor County   *Recording, Deed, Lien, Judgment, County Commissioner Records*
http://www2.myfloridacounty.com/wps/wcm/connect/taylorclerk
Access an index of recorded documents at www.myfloridacounty.com. Fees involved to order copies; save $1.50 per record by becoming a subscriber. Also, access to county commission records is free at http://taco.perryfl.com/search.htm. Online records go back to 1988.

Union County   *Real Estate, Lien, Recording, Property, GIS Records*
Access an index of recorded documents at www.myfloridacounty.com. Fees involved to order copies; save $1.50 per record by becoming a subscriber. Also, search the GIS-mapping site for property data for free at www.emapsplus.com/FLUnion/maps/.

Volusia County   *Property Appraiser, Real Estate, Lien, Vital Statistic, Recording, Citation Violation, Arrest, Property Sale, GIS, Inmate, Tax Deed Sale, Court, Personal Property Records*
www.clerk.org/index.html
Recording data is free at www.clerk.org/index.html. Click on Public Records. Recorder indices go back to 3/1996; soon back to 1990. Arrest ledger, tax deed sales and citations also at this website. County also offers full real estate, lien, court and vital records on a commercial site; set up is $100 with $25 monthly. For info, contact clerk. Search the inmate list free at http://volusia.org/corrections/search_page.htm. Access index of recorded documents at www.myfloridacounty.com; see section introduction. Also, search property appraiser database free at http://webserver.vcgov.org/vc_search.html. Also search property/GIS free at www.emapsplus.com/FLVolusia/maps/.

Wakulla County   *Real Estate, Lien, Recording Records*
http://www2.myfloridacounty.com/wps/wcm/connect/wakullaclerk
Access an index of recorded documents at www.myfloridacounty.com. Fees involved to order copies; save $1.50 per record by becoming a subscriber.

Walton County   *Real Estate, Lien, Vital Statistic, Grantor/Grantee, Property Tax Records*
http://clerkofcourts.co.walton.fl.us
Records back to 1/1976 on the County Clerk database are free at clerkofcourts.co.walton.fl.us/ORSearch/. Also, property appraiser records are free at www.qpublic.net/walton/search1.html. Also, search tax collector data free at http://fl-walton-taxcollector.governmaxa.com/collectmax/collect30.asp.

Washington County   *Recording, Deed, Judgment, Lien, Appraiser, Property Tax, Property Sale Records*
Access an index of recorded documents at www.mywashingtoncounty.com. Fees involved to order copies; save $1.50 per record by becoming a subscriber. Also, search the property appraiser sales and tax records for free at www.qpublic.net/washington/index-pa-search.html. Also, search the tax collector records for free at www.qpublic.net/wctc/index-tc-search.html.

Federal Courts in Florida...

Standards for Federal Courts: The universal PACER sign-up number is 800-676-6856. Find PACER and the Party/Case Index on the Web at http://pacer.psc.uscourts.gov. PACER dial-up access is $.60 per minute. Also, courts offering internet access via PACER, Web-PACER or the new CM-ECF charge $.08 per page fee ($.07 per page if record is pre-2005 or unless noted as free).

US District Court -- Middle District of Florida
www.flmd.uscourts.gov
PACER: Case records are available back to 1989-90. Records are purged 3 years after case closed. **PACER Online Access:** ECF replaces PACER. Document images available. **Electronic Filing:** CM/ECF data at https://ecf.flmd.uscourts.gov. **Opinions:** Selected notable opinions only. View court opinions at www.flmd.uscourts.gov. **Other Online Access:** Calendars free at www.flmd.uscourts.gov.
Fort Myers Division counties: Charlotte, Collier, De Soto, Glades, Hendry, Lee.

Jacksonville Div counties: Baker, Bradford, Clay, Columbia, Duval, Flagler, Hamilton, Nassau, Putnam, St. Johns, Suwannee, Union
Ocala Division counties: Citrus, Lake, Marion, Sumter.
Orlando Division counties: Brevard, Orange, Osceola, Seminole, Volusia.
Tampa Division counties: Hardee, Hernando, Hillsborough, Manatee, Pasco, Pinellas, Polk, Sarasota.

US Bankruptcy Court -- Middle District of Florida

www.flmb.uscourts.gov
PACER: Case records are available back to 1981. Records are purged yearly. New records are available online after 1 day. **PACER Online Access:** PACER online at http://pacer.flmb.uscourts.gov. **Electronic Filing:** CM/ECF data at https://ecf.flmb.uscourts.gov. **Opinions:** View court opinions at http://207.41.16.66/cgi/foxweb.exe/dcs-new/dcs. **Other Online Access:** Court now participates in the U.S. party case index. **Phone access:** Voice Case Information System, call 866-879-1286, 904-301-6490
Jacksonville Division counties: Baker, Bradford, Citrus, Clay, Columbia, Duval, Flagler, Hamilton, Marion, Nassau, Putnam, St. Johns, Sumter, Suwannee, Union, Volusia.
Orlando Division counties: Brevard, Lake, Orange, Osceola, Seminole.
Tampa Division counties: Charlotte, Collier, De Soto, Glades, Hardee, Hendry, Hernando, Hillsborough, Lee, Manatee, Pasco, Pinellas, Polk, Sarasota.

US District Court -- Northern District of Florida

www.flnd.uscourts.gov
PACER: Case records are available back to 1992. Records are purged 3 years after case closed. New records are available online after 1 day. **PACER Online Access:** ECF replaces PACER. **Electronic Filing:** CM/ECF data at https://ecf.flnd.uscourts.gov.
Gainesville Division counties: Alachua, Dixie, Gilchrist, Lafayette, Levy. Records for cases prior to 7/1996 are maintained at the Tallahassee Division.
Panama City Division counties: Bay, Calhoun, Gulf, Holmes, Jackson, Washington.
Pensacola Division counties: Escambia, Okaloosa, Santa Rosa, Walton.
Tallahassee Division counties: Franklin, Gadsden, Jefferson, Leon, Liberty, Madison, Taylor, Wakulla.

US Bankruptcy Court -- Northern District of Florida

www.flnb.uscourts.gov
PACER: Sign-up number is 904-435-8475. Case records are available back to 9/1985. Records are purged when case closed. **PACER Online Access:** ECF replaces PACER. **Electronic Filing:** CM/ECF data at https://ecf.flnb.uscourts.gov. **Opinions:** View court opinions at www.flnb.uscourts.gov/webapps/opinion_search/default.aspx. **Other Online Access:** Calendars at www.flnb.uscourts.gov/Calendar/calendar_ack.htm. **Phone access:** Voice Case Information System, call 850-435-8477.
Pensacola Division counties: Escambia, Okaloosa, Santa Rosa, Walton.
Tallahassee Division counties: Alachua, Bay, Calhoun, Dixie, Franklin, Gadsden, Gilchrist, Gulf, Holmes, Jackson, Jefferson, Lafayette, Leon, Levy, Liberty, Madison, Taylor, Wakulla, Washington.

US District Court -- Southern District of Florida

www.flsd.uscourts.gov
PACER: Case records are available back to 8/1990. Records are purged 3 years after case closed. New records are available online after 1 day. **PACER Online Access:** PACER online at http://pacer.flsd.uscourts.gov. Document images available. **Electronic Filing:** ECF to be available soon. CM/ECF data at https://ecf.flsd.uscourts.gov. **Opinions:** View filings and verdicts free at www.flsd.uscourts.gov/default.asp?file=fileverdicts.html.
View court opinions at www.flsd.uscourts.gov/default.asp?file=cases/index.html.
Fort Lauderdale Division counties: Broward.
Fort Pierce Division counties: Highlands, Indian River, Martin, Okeechobee, St. Lucie.
Key West Division counties: Monroe.
Miami Division counties: Dade, Miami-Dade.
West Palm Beach Division counties: Palm Beach. Not open to public - records at Ft Lauderdale Division.

US Bankruptcy Court -- Southern District of Florida

www.flsb.uscourts.gov
PACER: Case records are available back to 1986. Records are purged every 6 months. New records are available online after 1 day. **PACER Online Access:** PACER online at http://pacer.flsb.uscourts.gov. **Electronic Filing:** CM/ECF data at https://ecf.flsb.uscourts.gov. **Opinions:** View court opinions at www.flsb.uscourts.gov/FRAMES/court_opi.pl. **Other Online Access:** Judges calendars at www.flsb.uscourts.gov/FRAMES/judge_cal.pl. **Phone access:** Voice Case Information System, call 800-473-0226, 305-536-5979
Fort Lauderdale Division counties: Broward .
Miami Division counties: Dade, Miami-Dade, Monroe. Select Chapter 13 cases may be assigned to Fort Lauderdale judges.
West Palm Beach Division counties: Highlands, Indian River, Martin, Okeechobee, Palm Beach, St. Lucie.

Georgia

Capital: Atlanta
         Fulton County
Time Zone: EST
Population: 8,829,383
# of Counties: 159

Quick Links

Website: www.georgia.gov
Governor: www.ganet.org/governor/
Attorney General: www.law.state.ga.us
State Archives: www.sos.state.ga.us/archives/
State Statutes and Codes: www.legis.state.ga.us/cgi-bin/gl_codes_detail.pl?code=1-1-1
Legislative Bill Search: www.legis.state.ga.us
Bill Monitoring: www.gatrack.com
Unclaimed Funds: www.state.ga.us/dor/ptd/ucp/

State Level ... Major Agencies

Criminal Records

Georgia Bureau of Investigation, Attn: GCIC, PO Box 370748, Decatur, GA 30037-0748 (Courier: 3121 Panthersville Rd, Decatur, GA 30034); 404-244-2639, Fax-404-244-8417, 8AM-4PM.
www.ganet.org/gbi
Online search: There are three searchable databases found at www.cscj.org/crimjustinfo. They are for parolees, sexual offenders, and inmates. There is no online access to the criminal records database.

Statewide Court Records

Administrative Office of the Courts, 244 Washington St SW, #300, Atlanta, GA 30334-5900; 404-656-5171, Fax-404-651-6449, 8:30AM-5PM.
www.georgiacourts.org
Online search: Supreme Court docket information and opinions are available from the web, but there is no online access available statewide for trial courts, although statewide access is being planned. A certified copy of a Supreme Court Opinion can be purchased online for $5.00 at www2.state.ga.us/Courts/Supreme/main_pp.html.

Sexual Offender Registry

Georgia Bureau of Investigations, GCIC - Sexual Offender Registry, PO Box 370748, Decatur, GA 30037-0748 (Courier: 3121 Panthersville Rd, Decatur, GA 30037); 404-270-8465, 404-244-2600 (24 Hour Line to GBI), Fax-404-270-8452, 8AM-4PM.
http://services.georgia.gov/gbi/gbisor/disclaim.html
Online search: Records may be searched at http://services.georgia.gov/gbi/gbisor/disclaim.html. Earliest records go back to 07/01/96. Searches may be conducted for sex offenders, absconders, and predators.

Incarceration Records

Georgia Department of Corrections, Inmate Records Office - 6th Fl, East Tower, 2 Martin Luther King, Jr. Drive, S.E., Atlanta, GA 30334-4900; 404-656-4569, Fax-404-463-6232, 8AM-4:30PM.

www.dcor.state.ga.us
Online search: The website has an extensive array of search capabilities. Also, a private company offers free web access to DOC records at www.vinelink.com/index.jsp.

Corporation, Limited Partnership, Limited Liability Partnerships, Limited Liability Company Records

Sec of State - Corporation Division, Record Searches, 315 W Tower, #2 ML King Drive, Atlanta, GA 30334-1530; 404-656-2817, 9AM-5PM.
www.sos.state.ga.us/corporations
Online search: Records are available from the corporation database on the Internet site above. The corporate database can be searched by entity name or registered agent for no fee. Document Image and certificates are available for a $10.00 fee at www.ganet.org/services/corp/corpsearch.shtml. Other services include name reservation, filing procedures, downloading of forms/applications.

Trademarks/Servicemarks

Secretary of State, Trademark Division, 2 Martin Luther King, Room 315, W Tower, Atlanta, GA 30334; 404-656-2861, Fax-404-657-6380, 8AM-5PM.
www.sos.state.ga.us/corporations/trademarks.htm
Online search: A record database is searchable from the website at www.sos.state.ga.us/corporations/marksearch.htm. Search by registration #, mark name, description, connection, owner, or classification.

Uniform Commercial Code

Superior Court Clerks' Cooperative Authority, 1875 Century Blvd, #100, Atlanta, GA 30345; 404-327-9058, Fax-404-327-7877, 8:30AM-5PM.
www.gsccca.org
Online search: Online name searching is available free at the website. Also search by secured party, tax payer ID, date, or file number. For certified searches, there is a monthly charge of $9.95 and a $.25 fee per image. Billing is monthly. The system is open 24 hours daily. The website also includes real estate indexes and images, lien index, and notary index. **Other options:** The entire UCC Central Index System can be purchased on a daily, weekly, biweekly basis. For more information, contact the Director's office.

Birth Certificates

Department of Human Resources, Vital Records Unit, 2600 Skyland Dr NE, Atlanta, GA 30319; 404-679-4701, 877-572-6343 (Credit Card Line), Fax-404-679-4730, 8AM-4:45PM.
http://health.state.ga.us/programs/vitalrecords/index.asp
Online search: Records may be ordered online through an approved vendor - www.vitalchek.com. Additional fees apply.

Death Records

Department of Human Resources, Vital Records Unit, 2600 Skyland Dr NE, Atlanta, GA 30319; 404-679-4701, 877-572-6343 (Credit Card Line), Fax-404-679-4730, 8AM-4:45PM.
http://health.state.ga.us/programs/vitalrecords/index.asp
Online search: Records may be ordered online through an approved vendor - www.vitalchek.com. Acredit card fee applies. **Other options:** The death index is available for the years 1919-1998 on microfiche for $50.00.

Driver Records

Department of Driver Services, Driver's Services Section, MVR Unit, PO Box 80447, Conyers, GA 30013 (Courier: 2206 East View Parkway, Conyers, GA 30013); 678-413-8441, 8AM-3:30PM.
www.dds.ga.gov
Online search: Through the coordinated efforts of the GA Department of Motor Vehicle Safety and the Georgia Technology Authority, driving records are now available via the Internet for "certified users, including insurance, employers, and car rental companies. Requesters must complete several applications and user agreement forms. The fees are $5.00 for a three-year record and $7.00 for a seven-year record. For further information, visit: https://online.dmvs.ga.gov/mvr/cert.asp.

Vehicle Ownership, Vehicle Identification

Department of Revenue, Motor Vehicle Division, PO Box 740381, Atlanta, GA 30374-0381; 404-362-6500, Fax-404-362-2729, 8AM-4:30PM.
www.dmvs.ga.gov/motor/
Online search: Online access available only to Georgia dealers; registration is required.

Voter Registration

Secretary of State, Elections Division, 2 Martin Luther King Dr SE, Suite 1104, Atlanta, GA 30334; 404-656-2871, 888-265-1115, Fax-404-651-9531, 8AM-5PM.
www.sos.state.ga.us/elections/
Online search: Name and DOB needed to search registration information at the website. Go to "Poll Locator." The results will provide address and district-precinct information, no SSNs released. **Other options:** CDs, Internet files, disks, and paper lists are available for purchase for non-commercial purposes. Look at the website for pricing.

State Level ... Occupational Licensing

Acupuncturist	www.medicalboard.state.ga.us/bdsearch/index.html
Air Conditioning Contractor	https://secure.sos.state.ga.us/myverification/
Architect	https://secure.sos.state.ga.us/myverification/
Athletic Agent	https://secure.sos.state.ga.us/myverification/
Athletic Trainer	https://secure.sos.state.ga.us/myverification/
Auctioneer/Auction Dealer	https://secure.sos.state.ga.us/myverification/
Audiologist	https://secure.sos.state.ga.us/myverification/
Bank	www.ganet.org/dbf/other_institutions.html
Barber/Barber Shop	https://secure.sos.state.ga.us/myverification/
Charity	www.sos.state.ga.us/securities/charitysearch.htm
Check Casher/Seller	www.ganet.org/dbf/other_institutions.html
Chiropractor	https://secure.sos.state.ga.us/myverification/
Cosmetologist/Cosmetology Shop	https://secure.sos.state.ga.us/myverification/
Counselor	https://secure.sos.state.ga.us/myverification/
Credit Union	www.ganet.org/dbf/other_institutions.html
Dental Hygienist	https://secure.sos.state.ga.us/myverification/
Dentist	https://secure.sos.state.ga.us/myverification/
Detox Specialist	www.medicalboard.state.ga.us/bdsearch/index.html
Dietitian	https://secure.sos.state.ga.us/myverification/
Drug Whlse/Retail/Mfg (Hospital)	https://secure.sos.state.ga.us/myverification/
EDP - Electronic Data Processor	www.ganet.org/dbf/other_institutions.html
Electrical Contractor	https://secure.sos.state.ga.us/myverification/
Embalmer	https://secure.sos.state.ga.us/myverification/
Engineer	https://secure.sos.state.ga.us/myverification/
Esthetician	https://secure.sos.state.ga.us/myverification/
Family Therapist	https://secure.sos.state.ga.us/myverification/
Financial Statement (Ethics Dept.)	www.ethics.state.ga.us/GAEthics/Reports/Financial/Financial_byName.aspx
Forester	https://secure.sos.state.ga.us/myverification/
Funeral Director/Apprentice	https://secure.sos.state.ga.us/myverification/
Funeral Establishment	https://secure.sos.state.ga.us/myverification/
Geologist	https://secure.sos.state.ga.us/myverification/
Hearing Aid Dealer/Dispenser	https://secure.sos.state.ga.us/myverification/
Holding Company/Representative Office	www.ganet.org/dbf/other_institutions.html
Insurance Adjuster	www.gainsurance.org/INSURANCE/AgencyStatus.aspx
Insurance Agent	www.gainsurance.org/INSURANCE/AgentStatus.aspx
Insurance Company	www.gainsurance.org/INSURANCE/SearchCompanies.aspx
Insurance Counselor	www.gainsurance.org/INSURANCE/AgencyStatus.aspx
Interior Designer	https://secure.sos.state.ga.us/myverification/
Landscape Architect	https://secure.sos.state.ga.us/myverification/
Liquor Control	www.ganet.org/alcohol/
Liquor Retailers	www.ganet.org/alcohol/
Lobbyist	www.ethics.state.ga.us/gaethics/Reports/Lobbyist/Lobbyist_byName.aspx
Lobbyist Organization	www.ethics.state.ga.us/gaethics/Reports/Lobbyist/Lobbyist_byGroup.aspx
Low Voltage Contractor	https://secure.sos.state.ga.us/myverification/
Manicurist	https://secure.sos.state.ga.us/myverification/

Marriage Counselor	https://secure.sos.state.ga.us/myverification/
Medical Doctor	www.medicalboard.state.ga.us/bdsearch/index.html
Mortgage Institution	www.ganet.org/dbf/mortgage.html
Nail Care	https://secure.sos.state.ga.us/myverification/
Notary Public	www.gsccca.org/search/notary/search.asp
Nuclear Pharmacist	https://secure.sos.state.ga.us/myverification/
Nurse-LPN/RN	https://secure.sos.state.ga.us/myverification/
Nursing Home Administrator	https://secure.sos.state.ga.us/myverification/
Occupational Therapist/Assistant	https://secure.sos.state.ga.us/myverification/
Optician, Dispensing	https://secure.sos.state.ga.us/myverification/
Optometrist	https://secure.sos.state.ga.us/myverification/
Osteopathic Physician	www.medicalboard.state.ga.us/bdsearch/index.html
Perfusionist	www.medicalboard.state.ga.us/bdsearch/index.html
Pesticide Applicator	www.kellysolutions.com/ga/Applicators/index.htm
Pesticide Contr./Employee	www.kellysolutions.com/ga/Applicators/index.htm
Pharmacist	https://secure.sos.state.ga.us/myverification/
Pharmacy School, Clinic Researcher	https://secure.sos.state.ga.us/myverification/
Physical Therapist/Therapist Asst	https://secure.sos.state.ga.us/myverification/
Physician Assistant	www.medicalboard.state.ga.us/bdsearch/index.html
Plumber Journeyman/Contractor	https://secure.sos.state.ga.us/myverification/
Podiatrist	https://secure.sos.state.ga.us/myverification/
Poison Pharmacist	https://secure.sos.state.ga.us/myverification/
Private Detective	https://secure.sos.state.ga.us/myverification/
Psychologist	https://secure.sos.state.ga.us/myverification/
Public Accountant-CPA	https://secure.sos.state.ga.us/myverification/
Public Adjuster	www.gainsurance.org/INSURANCE/AgencyStatus.aspx
Real Estate Agent/Saller	www.grec.state.ga.us/clsweb/realestate.aspx
Real Estate Appraiser	www.grec.state.ga.us/clsweb/appraiser.aspx
Real Estate Broker	www.grec.state.ga.us/clsweb/realestate.aspx
Real Estate Community Assn. Mgr	www.grec.state.ga.us
Rebuilder (Motor Vehicle)	https://secure.sos.state.ga.us/myverification/
Respiratory Care Practitioner	www.medicalboard.state.ga.us/bdsearch/index.html
Salvage Pool Operator	https://secure.sos.state.ga.us/myverification/
Salvage Yard Dealer	https://secure.sos.state.ga.us/myverification/
School Librarian	https://secure.sos.state.ga.us/myverification/
Security Guard/Agency	https://secure.sos.state.ga.us/myverification/
Social Worker	https://secure.sos.state.ga.us/myverification/
Speech-Language Pathologist	https://secure.sos.state.ga.us/myverification/
Surplus Line Broker	www.gainsurance.org/INSURANCE/AgencyStatus.aspx
Surveyor, Land	https://secure.sos.state.ga.us/myverification/
Teacher	https://www.gapsc.com/certification/lookup.asp
Used Car Dealer	https://secure.sos.state.ga.us/myverification/
Used Car Parts Dist.	https://secure.sos.state.ga.us/myverification/
Utility Contractor	https://secure.sos.state.ga.us/myverification/
Veterinarian/Veterinary Technician	https://secure.sos.state.ga.us/myverification/
Waste Water Lab Analyst	https://secure.sos.state.ga.us/myverification/
Waste Water Operator	https://secure.sos.state.ga.us/myverification/
Waste Water System Operator	https://secure.sos.state.ga.us/myverification/
Water Distribution System Operator	https://secure.sos.state.ga.us/myverification/
Water Laboratory Operator	https://secure.sos.state.ga.us/myverification/
Water Operator Class 1-4	https://secure.sos.state.ga.us/myverification/

County Level ... Courts

Court Administration: Court Administrator, 244 Washington St SW, Suite 550, Atlanta, GA, 30334; 404-656-5171; www.georgiacourts.org/aoc/index.html

Court Structure: Georgia's Superior Courts are arranged in 49 circuits of general jurisdiction, and these also assume the role of a State Court if the county does not have one. The 69 State Courts, like Superior Courts, can conduct jury trials, but are limited jurisidiction. Each county has a Probate Court, a Juvenile Court, and a Magistrate Court. The latter has jurisdiction over civil actions under $15,000, also one type of misdemeanor related to passing bad checks.

Magistrate Courts also issue arrest warrants and set bond on all felonies. Magistrate Courts also have jurisdiction for bad checks, arrest warrants, preliminary hearings, and county ordinance violations. Probate Courts can, in certain cases, issue search and arrest warrants, and hear miscellaneous misdemeanors.

Online Access Note: Supreme Court docket information and opinions are available from the web. A certified copy of a Supreme Court Opinion can be purchased online for $5.00 at www2.state.ga.us/Courts/Supreme/main_pp.html. A limited number of county courts offer Internet access to court records, but there is no online access available statewide, although statewide access is being planned.

Bibb County

Superior Court – Civil and Criminal Records
www.co.bibb.ga.us/
Superior court calendars at www.co.bibb.ga.us/CalendarDirectory/CalendarDirectory.asp.

State Court – Civil Records
www.co.bibb.ga.us
Search civil court calendars online at www.co.bibb.ga.us/StateCourtClerk/Civil/Default.htm. Website will have access to full court record indexes in the future.

Chatham County

Superior Court – Civil and Criminal Records
www.chathamcourts.org/chatcourts.html
Search county court records at www.chathamcounty.org/jims/.

State Court – Civil and Criminal Records
www.statecourt.org
Search county dockets and records free at www.chathamcounty.org/jims/. Search by name or case number.

Clayton County

Superior Court – Civil and Criminal Calendars
Court calendars are online at www.co.clayton.ga.us/courtcalendars/index.htm.

Cherokee County

Magistrate Court – Civil Records
www.cccourt.com
Search the magistrate court database online at www.cccourt.com.

Cobb County

Superior Court – Civil and Criminal Records
www.cobbgasupctclk.com/index.htm
Civil or criminal indexes of Clerk of Superior Court are free at www.cobbgasupctclk.com/index.htm. Search by name, type or case number. Data updated Fridays.

De Kalb County

Superior Court – Civil and Criminal Records
www.co.dekalb.ga.us/superior/index.htm

Access is free at www.ojs.dekalbga.org. Jail and inmate records are also available.

State Court – Civil and Criminal Records
www.dekalbstatecourt.net
Access is free at www.ojs.dekalbga.org. Also, current court calendars free at www.dekalbstatecourt.net. Jail and inmate records also available.

Magistrate Court – Civil Records
http://dekalbstatecourt.net
Access is free at www.ojs.dekalbga.org.

Dougherty County

Superior & State Court – Civil, Probate, and Criminal Records
www.albany.ga.us/court_system/court_system.htm
Access pre-2003 civil and criminal court docket data free at www.albany.ga.us/court_system/court_clerk.htm. The same system permits access to probate, tax, deeds, death certificate records, and older civil/criminal records.

Magistrate Court – Civil Records
Access court records through the county clerk's system at www.albany.ga.us/court_system/court_clerk.htm. Records are pre-7/2002.

Gwinnett County

Superior & State Court – Civil and Criminal Records
www.gwinnettcourts.com/courts/Supcourt.htm
Access to court case party index is free at www.gwinnettcourts.com/misc/casendx.htm. Search by name or case number.

Magistrate Court – Civil Records
www.gwinnettcourts.com/courts/Magcourt.htm
Access to court case party index is free at www.gwinnettcourts.com/misc/casendx.htm.

Probate Court – Civil Records
www.gwinnettcourts.com/courts/Procourt.htm
Search Probate records by name free at www.gwinnettcourts.com/courts/Procourt.htm; click on "Data Search.".

Richmond County

Superior Court – Civil and Criminal Records
www.augustaga.gov/departments/clerk%5Fsup/
Access court dockets free at www.augustaga.gov/departments/clerk%5Fsup/disclaimer.asp for records 2001 forward.

State Court – Civil Records
www.augustaga.gov
Name search at www.augustaga.gov/WebDocket/.

County Level ... Recorders & Assessors

Recording Office Organization: 159 counties, 159 recording offices. The recording officer is the Clerk of Superior Court. All transactions are recorded in a "General Execution Docket." The entire state is in the Eastern Time Zone (EST). All tax liens on personal property are filed with the county Clerk of Superior Court in a "General Execution Docket" (grantor/grantee) or "Lien Index." Most counties will not perform tax lien searches. Copy fees are the same as for UCC.

Online Access Note: The Georgia Superior Court Clerk's Cooperative Authority (GSCCCA) at www.gsccca.org/search offers free access to three state indices. The Real Estate Index contains property transactions from all counties since January 1, 1999. The Lien Index includes liens filed on real and personal property. Throughput varies, but is generally from January 10, 2002. The UCC Index contains financing statement data from all counties since January, 1995 and can be searched by name, taxpayer ID, file date and file number. Additionally, the actual image of the corresponding UCC statement can be downloaded for a fee. Visit the GSCCCA website for details.

All Georgia Counties *RE Deed, Lien, UCC Records*

See www.gsccca.org for Deed, Lien and UCC indexes. Also, some counties offer plats on this system.

Bibb County *RE Deed, UCC, Property, Lien, Finance Statement, Property Tax, Ownership, Inmate Records*
See www.gsccca.org for Deed and UCC indexes. Also, search land, financing statements and liens on the Superior Court clerk search page for free at http://68.109.200.12/resolution. Also, search the assessors' property tax records for free at www.qpublic.net/bibb/digest_search1.html. Also, search for property ownership for free at www.co.bibb.ga.us/engineering/property/search.htm. Also, search property info at www.co.bibb.ga.us/gisonline/advancedsearch.asp and Ad Valorem tax statements at www.co.bibb.ga.us/TaxBills/Searchpage.asp; inmates at www.co.bibb.ga.us/BSOInmatesOnline/BSOSearchPage.asp

Chatham County *RE Deed, Lien, UCC, Assessor Records*
www.chathamcourts.org
See www.gsccca.org for Deed, Lien and UCC indexes. Search the assessor database at www.chathamcounty.org/prc.html.

Cherokee County *Grantor/Grantee, Lien, RE Deed, UCC, Sex Offender, Inmate Records*
www.cherokeega.com
See www.gsccca.org for Deed and UCC indexes. Also, access recording records free at http://deeds.cherokeega.com/Search.aspx. Also, search the sheriff's sex offender list at www.cherokeega-sheriff.org/offender/offender.htm. Also, search inmate info on private company website at www.vinelink.com/index.jsp.

Clarke County *RE Deed, UCC, Property Records*
See www.gsccca.org for Deed and UCC indexes. Also, you may view property information for free at https://athens-clarke.ga.ezgov.com/ezproperty/review_search.jsp; however, there is no name searching.

Clayton County *Real Estate, UCC, Lien, Property Tax Records*
www.co.clayton.ga.us/superior_court/clerk_of_courts/
See www.gsccca.org for Deed, Lien and UCC indexes. Also, search tax assessor records for free at www.qpublic.net/clayton/search.html.

Cobb County *Real Estate, Grantor/Grantee, UCC, Deed, Property Tax Records*
www.cobbgasupctclk.com
Property records on the County Superior Court Clerk website are free at www.cobbgasupctclk.com/index.htm. Search by name, address, land description, instrument type, or book & page. You may also search court records. Also, see www.gsccca.org for online access to Deed and UCC indexes. Also, search property tax records for free at www.cobbtax.org/Search/GenericSearch.aspx?mode=PARID. No name searching.

Columbia County *RE Deed, UCC, Lien, Sex Offender Records*
See www.gsccca.org for Deed, Lien and UCC indexes. Also, search the registered sex offender list at www.columbiacountyga.gov/home/index.asp?page=2391.

Dawson County *RE Deed, UCC, Lien, Property, Assessor, Property Sale Records*
See www.gsccca.org for Deed, Lien and UCC indexes. Also, search the assessor property information and sales for free at www.qpublic.net/ga/dawson/search1.html.

De Kalb County
RE Deed, UCC, Property Tax, Judgments, Most Wanted, Missing, Inmate, court cases Records
See www.gsccca.org for Deed and UCC indexes. Also, search tax commissioner property tax data for free at https://dklbweb.dekalbga.org/taxcommissioner/PropertyTaxMain2.htm. Click on "Make/View Property Tax Payment." No name searching. Also, search the civil and criminal cases, most wanted, registered sex offender list, missing children, and jail inmates at www.ojs.dekalbga.org.

Dougherty County
Real Estate, Tax, Court, Deed, Mortgage, Tax Assessor, UCC, Death, Divorce, Trade Name Records
www.albany.ga.us
Access to the clerk of courts Dept. of Deeds public menu is at www.albany.ga.us/court_system/court_clerk.htm. Click on "clerk of courts public records system page." Also, search the tax records system and sales lists free at www.qpublic.net/ga/dougherty/search1.html. Also, see www.gsccca.org for online access to Deed and UCC indexes.

Fayette County *Assessor, Real Estate, UCC, Lien Records*
www.admin.co.fayette.ga.us
Records on the County Assessor database are free on the GIS-mapping site at www.fayettecountymaps.com/disclaimer.htm. See www.gsccca.org for Deed and UCC indexes.

Forsyth County *RE Deed, Lien, UCC, Tax Assessor, Tax Digest Records*
www.forsythco.com
See www.gsccca.org for Deed, Lien and UCC indexes. Also, search the county tax digest pdf file free at www.forsythco.com/DeptPage.asp?DeptID=26&PageID=691.

Fulton County *RE Deed, Lien, UCC, Property Tax, Assessor, Delinquent Tax, Inmate Records*
www.fcclk.org
See www.gsccca.org for Deed, Lien and UCC indexes. Also, search assessor property data free at www.fultonassessor.org click on Property Search, but no name searching at this time. Also, search for property tax bills at https://www.fultoncountytaxes.org/fultoniwr/11a_depts_property_taxes.asp but no name searching. Also, search sheriff's jail inmate database free at www.fultonsheriff.org click on Inmate Information. Also, search tax commissioner's delinquent property pdf lists by district at https://www.fultoncountytaxes.org/fultoniwr/Delinquent_Properties.htm.

Glynn County *Assessor, Property, Recording, UCC, Lien Records*
Access the county assessor property tax records free on the GIS mapping website at http://glynn.binarybus.com. See www.gsccca.org for online access to Deed, Lien and UCC indexes.

Gwinnett County *Property, Deed, UCC, Plats, Judgment, Lien Records*
www.gwinnettcourts.com
See www.gsccca.org for Deed, Plat and UCC indexes. Deed records go back to 1870; UCCs to1995. Also, search for civil court judgments at www.gwinnettcourts.com/misc/casendx.htm.

Habersham County *RE Deed, UCC, Lien, Property, Assesor, GIS Records*
www.co.habersham.ga.us
See www.gsccca.org for Deed, Lien and UCC indexes. Also search property/GIS data free at www.emapsplus.com/GAHabersham/maps/. Click on Owner to name search.

Henry County *RE Deed, UCC, Property Tax, Assessor Records*
www.co.henry.ga.us
See www.gsccca.org for Deed, Lien and UCC indexes. Also, search property tax data free at https://hcwebb.boca.co.henry.ga.us/Henry_Tax/form.asp Also search tax assessor records for free at https://hcwebb.boca.co.henry.ga.us/Henry_Tax/index.html

Houston County *Assessor, RE, Plat, Lien Records*
www.houstoncountyga.com
Access to the assessor's Mapguide database is free at www.assessors.houstoncountyga.org. Download the Autodesk MapGuide viewer. Also, the clerks recording indices of plats, land records, liens is free at http://67.32.12.213/resolution/. Pre-1998 real estate and pre-1994 financing statements are also available. See www.gsccca.org for online access to Deed, Lien and UCC indexes.

McIntosh County *Deed (2000-present), UCC, Notary, Lien Records*
Call 800-304-5175 to subscribe to UCCs and Deed indexes online service. See www.gsccca.org for online access to Deed, Lien and UCC indexes.

Oglethorpe County *Real Estate, Deed, UCC Records*
County clerk UCC and real estate records available by monthly subscription; fee- $9.95 plus $.25 per printed page. Guest accounts available. For info and to open an account, call 404-327-9058. Also, see www.gsccca.org for online access to Deed, Lien and UCC indexes.

Whitfield County *Assessor, Property Tax, RE Deed, Lien, UCC, Sex Offender Records*
See www.gsccca.org for Deed, Lien and UCC indexes. Also, access to property tax data is available free at www.whitfieldcountyga.com/GIS/Public/searchassessor.asp. A subscription service is also available for professions who require full property data. Also, a sex offender search is online at www.whitfieldcountyga.com/wcso/searchsexoffender.asp.

Federal Courts in Georgia...

Standards for Federal Courts: The universal PACER sign-up number is 800-676-6856. Find PACER and the Party/Case Index on the Web at http://pacer.psc.uscourts.gov. PACER dial-up access is $.60 per minute. Also, courts offering internet access via PACER, Web-PACER or the new CM-ECF charge $.08 per page fee ($.07 per page if record is pre-2005 or unless noted as free).

US District Court -- Middle District of Georgia

www.gamd.uscourts.gov

PACER: Case records are available back to 1/1991. Records are purged never. New records are available online after 1 day. **PACER Online Access:** ECF replaces PACER. **Electronic Filing:** CM/ECF data at https://ecf.gamd.uscourts.gov.
Albany/Americus Division counties: Baker, Ben Hill, Calhoun, Crisp, Dougherty, Early, Lee, Miller, Mitchell, Schley, Sumter, Terrell, Turner, Webster, Worth. Ben Hill and Crisp were transferred from the Macon Division as of 10/1997.
Athens Division counties: Clarke, Elbert, Franklin, Greene, Hart, Madison, Morgan, Oconee, Oglethorpe, Walton. Closed cases before 4/1997 are located in the Macon Division.
Columbus Division counties: Chattahoochee, Clay, Harris, Marion, Muscogee, Quitman, Randolph, Stewart, Talbot, Taylor.
Macon Division counties: Baldwin, Ben Hill, Bibb, Bleckley, Butts, Crawford, Crisp, Dooly, Hancock, Houston, Jasper, Jones, Lamar, Macon, Monroe, Peach, Pulaski, Putnam, Twiggs, Upson, Washington, Wilcox, Wilkinson. Athens Division cases closed before 4/1997 are also located here. .
Thomasville Division counties: Brooks, Colquitt, Decatur, Grady, Seminole, Thomas. No criminal cases can be searched at this court, but trials held at Valdosta; see Macon Division for records.
Valdosta Division counties: Berrien, Clinch, Cook, Echols, Irwin, Lanier, Lowndes, Tift. No criminal cases can be searched at this court, but trials held at Valdosta; see Macon Division for records.

US Bankruptcy Court -- Middle District of Georgia

www.gamb.uscourts.gov

PACER: Case records are available back to 3/1990, some back to 1985. Records are purged every 12 months. New records are available online after 1 day. **PACER Online Access:** PACER online at http://pacer.gamb.uscourts.gov. **Electronic Filing:** May not be complete, as yet; read disclaimer at ECF site. CM/ECF data at https://ecf.gamb.uscourts.gov. **Opinions:** View court opinions at www.gamb.uscourts.gov/opinions.htm. **Other Online Access:** Calendars free at www.gamb.uscourts.gov/cgi-bin/crtcals.cgi. **Phone access:** Voice Case Information System, call 800-211-3015, 912-752-8183
Columbus Division counties: Berrien, Brooks, Chattahoochee, Clay, Clinch, Colquitt, Cook, Decatur, Echols, Grady, Harris, Irwin, Lanier, Lowndes, Marion, Muscogee, Quitman, Randolph, Seminole, Stewart, Talbot, Taylor, Thomas, Tift. This court has records for the Thomasville and Valdosta branches, also Chapter 11 & 12 records for the Albany branch.
Macon Division counties: Baldwin, Baker, Ben Hill, Bibb, Bleckley, Butts, Calhoun, Clarke, Crawford, Crisp, Dooly, Dougherty, Early, Elbert, Franklin, Greene, Hancock, Hart, Houston, Jasper, Jones, Lamar, Lee, Macon, Madison, Miller, Mitchell, Monroe, Morgan, Oconee, Oglethorpe, Peach, Pulaski, Putnam, Schley, Sumter, Terrell, Turner, Twiggs, Upson, Walton, Washington, Webster, Wilcox, Wilkinson, Worth. This court has records for the Athens branch as well as Chapter 7 & 13 records from the Albany branch. This branch also has criminal records for Valdosta and Thomasville Divisions.

US District Court -- Northern District of Georgia

www.gand.uscourts.gov

PACER: Case records are available back to 8/1992. Records are purged schedule varies. New records are available online after 1 day. **PACER Online Access:** ECF replaces PACER. Document images available. **Electronic Filing:** CM/ECF data at https://ecf.gand.uscourts.gov.
Atlanta Division counties: Cherokee, Clayton, Cobb, De Kalb, Douglas, Fulton, Gwinnett, Henry, Newton, Rockdale.
Gainesville Division counties: Banks, Barrow, Dawson, Fannin, Forsyth, Gilmer, Habersham, Hall, Jackson, Lumpkin, Pickens, Rabun, Stephens, Towns, Union, White.
Newnan Division counties: Carroll, Coweta, Fayette, Haralson, Heard, Meriwether, Pike, Spalding, Troup.
Rome Division counties: Bartow, Catoosa, Chattooga, Dade, Floyd, Gordon, Murray, Paulding, Polk, Walker, Whitfield.

US Bankruptcy Court -- Northern District of Georgia

www.ganb.uscourts.gov

PACER: Case records are available back to 8/1986. Records are purged never. New records are available online after 1 day. **PACER Online Access:** ECF replaces PACER. **Electronic Filing:** CM/ECF data at http://ecf.ganb.uscourts.gov. **Opinions:** View court opinions at www.ganb.uscourts.gov/judges/opn/opn_index.php. **Phone access:** Voice Case Information System, call 800-510-8284, 404-730-2866
Atlanta Division counties: Cherokee, Clayton, Cobb, DeKalb, Douglas, Fulton, Gwinnett, Henry, Newton, Rockdale.

Gainesville Division counties: Banks, Barrow, Dawson, Fannin, Forsyth, Gilmer, Habersham, Hall, Jackson, Lumpkin, Pickens, Rabun, Stephens, Towns, Union, White.
Newnan Division counties: Carroll, Coweta, Fayette, Haralson, Heard, Meriwether, Pike, Spalding, Troup.
Rome Division counties: Bartow, Catoosa, Chattooga, Dade, Floyd, Gordon, Murray, Paulding, Polk, Walker, Whitfield.

US District Court -- Southern District of Georgia

www.gasd.uscourts.gov

PACER: Case records are available back to 6/1995. New records are available online after 1 day. **PACER Online Access:** ECF replaces PACER. Document images available. **Electronic Filing:** CM/ECF data at https://ecf.gasd.uscourts.gov. **Other Online Access:** Opinions and calendars on PACER.
Augusta Division counties: Burke, Columbia, Dodge, Glascock, Jefferson, Johnson, Laurens, Lincoln, McDuffie, Montgomery, Richmond, Taliaferro, Telfair, Treutlen, Warren, Wheeler, Wilkes.
Brunswick Division counties: Appling, Camden, Glynn, Jeff Davis, Long, McIntosh, Wayne.
Savannah Division counties: Atkinson, Bacon, Bulloch, Brantley, Bryan, Candler, Charlton, Chatham, Coffee, Effingham, Emanuel, Evans, Jenkins, Liberty, Pierce, Screven, Tattnall, Toombs, Ware. Holds records for unstaffed Statesboro and Waycross Divisions. .

US Bankruptcy Court -- Southern District of Georgia

www.gas.uscourts.gov

PACER: Case records are available back to 8/1986. Records are purged yearly. **PACER Online Access:** ECF replaces PACER and RACER. Document images available. **Electronic Filing:** CM/ECF data at https://ecf.gasb.uscourts.gov. **Opinions:** View court opinions at http://207.41.17.136/bkcyorders/dtSearch.html. **Other Online Access:** Participates in the U.S. party case index. Search calendars at www.gasb.uscourts.gov/usbc/usbc.html click on Calendars.
Augusta Division counties: Bulloch, Burke, Candler, Columbia, Dodge, Emanuel, Evans, Glascock, Jefferson, Jenkins, Johnson, Laurens, Lincoln, McDuffie, Montgomery, Richmond, Screven, Taliaferro, Tattnall, Telfair, Toombs, Treutlen, Warren, Wheeler, Wilkes.
Savannah Division counties: Appling, Atkinson, Bacon, Brantley, Bryan, Camden, Charlton, Chatham, Coffee, Effingham, Glynn, Jeff Davis, Liberty, Long, McIntosh, Pierce, Ware, Wayne.

Hawaii

Capital: Honolulu
              Honolulu County
Time Zone: HT
Population: 1,262,840
# of Counties: 4

Quick Links

Website: www.hawaii.gov/portal/
Governor: www.hawaii.gov/gov/
Attorney General: www.hawaii.gov/ag/
State Archives: www.hawaii.gov/dags/divisions/archives_division
State Statutes and Codes: www.capitol.hawaii.gov/site1/docs/docs.asp?press1=docs
Legislative Bill Search: www.capitol.hawaii.gov/site1/docs/docs.asp?press1=docs
Unclaimed Funds: http://pahoehoe.ehawaii.gov/lilo/app

State Level ... Major Agencies

Criminal Records

Hawaii Criminal Justice Data Ctr, Criminal Record Request, 465 S King St, Room 101, Honolulu, HI 96813; 808-587-3106, 8-4PM.
http://hawaii.gov/ag/hcjdc/
Online search: Online access is available view eCrim at http://ecrim.ehawaii.gov/ahewa/. View the results of your search and have the option of purchasing a certified copy of the record. Registration is required. Questions are directed to 808-587-4220.

Statewide Court Records

Administrative Director of Courts, 417 S. King St, Honolulu, HI 96813; 808-539-4900, 808-539-4909 (Public Affairs Office), Fax-808-539-4855, 7:45AM-4:30PM.
www.courts.state.hi.us/index.jsp
Online search: Free online access to Circuit Court and Family Court records is available at www.courts.state.hi.us/index.jsp. Search by name or case number. These records are not considered "official" for FCRA compliant searches. The system is open daily - 3:30 a.m. to 12:00 midnight, Hawaii Standard Time. Also, opinions from the appellate court are available from the home web page site.

Sexual Offender Registry

Hawaii Criminal Justice Data Center, Sexual Offender Registry, 465 S King St, Room 101, Honolulu, HI 96813; 808-587-3106.
http://sexoffenders.hawaii.gov/index.html
Online search: Search at http://sexoffenders.hawaii.gov/search.jsp?. Search by name or ZIP Code.

Corporation, Trade Name, Assumed Name, Trademarks/Servicemarks, Limited Liability Company, Limited Liability Partnerships, Limited Partnership,

Business Registration Division, PO Box 40, Honolulu, HI 96810 (Courier: 335 Merchant St, 2nd Fl, Honolulu, HI 96813); 808-586-2727, 808-587-4220 (eHawaiiGov), Fax-808-586-2733, 7:45AM-4:30PM.
www.hawaii.gov/dcca/areas/breg

Online search: Online access to business names is available at www.ehawaii.gov/dcca/bizsearch/exe/bizsearch.cgi. There are no fees, the system is open 24 hours. For assistance during business hours, call 808-586-2727. Tax license searching is available free at http://pahoehoe.ehawaii.gov/tls/app. Search by name, ID number of DBA name. **Other options:** Bulk data can be purchased online through ehawaiigov.com. Visit the website or call 808-587-4220 for more information.

Uniform Commercial Code, Federal & State Tax Liens, Real Estate Recordings

UCC Division, Bureau of Conveyances, PO Box 2867, Honolulu, HI 96803 (Courier: Dept. of Land & Natural Resources, 1151 Punchbowl St, Honolulu, HI 96813); 808-587-0154, Fax-808-587-4380, 7:45AM-4:30PM.
www.hawaii.gov/dlnr/bc/bc.html
Online search: Search the indices from 1976 forward at http://bocweb.dlnrbc.hawaii.gov/boc/. Search by grantor, grantee, business name. Includes real estate recordings.

Birth, Marriage Certificates

State Department of Health, Vital Records Section, PO Box 3378, Honolulu, HI 96801 (Courier: 1250 Punchbowl St, Room 103, Honolulu, HI 96813); 808-586-4533, 7:45AM-2:30PM.
www.hawaii.gov/health/vital-records/
Online search: Records may requested from https://www.ehawaiigov.org/doh/vitrec/html/down.html. The records are returned by mail or by express delivery if paid for.

Driver Records

Traffic Violations Bureau, Abstract Section, 1111 Alakea St, 2nd Fl, Honolulu, HI 96813; 808-538-5530, 808-961-7470 (Hawaii Court), 808-244-2800 (Maui Court), 808-246-3330 (Kauai Court), Fax-808-538-5520, 7:45AM-9:PM.
www.hawaii.gov/dot/highways/
Online search: Online ordering by DPPA complaint requesters is available from the state-designated entity - Hawaii Information Consortium (HIC). The record fee is $9.00 per record, plus a $75.00 annual subscription fee is required. Record requests are accepted via FTP. Results, if clear, are returned via FTP. Results with hits on convictions on the record are returned on paper. Visit their website at http://pahoehoe.ehawaii.gov/portal/subscriber.html or call HIC at 808-587-4220 for more information. Note that the free online access described in the Statewide Court Records heading above gives the researcher the option to view motor vehicle tickets. **Other options:** Magnetic tape ordering is available in Hawaii for frequent or large orders. The fee is $9.00 per request. Turnaround time is 48 hours. Call HIC at 808-587-4220 for details.

State Level ... Occupational Licensing

Acupuncturist	www.ehawaiigov.org/serv/pvl
Architect	www.ehawaiigov.org/serv/pvl
Auction	http://pvl.ehawaii.gov/pvlsearch/app
Bank/Bank Agencies/Offices	www.hawaii.gov/dcca/areas/dfi/regulate/regulate/
Barber Shop/Barber/Barber Apprentice	www.ehawaiigov.org/serv/pvl
Beauty Instructor	www.ehawaiigov.org/serv/pvl
Beauty Operator/School/Shop	www.ehawaiigov.org/serv/pvl
Cemetery	http://pvl.ehawaii.gov/pvlsearch/app
Certified Public Accountant - CPA	www.ehawaiigov.org/serv/pvl
Chiropractor	www.ehawaiigov.org/serv/pvl
Collection Agency	http://pvl.ehawaii.gov/pvlsearch/app
Condominium Hotel Operator/Agent	www.ehawaiigov.org/serv/pvl
Contractor	www.ehawaiigov.org/serv/pvl
Credit Union	www.hawaii.gov/dcca/areas/dfi/regulate/regulate/
Dental Hygienist	www.ehawaiigov.org/serv/pvl
Dentist	http://pvl.ehawaii.gov/pvlsearch/app
Drug (Prescription) Dist./Whlse	www.ehawaiigov.org/serv/pvl
Elected Officials Financial Disclosure	www.state.hi.us/ethics/noindex/pubrec.htm
Electrician	www.ehawaiigov.org/serv/pvl

Electrologist .... http://pvl.ehawaii.gov/pvlsearch/app
Elevator Mechanic .... www.ehawaiigov.org/serv/pvl
Emergency Medical Personnel.................... www.ehawaiigov.org/serv/pvl
Employment Agency .... http://pvl.ehawaii.gov/pvlsearch/app
Engineer.. www.ehawaiigov.org/serv/pvl
Escrow Company.. www.hawaii.gov/dcca/areas/dfi/regulate/regulate/
Financial Services Loan Company.............. www.hawaii.gov/dcca/areas/dfi/regulate/regulate/
Hearing Aid Dealer/Fitter .... www.ehawaiigov.org/serv/pvl
Insurance Adjuster .... www.ehawaiigov.org/serv/hils
Insurance Agent/Producer/Solicitor .... www.ehawaiigov.org/serv/hils
Landscape Architect.................................... www.ehawaiigov.org/serv/pvl
Lobbyist.. www.state.hi.us/ethics/noindex/pubrec.htm
Marriage & Family Therapist .... http://pvl.ehawaii.gov/pvlsearch/app
Massage Therapist/Establishment............... http://pvl.ehawaii.gov/pvlsearch/app
Mechanic .... http://pvl.ehawaii.gov/pvlsearch/app
Medical Doctor .... www.ehawaiigov.org/serv/pvl
Mortgage Broker/Solicitor .... http://pvl.ehawaii.gov/pvlsearch/app
Motor Vehicle Dealer/Broker/Seller .... http://pvl.ehawaii.gov/pvlsearch/app
Motor Vehicle Repair Dealer...................... http://pvl.ehawaii.gov/pvlsearch/app
Naturopathic Physician .... www.ehawaiigov.org/serv/pvl
Nurse... www.ehawaiigov.org/serv/pvl
Nursing Home Administrator...................... www.ehawaiigov.org/serv/pvl
Occupational Therapist .... www.ehawaiigov.org/serv/pvl
Optician, Dispensing................................... www.ehawaiigov.org/serv/pvl
Optometrist .... www.ehawaiigov.org/serv/pvl
Osteopathic Physician................................. www.ehawaiigov.org/serv/pvl
Pest Control Field Rep./Operator................ http://pvl.ehawaii.gov/pvlsearch/app
Pharmacist/Pharmacy................................. www.ehawaiigov.org/serv/pvl
Physical Therapist...................................... www.ehawaiigov.org/serv/pvl
Physician Assistant .... www.ehawaiigov.org/serv/pvl
Pilot, Port .... http://pvl.ehawaii.gov/pvlsearch/app
Plumber.. www.ehawaiigov.org/serv/pvl
Podiatrist.. www.ehawaiigov.org/serv/pvl
Private Detective.. www.ehawaiigov.org/serv/pvl
Private Detective/Investigation Agency...... www.ehawaiigov.org/serv/pvl
Psychologist... www.ehawaiigov.org/serv/pvl
Public Accountant - PA .... www.ehawaiigov.org/serv/pvl
Real Estate Agent/Broker/Sales .... www.ehawaiigov.org/serv/pvl
Real Estate Appraiser................................. www.ehawaiigov.org/serv/pvl
Savings Bank/Savings & Loan Assoc......... www.hawaii.gov/dcca/areas/dfi/regulate/regulate/
Security Guard/Agency............................... www.ehawaiigov.org/serv/pvl
Social Worker .... http://pvl.ehawaii.gov/pvlsearch/app
Speech Pathologist/Audiologist .... www.ehawaiigov.org/serv/pvl
Surveyor, Land .... www.ehawaiigov.org/serv/pvl
Timeshare .... http://pvl.ehawaii.gov/pvlsearch/app
Travel Agency .... http://pvl.ehawaii.gov/pvlsearch/app
Trust Company .... www.hawaii.gov/dcca/areas/dfi/regulate/regulate/
Veterinarian .... www.ehawaiigov.org/serv/pvl

County Level ... Courts

Court Administration: Administrative Director of Courts, Judicial Branch, 417 S King St, Honolulu, HI, 96813; 808-539-4900; www.courts.state.hi.us

Court Structure: Hawaii's trial level is comprised of Circuit Courts (includes Family Courts) and District Courts. These trial courts function in four judicial circuits: First (Oahu), Second (Maui-Molokai-Lanai), Third (Hawaii County), and Fifth (Kauai-Niihau). The Fourth Circuit merged with the Third in 1943.

Circuit Courts are general jurisdiction and handle all jury trials, felony cases, and civil cases over $20,000, also probate and guardianship. The District Court handles criminal cases punishable by a fine and/or less than one year imprisonment and some civil cases up to $20,000, also landlord/tenant and DUI cases.

Online Access Note: Free online access to all Circuit Court and Family Court records, and civil records from the District Courts, is available at www.courts.state.hi.us (click on "Search Court Records"). Search by name or case number. These records are not considered "official" for FCRA compliant searches. Most courts have access back to mid 1980s. Also, opinions from the Appellate Court are available at www.courts.state.hi.us/index.jsp. Click on "Opinions."

Hawaii County

3rd Circuit Court Legal Documents Section – Civil and Criminal Records

District Court – Civil and Criminal Records
www.courts.state.hi.us/index.jsp
Free record searching at www.courts.state.hi.us/index.jsp. Click on "Search Court Records." Search by name or case number. Records go back to early 1900s.

Honolulu County

1st Circuit Court – Civil and Criminal Records

District Court – Civil and Criminal Records
www.courts.state.hi.us/index.jsp
Free record searching at www.courts.state.hi.us/index.jsp. Click on "Search Court Records." Search by name or case number.

Kauai County

5th Circuit Court – Civil and Criminal Records

District Court of the 5th Circuit – Civil and Criminal Records
www.courts.state.hi.us/index.jsp
Free record searching at www.courts.state.hi.us/index.jsp. Click on "Search Court Records." Search by name or case number.

Maui County

2nd Circuit Court – Civil and Criminal Records

District Court – Civil and Criminal Records
www.courts.state.hi.us/index.jsp
Access Circuit Court & Family Court records free at www.courts.state.hi.us/index.jsp. Click on "Search Court Records." Circuit Records go back to 1984. District court records go back to 12/03

County Level ... Recorders & Assessors

Recording Office Organization: All UCC financing statements, tax liens, and real estate documents are filed centrally with the Bureau of Conveyances located in Honolulu. The entire state is in the Hawaii Time Zone (HT).

Online Access Note: There is no statewide access to recorder or assessor information.

Bureau of Conveyances *Property Records*
www.hawaii.gov/dlnr/bc
Property records on the Hawaii County property assessor records are free at www.hawaiipropertytax.com. Also, search Honolulu real estate records at www.honolulupropertytax.com. No name searching. Maui Assessor Property records are free at www.mauipropertytax.com. Indices to all documents recorded in the Bureau of Conveyances from 1976 to current are online at http://132.160.239.151/boc/. Certified copies of documents may also be ordered.

Federal Courts in Hawaii...

Standards for Federal Courts: The universal PACER sign-up number is 800-676-6856. Find PACER and the Party/Case Index on the Web at http://pacer.psc.uscourts.gov. PACER dial-up access is $.60 per minute. Also, courts offering internet access via PACER, Web-PACER or the new CM-ECF charge $.08 per page fee ($.07 per page if record is pre-2005 or unless noted as free).

US District Court -- District of Hawaii
www.hid.uscourts.gov
PACER: Case records are available back to 10/1991. Records are purged never. New records are available online after 1 day. New criminal records are available online after 3 days. **PACER Online Access:** PACER online at http://pacer.hid.uscourts.gov. **Electronic Filing:** ECF may still be in testing stage; if so, do not use. CM/ECF data at https://ecf.hid.uscourts.gov. **Other Online Access:** Daily calendar at www.hid.uscourts.gov/calendar.
Honolulu Division counties: All counties.

US Bankruptcy Court -- District of Hawaii
www.hib.uscourts.gov
PACER: Case records are available back to 1987. New records are available online after 1 day. **Electronic Filing:** CM/ECF data at https://ecf.hib.uscourts.gov. **Opinions:** View court opinions at www.hib.uscourts.gov/opinions/index_opinions.htm. **Other Online Access:** Calendars are at www.hib.uscourts.gov/calendars/index_calendars.htm. **Phone access:** Voice Case Information System, call 808-522-8122.
Honolulu Division counties: All counties.

Idaho

Capital: Boise
                Ada County

Time Zone: MST

Idaho's ten northwestern-most counties are PST:
They are: Benewah, Bonner, Boundary, Clearwater,
Idaho, Kootenai, Latah, Lewis, Nez Perce, Shoshone.

Population: 1,393,262

# of Counties: 44

Quick Links

Website: www.state.is.us

Governor: http://gov.idaho.gov

Attorney General: www2.state.id.us/ag/

State Archives: www.idahohistory.net/library_archives.html

State Statutes and Codes: www.legislature.idaho.gov/statutesrules.htm

State Statutes and Codes: www.legis.state.ia.us/IowaLaw.html

Legislative Bill Search: www3.state.id.us/legislat/legtrack.html

Unclaimed Funds: http://tax.idaho.gov/ucp_search_idaho.htm

State Level ... Major Agencies

Statewide Court Records

Administrative Director of the Courts, Clerk of the Courts, PO Box 83720, Boise, ID 83720-0101 (Courier: 451 W State St, Boise, ID 83720); 208-334-2246, Fax-208-334-2146, 9AM-5PM.
www.isc.idaho.gov/
Online search: Although appellate and supreme court opinions are available from the web, there is no statewide computer system offering external access. ISTARS is a statewide intra-court/intra-agency system for all counties, enabling all courts to provide public access terminals on-site.

Sexual Offender Registry

State Repository, Central Sexual Offender Registry, PO Box 700, Meridian, ID 83680-0700 (Courier: 700 S Stratford Dr, Meridian, ID 83642); 208-884-7305, Fax-208-884-7193, 8AM-5PM.
www.isp.state.id.us
Online search: Access from the web page is available to the public. Inquires can be made by name, address, or by county or ZIP Code.

Incarceration Records

Idaho Department of Corrections, Records Bureau, 1299 N. Orchard Street, Suite 110, Boise, ID 83706; 208-658-2000, Fax-208-327-7444, 8AM-5PM.
www.corrections.state.id.us
Online search: This database search at https://www.accessidaho.org/public/corr/offender/search.html provides information about offenders currently under Idaho Department of Correction jurisdiction: those incarcerated, on probation, or on parole. Names of individuals who have served time and satisfied their sentence will appear - their convictions will not. Also, a private company offers free web access to Idaho DOC at www.vinelink.com/index.jsp.

Corporation, Limited Partnerships, Trademarks/Servicemarks, Limited Liability Companies, Limited Liability Partnerships, Assumed Names

Secretary of State, Corporation Division, PO Box 83720, Boise, ID 83720-0080 (Courier: 700 W Jefferson, Boise, ID 83720); 208-334-2301, Fax-208-334-2080, 8AM-5PM.
www.idsos.state.id.us
Online search: Business Entity Searches at www.accessidaho.org/public/sos/corp/search.html?SearchFormstep=crit. This is a free Internet service open 24 hours daily. Includes not-for-profit entities. Trademarks may be searched at www.accessidaho.org/public/sos/trademark/search.html. **Other options:** There are a variety of formats and media available for bulk purchase requesters. Requesters can subscribers to a monthly CD update.

Uniform Commercial Code, Federal Tax Liens, State Tax Liens

UCC Division, Secretary of State, PO Box 83720, Boise, ID 83720-0080 (Courier: 700 W Jefferson, Boise, ID 83720); 208-334-3191, Fax-208-334-2847, 8AM-5PM.
www.idsos.state.id.us
Online search: There is a free limited search at https://www.accessidaho.org/secure/sos/liens/search.html. We recommend professional searchers to subscribe to the extensive commercial service at this site. There is a $75 annual fee and possible transaction fees. **Other options:** A summary data file on current filing is available on CD.

Sales Tax Registrations

Revenue Operations Division, Records Management, PO Box 36, Boise, ID 83722 (Courier: 800 Park, Boise, ID 83722); 208-334-7660, 208-334-7792 (Records Management), Fax-208-334-7650, 8AM-5:00PM.
www.tax.idaho.gov/
Online search: Email requests are accepted at rmcmichael@tax.state.id.us.

Death Records

Vital Records, PO Box 83720, Boise, ID 83720-0036 (Courier: 450 W State St, 1st Floor, Boise, ID 83702); 208-334-5988, Fax-208-389-9096, 8AM-5PM.
www.healthandwelfare.idaho.gov
Online search: The agency has made the death index of records older than 50 available at http://abish.byui.edu/specialCollections/fhc/Death/searchForm.cfm. There is no fee.

Driver Records

Idaho Transportation Department, Driver's Services, PO Box 34, Boise, ID 83731-0034 (Courier: 3311 W State, Boise, ID 83703); 208-334-8736, Fax-208-334-8739, 8:30AM-5PM.
www.itd.idaho.gov/dmv/
Online search: Idaho offers online access (CICS) to the driver license files through its portal provider, Access Idaho. Fee is $5.50 per record. For more information, call 208-332-0102 or visit www.accessidaho.org. Idaho drivers can also order their own record from this site. **Other options:** Idaho offers bulk retrieval of basic drivers license information with a signed contract. For information, call 208-334-860.

Vehicle Ownership, Vehicle Identification, Vessel Ownership

Idaho Transportation Department, Vehicle Services, PO Box 34, Boise, ID 83731-0034 (Courier: 3311 W State St, Boise, ID 83707); 208-334-8773, 208-334-8663, Fax-208-334-8542, 8:30AM-5PM.
www.itd.idaho.gov/dmv/vehicleservices/vs.htm
Online search: Idaho offers online and batch access to registration and title files through its portal provider, Access Idaho. Records are $5.50 each or $3.50 for a lien search for subscribers. For more information, call 208-332-0102 or visit www.accessidaho.org. **Other options:** Idaho offers bulk retrieval of registration, ownership, and vehicle information with a signed contract. For more information, call 208-334-8601.

State Level ... Occupational Licensing

Acupuncturist..https://secure.ibol.idaho.gov/eIBOLPublic/LPRBrowser.aspx
Applicator, Commercial/Private ....www.agri.state.id.us/Categories/Pesticides/licensing/licenseLookUp.php
Appraiser, General/Resi/Trainee.................https://secure.ibol.idaho.gov/eIBOLPublic/LPRBrowser.aspx
Architect..https://secure.ibol.idaho.gov/eIBOLPublic/LPRBrowser.aspx
Assignees (Lender) ....http://finance.idaho.gov/CreditCodeLicence.aspx
Athlete Agent..https://secure.ibol.idaho.gov/eIBOLPublic/LPRBrowser.aspx
Athletic Trainer..www.accessidaho.org/public/bomed/license/search.html
Attorney ....http://www2.state.id.us/isb/mem/attorney_roster.asp
Audiologist ....https://secure.ibol.idaho.gov/eIBOLPublic/LPRBrowser.aspx
Backflow Assembly Tester ....https://secure.ibol.idaho.gov/eIBOLPublic/LPRBrowser.aspx
Bank...http://finance.idaho.gov/CreditCodeLicence.aspx
Barber School/Instructor............................https://secure.ibol.idaho.gov/eIBOLPublic/LPRBrowser.aspx
Barber/Barber Shop/Barber School.............https://secure.ibol.idaho.gov/eIBOLPublic/LPRBrowser.aspx
Chemigator ....www.agri.state.id.us/Categories/Pesticides/licensing/licenseLookUp.php
Chiropractor...https://secure.ibol.idaho.gov/eIBOLPublic/LPRBrowser.aspx
Collection Agency/Collector......................http://finance.idaho.gov/CollectionAgencyLicence.aspx
Community Action Program......................www.puc.state.id.us/consumer/helplist.pdf
Conselor, Debt/Credit ....http://finance.idaho.gov/CollectionAgencyLicence.aspx
Construction Manager, Public Works ....https://www.dbs.idaho.gov/edbspublic/lprbrowser.aspx
Consumer Loan Co & Credit Seller............http://finance.idaho.gov/CreditCodeLicence.aspx
Contracting Business ....https://secure.ibol.idaho.gov/eIBOLPublic/LPRBrowser.aspx
Contractor, Public Works...........................www.accessidaho.org/public/dbs/pubworks/search.html
Contractor, Registered ....https://secure.ibol.idaho.gov/eIBOLPublic/LPRBrowser.aspx
Cosmetics Dealer, Retail............................https://secure.ibol.idaho.gov/eIBOLPublic/LPRBrowser.aspx
Cosmetologist/Cosmo. Salon/School/Instr..https://secure.ibol.idaho.gov/eIBOLPublic/LPRBrowser.aspx
Counselor, Clinical ....https://secure.ibol.idaho.gov/eIBOLPublic/LPRBrowser.aspx
Counselor, Professional ....https://secure.ibol.idaho.gov/eIBOLPublic/LPRBrowser.aspx
Credit Seller...http://finance.idaho.gov/CreditCodeLicence.aspx
Credit Union ....http://finance.idaho.gov/CreditCodeLicence.aspx
Crematory ....https://secure.ibol.idaho.gov/eIBOLPublic/LPRBrowser.aspx
Dentist/Dental Hygienist............................http://www2.state.id.us/isbd/search.htm
Denturist/Denturist Intern/Establishment....https://secure.ibol.idaho.gov/eIBOLPublic/LPRBrowser.aspx
Dietitian ....www.accessidaho.org/public/bomed/license/search.html
Elections & Campaign Disclosure ....www.idsos.state.id.us/notary/npindex.htm
Electrical Apprentice/Journeyman..............https://www.dbs.idaho.gov/edbspublic/lprbrowser.aspx
Electrical Inspector/Contractor ....https://www.dbs.idaho.gov/edbspublic/lprbrowser.aspx
Electrolysis, Electrolysis Instructor ....https://secure.ibol.idaho.gov/eIBOLPublic/LPRBrowser.aspx
Engineer..www.ipels.idaho.gov/curroster.htm
Escrow Licensee ....http://finance.idaho.gov/EscrowLicense.aspx
Esthetician, Esthetician Instructor..............https://secure.ibol.idaho.gov/eIBOLPublic/LPRBrowser.aspx
Finance Company ....http://finance.idaho.gov/CreditCodeLicence.aspx
Funeral Director...https://secure.ibol.idaho.gov/eIBOLPublic/LPRBrowser.aspx
Funeral Director Trainee.............................https://secure.ibol.idaho.gov/eIBOLPublic/LPRBrowser.aspx
Funeral Establishment................................https://secure.ibol.idaho.gov/eIBOLPublic/LPRBrowser.aspx
Geologist..http://www2.state.id.us/ibpg/search.htm
Glamour Photography Studio......................https://secure.ibol.idaho.gov/eIBOLPublic/LPRBrowser.aspx
Guide ....www.oglb.idaho.gov/ofdirectory.htm
Hearing Aid Dealer/Fitter ....https://secure.ibol.idaho.gov/eIBOLPublic/LPRBrowser.aspx
Hearing Aid Fitter/Dealer ....https://secure.ibol.idaho.gov/eIBOLPublic/LPRBrowser.aspx
HVAC Contractor/Journeyman...................https://www.dbs.idaho.gov/edbspublic/lprbrowser.aspx
Insurance Agent/Corp./Partnership.............www.doi.idaho.gov/Insurance/search.aspx
Insurance Broker..www.doi.idaho.gov/Insurance/search.aspx
Insurer, Domestic/Mutual/Foreign..............www.doi.idaho.gov/Insurance/search.aspx

Investment Advisor	http://finance.idaho.gov/SecuritiesLicense.aspx
Landscape Architect	https://secure.ibol.idaho.gov/eIBOLPublic/LPRBrowser.aspx
Lobbyist	www.idsos.state.id.us/elect/lobbyist/lobinfo.htm
LPG Dealer/Facility	https://secure.ibol.idaho.gov/eIBOLPublic/LPRBrowser.aspx
Manufact'd Homes & Housing Related	https://www.dbs.idaho.gov/edbspublic/lprbrowser.aspx
Marriage & Family Counselor	https://secure.ibol.idaho.gov/eIBOLPublic/LPRBrowser.aspx
Medical Doctor	www.accessidaho.org/public/bomed/license/search.html
Medical Resident	www.accessidaho.org/public/bomed/license/search.html
Medical, Temporary	www.accessidaho.org/public/bomed/license/search.html
Money Transmitter	http://finance.idaho.gov/MoneytransmittersLicence.aspx
Mortgage Broker/Banker/Company	http://finance.idaho.gov/MortgageLicense.aspx
Mortgage Loan Originator	http://finance.idaho.gov/LoLicense.aspx
Mortician/Mortician Resident Trainee	https://secure.ibol.idaho.gov/eIBOLPublic/LPRBrowser.aspx
Nail Technician/Instructor	https://secure.ibol.idaho.gov/eIBOLPublic/LPRBrowser.aspx
Naturapath	https://secure.ibol.idaho.gov/eIBOLPublic/LPRBrowser.aspx
Notary Public	www.idsos.state.id.us/notary/npindex.htm
Nurse	http://www2.state.id.us/ibn/licenseesearch.htm
Nursing Home Administrator	https://secure.ibol.idaho.gov/eIBOLPublic/LPRBrowser.aspx
Occupational Therapist/Assistant	www.accessidaho.org/public/bomed/license/search.html
Optometrist	https://secure.ibol.idaho.gov/eIBOLPublic/LPRBrowser.aspx
Oral Surgeon	http://www2.state.id.us/isbd/search.htm
Orthodontist	http://www2.state.id.us/isbd/search.htm
Osteopathic Physician	www.accessidaho.org/public/bomed/license/search.html
Outfitter	www.oglb.idaho.gov/ofdirectory.htm
Payday Lender	http://finance.idaho.gov/CreditCodeLicence.aspx
Pest Control Consultant	www.agri.state.id.us/Categories/Pesticides/licensing/licenseLookUp.php
Pesticide Applicat'r/Operator/Dealer/Mfg	www.agri.state.id.us/Categories/Pesticides/licensing/licenseLookUp.php
Physical Therapist/Assistant	www.accessidaho.org/public/bomed/license/search.html
Physician Assistant	www.accessidaho.org/public/bomed/license/search.html
Plumbing Apprentice/Journeyman	https://www.dbs.idaho.gov/edbspublic/lprbrowser.aspx
Plumbing Inspector/Contractor	https://www.dbs.idaho.gov/edbspublic/lprbrowser.aspx
Podiatrist	https://secure.ibol.idaho.gov/eIBOLPublic/LPRBrowser.aspx
Polysomnography Technician/Trainee	www.accessidaho.org/public/bomed/license/search.html
Polysomnography Technologist	www.accessidaho.org/public/bomed/license/search.html
Psychologist	https://secure.ibol.idaho.gov/eIBOLPublic/LPRBrowser.aspx
Psychology Service Extender	https://secure.ibol.idaho.gov/eIBOLPublic/LPRBrowser.aspx
Public Accountant Firm	http://isba.idaho.gov/htm/databasesearch.htm
Public Accountant-CPA	http://isba.idaho.gov/htm/databasesearch.htm
Public Accountant-LPA	http://isba.idaho.gov/htm/databasesearch.htm
Real Estate Agent/Broker/Company	www.accessidaho.org/public/irec/licensing/search.html
Real Estate Appraiser	www.asc.gov/content/category1/appr_by_state.asp
Real Estate Appraiser	https://secure.ibol.idaho.gov/eIBOLPublic/LPRBrowser.aspx
Residential Care Administrator	https://secure.ibol.idaho.gov/eIBOLPublic/LPRBrowser.aspx
Respiratory Therapist	www.accessidaho.org/public/bomed/license/search.html
Savings & Loan Association	http://finance.idaho.gov/CreditCodeLicence.aspx
Securities Broker/Seller/Issuer	http://finance.idaho.gov/SecuritiesLicense.aspx
Social Worker	https://secure.ibol.idaho.gov/eIBOLPublic/LPRBrowser.aspx
Speech/Language Pathologist	https://secure.ibol.idaho.gov/eIBOLPublic/LPRBrowser.aspx
Surveyor, Land	www.ipels.idaho.gov/curroster.htm
Temporary Medical	www.accessidaho.org/public/bomed/license/search.html
Title Loan Lender	http://finance.idaho.gov/CreditCodeLicence.aspx
Trust Company	http://finance.idaho.gov/CreditCodeLicence.aspx
Utility Pay Station	www.puc.state.id.us/consumer/paystations.htm
Waste Water Treatment Operator	https://secure.ibol.idaho.gov/eIBOLPublic/LPRBrowser.aspx
Water Collection/Distribution Operator	https://secure.ibol.idaho.gov/eIBOLPublic/LPRBrowser.aspx
Water Treatment Operator	https://secure.ibol.idaho.gov/eIBOLPublic/LPRBrowser.aspx

County Level ... Courts

Court Administration: Administrative Director of Courts, Supreme Court Building, PO Box 83720, Boise, ID, 83720-0101; 208-334-2246; www.isc.idaho.gov

Court Structure: District judges hear felony criminal cases and civil actions if the amount involved is more than $10,000, and appeals of decisions of the Magistrate Division. The Magistrate Division hears probate matters, divorce proceedings, juvenile proceedings, initial felony proceedings through the preliminary hearing, criminal misdemeanors, infractions, civil cases when the amount in dispute does not exceed $10,000. Magistrates also hear Small Claims cases, established for disputes of $4,000 or less.

Online Access Note: Although appellate and supreme court opinions are available from the website, but there is no statewide computer system offering external access. ISTARS is a statewide intra-court/intra-agency system run and managed by the State Supreme Court. All counties are on ISTARS, and all courts provide public access terminals onsite.

Canyon County

District & Magistrate Courts *Civil Records*
www.canyoncounty.org
A daily court calendar is available at the website.

County Level ... Recorders & Assessors

Recording Office Organization: 44 counties, 44 recording offices. The recording officer is the County Recorder. Many counties utilize a grantor/grantee index containing all transactions recorded with them. 34 counties are in the Mountain Time Zone (MST), and 10 are in the Pacific Time Zone (PST). Until 07/01/98, state tax liens were filed at the local county recorder. Now they are filed with the Secretary of State who has all active case files. Federal tax liens on personal property of businesses are filed with the Secretary of State. Other federal tax liens are filed with the county recorder. Some counties will perform a combined tax lien search for $5.00 while others will not perform tax lien searches.

Online Access Note: Two counties offer web access to assessor records. Many Idaho counties property data is online via www.etitlesearch.com; fees and registration required. The Secretary of State's office offers online access to UCCs.

20 Idaho Counties *Real Estate Recording, Deed Records*

Access recording office land data at www.etitlesearch.com; registration required, fee based on usage.
Counties include- Bannock, Benewah, Bingham, Blaine, Bonner, Bonneville, Boundary, Butte, Camas, Clarke, Custer, Franklin, Fremont, Jerome, Madison, Power, Shoshone, Teton, Twin Falls, Valley.

Ada County *Assessor, Property, Inmate Records*

Search the property assessor database for property data for free at www.adacountyassessor.org. Click on "Online Property Information System". No name searching. Also, search inmate info on private company website at www.vinelink.com/index.jsp.

Canyon County *Assessor, Property Records*

www.canyoncounty.org
Access to the Assessor and Treasurer's databases requires $35 registration/setup fee and 150 yearly fee. For subscription information, email clane@canyoncounty.org or call 208-454-7401 or visit the website.

Kootenai County *Plats, Surveys, CPF's, Parcel Records*

www.co.kootenai.id.us/departments/recorder/
Access to the county mapping/recording database is free at www.co.kootenai.id.us/departments/mapping. No name searching.

Payette County *Real Estate, Recorder, Deed, Grantor/Grantee, Records*
www.payettecounty.org
Access to recorded documents is free at www.payettecounty.org/clerk/imagesilo.html.

Twin Falls County *Real Estate, Recorder, Deed Records*
www.twinfallscounty.org
Access recording office land data at www.etitlesearch.com; registration required, fee based on usage. Land records also available on CD-rom for $.10 per image.

Federal Courts in Idaho...

Standards for Federal Courts: The universal PACER sign-up number is 800-676-6856. Find PACER and the Party/Case Index on the Web at http://pacer.psc.uscourts.gov. PACER dial-up access is $.60 per minute. Also, courts offering internet access via RACER, PACER, Web-PACER or the new CM-ECF charge $.08 per page fee ($.07 per page if record is pre-2005 or unless noted as free).

US District Court -- District of Idaho

www.id.uscourts.gov
PACER: Sign-up number is . New records are available online after 2 days. New criminal records are available online after 1 day. **Electronic Filing:** CM/ECF data at https://ecf.idd.uscourts.gov. **Other Online Access:** The old, free RACER system no longer updated. To view calendars, click on Calendars at main website, choose type.
Boise Division counties: Ada, Adams, Blaine, Boise, Camas, Canyon, Cassia, Elmore, Gem, Gooding, Jerome, Lincoln, Minidoka, Owyhee, Payette, Twin Falls, Valley, Washington.
Coeur d' Alene Division counties: Benewah, Bonner, Boundary, Kootenai, Shoshone.
Moscow Division counties: Clearwater, Latah, Lewis, Nez Perce.
Pocatello Division counties: Bannock, Bear Lake, Bingham, Bonneville, Butte, Caribou, Clark, Custer, Franklin, Fremont, Idaho, Jefferson, Lemhi, Madison, Oneida, Power, Teton.

US Bankruptcy Court -- District of Idaho

www.id.uscourts.gov
PACER: Sign-up number is 208-334-9342. Case records are available back to 9/1990. Records are purged immediately when case closed. New records are available online after 1 day. **PACER Online Access:** No PACER online. **Electronic Filing:** CM/ECF data at https://ecf.idd.uscourts.gov. **Opinions:** Also, search archived bankruptcy cases free at www.id.uscourts.gov/cfCourt/CourtArchives/Archive_SearchForm.cfm. View court opinions at www.id.uscourts.gov/cfCourt/decisions/bk_decisionlist.cfm. **Other Online Access:** The old, free RACER system no longer updated. To view calendars, click on Calendars at main website, choose type. **Phone access:** Voice Case Information System, call 208-334-9386.
Boise Division counties: Ada, Adams, Blaine, Boise, Camas, Canyon, Cassia, Elmore, Gem, Gooding, Jerome, Lincoln, Minidoka, Owyhee, Payette, Twin Falls, Valley, Washington.
Coeur d' Alene - Nothern Division counties: Benewah, Bonner, Boundary, Kootenai, Shoshone.
Moscow - Northern Division counties: Clearwater, Idaho, Latah, Lewis, Nez Perce.
Pocatello Division counties: Bannock, Bear Lake, Bingham, Bonneville, Butte, Caribou, Clark, Custer, Franklin, Fremont, Jefferson, Lemhi, Madison, Oneida, Power, Teton.

Illinois

Capital: Springfield
            Sangamon County
Time Zone: CST
Population: 12,713,634
# of Counties: 102

Quick Links

Website: www100.state.il.us
Governor: www.illinois.gov/gov
Attorney General: www.ag.state.il.us
State Archives: www.sos.state.il.us/departments/archives/archives.html
State Statutes and Codes: www.ilga.gov/legislation/ilcs/ilcs.asp
Legislative Bill Search: www.ilga.gov/legislation/default.asp
Unclaimed Funds: www.cashdash.net

State Level ... Major Agencies

Criminal Records

Illinois State Police, Bureau of Identification, 260 N Chicago St, Joliet, IL 60432-4075; 815-740-5160, Fax-815-740-5215, 8AM-4PM
www.isp.state.il.us/crimhistory/crimhistoryhome.cfm
Online search: Online access costs $10.00 per name. Upon signing an interagency agreement with ISP and establishing an escrow account, users can submit inquiries by email. Responses are sent back in 24 to 48 hours by either email or fax.

Statewide Court Records

Administrative Office of Courts, 222 N. LaSalle - 13th Floor, Chicago, IL 60601; 312-793-3250, Fax-312-793-1335, 8AM-5PM.
www.state.il.us/court/
Online search: The web page offers access to supreme and appellate opinions. There is no statewide public online system for local court records. A few Circuit Courts offer online access. A vendor, Judici.com, offers free searching for a few counties with a fee service for multi-county searching.

Sexual Offender Registry

Illinois State Police, SOR Unit, 400 Iles Park Place, #300, Springfield, IL 62703-2978; 217-785-0653, 8AM-4PM M-F.
www.isp.state.il.us/sor/
Online search: The website provides an online listing of sex offenders required to register in the State of Illinois. The database is updated daily and allows searching by name, city, county, and ZIP Code. Note: the City of Chicago provides its own search site at http://12.17.79.4.

Incarceration Records

Illinois Department of Corrections, Public Information Office, PO Box 19277, Springfield, IL 62794-9277 (Courier: 1301 Concordia Court, Springfield, IL 62794); 217-522-2666 x2008, Fax-217-522-3568, 8:30AM-5PM M-F.
www.idoc.state.il.us
Online search: Click on Inmate Search at the website. Also, a private company offers free web access at www.vinelink.com/index.jsp. Includes state, DOC, and county jails.

Corporation, Limited Partnership, Trade Names, Assumed Name, Limited Liability Company Records

Department of Business Services, Corporate Department, 330 Howlett Bldg, 3rd Floor, Copy Section, Springfield, IL 62756 (Courier: 501 S 2nd St, Springfield, IL 62756); 217-782-7880, 217-782-9521 (Name Availability), 217-524-5248 (Expedited Srv), 217-524-8008 (Nmae Availability), Fax-217-782-4528, 8AM-4:30PM.
www.ilsos.net
Online search: The website gives free access to corporate and LLC records at http://cdsprod.ilsos.net/CorpSearchWeb/corpsrch.html. A commercial access program is also available. Fees vary. Potential users must submit in writing the purpose of the request. Submit your request to become involved in this program to the Director's Office. **Other options:** List or bulk file purchases are available. Contact the Director's office for details.

Birth Certificates

IL Department of Public Health, Division of Vital Records, 605 W Jefferson St, Springfield, IL 62702-5097; 217-782-6554, 217-782-6553 (Instructions), Fax-217-523-2648, 8:30AM-5PM M-F.
www.idph.state.il.us/vitalrecords/index.htm
Online search: Records may requested from www.vitalchek.com, a state-endorsed vendor. Also, detailed instructions are at the website above. Requests are processed within 2 days.

Death Records

IL Department of Public Health, Division of Vital Records, 605 W Jefferson St, Springfield, IL 62702-5097; 217-782-6554, 217-782-6553 (Instructions), Fax-217-523-2648, 8:30AM-4PM.
www.idph.state.il.us/vitalrecords/index.htm
Online search: Records may requested from www.vitalchek.com, a state-endorsed vendor. Detailed instructions are at the website above. Also, the state archives database of Illinois Death Certificates 1916-1950 is available free at www.cyberdriveillinois.com/departments/archives/genealogy/forms/idphdeathsrch.html.

Workers' Compensation Records

IL Workers' Compensation Commission, 100 W Randolph, 8th Floor, Chicago, IL 60601; 312-814-6611, 8:30AM-5PM.
www.iwcc.il.gov
Online search: Case info status for active cases only is available at the webpage. Click on the IIC box on the right side of the screen.

Driver Records

Abstract Information Unit, Drivers Services Department, 2701 S Dirksen Prky, Springfield, IL 62723; 217-782-2720, 8AM-4:30PM.
www.sos.state.il.us
Online search: A program for high volume, approved users may be available. Records are $12.00 each. Call 217-785-2384 for further information. **Other options:** Overnight cartridge batch processing may be available to high volume users (there is a 200 request minimum per day). Call 217-785-2384 for more information.

Accident Reports (Crash Reports)

Illinois State Police, Patrol Records Unit, 500 Iles Park Place, Ste 200, Springfield, IL 62703-2982; 217-785-0614, Fax-217-785-2325.
www.isp.state.il.us
Online search: Records can be requested and paid for online via E-Pay at the web page. The fee is $6.00 per report. Visit www.isp.state.il.us/traffic/crashreports.cfm.

State Level ... Occupational Licensing

Acupuncturist	https://www.idfpr.com/dpr/licenselookup/default.asp
Alarm Contractor	https://www.idfpr.com/dpr/licenselookup/default.asp
Amusement Attraction/Ride	www.state.il.us/agency/idol/Listings/Carnlist.htm
Architect	https://www.idfpr.com/dpr/licenselookup/default.asp
Armed Security Agent/Agency	https://www.idfpr.com/dpr/licenselookup/default.asp
Asbestos Contractor	www.idph.state.il.us/
Athletic Trainer	https://www.idfpr.com/dpr/licenselookup/default.asp
ATM Privately Owned	www.obre.state.il.us/CBT/REGENTY/ATMREG.pdf
Attorney	www.iardc.org/lawyersearch.asp

Auctioneer	www.obrelookupclear.state.il.us/default.asp
Audiologist	https://www.idfpr.com/dpr/licenselookup/default.asp
Bank	www.obrelookupclear.state.il.us/default.asp
Barber	https://www.idfpr.com/dpr/licenselookup/default.asp
Basic classr'm Training Course	https://www.idfpr.com/dpr/licenselookup/default.asp
Bilingual Teacher, Transitional	https://secqa1.isbe.net/otis/
Bull Ride	www.state.il.us/agency/idol/Listings/Carnlist.htm
Bungee Jump	www.state.il.us/agency/idol/Listings/Carnlist.htm
Carnival	www.state.il.us/agency/idol/Listings/Carnlist.htm
Check Seller/Distributor	www.obrelookupclear.state.il.us/default.asp
Chiropractor	https://www.idfpr.com/dpr/licenselookup/default.asp
Collection Agency	https://www.idfpr.com/dpr/licenselookup/default.asp
Controlled Substance Registrant	https://www.idfpr.com/dpr/licenselookup/default.asp
Corporate Fiduciary	www.obre.state.il.us/CBT/REGENTY/usa.asp?State=N
Cosmetologist	https://www.idfpr.com/dpr/licenselookup/default.asp
Counselor/Clinical Profess'l Counselor	https://www.idfpr.com/dpr/licenselookup/default.asp
CPA- Public Accountant	https://www.idfpr.com/dpr/licenselookup/default.asp
Dentist/Dental Hygienist	https://www.idfpr.com/dpr/licenselookup/default.asp
Design Firm	https://www.idfpr.com/dpr/licenselookup/default.asp
Dietitian/Nutrition Counselor	https://www.idfpr.com/dpr/licenselookup/default.asp
Doctor/Physician	https://www.idfpr.com/dpr/licenselookup/default.asp
Drug Distributor, Wholesale	https://www.idfpr.com/dpr/licenselookup/default.asp
Early Childhood Teacher	https://secqa1.isbe.net/otis/
Engineer, Structural	https://www.idfpr.com/dpr/licenselookup/default.asp
Engineer/Engineer Intern	https://www.idfpr.com/dpr/licenselookup/default.asp
Environmental Health Practitioner	https://www.idfpr.com/dpr/licenselookup/default.asp
Esthetician	https://www.idfpr.com/dpr/licenselookup/default.asp
Euthanasia Tech	https://www.idfpr.com/dpr/licenselookup/default.asp
Firearms Trainer	https://www.idfpr.com/dpr/licenselookup/default.asp
Funeral Director/Embalmer	https://www.idfpr.com/dpr/licenselookup/default.asp
Geologist	https://www.idfpr.com/dpr/licenselookup/default.asp
Go-kart track	www.state.il.us/agency/idol/Listings/Carnlist.htm
HMO/PPA	www.ins.state.il.us/PPA/PPA_list.asp
Home Inspector	www.obrelookupclear.state.il.us/default.asp
Home Medical Equip Provider	https://www.idfpr.com/dpr/licenselookup/default.asp
Insurance Producer	http://neonwebh.cmcf.state.il.us:8080/ins/imsfor
Interior Designer	https://www.idfpr.com/dpr/licenselookup/default.asp
Landscape Architect	https://www.idfpr.com/dpr/licenselookup/default.asp
Lead Contractor/Risk Assessor/Insp./Supr.	http://app.idph.state.il.us/Envhealth/Lead/LeadProfessionalListing.asp
Lead Training Provider	http://app.idph.state.il.us/Envhealth/lead/Leadinsp.asp
Liquor License, Retail/Dist./Mfg.	http://www2.state.il.us/lcc/license_search.asp
Lobbyist	www.cyberdriveillinois.com/departments/index/lobbyist/home.html
Locksmith	https://www.idfpr.com/dpr/licenselookup/default.asp
Long Term Care Insurance Co	http://neonwebh.cmcf.state.il.us:8080/ins/imsfor
Marriage & Family Therapist	https://www.idfpr.com/dpr/licenselookup/default.asp
Massage Therapist	https://www.idfpr.com/dpr/licenselookup/default.asp
Medical Corporation	https://www.idfpr.com/dpr/licenselookup/default.asp
Medical Doctor	https://www.idfpr.com/dpr/licenselookup/default.asp
Mortgage Banker/Broker	www.obre.state.il.us/MBLookup/MBList.htm
Nail Technician	https://www.idfpr.com/dpr/licenselookup/default.asp
Naprapath	https://www.idfpr.com/dpr/licenselookup/default.asp
Notary Public	www.cyberdriveillinois.com/departments/index/notary/home.html
Nurse	https://www.idfpr.com/dpr/licenselookup/default.asp
Nursing Home Administrator	www.medicare.gov/Nursing/Overview.asp
Occupational Therapist	https://www.idfpr.com/dpr/licenselookup/default.asp
Optometrist	https://www.idfpr.com/dpr/licenselookup/default.asp

Orthotist	https://www.idfpr.com/dpr/licenselookup/default.asp
Osteopathic Physician	https://www.idfpr.com/dpr/licenselookup/default.asp
Pawnbroker	www.obrelookupclear.state.il.us/default.asp
Pedorthist	https://www.idfpr.com/dpr/licenselookup/default.asp
Perfusionist	https://www.idfpr.com/dpr/licenselookup/default.asp
Pest Control Technician/Business	www.idph.state.il.us/
Pesticide Applicator	www.idph.state.il.us/
Pharmacist/Pharmacy	https://www.idfpr.com/dpr/licenselookup/default.asp
Physical Therapist	https://www.idfpr.com/dpr/licenselookup/default.asp
Physician Assistant	https://www.idfpr.com/dpr/licenselookup/default.asp
Podiatrist	https://www.idfpr.com/dpr/licenselookup/default.asp
Polygraph/Deception Detect'n Examiner	https://www.idfpr.com/dpr/licenselookup/default.asp
Private Detective/Private Security Cont'r	https://www.idfpr.com/dpr/licenselookup/default.asp
Psychologist/Psychology Business	https://www.idfpr.com/dpr/licenselookup/default.asp
Public Accountant-CPA	https://www.idfpr.com/dpr/licenselookup/default.asp
Real Estate Agent/Broker/Seller	www.obrelookupclear.state.il.us/default.asp
Real Estate Appraiser	www.obrelookupclear.state.il.us/default.asp
Respiratory Care Practitioner	https://www.idfpr.com/dpr/licenselookup/default.asp
Roofer	https://www.idfpr.com/dpr/licenselookup/default.asp
Roofing Contractor	https://www.idfpr.com/dpr/licenselookup/default.asp
Savings Bank/Savings & Loan Assoc	www.obrelookupclear.state.il.us/default.asp
Securities Salesperson/Dealer	www.nasd.com/web/idcplg?IdcService=SS_GET_PAGE&nodeId=6
Security Force/Guard Firm/Agency	https://www.idfpr.com/dpr/licenselookup/default.asp
Sewage System Contractor	www.idph.state.il.us/
Shorthand Reporter	https://www.idfpr.com/dpr/licenselookup/default.asp
Ski Lift, Tram	www.state.il.us/agency/idol/Listings/Carnlist.htm
Social Worker	https://www.idfpr.com/dpr/licenselookup/default.asp
Special Teacher	https://secqa1.isbe.net/otis/
Speech-Language Pathologist	https://www.idfpr.com/dpr/licenselookup/default.asp
Stock Broker	www.nasd.com/web/idcplg?IdcService=SS_GET_PAGE&nodeId=6
Substitute Teacher	https://secqa1.isbe.net/otis/
Surgical Technician	https://www.idfpr.com/dpr/licenselookup/default.asp
Surveyor, Land	https://www.idfpr.com/dpr/licenselookup/default.asp
Teacher	https://secqa1.isbe.net/otis/
Timeshare/Land Sales	www.obrelookupclear.state.il.us/default.asp
Trust Company	www.obre.state.il.us/CBT/REGENTY/Institution.asp?Inst=2
Veterinarian	https://www.idfpr.com/dpr/licenselookup/default.asp
Water Well & Pump Install Contr./IDHP	www.idph.state.il.us/

County Level ... Courts

Court Administration: Administrative Office of Courts, 222 N LaSalle 13th Floor, Chicago, IL, 60601;   312-793-3250. www.state.il.us/court/

Court Structure: Illinois is divided into 22 judicial circuits; 3 are single county: Cook, Du Page (18th Circuit) and Will (12th Circuit). The other 19 circuits consist of 2 or more contiguous counties. The Circuit Court of Cook County is the largest unified court system in the world. Its 2300-person staff handles approximately 2.4 million cases each year. The civil part of the various Circuit Courts in Cook County is divided as follows: under $30,000 are "civil cases" and over $30,000 are "civil law division cases." Probate is handled by the Circuit Court in all counties.

Online Access Note: While there is no statewide public online system available, other than Appellate Court and Supreme Court opinions from the website. A number of Illinois Circuit Courts offer online access, many through a vendor at www.judici.com

Adams County

Circuit Court – Civil and Criminal Records
www.co.adams.il.us
Access to 8th Circuit Clerk of Court records is free at www.judici.com/courts/cases/case_search.jsp?court=IL001025J. Search by name, case or docket number back to 1987. The county inmate list and warrant list is at the home page.

Bond County

Circuit Court – Civil and Criminal Records
www.johnkking.com
Access is free at www.judici.com/courts/cases/index.jsp?court=IL003015J. Premium/fee service is also available.

Boone County

Circuit Court – Civil and Criminal Records
www.boonecountyil.org/deptframeset.htm
Search cases free online at www.judici.com/courts/cases/case_search.jsp?court=IL004015J. Also, a more convenient premium fee service is available.

Bureau County

Circuit Court – Civil and Criminal Records
www.bccirclk.gov
Access to judicial circuit records is free at www.bccirclk.gov/remote.htm. Click on "JIMS". Index includes dates, defendants, record sheets and dispositions and goes back to 8/1988.

Carroll County

Circuit Court – Civil and Criminal Records
Access is free to criminal, civil, small claims, probate and traffic records at www.judici.com/courts/index.jsp?court=IL008015J. Records go back to 1988.

Champaign County

Circuit Court – Civil and Criminal Records
www.cccircuitclerk.com
Access to the circuit clerk's case query online system formerly called PASS is now free at https://secure.jtsmith.com/clerk/clerk.asp. Online case records go back to '92.

Coles County

Circuit Court – Civil and Criminal Records
Access criminal, civil, small claims, probate and traffic records free at www.judici.com/courts/index.jsp?court=IL015025J to 1989.

Cook County

Circuit Court - Chicago District 1 – Civil Records
www.cookcountyclerkofcourt.org
Search full case dockets free at www.cookcountyclerkofcourt.org/terms/full_docket_search/index.htm. Limited case snapshots are also online at www.cookcountyclerkofcourt.org/Terms/terms.htm. Search by name, number, or date. Data includes parties (up to 3), attorneys, case type, filing date, the ad damnum (amount of damages sought), division/district, and most current court date. An online search request form is at http://198.173.15.31/forms/pdf_files/CivilForm.pdf. Download criminal records search request form at http://198.173.15.31/forms/pdf_files/CriminalForm.pdf.

Bridgeview District 5 – Civil Records
Markham District 6 – Civil Records
Maywood District 4 – Civil Records
Rolling Meadows District 3 – Civil Records
Skokie District 2 – Civil Records
www.cookcountyclerkofcourt.org
Online case information is available; see Circuit Court - Chicago Division for details. Felony mail requests- download criminal search request form at http://198.173.15.31/forms/pdf_files/CriminalForm.pdf; mail to Clerk of Circuit Court, Criminal Div - Records, 2650 S California, Chicago, IL 60608, 773-869-3147. Misdemeanor records (county-wide) are also located at Circuit Court - Chicago District 1, Richard J. Daley Ctr, 50 W. Washington Ave, Rm 1006, Chicago, IL 60602.

De Kalb County

Circuit Court – Civil and Criminal Records
www.co.kane.il.us/judicial
Access to court records is via a internet subscription system. Fee is $240 per year for this county or $300 for Will, Madison, Sangamon, Winnebago, Kane, Kendall, DeKalb courts. Visit www.clericusmagnus.com/ or call 866-511-2892.

Henry County

Circuit Court – Civil and Criminal Records
Access is free to criminal, civil, small claims, probate and traffic records at www.judici.com/courts/index.jsp?court=IL037015J.

Iroquois County

Circuit Court – Civil and Criminal Records
www.judici.com/courts/index.jsp?court=IL038025J
Search cases free online at www.judici.com/courts/cases/case_search.jsp?court=IL038025J. Also, a more convenient premium fee service is available.

Jackson County

Circuit Court – Civil and Criminal Records
www.circuitclerk.co.jackson.il.us
Access civil, small claims, and traffic records free from the home page. Also, premiums service subscription with full info is available $77 per 6-months. Probate and genealogy records are free at www.iltrails.org/jackson/. Criminal records access is free at http://circuitclerk.co.jackson.il.us/. Click on "Case information." Also, premiums service subscription with full info is available $77 per 6-months.

Jo Daviess County

Circuit Court – Civil and Criminal Records
Access is free to criminal, civil, small claims, probate and traffic records at www.judici.com/courts/index.jsp?court=IL043015J.

Kane County and
Kendall County

Circuit Court – Civil and Criminal Records
Access to court records is via a internet subscription system. Fee is $240 per year for this county or $300 for Will, Madison, Sangamon, Winnebago, Kane, Kendall, DeKalb courts. Visit www.clericusmagnus.com/ or call 866-511-2892.

La Salle County

Circuit Court – Civil and Criminal Records
Access to Judicial Circuit records requires a $200 setup fee (waived for not-for-profits) and $.10 per minute usage fee. Call Clerk's office at 815-434-8671 for details.

Lee County

Circuit Court – Civil and Criminal Records
Access is free to criminal, civil, small claims, probate and traffic records at www.judici.com/courts/index.jsp?court=IL052025J.

Livingston County

Circuit Court – Civil Records
Search probate index 1837-1958 at www.cyberdriveillinois.com/departments/archives/pontiac.html.

Logan County

Circuit Court – Civil and Criminal Records
www.co.logan.il.us/circuit_clerk/
Access to criminal, civil, small claims, probate and traffic records is free at http://co.logan.il.us/circuit_clerk/. Click on search court cases. A subscription premium service with full records is available.

Macon County

Circuit Court – Civil and Criminal Records
www.court.co.macon.il.us
Access to court records is free at www.court.co.macon.il.us/Templates/SearchCaseInfo.htm. Search docket information back to 04/96. Includes criminal, traffic, probate, family, small claims.

Madison County

Circuit Court – Civil and Criminal Records
www.co.madison.il.us
Access to court records is via a internet subscription system. Fee is $240 per year for this county or $300 for Will, Sangamon, Madison, Winnebago, Kane, Kendall, DeKalb courts. For info, email bmulticourt@janojustice.com or call 866-511-2892.

McHenry County

Circuit Court – Civil and Criminal Records
www.mchenrycircuitclerk.org
Access to records on the remote online system requires $750 license fee and $53.50 access fee, plus $50 per month. Records date back to 1991 with Civil, probate, traffic, and domestic records, and 1990 for criminal. For more info, call 815-334-4193.

McLean County

Circuit Court – Criminal Records
www.mcleancountyil.gov
Public access is free at www.mcleancountyil.gov/circuitclerk/PA_main.htm. System has traffic as well as criminal index.

Mercer County

Circuit Court – Civil and Criminal Records
www.mercercountyil.org
Access is free to criminal, civil, small claims, probate and traffic records at www.judici.com/courts/index.jsp?court=IL066015J.

Montgomery County

Circuit Court – Civil and Criminal Records
www.montgomeryco.com/circlerk.htm
Access to court records is at www.courts.montgomery.k12.il.us/CaseInfo.htm.

Ogle County

Circuit Court – Civil and Criminal Records
www.oglecounty.org/marty/circuitclerk.html
Access is free to criminal, civil, small claims, probate and traffic records at www.oglecounty.org. Click on "Search for Case Information."

Pike County

Circuit Court – Civil and Criminal Records
Access is free to criminal, civil, small claims, probate and traffic records at www.judici.com/courts/index.jsp?court=IL075015J.

Rock Island County

Circuit Court – Civil and Criminal Records
www.co.rock-island.il.us/CirClk.asp?id=279
Full access to court records on the remote online system requires $300 setup fee plus a $1.00 per minute for access. Civil, criminal, probate, traffic, and domestic records can be accessed by name or case number. Also, access to criminal, civil, small claims, probate and traffic records is free at www.judici.com/courts/cases/index.jsp?court=IL081025J.

Sangamon County

Circuit Court – Civil and Criminal Records
www.co.sangamon.il.us/court
Access to court records is via a internet subscription system. Fee is $240 per year for this county or $300 for Will, Madison, Sangamon, Winnebago, Kane, Kendall, DeKalb courts. Visit www.clericusmagnus.com/ or call 866-511-2892.

Stephenson County

Circuit Court – Civil and Criminal Records
www.judici.com
Access is free to criminal, civil, small claims, probate and traffic records at www.judici.com/courts/index.jsp?court=IL089015J.

Union County

Circuit Court – Civil and Criminal Records
Access is free to criminal, civil, small claims, probate and traffic records at www.judici.com/courts/index.jsp?court=IL091015J.

Vermilion County

Circuit Court – Civil and Criminal Records
www.co.vermilion.il.us
Search the index at www.judici.com/courts/cases/case_search.jsp?court=IL092015J. Records are current to 1989.

Whiteside County

Circuit Court – Civil and Criminal Records
Access is free to criminal, civil, small claims, probate and traffic records at
www.judici.com/courts/cases/case_search.jsp?court=IL098015J.

Will County

Circuit Court – Civil and Criminal Records
www.cc.co.winnebago.il.us
Access to court records is via a internet subscription system. Fee is $240 per year for this county or $300 for Will, Madison,
Sangamon, Winnebago, Kane, Kendall, DeKalb courts. Visit www.clericusmagnus.com/ or call 866-511-2892.

County Level ... Recorders & Assessors

Recording Office Organization: 102 counties, 103 recording offices. Cook County had separate
offices for real estate recording and UCC filing until June 30, 2001. As of that date the UCC filing office only
searches for pre-existing UCCs and no longer takes new UCC filings. The recording officer is the Recorder
of Deeds. Many counties utilize a grantor/grantee index containing all transactions. The entire state is in the
Central Time Zone (CST). Federal tax liens on personal property of businesses are filed with the Secretary of
State. Other federal and all state tax liens on personal property are filed with the County Recorder. Some
counties will perform tax lien searches for $5.00-$10.00 per name (state and federal are separate searches in
many of these counties) and $1.00 per page of copy.

Online Access Note: A number of counties offer online access. There is no statewide system.

Adams County *Assessor, Real Estate Records*
Access property data free at www.emapsplus.com/ILAdams/maps/ including name searching.

Boone County *Real Estate, Property Tax, Land Sale Records*
www.boonecountyil.org
Access land data on commercial site - PropertyMax - at http://booneilpropertymax.governmaxa.com/propertymax/rover30.asp.
Subscription packages from $20.00 per month. Search property by owner, address, parcel number, property description, or GIS map.
Also, access to property data is free at www.helpillinois.net/boone/public.htm however there is no name searching

Cass County *Property, Assessor, GIS Records*
Search assessor property data for a fee on the GIS system at http://webgishome.promap.com/Default.aspx. Registration and username
required.

Champaign County *Recording, Real Estate, Deed, Lien Records*
Recorder office data by subscription on either the Laredo system using subscription and fees or the Tapestry System using credit card,
https://tapestry.fidlar.com/tapsearch.aspx; $3.99 search; $.50 per image.

Christian County *Real Estate, Recorder, Deed, Lien, UCC Records*
Recorder office data by subscription on either the Laredo system using subscription and fees or the Tapestry System using credit card,
https://tapestry.fidlar.com/tapsearch.aspx; $3.99 search; $.50 per image. From 1990 to present

Clinton County *Recording, Real Estate, Deed, Lien Records*
www.clintonco.org
Recorder office data by subscription on either the Laredo system using subscription and fees or the Tapestry System using credit card,
https://tapestry.fidlar.com/tapsearch.aspx; $3.99 search; $.50 per image. Index back to 1988; images to 1992.

Coles County *Real Estate, Recorder, Lien, UCC, Deed Records*
Records on the recorder's database are free at www.landaccess.com/proi/county.jsp?county=ilcoles

> **Editor's Note:** Cook County Assessor and the Cook County Recorder are listed as separate entries.

Cook County *Property Tax Records*
www.ccrd.info

Cook County Recorder
Real Estate, Recorder, Deed, Grantor/Grantee, Heir, Inmate, Wanted Sex Offender Records
www.ccrd.info
Search Grantor/Grantee index and locate property data at www.ccrd.info. Fee for documents. Search DIMS database of recordings since 10/1985; registration and fees apply. Includes Treasurer's Current Year Tax System (APIN) and DuPagerecorder. Sign-up information is at www.ccrd.info/CCRD/il031/index.jsp. Also, you may purchase the real estate transfer list; $100 per year on disk ($50 if you pick-up at agency.), Also search inmates and most wanted S.O.s at www.cookcountysheriff.org Also, search the treasurer's heirs database free at www.cookcountytreasurer.com/inheritance.aspx?ntopicid=238. Search assessor data at www.cookcountyassessor.com/ccao/online.html; however there is no name searching.

De Kalb County *Real Estate, Lien, Property Tax, Assessior Records*
www.dekalbcounty.org
The De Kalb County online system requires a $350 subscription fee, with a per minute charge of $.25, $.50 if printing. Records date back to 1980. Lending agency information is available. For further information, contact Sheila Larson at 815-895-7152. Also, search property assessor data free at http://gisweb.co.de-kalb.il.us/quicktaxsearch/quicksearch.asp. There is also a GIS mapping search page available through the county website.

Du Page County *Real Estate, Lien, Tax Assessor Records*
www.dupageco.org/recorder/
For access to the Du Page County database one must lease a live interface telephone line from a carrier to establish a connection. There is a fee of $.05 per transaction. Records date back to 1977. For info, contact Fred Kieltcka at 630-682-7030. Free internet access may soon be available. Access to sheriff's sex offenders, most wanted, and deadbeat parents lists are free at www.co.dupage.il.us/sheriff/. Search Wayne Township property records at www.waynetownshipassessor.com/disclaimer.html Search Bloomingdale Township property records at www.bloomingdaletownshipassessor.com/Assessor/Search.asp. Search Wheatland Township records at www.wheatlandtownship.com/Assessor/disclaim.html. No name searching in either Town.

Fulton County *Recording, Real Estate, Deed, Lien Records*
www.fultonco.org
Recorder office data by subscription on either the Laredo system using subscription and fees or the Tapestry System using credit card, https://tapestry.fidlar.com/tapsearch.aspx; $3.99 search; $.50 per image.

Gallatin County *Property Records*
Search for property information on the GIS-mapping site for free at www.gallatin.mt.gov/GIS/index.htm. No name searching.

Henry County *Assessor Records*
www.henrycty.com/codepartments/recorder/index.html
Access to the assessor database is free at www.henrycty.com/assessor/search.asp. Also, the county most wanted/fugitive list is at www.henrycty.com/sheriff/fugitives.html. Also, for county foreclosure go to www.foreclosure.com/search.html?rsp=6252&st=IL&cno=073

Kane County *Real Estate, Recording, Deed, Lien, Property Tax, Assessor Records*
www.co.kane.il.us
Access recorders real estate records free at www.kanecountyrecorder.net/searchrecords.aspx after downloading Citrix Plug-in which may or may not work. Search the treasurer's property tax info free at www.co.kane.il.us/treasurer/. Search by parcel number only; no name searching.

Kendall County *Real Estate Records*
Search property information at www.co.kendall.il.us/cidnet/public.htm. Search tax information by name or parcel number.

Lake County *Property, Assessor, GIS-mapping Records*
www.co.lake.il.us/recorder

Search the tax assessor's database at www.co.lake.il.us/assessor/assessments/default.asp. No name searching. Also, you may search property by address or legal description for free on the GIS-mapping site at http://gis1.co.lake.il.us/mapsonline/default.asp. Click on Search.

La Salle County   *Real Estate, Assessor Records*
www.lasallecounty.org/Final/contents2.htm
Assessor/property records on the County Assessor database are online at www.lasallecounty.org/cidnet/asrpfull.htm. Registration and password required; there is a $200.00 per year fee, plus per minute charges. For information, phone 815-434-8233. Also, last 2 years assessment data can be accessed online free at www.lasallecounty.org/contents3.htm. Parcel number is required.

Logan County   *Real Estate Records*
www.co.logan.il.us/county_clerk/
Search the tax assessor database at
http://loganilpropertymax.governmaxa.com/propertymax/rover30.asp?sid=671F91267FEE4E1CA02DA8587698C606.

McHenry County   *Assessor/Treasurer, Property, Foreclosure, Recording, Deed, Lien Records*
www.co.mchenry.il.us/countydpt/recorder
Records on the County Treasurer Inquiry site are free at http://taxweb2k.co.mchenry.il.us/cidnet/publictreasurer.htm. The sheriff's foreclosure list is free at www.co.mchenry.il.us. Also, recorder office data by subscription on either the Laredo system using subscription and fees or the Tapestry System using credit card, https://tapestry.fidlar.com/tapsearch.aspx; $3.99 search; $.50 per image.

McLean County   *Recorder, Deed, UCC, Lien, Immigration List, Assessor, Property, Treasurer Tax Bill, Assumed Name, Elected Official Records*
www.mcleancountyil.gov
Access to recorder official records and UCCs is free at www.mcleancountyil.gov/resolution/. Also, access assessor county parcel and mobile home lots free at www.mcleancountyil.gov/tax/; no name searching. Also, access Township of Normal assessor database free at www.normaltownship.org/assessor/parcelsearch.php. No name searching; parcel number or address required. Access immigration records at www.mcleancountyil.gov/CircuitClerk/imgrecs/imgrecs.html. Also, search restaurant data at www.mcleancountyil.gov/health/InspectionScores.asp. Also, search the assumed named list at www.mcleancountyil.gov/CountyClerk/CountyClerkAssumedNamesMain.asp. Search election officials by precinct at the website.

Madison County   *Recording, Real Estate, Deed, Lien Records*
www.co.madison.il.us
Recorder office data by subscription on either the Laredo system using subscription and fees or the Tapestry System using credit card, https://tapestry.fidlar.com/tapsearch.aspx; $3.99 search; $.50 per image.

Monroe County   *Recording, Real Estate, Deed, Lien Records*
Recorder office data by subscription on either the Laredo system using subscription and fees or the Tapestry System using credit card, https://tapestry.fidlar.com/tapsearch.aspx; $3.99 search; $.50 per image.

Morgan County   *Real Estate Recording, Deed Records*
Access recording office land data at www.etitlesearch.com; registration required, fee based on usage.

Ogle County   *Real Estate, Recorder, Deed, UCC, Property, Assessor, GIS Records*
Access to recorder data is free at https://www.illandrecords.com/illr/il141/index.jsp. Also, search assessor property data for a fee on the GIS system at http://webgishome.promap.com/Default.aspx but registration and username required for a name search. Also, the idex of recorded documents may be accessed from https://www.landaccess.com.

Peoria County   *Assessor, Property, Recording, Deed, Sheriff Warrant Records*
www.co.peoria.il.us
Access tax assessor records at www.co.peoria.il.us/frame.php?destination=66.99.203.101%2Fassessor%2Frealasp1.asp but no name searching. Also, the recorder's office has a subscription service with web access to land records and other official documents; call recorder for details. Also search sheriff warrants list at www.co.peoria.il.us/sheriff.php?dept=sheriff&page=warrants.

Randolph County   *Recording, Real Estate, Deed, Lien Records*
Recorder office data by subscription on either the Laredo system using subscription and fees or the Tapestry System using credit card, https://tapestry.fidlar.com/tapsearch.aspx; $3.99 search; $.50 per image. Images back to 1995; index to 1989.

Rock Island County *Property, Assessor, Recording, Real Estate, Deed, Lien Records*

www.co.rock-island.il.us
Recorder office data by subscription on either the Laredo system using subscription and fees or the Tapestry System using credit card, https://tapestry.fidlar.com/tapsearch.aspx; $3.99 search; $.50 per image. Index back to 1982, images 1992. Also, Moline Town assessor records are free at www.molinetownship.com/OnlineSearch/Search.asp. No name searching. Also, for the application for certified copy of vital records go to http://ricoclerk.revealed.net/.

St. Clair County *Recorder, Grantor/Grantee, Real Estate, Divorce, Lien, Judgment Records*

www.stclaircountyrecorder.com
Access to recorder records is free at www.stclaircountyrecorder.com/cgi-bin/display.cgi?file=search. Three search methods available.

Sangamon County *Recording, Real Estate, Deed, Lien Records*

www.co.sangamon.il.us
Recorder office data by subscription on either the Laredo system using subscription and fees or the Tapestry System using credit card, https://tapestry.fidlar.com/tapsearch.aspx; $3.99 search; $.50 per image. Records go back to 1992.

Stark County *Unclaimed Fund Records*

www.starkcourt.org
Access the county clerk of courts unclaimed funds database at www.starkcourt.org (click on "Unclaimed Funds"). File is in pdf format.

Vermilion County *Real Estate, Recorder, Lien, UCC, Deed Records*

Access to real estate records is free at https://www.illandrecords.com/illr/il183/index.jsp. Also visit https://www.landaccess.com for access to recorded documents.

Wayne County *Assessor, Property Records*

http://assessor.wayne.il.us
Records on the Wayne Township Assessor Office database are free at www.waynetownshipassessor.com/OPID.html. Also, you may subscribe to the advanced search feature for a fee. Access includes legal, assessment, sales history, buildings and other information.

Will County *Assessor, Appraiser, Property, Voter Registration, Deed, Lien, Mortgage Records*

www.willcountyrecorder.com
Access to the Recorder's real estate and lien records is free at www.willcountydata.com/rec/searchselect.htm; fees apply for full data and to print copies. Access to voter registration data is free at https://www.willcountydata.com/voterstatus/Voter_lookup_input.htm. The assessor offers a free parcel number inquiry at http://66.158.72.248:2080/cics/cwba/ccalm03; no name searching. Also, access Town of Manhattan assessor and appraiser records free at www.manhattantownship.net. No name searching.

Winnebago County *Property, UCC, Assessor, Court Records*

www.co.winnebago.il.us
Access county property and court data by subscription at www.co.winnebago.il.us; registration and $10.00 per month fee required. Also, access county land and UCC records free at https://www.illandrecords.com/illr/il201/index.jsp.

Federal Courts in Illinois...

Standards for Federal Courts: The universal PACER sign-up number is 800-676-6856. Find PACER and the Party/Case Index on the Web at http://pacer.psc.uscourts.gov. PACER dial-up access is $.60 per minute. Also, courts offering internet access via PACER, Web-PACER or the new CM-ECF charge $.08 per page fee ($.07 per page if record is pre-2005 or unless noted as free).

US District Court -- Central District of Illinois

www.ilcd.uscourts.gov
PACER: Case records are available back to 1995. Records are purged after 5-7 years. New records are available online after 1 day.
PACER Online Access: ECF replaces PACER. **Electronic Filing:** CM/ECF data at https://ecf.ilcd.uscourts.gov. **Opinions:** View court opinions at www.ilcd.uscourts.gov/orders&opinions.htm.
Peoria Division counties: Bureau, Fulton, Hancock, Knox, Livingston, McDonough, McLean, Marshall, Peoria, Putnam, Stark, Tazewell, Woodford.
Rock Island Division counties: Henderson, Henry, Mercer, Rock Island, Warren.

Springfield Division counties: Adams, Brown, Cass, Christian, De Witt, Greene, Logan, Macoupin, Mason, Menard, Montgomery, Morgan, Pike, Sangamon, Schuyler, Scott, Shelby.
Urbana Division counties: Champaign, Coles, Douglas, Edgar, Ford, Iroquois, Kankakee, Macon, Moultrie, Piatt, Vermilion.

US Bankruptcy Court -- Central District of Illinois

www.ilcb.uscourts.gov

PACER: Case records are available back to 1989-90. Records are purged immediately when case closed. New records are available online after 1 day. **PACER Online Access:** PACER online at http://pacer.ilcb.uscourts.gov for pre-2004 cases. **Electronic Filing:** CM/ECF data at https://ecf.ilcb.uscourts.gov. **Opinions:** View court opinions at www.ilcb.uscourts.gov/Opinions/opinions.asp. **Other Online Access:** Hearing calendars free at https://ecf.ilcb.uscourts.gov/cgi-bin/PublicCalendar.pl. **Phone access:** Voice Case Information System, call 800-827-9005, 217-492-4550

Danville Division counties: Champaign, Coles, Douglas, Edgar, Ford, Iroquois, Kankakee, Livingston, Moultrie, Piatt, Vermilion.
Peoria Division counties: Bureau, Fulton, Hancock, Henderson, Henry, Knox, Marshall, McDonough, Mercer, Peoria, Putnam, Rock Island, Stark, Tazewell, Warren, Woodford.
Springfield Division counties: Adams, Brown, Cass, Christian, De Witt, Greene, Logan, Macon, Macoupin, Mason, McLean, Menard, Montgomery, Morgan, Pike, Sangamon, Schuyler, Scott, Shelby.

US District Court -- Northern District of Illinois

www.ilnd.uscourts.gov

PACER: Case records are available back to 1988. New records are available online after 1 day. **PACER Online Access:** ECF replaces PACER. **Electronic Filing:** CM/ECF data at https://ecf.ilnd.uscourts.gov. **Opinions:** View court opinions at www.ilnd.uscourts.gov/RACER2/index.html. **Other Online Access:** Online ruling data at www.nysd.uscourts.gov/courtweb/public.htm. Daily calendar at www.ilnd.uscourts.gov/DAILYCAL/eventskd.htm.

Chicago (Eastern) Division counties: Cook, Du Page, Grundy, Kane, Kendall, Lake, La Salle, Will.
Rockford (Western) Division counties: Boone, Carroll, De Kalb, Jo Daviess, Lee, McHenry, Ogle, Stephenson, Whiteside, Winnebago.

US Bankruptcy Court -- Northern District of Illinois

www.ilnb.uscourts.gov

PACER: Case records are available back to 7/1993. Records are purged never. New records are available online after 1 day. **PACER Online Access:** Access to PACER/RACER is available at the website. Document images available. **Electronic Filing:** CM/ECF data at https://ecf.ilnb.uscourts.gov. **Other Online Access:** Case Image Viewing is available from 5AM to 11:59 p.m. CST at www.ilnb.uscourts.gov/casenotice.htm. Access fee is $.08 per page. **Phone access:** Voice Case Information System, call 888-232-6814, 312-408-5089

Chicago (Eastern) Division counties: Cook, Du Page, Grundy, Kane, Kendall, La Salle, Lake, Will.
Rockford Division counties: Boone, Carroll, De Kalb, Jo Daviess, Lee, McHenry, Ogle, Stephenson, Whiteside, Winnebago.

US District Court -- Southern District of Illinois

www.ilsd.uscourts.gov

PACER: Case records are available back to 1985. Records are purged as deemed necessary. New records are available online after 1 day. **PACER Online Access:** ECF replaces PACER. **Electronic Filing:** CM/ECF data at https://ecf.ilsd.uscourts.gov. **Opinions:** View court opinions at www.ilsd.uscourts.gov/opinions.cfm.

Benton Division counties: Alexander, Clark, Clay, Crawford, Cumberland, Edwards, Effingham, Franklin, Gallatin, Hamilton, Hardin, Jackson, Jasper, Jefferson, Johnson, Lawrence, Massac, Perry, Pope, Pulaski, Richland, Saline, Union, Wabash, Wayne, White, Williamson. Cases may also be allocated to the Benton Division. .
East St Louis Division counties: Bond, Calhoun, Clinton, Fayette, Jersey, Madison, Marion, Monroe, Randolph, St. Clair, Washington. Cases for these counties may also be allocated to the Benton Division.

US Bankruptcy Court -- Southern District of Illinois

www.ilsb.uscourts.gov

PACER: Case records are available back to 1/1989. Records are purged as deemed necessary. New records are available online after immediately. **PACER Online Access:** ECF replaces PACER. **Electronic Filing:** CM/ECF data at https://ecf.ilsb.uscourts.gov. **Opinions:** View court opinions at www.ilsb.uscourts.gov/search_main/opinionsearch.asp. **Phone access:** Voice Case Information System, call 800-726-5622, 618-482-9365

Benton Division counties: Alexander, Edwards, Franklin, Gallatin, Hamilton, Hardin, Jackson, Jefferson, Johnson, Massac, Perry, Pope, Pulaski, Randolph, Saline, Union, Wabash, Washington, Wayne, White, Williamson.
East St Louis Division counties: Bond, Calhoun, Clark, Clay, Clinton, Crawford, Cumberland, Effingham, Fayette, Jasper, Jersey, Lawrence, Madison, Marion, Monroe, Richland, St. Clair.

Indiana

Capital: Indianapolis
　　　　　Marion County

Time Zone: EST

> 11 western Indiana counties are CST and observe DST. They are: Gibson, Jasper, Laporte, Lake, Newton, Porter, Posey, Spencer, Starke, Vanderburgh, Warrick. The remainder are EST and do not observe DST except for Clark, Dearborn, Floyd, Harrison, Ohio.

Population: 6,237,659

# of Counties: 92

Quick Links

Website: www.state.in.us

Governor: www.in.gov/gov/

Attorney General: www.in.gov/attorneygeneral

State Archives: www.in.gov/icpr/archives/

State Statutes and Codes: www.in.gov/legislative/ic/code/

Legislative Bill Search: www.in.gov/apps/lsa/session/billwatch/billinfo

Bill Monitoring: www.in.gov/apps/lsa/session/billwatch/

Unclaimed Funds: https://secure.in.gov/apps/ag/ucp/

State Level ... Major Agencies

Criminal Records

Indiana State Police, Central Records, IGCN - 100 N Senate Ave, Rm N302, Indianapolis, IN 46204-2259; 317-232-5424, Fax-317-233-8813, 8AM-4PM.

www.IN.gov/isp/

Online search: A Limited Criminal History with only felonies and class A misdemeanor arrests is available at www.in.gov/ai/appfiles/isp-lch//. Using a credit card, the search fee is $16.32. Subscribers to accessIndiana can obtain records for $15.00 per search or for no charge if statutorily exempt, or $7.00 with a government exemption. Response of a "No Records Found" is considered an official search result.

Statewide Court Records

State Court Administrator, 200 W Washington St, #1080, Indianapolis, IN 46204; 317-232-2542, Fax-317-233-6586, 8:30-4:30PM.

www.in.gov/judiciary/

Online search: There is no statewide trial court records service available, but many counties offer an online subscription service at https://www.doxpop.com/prod/welcome.jsp. The website above gives free access to an index of docket information for Supreme, Appeals, and Tax Court cases.

Sexual Offender Registry

Sex and Violent Offender Directory Manager, Indiana Criminal Justice Institute, One North Capitol, Suite 1000, Indianapolis, IN 46204-2038; 317-232-1233, Fax-317-232-4979 .

www.insor.org/insasoweb/

Online search: The website has a searching capabilities by name and city or county at www.insor.org/insasoweb/. Email questions to svod@cji.state.in.us.

Incarceration Records

Indiana Department of Corrections, IGCS, Supervisor of Records, Room E-334, 302 W. Washington Street, Indianapolis, IN 46204; 317-232-5765, Fax-317-232-5728, 8AM-4:30PM.
www.in.gov/indcorrection
Online search: At the website, click on Offender Search.

Corporation, Limited Partnerships, Fictitious Name, Assumed Name, Limited Liability Company, Limited Liability Partnerships

Corporation Division, Secretary of State, 302 W Washington St, Room E018, Indianapolis, IN 46204; 317-232-6576, Fax-317-233-3387, 8AM-5:30PM M-F.
www.in.gov/sos/
Online search: You can conduct Business Entity Name Searches, Name Availability Checks and acquire official Certificates of Existence or Authorization at the website. The site also gives access to UCC records. Frequent users of Business Services Online should subscribe to accessIndiana at www.ai.org/ai/business/. **Other options:** Monthly lists of all new businesses are available online, as are bulk data and specialized searches. Look for Special Business Entity Search Orders at the website.

Trademarks/Servicemarks

Secretary of State, Trademark Division, 302 W Washington St, IGC-South, Room E018, Indianapolis, IN 46204; 317-232-6540, Fax-317-233-3675, 8:AM-4:30PM.
www.in.gov/sos/business/trademarks.html
Online search: Visit www.in.gov/apps/sos/trademarks/. This database contains information regarding the status of all trademarks on file with the state of Indiana. Access is free.

Uniform Commercial Code

UCC Division, Secretary of State, 302 West Washington St, Room E-018, Indianapolis, IN 46204; 317-233-3984, Fax-317-233-3387.
www.in.gov/sos/business/ucc.html
Online search: You may browse lien records at https://secure.in.gov/sos/bus_service/online_ucc/browse/default.asp. There is no charge. An official search may be performed for $4.40. If requester is subscriber to AccessIndiana then fee to obtain record is $3.00. Plans are underway to offer filing services also. Bulk downloads and special orders are available online.

Birth Certificates

State Department of Health, Vital Records Office, PO Box 7125, Indianapolis, IN 46206-7125 (Courier: 2 N. Meridian, Indianapolis, IN 46204); 317-233-2700, Fax-317-233-7210, 8:15AM-4:45PM.
www.in.gov/isdh/index.htm
Online search: Records may be ordered online via the website, but the requester must still fax a photo copy of an ID before the record request is processed. Also, records may requested from www.vitalchek.com, a state-endorsed vendor.

Death Records

State Department of Health, Vital Records Office, PO Box 7125, Indianapolis, IN 46206-7125 (Courier: 2 N. Meridian, Indianapolis, IN 46204); 317-233-2700, Fax-317-233-7210, 8:15AM-4:45PM.
www.in.gov/isdh/index.htm
Online search: Records may requested from www.vitalchek.com, a state-endorsed vendor.

Driver Records

BMV-Driving Records, 100 N Senate Ave, Indiana Government Ctr North, Room N405, Indianapolis, IN 46204; 317-232-6000 x2.
www.IN.gov/bmv/
Online search: AccessIndiana is the state owned interactive information and communication system which provides batch and interactive access to driving records. There is an annual $50.00 fee. Online access costs $6.00 per record. For more information, call 317-233-2010 or go to www.in.gov.

Vehicle & Vessel Ownership, Registration

Bureau of Motor Vehicles, Records, 100 N Senate Ave, Room N404, Indianapolis, IN 46204; 317-233-2513 (Titles), 317-233-6000 (Registration), 8:15AM-4:45PM.
www.in.gov/bmv/
Online search: AccessIndiana at 317-233-2010 is the state appointed vendor. Visit www.in.gov for more information. Search the Indiana Bureau of Motor Vehicles database for title and lien information by VIN number, title number, or social security number. Salvage titles included. The fee is $5.00 per record plus an annual fee of $50.00.

State Level ... Occupational Licensing

Acupuncturist	https://extranet.in.gov/WebLookup/Search.aspx
Alcoholic Bev. Dealer/Manufacturer	www.in.gov/ai/appfiles/atc-license-lookup/
Alcoholic Bev. Dist./Retailer/Employee	www.in.gov/ai/appfiles/atc-license-lookup/
Appraiser, Residential/General	https://extranet.in.gov/WebLookup/Search.aspx
Appraiser, Trainee/Temp	https://extranet.in.gov/WebLookup/Search.aspx
Architect	https://extranet.in.gov/WebLookup/Search.aspx
Asbestos Contractor	www.in.gov/idem/air/compliance/index.html
Asbestos Disposal Mgr/Worker	www.in.gov/idem/air/compliance/index.html
Asbestos Inspector/Supvr./Designer	www.in.gov/idem/air/compliance/index.html
Asbestos Training Course Provider	www.in.gov/idem/air/compliance/index.html
Athletic Trainer	https://extranet.in.gov/WebLookup/Search.aspx
Attorney	http://hostpub.courts.state.in.us/HostPublisher/rollatty/roa1_inp.jsp
Auctioneer	https://extranet.in.gov/WebLookup/Search.aspx
Audiologist	https://extranet.in.gov/WebLookup/Search.aspx
Bailbondsman/Agent	www.in.gov/idoi/bailbond/
Bank & Trust Company	http://extranet.dfi.in.gov/dfidb/deplist.aspx
Barber/Barber Instructor	https://extranet.in.gov/WebLookup/Search.aspx
Boxer	https://extranet.in.gov/WebLookup/Search.aspx
Boxing Occupation	https://extranet.in.gov/WebLookup/Search.aspx
Check Casher	http://extranet.dfi.in.gov/dfidb/nondeplist.aspx
Child Care Center	www.in.gov/apps/fssa/carefinder/
Child Care Home/Provider	www.in.gov/apps/fssa/carefinder/
Chiropractor	https://extranet.in.gov/WebLookup/Search.aspx
Clinical Nurse Specialist	https://extranet.in.gov/WebLookup/Search.aspx
Collection Agency	www.in.gov/serv/sos_securities
Cosmetologist	https://extranet.in.gov/WebLookup/Search.aspx
CPA-Public Accountant	https://extranet.in.gov/WebLookup/Search.aspx
Credit Union	http://extranet.dfi.in.gov/dfidb/deplist.aspx
Dental Anesthetist	https://extranet.in.gov/WebLookup/Search.aspx
Dental Hygienist	https://extranet.in.gov/WebLookup/Search.aspx
Dentist	https://extranet.in.gov/WebLookup/Search.aspx
Dietitian	https://extranet.in.gov/WebLookup/Search.aspx
Electrologist	https://extranet.in.gov/WebLookup/Search.aspx
Embalmer	https://extranet.in.gov/WebLookup/Search.aspx
EMS Providers	www.in.gov/dhs/fire/branches/ems/ems_provider.html
Engineer	https://extranet.in.gov/WebLookup/Search.aspx
Engineering Intern	https://extranet.in.gov/WebLookup/Search.aspx
Environmental Health Specialist	https://extranet.in.gov/WebLookup/Search.aspx
Esthetician	https://extranet.in.gov/WebLookup/Search.aspx
Funeral/Cemetery Director	https://extranet.in.gov/WebLookup/Search.aspx
Hazardous Waste Facility/Handler	www.in.gov/idem/land/permits/lists/index.html
Health Services Administrator	https://extranet.in.gov/WebLookup/Search.aspx
Hearing Aid Dealer	https://extranet.in.gov/WebLookup/Search.aspx
Hypnotist	https://extranet.in.gov/WebLookup/Search.aspx
Industrial Authority, State	http://extranet.dfi.in.gov/dfidb/deplist.aspx
Insurance Agent/Consultant	www.in.gov/idoi/agent_licensing
Investment Advisor	www.in.gov/serv/sos_securities
Landscape Architect	https://extranet.in.gov/WebLookup/Search.aspx
Lender, Small	http://extranet.dfi.in.gov/dfidb/nondeplist.aspx
Loan Broker	www.in.gov/serv/sos_securities
Lottery Retailer	www.in.gov/hoosierlottery/games/retailerlocator.asp
Manicurist	https://extranet.in.gov/WebLookup/Search.aspx
Marriage & Family Therapist	https://extranet.in.gov/WebLookup/Search.aspx

Medical Doctor	https://extranet.in.gov/WebLookup/Search.aspx
Medical Residency Permit	https://extranet.in.gov/WebLookup/Search.aspx
Mental Health Counselor	https://extranet.in.gov/WebLookup/Search.aspx
Midwife Nurse	https://extranet.in.gov/WebLookup/Search.aspx
Money Transmitter	http://extranet.dfi.in.gov/dfidb/nondeplist.aspx
Notary Public	www.ai.org/serv/sos_notary
Nurse	https://extranet.in.gov/WebLookup/Search.aspx
Nurse Midwife	https://extranet.in.gov/WebLookup/Search.aspx
Nurse-RN/LPN	https://extranet.in.gov/WebLookup/Search.aspx
Nursing Home Administrator	https://extranet.in.gov/WebLookup/Search.aspx
Occupational Therapist	https://extranet.in.gov/WebLookup/Search.aspx
Occupational Therapy Assistant	https://extranet.in.gov/WebLookup/Search.aspx
Optometrist	https://extranet.in.gov/WebLookup/Search.aspx
Optometrist Drug Certification	https://extranet.in.gov/WebLookup/Search.aspx
Osteopathic Physician	https://extranet.in.gov/WebLookup/Search.aspx
Pawnbroker	http://extranet.dfi.in.gov/dfidb/nondeplist.aspx
Pharmacist/Pharmacist Intern	https://extranet.in.gov/WebLookup/Search.aspx
Pharmacy Technician	https://extranet.in.gov/WebLookup/Search.aspx
Physical Therapist/Therapist Asst	https://extranet.in.gov/WebLookup/Search.aspx
Physician	https://extranet.in.gov/WebLookup/Search.aspx
Physician Assistant	https://extranet.in.gov/WebLookup/Search.aspx
PI Company Employee	https://extranet.in.gov/WebLookup/Search.aspx
Placement Officer, School	http://mustang.doe.state.in.us/TEACH/teach_inq.cfm
Plumber	https://extranet.in.gov/WebLookup/Search.aspx
Plumbing Contractor	https://extranet.in.gov/WebLookup/Search.aspx
Podiatrist	https://extranet.in.gov/WebLookup/Search.aspx
Polygraph Examiner	www.indianapolygraphassociation.com/members.html#top
Private Detective	https://extranet.in.gov/WebLookup/Search.aspx
Psychologist	https://extranet.in.gov/WebLookup/Search.aspx
Public Accountant	https://extranet.in.gov/WebLookup/Search.aspx
Real Estate Agent/Broker/Seller	https://extranet.in.gov/WebLookup/Search.aspx
Real Estate Appraiser	https://extranet.in.gov/WebLookup/Search.aspx
Recovery Agent	www.in.gov/idoi/bailbond/
Rental Purchase Lender	http://extranet.dfi.in.gov/dfidb/nondeplist.aspx
Respiratory Care Practitioner	https://extranet.in.gov/WebLookup/Search.aspx
Savings & Loan	http://extranet.dfi.in.gov/dfidb/deplist.aspx
School Administrator/Principal/Director	http://mustang.doe.state.in.us/TEACH/teach_inq.cfm
School Counselor	http://mustang.doe.state.in.us/TEACH/teach_inq.cfm
School Nurse	http://mustang.doe.state.in.us/TEACH/teach_inq.cfm
Securities Broker/Dealer	www.in.gov/serv/sos_securities
Securities Sales Agent	www.in.gov/serv/sos_securities
Shampoo Operator	https://extranet.in.gov/WebLookup/Search.aspx
Social Worker	https://extranet.in.gov/WebLookup/Search.aspx
Social Worker, Clinical	https://extranet.in.gov/WebLookup/Search.aspx
Solid Waste Facility	www.in.gov/idem/land/permits/lists/index.html
Speech Pathologist	https://extranet.in.gov/WebLookup/Search.aspx
Surveyor, Land	https://extranet.in.gov/WebLookup/Search.aspx
Teacher	http://mustang.doe.state.in.us/TEACH/teach_inq.cfm
Trust Company	http://extranet.dfi.in.gov/dfidb/deplist.aspx
Veterinarian	https://extranet.in.gov/WebLookup/Search.aspx
Veterinary Tech	https://extranet.in.gov/WebLookup/Search.aspx
Waste Tire Processor/Transporter	www.in.gov/idem/land/permits/lists/index.html
Yard Waste Composting Facility	www.in.gov/idem/land/permits/lists/index.html

County Level ... Courts

Court Administration: State Court Administrator, 115 W Washington St, #1080, Indianapolis, IN, 46204; 317-232-2542; www.IN.gov/judiciary

Court Structure: There are 92 judicial circuits with Circuit Courts or Combined Circuit and Superior Courts. In addition, there are 48 City Courts and 25 Town Courts. County Courts are gradually being restructured into divisions of the Superior Courts. Note that Small Claims in Marion County are heard at the townships and records are maintained at that level.

Online Access Note: There is no statewide trial court records service available, but many counties offer an online subscription service at https://www.doxpop.com/prod/welcome.jsp. The website above gives free access to an index of docket information for Supreme, Appeals, and Tax Court cases.

Bartholomew County

Circuit & Superior Court – Civil and Criminal Records
www.bartholomewco.com
Online subscription service at https://www.doxpop.com/prod/welcome.jsp. Fees involved. Records date from 5/85. A limited free search of open cases is available.

Brown County

Circuit Court – Civil and Criminal Records
Fee access to civil records back to 1993 is by subscription at https://www.doxpop.com/prod/welcome.jsp; free access limited to only current open cases.

Clinton County

Circuit & Superior Court – Civil and Criminal Records
Online subscription service at https://www.doxpop.com/prod/welcome.jsp. Fees involved. Records date from 01/91. A limited free search of open cases is available.

Daviess County

Circuit & Superior Court – Civil and Criminal Records
Online subscription service at https://www.doxpop.com/prod/welcome.jsp. Fees involved. Records date from 02/94. A limited free search of open cases is available.

Delaware County

Circuit Court – Civil and Criminal Records
www.dcclerk.org
Online subscription service at https://www.doxpop.com/prod/welcome.jsp. Fees involved. Records date from 01/89. A limited free search of open cases is available. Muncie City court is also available online. Access to criminal records from 1850 to 1950 only is free at www.munpl.org/Main_Pages/documents.htm, the Muncie Public Library website.

Elkhart County

Elkhart Superior Courts 1, 2, 5, 6 – Civil and Criminal Records
www.elkhartcountyindiana.com/administrative/clerk.html
Online subscription service at https://www.doxpop.com/prod/welcome.jsp. Fees involved. Records date from 1/92. A limited free search of open cases is available.

Goshen Circuit & Superior Courts 3, 4 – Civil and Criminal Records
www.elkhartcountyindiana.com/administrative/clerk.html
Online subscription service at https://www.doxpop.com/prod/welcome.jsp. Fees involved; $39.00 per month. Records date from 01/92. A limited free search of open cases is available.

Floyd County

Circuit, Superior & County Court – Civil Records
Access is the same as criminal, see below. Access to court records is free at www.floydcounty.in.gov/court_rec_menu.asp. Name search or view calendars or case summaries.

Fulton County

Circuit Court – Civil and Criminal Records

Online subscription service at https://www.doxpop.com/prod/welcome.jsp. Fees involved. Records date back to 1/1999. A limited free search of open cases is available.

Grant County

Circuit & Superior Court – Civil and Criminal Records

www.grantcounty.net

Online subscription service at https://www.doxpop.com/prod/welcome.jsp. Fees involved. Records date back to 8/1989. A limited free search of open cases is available. Gas City City Court is also available.

Henry County

Circuit & Superior Courts I & II – Civil and Criminal Records

Online subscription service at https://www.doxpop.com/prod/welcome.jsp. Fees involved. Records date back to 1/1991. A limited free search of open cases is available.

Howard County

Circuit & Superior Court – Civil and Criminal Records

http://co.howard.in.us/clerk1

Online subscription service at https://www.doxpop.com/prod/welcome.jsp. Fees involved. Records date from 07/94. A limited free search of open cases is available.

Jay County

Circuit & Superior Court – Civil and Criminal Records

www.co.jay.in.us

Online subscription service at https://www.doxpop.com/prod/welcome.jsp. Fees involved. Records date from 03/94. A limited free search of open cases is available.

Johnson County

Circuit & Superior Court – Civil and Criminal Records

Online subscription service at https://www.doxpop.com/prod/welcome.jsp. Fees involved. Records date from 08/89. A limited free search of open cases is available.

LaGrange County

Circuit & Superior Court – Civil and Criminal Records

Online subscription service at https://www.doxpop.com/prod/welcome.jsp. Fees involved. Records date back to 1/1990. A limited free search of open cases is available.

Lake County

Circuit & Superior Court – Civil and Criminal Records

www.lakecountyin.org/index.jsp

Online searching for docket records available at https://www.lakecountyin.org/portal/media-type/html/user/anon/page/online-docket. Search free but $.25 per page copy fee with $1.00 minimum.

Madison County

Circuit, Superior & County Court – Civil and Criminal Records

http://madisoncty.com/courts/index.html

Online subscription service at https://www.doxpop.com/prod/welcome.jsp. Fees involved. Records date back to 8/1989. A limited free search of open cases is available. Access to criminal is the same as civil except there are no criminal case records from the Circuit Court available.

Marion County

Circuit & Superior Court – Civil and Criminal Records

www.indygov.org/eGov/County/Clerk/home.htm

Search names online for free at www.civicnet.net. There is a $7.50 charge assessed to view each Case Summary. Online records go back to 1991. Access to online criminal records at https://www.civicnet.net/criminal/ requires a subscription or you may search at rate of $4.50 per name and pay with credit card. Criminal records go back to 1988.

Marshall County

Circuit & Superior Court 1 & 2 – Civil and Criminal Records

Online subscription service at https://www.doxpop.com/prod/welcome.jsp. Fees involved. Records date from 09/88. A limited free search of open cases is available.

Miami County

Circuit & Superior Court – Civil and Criminal Records

Online subscription service at https://www.doxpop.com/prod/welcome.jsp. Fees involved. Records date from 03/98. A limited free search of open cases is available.

Monroe County

Circuit Court – Civil and Criminal Records

www.co.monroe.in.us

Online subscription service at https://www.doxpop.com/prod/welcome.jsp. Fees involved. Records date from 08/93. A limited free search of open cases is available.

Montgomery County

Circuit, Superior & County Court – Civil and Criminal Records

www.montgomeryco.net

Online subscription service at https://www.doxpop.com/prod/welcome.jsp. Fees involved. Records date from 01/90. A limited free search of open cases is available.

Morgan County

Circuit & Superior Court – Civil and Criminal Records

Online subscription service at https://www.doxpop.com/prod/welcome.jsp. Fees involved. Records date from 01/1997. A limited free search of open cases is available. In some instances, limited information is given over the phone if the docket number is known.

Perry County

Circuit Court – Civil and Criminal Records

Online subscription service at https://www.doxpop.com/prod/welcome.jsp. Fees involved. Records date back to July 1997.

Putnam County

Circuit & Superior Court – Civil and Criminal Records

Online subscription service at https://www.doxpop.com/prod/welcome.jsp. Fees involved. Records date from 01/92. A limited free search of open cases is available.

Randolph County

Circuit & Superior Court – Civil and Criminal Records

Online subscription service at https://www.doxpop.com/prod/welcome.jsp. Fees involved. Records date from 06/94. A limited free search of open cases is available.

Spencer County

Circuit Court – Civil and Criminal Records

Fee access to civil records back to 2002 is by subscription at www.doxpop.com/prod/welcome.jsp; Free access limited to only current open cases.

Starke County

Circuit Court – Civil and Criminal Records

Online subscription service at https://www.doxpop.com/prod/welcome.jsp. Fees involved. Records date back to 9/2005 A limited free search of open cases is available.

Sullivan County

Circuit & Superior Court – Civil and Criminal Records

Online subscription service at https://www.doxpop.com/prod/welcome.jsp. Fees involved. Records date from 04/1999. A limited free search of open cases is available.

Tippecanoe County

Circuit, Superior & County Court – Civil and Criminal Records

www.tippecanoe.in.gov

Access to court records through CourtView are free online at www.county.tippecanoe.in.us/court/pa.urd/pamw6500-display.

Vigo County

Circuit Court – Civil and Criminal Records

http://vigocountyin.com
Online subscription service at https://www.doxpop.com/prod/welcome.jsp. Fees involved. Records date from 04/96. A limited free search of open cases is available.

Wabash County

Circuit & Superior Court – Civil and Criminal Records
Online subscription service at https://www.doxpop.com/prod/welcome.jsp. Fees involved. Records date from 08/89. A limited free search of open cases is available.

Wayne County

Circuit & Superior Court – Civil and Criminal Records

www.co.wayne.in.us/courts
Access records via subscription service at https://www.doxpop.com/prod/welcome.jsp. Fees involved. Records date from 3/90; a limited free search of open cases is available.

Whitley County

Circuit & Superior Court – Civil and Criminal Records
Online subscription service at https://www.doxpop.com/prod/welcome.jsp. Fees involved. Records date from 01/1999. A limited free search of open cases is available.

County Level ... Recorders & Assessors

Recording Office Organization: 92 counties, 92 recording offices. The recording officer is the County Recorder (or the Circuit Clerk for state tax liens on personal property). Many counties utilize a "Miscellaneous Index" for tax and other liens. 81 counties are in the Eastern Time Zone (EST), and 11 are in the Central Time Zone (CST). All federal tax liens on personal property are filed with the County Recorder. State tax liens on personal property are filed with the Circuit Clerk who is in a different office from the Recorder. Refer to the County Court section for information about Indiana Circuit Courts. Most counties will not perform tax lien searches.

Online Access Note: A growing number of county agencies offer online access. The most notable is the subscription service offered by Marion County at www.civicnet.net.

Bartholomew County   *Property, GIS Records*

www.bartholomewco.com
Access to county Public Access Geographic Information System is free at http://gis.bartholomewco.com/pagis/login.aspx; you must have an email for free registration and login.

Clinton County   *Property, Assessor, GIS Records*

Search assessor property data for a fee on GIS system at http://webgishome.promap.com/Default.aspx. Registration username required

Elkhart County   *Real Estate, Lien, Tax Assessor Records*

www.elkhartindiana.org
Access Elkhart County records for an annual fee of $50. plus a minimum of $20. per month of use. The minimum fee allows for 2 hours access, and add'l use is billed at $10 per hour. Lending agency information available. For information, call at 574-535-6777.

Fayette County   *Property, Assessor Records*

www.co.fayette.in.us
Access assessor property data free at www.co.fayette.in.us/auditor.htm.

Floyd County   *Recording, Real Estate Records*

www.floydcounty.in.gov
Computerized versions of microfiche cards will be on the internet sometime; call clerk at 812-948-5430 for update information.

Gibson County *Assessor, Property Records*
Access assessor property data free at http://in-gibson-assessor.governmaxa.com. Click on "Start your search"

Grant County
Recorder, Deed, UCC, Mortgage, Assessor, Property Tax, Voter Registration, Sex Offender Records
www.grantcounty.net
Access to recorder data is free at http://recorder.grant.in.uinquire.us/. Click on "Recorder Information." Tax information is free at http://auditor.grant.in.uinquire.us/. Click on "Tax Information." Access to assessor property information is free at http://in27.plexisgroup.com/ecama/index.cfm. Click on "Property Information." The sheriff's sex offender list is at http://sheriff.grant.in.uinquire.us/. Click on "Sex Offenders." Also, voter registration is at http://voters.grant.in.uinquire.us/nxweb.exe; registration, login, and password required.

Hamilton County *Inmate, Offender Records*
Search inmate information for free on private company website at www.hamiltoncountyauditor.org/realestate/.

Hancock County *Sale Disclosure Records*
www.hancockcoingov.org/recorder
Access to the assessor's sales disclosure data is free at www.hancockcoingov.org/assessor/sales_disclosure_search.asp.

Hendricks County *Property, GIS-Mapping, Assessor Records*
www.co.hendricks.in.us
Access to county property data on the GIS mapping site is free at http://in32.plexisgroup.com/map/index.html. Click on "Query" to select query by owner name. Also, search the assessor's property data free at www.co.hendricks.in.us/DWLookup/Disclaimer.asp.

Howard County *Property, Assessor, GIS Records*
Search assessor property data for a fee on the GIS system at http://webgishome.promap.com/Default.aspx. Registration and username required.

Kosciusko County *Property, GIS Mapping Records*
http://kcgov.com/countyOfficeSelect.asp
Recorded documents are not online. But access to property records on the searchable GIS mapping site is free at http://kcgov.com/application/gis/viewer.htm. Click on "Search" to get to name search mode.

Lake County *Assessor, Property Tax Records*
Access property tax data online at www.lakecountyin.org/index.jsp; click on "online property tax information" and follow links. Search free as Guest, but no name searching. Subscription service allows name searching; sub fee is $19.95 per month.

La Porte County *Recording, Real Estate, Deed, Lien Records*
www.laportecounty.org
Recorder office data by subscription on either the Laredo system using subscription and fees or the Tapestry System using credit card, https://tapestry.fidlar.com/tapsearch.aspx; $3.99 search; $.50 per image. Index back to 8/1988; images to 8/1999.

Marion County *Real Estate, Lien, Deed, UCC, Inmate Records*
www.indygov.org/eGov/County/Recorder/home.htm
Access to Marion County online records requires a $200 set up fee, plus an escrow balance of at least $100 must be maintained. add'l charges are $.25 per minute, $.05 display charge for 1st page; $.05 each add'l page. Records date back to 1964; images from 1964. Federal tax liens and UCC information are available. For information, contact Mike Kerner at 317-327-4587. Also, acquire recording information on customized CD-rom and in specialized online reports. Also, access recording office land data at www.etitlesearch.com; registration required, fee based on usage. Also, search inmate info on private company website at www.vinelink.com/index.jsp.

St. Joseph County *Recording, Real Estate, Deed, Lien, Most Wanted Records*
Recorder office data by subscription on either the Laredo system using subscription and fees or the Tapestry System using credit card, https://tapestry.fidlar.com/tapsearch.aspx; $3.99 search; $.50 per image. Index back to 12/1992; images 1998 to 2005.

Tippecanoe County *Assessor, Real Estate, GIS Mapping Records*
http://county.tippecanoe.in.us
A subscription fee of $10 per month plus a one-time set-up fee of $50 allows full access to both the tax database and the assessment database. Click on Access Property Tax & Assessment Records. Free access to mapping at www.tippecanoe.in.gov/gis/.

Tipton County *Assessor, Property, GIS Records*
Search assessor property data for a fee on the GIS system at http://webgishome.promap.com/Default.aspx. Registration and account required.

Vanderburgh County *Property Records*
www.assessor.evansville.net
Records on the County Assessor Property database are free at www.assessor.evansville.net/disclaim.htm.

Vigo County *Assessor, Property, Tax Sale Records*
www.vigocounty.org/recorder/
Search Vigo County property information by parcel, name or address at www.vigocounty.org/assessor/.

Wabash County *Property, Assessor, Warrant, Sex Offender Records*
www.wabashcounty.in.gov
Access property information free from the Property List at http://assessor.wabash.in.datapitstop.us. Click on Property Information. Also, search sheriff's warrants and sex offender data free at www.geocities.com/Pentagon/7155/.

Warrick County *Assessor, Property, Tax Bill Records*
www.warrickcounty.gov/departments/recorder.htm
Access to the assessors property tax data is free at www.pvdnetwork.com/Search/Search.asp. Also, access to tax bill records is free at www.pvdnetwork.com/Search/TaxSearch.asp.

Wayne County *Property, Assessor, Marriage Records*
http://co.wayne.in.us/recorder/
Access to the county property records database is free at http://prc.co.wayne.in.us. Marriage records are being added irregularly to the website at www.co.wayne.in.us/marriage/retrieve.cgi. Records are from 1811 forward, with recent years being added. Access tor recorded document indexes through doxpop go to www.doxpop.com

Whitley County *Property, Assessor, GIS Records*
Search assessor property data for a fee on the GIS system at http://webgishome.promap.com/Default.aspx. Registration and username required.

Federal Courts in Indiana...

Standards for Federal Courts: The universal PACER sign-up number is 800-676-6856. Find PACER and the Party/Case Index on the Web at http://pacer.psc.uscourts.gov. PACER dial-up access is $.60 per minute. Also, courts offering internet access via PACER, Web-PACER or the new CM-ECF charge $.08 per page fee ($.07 per page if record is pre-2005 or unless noted as free).

US District Court -- Northern District of Indiana

www.innd.uscourts.gov

PACER: Case records are available back to 1994. Records are purged as deemed necessary. New records are available online after 1 day. **PACER Online Access:** ECF replaces PACER. **Electronic Filing:** CM/ECF data at https://ecf.innd.uscourts.gov. **Opinions:** View court opinions at www.innd.uscourts.gov/opinions.asp.

Fort Wayne Division counties: Adams, Allen, Blackford, DeKalb, Grant, Huntington, Jay, Lagrange, Noble, Steuben, Wells, Whitley.

Hammond Division counties: Lake, Porter.

Lafayette Division counties: Benton, Carroll, Jasper, Newton, Tippecanoe, Warren, White.

South Bend Division counties: Cass, Elkhart, Fulton, Kosciusko, La Porte, Marshall, Miami, Pulaski, St. Joseph, Starke, Wabash.

US Bankruptcy Court -- Northern District of Indiana

www.innb.uscourts.gov

PACER: Case records are available back to 1992. Records are purged every 6 months. New records are available online after 1 day. **PACER Online Access:** ECF replaces PACER. **Electronic Filing:** CM/ECF data at https://ecf.innb.uscourts.gov. **Opinions:** View court opinions at www.innb.uscourts.gov/opinions/. **Other Online Access:** Judges calendars at www.innb.uscourts.gov/courtcal.htm.

Phone access: Voice Case Information System, call 800-755-8393, 574-236-8814

Fort Wayne Division counties: Adams, Allen, Blackford, DeKalb, Grant, Huntington, Jay, Lagrange, Noble, Steuben, Wells, Whitley.

Hammond at Gary Division counties: Lake, Porter.

Hammond at Lafayette Division counties: Benton, Carroll, Jasper, Newton, Tippecanoe, Warren, White. All files for the Hammond Division at Lafayette are physically kept in the Fort Wayne office. All papers pertaining to Hammond Division at Lafayette cases after the initial filing, including claims, should be sent to the Fort Wayne office. .

South Bend Division counties: Cass, Elkhart, Fulton, Kosciusko, La Porte, Marshall, Miami, Pulaski, St. Joseph, Starke, Wabash.

US District Court -- Southern District of Indiana

www.insd.uscourts.gov

PACER: Electronic Filing: CM/ECF data at https://ecf.insd.uscourts.gov. **Other Online Access:** Search case records free at www.insd.uscourts.gov/Search/case_search.htm; all Criminal cases but civil 1991-2002 only.

Evansville Division counties: Daviess, Dubois, Gibson, Martin, Perry, Pike, Posey, Spencer, Vanderburgh, Warrick.

Indianapolis Division counties: Bartholomew, Boone, Brown, Clinton, Decatur, Delaware, Fayette, Fountain, Franklin, Hamilton, Hancock, Hendricks, Henry, Howard, Johnson, Madison, Marion, Monroe, Montgomery, Morgan, Randolph, Rush, Shelby, Tipton, Union, Wayne.

New Albany Division counties: Clark, Crawford, Dearborn, Floyd, Harrison, Jackson, Jefferson, Jennings, Lawrence, Ohio, Orange, Ripley, Scott, Switzerland, Washington.

Terre Haute Division counties: Clay, Greene, Knox, Owen, Parke, Putnam, Sullivan, Vermillion, Vigo.

US Bankruptcy Court -- Southern District of Indiana

www.insb.uscourts.gov

PACER: Sign-up number is 317-229-3845. Case records are available back to 1988. Records are purged every 3 months. New records are available online after 1 day. **PACER Online Access:** PACER at www.insb.uscourts.gov. Click on "Case Search." Registration and fees required. Document images available. The free case lookup system is no longer found. **Electronic Filing:** CM/ECF data at https://ecf.insb.uscourts.gov. **Opinions:** Includes judge calendars as well. View court opinions at http://pacer.insb.uscourts.gov/public/default.asp. **Phone access:** Voice Case Information System, call 800-335-8003.

Evansville Division counties: Daviess, Dubois, Gibson, Martin, Perry, Pike, Posey, Spencer, Vanderburgh, Warrick.

Indianapolis Division counties: Bartholomew, Boone, Brown, Clinton, Decatur, Delaware, Fayette, Fountain, Franklin, Hamilton, Hancock, Hendricks, Henry, Howard, Johnson, Madison, Marion, Monroe, Montgomery, Morgan, Randolph, Rush, Shelby, Tipton, Union, Wayne.

New Albany Division counties: Clark, Crawford, Dearborn, Floyd, Harrison, Jackson, Jefferson, Jennings, Lawrence, Ohio, Orange, Ripley, Scott, Switzerland, Washington.

Terre Haute Division counties: Clay, Greene, Knox, Owen, Parke, Putnam, Sullivan, Vermillion, Vigo.

Iowa

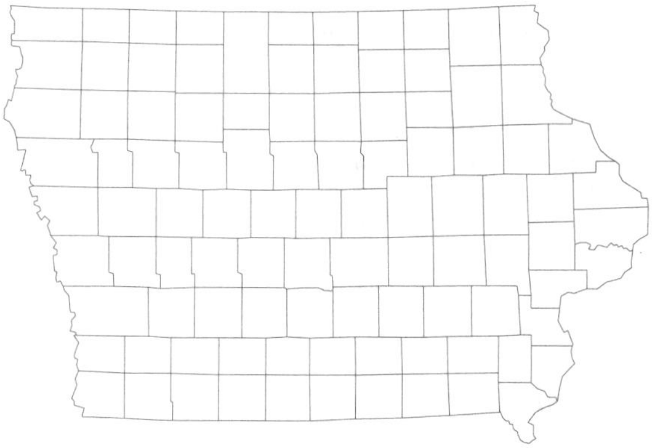

Capital: Des Moines
      Polk County
Time Zone: CST
Population: 2,954,451
# of Counties: 99

Quick Links

Website: www.iowa.gov/state/main/index.html
Governor: www.governor.state.ia.us
Attorney General: www.state.ia.us/government/ag
State Archives: www.iowahistory.org
Legislative Bill Search:
    http://coolice.legis.state.ia.us/Cool-ICE/default.asp?category=billinfo&Service=Billbook
Bill Monitoring:
    http://coolice.legis.state.ia.us/Cool-ICE/default.asp?Category=BillWatch&Service=BWSignIn
Unclaimed Funds: http://greatiowatreasurehunt.com/dsp_search.cfm

State Level ... Major Agencies

Statewide Court Records

Clerk of Supreme Court, Judicial Branch Bldg, 111 East Court Ave, Des Moines, IA 50319; 515-281-5911, Fax-515-242-6164.
www.judicial.state.ia.us
Online search: Criminal, civil, probate, traffic and appellate information is available from all 99 counties in Iowa at www.judicial.state.ia.us/online_records/. There is no fee for basic information, and a pay system is available for more detailed requests. Name searches are available on a statewide or specific county basis. Although records are updated daily, the historical records offered are not from the same starting date on a county-by-county basis. Also, from the home page one may access supreme and appellate court opinions. **Other options:** The State Law Library (515-281-5124) has case information. A list of licensed attorneys may be purchased from the Client Security Commission (515-725-8029).

Sexual Offender Registry

Division of Criminal Investigations, SOR Unit, Wallace State Office Bldg, Des Moines, IA 50319; 515-281-8716, Fax-515-281-4898.
www.iowasexoffender.com/
Online search: The website contains the majority of sex offenders registered in Iowa. Instant access is available.

Incarceration Records

Iowa Department of Corrections, 420 Watson Powell Jr. Way,, Des Moines, IA 50309-1639; 515-242-5708, 515-281-4062 (Second fax number), Fax-515-281-7345, 8AM-4:30PM.
www.doc.state.ia.us
Online search: Click on Public Info for an inmate search. This site seems to be under construction at times. **Other options:** Bulk records are not available, but should be in the future.

Corporation, Limited Liability Company, Fictitious Name, Limited Partnership, Trademarks/Servicemarks

Secretary of State - Corporation Division, 321 E 12th Street, 1st Floor, Lucas Bldg, Des Moines, IA 50319; 515-281-5204, Fax-515-242-5953, 8AM-4:30PM.

www.sos.state.ia.us
Online search: For free searching, go to www.sos.state.ia.us/corp/corp_search.asp. **Other options:** This agency will sell the records in database format. Call the number listed above and ask for Karen Ubaldo for more information.

Uniform Commercial Code, Federal Tax Liens

UCC Division, Secretary of State, 1st Floor, Lucas Bldg, Des Moines, IA 50319; 515-281-5204, Fax-515-242-6556, 8AM-4:30PM.
www.sos.state.ia.us
Online search: All computerized data on or before June 30, 2001 is available www.sos.state.ia.us/Ucc_Search/UccOld_Search.html. There is no fee at this "UCC Archive" site. For most computerized records from July 1, 2001 to present, search at www.sos.state.ia.us/UCC_Search/UCC_Search.asp. Effective 11/05, A fee is required to view images on lien documents that include debtors who are individuals. There is a $25.00 annual subscription, prorated by year, to obtain a PIN. Visit www.sos.state.ia.us/Ucc_Search/Ucc_Search.asp.

Driver Records

Department of Transportation, Driver Service Records Section, PO Box 9204, Des Moines, IA 50306-9204 (Courier: Park Fair Mall, 100 Euclid, Des Moines, IA 50306); 515-244-9124, 800-532-1121 (Iowa only), Fax-515-237-3152, 8AM-4:30PM.
www.dot.state.ia.us/mvd
Online search: The state requires that all ongoing requesters/users access records via IowaAccess. The fee is $8.50 per record, the service is interactive or batch. Requesters must be approved and open an account. The records contain personal information, so requesters must comply with DPPA. For more information, contact IowaAccess at 515-323-3468 or 866-492-3468.

Vehicle Ownership, Vehicle Identification

Department of Transportation, Office of Vehicle Services, PO Box 9278, Des Moines, IA 50306-9278 (Courier: Park Fair Mall, 100 Euclid, Des Moines, IA 50306); 515-237-3148, 515-237-3049, Fax-515-237-3181, 8AM-4:30PM.
www.dot.state.ia.us/mvd
Online search: Online access is available to dealers, Iowa licensed investigators and security companies. There is no fee. All accounts must register and be pre-approved. Write to the Office of Motor Vehicle, explaining purpose/use of records. **Other options:** Iowa makes the entire vehicle file or selected data available for purchase. Weekly updates are also available for those purchasers. Requesters subject to DPPA requirements. For more information, call 515-237-3110.

State Level ... Occupational Licensing

Acupuncturist	www.docboard.org/ia/df/iasearch.htm
Anesthesiologist	www.docboard.org/ia/df/iasearch.htm
Architect	www.state.ia.us/government/com/prof/search/index.html
Bank	www.idob.state.ia.us
Debt Management Company	www.idob.state.ia.us/license/lic_default.htm
Delayed Deposit Service Business	www.idob.state.ia.us/license/lic_default.htm
Engineer	www.state.ia.us/government/com/prof/search/index.html
Excursion Gambling Boat	www.iowa.gov/irgc/
Finance Company	www.idob.state.ia.us/license/lic_default.htm
Hypnotist	www.docboard.org/ia/df/iasearch.htm
Landscape Architect	www.state.ia.us/government/com/prof/search/index.html
Lobbyist	www.legis.state.ia.us/Lobbyist.html
Medical Doctor	www.docboard.org/ia/df/iasearch.htm
Money Transmitter	www.idob.state.ia.us/license/lic_default.htm
Mortgage Banker/Broker/Loan Service	www.idob.state.ia.us/license/lic_default.htm
Notary Public	www.sos.state.ia.us/notaries/notary_search.asp
Nurse/Nurse LPN	www.state.ia.us/nursing/Licensure.html
Nurse, Advance Registered Practice	www.state.ia.us/nursing/Licensure.html
Optometrist	www.arbo.org/index.php?action=findanoptometrist
Orthopedic Doctor	www.docboard.org/ia/df/iasearch.htm
Osteopathic Physician	www.docboard.org/ia/df/iasearch.htm
Pari-Mutuel Race Track Enclosure	www.iowa.gov/irgc/
Pediatrician	www.docboard.org/ia/df/iasearch.htm
Pesticide Dealer/Applicator	www.kellysolutions.com/ia/dealers/index.asp

Psychiatrist.. www.docboard.org/ia/df/iasearch.htm
Real Estate Agent/Broker/Sales .... www.state.ia.us/government/com/prof/search/index.html
Real Estate Appraiser................................. www.state.ia.us/government/com/prof/search/index.html
Surveyor, Land .... www.state.ia.us/government/com/prof/search/index.html

County Level ... Courts

Court Administration: State Court Administrator, Judicial Branch Bldg, 1111 East Court Ave, Des Moines, IA, 50319; 515-281-5241; www.judicial.state.ia.us

Court Structure: The District Court is the court of general jurisdiction. Effective 7/1/95, the Small Claims limit increased to $4000 from $3000.

Vital records were moved from courts to the County Recorder s office in each county.

Online Access Note: Criminal, civil, probate, traffic and appellate information is now available from all 99 Iowa counties at www.judicial.state.ia.us/online_records. There is no fee for basic information and a pay system is offered for more detailed requests. Name searches are available on either a statewide or specific county basis. While this is an excellent site with much information, there is one important consideration to keep in mind– although records are updated daily, the historical records offered are not from the same starting date on a county-by-county basis. Also, from the home page one may access Supreme Court and Appellate Court opinions.

County Level ... Recorders & Assessors

Recording Office Organization: 99 counties, 100 recording offices. Lee County has two recording offices. The recording officer is the County Recorder. Many counties utilize a grantor/grantee index containing all transactions recorded with them. The entire state is in the Central Time Zone (CST). Federal tax liens on personal property of businesses are filed with the Secretary of State. Other federal and all state tax liens on personal property are filed with the County Recorder. County search practices vary widely but most provide some sort of tax lien search for $6.00 per name.

Online Access Note: As yet there is no fully operational statewide access to county recorder data, however 87-plus counties' land records are available at http://iowalandrecords.org after you register. New in 2005, this County Land Record Information System offers free searching and pdf images of deeds, liens, even UCCs and judgments, though this state-sponsored service may begin charging at any time. There is also features for monitoring for new documents and saving documents.

Assessor records for 58 counties plus cities of Ames, Cedar Rapids, Dubuque, Iowa City, and Souix City are available free at www.iowaassessors.com. A statewide Property Tax lookup and payment page is at www.iowatreasurers.org/county_locator.cfm?ID=1. First, select the county then follow prompts to the search page where you can first look-up the name, then parcel information.

Adair County   *Assessor, Property Records*
Access to the assessor database of property and sales data is free at www.adair.iowaassessors.com. At http://iowalandrecords.org/portal/clris/SwitchToCountiesTab, an index of recorded land records is available from 1/1991; images from 1/2004.

Adams County   *Real Estate, Deed, Lien, UCC, Judgment Records*
At http://iowalandrecords.org/portal/clris/SwitchToCountiesTab, an index of recorded land records is available from 1/1995; images from 1/2005.

Allamakee County   *Real Estate, Deed, Lien, Judgment, Assessor, Property, GIS Records*
At http://iowalandrecords.org/portal/clris/SwitchToCountiesTab an index and images of recorded land records are available from 4/1991. Also, search assessor property data free on the GIS system at http://webgishome.promap.com/Default.aspx.

Appanoose County *Real Estate, Deed, Lien, UCC, Judgment Records*
At http://iowalandrecords.org/portal/clris/SwitchToCountiesTab, an index of land records and images are available from 06/2001.

Audubon County *Property, Assessor, GIS Records*
Search assessor property data for a fee on GIS system at http://webgishome.promap.com/Default.aspx. Registration/username required

Benton County *Real Estate, Deed, Lien, UCC, Judgment, Property, Assessor, GIS Records*
At http://iowalandrecords.org/portal/clris/SwitchToCountiesTab, an index of recorded land records and images are available from 2/26/2004. Also, search assessor property data free on the GIS system at http://webgishome.promap.com/Default.aspx.

Black Hawk County *Assessor, Property Records*
Access to the assessor database of property and sales data is free at www.co.black-hawk.ia.us/depts/bhentry.htm.

Boone County *Assessor, Property, Real Estate, Deed, Lien, UCC, Judgment, GIS Records*
www.co.boone.ia.us
Access to the assessor GIS database of property and sales data is free at http://webgishome.promap.com/default.aspx. At http://iowalandrecords.org/portal/clris/SwitchToCountiesTab, an index of land records and their images are available from 08/2002.

Bremer County *Real Estate, Deed, Assessor, Property Tax Records*
At http://iowalandrecords.org/portal/clris/SwitchToCountiesTab, an index of recorded land records and their images are available from 08/2002. Search assessor property records at http://bremer.iowaassessors.com.

Buena Vista County
Property, Assessor, Real Estate, Deed, Lien, UCC, Judgment, Ag Sale, Inmate, Accident, Incident Records
At http://iowalandrecords.org/portal/clris/SwitchToCountiesTab, an index of recorded land records and their images are available from 1/1999. Also, search the property assessor and Ag sales databases for free at www.co.buena-vista.ia.us/assessors/. No name searching. Also, search the jail inmates list for free at www.bvsheriff.com/jailroster/index.html. Also, search accident/incident reports for free at www.bvsheriff.com/accident-incident/index.html.

Butler County *Real Estate, Recorded land Document Records*
At http://iowalandrecords.org/portal/clris/SwitchToCountiesTab, an index of recorded land records and their images are available from 1/2004.

Calhoun County *Real Estate, Deed, Treasurer, Property, Death, Assessor, Real Estate Sale Records*
www.calhouncountyiowa.com
Access to the treasurers property database is free; see Online Access note at beginning of section. Also, access to Death records for genealogists is free at www.rootsweb.com/~usgenweb/ia/calhoun/deaths.html. At http://iowalandrecords.org/portal/clris/SwitchToCountiesTab, an index of recorded land records and their images are available from 1/2003. Also, access to the assessor database of property and sales data is free at www.calhoun.iowaassessors.com.

Carroll County *Real Estate, Deed, Assessor, Property Tax Records*
Access to the assessor database of property and sales data is free at www.co.carroll.ia.us/Assessor/property_records.htm. At http://iowalandrecords.org/portal/clris/SwitchToCountiesTab, an index of recorded land records is available from 1/2001.

Cass County *Real Estate, Deed, Lien, UCC, Judgment, Warrant Records*
www.casscountyiowa.org
At http://iowalandrecords.org/portal/clris/SwitchToCountiesTab, an index of recorded land records and their images are available from 1/1991. Also, search sheriff's warrants free at www.sheriffcass.com/warrants.html.

Cedar County *Real Estate, Deed, Lien, UCC, Judgment Records*
At http://iowalandrecords.org/portal/clris/SwitchToCountiesTab, an index of recorded land records is available from 01/04, their images are available from 01/05.

Cerro Gordo County *Real Estate Sale, Property, Assessor Records*
www.co.cerro-gordo.ia.us
Access to the County and Mason City property records is free at www.co.cerro-gordo.ia.us/property_search/property_search.cfm. Also, access to recorded documents at www.co.cerro-gordo.ia.us/document_indexing_inquiry/docindex_inquiry.cfm.

Cherokee County   *Real Estate, Deed, Lien, UCC, Judgment Records*

At http://iowalandrecords.org/portal/clris/SwitchToCountiesTab, an index of recorded land records is available from 1/2000, images available from 03/2002.

Chickasaw County   *Real Estate, Deed, Lien, UCC, Judgment, Assessor, Property, GIS Records*

www.chickasawcoia.org/Recorder

At http://iowalandrecords.org/portal/clris/SwitchToCountiesTab, an index of recorded land records and their images are available from 1/2004. Access to the assessor database of property and sales data is free at www.iowaassessors.com. Also, search property data free on the GIS system at http://webgishome.promap.com/Default.aspx but name searching requires you to have an account.

Clarke County   *Real Estate, Deed, Assessor, Property Tax Records*

www.clarkecountyia.org/recorder/index.html

Access to the assessor database of property and sales data is free at www.clarkecountyiowa.org/assessor/index.html. At http://iowalandrecords.org/portal/clris/SwitchToCountiesTab, an index of land records and their images are available from 1/2004.

Clay County   *Real Estate, Recording, Grantor/Grantee, Lien, Judgment, UCC, Tax Sale Certificate, Mortgage, Assessor, Property Records*

www.co.clay.ia.us

At the main website, click to choose database to search; name search on all except the real estate/tax inquiry. At http://iowalandrecords.org/portal/clris/SwitchToCountiesTab, an index of recorded land records and their images are available from 1/2004. Also, access to the assessor database of property and sales data is free at http://clay.iowaassessors.com.

Clinton County   *Real Estate, Deed, Assessor, Property Tax Records*

www.clintoncountyiowa.com/recorder/default.asp

Access to the assessor database of property and sales data is free at www.qpublic.net/clinton/search1.html. At http://iowalandrecords.org/portal/clris/SwitchToCountiesTab, an index of land records and their images are available from 1/1998.

Crawford County   *Real Estate, Deed, Lien, UCC, Judgment Records*

http://crawfordcounty.org

At http://iowalandrecords.org/portal/clris/SwitchToCountiesTab, view an index of land records from 1/1999, images from 1/2004.

Dallas County   *Assessor, Property Records*

Access to the assessor database of property and sales data is free at www.dallas.iowaassessors.com. At http://iowalandrecords.org/portal/clris/SwitchToCountiesTab, view an index of recorded land records from 1/2004.

Davis County   *Real Estate, Assessor, Property Tax, Deed, Lien, UCC, Judgment, GIS Records*

www.daviscountyrecorder.org

At http://iowalandrecords.org/portal/clris/SwitchToCountiesTab, view an index of recorded land records from 1/1980, images from 03/15/2002. Also, access to the assessor GIS database of property and sales data is free at http://webgishome.promap.com/?site=DavisCountyIA.

Decatur County   *Real Estate, Deed Records*

At http://iowalandrecords.org/portal/clris/SwitchToCountiesTab, view an index of land records from 1/2004, images from 1/2004.

Delaware County   *Real Estate, Deed, Property, Assessor, GIS Records*

At http://iowalandrecords.org/portal/clris/SwitchToCountiesTab, view an index of recorded land records from 1/2004, images from 1/2004. Also, search assessor property data for a fee on the GIS system at http://webgishome.promap.com/Default.aspx. Registration and username required.

Des Moines County   *Real Estate, Deed, Assessor, Property Tax Records*

www.co.des-moines.ia.us

Access to the assessor database of property and sales data is free at www.dmcgis.com/. At http://iowalandrecords.org/portal/clris/SwitchToCountiesTab, view an index of recorded land records from 1/2000, images from 1/2004.

Dickinson County   *Assessor, Property Records*

Access to the assessor database of property and sales data is free at http://dickinson.iowaassessors.com.

Dubuque County *Real Estate, Deed, Assessor, Property, GIS Records*
www.dubuquecounty.org
Access to the assessor database of property and sales data is free at http://beacon.schneidercorp.com/?site=DubuqueCountyIA. At http://iowalandrecords.org/portal/clris/SwitchToCountiesTab, view index of recorded land records from 1/2004, images from 1/2004. Also, search assessor property data free on GIS system at http://webgishome.promap.com/Default.aspx but no name search.

Emmet County *Real Estate, Deed, Assessor, Property, GIS Records*
Access the assessor GIS database of property and sales data free at http://webgishome.promap.com/default.aspx?site=EmmetCountyIA. At http://iowalandrecords.org/portal/clris/SwitchToCountiesTab, view an index of recorded land records from 1/2003, images from 1/2004.

Fayette County *Real Estate, Deed, Most Wanted, Property, Assessor, GIS Records*
www.fayettecounty.ia.com
At http://iowalandrecords.org/portal/clris/SwitchToCountiesTab, view an index of recorded land records from 1/2004, images from 1/2004. Search for Fayette County most wanted at www.fayettecountysheriff.com/mostwanted.htm. Access to the assessor GIS database of property and sales data is free at http://webgishome.promap.com/?site=FayetteCountyIA.

Floyd County *Assessor, Property, Real Estate, Deed, Lien, UCC, Judgment, GIS Records*
www.floydcoia.org
Access to the assessor database of property and sales data is free at www.floydcoia.org/features/gis.asp. Also, search assessor property data free on the GIS system at http://webgishome.promap.com/Default.aspx but name searching; requires registration and password. At http://iowalandrecords.org/portal/clris/SwitchToCountiesTab, view an index of recorded land records from 3/1995, images from 8/22/1996.

Franklin County *Real Estate, Deed, Lien Records*
At http://iowalandrecords.org/portal/clris/SwitchToCountiesTab, view an index of land records from 10/2001, images from 10/2004.

Fremont County *Real Estate, Deed, Lien, UCC, Judgment Records*
www.co.fremont.ia.us
At http://iowalandrecords.org/portal/clris/SwitchToCountiesTab, view an index of recorded land records from 1/1990, images from 1/1990.

Greene County *Assessor, Property, Real Estate, Deed, Lien, UCC, Judgment Records*
www.co.greene.ia.us
Access to the assessor database of property and sales data is free at http://greene.iowaassessors.com. At http://iowalandrecords.org/portal/clris/SwitchToCountiesTab, view an index of land records from 1/1988, images from 1/1988.

Grundy County *Real Estate, Deed, Assessor, Property, GIS Records*
Access to the assessor GIS database of property and sales data is free at http://webgishome.promap.com/?site=GrundyCountyIA. At http://iowalandrecords.org/portal/clris/SwitchToCountiesTab, view an index of land records from 1/2004, images from 1/2004.

Guthrie County *Real Estate, Deed, Assessor, Property Tax Records*
Access to the assessor database of property and sales data is free at www.guthrie.iowaassessors.com. At http://iowalandrecords.org/portal/clris/SwitchToCountiesTab, view an index of land records from 1/2004, images from 1/2004.

Hamilton County *Assessor, Property, Real Estate, Sales, Deed, Lien, UCC, Judgment Records*
www.hamiltoncounty.org
At http://iowalandrecords.org/portal/clris/SwitchToCountiesTab, view an index of recorded land records from 1/2004, images from 1/2004. Also, assessor property records free at http://hamilton.iowaassessors.com.

Hancock County *Real Estate, Deed Records*
At http://iowalandrecords.org/portal/clris/SwitchToCountiesTab, view an index of land records from 1/2004, images from 1/2004.

Hardin County *Real Estate, Recorder, Deed, Assessor, GIS Records*
At http://iowalandrecords.org/portal/clris/SwitchToCountiesTab, view an index of recorded land records from 1/2004, images from 1/2004. Also, search City of Iowa Falls assessor property data for a fee on the GIS system at http://webgishome.promap.com/Default.aspx. Registration and username required.

Harrison County *Real Estate, Deed, Assessor, Property, GIS Records*

Access to the assessor database of property and sales data and maps is free at http://maps.harrisoncountyia.org. Also, search assessor property data free on the GIS system at http://webgishome.promap.com/Default.aspx. At http://iowalandrecords.org/portal/clris/SwitchToCountiesTab, view an index of recorded land records from 1/2004.

Henry County *Real Estate, Deed, Assessor, Property Tax, GIS Records*

At http://iowalandrecords.org/portal/clris/SwitchToCountiesTab, view an index of recorded land records from 1/2002, images from 1/2002. Assessor records available at www.henrycountyiowa.us/Assessor.html. Also, search assessor property data for a fee on the GIS system at http://webgishome.promap.com/Default.aspx. Registration and username required.

Howard County *Real Estate, Deed, Lien, UCC, Judgment Records*

At http://iowalandrecords.org/portal/clris/SwitchToCountiesTab, view an index of recorded land records from 1/2004.

Humboldt County *Real Estate, Deed, Property Assessor Records*

At http://iowalandrecords.org/portal/clris/SwitchToCountiesTab, view an index of recorded land records from 1/2004, images from 1/2004. Assessor records at www.humboldt.iowaassessors.com.

Ida County *Real Estate, Deed Records*

At http://iowalandrecords.org/portal/clris/SwitchToCountiesTab, view an index of recorded land records from 1/2003.

Iowa County *Real Estate, Grantor/Grantee, Deed, Assessor, Property Records*

www.co.iowa.ia.us/recorder.htm
Access real estate records free at http://65.240.48.153/index.html. At http://iowalandrecords.org/portal/clris/SwitchToCountiesTab, view an index of recorded land records from 1/2004, images from 1/2004. Access to the assessor database of property and sales data is free at http://iowa.iowaassessors.com.

Jackson County *Real Estate, Deed, Lien, UCC, Judgment, GIS Records*

www.jacksoncountyiowa.com
At http://iowalandrecords.org/portal/clris/SwitchToCountiesTab, view an index of recorded land records from 1/1998, images from 1/1998. Also, search assessor property data for a fee on the GIS system at http://webgishome.promap.com/Default.aspx. Registration and username required.

Jasper County *Real Estate, Deed, Assessor, Property Tax Records*

Access to the assessor database of property and sales data is free at http://beacon.schneidercorp.com/?site=JohnsonCountyIA. At http://iowalandrecords.org/portal/clris/SwitchToCountiesTab, view an index of recorded land records from 1/2004, images from 1/2004.

Jefferson County *Assessor, Property Records*

Access to the assessor database of property and sales data is free at www.iowaassessors.com.

Johnson County *Real Estate, Recorder, Deed, Assessor, Property, GIS Records*

www.johnson-county.com/recorder
Access to the assessor database of property and sales data is free at http://beacon.schneidercorp.com/?site=JohnsonCountyIA. Also, access to Iowa City assessor and property data is free at http://iowacity.iowaassessors.com. At http://iowalandrecords.org/portal/clris/SwitchToCountiesTab, view index of recorded land records from 2004, images from 2/27/2004. Also, search assessor property data free on GIS system at http://webgishome.promap.com/Default.aspx but no name search.

Jones County *Real Estate, Deed Records*

www.co.jones.ia.us/recorder.html
At http://iowalandrecords.org/portal/clris/SwitchToCountiesTab, view an index of recorded land records from 1/1999, images from 1/1999.

Keokuk County *Real Estate, Deed, Lien, UCC, Judgment, Assessor, Property, GIS Records*

www.keokukcountyia.com
At http://iowalandrecords.org/portal/clris/SwitchToCountiesTab, view an index of recorded land records from 1/1991, images from 1/1996. Access to the assessor GIS database of property and sales data is free at http://webgishome.promap.com/?site=KeokukCountyIA.

Kossuth County *Assessor, Property, Real Estate, Deed, Lien, UCC, Judgment Records*
Access to the assessor database of property and sales data is free at www.co.kossuth.ia.us/assessor/assessor.htm. At
http://iowalandrecords.org/portal/clris/SwitchToCountiesTab, view an index of land records from 1/2004, images from 1/2004.

Lee County (Northern District) *Real Estate, Deed, Lien, UCC, Judgment Records*
www.leecounty.org
At http://iowalandrecords.org/portal/clris/SwitchToCountiesTab, view an index of recorded land records from 1/2003, images from
1/2003.

Lee County (Southern District) *Real Estate, Deed, Lien, UCC, Judgment Records*
www.leecounty.org
At http://iowalandrecords.org/portal/clris/SwitchToCountiesTab, view an index of land records from 1/2004, images from 1/2004.

Linn County *Assessor, Property, Real Estate, Deed, Lien, UCC, Judgment Records*
www.linncountyrecorder.com
Access to the assessor database of property and sales data is free at www.linn.iowaassessors.com/search.php. Also, access to City of
Cedar Rapids property information is free at www.cedar-rapids-assessor.org/pmc/. No name searching. At
http://iowalandrecords.org/portal/clris/SwitchToCountiesTab, view an index of land records from 1/1990, images from 1/1990.

Louisa County *Real Estate, Deed Records*
At http://iowalandrecords.org/portal/clris/SwitchToCountiesTab, view an index of land records from 1/1992, images from 11/2003.

Lucas County *Real Estate, Deed Records*
At http://iowalandrecords.org/portal/clris/SwitchToCountiesTab, view an index of land records from 1/2004, images from 1/2004.

Lyon County *Real Estate, Deed, Assessor, Property Tax Records*
Access to the assessor database of property and sales data is free at http://lyon.iowaassessors.com/links.php. At
http://iowalandrecords.org/portal/clris/SwitchToCountiesTab, view an index of land records from 1/2004, images from 1/2004.

Madison County *Real Estate, Deed, Assessor, Property Tax Records*
www.madisoncoia.us
Access to the assessor database of property and sales data is free at http://madison.iowaassessors.com. At
http://iowalandrecords.org/portal/clris/SwitchToCountiesTab, view an index of recorded land records from 1/1999, images from
1/1999.

Mahaska County *Assessor, Property, GIS Records*
Access to the assessor GIS database of property and sales data is free at http://webgishome.promap.com/?site=MahaskaCountyIA. At
http://iowalandrecords.org/portal/clris/SwitchToCountiesTab, view an index of recorded land records from 1/2004.

Marion County *Real Estate, Deed, Assessor, Property, GIS Records*
Access to the assessor GIS database of property and sales data is free at http://webgishome.promap.com/?site=MarionCountyIA. At
http://iowalandrecords.org/portal/clris/SwitchToCountiesTab, view an index of recorded land records from 06/2003, images from
06/2003.

Marshall County *Assessor, Property Records*
www.co.marshall.ia.us
Access to the assessor's property record card system is free at www.co.marshall.ia.us/departments/assessor/disclaimer_html. Also,
access to the assessor database of property and sales data is free at www.co.marshall.ia.us/departments/assessor/disclaimer_html.

Mills County *Assessor, Property, Real Estate, Deed, Lien, UCC, Judgment Records*
Access to the assessor database of property and sales data is free at http://65.240.48.154/index.html. At
http://iowalandrecords.org/portal/clris/SwitchToCountiesTab, view an index of recorded land records from 2/1995, images from
1/2004.

Mitchell County *Real Estate, Deed, Lien, UCC, Judgment Records*
At http://iowalandrecords.org/portal/clris/SwitchToCountiesTab, view an index of recorded land records from 1/2000, images from
03/09/2004.

Monona County *Real Estate, Deed, Assessor, Property, GIS Records*

Access to the assessor GIS database of property and sales data is free at http://webgishome.promap.com. At http://iowalandrecords.org/portal/clris/SwitchToCountiesTab, view an index of land records from 03/2004, images from 03/2004.

Monroe County *Real Estate, Deed Records*

At http://iowalandrecords.org/portal/clris/SwitchToCountiesTab, view an index of land records from 1/2004, images from 1/2004.

Montgomery County *Assessor, Property, Real Estate, Deed, Lien, UCC, Judgment, GIS Records*

Access to the assessor GIS database of property and sales data is free at http://webgishome.promap.com/?site=MontgomeryCountyIA but no name searching. At http://iowalandrecords.org/portal/clris/SwitchToCountiesTab, view an index of land records from 1/2004.

Muscatine County *Real Estate, Deed, GIS-mapping, Assessor, Property, GIS Records*

www.co.muscatine.ia.us

At http://iowalandrecords.org/portal/clris/SwitchToCountiesTab, view an index of recorded land records from 1/1989, images from 1/1989. Also, search area property and sales data free on GIS system at http://webgishome.promap.com/?site=MuscatineCountyIA, registration required to name search.

O'Brien County *Real Estate, Deed, Lien, UCC Records*

www.obriencounty.com/government/recorder.htm

At http://iowalandrecords.org/portal/clris/SwitchToCountiesTab, view an index of land records from 1/1988, images from 1/2004.

Osceola County *Real Estate, Deed, Lien, UCC, Judgment Records*

At http://iowalandrecords.org/portal/clris/SwitchToCountiesTab, view an index of recorded land records from 1/2004, images back to 2000 being added during 2006.

Page County *Real Estate, Deed, Lien, UCC, Judgment Records*

At http://iowalandrecords.org/portal/clris/SwitchToCountiesTab, view an index of land records from 1/2004, images from 1/2004.

Palo Alto County *Real Estate, Deed, Lien, UCC, Judgment Records*

At http://iowalandrecords.org/portal/clris/SwitchToCountiesTab, view an index of recorded land records from 1/2004, images are being added weekly.

Plymouth County *Assessor, Property, Real Estate, Deed, Lien, UCC, Judgment Records*

www.co.plymouth.ia.us

Access to the assessor database of property and sales data is free at http://plymouth.iowaassessors.com. At http://iowalandrecords.org/portal/clris/SwitchToCountiesTab, view an index of land records from 1/2001, images from 1/2001.

Pocahontas County *Real Estate, Deed, Lien, UCC, Judgment Records*

At http://iowalandrecords.org/portal/clris/SwitchToCountiesTab, view an index of recorded land records from 07/1991.

Polk County *Assessor, Property, Real Estate Sale, Recording, Deed, Lien, UCC Records*

http://recorder.co.polk.ia.us

Access to the Recorder's Index Search is free at http://216.81.134.113/resolution/. Also includes trade names, financing statements, and plats as well as recordings. Also, access to the Polk County assessor database is free at www.assess.co.polk.ia.us/web/basic/search.html. Search by property or by sales. Also, download resi., commercial, or agricultural data free at www.assess.co.polk.ia.us/web/basic/exports.html.

Pottawattamie County *Real Estate, Property, Residential Sale, Assessor Records*

www.pottcounty.com

Records on the County Courthouse/Council Bluffs property database are free at www.pottco.org. Search by owner name, address, or parcel number. Records since 7/1/89, images since 10/20/2002.

Poweshiek County *Assessor, Property Records*

Access to the assessor database of property and sales data is free at http://poweshiek.iowaassessors.com. At http://iowalandrecords.org/portal/clris/SwitchToCountiesTab, view an index of land records from 12/2003, images from 12/2003.

Sac County *Real Estate, Deed, Lien, UCC, Judgment, GIS Records*

www.saccounty.org

Assessor's property records online for a small fee; contact the Auditors Office at 712-662-7310 or visit www.saccounty.org/features/gis.asp. Also, search property data after registration on the GIS system at http://webgishome.promap.com/Default.aspx - a fee applies. At http://iowalandrecords.org/portal/clris/SwitchToCountiesTab, view an index of recorded land records from 1/2002, images from 1/2003.

Scott County *Assessor, Property, Real Estate, Deed, Lien, UCC, Judgment, Restaurant Inspection, Most Wanted, Sheriff Sale Records*

www.scottcountyiowa.com
At http://iowalandrecords.org/portal/clris/SwitchToCountiesTab, view an index of recorded land records from 1/2003, images from 1/2003. Also, access to assessor property records is free at www.scottcountyiowa.com/query.php. Also search restaurant inspections at www.scottcountyiowa.com/health/food.php. Also, view the sheriff's most wanted list at www.scottcountyiowa.com/sheriff/mostwanted.php. Sheriff sales lists free at www.scottcountyiowa.com/sheriff/sales.php

Shelby County *Real Estate, Deed, Lien, UCC, Judgment, Property, GIS Records*

www.shco.org
At http://iowalandrecords.org/portal/clris/SwitchToCountiesTab, view an index of recorded land records from 1/2000, images from 1/2000. Also, access the county GIS parcel search free at http://webgishome.promap.com/?site=ShelbyCountyIA. Also, access recording office land data at www.etitlesearch.com; registration required, fee based on usage.

Sioux County *Real Estate, Deed, Treasurer, Property Tax Records*

www.siouxcounty.org
Search the treasurer's property tax records online by subscription; for information please contact Micah Van Maanen at 712-737-6818, http://siouxcounty.org/treasurer.htm. At http://iowalandrecords.org/portal/clris/SwitchToCountiesTab, view an index of recorded land records from 1/2004.

Story County *Real Estate, Grantor/Grantee, Deed, Mortgage, UCC, Assessor, Property Tax, Sheriff Sale, Most Wanted, Accident Records*

www.storycounty.com/
Records on the county assessor database are free at www.storyassessor.org/pmc/ but no name searching. Also, at http://iowalandrecords.org/portal/clris/SwitchToCountiesTab, view an index of recorded land records from 09/2000, images from 09/2000. Also, City of Ames property assessor data is free at www.amesassessor.org/pmc/ but no name searching. Also, City of Ames accident reports are free at http://webgishome.promap.com/Default.aspx, search by location.

Tama County *Real Estate, Deed, Assessor, Property Tax Records*

Access to the assessor database of property and sales data is free at http://tama.iowaassessors.com. At http://iowalandrecords.org/portal/clris/SwitchToCountiesTab, view an index of land records from 1/2003, images from 6/16/2004.

Taylor County *Real Estate, Deed Records*

At http://iowalandrecords.org/portal/clris/SwitchToCountiesTab, view an index of recorded land records from 1/2004.

Union County *Real Estate, Deed Records*

At http://iowalandrecords.org/portal/clris/SwitchToCountiesTab, view an index of land records from 1/2005, images from 1/2005.

Van Buren County *Real Estate, Deed, Lien, UCC, Judgment Records*

At http://iowalandrecords.org/portal/clris/SwitchToCountiesTab, view an index of recorded land records from 1/2004.

Wapello County *Real Estate, Deed Records*

At http://iowalandrecords.org/portal/clris/SwitchToCountiesTab, view an index of land records from 1/2004, images from 1/2004.

Warren County *Real Estate, Deed, Assessor, Property, GIS Records*

Access to the assessor GIS database of property and sales data is free at http://webgishome.promap.com/?site=WarrenCountyIA. At http://iowalandrecords.org/portal/clris/SwitchToCountiesTab, view an index of land records from 1/1994, images from 1/1995.

Washington County *Real Estate, Deed, Assessor, Property Tax Records*

Access to the assessor database of property and sales data is free at http://washington.iowaassessors.com.
At http://iowalandrecords.org/portal/clris/SwitchToCountiesTab, view an index of recorded land records from 1/1992, images from 1/1992.

Wayne County *Real Estate, Deed, Lien, UCC, Judgment Records*
At http://iowalandrecords.org/portal/clris/SwitchToCountiesTab, view an index of land records from 1/2004, images from 1/2004.

Webster County *Assessor, Property, Real Estate, Deed, Lien, UCC, Judgment Records*
www.webstercountyia.org
Access to the assessor database of property and sales data is free at http://webster.iowaassessors.com. Also, property data is free at www.webstercountyia.org At http://iowalandrecords.org/portal/clris/SwitchToCountiesTab, view an index of recorded land records from 1/2002, images from 1/2002.

Winnebago County *Real Estate, Deed, Assessor, Property, GIS Records*
Access to the assessor GIS database of property and sales data is free at http://webgishome.promap.com/?site=WinnebagoCountyIA. At http://iowalandrecords.org/portal/clris/SwitchToCountiesTab, view an index of land records from 1/2003, images from 1/2003.

Winneshiek County *Real Estate, Deed, Assessor, Property Tax Records*
Access to the assessor database of property and sales data is free at www.winneshiek.us/. At http://iowalandrecords.org/portal/clris/SwitchToCountiesTab, view an index of recorded land records from 1/2004, images from 1/2004.

Woodbury County *Assessor, Property, Real Estate, Deed, Lien, UCC, Judgment, GIS Records*
Access to the assessor GIS database of property and sales data is free at http://webgishome.promap.com/?site=WoodburyCountyIA. Also, search Sioux City property data for free at http://sidwellmaps.com/website/siouxcity/eula1.asp. No name searching. At http://iowalandrecords.org/portal/clris/SwitchToCountiesTab, view an index of land records from 1/2004, images from 1/2004.

Worth County *Real Estate, Deed, Lien, UCC, Judgment Records*
At http://iowalandrecords.org/portal/clris/SwitchToCountiesTab, view an index of land records from 1/2004, images from 1/2004.

Wright County *Real Estate, Deed, Lien, UCC, Judgment, Assessor Records*
www.wrightcounty.org/county_offices.htm
At http://iowalandrecords.org/portal/clris/SwitchToCountiesTab, view an index of recorded land records from 1/2004, images from 1/2004. Assessor data is at www.wright.iowaassessors.com.

Federal Courts in Iowa...

Standards for Federal Courts: The universal PACER sign-up number is 800-676-6856. Find PACER and the Party/Case Index on the Web at http://pacer.psc.uscourts.gov. PACER dial-up access is $.60 per minute. Also, courts offering internet access via PACER, Web-PACER or the new CM-ECF charge $.08 per page fee ($.07 per page if record is pre-2005 or unless noted as free).

US District Court -- Northern District of Iowa
www.iand.uscourts.gov
PACER: Sign-up number is 800-676-5856. Case records are available back to 11/1992. New records are available online after 1 day.
PACER Online Access: PACER online at http://pacer.iand.uscourts.gov. **Electronic Filing:** CM/ECF data at https://ecf.iand.uscourts.gov. **Opinions:** Click on Decisions/Opinions and Jury Verdicts. View court opinions at www.iand.uscourts.gov.
Cedar Rapids (Eastern) Division counties: Allamakee, Benton, Black Hawk, Bremer, Buchanan, Cedar, Chickasaw, Clayton, Delaware, Dubuque, Fayette, Floyd, Grundy, Hardin, Howard, Iowa, Jackson, Jones, Linn, Mitchell, Tama, Winneshiek.
Sioux City (Western) Division counties: Buena Vista, Butler, Calhoun, Carroll, Cerro Gordo, Cherokee, Clay, Crawford, Dickinson, Emmet, Franklin, Hamilton, Hancock, Humboldt, Ida, Kossuth, Lyon, Monona, O'Brien, Osceola, Palo Alto, Plymouth, Pocahontas, Sac, Sioux, Webster, Winnebago, Woodbury, Worth, Wright. This court also has records for the Ft. Dodge, Independence, and Mason City Divisions, but not Green, Boone or Marshall counties. Court is held occasionally held at Ft. Dodge, but records are here at Sioux City.

US Bankruptcy Court -- Northern District of Iowa

www.ianb.uscourts.gov

PACER: Sign-up number is . **PACER Online Access:** ECF replaces PACER. Document images available. **Electronic Filing:** CM/ECF data at https://ecf.ianb.uscourts.gov. **Opinions:** View court opinions at www.ianb.uscourts.gov/decframe.html. **Other Online Access:** Calendars free at www.ianb.uscourts.gov/cal/index.html. **Phone access:** Voice Case Information System, call 800-249-9859, 319-362-9906

Cedar Rapids (Eastern) Division counties: Allamakee, Benton, Black Hawk, Bremer, Buchanan, Cedar, Chickasaw, Clayton, Delaware, Dubuque, Fayette, Floyd, Grundy, Howard, Iowa, Jackson, Jones, Linn, Mitchell, Tama, Winneshiek. Also has electronic records of cases from the Sioux City Division.

Sioux City (Western) Division counties: Buena Vista, Calhoun, Carroll, Cerro Gordo, Cherokee, Clay, Crawford, Dickinson, Emmet, Floyd, Franklin, Hamilton, Hancock, Hardin, Humboldt, Ida, Kossuth, Lyon, Mitchell, Monona, O'Brien, Osceola, Palo Alto, Plymouth, Pocahontas, Sac, Sioux, Webster, Winnebago, Woodbury, Worth, Wright. Case records are also available electronically at the Cedar Rapids Division.

US District Court -- Southern District of Iowa

www.iasd.uscourts.gov

PACER: Case records are available back to mid 1989. Records are purged 3 years after case closed. New records are available online after 1 day. **PACER Online Access:** ECF replaces PACER. Document images available. **Electronic Filing:** Required as of 4/2005. CM/ECF data at https://ecf.iasd.uscourts.gov. **Opinions:** View court opinions at www.iasd.uscourts.gov/iasd/opinions.nsf/main/page. **Other Online Access:** Court calendars free at www.iasd.uscourts.gov/iasd/judgecal.nsf/main/page.

Council Bluffs (Western) Division counties: Audubon, Cass, Fremont, Harrison, Mills, Montgomery, Page, Pottawattamie, Shelby.

Davenport (Eastern) Division counties: Henry, Johnson, Lee, Louisa, Muscatine, Scott, Van Buren, Washington. Court is temporarily located at US District Court in Rock Island, Illinois, and will return to 131 E 4th St in Davenport, IA in 2006.

Des Moines (Central) Division counties: Adair, Adams, Appanoose, Boone, Clarke, Clinton, Dallas, Davis, Decatur, Des Moines, Greene, Guthrie, Jasper, Jefferson, Keokuk, Lucas, Madison, Mahaska, Marion, Marshall, Monroe, Polk, Poweshiek, Ringgold, Story, Taylor, Union, Wapello, Warren, Wayne.

US Bankruptcy Court -- Southern District of Iowa

www.iasb.uscourts.gov

PACER: Case records are available back to 6/1987. Records are purged every 6 months. New records are available online after 1 day. **PACER Online Access:** New CM/ECF online system access only. **Electronic Filing:** CM/ECF data at https://ecf.iasb.uscourts.gov. **Other Online Access:** The RACER system has been replaced by the ECF/PACER system. Access fee is $.08 per page. **Phone access:** Voice Case Information System, call 888-219-5534, 515-284-6427

Des Moines Division counties: Adair, Adams, Appanoose, Audubon, Boone, Cass, Clarke, Clinton, Dallas, Davis, Decatur, Des Moines, Fremont, Greene, Guthrie, Harrison, Henry, Jasper, Jefferson, Johnson, Keokuk, Lee, Louisa, Lucas, Madison, Mahaska, Marion, Marshall, Mills, Monroe, Montgomery, Muscatine, Page, Polk, Pottawattamie, Poweshiek, Ringgold, Scott, Shelby, Story, Taylor, Union, Van Buren, Wapello, Warren, Washington, Wayne.

Kansas

Capital: Topeka
      Shawnee County
Time Zone: CST

> Kansas' five western-most counties are MST:
> They are: Greeley, Hamilton, Kearny, Sherman, Wallace.

Population: 2,735,502
# of Counties: 105

Quick Links

Website: www.accesskansas.org
Governor: www.ksgovernor.org
Attorney General: www.ksag.org
State Archives: www.kshs.org
State Statutes and Codes: www.kslegislature.org/legsrv-statutes/index.do
Legislative Bill Search: www.kslegislature.org/legsrv-legisportal/bills.do
Bill Monitoring: https://www.accesskansas.org/lobbyist/demo.html
Unclaimed Funds: www.kansascash.com/prodweb/up/disclaimer_page.php

State Level ... Major Agencies

Criminal Records

Kansas Bureau of Investigation, Criminal Records Division, 1620 SW Tyler, Crim. History Record Sec., Topeka, KS 66612-1837; 785-296-8200, Fax-785-368-7162, 8AM-5PM.
www.accesskansas.org/kbi/
Online search: Anyone may obtain non-certified criminal records online at www.accesskansas.org/kbi/criminalhistory/. The system is also available for premium subscribers of accessKansas. The fee is $17.50 per record; credit cards accepted online. The system is unavailable between the hours of midnight and 4 AM daily. A Kansas "Most Wanted" list is available at www.accesskansas.org/kbi/mw.htm.

Statewide Court Records

Judicial Administrator, Kansas Judicial Center, 301 SW 10th St, Topeka, KS 66612-1507; 785-296-3229, Fax-785-296-1028.
www.kscourts.org
Online search: The website above offers free online access to published opinions of the Supreme and Appellate courts, as well as case information for the Appellate courts. Five counties have record index access from www.accesskansas.org. Fees are involved.

Sexual Offender Registry

Kansas Bureau of Investigation, Offender Registration, 1620 SW Tyler, Topeka, KS 66612-1837; 785-296-8200, Fax-785-296-6781.
https://www.accesskansas.org/ssrv-registered-offender/index.do
Online search: Searching is available at the website. All open registrants are searchable.

Incarceration Records

Kansas Department of Corrections, Public Information Officer, 900 SW Jackson, 4th floor, Topeka, KS 66612-1284; 785-296-3310, Fax-785-296-0014, 8AM-5PM.
http://docnet.dc.state.ks.us

Online search: Web access to the database known as KASPER gives information on offenders who are: currently incarcerated; under post-incarceration supervision; and, who have been discharged from a sentence. The database does not have information available about inmates sent to Kansas under the provisions of the interstate compact agreement. Go to http://docnet.dc.state.ks.us/kasper2/kasperexpl.htm.

Corporation, Limited Partnerships, Limited Liability Company Records

Secretary of State, Memorial Hall, 1st Floor, 120 SW 10th Ave, Topeka, KS 66612-1594; 785-296-4564, Fax-785-296-4570, 8-5PM. www.kssos.org/main.html
Online search: Free entity searching is available at www.accesskansas.org/srv-corporations/index.do. Search by individual or company name, key word, date, or organizational number. There is no fee to search records, but there is a fee to order copies of certificates of good standings.

Uniform Commercial Code, Federal Tax Liens, State Tax Liens

Secretary of State - UCC Searches, Memorial Hall, 1st Fl, 120 SW 10th Ave, Topeka, KS 66612; 785-296-4564, Fax-785-296-3659,. www.kssos.org/business/business_ucc.html
Online search: Online service is provided by accessKansas at www.accesskansas.org. The system is open 24 hours daily. There is an annual fee. UCC records are $10.00 per record. This is the same online system used for corporation records. For more information, call at 800-4-KANSAS. **Other options:** Records in a bulk or database format is available from accessKansas.com.

Birth, Death, Marriage, Divorce Certificates

Kansas Department of Health & Environment, Office of Vital Statistics, 1000 SW Jackson, #120, Topeka, KS 66612-2221; 785-296-1400, 785-296-3253 (Phone Credit Card Orders), Fax-785-357-4332, 8AM-5PM. www.kdheks.gov/vital
Online search: Records may be ordered online via a state designated vendor VitalChek at www.vitalchek.com.

Driver Records, Accident Reports

Department of Revenue, Driver Control Bureau, PO Box 12021, Topeka, KS 66612-2021 (Courier: Docking State Office Building, 915 Harrison, Rm 100, Topeka, KS 66612); 785-296-3671, Fax-785-296-6851, 8AM-4:45PM. www.ksrevenue.org/vehicle.htm
Online search: Kansas has contracted with the AccessKansas (800-452-6727) to service all electronic media requests of driver license histories at www.accesskansas.org. The fee per record is $6.00 for batch requests or $6.50 for immediate inquiry. There is an initial $75 subscription fee and an annual $60 fee. The system is open 24 hours a day, 7 days a week. Batch requests are available at 7:30 am (if ordered by 10 pm the previous day).

Vehicle Ownership, Vehicle Identification

Division of Vehicles, Title and Registration Bureau, 915 Harrison, Rm 155, Topeka, KS 66626-0001; 785-296-3621, 785-271-3127 (Motor Carrier Srvs), Fax-785-296-3852, 8AM-4:45PM. www.ksrevenue.org/vehicle.htm
Online search: Online batch inquires are $6.00 per record; online interactive requests are $6.50 per record. Visit www.accesskansas.org for a complete description of accessKansas (800-452-6727), the state authorized vendor. There is an initial $75 subscription fee and an annual $60 fee to access records from AccessKansas.

State Level ... Occupational Licensing

Alcohol/Drug Counselor	www.ksbsrb.org/verification.html
Architect	www.accesskansas.org/roster-search/index.html
Athletic Trainer	www.ksbha.org
Body Piercer	www.accesskansas.org/kboc/LicenseeDatabase.htm
Charity Organization	www.kscharitycheck.org/search.asp
Chiropractor	www.ksbha.org
Cosmetologist/Cosmetic Facility	www.accesskansas.org/kboc/LicenseeDatabase.htm
Cosmetology School Instructor	www.accesskansas.org/kboc/LicenseeDatabase.htm
Cosmetology-related School	www.accesskansas.org/kboc/SchoolListing.htm
Counselor, Professional	www.ksbsrb.org/verification.html
Crematories	www.accesskansas.org/ksbma/listings.html
Dental Hygienist	www.accesskansas.org/srv-dental-verification/start.do

Dentist..	www.accesskansas.org/srv-dental-verification/start.do
Electrologist..	www.accesskansas.org/kboc/LicenseeDatabase.htm
Embalmer...	www.accesskansas.org/ksbma/listings.html
Engineer...	www.accesskansas.org/roster-search/index.html
Esthetician...	www.accesskansas.org/kboc/LicenseeDatabase.htm
Funeral Director/Assist. Finan'l Director....	www.accesskansas.org/ksbma/listings.html
Funeral Establishments	www.accesskansas.org/ksbma/listings.html
Geologist..	www.accesskansas.org/roster-search/index.html
Insurance Agent	http://towerii.ksinsurance.org/agent/agent.jsp?pagnam=agentsearch
Insurance Company	http://towerii.ksinsurance.org/agent/agency.jsp?pagnam=agencysearch
Landscape Architect.....................................	www.accesskansas.org/roster-search/index.html
Lobbyist...	www.kssos.org/elections/elections_lobbyists.html
Marriage & Family Therapist	www.ksbsrb.org/verification.html
Medical Doctor	www.ksbha.org
Nail Technician...	www.accesskansas.org/kboc/LicenseeDatabase.htm
Nurse...	https://www.accesskansas.org/app/nursing/verification/
Occupational Therapist/Assistant................	www.ksbha.org
Optometrist	www.arbo.org/index.php?action=findanoptometrist
Osteopathic Physician..................................	www.ksbha.org
Permanent Cosmetic Technician.................	www.accesskansas.org/kboc/LicenseeDatabase.htm
Pharmacist...	https://www.accesskansas.org/pharmacy_verification/index.html
Physical Therapist/Assistant	www.ksbha.org
Physician Assistant	www.ksbha.org
Podiatrist...	www.ksbha.org
Private Investigator	https://www.accesskansas.org/kbi-pi-verify/index.html
Psychologist..	www.ksbsrb.org/verification.html
Psychologist, Masters Level	www.ksbsrb.org/verification.html
Public Accountant-CPA...............................	www.ksboa.org/permit_list.htm
Real Estate Agent/Salesperson/Broker........	https://www.accesskansas.org/krec/verification/index.html
Real Estate Appraiser..................................	www.accesskansas.org
Respiratory Therapist..................................	www.ksbha.org
Social Worker	www.ksbsrb.org/verification.html
Surveyor, Land	www.accesskansas.org/roster-search/index.html
Tanning Facility..	www.accesskansas.org/kboc/LicenseeDatabase.htm
Tattoo Artist..	www.accesskansas.org/kboc/LicenseeDatabase.htm
Teacher	www.ksbe.state.ks.us/cert/cert_search.html
Veterinarian	www.accesskansas.org/veterinary/listing.html

County Level ... Courts

Court Administration: Judicial Administrator, Kansas Judicial Center, 301 SW 10th St, Topeka, KS, 66612; 785-296-3229; www.kscourts.org

Court Structure: The District Court is the court of general jurisdiction. There are 110 courts in 31 districts in 105 counties.

Online Access Note: Commercial online access for civil and criminal records is available for District Court Records in eight counties – Anderson, Coffey, Franklin, Johnson, Osage, Sedgwick, Shawnee, and Wyandotte. Access is web-based at www.accesskansas.org. An initial $75.00 subscription is required, access fees are involved. The system also provides state criminal records and motor vehicle records among other records. For additional information or a registration packet, telephone 800-4-KANSAS (800-452-6727) or visit the web page.

The Kansas Appellate Courts offer free online access to case information at www.kscourts.org. Published opinions from the Appellate Courts and Supreme Court are also available.

Anderson County

District Court – Civil and Criminal Records

www.kscourts.org/dstcts/4anco.htm

Current court calendars are free online at www.kscourts.org/dstcts/4andckt.htm. Also, access to probate court records is free at www.kscourts.org/dstcts/4anprrec.htm Access is web-based at www.accesskansas.org. An initial $75.00 subscription is required, access fees are involved. The system has 8 county District Courts, state criminal records, motor vehicle records, and others. Records go back to 11/01/2001.

Coffey County

District Court – Civil and Criminal Records

www.kscourts.org/dstcts/4coco.htm

Current court calendars are free online at www.franklincoks.org/4thdistrict/coffeybydate.html. Probate and marriage records are accessible at this website. Access is web-based at www.accesskansas.org. An initial $75.00 subscription is required, access fees are involved. The system has 8 county District Courts, state criminal records, motor vehicle records, and others. Also, access to probate court records is free at www.kscourts.org/dstcts/4coprrec.htm.

Douglas County

District Court – Civil and Criminal Records

www.douglas-county.com/District_Court/dc.asp

Internet access to the new court records system will require registration, password, and yearly fee; online records go back to 1986. Call the District Court for sign-up info at 785-832-5356.

Franklin County

District Court – Civil and Criminal Records

www.kscourts.org/dstcts/4frco.htm

Index online through Access Kansas; see www.accesskansas.org for subscription information. Current court calendars are free at www.franklincoks.org/4thdistrict/franklinbydate.html. Also, access to probate court records is free at www.kscourts.org/dstcts/4frprrec.htm.

Johnson County

District Court – Civil and Criminal Records

http://rta.jocogov.org

Access is web-based at www.accesskansas.org. An initial $75.00 subscription is required, access fees are involved. The system has 8 county District Courts, state criminal records, motor vehicle records, and others.

Osage County

District Court – Civil and Criminal Records

www.kscourts.org/dstcts/4osco.htm

Current court calendars are free online at www.franklincoks.org/4thdistrict/osagebydate.html. Also, access to old probate court and marriage records is free at www.kscourts.org/dstcts/4osprrec.htm. Access is web-based at www.accesskansas.org. An initial $75.00 subscription is required, access fees are involved. The system has 9 county District Courts, state criminal records, motor vehicle records, and others.

Sedgwick County

District Court – Civil and Criminal Records

www.dc18.org

Access is web-based at www.accesskansas.org. An initial $75.00 subscription is required, access fees are involved. The system has 8 county District Courts, state criminal records, motor vehicle records, and others. The system also includes probate, traffic, domestic, and criminal cases. For more information, call 316-383-7563 or visit www.accesskansas.org/online-services.html.

Shawnee County

District Court – Civil and Criminal Records

www.shawneecourt.org

Access is web-based at www.accesskansas.org. An initial $75.00 subscription is required, access fees are involved. The system has 8 county District Courts, state criminal records, motor vehicle records, and others. Also, access to court record images is free at www.shawneecourt.org/img_temp.htm. Also find "viewing restricted" domestic documents here. Also, daily dockets lists free at www.shawneecourt.org/docket/.

Wyandotte County
District Court – Civil and Criminal Records
Access is web-based at www.accesskansas.org. An initial $75.00 subscription is required, access fees are involved. The system has 8 county District Courts, state criminal records, motor vehicle records, and others.

County Level ... Recorders & Assessors

Recording Office Organization: 105 counties, 105 recording offices. The recording officer is the Register of Deeds. Many counties utilize a "Miscellaneous Index" for tax and other liens, separate from real estate records. 100 counties are in the Central Time Zone (CST) and 5 are in the Mountain Time Zone (MST). Federal tax liens on personal property of businesses are filed with the Secretary of State. Other federal tax liens and all state tax liens on personal property are filed with the county Register of Deeds. Most counties automatically include tax liens on personal property with a UCC search. Tax liens on personal property may usually be searched separately for $8.00 per name.

Online Access Note: A number of counties have online access, there is no statewide system.

Anderson County *Marriage Records*
Access to marriage records is by alpha search for free at www.kscourts.org/dstcts/4anmarec.htm. Updated to 2/15/2001 only.

Barton County *Assessor, Property Records*
www.bartoncounty.org
Access to the County Property value list by address and name is at www.bartoncounty.org/propvals.pdf.

Bourbon County *Real Estate, Appraiser, Property Tax, Deed Records*
http://bourboncountyks.org
Access to property data index is free at www.bourbon.kansasgov.com/parcel/. Subscription is required for full data. These is also a separate level for fee appraisers. Contact Appraiser's office at 620-223-3800 x36. Also, search property tax data at www.bourbon.kansasgov.com/tax/ or subscribe for full data; contact the Treasurer's office. Also the Deeds Management System subscription service at http://bourboncountyks.org/dms_online_search.htm. User name and password required; contact Sharon Elder, Register of Deeds, to register.

Butler County *Real Estate Recordings, Appraiser of Real Estate Value Records*
www.bucoks.com/depts/regdeeds/register_of_deeds.htm
An index of recorded real estate records from 1993 forward is available at www.bucoks.com/depts/regdeeds/disclaimer.htm. Access to the appraiser's Real Estate Market Values data is free at www.bucoks.com/depts/appr/values/values.htm. No name searching.

Cloud County *Assessor, Property Records*
www.cloudcountyks.org
Access to assessor property data is free at www.cloudcountyks.org/V2RunLev2.asp?submit1=OK. Search by registering or without.

Coffey County *Marriage Records*
www.coffeycountyks.org
Access to marriage records is by alpha search up to 1/18/2001 for free at www.kscourts.org/dstcts/4osmarec.htm.

Dickinson County *Property, Assessor Records*
Access to county property tax data is free at www.dickinson.kansasgov.com/disclaimerlev2.asp

Douglas County *Appraiser, Real Estate, Recording, Deed, Lien, Voter Registration Records*
www.douglas-county.com
Two non-government sites provide free access to records from the Douglas County Assessor. Find County Property Appraiser records at www.douglas-county.com/value/disclaimer.asp. Property valuations also free at http://old.hometown.lawrence.com/valuation/valuation.cgi. Check voter registration names at www.douglas-county.com/clerk/regvoters.asp. Also, Register of Deeds Records data is by subscription; for info and subscription call 785-832-5183.

Ellis County *Property, Asessor, Land, Sherif Sales, Most Wanted Records*
www.ksrods.org

Access to assessor property data is available free at www.ellisco.net/index.asp?page=app_search. Also, search sheriff's most wanted and sheriff sales lists free at www.ellisco.net/index.asp?DocumentID=230.

Franklin County *Marriage Records*

Access to county marriage records is by alpha search for free at www.kscourts.org/dstcts/4frmarec.htm.

Geary County *Recorded Documents Records*

www.geary.kansasgov.com/MV2Base.asp?VarCN=171

The county offers a fee system to access the recorded document index and images. From January 2001 to present images are available online using the DMS On-line Access Module. The web page has limited information about this registering for this system; you must call the office for an information packet.

Johnson County *Property Appraiser, Land, Marriage Records*

www.jocoks.com

Records on the Johnson County Kansas Land Records database are free at http://appraiser.jocogov.org/disclaimer.htm. At the bottom of the Disclaimer page, click on "Yes". No name searching. Marriages are accessible via the Accesskansas subscription service at www.accesskansas.org

McPherson County *Real Estate Recoding, Deed Records*

www.mcphersoncountyks.us

Access recording office land data at www.etitlesearch.com; registration required, fee based on usage.

Nemaha County *Property, Assessor, Surname Records*

www.nemaha.kansasgov.com

Access property data free or by registering for full subscription access at www.nemaha.kansasgov.com/parcel/. Click on 'Parcel Search Level One' for free access and name search. Subscription service for full data is $200 per year. Also, search a limited list of county surnames free at http://skyways.lib.ks.us/genweb/nemaha/.

Osage County *Appraiser, Property Records*

www.osageco.org

Online access to property appraiser is free at www.osageco.org/MV2Base.asp?VarCN=34. There are two levels- public and registered user. The latter can see sales information as well as property data.

Osborne County *Property, Appraiser Records*

www.osbornecounty.org

Access to property appraisal land data is free at www.osbornecounty.org. Search field is at bottom right of page. CAMA Records found at www.osbornecounty.org

Ottawa County *Appraiser, Property Tax Records*

www.ottawacounty.org

Access to the appraiser property data is free at www.ottawacounty.org/index.asp?DocumentID=283.

Riley County *Real Estate, Deed, Lien, UCC Records*

www.rileycountyks.gov

Access to recorder office land data is by subscription; Fee is $100 per year plus $.50 per page printed. Records go back to 1850. Registration through the Recorder's Office

Russell County *Property, Appraiser Records*

www.russellcounty.org

Access property data free at the righthand side of the main website at www.russellcounty.org

Sedgwick County *Real Estate, Lien, Recorder, Assessor, Property Sale, Property Tax, Treasurer, Delinquent Tax, Marriage, Probate Records*

www.sedgwickcounty.org/deeds/

Access to the exhaustive County online system (all departments) require a $225 set up fee, $49 monthly fee and a per transaction fee of $.09. For information on this and county record access generally, call Cindy Kirkland at 316-660-9860. Also, access recorder deeds free at https://rod.sedgwickcounty.org. Also, search property appraisal/tax data at www.sedgwickcounty.org/realpropertyinfo/realproperty.html. Also, access marriage, courts, probate records with sub at www.accesskansas.org.

Shawnee County *Property Appraiser, Personal Property Records*
www.co.shawnee.ks.us
Search residential or commercial property appraisal data at www.co.shawnee.ks.us/Appraiser/appr_home.shtm. Search residential by name; commercial by address.

Wabaunsee County *Property Tax, Treasurer, Property, Assessor Records*
www.wabaunsee.kansasgov.com
Access to the treasurer's property tax data is free at www.wabaunsee.kansasgov.com/TaxSearch.asp. Also, access to the assessor parcel search data is at www.wabaunsee.kansasgov.com/v2loginreg.asp; registration is asked for, but you may search basic data for free. To subscribe, phone 785-765-3508.

Woodson County *Property, Assessor Records*
www.woodsoncounty.net
Access property data free or by registering for full subscription access at http://woodson.kansasgov.com/parcel/V2LoginReg.asp. Click on 'Parcel Search Level One' for free access and name search. Subscription service for full data is $200 per year.

Wyandotte County
Real Estate, Lien, Property Appraisal, Personal Property, Recording, Deed, Judgment Records
County records are online and property tax records are on dial-up. The property dial-up services requires a $20 set up fee, $5 monthly minimum and $.05 each transaction. Lending agency info also available. Contact Louise Sachen 913-573-2885 for signup. Also, Register has online subscription services named Laredo and Tapestry; index goes back to 1975, images to 1991. Tapestry accepts credit card searches $3.99 a search, $.50 per image. Also, Judgments and Liens via subscription at www.accesskansas.org. Records from the County Treasurer Tax database are free at https://www.accesskansas.org/wyandotte-propertytax/index.html. Name search for personal property only; property searches require street number/ name; no name searching.

Federal Courts in Kansas...

Standards for Federal Courts: The universal PACER sign-up number is 800-676-6856. Find PACER and the Party/Case Index on the Web at http://pacer.psc.uscourts.gov. PACER dial-up access is $.60 per minute. Also, courts offering internet access via PACER, Web-PACER or the new CM-ECF charge $.08 per page fee ($.07 per page if record is pre-2005 or unless noted as free).

US District Court -- District of Kansas
www.ksd.uscourts.gov
PACER: Case records are available back to 1991. Records are purged never. New records are available online after 1 day. **PACER Online Access:** ECF replaces PACER. **Electronic Filing:** CM/ECF data at https://ecf.ksd.uscourts.gov.
Kansas City Division counties: Atchison, Bourbon, Brown, Cherokee, Crawford, Doniphan, Johnson, Labette, Leavenworth, Linn, Marshall, Miami, Nemaha, Wyandotte.
Topeka Division counties: Allen, Anderson, Chase, Clay, Cloud, Coffey, Dickinson, Douglas, Franklin, Geary, Jackson, Jewell, Lincoln, Lyon, Marion, Mitchell, Morris, Neosho, Osage, Ottawa, Pottawatomie, Republic, Riley, Saline, Shawnee, Wabaunsee, Washington, Wilson, Woodson.
Wichita Division counties: All counties in Kansas. Cases may be heard from counties in the other division.

US Bankruptcy Court -- District of Kansas
www.ksb.uscourts.gov
PACER: Case records are available back to 1988. Records are purged every 6 months. New records are available online after 1 day. **PACER Online Access:** ECF replaces PACER. **Electronic Filing:** Document images available. CM/ECF data at https://ecf.ksb.uscourts.gov. **Other Online Access:** Motion dockets and calendars free at www.ksb.uscourts.gov/motion.html. **Phone access:** Voice Case Information System, call 800-827-9028, 316-269-6668
Kansas City Division counties: Atchison, Bourbon, Brown, Cherokee, Comanche, Crawford, Doniphan, Johnson, Labette, Leavenworth, Linn, Marshall, Miami, Nemaha, Wyandotte.
Topeka Division counties: Allen, Anderson, Chase, Clay, Cloud, Coffey, Dickinson, Douglas, Franklin, Geary, Jackson, Jewell, Lincoln, Lyon, Marion, Mitchell, Morris, Neosho, Osage, Ottawa, Pottawatomie, Republic, Riley, Saline, Shawnee, Wabaunsee, Washington, Wilson, Woodson.
Wichita Division counties: Barber, Barton, Butler, Chautauqua, Cheyenne, Clark, Comanche, Cowley, Decatur, Edwards, Elk, Ellis, Ellsworth, Finney, Ford, Gove, Graham, Grant, Gray, Greeley, Greenwood, Hamilton, Harper, Harvey, Haskell, Hodgeman, Jefferson, Kearny, Kingman, Kiowa, Lane, Logan, McPherson, Meade, Montgomery, Morton, Ness, Norton, Osborne, Pawnee, Phillips, Pratt, Rawlins, Reno, Rice, Rooks, Rush, Russell, Scott, Sedgwick, Seward, Sheridan, Smith, Stafford, Stanton, Stevens, Sumner, Thomas, Trego, Wallace, Wichita.

Kentucky

Capital: Frankfort
         Franklin County

Time Zone: EST

> Kentucky's forty western-most counties are CST.
> CST counties are– Adair, Allen, Ballard, Barren, Breckinridge, Butler, Caldwell, Calloway, Carlisle, Christian, Clinton, Crittenden, Cumberland, Daviess, Edmonson, Fulton, Graves, Grayson, Hancock, Hart, Henderson, Hickman, Hopkins, Livingstone, Logan, Marshall, McCracken, McLean, Metcalfe, Monroe, Muhlenberg, Ohio,Russell, Simpson, Todd, Trigg, Union, Warren, Wayne, and Webster.

Population: 4,145,922
# of Counties: 120

Quick Links

Website: www.kentucky.gov/
Governor: http://governor.ky.gov
Attorney General: http://ag.ky.gov
State Archives: www.kdla.ky.gov/index.htm
State Statutes and Codes: http://lrc.ky.gov/statrev/frontpg.htm
Legislative Bill Search: http://lrc.ky.gov/legislat/legislat.htm
Unclaimed Funds: www.kytreasury.com/html/kyt_uprop.asp#Unclaimed%20Tax%20Refunds

State Level ... Major Agencies

Statewide Court Records

Administrative Office of the Courts, Pre-Trial Services Records Unit, 100 Millcreek Park, Frankfort, KY 40601; 502-573-1682, 800-928-6381 (Set-up Account), Fax-502-573-1669, 7:30AM-5PM.
www.kycourts.net
Online search: District court records may be searched at www.kycourts.net/CourtRecords/Court_Records.shtm. The disclaimer states this data should not be used for employment purposes. You may search six days of daily court calendars by county for free at www.kycourts.net/dockets/. From the home web page above search Supreme Court docket info and Appellate opinions.

Sexual Offender Registry

Kentucky State Police, Criminal Identification and Records Branch, 1250 Louisville Rd, Frankfort, KY 40601; 502-227-8700, 866-564-5652 (Alert Line), Fax-502-226-7419, 8AM-4PM.
http://kspsor.state.ky.us
Online search: Access is available via the website. Search by Last Name, City, ZIP, or County.

Incarceration Records

Kentucky Department of Corrections, Offender Information Services, PO Box 2400, Frankfort, KY 40602-2400 (Courier: 275 E. Main, Room 619, Frankfort, KY 40602); 502-564-2433, 800-511-1670 (Victim Notification Line), Fax-502-564-1471, 8AM-4:30PM.
www.corrections.ky.gov
Online search: The website provides current inmate information on the Kentucky Online Offender Lookup (KOOL) system as a service to the public. It can take as long as 120 days for the data to be current. Also, a private company offers free web access at

www.vinelink.com/index.jsp. Include state, DOC, and county jails **Other options:** The IT Department has the database on CD available for $50.00; call 502-564-4360.

Corporation, Limited Partnerships, Assumed Name, Limited Liability Company Records

Secretary of State, Corporate Records, PO Box 718, Frankfort, KY 40602-0718 (Courier: 700 Capitol Ave, Room 156, Frankfort, KY 40601); 502-564-2848, Fax-502-564-4075, 8AM-4:30PM.
http://sos.ky.gov/business/
Online search: The Internet site, open 24 hours, has a searchable database with over 340,000 KY businesses. A Request Form for copies or documents may be downloaded from the web. The site also offers downloading of filing forms. Go to http://sos.ky.gov/business/filings/online/. **Other options:** Monthly lists of new corporations are available for $50.00 per month.

Trademarks/Servicemarks

Secretary of State, Trademarks Section, 700 Capitol Ave, Suite 152, Frankfort, KY 40601; 502-564-2848 x442, Fax-502-564-1484.
http://sos.ky.gov/business/trademarks/
Online search: Free, searchable database at http://apps.sos.ky.gov/business/trademarks/.

Uniform Commercial Code

UCC Branch, Secretary of State, PO Box 1470, Frankfort, KY 40601; 502-564-3490, Fax-502-564-5687, 8AM-4:30PM.
http://sos.ky.gov/business/ucc/
Online search: UCC record searching is offered free of charge at the website. Search by debtor name, or file number. SSNs are withheld from the online system. Pre-paid accounts may be established for those requiring copies or certified documents.

Birth Certificates

Department for Public Health, Vital Statistics, 275 E Main St - IE-A, Frankfort, KY 40621-0001; 502-564-4212, 877- 817-3632 (Order), Fax-502-227-0032, 8AM-4PM.
http://chfs.ky.gov/dph/vital/
Online search: Records may be ordered online via a state designated vendor at www.vitalchek.com.

Death Records

Department for Public Health, Vital Statistics, 275 E Main St - IE-A, Frankfort, KY 40621-0001; 502-564-4212, 877- 817-3632 (Order), Fax-502-227-0032, 8AM-3PM.
http://chfs.ky.gov/dph/vital/
Online search: In cooperation with the University of Kentucky, there is a searchable death index at http://ukcc.uky.edu:80/~vitalrec/. This is for non-commercial use only. Records are from 1911 through 1992. Also, there is a free genealogy site at http://vitals.rootsweb.com/ky/death/search.cgi. Death Indexes from 1911-2000 are available. You may search by surname, given name, place of death, residence, or year. Records may be ordered online via a state designated vendor at www.vitalchek.com.

Marriage Certificates

Department for Public Health, Vital Statistics, 275 E Main St - IE-A, Frankfort, KY 40621-0001; 502-564-4212, 877- 817-3632 (Order), Fax-502-227-0032, 8AM-3PM.
http://chfs.ky.gov/dph/vital/
Online search: In cooperation with the University of Kentucky, a searchable index is available on the Internet at http://ukcc.uky.edu:80/~vitalrec/. The index runs from 1973 through 1993. This is for non-commercial use only. Records may be ordered online via a state designated vendor at www.vitalchek.com. **Other options:** Contact Libraries and Archives.

Divorce Records

Department for Public Health, Vital Statistics, 275 E Main St - IE-A, Frankfort, KY 40621-0001; 502-564-4212, 877- 817-3632 (Order), Fax-502-227-0032, 8AM-3PM.
http://chfs.ky.gov/dph/vital/
Online search: In cooperation with the University of Kentucky, there is a searchable index on the Internet at http://ukcc.uky.edu:80/~vitalrec/. This is for non-commercial use only. The index is for 1973-1993. Records may be ordered online via a state designated vendor at www.vitalchek.com. **Other options:** Contact Libraries and Archives.

Driver Records

Division of Driver Licensing, KY Transportation Cabinet, 200 Mero Street, Frankfort, KY 40622; 502-564-6800 x2250, Fax-502-564-5787, 8AM-4:30PM.

http://transportation.ky.gov/drlic/

Online search: There are 2 systems. Permissible use requesters who need personal information can order by batch, minimum order is 150 requests per batch. Input received by 3 PM will be available the next morning. Fee is $4.50 per record and billing is monthly. Call for details to subscribe. Records without personal information can be obtained at http://dhr.ky.gov/DHRWeb/. The same $4.50 fee applies and up to 50 records can be ordered and received immediately.

Vehicle & Vessel Ownership, Registration

Department of Motor Vehicles, Division of Motor Vehicle Licensing, PO Box 2014, Frankfort, KY 40622; 502-564-3298, 502-564-2737 (Questions), Fax-502-564-1686, 8AM-4:30PM.

www.kytc.state.ky.us

Online search: Online access costs $2.00 per record. The online mode is interactive. Title, lien and registration searches are available. Records include those for mobile homes. For more information, contact Gale Warfield at 502-564-4076. **Other options:** Kentucky has the ability to supply customized bulk delivery of vehicle registration information. The request must be in writing with the intended use outlined. For more information, call 502-564-3298.

Voter Registration

State Board of Elections, 140 Walnut, Frankfort, KY 40601; 502-573-7100, Fax-502-573-4369, 8AM-4:30PM.

http://elect.ky.gov/registrationinfo/

Online search: The agency offers a voter information status search at https://cdcbp.ky.gov/VICWeb/index.jsp. First name, last name and DOB are required. **Other options:** Data is available on CD-Rom, labels or lists for eligible persons, pursuant to state statutes

State Level ... Occupational Licensing

Addiction Psychiatrist	http://weba.state.ky.us/genericsearch/LicenseSearch.asp?AGY=5
Agent of Issuer, Securities	http://dfi.ky.gov/scr/ifs/old/sec/
Alcohol/Drug Counselor	https://kyeasupt1.state.ky.us/OPB/BrdWebSearch.asp?BRD=4
Anesthesiologist	http://weba.state.ky.us/genericsearch/LicenseSearch.asp?AGY=5
Architect	http://kybera.com/roster.shtml
Art Therapist	https://kyeasupt1.state.ky.us/OPB/BrdWebSearch.asp?BRD=5
Athlete Agent	https://kyeasupt1.state.ky.us/OPB/BrdWebSearch.asp?BRD=19
Athletic Manager/Athletic Trainer	https://kyeasupt1.state.ky.us/OPB/BrdWebSearch.asp?BRD=17
Athletic Trainer, Medical	http://weba.state.ky.us/genericsearch/LicenseSearch.asp?AGY=5
Auctioneer/Auctioneer Apprentice	http://weba.state.ky.us/genericsearch/LicenseSearch.asp?AGY=3
Bank	http://dfi.ky.gov/scr/ifs/old/fi/
Blood Banking/Transfusion Med	http://weba.state.ky.us/genericsearch/LicenseSearch.asp?AGY=5
Boxer/Boxing Professional	https://kyeasupt1.state.ky.us/OPB/BrdWebSearch.asp?BRD=17
Check Casher	http://dfi.ky.gov/whoweregulate/check%20casher%20recap.pdf
Counselor, Pastoral	https://kyeasupt1.state.ky.us/OPB/BrdWebSearch.asp?BRD=3
Counselor, Professional	https://kyeasupt1.state.ky.us/OPB/BrdWebSearch.asp?BRD=6
Credit Union	http://dfi.ky.gov/scr/ifs/old/fi/
Dental Hygienist	http://dentistry.state.ky.us/search.htm
Dentist	http://dentistry.state.ky.us/search.htm
Dietitian/Nutritionist	https://kyeasupt1.state.ky.us/OPB/BrdWebSearch.asp?BRD=8
EDP Servicer	http://dfi.ky.gov/scr/ifs/old/fi/
Engineer	http://kyboels.state.ky.us/SearchRoster.asp
Engineer/Land Surveyor Firm	http://kyboels.state.ky.us/SearchRoster.asp
Geologist	https://kyeasupt1.state.ky.us/OPB/BrdWebSearch.asp?BRD=1
Hearing Instrument Specialist	https://kyeasupt1.state.ky.us/OPB/BrdWebSearch.asp?BRD=15

Insurance Agent .... www.doi.state.ky.us/kentucky/search/agent/
Insurance CE Provider .... www.doi.state.ky.us/kentucky/search/provider/
Insurance Company/Insurer .... www.doi.state.ky.us/kentucky/search/company/
Interior Designer .... www.kybera.com/idlist.shtml
Investment Advisor/Company .... http://dfi.ky.gov/scr/ifs/old/sec/
Legislative Employers of Lobbyists .... www.lrc.state.ky.us/otherweb/ethics/agents.htm
Loan Company, Comm./Industrial   ... http://dfi.ky.gov/whoweregulate/Small%20Industrial%20Loan%20Recap.pdf
Lobbyist .... www.lrc.state.ky.us/otherweb/ethics/agents.txt
Marriage & Family Therapist .... https://kyeasupt1.state.ky.us/OPB/BrdWebSearch.asp?BRD=9
Medical Doctor/Surgeon .... http://weba.state.ky.us/genericsearch/LicenseSearch.asp?AGY=5
Medical Specialist .... http://weba.state.ky.us/genericsearch/LicenseSearch.asp?AGY=5
Mortgage Broker .... http://dfi.ky.gov/whoweregulate/mort_brokers.asp
Mortgage Loan Company .... http://dfi.ky.gov/whoweregulate/mort_company.asp
Nurse-RN/LPN .... https://ssla.state.ky.us/KBN/kbnknar.asp
Nurses Aide .... https://ssla.state.ky.us/KBN/kbnknar.asp
Nursing Home Administrator .... https://kyeasupt1.state.ky.us/OPB/BrdWebSearch.asp?BRD=10
Occupational Therapist/Assistant .... https://kyeasupt1.state.ky.us/OPB/BrdWebSearch.asp?BRD=16
Ophthalmic Dispenser/Optician/Apprentice ...... https://kyeasupt1.state.ky.us/OPB/BrdWebSearch.asp?BRD=11
Optometrist .... http://weba.state.ky.us/GenericSearch/LicenseSearch.asp?AGY=8
Osteopathic Physician .... http://weba.state.ky.us/genericsearch/LicenseSearch.asp?AGY=5
Pediatrist .... http://weba.state.ky.us/genericsearch/LicenseSearch.asp?AGY=5
Physical Therapist/ Therapist Assistant .... http://weba.state.ky.us/genericsearch/LicenseSearch.asp?AGY=5
Physician Assistant .... http://weba.state.ky.us/genericsearch/LicenseSearch.asp?AGY=5
Proprietary Education School .... https://kyeasupt1.state.ky.us/OPB/BrdWebSearch.asp?BRD=18
Psychiatrist .... http://weba.state.ky.us/genericsearch/LicenseSearch.asp?AGY=5
Psychologist .... https://kyeasupt1.state.ky.us/OPB/BrdWebSearch.asp?BRD=7
Public Accountant-CPA .... http://cpa.state.ky.us/Locate.html
Radiation Operator .... http://weba.state.ky.us/genericsearch/LicenseSearch.asp?AGY=5
Real Estate Agent/Broker/Sales .... http://weba.state.ky.us/realestate/LicenseeLookUp.asp
Real Estate Appraiser .... www.asc.gov
Real Estate Brokerage/Firm .... http://weba.state.ky.us/realestate/FirmLookUp.asp
Savings & Loan .... http://dfi.ky.gov/scr/ifs/old/fi/
School Admin/Counselor/Nurse/Librarian .... www.kyepsb.net
School Social Worker/Psychologist .... www.kyepsb.net
Securities Agent/Broker/Dealer .... http://dfi.ky.gov/scr/ifs/old/sec/
Social Worker .... https://kyeasupt1.state.ky.us/OPB/BrdWebSearch.asp?BRD=2
Speech-Language Pathologist/Audiologist .... https://kyeasupt1.state.ky.us/OPB/BrdWebSearch.asp?BRD=13
Surveyor, Land .... http://kyboels.state.ky.us/SearchRoster.asp
Teacher .... www.kyepsb.net
Trust Company .... http://dfi.ky.gov/scr/ifs/old/fi/
Veterinarian .... https://kyeasupt1.state.ky.us/OPB/BrdWebSearch.asp?BRD=14
Wrestler/Wrestling Professional .... https://kyeasupt1.state.ky.us/OPB/BrdWebSearch.asp?BRD=17

County Level ... Courts

Court Administration: Administrative Office of Courts, 100 Mill Creek Park, Frankfort, KY, 40601; 502-573-1682; www.kycourts.net

Court Structure: The Circuit Court is the court of general jurisdiction and the District Court is the limited jurisdiction court. Most of Kentucky's counties combined the courts into one location and records are co-mingled. Circuit Courts have jurisdiction over cases involving capital offenses and felonies, divorces, adoptions, terminations of parental rights, land dispute title problems, and contested probates of will. Juvenile matters, city and county ordinances, misdemeanors, traffic offenses, uncontested probate of wills, felony preliminary hearings, and civil cases involving $4,000 or less are heard in District Court. Ninety percent of all Kentuckians involved in court proceedings appear in District Court.

Online Access Note: There is a free access system at www.kycourts.net/CourtRecords/Court_Record s.shtm, but limited info is released. Also, you may search daily court calendars by county for free at www.kycourts.net/dockets/. KY Bar attorneys may register to use the KCOJ court records data at www.kycourts.net/CourtRecordsKBA/. There are statewide, online computer systems called SUSTAIN and KyCourts available for internal judicial/state agency use only. Also, you may search online for open dockets (Limited) of the Supreme Court at the home page.

Caldwell County

Circuit & District Court – Civil and Criminal Records
www.sangamoncountycircuitclerk.org
Access by subscription available at www.janojustice.com/products/magnus_dot_com/cm.htm. Email sales@janojustice.com for information, fees and set-up.

County Level ... Recorders & Assessors

Recording Office Organization: 120 counties, 122 recording offices. The recording officer is the County Clerk. Kenton County has two recording offices. Jefferson County had a separate office for UCC filing until June 30, 2001; that office now only searches for filings up to that date. 80 counties are in the Eastern Time Zone (EST) and 40 are in the Central Time Zone (CST). All federal and state tax liens on personal property are filed with the County Clerk, often in an "Encumbrance Book." Most counties will not perform tax lien searches.

Online Access Note: A number of counties offer free access to assessor records. Several other counties offer commercial systems. There is no statewide system.

Boone County *Real Estate, Lien, UCC, Assessor, Marriage Records*
www.boonecountyclerk.com
Access the county clerk database through eCCLIX, a fee-based service; $200.00 sign-up and $65.00 monthly. Records go back to 1989; images to 1998. For information, see the website or call 502-266-9445.

Boyd County *Real Estate, Lien Records*
Access to the County Clerk online records requires a $10 monthly usage fee. The system operates 24 hours daily; records date back to 1/1979. Lending agency information is available. For info, contact Doris Stephen Hallan-Clerk or Kathy Fisher at 606-739-5116.

Calloway County *Assessor, Property, Subdivisions Records*
Access to property data is free at www.ccpva.org/searchdb/default.htm.

Campbell County *Property, Appraiser Records*
Access to the Property Valuation Administrator property value is free at
http://campbellpropertymax.governmax.com/propertymax/rover30.asp.

Christian County   *Property, Assessor, Recorder, Real Estate, Deed, Marriage, Tax Lien, UCC Records*

Access recorder records free at http://66.112.71.165/resolution/. Access property tax data by subscription at http://christianpva.com/wps-html/TaxRoll/; fees starts as low as $50 for 60 records.

Fayette County   *Property, Crime Map Records*

www.fayettecountyclerk.com/fccweb/

Search property evaluations at www.pvdnetwork.com/PVDNet.asp?SiteID=116. Also, search the interactive crime map at http://crimewatch.lfucg.com.

Hardin County   *Recording, Will, Deed, Mortgage, Real Estate, Marriage, Assumed Name Records*

www.hccoky.org

Access the Clerk's permanent and temporary records search page free at www.hccoky.org/recordsearch/. Deeds go back to 1982; mortgages to 1975; most other records all available.

Jefferson County Clerk

Real Estate, Recorder, Grantor/Grantee, Deed, Lien, Will, Property, Assessor, Voter Registration Records

www.jeffersoncountyclerk.org

Access county land records free at www.landrecords.jcc.ky.gov; 8AM-midnight. Images go back to 6/1992. Check voter registration by name free at https://cdcbp.ky.gov/VICWeb/index.jsp. Also, access to the county property valuation administrator's assessment roll is free at www.pvalouky.org. Click on 'Assessment Roll.' No name searching. There is also a subscription service, call 502-574-6380 for info and signup.

Kenton County (1st District)   *Property Appraiser, Real Estate, , Deed, County Clerk Official Records*

www.kcor.org

Access the county clerks official data or the Property Valuation database at www.kcor.org. To search the summarized guest access, click "Property Data" and click "Guest Access" and "PVA Real Estate". Records go back to 5/15/1991. For full, professional property data you may subscribe; fee for clerk only- $75.00; PVA only $50.00; PVA plus clerk official records- $100 per month. $5.00 per hour and 12-hr for $25 accounts also available.

Kenton County (2nd District)   *Property Appraiser Records*

www.kentonpva.com

Access the county Property Valuation database at www.kcor.org. Search for free by using "Guest Access." For full, professional property data you may subscribe; fee for username and password is $50. per month, or use hourly account.

Laurel County   *Property Appraiser Records*

Access to the county Property Valuation database is free at www.pvdnetwork.com/PVDNet.asp?SiteID=107.

Meade County   *Real Estate, Recording, Deed, Lien, Judgment, Marriage, Will Records*

Access to recorder office records is by internet subscription; fee is $50 monthly; signup through recorder office, contact Katrina. Index back to 1828, images to late 1960's. No images of wills.

Oldham County   *Real Estate, Lien, UCC, Assessor, Marriage Records*

http://oldhamcounty.state.ky.us

Access to the database is through eCCLIX database, a fee-based service; $200.00 sign-up & $65.00 monthly. Records go back, to 1980. UCC images to 2/97. Real estate instruments back to 1/95. Marriages back to 1980. For information, see the website http://oldhamcounty.state.ky.us/ecclix.stm or call 502-266-9445.

Shelby County   *Real Estate, Deed, Recording Records*

www.shelbycountyclerk.com

Access is via the eCCLIX subscription system at www.shelbycountyclerk.com/ecclix.stm. Images go back to 1998; index to 1995. Sign-up fee is $100 plus $65 per month for unlimited access. For more information, phone 502-266-9445 or email sales@softwaremanagementinc.com.

Warren County   *Real Estate, Lien, UCC, Assessor, Marriage Records*

http://warrencounty.state.ky.us

Access the county clerk database through eCCLIX, a fee-based service; $200.00 sign-up and $65.00 monthly. Records go back to 1989; images to 1998. For information, see the website or call 502-266-9445.

Federal Courts in Kentucky...

Standards for Federal Courts: The universal PACER sign-up number is 800-676-6856. Find PACER and the Party/Case Index on the Web at http://pacer.psc.uscourts.gov. PACER dial-up access is $.60 per minute. Also, courts offering internet access via PACER, Web-PACER or the new CM-ECF charge $.08 per page fee ($.07 per page if record is pre-2005 or unless noted as free).

US District Court -- Eastern District of Kentucky

www.kyed.uscourts.gov

PACER: Case records are available back to 9/1991. Records are purged never. New records are available online after 1 day. **PACER Online Access:** ECF replaces PACER. **Electronic Filing:** CM/ECF data at https://ecf.kyed.uscourts.gov. **Other Online Access:** For calendars, click on "Hearing Schedule" at www.kyed.uscourts.gov.
Ashland Division counties: Boyd, Carter, Elliott, Greenup, Lawrence, Lewis, Morgan, Rowan.
Covington Division counties: Boone, Bracken, Campbell, Gallatin, Grant, Kenton, Mason, Pendleton, Robertson.
Frankfort Division counties: Anderson, Carroll, Franklin, Henry, Owen, Shelby, Trimble.
Lexington Division counties: Bath, Bourbon, Boyle, Breathitt, Clark, Estill, Fayette, Fleming, Garrard, Harrison, Jessamine, Lee, Lincoln, Madison, Menifee, Mercer, Montgomery, Nicholas, Perry, Powell, Scott, Wolfe, Woodford.
London Division counties: Bell, Clay, Harlan, Jackson, Knox, Laurel, Leslie, McCreary, Owsley, Pulaski, Rockcastle, Wayne, Whitley.
Pikeville Division counties: Floyd, Johnson, Knott, Letcher, Magoffin, Martin, Pike.

US Bankruptcy Court -- Eastern District of Kentucky

www.kyeb.uscourts.gov

PACER: Case records are available back to 7/1992. **PACER Online Access:** ECF replaces PACER. **Electronic Filing:** CM/ECF data at https://ecf.kyeb.uscourts.gov. **Opinions:** View court opinions at www.kyeb.uscourts.gov/opin/queryopin.asp. **Other Online Access:** Access calendars free at www.kyeb.uscourts.gov/calendar.htm **Phone access:** Voice Case Information System, call 800-998-2650, 859-233-2650
Lexington Division counties: Anderson, Bath, Bell, Boone, Bourbon, Boyd, Boyle, Bracken, Breathitt, Campbell, Carroll, Carter, Clark, Clay, Elliott, Estill, Fayette, Fleming, Floyd, Franklin, Gallatin, Garrard, Grant, Greenup, Harlan, Harrison, Henry, Jackson, Jessamine, Johnson, Kenton, Knott, Knox, Laurel, Lawrence, Lee, Leslie, Letcher, Lewis, Lincoln, Madison, Magoffin, Martin, Mason, McCreary, Menifee, Mercer, Montgomery, Morgan, Nicholas, Owen, Owsley, Pendleton, Perry, Pike, Powell, Pulaski, Robertson, Rockcastle, Rowan, Scott, Shelby, Trimble, Wayne, Whitley, Wolfe, Woodford.

US District Court -- Western District of Kentucky

www.kywd.uscourts.gov

PACER: Case records are available back to 1992. New records are available online after 1 day. **PACER Online Access:** Court is converting online WebPACER/PACER service over to ECF. **Electronic Filing:** CM/ECF data at https://ecf.kywd.uscourts.gov. **Opinions:** View court opinions at www.kywd.uscourts.gov/judicialOpinionsSearch.php. **Other Online Access:** Calendars at www.kywd.uscourts.gov/CourtCalendars.php.
Bowling Green Division counties: Adair, Allen, Barren, Butler, Casey, Clinton, Cumberland, Edmonson, Green, Hart, Logan, Metcalfe, Monroe, Russell, Simpson, Taylor, Todd, Warren.
Louisville Division counties: Breckinridge, Bullitt, Hardin, Jefferson, Larue, Marion, Meade, Nelson, Oldham, Spencer, Washington.
Owensboro Division counties: Daviess, Grayson, Hancock, Henderson, Hopkins, McLean, Muhlenberg, Ohio, Union, Webster.
Paducah Division counties: Ballard, Caldwell, Calloway, Carlisle, Christian, Crittenden, Fulton, Graves, Hickman, Livingston, Lyon, McCracken, Marshall, Trigg.

US Bankruptcy Court -- Western District of Kentucky

www.kywb.uscourts.gov

PACER: Case records are available back to 7/1992. New records are available online after 1 day. **PACER Online Access:** ECF replaces PACER. **Electronic Filing:** CM/ECF data at https://ecf.kywb.uscourts.gov. **Opinions:** View court opinions at www.kywb.uscourts.gov/opinions/main.php. **Phone access:** Voice Case Information System, call 800-263-9385, 502-627-5660
Louisville Division counties: Adair, Allen, Ballard, Barren, Breckinridge, Bullitt, Butler, Caldwell, Calloway, Carlisle, Casey, Christian, Clinton, Crittenden, Cumberland, Daviess, Edmonson, Fulton, Graves, Grayson, Green, Hancock, Hardin, Hart, Henderson, Hickman, Hopkins, Jefferson, Larue, Livingston, Logan, Lyon, Marion, Marshall, McCracken, McLean, Meade, Metcalfe, Monroe, Muhlenberg, Nelson, Ohio, Oldham, Russell, Simpson, Spencer, Taylor, Todd, Trigg, Union, Warren, Washington, Webster.

Louisiana

Capital:　Baton Rouge
　　　　　East　Baton Rouge Parish
Time Zone: CST
Population: 4,496,334
of　Parishes: 64

Quick Links

Website:　http://www.louisiana.gov/wps/portal/
Governor:　www.gov.state.la.us
Attorney General:　www.ag.state.la.us
State Archives:　www.sec.state.la.us/archives/archives/archives-index.htm
State Statutes and Codes:　www.legis.state.la.us/searchlegis.htm
Legislative Bill Search:　www.legis.state.la.us
Unclaimed Funds:　www.treasury.state.la.us/ucpm/index.htm

State Level ... Major Agencies

Statewide Court Records

Judicial Administrator, Judicial Council of the Supreme Court, 400 Royal Street, Suite 1190, New Orleans, LA 70130-8101; 504-310-2550, Fax-504-310-2587, 9AM-5PM.　www.lasc.org
Online search: Search opinions from the state Supreme Court at www.lasc.org/opinion_search.asp. Online records go back to 1995.

Sexual Offender Registry

State Police, Sex Offender and Child Predator Registry, PO Box 66614, Box A-6, Baton Rouge, LA 70896; 225-925-6100, 800-858-0551, Fax-225-925-7005, 8AM-4:30PM.
http://lasocpr1.lsp.org
Online search: Search by name, ZIP Code, or view the entire list at the website. Also search by city, school area or parish.

Incarceration Records

Department of Public Safety and Corrections, P.O. Box 94304, Attn: Office of Adult Services, Baton Rouge, LA 70804-9304; 225-342-6642, 225-342-9711 (Locator), Fax-225-342-3349, 8AM-4:30PM.
www.corrections.state.la.us
Online search: Access is limited to schedules for upcoming Parole Board hearings, as well as decisions from previous Parole Board hearings. Go to www.corrections.state.la.us/Offices/paroleboard/paroledockets.htm. Also, a private company offers free web access at www.vinelink.com/index.jsp including state, DOC, and most county jail systems

Corporation, Limited Partnership, Limited Liability Company, Trademarks/Servicemarks

Commercial Division, Corporation Department, PO Box 94125, Baton Rouge, LA 70804-9125 (Courier: 8549 United Plaza Blvd, Baton Rouge, LA 70809); 225-925-4704, Fax-225-925-4726, 8AM-4:30PM.
www.sos.louisiana.gov
Online search: There are 2 ways to go: free on the Internet or pay. To view limited information on the website, go to "Commercial Division, Corporations Section," then "Search Corporations Database." The pay system is $360 per year for unlimited access. Almost any communications software will work. The system is open from 6:30 am to 11pm. For more information, call Carolyn Vogelaar at 225-925-4792. **Other options:** This agency offers corporation, LLC, partnership, and trademark information on tape cartridges. For more info, call 225-925-4792.

Uniform Commercial Code

Secretary of State, UCC Records, PO Box 94125, Baton Rouge, LA 70804-9125; 800-256-3758, Fax-225-342-7011, 8AM-4:30PM. www.sos.louisiana.gov/comm/ucc/ucc-index.htm
Online search: An annual $400 fee gives unlimited access to UCC filing information at Direct Access. This dial-up service is open from 6:30 AM to 11 PM daily. Most any software communications program can be configured to work. For further information, call Carolyn Vogelaar at 225-925-4792, or e-mail cvogelaar@sos.louisiana.gov or visit the website.

Birth, Death Certificates

Vital Records Registry, Office of Public Health, PO Box 60630, New Orleans, LA 70160 (Courier: 325 Loyola Ave Room 102, New Orleans, LA 70112); 504-568-5152, 504-568-8353, 800-454-9570, 877-605-8562 (VitalChek), Fax-866-761-1855, 8AM-4PM. www.dhh.louisiana.gov/offices/page.asp?id=252&detail=6489
Online search: Orders can be placed online at www.vitalchek.com, a state-approved vendor.

Driver Records

Dept of Public Safety and Corrections, Office of Motor Vehicles, PO Box 64886, Baton Rouge, LA 70896 (Courier: 109 S Foster Dr, Baton Rouge, LA 70806); 877-368-5463, 225-925-6388, Fax-225-925-6915, 8AM-4:30PM.
www.expresslane.org
Online search: There are two methods. The commercial requester, interactive mode is available from 7 AM to 9:30 PM daily. There is a minimum order requirement of 2,000 requests per month. A bond or large deposit is required. Fee is $6.00 per record. For more information, call 225-925-6335. The 2nd method is for individuals to order their own record from the Internet site at www.expresslane.org. The fee is $17.00 and requires a credit card. **Other options:** Tape ordering is available for batch delivery. Bulk database sales are available to permissible users.

State Level ... Occupational Licensing

Acupuncturist	www.lsbme.org/verifications.htm
Alcoholic Beverage Vendor	http://atcpub1.license.louisiana.gov/
Architect	www.lastbdarchs.com/search_reg.htm
Architect Firm/Architectural Firm	www.lastbdarchs.com/search_firms.htm
Athletic Trainer	www.lsbme.org/verifications.htm
Bank	www.ofi.state.la.us
Bond For Deed Agency	www.ofi.state.la.us
Check Casher	www.ofi.state.la.us
Chemical Engineer	www.lapels.com/indiv_search.asp
Child Residential Care	www.dss.state.la.us/departments/os/child_care_facilities_by_parish.html
Chiropractor	www.lachiropracticboard.com/lic-drs.htm
Clinical Lab Personnel	www.lsbme.org/verifications.htm
Collection Agency	www.ofi.state.la.us
Construction Project, Commer'l +$50,000	www.lslbc.louisiana.gov/findcontractor_type.htm
Consumer Credit Grantor	www.ofi.state.la.us
Contractor, General/Subcontractor	www.lslbc.louisiana.gov/findcontractor_type.htm
Counselor, Professional (LPC)	www.lpcboard.org/lpc_alpha_list.htm
Credit Repair Agency	www.ofi.state.la.us
Credit Union	www.ofi.state.la.us
Day Care Facility	www.dss.state.la.us/departments/os/child_care_facilities_by_parish.html
Dentist/Dental Hygienist	www.lsbd.org/DentistSearch.aspx
Dietitian	www.lbedn.org/licensee_database.asp
Drug Distributor, Wholesale	www.lsbwdd.org
Electrical Engineer	www.lapels.com/indiv_search.asp
Emergency Shelter	www.dss.state.la.us/departments/os/child_care_facilities_by_parish.html
Engineer/Engineer Intern	www.lapels.com/indiv_search.asp
Engineering Firm	www.lapels.com/firm_search.asp
Environmental Engineer	www.lapels.com/indiv_search.asp
Exercise Physiologist, Clinical	www.lsbme.org/verifications.htm
Family Support	www.dss.state.la.us/departments/os/child_care_facilities_by_parish.html
Foster Care/Adoption Care	www.dss.state.la.us/departments/os/child_care_facilities_by_parish.html

Home Improvement Contr'ting +$75,000... www.lslbc.louisiana.gov/findcontractor_type.htm
Infant Intervention Service.......................... www.dss.state.la.us/departments/os/child_care_facilities_by_parish.html
Insurance Agent, LHA/PC .... www.ldi.state.la.us/search_forms/searchforms.htm
Insurance Agent/Broker/Producer............... www.ldi.state.la.us/search_forms/searchforms.htm
Land Surveyor Firm.................................... www.lapels.com/firm_search.asp
Land Surveyor/Surveyor Intern .... www.lapels.com/indiv_search.asp
Lender.. www.ofi.state.la.us
Lobbyist... www.ethics.state.la.us/lobs.htm
Medical Doctor .... www.lsbme.org/verifications.htm
Midwife .... www.lsbme.org/verifications.htm
Mold Remediation .... www.lslbc.louisiana.gov/findcontractor_type.htm
Mortgage Lender/Broker, Residential......... www.ofi.state.la.us/newrml.htm
Notary Public... www.sos.louisiana.gov/
Notification Filer....................................... www.ofi.state.la.us/newnotif.htm
Nuclear Engineer .... www.lapels.com/indiv_search.asp
Nutritionist.. www.lbedn.org/licensee_database.asp
Occupational Therapist/Technologist .... www.lsbme.org/verifications.htm
Optometrist .... www.arbo.org/index.php?action=findanoptometrist
Osteopathic Physician............................... www.lsbme.org/verifications.htm
Pawnbroker.. www.ofi.state.la.us/newpawn.htm
Pharmacist/Pharmacy/Techs/Interns .... www.labp.com/pbs.html
Physician Assistant .... www.lsbme.org/verifications.htm
Podiatrist... www.lsbme.org/verifications.htm
Psychologist.. www.onesimuswebs.com/lsbep_db.asp
Radiologic Technologist, Private............... www.lsbme.org/verifications.htm
Real Estate Agent/Broker/Sales .... www.lrec.state.la.us/sblist/csblistmain.asp
Real Estate Appraiser................................. www.lreasbc.state.la.us/dbfiles/appraiserinfo.htm
Residential Construction +$50,000............. www.lslbc.louisiana.gov/findcontractor_type.htm
Respiratory Therapist/Therapy Tech........... www.lsbme.org/verifications.htm
Savings & Loan .... www.ofi.state.la.us/newcus.htm
Solicitor .... www.ldi.state.la.us/search_forms/searchforms.htm
Speech Pathologist/Audiologist .... www.lbespa.org
Thrift & Loan Company .... www.ofi.state.la.us/newthrift.htm
Vocational Rehabilitation Counselor .... www.lrcboard.org/licensee_database.asp

County Level ... Courts

Court Administration:　　　Judicial Administrator, Judicial Council of the Supreme Court, 400 Royal Street, Suite 1190, New Orleans, LA, 70130; 504-310-2550, www.lasc.org

Court Structure:　　　The trial court of general jurisdiction in Louisiana is the District Court. A District Court Clerk in each Parish holds all the records for that Parish. Each Parish has its own clerk and courthouse. City Courts are courts of record and generally exercise concurrent jurisdiction with the District Court in civil cases where the amount in controversy does not exceed $15,000. In criminal matters, City Courts generally have jurisdiction over ordinance violations and misdemeanor violations of state law. City judges also handle a large number of traffic cases. Parish Courts exercise jurisdiction in civil cases worth up to $10,000 and criminal cases punishable by fines of $1,000 or less, or imprisonment of six months or less. Cases are appealable from the Parish Courts directly to the courts of appeal. A municipality may have a Mayor's Court; the mayor may hold trials, but nothing over $30.00, and there are no records.

Online Access Note:　　　The online computer system, Case Management Information System (CMIS), is operating and development is continuing. It is for internal use only; there is no plan to permit online public access. However, Supreme Court and Appellate opinions are currently available.

Bossier Parish

26th District Court – Civil and Criminal Records

www.bossierclerk.com

Access to the Parish Clerk of Court online records requires $50 setup fee and a $35 monthly flat fee. Civil, criminal, probate (1982 forward), traffic and domestic index information is by name or case number. Call 318-965-2336 for more information.

Caddo Parish

1st District Court – Civil and Criminal Records

www.caddoclerk.com

Access to civil records back to 1994 and name index back to 1984 is through county dial-up service. Registration and $50 set-up fee and $30 monthly usage fee is required. Marriage and recording information is also available. For information and sign-up, call 318-226-6523. Online criminal name index goes back to '80; minutes to '84. Current calendar is also available.

Calcasieu Parish

14th District Court – Civil and Criminal Records

www.calclerkofcourt.com

Access to civil records is the same as criminal, see below. Access to court record indices is free at www.calclerkofcourt.com/resolution/. Registration and password required. Full documents requires $100.00 per month subscription.

De Soto Parish

11th District Court – Civil and Criminal Records

www.desotoparishclerk.org

There is a web-based subscription service to records. Seach indexes only id$50.00 per month, search index, view, & print Image is $100.00 per month. Therei s a one-time setup fee of $50.00 Please contact Janet or Lindsey at 318-872-3110 to set-up an account.

East Baton Rouge Parish

19th District Court – Civil and Criminal Records

www.ebrclerkofcourt.org

Access to the clerk's database is by subscription. Civil record indexes go back to '88; case tracking of civil and probate back to 1991. Setup fee is $100.00 plus $15.00 per month plus per-minute usage charges. Call MIS Dept at 225-389-5295 for info or visit the website. Criminal case tracking goes back to 8/1990.

Baton Rouge City Court – Civil and Criminal Records

www.brgov.com/dept/citycourt

Access city court's database including attorneys and warrants free at http://brcc.ci.baton-rouge.la.us/. Access city court's criminal dockets database and warrants free at http://brcc.ci.baton-rouge.la.us/.

East Feliciana Parish

20th District Court – Civil Records

www.eastfelicianaclerk.org/court.html

Online subscription service is available. $400.00 per quarter permits access to viewable documents; $250 per quarter permits access in indices. This database also includes recordings, conveyances, mortgages, and marriage records.

Jefferson Parish

24th District Court – Civil and Criminal Records

www.jpclerkofcourt.us

Access is through dial-up service; initiation fee is $200, plus $85.00 monthly and $.25 per minute usage. Includes recordings, marriage index, and assessor rolls. For further information and sign-up, call 504-364-2908 or visit the website and click on "Jeffnet."

Lafayette Parish

15th District Court – Civil and Criminal Records

www.lafayetteparishclerk.com

Access to the remote online system requires $100 setup fee plus $15 per month and $.50 per minute. Civil index goes back to 1986. For more information, call Derek Comeaux at 337-291-6433.

Orleans Parish

Civil District Court – Civil Records

www.orleanscdc.com/   more…

CDC Remote provides access to civil cases from 1985 and First City Court cases as well as parish mortgage and conveyance indexes. The fee is $250 or $300 per year. Call 504-592-9264 for more information.

New Orleans City Court – Civil Records
CDC Remote provides access to First City Court cases from 1988 as well as civil cases, parish mortgage and conveyance indexes. The fee is $250 or $300 per year. Call 504-592-9264 for more information.

St. Landry Parish

27th District Court – Civil Records
www.stlandry.org
Online subscription access program to civil cases is available. The fee is $50.00 per month. Includes civil court records back to 1997, also land indexes and images. Contact the court or visit the web page for details.

St. Martin Parish

16th District Court – Civil Records
www.stmartinparishclerkofcourt.com
Court indices to be available at www.stmartinparishclerkofcourt.com.

St. Tammany Parish

22nd District Court – Civil and Criminal Records
www.sttammanyclerk.org
Remote access to civil records is from the Clerk of Court. $50 initial setup fee, $50.00 per month and $.20 to print a page. For information, call Kristie Howell at 985-809-8787. A non-Internet dial-up service is also available; $100 setup and $.20 per minute. Civil index goes back to 1992; images to 1995. Dialup criminal indices go back to 1988. Search index free at https://www.sttammanyclerk.org/liveapp/default.asp.

Tangipahoa Parish

21st District Court – Civil Records
www.tangiclerk.org
Access to Parish notaries index records is by free subscription (subject to change); fee is $1.00 to print a document. Images go back to 1/1990; index to 1974. Visit www.tangiclerk.org/OnlineServices/onlineservices.asp for info or call Alison Theard: 985-748-4146.

County Level ... Recorders & Assessors

Recording Office Organization: 64 parishes (not counties), 64 recording offices. One parish, St. Martin, has two non-contiguous segments. The recording officer is the Clerk of Court. Many parishes include tax and other non-UCC liens in their mortgage records. The entire state is in the Central Time Zone (CST). All federal and state tax liens are filed with the Clerk of Court. Parishes usually file tax liens on personal property in their UCC or mortgage records, and most will perform tax lien searches for varying fees. Some parishes will automatically include tax liens on personal property in a mortgage certificate search.

Online Access Note: A number of Parishes offer online access to recorded documents; most are commercial fee systems. A statewide system (excluding parishes of East Feliciano, Jefferson Davis, Orleans, Sabine, St. Bernard, St. Tammany, Terrebonne, and Winn) at www.latax.state.la.us/TaxRoll_ParishSelect.asp offers free access to assessor parish tax roll data.

Caddo Parish *Real Estate, Lien, Marriage, Assessor, Property Records*
www.caddoclerk.com
Access to the Parish online records requires a $100 set up fee plus $30 monthly fee; $.25 per image. Mortgages and indirect conveyances date back to 1981; direct conveyances date back to 1914. Lending agency information available. Marriage licenses free back to 1937; use username "muser" and password "caddo." Signup and info at www.caddoclerk.com/remote.htm or call 318-226-6523. Also, search assessor property free at www.caddoassessor.org/cgi-bin/pub_search.pl; no name searching for free; Annual sub for full data-$1.00 per day.

Calcasieu Parish *Real Estate, Recording, Deed, Mortgage, Marriage, Court, UCC Records*
Online access to court record indices is free at http://207.191.42.34/resolution/. Registration and password required. Full documents requires $100.00 per month subscription.

De Soto Parish *Real Estate, Recorder, Deed, Judgment, Lien, Mortgage Records*
www.desotoparishclerk.org
Access Clerk of Court records index by subscription at www.desotoparishclerk.org/online.html; set-up fee is $50.00 plus either $50 per month for index only searching or $100 per month for index, doc viewing, and images.

East Baton Rouge Parish *Real Estate, Lien, Marriage, Probate, Court, Judgment, Map Data Index Records*
www.ebrclerkofcourt.org
Access to online records requires a $100 set up fee with a $5 monthly fee and $.33 per minute of use. Four years worth of data is kept active on the system. Lending agency information is available. For information, contact Wendy Gibbs at 225-398-5295. UCC information is located at the Secretary of State.

East Feliciana Parish *Real Estate, Lien, Mortgage, Marriage, Civil Court Records*
www.eastfelicianaclerk.com
Access to online records requires a subscription, $100 set up fee with a $50 monthly usage fee for indices or $100.00 per month for indices plus images, in quarterly advances. Conveyances go back to 1962, mortgages to 1981; viewable back to 6/18/1982. Marriages go back to 1987, viewable to 1995, and miscellaneous index goes back to 1984. For information, contact clerk's office at 225-683-5145 or visit www.eastfelicianaclerk.com/.

Iberia Parish *Real Estate, Lien, Marriage, Divorce Records*
Access to the Parish online records requires a $50 monthly usage fee. Records date back to 1959. Lending agency information is available. For information, contact Mike Thibodeaux at 337-365-7282.

Iberville Parish *Real Estate, Recorder, Deed, Property Tax, Assessor Records*
www.ibervilleparish.com
Office is in the process of implementing an online system; records are to be accessible free on the Internet; call clerk office for detail, 225-687-5160. Also, access assessor property tax records free at www.ibervilleassessor.org/Search.aspx.

Jefferson Parish *Real Estate, Assessor, Marriage, Civil, Assessor, Property Tax Records*
www.jpclerkofcourt.us
Access to the clerk's JeffNet database is by subscription; set-up fee is $200.00 plus $8.50 monthly and $.25 per minute. Mortgage and conveyance images go back to 1971 and changing; index to 1967. Marriage and assessor records go back to 1992. For information, visit https://ssl.jpclerkofcourt.us/JeffnetSetup/default.asp. Also, search the assessor property rolls free at www.jpassessor.com. Call Donna Richoux at 504-364-2900 for fees.

Lafayette Parish *Real Estate, Lien Records*
www.lafayetteparishclerk.com
Access to Parish online records requires a $100 set up fee plus $15 per month and $.50 per minute. Conveyances date back to 1936; mortgages to 1948; other records to 1986. Lending agency information is available. For information, contact Derek Comeaux at 337-291-6433. Tax and UCC lien information is for this parish only. Also, assessor property data is free at www.lafayetteassessor.com/search.html, but no name searching.

Orleans Parish *Real Estate, Mortgage, Lien, Birth, Death, City Property Records*
www.orleanscdc.com
Access to the Parish online records requires a $300 yearly subscription fee, pro-rated. Records date back to 1989. Access includes real estate, liens, civil and 1st city court records. For information, contact at 504-592-9264. Access City of New Orleans property data free at https://secure.cityofno.com/portal.aspx?portal=1&load=~/Services/Assessor/PropertyDatabase/PropertySearch.ascx. Also, unofficial birth records to 1900 and death records to 1950 are free at www.rootsweb.com/~usgenweb/la/orleans.htm. Also includes limited marriage lists.

St. Landry Parish *Real Estate, Deed Records*
www.stlandry.org/index.htm
Access to recorder office land records is by subscription; fee is $35-50 per month. Data includes mortgages and conveyances, also perhaps court records. For registration and password contact Ms Lisa at Clerk of Court office, extension 103.

St. Tammany Parish *Recorder, Real Estate, Mortgage, Lien, Assessor, Property Tax Records*
www.sttammanyclerk.org
Access to online records requires a $50 per month plus $50.00 start-up fee, plus $.20 per printed page. Records date back to 1961; viewable images on conveyances back to 1980. For information, contact Eli Wilson or Kristie Howell at 985-809-8787. A dialup

service is also available; $100 setup and $.10 per minute. Free public access is also at https://www.sttammanyclerk.org/livea pp/default.asp; includes marriages, land, and court cases. UCC lien information is with the Secretary of State.

Tangipahoa Parish *Real Estate, Lien, Recording, Civil, Marriage, Mortgage Records*
www.tangiclerk.org
Access to Parish online records requires registration and a trial membership. Print documents for $1.00 each. They may later charge a $55 monthly fee. Record dates vary though most indexes go back before 1990. Lending agency information is available. For information, contact Alison Carona at 504-549-1611. Also, a mapping feature is being developed that includes assessor basic information; access will be free.

West Baton Rouge Parish *Property, Assessor, GIS Records*
Access property data via GIS site for free at www.geoportalmaps.com/atlas/wbr/viewer.htm. Click on Search Parcels by owner name.

Federal Courts in Louisiana...

Standards for Federal Courts: The universal PACER sign-up number is 800-676-6856. Find PACER and the Party/Case Index on the Web at http://pacer.psc.uscourts.gov. PACER dial-up access is $.60 per minute. Also, courts offering internet access via PACER, Web-PACER or the new CM-ECF charge $.08 per page fee ($.07 per page if record is pre-2005 or unless noted as free).

US District Court -- Eastern District of Louisiana
www.laed.uscourts.gov
PACER: Case records are available back to 1989. Records are purged every 6 months. New records are available online after 1 day. **PACER Online Access:** ECF replaces PACER. Document images available. **Electronic Filing:** CM/ECF data at https://ecf.laed.uscourts.gov.
New Orleans Division parishes: Assumption, Jefferson, Lafourche, Orleans, Plaquemines, St. Bernard, St. Charles, St. James, St. John the Baptist, St. Tammany, Tangipahoa, Terrebonne, Washington.
Baton Rouge Division parishes: Ascension, East Baton Rouge, East Feliciana, Iberville, Livingston, Pointe Coupee, St. Helena, West Baton Rouge, West Feliciana.

US Bankruptcy Court -- Middle District of Louisiana
www.lamb.uscourts.gov
PACER: Case records are available back to 5/15/1992. New records are available online after 1 day. **PACER Online Access:** ECF replaces PACER. **Electronic Filing:** CM/ECF data at https://ecf.lamb.uscourts.gov. **Opinions:** View court opinions at www.lamb.uscourts.gov/opinions.htm. **Phone access:** Voice Case Information System, call 225-382-2175.
Baton Rouge Division parishes: Ascension, East Baton Rouge, East Feliciana, Iberville, Livingston, Pointe Coupee, St. Helena, West Baton Rouge, West Feliciana.

US District Court -- Western District of Louisiana
www.lawd.uscourts.gov
PACER: Case records are available back to 10/1993. Records are purged as deemed necessary. **PACER Online Access:** ECF replaces PACER. Document images available. **Electronic Filing:** CM/ECF data at https://ecf.lawd.uscourts.gov.
Alexandria Division parishes: Avoyelles, Catahoula, Concordia, Grant, La Salle, Natchitoches, Rapides, Winn.
Lafayette Division parishes: Acadia, Evangeline, Iberia, Lafayette, St. Landry, St. Martin, St. Mary, Vermilion.
Lake Charles Division parishes: Allen, Beauregard, Calcasieu, Cameron, Jefferson Davis, Vernon.
Monroe Division parishes: Caldwell, East Carroll, Franklin, Jackson, Lincoln, Madison, Morehouse, Ouachita, Richland, Tensas, Union, West Carroll.
Shreveport Division parishes: Bienville, Bossier, Caddo, Claiborne, De Soto, Red River, Sabine, Webster.

US Bankruptcy Court -- Western District of Louisiana
www.lawb.uscourts.gov
PACER: Case records are available back to 1992. New records are available online after 1 day. **PACER Online Access:** ECF replaces PACER. Document images available. **Electronic Filing:** CM/ECF data at https://ecf.lawb.uscourts.gov. **Opinions:** View court opinions at www.lawb.uscourts.gov. **Phone access:** Voice Case Information System, call 800-326-4026, 318-676-4234
Alexandria Division parishes: Avoyelles, Catahoula, Concordia, Grant, La Salle, Natchitoches, Rapides, Vernon, Winn.
Lafayette-Opelousas Division parishes: Acadia, Evangeline, Iberia, Lafayette, St. Landry, St. Martin, St. Mary, Vermilion.
Lake Charles Division parishes: Allen, Beauregard, Calcasieu, Cameron, Jefferson Davis.
Monroe Division parishes: Caldwell, East Carroll, Franklin, Jackson, Lincoln, Madison, Morehouse, Ouachita, Richland, Tensas, Union, West Carroll.
Shreveport Division parishes: Bienville, Bossier, Caddo, Claiborne, De Soto, Red River, Sabine, Webster.

Maine

Capital: Augusta
           Kennebec County
Time Zone: EST
Population: 1,305,728
# of Counties: 16

Quick Links

Website: www.maine.gov/
Governor: www.maine.gov/portal/government/governor.html
Attorney General: www.maine.gov/ag/
State Archives: www.state.me.us/sos/arc
State Statutes and Codes: http://janus.state.me.us/legis/statutes/
Legislative Bill Search: http://janus.state.me.us/legis/LawMakerWeb/search.asp
Unclaimed Funds: www.maine.gov/treasurer/unclaimed_property/

State Level ... Major Agencies

Criminal Records

Maine State Police, State Bureau of Identification, 45 Commerce Dr #1, Augusta, ME 04333; 207-624-7240, Fax-207-287-3421, 8AM-5PM.
www10.informe.org/PCR/
Online search: One may request a record search form the website. Results are usually returned via e-mail in 2 hours. Fee is $25.00, unless requester is an in-state subscriber to InforME, then fee is $15.00 per record. There is a $75.00 annual fee to be a subscriber.

Statewide Court Records

State Court Administrator, PO Box 4820, Portland, ME 04112; 207-822-0792, Fax-207-822-0781, 8AM-4PM.
www.courts.state.me.us
Online search: The website offers access to Maine Supreme Court opinions and administrative orders, but not all documents are available online. Also, the site offers online access to trial court schedules by region and case type.

Sexual Offender Registry

State Bureau of Investigation, 45 Commerce Drive, #1, Attn: SOR, Augusta, ME 04330; 207-624-7009, Fax-207-624-7088, 8AM-5PM.
http://sor.informe.org/sor/
Online search: Search at http://sor.informe.org/sor/. Search by name, town or ZIP Code. Information is only provided for those individuals that are required to register pursuant to Title 34-A MRSA, Chapter 15. Records date to 06/30/92 and forward. The date of the last address verification is indicated next to the registrant's address. **Other options:** The entire database is for sale.

Incarceration Records

Maine Department of Corrections, Inmate Records, 111 State House Station, Augusta, ME 04333; 207-287-2711, 207-287-4381 (Probation info), 800-968-6909 (Victim Services info), Fax-207-287-4370, 8AM-4:30PM.
www.state.me.us/corrections
Online search: No direct online access available at this time (check website for updated information). Email requesting is available at Corrections.Webdesk@maine.gov. **Other options:** Database sales/bulk records can be requested and will be reviewed.

Corporation, Limited Partnerships, Trademarks/Servicemarks, Assumed Name, Limited Liability Company Records, Limited Liability Partnerships

Secretary of State, Reports & Information Division, 101 State House Station, Augusta, ME 04333-0101; 207-624-7752, 207-624-7736 (Main Number), Fax-207-287-5874, 8AM-5PM.
www.maine.gov/sos/cec/corp/
Online search: Basic information about the entity including address, corporate ID, agent, and status is found at http://icrs.informe.org/nei-sos-icrs/ICRS. A commercial subscriber account gives extensive information and ability to download files.
Other options: Lists of new entities filed with this office are available monthly.

Uniform Commercial Code, Federal Tax Liens, State Tax Liens

Secretary of State, UCC Records Section, 101 State House Station, Augusta, ME 04333-0101 (Courier: Burton M. Cross State Office Bldg, 109 Sewell St, 4th Fl, Augusta, ME 04333); 207-624-7760, Fax-207-287-5874, 8AM-5PM.
www.maine.gov/sos/cec/ucc/index.html
Online search: Online access for official records is available at https://www.informe.org/ucc/search/begin.shtml. Fees are involved. However, there is a free search of the index to search only the names or name variations at www.state.me.us/sos/cec/corp/debtor_index.shtml. **Other options:** Farm products - buyers reports, secured party available in bulk.

Death Records

Maine Department of Human Services, Vital Records, 244 Water St, Station 11, Augusta, ME 04333-0011; 207-287-3181, 877-523-2659 (VitalChek), Fax-207-287-1093, 8AM-5PM.
www.maine.gov/dhhs/vitalrecords.htm
Online search: Search death records for 1960 thru 1997 from the web page at http://portalx.bisoex.state.me.us/pls/archives_mhsf/archdev.death_archive.search_form. Also, a free genealogy site at http://vitals.rootsweb.com/me/death/search.cgi has Death Indexes from 1960-1997. Search by surname, given name, place or year.
Other options: Bulk file purchases are available, with the exclusion of restricted data.

Marriage Certificates

Maine Department of Human Services, Vital Records, 244 Water St, Station 11, Augusta, ME 04333-0011; 207-287-3181, 877-523-2659 (VitalChek), Fax-207-287-1093, 8AM-5PM.
www.maine.gov/dhhs/vitalrecords.htm
Online search: Records are available at the web page from 1892- thru 1996. **Other options:** Bulk file purchasing is available, with restricted data excluded.

Driver Records

BMV - Driver License Services, 101 Hospital Street, 29 State House Station, Augusta, ME 04333-0029; 207-624-9000 x52116, Fax-207-624-9090, 8AM-5PM.
www.state.me.us/sos/bmv
Online search: Access is through InforME via the Internet. There are two access systems. Casual requesters can obtain records that have personal information cloaked. There is a subscription service for approved requesters, records contain personal information. Records are released per DPPA. Records are $7.00 per request and go back three years. Visit www.informe.org/bmv/drc/ or call 207-621-2600. There is a $75.00 annual fee for the subscription service. A myriad of other state government records are available. **Other options:** The state offers "Driver Cross Check" - a program for employers - to provide notification when activity occurs on a specific record.

Vehicle Ownership, Vehicle Identification

Department of Motor Vehicles, Registration Section, 29 State House Station, Augusta, ME 04333-0029; 207-624-9000 x52149 (Registration), 207-624-9000 x52138 (Titles), Fax-207-624-9204, 8AM-5PM M-F.
www.state.me.us/sos/bmv/
Online search: Maine offers online access to title and registration records via InfoME. Fee is $5.00 per record. Records are available as interactive online or FTP with a subscription account. Contact InfoME at info@informe.org.

Accident Reports

Maine State Police, Traffic Division, Station 20, Augusta, ME 04333-0020 (Courier: 397 Water St, Gardiner, ME 04345); 207-624-8944, Fax-207-624-8945, 8AM-5PM.
www.informe.org/mcrs/

Online search: Records from 01/2003 forward may be ordered from www.informe.org/mcrs for $10.00 per record. If you do not have a subscription to InforME, then a credit card must be used. Resulting reports is either returned by mail, or emailed in a PDF format. You can search by name, date of birth, crash location, crash date, or investigating agency (police department). These reports may include officer narratives, witness statements, photographs or other recordings.

GED Certificates

Dept of Education, GED Office, 23 State House Station, Augusta, ME 04333; 207-624-6752, Fax-207-624-6731, 8AM-5PM. www.maine.gov/education/aded/dev/ged/transcript.htm
Online search: Email requests can be made by sending email to: lisa.perry@maine.gov

State Level ... Occupational Licensing

Adult Day Service	http://beas.dhs.maine.gov/rcare/
Aesthetician	http://pfr0.informe.org/almsquery/LicLookup.aspx
Alcohol/Drug Abuse Counselor	http://pfr0.informe.org/almsquery/LicLookup.aspx
Ambulatory Surgical Center	http://licert.dhs.state.me.us/pgGenSearch.asp
Animal Medical Technician	http://pfr0.informe.org/almsquery/LicLookup.aspx
Appraiser, Residential Real Estate	http://pfr0.informe.org/almsquery/LicLookup.aspx
Architect	http://pfr0.informe.org/almsquery/LicLookup.aspx
Assisted Living Facility	http://beas.dhs.maine.gov/rcare/
Athletic Trainer	http://pfr0.informe.org/almsquery/LicLookup.aspx
Auctioneer	http://pfr0.informe.org/almsquery/LicLookup.aspx
Barber	http://pfr0.informe.org/almsquery/LicLookup.aspx
Boiler	http://pfr0.informe.org/almsquery/LicLookup.aspx
Boxer	http://pfr0.informe.org/almsquery/LicLookup.aspx
Charitable Solicitation	http://pfr0.informe.org/almsquery/LicLookup.aspx
Chiropractor	http://pfr0.informe.org/almsquery/LicLookup.aspx
Cosmetologist	http://pfr0.informe.org/almsquery/LicLookup.aspx
Counselor	http://pfr0.informe.org/almsquery/LicLookup.aspx
Dental Hygienist	www.mainedental.org/search.htm
Dental Radiographer	www.mainedental.org/search.htm
Dentist/Denturist	www.mainedental.org/search.htm
Dietitian	http://pfr0.informe.org/almsquery/LicLookup.aspx
Electrician	http://pfr0.informe.org/almsquery/LicLookup.aspx
Elevator/Tramway	http://pfr0.informe.org/almsquery/LicLookup.aspx
Employee Leasing Company	www.state.me.us/pfr/ins/emplease.htm
Engineer	https://www.maine.gov/professionalengineers/database.shtml
Forester	http://pfr0.informe.org/almsquery/LicLookup.aspx
Fund Raiser	http://pfr0.informe.org/almsquery/LicLookup.aspx
Funeral Service	http://pfr0.informe.org/almsquery/LicLookup.aspx
Geologist	http://pfr0.informe.org/almsquery/LicLookup.aspx
Hearing Aid Dealer/Fitter	http://pfr0.informe.org/almsquery/LicLookup.aspx
HMO	www.state.me.us/pfr/ins/inshmo.htm
Home Health Agency	http://licert.dhs.state.me.us/pgGenSearch.asp
Home Health Care Svc Agency	http://licert.dhs.state.me.us/pgGenSearch.asp
Hospice	http://licert.dhs.state.me.us/pgGenSearch.asp
Hospital	http://licert.dhs.state.me.us/pgGenSearch.asp
Insurance Adjuster/Advisor	http://pfr0.informe.org/almsquery/LicLookup.aspx
Insurance Agent/Company	http://pfr0.informe.org/almsquery/LicLookup.aspx
Insurance Consultant/Producer	http://pfr0.informe.org/almsquery/LicLookup.aspx
Interior Designer	http://pfr0.informe.org/almsquery/LicLookup.aspx
Intermediate Care Facil'y, Mental Ret'd	http://licert.dhs.state.me.us/pgGenSearch.asp
Interpreter	http://pfr0.informe.org/almsquery/LicLookup.aspx
Investment Advisor	http://pfr0.informe.org/almsquery/LicLookup.aspx
Kickboxer	http://pfr0.informe.org/almsquery/LicLookup.aspx

Landscape Architect	http://pfr0.informe.org/almsquery/LicLookup.aspx
Licensed Practical Nurse	https://portalx.bisoex.state.me.us/pls/msbn_nlv/bnxdev.license_search.main_page
Lobbyist	www.mainecampaignfinance.com/public/entity_list.asp?TYPE=LOB
Manicurist	http://pfr0.informe.org/almsquery/LicLookup.aspx
Manufactured Housing	http://pfr0.informe.org/almsquery/LicLookup.aspx
Marriage & Family Therapist	http://pfr0.informe.org/almsquery/LicLookup.aspx
Massage Therapist	http://pfr0.informe.org/almsquery/LicLookup.aspx
Medical Doctor	www.docboard.org/me/df/mesearch.htm
Naturopathic Physician	http://pfr0.informe.org/almsquery/LicLookup.aspx
Notary Public	http://portalx.bisoex.state.me.us/pls/sos_bc/bcdev.notaries.search
Nurse	https://portalx.bisoex.state.me.us/pls/msbn_nlv/bnxdev.license_search.main_page
Nursing Home	http://licert.dhs.state.me.us/pgGenSearch.asp
Nursing Home Administrator	http://pfr0.informe.org/almsquery/LicLookup.aspx
Occupational Therapist	http://pfr0.informe.org/almsquery/LicLookup.aspx
Oil & Solid Fuel Profession'l/Company	http://pfr0.informe.org/almsquery/LicLookup.aspx
Optometrist	http://pfr0.informe.org/almsquery/LicLookup.aspx
Osteopathic Physician/Phys. Assist.	www.docboard.org/me-osteo/df/index.htm
Osteopathic Resident/Intern	www.docboard.org/me-osteo/df/index.htm
Pastoral Counselor	http://pfr0.informe.org/almsquery/LicLookup.aspx
Pharmacist	http://pfr0.informe.org/almsquery/LicLookup.aspx
Physical Therapist	http://pfr0.informe.org/almsquery/LicLookup.aspx
Physician Assistant	www.docboard.org/me/df/mesearch.htm
Pilot	http://pfr0.informe.org/almsquery/LicLookup.aspx
Plumber	http://pfr0.informe.org/almsquery/LicLookup.aspx
Podiatrist	http://pfr0.informe.org/almsquery/LicLookup.aspx
Preferred Provider Organization	www.state.me.us/pfr/ins/insppo.htm
Psychologist	http://pfr0.informe.org/almsquery/LicLookup.aspx
Public Accountant-CPA	http://pfr0.informe.org/almsquery/LicLookup.aspx
Radiologic Technician	http://pfr0.informe.org/almsquery/LicLookup.aspx
Real Estate Appraiser	http://pfr0.informe.org/almsquery/LicLookup.aspx
Real Estate Broker	http://pfr0.informe.org/almsquery/LicLookup.aspx
Registered Professional Nurse	https://portalx.bisoex.state.me.us/pls/msbn_nlv/bnxdev.license_search.main_page
Reinsurance Intermediary	http://pfr0.informe.org/almsquery/LicLookup.aspx
Re-insurer, Approved	http://pfr0.informe.org/almsquery/LicLookup.aspx
Renal Disease (End Stage) Facility	http://licert.dhs.state.me.us/pgGenSearch.asp
Respiratory Care Therapist	http://pfr0.informe.org/almsquery/LicLookup.aspx
RN, Advanced Practice	https://portalx.bisoex.state.me.us/pls/msbn_nlv/bnxdev.license_search.main_page
RN, Professional	https://portalx.bisoex.state.me.us/pls/msbn_nlv/bnxdev.license_search.main_page
Securities Agent/Broker	http://pfr0.informe.org/almsquery/LicLookup.aspx
Social Worker	http://pfr0.informe.org/almsquery/LicLookup.aspx
Soil Scientist	http://pfr0.informe.org/almsquery/LicLookup.aspx
Speech Pathologist/Audiologist	http://pfr0.informe.org/almsquery/LicLookup.aspx
Substance Abuse Counselor	http://pfr0.informe.org/almsquery/LicLookup.aspx
Surplus Lines Company	http://pfr0.informe.org/almsquery/LicLookup.aspx
Surveyor, Land	http://pfr0.informe.org/almsquery/LicLookup.aspx
Tattoo Artist	http://mainegov-images.informe.org/dhhs/eng/el/tattooist.pdf
Third Party Administrator	http://pfr0.informe.org/almsquery/LicLookup.aspx
Utilization Review Entity	www.state.me.us/pfr/ins/insmedur.htm
Vendor, Itinerant/Transient	http://pfr0.informe.org/almsquery/LicLookup.aspx
Veterinarian/Veterinary Technician	http://pfr0.informe.org/almsquery/LicLookup.aspx
Wrestler	http://pfr0.informe.org/almsquery/LicLookup.aspx

County Level ... Courts

Court Administration: State Court Administrator, PO Box 4820, Portland, ME, 04112; 207-822-0792;
www.state.me.us/courts

Court Structure: A Superior Court – the court of general jurisdiction – is located in each of
Maine's sixteen counties, except for Aroostook County which has two Superior Courts. Both Superior and
District Courts handle misdemeanor and felony cases, with jury trials being held in Superior Court only. The
District Court hears both civil and criminal and always sits without a jury.

Within the District Court is the Family Division, which hears all divorce and family matters, including child
support and paternity cases. The District Court also hears child protection cases, and serves as Maine's
juvenile court. Actions for protection from abuse or harassment, mental health, small claims cases, and
money judgments are filed in the District Court. Traffic violations are processed primarily through a
centralized Violations Bureau, part of the District Court system. Prior to year 2001, District Courts accepted
civil cases involving claims less than $30,000. Now, District Courts have jurisdiction concurrent with that of
the Superior Court for all civil actions, except cases vested in the Superior Court by statute.

Online Access Note: The website offers access to Maine Supreme Court opinions and administrative
orders, but not all documents are available online. Also, the website offers online access to trial court
schedules by region and case type. Some county level courts are online through a private vendor.

County Level ... Recorders & Assessors

Recording Office Organization: 16 counties, 17 recording offices. The recording officer is the County
Register of Deeds. Counties maintain a general index of all transactions recorded. Aroostock and Oxford
Counties each have two recording offices. There are no county assessors; each town has its own. The entire
state is in the Eastern Time Zone (EST). All tax liens on personal property are filed with the Secretary of
State. All tax liens on real property are filed with the Register of Deeds.

Online Access Note: There is no statewide system. Several counties have developed their own, and a
private vendor has placed a number of towns assessor records online at www.visionappraisal.com/databases.

Androscoggin County *Real Estate, Deed, Tax Lien, Assessor Records*
http://androscoggindeeds.com
Access the Registry index by subscription for a $140.00 annual fee plus $1.00 per page/image printed. Indexes go back to 1976. For
information and sign-up, contact Tina at 207-782-0191. Search for free at http://androscoggindeeds.com/ALIS/WW400R.PGM. Index
goes back to 1976; images to 1/1976. Also, Town of Lisbon Assessor data is free at
www.mygovnow.com/lisbto/Invision/assessing/index.htm. No name searching. Also City of Auburn tax assessor data is free at
www.auburnmaine.org/html/webgis.htm.

Aroostook County (Northern District) *Real Estate, Recordings, Deed, Lien, Judgment Records*
www.aroostook.me.us/deeds.html
Remote access via a commercial online system has been replaced by a subscription internet-based system. Data on the internet system
includes deeds, mortgages, liens, judgment, and land recording generally. Records go back to 1985. Subscription fee is $100 for North
District, $150 for both North and South. For more info and signup, see www.aroostookdeedsnorth.com then click on Access
Information button on left side of page.

Aroostook County (Southern District) *Real Estate, Recordings, Deed, Lien, Judgment Records*
www.aroostook.me.us/indexhome.html
Remote access via a commercial online system has been replaced by a subscription internet-based system. Data on the internet system
includes deeds, mortgages, liens, judgment, and land recording generally. Records go back to 1985. Subscription fee is $100 for South
District, $150 for both North and South. For more info and signup, see www.aroostookdeedsnorth.com then click on Access
Information button on left side of page.

Cumberland County *Assessor, Property Sale Records*
www.cumberlandcounty.org/DEEDSmain.html
Search Register of Deeds fee site at https://www.mainelandrecords.com. Cape Elizabeth Town assessor data free-www.capeelizabeth.com/taxdata.html. Gray Town assessor data- www.graymaine.org/vclerk/index.htm. Portland assessor-www.portlandassessor.com. Scarborough-www.scarborough.me.us/townhall/assessing/search.html. Cumberland, Raymond, Freeport, Gorham, Harpswell, Standish and S. Portland town assessors at www.visionappraisal.com/databases/maine/index.htm Also Westbrook assessor data at http://data.visionappraisal.com/WestbrookME. Falmouth assessor data at www.town.falmouth.me.us/assessing/home.html. Yarmouth property info: http://data.visionappraisal.com/YarmouthME/.

Hancock County *Real Estate, Deed, Lien, UCC, Recording Records*
www.co.hancock.me.us
Access to the county registry of deeds database at www.registryofdeeds.com requires registration. Viewing of records back to 1790 is free, but $2.00 per page to print. Register online. For info see website or call 888-833-3979. Also, City of Ellsworth real estate data is free at www.ci.ellsworth.me.us/realestatedb.html. Also, access to Bar Harbor property data is at http://data.visionappraisal.com/BarHarborME/. Free registration required.

Kennebec County *Assessor, Property, Deed, Recording Records*
Register free and search recorder index free at www.kennebec.me.us.landata.com. Fee for images by sub or pay-per-view. Also, records on the Winslow Town Property Records database are free at www.winslowmaine.org. Records on the Town of Waterville Assessor's database are free at http://data.visionappraisal.com/WatervilleME/. For full data, user ID is required; registration is free. Also, search the City of Augusta assessor database at http://data.visionappraisal.com/AugustaME/. Free registration for full data.

Knox County *Property, Assessor Records*
www.knoxcounty.midcoast.com
For property records go to mainelandrecords.com. The indexes are available from 1966 to present. Document images are available from 1980 to present. There are fees for images. Search Camden, Rockland and Rockport town assessor data at www.visionappraisal.com/databases/maine/index.htm.

Lincoln County *Deed, Property, Recording Records*
Search Register of Deeds index back to 1954 for free at www.lincolncomeregofdeeds.com. Click on Free Access at left. Images for a fee go back to 9/1999. Also Town of Boothbay property data is free at http://data.visionappraisal.com/BoothbayME/.

Oxford County *Real Estate, Deed Records*
Search the Eastern portion of the county at https://www.mainelandrecords.com/melr/MelrApp/index.jsp.

Penobscot County *Real Estate, Deed, Recording, Assessor, Property Records*
www.penobscotdeeds.com
Search the Register of Deeds index back to 1967 and images back to 1976 for free at www.penobscotdeeds.com. A fee is charged for copies and you may not download with registering. Also, search the City of Old Town real estate database for free at www.old-town.me.us/assessor/rev.asp.

Piscataquis County *Deed, Land, Judgment Records*
In the process of developing a searchable website. Online searching expected in late 2005.

Sagadahoc County *Recording, Grantor/Grantee, Real Estate, Assessor Records*
Register of Deeds records are online for a $50.00 per year fee plus $.25 per minute access fee. Records go back to 1964 on Grantor/Grantee index. For more info and registration, call the Register of Deeds. Also, records on the City of Bath Assessor database are free at http://assessdb.cityofbath.com.

Somerset County *Real Estate, Deed Records*
Access real estate records free at https://www.mainelandrecords.com/melr/MelrApp/index.jsp. Subscription required for full data and images.

Waldo County *Real Estate, Deed Records*
Access real estate records by subscription at https://www.mainelandrecords.com/melr/MelrApp/index.jsp. Index back to 1985, images back to 1992.

York County *Real Estate, Deed, Recording, Assessor, Property Records*
www.york.me.us.landata.com/
Search Register of Deeds records at www.york.me.us.landata.com. Register & search basic index free; get doc copies either by sub @ $1.25 per pg or non-sub @$2.00. Kennebunk Town data free at www.kennebunkmaine.org; click on Dept then Tax Assessment. Also, Berwick, Eliot, Kittery, Old Orchard Beach, Saco, Wells, and York Town assessor data at www.visionappraisal.com/databases/maine/index.htm. Free registration required.

Federal Courts in Maine...

Standards for Federal Courts: The universal PACER sign-up number is 800-676-6856. Find PACER and the Party/Case Index on the Web at http://pacer.psc.uscourts.gov. PACER dial-up access is $.60 per minute. Also, courts offering internet access via PACER, Web-PACER or the new CM-ECF charge $.08 per page fee ($.07 per page if record is pre-2005 or unless noted as free).

US District Court -- District of Maine

www.med.uscourts.gov
PACER: Case records are available back to 8/1991. Records are purged every 6 months. New records are available online after 1 day.
PACER Online Access: ECF replaces PACER. **Electronic Filing:** CM/ECF data at https://ecf.med.uscourts.gov. **Opinions:** View court opinions at www.med.uscourts.gov/rulesandopinions.htm.
Bangor Division counties: Aroostook, Franklin, Hancock, Kennebec, Penobscot, Piscataquis, Somerset, Waldo, Washington.
Portland Division counties: Androscoggin, Cumberland, Knox, Lincoln, Oxford, Sagadahoc, York.

US Bankruptcy Court -- District of Maine

www.meb.uscourts.gov
PACER: Case records are available back to 12/1988. Records are purged every 2 years. New records are available online after 1 day.
PACER Online Access: ECF replaces PACER. **Electronic Filing:** CM/ECF data at https://ecf.meb.uscourts.gov. **Opinions:** View court opinions at www.meb.uscourts.gov/w_judges.html. **Phone access:** Voice Case Information System, call 800-650-7253, 207-780-3755
Bangor Division counties: Aroostook, Franklin, Hancock, Kennebec, Knox, Lincoln, Penobscot, Piscataquis, Somerset, Waldo, Washington.
Portland Division counties: Androscoggin, Cumberland, Oxford, Sagadahoc, York.

Maryland

Capital: Annapolis
              Anne Arundel County
Time Zone: EST
Population: 5,558,058
# of Counties: 23

Quick Links

Website: www.maryland.gov
Governor: www.gov.state.md.us
Attorney General: www.oag.state.md.us
State Archives: www.mdarchives.state.md.us
State Statutes and Codes: http://mlis.state.md.us/#stat
Legislative Bill Search: http://mlis.state.md.us/#gena
Unclaimed Funds: https://interactive.marylandtaxes.com/unclaim/default.asp

State Level ... Major Agencies

Statewide Court Records

Administrative Office of the Courts, 580 Taylor Ave, Annapolis, MD 21401; 410-260-1400, 8AM-5PM.
www.courts.state.md.us
Online search: There are two systems offered by this agency for court records, however case information from the Circuit Courts for Montgomery and Prince George's Counties is not included in either system. A dial-up (non-Internet) system is being phased out, more court data will be removed in 2006, including Baltimore criminal records. All case information may be searched by party name or case number. For info call 410-260-1031 or visit the website. The free Internet search at http://casesearch.courts.state.md.us/inquiry/inquiry-index.jsp is new, but includes basic summary information and not the details found on the dial-up system. Bulk data of civil record information can be requested for a fee at www.courts.state.md.us/district/forms/acct/dca107.pdf. Appellate opinions are available from www.courts.state.md.us/opinions.html.

Sexual Offender Registry

Criminal Justice Information System, PO Box 5743, SOR Unit, Pikeville, MD 21282-5743 (Courier: 6776 Reistertown Rd, Baltimore, MD); 410-585-3649, 866-368-8657, Fax-410-653-5690, 7:30AM-5:00PM.
www.dpscs.state.md.us/onlineservs/sor/
Online search: Online access is free at www.dpscs.state.md.us/sorSearch/. Search by name or ZIP Code.

Incarceration Records

Dept of Public Safety and Correctional Services, Maryland Division of Corrections, 6776 Reistertown Road, Suite 310, Baltimore, MD 21215-2342; 410-585-3351, Fax-410-764-4182, 8AM-4:30PM.
www.dpscs.state.md.us
Online search: Search inmates online at www1.dpscs.state.md.us/inmate/. The Locator may not list some short sentenced inmates who, although committed to the Commissioner of Correction, are in fact housed at Division of Pretrial and Detention Services facilities. Also, a private company offers free web access at www.vinelink.com/index.jsp, including state, DOC, and a few county jails.

Corporation, Limited Partnerships, Trade Names, Limited Liability Company, Fictitious Name, Limited Liability Partnerships

Department of Assessments and Taxation, Corporations Division, 301 W Preston St, Room 801, Baltimore, MD 21201; 410-767-1340, 410-767-1330 (Charter Information), Fax-410-333-7097, 8AM-4:30PM.
www.dat.state.md.us
Online search: Search for corporate name and trade name records for free at the main website (see above); also includes real estate statewide (cannot search by name) and UCC records. A Certificate of Good Standing is available online at http://sdatcert1.resiusa.org/certificate/. **Other options:** This agency will release information in a bulk output format. Contact 410-561-9600 for details.

Trademarks/Servicemarks

Secretary of State, Trademarks Division, State House, Annapolis, MD 21401; 410-974-5521, Fax-410-974-5527, 9AM-5PM.
www.marylandsos.gov
Online search: Online searching is available at the Internet site. Search can be by keyword in the description field, the service or product, the owner, the classification, or the mark name or keyword in the mark name. Site offers application forms to register, renew, or assign trade and service marks, and general info about registration. Click on "Trade & Service Marks" or search at www.sos.state.md.us/Registrations/Trademarks/TMSearch.htm. **Other options:** A computer printout of all marks registered, renewed or assigned within a 3 month period is available for $.05 per trademark.

Uniform Commercial Code

UCC Division-Taxpayer's Services, Department of Assessments & Taxation, 301 West Preston St, Baltimore, MD 21201; 410-767-1340, Fax-410-333-7097, 8:30AM-5PM.
http://sdatcert3.resiusa.org/ucc-charter/
Online search: The Internet site above offers free access to UCC index information. Also, there is a related site offering access to real property data for the whole state at www.dat.state.md.us/. **Other options:** The agency has available for sale copies of public release master data files including corporation, real estate, and UCC. In addition, they can produce customized files on paper or disk. Visit the website for more information.

Sales Tax Registrations

Taxpayer Services, Revenue Administration Division, 301 W Preston St #206, Baltimore, MD 21201; 410-767-1313, 410-767-1300, Fax-410-767-1571, 8AM-5PM.
www.comp.state.md.us
Online search: Using the web, one can determine if a MD sales tax account number is valid.

Birth, Death, Marriage, Divorce Certificates

Department of Health, Division of Vital Records, PO Box 68760, Baltimore, MD 21215-0020 (Courier: 6550 Reisterstown Plaza, Baltimore, MD 21215); 410-764-3038, 410-764-3170 (Order), 410-318-6119 (Recording), Fax-410-358-7381, 8AM-4PM M-F; 3rd Saturday of each month.
www.dhmh.state.md.us
Online search: Records may be ordered over the web at www.vitalchek.com. Use of credit card is required.

Workers' Compensation Records

Workers Compensation Commission, 10 E Baltimore St, Baltimore, MD 21202; 410-864-5100, 410-864-5120 (Information Technology), 8AM-4:30PM.
www.wcc.state.md.us
Online search: Request for online hook-up must be in writing on letterhead. There is no search fee, but there is a $7.00 set-up fee, $5.00 monthly fee and a $.01-03 per minute connect fee assessed by Verizon or other provider. The system is open 24 hours a day to only in-state accounts. Write to the Commission at address above, care of Information Technology Division, or at 410-864-5170. **Other options:** This agency will sell its entire database depending on the use of the purchaser. Contact the commission for further information.

Driver Records

MVA, Driver Records Unit, Rm 145, 6601 Ritchie Hwy, NE, Glen Burnie, MD 21062; 410-787-7758, Fax-410-424-3678, 8:15AM-4:30PM.
www.mva.state.md.us
Online search: Under the Direct Access Record System (DARS), participants access driver and vehicle record information via an Internet connection. The systems is open 24/6 to qualified and bonded individuals and businesses. Inquiries are processed interactive

and may be accessed using either the driver's license number, name and date of birth, VIN or tag number. Fee is $9.00 per record. Call Ms. Barbara Bentley at 410-768-7234 for account information. **Other options:** Drivers may order their own record online via the website. Records are not mailed out-of-state unless signature given. Also, under the new License Monitoring System (LMS), transfers of record information to employers occur via an FTP server.

Vehicle Ownership, Identification

Department of Motor Vehicles, Vehicle Registration Division, Room 204, 6601 Ritchie Hwy, NE, Glen Burnie, MD 21062; 410-768-7250, Fax-410-768-7653, 8:15AM-4:30PM.
www.mva.state.md.us
Online search: The state offers vehicle and ownership data over the same online network (DARS) utilized for driving record searches. Fee is $9.00 per record. Access by VIN, tag # or full name. The network is available six days a week, twenty-four hours a day to qualified bonded accounts. Call 410-768-7234 for details.

State Level ... Occupational Licensing

Architect	https://www.dllr.state.md.us/secdocs/pq/arch.cfm?board=Architects
Architectural Partnership/Corporation	www.dllr.state.md.us/license/occprof/
Attorney	www.courts.state.md.us/cpf/attylist.html
Barber	https://www.dllr.state.md.us/secdocs/pq/barber.cfm?board=Barbers
Business, Any Licensed	www.blis.state.md.us/
Charity	www.sos.state.md.us/charity/charityhome.htm
Condominium/Timeshare	www.sos.state.md.us/Registrations/condo_TS.htm
Contractor	https://www.dllr.state.md.us/secdocs/pq/home_imprv.cfm?board=HomeImprovement
Cosmetologist	https://www.dllr.state.md.us/secdocs/pq/cosmet.cfm?board=Cosmetologists
CPA-Public Accountant	https://www.dllr.state.md.us/secdocs/pq/cpa.cfm?board=CertifiedPublicAccountants
Election	www.sos.state.md.us/ElectionsInfo.htm
Electrician, Master	www.dllr.state.md.us/license/occprof/
Engineer, Examining	www.dllr.state.md.us/license/occprof/
Engineer, Professional	www.dllr.state.md.us/license/occprof/
Esthetician	https://www.dllr.state.md.us/secdocs/pq/cosmet.cfm?board=Cosmetologists
Extradition/Requisition	www.sos.state.md.us/Services/Extradit.htm
Forester	www.dllr.state.md.us/license/occprof/
Fund Raising Counsel	www.sos.state.md.us/charity/RegisterProfSol.htm
Gem Dealer	https://www.dllr.state.md.us/secdocs/pq/sec_hand_deal.cfm?board=PreciousMetalDealers
Grain Dealer	www.mda.state.md.us/pdf/grainbrochure2005.pdf
Home Improvement Contractor	https://www.dllr.state.md.us/secdocs/pq/home_imprv.cfm?board=HomeImprovement
Home Improvement Salesperson	https://www.dllr.state.md.us/secdocs/pq/home_imprv.cfm?board=HomeImprovement
Home Inspector	https://www.dllr.state.md.us/secdocs/pq/real_est_app.cfm?board=RealEstateAppraisers
HVACR Contractor	www.dllr.state.md.us/license/occprof/
Interior Designer	www.dllr.state.md.us/license/occprof/
Land Surveyor	www.dllr.state.md.us/license/occprof/
Landscape Architect	www.dllr.state.md.us/license/occprof/
Limousine Driver	www.psc.state.md.us/psc/
Lobbyist	http://ethics.gov.state.md.us/listing.htm
Lobbyist Employer	http://ethics.gov.state.md.us/listing.htm
Makeup Artist	https://www.dllr.state.md.us/secdocs/pq/cosmet.cfm?board=Cosmetologists
Medical Doctor	www.mbp.state.md.us/
Mortgage Broker	www.dllr.state.md.us/license/fin_reg/mortlend/mdfinreg.html
Nail Technician	https://www.dllr.state.md.us/secdocs/pq/cosmet.cfm?board=Cosmetologists
Notary Public	www.sos.state.md.us/notary/notary.htm
Nurse-RN/LPN	https://12.153.47.224/
Nursery, Plant	www.mda.state.md.us/plants-pests/plant_protection_weed_mgmt/nurseries_plant_dealers/
Nursing Assistant	https://12.153.47.224/
Nursing Occupation	https://12.153.47.224/

Optometrist .... www.arbo.org/index.php?action=findanoptometrist
Pardon/Commutation .... www.sos.state.md.us/Services/Pardons.htm
Pawnbroker ... ...   https://www.dllr.state.md.us/secdocs/pq/sec_hand_deal.cfm?board=PreciousMetalDealers
Pesticide Applicator/Operator .... www.mda.state.md.us/plants-pests/pesticide_regulation/pesticide_db.php
Pesticide Business/Dealer .... www.mda.state.md.us/plants-pests/pesticide_regulation/pesticide_db.php
Pesticide Consultant................................. www.mda.state.md.us/plants-pests/pesticide_regulation/pesticide_db.php
Pesticide, Private Applicator...................... www.mda.state.md.us/plants-pests/pesticide_regulation/pesticide_db.php
Plant Broker/Dealer   ...   www.mda.state.md.us/plants-pests/plant_protection_weed_mgmt/nurseries_plant_dealers/
Plumber... https://www.dllr.state.md.us/secdocs/pq/plumb.cfm?board=Plumbers
Polygraph Examiner .... www.mpapolygraph.org/
Precious Metal & Gem Dealer
 https://www.dllr.state.md.us/secdocs/pq/sec_hand_deal.cfm?board=PreciousMetalDealers
Public Accountant-CPA   ... ...   https://www.dllr.state.md.us/secdocs/pq/cpa.cfm?board=CertifiedPublicAccountants
Radiation Therapy Technician .... www.mbp.state.md.us/
Real Estate Agent.. https://www.dllr.state.md.us/secdocs/pq/real_est.cfm?board=RealEstate
Real Estate Appraiser   ... ...   https://www.dllr.state.md.us/secdocs/pq/real_est_app.cfm?board=RealEstateAppraisers
Respiratory Care Practitioner..................... www.mbp.state.md.us/
Solicitor, Professional................................ www.sos.state.md.us/charity/RegisterProfSol.htm#ps
Special Police/Railroad Police .... www.sos.state.md.us/Services/Police.htm
Subcontractor   ... ...   https://www.dllr.state.md.us/secdocs/pq/home_imprv.cfm?board=HomeImprovement
Taxi Driver... www.psc.state.md.us/psc/

County Level ... Courts

Court Administration: Court Administrator, Administrative Office of the Courts, 580 Taylor Ave, Annapolis, MD, 21401; 410-260-1400; www.courts.state.md.us

Court Structure: The Circuit Court is the highest court of record. There is a Circuit Court with an elected clerk in each county of Maryland and Baltimore City.

The jurisdiction of the District Court includes all landlord/tenant cases, replevin actions, motor vehicle violations, misdemeanors and certain felonies. In civil cases the District Court has exclusive jurisdiction in claims for amounts up to $5,000, and concurrent jurisdiction with the circuit courts in claims for amounts above $5,000 but less than $25,000. The jurisdiction of the court in criminal cases is concurrent with the Circuit Court for offenses in which the penalty may be confinement for three years or more or a fine of $2,500 or more; or offenses which are felonies.

Online Access Note: **There are two systems offered by this agency for court records**, however case information from the Circuit Courts for Montgomery and Prince George's Counties is not included in either system. A dial-up (non-Internet) system is being phased out and existing court data is being removed in 2006, including Baltimore criminal records. All case information may be searched by party name or case number. For info call 410-260-1031 or visit the website. The free Internet search at http://casesearch.courts.state.md.us/inquiry/inquiry-index.jsp is new, but includes basic summary information and not the details found on the dial-up system. Bulk data of civil record information can be requested for a fee at www.courts.state.md.us/district/forms/acct/dca107.pdf. Appellate opinions are available from www.courts.state.md.us/opinions.html

Montgomery County

Circuit Court – Civil Records
www.montgomerycountymd.gov/mc/judicial
Access is through JIS. See state introduction or visit www.courts.state.md.us. The daily calendar is free at www.montgomerycountymd.gov/mc/judicial/circuit/docket.html. Will not provide name searches, only copies of specific documents.

County Level ... Recorders & Assessors

Recording Office Organization: 23 counties and one independent city -- 24 total recording offices. The recording officer is the Clerk of the Circuit Court. Baltimore City has a recording office separate from the county of Baltimore. See the City/County Locator section at the end of this chapter for ZIP Codes that include both the city and the county. The entire state is in the Eastern Time Zone (EST). All tax liens are filed with the county Clerk of Circuit Court. Counties will not perform tax lien name searches.

Online Access Note: Search   statewide   property   records   data   free   at http://sdatcert3.resiusa.org/rp_rewrite/. There is no name searching. Also, the Maryland State Dept. of Planning offers MDPropertyview with property maps/parcels and assessments on the web or CD-rom. Registration required; visit www.mdp.state.md.us or call 410-767-4614 or 410-767-4474. There is no name searching. Also, vendors provide online access in several places. County tax records are at www.taxrecords.com. Land survey, condominium, and survey plats are available free by county at www.plats.net. Use username "Plato" and password "plato#". No name searching.

All Counties and Baltimore City   *Real Property, Land Survey/Plat Records*

Search real property data free at http://sdatcert3.resiusa.org/rp_rewrite/. No name searching. Land records available from www.plats.net (use username "Plato" and password "plato#") and MDPropertyview at www.mdp.state.md.us/data/mdview.htm or www.dat.state.md.us. No name searching.

Baltimore City   *Real Property, Land Survey/Plat, Property Tax Records*

www.courts.state.md.us/clerks/baltimorecity
Search real property tax account information at http://cityservices.baltimorecity.gov/realproperty/default.aspx. Also, see state introduction for add'l land records

Carroll County   *Real Property, Land Survey/Plat Records*

Access digital image land records at www.mdlandrec.net. Registration and password required. Also, see state introduction for add'l land records.

Charles County   *Real Property, Land Survey/Plat, Treasurer, Property Tax, Tax Sale Records*

www.courts.state.md.us/clerks/charles
Access to property tax data is free at www.charlescounty.org/treas/taxes/acctinquiry/selection.jsp. Tax sale list search free at www.charlescounty.org/treas/taxes/taxSale/selection.jsp. Also, see state introduction for add'l land records.

Dorchester County   *Real Property, Land Survey/Plat Records*

An online records system is planned for MDlandRec.net. Until then, Also, see state introduction for add'l land records.

Montgomery County   *Real Property, Land Survey/Plat, Property Tax, Assessor Records*

www.montgomerycountymd.gov/mc/judicial/
Access to clerk records is via JIS Dialup Access; contact Mary Hutchins 410-260-1031. Also, access to the assessor's property tax account database is free at https://www.montgomerycountymd.gov/apps/tax/index.asp. Also, see state introduction for add'l land records.

Prince George's County   *Real Property, Land Survey/Plat, Property Tax Records*

www.co.pg.md.us
Search the Treasurer's property tax inquiry system at http://tax-acct-info.goprincegeorgescounty.com/servlets/resqportal?rqs_custom_dir=taxes&rqs_cleancache=0. No name searching. Also, see state introduction for add'l land records.

Federal Courts in Maryland...

Standards for Federal Courts: The universal PACER sign-up number is 800-676-6856. Find PACER and the Party/Case Index on the Web at http://pacer.psc.uscourts.gov. PACER dial-up access is $.60 per minute. Also, courts offering internet access via RACER, PACER, Web-PACER or the new CM-ECF charge $.07 per page fee unless noted as free.

US District Court -- Northern District of Maryland

www.mdd.uscourts.gov

PACER: Case records are available back to 10/1990. Records are purged every 6 months. New records are available online after 1 day. **PACER Online Access:** ECF replaces PACER. **Electronic Filing:** CM/ECF data at https://ecf.mdd.uscourts.gov. **Opinions:** Selected opinions only. View court opinions at www.mdd.uscourts.gov/Opinions152/SelectOpsMenu.asp. **Other Online Access:** Access calendars free at www.mdd.uscourts.gov/weeklycalnew/.

Baltimore Division counties: Allegany, Anne Arundel, Baltimore, City of Baltimore, Caroline, Carroll, Cecil, Dorchester, Frederick, Garrett, Harford, Howard, Kent, Queen Anne's, Somerset, Talbot, Washington, Wicomico, Worcester.

US Bankruptcy Court -- Northern District of Maryland

www.mdb.uscourts.gov

PACER: Case records are available back to mid 1991. Records are purged every 6 months. New records are available online after 1 day. **PACER Online Access:** ECF replaces PACER. **Electronic Filing:** CM/ECF data at https://ecf.mdb.uscourts.gov. **Opinions:** View court opinions at http://207.41.17.84/QryOpinion.aspx?qTarget=Opinion. **Other Online Access:** Search judgments back through 2002 free at http://207.41.17.84/QryJudgment.aspx?qTarget=Judgment. Access calendars free at https://ecf.mdb.uscourts.gov/cgi-bin/PublicCalendar4.pl. **Phone access:** Voice Case Information System, call 800-829-0145, 410-962-0733

Baltimore Division counties: Anne Arundel, Baltimore, City of Baltimore, Caroline, Carroll, Cecil, Dorchester, Harford, Howard, Kent, Queen Anne's, Somerset, Talbot, Wicomico, Worcester.

US District Court -- Southern District of Maryland

www.mdd.uscourts.gov

PACER: Case records are available back to 10/1990. Records are purged every 6 months. New records are available online after immediately. New criminal records are available online after immediate. **PACER Online Access:** ECF replaces PACER. **Electronic Filing:** CM/ECF data at https://ecf.mdd.uscourts.gov. **Opinions:** Selected opinions only. View court opinions at www.mdd.uscourts.gov/Opinions152/SelectOpsMenu.asp. **Other Online Access:** Access calendars free at www.mdd.uscourts.gov/weeklycalnew/.

Greenbelt Division counties: Calvert, Charles, Montgomery, Prince George's, St. Mary's.

US Bankruptcy Court -- Southern District of Maryland

www.mdb.uscourts.gov

PACER: Case records are available back to mid 1991. Records are purged every 6 months. New records are available online after 1 day. **PACER Online Access:** ECF replaces PACER. **Electronic Filing:** CM/ECF data at https://ecf.mdb.uscourts.gov. **Opinions:** View court opinions at http://207.41.17.84/QryOpinion.aspx?qTarget=Opinion. **Other Online Access:** Search judgments back through 2002 free at http://207.41.17.84/QryJudgment.aspx?qTarget=Judgment. Access calendars free at https://ecf.mdb.uscourts.gov/cgi-bin/PublicCalendar4.pl. **Phone access:** Voice Case Information System, call 800-829-0145, 410-962-0733

Greenbelt Division counties: Allegany, Calvert, Charles, Frederick, Garrett, Montgomery, Prince George's, St. Mary's, Washington.

Massachusetts

Capital: Boston
　　　　　Suffolk County
Time Zone: EST
Population: 6,416,505
# of Counties: 14

Quick Links

Website: www.mass.gov/gov
Governor: http://mass.gov/gov
Attorney General: www.ago.state.ma.us
State Archives: www.sec.state.ma.us/arc/
State Statutes and Codes: www.mass.gov/legis/laws/mgl/index.htm
Legislative Bill Search: www.mass.gov/legis/ltsform.htm
Unclaimed Funds: http://abpweb.tre.state.ma.us/abp/frmNewSrch.aspx

State Level ... Major Agencies

Statewide Court Records

Chief Justice for Administration & Management, 2 Center Plaza, Room 540, Boston, MA 02108; 617-742-8575, Fax-617-742-0968. www.mass.gov/courts/admin/index.html
Online search: Opinions to the Mass Supreme and Appellate courts can be found at http://massreports.com/. Online access to records on the statewide Trial Courts Information Center website is available to attorneys and law firms at www.ma-trialcourts.org/tcic/welcome.jsp. Contact Peter Nylin by email at nylin_p@jud.state.ma.us. Site is updated daily.

Sexual Offender Registry

Sex Offender Registry Board, PO Box 4547, Salem, MA 01970; 978-740-6400, Fax-978-740-6464, 8:45AM-5PM. www.mass.gov/sorb/
Online search: Search free at http://ma-sorb.gis.net/intro.htm. Pursuant to M.G.L. C. 6, §§ 178C - 178P, the individuals who appear on the web page have been designated a Level 3 Sex Offenders by the Sex Offender Registry Board.

Incarceration Records

Massachusetts Executive Office of Public Safety, Criminal History Systems Board, 200 Arlington #2200, Chelsea, MA 02150; 617-660-4600, 877-421-8463 (Locator), 617-660-4690 (Criminal Histories Systems Board), 8AM-5PM. www.mass.gov/doc/
Online search: No searching online is offered by this agency; however this agency promotes a private company offers free web access to DOC offenders at www.vinelink.com/index.jsp.

Corporation, Trademarks/Servicemarks, Limited Liability Partnerships, Limited Partnerships, Limited Liability Companies

Secretary of the Commonwealth, Corporation Division, One Ashburton Pl, 17th Floor, Boston, MA 02108; 617-727-9640 (Corporations), 617-727-2850 (Records), 617-727-8329 (Trademarks), 617-727-9440 (Forms Requests), Fax-617-742-4538, 8:45-5pm www.sec.state.ma.us/cor/coridx.htm
Online search: There is a free Internet lookup from the website. This site also provides UCC information. **Other options:** Bulk sale on CD is available.

Uniform Commercial Code, State Tax Liens

UCC Division, Secretary of the Commonwealth, One Ashburton Pl, Room 1711, Boston, MA 02108; 617-727-2860, 900-555-4500 (Computer Prints), 900-555-4600 (Copies), 8:45AM-5PM.
www.sec.state.ma.us/cor/ucc/uccmain.htm
Online search: There is free access to record index from the website. Search by name, organization or file number. There is another site at www.state.me.us/sos/cec/corp/debtor_index.shtml. **Other options:** Microfiche may be purchased.

Birth, Death, Marriage Certificates

Registry of Vital Records and Statistics, 150 Mt Vernon St, 1st FL, Dorchester, MA 02125; 617-740-2600, 617-740-2606, Fax-617-825-7755, 8:45AM-4:45PM.
www.mass.gov/dph/bhsre/rvr/vrcopies.htm
Online search: One may order online at www.uscerts.com, a state designated vendor.

Driver Records-Registry

Registry of Motor Vehicles, Driver Control Unit, Box 199150, Boston, MA 02119-1950; 617-351-9213 (Registry), Fax-617-351-9219, 8AM-4:30PM M-T-W-F; 8AM-7PM TH.
www.mass.gov/rmv/
Online search: Access from the Registry is available for approved entities for $6.00 per record. Call the above number for details.

Driver Records-Insurance

Merit Rating Board, Attn: Driving Records, PO Box 199100, Boston, MA 02119-9100; 617-351-4400, Fax-617-351-9660, 8:45-5PM.
www.mass.gov/rmv/
Online search: The Merit Rating Board provides both online and tape inquiry to the insurance industry for rating and issuance of new and renewal automobile insurance policies. Per statute, this method of retrieval is not open to the general public.

Vehicle Ownership, Vehicle Identification

Registry of Motor Vehicles, Document Control, PO Box 199100, Boston, MA 02119-9100; 617-351-9458, Fax-617-351-9524, 8-4:30.
www.mass.gov/rmv/
Online search: Searching is limited to Massachusetts based insurance companies and agents for the purpose of issuing or renewing insurance. This system is not open to the public. There is no fee, but line charges will be incurred. **Other options:** This agency offers an extensive array of customized bulk record requests to authorized users. For further info, contact the Production Control Office.

State Level ... Occupational Licensing

Adjuster, Fire Loss....................................... www.mass.gov/doi/Producer/Producer_list.html
Adoption Center   ...   ...   www.eec.state.ma.us/adoptSearchResult.aspx?city=&zipcode=&type=ADOPT
Aesthetician .... http://license.reg.state.ma.us/pubLic/licque.asp?color=red&Board=HD
Alarm Installer, Burglar/Fire....................... http://license.reg.state.ma.us/pubLic/licque.asp?color=red&Board=EL
Ambulance Service .... http://db.state.ma.us/dph/amb/amb_search.asp
Amusement Device Inspector .... www.mass.gov/dps/inspectors.htm
Appraiser, MVR Damage .... www.mass.gov/doi/Producer/Producer_list.html
Architect .... http://license.reg.state.ma.us/pubLic/licque.asp?color=red&Board=AR
Athletic Trainer.. http://license.reg.state.ma.us/pubLic/licque.asp?color=red&Board=AH
Attorney .... http://massbbo.org
Auctioneer School
   www.mass.gov/?pageID=ocaterminal&&L=6&L0=Home&L1=Government&L2=Our+Agencies+and+Divisions&L3
   =Division+of+Standards&L4=Licensing+(DOS)&L5=Auctioneers&sid=Eoca&b=terminalcontent&f=dos_auc-
   sch&csid=Eoca
Auto Repair Shop, Registered..................... www.aib.org/BDYSHOP/bdshind.htm
Automobile Sales Finance Company .... www.mass.gov/Eoca/docs/dob/mvlist.xls
Bank & Savings Institution .... http://db.state.ma.us/dob/in-choose.asp
Bank, Cooperative .... http://db.state.ma.us/dob/in-choose.asp
Barber/Barber Shop .... http://license.reg.state.ma.us/pubLic/licque.asp?color=red&Board=BR
Boiler Engineer/Pressure Vessels Inspect'r www.mass.gov/dps/LIC_SRCH.HTM
Boxer .... www.mass.gov/mbc/ranking.htm

Brokerage Firm .... www.nasd.com/web/idcplg?IdcService=SS_GET_PAGE&nodeId=6
Building Inspector/Local Inspector .... www.mass.gov/bbrs/bocert.PDF
Building Producer www.mass.gov/bbrs/mfg98.pdf
Check Casher .... www.mass.gov/Eoca/docs/dob/cclist.xls
Check Casher/Seller
    www.mass.gov/?pageID=ocaterminal&&L=4&L0=Home&L1=Consumer&L2=Banks+%26+Banking&L3=Loans+%
    26+Mortgages&sid=Eoca&b=terminalcontent&f=dob_liclist&csid=Eoca
Chiropractor .... http://license.reg.state.ma.us/pubLic/licque.asp?color=red&Board=CH
Collection Agency
    www.mass.gov/?pageID=ocaterminal&&L=4&L0=Home&L1=Consumer&L2=Banks+%26+Banking&L3=Loans+%
    26+Mortgages&sid=Eoca&b=terminalcontent&f=dob_liclist&csid=Eoca
Concrete Technician .... www.mass.gov/bbrs/programs.htm
Concrete Testing Laboratory .... www.mass.gov/bbrs/programs.htm
Construction Supervisor .... www.mass.gov/bbrs/cslsearch.htm
Construction Supervisor (Resid'l) .... www.mass.gov/bbrs/programs.htm
Consumer Credit Grantor
    www.mass.gov/?pageID=ocaterminal&&L=4&L0=Home&L1=Consumer&L2=Banks+%26+Banking&L3=Loans+%
    26+Mortgages&sid=Eoca&b=terminalcontent&f=dob_liclist&csid=Eoca
Contractor, Home Improvement .... www.mass.gov/bbrs/Hicsearch.htm
Cosmetologist/Manicurist/Aesthetician ...... http://license.reg.state.ma.us/pubLic/licque.asp?color=red&Board=HD
Credit Union .... http://db.state.ma.us/dob/in-choose.asp
Day Care Center .... www.eec.state.ma.us/oo_licensing.aspx
Debt Collector .... www.mass.gov/Eoca/docs/dob/dclist.xls
Dental Hygienist .... http://license.reg.state.ma.us/pubLic/licque.asp?color=red&Board=DN
Dentist .... http://license.reg.state.ma.us/pubLic/licque.asp?color=red&Board=DN
Electrician .... http://license.reg.state.ma.us/pubLic/licque.asp?color=red&Board=EL
Electrologist .... http://license.reg.state.ma.us/pubLic/licque.asp?color=red&Board=ET
Embalmer .... http://license.reg.state.ma.us/pubLic/licque.asp?color=red&Board=EM
Emergency Medical Technician .... http://db.state.ma.us/dph/emtcert/cert_search.asp
Engineer .... http://license.reg.state.ma.us/pubLic/licque.asp?color=red&Board=EN
Engineers/Fireman School .... www.mass.gov/dps/schools.htm
Family Child Care Provider .... www.eec.state.ma.us/childCareSearchResult.aspx?city=&zipcode=&type=FCC
Finfishing, Commercial .... www.mass.gov/dfwele/dmf/
Fire Sprinkler Contr./Fitter .... www.mass.gov/dps/LIC_SRCH.HTM
Fireman, 1st/2nd Class .... www.mass.gov/dps/LIC_SRCH.HTM
Firemen / Engineer .... www.mass.gov/dps/LIC_SRCH.HTM
Foreign Transmittal Agency
    www.mass.gov/?pageID=ocaterminal&&L=4&L0=Home&L1=Consumer&L2=Banks+%26+Banking&L3=Loans+%
    26+Mortgages&sid=Eoca&b=terminalcontent&f=dob_liclist&csid=Eoca
Foster Care Provider .... www.eec.state.ma.us/fosterSearchResult.aspx?city=&zipcode=&type=FOSTER
Funeral Director .... http://license.reg.state.ma.us/pubLic/licque.asp?color=red&Board=EM
Fur Buyer .... www.mass.gov/dfwele/dfw/
Gas Fitter .... http://license.reg.state.ma.us/pubLic/licque.asp?color=red&Board=PL
Health Insurer .... www.mass.gov/doi/Companies/companies_lists.html
Health Officer, Certified .... http://license.reg.state.ma.us/public/licque.asp?color=blue
Health Profession, Allied .... http://license.reg.state.ma.us/pubLic/licque.asp?color=red&Board=AH
HMO .... www.mass.gov/doi/Consumer/CSS_health_HMO_Licensed.HTML
Hoisting Machinery Operator .... www.mass.gov/dps/LIC_SRCH.HTM
Home Improvement Contractor/Supvr. .... www.mass.gov/bbrs/Hicsearch.htm
Home Inspector .... http://license.reg.state.ma.us/pubLic/v_list_hi.asp
Inspection Agency, 3rd Party .... www.mass.gov/bbrs/MFB.htm
Insurance Advisor/Adjuster/Agent/Broker . www.mass.gov/doi/Producer/Producer_list.html
Insurance Premium Financer
    www.mass.gov/?pageID=ocaterminal&&L=4&L0=Home&L1=Consumer&L2=Banks+%26+Banking&L3=Loans+%
    26+Mortgages&sid=Eoca&b=terminalcontent&f=dob_liclist&csid=Eoca
Insurance, Domestic/Foreign Company ...... www.mass.gov/doi/Companies/companies_lists.html

Investment Advisor..................................... www.nasd.com/web/idcplg?IdcService=SS_GET_PAGE&nodeId=6
Land Surveyor .... http://license.reg.state.ma.us/pubLic/licque.asp?color=red&Board=EN
Landscape Architect.................................... http://license.reg.state.ma.us/pubLic/licque.asp?color=red&Board=LA
Loan Company, Small .... www.mass.gov/Eoca/docs/dob/sllist.xls
Loan Servicer... www.mass.gov/Eoca/docs/dob/lslist.xls
Lobbyist/Lobbyist Employer .... http://db.state.ma.us/SEC/PRE/search.asp
Lobstering.. www.mass.gov/dfwele/dmf/
Lumber Producer, Native............................ www.mass.gov/bbrs/lumber.pdf
Mammography Radiologic Technologist.... http://db.state.ma.us/dph/Radtechs/
Manufactured Building Producer................ www.mass.gov/bbrs/MFB.htm
Marriage & Family Therapist   http://license.reg.state.ma.us/pubLic/licque.asp?query=personal&color=red&board=MH
Medical Doctor ... ...   http://profiles.massmedboard.org/Profiles/MA-Physician-Profile-Find-Doctor.asp
Mental Health & Human Svcs Prof, Allied
  http://license.reg.state.ma.us/pubLic/licque.asp?query=personal&color=red&board=MH
Mental Health Counselor ... http://license.reg.state.ma.us/pubLic/licque.asp?query=personal&color=red&board=MH
Mortgage Broker... www.mass.gov/Eoca/docs/dob/mblist.xls
Mortgage Broker/Lender .... www.mass.gov/Eoca/docs/dob/mclist.xls
Mortgage Lender... www.mass.gov/Eoca/docs/dob/mllist.xls
Motor Vehicle Sales Financer
  www.mass.gov/?pageID=ocaterminal&&L=4&L0=Home&L1=Consumer&L2=Banks+%26+Banking&L3=Loans+%
  26+Mortgages&sid=Eoca&b=terminalcontent&f=dob_liclist&csid=Eoca
Nuclear Power Plant Engineer/Operator ..... www.mass.gov/dps/LIC_SRCH.HTM
Nurse, LPN/RN/Midwife............................ http://license.reg.state.ma.us/pubLic/licque.asp?color=red&Board=RN
Nursing Home Administrator...................... http://license.reg.state.ma.us/public/licque.asp?color=blue
Occupational Therapist/Assistant................ http://license.reg.state.ma.us/pubLic/licque.asp?color=red&Board=AH
Oil Burner Technician/Contr. .... www.mass.gov/dps/LIC_SRCH.HTM
Optician   ... ...   http://license.reg.state.ma.us/pubLic/licque.asp?query=personal&color=red&board=DO
Optician, Dispensing.................................. http://license.reg.state.ma.us/pubLic/licque.asp?color=red&Board=DO
Optometrist .... http://license.reg.state.ma.us/pubLic/licque.asp?color=red&Board=OP
P&C Insurance Agency............................... www.mass.gov/doi/Producer/Producer_list.html
Perfusionist .... http://license.reg.state.ma.us/pubLic/licque.asp?color=red&Board=PF
Pharmacist.. http://license.reg.state.ma.us/pubLic/licque.asp?color=red&Board=PH
Physical Therapist/Assistant .... http://license.reg.state.ma.us/pubLic/licque.asp?color=red&Board=AH
Physician Assistant .... http://license.reg.state.ma.us/pubLic/licque.asp?color=red&Board=AP
Pipefitter .... www.mass.gov/dps/LIC_SRCH.HTM
Pipefitter School .... www.mass.gov/dps/schools.htm
Plumber.. http://license.reg.state.ma.us/pubLic/licque.asp?color=red&Board=PL
Podiatrist.. http://license.reg.state.ma.us/pubLic/licque.asp?color=red&Board=PD
Psychologist, Educational   ... http://license.reg.state.ma.us/pubLic/licque.asp?query=personal&color=red&board=MH
Psychologist/Provider .... http://license.reg.state.ma.us/public/licque.asp?color=blue
Public Accountant-CPA.............................. http://license.reg.state.ma.us/pubLic/licque.asp?color=red&Board=PA
Radiation Therapy/Radiologic Technolog't http://db.state.ma.us/dph/Radtechs/
Radio & TV Repair Technician .... http://license.reg.state.ma.us/pubLic/licque.asp?color=red&Board=TV
Radiographer/Radiologic Technologist....... http://db.state.ma.us/dph/Radtechs/
Real Estate Agent/Broker/Sales .... http://license.reg.state.ma.us/pubLic/licque.asp?color=red&Board=RE
Real Estate Appraiser................................. http://license.reg.state.ma.us/pubLic/licque.asp?color=red&Board=RA
Refrigeration Technician School................. www.mass.gov/dps/schools.htm
Refrigeration Technician/Contr. .... www.mass.gov/dps/LIC_SRCH.HTM
Rehabilitation Therapist ... http://license.reg.state.ma.us/pubLic/licque.asp?query=personal&color=red&board=MH
Residential Care, Youth............................. www.eec.state.ma.us
Respiratory Care Therapist .... http://license.reg.state.ma.us/pubLic/licque.asp?color=red&Board=RC
Retail Installment Financer
  www.mass.gov/?pageID=ocaterminal&&L=4&L0=Home&L1=Consumer&L2=Banks+%26+Banking&L3=Loans+%
  26+Mortgages&sid=Eoca&b=terminalcontent&f=dob_liclist&csid=Eoca
Sales Finance Company.............................. www.mass.gov/Eoca/docs/dob/mvlist.xls
Sanitarian .... http://license.reg.state.ma.us/pubLic/licque.asp?color=red&Board=SA

Seafood Dealer... www.mass.gov/dfwele/dmf/
Securities Agent/Broker/Dealer .... www.nasd.com/web/idcplg?IdcService=SS_GET_PAGE&nodeId=6
Shellfishing, Commercial .... www.mass.gov/dfwele/dmf/
Social Worker .... http://license.reg.state.ma.us/pubLic/licque.asp?color=red&Board=SW
Speech-Language Pathologist/Audiologist . http://license.reg.state.ma.us/pubLic/licque.asp?color=red&Board=SP
Sprinkler Fitting School.............................. www.mass.gov/dps/schools.htm
Surplus Lines Broker .... www.mass.gov/doi/Producer/Producer_list.html
Taxidermist.. www.mass.gov/dfwele/dfw/
Trapping... www.mass.gov/dfwele/dfw/
Trust Company .... http://db.state.ma.us/dob/in-choose.asp
Veterinarian .... http://license.reg.state.ma.us/pubLic/licque.asp?color=red&Board=VT
Water Supply Facility Operator .... http://license.reg.state.ma.us/pubLic/licque.asp?color=red&Board=DW

County Level ... Courts

Court Administration: Chief Justice for Administration and Management, 2 Center Plaza, Room 540, Boston, MA, 02108; 617-742-8575; www.mass.gov/courts/admin/index.html

Court Structure: The various court sections are called "Departments." While Superior Courts and District Courts have concurrent jurisdiction in civil cases, the practice is to assign cases less than $25,000 to the District Court and those over $25,000 to Superior Court. In addition to misdemeanors, District Courts and Boston Municipal Courts have jurisdiction over certain minor felonies. In Massachusetts courts, "attestation" is the term for what is known as certification in other states. In Massachusetts, a "certificate" is a separate authentification page with a gold seal. In July 2003, the state mandated the attestation fee be $2.50 per page (includes copy fee) and the copy fee be $1.00 per page for all Superior and District Courts.

Eviction cases may be filed at a county District Court or at the regional "Housing Court." A case may be moved from a District Court to a Housing Court, but never the reverse. Housing Courts also hear misdemeanor "Code Violation" cases and prelims for these. There are five Housing Court Regions - Boston (Suffolk County), Worcester (County), Southeast (Plymouth and Bristol Counties), Northeast (Essex County), and Western (Berkshire, Franklin, Hampden and Hampshire Counties). The Southeast Housing Court has three branches - Brockton, Fall River, and New Bedford.

Online Access Note: Opinions from the Supreme Court and Appellate Courts can be found at http://massreports.com. An online access to records on the statewide Trial Courts Information Center website is only available to attorneys and law firms. For more information, contact Peter Nylin by email at nylin_p@jud.state.ma.us. Site updated daily.

County Level ... Recorders & Assessors

Recording Office Organization: 14 counties, 312 towns, and 39 cities; 21 recording offices and 365 UCC filing offices. Each town/city profile indicates the county in which the town/city is located. Filing locations vary depending upon the type of document, as noted below. Berkshire and Bristol counties each have three recording offices. Essex, Middlesex and Worcester counties each have two recording offices. Cities/towns bearing the same name as a county are Barnstable, Essex, Franklin, Hampden, Nantucket, Norfolk, Plymouth, and Worcester. Some UCC financing statements on personal property collateral were submitted to cities/towns until June 30, 2001, while real estate recording continues to be handled by the counties. The recording officers are Town/City Clerk (UCC), County Register of Deeds (real estate), and Clerk of US District Court (federal tax liens). The entire state is in the Eastern Time Zone (EST). Federal tax liens on personal property were filed with the Town/City Clerks prior to 1970. Since that time federal tax liens on personal property are filed with the US District Court in Boston as well as with the towns/cities. Following is how to search the central index for federal tax liens - Address:

US District Court, 1 Courthouse Way, Boston, MA 02110   (617-748-9152)

The federal tax liens are indexed here on a computer system. Searches are available by mail or in person. Do not use the telephone. The court suggests including the Social Security number and/or address of individual names in your search request in order to narrow the results. You can do the search yourself at no charge on their public computer terminal.

State tax liens on personal property are filed with the Town/City Clerk or Tax Collector. All tax liens against real estate are filed with the county Register of Deeds. Some towns file state tax liens on personal property with the UCC index and include tax liens on personal property automatically with a UCC search. Others will perform a separate state tax lien search usually for a fee of $10.00 plus $1.00 per page of copies.

Online Access Note:

A large number of towns and several counties offer online access to assessor records via the Internet for no charge. Also, a private vendor has placed assessor records from a number of towns on the Internet. Visit http://data.visionappraisal.com.

> **Editor's Tip:** Towns and cities that offer online access are listed under their county location.

Barnstable County *Real Estate, Lien, Deed Records*
www.bcrd.co.barnstable.ma.us
Access to County records is free at http://199.232.150.242/ALIS/WW400R.PGM. Search for free, but to print requires a $50 annual fee. Records date back to 1940. Lending agency information is available.

Barnstable Town *Assessor Records*
www.town.barnstable.ma.us
Access town assessor records free at www.town.barnstable.ma.us/VsApps/ParcelLoopUp/LookUp.aspx. Email questions or comments to webadm@town.barnstable.ma.us or call the Assessing Dept. at 508-862-4022.

Chatham Town *Assessor, Property Records*
www.town.chatham.ma.us
Free access to assessor database at http://data.visionappraisal.com/ChathamMA/.

Dennis Town *Assessor, Property Records*
www.town.dennis.ma.us
Access to assessor property records is free at http://townofdennis.bonsailogic.com/.

Falmouth Town *Assessor, Property, Dog Tag Records*
www.town.falmouth.ma.us
Access property data free at http://falmouth.patriotproperties.com/default.asp. Also, find lost dog owners at www.town.falmouth.ma.us/lostdog.php.

Mashpee Town *Assessor Records*
www.ci.mashpee.ma.us
Records on the Town of Mashpee Assessor database are free at www.capecode.com/mashpee/search.asp

Provincetown Town *Assessor, Property Sale Records*
www.provincetowngov.org
Records on the Provincetown Assessor database are free at www.provincetowngov.org/assessor.html.

Yarmouth Town *Assessor, Property Records*
http://yarmouth.ma.us
Records on the Assessor's database are free at http://data.visionappraisal.com/yarmouthma. Free registration for full data. Non-registered users can access a limited set of data.

Berkshire County (Middle District or Northern District) *Real Estate, Lien Records*
Berkshire County (Southern Dist.) *Real Estate, Recording, Judgment, Deed, Lien, Judgment, Will Records*
www.berkshiresouthdeeds.com
Access to Southern District Recorder's records is now free at www.masslandrecords.com/malr/controller; records date back to 1971. Searchable indices include recorded land, plans, registered land. Lending agency information available. Also, search Register of Deeds Records for all Berkshire districts free at www.masslandrecords.com. Click on appropriate Division on map.

Alford Town *Property, Assessor Records*
Access property data free at http://csc-ma.us/AlfordPubAcc/jsp/Home.jsp.

Egremont Town *Property, Assessor Records*
http://egremont-ma.gov/index.html
Access to property data is free at http://csc-ma.us/PropertyContent/jsp/Home.jsp?Page=1. Select Egremont Town.

Great Barrington Town *Property, Assessor Records*
Access to property data is free at http://csc-ma.us/PropertyContent/jsp/Home.jsp?Page=1.

Lee Town *Property, Assessor Records*
Access to property data is free at http://csc-ma.us/PropertyContent/jsp/Home.jsp?Page=1.

Otis Town *Property, Assessor Records*
Access to assessor property record cards is to be available in Summer, 2006. Call the assessor office for details or check www.noticeotis.com.

Richmond Town *Property, Assessor Records*
Access to property data is free at http://csc-ma.us/PropertyContent/jsp/Home.jsp?Page=1.

Bristol County (Fall River District) *Real Estate, Deed, Lien, Judgment, Death, Marriage, Will Records*
www.fallriverdeeds.com
Access registry documents at https://www.fallriverdeeds.com/malr_ecom/MalrApp/index.jsp. Search index free - click on Free Search - but a subscription is required for a pay-per view of images, $1.00 per page, maximum of $5.00 per doc. For add'l online search see Bristol County Southern District. Indexes are 1982 to present.

Bristol County (Northern District) *Real Estate, Lien Records*
www.tauntondeeds.com
Online search: see Bristol County Southern District.

Bristol County (Southern District) *Real Estate, Lien Records*
www.newbedforddeeds.com
Access to County records requires a $100 set up fee and $.50 per minute of use. All three districts are on this system; the record dates vary by district. Lending agency information is available. For information, contact Sherrilynn at 508-993-2605 x17. Real Estate searches found at www.newbedforddeeds.com/mason/main/search/.

Berkley Town *Property, Assessor Records*
Access to property data is free at http://csc-ma.us/PropertyContent/jsp/Home.jsp?Page=1. Click on Berkley Town.

Dartmouth Town *Assessor Records*
www.town.dartmouth.ma.us/town_hall.htm
Search the town assessor database at http://data.visionappraisal.com/DartmouthMA/. Free registration for full data.

Fall River City *Assessor, Property Records*
Access property data free at http://fallriver.patriotproperties.com/default.asp.

Mansfield Town *Assessor Records*
Search town assessor database at http://data.visionappraisal.com/MansfieldMA/. Free registration for full data.

New Bedford City *Property, Assessor Records*
www.ci.new-bedford.ma.us/Nav3.htm
Access to the assessor's property database is free at www.ci.new-bedford.ma.us/Assessors/RealPropertyLookup.htm.

North Attleborough Town *Assessor Records*
Search the town assessor database at http://data.visionappraisal.com/NorthAttleboroMA/. Free registration for full data.

Somerset Town *Property, Assessor Records*
Access to property data is free at http://csc-ma.us/PropertyContent/jsp/Home.jsp?Page=1. Select Somerset Town.

Swansea Town *Property, Assessor Records*
Access to property data is free at http://csc-ma.us/PropertyContent/jsp/Home.jsp?Page=1. Select Swansea Town.

Taunton City *Assessor Records*
www.ci.taunton.ma.us
Access assessor data at http://data.visionappraisal.com/TauntonMA/. Does not require a username & password. Click on link.

Dukes County

Edgartown Town *Real Estate, Property Tax Records*
Search the Town assessor's database at http://data.visionappraisal.com/EdgartownMA. Free registration for full data.

Oak Bluffs Town *Assessor Records*
www.ci.oak-bluffs.ma.us
Search the town assessor database at http://data.visionappraisal.com/OakBluffsMA/. Free registration for full data.

Tisbury Town *Assessor Records*
www.tisburygov.org
Search the town assessor database at http://data.visionappraisal.com/TisburyMA/. Free registration for full data.

West Tisbury Town *Assessor Records*
www.town.west-tisbury.ma.us
Access assessor data at http://data.visionappraisal.com/WestTisburyMA/. Free registration for full data.

Essex County (Northern District) *Real Estate, Lien, Grantor/Grantee, Recording Records*
www.lawrencedeeds.com
Search the recorder database for free at www.lawrencedeeds.com/dsSearch.asp. Also see Andover Town and Essex County Southern District.

Essex County (Southern District) *Real Estate, Lien, Deed Records*
www.salemdeeds.com
Records on the Essex County South Registry of Deeds database are free at www.salemdeeds.com. Click on "Deeds online". Images start 1/1992; records back to 1/1984. Search by grantee/grantor, town & date, street, or book & page.

Amesbury Town *Assessor Records*
www.amesburyma.gov
Search the town assessor data at http://data.visionappraisal.com/AmesburyMA/. Free registration for full data.

Andover Town *Assessor, Land, Grantor/Grantee, Recording Records*
http://andoverma.gov/clerk/
Property tax records on the Assessor's database are free at http://andoverma.gov/assessors/values.php. Also, search the recorder database for free at www.lawrencedeeds.com/dsSearch.asp.

Beverly City *Assessor, Property Records*
www.beverlyma.gov
Access city property data free at http://beverly.patriotproperties.com/default.asp.

Danvers Town *Assessor, Property Records*
www.danvers.govoffice.com
Access property data free at http://danvers.patriotproperties.com/default.asp.

Georgetown Town *Assessor, Property Records*
www.georgetownma.gov
Free access to assessor database at http://data.visionappraisal.com/GeorgetownMA. Registration required.

Haverhill City *Assessor, Property Records*
www.ci.haverhill.ma.us
Access property data free at http://haverhill.patriotproperties.com/default.asp.

Ipswich Town *Assessor, Property Records*
www.town.ipswich.ma.us
Access property data free at http://ipswich.patriotproperties.com/default.asp.

Lawrence City *Land, Grantor/Grantee, Recording Records*
www.cityoflawrence.com/Departments.asp
Search the recorder database for free at www.lawrencedeeds.com/dsSearch.asp.

Lynn City *Assessor, Property Records*
Access property data free at http://lynn.patriotproperties.com/default.asp.

Lynnfield Town *Assessor, Property Records*
www.town.lynnfield.ma.us
Access property data free at http://lynnfield.patriotproperties.com/default.asp.

Manchester-by-the-Sea Town *Property Assessor Records*
www.manchester.ma.us
Search the property assessment data at http://manchester.patriotproperties.com/default.asp.

Marblehead Town *Assessor, Property Records*
www.marblehead.org
Access property data free at http://marblehead.patriotproperties.com/default.asp?br=exp&vr=6.

Methuen City *Property Assessor, Land, Grantor/Grantee, Recording Records*
www.ci.methuen.ma.us
Search the property assessment data free at http://host229.ci.methuen.ma.us. Also, search the recorder database for free at www.lawrencedeeds.com/dsSearch.asp.

Nahant Town *Assessor, Property Records*
www.nahant.org/townhall/clerk.shtml
Access property data free at http://nahant.patriotproperties.com/default.asp.

Newbury Town *Assessor, Property Tax Records*
www.townofnewbury.org
Access property tax data free at http://newbury.patriotproperties.com/default.asp.

Newburyport City *Assessor Records*
Search the city assessor database at http://data.visionappraisal.com/NewBURYPORTMA/. Free registration for full data.

North Andover Town *Land, Grantor/Grantee, Recording, Property, Assessor Records*
Search the recorder database for free at www.lawrencedeeds.com/dsSearch.asp. Also, access to property data is free at http://csc-ma.us/PropertyContent/jsp/Home.jsp?Page=1.

Peabody City *Assessor, Property Records*
www.peabody-ma.gov
Access property data free at http://207.234.185.50/assessorasp/.

Rowley Town *Assessor Records*
Search the town assessor data at http://data.visionappraisal.com/RowleyMA/. Free registration for full data.

Salem City *Assessor, Property Records*
Access property data free at http://salem.patriotproperties.com/default.asp. No name searching.

Salisbury Town *Property, Assessor Records*
www.salisburyma.gov
Access town property data free at http://salisbury.patriotproperties.com/default.asp.

Saugus Town *Property, Assessor Records*
www.saugus.net
Access property data free at http://csc-ma.us/SaugusPubAcc/jsp/Home.jsp.

Swampscott Town *Assessor, Property Records*
www.town.swampscott.ma.us
Access property data free at http://swampscott.patriotproperties.com/default.asp.

Franklin County *Real Property, Recording, Lien, Deed, Judgment, Will Records*
http://franklindeeds.com
Access to Registry of Deeds data is free at www.masslandrecords.com. Select Franklin County on map.

Bernardston Town *Property Assessor Records*
Access to property data is free at http://csc-ma.us/PropertyContent/jsp/Home.jsp?Page=1. Select Bernardston Town.

Charlemont Town *Assessor, Property Tax Records*
www.charlemont-ma.us/Town/TownClerk.shtml
Access is free at http://csc-ma.us/Charlemont.

Deerfield Town *Property, Assessor Records*
www.town.deerfield.ma.us
Access property data free at http://deerfield.patriotproperties.com/default.asp.

Franklin Town *Assessor, Property Records*
Access property data free at http://franklin.patriotproperties.com/default.asp.

Gill Town *Property, Assessor Records*
Access to property data is free at http://csc-ma.us/PropertyContent/jsp/Home.jsp?Page=1.

Heath Town *Property, Assessor Records*
Access to property data is free at http://csc-ma.us/PropertyContent/jsp/Home.jsp?Page=1. Select Heath Town.

Hampden County *Real Estate, Lien, Recording Records*
http://registryofdeeds.co.hampden.ma.us
Access to the county index of land records is free or via subscription at http://204.213.242.147/alis/ww400r.pgm. Images can be viewed free, but cannot be printed unless you subscribe. Access to images via dial-up or web requires a $100 annual fee and $.50 per minute of use. Records go back to 1962. Lending agency info is available. Searchable indexes are bankruptcy (from PACER), unregistered land site and registered land site. For information, contact Mary Caron at 413-755-1722 x121.

Agawam Town *Property Assessor, Real Estate, Recording, Lien Records*
www.agawam.ma.us
Access Property Assessment Data free at http://agawam.patriotproperties.com/default.asp. See Hampden County for recording records searching.

Blandford Town *Real Estate, Recording, Lien Records*
See Hampden County for recording records searching.

Brimfield Town *Real Estate, Recording, Lien Records*
See Hampden County for recording records searching.

Chester Town *Property, Assessor, Real Estate, Recording, Lien Records*
Access to property data is free at http://csc-ma.us/PropertyContent/jsp/Home.jsp?Page=1. Select Chester Town. Also, see Hampden County for recording records searching.

Chicopee City *Real Estate, Recording, Lien Records*
See Hampden County for recording records searching.

East Longmeadow Town *Real Estate, Recording, Lien Records*
www.eastlongmeadow.org
See Hampden County for recording records searching.

Granville Town *Real Estate, Recording, Lien Records*
See Hampden County for recording records searching.

Hampden Town *Real Estate, Recording, Lien Records*
www.hampden.org
See Hampden County for recording records searching.

Holland Town *Real Estate, Recording, Deed, Lien Records*
See Hampden County for recording records searching.

Holyoke City *Assessor, Property, Real Estate, Recording, Lien Records*
www.ci.holyoke.ma.us
Access to property valuations on the tax assessor database are free at www.ci.holyoke.ma.us/legend.htm. No name searching, but you can search by property types. Also, see Hampden County for recording records searching.

Longmeadow Town *Assessor, Real Estate, Recording, Lien Records*
www.longmeadow.org
Access to tax records is at http://data.visionappraisal.com/LONGMEADOWMA/. Free registration for full data. Also, see Hampden County for recording records searching.

Ludlow Town *Real Estate, Recording, Lien Records*
www.ludlow.ma.us/clerk/
See Hampden County for recording records searching.

Monson Town *Real Estate, Recording, Lien Records*
www.monson-ma.gov
See Hampden County for recording records searching.

Montgomery Town *Real Estate, Recording, Lien Records*
See Hampden County for recording records searching.

Palmer Town *Real Estate, Recording, Lien Records*
See Hampden County for recording records searching.

Russell Town *Real Estate, Recording, Lien Records*
See Hampden County for recording records searching.

Southwick Town *Assessor, Real Estate, Recording, Lien Records*
www.southwickma.org
Search the town assessor database at http://data.visionappraisal.com/SouthwickMA/. Free registration for full data. Also, see Hampden County for recording records searching.

Springfield City *Real Estate, Recording, Lien, Assessor, Property Tax, GIS Records*
www.springfieldcityhall.com
See Hampden County for recording records searching. Assess to city assessor property valuations is free at http://springfield.univers-clt.com/index.php. Also, search the city GIS-mapping site for property data at http://www2.springfieldcityhall.com/gis/ but no name searching.

Tolland Town *Real Estate, Recording, Lien, Property, Assessor Records*
See Hampden County for recording records searching. Also, access to property data is free at http://csc-ma.us/PropertyContent/jsp/Home.jsp?Page=1.

Wales Town *Real Estate, Recording, Lien Records*
See Hampden County for recording records searching.

West Springfield Town *Assessor, Real Estate, Recording, Lien Records*
www.west-springfield.ma.us
Search the town assessor database at http://data.visionappraisal.com/WestSpringfieldMA/. Free registration for full data. Also, see Hampden County for recording records searching.

Westfield City *Real Estate, Recording, Lien, Assessor Records*
www.cityofwestfield.org
Assessor records can be found online for Westfield City at http://data.visionappraisal.com/WestfieldMA/. Does not require a username & password. Simply click on link. Also see the Hampden County Register of Deeds for online recorded property data.

Wilbraham Town *Real Estate, Recording, Lien Records*
See Hampden County for recording records searching.

Hampshire County *Real Estate, Lien, Recorder, Deed, Judgment, Will Records*
Access to property records is available; records date back to 9/2/1983. Lending agency information is available. For information, contact Marianne Foster at 413-584-3637. Also, Registry of Deeds records are searchable at www.masslandrecords.com. Click on Hampshire on map.

Amherst Town *Assessor Records*
Search the town assessor data at http://data.visionappraisal.com/AmherstMA/. Free registration for full data.

Belchertown Town *Property, Assessor Records*
www.belchertown.org
Access property data free at http://belchertown.patriotproperties.com/default.asp.

Middlesex County *Recorder, Deed, Lien, Judgment, UCC, Will Records*
www.lowelldeeds.com
Access Register of Deeds data free at www.masslandrecords.com. Click on North Middlesex on map for North District, South for South District.

Arlington Town *Assessor Records*
www.town.arlington.ma.us
Search the town assessor database for free at http://arlserver.town.arlington.ma.us/property.html. There is also a website at http://arlingtonma.virtualtownhall.net/Search for searching for names on town public records.

Ashby Town *Property, Assessor Records*
Access to property data is free at http://csc-ma.us/PropertyContent/jsp/Home.jsp?Page=1. Click on Ashby Town.

Ayer Town *Property, Assessor Records*
www.ayer.ma.us
Access to property data is free at http://csc-ma.us/PropertyContent/jsp/Home.jsp?Page=1. Click on Ayer Town.

Bedford Town *Property, Assessor Records*
www.town.bedford.ma.us
Access to property data is free at http://csc-ma.us/PropertyContent/jsp/Home.jsp?Page=1.

Belmont Town *Assessor, Property Records*
www.town.belmont.ma.us
Access to the town assessor data is free at http://24.61.156.140/Belmont/.

Billerica Town *Assessor, Property Records*
Access property data free at http://billerica.patriotproperties.com/default.asp. No name searching.

Burlington Town   *Property, Assessor Records*
www.burlington.org/clerk
Access property data free at http://burlington.patriotproperties.com/default.asp.

Cambridge City   *Assessor Records*
www.cambridgema.gov/CityClrk/
Records on the City of Cambridge Assessor database are free at www.cambridgema.gov/fiscalaffairs/PropertySearch.cfm. No name searching. Also, search town assessor database at www.cambridgema.gov/fiscalaffairs/PropertySearch.cfm. Does not require a username and password. Simply click on link.

Chelmsford Town   *Assessor Records*
www.townofchelmsford.us
Search town assessor database at http://data.visionappraisal.com/ChelmsfordMA/. Free registration for full data.

Concord Town   *Property Assessor Records*
www.concordnet.org
Alpha search residential and commercial assessments at www.concordnet.org/assessor/.

Dracut Town   *Assessor Records*
Search the town assessor database at http://data.visionappraisal.com/DracutMA/. Free registration for full data.

Groton Town   *Map Browser, Property, Sex Offender Registry Records*
http://townofgroton.org
Access the free map browser at www.geozone.com/Groton/. Also, access the property search site for free at http://host.appgeo.com/groton/. For name searching, you must be a registered user and know the password. Also, access the Mass. State and Groton police sex offender registry websites at www.grotonpd.org/GrotonPD/Helpful_links.html.

Holliston Town   *Property, Assessor Records*
www.townofholliston.us
Access to property data is free at http://csc-ma.us/PropertyContent/jsp/Home.jsp?Page=1. Select Holliston Town.

Hopkinton Town   *Property Records*
www.hopkinton.org
Access Board of Assessors maps at www.hopkinton.org/gov/assessor/listing.htm; no name searching.

Hudson Town   *Property, Assessor, Deed Records*
www.townofhudson.org
Access Town Assessor records free at www.townofhudson.org/Public_Documents/HudsonMA_Assessor/index; click on FY05 Online Assessment Information. To deed search, see www.masslandrecords.com/malr/index.htm and search at Middlesex County.

Lexington Town   *Assessor Records*
http://ci.lexington.ma.us
Assessor data is at http://data.visionappraisal.com/LexingtonMA/. Does not require a username & password. Click on link.

Marlborough City   *Property Assessor Records*
Search the city assessor data at http://data.visionappraisal.com/MarlboroughMA/. Free registration for full data.

Medford City   *Assessor Records*
www.medford.org
Search the city assessor database at http://data.visionappraisal.com/MedfordMA/. Free registration for full data.

Melrose City   *Assessor, Property Records*
www.cityofmelrose.org
Access property data free at http://melrose.patriotproperties.com/default.asp.

Natick Town   *Assessor, Property Records*
www.natickma.org
Search town assessments free at www.natickma.org/assess/assessinfo.asp. Includes name searches.

Newton City   *Assessor Records*
www.ci.newton.ma.us
Records on the City of Newton Fiscal 1998 Assessment database are free at www.ci.newton.ma.us/assessors2003/Search.asp. Data represents market value as of January of current year.

North Reading Town   *Assessor, Property Records*
www.northreadingma.gov
Access property data free at http://csc-ma.us/NreadingPubAcc/jsp/Home.jsp?Page=1 but no name searching.

Reading Town   *Assessor Records*
www.ci.reading.ma.us
Records on the Town of Reading Assessor database are free at www.ziplink.net/~reading1/assessor.htm but no name searching.

Shirley Town   *Assessor, Property Records*
www.shirley-ma.gov/controller.action?mod=10&submod=15
Access property data free at http://shirley.patriotproperties.com/default.asp.

Somerville City   *Assessor Records*
www.ci.somerville.ma.us
Search the city assessor database at http://data.visionappraisal.com/SomervilleMA/. Free registration for full data.

Sudbury Town   *Assessor, Property Records*
www.town.sudbury.ma.us/services
Access to the property valuations list for current year is free at www.town.sudbury.ma.us/services/department_home.asp?dept=Assessors. No name searching on this address index list.

Tewksbury Town   *Assessor, Property Tax, Sale Records*
www.tewksbury.net
Access lists of yearly tax assessments free at www.tewksbury.info/assessor/FY2006Assessments.html. Also, address search recent property sales list free at www.tewksbury.net/assessor/sales.html; link to the pdf list is at the bottom of page.

Wakefield Town   *Assessor, Property Records*
Access property data free at http://wakefield.patriotproperties.com/default.asp.

Waltham City   *Assessor, Property Records*
www.city.waltham.ma.us
Access property data free at http://waltham.patriotproperties.com/default.asp.

Watertown Town   *Assessor, Property Records*
www.ci.watertown.ma.us
Access property data free at http://watertown.patriotproperties.com/default.asp.

Wayland Town   *Assessor Records*
www.wayland.ma.us
Assessment records on the Assessor's database are free at www.wayland.ma.us/assessors/index.htm. No name searching; street name required.

Winchester Town   *Assessor, Property Records*
Access property data free at http://winchester.patriotproperties.com/default.asp.

Woburn City   *Assessor Records*
www.cityofwoburn.com
Search the city assessor data at http://data.visionappraisal.com/WoburnMA/. Free registration for full data.

Nantucket County   *Real estate, Deed, Recording, Lien Records*
County deed records may possibly be available by subscription, call 508-228-7250.

Norfolk County *Real Estate, Lien, Deed, Judgment Records*
www.norfolkdeeds.org
Access to county online records is on two levels, both accessible via http://research.norfolkdeeds.org/ALIS/WW400R.PGM. You may search images and indices free, however, to print requires a subscription; $100 per year plus $1.00 per page. Land records go back to 1974; images to 1974. Land court records go back to 9/1984, with images back to 1901. This replaces the old subscription system.

Bellingham Town *Assessor, Property Records*
www.bellinghamma.org
Access property data free at http://bellingham.patriotproperties.com/default.asp.

Braintree Town *Assessor, Property Records*
Access property data free at http://braintree.patriotproperties.com/default.asp.

Brookline Town *Assessor, Property Records*
www.town.brookline.ma.us/Assessors
Records on the Town of Brookline Assessors database are free at www.townofbrooklinemass.com/assessors/propertylookup.asp.

Dedham Town *Assessor Records*
Property records on the Assessor's database are free at http://data.visionappraisal.com/dedhamma/. Does not require a username & password. Simply click on link.

Dover Town *Property, Assessor Records*
http://doverma.org/townclerk.php
Access to the assessor's property values data is free at www.doverma.org/assessorsproposedvaluesnew.php. You must open individual tables to search by name.

Holbrook Town *Assessor, Property Records*
Access property data free at http://holbrook.patriotproperties.com/default.asp.

Medfield Town *Assessor, Property Records*
www.town.medfield.net
Access town property data free at http://medfield.patriotproperties.com/default.asp?br=exp&vr=6.

Needham Town *Property, Assessor Records*
www.town.needham.ma.us
Access to property data is free at http://csc-ma.us/PropertyContent/jsp/Home.jsp?Page=1. Select Needham Town.

Quincy City *Assessor, Property Records*
www.ci.quincy.ma.us
Access assessor property data free at http://data.visionappraisal.com/QuincyMA/. No name searching. Also a sales look-up.

Walpole Town *Property Assessor Records*
www.walpole-ma.gov
Search the town assessor database at http://data.visionappraisal.com/WalpoleMA/. Free registration for full data.

Wellesley Town *Assessor, Town By-Law, Zoning By-Law, Election results Records*
www.wellesleyma.gov/Pages/index
Property tax records on the Assessor's database are free at www.ci.wellesley.ma.us/Pages/WellesleyMA_Assessor/FISCAL%20YEAR%202006%20Values. This site will be under a new name in subsequent years.

Weymouth Town *Property, Assessor Records*
www.weymouth.ma.us
Access to property data is free at www.weymouth.ma.us/propview/.

Plymouth County *Real Estate, Lien, Judgment Records*

www.regdeeds.co.plymouth.ma.us
Access to Online Titleview for Plymouth County records requires a usage charge of $.60 per minute of use. Indices date back to 1971. Lending agency information is available. Unlimited viewing and printing of documents available for $30.00 per month. A fax back service is $3 plus $1 per page in county, $5. plus $1 per page, outside. For info, call 508-830-9287.

Abington Town *Assessor Records*

www.abingtonmass.com
Search town assessor database at http://data.visionappraisal.com/AbingtonMA/. Does not require a username & password. Simply click on link.

Duxbury Town *Property, Assessor Records*

Search the town public documents free at http://duxburyma.virtualtownhall.net/Public_Documents/Search. Also, access to property data is free at http://csc-ma.us/PropertyContent/jsp/Home.jsp?Page=1.

Hanson Town *Property, GIS-mapping Records*

www.hanson-ma.gov
Access property records free at http://gis.virtualtownhall.net/hanson/index.htm; no name searching.

Hingham Town *Property, Assessor, Sale Records*

Search assessor rolls and property sales free at http://csc-ma.us/HinghamPubAcc/jsp/Home.jsp?. Click on "New Search" or Sales

Lakeville Town *Property Records*

Property information is listed on a private site at http://69.95.33.2/Newdatabases.html.

Marion Town *Assessor Records*

www.townofmarion.org
Search town assessor data at http://data.visionappraisal.com/MarionMA/. Free registration for full data.

Marshfield Town *Assessor Records*

Search town assessor database at http://data.visionappraisal.com/MarshfieldMA/. Does not require a username & password. Simply click on link.

Mattapoisett Town *Property, Assessor Records*

www.mattapoisett.net
Access to property data is free at http://csc-ma.us/PropertyContent/jsp/Home.jsp?Page=1. Select Mattapoisett Town.

Middleborough Town *Assessor, Property Records*

www.middleborough.com
Search town assessor database at http://data.visionappraisal.com/MiddleboroMA/. Does not require a username & password. Simply click on link.

Pembroke Town *Assessor, Property Records*

www.townofpembrokemass.org
Access assessor data free at http://pembroke.patriotproperties.com/default.asp?br=exp&vr=6.

Plymouth Town *Assessor, Property Records*

www.townofplymouth.org
Access property data free at http://plymouth.patriotproperties.com/default.asp.

Wareham Town *Assessor Records*

Search town assessor database at http://data.visionappraisal.com/WarehamMA/. Free registration for full data.

Suffolk County *Real Estate, Lien, Deed, Judgment, Property Assessor Records*

www.suffolkdeeds.com
Searches on Registry of Deeds site are free; real estate/liens on the county online system is not. Access to the County online system requires a written request submitted to Register of Deeds, POB 9660, Boston. Online charges are $.50 per minute. Also, Records on the County Registry of Deeds database are free at www.suffolkdeeds.com/search/default.asp. Search by name, corporation, and

grantor/grantee. Recorded land records begin 1979; Registered land, 1983. Also, Registry of Deeds data is free at www.masslandrecords.com; click on Suffolk on the map. Also, search Boston assessor property records free at www.cityofboston.gov/assessing/search.asp. City property taxes also available, but no name searching.

Boston City *Assessor Records*
www.cityofboston.gov/cityclerk/default.asp
Records on the City of Boston Assessor database are free at www.cityofboston.gov/assessing/search/. Also, property tax bill and payment is searchable by parcel number for free at www.cityofboston.gov/assessing/paysearch.asp.

Chelsea City *Assessor Records*
Search the city assessor database at http://data.visionappraisal.com/ChelseaMA/. Free registration for full data.

Revere City *Assessor, Property Records*
www.revere.org/greeting.htm
Access property data free at http://revere.patriotproperties.com/default.asp. Free registration for full data.

Worcester County (Northern District) *Real Estate, Lien, Recording, Land Court, Assessor Records*
www.fitchburgdeeds.com
Access to Registry of Deeds is now free at http://151.203.96.11/alis/ww400r.pgm. Small fee to copy or certify documents. Land index back to 1982; images to 1983. Also, county recorded land images from 1731 to 1974 are free at www.worcesterdeeds.com/worcester/dsbppagelist.asp; book and page number required.

Worcester County (Worcester District) *Real Estate, Deed, Lien, Grantor/Grantee, Judgment, Will, Property Tax Records*
www.worcesterdeeds.com
Access to the Register of Deeds database is free at www.masslandrecords.com. Click on South Worcester on map. Also, county recorded land images from 1731 to 1974 are free at www.worcesterdeeds.com/worcester/dsbppagelist.asp

Bolton Town *Real Estate, Deed, Property, Assessor Records*
www.townofbolton.com
See Worcester County Southern District for online information. Also, access to assessor property data is free at http://csc-ma.us/PropertyContent/jsp/Home.jsp?Page=1.

Brookfield Town *Property, Assessor Records*
www.brookfieldma.us
Access to property data is free at http://csc-ma.us/PropertyContent/jsp/Home.jsp?Page=1. Select Brookfield Town.

Charlton Town *Assessor, Property Records*
Access property data free at http://charlton.patriotproperties.com/default.asp.

Dudley Town *Assessor Records*
www.dudleyma.gov
Search the town assessor database at http://data.visionappraisal.com/DudleyMA/. Free registration for full data.

East Brookfield Town *Assessor, Property Records*
Access to property data is free at http://csc-ma.us/PropertyContent/jsp/Home.jsp?Page=1. Select East Brookfield Town.

Gardner City *Property Assessor Records*
Search the city assessor data at http://data.visionappraisal.com/GardnerMA/. Free registration for full data.

Grafton Town *Property, Assessor Records*
www.town.grafton.ma.us/Home/
Access to property data is free at http://csc-ma.us/GraftonPubAcc/jsp/Home.jsp?Page=1; also at http://csc-ma.us/PropertyContent/jsp/Home.jsp?Page=1. Select Grafton Town.

Hardwick Town *Property, Assessor Records*
Access to property data is free at http://csc-ma.us/PropertyContent/jsp/Home.jsp?Page=1. Select Harwick Town.

Harvard Town *Assessor Records*
www.harvard.ma.us/townclerk.htm
Search town assessor database at http://data.visionappraisal.com/HARVARDMA/. Free registration for full data.

Holden Town *Real Estate, Property Tax Records*
Search the Town assessor's database free at http://data.visionappraisal.com/HOLDENMA. Free registration for full data.

Lancaster Town *Property, Assessor Records*
www.ci.lancaster.ma.us
Access to property data is free at http://csc-ma.us/PropertyContent/jsp/Home.jsp?Page=1. Select Lancaster Town.

Leicester Town *Assessor, Property Records*
Access property data free at http://leicester.patriotproperties.com/default.asp.

Leominster City *Assessor Records*
www.ci.leominster.us
Search the assessor's database at http://data.visionappraisal.com/leominsterma. Free registration for full data.

Lunenburg Town *Property, Assessor Records*
www.lunenburgonline.com
Access to property data is free at http://csc-ma.us/PropertyContent/jsp/Home.jsp?Page=1.

Milford Town *Assessor, Property Records*
Access property data free at http://milford.patriotproperties.com/default.asp.

Millbury Town *Assessor Records*
Access to the town tax assessor info is free at http://data.visionappraisal.com/MillburyMA/.

Millville Town *Real Estate, Deed, Tax Lien Records*
http://millvillema.org
Access the index at www.worcesterdeeds.com/worcester/dsbppagelist.asp.

North Brookfield Town *Property, Assessor Records*
Access to property data is free at http://csc-ma.us/PropertyContent/jsp/Home.jsp?Page=1. Select North Brookfield Town.

Northborough Town *Property, Assessor Records*
www.town.northborough.ma.us
Access to property data is free at http://csc-ma.us/PropertyContent/jsp/Home.jsp?Page=1.

Oakham Town *Property, Assessor Records*
Access to property data is free at http://csc-ma.us/PropertyContent/jsp/Home.jsp?Page=1. Select Oakham Town.

Oxford Town *Property Assessor Records*
www.town.oxford.ma.us
Search the property assessments by street name for free at www.town.oxford.ma.us/Assessor/Assessor.htm.

Paxton Town *Assessor Records*
Search town assessor database at http://data.visionappraisal.com/PaxtonMA/. Does not require a username & password. Simply click on link.

Royalston Town *Assessor, Property Records*
Access to property data is free at http://csc-ma.us/PropertyContent/jsp/Home.jsp?Page=1. Select Royalston Town.

Rutland Town *Assessor, Property Records*
Access to Rutland town assessor records is free at http://data.visionappraisal.com/RutlandMA/.

Southborough Town *Assessor, Property Records*
Access property tax data free at http://csc-ma.us/SouthboroughPubAcc/jsp/Home.jsp?Page=1. No name searching.

Sturbridge Town *Real Estate, Deed Records*
www.town.sturbridge.ma.us
See Worcester County Southern District for online information.

Templeton Town *Assessor Records*
Access assessor data at http://data.visionappraisal.com/TempletonMA/. Free registration for full data.

Uxbridge Town *GIS Records*
www.uxbridge-ma.gov
Search maps by owner's name at www.mapsonline.net/uxbridgema/.

West Brookfield Town *Property, Assessor Records*
Access to property data is free at http://csc-ma.us/PropertyContent/jsp/Home.jsp?Page=1.

Westborough Town *Assessor, Property Records*
Access property data free at http://westborough.patriotproperties.com/default.asp.

Worcester City *Real Estate, Lien, Assessor Records*
Data is online in 2 ways. Online access to the City Assessor Valuation Search database is free at www.ci.worcester.ma.us/aso/value_search.htm. And, access to the Landtrack System for Worcester District records requires a $50 annual fee plus $.25 per minute of use. Index records date back to 1966. Images are viewable from 1974 onward. Lending agency info is available. Fax back service: $.50 per page. For information, contact Joe Ursoleo at 508-798-7713 X233.

Federal Courts in Massachusetts...

Standards for Federal Courts: The universal PACER sign-up number is 800-676-6856. Find PACER and the Party/Case Index on the Web at http://pacer.psc.uscourts.gov. PACER dial-up access is $.60 per minute. Also, courts offering internet access via PACER, Web-PACER or the new CM-ECF charge $.08 per page fee ($.07 per page if record is pre-2005 or unless noted as free).

US District Court -- District of Massachusetts
www.mad.uscourts.gov
PACER: Case records are available back to 1/1990. Records are purged every 12 months. New records are available online after 1 day. **PACER Online Access:** PACER online at http://pacer.mad.uscourts.gov. Document images available. **Electronic Filing:** CM/ECF data at https://ecf.mad.uscourts.gov. **Opinions:** View court opinions at http://pacer.mad.uscourts.gov/opinion.html. **Other Online Access:** Access calendars free at www.mad.uscourts.gov/Calendar/calendar.htm.
Boston Division counties: Barnstable, Bristol, Dukes, Essex, Middlesex, Nantucket, Norfolk, Plymouth, Suffolk.
Springfield Division counties: Berkshire, Franklin, Hampden, Hampshire.
Worcester Division counties: Worcester.

US Bankruptcy Court -- District of Massachusetts
www.mab.uscourts.gov
PACER: Case records are available back to 4/1987. Records are purged every 12 months. New records are available online after immediately. **PACER Online Access:** ECF replaces PACER. Document images available. **Electronic Filing:** CM/ECF data at https://ecf.mab.uscourts.gov. **Opinions:** View court opinions at www.mab.uscourts.gov/opinions.htm. **Phone access:** Voice Case Information System, call 888-201-3572, 617-565-6025
Boston Division counties: Barnstable, Bristol, Dukes, Essex (except towns assigned to Worcester Division), Nantucket, Norfolk (except towns assigned to Worcester Division), Plymouth, Suffolk, and the following towns in Middlesex: Arlington, Belmont, Burlington, Everett, Lexington, Malden, Medford, Melrose, Newton, North Reading, Reading, Stoneham, Wakefield, Waltham, Watertown, Wilmington, Winchester and Woburn.
Worcester Division counties: Berkshire, Franklin, Hampden, Hampshire, Middlesex (except the towns assigned to the Boston Division), Worcester and the following towns: in Essex-Andover, Haverhill, Lawrence, Methuen and North Andover; in Norfolk-Bellingham, Franklin, Medway, Millis and Norfolk.

Michigan

Capital: Lansing
Ingham County

Time Zone: EST

Four NW Michigan counties are in the CST:

They are: Dickinson, Gogebic, Iron, Menominee.

Population: 10,112,620

# of Counties: 83

Quick Links

Website: www.michigan.gov

Governor: www.michigan.gov/gov

Attorney General: www.michigan.gov/ag

State Archives: www.michigan.gov/hal/0,1607,7-160-17445_19273_19313---,00.html

State Statutes and Codes:
www.legislature.mi.gov/(akl2lgy414wpnie0dcmcb4bq)/mileg.aspx?page=mclbasicsearch

Legislative Bill Search:
www.legislature.mi.gov/(nywb32iqibn11d2s2o1kzlez)/mileg.aspx?page=home

Unclaimed Funds: www.michigan.gov/treasury/0,1607,7-121-1748_1876_1912-7924--,00.html

State Level ... Major Agencies

Criminal Records

Michigan State Police, Criminal History Section, Criminal Justice Information Center, 7150 Harris Dr, Lansing, MI 48913; 517-322-1956, Fax-517-322-0635, 8AM-5PM.
www.michigan.gov/msp
Online search: Online access is available at www.michigan.gov/ichat. Results are available in seconds; fee is $10.00 per name. Call 517-322-1377. This is a non-fingerprint search. You are also allowed up to three variations on one name search. Use of a MasterCard or VISA is required.

Statewide Court Records

State Court Administrative Officer, PO Box 30048, Lansing, MI 48909 (Courier: 925 W Ottawa St, Lansing, MI 48909); 517-373-0130, Fax-517-373-9831, 8:30AM-5PM.
http://courts.michigan.gov/scao/
Online search: Subscribe to email updates of appellate opinions at http://courtofappeals.mijud.net/resources/subscribe.htm. There is no fee. There is a wide range of online computerization of the judicial system from "none" to "fairly complete," but there is no statewide court records network for record of local courts. **Other options:** Zip files are provided for recent Supreme Court and Court of Appeals releases.

Sexual Offender Registry

Michigan State Police, SOR Unit, 7150 Harris Dr, Lansing, MI 48913; 517-322-5098, Fax-517-322-4957, 8AM-5PM.
www.mipsor.state.mi.us
Online search: One may search the registry at the website, there is no charge.

Incarceration Records

Michigan Department of Corrections, Central Records Office, PO Box 30003, Lansing, MI 48909 (Courier: 206 E. Michigan Ave., Lansing, MI 48909); 517-373-0284, Fax-517-373-2628, 8AM-4:30PM.
www.michigan.gov/corrections
Online search: The online access through the main website and at www.state.mi.us/mdoc/asp/otis2.html has many search criteria capabilities. There is also a DOC Most Wanted list at www.state.mi.us/mdoc/MostWanted/MostWanted.asp. **Other options:** Bulk sales of database information is available.

Corporation, Limited Liability Company, Limited Partnership, Assumed Name

Department of Labor & Economic Growth, Bureau of Commercial Services, PO Box 30054, Lansing, MI 48909-7554 (Courier: 7150 Harris Dr, Lansing, MI 48909); 517-241-6470, Fax-517-241-0538, 8AM-noon, 1-5PM.
http://michigan.gov/cis/0,1607,7-154-10557_12901---,00.html
Online search: At the website, search by company name or file number for records of domestic corporations, limited liability companies, and limited partnerships and of foreign corporations, and limited partnerships qualified to transact business in the state. **Other options:** The database is for sale by contract.

Trademarks/Servicemarks

Corporation Division, Trademarks & Service Marks, PO Box 30054, Lansing, MI 48909-7554 (Courier: 7150 Harris Dr, Lansing, MI 48909); 517-241-6470, 8AM-5PM (closed at noon for 1 hr).
www.michigan.gov/cis/0,1607,7-154-10557_21107---,00.html
Online search: Free searching is available at www.cis.state.mi.us/bcsc/forms/corp/mark/markcom.pdf. This is a search of a PDF file of their system. It is very tricky to get to on the web.

Uniform Commercial Code, Federal Tax Liens, State Tax Liens

MI Department of State, UCC Section, PO Box 30197, Lansing, MI 48909-7697 (Courier: 7064 Crowner Dr, Dimondale, MI 48821); 517-322-1144, Fax-517-322-5434, 8AM-5PM.
www.michigan.gov/sos
Online search: From the website, click on UCC Online Service. Conducting a Debtor Name Quick Search is free. No login is needed. Documents may be ordered for a fee. Registration and credit card are required. **Other options:** A monthly subscription service is available for the bulk purchase of UCC filings on microfilm. The fee is $50 or actual cost, whichever is greater. Call 517-322-1144 for additional information.

Birth, Death, Marriage, Divorce Records

Department of Health, Vital Records Requests, PO Box 30721, Lansing, MI 48909 (Courier: 3423 N Martin Luther King, Jr Blvd, Lansing, MI 48906); 517-335-8656 (Instructions), 517-335-8666 (Request Unit), Fax-517-321-5884, 8AM-5PM.
www.michigan.gov/mdch
Online search: Records may be ordered from the web. Use of a credit card is required. Records are returned by mail or express delivery. If problems, call 800-255-2414.

Workers' Compensation Records

Department of Labor & Economic Dev., Workers' Compensation Agency, 7150 Harris Dr, Lansing, MI 48909; 888-396-5041, Fax-517-322-1808, 8AM-5PM.
www.michigan.gov/wca
Online search: Go to the website and follow the links to see if an employer has coverage. The site does not allow searching by employee name.

Driver Records

Department of State, Record Lookup Unit, 7064 Crowner Dr, Lansing, MI 48918; 517-322-1624 (Look-up Unit), Fax-517-322-1181, 8AM-4:45PM.
www.michigan.gov/sos
Online search: Online ordering is available on an interactive basis. The system is open 7 days a week. Ordering is by DL or name and DOB. An account must be established and billing is monthly. Access is also available from the Internet. Fee is $7.00 per record. A $25,000 surety bond is required. Also, the agency offers an activity notification service for employers who register their drivers. For more information on either program, call 517-322-6281. **Other options:** Magnetic tape inquiry is available. Also, the state offers the license file for bulk purchase. Customized runs are $64.00 per thousand records; complete database can be purchased for $16.00 per thousand. A $10,000 surety bond is required. Call 322-1042.

Vehicle & Vessel Ownership, Registration

Department of State, Record Lookup Unit, 7064 Crowner Dr, Lansing, MI 48918; 517-322-1624, Fax-517-322-1181, 8AM-4:45PM.
www.michigan.gov/sos
Online search: Online searching via the Internet is single inquiry and requires a VIN or plate number. (no name searches). A $25,000 surety bond is required. Fee is $7.00 per record. For more information, call 517-322-6281. **Other options:** Michigan offers bulk retrieval from the VIN and plate database. A written request letter, stating purpose, must be submitted and approved. A $10,000 surety bond is required upon approval. Please call 517-322-1042.

Accident Reports

Department of State Police, Criminal Justice Information Center, 7150 Harris Dr, Lansing, MI 48913; 517-322-5509 (FOIA), 517-322-1150 (Online Questions), Fax-517-323-5350, 8AM-5PM.
www.michigan.gov/msp/0,1607,7-123--28578--,00.html
Online search: Records may be requested from the Traffic Crash Purchasing System at https://mdotwas1.mdot.state.mi.us/TCPS/login/welcome.jsp. There is a fee and credit cards are accepted. Records are available going back 10 years. For specific questions email CrashPurchaseTCPS@michigan.gov.

GED Certificates

MI Department of Labor & Econ Growth, Adult Education - GED Testing, 201 N Washington Square, 3rd Fl, Lansing, MI 48913; 517-373-1692, Fax-517-335-3461, 7AM-5PM.
www.michigan.gov/mdcd/0,1607,7-122-1680_2798---,00.html
Online search: Will accept e-mail requests with a scanned signature.

State Level ... Occupational Licensing

Adoption Service	www.michigan.gov/dhs/1,1607,7-124-5452_7116---,00.html
Airport Manager	www.michigan.gov/documents/MGRLST_17899_7.pdf
Alarm System Service	http://cis.state.mi.us/bcs_free/default.asp
Ambulance Attendant	www.cis.state.mi.us/free/default.asp
Amusement Ride	http://cis.state.mi.us/verify.htm
Appraiser, Real Estate/General/Resident'l	http://cis.state.mi.us/verify.htm
Architect	http://cis.state.mi.us/verify.htm
Assessor	www.michigan.gov/documents/CertificationLevel_3022_7.pdf
Attorney, State Bar	www.michbar.org/memberdirectory/
Auto Dealer/Mechanic/Repair Facility	www.michigan.gov/sos/0,1607,7-127-1631_8849-51047--,00.html
Bank & Trust Company	www.michigan.gov/cis/1,1607,7-154--22352--,00.html
Barber/Barber Shop/School	http://cis.state.mi.us/verify.htm
Boxing/Wrestling Occupation	http://cis.state.mi.us/verify.htm
Builder, Residential	http://cis.state.mi.us/verify.htm
Camp, Children/Adult Foster Care	www.cis.state.mi.us/brs_cwl/sr_cac.asp
Carnival	http://cis.state.mi.us/verify.htm
Casino Interest Personnel/Company	http://miboecfr.nicusa.com/cgi-bin/cfr/casino_srch.cgi
Cemetery	http://cis.state.mi.us/verify.htm
Check Seller	www.michigan.gov/cis/0,1607,7-154-10555_13251_13257---,00.html
Child Care Institution	www.dleg.state.mi.us/brs_cwl/sr_cwl.asp
Child Day Care	www.cis.state.mi.us/brs_cdc/sr_lfl.asp
Child Facility, Court Operated	www.dleg.state.mi.us/brs_cwl/sr_cwl.asp
Child Welfare/Child Placing Agency	www.dleg.state.mi.us/brs_cwl/sr_cwl.asp
Chiropractor	www.cis.state.mi.us/free/default.asp
Collection Manager	http://cis.state.mi.us/verify.htm
Community Planner	http://cis.state.mi.us/verify.htm
Community Planner (Mfg. Home)	www.cis.state.mi.us/bcs_free/
Consumer Financial Service	www.michigan.gov/cis/0,1607,7-154-10555_13251_13257---,00.html
Contractor, Residential	http://cis.state.mi.us/verify.htm
Cosmetologist/Cosmetology Shop/School	http://cis.state.mi.us/verify.htm
Counselor	www.cis.state.mi.us/free/default.asp

Credit Card Issuer	www.michigan.gov/cis/0,1607,7-154-10555_13251_13257---,00.html
Credit Union	www.michigan.gov/cis/1,1607,7-154--22352--,00.html
Debt Management Firm	www.michigan.gov/documents/cis_ofis_debtlist_25540_7.pdf
Dentist/Dental Assistant/Dental Hygienist	www.cis.state.mi.us/free/default.asp
Election Campaign Finance Committee	http://miboecfr.nicusa.com/cgi-bin/cfr/mi_com.cgi
Election Candidate Committee	http://miboecfr.nicusa.com/cgi-bin/cfr/can_search.cgi
Emergency Medical Personnel	www.cis.state.mi.us/free/default.asp
Employment Agency, fee only	http://cis.state.mi.us/verify.htm
EMT Advanced/Specialist/Instr.	www.cis.state.mi.us/free/default.asp
Engineer	http://cis.state.mi.us/verify.htm
Flight School	www.michigan.gov/aero/0,1607,7-145-6774_6887---,00.html
Forester	http://cis.state.mi.us/verify.htm
Foster Care Facility/Adult Camp	www.cis.state.mi.us/brs_cwl/sr_cac.asp
Foster Care Program	www.dleg.state.mi.us/brs_afc/sr_afc.asp
Foster Care, Adult	www.cis.state.mi.us/brs_afc/sr_afc.asp
Foster Care, Child	www.cis.state.mi.us/brs_cwl/sr_cf.asp
Foster Family Home	www.dleg.state.mi.us/brs_cwl/sr_cac.asp
Funeral Home/Salesperson	http://cis.state.mi.us/verify.htm
Funeral, Prepaid Contract Regis.	http://cis.state.mi.us/verify.htm
Grain Dealer	www.mda.state.mi.us/prodag/GrainDealers/dealers.html
Health Facility/Laboratory	www.cis.state.mi.us/free/default.asp
Hearing Aid Dealer	http://cis.state.mi.us/verify.htm
HMO	www.michigan.gov/cis/0,1607,7-154-10555_13251_13262---,00.html
Insurance Adjuster	www.michigan.gov/cis/0,1607,7-154-10555_13251_13262---,00.html
Insurance Agent/Counselor/Solic'r/Admin.	www.michigan.gov/cis/0,1607,7-154-10555_13251_13262---,00.html
Insurance Counselor/Solicitor	www.cis.state.mi.us/fis/ind_srch/ins_agnt/insurance_agent_criteria.asp
Insurance-related Entity	www.michigan.gov/cis/0,1607,7-154-10555_13251_13262---,00.html
Investment Adviser	www.nasd.com/web/idcplg?IdcService=SS_GET_PAGE&nodeId=469
Landscape Architect	http://cis.state.mi.us/verify.htm
Liquor Dist./Whlse./Mfg./License	http://cis.state.mi.us/bcs_free/default.asp
Liquor Licensing Director	http://cis.state.mi.us/bcs_free/default.asp
Living Care Facility	www.michigan.gov/documents/cis_ofis_lclist_25541_7.pdf
Lobbyable Public Official	www.michigan.gov/sos/0,1607,7-127-1633_11945-30499--,00.html
Lobbyist/Lobbyist Agent	http://miboecfr.nicusa.com/cgi-bin/cfr/lobby_srch.cgi
Long Term Care Company	www.michigan.gov/cis/0,1607,7-154-10555_13251_13262---,00.html
Mammography Facility	www.cis.state.mi.us/free/default.asp
Marriage & Family Therapist	www.cis.state.mi.us/free/default.asp
Medical Doctor	www.cis.state.mi.us/free/default.asp
Medical First Responder	www.cis.state.mi.us/free/default.asp
Mortgage Licensee	www.michigan.gov/cis/0,1607,7-154-10555_13251_13257---,00.html
Mortuary Science	http://cis.state.mi.us/verify.htm
Motor Vehicle Loan Seller/Financer	www.michigan.gov/cis/0,1607,7-154-10555_13251_13257---,00.html
Nurse	www.cis.state.mi.us/free/default.asp
Nursery Dealer/Grower	www.mda.state.mi.us/industry/Nursery/license/index.html
Nurses' Aide	www.cis.state.mi.us/free/default.asp
Nursing Home	www.cis.state.mi.us/bhs_car/sr_car.asp
Nursing Home Administrator	www.cis.state.mi.us/free/default.asp
Ocularist	http://cis.state.mi.us/verify.htm
Optometrist	www.cis.state.mi.us/free/default.asp
Osteopathic Physician	www.cis.state.mi.us/free/default.asp
Paramedic	www.cis.state.mi.us/free/default.asp
Personnel Agency	http://cis.state.mi.us/verify.htm
Pesticide Applicator Company	www.michigan.gov/mda/0,1607,7-125-1569_2459-13075--,00.html
Pharmacist	www.cis.state.mi.us/free/default.asp
Physical Therapist	www.cis.state.mi.us/free/default.asp
Physician Assistant	www.cis.state.mi.us/free/default.asp

Podiatrist .... www.cis.state.mi.us/free/default.asp
Political Action Committee......................... http://miboecfr.nicusa.com/cgi-bin/cfr/pac_search.cgi
Political Party Committee .... http://miboecfr.nicusa.com/cgi-bin/cfr/mi_com.cgi?com_type=PPY
Polygraph Examiner .... http://cis.state.mi.us/verify.htm
Potato Dealer .... www.michigan.gov/mda/0,1607,7-125-1566_1733_2321-11149--,00.html
Private Detective....................................... http://cis.state.mi.us/bcs_free/default.asp
Private Investigator .... http://cis.state.mi.us/verify.htm
Private Security/Security Arrest Authority . http://cis.state.mi.us/bcs_free/default.asp
Psychologist.. www.cis.state.mi.us/free/default.asp
Public Accountant-CPA............................. http://cis.state.mi.us/verify.htm
Pump Installer ... ...   www.deq.state.mi.us/documents/deq-dwrpd-gws-wcu-Reg-Contractors-By-County.pdf
Real Estate Agent/Broker/Seller .... http://cis.state.mi.us/verify.htm
Regulatory Loan Licensee .... www.michigan.gov/cis/0,1607,7-154-10555_13251_13257---,00.html
Sanitarian .... www.cis.state.mi.us/free/default.asp
Savings Bank www.michigan.gov/cis/1,1607,7-154--22352--,00.html
Securities Agent/Broker/Dealer .... www.nasd.com/web/idcplg?IdcService=SS_GET_PAGE&nodeId=469
Security Agency/Alarm Installer/Guard...... http://cis.state.mi.us/verify.htm
Social Worker .... www.cis.state.mi.us/free/default.asp
Surety Company .... www.michigan.gov/cis/0,1607,7-154-10555_13251_13262---,00.html
Surplus Line Broker................................... www.michigan.gov/cis/0,1607,7-154-10555_13251_13262---,00.html
Surveyor, Professional .... http://cis.state.mi.us/verify.htm
Teacher .... https://mdoe.state.mi.us/teachercert/
Third-Party Administrator .... www.michigan.gov/cis/0,1607,7-154-10555_13251_13262---,00.html
Veterinarian/Veterinary Technician............ www.cis.state.mi.us/free/default.asp
Well Contractor   ... ...   www.deq.state.mi.us/documents/deq-dwrpd-gws-wcu-Reg-Contractors-By-County.pdf

County Level ... Courts

Court Administration: State Court Administrator, PO Box 30048 (309 N Washington Sq), Lansing, MI, 48909; 517-373-0130; http://courts.michigan.gov/scao/

Court Structure: The Circuit Court is the court of general jurisdiction. District Courts and Municipal Courts have jurisdiction over certain minor felonies and handle all preliminary hearings.

There is a Court of Claims in Lansing that is a function of the 30th Circuit Court with jurisdiction over claims against the state of Michigan. A Recorder's Court in Detroit was abolished as of October 1, 1997.

As of January 1, 1998, the Family Division of the Circuit Court was created. Domestic relations actions and juvenile cases, including criminal and abuse/neglect, formerly adjudicated in the Probate Court, were transferred to the Family Division of the Circuit Court. Mental health and estate cases continue to be handled by Probate Courts. Several counties (Barry, Berrien, Iron, Isabella, Lake, and Washtenaw) and the 46th Circuit Court are participating in a "Demonstration" pilot project designed to streamline court services and consolidate case management. These courts may refer to themselves as County Trial Courts.

Online Access Note: There is a wide range of online computerization of the judicial system from "none" to "fairly complete," but there is no statewide court records network. Some Michigan courts provide public access terminals in clerk's offices, and some courts are developing off-site electronic filing and searching capability. A few offer remote online to the public. The Criminal Justice Information Center (CJIC), the repository for MI criminal record info, offers online access. Results are available in seconds; fee is $10.00 per name. Go to www.michigan.gov/ichat or call 517-322-5546. Subscribe to email updates of appellate opinions at http://courtofappeals.mijud.net/resources/subscribe.htm. There is no fee.

Crawford County

46th Circuit Court – Civil and Criminal Records
www.Circuit46.org
Access to court case records (closed cases for 90 days only) is free at www.circuit46.org/Cases/cases.html.

46th Circuit Trial Court - District Division – Civil, Probate, and Criminal Records
Access to limited index of court records is free at http://66.129.39.149/c46_Cases.php. There are limitations, system is not meant to be used for background checks, it is supplemental only.

Eaton County

56th Circuit Court – Criminal Records
www.eatoncountycourts.org/courts.html
Last 12-13 months of criminal case dispositions listed at www.eatoncounty.org/County_Services/criminal/Criminal.htm.

Genesee County

7th Circuit Court – Civil and Criminal Records
www.co.genesee.mi.us
Access to court records is free at www.co.genesee.mi.us/clerk/#; click on "Circuit Court Records."

67th District Court – Civil and Criminal Records
www.co.genesee.mi.us/districtcourt/
Search by name or case number at www.co.genesee.mi.us/districtcourt/recordschk.htm. Also includes traffic.

Grand Traverse County

13th Circuit Court – Civil and Criminal Records
www.co.grand-traverse.mi.us
Search civil records free at www.co.grand-traverse.mi.us; 1981 through 1985 contain only index information.1986 to present include case information and register of actions. Search criminal records index 1967 through 1985. 1986 to present include case information and register of actions. Database updated nightly.

Kalkaska County

46th Circuit Court – Civil and Criminal Records
www.Circuit46.org
Access to court case records (open or closed cases for 90 days only) is free at www.circuit46.org/Cases/cases.html.

46th Circuit Trial Court - District Court – Civil, Probate and Criminal Records
www.Circuit46.org
Access to limited index of court records is free at http://66.129.39.149/c46_Cases.php. There are limitations, system is not meant to be used for background checks, it is supplemental only.

Kent County

17th Circuit Court – Civil and Criminal Records
www.accesskent.com/CourtsAndLawEnforcement
Search for $6.00 per name at https://www.accesskent.com/CourtNameSearch/. DOB not required but credit card is for record found. Also, search hearings schedule free at https://www.accesskent.com/CCHearing/ Also, search for accident reports at $3.00 per name at https://www.accesskent.com/AccidentReports/.

61st District Court - Grand Rapids – Civil and Criminal Records
www.ci.grand-rapids.mi.us/197
Search online at www.ci.grand-rapids.mi.us/index.pl?page_id=645.

Macomb County

16th Circuit Court – Civil and Criminal Records
www.macombcountymi.gov/circuitcourt
Online records includes divorces. Access Circuit Court index for free at http://209.131.29.171/pa/pa.urd/pamw6500.display. Fee to copy and view documents.

Otsego County

46th Circuit Court – Civil and Criminal Records
www.Circuit46.org
Access to court case records (closed cases for 90 days only) is free at www.circuit46.org/Cases/cases.html.

46th Circuit Trial Court - District Court – Civil, Probate, and Criminal Records
www.circuit46.org
Access to limited index of court records is free at http://66.129.39.149/c46_Cases.php. There are limitations, system is not meant to be used for background checks, it is supplemental only.

County Level ... Recorders & Assessors

Recording Office Organization: 83 counties, 83 recording offices. The recording officer is the County Register of Deeds. 79 counties are in the Eastern Time Zone (EST) and 4 counties that border on Wisconsin (Gogebic, Iron, Dickinson, and Menominee) are in the Central Time Zone (CST). Federal and state tax liens on personal property of businesses are filed with the Secretary of State. Other federal and state tax liens are filed with the Register of Deeds. Most counties search each tax lien index separately. Some charge one fee to search both, while others charge a separate fee for each one. When combining a UCC and tax lien search, total fee is usually $9.00 for all three searches. Some counties require tax identification number as well as name to do a search. Copy fees are usually $1.00 per page.

Online Access Note: There is no statewide online access, but a number of counties, including Wayne, offer free access to assessor and register of deeds records.

Allegan County   *Real Estate, Property Tax, Delinquent Tax Records*
www.allegancounty.org
Search by name or address at www.allegancounty.org/prdwebeq/ or https://is.bsasoftware.com/bsa.is/. The latter site includes Cities of Otsego, Plainwell, Saugatuck, and Saugatuck Township.

Antrim County   *Most Wanted Records*
www.antrimcounty.org
Access to the sheriff's most wanted list is free at www.torchlake.com/acsd/.

Barry County   *Property, Assessor, Delinquent Tax Records*
www.barrycounty.org
Access to county parcel data is free at www.barrycounty.org/ParcelData.htm. County property Index is from 12/95 to 1/04.

Bay County   *Real Estate, Deed, Lien, Property Tax Records*
www.co.bay.mi.us
Access the register's land records data, click on Internet Land Records Search at the bottom of www.co.bay.mi.us/bay/home.nsf/Public/Bay_County_Register_Of_Deeds.htm. Log-in as Guest. Index goes back to 1985; no images. Access county property tax data for free at www.co.bay.mi.us/bay/ptq.nsf. Also, access City of Essexville and Hampton Township at https://is.bsasoftware.com/bsa.is/

Benzie County   *Recording, Real Estate, Deed, Lien, Property Tax Records*
Recorder office data by subscription on either the Laredo system using subscription and fees or the Tapestry System using credit card, https://tapestry.fidlar.com/tapsearch.aspx; $3.99 search; $.50 per image. Also, access land and proeprty tax data fee for Almira Township at https://is.bsasoftware.com/bsa.is/.

Berrien County   *Property Records*
www.berriencounty.org
Access to City of Niles property data is free with registration at https://is.bsasoftware.com/bsa.is/.

Branch County   *Real Estate, Recorder, Deed, Vital Statistic, Business Name Records*
www.co.branch.mi.us
Access to recorder records is to be available Summer 2006. See www.fidlar.com; typically this offers access via Laredo with free access and sale of docs per item with credit card, or by subscription to the Tapestry system with monthly fee. Currently, search the county vital records free at www.co.branch.mi.us/vital/vital.html. Search business names and DBAs at www.co.branch.mi.us/dbasearch.taf. Also, access City of Coldwater property, tax, and speecial assessments free after registration at https://is.bsasoftware.com/bsa.is/.

Calhoun County   *Property, Land, Tax, Special Assessments Records*
http://co.calhoun.mi.us
Access to data for Cities of Albion, Battle Creek, Marshall, Springfield and Townships of Marshall, Newton, and Sheridan is free with registration at https://is.bsasoftware.com/bsa.is/.

Charlevoix County   *Birth, Marriage, Obituary, Cemetery, Birth, Property, Tax, Delinquent Tax Records*
Access to these unofficial records is courtesy of genealogical researcher at www.rootsweb.com/~micharle/charlevx.htm. Also, access to county and Township of Evangeline data is free with registration at https://is.bsasoftware.com/bsa.is/.

Clare County   *Property, Tax, Building, Utility Bill Records*
www.clareco.net
Access to City of Clare data is free with registration at https://is.bsasoftware.com/bsa.is/.

Clinton County   *Property Tax, Assessor, Recording, Deed, Judgment, Lien, Fictitious Business Name Records*
www.clinton-county.org/rod/register_of_deeds.htm
Register to search free on the recorders database at www.clinton-county.org/rod/index_search.htm. Username and password is required. Also, search fictitious business names free at www.clinton-county.org/clerk/dba_search.asp. Also, access property tax data by subscription; see www.clinton-county.org/treasurer/delq_tax_search.htm. $20 processing fee plus $.25 per parcel. Also, gis-mapping site property data at http://maps.clinton-county.org/ClintonCountyCX/Disclaimer.htm; does not appear to have name searching. Access DeWitt, Eagle, Victor, and Watertown property, tax data, utility bills, and assessments free with registration at https://is.bsasoftware.com/bsa.is/.

Dickinson County   *Land, Property Tax Records*
Access City of Iron Mountain land and property tax data free with registration at https://is.bsasoftware.com/bsa.is/.

Eaton County   *Assessor, Tax, Recorder, Marriage, Divorce Records*
www.eatoncounty.org/County_Clerk/CountyClerk.htm
Two levels of service are available on the County Online Data Service site at www.eatoncounty.org/County_Services/Online.htm. There is a limited free service and a full-access subscription service. Other county records, including Marriages and Divorces back to early 2005 are accessible at www.eatoncounty.org/County_Services/County_Service.htm. Also, access property and tax data for Cities of Charlotte, Eaton Rapids, Grand Ledge, and Townships of Carmel and Delta for free with registration at https://is.bsasoftware.com/bsa.is/.

Emmet County
Real Estate, Recorder, Deed, Lien, Property Tax, Assessor, Marriage, Death, Fictitious Name Records
www.co.emmet.mi.us/deeds/
Access the recorder land records at www.co.emmet.mi.us:8080/icris/Login.jsp; registration, logon and password required to view full data; full access to all images back to 1982 is $1,000.00 per month. Also, access assessor property records free at www.co.emmet.mi.us/equalization/propsrcheq.htm. Use username "general" and password "general." Also, search marriages, deaths, and assumed names free at www.co.emmet.mi.us/clerk/. Also, access county porperty tax, land, animal licenses, and delinquent taxes free with registration at https://is.bsasoftware.com/bsa.is/.

Genesee County   *Real Estate, Recording, Property Tax, Deed, Marriage, Death Records*
www.co.genesee.mi.us
Access to Register of Deeds database is free at www.co.genesee.mi.us/rod/. But to view documents back to 10/2000, there is a fee, and user ID and password required. Also, online access to the county clerk's marriage (back to 1963) and death (back to 1930) indexes are free at www.co.genesee.mi.us/vitalrec. Search property index at www.co.genesee.mi.us/cgi-bin/gweb.exe?mode=7800&sessionname=gentax&command=connect. Also, access property data for the county and for Cities of Burton, Linden and townships of Fenton, Davison, and Grand Blanc free with registration at https://is.bsasoftware.com/bsa.is/.

Gladwin County   *Land, Property Records*
www.gladwinco.com
Access City of Gladwin property data free with registration at https://is.bsasoftware.com/bsa.is/.

Grand Traverse County   *Recording, Deed, Real Estate, Tax Lien, Judgment, Assumed Name, Construction Permit, Marriage, Death Records*
www.co.grand-traverse.mi.us
Except for document images, all searches are free at www.co.grand-traverse.mi.us; click on "Online Records." Recorder's document index search is free but images require fee; pay by credit card. Recording records go back to 1986. Deaths back to 1867; marriages to 1853; District civil court judgments go back to 1966; images mid-1980s. Criminal records available. Also, access death and marriage indices free at www.tcnet.org/gtcounty/index.html. Also, recording data by sub on Laredo system or Tapestry credit card system at https://tapestry.fidlar.com/tapsearch.aspx; $3.99 search; $.50 per image. Also, access tax and special assessments free at https://is.bsasoftware.com/bsa.is/.

Hillsdale County
Recording, Deed, Judgment, Lien, UCC, Parcel, Tax Sale, Property Tax, Most Wanted Records
www.co.hillsdale.mi.us
Access to the recorder's index is free but images available only by sub. Records go back to 9/1984 and more being added. Fee is $300.00 for recorder, or $50.00 for just the assessor's equalization records. Copies included. Call recorder for signup. Also, search complete recorder index free at www.deeds.hillsdale.us/LandWeb.dll. Treasurer's tax sale lists at www.co.hillsdale.mi.us/hc-treasurer.htm. Search Parcels free at www.hillsdalecounty.info/parcelsearch.asp but no name searching. Also, access City of Hillsdale tax records free with registration at https://is.bsasoftware.com/bsa/. Also, search sheriff's most wanted list at www.hillsdalecountysheriff.com/most-wanted/most-wanted2.html.

Ingham County *Assumed Business Name, Recording, Deed, Grantor/Grantee, Assessor, Property, Delinquent Tax, Marriage Applicant Records*
www.ingham.org/rd/rodindex.htm
Access the Register of Deeds database after free registration at https://qdocs.ingham.org/recorder/eagleweb/login.jsp. Also, county DBA and co-partnership listings are free at www.ingham.org/CL/dbalists.htm. Also, marriage applicants can be searched by the week for free at www.ingham.org/CL/marrind.htm. Access land, tax, utility records and more free with registration for Cities of East Lansing, Lansing, Leslie, Mason and townships of Aurelius, Lansing, Vevay, and Village of Stockbridge at https://is.bsasoftware.com/bsa.is/.

Ionia County *Real Estate, Recorder, Deed, Judgment, Lien, Will, Death, Property Tax, Assessor Records*
www.ioniacounty.org
Access recorder records free at http://66.39.252.38/cland2/landweb.dll. Also, access county property data free at www.ioniacounty.org/taxweb/viewparcels.asp. Also, access Lyons Township land and proeprty records free with registration at https://is.bsasoftware.com/bsa.is/.

Isabella County *Real Estate, Recorder, Deed, Property Tax Records*
www.isabellacounty.org
Access to recorder land data is to be available online by Summer 2006. Visit www.isabellacounty.org/Dept/Deeds/deeds.html. Access to City of Mt Pleasant property and tax data is free with registration at https://is.bsasoftware.com/bsa.is/.

Jackson County *Real Estate, Lien, Deed, Grantor/Grantee, Foreclosed Property Sale Records*
www.co.jackson.mi.us/rod/
Search recorded documents at http://70.227.252.194/icris/documentSearch.jsp. Search foreclosed property sales lists at www.jacksoncountytaxsale.com/local_units.htm but no name searching. Also, access property, tax and land data for City of Jackson and townships of Columbia and Rives for free with registration at https://is.bsasoftware.com/bsa.is/. Search for Columbia utility bills as well.

Kalamazoo County *Assessor, Property Records*
www.kalcounty.com
Access property assessor data free at www.kalcounty.com/equalization/parcel_search.php. Also, access property, land, and tax data for Cities of Kalamazoo, Parchment, Portage and the townships of Alamo, Brady, Comstock, Kalamazoo, Oshtemo, Pavilion, Ross, Schoolcraft, and Wakeshma for free with registration at https://is.bsasoftware.com/bsa.is/. Also includes special assessments data for Cooper and Oshtemo Townships.

Kent County
Recording, Deed, Lien, Assessor, Property, Accident Report, Vital Statistic, Treasurer, Inmate Records
www.accesskent.com/YourGovernment/RegisterofDeeds/deeds_index.htm
Search county parcel data free at https://www.accesskent.com/Property/. With username, password & credit card, view records for $1. or subscribe for $75. per year at 616-632-6516. Accident reports $3.00 at https://www.accesskent.com/AccidentReports/. Kent deeds index free at https://www.accesskent.com/deeds/. Walker City assessor- https://is.bsasoftware.com/bsa.is/ free registration. Search assessment-Ada, Bowne, Caledonia, Courtland, Grand Rapids, Lowell, Vergennes at www.addorio.com/netparcel.htm. For more, see https://is.bsasoftware.com/bsa.is/. Alpine assessments at http://alpine.data-web.net. No name search. Order vital statistic records $7 at https://www.accesskent.com/servlet/VitalRec. Grand Rapids property at www.ci.grand-rapids.mi.us/22.

Lapeer County *Real Estate, Recorder, Deed, Lien, Judgment Records*
www.county.lapeer.org/deeds
Access recorder data free by name by clicking on "Guest Login" at http://207.72.70.14/scripts/landweb.dll. Registration and fees required for full search. Pop-up blocker must be off. Images to be available soon. Also, access property, land and tax data for City of Lapeer and townships of Almont, Imlay, and Mayfield for free with registration at https://is.bsasoftware.com/bsa.is/. Also has special assessment records for City of Lapeer.

Lenawee County   *Real Estate, Recording, Deed, Will, Probate Order, Lien, Personal Property, Assessor, Property Tax Records*
www.lenawee.mi.us/regdeeds.html
Recording records available by subscription, call 517-264-4539 (Register of Deeds) for info and fees. Also, search assessing/property data free at http://lenawee.zenacomp.com. Also, access to City of Tecumseh data including animal licensings is free with registration at https://is.bsasoftware.com/bsa.is/.

Livingston County   *Real Estate, Lien, Tax Assessor, Death Records*
www.co.livingston.mi.us/RegisterofDeeds/
Web access to county records is available for occasional users and a dedicated line is available for $1200 for professionals. Annual fee for occasional use- $400, plus $.000043 per second. Records date back to 1984. Lending agency information available. For information, contact IT Dept at 517-548-3230. Also, search the county death indices to 1948 for free at www.livgenmi.com/deathlisting.htm. Also, acess to property, tax, and other civil data for Cities of Brighton, Howell, and Townships of Brighton, Handy, hartland, and Putnam is free with registration at https://is.bsasoftware.com/bsa.is/. Includes Village of Fowler proeprty tax data.

Macomb County   *Recorder, Deed, Business Registration, Death, Campaign Committee/Candidate, Most Wanted, Sex Offender Records*
http://macombcountymi.gov/clerksoffice/index.asp
13 cities' and towns' property, tax, and certain other civil records are free with registration at https://is.bsasoftware.com/bsa.is/. County business registration info is free at http://macomb.mcntv.com/businessnames. Search by full or partial name. County death records are at http://macomb.mcntv.com/deathrecords. Search by name or approx. date. Also, county recorder images are from a private source at www.courthousedirect.com; Fees/registration required. Search sex offender and most wanted lists at sheriff site at www.macombsheriff.com. Also, Land records from the assessor database found at www.landaccess.com/index.jsp?content=register. Free registration for password and user name.

Marquette County   *Assessor, Property, Building Records*
www.co.marquette.mi.us/register.htm
Access City of Marquette only property, tax, and building records free with registration at https://is.bsasoftware.com/bsa.is/.

Mason County   *Parcel, Property Tax, Utility Bill Records*
Access to City of Ludington parcels and tax data is free with registration at https://is.bsasoftware.com/bsa.is/. Ditto for Hamlin Township property, and ditto for Pere Marquette Township property and utility bills.

Mecosta County   *Assessor, Property, Animal License, Special Assessments, Delinquent Tax Records*
Access to the county property, land, and tax data index is free with registration at https://is.bsasoftware.com/bsa.is/. May have fees to view images. Also search the City of Big Rapids assessing and tax page - including special assessments and animal license search - for free at that website.

Menominee County   *Land, Recording, Deed, Property Tax Records*
www.menomineecounty.com/rod/rgstr1.html
Access to land records is free at http://66.84.189.207/landweb.dll. Search is free - use "Guest Login" - but document images may be ordered by fax for $1.50 each or mail for $1.00 each. Subscriptions available for full data. Also, access property tax and land data for City of Menominee for free with registration at https://is.bsasoftware.com/bsa.is/.

Midland County   *Land, Property Tax, Delinquent Tax, Animal License Records*
www.co.midland.mi.us
Access to the county and City of Midland property data is free with registration at https://is.bsasoftware.com/bsa.is/. The county access also includes delinquent tax and animal license data.

Monroe County   *Real Estate, Recorder, Deed, Fictitious Name, Voter Registration Records*
www.co.monroe.mi.us
Access recorder land index free at https://www.co.monroe.mi.us/egov/landrecords/. Access to images requires credit card payment. Access fictitious business names free at https://www.co.monroe.mi.us/egov/searchdbanames.aspx. Also, order voter registration lists at https://www.co.monroe.mi.us/egov/ordervoterlist.aspx; fee is $20 per copy on CD-rom. Also, access county tax bill and delinquent tax data for free with registration at https://is.bsasoftware.com/bsa.is/. This also offers access to City of Monroe Property, tax, and utility bill information.

Montcalm County
Real Estate, Recorder, Deed, Lien, Judgment, Assessor, Treasurer, Tax Roll, Tax Sale, Inmate Records
No fee to view the index at http://65.118.226.83/landweb.dll, but a $50 monthly fee for details. Unlimited access is $300 monthly. Access plus printable document images is $700 monthly. Records date back to 1/1/1988. Lending agency info is available. For singup, call Register of Deeds office. Also, assessor property tax data is free at www.montcalm.org/taxweb/viewparcels.asp. Also, search tax roll, tax sale online free at www.co.whatcom.wa.us/treasurer/index.jsp. Access to Cities of Greenville property, tax, and land data is free with registration at https://is.bsasoftware.com/bsa.is/. Also, search county jail roster at www.co.whatcom.wa.us/sheriff/jail/roster.jsp.

Muskegon County *Property, Tax, Land, Death Records*
www.co.muskegon.mi.us/deeds/
Access the county genealogical death index system for free at www.co.muskegon.mi.us/clerk/websearch.cfm. Records 1867-1965. Also, access to the city of Norton Shores tax data is free with registration at https://is.bsasoftware.com/bsa.is/. Also at this site you may access City of Roosevelt property and tax data.

Newaygo County *Land, Property Tax Records*
Access to City of Fremont land and property data is free with registration at https://is.bsasoftware.com/bsa.is/.

Oakland County *Real Estate, Property Tax, Tax Lien, Most Wanted, Foreclosure, Assumed Name Records*
www.oakgov.com/clerkrod/
Access to Oakland property information is by subscription, available monthly or per use. For information or sign-up, visit www.oakgov.com (click on "Access Oakland") or call Information Services at 248-858-0861. Search foreclosure property lists at www.oakgov.com/fcloser/fmain?cmd=fcvt. Also, search the county sheriff's most-wanted list at www.oakgov.com/sheriff/most_wanted/. Also search fictitious, assumed names for free at www.oakgov.com/crts0003/main. Search Rochester Hills tax assessor data at http://64.7.183.246/Services/TaxandAssessing/SearchOverview.asp. No name searching. Also access 8 municipalities land, property tax records and more free with registration at https://is.bsasoftware.com/bsa.is/

Oceana County *Real Estate, Recorder, Deed, Property Tax Records*
www.oceana.mi.us/
Access the record index back to 1/2002 free at http://mi-oceana-recorder.governmaxa.com/recordmax/record40.asp. No images currently available. Also, access property tax and land records for Hart Township for free with registration at https://is.bsasoftware.com/bsa.is/.

Otsego County *Real Estate, Recorder, Deed, Subdivision, Plat, Assessor Records*
Access recorder data free at http://66.84.47.80/otsearch.htm. Includes assessment data.

Ottawa County *Property, Mapping, Deed, UCC, Judgment, Accident Report Records*
www.co.ottawa.mi.us
Search property data free at https://www.miottawa.org/Property/noLogin.do. Also, free online mapping service with parcel ID at www.gis.co.ottawa.mi.us/ottawa/. No name searching. Holland City land and tax data free at https://is.bsasoftware.com/bsa.is/. Also, access recorder records by subscription at https://www.landaccess.com/ottawa/sub.jsp?county=miottawa. Fee- $200.00 per month plus $1.00 per page to view and print; maximum $10.00 per doc. Credit cards search only. Also, access accident reports at https://www.miottawa.org/AccidentReports/ there is a $5.00 per 2-page document fee. Also, access property and tax records for 8 municipalities for free with registration at https://is.bsasoftware.com/bsa.is/. Includes some building and assessment data.

Saginaw County *Assessor, Assumed Business Name, Marriage, Death, Election, Notary, Grantor/Grantee, Recording, Obituary Records*
www.saginawcounty.com
Access to the county clerks database is free at www.saginawcounty.com/clerk/search/index.html. Vital statistic records go back to 1995. Search the Register of Deeds index at www.saginawcounty.com/ROD/Simple.htm. Also, a general property search is free at www.sagagis.org/search/. Also, search equalization board tax records at www.saginawcounty.com/equ/prop_info.htm.

St. Clair County
Real Estate, Recorder, Deed, Lien, Marriage, Death, Property, Assessor, GIS-map, Utility Bill, Buildings Records
www.stclaircounty.org/Offices/register_of_deeds/
Access register of deeds database free at https://publicdeeds.stclaircounty.org:444/. Click on OPR. Online records go back to 10/1993. Search tax equalization data free at www.stclaircounty.org/offices/equalization/search.asp. Also, data may be available at http://gis.stclaircounty.org/landmanagement on the map site. Access to unofficial death records up to 1974 are free at www.rootsweb.com/~mistcla2/. 19th century marriages are also available. Also, access land and property tax data for Cities of

Algonac, Marysville, St Clair also Townships of Clay, Cottleville, East China, and Ira for free with registration at https://is.bsasoftware.com/bsa.is/. Includes some Utility Bill and building data.

St. Joseph County *Land, Assessor, Property Tax, Delinquent Tax Records*
www.stjosephcountymi.org
Search assessor records for free at www.stjosephcountymi.org/taxsearch/default.asp. Also, search county land, property tax and delinquent tax data and City of Sturgis land data for free with registration at https://is.bsasoftware.com/bsa.is/.

Sanilac County *Real Estate, Property Records*
www.sanilaccounty.net
Access to property and tax data is available by subscription or CD-rom. CD-rom is $100; internet subscription is $204.00 per year. For signup, phone 810-648-4114 or visit www.sanilaccounty.net/subinfo.asp. Also, access county land and property tax records free with registration at https://is.bsasoftware.com/bsa.is/ Access Argyle Township property records for free there also.

Shiawassee County *Land, Property Tax Records*
Access land and property tax data for Cities of Laingsburg and Perry, and Caledonia Township for free with registration at https://is.bsasoftware.com/bsa.is/. Also at this site is property tax data for Venice Township.

Tuscola County *Land, Tract Records*
www.tuscolacounty.org
Access to the county land tract index is free at www.landaccess.com/sites/mi/tuscola/index.php?mituscola.

Van Buren County *Real Estate, Property Tax, Special Assessment Records*
www.vbco.org/government0104.asp
Free search for ownership of real property at www.vbco.org/mapsearch.asp. Aslo, access property tax, land, and special assessment data for free with registration at https://is.bsasoftware.com/bsa.is/. Also includes property records for Townships of Antwerp and Paw Paw.

Washtenaw County *Real Estate, Deed, Lien, Judgment, Parcel, Property Tax, Vital Statistic, Business Name, Accident Report Records*
www.ewashtenaw.org/government/clerk_register
Access a menu of searchable databases for free at www.ewashtenaw.org/online. Also, search land and property tax data and more for Cities of Ann Arbur, Chelsea, Milan, Saline, and townships of Ann Arbor, Augusta, Bridgewater, Dexter, Lodi, Pittsfield, Superior, Webster, York, Ypsilanti and Village of Dexter for free with registration at https://is.bsasoftware.com/bsa.is/.

Wayne County *Assessor, Recording, Deed, Judgment, Lien, Assumed Name, Delinquent Tax Records*
www.waynecounty.com/register/
Search the recorders land records database for free at www.waynecountylandrecords.com/. A full data on-demand or business service is also available; call 313-967-6857 for info or sign-up or visit www.waynecountylandrecords.com/RODC/Default.asp. Search assumed names at www.waynecounty.com/clerk/AssumedNames/search.asp. Search delinquent tax list at www.waynecounty.com/pta/Disclaimer.asp. Also, property and tax data and more for 16 munipalities is free at https://is.bsasoftware.com/bsa.is/. Also, City of Dearborn property data is free at www.dearbornfordcenter.com/dbnassessor/. No name searching. Also, City of Livona property data is free at http://livonia.zenacomp.com/bins/site/templates/splash.asp. No name searching.

Wexford County *Real Estate Records*
www.wexfordcounty.org/services_deeds.php
Search treasurer's records at www.wexfordcounty.org/treas/search.htm.

Federal Courts in Michigan...

Standards for Federal Courts: The universal PACER sign-up number is 800-676-6856. Find PACER and the Party/Case Index on the Web at http://pacer.psc.uscourts.gov. PACER dial-up access is $.60 per minute. Also, courts offering internet access via PACER, Web-PACER or the new CM-ECF charge $.08 per page fee ($.07 per page if record is pre-2005 or unless noted as free).

US District Court -- Eastern District of Michigan

www.mied.uscourts.gov

PACER: Case records are available back to 1988. New records are available online after 1 day. **PACER Online Access:** ECF replaces PACER. **Electronic Filing:** CM/ECF data at https://ecf.mied.uscourts.gov. **Opinions:** View court opinions at www.mied.uscourts.gov/_opinions/opinion.htm.

Ann Arbor Division counties: Jackson, Lenawee, Monroe, Oakland, Washtenaw. Many Oakland cases are heard in Detroit Division. Civil cases in these counties are assigned randomly to Detroit, Flint, Ann Arbor, or Port Huron Divisions. Case files maintained where case is assigned. However, all cases can be accessed electronically in the District index.

Bay City Division counties: Alcona, Alpena, Arenac, Bay, Cheboygan, Clare, Crawford, Gladwin, Gratiot, Huron, Iosco, Isabella, Midland, Montmorency, Ogemaw, Oscoda, Otsego, Presque Isle, Roscommon, Saginaw, Tuscola.

Detroit Division counties: Macomb, St. Clair, Sanilac, Wayne (and Oakland County). Civil cases for these counties are assigned randomly among the Flint, Ann Arbor and Detroit divisions. Port Huron cases may also be assigned here. Case files are kept where the case is assigned. However, all cases can be accessed electronically in the District index.

Flint Division counties: Genesee, Lapeer, Livingston, Shiawassee. This office handles all criminal cases for these counties. Civil cases are assigned randomly among the Detroit, Ann Arbor and Flint divisions. However, all cases can be accessed electronically in the District index.

US Bankruptcy Court -- Eastern District of Michigan

www.mieb.uscourts.gov

PACER: Case records are available back to 10/1992. New records are available online after 1 day. **PACER Online Access:** ECF replaces PACER. **Electronic Filing:** CM/ECF data at https://ecf.mieb.uscourts.gov. **Opinions:** View court opinions at www.mieb.uscourts.gov/courtOpinions/index.html. **Other Online Access:** PDF versions of daily dockets free at www.mieb.uscourts.gov/courtDocket/index.html. **Phone access:** Voice Case Information System, call 877-422-3066, 313-961-4940

Bay City Division counties: Alcona, Alpena, Arenac, Bay, Cheboygan, Clare, Crawford, Gladwin, Gratiot, Huron, Iosco, Isabella, Midland, Montmorency, Ogemaw, Oscoda, Otsego, Presque Isle, Roscommon, Saginaw, Tuscola.

Detroit Division counties: Jackson, Lenawee, Macomb, Monroe, Oakland, Sanilac, St. Clair, Washtenaw, Wayne.

Flint Division counties: Genesee, Lapeer, Livingston, Shiawassee.

US District Court -- Western District of Michigan

www.miwd.uscourts.gov

PACER: Case records are available back to 9/1989. Records are purged never. **PACER Online Access:** ECF replaces PACER. **Electronic Filing:** CM/ECF data at https://ecf.miwd.uscourts.gov.

Grand Rapids Division counties: Antrim, Barry, Benzie, Charlevoix, Emmet, Grand Traverse, Ionia, Kalkaska, Kent, Lake, Leelanau, Manistee, Mason, Mecosta, Missaukee, Montcalm, Muskegon, Newaygo, Oceana, Osceola, Ottawa, Wexford. The Lansing and Kalamazoo Divisions also handle cases from these counties. Cases in these counties may also be tried in the Kalamazoo or Lansing courts.

Kalamazoo Division counties: Allegan, Berrien, Calhoun, Cass, Kalamazoo, St. Joseph, Van Buren. Also handle cases from the counties in the Grand Rapids Division.

Lansing Division counties: Branch, Clinton, Eaton, Hillsdale, Ingham. Also handle cases from the counties in the Grand Rapids Division.

Marquette-Northern Division counties: Alger, Baraga, Chippewa, Delta, Dickinson, Gogebic, Houghton, Iron, Keweenaw, Luce, Mackinac, Marquette, Menominee, Ontonagon, Schoolcraft.

US Bankruptcy Court -- Western District of Michigan

www.miwb.uscourts.gov

PACER: Case records are available back to 9/1989. Records are purged 6 months after case closed. New records are available online after 1 day. **PACER Online Access:** ECF replaces PACER. **Electronic Filing:** CM/ECF data at https://ecf.miwb.uscourts.gov. **Opinions:** Opinions can also be mailed to annual subscribers, $30.00 per year. View court opinions at www.miwb.uscourts.gov/content/opinions/query_all.asp. **Other Online Access:** Active motional calendars free at www.miwb.uscourts.gov/content/calendars/. **Phone access:** Voice Case Information System, call 866-729-9098, 616-456-2075

Grand Rapids Division counties: Allegan, Antrim, Barry, Benzie, Berrien, Branch, Calhoun, Cass, Charlevoix, Clinton, Eaton, Emmet, Grand Traverse, Hillsdale, Ingham, Ionia, Kalamazoo, Kalkaska, Kent, Lake, Leelanau, Manistee, Mason, Mecosta, Missaukee, Montcalm, Muskegon, Newaygo, Oceana, Osceola, Ottawa, St. Joseph, Van Buren, Wexford. Marquette cases are also available electronically on the Grand Rapids Division public access terminal.

Marquette Division counties: Alger, Baraga, Chippewa, Delta, Dickinson, Gogebic, Houghton, Iron, Keweenaw, Luce, Mackinac, Marquette, Menominee, Ontonagon, Schoolcraft. Marquette cases are also available electronically on the Grand Rapids Division public access terminal, but Grand Rapids cases are not available on Marquette's pub access computer as yet.

Minnesota

Capital: St. Paul
                Ramsey County
Time Zone: CST
Population: 5,100,958
# of Counties: 87

Quick Links

Website: www.state.mn.us
Governor: www.governor.state.mn.us
Attorney General: www.ag.state.mn.us
State Archives: www.mnhs.org
State Statutes and Codes: www.leg.state.mn.us/leg/statutes.asp
Legislative Bill Search: www.leg.state.mn.us/leg/legis.asp
Bill Monitoring: www.house.leg.state.mn.us/leg/billsublogin.asp
Unclaimed Funds:
        www.state.mn.us/cgi-bin/portal/mn/jsp/content.do?id=-536881373&agency=Commerce

State Level ... Major Agencies

Criminal Records

Bureau of Criminal Apprehension, Criminal Justice Information Systems, 1430 Maryland Ave E, St Paul, MN 55106; 651-793-2400, Fax-651-793-2401, 8:15AM-4PM.
www.bca.state.mn.us
Online search: Access to the public criminal history system is available from the web. The fee is $5.00 per name searched, use of a credit card is required. **Other options:** A public database is available on CD-ROM. Monthly updates can be purchased. Data is in ASCII format and is raw data. Fee is $40.00

Statewide Court Records

State Court Administrator, 135 Minnesota Judicial Center, 25 Rev ML King Blvd, St Paul, MN 55155; 651-296-2474, Fax-651-297-5636, 8AM-4:30PM.
www.courts.state.mn.us/default.aspx
Online search: Appellate and Supreme Court opinions are available from the website. There is an online system in place that allows internal and external access for government personnel only.

Sexual Offender Registry

Bureau of Criminal Apprehension, Minnesota Predatory Offender Program, 1430 Maryland Ave E, St Paul, MN 55106; 651-793-7070, 888-234-1248, Fax-651-793-7071, 8AM-4:30PM.
www.dps.state.mn.us/bca/
Online search: Level 3 offenders may be searched at www.doc.state.mn.us/level3/Search.asp. Also, you can bring up lists by city, county, or ZIP Code.

Incarceration Records

Minnesota Department of Corrections, Records Management Unit, 450 Energy Park Drive, Suite 200, St. Paul, MN 55108; 651-642-0200, Fax-651-643-3588, 8AM-5PM.
www.corr.state.mn.us
Online search: Search at the web to retrieve public information about adult offenders who have been committed to the Commissioner of Corrections, and who are still under our jurisdiction (i.e. in prison, or released from prison and still under supervision). Search by name, with or without DOB, or by OID number. Also, there is a separate search for Level 3 offender/predatory information. Also, a private company offers free web access at www.vinelink.com/index.jsp, including state, DOC, and most county jail systems.

Corporation, Limited Liability Company, Assumed Name, Trademarks/Servicemarks, Limited Partnerships

Business Records Services, Secretary of State, 180 State Office Bldg, 100 Martin Luther King Blvd, St Paul, MN 55155-1299; 651-296-2803 (Information), Fax-651-297-7067, 8AM-4:30PM.
www.sos.state.mn.us
Online search: Go to www.sos.state.mn.us/home/index.asp?page=6 This Internet site permits free look-ups of business names and corporation files. Also, a commercial program called Direct Access is available 24 hours. There is an annual subscription fee of $75.00. Record copies or certificates may be ordered for an additional $10.00 fee using Express Service. **Other options:** Information can be purchased in bulk format. Call for more information.

Uniform Commercial Code, Federal Tax Liens, State Tax Liens

UCC Division, Secretary of State, 60 Empire Dr, St Paul, MN 55103; 651-296-2803, Fax-651-215-1009, 8AM-4:30PM.
www.sos.state.mn.us/home/index.asp?page=89
Online search: There is a free look-up by filing number available from the website. A fee is charged for a name search. A comprehensive commercial program called Direct Access is available 24 hours. There is an annual subscription fee of $75.00 per year, plus $5.00 per debtor name. Call 651-296-2803 for more information. **Other options:** This agency will provide information in bulk form on paper, CD or disk. Call 651-296-2803 or 877-551-6767 for more information.

Sales Tax Registrations

Minnesota Revenue Dept, Sale and Use Tax, 600 N Robert St, MS:6330, St Paul, MN 55146-6330; 651-282-5225, Fax-651-556-3124.
www.taxes.state.mn.us
Online search: Email requests are accepted at sales.use@state.mn.us@state.mn.us. Lists of delinquent taxpayers including companies is free at www.taxes.state.mn.us/collection/delinqnet/delinqnet_overview.shtml.

Death Records

Minnesota Department of Health, Section of Vital Records, PO Box 9441, Minneapolis, MN 55440-9441 (Courier: 717 Delaware St SE, Minneapolis, MN 55414); 612-676-5120, Fax-612-331-5776, 8AM-4:30PM.
www.health.state.mn.us
Online search: No official online access available however the State Historical Society offers a free Death Certificate Search at http://people.mnhs.org/dci/Search.cfm. Records are from 1906 to 1996. **Other options:** The State Health agency offers bulk lists and files of information, if public record, on paper and in electronic format. Call Linda Salkowicz at 612-676-5120 for details.

Driver Records

Driver & Vehicle Services, Records Section, 445 Minnesota St, #161, St Paul, MN 55101; 651-215-1335, 8AM-4:30PM.
www.mndriveinfo.org
Online search: Online access costs $2.50 per record. Online inquiries can be processed either as interactive or as batch files (overnight) 24 hours a day, 7 days a week. Requesters operate from a "bank." Records are accessed by either DL number or full name and DOB. Call Data Services at 651-297-5352 for more information. Also, with a PIN at the web page, drivers may view their own record. For a certified copy mailed, there is a $5.00 fee. Also, at https://dutchelm.dps.state.mn.us/dvsinfo/mainframepublic.asp one may view a Status Report of a driver; the DL# is needed. **Other options:** Minnesota will sell its entire database of driving record information with monthly updates. Customized request sorts are available. Fees vary by type with programming and computer time and are quite reasonable.

Vehicle Ownership, Identification

Driver & Vehicle Services, Vehicle Record Requests, 445 Minnesota St, #161, St Paul, MN 55101; 651-215-1335, 8AM-4:30PM.
www.dps.state.mn.us/dvs/index.html
Online search: Online access costs $2.50 per record. There is an additional monthly charge for dial-in access. The system is the same as described for driving record requests. It is open 24 hours a day, 7 days a week. Lien holder information is included. Users, who

must qualify per DPPA, will receive address information. Call Data Services 651-297-5352 for more information. Also, enter a Minn plate or VIN at http://dutchelm.dps.state.mn.us/dvsinfo/mainframepublic.asp to get a status report.

State Level ... Occupational Licensing

Abstractor	https://www.egov.state.mn.us/Commerce/license_lookup.do?action=lookupForm
Abstractor/Abstractor Company	https://www.egov.state.mn.us/Commerce/license_lookup.do?action=lookupForm
Acupuncturist	www.docboard.org/mn/df/mndf.htm
Adjuster	https://www.egov.state.mn.us/Commerce/license_lookup.do?action=lookupForm
Alarm System Contr./Installer	www.electricity.state.mn.us/Elec_lic/index.html
Alcohol/Drug Counselor	www.health.state.mn.us/divs/hpsc/hop/adc/index.html
Ambulance Service/Personnel	www.emsrb.state.mn.us/cert.asp?p=s
Appraiser	https://www.egov.state.mn.us/Commerce/license_lookup.do?action=lookupForm
Architect	www.aelslagid.state.mn.us/roster.html
Athletic Trainer	www.docboard.org/mn/df/mndf.htm
Attorney	www.courts.state.mn.us/mars/default.aspx
Attorney Specialist	http://mail.statebar.gen.mn.us/search/search.asp
Auditor	www.boa.state.mn.us/Licensees/LicenseeList.aspx
Bingo Operation	www.gcb.state.mn.us/
Campground Membership Agent	https://www.egov.state.mn.us/Commerce/license_lookup.do?action=lookupForm
Chiropractor	https://www.hlb.state.mn.us/chi/publicaccess/search.asp
Collection Agency	https://www.egov.state.mn.us/Commerce/license_lookup.do?action=lookupForm
Consumer Credit/Payday Lender	www.state.mn.us/ebranch/commerce/pages/FinService/FSLicensees/sl.html
Contract'r/Remodeler, Residential	https://www.egov.state.mn.us/Commerce/license_lookup.do?action=lookupForm
Cosmetologist	https://www.egov.state.mn.us/Commerce/license_lookup.do?action=lookupForm
Cosmetology School/Shop	https://www.egov.state.mn.us/Commerce/license_lookup.do?action=lookupForm
CPA Firm	www.boa.state.mn.us/Licensees/FirmList.aspx
Credit Union	www.state.mn.us/ebranch/commerce/pages/FinService/FSLicensees/cu.html
Crematory	www.health.state.mn.us/divs/hpsc/mortsci/mortsciselect.cfm
Currency Exchange	https://www.egov.state.mn.us/Commerce/license_lookup.do?action=lookupForm
Debt Collector	https://www.egov.state.mn.us/Commerce/license_lookup.do?action=lookupForm
Debt Prorate Company	www.state.mn.us/ebranch/commerce/pages/FinService/FSLicensees/dp.html
Dentist/Dental Assistant/Hygienist	https://www.hlb.state.mn.us/mnbod/glsuiteweb/homeframe.aspx
Electrician	www.electricity.state.mn.us/Elec_lic/index.html
Emergency Medical Technician	www.emsrb.state.mn.us/cert.asp?p=s
EMS Examiner	www.emsrb.state.mn.us/examiner.asp?p=s
Engineer	www.aelslagid.state.mn.us/roster.html
Esthetician	https://www.egov.state.mn.us/Commerce/license_lookup.do?action=lookupForm
Funeral Director/ Establishment	www.health.state.mn.us/divs/hpsc/mortsci/mortsciselect.cfm
Gambling Equipment Dist./Mfg	www.gcb.state.mn.us/
Gambling, Lawful Organization	www.gcb.state.mn.us/
Geologist	www.aelslagid.state.mn.us/roster.html
Grain Licensing	http://www2.mda.state.mn.us/webapp/lis/default.jsp
Insurance Agency	https://www.egov.state.mn.us/Commerce/license_lookup.do?action=lookupForm
Insurance Agent/Salesman	https://www.egov.state.mn.us/Commerce/license_lookup.do?action=lookupForm
Interior Designer	www.aelslagid.state.mn.us/roster.html
Landscape Architect	www.aelslagid.state.mn.us/roster.html
Lender, Small	www.state.mn.us/ebranch/commerce/pages/FinService/FSLicensees/sl.html
Liquor On-sale Retail/Munic	www.dps.state.mn.us/alcgamb/alcenf/liquorlic/liquorlic.html
Livestock Dealer/Market	http://www2.mda.state.mn.us/webapp/lis/default.jsp
Livestock Weigher	http://www2.mda.state.mn.us/webapp/lis/default.jsp
Loan Company	www.state.mn.us/ebranch/commerce/pages/FinService/FSLicensees/rl.html
Lobbyist	www.cfboard.state.mn.us/Lobby.htm
LPA	www.boa.state.mn.us/Licensees/LicenseeList.aspx
Managing General Agent	https://www.egov.state.mn.us/Commerce/license_lookup.do?action=lookupForm

Manicurist .... https://www.egov.state.mn.us/Commerce/license_lookup.do?action=lookupForm
Medical Doctor .... www.docboard.org/mn/df/mndf.htm
Medical Professional Firm .... www.docboard.org/mn/df/mndf.htm
Midwife .... www.docboard.org/mn/df/mndf.htm
Money Transmitter .... www.commerce.state.mn.us/pages/FinService/FSLicensees/MoneyTransmitList.pdf
Mortgage Originator/Servc'r, Resid'l. https://www.egov.state.mn.us/Commerce/license_lookup.do?action=lookupForm
Mortician .... www.health.state.mn.us/divs/hpsc/mortsci/mortsciselect.cfm
Notary Public .... https://www.egov.state.mn.us/Commerce/license_lookup.do?action=lookupForm
Nurse-LPN, RN ... ... https://www.hlb.state.mn.us/mbn/Portal/DesktopDefault.aspx?tabindex=0&tabid=41
Occupational Therapist/Assistant....... www.health.state.mn.us/divs/hpsc/hop/otp/licprac.html
Optometrist .... www.optometryboard.state.mn.us/Default.aspx?tabid=799
Pesticide Applicator Company........... http://www2.mda.state.mn.us/webapp/lis/pestappdefault.jsp
Pesticide Applicator, Private.............. http://www2.mda.state.mn.us/webapp/PrivApp/default.jsp
Physical Therapist............................. www.docboard.org/mn/df/mndf.htm
Physician Assistant .... www.docboard.org/mn/df/mndf.htm
Political Action Committee................ www.cfboard.state.mn.us/campfin/pcfatoz.html
Political Candidate .... www.cfboard.state.mn.us/cand_lists.html
Public Accountant Firm .... www.boa.state.mn.us/Licensees/FirmList.aspx
Public Accountant-CPA..................... www.boa.state.mn.us/Licensees/LicenseeList.aspx
Real Estate Agent/Broker/Dealer....... https://www.egov.state.mn.us/Commerce/license_lookup.do?action=lookupForm
Re-Insurance Intermediary................. https://www.egov.state.mn.us/Commerce/license_lookup.do?action=lookupForm
Respiratory Care Practitioner............. www.docboard.org/mn/df/mndf.htm
Soil Scientist .... www.aelslagid.state.mn.us/roster.html
Surgeon... www.docboard.org/mn/df/mndf.htm
Surveyor, Land .... www.aelslagid.state.mn.us/roster.html
Teacher
 http://education.state.mn.us/mde/Teacher_Support/Educator_Licensing/View_an_Individual_Educators_License/index.html
Telemedicine..................................... www.docboard.org/mn/df/mndf.htm
Thrift/Industrial Loan Company .... www.state.mn.us/ebranch/commerce/pages/FinService/FSLicensees/il.html
Underground Tank Contr./Spvr. .... www.pca.state.mn.us/cleanup/ust.html#certification
Weather Modifier............................... http://www2.mda.state.mn.us/webapp/lis/default.jsp

County Level ... Courts

Court Administration: State Court Adminstrator, 135 Minn. Judicial Center, 25 Constitution Ave, St Paul, MN, 55155; 651-296-2474; www.courts.state.mn.us

Court Structure: There are 97 District Courts (some counties gave divisional courts) comprising 10 judicial districts. Effective July 1, 1994, the limit for small claims was raised from $5000 to $7500. The limit is $4,000 if it involves a consumer credit transaction.

Online Access Note: Appellate and Supreme Court opinions are available from the website. There is an online system in place that allows internal and external access, but only for government personnel.

Hennepin County

4th Judicial District Court - Division 3 Ridgedale – Civil Records
www.courts.state.mn.us/districts/fourth/
Plaintiff, defendant search of small claims is free at www2.co.hennepin.mn.us/ccourt/ccsrch.jsp.

Olmsted County

Olmsted County District Court – Civil Records
www.courts.state.mn.us/districts/third/counties/olmsted.htm
Access is to probate records only, and these are from a private library source at www.selco.lib.mn.us/apps/ochs/probate.cfm. Files vary greatly, but most contain date and place of death, list of heirs, copy of will (if one was written), inventory of personal property, and final disposition of the estate .

County Level ... Recorders & Assessors

Recording Office Organization: 87 counties, 87 recording offices. The recording officer is the County Recorder. The entire state is in the Central Time Zone (CST). Federal and state tax liens on personal property of businesses are filed with the Secretary of State. Other federal and state tax liens are filed with the County Recorder. A special search form UCC-12 is used for separate tax lien searches. Some counties search each tax lien index separately. Some charge one $15.00 or $20.00 fee to search both indexes, but others charge a separate fee for each index searched. Search and copy fees vary widely.

Online Access Note: There is no statewide system, but a number of counties offer web access to assessor data and recorded deeds.

18 Minnesota Counties *Recording, Real Estate, Lien, Deed, RE UCC Records*
https://tapestry.fidlar.com/tapsearch.aspx
Access recorder office data by subscription on either the Laredo system using subscription and fees (usually $50.00 per month) or the Tapestry System using credit card, https://tapestry.fidlar.com/tapsearch.aspx; $3.99 search; $.50 an image. More counties being added.

Anoka County *Real Estate, Tax Assessor Records*
www.co.anoka.mn.us
Access to the County online records requires an annual fee of $35 and a $25 monthly fee and $.25 per transaction. Records date back to 1995. Lending agency information is available. For information, contact Pam LeBlanc at 763-323-5424. There is also a dial-up property information system at 763-323-5400. Also, you may access property information at https://prtinfo.co.anoka.mn.us/(2sqvv055oxsegqmkh22u4nvx)/search.aspx. No name searching.

Becker County *Property Tax, Assessor Records*
www.beckercounty.com
Access to the assessor property data is free at www.co.becker.mn.us/.

Beltrami County *Recording, Real Estate, Lien, Deed Records*
For Recorder office data by subscription see note at beginning of section.

Blue Earth County *Property, Assessor Records*
www.co.blue-earth.mn.us
Access to the property information search database is free at www.co.blue-earth.mn.us/tax/. Also, you may search at www.blueearth.minnesotaassessors.com. No name searching at either site, but a subscription service is available at the latter.

Carlton County *Real Estate, Deed, Lien, RE UCC Records*
www.co.carlton.mn.us
For Recorder data by subscription see note at beginning of section; index goes back to 1989, images to 2003 with earlier being added.

Carver County *Real Estate, Grantor/Grantee, Lien, Property Tax Records*
www.co.carver.mn.us
Access to recorder land records and property tax records is free at www.co.carver.mn.us/egov.html. Select Land Title Information or Property Tax Information.

Cass County *Property, GIS, Warrant, Most Wanted, Recording, Real Estate, Deed Records*
www.co.cass.mn.us
Access to parcel, tax, and limited real estate data is free at the GIS-mapping site at www.co.cass.mn.us/maps/map_parcel_info.html. No name searching. Also, search the sheriff's warrant list for free at www.co.cass.mn.us/sheriff/sheriff_warrants.html; most wanted list is at www.co.cass.mn.us/sheriff/sheriff_most_wanted.html. Also, for Recorder office data by subscription see note at beginning of section.; index is 4-1-87 to present.

Chippewa County *Recorder, Real Estate, Deed, Lien Records*
For Recorder office data by subscription see note at beginning of section.

Chisago County *Real Estate, Deed, Property, Assessor Records*
www.co.chisago.mn.us
Access property data free at www.co.chisago.mn.us/chisagocountyrecap/ but no name searching. Also, recording office records to be available online Summer 2006 at www.co.chisago.mn.us/Recorder/recorder.htm. Also, search the GIS data map at www.co.chisago.mn.us/website/chisagoGDBpublic/main.php. Zoom in on map and click on "I" in black dot to identify parcel owner.

Clay County *Real Estate, Deed, Recording, Lien Records*
www.co.clay.mn.us
The county online GIS mapping service at www.gis.co.clay.mn.us/map/Clay/disclaimer.htm provides property record searching, but by parcel number only. recorder records may be searched at the website in the near future. Plats and corner certificates online free at www.co.clay.mn.us/depts/recorder/laredo/rerrol.htm. For Recorder office data by subscription see note at beginning of section.

Cook County *Recording, Real Estate, Deed, Lien Records*
For Recorder office data by subscription see note at beginning of section.

Crow Wing County *Real Estate, Recorder, Deed, Lien, Surveyor Records*
www.co.crow-wing.mn.us
Access to recorder data is available by subscription, $50.00 per month and $.25 per image. Email the County Recorder at kathyl@co.crow-wing.mn.us for more information and signup. Access the county list of surveyors free at www.co.crow-wing.mn.us/docs/Surveyor_s_List.pdf.

Dakota County *Real Estate, Assessor Records*
www.co.dakota.mn.us
Records on the County Real Estate Inquiry database are free at www.co.dakota.mn.us/assessor/real_estate_inquiry.htm. Information includes items such as address, estimated value, taxes, last sale price, building details.

Douglas County *Assessor Records*
www.co.douglas.mn.us
Look-up assessor property tax data free at http://morris.state.mn.us/tax/.

Faribault County *Recording, Real Estate, Lien, Deed Records*
For Recorder office data by subscription see note at beginning of section. index goes back to 1995; images to 9/2003.

Hennepin County *Real Estate, Lien, Most Wanted Records*
www.co.hennepin.mn.us
Three sources available. Access to Hennepin County online records requires a $35 annual fee with a charge of $5 per hour from 7AM-7PM, or $4.15 per hour at other times. Records date back to 1988. Only lending agency information is available. Property tax info is at Treasurer office; call 612-348-3011. Also, search records on county Property Information Search database free at http://www2.co.hennepin.mn.us/pins/. Or, search at www.co.hennepin.mn.us/ Click on Property Info Search. Search by Property ID #, address, or addition name. An Automated phone system is also available; 612-348-3011.

Hubbard County *Property, GIS, Real Estate, Recording, Deed, Lien Records*
www.co.hubbard.mn.us/Recorder.htm
Access to parcel data is free at www.co.hubbard.mn.us/website/hubbard/disclaimer.htm.. For Recorder office data by subscription see note at beginning of section.

Itasca County *Property, Auditor, Real Estate, Recorder, Deed, Lien Records*
www.co.itasca.mn.us
Access to property and parcel data is from a private company at www.parcelinfo.com; click on Itasca County Public Access. Also, for Recorder office data by subscription see note at beginning of section.

Kandiyohi County *Property, Assessor, Recording, Real Estate, Deed, Lien Records*
www.co.kandiyohi.mn.us
Access to county property tax data is free at http://morris.state.mn.us/tax/. Also, for Recorder office data by subscription see note at beginning of section; index goes back to 3/1987; images to 1/1998.

Koochiching County *Property, Auditor, Recording, Real Estate, Deed, Lien Records*
www.co.koochiching.mn.us
Access to property and parcel data is from a private company at www.parcelinfo.com. Subscriptions are as low as $15 per month - $50 if you require weekly updates. A limited free guest account is available. Also, for Recorder office data by subscription see note at beginning of section.

Lake County *Assessor, Property, Recording, Real Estate, Deed, Lien Records*
www.co.lake.mn.us
Access property data free at www.parcelinfo.com; click on Lake County Users Click Here. Also, for Recorder office data by subscription see note at beginning of section.

Lincoln County *Recording, Real estate, Deed, Lien Records*
For Recorder office data by subscription see note at beginning of section.

Lyon County *Recording, Real Estate, Deed, Lien Records*
For Recorder office data by subscription see note at beginning of section; index goes back to 1987; images to 1988.

McLeod County *Real Estate, Recording, Deed Records*
www.co.mcleod.mn.us
Access recorder data by subscription at http://landshark.co.mcleod.mn.us/eddie/. Set-up $50 plus $50.00 per month, plus $2.00 per image.

Martin County *Recording, Real Estate, Deed, Lien Records*
www.co.martin.mn.us
For Recorder office data by subscription see note at beginning of section; index goes back to 1987; images to 1992.

Morrison County *Real Estate, Recorder, Assessor, Deed, Lien Records*
www.co.morrison.mn.us/wsite/index.htm
Access is presently by subscription dial-up; $100 setup plus $40 monthly charged annually. Also $25 de-activation fee if you quit. Available business hours; Powerterm software recommended but TelNet will work. Signup with Irene at 320-631-0830. Data is to be available via internet later in 2006; check website.

Mower County *Property, Assessor, Recording, Grantor/Grantee, Deed, Lien Records*
www.co.mower.mn.us/Recorder01.htm
Search property assessor data free at www.mower.minnesotaassessors.com. No name searching for free, but a sub service is also available. Also, for Recorder office data by subscription see note at beginning of section; index goes back to 1988; images to 8/1999.

Norman County *Assessor Records*
Look-up assessor property tax data free at http://morris.state.mn.us/tax/.

Olmsted County *Probate, Property Records*
www.olmstedcounty.com
Access to county probate records is free at www.selco.lib.mn.us/apps/ochs/probate.cfm. Files vary greatly, but most contain date and place of death, list of heirs, copy of will (if one was written), inventory of personal property, and final disposition of the estate. Also, a Tract Index of recorded documents is available from a contract vendor; call for details.

Otter Tail County *Property Tax, Assessor, Real Estate, Recorder Records*
www.co.otter-tail.mn.us
Access recorder office real estate data by a LandShark subscription at www.co.otter-tail.mn.us/eddie/login.jsp. User name and login required. Call recorder office for details and sign-up. Also, search property tax data at www.co.otter-tail.mn.us/taxes/. Parcel searching or map searching only.

Pope County *Property, Assessor, Recording, Real Estate, Lien, Deed Records*
www.mncounties3.org/pope/
Look-up assessor property tax data free at http://morris.state.mn.us/tax/searchinput.asp. Also, for Recorder office data by subscription see note at beginning of section; index and images goes back to 11/1996

Ramsey County *Property Assessor, Recorded Documents Records*
http://rrinfo.co.ramsey.mn.us
Search the property assessment rolls free at www.rrinfo.co.ramsey.mn.us, but no name searching. The agency offers a more extensive search product on a subscription basis that includes recorded documents.

Renville County *Assessor Records*
www.co.renville.mn.us
Look-up assessor property tax data free at http://morris.state.mn.us/tax/.

Rice County *Property, Assessor, Property Sale, GIS Records*
www.co.rice.mn.us
Search parcel information and residential/commercial sales data free at www.rice.minnesotaassessors.com. No name searching for free but a sub service is also available. Also, search assessor property data free on the GIS system at http://webgishome.promap.com/Default.aspx but no name searching.

Rock County *Assessor, Property, Warrants Records*
www.co.rock.mn.us
Look-up assessor property tax data free at http://morris.state.mn.us/tax/. Also, sheriff's warrant list is online at www.sheriff.co.rock.mn.us.

St. Louis County *Real Estate, Property Tax, Auditor Records*
www.co.st-louis.mn.us/
Access to the auditor and recorder's tax records for tax professionals database is by subscription. Fee is $100 monthly; password provided. For info or sign-up, contact Pam Palen at 218-726-2380 or email to palenp@co.st-louis.mn.us or visit www.co.st-louis.mn.us/auditorsoffice/subscription.pdf. Also, search auditor info for free at www.co.st-louis.mn.us/auditor/parcelinfo/. Also, search the City of Duluth property assessor data free at www.ci.duluth.mn.us/city/assessor/index.htm.

Scott County *Real Estate, Recorder, Property Tax, Assessor, GIS Records*
www.co.scott.mn.us
Search the county property databases free at www.co.scott.mn.us/xpedio/groups/public/documents/web_files/scottcountywebframe.hcsp. There is also a free online document subscription service and GIS mapping. At left hand side, click on land records for recordings, or property tax for assessor records.

Sherburne County *Real Estate, Tax Assessor, Most Wanted Records*
www.co.sherburne.mn.us
Property records from the county tax assessor database are free at www.sherburne.mn.promap.com. However, to perform a name search, you must subscribe; fee is $25.00 setup and $300.00 per year. A free 30-day trial is offered. Call 763-241-2880 for information on how to subscribe, or visit website. Also, search the sheriff's most wanted list at www.co.sherburne.mn.us/sheriff/mostwanted.htm.

Stearns County *Real Estate, Tax Assessor Records*
www.co.stearns.mn.us
Records from the county tax assessor database are free at http://secure.co.stearns.mn.us/. No name searching.

Steele County *Property Tax, Recording, Real Estate, Deed, Lien Records*
www.co.steele.mn.us
Search using parcel data at www.co.steele.mn.us/auditor/auditor.html. Also, for Recorder office data by subscription see note at beginning of section.

Stevens County *Assessor Records*
Look-up assessor property tax data free at http://morris.state.mn.us/tax/.

Todd County *Property, GIS-Mapping Records*
www.co.todd.mn.us/Recorder/recorder.htm
Access to property information on the GIS-mapping site is free at www.co.todd.mn.us/toddcounty/propertyinfo0009.asp, although search options are limited; no name or address searching.

Washington County *Real Estate Tract Records*
www.co.washington.mn.us
Access to county online records requires a monthly set up fee; UCC information is on a state system. Online access to property tax records is free at http://www2.co.washington.mn.us/opip/; no name searching - property ID or address required.

Wright County *Recorder, Land, Lien, Grantor/Grantee, Property Tax Records*
www.co.wright.mn.us
Access to Land Title database is free at www.co.wright.mn.us/department/recorder/landtitle/index.htm. Also, search the property tax database for free at www.co.wright.mn.us/department/audtreas/proptax/default.asp

Federal Courts in Minnesota...

Standards for Federal Courts: The universal PACER sign-up number is 800-676-6856. Find PACER and the Party/Case Index on the Web at http://pacer.psc.uscourts.gov. PACER dial-up access is $.60 per minute. Also, courts offering internet access via PACER, Web-PACER or the new CM-ECF charge $.08 per page fee ($.07 per page if record is pre-2005 or unless noted as free)

US District Court -- District of Minnesota

www.mnd.uscourts.gov
PACER: Case records are available back to 2/1990. New records are available online after 1 day. **PACER Online Access:** PACER online at http://pacer.mnd.uscourts.gov. **Electronic Filing:** CM/ECF data at https://ecf.mnd.uscourts.gov. **Opinions:** View court opinions at www.nysd.uscourts.gov/courtweb/PubMain.htm. **Other Online Access:** Search recent filings at www.mnd.uscourts.gov/ncs/caselist.html.
Duluth Division counties: Aitkin, Becker*, Beltrami*, Benton, Big Stone*, Carlton, Cass, Clay*, Clearwater*, Cook, Crow Wing, Douglas*, Grant*, Hubbard*, Itasca, Kanabec, Kittson*, Koochiching, Lake, Lake of the Woods*, Mahnomen*, Marshall*, Mille Lacs, Morrison, Norman*, Otter Tail,* Pennington*, Pine, Polk*, Pope*, Red Lake*, Roseau*, Stearns*, Stevens*, St. Louis, Todd*, Traverse*, Wadena*, Wilkin*. From 3/1995, to 1998, cases from the counties marked with an asterisk (*) were heard here. Before and after that period, cases were and are allocated between St. Paul and Minneapolis.
Minneapolis Division counties: Cases are allocated between Minneapolis and St Paul.
St Paul Division counties: All counties not covered by the Duluth Division. Cases are allocated between Minneapolis and St Paul.

US Bankruptcy Court -- District of Minnesota

www.mnb.uscourts.gov
PACER: Case records are available back to 1/1993. New records are available online after 1 day. **PACER Online Access:** PACER online not available. **Electronic Filing:** May still be in testing stage; if so, do not use. CM/ECF data at https://ecf.mnb.uscourts.gov. **Opinions:** View court opinions at www.mnb.uscourts.gov/WebDir/Html/judge_opinions.html. **Other Online Access:** Search records free at www.mnb.uscourts.gov/ers-bin/mnb-651-main.pl. Images go back to 1997. Judges calendars at www.mnb.uscourts.gov/Calendar/CalSelect2.html. **Phone access:** Voice Case Information System, call 800-959-9002, 612-664-5302
Duluth Division counties: Aitkin, Benton, Carlton, Cass, Cook, Crow Wing, Itasca, Kanabec, Koochiching, Lake, Mille Lacs, Morrison, Pine, St. Louis. A petition commencing Chapter 11 or 12 proceedings may initially be filed in any of the 4 divisions, but may be assigned to another division.
Fergus Falls Division counties: Becker, Beltrami, Big Stone, Clay, Clearwater, Douglas, Grant, Hubbard, Kittson, Lake of the Woods, Mahnomen, Marshall, Norman, Otter Tail, Pennington, Polk, Pope, Red Lake, Roseau, Stearns, Stevens, Todd, Traverse, Wadena, Wilkin. A petition commencing Chapter 11 or 12 proceedings may be filed initially in any of the four divisions, but may then be assigned to another division.
Minneapolis Division counties: Anoka, Carver, Chippewa, Hennepin, Isanti, Kandiyohi, McLeod, Meeker, Renville, Sherburne, Swift, Wright. Initial petitions for Chapter 11 or 12 may be filed initially at any of the 4 divisions, but may then be assigned to a judge in another division.
St Paul Division counties: St Paul court re-located to Minneapolis courthouse 7/15/2005. Blue Earth, Brown, Chisago, Cottonwood, Dakota, Dodge, Faribault, Fillmore, Freeborn, Goodhue, Houston, Jackson, Lac qui Parle, Le Sueur, Lincoln, Lyon, Martin, Mower, Murray, Nicollet, Nobles, Olmsted, Pipestone, Ramsey, Redwood, Rice, Rock, Scott, Sibley, Steele, Wabasha, Waseca, Washington, Watonwan, Winona, Yellow Medicine. Cases from Benton, Kanabec, Mille Lacs, Morrison and Pine may also be heard here. A petition commencing Chapter 11 or 12 proceedings may be filed initially with any of the four divisions, but may then be assigned to another division.

Mississippi

Capital: Jackson
          Hinds County
Time Zone: CST
Population: 2,902,966
# of Counties: 82

Quick Links

Website: www.ms.gov/index.jsp
Governor: www.governor.state.ms.us
Attorney General: www.ago.state.ms.us
State Archives: www.mdah.state.ms.us
State Statutes and Codes: www.sos.state.ms.us/ed_pubs/mscode/
Legislative Bill Search: www.ls.state.ms.us
Unclaimed Funds: www.treasury.state.ms.us/

State Level ... Major Agencies

Statewide Court Records

Administrative Office of Courts, PO Box 117, Jackson, MS 39205 (Courier: 450 High St, Jackson, MS 39205); 601-354-7406, Fax-601-354-7459, 8AM-5PM.
www.mssc.state.ms.us
Online search: The website offers searching of the MS Supreme Court and Court of Appeals Decisions, and dockets of the trial courts. It is difficult to do a name search in the trial courts because the sequence number of the docket must be included in request.

Sexual Offender Registry

Dept. of Public Safety, Sexual Offender Registry, PO Box 958, Jackson, MS 39205; 601-368-1740, 8AM-5PM.
www.sor.mdps.state.ms.us
Online search: The state Sex Offender Registry can be accessed at the website. Search by last name, city, county, or ZIP Code.

Incarceration Records

Mississippi Department of Corrections, Records Department, 723 N President Street, Jackson, MS 39202;, 601-359-5600, 8AM-5PM.
www.mdoc.state.ms.us
Online search: Search online by name only from the website. Click on Inmate Search. Also, search the Parole Board records (click on Parole Board and follow instructions).

Corporation, Limited Partnership, Limited Liability Company, Trademarks/Servicemarks

Secretary of State, Business Services, PO Box 136, Jackson, MS 39205-0136; 601-359-1633, 800-256-3494, Fax-601-359-1607, 8AM-5PM.
www.sos.state.ms.us
Online search: A variety of online search services are available at www.sos.state.ms.us/busserv/corp/soskb/csearch.asp. There is no fee to view records, including officers and registered agents. A Good Standing can be ordered. You can download images for no charge. **Other options:** The Data Division offers bulk release of information on paper or disk. Monthly subscription to list of new corporations and new qualifications is $25.00.

Uniform Commercial Code, Federal Tax Liens, State Tax Liens

Secretary of State, Business Services - UCC, PO Box 136, Jackson, MS 39205-0136 (Courier: 700 N Jackson St, Jackson, MS 39202); 601-359-1633, 800-256-3494, Fax-601-359-1607, 8AM-5PM.
www.sos.state.ms.us/busserv/ucc/ucc.asp
Online search: Two systems available. Free searching for UCC debtors is at www.sos.state.ms.us/busserv/ucc/soskb/SearchStandardRA9.asp. **Other options:** A monthly list of farm liens is available for purchase.

Sales Tax Registrations

Office of Revenue, Sales and Use Tax Bureau, PO Box 1033, Jackson, MS 39215-1033 (Courier: 1577 Springridge Rd, Raymond, MS 39154); 601-923-7000, Fax-601-923-7034, 8AM-5PM.
www.mstc.state.ms.us
Online search: Requests may be emailed to sales@mstc.state.ms.us.

Birth, Death, Marriage, Divorce Certificates

State Department of Health, Vital Statistics & Records, PO Box 1700, Jackson, MS 39215-1700 (Courier: 571 Stadium Dr, Jackson, MS 39216); 601-576-7960, 601-576-7988, Fax-601-576-7505, 8AM-5PM.
www.msdh.state.ms.us/phs/index.htm
Online search: Records may be ordered online via a designated vendor - www.uscerts.com.

Workers' Compensation Records

Workers Compensation Commission, PO Box 5300, Jackson, MS 39296-5300 (Courier: 1428 Lakeland Dr, Jackson, MS 39216); 601-987-4200, 8AM-5PM.
www.mwcc.state.ms.us
Online search: The First Report of Injury and other documents are available via the web. There is no fee, but users must register. **Other options:** A first report of injury database is available on CD-ROM for $500.00.

Driver Records

Department of Public Safety, Driver Services, PO Box 958, Jackson, MS 39205 (Courier: 1900 E Woodrow Wilson, Jackson, MS 39216); 601-987-1274, 8AM-5PM.
www.dps.state.ms.us/dps/dps.nsf/main?OpenForm
Online search: Both interactive and batch delivery is offer for high volume users only. Billing is monthly. Hook-up is through the Advantis System, fees apply. Lookup is by name only; not by driver license number. Fee is $11.00 per record. For more information, call the Director's office. Another service is available. Drivers may view their own record online at https://www.ms.gov/hp/drivers/license/motorVehicleReportBegin.do. The MVR shows the current status of the license and the moving violations on record. **Other options:** Overnight batch delivery by tape is available.

Vehicle Ownership, Vehicle Identification

Mississippi State Tax Commission, Registration Department, PO Box 1140, Jackson, MS 39215 (Courier: 1577 Springridge Rd, Raymond, MS 39154); 601-923-7100 (Registration), 601-923-7200 (Titles), Fax-601-923-7134, 8AM-5PM.
www.mstc.state.ms.us/mvl/main.htm
Online search: Internet access to vehicle records is available to approved, DPPA compliant entities. Accounts must pay an initial $25.00 registration fee, record search fees are the same as listed above. **Other options:** Mississippi offers some standardized files as well as some customization for bulk requesters of VIN and registration information. For more information, contact MLVB at the address listed above.

State Level...Occupational Licensing

Architect	www.archbd.state.ms.us/roster.html
Attorney/Attorney Firm	www.msbar.org/lawyerdirectory.php
Camp, Youth	www.msdh.state.ms.us/msdhsite/index.cfm/30,332,183,html
Charity	www.sos.state.ms.us/regenf/charities/charannrpt/index.asp
Child Care Facility	www.msdh.state.ms.us/msdhsite/index.cfm/30,332,183,html
Chiropractor	www.msbce.ms.gov/msbce/msbce.nsf/Search?OpenForm
Contractor, General	www.msboc.state.ms.us/Search.cfm
CPA-Certified Public Accountant	www.msbpa.state.ms.us/licsearch.html
Dentist/Dental Hygienist/Radiologist	www.msbde.state.ms.us

Domestic Insurance Company	www.doi.state.ms.us/pdf/domesticlist.pdf
Engineer	http://dsitspe01.its.state.ms.us/pepls/EngSurveyors.nsf
Fund Raiser	www.sos.state.ms.us/regenf/charities/charannrpt/index.asp
Funeral Pre-Need Contractor	www.sos.state.ms.us
Geologist	www.msbrpg.state.ms.us/rpg.htm
HMO	www.doi.state.ms.us/pdf/hmolist.pdf
Home Inspector	www.mrec.state.ms.us/asp/findrealtor.asp
Insurance Agent/Solicitor/Advisor/Corp	www.doi.state.ms.us/licapp/
Investment Advisor	www.sos.state.ms.us
Landscape Architect	www.archbd.state.ms.us/roster.html
Lobbyist	www.sos.state.ms.us/elections/Lobbying/Lobbyist_Dir.asp
Long Term Care Insurance Company	www.doi.state.ms.us/pdf/ltclist.pdf
Medical Doctor	www.msbml.state.ms.us
Notary Public	www.sos.state.ms.us/busserv/notaries/notaries.asp
Optometrist	www.arbo.org/index.php?action=findanoptometrist
Osteopathic Physician	www.msbml.state.ms.us
Pharmacist/Pharmacy/Intern/Technician	www.mbp.state.ms.us
Podiatrist	www.msbml.state.ms.us
Psychologist	www.psychologyboard.state.ms.us/msbp/msbp.nsf/Search?OpenForm
Real Estate Agent/Sales	www.mrec.state.ms.us/asp/findrealtor.asp
Real Estate Appraiser	www.mrec.state.ms.us/asp/findappraiser.asp
Real Estate Broker	www.mrec.state.ms.us/asp/findrealtor.asp
Securities Agent/Broker/Dealer/Offering	www.sos.state.ms.us
Surplus Lines Insurer	www.doi.state.ms.us/licapp/downloadlist.aspx
Surveyor, Land	http://dsitspe01.its.state.ms.us/pepls/EngSurveyors.nsf
Youth Home, Residential	www.msdh.state.ms.us/msdhsite/index.cfm/30,332,183,html

County Level ... Courts

Court Administration: Court Administrator, Supreme Court, Box 117, Jackson, MS, 39205; 601-354-7406; www.mssc.state.ms.us

Court Structure: The court of general jurisdiction is the Circuit Court with 70 courts in 22 districts. Justice Courts were first created in 1984, replacing the Justice of the Peace. Prior to 1984, records were kept separately by each Justice of the Peace, so the location of such records today is often unknown. Probate is handled by the Chancery Courts, as are property matters.

Online Access Note: A statewide online computer system is in use internally for court personnel. There are plans underway to make this system available to the public, however this has been put on hold. The website offers searching of Mississippi Supreme Court and Court of Appeals decisions, also dockets of the trial courts. It is difficult to do a name search in the trial courts because the sequence number of the docket must be included in request.

De Soto County

Circuit & County Court – Civil and Criminal Records
www.desotoms.com
Search docket information at www.desotoms.info/.

Harrison County

Circuit Court – Civil Records
Access to Judicial District judgments are free at http://co.harrison.ms.us/departments/circlerk/rolls/. Search current court dockets free at http://co.harrison.ms.us/dockets/.

Gulfport Chancery Court – Civil Records
http://co.harrison.ms.us/departments/chanclerk/court.asp
Search Chancery Court dockets for free at http://co.harrison.ms.us/dockets/.

Jackson County

Circuit Court – Civil and Criminal Records

Chancery Court – Civil Records
Access to Circuit and Chancery Court monthly dockets is free at www.co.jackson.ms.us/DS/CircuitDockets.html.

County Level ... Recorders & Assessors

Recording Office Organization: 82 counties, 92 recording offices. The recording officers are the Chancery Clerk and the Clerk of Circuit Court (state tax liens). Ten counties have two separate recording offices - Bolivar, Carroll, Chickasaw, Craighead, Harrison, Hinds, Jasper, Jones, Panola, Tallahatchie, and Yalobusha. See the notes under each county for how to determine which office is appropriate to search. The entire state is in the Central Time Zone (CST). Federal tax liens on personal property of businesses are filed with the Secretary of State. Federal tax liens on personal property of individuals are filed with the county Chancery Clerk. State tax liens on personal property are filed with the county Clerk of Circuit Court. Refer to the County Court section for information about Mississippi Circuit Courts. State tax liens on real property are filed with the Chancery Clerk. Most Chancery Clerk offices will perform a federal tax lien search for a fee of $5.00 per name. Copy fees vary.

Online Access Note: A number of counties offer online access to records. There is no statewide system except for the Secretary of State's UCC access - see State Agencies section.

Adams County *Judgment, Circuit Court, Voter Registration Records*
Access judgments, voter registration, circuit courts (go back to 1997, scanned 12/02 to present) for a fee go to www.deltacomputersystems.com/search.html.

Alcorn County *Property Tax, Appraisal Records*
Access is free at www.deltacomputersystems.com/MS/MS02/index.html

De Soto County *Property Tax, Assessor, Grantor/Grantee, Deed, Recording, Voter Registration Records*
www.desotoms.info
Access to assessor property data is free at www.desotoms.info. Click on "Tax Assessor." GIS-mapping site is also available. Also, access to Chancery Clerk grantor/grantee index is also available; click on "Chancery Clerk." For voter registration data, click on Circuit Clerk and then Voter Registration tab. GIS mapping site is also available, also county board and planning commission minutes.

Forrest County *Property Tax, Appraisal Records*
Access property tax or appraisal records free at www.deltacomputersystems.com/search.html.

George County *Assessor, Property Records*
Access to the property tax records is free at www.deltacomputersystems.com/MS/MS20/plinkquerym.html.

Harrison County (1st District) *Property, Deed, Recording, UCC, Voter Registration, Deed, Grantor/Grantee, Marriage, Inmate, Court, Property Tax Records*
http://co.harrison.ms.us
Access all records through the county portal at http://co.harrison.ms.us. Also, access to property tax data is free at www.deltacomputersystems.com/MS/MS24DELTA/DATALINK.html or http://co.harrison.ms.us/departments/chanclerk/proplink.asp. Also, search chancery clerk Deed & Record index back 20 years. Also, search voter registration and marriage licenses. Also, the delinquent tax sales list no longer appears on the web. Access to the jail docket is free at www.harrisoncountysheriff.com/docket/. Also, search circuit court judgment rolls at http://co.harrison.ms.us/departments/circlerk/rolls/ and chancery court dockets at http://co.harrison.ms.us/dockets/.

Harrison County (2nd District) *Property, Deed, Recording, UCC, Voter Registration, Deed, Grantor/Grantee, Marriage, Inmate, Court Records*
http://co.harrison.ms.us
Access to property tax data is free at www.deltacomputersystems.com/MS/MS24DELTA/DATALINK.html or http://co.harrison.ms.us. You may also choose to search chancery clerk Deed & Record index back 15 years. Also search voter registration and marriage licenses. Also, the delinquent tax sales list no longer appears on the web. Access to the jail docket is free at

www.harrisoncountysheriff.com/docket/. Also, search circuit court judgment rolls at http://co.harrison.ms.us/departments/circlerk/rolls/ and chancery court dockets at http://co.harrison.ms.us/dockets/.

Hinds County   *Real Estate, Grantor/Grantee, Judgment, Lien, Assessor, Condominium, Acreage Records*
www.co.hinds.ms.us/pgs/elected/chanceryclerk.asp
Access to the county records databases are free at www.co.hinds.ms.us/pgs/apps/gindex.asp. Also, search the assessor land rolls for free at www.co.hinds.ms.us/pgs/apps/landroll_query.asp.

Lafayette County   *Property Tax, Appraisal Records*
Access to property data is free at www.deltacomputersystems.com/ms/ms36/plinkquerym.html

Lamar County   *Property Tax, Appraisal Records*
Access to property data is free at www.deltacomputersystems.com/MS/MS37/INDEX.html

Lauderdale County   *Property Tax, Appraisal Records*
www.lauderdalecounty.org
Access property data free at www.deltacomputersystems.com/MS/MS38/INDEX.html.

Lee County   *Property Tax, Appraisal Records*
Access is to property records is free at www.deltacomputersystems.com/MS/MS41/INDEX.html.

Lincoln County   *Real Estate, Grantor/Grantee, Deed Records*
Access to county deed records is free at www.deltacomputersystems.com/MS/MS43/drlinkquerym.html.

Lowndes County   *Assessor, Property Records*
Access property assessor data free at www.lowndesassessor.com/propsearch.asp.

Madison County   *Real Estate, Recorder, Deed, Land Roll, Assessor Records*
www.madison-co.com/elected_offices/chancery_clerk/
Access the Chancery clerks recorded land records free at http://spyweb.madison-co.com/spyweb/spyweb.exe/entry/chancery. Username and password is madpublic, then click on SpyLinks then click LandDocs Access Land Roll data free at www.madison-co.com/elected_offices/tax_assessor/real_property_search.php.

Marion County   *Real Estate, Recorder, Property Tax, Probate, Judgment, Redemption, Landroll Records*
Access county records free at www.deltacomputersystems.com/MS/MS46/INDEX.HTML. Says it is a subscription service, but searching is free.

Marshall County   *Property Tax, Appraisal Records*
Access to property tax records is free at www.deltacomputersystems.com/MS/MS47/INDEX.html.

Neshoba County   *Property Tax, Appraisal Records*
Access to property data is free at www.deltacomputersystems.com/MS/MS50/index.html.

Pearl River County   *Property Tax, Appraisal Records*
Access to property data is free at www.deltacomputersystems.com/MS/MS55/INDEX.html

Pike County   *Real Estate, Grantor/Grantee, Deed Records*
www.co.pike.ms.us
Access to the county Deeds & Records Link is free at www.co.pike.ms.us/drlinkquery.html. Also property assessor records may soon be at www.co.pike.ms.us/tax.html.

Rankin County   *Real Estate, Tax Assessor, Voter Registration Records*
www.rankincounty.org
Records on the county Land Roll database are free at www.rankincounty.org/ta/interact.html. Also, voter registration files can be downloaded at www.rankincounty.org/ci.

Stone County   *Property Tax, Appraisal Records*
Access property tax records free at www.deltacomputersystems.com/search.html.

Warren County   *Property Tax, Appraisal Records*
www.co.warren.ms.us
Access is free at www.deltacomputersystems.com/MS/MS75/INDEX.html.

Washington County   *Property Tax, Appraisal Records*
Access is free at www.deltacomputersystems.com/MS/MS76/INDEX.html.

Federal Courts in Mississippi...

Standards for Federal Courts: The universal PACER sign-up number is 800-676-6856. Find PACER and the Party/Case Index on the Web at http://pacer.psc.uscourts.gov. PACER dial-up access is $.60 per minute. Also, courts offering internet access via PACER, Web-PACER or the new CM-ECF charge $.08 per page fee ($.07 per page if record is pre-2005 or unless noted as free)

US District Court -- Northern District of Mississippi

www.msnd.uscourts.gov
PACER: Case records are available back to 1990. Records are purged every 6 months. New records are available online after 1 day.
PACER Online Access: ECF replaces PACER. **Electronic Filing:** CM/ECF data at https://ecf.msnd.uscourts.gov. **Opinions:** Also, search opinions by year back to 1994 at http://home.olemiss.edu/~llibcoll/ndms/#OPINIONS. View court opinions at www.msnd.uscourts.gov/opinions/index.htm.
Aberdeen-Eastern Division counties: Alcorn, Attala, Chickasaw, Choctaw, Clay, Itawamba, Lee, Lowndes, Monroe, Oktibbeha, Prentiss, Tishomingo, Winston.
Clarksdale/Delta Division counties: Bolivar, Coahoma, De Soto, Panola, Quitman, Tallahatchie, Tate, Tunica.
Greenville Division counties: Carroll, Humphreys, Leflore, Sunflower, Washington.
Oxford-Northern Division counties: Benton, Calhoun, Grenada, Lafayette, Marshall, Montgomery, Pontotoc, Tippah, Union, Webster, Yalobusha.

US Bankruptcy Court -- Northern District of Mississippi

www.msnb.uscourts.gov
PACER: Case records are available back to 4/1987. Records are purged every 6 months. New records are available online after 1 day.
PACER Online Access: ECF replaces PACER. **Electronic Filing:** CM/ECF data at https://ecf.msnb.uscourts.gov. **Phone access:** Voice Case Information System, call 800-392-8653, 662-369-8147
Aberdeen Division counties: Alcorn, Attala, Benton, Bolivar, Calhoun, Carroll, Chickasaw, Choctaw, Clay, Coahoma, De Soto, Grenada, Humphreys, Itawamba, Lafayette, Lee, Leflore, Lowndes, Marshall, Monroe, Montgomery, Oktibbeha, Panola, Pontotoc, Prentiss, Quitman, Sunflower, Tallahatchie, Tate, Tippah, Tishomingo, Tunica, Union, Washington, Webster, Winston, Yalobusha.

US District Court -- Southern District of Mississippi

www.mssd.uscourts.gov
PACER: Case records are available back to 1992. **PACER Online Access:** ECF replaces PACER. **Electronic Filing:** CM/ECF data at https://ecf.mssd.uscourts.gov.
Biloxi-Southern Division counties: George, Hancock, Harrison, Jackson, Pearl River, Stone.
Eastern Division counties: Clarke, Jasper, Kemper, Lauderdale, Neshoba, Newton, Noxubee, Wayne.
Hattiesburg Division counties: Covington, Forrest, Greene, Jefferson Davis, Jones, Lamar, Lawrence, Marion, Perry, Walthall.
Jackson Division counties: Amite, Copiah, Franklin, Hinds, Holmes, Leake, Lincoln, Madison, Pike, Rankin, Scott, Simpson, Smith.
Western Division counties: Adams, Claiborne, Issaquena, Jefferson, Sharkey, Warren, Wilkinson, Yazoo.

US Bankruptcy Court -- Southern District of Mississippi

www.mssb.uscourts.gov
PACER: Case records are available back to 1986. New records are available online after 1 day. **PACER Online Access:** PACER online at https://pacer.login.uscourts.gov/cgi-bin/login.pl?court_id=mssbk. **Electronic Filing:** CM/ECF data at http://ecf.mssb.uscourts.gov. **Opinions:** View court opinions at www.mssb.uscourts.gov/Opinions/OpinionsList.htm. **Other Online Access:** Judges calendars free at www.mssb.uscourts.gov/Calendars.htm. **Phone access:** Voice Case Information System, call 800-601-8859, 601-965-6106
Biloxi Division counties: Formerly located in Biloxi. Clarke, Covington, Forrest, George, Greene, Hancock, Harrison, Jackson, Jasper, Jefferson Davis, Jones, Kemper, Lamar, Lauderdale, Lawrence, Marion, Neshoba, Newton, Noxubee, Pearl River, Perry, Stone, Walthall, Wayne.
Jackson Division counties: Adams, Amite, Claiborne, Copiah, Franklin, Hinds, Holmes, Issaquena, Jefferson, Leake, Lincoln, Madison, Pike, Rankin, Scott, Sharkey, Simpson, Smith, Warren, Wilkinson, Yazoo.

Missouri

Capital: Jefferson City
           Cole County
Time Zone: CST
Population: 5,754,618
# of Counties: 114

Quick Links

Website: www.state.mo.us
Governor: www.mo.gov/mo/govoffices.htm
Attorney General: www.mo.gov/mo/govoffices.htm
State Archives: www.sos.mo.gov/archives/Default.asp
State Statutes and Codes: www.moga.state.mo.us/STATUTES/STATUTES.HTM
Legislative Bill Search: www.house.state.mo.us/jointsearch/
Unclaimed Funds: www.treasurer.mo.gov/ucp/search.asp

State Level ... Major Agencies

Statewide Court Records

Court Administrator, 2112 Industrial Drive - PO Box 104480, Jefferson City, MO 65110; 573-751-4377, Fax-573-751-5540, 8-5PM.
www.courts.mo.gov
Online search: Available at www.courts.mo.gov/casenet/base/welcome.do is Missouri Casenet, a limited but growing online system. The system includes at least 88 counties (with more projected) as well as the Eastern, Western, and Southern Appellate Courts, the Supreme Court, and Fine Collection Center. Cases can be searched case number, filing date, or litigant name. Also, search Supreme Court and Appellate Court opinions at www.courts.mo.gov/.

Sexual Offender Registry

Missouri State Highway Patrol, Sexual Offender Registry, PO Box 9500, Jefferson City, MO 65102-0568 (Courier: 1510 E Elm St, Jefferson City, MO 65102); 573-526-6153, Fax-573-751-9382, 8AM-5PM.
www.mshp.dps.missouri.gov
Online search: The name index can be searched at the website, by name, county or ZIP Code. The web page also gives links lists to the county sheriffs that have online access.

Incarceration Records

Missouri Department of Corrections, Probation and Parole, 1511 Christy Dr., Jefferson City, MO 65101; 573-751-8488, Fax-573-751-8501, 8AM-5PM.
www.doc.missouri.gov
Online search: No Internet searching is available from this agency. However, you may email a single request to probation&parole@doc.mo.gov or constituentservices@doc.mo.gov. Spell the full name correctly. An email response will be provided to you, usually within 24 hours of receipt during regular business hours. This only provides general search information and policy information. Department does not provide search information to companies conducting employee background checks. Although this agency provides no direct internet access, a private company offers free web access at www.vinelink.com/index.jsp.

Corporation, Fictitious Name, Limited Partnership, Assumed Name, Trademarks/Servicemarks, Limited Liability Company Records

Secretary of State, Corporation Services, PO Box 778, Jefferson City, MO 65102 (Courier: 600 W Main, Jefferson City, MO 65101); 573-751-4153, 866-223-6535, Fax-573-751-5841, 8AM-5PM.
www.sos.mo.gov/business/corporations/
Online search: Search free online at https://www.sos.mo.gov/BusinessEntity/soskb/csearch.asp. The corporate name, agent name or the charter number is required to search. The site will indicate the currency of the data. Many business entity type searches available.

Uniform Commercial Code

UCC Division, Attn: Records, PO Box 1159, Jefferson City, MO 65102 (Courier: 600 W Main St, Rm 302, Jefferson City, MO 65101); 866-223-6565, 8AM-5PM.
www.sos.mo.gov/ucc/
Online search: Free searching for debtor names is available on the Internet at www.sos.mo.gov/ucc/soskb/searchstandardRA9.asp. Search by name or file number. Images are available for a fee. **Other options:** The agency will release information for bulk purchase, call for procedures and pricing.

Birth, Death Certificates

Department of Health & Senior Srvs, Bureau of Vital Records, PO Box 570, Jefferson City, MO 65102-0570 (Courier: 930 Wildwood, Jefferson City, MO 65109); 573-751-6387, 573-751-6400 (Message Number), 877-817-7363 (Orders), Fax-573-526-3846, www.dhss.mo.gov
Online search: Orders may be placed online at www.vitalchek.com. Records prior to 1910 are available by county at www.sos.mo.gov/archives/resources/birthdeath/.

Driver Records

Department of Revenue, Driver License Bureau, PO Box 200, Jefferson City, MO 65105-0200 (Courier: Harry S Truman Bldg, 301 W High St, Room 470, Jefferson City, MO 65105); 573-751-4300, Fax-573-526-7367, 7:30AM-5PM.
http://dor.mo.gov/mvdl/drivers/
Online search: Online access of Information Exchange costs $1.25 per record. Online inquiries can be put in Missouri's "mailbox" any time of the day. These inquiries are then picked up at 2 AM the following morning, and the resulting MVR's are sent back to each customer's "mailbox" approx. 2 hours later. **Other options:** The entire license file can be purchased, with updates. Call 573-751-5579 for more information.

Vehicle and Vessel Ownership, Registration

Department of Revenue, Motor Vehicle Bureau, PO Box 100, Jefferson City, MO 65105-0100 (Courier: Harry S Truman Bldg, 301 W High St, Jefferson City, MO 65105); 573-526-3669, 573-751-4509, Fax-573-751-7060, 7:30AM-5:30PM.
www.dor.mo.gov
Online search: Online record searches are available to registered entities who have a DPPA security access code issued by the Department. The fee is $1.25 per record and is automatically withdrawn through the requestor's ACH account. Access is via the Internet. Visit www.dor.mo.gov for more information. **Other options:** Missouri has an extensive range of records and information available on magnetic tape, labels or paper. Besides offering license, vehicle, title, dealer, and marine records, specific public report data is also available.

State Level ... Occupational Licensing

Acupuncturist	http://pr.mo.gov/licensee-search.asp
Alcohol Brand/Label	www.atc.dps.mo.gov/BrandLabelRegistrationLog2006.xls
Alcohol Suspensions	www.atc.dps.mo.gov/suspensionnotice.htm
Anesthesia Permit, Dental	http://pr.mo.gov/licensee-search.asp
Animal Technician	http://pr.mo.gov/licensee-search.asp
Ankle Specialist	http://pr.mo.gov/licensee-search.asp
Announcer, Ring	http://pr.mo.gov/licensee-search.asp
Architect	http://pr.mo.gov/licensee-search.asp
Athletic Trainer	http://pr.mo.gov/licensee-search.asp
Attorney	www.mobar.org/directory/index.htm
Audiologist/Audiologist, Clinical	http://pr.mo.gov/licensee-search.asp
Audiologist/Speech Pathologist, Clinical	http://pr.mo.gov/licensee-search.asp

Barber/Barber Shop/Instructor/School .... http://pr.mo.gov/licensee-search.asp
Beauty Shop .... http://pr.mo.gov/licensee-search.asp
Body Piercing/Branding Estab. .... http://pr.mo.gov/licensee-search.asp
Boxer/Boxing Professional .... http://pr.mo.gov/licensee-search.asp
Brander, Cosmetic .... http://pr.mo.gov/licensee-search.asp
Cemetery .... http://pr.mo.gov/licensee-search.asp
Chiropractor .... http://pr.mo.gov/licensee-search.asp
Cosmetologist/School/Instruct'r/Shop .... http://pr.mo.gov/licensee-search.asp
Counselor, Professional/Trainee .... http://pr.mo.gov/licensee-search.asp
Dentist/Dental Specialist/Hygienist .... http://pr.mo.gov/licensee-search.asp
Drug Distributor .... http://pr.mo.gov/licensee-search.asp
Embalmer .... http://pr.mo.gov/licensee-search.asp
Engineer .... http://pr.mo.gov/licensee-search.asp
Esthetician .... http://pr.mo.gov/licensee-search.asp
Funeral Director/Establishment .... http://pr.mo.gov/licensee-search.asp
Funeral Pre-Need Provider/Seller .... http://pr.mo.gov/licensee-search.asp
Geologist/Geologist in Training .... http://pr.mo.gov/licensee-search.asp
Hairdresser .... http://pr.mo.gov/licensee-search.asp
Hearing Instrument Specialist .... http://pr.mo.gov/licensee-search.asp
Insurance Agent/Broker .... www.insurance.mo.gov/industry/producer/agtstatus.htm
Insurance Consultant, Chiropractic .... http://pr.mo.gov/licensee-search.asp
Interior Designer .... http://pr.mo.gov/licensee-search.asp
Interpreter for the Deaf .... http://pr.mo.gov/licensee-search.asp
Landfill Operator .... www.dnr.mo.gov/alpd/swmp/forms/form_permit.htm
Landscape Architect .... http://pr.mo.gov/licensee-search.asp
Manicurist .... http://pr.mo.gov/licensee-search.asp
Marital & Family Therapist .... http://pr.mo.gov/licensee-search.asp
Martial Artist/Martial Arts Occupation .... http://pr.mo.gov/licensee-search.asp
Massage Therapist, Individual/Business ..... http://pr.mo.gov/licensee-search.asp
Medical Doctor .... http://pr.mo.gov/licensee-search.asp
Nurse Midwife .... http://pr.mo.gov/licensee-search.asp
Nurse .... http://pr.mo.gov/licensee-search.asp
Nursing School .... http://pr.mo.gov/licensee-search.asp
Occupational Therapist/Therapist Assist .... http://pr.mo.gov/licensee-search.asp
Optometrist .... http://pr.mo.gov/licensee-search.asp
Osteopathic Physician .... http://pr.mo.gov/licensee-search.asp
Perfusionist .... http://pr.mo.gov/licensee-search.asp
Pesticide Applicator/Technician/Dealer ...... www.kellysolutions.com/MO/
Pharmacist/Pharmacy Intern/Technician ..... http://pr.mo.gov/licensee-search.asp
Pharmacy .... http://pr.mo.gov/licensee-search.asp
Physical Therapist, Assistant .... http://pr.mo.gov/licensee-search.asp
Physician Assistant .... http://pr.mo.gov/licensee-search.asp
Physician, Athletic Event .... http://pr.mo.gov/licensee-search.asp
Podiatrist .... http://pr.mo.gov/licensee-search.asp
Pre-Need Provider/Seller, Funeral .... http://pr.mo.gov/licensee-search.asp
Psychologist .... http://pr.mo.gov/licensee-search.asp
Public Accountant Partnership .... http://pr.mo.gov/licensee-search.asp
Public Accountant-CPA .... http://pr.mo.gov/licensee-search.asp
Real Estate Agent/Seller/Broker/Partner ..... http://pr.mo.gov/licensee-search.asp
Real Estate Appraiser .... http://pr.mo.gov/licensee-search.asp
Real Estate Instructor/School .... http://pr.mo.gov/licensee-search.asp
Real Estate Officer/Corp/Association .... http://pr.mo.gov/licensee-search.asp
Respiratory Care Practitioner .... http://pr.mo.gov/licensee-search.asp
School Nurse .... http://pr.mo.gov/licensee-search.asp
Social Worker, Clinical .... http://pr.mo.gov/licensee-search.asp
Speech-Language Pathologist/Audiolog't... http://pr.mo.gov/licensee-search.asp

Surveyor, Land .... http://pr.mo.gov/licensee-search.asp
Tattoo Artist.. http://pr.mo.gov/licensee-search.asp
Teacher .... https://k12apps.dese.mo.gov/webapps/tcertsearch/tc_search1.asp
Timekeeper, Athletic Event .... http://pr.mo.gov/licensee-search.asp
Transfer Station.. www.dnr.mo.gov/alpd/swmp/facilities/tranlist.htm
Veterinarian/Veterinary Tech/Facility .... http://pr.mo.gov/licensee-search.asp
Waste Tire End User/Site............................ www.dnr.mo.gov/env/swmp/tires/tireend.htm
Waste Tire Processor/Hauler .... www.dnr.mo.gov/alpd/swmp/tires/tirehaul.htm
Wrestler/Wrestling Professional .... http://pr.mo.gov/licensee-search.asp

County Level ... Courts

Court Administration: State Court Administrator, 2112 Industrial Dr., PO Box 104480, Jefferson City, MO, 65109; 573-751-4377; www.courts.mo.gov

Court Structure: The Circuit Court is the court of general jurisdiction. There are 45 circuits comprised of 114 county Circuit Courts and one independent City Court. There are also Associate Circuit Courts with limited jurisdiction. Many counties have Combined Courts, a growing trend (23 consolidated in 2005/2006). Municipal Courts only have jurisdiction over traffic and ordinance violations.

Online Access Note: Available at www.courts.mo.gov/casenet/base/welcome.do is Missouri Casenet, a limited but growing online system. The system includes at least 88 counties (with more projected) as well as the Eastern, Western, and Southern Appellate Courts, the Supreme Court, and Fine Collection Center. Cases can be searched case number, filing date, or litigant name. Also, search Supreme Court and Appellate Court opinions at www.courts.mo.gov/

The counties listed on the following three pages participate in the free state online civil and criminal court record system CaseNet at http://casenet.osca.state.mo.us/casenet. Please note that each county may or may not include the Associate Circuit Court and the Circuit Court, or vice versa. Online access to Probate records may also be noted. **Also see end of this County Level Courts section for counties offering online access to non-CaseNet courts.**

Adair County
Circuit Court –Associate Circuit Division – Civil and Criminal Records. Online records go back to 9/6/2005.

Andrew County
Circuit Court – Associate Circuit Division – Civil and Criminal Records. Online records go back to 1993.

Audrain County
Circuit Court –Associate Circuit Division – Civil and Criminal Records

Barry County
Circuit Court –Associate Circuit Division – Civil and Criminal Records. Online records go back to 7/11/2005.

Barton County
Circuit Court – Civil and Criminal Records. Online records go back to 4/1/1999.

Bates County
Circuit Court – Associate Circuit Division – Civil and Criminal Records

Benton County
Circuit Court – Civil and Criminal Records

Bollinger County
Circuit Court –Associate Circuit Division – Civil and Criminal Records
Online records go back to 7/1/2001; judgments to 8/23/1993.

Boone County
Circuit Court – Civil and Criminal Records
Online civil records go back to 1986. Probate records back to 1986. Criminal records go back to 1983.

Buchanan County
Circuit Court – Civil and Criminal Records
Civil online records go back to 2000. Criminal records go back to 1992.

Callaway County
Circuit Court – Civil and Criminal Records. Online public cases go back to 2000; online probate to 1977.

Camden County
Circuit Court –Associate Circuit Division – Civil and Criminal Records

Cape Girardeau County
Circuit Court - Circuit Court - Criminal Division I & II – Civil and Criminal Records
Online public case records go back to 7/1/01; Circuit court judgments to 8/23/1993.

Carroll County
Circuit Court –Associate Circuit Division – Civil and Criminal Records. Online records go back to 09/19/01.

Carter County
Circuit Court –Associate Circuit Division – Civil and Criminal Records. Online records go back to 4/17/2000.

Cass County
Circuit Court –Associate Circuit Division – Civil and Criminal Records. Online records go back to 6/6/2005.

Cedar County
Circuit Court – Civil and Criminal Records. Online records go back to 9/11/2000. Online records include Probate Court.

Chariton County
Circuit Court – Civil and Criminal Records

Christian County
Circuit Court – Associate Circuit Division – Civil and Criminal Records. Online records are from 6/13/03 forward only.

Clark County
Circuit Court –Associate Circuit Division – Civil and Criminal Records. Online records go back to 09/19/01.

Cole County
Circuit Court – Civil and Criminal Records. Online records go back to 1/1980; probate to 6/2/72.

Cooper County
Circuit Court –Associate Circuit Division – Civil and Criminal Records. Online records go back to 4/2001.

Crawford County
Circuit Court –Associate Circuit Division – Civil and Criminal Records

Dade County
Circuit Court – Civil and Criminal Records. Online records go back to 9/20/1999. Online records include Probate Court.

Dallas County
Circuit Court –
Associate Circuit Division – Civil and Criminal Records. Associate court records go back to 1992.

Dent County
Circuit Court –Associate Circuit Division – Civil and Criminal Records

Dunklin County
Circuit Court – Civil and Criminal Records. Online records go back to 7/1/2001.

Franklin County
Circuit Court –Associate Circuit Division – Civil and Criminal Records.
Online records go back to 1/1995, probate back to 10/14/1967.

Gasconade County
Circuit Court –Associate Circuit Division – Civil and Criminal Records. Online Associate court records go back to 7/31/2000.

Grundy County
Circuit Court – Associate Circuit Division – Civil and Criminal Records
Online Circuit court records go back to 3/2000. Online Associate court records go back to 3/29/2000.

Harrison County
Circuit Court – Civil and Criminal Records. Online records go back to 3/29/2000.

Henry County
Circuit Court – Civil and Criminal Records

Hickory County
Circuit Court –Associate Circuit Division – Civil and Criminal Records

Howard County
Circuit Court – Associate Circuit Division – Civil and Criminal Records
Circuit Court cases include those filed from 10/01 to present. Associate court includes Probate and Traffic records.

Howell County
Circuit Court – Associate Circuit Division – Civil and Criminal Records
Circuit Court online records go back to 8/2000; pending cases back to 1990. Associate Court records go back to 1990.

Iron County
Circuit Court –Associate Circuit Division – Civil and Criminal Records

Jasper County
Circuit Court –Associate Division Court – Civil and Criminal Records
Online records go back to 6/26/2000.

Johnson County
Circuit Court –Associate Circuit Division – Civil and Criminal Records. Online records go back to 6/6/2005.

Knox County
Circuit Court – Civil and Criminal Records. Online records go back to 9/6/2005.

Laclede County
Circuit Court – Civil and Criminal Records

Lafayette County
Circuit Court – Civil and Criminal Records. Online records go back to 04/01/02.

Lawrence County
Circuit Court –Associate Circuit Division – Civil and Criminal Records. Online records go back to 7/11/2005.

Lewis County
Circuit Court – Civil and Criminal Records. Online records go back to 9/6/2005.

Lincoln County
Circuit Court – Civil and Criminal Records. Records from 04/03/02 forward.

Linn County
Consolidated Circuit Court – Civil and Criminal Records

Macon County
Circuit Court –Associate Circuit Division – Civil and Criminal Records. Online records go back to 4/17/2000.

Madison County
Circuit Court – Civil and Criminal Records. Records from 11/01/00 forward.

Marion County
Circuit Court – Civil and Criminal Records. Online records go back to 9/12/2005.

McDonald County
Circuit Court – Civil and Criminal Records

Mercer County
Circuit Court – Civil and Criminal Records. Online records go back to 3/29/2000.

Miller County
Circuit Court – Civil and Criminal Records

Mississippi County
Circuit Court – Civil and Criminal Records. Online records go back to 6/15/2001.

Moniteau County
Circuit Court –Associate Circuit Division – Civil and Criminal Records

Monroe County
Circuit Court –Associate Circuit Division – Civil and Criminal Records. Online records go back to 9/12/2005.

Montgomery County
Circuit Court – Associate Circuit Division – Civil and Criminal Records
Circuit Court civil records go back to 6/25/1997. Circuit criminal records go back to 12/10/1996. Associate civil records go back to 6/25/1997. Associate criminal records go back to 8/29/1950.

Morgan County
Circuit Court – Civil and Criminal Records

New Madrid County
Circuit Court – Civil and Criminal Records. Online records go back to 2/7/2001.

Newton County
Circuit Court – Civil and Criminal Records

Oregon County
Circuit Court – Associate Circuit Division – Civil and Criminal Records. Online records go back to 1991.

Osage County
Circuit Court – Civil and Criminal Records. Online civil records go back to 9/01/2000. Criminal records go back to 8/28/1992.

Pemiscot County
Circuit Court –Associate Circuit Division – Civil and Criminal Records.
Online Civil records go back to 2/14/2001. Access to criminal records back to 1990.

Perry County
Circuit Court – Associate Circuit Division – Civil and Criminal Records
Civil records go back to 7/1/2001; Circuit criminal records go back to 1993; Associate criminal records go back to 7/1/2001.

Pettis County
Circuit Court – Associate Circuit Division – Civil, Probate, and Criminal Records
Online civil records go back to 4/2001. Online Circuit criminal records go back to 1/1992. Online Associate criminal records go back to 1/1993.

Pike County
Circuit Court –Associate Circuit Division – Civil and Criminal Records. Online records go back to 04/03/02.

Platte County
Circuit Court – Associate Circuit Division – Civil and Criminal Records

Polk County
Circuit Court – Civil and Criminal Records

Putnam County
Circuit Court –Associate Circuit Division – Civil and Criminal Records. Online records go back to 3/29/2000.

Ralls County
Circuit Court – Associate Circuit Division – Civil and Criminal Records. Online records go back to 9/12/2005.

Ray County
Circuit Court – Civil and Criminal Records. Online records only go back to 2001.

Reynolds County
Circuit Court –Associate Circuit Division – Civil and Criminal Records

Saline County
Circuit Court – Associate Circuit Division – Civil and Criminal Records. Circuit Court records only go back to 4/2002.

Schuyler County
Circuit Court –Associate Circuit Division – Civil and Criminal Records. Online records go back to 09/19/01.

Scotland County
Circuit Court –Associate Circuit Division – Civil and Criminal Records. Online records go back to 09/19/01.

Scott County
Circuit Court –Associate Circuit Division – Civil and Criminal Records. Online records go back to 6/15/2001.

Shannon County
Circuit Court –Associate Circuit Division – Civil and Criminal Records. Online records go back to 1992.

Shelby County
Circuit Court – Civil and Criminal Records. Online criminal records go back to 4/17/2000.

St. Charles County
Circuit Court – Civil and Criminal Records. Online civil records go back to 1982. Online criminal records go back to 10/1992.

St. Clair County
Circuit Circuit Court – Civil and Criminal Records

St. Francois County
Circuit Court - Associate Circuit Division – Civil and Criminal Records
Circuit records go back to 11/01/00. Associate records go back to 1992, probate records to 11/06/00.

St. Louis County
Associate Circuit - Civil Division – Civil Records

Ste. Genevieve County
Circuit Court –Associate Circuit Division – Civil and Criminal Records. Online records go back to 11/06/00.

Stoddard County
Circuit Court – Associate Circuit Division - Civil and Criminal Records. Online records go back to 7/1/2001.

Stone County
Circuit Court – Civil and Criminal Records. Online records go back to 7/11/2005.

Sullivan County
Circuit Court – Civil and Criminal Records

Taney County
Circuit Court – Associate Circuit Court – Civil and Criminal Records. Online records include probate court.

Vernon County
Circuit Court – Civil and Criminal Records. Online records go back to 9/11/2001. Online records include probate court.

Warren County
Circuit Court – Associate Circuit Division – Civil and Criminal Records
Circuit Court online records go back to 9/20/1999.

Washington County
Circuit Court – Associate Circuit Division – Civil and Criminal Records. Online records go back to 11/09/00.

Wayne County
Circuit Court – Civil and Criminal Records
Criminal online records go back to 09/19/01.

Webster County
Circuit Court –Associate Circuit Division – Civil and Criminal Records
- - - - - - - - - - - - -

The following courts offer records directly (these courts may or may not participate in CaseNet)

Clay County
Circuit Court – Associate Circuit Division – Civil and Criminal Records
www.circuit7.net
Access to Circuit record index s is free at www.circuit7.net/pages/publicaccess/publicaccess.asp. Includes traffic. Also, participates in the free state online court record system at www.courts.mo.gov/casenet/base/welcome.do.

Greene County
Circuit Court – Associate Circuit Division – Civil and Criminal Records
www.greenecountymo.org/web/Assoc_Cir_Court/
Access records at the court's website free at www.greenecountymo.org/ccourt31/search.htm.

Jackson County

Circuit Court - Civil Division – Civil Records
www.16thcircuit.org
Participates in the free state online court record system at www.courts.mo.gov/casenet/base/welcome.do. Jackson Casenet records go back to 1/89. The Probate Court also participates in the Casenet system; also, probate records are free at www.16thcircuit.org/publicaccess.asp. This includes private process servers, jury verdicts, criminal traffic, and criminal sureties.

Circuit Court - Criminal Division – Criminal Records
www.16thcircuit.org
Participates in the free state online court record system at www.courts.mo.gov/casenet/base/welcome.do. Jackson Casenet records go back to 1/89. Also, Access to criminal traffic dockets is at www.16thcircuit.org/trafficdockets.asp. Also, search surety bonding agents at www.16thcircuit.org/suretyqualifications.asp.

St. Louis City

Circuit Courts - Civil – Civil Records
www.stlcitycircuitcourt.com
Access to civil records is free at https://www.stlcitycircuitcourt.com/SSL/getCivil.cfm. Remote access is also through MoBar Net and is open only to attorneys. Call 314-535-1950 for information. Also, probate records are free online at www.courts.mo.gov/casenet/base/welcome.do. Online probate records go back to 5/31/2000.

City of St Louis Circuit Court - Criminal Records
www.stlcitycircuitcourt.com/PDF/TelephoneList/TeleDirectory.pdf
Access to criminal records is free at https://www.stlcitycircuitcourt.com/SSL/getCriminal.cfm.

County Level ... Recorders & Assessors

Recording Office Organization: 114 counties and one independent city -- 115 recording offices. The recording officer is the Recorder of Deeds. The City of St. Louis has its own recording office. The entire state is in the Central Time Zone (CST). All federal and state tax liens are filed with the county Recorder of Deeds. They are usually indexed together. Some counties will perform tax lien searches. Search and copy fees vary widely.

Online Access Note: A number of counties offer online access. UCCs are available from Secretary of State.

Adair County *Death Records*
Search the historical society indexes of deaths for free at http://homepage.mac.com/ggl1/ObitAnchor.html.

Audrain County *Property, Assessor, GIS Records*
Search assessor property data for a fee on the GIS system at http://webgishome.promap.com/Default.aspx. Registration and username required.

Boone County *Real Estate, Lien, Marriage, UCC, Real Property, Personal Property Records*
www.showmeboone.com/RECORDER/
Access to the recorder database is free at www.showmeboone.com/recorder. Also, the assessor data is free at www.showmeboone.com/assessor/. Free registration and password are required for access.

Buchanan County *Real Estate, Recording, Deed, Lien, UCC, Marriage, Divorce, Judgment, Will, Military Discharge, Property, GIS Records*
www.co.buchanan.mo.us
Access the recorder database free at http://67.98.136.123/or_wb1/or_sch_1.asp. Also, search the GIS-mapping site for property data free at www.buchanancomogis.com but no name searching. Also, search sheriff sex offenders list at www.ecountywatch.net/sexoffenders_interface/SEX_OFFENDERS/editor/sosearch.asp.

Butler County *Death Index Records*
Search the county death index at www.rootsweb.com/~mobutle2/dndx/bc-death.htm?.

Cape Girardeau County *Recording, Real Estate, Deed, Lien Records*

Recorder office data by subscription on either the Laredo system using subscription and fees or the Tapestry System using credit card, https://tapestry.fidlar.com/tapsearch.aspx; $3.99 search; $.50 per image.

Clay County *Real Estate, Marriage, Military Discharge, UCC, Recording Records*

http://recorder.claycogov.com/pages/index.asp
Access to the recorder's database is free at http://recorder.claycogov.com/pages/online_access.asp. Overall index goes back to 1986; images back to 1986. Real estate only UCCs back to 1986. No images for marriages, discharges, just data. Also, access real estate records from Collector's Office free at www.claycogov.com/county/offices/collector/realprop.php.

Cole County *Death Records*

Access to unofficial death records up to 1907 are free from a private company at www.ancestry.com/ancestry/search/3074.htm.

De Kalb County *Property, Assessor, GIS Records*

Search assessor property data for a fee on the GIS system at http://webgishome.promap.com/Default.aspx. Registration and username required.

Franklin County *Real Estate, Recorder, Deed Records*

www.franklinmo.org.
Recorder office data by subscription on either the Laredo system using subscription and fees or the Tapestry System using credit card, https://tapestry.fidlar.com/tapsearch.aspx; $3.99 search; $.50 per image.

Greene County *Assessor, Property, Deed, Lien, UCC, Recording, Death, Divorce Records*

www.greenecountymo.org
Search the recorder database for free at www.greenecountymo.org/Recorder/search.php. Search UCCs & tax liens at www.greenecountymo.org/Recorder/ucctaxsearch.php. Records for divorces that occurred 1837 to 1920 in Greene County are free at http://userdb.rootsweb.com/divorces.

Howell County *Real Estate, Recorder, Deed Records*

Also, recorder office data by subscription on either the Laredo system using subscription and fees or the Tapestry System using credit card, https://tapestry.fidlar.com/tapsearch.aspx; $3.99 search; $.50 per image.

Jackson County (Kansas City) *Property, Tax Assessor, Recording, Marriages, Grantor/Grantee, Deed, Lien, Judgment, UCC Records*

www.jackson.gov.org
Search the recorder Grantor/Grantee database for free at http://records.co.jackson.mo.us/search.asp?cabinet=opr. Search property tax data free at www.jacksongov.org/ser_os_ta_SrchIntro.asp. Also, access recording office land data at www.etitlesearch.com; registration required, fee based on usage. Also, search Kansas City land data free at http://kivaweb.kcmo.org/kivanet/2/land/lookup/index.cfm?fa=dslladdr. Search the marriage records free at http://records.co.jackson.mo.us/search.asp?cabinet=marriage. Search the UCC database at http://records.co.jackson.mo.us/search.asp?cabinet=ucc.

Jefferson County *Real Estate Recording, Deed, Judgment, Assessor, Property Tax Records*

www.jeffcomo.org
Search assessor property data for free at www.jcao.org/myinfo.htm. Access recording office land data at www.etitlesearch.com; registration required, fee based on usage; call 870-856-3055 for info. Also, recorder office data by subscription on either the Laredo system using subscription and fees or the Tapestry System using credit card, https://tapestry.fidlar.com/tapsearch.aspx; $3.99 search; $.50 per image.

Lincoln County *Recording, Real Estate, Tax Lien Records*

Access recording records with subscription; details not yet available; call Recorder.

Miller County *Property Data Records*

http://millercountymissouri.org
Property data is available on CD-rom; fees vary. Call either the Recorder 573-369-1935 or Assessor office 573-369-1960 to order.

Mississippi County *Real Estate Recording Records*

Access land records at http://etitlesearch.com. You can do a name search; choose from $200.00 monthly subscription or per click account.

New Madrid County   *Real Estate Recording Records*
Land records may be available at http://etitlesearch.com. You can do a name search; choose from $200.00 monthly subscription or per click account.

Newton County   *Deed, Mortgage, UCC, Lien, Vital Statistic Records*
Access to the Recorder's database requires a $200 sign-up fee; images go back to 1999; index to 1994. System may be temporarily down.

Pemiscot County   *Real Estate Recording, Deed Records*
Access land records at http://etitlesearch.com. Name searching; choose from $200.00 monthly subscription or per click account.

Perry County   *Real Estate, Recorder, Deed Records*
Recorder office data by subscription on either the Laredo system using subscription and fees or the Tapestry System using credit card, https://tapestry.fidlar.com/tapsearch.aspx; $3.99 search; $.50 per image.

Pettis County   *Property, Assessor, GIS Records*
www.pettiscomo.com
Search assessor property data for a fee on the GIS system at http://webgishome.promap.com/Default.aspx. Registration and username is required.

St. Charles County   *Assessor, Property Records*
www.saintcharlescounty.org
Access recorder records free at http://65.125.29.166/scweb/. Search index free; images -$1.00 per page. Also, search Property Assessment data free at www.win.org/library/library_office/assessment. No name searching; search by address, street or map ID.

St. Francois County   *Assessor, Property Records*
Access property assessor data free at www.sfcassessor.org/parcel_search.html.

St. Louis City   *Recording, Real Estate, Deed, Lien Records*
Recorder office data by subscription on either the Laredo system using subscription and fees or the Tapestry System using credit card, https://tapestry.fidlar.com/tapsearch.aspx; $3.99 search; $.50 per image.

St. Louis County   *Assessor, Property, Recorder, Deed, Licensing Records*
www.co.st-louis.mo.us
Access county data free at http://revenue.stlouisco.com/ias/.

Scott County   *Real Estate Recording, Deed Records*
Access recording office land data at www.etitlesearch.com; registration required, fee based on usage.

Stone County   *Property, Assessor Records*
Access property data from the GIS interactive map at www.stoneco-mo.us/disclaim.htm. Download the MapGuide viewer first.

Taney County   *Real Estate, Recorder, Deed, Lien, Sexual Offender, Assessor, Property Tax, GIS Records*
www.co.taney.mo.us
Recorder office data is by subscription on the Laredo System for $100 monthly; call 309-794-3200 for information and sign-up. Index goes back to 1994. Search the sheriff's sex offender list free at www.co.taney.mo.us/Files/offenders.pdf updated weekly. Also, search assessor property data free on the GIS system at http://webgishome.promap.com/Default.aspx.

Federal Courts in Missouri...

Standards for Federal Courts: The universal PACER sign-up number is 800-676-6856. Find PACER and the Party/Case Index on the Web at http://pacer.psc.uscourts.gov. PACER dial-up access is $.60 per minute. Also, courts offering internet access via PACER, Web-PACER or the new CM-ECF charge $.08 per page fee ($.07 per page if record is pre-2005 or unless noted as free)

US District Court -- Eastern District of Missouri

www.moed.uscourts.gov

PACER: Case records are available back to 1992. Records are purged never. New records are available online after 1 day. **PACER Online Access:** ECF replaces PACER. **Electronic Filing:** CM/ECF data at https://ecf.moed.uscourts.gov. **Opinions:** View court opinions at https://ecf.moed.uscourts.gov/documents/index.html.
Cape Girardeau Division counties: Bollinger, Butler, Cape Girardeau, Carter, Dunklin, Madison, Mississippi, New Madrid, Pemiscot, Perry, Reynolds, Ripley, Scott, Shannon, Stoddard, Wayne.
St Louis Division counties: Adair, Audrain, Chariton, Clark, Crawford, Dent, Franklin, Gasconade, Iron, Jefferson, Knox, Lewis, Lincoln, Linn, Macon, Maries, Marion, Monroe, Montgomery, Phelps, Pike, Ralls, Randolph, Schuyler, Scotland, Shelby, St. Charles, St. Francois, St. Louis, St. Louis City, Ste. Genevieve, Warren, Washington, This court also holds records for the Hannibal Division.

US Bankruptcy Court -- Eastern District of Missouri

www.moeb.uscourts.gov

PACER: Case records are available back to 1/1991. Records are purged every 6 months. New records are available online after 1 day. **PACER Online Access:** ECF replaces PACER. Document images available. **Electronic Filing:** CM/ECF data at https://ecf.moeb.uscourts.gov. **Opinions:** View court opinions at www.moeb.uscourts.gov/opin_search/opin_search.html. **Other Online Access:** Search records on the Internet using RACER at http://racer.moeb.uscourts.gov/perl/bkplog.html. Access fee is $.08 per page. Also, access calendars free at www.moeb.uscourts.gov/calendar.htm. **Phone access:** Voice Case Information System, call 888-223-6431, 314-244-4999
St Louis Division counties: Adair, Audrain, Bollinger, Butler, Cape Girardeau, Carter, Chariton, Clark, Crawford, Dent, Dunklin, Franklin, Gasconade, Iron, Jefferson, Knox, Lewis, Lincoln, Linn, Macon, Madison, Maries, Marion, Mississippi, Monroe, Montgomery, New Madrid, Pemiscot, Perry, Phelps, Pike, Ralls, Randolph, Reynolds, Ripley, Schuyler, Scotland, Scott, Shannon, Shelby, St. Charles, St. Francois, St. Louis, St.Louis City, Ste. Genevieve, Stoddard, Warren, Washington, Wayne.

US District Court -- Western District of Missouri

www.mow.uscourts.gov

PACER: Case records are available back to 5/1989. Records are purged as deemed necessary. **PACER Online Access:** ECF replaces PACER. **Electronic Filing:** CM/ECF data at https://ecf.mowd.uscourts.gov. **Opinions:** View court opinions at www.mow.uscourts.gov/New_Opinions.html.
Jefferson City-Central Division counties: Benton, Boone, Callaway, Camden, Cole, Cooper, Hickory, Howard, Miller, Moniteau, Morgan, Osage, Pettis.
Joplin-Southwestern Division counties: Barry, Barton, Jasper, Lawrence, McDonald, Newton, Stone, Vernon.
Kansas City - Western Division counties: Bates, Carroll, Cass, Clay, Henry, Jackson, Johnson, Lafayette, Ray, St. Clair, Saline.
Springfield-Southern Division counties: Cedar, Christian, Dade, Dallas, Douglas, Greene, Howell, Laclede, Oregon, Ozark, Polk, Pulaski, Taney, Texas, Webster, Wright.
St Joseph Division counties: Andrew, Atchison, Buchanan, Caldwell, Clinton, Daviess, De Kalb, Gentry, Grundy, Harrison, Holt, Livingston, Mercer, Nodaway, Platte, Putnam, Sullivan, Worth.

US Bankruptcy Court -- Western District of Missouri

www.mow.uscourts.gov

PACER: PACER Online Access: ECF replaces PACER. **Electronic Filing:** CM/ECF data at https://ecf.mowb.uscourts.gov. **Opinions:** View court opinions at www.mow.uscourts.gov/New_Opinions.html. **Phone access:** Voice Case Information System, call 888-205-2527, 816-512-5110
Kansas City - Western Division counties: Andrew, Atchison, Barry, Barton, Bates, Benton, Boone, Buchanan, Caldwell, Callaway, Camden, Carroll, Cass, Cedar, Christian, Clay, Clinton, Cole, Cooper, Dade, Dallas, Daviess, De Kalb, Douglas, Gentry, Greene, Grundy, Harrison, Henry, Hickory, Holt, Howard, Howell, Jackson, Jasper, Johnson, Laclede, Lafayette, Lawrence, Livingston, McDonald, Mercer, Miller, Moniteau, Morgan, Newton, Nodaway, Oregon, Osage, Ozark, Pettis, Platte, Polk, Pulaski, Putnam, Ray, Saline, St. Clair, Stone, Sullivan, Taney, Texas, Vernon, Webster, Worth, Wright.

Montana

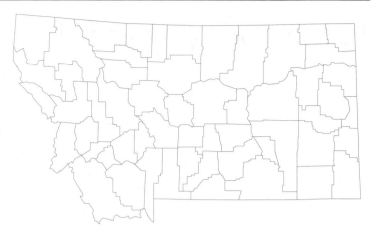

Capital: Helena
           Lewis and Clark County
Time Zone: MST
Population: 926,865
# of Counties: 56

Quick Links

Website: http://mt.gov/
Governor: http://mt.gov/gov2/default.asp
Attorney General: www.doj.mt.gov/department/attorneygeneral.asp
State Archives: www.montanahistoricalsociety.org
State Statutes and Codes: http://data.opi.state.mt.us/bills/mca_toc/index.htm
Legislative Bill Search: www.leg.state.mt.us/css/research/laws.asp
Unclaimed Funds: http://mt.gov/revenue/programsandservices/unclaimedproperty.asp

State Level ... Major Agencies

Statewide Court Records

Court Administrator, PO Box 203002, Helena, MT 59620-3002 (Courier: 215 N Sanders, Justice Bldg Rm 315, Helena, MT 59620); 406-444-2621, Fax-406-444-0834, 8AM-5PM.
www.lawlibrary.state.mt.us
Online search: Montana Supreme Court opinions and orders are found at the website. This is no statewide system for obtaining local court records online.

Sexual Offender Registry

Department of Justice, Sexual and Violent Offender Registry, PO Box 201417, Helena, MT 59620; 406-444-2497, Fax-406-444-2759, 8AM-5PM.
http://doj.state.mt.us/svor/search.asp
Online search: The state sexual offender list is available at the website. You can search for this information by name, by city or county, or by the type of offense committed.

Incarceration Records

Montana Department of Corrections, Directors Office, PO Box 201301, Helena, MT 59620-1301 (Courier: 1539 11th Ave, Helena, MT 59620); 406-444-3930, 406-444-7461 (Information Officer), Fax-406-444-4920, 8:30AM-4:30PM.
www.cor.state.mt.us
Online search: Search current or former inmates on the ConWeb system at http://app.discoveringmontana.com/conweb/index.html. Search by ID# or name. Also, a private company offers free web access to DOC records at www.vinelink.com/index.jsp. **Other options:** Entire offender database is available for purchase for $100.00; call Discovering Montana, 406-449-3468. Academic or social researchers can acquire the same database for no charge.

Corporation, Limited Liability Company, Fictitious Name, Limited Partnerships, Assumed Name, Trademarks/Servicemarks

Business Services Bureau, Secretary of State, PO Box 202801, Helena, MT 59620-2801 (Courier: 1236 East 6th Ave, Helena, MT 59620); 406-444-3665, Fax-406-444-3976, 8AM-5PM.
http://sos.state.mt.us/css/index.asp
Online search: Visit http://app.discoveringmontana.com/bes/ for free searches of MT business entities. There is a commercial service for finding registered principles, the fee is $4.00 per search. Go to http://app.discoveringmontana.com/walkthrough/rps/. **Other options:** Lists of the new corporations per month are available.

Uniform Commercial Code, Federal Tax Liens

Business Services Bureau, Secretary of State, Rm 260, PO Box 202801, Helena, MT 59620-2801 (Courier: 1236 East 6th Ave, Helena, MT 59620); 406-444-1212, Fax-406-444-3976, 8AM-5PM.
www.sos.mt.gov/css/index.asp
Online search: This web-based subscription service provides information about all active liens filed with the office. To use the service, you need to establish an with Discovering Montana for a fee of $25 per month. Contact Discovering Montana at 101 N Rodney #3, Helena MT 59601, or call 406-449-3468, or visit their web site at http://mt.gov/default.asp. **Other options:** The agency offers farm bill filings lists on a monthly basis for $5.00 per category on paper or microfiche. A CD-Rom for all Farm Products is available for $20.00.

Birth, Death Certificates

Montana Department of Health, Vital Records, PO Box 4210, Helena, MT 59604 (Courier: 111 N Sanders, Rm 209, Helena, MT 59601); 406-444-4228 (Recording), 406-444-2685, Fax-406-444-1803, 8AM-5PM.
http://vhsp.dphhs.mt.gov/certificates/ordercertificates.shtml
Online search: Order records via state designated vendor at www.vitalchek.com or www.uscerts.com.

Driver Records

Motor Vehicle Division, Driver's Services, PO Box 201430, Helena, MT 59620-1430 (Courier: Records Unit, 303 N Roberts, Room 260, Helena, MT 59620); 406-444-3292, Fax-406-444-7623, 8AM-5PM.
www.doj.mt.gov/driving/default.asp
Online search: A Restricted Use Agreement and a Requestor Services Agreement must be completed and approved in advance. Both interactive and batch delivery is offered ($6.50 per record) to users who sign up in advance and pay a $50.00 annual registration fee. Online services also include a License Status Conviction Activity batch search, at a reduced price. This is a monitoring service, for a small fee users may submit a monthly query. For more information, visit https://app.mt.gov/dojdrs/ or call 406-449-3468.

Vehicle & Vessel Ownership, Registration

Department of Justice, Title and Registration Bureau, 1003 Buckskin Drive, Deer Lodge, MT 59722; 406-846-6000, Fax-406-846-6039, 8AM-5PM.
www.doj.state.mt.us/driving/vehicletitleregistration.asp
Online search: Online access to vehicle records is available at https://app.discoveringmontana.com/dojvs/. Requesters must pay an annual $50.00 registration fee, and the purpose of the requests must pass DPPA muster. The following is available (authority level determined by DOJ): Vehicle Information, License Plate Information, Vehicle Owner Information, Lien History, Title History and Registration Information. Call 866-449-3468 for more information. **Other options:** Bulk or batch ordering of registration information is available on tape, disk, or paper. The user must fill out a specific form, which gives the user the capability of customization. For further information, contact the Registrar at address above.

Voter Registration

Secretary of State, Elections Bureau, PO Box 202801, Helena, MT 59620-2801; 406-444-5376, Fax-406-444-2023, 8AM-5PM.
http://sos.mt.gov/ELB/index.asp
Online search: Access records at http://app.mt.gov/voterfile/select_criteria.html. Customized lists are available for $.04 per record. Records can be purchased for non-commercial use only. **Other options:** This agency database can be purchased on disk or CD-ROM, or downloaded from the web site mentioned above. Fee of $.012 per record will be assessed. For more information, contact Elaine Graveley.

State Level ... Occupational Licensing

Acupuncturist .... http://app.mt.gov/lookup/
Architect .... http://app.mt.gov/lookup/
Athletic Event/Event Timekeeper .... http://app.mt.gov/lookup/
Audiologist .... http://app.mt.gov/lookup/
Barber/Barber Instructor .... http://app.mt.gov/lookup/
Boxer/Boxing Professional .... http://app.mt.gov/lookup/
Boxing Manager/Promoter/Judge .... http://app.mt.gov/lookup/
Cemetery, Privately Owned .... http://app.mt.gov/lookup/
Chemical Dependency Counselor .... http://app.mt.gov/lookup/
Child Care Provider .... http://oraweb.hhs.state.mt.us:9999/ccrd/plsql/ccrd_provider.startup
Chiropractor .... http://app.mt.gov/lookup/
Clinical Nurse Specialist .... http://app.mt.gov/lookup/
Clinical Social Worker .... http://app.mt.gov/lookup/
Construction Blaster .... http://app.mt.gov/lookup/
Contractor, Public/Independent .... http://erdcr.dli.mt.gov:8910/IC_Parms.htm
Contractor, Revoked License http://erdcr.dli.mt.gov:8910/ICRevoke.htm
Cosmetologist/Cosmetology Instr./School .. http://app.mt.gov/lookup/
CP Installer/Designer .... http://deq.mt.gov/UST/licensees.asp
Crematory/Crematory Operator/Technic'n . http://app.mt.gov/lookup/
Day Care Center .... http://oraweb.hhs.state.mt.us:9999/ccrd/plsql/ccrd_provider.startup
Dental Hygienist .... http://app.mt.gov/lookup/
Dentist/Dental Assistant .... http://app.mt.gov/lookup/
Denturist .... http://app.mt.gov/lookup/
Drug Registration, Dangerous...,................ http://app.mt.gov/lookup/
Drug Wholesaler .... http://app.mt.gov/lookup/
Electrician .... http://app.mt.gov/lookup/
Electrologist .... http://app.mt.gov/lookup/
Emergency Medical Technician .... http://app.mt.gov/lookup/
Engineer .... http://app.mt.gov/lookup/
Esthetician .... http://app.mt.gov/lookup/
Firearms Instructor .... http://app.mt.gov/lookup/
Funeral Director .... http://app.mt.gov/lookup/
Guide .... http://app.mt.gov/lookup/
Hairstylist .... http://app.mt.gov/lookup/
Hearing Aid Dispenser .... http://app.mt.gov/lookup/
Insurance Adjuster .... http://sao.mt.gov/insurance/findagent.asp
Insurance Producer .... http://sao.mt.gov/insurance/findagent.asp
Land Surveyor .... http://app.mt.gov/lookup/
Landscape Architect .... http://app.mt.gov/lookup/
Manicurist .... http://app.mt.gov/lookup/
Medical Doctor .... http://app.mt.gov/lookup/
Midwife Nurse .... http://app.mt.gov/lookup/
Midwife, Direct Entry/Apprentice .... http://app.mt.gov/lookup/
Monitoring Well Installer .... http://deq.mt.gov/UST/licensees.asp
Mortuary/Mortician .... http://app.mt.gov/lookup/
Naturopathic Physician .... http://app.mt.gov/lookup/
Nurse Anesthetist .... http://app.mt.gov/lookup/
Nurse Practitioner .... http://app.mt.gov/lookup/
Nurse-RN/LPN .... http://app.mt.gov/lookup/
Nutritionist .... http://app.mt.gov/lookup/
Occupational Therapist .... http://app.mt.gov/lookup/
Optometrist .... http://app.mt.gov/lookup/
Osteopathic Physician .... http://app.mt.gov/lookup/

Outfitter, Hunting/Fishing........................ http://app.mt.gov/lookup/
Pharmacist.. http://app.mt.gov/lookup/
Physical Therapist.................................... http://app.mt.gov/lookup/
Physician Assistant .... http://app.mt.gov/lookup/
Plumber.. http://app.mt.gov/lookup/
Podiatrist.. http://app.mt.gov/lookup/
Private Investigator .... http://app.mt.gov/lookup/
Private Security Guard.............................. http://app.mt.gov/lookup/
Process Server... http://app.mt.gov/lookup/
Property Manager .... http://app.mt.gov/lookup/
Psychologist.. http://app.mt.gov/lookup/
Public Accountant.................................... http://app.mt.gov/lookup/
Radiologic Technologist .... http://app.mt.gov/lookup/
Real Estate Agent/Broker/Sales .... http://app.mt.gov/lookup/
Real Estate Appraiser............................... http://app.mt.gov/lookup/
Referee... http://app.mt.gov/lookup/
Respiratory Care Practitioner.................... http://app.mt.gov/lookup/
Sanitarian... http://app.mt.gov/lookup/
Security Alarm Installer............................ http://app.mt.gov/lookup/
Security Company/Organization................. http://app.mt.gov/lookup/
Security Guard... http://app.mt.gov/lookup/
Social Worker, LSW .... http://app.mt.gov/lookup/
Speech Pathologist................................... http://app.mt.gov/lookup/
Surveyor, Land .... http://app.mt.gov/lookup/
Teacher .... http://data.opi.state.mt.us/certification/
Timeshare Broker/Salesperson .... http://app.mt.gov/lookup/
Underground Storage Tank Inspector .... http://deq.mt.gov/UST/licensees.asp
Underground Tank Installer/Remover .... http://deq.mt.gov/UST/licensees.asp
Veterinarian .... http://app.mt.gov/lookup/
Wrestler .... http://app.mt.gov/lookup/
X-ray Technician .... http://app.mt.gov/lookup/

County Level ... Courts

Court Administration: Court Administrator, Justice Building, 215 N Sanders, Room 315 (PO Box 203002), Helena, MT, 59620; 406-444-2621. www.lawlibrary.state.mt.us

Court Structure: The District Courts have no maximum amount for civil judgment cases. Most District Courts handle civil over $7,000; there are exceptions that handle a civil minimum as low as $5,000. Limited Jurisdiction Courts, which are also known as Justice Courts, may handle civil actions up to $7,000. The Small Claims limit is $3,000. Many Montana Justices of the Peace maintain case record indexes on their personal PCs, which does speed the retrieval process.

Online Access Note: Supreme Courts Opinions, Orders, and recently Filed Briefs may be found at www.lawlibrary.state.mt.us/dscgi/ds.py/View/Collection-36. Federal District court records are also available here.

Lewis and Clark County

District Court – Civil and Criminal Records
www.co.lewis-clark.mt.us
Will accept email record requests to kallio@co.lewis-clark.mt.us.

County Level ... Recorders & Assessors

Recording Office Organization: 57 counties, 56 recording offices. The recording officer is the County Clerk and Recorder (it is the Clerk of District Court for state tax liens). Yellowstone National Park is considered a county but is not included as a filing location. The entire state is in the Mountain Time Zone (MST). Federal tax liens on personal property of businesses are filed with the Secretary of State. Other federal tax liens are filed with the county Clerk and Recorder. State tax liens are filed with the Clerk of District Court. Usually tax liens on personal property filed with the Clerk and Recorder are in the same index with UCC financing statements. Most counties will perform tax lien searches, some as part of a UCC search and others for a separate fee, usually $7.00 per name. Copy fees vary.

Online Access Note: Search for a for a Montana property owner by name and county on the Montana Cadastral Mapping Project GIS mapping database at http://gis.doa.state.mt.us.

All Montana Counties *Property Records*
Name search on the statewide Cadastral database free at http://gis.mt.gov (incomplete revenue tax records).

Cascade County *Property, Real Estate Recording, Deed Records*
www.co.cascade.mt.us
Access recorded land data at www.etitlesearch.com; registration required, fee based on usage. Also, see note at beginning of section.

Deer Lodge County *Property, Real Estate Recording, Deed Records*
Access recorded land data at www.etitlesearch.com; registration required, fee based on usage. Also, see note at beginning of section.

Fergus County *Property, Real estate Recording, Deed Records*
Access recorded land data at www.etitlesearch.com; registration required, fee based on usage. Also, see note at beginning of section.

Gallatin County *Property, Assessor, Treasurer, Real Estate Recording, Deed Records*
www.gallatin.mt.gov/index.htm
Name search at the county site at www.gallatin.mt.gov/GIS/index.htm or on the statewide Cadastral database free at http://gis.mt.gov (incomplete revenue tax records). Also, access to the treasurer's property tax data is free at www.gallatin.mt.gov/webtax/default.asp. Also, access recording office land data at www.etitlesearch.com; registration required, fee based on usage.

Granite County *Property, Real Estate Recording, Deed Records*
Access recorded land data at www.etitlesearch.com; registration required, fee based on usage. Also, see note at beginning of section.

Judith Basin County *Property, Real Estate Recording, Deed Records*
Access recorded land data at www.etitlesearch.com; registration required, fee based on usage. Also, see note at beginning of section.

Lake County *Property, Real Estate Recording, Deed Records*
www.lakecounty-mt.org
Access recorded land data at www.etitlesearch.com; registration required, fee based on usage. Also, see note at beginning of section.

Lewis and Clark County *Grantor/Grantee, Real Estate, Lien, Recording, Property Records*
www.co.lewis-clark.mt.us
Search Grantor/Grantee index and recorder records free at http://records.co.lewis-clark.mt.us/icris/splash.jsp. Registration, logon and password required. This new automation includes document imaging via subscription online service. Records go back to 4/2001. Also, see note at beginning of section.

Lincoln County *Property, Real Estate Recording, Deed Records*
Access recorded land data at www.etitlesearch.com; registration required, fee based on usage. Also, see note at beginning of section.

Madison County *Property, Real Estate Recording, Deed Records*
Access recorded land data at www.etitlesearch.com; registration required, fee based on usage. Also, see note at beginning of section.

Mineral County *Property, Real Estate Recording, Deed Records*
Access recorded land data at www.etitlesearch.com; registration required, fee based on usage. Also, see note at beginning of section.

Missoula County *Property, Assessor, Real Estate Recording, Deed Records*
www.co.missoula.mt.us
Access the county property information system free at www.co.missoula.mt.us/owner/. No name searching at this time. Also, access recording office land data at www.etitlesearch.com; registration required, fee based on usage. Also, see note at beginning of section.

Ravalli County *Property, Real Estate, Recording, Deed Records*
www.ravallicounty.mt.gov/county/clerk&recorder.htm
Access property tax/recorded document info at www.ravallicounty.mt.gov/clerkrecorder/access.htm. Also, access recording office land data at www.etitlesearch.com; registration required, fee based on usage. Also, see note at beginning of section.

Sheridan County *Property, Parcel Records*
www.co.sheridan.mt.us
Access the parcel look-ups page at http://gis.doa.state.mt.us/index.html. Also, see note at beginning of section.

Yellowstone County *Assessor, Tax, Grantor/Grantee, Property Records*
www.co.yellowstone.mt.us/clerk
Access the county clerk & recorder document searches free at https://secure.co.yellowstone.mt.us/clerk/secure_search.asp. Also, access tax assessor records free at www.co.yellowstone.mt.us/gis. Also, see note at beginning of section.

Federal Courts in Montana...

Standards for Federal Courts: The universal PACER sign-up number is 800-676-6856. Find PACER and the Party/Case Index on the Web at http://pacer.psc.uscourts.gov. PACER dial-up access is $.60 per minute. Also, courts offering internet access via PACER, Web-PACER or the new CM-ECF charge $.08 per page fee ($.07 per page if record is pre-2005 or unless noted as free).

US District Court -- District of Montana
www.mtd.uscourts.gov
PACER: Case records are available back to 1992. Records are purged never. New records are available online after 1 day. **Electronic Filing:** CM/ECF data at https://ecf.mtd.uscourts.gov. **Other Online Access:** Access calendars at www.mtd.uscourts.gov.
Billings Division counties: Big Horn, Carbon, Carter, Custer, Daniels, Dawson, Fallon, Garfield, Golden Valley, McCone, Musselshell, Park, Petroleum, Powder River, Prairie, Richland, Rosebud, Sheridan, Stillwater, Sweet Grass, Treasure, Wheatland, Wibaux, Yellowstone, Yellowstone National Park.
Butte Division counties: Beaverhead, Deer Lodge, Gallatin, Madison, Silver Bow.
Great Falls Division counties: Blaine, Cascade, Chouteau, Daniels, Fergus, Glacier, Hill, Judith Basin, Liberty, Phillips, Pondera, Roosevelt, Sheridan, Teton, Toole, Valley.
Helena Division counties: Broadwater, Jefferson, Lewis and Clark, Meagher, Powell.
Missoula Division counties: Flathead, Granite, Lake, Lincoln, Mineral, Missoula, Ravalli, Sanders.

US Bankruptcy Court -- District of Montana
www.mtb.uscourts.gov
PACER: Case records are available back to 1986. New records are available online after 1 day. **PACER Online Access:** ECF replaces PACER. **Electronic Filing:** Calendars on ECF. CM/ECF data at https://ecf.mtb.uscourts.gov. **Opinions:** Judge's Decisions posted here are selected by the judges to inform the public. View court opinions at www.mtb.uscourts.gov/mtb_opinions.asp. **Other Online Access:** Court now participates in the U.S. party case index. **Phone access:** Voice Case Information System, call 888-879-0071, 406-782-1060.
All counties in Montana.

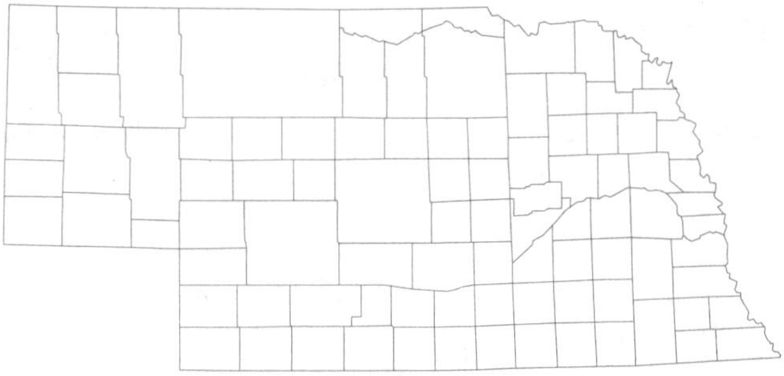

Nebraska

Capital: Lincoln
                 Lancaster County
Time Zone: CST
> Nebraska's nineteen western-most counties are MST. They are:
> Arthur, Banner, Box Butte, Chase, Cherry, Cheyenne, Dawes, Deuel, Dundy, Garden, Grant,
> Hooker, Keith, Kimball, Morrill, Perkins, Scotts Bluff, Sheridan, Sioux.

Population: 1,747,214
# of Counties: 93

Quick Links

Website: www.nebraska.gov/index.phtml

Governor: http://gov.nol.org

Attorney General: www.ago.state.ne.us

State Archives: www.nebraskahistory.org

State Statutes and Codes: http://statutes.unicam.state.ne.us/

Legislative Bill Search: www.unicam.state.ne.us

Bill Monitoring: www.nebraska.gov/billtracker/

Unclaimed Funds: www.treasurer.state.ne.us/ie/uphome2.asp

State Level ... Major Agencies

Statewide Court Records

Court Administrator, PO Box 98910, Lincoln, NE 68509-8910 (Courier: 1213 State Capitol Building, Lincoln, NE 68509); 402-471-3730, Fax-402-471-2197, 8AM-4:30PM.
http://court.nol.org/AOC/index.html
Online search: An online access subscription service is available for NE District and County courts, except Douglas County District Court. Case details, all party listings, payments and actions taken for criminal, civil, probate, juvenile, and traffic is available. Users must be registered with Nebraska.gov, there is a start-up fee. The fee is $.60 per record or a flat rate of $300.00 per month. Go to www.nebraska.gov/faqs/justice/ for more info and how far back records go per county. Supreme Court opinions are available from http://court.nol.org/opinions/.

Sexual Offender Registry

Nebraska State Patrol, Sexual Offender Registry, PO Box 94907, Lincoln, NE 68509-4907 (Courier: 1500 Nebraska Highway 2, Lincoln, NE 68502); 402-471-8647, Fax-402-471-8496, 8AM-5PM.
www.nsp.state.ne.us/sor/
Online search: A Level 3 sexual offender registry search is available at the website. The records may be searched by either ZIP Code, last name, city, or county. Search or review the entire list of names.

Incarceration Records

Nebraska Department of Correctional Services, Central Records Office, PO Box 94661, Lincoln, NE 68509-4661; 402-479-5765, Fax-402-479-5913, 8AM-5PM.
www.corrections.state.ne.us
Online search: Click on Inmate Records at the website for a search of inmates incarcerated after 1977. Also, a private company offers free web access at www.vinelink.com/index.jsp; includes state, DOC, and county jails.

Corporation, Limited Liability Company, Limited Partnerships, Trade Names, Trademarks/Servicemarks

Secretary of State, Corporation Commission, 1301 State Capitol Bldg, Lincoln, NE 68509; 402-471-4079, Fax-402-471-3666, 8-5PM. www.sos.state.ne.us/business/corp_serv/
Online search: There are two levels of service. The free lookup at https://www.nebraska.gov/sos/corp/corpsearch.cgi?nav=search provides general information to obtain information on the status of corporations and other business entities registered in this state. The state has designated Nebraska.gov (800-747-8177) to facilitate online retrieval of records. This access to records requires fees and the lookup can be accessed from the same webpage. **Other options:** Nebrask@ Online has the capability of offering database purchases.

Uniform Commercial Code, Federal Tax Liens, State Tax Liens

UCC Division, Secretary of State, Rm 1301, PO Box 95104, Lincoln, NE 68509-5104 (Courier: 1301 State Capitol Bldg, 1445 "K" Street, Lincoln, NE 68509); 402-471-4080, Fax-402-471-4429, 7:30AM-5PM.
www.sos.state.ne.us/business/ucc/
Online search: Access is outsourced to Nebraska.gov To set an account, go to www.nebraska.gov/subscribe.phtml. The system is available 24 hours daily. There is an annual $50.00 fee in addition to charges to view records. Call 800-747-8177 for more information. **Other options:** Check with Nebrask@ Online for bulk purchase programs.

Birth, Death, Marriage, Divorce Certificates

Health & Human Services System, Vital Statistics Section, PO Box 95065, Lincoln, NE 68509-5065 (Courier: 1050 N St, Lincoln, NE 68508-2126); 402-471-2871, 402-471-6440, Fax-402-471-8230, 8AM-5PM.
www.hhs.state.ne.us/ced/nevrinfo.htm
Online search: Records may be ordered online from the Internet site or from www.vitalchek.com .

Workers' Compensation Records

Workers' Compensation Court, PO Box 98908, Lincoln, NE 68509-8908 (Courier: State Capitol, 13th Floor, Lincoln, NE 68509); 402-471-6468, 800-599-5155 (In-state), Fax-402-471-2700, 8AM-5PM.
www.wcc.ne.gov
Online search: Access to this Court's orders and decisions is available from the website. Note this is not access to records. Email requests accepted at newcc@wcc.ne.gov.

Driver Records

Department of Motor Vehicles, Driver & Vehicle Records Division, PO Box 94789, Lincoln, NE 68509-4789 (Courier: 301 Centennial Mall, S, Lincoln, NE 68509); 402-471-3918, Fax-402-471-8694, 8AM-5PM.
www.dmv.state.ne.us
Online search: Nebraska outsources all online and tape record requests through Nebrask.gov at www.nebraska.gov/subscribe.phtml or call 800-747-8177. The system is interactive and open 24 hours a day, 7 days a week. Fee is $3.00 per record. There is an annual fee of $50.00 and a $.12 per minute connect fee or no connect fee if through the Internet.

Vehicle Ownership, Vehicle Identification, Vessel Ownership

Department of Motor Vehicles, Driver & Vehicle Records Division, PO Box 94789, Lincoln, NE 68509-4789 (Courier: 301 Centennial Mall, S, Lincoln, NE 68509); 402-471-3918, Fax-402-471-8694, 8AM-5PM.
www.dmv.state.ne.us
Online search: Electronic access is through Nebraska.gov at www.nebraska.gov/subscribe.phtml. There is a start-up fee addition to the $1.00 per record fee. The system is open 24 hours a day, 7 days a week. Call 800-747-8177 for more information. **Other options:** Bulk requesters must be authorized by state officials. Purpose of the request and subsequent usage are reviewed. For more information, call 402-471-3885.

Voter Registration

Secretary of State, Elections Division-Records, PO Box 94608, Lincoln, NE 68509; 402-471-2554 x2, 402-471-3237 (Fax), 8-5PM.
www.sos.state.ne.us/Elections/election.htm
Online search: No online access available.   **Other options:** Current law dictates the database can only be sold for political purposes and not for commercial purposes. A CD can be purchased for $500.

State Level ... Occupational Licensing

Abstracting Company	www.abe.state.ne.us/local/company_search.phtml
Abstractor	www.abe.state.ne.us/local/license_search.phtml
Adult Day Care	www.hhs.state.ne.us/crl/rosters.htm
Alcohol/Drug Testing	www.hhs.state.ne.us/lis/lis.asp
Animal Technician	www.hhs.state.ne.us/lis/lis.asp
Architect	www.ea.state.ne.us/search/arch.htm
Asbestos-related Occupation	www.hhs.state.ne.us/lis/lis.asp
Assisted Living Facility	www.hhs.state.ne.us/crl/rosters.htm
Athletic Trainer	www.hhs.state.ne.us/lis/lis.asp
Attorney	www.nebar.com/index.htm
Bank	www.ndbf.org/searches/fisearch.shtml
Barber School	www.barbers.state.ne.us/
Check Sales	www.ndbf.org/searches/fisearch.shtml
Child Care Ctr/Child Placing Agency	www.hhs.state.ne.us/crl/rosters.htm
Chiropractor	www.hhs.state.ne.us/lis/lis.asp
Collection Agency	www.sos.state.ne.us/business/collection/col_agn.html
Cosmetologist/Cosmetology Salon/School	www.hhs.state.ne.us/lis/lis.asp
Credit Union	www.ndbf.org/searches/fisearch.shtml
Debt Management Agency	www.sos.state.ne.us/business/debt_list.html
Delayed Deposit Service	www.ndbf.org/searches/fisearch.shtml
Dental Anesthesia Permit	www.hhs.state.ne.us/lis/lis.asp
Dentist/Dental Hygienist	www.hhs.state.ne.us/lis/lis.asp
Developmentally Disabled Center	www.hhs.state.ne.us/crl/rosters.htm
Drug Distributor, Wholesale	www.hhs.state.ne.us/crl/rosters.htm
Drug Wholesale Facility	www.hhs.state.ne.us/crl/rosters.htm
Electrologist	www.hhs.state.ne.us/lis/lis.asp
Electrology Facility	www.hhs.state.ne.us/lis/lis.asp
Embalmer	www.hhs.state.ne.us/lis/lis.asp
Emergency Medical Care Facility	www.hhs.state.ne.us/lis/lis.asp
Engineer	www.ea.state.ne.us/search/
Environmental Health Specialists	www.hhs.state.ne.us/lis/lis.asp
Esthetician/Esthetician Establishment	www.hhs.state.ne.us/lis/lis.asp
Fund Transmission	www.ndbf.org/searches/fisearch.shtml
Funeral Director/Establishment	www.hhs.state.ne.us/lis/lis.asp
Geologist	www.geology.state.ne.us/board/roster.pdf
Health Clinic	www.hhs.state.ne.us/lis/lis.asp
Hearing Aid Dispenser/Fitter	www.hhs.state.ne.us/lis/lis.asp
Home Health Agency	www.hhs.state.ne.us/crl/rosters.htm
Hospice	www.hhs.state.ne.us/crl/rosters.htm
Hospital	www.nlc.state.ne.us/docs/pilot/pubs/h.html
Insurance Agency/Agent/Broker/Producer	www.doi.ne.gov/appointments/search/index.cgi
Insurance Company/Consultant	www.doi.ne.gov/appointments/search/index.cgi
Intermediate Care Facility (Mental Ret'd)	www.hhs.state.ne.us/crl/rosters.htm
Investigator, Plainclothes	www.sos.state.ne.us/business/private_eye/pi_list.html
Investment Advisor/Advisor Rep	www.ndbf.org/searches/fisearch.shtml
Labor/Delivery Service/Clinic	www.hhs.state.ne.us/crl/rosters.htm
Laboratory	www.hhs.state.ne.us/crl/rosters.htm
Landscape Architect	www.landarch.state.ne.us/registrants.pdf
Lead Abatement Worker, etc.	www.hhs.state.ne.us/lis/lis.asp
Liquor Retailers/ Wholse/ Shippers	www.lcc.ne.gov/license_search/licsearch.cgi
Lobbyist	www.unicam.state.ne.us
Local Anesthesia Certification	www.hhs.state.ne.us/lis/lis.asp
Long Term Care Center	www.hhs.state.ne.us/crl/rosters.htm

Marriage & Family Therapist .... www.hhs.state.ne.us/lis/lis.asp
Massage Establishment/Therapy School..... www.hhs.state.ne.us/lis/lis.asp
Medical Doctor .... www.hhs.state.ne.us/lis/lis.asp
Mental Health Center................................. www.hhs.state.ne.us/lis/lis.asp
Mentally Retarded Care Service .... www.hhs.state.ne.us/crl/rosters.htm
Nail Technologist...................................... www.hhs.state.ne.us/lis/lis.asp
Notary Public .... www.sos.state.ne.us
Nurse... www.hhs.state.ne.us/lis/lis.asp
Nursing Home... www.hhs.state.ne.us/lis/lis.asp
Nursing Home Administrator...................... www.hhs.state.ne.us/lis/lis.asp
Nutrition Therapy, Medical......................... www.hhs.state.ne.us/lis/lis.asp
Occupational Therapist .... www.hhs.state.ne.us/lis/lis.asp
Optometrist .... www.hhs.state.ne.us/lis/lis.asp
Osteopathic Physician................................ www.hhs.state.ne.us/lis/lis.asp
Pesticide Applicator/Dealer .... www.kellysolutions.com/ne/
Pharmacist/Pharmacy................................. www.hhs.state.ne.us/lis/lis.asp
Physical Therapist..................................... www.hhs.state.ne.us/lis/lis.asp
Physician.. www.hhs.state.ne.us/lis/lis.asp
Physician Assistant .... www.hhs.state.ne.us/lis/lis.asp
Podiatrist.. www.hhs.state.ne.us/lis/lis.asp
Polygraph Examiner, Private .... www.sos.state.ne.us/business/poly_pri.html
Polygraph Examiner, Public .... www.sos.state.ne.us/business/poly_pub.html
Preschool .... www.hhs.state.ne.us/crl/rosters.htm
Private Detective....................................... www.sos.state.ne.us/business/private_eye/pd_list.html
Private Detective Agency .... www.sos.state.ne.us/business/private_eye/pd_agenci.html
Psychologist.. www.hhs.state.ne.us/lis/lis.asp
Public Accountant-CPA.............................. www.nbpa.ne.gov/search/index.phtml
Radiographer... www.hhs.state.ne.us/lis/lis.asp
Radon Mitigation Specialist/Technician ..... www.hhs.state.ne.us/lis/lis.asp
Real Estate Agent/Sales/Broker .... http://nrec.nol.org/licinfodb/
Real Estate Appraiser................................. www.appraiser.ne.gov/appraiser/listing/
Rehabilitation Agency .... www.hhs.state.ne.us/crl/rosters.htm
Respiratory Care Practitioner...................... www.hhs.state.ne.us/lis/lis.asp
Respite Care Service .... www.hhs.state.ne.us/crl/rosters.htm
Sales Finance Company .... www.ndbf.org/searches/fisearch.shtml
Saving & Loan... www.ndbf.org/searches/fisearch.shtml
Securities Agent.. www.ndbf.org/searches/fisearch.shtml
Securities Broker/Dealer............................ www.ndbf.org/searches/fisearch.shtml
Social Worker .... www.hhs.state.ne.us/lis/lis.asp
Speech-Language Pathologist/Audiologist . www.hhs.state.ne.us/lis/lis.asp
Substance Abuse Treatment Center .... www.nlc.state.ne.us/docs/pilot/pubs/h.html
Surplus Lines Seller .... www.doi.ne.gov/appointments/search/index.cgi
Surveyor, Land .... www.sso.state.ne.us/bels/
Swimming Pool Operator .... www.hhs.state.ne.us/lis/lis.asp
Trust Company .... www.ndbf.org/searches/fisearch.shtml
Veterinarian/Veterinary Technician............ www.hhs.state.ne.us/lis/lis.asp
Voice Stress Examiner/Analyzer .... www.sos.state.ne.us/business/voice.html
Water Operator .... www.hhs.state.ne.us/lis/lis.asp
Water Treatment Plant Operator .... www.hhs.state.ne.us/lis/lis.asp
Well Driller/Pump Installer......................... www.hhs.state.ne.us/lis/lis.asp
X-ray Unit Portable.................................... www.hhs.state.ne.us/lis/lis.asp

County Level ... Courts

Court Administration: Court Administrator, PO Box 98910, Lincoln, NE, 68509-8910; 402-471-3730;
http://court.nol.org/AOC/

Court Structure: The District Court is the court of general jurisdiction. The minimum on civil judgment matters for District Courts is $51,000. Prior to the current level, historically the state raised the County Court limit on civil matters from $15,000 to $45,000 Sept. 1, 2001. As it is less expensive to file civil cases in County Court than in District Court, civil cases in the $15,000 to $45,000 range are more likely to be found in County Court, after Sept. 1, 2001.

The number of judicial districts went from 21 to the current 12 in July, 1992. County Courts have juvenile jurisdiction in all but 3 counties. Douglas, Lancaster, and Sarpy counties have separate Juvenile Courts.

Online Access Note: An online access subscription service is available for Nebraska District Courts and County courts, except Douglas County District Court. Case details, all party listings, payments, and actions taken for criminal, civil, probate, juvenile, and traffic is available. Users must be registered with Nebrask@Online; there is a start-up fee. The fee is $.60 per record or a flat rate of $300.00 per month. Go to www.nebraska.gov/faqs/justice for more info and how far back records go per county. Supreme Court opinions are available from http://court.nol.org/opinions/ Also, Douglas, Lancaster, and Sarpy county courts offer Internet access with registration and password required; details follow.

All Nebraska Counties (except Douglas, Lancaster, Sarpy Counties)

District Court – County Court – Civil and Criminal Records
Subscribe to NOL at www.nebraska.gov/service_info.phtml?service_id=147 for court access. $.60 a record fee or $300 per month flat rate. Throughput dates for courts varies by jurisdiction. Most County Courts offer traffic records online as well civil and criminal.

Douglas County

District Court – Civil and Criminal Records   www.co.douglas.ne.us
Access to the Internet system at www.co.douglas.ne.us/cpan/index.htm requires registration and password. Call CPAN at 402-444-7117 for more information. System can be searched by name or case number.

Douglas County Court – Civil and Criminal Records   www.co.douglas.ne.us
Access to the Internet system at www.co.douglas.ne.us/cpan/index.htm requires registration and password. Call CPAN at 402-444-7117 for more information. System can be searched by name or case number. Also, subscribe to NOL at www.nebraska.gov/service_info.phtml?service_id=147 for online court access; online criminal and traffic records date from 4/96. Online civil records go back to 10/18/99, probate back to 3/2000.

Lancaster County

District Court – Civil and Criminal Records
www.ci.lincoln.ne.us/cnty/discrt/index.htm
Online on the statewide system; requires a subscription. Visit www.nebraska.gov/service_info.phtml?service_id=147. See note at beginning of section.
Lancaster County Court – Civil and Criminal Records
Access to the Internet system requires registration and password. Call John at 402-471-3049 for more information. Also, there is access via the statewide online system; visit www.nebraska.gov/service_info.phtml?service_id=147. Criminal and traffic records go back to 2/28/95. Civil records go back to 11/16/98, probate back to 5/98.

Sarpy County

District Court – Civil and Criminal Records
Online on the statewide system; requires a subscription. Visit www.nebraska.gov/service_info.phtml?service_id=147. See note at beginning of section.

Sarpy County Court – Civil and Criminal Records
www.sarpy.com
Access to internet system requires registration and password. Call John at 402-471-3049 for more information. System can be searched by name or case number. Also, you may subscribe to NOL at www.nebraska.gov/service_info.phtml?service_id=147 for online court access; criminal and traffic records go back to 8/97. Civil records go back to 10/2000, probate back to 4/99.

County Level ... Recorders & Assessors

Recording Office Organization: 93 counties, 109 recording offices. The recording officers are County Clerk (UCC and some state tax liens) and Register of Deeds (real estate and most tax liens). Most counties have a combined Clerk/Register office, which are designated "County Clerk" in this section. Sixteen counties have separate offices for County Clerk and for Register of Deeds - Adams, Cass, Dakota, Dawson, Dodge, Douglas, Gage, Hall, Lancaster, Lincoln, Madison, Otoe, Platte, Sarpy, Saunders, and Scotts Bluff. In combined offices, the Register of Deeds is frequently a different person from the County Clerk. 74 counties are in the Central Time Zone (CST) and 19 are in the Mountain Time Zone (MST). All federal and some state tax liens are filed with the County Register of Deeds. Some state tax liens on personal property are filed with the County Clerk. Most counties will perform tax lien searches, some as part of a UCC search, and others for a separate fee, usually $3.50 per name in each index. Copy fees vary.

Online Access Note: Nebrask@online offers online access to Secretary of State's UCC database; registration and a usage fee is required. For information, visit www.nebraska.gov/business/egov.phtml.

24 Nebraska Counties *Assessor, Property, Treasurer Records*
Access real estate or personal property data for free at www.nebraskataxesonline.us/. Click on map or Select a County.
Counties Include- Adams, Boone, Box Butte, Cass, Chase, Colfax, Cuming, Dawes, Dawson, Dundy, Gage. Greeley, Hamilton, Keith, Kimball, Lincoln, Madison, Otoe, Phelps, Platte, Scotts Bluff, Seward, Stanton, Thayer.

Butler County *Assessor, Property, GIS Records*
www.co.butler.ne.us/clerk.html
Search Butler County Assessor property data on the GIS site free at http://butler.gisworkshop.com/ButlerIMS/.

Cass County *Assessor, Property, Treasurer, GIS Records*
www.cassne.org
Access county property assessor search site free at www.gis-srv.cassne.org/CassIMSPublic/index.jsp. Also see not at start of section.

Clay County *Sheriff Warrant Records*
www.claycounty.ne.gov
Search county sheriff's warrant list at www.claycounty.ne.gov/content/warrant_list.htm,

Dodge County *Real Estate, Mortgage Records*
www.registerofdeeds.com
Access to Register of Deeds mortgages database is at the website. Registration is required. The site is under development.

Douglas County *Property, Assessor, Marriage Records*
www.co.douglas.ne.us
Assessor to the county assessor property valuation lookup is free at www.dcassessor.org/valuation.html. Search the clerk/comptroller marriage database free at www.co.douglas.ne.us/dept/Clerk/marriagelicense.htm.

Gage County Clerk *Property, Assessor, Treasurer Records*
www.co.gage.ne.us/clerk.html
Access to property information via the county Assessor CIS service is free at http://gage.gisworkshop.com/GageIMS/. Also see not at beginning of section.

Hall County *Real Estate, Grantor/Grantee, Deed, Lien, Judgment, Assessor, Property Tax Records*
www.hcgi.org
Access to the county Register of Deeds Document Search is free at http://deeds.hallcountyne.gov. Also, assessor property data is available free at http://mapsifter.grand-island.com/taxsifter/T-Parcelsearch.asp.

Lancaster County Clerk *Assessor, Property Tax, Dog Tag, Treasurer, Marriage, Accident, Parking Ticket, Building Permit, Warranty Bond, City Clerk Records*
http://interlinc.ci.lincoln.ne.us
Records on the county Assessor Property Information Search database are free at www.dcassessor.org/valuation.html. Search parking tickets at www.ci.lincoln.ne.us/city/finance/treas/tickets.htm. See also Register of Deeds. Also search warranty bonds free by name at

http://ims.lincoln.ne.gov/planning/fwb.jsp. Search Lincoln City accident reports at www.ci.lincoln.ne.us/city/police/stats/acc.htm. Search Lincoln clerk records a www.ci.lincoln.ne.us/asp/city/clerk/DocMan.asp. Also, search treasurer' property info at www.ci.lincoln.ne.us/cnty/treas/property.htm. Search dog tag registrations at www.ci.lincoln.ne.us/city/health/animal/acttag.htm. Search marriages at www.ci.lincoln.ne.us/cnty/clerk/marrsrch.htm

Lancaster County Register of Deeds *Recorder, Deed, Grantor/Grantee, Lien, Judgment Records*
www.mynevadacounty.com/recorder
Search register of deeds Grantor/Grantee index free at http://deeds.lincoln.ne.gov/recorder/eagleweb/login.jsp. Use Public Login or you may register. See also County Clerk for other databases online.

Phelps County *Assessor, Property, GIS Records*
www.phelpsgov.org
Search property records free on the GIS mapping site at www.phelps.gisworkshop.com. Also see not at beginning of section.

Platte County Clerk *Assessor, Property, Treasurer, Warrant Records*
www.plattecounty.net
Access to the sheriff warrant list is free at www.megavision.net/pcsher/Warrant%20List.htm. Also see not at beginning of section.

Sarpy County Clerk *Assessor, Property Records*
www.sarpy.com
Records on the county Property Lookup database are free at www.sarpy.com/assessor/property-search.htm.

Wayne County *Sheriff Sale, Warrant List Records*
http://county.waynene.org
Search the sheriff's sales list and warrant list for free at http://county.waynene.org/County_Offices/Sheriff/.

Federal Courts in Nebraska...

Standards for Federal Courts: The universal PACER sign-up number is 800-676-6856. Find PACER and the Party/Case Index on the Web at http://pacer.psc.uscourts.gov. PACER dial-up access is $.60 per minute. Also, courts offering internet access via PACER, Web-PACER or the new CM-ECF charge $.08 per page fee ($.07 per page if record is pre-2005 or unless noted as free).

US District Court -- District of Nebraska   www.ned.uscourts.gov
PACER: Case records are available back to late 1990. Records are purged yearly. New records are available online after 1 day. **PACER Online Access:** ECF replaces PACER. **Electronic Filing:** CM/ECF data at https://ecf.ned.uscourts.gov. **Opinions:** View court opinions at www.nebar.com/resources/opinions/usdist/index.htm.
Lincoln Division counties: Nebraska cases may be filed in any of 3 courts at the attorney's option, except filings in North Platte Division must be during trial session.
North Platte Division counties: Nebraska cases may be filed in any of 3 courts at the attorney's option, except filings in North Platte Division must be during trial session. Some case records may be in the Omaha Division as well as Lincoln Division.
Omaha Division counties: Nebraska cases may be filed in any of 3 courts at the attorney's option, except filings in North Platte Division must be during trial session.

US Bankruptcy Court -- District of Nebraska   www.neb.uscourts.gov
PACER: Case records are available back to 9/1989. Records are purged every 6 months. New records are available online after 1 day. **PACER Online Access:** ECF replaces PACER. **Electronic Filing:** CM/ECF data at https://ecf.neb.uscourts.gov. **Opinions:** Click on Case Info, then Nebraska Bankruptcy Opinions. View court opinions at www.neb.uscourts.gov. **Phone access:**   Voice Case Information System, call 800-829-0112, 402-221-3757
Lincoln Division counties: Adams, Antelope, Boone, Boyd, Buffalo, Butler, Clay, Colfax, Fillmore, Franklin, Gage, Greeley, Hall, Hamilton, Harlan, Holt, Howard, Jefferson, Johnson, Kearney, Lancaster, Madison, Merrick, Nance, Nemaha, Nuckolls, Otoe, Pawnee, Phelps, Platte, Polk, Richardson, Saline, Saunders, Seward, Sherman, Stanton, Thayer, Webster, Wheeler, York. Cases from the North Platte Division assigned here.
North Platte Division counties: Arthur, Banner, Blaine, Box Butte, Brown, Chase, Cherry, Cheyenne, Custer, Dawes, Dawson, Deuel, Dundy, Frontier, Furnas, Garden, Garfield, Gosper, Grant, Hayes, Hitchcock, Hooker, Keith, Keya Paha, Kimball, Lincoln, Logan, Loup, McPherson, Morrill, Perkins, Red Willow, Rock, Scotts Bluff, Sheridan, Sioux, Thomas, Valley. Cases assigned to Lincoln Division.
Omaha Division counties: Burt, Cedar, Cass, Cuming, Dakota, Dixon, Dodge, Douglas, Knox, Pierce, Sarpy, Thurston, Washington, Wayne.

Nevada

Capital: Carson City
          Carson City County
Time Zone: PST
Population: 2,334,771
# of Counties: 17

Quick Links

Website: www.nv.gov
Governor: http://gov.state.nv.us
Attorney General: http://ag.state.nv.us
State Archives: http://dmla.clan.lib.nv.us/docs/nsla
State Statutes and Codes: www.leg.state.nv.us/NRS/
Legislative Bill Search: www.leg.state.nv.us
Bill Monitoring: https://www.leg.state.nv.us/73rd/Subscriber/
Unclaimed Funds: https://nevadatreasurer.gov/unclaimed/search/

State Level ... Major Agencies

Statewide Court Records

Supreme Court of Nevada, Administrative Office of the Courts, 201 S Carson St, #250, Carson City, NV 89701-4702; 775-684-1700, Fax-775-684-1723, 8AM-5PM.
www.nvsupremecourt.us/index.php
Online search: The Supreme Court website gives access to opinions and decisions. Some Nevada Courts have internal online computer systems, but only Clark and Washoe counties offer online access of a record index to the public. A statewide court automation system is being implemented.

Sexual Offender Registry

Records and Identification Bureau, Sex Offender Registry, 808 W Nye Lane, Carson City, NV 89703; 775-687-1600 x253, Fax-775-687-1844, 8AM-5PM.
www.nvsexoffenders.gov
Online search: Information on the website will include the name, aliases, photograph (where available), conviction information and ZIP Code based on the latest registered address. The website does not contain information on all convicted sex offenders. Information is only provided for sex offenders with a risk assessment score of a TIER Level 3 and certain information regarding a TIER Level 2. Search by name, ZIP Code, or even license plate number.

Incarceration Records

Nevada Department of Corrections, Attn: Records, PO Box 7011, Carson City, NV 89702 (Courier: 5500 Snyder Ave, Bldg 89, Carson City, NV 89701); 775-887-3285, Fax-775-687-6715, 8AM-5PM.
www.doc.nv.gov/ncis/
Online search: There are two ways to access information at the web page. The first is by clicking on Online Inmate Search or www.doc.nv.gov/ncis/search.php. This will allow you to look up information about a particular individual. If you prefer, you may click on Download Information to obtain text files of all the information available via the Inmate Search. This system contains information about current inmates and those discharged in the past 18 months.

Corporation, Limited Partnerships, Limited Liability Company,

Secretary of State, Records, 202 N Carson City, Carson City, NV 89701-4707; 775-684-5708 (Expedite), 800-486-2880 (Customer Srv), Fax-775-684-5645, 8AM-5PM.
www.sos.state.nv.us
Online search: Online access is offered on the Internet site for no charge. You can search by corporate name, resident agent, corporate officers, or by file number.

Uniform Commercial Code, Federal Tax Liens, State Tax Liens

UCC Division, Secretary of State, 200 N Carson St, Carson City, NV 89701-4069; 775-684-5708, Fax-775-684-5630, 8AM-5PM.
www.sos.state.nv.us
Online search: Searching is available from the web, fee is $20.00, an order form may be downloaded. A commercial system is also available. The PC dial-up system fee is based on hourly rate - $6.50 peak time, $4.50 non-peak time. Includes unlimited access. There is a $50.00 minimum deposit. The system is up from 7 AM to 5 PM.

Birth, Death Certificates

Nevada Department of Health, Office of Vital Statistics, 505 E King St, Rm 102, Carson City, NV 89701-4749; 775-684-4242, 775-684-4280 (Message Phone), 877-456-5410 (Orders), Fax-775-684-4156, 8AM-4PM.
http://health2k.state.nv.us
Online search: Expedited service is available from state designated vendor at www.vitalchek.com.

Driver Records

Department of Motor Vehicles, Records Section, 555 Wright Way, Carson City, NV 89711-0250; 775-684-4590, 877-368-7828 (In-state), Fax-775-684-4899, 8AM-5PM.
www.dmvstat.com
Online search: The state has an FTP type online system available for high volume users. All files received by 5:30 PM are processed and returned at 6:30 PM. Fee is $7.00 per record. Call 775-684-4702 for details. A person may order his or her own record at online. Go to https://dmvapp.state.nv.us/OL_DH/Drvr_Usr_Info.aspx. The fee is $7.00.

State Level ... Occupational Licensing

Ambulatory Surgery Ctr. (Pharm)	https://nvbop.glsuite.us/renewal/glsweb/homeframe.aspx
Architect	http://nsbaidrd.state.nv.us/directory.htm
Athletic Promoter, Profess'l/Amateur)	www.boxing.nv.gov/teledir.htm
Attorney	www.nvbar.org/find_a_lawyer.asp
Bank	http://fid.state.nv.us/banks.htm
Boxing Gym	www.boxing.nv.gov/gyms.htm
Boxing Organization	www.boxing.nv.gov/teledir.htm
Building Mover	http://nscb.sierracat.com
Carpentry Contractor	http://nscb.sierracat.com
Check Casher	http://fid.state.nv.us/check-cashing.htm
Chiropractor	http://chirobd.nv.gov/
Collection Agency	http://fid.state.nv.us/collection%20agency.htm
Contractor, General	http://nscb.sierracat.com
Court Reporter, Certified	http://crptr.state.nv.us/contact.htm
Credit Union	http://fid.state.nv.us/credit%20union.htm
Debt Adjuster	http://fid.state.nv.us/debt-adjuster.htm
Deferred Deposit Company	http://fid.state.nv.us/check-cashing.htm
Denied/Unsuitable Gaming Individual	http://gaming.nv.gov/unsuitable.htm
Dentist/Dental Hygienist	www.nvdentalboard.org/database/search.html
Doctor	http://medboard.nv.gov/default.asp
Doctor, Disciplinary Action	http://medboard.nv.gov/Disciplinary%20Actions/disciplinary_list.htm
Drug Wholesaler/Dist./Mfg.	https://nvbop.glsuite.us/renewal/glsweb/homeframe.aspx
Electrical Contractor	http://nscb.sierracat.com
Elevator/Conveyor Related Occupation	http://nscb.sierracat.com
Engineer	http://boe.state.nv.us/ROST_HOME.HTM

Engineering, General .... http://nscb.sierracat.com
Euthanasia Technician (Animal)................ https://nvbop.glsuite.us/renewal/glsweb/homeframe.aspx
Financial Development Company............... http://fid.state.nv.us/development%20co.htm
Fire Protection Contractor.......................... http://nscb.sierracat.com
Fishing Guide... www.ndow.org/about/contacts/
Floor/Tile/Carpet Layer .... http://nscb.sierracat.com
Fur Dealer... www.ndow.org/about/contacts/
Gas Fitter .... http://nscb.sierracat.com
GCB Most-Wanted & Banned List .... http://gaming.nv.gov/unsuitable.htm
Glazier Contractor...................................... http://nscb.sierracat.com
Heating & Air Conditioning Mechanic....... http://nscb.sierracat.com
Hospital Pharmacy, Institutional................ https://nvbop.glsuite.us/renewal/glsweb/homeframe.aspx
Installment Loan Company......................... http://fid.state.nv.us/installment%20loan.htm
Insulation Installer Contr. .... http://nscb.sierracat.com
Insurance Agent .... www.doi.state.nv.us/PL-ContactUs.htm
Interior Designer.. http://nsbaidrd.state.nv.us/directory.htm
Landscape Contractor .... http://nscb.sierracat.com
Lobbyist... www.leg.state.nv.us/lobbyistdb/index.cfm
Marriage & Family Therapist .... http://marriage.state.nv.us/
Mason .... http://nscb.sierracat.com
Medical Device, Equipment or Gas .... https://nvbop.glsuite.us/renewal/glsweb/homeframe.aspx
Medical Doctor .... http://medboard.nv.gov/default.asp
Money Transmitter Agent........................... http://fid.state.nv.us/Qry_MTALicensee.asp
Money Transmitter Company http://fid.state.nv.us/money%20transmitter.htm
Narcotic Treatment Center.......................... https://nvbop.glsuite.us/renewal/glsweb/homeframe.aspx
Nurse Anesthetist.. www.nursingboard.state.nv.us/Verification/formLicense.html
Nurse Assistant .... www.nursingboard.state.nv.us/Verification/formLicense.html
Nurse, Advanced Practitioner (Pharm) .... https://nvbop.glsuite.us/renewal/glsweb/homeframe.aspx
Nurse, Adverse Action Report .... www.nursingboard.state.nv.us/dactions/
Nurse, RN/LPN/Advanced Practice............ www.nursingboard.state.nv.us/Verification/formLicense.html
Optometrist .... http://optometry.nv.gov/roster/licenseeinfo.pdf
Osteopathic Physician................................ https://nvboo.glsuite.us/renewal/glsweb/homeframe.aspx
Osteopathic Physician Assistant .... https://nvboo.glsuite.us/renewal/glsweb/homeframe.aspx
Painter/Paper Hanger .... http://nscb.sierracat.com
Pharmacist/Pharmaceutical Technician....... https://nvbop.glsuite.us/renewal/glsweb/homeframe.aspx
Pharmacy .... https://nvbop.glsuite.us/renewal/glsweb/homeframe.aspx
Physician Assistant .... http://medboard.nv.gov/default.asp
Physician Assistant (Pharm) .... https://nvbop.glsuite.us/renewal/glsweb/homeframe.aspx
Plasterer/Drywall Installer .... http://nscb.sierracat.com
Playground Builder .... http://nscb.sierracat.com
Plumber.. http://nscb.sierracat.com
Podiatrist.. http://podiatry.state.nv.us/
Prison Pharmacy .... https://nvbop.glsuite.us/renewal/glsweb/homeframe.aspx
Private Investigator
  http://ag.state.nv.us/menu/top/who_are_we/faqs/pilb/PUBLIC%20LIST%20FOR%20INTERNET.pdf
Pump Installer.. http://nscb.sierracat.com
Refractory/Firebrick Contr.......................... http://nscb.sierracat.com
Residential Designer .... http://nsbaidrd.state.nv.us/directory.htm
Respiratory Care Practitioner..................... http://medboard.nv.gov/default.asp
Roofer .... http://nscb.sierracat.com
Savings & Loan http://fid.state.nv.us/savings%20and%20loan.htm
Scientific Collector .... www.ndow.org/about/contacts/
Sewerage Contractor .... http://nscb.sierracat.com
Sheet Metal Fabricator............................... http://nscb.sierracat.com
Sign Erector .... http://nscb.sierracat.com
Steel Contractor .... http://nscb.sierracat.com

Surveyor, Land .... http://boe.state.nv.us/ROST_HOME.HTM
Tank Installer, Pressure/Storage .... http://nscb.sierracat.com
Thrift/Trust Company http://fid.state.nv.us/thrift%20company.htm
Water Well Driller .... http://water.nv.gov/Engineering/wd/wd_queries.cfm
Well Driller... http://nscb.sierracat.com
Well Driller/Monitor................................... http://water.nv.gov/Engineering/wd/wd_queries.cfm
Wrecker/Demolisher.................................... http://nscb.sierracat.com

County Level ... Courts

Court Administration: Supreme Court of Nevada, Administrative Office of the Courts, Capitol Complex, 201 S Carson St #250, Carson City, NV, 89701; 775-684-1700; www.nvsupremecourt.us

Court Structure: 17 District Courts are the courts of general jurisdiction and are within 9 judicial districts. Their minimum civil limit raised from $7,500 to $10,000 on Jan 1, 2005. The Justice Courts are named for the township of jurisdiction. Due to their small populations, some townships no longer have Justice Courts. The Justice Courts handle misdemeanor crime and traffic matters, small claims disputes, evictions, and other civil matters less than $10,000. The Justices of the Peace also preside over felony and gross misdemeanor arraignments and conduct preliminary hearings to determine if sufficient evidence exists to hold criminals for trial at District Court.

Probate is handled by the District Courts.

Online Access Note: Some Nevada courts have internal online computer systems, but only Clark and Washoe counties offer online access to the public. A statewide court automation system is being implemented. The Supreme Court website gives access to opinions.

Many Clark County Justice Courts and Municipal Courts offer current court calendars at http://redrock.co.clark.nv.us/jcCalendar/CalendarSearch.aspx

Clark County

8th Judicial District Court – Civil and Criminal Records
www.co.clark.nv.us/district_court/courthome.htm
Records from the court are free online at http://courtgate.coca.co.clark.nv.us:8490. Search by case number or party name. Family Law and Probate also available.

Washoe County

2nd Judicial District Court – Civil and Criminal Records
www.washoecourts.com
CourtConnect online access is at the website. Data in CourtConnect limited to cases filed after 1/2000. Calendars also free at website.

County Level ... Recorders & Assessors

Recording Office Organization: 16 counties and one independent city, 17 recording offices. The recording officer is the County Recorder. Carson City has a separate filing office. The entire state is in the Pacific Time Zone (PST). Federal tax liens on personal property of businesses are filed with the Secretary of State. Federal tax liens on personal property of individuals are filed with the County Recorder. Although not called state tax liens, employment withholding judgments have the same effect and are filed with the County Recorder. Most counties will provide tax lien searches for a fee of $15.00 per name - $20.00 if the standard UCC request form is not used.

Online Access Note: A number of counties have searchable databases online. A private company, GoverNet, offers online access to Assessor, Treasurer, Recorder and other county databases. Registration is required; sliding monthly and per-hit fees apply. Counties online are Churchill, Clark, Elko, Esmeralda, Eureka, Humboldt, Lander, Lyon, Mineral, Nye, Pershing, Storey, Washoe, and White Pine. System includes access to Secretary of State's Corporation, Partnership, UCC, Fictitious Name, and Federal Tax Lien records. For more information, visit www.governet.net/SurfNV/ or call 208-522-1225.

Editor's Note: While several Nevada state agencies have offices in both Las Vegas and in the Carson City area, the agencys' online records include the entire state.

Carson City *Assessor, Recorder, Treasurer, Real Estate, Marriage, Vital Statistic Records*
www.carson-city.nv.us/clerk
Access is on goverNet (www.governet.net/surfnv) 208-522-1225; requires registration and fees; see beginning of this section. Also, you may search the city clerk-recorder documents for free at http://207.228.41.46/jwalk/docindex.html. Marriage records are free at http://207.228.41.46/jwalk/marriage.html.

Churchill County *Assessor, Property, Recording, Grantor/Grantee, Deed, Judgment, UCC, Lien Records*
www.churchillcounty.org/recorder/
Access recorder records at www.churchillcounty.org/recorder/. Also, access assessor property records free at www.churchillcounty.org/assessor/ Go to www.vitalchek.com for vital records.

Clark County *Real Estate, Lien, Deed, UCC, Vital Statistic, Marriage, Property Assessor, Fictitious Name, Business License, Inmate, Voter Registration Records*
www.co.clark.nv.us/recorder/recindex.htm
Property records, assessor maps, manufactured housing and road documents on the county Assessor database are free at www.co.clark.nv.us/assessor/Disclaim.htm. Search inmates at www.vinelink.com/welcome.jsp?siteID=29004. Marriages: www.co.clark.nv.us/recorder/mar_srch.htm. Property owners on GIS at http://gisgate.co.clark.nv.us. Business licenses: http://sandgate.co.clark.nv.us/businessLicense/businessSearch/blindex.asp. Voters at www.co.clark.nv.us/election/Lookup.asp. Recorder's real estate, UCC and vital records are free at www.co.clark.nv.us/recorder/recindex.htm. UCCs go back to 1986; liens to '84. Search county fictitious names at http://sandgate.co.clark.nv.us:8498/clarkcounty/clerk/clerkSearch.html.

Douglas County *Assessor, Real Estate, Property Tax, Recorder, Deed Records*
http://recorder.co.douglas.nv.us
Property records on the Assessor's database are free at www.co.douglas.nv.us/databases/assessors. Also, the clerk/treasurer property tax database is free at www.co.douglas.nv.us/databases/treasurers/. Also, search the recorder's document files for free at www.co.douglas.nv.us/databases/recorders/ Records go back to 1/1/1983.

Elko County *Assessor, Treasurer, Recording, Marriage, Personal Property, Property Tax Records*
Access to the recorder database including marriages is free at www.elkocountynv.net/recorder.htm. Recording records go back to 1984. Access to the assessors database including personal property is free at www.elkocountynv.net/assessor.htm. Also, access no longer via the GoverNet system.

Esmeralda County *Assessor, Treasurer, Recording, State UCC, Assessor, Proeprty Tax Records*
Access is on goverNet (www.governet.net/surfnv) 208-522-1225; requires registration and fees; see beginning of this section. Also, access the assessment roll free at www.accessesmeralda.com/Assessor.htm. Click on Assessment Roll.

Eureka County *Assessor, Treasurer, Recorder, Deed, Lien, Judgment, Vital Statistic Records*
www.co.eureka.nv.us
Assess to the recorders index is free at http://207.212.113.130/docindex.html. Search the treasurer's secured property tax roll at http://207.212.113.130/taxcoll.html. Search the assessor property data at http://207.212.113.130/assessor.html. Also, access is on goverNet (www.governet.net/surfnv) 208-522-1225; requires registration, fees; see beginning of this section. Not updated regularly.

Humboldt County *Inmate Records*
www.hcnv.us
Access the Sheriff's inmate list is free at www.hcsonv.com.

Lander County *Assessor, Recorder Records*
Access is on goverNet (www.governet.net/surfnv) 208-522-1225; requires registration and fees; see note at beginning of this section.

Lyon County   *Assessor, Recorder, Treasurer, Real Estate, UCC Records*

www.lyon-county.org/recorder/

Access recorder records free at www.lyon-county.org/recorder/; records go back to 11/15/1999. Also, access is on goverNet (www.governet.net/surfnv) 208-522-1225; requires registration and fees; see beginning of this section.

Mineral County   *Assessor, Treasurer, Recording Records*

Access is on goverNet (www.governet.net/surfnv) 208-522-1225; requires registration and fees; see beginning of this section.

Nye County   *Assessor, Treasurer, Recording, Deed Records*

Access is on goverNet at www.governet.net/surfnv, phone 208-522-1225; requires registration and fees; see beginning of this section. Also, search for property assessor data for free at www.nyecounty.net/assess/ver2/.

Pershing County
Assessor, Treasurer, Recording, Real Estate, Deed, Lien, UCC, Building Permit, Occ. License Records
Access is on goverNet at www.governet.net/surfnv - 208-522-1225; requires registration and fees; see beginning of this section.

Storey County   *Assessor, Treasurer, Recording Records*

Access is on goverNet (www.governet.net/surfnv) 208-522-1225; requires registration and fees; see beginning of this section. This office warns that the database is information only, is not up-to-date nor is audited.

Washoe County   *Assessor, Treasurer, Recording, Grantor/Grantee, Real Estate, Inmate, Voter Registration, Property Sales, Property Tax, Aircraft, Business Personal Property, Mobile/Manufactured Home Records*

www.co.washoe.nv.us/recorder

Access is on goverNet (www.governet.net/surfnv) 208-522-1225; requires registration & fees, copies made for free; see beginning of this section. Search aircraft, business property, mobile home data free at www.co.washoe.nv.us/assessor/index.htm Also, access grantor/grantee index free at www.co.washoe.nv.us/recorder/icrisdisclaimer.html; a $1.00 per page fee for documents. Download property sales 2003-2005 data free at www.co.washoe.nv.us/assessor/SalesRpt.htm. Search inmate info on private website-www.vinelink.com/index.jsp. Search voter registration roll at www.co.washoe.nv.us/voters/regsearch.php~color=grey&text_version=. Property tax data at www.co.washoe.nv.us/assessor/cama/search.php.

White Pine County   *Assessor, Recorder Records*

Access is on goverNet (www.governet.net/surfnv) 208-522-1225; requires registration and fees; see beginning of this section.

Federal Courts in Nevada...

Standards for Federal Courts: The universal PACER sign-up number is 800-676-6856. Find PACER and the Party/Case Index on the Web at http://pacer.psc.uscourts.gov. PACER dial-up access is $.60 per minute. Also, courts offering internet access via PACER, Web-PACER or the new CM-ECF charge $.08 per page fee ($.07 per page if record is pre-2005 or unless noted as free).

US District Court -- District of Nevada

www.nvd.uscourts.gov

PACER: PACER Online Access: PACER online at https://pacer.psc.uscourts.gov/cgi-bin/login/login.pl?court_id=nvdc. Document images available. **Electronic Filing:** CM/ECF data at (Currently in the process of implementing CM/ECF).
Las Vegas Division counties: Clark, Esmeralda, Lincoln, Nye.
Reno Division counties: Carson City, Churchill, Douglas, Elko, Eureka, Humboldt, Lander, Lyon, Mineral, Pershing, Storey, Washoe, White Pine.

US Bankruptcy Court -- District of Nevada

www.nvb.uscourts.gov

PACER: Case records are available back to 9/1993. Records are purged every 16 months. New records are available online after 1 day. **PACER Online Access:** ECF replaces PACER. **Electronic Filing:** CM/ECF data at https://ecf.nvb.uscourts.gov. **Other Online Access:** Searching records online using RACER has been phased out; ECF account is now required. **Phone access:** Voice Case Information System, call 800-314-3436, 702-388-6708
Las Vegas Division counties: Clark, Esmeralda, Lincoln, Nye.
Reno Division counties: Carson City, Churchill, Douglas, Elko, Eureka, Humboldt, Lander, Lyon, Mineral, Pershing, Storey, Washoe, White Pine.

New Hampshire

Capital: Concord
            MerrimackCounty
Time Zone: EST
Population: 1,299,500
# of Counties: 10

Quick Links

Website: www.state.nh.us
Governor: www.nh.gov/governor/
Attorney General: http://doj.nh.gov
State Archives: www.sos.nh.gov/archives/
State Statutes and Codes: http://gencourt.state.nh.us/rsa/html/indexes/default.html
Legislative Bill Search: http://gencourt.state.nh.us/index/
Unclaimed Funds: www.state.nh.us/treasury/Divisions/AP/APsearch2.htm

State Level ... Major Agencies

Statewide Court Records

Administrative Office of Courts, 2 Noble Dr, Supreme Ct Bldg, Concord, NH 03301-6160; 603-271-2521, Fax-603-271-3977, 8-5PM.
www.courts.state.nh.us
Online search: While there is no statewide access available for trial court records, the web page has a lot of useful information. Opinions and directives from the Supreme Court, Superior Courts, and District Courts can be accessed from www.courts.state.nh.us/supreme/index.htm

Sexual Offender Registry

State Police Headquarters, Special Investigations Unit-SOR, James H. Hayes Bldg, 33 Hazen Dr, Concord, NH 03305; 603-271-2538, Fax-603-271-6479, 8:15AM-4:15PM.
www.egov.nh.gov/nsor/
Online search: For web access, click on the Offenders Against Children link. This list only contains certain information about registered offenders who have committed certain criminal offenses against children. The list also contains outstanding arrest warrants for any sexual offender or offender against children who did not register.

Corporation, Limited Partnership, Limited Liability Company, Trademarks/Servicemarks, Trade Names, Limited Liability Partnerships, Not For Profit Entities

Secretary of State, Corporation Division, 107 N Main St, Concord, NH 03301-4989 (Courier: State House Annex Room 341, 25 Capitol Street, 3rd Floor, Concord, NH 03301); 603-271-3246, 603-271-3244, 603-271-8200 (Order Annual Report), Fax-603-271-3247, 8:30AM-3:30PM.
www.sos.nh.gov/corporate
Online search: A free business name lookup is available at the website. The agency may convert to a new system that will allow purchase of copies and certificates online. **Other options:** Corporation, LLC, or trade name monthly Excel files are $50.00 each or $500.00 for a 1 year subscription. A list of all non-profits on file is available for $250.00.

Uniform Commercial Code, Federal Tax Liens, State Tax Liens

UCC Division, Secretary of State, 107 N Main St, Concord, NH 03301-4989 (Courier: 25 Capitol St, State House Annex, 3rd Floor, Concord, NH 03301); 603-271-3276, 9AM-3:30PM (searches).
www.sos.nh.gov/ucc/index.html
Online search: Visit https://www.sos.nh.gov/uccegov/ for commercial online access to records. Accounts may be established using either automated clearing house (ACH) debit account or credit card. The fee is $27.00 per debtor name, or for $5,000.00 subscription fee unlimited online searches for available for one full year. Users can apply for an ACH (Automated Clearing House) account to be used as a payment option for filings or search.

Birth Death, Marriage, Divorce Certificates

Office of Community and Public Health, Bureau of Vital Records, 29 Hazen Dr, Concord, NH 03301-6527; 603-271-4650, 603-271-4654 (Recording), 800-852-3345 x4651 (In-state), Fax-603-223-6614, 8:30AM-4PM.
www.sos.nh.gov/vitalrecords/index.html
Online search: Records may be ordered online from www.vitalchek.com.

Driver Records

Department of Motor Vehicles, Driving Records, 23 Hazen Dr, Concord, NH 03305; 603-271-2322, 8:15AM-4:15PM.
www.nh.gov/safety/dmv/
Online search: Online access and FTP (file transfer protocal) is offered for approved commercial accounts. Searches are by license number or by name and DOB. Fee is $8.00 per record. For more information, call the Director's Office.

State Level ... Occupational Licensing

Architect	www.state.nh.us/jtboard/arlist.htm
Bank/Bank Holding Company	www.nh.gov/banking/banking.html
Bank, Cooperative	www.nh.gov/banking/banking.html
Banking Service Unit	www.nh.gov/banking/banking.html
Cash Dispensing Machine, Non-bank	www.nh.gov/banking/banking.html
Credit Union	www.nh.gov/banking/banking.html
Debt Adjuster	www.nh.gov/banking/consumer.html
Drug Wholesaler/Manufacturer	www.state.nh.us/pharmacy/NH%20Wholesaler%20List.html
Electrician, Master/Journey'n/Apprentice	http://nhlicenses.nh.gov/WebLookUp/
Engineer	http://nh.neinetwork.com/cgi-bin/professional/nhprof/search.pl
Forester	www.state.nh.us/jtboard/forlist.htm
Geologist	http://nh.neinetwork.com/cgi-bin/professional/nhprof/search.pl
High/Medium Voltage Electrician/Trainee	http://nhlicenses.nh.gov/WebLookUp/
Liquor Keg Shipper, Direct	www.nh.gov/liquor/direct_shippers.shtml
Liquor Product	www.nh.gov/liquor/pllicen.shtml
Liquor Stores	www.state.nh.us/liquor/stores.shtml
Loan Company, Small	www.nh.gov/banking/consumer.html
Lobbyist	www.sos.nh.gov/lobbyist%20information.htm
Marital Mediator	www.nh.gov/marital/mediators.htm
Midwife	www.cfmidwifery.org/states/states.asp?ST=38
Mortgage (1st) Banker, Non-Depository	www.nh.gov/banking/consumer.html
Mortgage Servicer	www.nh.gov/banking/consumer.html
Motor Vehicle Financer	www.nh.gov/banking/consumer.html
Motor Vehicle Retailer	www.nh.gov/banking/consumer.html
Nurse, LPN/Practical/Advanced	www.nhlicenses.nh.gov/WebLookUp/
Nursing Assistant	www.nhlicenses.nh.gov/WebLookUp/
Optometrist	www.arbo.org/index.php?action=findanoptometrist
Pharmacist	www.state.nh.us/pharmacy/NH%20Pharmacist%20List.html
Pharmacy	www.state.nh.us/pharmacy/NH%20Pharmacy%20List.html
Pharmacy Technician	www.state.nh.us/pharmacy/NH%20Tech%20List.html
Pharmacy, Mail Order	www.state.nh.us/pharmacy/NH%20Mail-Order%20List.html

Physician.. http://pierce.state.nh.us/MedicineBoard/licensecode.asp
Public Health Clinic.................................... www.state.nh.us/pharmacy/NH%20Clinic%20List.html
Real Estate Agent/Sales/Broker/Firm .... www.nhlicenses.nh.gov/WebLookUp/
Real Estate Appraiser................................. www.asc.gov
Savings Bank .... www.nh.gov/banking/banking.html
Scientist, Natural....................................... http://nh.neinetwork.com/cgi-bin/professional/nhprof/search.pl
Scientist, Wetlands.................................... http://nh.neinetwork.com/cgi-bin/professional/nhprof/search.pl
Surveyor, Land .... www.state.nh.us/jtboard/lsis.htm
Trust Company .... www.nh.gov/banking/banking.html

County Level ... Courts

Court Administration: Administrative Office of the Courts, Supreme Court Bldg, Noble Dr, Concord, NH, 03301; 603-271-2521; www.courts.state.nh.us

Court Structure: The Superior Court is the court of General Jurisdiction. Felony cases include Class A misdemeanors.

The District Court upper civil limit was increased to $25,000 from $10,000 on 1/1/93. Filing a civil case in the monetary "overlap" area between the Superior Court minimum and the District Court maximum is at the discretion of the filer.

The municipal courts have been closed as the judges retire. The caseload and records are absorbed by the nearest District Court.

Online Access Note: While there is no statewide access available for trial court records, www.courts.state.nh.us has useful information including opinions and directives from the Supreme Court, Superior Courts, and District Courts; search at www.courts.state.nh.us/search/index.htm

There are no known courts that independently offer access to their records.

County Level ... Recorders & Assessors

Recording Office Organization: 238 cities/towns and 10 counties, 10 recording offices and 242 UCC filing offices. The recording officers are Town/City Clerk (UCC) and Register of Deeds (real estate only). Each town/city profile indicates the county in which the town/city is located. Be careful to distinguish the following names that are identical for both a town/city and a county - Grafton, Hillsborough, Merrimack, Strafford, and Sullivan. Many towns are so small that their mailing addresses are within another town. The following unincorporated towns do not have a Town Clerk, so all liens are located at the corresponding county: Cambridge (Coos), Dicksville (Coos), Green's Grant (Coos), Hale's Location (Carroll), Millsfield (Coos), and Wentworth's Location (Coos). Federal and state tax liens on personal property of businesses are filed with the Secretary of State. Other federal and state tax liens on personal property are filed with the Town/City Clerk. Federal and state tax liens on real property are filed with the county Register of Deeds. There is wide variation in indexing and searching practices among the recording offices.

Online Access Note: The New Hampshire Counties Registry of Deeds website at www.nhdeeds.com allows free searching of real estate related records for Belknap, Cheshire, Coos, Hillsborough, Rockingham, Strafford and Sullivan counties. Also, a private vendor has placed assessor records from a number of towns on the internet, visit www.visionappraisal.com/databases/nh/index.htm. An additional vendor offers Property Card data for 70+ NH Towns, see www.avitarofneinc.com. Fees apply.

Belknap County   *Real Estate, Deed, Mortgage, Lien Records*
Access to county register of deeds data is free at www.nhdeeds.com/belk/web/agree5.htm. Online records go back to 1765. To establish an account for copies of documents on line go to www.nhdeeds.com/belk/web/start.htm for account form.

Alton Town *Assessor, Property Records*
www.alton.nh.gov
Search the assessor database at http://data.visionappraisal.com/AltonNH/.

Belmont Town *Assessor, Property Records*
Access to property assessor data is at http://data.visionappraisal.com/BelmontNH/. Does not require a username & password; simply click on link.

Gilford Town *Assessor, Property Records*
www.gilfordnh.org
Access assessor and other town online documents free at www.gilfordnh.org/Public_Documents/GilfordNH_BBoard/Document%20Index. Click on Alpha with Addresses.

Laconia City *Property Assessor Records*
Records on the town assessor database are online at http://data.visionappraisal.com/LaconiaNH. Free registration is required for full access.

Meredith Town *Assessor, Property Card Records*
http://meredithnh.org
Access to Belknap County Registry of Deeds records is at www.nhdeeds.com.

Sanbornton Town *Assessor, Property Records*
Access to assessor property data is at http://data.visionappraisal.com/SanborntonNH/. Free registration for full data.

Tilton Town *Assessor, Property Records*
www.tiltonnh.org
Search the assessor database at http://data.visionappraisal.com/TiltonNH/, there is no charge. For UCC's go to www.sos.nh.gov/ucc/index.html

Carroll County
Albany Town *Assessor, Property Card Records*
Access assessor property card data by subscription at www.avitarofneinc.com or call 603-798-4419. Annual subscription fee is $150 for 1st Town, $50.00 for each add'l town, or $500 for all 70+ Towns.

Brookfield Town *Assessor, Property Records*
Access to property records is to be available via a private company upon Selectmen approval sometime in 2006. Also, check access to assessor property card data by subscription at www.avitarofneinc.com or call 603-798-4419. Annual subscription fee is $150 for 1st Town, $50.00 for each add'l town, or $500 for all 70+ Towns.

Effingham Town *Assessor, Property Card Records*
Access assessor property card data by subscription at www.avitarofneinc.com or call 603-798-4419. Annual subscription fee is $150 for 1st Town, $50.00 for each add'l town, or $500 for all 70+ Towns.

Hart's Location Town *Property Records*
www.hartslocation.com
The town is intending on posting property data on the internet in the future.

Jackson Town *Assessor, Property Card Records*
Access assessor property card data by subscription at www.avitarofneinc.com or call 603-798-4419. Annual subscription fee is $150 for 1st Town, $50.00 for each add'l town, or $500 for all 70+ Towns.

Madison Town *Assessor, Property Card Records*
Access assessor property card data by subscription at www.avitarofneinc.com or call 603-798-4419. Annual subscription fee is $150 for 1st Town, $50.00 for each add'l town, or $500 for all 70+ Towns.

Moultonborough Town *Assessor, Property Card Records*
Search town assessor database at http://data.visionappraisal.com/MoultonboroughNH/. Free registration for full data.

Sandwich Town *Assessor, Property Card Records*

Access assessor property card data by subscription at www.avitarofneinc.com or call 603-798-4419. Annual subscription fee is $150 for 1st Town, $50.00 for each add'l town, or $500 for all 70+ Towns.

Tuftonboro Town *Assessor, Property Card Records*

www.tuftonboro.org
Access assessor property card data by subscription at www.avitarofneinc.com or call 603-798-4419. Annual subscription fee is $150 for 1st Town, $50.00 for each add'l town, or $500 for all 70+ Towns.

Wakefield Town *Assessor, Property Card Records*

www.wakefieldnh.com
Access assessor property card data by subscription at www.avitarofneinc.com or call 603-798-4419. Annual subscription fee is $150 for 1st Town, $50.00 for each add'l town, or $500 for all 70+ Towns.

Wolfeboro Town *Assessor, Property Records*

Access to assessor property data is at http://data.visionappraisal.com/wolfeboroNH/. Free registration for full data.

Cheshire County *Real Estate, Deed, Mortgage, Lien Records*

Access to county register of deeds data is free at www.nhdeeds.com/chsr/web/agree2.htm. Online records go back to 1980.

Dublin Town *Assessor, Property Card Records*

Access assessor property card data by subscription at www.avitarofneinc.com or call 603-798-4419. Annual subscription fee is $150 for 1st Town, $50.00 for each add'l town, or $500 for all 70+ Towns.

Fitzwilliam Town *Assessor, Property Records*

www.fitzwilliam-nh.gov
Search the assessor database at http://data.visionappraisal.com/FitzwilliamNH. Registration required, but search is free.

Gilsum Town *Assessor, Property Card Records*

Access assessor property card data by subscription at www.avitarofneinc.com or call 603-798-4419. Annual subscription fee is $150 for 1st Town, $50.00 for each add'l town, or $500 for all 70+ Towns.

Harrisville Town *Assessor, Property Card Records*

Access assessor property card data by subscription at www.avitarofneinc.com or call 603-798-4419. Annual subscription fee is $150 for 1st Town, $50.00 for each add'l town, or $500 for all 70+ Towns.

Jaffrey Town *Assessor, Property Records*

Search town assessor database at http://data.visionappraisal.com/JaffreyNH/. Does not require a username & password. Simply click on link.

Rindge Town *Assessor, Property Records*

www.town.rindge.nh.us
Search town assessor database at http://data.visionappraisal.com/RindgeNH/. Does not require a username & password. Simply click on link.

Roxbury Town *Assessor, Property Card Records*

Access assessor property card data by subscription at www.avitarofneinc.com or call 603-798-4419. Annual subscription fee is $150 for 1st Town, $50.00 for each add'l town, or $500 for all 70+ Towns.

Sullivan Town *Assessor, Property Card Records*

Access assessor property card data by subscription at www.avitarofneinc.com or call 603-798-4419. Annual subscription fee is $150 for 1st Town, $50.00 for each add'l town, or $500 for all 70+ Towns.

Surry Town *Assessor, Property Card Records*

Access assessor property card data by subscription at www.avitarofneinc.com or call 603-798-4419. Annual subscription fee is $150 for 1st Town, $50.00 for each add'l town, or $500 for all 70+ Towns.

Swanzey Town *Assessor, Property Records*

Access assessor data at http://data.visionappraisal.com/SwanzeyNH/. Free registration for full data.

Walpole Town *Assessor, Property Card Records*

Access assessor property card data by subscription at www.avitarofneinc.com or call 603-798-4419. Annual subscription fee is $150 for 1st Town, $50.00 for each add'l town, or $500 for all 70+ Towns.

Westmoreland Town *Assessor, Property Card Records*

Access assessor property card data by subscription at www.avitarofneinc.com or call 603-798-4419. Annual subscription fee is $150 for 1st Town, $50.00 for each add'l town, or $500 for all 70+ Towns.

Winchester Town *Assessor, Property Card Records*

Access assessor property card data by subscription at www.avitarofneinc.com or call 603-798-4419. Annual subscription fee is $150 for 1st Town, $50.00 for each add'l town, or $500 for all 70+ Towns.

Coos County *Real Estate, Deed, Mortgage, Lien Records*

Access to county register of deeds data is free at www.nhdeeds.com/coos/web/start.htm. A subscription is required to print images.

Berlin City *Assessor, Property Card Records*

Access assessor property card data by subscription at www.avitarofneinc.com or call 603-798-4419. Annual subscription fee is $150 for 1st Town, $50.00 for each add'l town, or $500 for all 70+ Towns.

Colebrook Town *Assessor, Property Card Records*

www.colebrook-nh.com
Access assessor property card data by subscription at www.avitarofneinc.com or call 603-798-4419. Annual subscription fee is $150 for 1st Town, $50.00 for each add'l town, or $500 for all 70+ Towns.

Columbia Town *Assessor, Property Card Records*

Access assessor property card data by subscription at www.avitarofneinc.com or call 603-798-4419. Annual subscription fee is $150 for 1st Town, $50.00 for each add'l town, or $500 for all 70+ Towns.

Dummer Town *Assessor, Property Card Records*

Access assessor property card data by subscription at www.avitarofneinc.com or call 603-798-4419. Annual subscription fee is $150 for 1st Town, $50.00 for each add'l town, or $500 for all 70+ Towns.

Milan Town *Assessor, Property Card Records*

Access assessor property card data by subscription at www.avitarofneinc.com or call 603-798-4419. Annual subscription fee is $150 for 1st Town, $50.00 for each add'l town, or $500 for all 70+ Towns.

Pittsburg Town *Assessor, Property Card Records*

Access assessor property card data by subscription at www.avitarofneinc.com or call 603-798-4419. Annual subscription fee is $150 for 1st Town, $50.00 for each add'l town, or $500 for all 70+ Towns.

Stark Town *Assessor, Property Card Records*

Access assessor property card data by subscription at www.avitarofneinc.com or call 603-798-4419. Annual subscription fee is $150 for 1st Town, $50.00 for each add'l town, or $500 for all 70+ Towns.

Stewartstown Town *Assessor, Property Card Records*

Access assessor property card data by subscription at www.avitarofneinc.com or call 603-798-4419. Annual subscription fee is $150 for 1st Town, $50.00 for each add'l town, or $500 for all 70+ Towns.

Grafton County *Real Estate, Lien Records*

Access to the County dial-up service requires a $100 set up fee and $40 per month access fee. Two years of data are kept on system; prior years on CD. Lending agency information available. A fax-back service is in-state only. For further info, call 603-787-6921.

Alexandria Town *Assessor, Property Card Records*

Access assessor property card data by subscription at www.avitarofneinc.com or call 603-798-4419. Annual subscription fee is $150 for 1st Town, $50.00 for each add'l town, or $500 for all 70+ Towns.

Canaan Town   *Assessor, Property Card Records*

Access assessor property card data by subscription at www.avitarofneinc.com or call 603-798-4419. Annual subscription fee is $150 for 1st Town, $50.00 for each add'l town, or $500 for all 70+ Towns.

Dorchester Town   *Assessor, Property Card Records*

Access assessor property card data by subscription at www.avitarofneinc.com or call 603-798-4419. Annual subscription fee is $150 for 1st Town, $50.00 for each add'l town, or $500 for all 70+ Towns.

Ellsworth Town   *Assessor, Property Card Records*

Access assessor property card data by subscription at www.avitarofneinc.com or call 603-798-4419. Annual subscription fee is $150 for 1st Town, $50.00 for each add'l town, or $500 for all 70+ Towns.

Franconia Town   *Assessor, Property Card Records*

Access assessor property card data by subscription at www.avitarofneinc.com or call 603-798-4419. Annual subscription fee is $150 for 1st Town, $50.00 for each add'l town, or $500 for all 70+ Towns.

Groton Town   *Assessor, Property Card Records*

Access assessor property card data by subscription at www.avitarofneinc.com or call 603-798-4419. Annual subscription fee is $150 for 1st Town, $50.00 for each add'l town, or $500 for all 70+ Towns.

Hebron Town   *Assessor, Property Card Records*

www.hebronnh.org
Access assessor property card data by subscription at www.avitarofneinc.com or call 603-798-4419. Annual subscription fee is $150 for 1st Town, $50.00 for each add'l town, or $500 for all 70+ Towns.

Lebanon City   *Property Assessor Records*

www.lebcity.com
Records from the city assessor database are free at http://data.visionappraisal.com/LEBANONNH/. Free registration is required to view full data.

Littleton Town   *Assessor, Property Records*

www.townoflittleton.org
Search town assessor database at http://data.visionappraisal.com/LittletonNH/. Does not require a username & password. Simply click on link.

Lyman Town   *Assessor, Property Card Records*

Access assessor property card data by subscription at www.avitarofneinc.com or call 603-798-4419. Annual subscription fee is $150 for 1st Town, $50.00 for each add'l town, or $500 for all 70+ Towns.

Orford Town   *Assessor, Property Card Records*

Access assessor property card data by subscription at www.avitarofneinc.com or call 603-798-4419. Annual subscription fee is $150 for 1st Town, $50.00 for each add'l town, or $500 for all 70+ Towns.

Thornton Town   *Assessor, Property Card Records*

Access assessor property card data by subscription at www.avitarofneinc.com or call 603-798-4419. Annual subscription fee is $150 for 1st Town, $50.00 for each add'l town, or $500 for all 70+ Towns.

Hillsborough County   *Real Estate, Deed, Mortgage, Lien, Grantor/Grantee Records*

Access to county register of deeds data is free at www.nhdeeds.com/hils/web/argthc.htm. Online records go back to 1966.

Amherst Town   *Assessor, Property Records*

Records on the town assessor database are free at http://data.visionappraisal.com/AmherstNH/. Registration is required to view full data.

Bedford Town   *Assessor, Property Records*

www.ci.bedford.nh.us
Access assessor data at http://data.visionappraisal.com/BedfordNH/. Free registration for full data.

Deering Town *Assessor, Property Card Records*
www.deering.nh.us
Access assessor property card data by subscription at www.avitarofneinc.com or call 603-798-4419. Annual subscription fee is $150 for 1st Town, $50.00 for each add'l town, or $500 for all 70+ Towns.

Francestown Town *Assessor, Property Card Records*
Access assessor property card data by subscription at www.avitarofneinc.com or call 603-798-4419. Annual subscription fee is $150 for 1st Town, $50.00 for each add'l town, or $500 for all 70+ Towns.

Greenfield Town *Assessor, Property Card Records*
http://greenfieldnh.org
Access assessor property card data by subscription at www.avitarofneinc.com or call 603-798-4419. Annual subscription fee is $150 for 1st Town, $50.00 for each add'l town, or $500 for all 70+ Towns.

Greenville Town *Assessor, Property Card Records*
Access assessor property card data by subscription at www.avitarofneinc.com or call 603-798-4419. Annual subscription fee is $150 for 1st Town, $50.00 for each add'l town, or $500 for all 70+ Towns.

Hollis Town *Assessor, Property Records*
www.hollis.nh.us
Access assessor data at http://data.visionappraisal.com/HollisNH/. Does not require a username & password. Simply click on link.

Hudson Town *Assessor, Property Records*
Access property data free at http://hudsonnh.patriotproperties.com.

Litchfield Town *Assessor, Property Card Records*
Access assessor property card data by subscription at www.avitarofneinc.com or call 603-798-4419. Annual subscription fee is $150 for 1st Town, $50.00 for each add'l town, or $500 for all 70+ Towns.

Manchester City *Property, Assessor Records*
www.manchesternh.gov
Search Property valuations lists manually for free at www.manchesternh.gov/CityGov/Asr/RevalInfo.html. Also, search Tax Collector accounts free at http://216.204.100.85/Click2GovTX/Index.jsp but no name searching.

Nashua City *Property Assessor Records*
Search the City Assessor database for free at www.ci.nashua.nh.us/content/51/53/114/default.aspx.

New Boston Town *Assessor, Property Card Records*
http://www2.new-boston.nh.us/Pages/NewBostonNH_Clerk/index
Access assessor property card data by subscription at www.avitarofneinc.com or call 603-798-4419. Annual subscription fee is $150 for 1st Town, $50.00 for each add'l town, or $500 for all 70+ Towns.

New Ipswich Town *Assessor, Property Card Records*
Access assessor property card data by subscription at www.avitarofneinc.com or call 603-798-4419. Annual subscription fee is $150 for 1st Town, $50.00 for each add'l town, or $500 for all 70+ Towns.

Sharon Town *Assessor, Property Card Records*
Access assessor property card data by subscription at www.avitarofneinc.com or call 603-798-4419. Annual subscription fee is $150 for 1st Town, $50.00 for each add'l town, or $500 for all 70+ Towns.

Temple Town *Assessor, Property Card Records*
Access assessor property card data by subscription at www.avitarofneinc.com or call 603-798-4419. Annual subscription fee is $150 for 1st Town, $50.00 for each add'l town, or $500 for all 70+ Towns.

Windsor Town *Assessor, Property Card Records*
Access assessor property card data by subscription at www.avitarofneinc.com or call 603-798-4419. Annual subscription fee is $150 for 1st Town, $50.00 for each add'l town, or $500 for all 70+ Towns.

Merrimack County *Real Estate, Grantor/Grantee, Deed Records*
www.merrimackcounty.nh.us.landata.com
Access records on the county Registry of Deeds index for free after registration; images require subscription at
www.merrimackcounty.nh.us.landata.com.. Indexes are 1920-present, document images, 1945-present.

Andover Town *Assessor, Property Card Records*
Access assessor property card data by subscription at www.avitarofneinc.com or call 603-798-4419. Annual subscription fee is
$150 for 1st Town, $50.00 for each add'l town, or $500 for all 70+ Towns.

Boscawen Town *Real Estate, Grantor/Grantee, Deed, Assessor, Property Card Records*
Access records on the county Registry of Deeds index for free after registration; images require subscription at
www.merrimackcounty.nh.us.landata.com. Also, access assessor property card data by subscription at www.avitarofneinc.com or
call 603-798-4419. Annual subscription fee is $150 for 1st Town, $50.00 for each add'l town, or $500 for all 70+ Towns.

Bow Town *Property Assessor Records*
Records on town assessor database are free at http://data.visionappraisal.com/BowNH/. Registration is required to view full data.

Bradford Town *Assessor, Property Card Records*
Access assessor property card data by subscription at www.avitarofneinc.com or call 603-798-4419. Annual subscription fee is
$150 for 1st Town, $50.00 for each add'l town, or $500 for all 70+ Towns.

Canterbury Town *Assessor, Property Records*
Access assessor property card data by subscription at www.avitarofneinc.com or call 603-798-4419. Annual subscription fee is
$150 for 1st Town, $50.00 for each add'l town, or $500 for all 70+ Towns.

Chichester Town *Assessor, Property Card Records*
Access assessor property card data by subscription at www.avitarofneinc.com or call 603-798-4419. Annual subscription fee is
$150 for 1st Town, $50.00 for each add'l town, or $500 for all 70+ Towns.

Concord City *Property Assessor Records*
www.onconcord.com
Records on city assessor database are free at http://data.visionappraisal.com/ConcordNH/. Registration required to view full data.

Dunbarton Town *Assessor, Property Records*
Search town assessor database at http://data.visionappraisal.com/DunbartonNH/. Does not require a username & password.
Simply click on link.

Epsom Town *Assessor, Property Card Records*
Access assessor property card data by subscription at www.avitarofneinc.com or call 603-798-4419. Annual subscription fee is
$150 for 1st Town, $50.00 for each add'l town, or $500 for all 70+ Towns.

Henniker Town *Assessor, Property Records*
Search the assessor database free at http://data.visionappraisal.com/HennikerNH/.

Hill Town *Assessor, Property Card Records*
Access assessor property card data by subscription at www.avitarofneinc.com or call 603-798-4419. Annual subscription fee is
$150 for 1st Town, $50.00 for each add'l town, or $500 for all 70+ Towns.

Loudon Town *Assessor, Property Card Records*
Access assessor property card data by subscription at www.avitarofneinc.com or call 603-798-4419. Annual subscription fee is
$150 for 1st Town, $50.00 for each add'l town, or $500 for all 70+ Towns.

New London Town *Property Appraiser Records*
Search the town assessor database at http://data.visionappraisal.com/NEWLONDONNH/.

Newbury Town *Assessor, Property Records*
Access to property assessor data is at http://data.visionappraisal.com/NorthHamptonNH/. Free registration required.

Northfield Town *Assessor, Property Card Records*

Access assessor property card data by subscription at www.avitarofneinc.com or call 603-798-4419. Annual subscription fee is $150 for 1st Town, $50.00 for each add'l town, or $500 for all 70+ Towns.

Pembroke Town *Assessor, Property Records*

Access assessor data at http://data.visionappraisal.com/PembrokeNH/.

Rockingham County *Real Estate, Most Wanted, Inmate Records*

Access to the register of deeds database is free at www.nhdeeds.com/rock/web/start.htm. Index goes back to 1980. Also, search inmate info on private company website at www.vinelink.com/index.jsp.

Atkinson Town *Property, Real Estate Transfer, Property Card Records*

www.town-atkinsonnh.com

Access town property values for free at www.town-atkinsonnh.com/values.htm. Also, access assessor property card data by subscription at www.avitarofneinc.com or call 603-798-4419. Annual subscription fee is $150 for 1st Town, $50.00 for each add'l town, or $500 for all 70+ Towns. Also, search the last 3 months of real estate transfers and 4 months of building permits for free via www.town-atkinsonnh.com.

Auburn Town *Assessor, Property Card Records*

Access assessor property card data by subscription at www.avitarofneinc.com or call 603-798-4419. Annual subscription fee is $150 for 1st Town, $50.00 for each add'l town, or $500 for all 70+ Towns.

Candia Town *Assessor, Property Records*

www.townofcandianh.org

Access assessor data at http://data.visionappraisal.com/CandiaNH/. Free registration for full data.

Deerfield Town *Assessor, Property Card Records*

www.ci.deerfield-nh.us

Access assessor property card data by subscription at www.avitarofneinc.com or call 603-798-4419. Annual subscription fee is $150 for 1st Town, $50.00 for each add'l town, or $500 for all 70+ Towns.

Derry Town *Assessor, Property Records*

www.derry.nh.us

Access Derry assessed values database free at http://derry.univers-clt.com.

East Kingston Town *Assessor, Property Card Records*

www.eastkingston.org

Access assessor property card data by subscription at www.avitarofneinc.com or call 603-798-4419. Annual subscription fee is $150 for 1st Town, $50.00 for each add'l town, or $500 for all 70+ Towns.

Epping Town *Assessor, Property Records*

Search the assessor database at http://data.visionappraisal.com/EppingNH/.

Fremont Town *Assessor, Property Records*

http://fremont.nh.gov

Search town assessor database at http://data.visionappraisal.com/FremontNH/. Does not require a username & password. Simply click on link.

Greenland Town *Property Assessor Records*

www.greenland-nh.com/?dept=clerk

Access is via a private company at http://data.visionappraisal.com/GreenlandNH/. Free registration is required to view full data.

Londonderry Town *Assessor, Property Records*

www.londonderrynh.org

Access property data free at http://londonderrynh.patriotproperties.com/default.asp.

New Castle Town *Assessor, Property Card Records*
Access assessor property card data by subscription at www.avitarofneinc.com or call 603-798-4419. Annual subscription fee is $150 for 1st Town, $50.00 for each add'l town, or $500 for all 70+ Towns.

Newmarket Town *Assessor, Property Records*
www.visionappraisal.com
Access is via a private company at http://data.visionappraisal.com/NewMarketNH/. Apply for a free registered user ID (more data) or search anonymously (less data, no name searching).

Newton Town *Assessor, Property Card Records*
Access assessor property card data by subscription at www.avitarofneinc.com or call 603-798-4419. Annual subscription fee is $150 for 1st Town, $50.00 for each add'l town, or $500 for all 70+ Towns.

North Hampton Town *Assessor, Property Records*
www.northhampton-nh.gov
Access to property assessor data is at http://data.visionappraisal.com/NorthHamptonNH/. Does not require a username & password. Simply click on link.

Northwood Town *Assessor, Property Card Records*
www.town.northwood.nh.us
Access assessor property card data by subscription at www.avitarofneinc.com or call 603-798-4419. Annual subscription fee is $150 for 1st Town, $50.00 for each add'l town, or $500 for all 70+ Towns.

Nottingham Town *Assessor, Property Card Records*
Access assessor property card data by subscription at www.avitarofneinc.com or call 603-798-4419. Annual subscription fee is $150 for 1st Town, $50.00 for each add'l town, or $500 for all 70+ Towns.

Pelham Town *Assessor, Property Records*
Search town assessor database at http://data.visionappraisal.com/PelhamNH/. Free registration for full data.

Portsmouth City *Property Assessor Records*
www.cityofportsmouth.com/cityclerk/index.htm
Records on the Portsmouth Assessed Property Values database are free at www.portsmouthnh.com/realestate/index.cfm.

Raymond Town *Property Assessor Records*
Search the town assessor database at http://data.visionappraisal.com/RaymondNH. Free registration is required to view full data.

Rye Town *Property Assessor Records*
Access is via a private company at http://data.visionappraisal.com/RyeNH. Free registration is required to view full data.

Salem Town *Property Assessor Records*
www.ci.salem.nh.us
Records from the town database are free at http://data.visionappraisal.com/SalemNH/. Free registration for full data.

Stratham Town *Assessor, Property Card Records*
www.strathamnh.org
Access assessor property card data by subscription at www.avitarofneinc.com or call 603-798-4419. Annual subscription fee is $150 for 1st Town, $50.00 for each add'l town, or $500 for all 70+ Towns.

Windham Town *Parcel, Sales Records*
www.windhamnewhampshire.com
Access to lists of parcels and sales data is available free at http://windhamnewhampshire.com/depts/assess(3).htm,

Strafford County   *Real Estate, Deed, Mortgage, Lien, Grantor/Grantee Records*

Access to county register of deeds data is free at www.nhdeeds.com/stfd/web/agree3.htm. Online records go back to 1970.

Barrington Town   *Property, Deed, Grantor/Grantee Records*

Records are free on the Stafford county-wide system at www.nhdeeds.com/stfd/web/agree3.htm. Use the subscription service for full data.

Dover City   *Property, Deed, Grantor/Grantee Records*

www.ci.dover.nh.us
Records are free on the Stafford county-wide system at www.nhdeeds.com/stfd/web/agree3.htm. Use the subscription service for full data.

Durham Town   *Property, Deed, Grantor/Grantee, Assessor Records*

www.ci.durham.nh.us/departments/town_clerk/clerk.html
Records are free on the Stafford county-wide system at www.nhdeeds.com/stfd/web/agree3.htm. Use the subscription service for full data. Also, Assessor data is free at http://data.visionappraisal.com/DurhamNH/.

Farmington Town   *Property, Deed, Grantor/Grantee Records*

Records are free on the Stafford county-wide system at www.nhdeeds.com/stfd/web/agree3.htm. Use the subscription service for full data.

Lee Town   *Property, Deed, Grantor/Grantee, Assessor, Property Card Records*

www.leenh.org
Records are free on the Stafford county-wide system at www.nhdeeds.com/stfd/web/agree3.htm. Use the subscription service for full data. Also, access assessor property card data by subscription at www.avitarofneinc.com or call 603-798-4419. Annual subscription fee is $150 for 1st Town, $50.00 for each add'l town, or $500 for all 70+ Towns.

Madbury Town   *Property, Deed, Grantor/Grantee, Assessor, Property Card Records*

Records are free on the Stafford county-wide system at www.nhdeeds.com/stfd/web/agree3.htm. Use the subscription service for full data. Access assessor property card data by subscription at www.avitarofneinc.com or call 603-798-4419. Annual subscription fee is $150 for 1st Town, $50.00 for each add'l town, or $500 for all 70+ Towns.

Middleton Town   *Property, Deed, Grantor/Grantee, Assessor, Property Card Records*

Records are free on the Stafford county-wide system at www.nhdeeds.com/stfd/web/agree3.htm. Use the subscription service for full data. Also, access assessor property card data by subscription at www.avitarofneinc.com or call 603-798-4419. Annual subscription fee is $150 for 1st Town, $50.00 for each add'l town, or $500 for all 70+ Towns.

Milton Town   *Property, Deed, Grantor/Grantee, Assessor, Property Card Records*

www.miltonnh-us.com
Records are free on the Stafford county-wide system at www.nhdeeds.com/stfd/web/agree3.htm. Use the subscription service for full data. Also, access assessor property card data by subscription at www.avitarofneinc.com or call 603-798-4419. Annual subscription fee is $150 for 1st Town, $50.00 for each add'l town, or $500 for all 70+ Towns.

New Durham Town   *Property, Deed, Grantor/Grantee Records*

Records are free on the Stafford county-wide system at www.nhdeeds.com/stfd/web/agree3.htm. Use the subscription service for full data. Assessor data is at http://data.visionappraisal.com/NewDurhamNH/. Does not require a username & password. Simply click on link.

Rochester City   *Property, Deed, Grantor/Grantee, Assessor Records*

www.rochesternh.net
Records are free on the Stafford county-wide system at www.nhdeeds.com/stfd/web/agree3.htm. Use the subscription service for full data. Also, access property data free at http://rochesternh.patriotproperties.com/default.asp.

Rollinsford Town   *Property, Deed, Grantor/Grantee, Assessor, Property Card Records*

Access records free on the Stafford county-wide system at www.nhdeeds.com/stfd/web/agree3.htm. Use the subscription service for full data. Also, access assessor property card data by subscription at www.avitarofneinc.com or call 603-798-4419. Annual subscription fee is $150 for 1st Town, $50.00 for each add'l town, or $500 for all 70+ Towns.

Somersworth City *Property, Deed, Grantor/Grantee Records*
Records are free on the Stafford county-wide system at www.nhdeeds.com/stfd/web/agree3.htm. Use the subscription service for full data.

Strafford Town *Property, Deed, Grantor/Grantee Records*
Records are free on the Stafford county-wide system at www.nhdeeds.com/stfd/web/agree3.htm. Use the subscription service for full data.

Sullivan County *Real Estate, Grantor/Grantee, Deed Records*
Access to the county Register of Deeds database is free at www.nhdeeds.com/slvn/web/agree7.htm.

Croydon Town *Real Estate, Deed, Recorder, Grantor/Grantee Records*
Access the clerks recording database free at www.nhdeeds.com/slvn/web/start.htm. Online index goes back to 1827.

Lempster Town *Assessor, Property Card Records*
Access assessor property card data by subscription at www.avitarofneinc.com or call 603-798-4419. Annual subscription fee is $150 for 1st Town, $50.00 for each add'l town, or $500 for all 70+ Towns.

Newport Town *Assessor, Property Card Records*
Access assessor property card data by subscription at www.avitarofneinc.com or call 603-798-4419. Annual subscription fee is $150 for 1st Town, $50.00 for each add'l town, or $500 for all 70+ Towns.

Springfield Town *Assessor, Property Card Records*
Access assessor property card data by subscription at www.avitarofneinc.com or call 603-798-4419. Annual subscription fee is $150 for 1st Town, $50.00 for each add'l town, or $500 for all 70+ Towns.

Sunapee Town *Assessor, Property Records*
Search town assessor database at http://data.visionappraisal.com/SunapeeNH/. Free registration for full data.

Washington Town *Assessor, Property Card Records*
www.washingtonnh.org
Access assessor property card data by subscription at www.avitarofneinc.com or call 603-798-4419. Annual subscription fee is $150 for 1st Town, $50.00 for each add'l town, or $500 for all 70+ Towns.

Federal Courts in New Hampshire...

Standards for Federal Courts: The universal PACER sign-up number is 800-676-6856. Find PACER and the Party/Case Index on the Web at http://pacer.psc.uscourts.gov. PACER dial-up access is $.60 per minute. Also, courts offering internet access via PACER, Web-PACER or the new CM-ECF charge $.08 per page fee ($.07 per page if record is pre-2005 or unless noted as free).

US District Court -- District of New Hampshire
www.nhd.uscourts.gov
PACER: Case records are available back to 1980. Records are purged every 2 years. New records are available online after 1 day.
PACER Online Access: ECF replaces PACER. **Electronic Filing:** CM/ECF data at https://ecf.nhd.uscourts.gov. **Opinions:** Includes orders and standing orders as well. View court opinions at www.nhd.uscourts.gov/oo/default.asp.
Concord Division counties: Belknap, Carroll, Cheshire, Coos, Grafton, Hillsborough, Merrimack, Rockingham, Strafford, Sullivan.

US Bankruptcy Court -- District of New Hampshire
www.nhb.uscourts.gov
PACER: Case records are available back to 1989. Records are purged every 6 months. **PACER Online Access:** ECF replaces PACER. **Electronic Filing:** CM/ECF data at https://ecf.nhb.uscourts.gov. **Opinions:** View court opinions at www.nhb.uscourts.gov/Court_Opinions/court_opinions.html. **Phone access:** Voice Case Information System, call 800-851-8954, 603-666-7424
Manchester Division counties: Belknap, Carroll, Cheshire, Coos, Grafton, Hillsborough, Merrimack, Rockingham, Strafford, Sullivan.

New Jersey

Capital: Trenton
           Mercer County
Time Zone: EST
Population: 8,698,879
# of Counties: 21

Quick Links

Website: www.state.nj.us
Governor: www.state.nj.us/governor
Attorney General: www.state.nj.us/lps
State Archives: www.state.nj.us/state/darm/index.html
State Statutes and Codes: http://lis.njleg.state.nj.us/cgi-bin/om_isapi.dll?clientID=202576587
Legislative Bill Search: www.njleg.state.nj.us
Bill Monitoring: www.njleg.state.nj.us/bills/BillsSubscriptionLogin.asp
Unclaimed Funds: https://www1.state.nj.us/treasury/taxation/unclaimsrch.htm

State Level ... Major Agencies

Statewide Court Records

Administrative Office of Courts, RJH Justice Complex, 7th Fl, PO Box 037, Trenton, NJ 08625; 609-984-0275, Fax-609-984-6968, 8:30AM-4:30PM.
www.judiciary.state.nj.us/admin.htm
Online search: Online access to all civil records is available through the ACMS, AMIS, and FACTS systems. The fee is $1.00 per minute of use. For more information, contact the Superior Court Clerk's Office, Electronic Access Program. Write to 25 Market St, CN971, Trenton NJ 08625, or fax 609-292-6564, or call 609-292-4987. Ask for the Inquiry System Guidebook containing hardware and software requirements and an enrollment form. A Superior Court Civil Motion Calendar is at www.judiciary.state.nj.us/acms/MOTN/CV0390W0E.ASP. And, http://lawlibrary.rutgers.edu/search.shtml.

Sexual Offender Registry

Division of State Police, Sexual Offender Registry, PO Box 7068, West Trenton, NJ 08628-0068; 609-882-2000 x2886, Fax-609-538-0544, 9AM-5PM.
www.njsp.org
Online search: Data can be searched online at the website. Click on NJ Sex Offender Registry. Search can be done by name, by county or by physical characteristics.

Incarceration Records

New Jersey Department of Corrections, Central Reception & Assignment Facility, PO Box 7450, Trenton, NJ 08628; 609-777-5753, 609-984-2695, Fax-609-777-8369, 8AM-5PM.
www.state.nj.us/corrections/index.html
Online search: Extensive search capabilities are offered from the website; click on "Offender Search". Offenders on Work Release, Furlough, or in a Halfway House are not necessarily reflected as such in their profile.

Corporation, Limited Liability Company, Fictitious Name, Limited Partnerships

Division of Revenue, Records Unit, PO 450, Trenton, NJ 08646 (Courier: 225 W State St, 3rd Fl, Trenton, NJ 08608); 609-292-9292, Fax-609-984-6855, 8:30AM-4:30PM.
www.state.nj.us/treasury/revenue/certcomm.htm
Online search: Business entities may be searched at https://accessnet.state.nj.us/home.asp. Records are available from the New Jersey Business Gateway Service (NJBGS) website at www.state.nj.us/njbgs. There is no fee to browse the site to locate a name; however fees are involved for copies or status reports. There is also a business list search function at www.state.nj.us/treasury/revenue/searchfile.htm.

Trademarks/Servicemarks

Department of Treasury, Trademark Division, PO Box 453, Trenton, NJ 08625-0453 (Courier: 225 W State St, 3rd Floor, Trenton, NJ 08608); 609-292-9292, Fax-609-984-6681, 8:30AM-5PM.
www.state.nj.us/treasury/revenue/
Online search: Search the trade names list for free at www.state.nj.us/treasury/revenue/checkbusiness.htm for name availability.

Uniform Commercial Code

UCC Section, Certification and Status Unit, PO 303, Trenton, NJ 08625 (Courier: 225 West State St, Trenton, NJ 08618); 609-292-9292, 8AM-5PM.
www.state.nj.us/njbgs
Online search: Go to https://www.state.nj.us/treasury/revenue/dcr/filing/ucc_lead.htm to search the UCC index. Go to https://accessnet.state.nj.us/home.asp to find a business entity, UCC debtor, or other business name without accruing a service charge with the Division of Revenue. However, if you wish to receive status reports or other information services, you will need to pay the applicable statutory fee.

Birth, Death, Marriage, Divorce Certificates

Department of Health, Bureau of Vital Statistics, PO Box 370, Trenton, NJ 08625-0370 (Courier: S Warren St, Room 504, Health & Agriculture Building, Trenton, NJ 08625); 609-292-4087, 877-622-7549 (Credit Card Requests), Fax-609-392-4292, 8:30AM-4PM.
www.state.nj.us/health/vital/vital.htm
Online search: Online ordering is available via www.vitalchek.com, a state approved vendor.

Workers' Compensation Records

Labor Department, Division of Workers Compensation, PO Box 381, Trenton, NJ 08625-0381 (Courier: Labor Building, 6th Floor, John Fitch Plaza, Trenton, NJ 08625); 609-292-6026, 609-292-2515 (General Hotline), Fax-609-984-2515, 8:30AM-4:30PM.
www.nj.gov/labor/wc/wcindex.html
Online search: COURTS on-line is a secure Internet website that provides authorized subscribers access to the Division's database. Possible subscribers include: Insurance Carrier/Law Firms; Court Reporting Firms; and WC Forensic Experts (Physicians).

Driver Records

Motor Vehicle Commission, Driver History Abstract Unit, PO Box 142, Trenton, NJ 08666; 609-984-7771, 609-292-6500 (Forms request), 609-292-7500 (Suspensions), 8AM-4:30PM.
www.state.nj.us/mvc/
Online search: Fee is $10.00 per record. Access is limited to insurance, bus and trucking companies, parking authorities, and approved vendors. For more information, call 609-292-4572. NJ drivers may order their own record online at www.state.nj.us/mvc/d_driver_history.html. A user ID number must be obtained first. The fee is $10.00 per record.

Vehicle and Vessel Ownership, Registration

Motor Vehicle Commission, Certified Information Unit, PO Box 146, Trenton, NJ 08666; 609-292-6500, 888-486-3339 (In-state), 8:30AM-4:30PM.
www.state.nj.us/mvc/cit_title/v_title.html
Online search: Limited online access is available for insurance companies, bus and trucking companies, highway/parking authorities, and approved vendors for these businesses. Fees are $4.00 per request for registration record and $8.00 for ownership history. Call 609-292-4572 for more information. **Other options:** There is no program for massive/customized bulk look-ups. Each request is looked at on an individual basis. Records are not sold for commercial or political reasons.

Accident Reports

New Jersey State Police, CJRB - Traffic, PO Box 7068, West Trenton, NJ 08628-0068; 609-882-2000 x2234, 8AM-5PM. www.njsp.org
Online search: No online access to accidents reports is available, however, you may access the Insurance Company Name Codes free online at www.state.nj.us/mvc/cit_insurance/v_insurance_codes.html. By reading the code on the accident report, you can then use this website to determine the insurance company involved.

State Level ... Occupational Licensing

Acupuncturist ... ... www.state.nj.us/cgi-bin/consumeraffairs/search/searchentry.pl?searchprofession=3251
Alcohol/Drug Counselor ... www.state.nj.us/cgi-bin/consumeraffairs/search/searchentry.pl?searchprofession=3703
Appraiser, General/Residential www.state.nj.us/cgi-bin/consumeraffairs/search/searchentry.pl?searchprofession=4202
Architect .... www.state.nj.us/cgi-bin/consumeraffairs/search/searchentry.pl
Athletic Trainer.. www.state.nj.us/cgi-bin/consumeraffairs/search/searchentry.pl
Audiologist .... www.state.nj.us/cgi-bin/consumeraffairs/search/search.pl
Barber/Barber Shop .... www.state.nj.us/cgi-bin/consumeraffairs/search/searchentry.pl
Beautician .... www.state.nj.us/cgi-bin/consumeraffairs/search/searchentry.pl
Candidate report... www.elec.state.nj.us/publicinformation.htm
Cemetery/Cemetery Salesperson www.state.nj.us/cgi-bin/consumeraffairs/search/searchentry.pl?searchprofession=4701
Certificate of Authorization .... www.state.nj.us/cgi-bin/consumeraffairs/search/searchentry.pl
Charities... www.state.nj.us/lps/ca/charfrm.htm
Chiropractor... www.state.nj.us/cgi-bin/consumeraffairs/search/searchentry.pl
Contributor, Political .... www.elec.state.nj.us/publicinformation.htm
Cosmetologist/Hairstylist/Shop .... www.state.nj.us/cgi-bin/consumeraffairs/search/searchentry.pl
Counselor, Professional .... www.state.nj.us/cgi-bin/consumeraffairs/search/searchentry.pl
Court Reporter ... ... www.state.nj.us/cgi-bin/consumeraffairs/search/searchentry.pl?searchprofession=3000
CPA/Public Accountant
   www.state.nj.us/cgi-bin/consumeraffairs/search/searchentry.pl?searchprofession=2000
Dental Assistant, Ltd/Registered................. www.state.nj.us/cgi-bin/consumeraffairs/search/searchentry.pl
Dentist/Dental Hygienist............................. www.state.nj.us/cgi-bin/consumeraffairs/search/searchentry.pl
Dental Radiation Technologist
   http://datamine.state.nj.us/DEP_OPRA/OpraMain/report?report=Radiologic+Technologist+License+Status+by+First+
   and+Last+Name+and+Date+of+Birth
Electrical Contractor ... www.state.nj.us/cgi-bin/consumeraffairs/search/searchentry.pl?searchprofession=3400
Embalmer ... ... www.state.nj.us/cgi-bin/consumeraffairs/search/searchentry.pl?searchprofession=2
Engineer... www.njconsumeraffairs.com/nonmedical/pels.htm
Funeral Home .... www.state.nj.us/cgi-bin/consumeraffairs/search/searchentry.pl
Funeral Practitioner ... ... www.state.nj.us/cgi-bin/consumeraffairs/search/searchentry.pl?searchprofession=2
Hearing Aid Dispenser/Fitter ... www.state.nj.us/cgi-bin/consumeraffairs/search/searchentry.pl?searchprofession=2253
Home Health Aide .... www.state.nj.us/cgi-bin/consumeraffairs/search/searchentry.pl
Home Inspection... www.njconsumeraffairs.com/nonmedical/pels.htm
Insurance Agent .... www.nj.gov/dobi/licenseesearch/insurancelicensee.htm
Insurance Public Adjuster .... www.nj.gov/dobi/licenseesearch/insurancelicensee.htm
Lab Director, Bio-Analytical ... www.state.nj.us/cgi-bin/consumeraffairs/search/searchentry.pl?searchprofession=2505
Landscape Architect...................................... www.state.nj.us/cgi-bin/consumeraffairs/search/searchentry.pl
Lobbyist... www.elec.state.nj.us/PublicInformation/GAA_Annual.htm
Manicurist/Manicurist Shop......................... www.state.nj.us/cgi-bin/consumeraffairs/search/searchentry.pl
Marriage & Family Counselor www.state.nj.us/cgi-bin/consumeraffairs/search/searchentry.pl?searchprofession=3703
Midwife ... ... www.state.nj.us/cgi-bin/consumeraffairs/search/searchentry.pl?searchprofession=2510
Mortician ... ... www.state.nj.us/cgi-bin/consumeraffairs/search/searchentry.pl?searchprofession=2
Nuclear Medicine Technologist
   http://datamine.state.nj.us/DEP_OPRA/OpraMain/report?report=Radiologic+Technologist+License+Status+by+First+
   and+Last+Name+and+Date+of+Birth
Nurse, LPN, RN, Advance Practice .... www.state.nj.us/cgi-bin/consumeraffairs/search/searchentry.pl
Occupational Therapist ... ... www.state.nj.us/cgi-bin/consumeraffairs/search/searchentry.pl?searchprofession=4601

Occupational Therapy Asst. .... www.state.nj.us/cgi-bin/consumeraffairs/search/searchentry.pl
Opthalmic Dispenser................................. www.state.nj.us/cgi-bin/consumeraffairs/search/searchentry.pl
Optician/Opthalmic Technician www.state.nj.us/cgi-bin/consumeraffairs/search/searchentry.pl?searchprofession=3102
Optometrist ... ... www.state.nj.us/cgi-bin/consumeraffairs/search/searchentry.pl?searchprofession=2701
Orthotist/Prosthetist .... www.state.nj.us/lps/ca/medical/orthotic.htm
Pharmacist ... ... www.state.nj.us/cgi-bin/consumeraffairs/search/searchentry.pl?searchprofession=2801
Physical Therapist/Assistant   www.state.nj.us/cgi-bin/consumeraffairs/search/searchentry.pl?searchprofession=4001
Physician ... ... www.state.nj.us/cgi-bin/consumeraffairs/search/searchentry.pl?searchprofession=2501
Physician Assistant .... www.state.nj.us/cgi-bin/consumeraffairs/search/searchentry.pl
Planner, Professional ... . www.state.nj.us/cgi-bin/consumeraffairs/search/searchentry.pl?searchprofession=3300
Plumber/Master Plumber ... www.state.nj.us/cgi-bin/consumeraffairs/search/searchentry.pl?searchprofession=3601
Podiatrist ... ... www.state.nj.us/cgi-bin/consumeraffairs/search/searchentry.pl?searchprofession=2507
Psychologist ... ... www.state.nj.us/cgi-bin/consumeraffairs/search/searchentry.pl?searchprofession=3
Radiation Reports .... http://datamine.state.nj.us/dep/DEP_OPRA/keyword_index.html
Radiation Therapist/Radiation Technologist/Radiation Technologist, Limited
   http://datamine.state.nj.us/DEP_OPRA/OpraMain/report?report=Radiologic+Technologist+License+Status+by+First+
   and+Last+Name+and+Date+of+Birth
Radon Tester... www.nj.gov/dep/rpp/radon/CERTMES2.HTM
Real Estate Agent/Broker/Sales .... www.state.nj.us/dobi/licenseesearch/realestatelicensee.htm
Real Estate Appraiser/Apprentice ....
   www.state.nj.us/cgi-bin/consumeraffairs/search/searchentry.pl?searchprofession=4202
Real Estate School/ Instructor..................... www.state.nj.us/dobi/recskool.htm
Respiratory Therapist ... ... www.state.nj.us/cgi-bin/consumeraffairs/search/searchentry.pl?searchprofession=4301
Shorthand Reporter   ... ... www.state.nj.us/cgi-bin/consumeraffairs/search/searchentry.pl?searchprofession=3000
Skin Care Specialist/Shop........................... www.state.nj.us/cgi-bin/consumeraffairs/search/searchentry.pl
Social Worker ... ... www.state.nj.us/cgi-bin/consumeraffairs/search/searchentry.pl?searchprofession=4401
Speech-Language Pathologist..................... www.state.nj.us/cgi-bin/consumeraffairs/search/search.pl
Surveyor, Land .... www.njconsumeraffairs.com/nonmedical/pels.htm
Tree Expert .... www.state.nj.us/dep/parksandforests/forest/community/cte.html
Veterinarian ... ... www.state.nj.us/cgi-bin/consumeraffairs/search/searchentry.pl?searchprofession=2901
Viatical Settlement Broker.......................... www.nj.gov/dobi/licenseesearch/insurancelicensee.htm

County Level ... Courts

Court Administration: Administrative Office of the Courts, RJH Justice Complex, Courts Bldg 7th
Floor, CN 037, Trenton, NJ, 08625; 609-984-0275; www.judiciary.state.nj.us

Court Structure: Each Superior Court has 2 divisions; one for the Civil Division and another for
the Criminal Division. Search requests should be addressed separately to each division.

Civil cases in which the amounts in controversy exceeds $15,000 are heard in the Civil Division of Superior
Court. Cases in which the amounts in controversy are between $3,000 and $15,000 are heard in the Special
Civil Part of the Civil Division. Those in which the amounts in controversy are less than $3,000 also are
heard in the Special Civil Part and are known as small claims cases. Probate is handled by Surrogates.

Online Access Note: The Judiciary's civil motion calendar is searchable at www.judiciary.
state.nj.us/calendars.htm. The database includes all Superior Court Motion calendars for the Civil Division
(Law-Civil Part, Special CivilPart and Chancery-General Equity), and proceeding information for a six-week
period (two weeks prior to the current date and four weeks following the current date). Another useful
website giving decisions is maintained by the Rutgers Law School at
http://lawlibrary.rutgers.edu/search.shtml

Also, the state has three computerized case management systems - ACMS, AMIS, and FACTS - which are
not open to the general public–

- ACMS (Automated Case Management System) contains data on all active civil cases statewide from the Law Division-Civil Part, Chancery Division-Equity Part, the Special Civil Part statewide, and the Appellate Division.
- AMIS (Archival Management Information System) contains closed civil case information. Records go back to the late 1980s.
- FACTS (Family Automated Case Tracking System) contains information on dissolutions from all counties.

The fee is $1.00 per minute of use, and a $500 collateral account is required. For information or a guidebook containing requirements and an enrollment form, write to: Superior Court Clerk's Office, Electronic Access Program, 25 Market St, CN971, Trenton NJ 08625, fax 609-292-6564 or telephone 609-292-4987.

The following county courts participate in the civil court records statewide Electronic Access Program–

> **Atlantic - Bergen - Burlington - Camden - Cape May - Cumberland - Essex - Gloucester - Hudson - Hunterdon - Mercer - Monmouth - Morris - Ocean - Passaic - Salem - Somerset - Sussex - Union - Warren**

There are no known courts that independently offer access to their records.

County Level ... Recorders & Assessors

Recording Office Organization: 21 counties, 21 recording offices. The recording officer title varies depending upon the county. It is either Register of Deeds or County Clerk. The Clerk of Circuit Court records the equivalent of some state's tax liens. The entire state is in the Eastern Time Zone (EST). All federal tax liens are filed with the County Clerk/Register of Deeds and are indexed separately from all other liens. State tax liens comprise two categories - certificates of debt are filed with the Clerk of Superior Court (some, called docketed judgments are filed specifically with the Trenton court), and warrants of execution are filed with the County Clerk/Register of Deeds. Few counties will provide tax lien searches. Refer to the County Court section for information about New Jersey Superior Courts.

Online Access Note: There are two statewide systems. A statewide database of property tax records can be accessed at http://taxrecords.com. The site is operated by a private company. You may also search property data for New Jersey counties for free at http://tax1.co.monmouth.nj.us/cgi-bin/prc6.cgi. Use username "monm" and password "data" then select county. Also, several county's property assessor and other info is available through a private company; for information, call Infocon at 814-472-6066 or www.ic-access.com

Note: Counties on the statewide systems are only listed below if other sites are available within that county.

Atlantic County *Property, Assessor, Inmate Records*
www.atlanticcountyclerk.org
Search inmate info on private company website at www.vinelink.com/index.jsp. See notes at beginning of section for property data.

Cape May County *Real Estate, Recording, Property Records*
www.capemaycountygov.net
Property records for Cape May county are free to view online at http://209.204.84.120/ALIS/WW400R.PGM. To print and have full access to documents, registration and login is required. $1.00 per page copy and/or $10.00 certification fees apply to documents. Online documents go back to 1996, images to 2000. For assistance, telephone 609-465-1010. Land Records found at www.capemaycountygov.net. Also, see notes at beginning of section for more property data.

Gloucester County *Recording, Real Estate, Deed, Lien, UCC, Mortgage, Assessor, Property Tax Records*
www.co.gloucester.nj.us
Access the land index of the assessor database for free at https://www.landaccess.com/sites/nj/gloucester/. Subscription fee of $250 per month for full data, or a $2.00 per search/view fee applies. Also, see notes at beginning of section for more property data.

Middlesex County   *Recording, Deed, Lien, Mortgage, Property Records*
www.co.middlesex.nj.us/countyclerk
Access to the county public access system requires registration and password at http://mcrecords.co.middlesex.nj.us/. There is a sign up fee plus $.25 per page, call Bob Receine at 732-745-3769 for more details. Also, see notes at beginning of section for more property data.

Ocean County   *Property Tax, Real Estate, Deed Records*
www.oceancountyclerk.com
Access to land records on the County Clerk database are free at www.oceancountyclerk.com/search.htm. Search by parties, document or instrument type, or township. Tax records for Ocean county are also on a private company site at http://imac.taxrecords.com/login/signup.html?url=ww1.taxrecords.com. Free index search, but fees for deeper info. Search by name, address or property description. Also, see notes at beginning of section for more property data..

Somerset County   *Real Estate, Recording, Deed, Property Tax, Assessor Records*
www.co.somerset.nj.us
Access to the County Clerk's recordings database is free at http://204.8.192.169/search.asp?cabinet=opr. Registration required for deeper data. Free index goes back to 1/93; images back to 6/11/01. Also, see notes at beginning of section for more property data.

Sussex County   *Property, Assessor, Real Estate, Deed Records*
www.sussexcountyclerk.com
Access to recorder records back to 1/1964 is at www.landaccess.com/proi/county.jsp?county=njsussex. They may begin charging a $250 sub fee. Also, see notes at beginning of section for more property data..

Union County   *Real Estate, Deed, Property Tax, Assessor Records*
http://clerk.ucnj.org
Search recorded real estate related documents at http://clerk.ucnj.org/UCPA/DocIndex. Also, see notes at beginning of section for more property data.

Federal Courts in New Jersey...

Standards for Federal Courts: The universal PACER sign-up number is 800-676-6856. Find PACER and the Party/Case Index on the Web at http://pacer.psc.uscourts.gov. PACER dial-up access is $.60 per minute. Also, courts offering internet access via PACER, Web-PACER or the new CM-ECF charge $.08 per page fee ($.07 per page if record is pre-2005 or unless noted as free).

US District Court -- District of New Jersey
www.njd.uscourts.gov
PACER: Case records are available back to 5/1991. Records are purged never. New records are available online after 1 day. **PACER Online Access:** PACER online at http://pacer.njd.uscourts.gov. **Electronic Filing:** CM/ECF data at https://ecf.njd.uscourts.gov. **Opinions:** View court opinions at http://lawlibrary.rutgers.edu/fed/search.html.
Camden Division counties: Atlantic, Burlington, Camden, Cape May, Cumberland, Gloucester, Salem.
Newark Division counties: Bergen, Essex, Hudson, Middlesex, Morris, Passaic, Sussex, Union. Monmouth County cases here from late 1997-200?; Pre-1997 closed cases remain in Trenton.
Trenton Division counties: Hunterdon, Mercer, Monmouth, Ocean, Somerset, Warren. 1997-200? Monmouth County may be found at Newark Division. Pre-1997 closed Monmouth cases remain in Trenton.

US Bankruptcy Court -- District of New Jersey
www.njb.uscourts.gov
PACER: Case records are available back to 1991. Records are purged every 6 months. **PACER Online Access:** ECF replace PACER. Document images available. **Electronic Filing:** CM/ECF data at https://ecf.njb.uscourts.gov. **Opinions:** Opinions lists are not complete. View court opinions at www.njb.uscourts.gov/chambers2/index.shtml. **Other Online Access:** Calendars free at www.njb.uscourts.gov/hearingdate/index.pl. **Phone access:** Voice Case Information System, call 877-239-2547, 973-645-6044
Camden Division counties: Atlantic, Burlington (partial), Camden, Cape May, Cumberland, Gloucester, Salem. See Trenton Division for remainder of Burlington County .
Newark Division counties: Bergen, Essex, Hudson, Morris, Passaic, Sussex, Union.
Trenton Division counties: Burlington (partial), Hunterdon, Mercer, Middlesex, Monmouth, Ocean, Somerset, Warren. See Camden Division for remainder of Burlington County.

New Mexico

Capital: Santa Fe
           Santa Fe County
Time Zone: MST
Population: 1,903,289
# of Counties: 33

Quick Links

Website: www.newmexico.gov/
Governor: www.governor.state.nm.us
Attorney General: www.ago.state.nm.us
State Archives: www.nmcpr.state.nm.us
State Statutes and Codes: www.conwaygreene.com/NewMexico.htm
Legislative Bill Search: http://legis.state.nm.us/lcs/BillFinder.asp
Bill Monitoring: http://legis.state.nm.us:8080/billwatcher/
Unclaimed Funds: https://ec3.state.nm.us/ucp/SearchUCP.htm

State Level ... Major Agencies

Criminal Records

Department of Public Safety, Criminal Records Bureau, PO Box 1628, Santa Fe, NM 87504-1628 (Courier: 4491 Cerrillos Rd, Santa Fe, NM 87504); 505-827-9181, Fax-505-827-3388, 8AM-5PM.
www.dps.nm.org
Online search: Online access is available from www.osogrande.com/online-services.html, a state-supported agency. The fee is $10.00. You must set up an account to receive a password. When a record is found, a signed release from the subject must then be presented (faxed) to DPS in order to receive the detail page. For more information visit the website mentioned or call 505-345-6555.

Statewide Court Records

Administrative Office of the Courts, 237 Don Gaspar, Rm 25, Santa Fe, NM 87501; 505-827-4800, Fax-505-827-4824, 8AM-5PM.
www.nmcourts.com
Online search: The www.nmcourts.com website offers free access to District and Magistrate Court case information, except Bernalillo Metro which has its own system. In general, records are available from June 1997 forward. Search by name or case #. The search is inclusive of all participating counties. The website also offers a DWI Offender History tool for researching an individual's DWI history. Search by name or SSN. Supreme Court opinions may be researched at www.supremecourt.nm.org/.

Sexual Offender Registry

Department of Public Safety, Records Bureau, PO Box 1628, Santa Fe, NM 87504-1628 (Courier: 4491 Cerrillos Rd, Santa Fe, NM 87504); 505-827-9297, 505-827-9193, Fax-505-827-3399, 8AM-5PM.
www.nmsexoffender.dps.state.nm.us
Online search: The website offers a variety of search methods including by name, county, city, and ZIP Code. The site also offers a complete state list, also an absconder list.

Incarceration Records

New Mexico Corrections Department, Central Records Unit, PO Box 27116, Santa Fe, NM 87502; 505-827-8674, Fax-505-827-8801. http://corrections.state.nm.us
Online search: To search at the website, you must first click on Offender Information, then on Offender Search.

Corporation, Limited Liability Company Records

New Mexico Public Regulation Commission, Corporations Bureau, PO Box 1269, Santa Fe, NM 87504-1269 (Courier: 1120 Paseo de Peralta, Pera Bldg 4th Fl, Rm 413, Santa Fe, NM 87501); 505-827-4502 (Main Number), 800-947-4722 (In-state Only), 505-827-4510 (Good Standing), 505-827-4513 (Copy Request), Fax-505-827-4387, 8AM-12:00: 1PM-5PM.
www.nmprc.state.nm.us/corporations/corpshome.htm
Online search: There is no charge to view records at the Internet site, www.nmprc.state.nm.us/corporations/corpsinquiry.htm. Records can be searched by company name or by director name. **Other options:** This agency makes the database available on electronic format using a 3480 tape cartridge. Fee is $3,600, monthly updates available for $600.

Uniform Commercial Code

UCC Division, Secretary of State, 325 Don GasparSt #301, Santa Fe, NM 87503; 505-827-3615, Fax-505-827-3611, 8AM-5PM.
http://secure.sos.state.nm.us/ucc/default.asp
Online search: The website permits searching and provides a form to use to order copies of filings. You can also request records via email. **Other options:** Microfilm and images (from 7/99) on disk may be purchased.

Birth Certificates

Department of Health, Bureau of Vital Records, PO Box 26110, Santa Fe, NM 87502 (Courier: 1105 South St Francis Dr, Santa Fe, NM 87502); 505-827-0121, 505-827-2338 (Information), 877-284-0963 (Order), Fax-505-984-1048, 8AM-5:00PM.
www.health.state.nm.us
Online search: Records can be ordered at www.vitalchek.com, a state designated vendor.

Death Records

Department of Health, Bureau of Vital Records, PO Box 26110, Santa Fe, NM 87502 (Courier: 1105 South St Francis Dr, Santa Fe, NM 87502); 505-827-0121, 505827-2338 (Information), 877-284-0963 (Order), Fax-505-984-1048, 8AM-5PM.
www.health.state.nm.us
Online search: A free lookup is available at www.rootsweb.com/~usgenweb/nm/nmdi.htm. Records date from 1899 to 1940. Expedited records can be ordered at www.vitalchek.com, a state designated vendor.

Driver Records

Motor Vehicle Division, Driver Services Bureau, PO Box 1028, Santa Fe, NM 87504-1028 (Courier: Joseph M. Montoya Bldg, 1100 S St. Francis Dr, 2nd Floor, Santa Fe, NM 87504); 505-827-2241, 888-683-4636 (Toll Free-Automated), 505-827-4636 (Local-Automated), Fax-505-827-2792, 8AM-5PM.
www.state.nm.us/tax/mvd
Online search: Records are available, for authorized users, from the state's designated vendors - Oso Grande (505-343-7639) www.osogrande.com and Samba (888-94-samba) www.samba.biz. In general, subscription fees are $1.49 to $3.50 depending on the type of record ordered, plus possible network or access fees. Systems are open 24 hours a day, batch requesters must wait 24 hours.

Vehicle and Vessel Ownership, Identification, Registration

Motor Vehicle Division, Vehicle Services Bureau, PO Box 1028, Santa Fe, NM 87504-1028 (Courier: Joseph M. Montoya Bldg, 1100 S St. Francis Dr, 2nd Floor, Santa Fe, NM 87504); 505-827-4636, 888-683-4636, Fax-505-827-0395, 8AM-5PM.
www.state.nm.us/tax/mvd
Online search: Records are available, for authorized users, from two state designated vendor - Oso Grande (505-343-7639). Go to www.osogrande.com. In general, fees are $2.50 to $3.50 per record. Authorization must come from the state agency. **Other options:** Bulk requests for vehicle or ownership information must be approved by the Director's office. Once a sale is made, further resale is prohibited.

Accident Reports

Department of Public Safety, Attn: Records, PO Box 1628, Santa Fe, NM 87504-1628 (Courier: New Mexico State Police Complex, 4491 Cerrillos Rd, Santa Fe, NM 87504); 505-827-9181, Fax-505-827-9189, 8AM-5PM.
www.dps.nm.org
Online search: Reports are available at https://www.nmaccidentreports.com/index.jsp. The officer's diagram and narrative is included. There is a $1.00 fee. Credit cards are accepted.

State Level ... Occupational Licensing

Acupuncturist............................www.rld.state.nm.us/b&c/Acupuncture/Licensee%20Search/licensee_search.asp

Alcohol Server..........................www.rld.state.nm.us/AGD/Licensee%20Search/licensee_search_servers.asp

Announcer, Athletic Event........www.rld.state.nm.us/b&c/Athletic%20Comm/Licensee%20Search/licensee_search.asp

Architect ....www.nmbea.org/People/Aroster.htm

Art Therapist.............................www.rld.state.nm.us/b&c/counseling/Licensee%20Search/licensee_search.asp

Athletic Promoter/Matchmaker.www.rld.state.nm.us/b&c/Athletic%20Comm/Licensee%20Search/licensee_search.asp

Athletic Trainer.........................www.rld.state.nm.us/b&c/Athletic%20Trainers/Licensee%20Search/licensee_search.asp

Attorney ....www.nmbar.org/template.cfm?section=attorney_firm_finder

Audiologist ....www.rld.state.nm.us/b&c/speech/Licensee%20Search/licensee_search.asp

Bank...www.rld.state.nm.us/fid/Licensee%20Search/licensee_search_index.htm

Barber/Barber Shop/School ......www.rld.state.nm.us/b&c/Barber%20&%20Cosmo/Licensee%20Search/licensee_search.asp

Boiler Operator Journeyman.....www.contractorsnm.com:8080/search/

Booking Agent...........................www.rld.state.nm.us/b&c/Athletic%20Comm/Licensee%20Search/licensee_search.asp

Boxer/Boxer Manager...............www.rld.state.nm.us/b&c/Athletic%20Comm/Licensee%20Search/licensee_search.asp

Boxing Judge/Timekeeper ....www.rld.state.nm.us/b&c/Athletic%20Comm/Licensee%20Search/licensee_search.asp

Cemetery, Endowed/Perp. Care www.rld.state.nm.us/fid/Licensee%20Search/licensee_search_index.htm

Chiropractor..............................www.rld.state.nm.us/b&c/Chiropractic/Licensee%20Search/licensee_search.asp

Clinical Nurse Specialist...........www.state.nm.us/nursing/lookup.html

Collection Agency/Manager .....www.rld.state.nm.us/fid/Licensee%20Search/licensee_search_index.htm

Consumer Credit Loaner...........www.rld.state.nm.us/fid/Licensee%20Search/licensee_search_index.htm

Contractor www.contractorsnm.com:8080/search/

Cosmetologist/Shop/School......www.rld.state.nm.us/b&c/Barber%20&%20Cosmo/Licensee%20Search/licensee_search.asp

Counseling/Therapy Practice ....www.rld.state.nm.us/b&c/counseling/Licensee%20Search/licensee_search.asp

Credit Union ....www.rld.state.nm.us/fid/Licensee%20Search/licensee_search_index.htm

Crematory ....www.rld.state.nm.us/b&c/thanato/Licensee%20Search/licensee_search_index.asp

Dental Assistant ....www.rld.state.nm.us/b&c/dental/

Dentist/Dental Hygienist...........www.rld.state.nm.us/b&c/dental/

Dietitian/Nutritionist................www.rld.state.nm.us

Direct Disposer (Funerary) ....www.rld.state.nm.us/b&c/thanato/Licensee%20Search/licensee_search_index.asp

Electrologist..............................www.rld.state.nm.us/b&c/Barber%20&%20Cosmo/Licensee%20Search/licensee_search.asp

Electrophysician........................www.rld.state.nm.us/b&c/Barber%20&%20Cosmo/Licensee%20Search/licensee_search.asp

Engineer....................................www.state.nm.us/java-bin/peps/PEPSBoard/PEPSBoard.jsp

Escrow Company......................www.rld.state.nm.us/fid/Licensee%20Search/licensee_search_index.htm

Esthetician.................................www.rld.state.nm.us/b&c/Barber%20&%20Cosmo/Licensee%20Search/licensee_search.asp

Funeral Director/Practitioner ....www.rld.state.nm.us/b&c/thanato/Licensee%20Search/licensee_search_index.asp

Funeral Home/FSI/Intern ....www.rld.state.nm.us/b&c/thanato/Licensee%20Search/licensee_search_index.asp

Hearing Aid Specialist..............www.rld.state.nm.us/b&c/speech/Licensee%20Search/licensee_search.asp

Hemodialysis Technician..........www.state.nm.us/nursing/lookup.html

Insurance Agent ....www.nmprc.state.nm.us/insurance/agents/agentshome.htm

Interior Designer.......................www.rld.state.nm.us/b&c/Interior/Licensee%20Search/licensee_search.asp

Journeyman Contractor.............www.contractorsnm.com:8080/search/

Landscape Architect..................www.rld.state.nm.us/b&c/landscape/Licensee%20Search/licensee_search.asp

Loan Company, Small ....www.rld.state.nm.us/fid/Licensee%20Search/licensee_search_index.htm

Lobbying Organization ....http://ethics.sos.state.nm.us/LOBBY/ORG.htm

Lobbyist ....http://ethics.sos.state.nm.us/LOBBY/LOB.htm

LPG Gas License www.contractorsnm.com:8080/search/

Manicurist ....www.rld.state.nm.us/b&c/Barber%20&%20Cosmo/Licensee%20Search/licensee_search.asp

Marriage & Family Therapist ...www.rld.state.nm.us/b&c/counseling/Licensee%20Search/licensee_search.asp

Martial Arts Contest..................www.rld.state.nm.us/b&c/Athletic%20Comm/Licensee%20Search/licensee_search.asp

Massage Instr./Practitioner/School

....www.rld.state.nm.us/b&c/massage/Licnesee%20Search/licensee_search.asp

Massage Therapist ....www.rld.state.nm.us/b&c/massage/Licnesee%20Search/licensee_search.asp

Medical Doctor ....www.docboard.org/nm/

Medication Aide ....www.state.nm.us/nursing/lookup.html

Mental Health Counselor ....www.rld.state.nm.us/b&c/counseling/Licensee%20Search/licensee_search.asp

Midwife ....www.health.state.nm.us/midwife-roster.html

Money Order Agent ....www.rld.state.nm.us/fid/Licensee%20Search/licensee_search_index.htm

Mortgage Company/Loaner ......www.rld.state.nm.us/fid/Licensee%20Search/licensee_search_index.htm

Motor Vehicle Sales Financier..www.rld.state.nm.us/fid/Licensee%20Search/licensee_search_index.htm

Nurse Anesthetist......................www.state.nm.us/nursing/lookup.html

Nurse-LPN, RN, Practitioner....www.state.nm.us/nursing/lookup.html

Nursing Home Administrator....www.rld.state.nm.us/b&c/nhab/Licensee%20Search/licensee_search.asp

Occupational Therapist/Assist. .www.rld.state.nm.us/b&c/otb/Licensee%20Search/licensee_search.asp

Optometrist ....www.rld.state.nm.us/b&c/optometry/Licensee%20Search/licensee_search.asp

Oriental Medicine Doctor ....www.rld.state.nm.us/b&c/Acupuncture/Licensee%20Search/licensee_search.asp

Osteopathic Physician...............www.rld.state.nm.us/b&c/osteo/Licensee%20Search/licensee_search.asp

Pharmacist/Pharmacy................http://ec4.state.nm.us/pharmacy/

Physical Therapist/Assistant ....www.rld.state.nm.us/b&c/ptb/Licensee%20Search/licensee_search.asp

Physician Assistant ....www.docboard.org/nm/

Podiatrist..................................www.rld.state.nm.us/b&c/Podiatry/Licensee%20Search/licensee_search.asp

Psychologist.............................www.rld.state.nm.us/b&c/psychology/Licensee%20Search/licensee_search.asp

Psychologist Associate.............www.rld.state.nm.us/b&c/psychology/Licensee%20Search/licensee_search.asp

Public Accountant-CPA............www.rld.state.nm.us/b&c/accountancy/Licensee%20Search/licensee_search.asp

Real Estate Agent/Salesperson..http://rld.state.nm.us/b&c/recom/Licensee%20Search/licensee_search.asp

Real Estate Appraiser................www.rld.state.nm.us/b&c/reappraisers/Licensee%20Search/licensee_search.asp

Real Estate Broker ....http://rld.state.nm.us/b&c/recom/Licensee%20Search/licensee_search.asp

Referee......................................www.rld.state.nm.us/b&c/Athletic%20Comm/Licensee%20Search/licensee_search.asp

Respiratory Care Therapist ....www.rld.state.nm.us/b&c/rcb/Licensee%20Search/licensee_search.asp

Savings & Loan ....www.rld.state.nm.us/fid/Licensee%20Search/licensee_search_index.htm

School Administrator................www.ped.state.nm.us/

School Counselor......................www.ped.state.nm.us/

Social Worker (LBSW, LI, LM)..www.rld.state.nm.us/b&c/socialwk/index.htm

Speech-Language Pathologist...www.rld.state.nm.us/b&c/speech/Licensee%20Search/licensee_search.asp

Substance Abuse Counselor......www.rld.state.nm.us/b&c/counseling/Licensee%20Search/licensee_search.asp

Surveyor, Land ....www.state.nm.us/java-bin/peps/PEPSBoard/PEPSBoard.jsp

Teacher ....www.ped.state.nm.us/

Trust Company ....www.rld.state.nm.us/fid/Licensee%20Search/licensee_search_index.htm

Veterinarian/Veterinary Tech ...www.newmexicoveterinaryboard.us/

Veterinary Facility ....www.newmexicoveterinaryboard.us/

Wrestler ....www.rld.state.nm.us/b&c/Athletic%20Comm/Licensee%20Search/licensee_search.asp

County Level ... Courts

Court Administration: Administrative Office of the Courts, Supreme Court Building, 237 Don Gaspar, Rm 25, Santa Fe, NM, 87501; 505-827-4800; www.nmcourts.com

Court Structure: The 30 District Courts in 13 districts are the courts of general jurisdiction. The Magistrate Courts handle civil cases up to $10,000, and are referred to as Small Claims. The Bernalillo Metropolitan Court has jurisdiction in cases up to $10,000. Municipal Courts handle petty misdemeanors, DWI/DUI, traffic violations, and other municipal ordinance violations.

Online Access Note: The www.nmcourts.com website offers free access to District Courts and Magistrate Courts case information (except Bernalillo Metropolitan Court, see below). In general, records are available from June, 1997 forward. The website also offers a DWI Offender History tool for researching an individual's DWI history. Search by name or SSN.

Supreme Court opinions may be researched at www.supremecourt.nm.org

A commercial online service is available for the Metropolitan Court of Bernalillo County. There is a $35.00 set up fee, a connect time fee based on usage. The system is available 24 hours daily. Call 505-345-6555 for more information.

Bernalillo County

2nd Judicial District Court – Civil and Criminal Records
www.seconddistrictcourt.com
Access is free at www.nmcourts.com. Most data goes back to 6/1997. Access to criminal records is free at www.nmcourts.com. Most data goes back to 6/1997.

Metropolitan Court – Civil and Criminal Records
www.metrocourt.state.nm.us
Access Metropolitan court civil records online at www.osogrande.com. There is set up fee plus a per minute charge based on usage. For information or to obtain an account call 505-345-6555. Also, search Metro Court civil case records free at www.metrocourt.state.nm.us. Search Metro Court criminal case records free at www.metrocourt.state.nm.us/docket_help.htm.

Catron -Chaves -Cibola -Colfax -Curry -De Baca -Dona Ana -Eddy -Grant -Guadalupe -Harding -Hidalgo -Lea -Lincoln -Los Alamos -Luna -McKinley -Mora -Otero -Quay -Rio Arriba -Roosevelt -San Juan -San Miguel -Sandoval -Santa Fe -Sierra -Socorro -Taos -Torrance -Union –Valencia.
Access to court records from 1997 forward is free at www.nmcourts.com.

County Level ... Recorders & Assessors

Recording Office Organization: 33 counties, 33 recording offices. The recording officer is the County Clerk. Most counties maintain a grantor/grantee index and a miscellaneous index. The entire state is in the Mountain Time Zone (MST). All federal and state tax liens are filed with the County Clerk. Most counties will not provide tax lien searches.

Online Access Note: A handful of counties offer online access, but there is no statewide system.

Bernalillo County
Real Estate, Recording, Deed, Lien, Judgment, Death, Marriage, UCC, Property Assessor Records
www.bernco.gov
The recorders data and Grantor/Grantee index is free at http://augery.bernco.gov:8080/icris/documentSearch.jsp. Free registration and password required. Also search assessor records at www.bernco.gov/property/default.asp?qpaction=search_form&type=situs.

Dona Ana County *Assessor, Real Estate, Deed, Personal Property Records*
www.co.dona-ana.nm.us
Access the deeds database free at www.co.dona-ana.nm.us/search/deeds/. Also, access the Real Property database free at www.co.dona-ana.nm.us/search/realprop/.

Lincoln County *Assessor, Property Records*
Access to the assessor property records is free at www.lincolncountynm.net/ACCESS[1].htm. Registration, software, username and password is required. Follow prompts at website.

San Juan County *Real Estate, Assessor Records*
www.sjcounty.net/Dpt/Clerk/_Default.asp
Access to county real estate tax data is free at www.sjcounty.net/SJCTaxes/.

Santa Fe County *Assessor, Property, Real Estate, Grantor/Grantee, Deed Records*
www.co.santa-fe.nm.us
Access to county property data at http://216.161.39.9/wick/Query1CompactHTMLInput.html requires Location ID or Tax Account ID that is found on a county tax bill. Also, access to recorder's grantor/grantee index available by subscription; call Mary Quintana at 505-986-6375 or 6329. $30.00 setup fee and $25.00 monthly and $7.00 per hour usage fee. With username and password you may search the WEBXtender Document Imaging System at www.co.santa-fe.nm.us/web_X.php.

Federal Courts in New Mexico...

Standards for Federal Courts: The universal PACER sign-up number is 800-676-6856. Find PACER and the Party/Case Index on the Web at http://pacer.psc.uscourts.gov. PACER dial-up access is $.60 per minute. Also, courts offering internet access via PACER, Web-PACER or the new CM-ECF charge $.08 per page fee ($.07 per page if record is pre-2005 or unless noted as free).

US District Court -- District of New Mexico
www.nmcourt.fed.us/dcdocs
PACER: Sign-up number is . Case records are available back to 1990. Records are purged every 6 months. New records are available online after 2 weeks. **PACER Online Access:** Register for free online searching. **Electronic Filing:** This utilizes ACE (Advanced Court Engineering), not the US Courts standard CM/ECF system. CM/ECF data at www.nmcourt.fed.us/dcdocs - click on Electronic Filing. **Other Online Access:** Submit a written request for an ACE (Advanced Court Engineering) user name and password in order to freely access court records, docket reports, and court opinions. See www.nmcourt.fed.us/web/DCDOCS/files/accountrequest.html.
Albuquerque Division counties: All counties in New Mexico. Cases may be assigned to any of 3 divisions - Santa Fe (505-988-6481), Las Cruces (505-528-1400), and Roswell (505-625-2388). Santa Fe and Las Cruces have searchable records; Roswell does not.

US Bankruptcy Court -- District of New Mexico
www.nmcourt.fed.us/bkdocs
PACER: Case records are available back to 7/1991. New records are available online after 1 day. **PACER Online Access:** PACER online at http://pacer.nmb.uscourts.gov. **Electronic Filing:** CM/ECF data at (Currently in the process of implementing CM/ECF). **Other Online Access:** Submit a written request for an ACE (Advanced Court Engineering) user name and password in order to freely access court records, docket reports, and court opinions. See www.nmcourt.fed.us/web/BCDOCS/bcindex.html. **Phone access:** Voice Case Information System, call 888-435-7822, 505-348-2444
Albuquerque Division counties: All counties in New Mexico. Judges do travel to Los Cruces and Roswell, however, bankruptcy records are not searchable at those courthouses.

New York

Capital: Albany
          AlbanyCounty
Time Zone: EST
Population: 19,227,088
# of Counties: 62

Quick Links

Website: www.state.ny.us
Governor: www.ny.gov/governor/
Attorney General: www.oag.state.ny.us
State Archives: www.nysarchives.org/gindex.shtml
State Statutes and Codes: http://assembly.state.ny.us/leg/?cl=0
Legislative Bill Search: http://public.leginfo.state.ny.us/menuf.cgi
Unclaimed Funds: http://wwe1.osc.state.ny.us/ouf/oufSearchForm.html

State Level ... Major Agencies

Statewide Court Records

NY State Office of Court Administration, New York City Office, 25 Beaver St, New York, NY 10004; 212-428-2100, 212-428-2990, Fax-212-428-2190, 9AM-5PM.
www.courts.state.ny.us
Online search: The OCA offers online or email access to approved requesters for statewide criminal records. Call the OCA for details on how to set up an account. The fee is $52.00 per record. Civil Supreme Court case information for open cases is available for all 62 New York counties through https://iapps.courts.state.ny.us/caseTrac/jsp/ecourt.htm. Go to www.nycourts.gov/ctapps for appellate case summaries. Also, state Civil Court Commercial Division decisions are searchable at http://decisions.courts.state.ny.us/nyscomdiv/search/comdivintro.htm.

Sexual Offender Registry

Division of Criminal Justice Srvs, Sexual Offender Registry, 4 Tower Place, Rm 604, Albany, NY 12203; 518-457-6326 x1, 800-262-3257 x2 (Verification), Fax-518-485-5805, 8AM-5PM.
www.criminaljustice.state.ny.us/nsor/index.htm
Online search: The sex offender registry Level 3 can be searched at the website. Requesters are required to register. Please note that a federal court injunction currently prohibits the release of information on this web site concerning sex offenders who committed their crime prior to January 21, 1996 and were assigned a risk level prior to January 1, 2000.

Incarceration Records

New York Department of Correctional Services, Building 2 - Central Files, 1220 Washington Ave, Albany, NY 12226-2050; 518-457-5000, 518-457-8126 (Contact phone), Fax-518-457-4966, 8AM-4PM.
www.docs.state.ny.us
Online search: Computerized inmate information is available from the Inmate Lookup at http://nysdocslookup.docs.state.ny.us/kinqw00 or follow "inmate lookup" link at main site. Records go back to early 1970s. To acquire inmate DIN number, you may call 518-457-5000. The site is open, in general, from Mon. thru Sat. 2:00 a.m.-11:00 p.m. & Sun. 4:00 a.m. thru 11:00 p.m.

Corporation, Limited Partnership, Limited Liability Company, Limited Liability Partnerships

Division of Corporations, Department of State, 41 State St, Albany, NY 12231; 518-473-2492 (General Information), 900-835-2677 (Corporate Searches), Fax-518-474-1418, 8AM-4:30PM.
www.dos.state.ny.us
Online search: A commercial account can be set up for direct access. Fee is $.75 per transaction through a drawdown account. There is an extensive amount of information available including historical information. Also, the Division's corporate and business entity database may be accessed at http://appsext5.dos.state.ny.us/corp_public/CORPSEARCH.ENTITY_SEARCH_ENTRY. The web has not-for-profit corporations, limited partnerships, limited liability companies and limited liability partnerships as well. **Other options:** You may submit an email search request at corporations@dos.state.ny.us.

Uniform Commercial Code, Federal Tax Liens, State Tax Liens

Department of State, UCC Unit - Records, 41 State Street, Albany, NY 12231-0001; 518-474-4763, 518-474-5418, Fax-518-474-4478, 8AM-4:30PM.
www.dos.state.ny.us/corp/uccfaq.html
Online search: Free access is available at http://appsext4.dos.state.ny.us/pls/ucc_public/web_search.main_frame. Search financing statements and federal tax lien notices by debtor name, or secured party name, or by filing number and date. Document images can be provided. **Other options:** This agency offers its database for sale on microfilm.

Death, Marriage Divorce Records

Vital Records Section, Certification Unit, 800 N Pearl St, Albany, NY 12204-1842 (Courier: PO Box 2602, Albany, NY 12220-2602); 518-474-3038, 518-474-3077, Fax-518-474-9168, 8:30AM-4:30PM.
www.health.state.ny.us/vital_records/
Online search: Online ordering is available via an approved third party vendor, go to www.vitalchek.com.

Birth and Death Records-New York City

Department of Health, Bureau of Vital Records, 125 Worth St, Box 4, Rm 133, New York, NY 10013; 212-788-4520, 212-442-1999, Fax-212-962-6105, 9AM-4PM.
www.nyc.gov/html/doh/
Online search: Records may be requested via www.vitalchek.com. Use of credit card is required.

Workers' Compensation Records

NY Workers' Compensation Board, Office of General Counsel, 20 Park Street # 401, Albany, NY 12207; 518-474-6670, 9AM-5PM.
www.wcb.state.ny.us
Online search: Proof of coverage is available at www.wcb.state.ny.us/design/framework/ebiz.htm.

Driver Records

Department of Motor Vehicles, MV-15 Processing, 6 Empire State Plaza, Room 430, Albany, NY 12228; 518-473-5595, 800-225-5368 (In-state), 8AM-5PM.
www.nydmv.state.ny.us
Online search: NY has implemented a "Dial-In Display" system which enables customers to obtain data online 24 hours a day. The DL# or name, DOB and sex are required to retrieve. The systems works off of a pre-paid bank. The fee is $7.00 per record. For more information, visit www.nysdmv.com/dialin.htm. Note: drivers may use the Dial-in Search Account to request their own DMV records; however, records are returned by mail. **Other options:** This agency offers a program to employers whereby the agency will notify the employers when an event is posted to an employee's record. To find out about the "LENS" program, visit www.nysdmv.com/lens.htm.

Vehicle and Vessel Ownership, Vessel Registration

Department of Motor Vehicles, MV-15 processing, 6 Empire State Plaza, Room 430, Albany, NY 12228; 518-474-0710, 518-474-8510, 8AM-5PM.
www.nydmv.state.ny.us
Online search: New York offers plate, VIN and ownership data through the same network discussed in the Driving Records Section. The system is interactive and open 24 hours a day. The fee is $5.00 per record. All accounts must be approved, requesters must follow DPPA guidelines. Call 518-474-4293 or visit www.nysdmv.com/dialin.htm for more information.

State Level ... Occupational Licensing

Accountant, CPA/Public .... www.op.nysed.gov/opsearches.htm#nme
Acupuncturist/Acupuncturist Assistant. www.op.nysed.gov/opsearches.htm#nme
Addiction Counselor .... www.oasas.state.ny.us/credentialingVerification/verification/home.cfm
Addiction Treatment Center................. www.oasas.state.ny.us/credentialingVerification/verification/home.cfm
Adult Care Med. Facility .... www.health.state.ny.us/facilities/adult_care/
Adult Care Suspended List .... www.health.state.ny.us/facilities/adult_care/memorandum.htm
Alarm Installer .... http://appsext5.dos.state.ny.us/lcns_public/lcns_query.lic_name_search_frm
Alcohol Abuse Provider........................ www.oasas.state.ny.us/credentialingVerification/verification/home.cfm
Alcohol Beverage Bond Company........ http://abc.state.ny.us/JSP/content/bonds.jsp
Alcohol Distiller/Whlser/Mfg .... http://abc.state.ny.us/JSP/query/PublicQueryInstructPage.jsp
Alcohol Service Establishment .... http://abc.state.ny.us/JSP/query/PublicQueryInstructPage.jsp
Alcohol/Substance Abuse Counselor .... www.oasas.state.ny.us/credentialingVerification/verification/home.cfm
Apartment Information Vendor .... http://appsext5.dos.state.ny.us/lcns_public/lcns_query.lic_name_search_frm
Apartment Manager/Vendor/Agent ...... http://appsext5.dos.state.ny.us/lcns_public/lcns_query.lic_name_search_frm
Appearance Enhancement Professional http://appsext5.dos.state.ny.us/lcns_public/lcns_query.lic_name_search_frm
Architect .... www.op.nysed.gov/opsearches.htm#nme
Armored Car/Car Carrier .... http://appsext5.dos.state.ny.us/lcns_public/lcns_query.lic_name_search_frm
Athlete Agent...................................... http://appsext5.dos.state.ny.us/lcns_public/lcns_query.lic_name_search_frm
Athletic Trainer................................... www.op.nysed.gov/opsearches.htm#nme
Attorney .... www.nycourts.gov/attorneys/registration/index.shtml
Audiologist .... www.op.nysed.gov/opsearches.htm#nme
Bail Enforcement Agent .... http://appsext5.dos.state.ny.us/lcns_public/lcns_query.lic_name_search_frm
Bank Representative Office, Foreign .... www.banking.state.ny.us/silicrepo.htm
Bank.. www.banking.state.ny.us/sifagen.htm
Banker, Private .... www.banking.state.ny.us/siprivat.htm
Banking Regulatory Action .... www.banking.state.ny.us/ea.htm
Barber Apprentice................................ http://appsext5.dos.state.ny.us/lcns_public/lcns_query.lic_name_search_frm
Barber/Barber Shop .... http://appsext5.dos.state.ny.us/lcns_public/lcns_query.lic_name_search_frm
Bottled Water Facility.......................... www.health.state.ny.us
Budget Planner..................................... www.banking.state.ny.us/sibudget.htm
Bulk Water Facility.............................. www.health.state.ny.us
Check Casher .... www.banking.state.ny.us/sicheckc.htm
Chemical Dependence Operation.......... www.oasas.state.ny.us/credentialingVerification/verification/home.cfm
Chiropractor.. www.op.nysed.gov/opsearches.htm#nme
Cigarette/Tobacco Whlse/Retail/Agent. http://www7.nystax.gov/CGTX/cgtxHome
Cosmetologist .... http://appsext5.dos.state.ny.us/lcns_public/lcns_query.lic_name_search_frm
Court Reporter .... www.op.nysed.gov/opsearches.htm#nme
Credit Union .... www.banking.state.ny.us/sicredit.htm
Day Care, Farm Worker (ABCD) .... www.agmkt.state.ny.us/programs/childdev.html
DEC Permit Application...................... www.dec.state.ny.us/cfmx/extapps/envapps/index.cfm?view=wizard
Dental Hygienist .... www.op.nysed.gov/opsearches.htm#nme
Dentist/Dental Assistant....................... www.op.nysed.gov/opsearches.htm#nme
Dietitian .... www.op.nysed.gov/opsearches.htm#nme
Dispatch Facility (Alarm/Security/Fire) http://appsext5.dos.state.ny.us/lcns_public/lcns_query.lic_name_search_frm
Dog License... www.agmkt.state.ny.us/AI/dog_pwd.htm
Domestic Out of State Bank Rep. Ofc. . www.banking.state.ny.us/sioosrep.htm
Engineer.. www.op.nysed.gov/opsearches.htm#nme
Environmental Permit .... www.dec.state.ny.us/cfmx/extapps/envapps/index.cfm?view=wizard
Esthetics Specialist .... http://appsext5.dos.state.ny.us/lcns_public/lcns_query.lic_name_search_frm
Farm Products Dealer .... www.agmkt.state.ny.us/AP/LicFarmProdDealersList.asp
Foreign Banking Agency .... www.banking.state.ny.us/sifagen.htm
Greenhouse .... www.agmkt.state.ny.us/nurseryDealers.html
Guard Dog Agency .... http://appsext5.dos.state.ny.us/lcns_public/lcns_query.lic_name_search_frm

Guard/Patrol Agency .... http://appsext5.dos.state.ny.us/lcns_public/lcns_query.lic_name_search_frm
Hair Styling, Natural............................ http://appsext5.dos.state.ny.us/lcns_public/lcns_query.lic_name_search_frm
Hearing Aid Dealer .... http://appsext5.dos.state.ny.us/lcns_public/lcns_query.lic_name_search_frm
HMO (Insurance) www.ins.state.ny.us/tocol4.htm
Holding Company .... www.banking.state.ny.us/siholdmu.htm
Hospital .... www.health.state.ny.us/nysdoh/hospital/index.htm
Insurance Company www.ins.state.ny.us/tocol4.htm
Interior Designer .... www.op.nysed.gov/opsearches.htm#nme
Investment Company Article XII .... www.banking.state.ny.us/siinvest.htm
Landscape Architect............................. www.op.nysed.gov/opsearches.htm#nme
Lender, Licensed .... www.banking.state.ny.us/silicend.htm
Lobbyist .... www.nylobby.state.ny.us/lobby_data.html
Lottery Claim Center   ... ...   www.nylottery.org/ny/nyStore/cgi-bin/ProdSubEV_Cat_333605_NavRoot_306.htm#lcc
Mammography Facility......................... www.accessdata.fda.gov/scripts/cdrh/cfdocs/cfMQSA/mqsa.cfm
Massage Therapist .... www.op.nysed.gov/opsearches.htm#nme
Medical Doctor .... www.op.nysed.gov/opsearches.htm#nme
Medical Examiner, Independent .... www.wcb.state.ny.us/content/main/hcpp/ListofAuthIME.jsp
Mentally Retarded Facility/Service....... www.omr.state.ny.us/ws/servlets/WsAdminServlet
Midwife .... www.op.nysed.gov/opsearches.htm#nme
Minority/Woman-owned Business........ http://205.232.252.35/
Money Transmitter .... www.banking.state.ny.us/simoneyt.htm
Mortgage Banker .... www.banking.state.ny.us/simbanke.htm
Mortgage Broker.................................. www.banking.state.ny.us/simbroke.htm
Nail Technologist................................. http://appsext5.dos.state.ny.us/lcns_public/lcns_query.lic_name_search_frm
Notary Public .... http://appsext5.dos.state.ny.us/lcns_public/lcns_query.lic_name_search_frm
Nurse-LPN, RPN .... www.op.nysed.gov/opsearches.htm#nme
Nursery, Plant .... www.agmkt.state.ny.us/nurseryDealers.html
Nursing Home....................................... www.health.state.ny.us/facilities/nursing/
Nutritionist... www.op.nysed.gov/opsearches.htm#nme
Occupational Therapist/Assistant.......... www.op.nysed.gov/opsearches.htm#nme
Off-Track Betting .... http://licensing.racing.state.ny.us/license.cfm
Ophthalmic Dispenser........................... www.op.nysed.gov/opsearches.htm#nme
Optometrist .... www.op.nysed.gov/opsearches.htm#nme
Pesticide Business/Distributor .... www.dec.state.ny.us/website/dshm/pesticid/appman.htm#top
Pesticide/Commercial Applicator .... www.dec.state.ny.us/website/dshm/pesticid/appman.htm#top
Pharmacist... www.op.nysed.gov/opsearches.htm#nme
Physical Therapist/Assistant .... www.op.nysed.gov/opsearches.htm#nme
Physician... www.op.nysed.gov/opsearches.htm#nme
Physician Assistant .... www.op.nysed.gov/opsearches.htm#nme
Plant Dealer .... www.agmkt.state.ny.us/nurseryDealers.html
Podiatrist.. www.op.nysed.gov/opsearches.htm#nme
Premium Finance Company.................. www.banking.state.ny.us/sipremfi.htm
Private Investigator .... http://appsext5.dos.state.ny.us/lcns_public/lcns_query.lic_name_search_frm
Psychiatrist... www.nyspsych.org
Psychologist.. www.op.nysed.gov/opsearches.htm#nme
Public Accountant-CPA........................ www.op.nysed.gov/opsearches.htm#nme
Racing Occupation............................... http://licensing.racing.state.ny.us/license.cfm
Radiologic Technology School............. www.health.state.ny.us/nysdoh/radtech/schlist2.htm
Radon Testing Lab................................ www.wadsworth.org/labcert/elap/radon.html
Real Estate Agent/Broker/Office .... http://appsext5.dos.state.ny.us/lcns_public/lcns_query.lic_name_search_frm
Real Estate Appraiser............................ http://appsext5.dos.state.ny.us/lcns_public/lcns_query.lic_name_search_frm
Respiratory Therapist/Therapy Tech..... www.op.nysed.gov/opsearches.htm#nme
Safe Deposit Company .... www.banking.state.ny.us/sisafede.htm
Sales Finance Company........................ www.banking.state.ny.us/sisalesf.htm
Savings Bank, Savings & Loan............. www.banking.state.ny.us/sisavloa.htm
School, Non-Degree Proprietary........... www.highered.nysed.gov/bpss/directory_main_page.htm

Security & Fire Alarm Installer .... http://appsext5.dos.state.ny.us/lcns_public/lcns_query.lic_name_search_frm
Security Guard .... http://appsext5.dos.state.ny.us/lcns_public/lcns_query.lic_name_search_frm
Social Worker .... www.op.nysed.gov/opsearches.htm#nme
Speech Pathologist/Audiologist .... www.op.nysed.gov/opsearches.htm#nme
State Telecommunication Contractor.... www.ogs.state.ny.us/purchase/telecomContracts.asp
Substance Abuse Provider .... www.oasas.state.ny.us/credentialingVerification/verification/home.cfm
Summer Camp for Mental Retarded ..... www.omr.state.ny.us//hp_camp_directory.jsp
Surveyor, Land .... www.op.nysed.gov/opsearches.htm#nme
Teacher .... www.highered.nysed.gov/tcert/respublic/ocvs.htm
Telemarketer Business .... http://appsext5.dos.state.ny.us/lcns_public/lcns_query.lic_name_search_frm
Trust Company .... www.banking.state.ny.us/sibank.htm
Uniform Procedures Act Permit............ www.dec.state.ny.us/cfmx/extapps/envapps/index.cfm?view=wizard
Upholster & Bedding Industry.............. http://appsext5.dos.state.ny.us/lcns_public/lcns_query.lic_name_search_frm
Vendor, New York City........................ http://slnx-prd-web.nyc.gov/cfb/cfbSearch.nyc?method=search
Veteran Home...................................... www.nysvets.org/
Veterinarian/Veterinary Technician...... www.op.nysed.gov/opsearches.htm#nme
Water Supply Permit............................ www.dec.state.ny.us/cfmx/extapps/envapps/index.cfm?view=wizard
Water Treatment Plant Operator .... www.health.state.ny.us
Waxing Establishment/Oper/Tech .... http://appsext5.dos.state.ny.us/lcns_public/lcns_query.lic_name_search_frm
Weights/Measures Local Office............ www.agmkt.state.ny.us/WM/wmdirlst.html
Woman-owned Business....................... http://205.232.252.35/
Workers Comp Appr'v'd Health Provider .. www.wcb.state.ny.us/hps/HPSearch.jsp
Workers Comp Claim Representative... www.wcb.state.ny.us/content/main/SiLr/sec24a.pdf
Workers Comp PPO Applicant www.wcb.state.ny.us/content/main/PrefProviderOrg/ppotrak1.pdf

County Level ... Courts

Court Administration: New York State Unified Court System, Office of Court Administration, 4 ESP, Suite 201, Empire State Plaza, Albany, NY 12223. There is also a New York City Office of Court Administration, 25 Beaver St, New York, NY 10004, 212-428-2700; www.courts.state.ny.us

Court Structure:
"Supreme and County Courts" are the highest trial courts in the state, equivalent to Circuit or District Courts in other states. New York's Supreme and County Courts may be administered together or separately. When separate, there is a clerk for each. Supreme and/or County Courts are not appeals courts. Supreme Courts handle civil cases – usually civil cases over $25,000 but there are many exceptions. County Courts handle felony cases and, in many counties, these County Courts also handle misdemeanors.

Records for Supreme and County Courts are maintained by the County Clerks, who are county employees. There are exceptions. In New York City - with its five boroughs - the courts records are administered directly by the state OCA – Office of Court Administration. Also, there are a small number of upstate counties where the Supreme Court OR County Court records are maintained by their court clerk (state employee), and only an index list of cases and defendants is provided to the County Clerk (county employee).

In at least 20 New York Counties, misdemeanor records are only available at city, town, or village courts. This is also true of small claims and eviction records.

Online Access Note: In addition to the standard $52.00 statewide mail or in-person record search, the state OCA offers online access to "approved requesters" for criminal records. Requesters receive information back via email. Call the OCA for details on how to set up an account. The fee is the same $52.00 per record.

Civil Supreme Court case information is available for all 62 New York counties through the court system's website - http://e.courts.state.ny.us. Select decisions from New York Supreme Criminal Court and other criminal courts are also available. There is no charge for this information.

Also, at http://e.courts.state.ny.us you may search for future court dates for defendants in these 21 criminal courts: Bronx Criminal Court, Bronx Supreme Court, Dutchess County Court, Buffalo City Court, Erie County Court, Kings Criminal Court, Kings Supreme Court, Nassau County Court, Nassau District Court,

New York Criminal Court, New York Supreme Court, Orange County Court, Putnam County, Queens Criminal Court, Queens Supreme Court, Richmond Criminal Court, Richmond Supreme Court, Rockland County Court, Suffolk County Court, Suffolk District Court, Westchester County Court.

Broome County

County Clerk – Civil and Criminal Records

www.gobcclerk.com

Access the clerk's court and judgment indexes free at www.gobcclerk.com/cgi/Official_Search_Types.html/input; records go back to 1987. Also, access to civil (judgment) records are available; for registration information on the county clerk online system, call Danielle at 607-778-2377.

Erie County

County Clerk – Civil and Criminal Records

www.erie.gov/depts/government/clerk/civil_criminal.phtml

Access to the county clerk's database of civil matters is free at http://ecclerk.erie.gov. Records go back to 2/1994. Also, see note at beginning of section.

Monroe County

Supreme & County Court – Civil and Criminal Records

www.clerk.co.monroe.ny.us

Access to felony, civil, and divorce records free online at www.clerk.co.monroe.ny.us. Records go back to 6/1993, and earlier film images are being added. Call 585-428-5151 for username, password, or more information. Also, access to current Supreme court cases and some closed cases is at http://e.courts.state.ny.us/.

New York County

Supreme Court - Civil Division – Civil Records

www.nycourts.gov/supctmanh

Search decisions at http://portal.courts.state.ny.us/pls/portal30/CMS_DEV.DECISIONS_NDAWCASE.show_parms. Also, see note at beginning of section.

Rockland County

County Clerk – Civil and Criminal Records

www.rocklandcountyclerk.com

Access to county clerk index is free at www.rocklandcountyclerk.com/court_records.html. Online includes civil judgments, real estate records, tax warrants. Free registration required. Call 845-638-5221 for info. Also, see note at beginning of section.

County Level ... Recorders & Assessors

Recording Office Organization: 62 counties, 62 recording offices. The recording officer is the County Clerk (it is the New York City Register in the counties of Bronx, Kings, New York, and Queens). The entire state is in the Eastern Time Zone (EST). Federal tax liens on personal property of businesses are filed with the Secretary of State. Other federal tax liens are filed with the County Clerk. State tax liens are filed with the County Clerk, with a master list - called state tax warrants - available at the Secretary of State's office. Federal tax liens are usually indexed with UCC Records. State tax liens are usually indexed with other miscellaneous liens and judgments. Some counties include federal tax liens as part of a UCC search, and others will search tax liens for a separate fee or not at all. Search fees and copy fees vary.

Online Access Note: A many counties and towns offer free internet access to assessor records and the number is growing. The New York City Register now offers free access to all borough's real estate records (also including Staten Island) at http://nyc.gov/html/dof/html/home/home.shtml. Search by address or legal description.

New York Counties *Property Records*

A private company offers property assessment data for most New York Counties online at www.uspdr.com/consumer/ownersearch.asp.

Albany County *Real Estate, Deed, Mortgage, Recording, Assessor, Property Tax, Naturalization Records*

www.albanycounty.com/clerk
Access deeds and mortgages free at https://access.albanycounty.com/clerk/deedsandmortgages/. Also, search county naturalization records free at www.albanycounty.com/departments/achor/. Also, see note at beginning of section for more online property searches.

Bronx County *Real Estate, Lien, Deed, Judgment, UCC, Deed, Mortgage, Tax Assessor, Property Records*
Recording data from the City Register are free at http://a836-acris.nyc.gov/scripts/docsearch.dll/index. Also, for deeper financial data back 10 years, subscribe to the NYC Dept of Finance dial-up system; fee-$250 monthly and $5.00 per item. For info/signup, call Richard Reskin 718-935-6523. Also, property assessment rolls from NYC's Dept. of Finance are free at http://nyc.gov/html/dof/html/home/home.shtml. No name searching. Also, they offer daily downloads for borough-wide transactions of UCCs, Fed Liens, deeds, real estate. Also, see note at beginning of section for more online property searches.

Broome County *Property, Deed, Mortgage, Recording, Real Estate, Lien, Judgment, Court Index Records*
www.gobroomecounty.com/clerk/index.php
Search the clerk's indexes free at www.gobcclerk.com/cgi/Official_Search_Types.html/input. Online miscellaneous and lien records go back to 1989, deeds & mortgages go back to 1963 and court records (civil and criminal) from 1985 to present. Also, see note at beginning of section for moe online property searches.

Cattaraugus County *Tax Assessor, Property, Most Wanted, Warrant Records*
www.cattco.org
Records on the City of Olean assessor database are free at www.cityofolean.com/Assessor/main.htm. Also, you may search for property info on the interactive map at www.cattco.org/real_property/parcel_news.asp. Also, search sheriff's warrants and wanted at www.sheriff.cattco.org. Also, see note at beginning of section for more online property searches.

Cayuga County *Property, Assessor, Real Estate, Deed, Lien Records*
www.co.cayuga.ny.us/clerk
Search real estate, deeds and liens at www.landaccess.com/proi/county.jsp?county=nycayuga. Subscription fee is $440 per year or $40 per month, plus $5.00 per image, credit cards accepted. Index goes back to 1972; images back to 1993.

Chenango County *Property Records*
www.co.chenango.ny.us
A private company offers property assessment data online at www.uspdr.com/consumer/ownersearch.asp.

Cortland County *Property, Deed, Mortgage, Civil, Judgment, UCC, Lien, Fictitious Business Name Records*
http://www2.cortland-co.org
Online access at https://cclerk.cortland-co.org/index.asp gives judgments and other county clerk records. Login using "public" as user name and password. A subscription service is also available. Also, see note at beginning of section for online property searches.

Delaware County *Property Records*
A private company offers property assessment data online at www.uspdr.com/consumer/ownersearch.asp.

Erie County *Recording, Deed, Mortgage, Judgment, Property Records*
http://ecclerk.erie.gov
Access to the county clerk's database index and images is at http://ecclerk.erie.gov/CGI-BIN/DB2WWW/RECORDS.mbr/RECORDS. A private company offers property assessments at www.uspdr.com/consumer/ownersearch.asp. Also, find property data on the mapping site at www.co.chautauqua.ny.us.

Essex County *Property Records*
www.co.essex.ny.us
A private company offers property assessment data online at www.uspdr.com/consumer/ownersearch.asp.

Fulton County *Auditor, Real Estate, Deed, UCC Records*
Search county auditor information at http://66.194.132.76/. Search recorder documents at www.landaccess.com/sites/oh/disclaimer.php?county=ohfulton.

Genesee County - Green County - Hamilton County - Herkimer County *Property Records*
A private company offers property assessment data online at www.uspdr.com/consumer/ownersearch.asp.

Jefferson County *Property Records*
Property assessment data offered online at www.co.jefferson.ny.us. Also, see note at beginning of section for more property searches.

Kings County *Real Estate, Lien, Deed, Judgment, UCC, Deed, Mortgage, Tax Assessor, Property Records*
Recording data from the City Register free at http://a836-acris.nyc.gov/scripts/docsearch.dll/index. Also, for deeper financial data back 10 years, subscribe to the NYC Dept of Finance dial-up system; fee-$250 monthly and $5.00 per item. For info/signup, call Richard Reskin 718-935-6523. Also, property assessment rolls from NYC's Dept. of Finance are free at http://nyc.gov/html/dof/html/home/home.shtml. No name searching. Also, see note at beginning of section for online property searches.

Lewis County *Property, Assessor Records*
Madison County *Property Records*
A private company offers property assessment data online at www.uspdr.com/consumer/ownersearch.asp.

Monroe County *Land, Judgment, UCC, Lien, Court, Property Records*
www.monroecounty.gov/org34.asp
Access the county clerk database online at www.clerk.co.monroe.ny.us. Includes mortgages, deeds, court records; free registration. Land records back to 1984. Liens, judgments, UCCS back to 5/1989. Court records - civil, felony, divorce - go back to June, 1993. Earlier microfilm images are being added as time permits. Also, see note at beginning of section for more online property searches.

Montgomery County *Property Records*
A private company offers property assessment data online at www.uspdr.com/consumer/ownersearch.asp.

Nassau County *Real Estate, Assessor, Recording, Property Records*
www.nassaucountyny.gov/
Access to the county assessor tax data for free at www.nassaucountyny.gov/ncasmt/index.jsp. No name searching. Also, access to recorder images is through a private company at www.courthousedirect.com. Fee for data.

New York County *Real Estate, Lien, Judgment, UCC, Deed, Mortgage, Tax Assessor, Most Wanted, Missing Person, Restaurant Insp. Records*
Recording data from the City Register are free at http://a836-acris.nyc.gov/scripts/docsearch.dll/index. Also, for deeper financial data back 10 years, subscribe to the NYC Dept of Finance dial-up system; fee-$250 monthly and $5.00 per item. For info/signup, call Rich Reskin 718-935-6523. Also, assessment roll searches are free at http://nycserv.nyc.gov/nycproperty/nynav/jsp/selectbbl.jsp; no name searching. Also, search assessments free at www.uspdr.com/consumer/ownersearch.asp. Search most wanted list at www.ci.nyc.ny.us/html/nypd/html/wanted/mwant.html; missing persons- www.nyc.gov/html/nypd/html/missing.html; restaurant insp.- www.nyc.gov/html/doh/html/rii/index.shtml.

Niagara County *Real Estate, Recording, Deed, Mortgage, Lien, Judgment Records*
A private company offers access to recorder documents at http://www2.landaccess.com/niagara_ny. Username and password required; register online.

Oneida County *Property Records*
www.oneidacounty.org/index1.htm
A private company offers property assessment data online at www.uspdr.com/consumer/ownersearch.asp.

Onondaga County *Assessor, Property, GIS-mapping, Inmate Records*
www.ongov.net
Access county property data free at www.ongov.net/Realproptax/taxinformation.html, includes access to City of Syracuse property data free at http://ocfintax.ongov.net/imateSyr/search.aspx. Also, search for property data free on the GIS-mapping page at www.maphost.com/syracuse%2Donondaga/main.asp. Click on "Query" and then "Find Tax Parcels." Also, access sheriff's county inmate list at http://w3cor.ongov.net:26001/inmate_lookup.

Ontario County *Property Records*
Orleans County *Property, Assessor Records*
A private company offers property assessment data online at www.uspdr.com/consumer/ownersearch.asp.

Oswego County *Real Estate, Deed Records*
www.oswegocounty.com/clerk/index.html
Access county clerk records 1963 to present at http://72.43.24.100/. Username and password required. You may email sales@InfoQuickSolutions.com for a free trial account or for info, or call Info Quick Solutions at 800-320-2617.

Otsego County *Property Records*
A private company offers property assessment data online at www.uspdr.com/consumer/ownersearch.asp.

Putnam County *Real Estate, UCC, Lien, Property Records*
Recorder records are accessible through a private online service at www.landaccess.com. This is a subscription service only, registration is required.

Queens County *Real Estate, Lien, Deed, Judgment, UCC, Deed, Mortgage, Tax Assessor Records*
Recording data from the City Register are free at http://a836-acris.nyc.gov/scripts/docsearch.dll/index. Also, for deeper financial data back 10 years, subscribe to the NYC Dept of Finance dial-up system; fee-$250 monthly and $5.00 per item. For info/signup, call Richard Reskin 718-935-6523. Also, property assessment rolls from NYC's Dept. of Finance are free at http://nyc.gov/html/dof/html/home/home.shtml. No name searching.

Rensselaer County *Property, Assessor, Deed, Lien, Real Estate Records*
Search real estate deeds and liens at www.nylandrecords.com. Click on Rensselaer. Registration required. Commercial users can subscribe for $25.00 per month and $.25 per search; Personal users can purchase documents for $5.00 each, no monthly fee.

Richmond County *Real Estate, Lien, Deed, Judgment, UCC, Deed, Mortgage, Tax Assessor Records*
Recording data from the City Register are free at http://a836-acris.nyc.gov/scripts/docsearch.dll/index. Also, for deeper financial data back 10 years, subscribe to the NYC Dept of Finance dial-up system; fee-$250 monthly and $5.00 per item. For info/signup, call Richard Reskin 718-935-6523. Also, property assessment rolls from NYC's Dept. of Finance are free at http://nycserv.nyc.gov/nycproperty/nynav/jsp/selectbbl.jsp. No name searching.

Rockland County *Real Estate, Lien, Deed, Court, Recording Records*
www.rocklandcountyclerk.com
Access is the county clerk's records index is free at www.rocklandcountyclerk.com/court_records.html. Includes criminal records back to 1982, civil judgments, real estate records, tax warrants. View images back to 6/96, and more are being added. Call Paul Pipearto at 845-638-5221 for more information. Also, see note at beginning of section for online property searches.

Saratoga County - Schoharie County - Schuyler County - Seneca County *Property Records*
A private company offers property assessment data online at www.uspdr.com/consumer/ownersearch.asp.

Steuben County *Property Records*
www.steubencony.org
Search Town of Erwin Real Property Assessment Roll free online at www.erwinny.org/ertxsrch.htm.

Suffolk County *Most Wanted Records*
Access the county most wanted list at www.co.suffolk.ny.us/police/cs/mwindex.asp.

Sullivan County *Property Records*
A private company offers property assessment data online at www.uspdr.com/consumer/ownersearch.asp.

Tompkins County *Real Estate, Assessor Records*
www.tompkins-co.org
Access to property records on the ImageMate system at www.tompkins-co.org/assessment/online.html has two levels: basic free and a registration/password fee-based full system. There is no name searching on the free version. The fee service is $20 monthly or $200 per year. For info or registration for the latter, email assessment@tompkins-co.org. Also, see note at beginning of section for more online property searches.

Ulster County *Real Estate, Lien, Property Tax, Voter Registration, Court Records*
www.co.ulster.ny.us
Two sources exist. Access to county online records requires a $33.33 (under 25 transactions) or $44.55 monthly fee; 12 month agreement required. Land Records date back to 1984. Includes county court records back to 7/1987. Lending agency information is available. For info, contact Valerie Harris at 845-334-5367. Also, see note at beginning of section for more online property searches.

Warren County *Property Records*
A private company offers property assessment data online at www.uspdr.com/consumer/ownersearch.asp.

Wayne County *Property Tax, Treasurer Records*
www.co.wayne.ny.us
Access real property tax data free at www.co.wayne.ny.us/warnicktreasurer/PropertyTaxSite.ASP?WCI=frmSearch&WCU.

Westchester County *Property, Recordings, Deed, Land, Fictitious Names, Judgment, Lien, UCC Records*
Access to the clerk's land record database is free at http://ccpv.westchesterclerk.com/WCCLogin.asp. There is also an advanced search that features images; registration is required.

Wyoming County *Real Estate, Recording, Property, Registered Sex Offenders Records*
www.wyomingco.net
Recorder records are accessible through a private online service at www.landaccess.com. This is a subscription service, fees and registration are required. Also, Registered Sex Offenders list is accessible at www.geocities.com/wyomingso1/. Also, see note at beginning of section for more online property searches.

Yates County *Property Records*
www.yatescounty.org
A private company offers property assessment data online at www.uspdr.com/consumer/ownersearch.asp.

Federal Courts in New York...

Standards for Federal Courts: The universal PACER sign-up number is 800-676-6856. Find PACER and the Party/Case Index on the Web at http://pacer.psc.uscourts.gov. PACER dial-up access is $.60 per minute. Also, courts offering internet access via PACER, Web-PACER or the new CM-ECF charge $.08 per page fee ($.07 per page if record is pre-2005 or unless noted as free).

US District Court -- Eastern District of New York
www.nyed.uscourts.gov
PACER: Case records are available back to 1/1990. Records are purged never. New records are available online after 1 day. **PACER Online Access:** ECF replaces PACER. This system includes electronic records from Suffolk and Nassau Counties, Long Island. **Electronic Filing:** CM/ECF data at https://ecf.nyed.uscourts.gov. **Other Online Access:** Access to court calendars at www.nyed.uscourts.gov/cgi-bin/caldir.pl.
Brooklyn Division counties: Kings, Queens, Richmond. Cases from Nassau and Suffolk may also be filed here (but paper records and cases are heard in Central Islip Div.), but all records are available electronically through PACER from this Brooklyn Division.
Central Islip Division counties: Nassau, Suffolk. Cases from these counties may be filed in Brooklyn Division, but heard in Central Islip. Central Islip cases can be found on Brooklyn's PACER system.

US Bankruptcy Court -- Eastern District of New York
www.nyeb.uscourts.gov
PACER: Case records are available back to 1991. Records are purged yearly. New records are available online after 1 day. **PACER Online Access:** ECF replaces PACER. **Electronic Filing:** CM/ECF data at https://ecf.nyeb.uscourts.gov. **Opinions:** Opinions date back to 4/2004. View court opinions at www.nyeb.uscourts.gov/jud_opinions/search.php. **Other Online Access:** Access calendars free at www.nyeb.uscourts.gov/calendars.htm. **Phone access:** Voice Case Information System, call 800-252-2537, 718-852-5726
Brooklyn Division counties: Kings, Queens, Richmond. Kings and Queens County Chapter 11 cases may also be assigned to Westbury. Other Queens County cases may be assigned to Westbury Division. Nassau County Chapter 11 cases may be assigned here. This office relocating to 271 Cadman Plaza East on Sept. 23, 2005.
Central Islip Division counties: Suffolk, Nassau.

US District Court -- Northern District of New York
www.nynd.uscourts.gov
PACER: Case records are available back to 6/1991. New records are available online after 1 day. **PACER Online Access:** ECF replaces PACER. **Electronic Filing:** CM/ECF data at https://ecf.nynd.uscourts.gov. **Opinions:** Selected Rulings only. View court opinions at www.nysd.uscourts.gov/courtweb/PubMain.htm.
Albany Division counties: Albany, Clinton, Columbia, Essex, Greene, Rensselaer, Saratoga, Schenectady, Schoharie, Ulster, Warren, Washington. This court provides the judges (and physical case records) for Plattsburgh Division - Clinton, Essex, Franklin counties - although cases are often assigned to Syracuse, Utica or Binghamton Divisions on occasion.
Binghamton Division counties: Broome, Chenango, Delaware, Jefferson, Lewis, Otsego, St. Lawrence, Tioga. This court provides the judges (and physical case records) for the Watertown Division - Jefferson, Lewis and St Lawrence counties - although cases are often assigned to Syracuse, Utica or especially Albany Divisions.

Syracuse Division counties: Cayuga, Cortland, Madison, Onondaga, Oswego, Tompkins. May also have some cases from Watertown Division - Jefferson, Lewis, or St Lawrence counties - and rarely from Clinton, Essex, Franklin counties.
Utica Division counties: Fulton, Hamilton, Herkimer, Montgomery, Oneida. May also have some cases from Watertown Division - Jefferson, Lewis, or St Lawrence counties - and rarely from Clinton, Essex, Franklin counties.

US Bankruptcy Court -- Northern District of New York

www.nynb.uscourts.gov

PACER: Case records are available back to 1992. New records are available online after 1 day. **PACER Online Access:** ECF replaces PACER. **Electronic Filing:** CM/ECF data at https://ecf.nynb.uscourts.gov. **Opinions:** View court opinions at www.nynb.uscourts.gov/decisions.htm. **Other Online Access:** Access weekly calendars free at www.nynb.uscourts.gov/usbc/calendar/calendar.html. **Phone access:** Voice Case Information System, call 800-206-1952.
Albany Division counties: Albany, Clinton, Essex, Franklin, Fulton, Jefferson, Montgomery, Rensselaer, Saratoga, Schenectady, Schoharie, St. Lawrence, Warren, Washington.
Utica Division counties: Broome, Cayuga, Chenango, Cortland, Delaware, Hamilton, Herkimer, Lewis, Madison, Oneida, Onondaga, Otsego, Oswego, Tioga, Tompkins.

US District Court -- Southern District of New York

www.nysd.uscourts.gov

PACER: Case records are available back to early 1990. Records are purged every 6 months. New records are available online after 1 day. **PACER Online Access:** ECF replaces PACER. **Electronic Filing:** CM/ECF data at https://ecf.nysd.uscourts.gov. **Opinions:** Search selected rulings online using CourtWeb. View court opinions at www.nysd.uscourts.gov/courtweb.
New York City Division counties: Bronx, New York. A 2nd courthouse at 40 Centre St is an Appellate Division with some District Cases heard there; search both at Pearl St location. Some cases from counties in the White Plains Division are also assigned to this New York Division.
White Plains Division counties: Dutchess, Orange, Putnam, Rockland, Sullivan, Westchester. Some cases may be assigned to New York Division.

US Bankruptcy Court -- Southern District of New York

www.nysb.uscourts.gov

PACER: Case records are available back to 6/1991. Records are purged every 6 months. New records are available online after 1 day. **PACER Online Access:** ECF replaces PACER. **Electronic Filing:** CM/ECF data at http://ecf.nysb.uscourts.gov. **Other Online Access:** Judges Bernstein, Gerber, Gonzales calendars at http://216.220.101.146/calendar/. All other judge calendars on ECF system. **Phone access:** Voice Case Information System, call 212-668-2772.
New York Division counties: Bronx, New York.
Poughkeepsie Division counties: Columbia, Dutchess, Greene, Orange, Putnam, Sullivan, Ulster.
White Plains Division counties: Rockland, Westchester.

US District Court -- Western District of New York

www.nywd.uscourts.gov

PACER: Case records are available back to 1992. Records are purged never. New records are available online after 1 day. **PACER Online Access:** ECF replaces PACER. **Electronic Filing:** CM/ECF data at https://ecf.nywd.uscourts.gov. **Opinions:** View court opinions at www.nywd.uscourts.gov/decision/decision.php.
Buffalo Division counties: Allegany, Cattaraugus, Chautauqua, Erie, Genesee, Niagara, Orleans, Wyoming. Prior to 1982, this division included what is now the Rochester Division.
Rochester Division counties: Chemung, Livingston, Monroe, Ontario, Schuyler, Seneca, Steuben, Wayne, Yates.

US Bankruptcy Court -- Western District of New York

www.nywb.uscourts.gov

PACER: Case records are available back to 8/1987. Records are purged never. New records are available online after 1 day. **PACER Online Access:** ECF replaces PACER. **Electronic Filing:** CM/ECF data at https://ecf.nywb.uscourts.gov. **Opinions:** View court opinions at www.nywb.uscourts.gov/decisions/. **Other Online Access:** Calendars free at www.nywb.uscourts.gov/calendars.php. **Phone access:** Voice Case Information System, call 800-776-9578, 716-551-5311
Buffalo Division counties: Allegany, Cattaraugus, Chautauqua, Erie, Genesee, Niagara, Orleans, Wyoming.
Rochester Division counties: Chemung, Livingston, Monroe, Ontario, Schuyler, Seneca, Steuben, Wayne, Yates.

North Carolina

Capital: Raleigh
           Wake County
Time Zone: EST
Population: 8,451,221
# of Counties: 100

Quick Links

Website: www.ncgov.com
Governor: www.governor.state.nc.us
Attorney General: www.ncdoj.com/default.jsp
State Archives: www.ah.dcr.state.nc.us
State Statutes and Codes: www.ncleg.net/gascripts/Statutes/Statutes.asp
Legislative Bill Search: www.ncleg.net
Unclaimed Funds:
     https://www.treasurer.state.nc.us/dsthome/AdminServices/UnclaimedProperty

State Level ... Major Agencies

Statewide Court Records

Administrative Office of Courts, PO Box 2448, Raleigh, NC 27602-2448 (Courier: 227 Fayatteville St Mall, Raleigh, NC 27601); 919-733-7107, Fax-919-715-5779, 8AM-5PM.
www.nccourts.org/Courts/
Online search: The agency has public access (Virtual Private Network) to approved requesters. Charges are based on screens viewed, rather than a specific fee per name. As we go to press, there is a question if the DOB will be taken off this system. A lesser valued product known as the Criminal Extract is available, but does not have the depth and quality of data as the network described above. Call 919-716-5088 for details on the programs. Go to www1.aoc.state.nc.us/www/calendars/Civil.html for current civil court calendars. Most current criminal calendars on a county or statewide basis is at www1.aoc.state.nc.us/www/calendars/Criminal.html. Also, Appellate Court and Supreme Court opinions are available www.aoc.state.nc.us/www/public/html/opinions.htm.

Sexual Offender Registry

State Bureau of Investigation, Criminal Information & Ident Sect - SOR Unit, PO Box 29500, Raleigh, NC 27626-0500 (Courier: 3320 Garner Rd, Raleigh, NC 27626-0500); 919-662-4500 x6257, Fax-919-662-4619, 8AM-5PM.
http://sbi.jus.state.nc.us
Online search: Search Level 3 records at the website. Search by name or geographic region. **Other options:** Agency can provide data on CD-Rom.

Incarceration Records

North Carolina Department of Corrections, Combined Records, 2020 Yonkers Road, 4226 MSC, Raleigh, NC 27699-4226; 919-716-3200, Fax-919-716-3986, 8AM-4:30PM.
www.doc.state.nc.us
Online search: The web access allows searching by name or ID number for public information on inmates, probationers, or parolees since 1973. Also, a private company offers free web access to inmates at www.vinelink.com/index.jsp including state, DOC, and county jail systems.

Corporation, Limited Partnerships, Limited Liability Company, Trademarks/Servicemarks

Secretary of State, Corporations Division, PO Box 29622, Raleigh, NC 27626-0622 (Courier: 2 S Salisbury, Raleigh, NC 27601); 919-807-2225 (Corporations), 919-807-2162 (Trademarks), 888-246-7636, Fax-919-807-2039, 8AM-5PM.
www.sosnc.com
Online search: The website offers a free search of status, corporate documents, and search by registered agent. The trademark database is not available online. **Other options:** This agency makes database information available for purchase via an FTP site. Contact Bonnie Elek at 919-807-2196 for details.

Uniform Commercial Code, Federal Tax Liens

UCC Division, Secretary of State, PO Box 29626, Raleigh, NC 27626-0626 (Courier: 2 South Salisbury St, Raleigh, NC 27602); 919-807-2111, 919-807-2119, Fax-919-807-2120, 8AM-5PM.
www.secretary.state.nc.us/UCC
Online search: Free access is available at www.secretary.state.nc.us/ucc/. Click on "UCC research" or "Tax Liens." Search by ID number or debtor name. Also, you may search tax liens at www.secretary.state.nc.us/taxliens. **Other options:** The UCC or tax lien database can be purchased on either a weekly or monthly basis via an FTP site. For more information, call 919-807-2196.

Sales Tax Registrations

Revenue Department, Sales & Use Tax Division, PO Box 25000, Raleigh, NC 27640 (Courier: 501 N Wilmington Street, Raleigh, NC 27604); 877-252-3052, Fax-919-733-5750, 8AM-5PM.
www.dor.state.nc.us
Online search: Delinquent debtors are shown on the web at www.dor.state.nc.us/collect/delinquent.html.

Birth, Death, Marriage, Divorce Certificates

Center for Health Statistics, Vital Records Branch, 1903 Mail Service Center, Raleigh, NC 27699-1903 (Courier: 225 N McDowell St, Raleigh, NC 27603); 919-733-3526, 800-669-8310 (Credit Card Orders), Fax-919-829-1359, 8AM-4PM.
http://vitalrecords.dhhs.state.nc.us/vr/index.html
Online search: Online ordering is available using a credit card via a state-designated vendor - www.vitalchek. Total fee is $55.45 and includes use of credit card and express delivery.

Workers' Compensation Records

NC Industrial Commission, Worker's Comp Records, 4340 Mail Service Center, Raleigh, NC 27699-4340; 919-807-2500, 800-688-8349 (Claims Questions), Fax-919-715-0282, 8AM-5PM.
www.comp.state.nc.us
Online search: Extensive information about employers and insurers may be searched online at www.comp.state.nc.us/iwcnss/. This site also gives access to court decisions involving worker's comp.

Driver Records

Division of Motor Vehicles, Driver License Records, 3113 MSC, Raleigh, NC 27699; 919-715-7000, 8AM-5PM.
www.ncdot.org/dmv/driver_services/
Online search: To qualify for online availability, a client must be an insurance agent or insurance company support organization. The mode is interactive and is open from 7 AM to 10 PM. The DL# and name are needed when ordering. Records are $8.00 each. A minimum $500 security deposit is required. Call 919-861-3062 for details. **Other options:** Magnetic tape for high volume batch users is available. Requests must be pre-paid.

Voter Registration

State Board of Elections, PO Box 27255, Raleigh, NC 27611-7255; 919-733-7173, Fax-919-715-0135, 8AM-5PM.
www.sboe.state.nc.us
Online search: Online access to voter registration records is available free at www.app.sboe.state.nc.us/votersearch/seimsvot.htm. A DOB is needed. **Other options:** Most records are sold in CD format or sent via email. The maximum fee is $25.00. Request forms are available at the webpage. This is the most prompt access to records, other than in person.

State Level ... Occupational Licensing

Acupuncturist	http://ncaaom.org/directory.php
Amusement Device	www.nclabor.com/elevator/elevator.htm
Architect	www.member-base.com/ncbarch/public/lic/searchdb.asp
Architectural Firm	www.member-base.com/ncbarch/public/firms/searchdb.asp
Athletic Trainer	www.ncbate.org/trainers.html
Attorney	www.ncbar.com/home/member_directory.asp
Auction Company	www.ncalb.org/scripts/members.asp
Auctioneer Disciplinary Action	www.ncalb.org/scripts/disciplinaryaction.asp
Auctioneer/Auctioneer Apprentice	www.ncalb.org/scripts/members.asp
Bank	https://www.nccob.org/Online/brts/BanksAndTrusts.aspx
Bank Branch	https://www.nccob.com/Online/brts/BankBranchSearch.aspx
Bodywork Therapist	www.bmbt.org/MTSEARCH.ASP
Boiler/Pressure Vessel Inspector	www.nclabor.com/boiler/boiler.htm
Building Inspector	www.ncdoi.com/OSFM/Engineering/COQB/engineering_coqb_inspectors.asp
Charitable/Sponsor Organization	www.secretary.state.nc.us/csl/Search.aspx
Check Casher	https://www.nccob.org/Online/CCS/CompanyListing.aspx
Clinical Social Worker	www.ncswboard.org/search.asp
Consumer Financer	https://www.nccob.org/online/CFS/CFSCompanyListing.aspx
Contractor, General	www.nclbgc.org/lic_fr.html
Cosmetology Disciplinary Action	www.cosmetology.state.nc.us/newsletter/Disciplinary.pdf
Counselor, Professional	www.ncblpc.org/search.php
Crematory	www.ncbfs.org/dir_crematoriesdb.htm
Dentist/Dental Hygienist	www.ncdentalboard.org/ncdbe_search.asp
Electrical Contractor/Inspector	www.ncbeec.org/LicSearch.asp
Elevator Inspector	www.nclabor.com/elevator/elevator.htm
Embalmer	www.ncbfs.org/dir_licenseedb.htm
Engineer	www.member-base.com/ncbels-vs/public/searchdb.asp
Engineering/Surveying Firm	www.member-base.com/ncbels-vs/public/searchdb.asp
Fire Sprinkler Contractor/Technician	www.nclicensing.org/OnlineReg.htm
Forester	http://members.aol.com/ncbrf/roster_index.htm
Fund Raiser Consultant/Solicitor	www.secretary.state.nc.us/csl/Search.aspx
Funeral Chapel	www.ncbfs.org/dir_chapeldb.htm
Funeral Director/Service	www.ncbfs.org/dir_licenseedb.htm
Funeral Home	www.ncbfs.org/dir_funeralhomedb.htm
Funeral Trainee	www.ncbfs.org/dir_traineesdb.htm
Funeral Transport/Removal Svc	www.ncbfs.org/Transport%20and%20Removal%20Services.doc
Geologist	www.ncblg.org/licensees.html
Hearing Aid Dispenser/Fitter	http://default.1dis.com/webapplication1/queryname.aspx
Heating Contractor	www.nclicensing.org/OnlineReg.htm
HMO	http://infoportal.ncdoi.net/cmp_lookup.jsp
Home Inspector	www.ncdoi.com/OSFM/Engineering/hilb/engineering_hilb_directories.asp
Insurance Company	http://infoportal.ncdoi.net/cmp_lookup.jsp
Insurer, Life/Health	http://infoportal.ncdoi.net/filelookup.jsp?divtype=3
Insurer, Property/Casualty	http://infoportal.ncdoi.net/filelookup.jsp?divtype=2
Investment Representative/Advisor	www.sosnc.com/
Landscape Architect	www.ncbola.org/licensees.htm
Lobbyist	www.secretary.state.nc.us/Lobbyists/LSearch.aspx
Manuf'd Housing Retailer/Mfg/Contr.	www.ncdoi.com/osfm/manufacturedbuilding/licensees/mainmenu.asp
Manuf'd Housing Seller/Qualifier	www.ncdoi.com/osfm/manufacturedbuilding/licensees/mainmenu.asp
Massage Therapist	www.bmbt.org/MTSEARCH.ASP
Medical Doctor/Physician	www.ncmedboard.org/Clients/NCBOM/Public/NCBOMLicenseeSearch.aspx
Money Transmitter	https://www.nccob.org/Online/MTS/MTSCompanyListing.aspx
Nurse Practitioner	www.ncmedboard.org/Clients/NCBOM/Public/NCBOMLicenseeSearch.aspx

Nurse-LPN .... https://www.ncbon.com/Lic-verif.asp
Nursing Home Administrator .... www.ncbenha.org/searchdb.asp
Occupational Therapist/Therap't Assist www.ncbot.org/fpdb/otimport.html
Optometrist .... www.ncoptometry.org/verify.aspx
Osteopathic Physician .... www.ncmedboard.org/Clients/NCBOM/Public/NCBOMLicenseeSearch.aspx
Pesticide Applicator .... www.ncagr.com/aspzine/Fooddrug/data/advsearch.asp
Pesticide Dealer/Consultant .... www.ncagr.com/aspzine/Fooddrug/data/advsearch.asp
Pharmacist .... www.ncbop.org/namesAA.asp
Pharmacy Technician www.ncbop.org/Names01.asp
Pharmacy/Physician Pharmacy .... www.ncbop.org/pharmacyAA.asp
Physical Therapist .... www.ncptboard.org/search.asp
Physical Therapist Assistant .... www.ncptboard.org/search.asp
Physician Assistant .... www.ncmedboard.org/Clients/NCBOM/Public/NCBOMLicenseeSearch.aspx
Plumber .... www.nclicensing.org/OnlineReg.htm
Podiatrist .... www.ncbpe.org/search.php
Psychological Associate .... www.ncpsychologyboard.org/search.htm
Psychologist .... www.ncpsychologyboard.org/search.htm
Public Accountant-CPA .... www.nccpaboard.gov/Clients/NCBOA/Public/Static/search_the_database.htm
RAL .... https://www.nccob.org/online/RALS/RALSCompanyListing.aspx
Real Estate Agent/Broker/Dealer .... www.memberbase.com/ncrec-new/licdb/indv/searchdb.asp
Real Estate Firm .... www.memberbase.com/ncrec-new/licdb/firms-new/searchdb.asp
Sanitarian .... www.rsboard.com/rsweb/directory/directory.htm
Securities Agent/Broker .... www.sosnc.com/
Social Worker .... www.ncswboard.org/search.asp
Social Worker Manager .... www.ncswboard.org/search.asp
Soil Scientist .... www.ncblss.org/director.html
Speech Pathologist/Audiologist .... www.ncboeslpa.org
Surveyor, Land .... www.member-base.com/ncbels-vs/public/searchdb.asp
Therapist, Bodywork-Massage .... www.bmbt.org/MTSEARCH.ASP
Trust Company .... https://www.nccob.org/Online/brts/BanksAndTrusts.aspx

County Level ... Courts

Court Administration: Administrative Office of the Courts, Justice Bldg, PO Box 2448, Raleigh, NC, 27602; 919-733-7107, Fax: 919-715-5779. www.nccourts.org

Court Structure: The Superior Court is the court of general jurisdiction; the District Court is limited jurisdiction. The counties combine the courts, thus searching is done through one court, not two, within the county. Small Claims Court is part of the District Court Division and handles civil cases where a plaintiff requests assignment to a magistrate and the amount in controversy is $5000 or less (raised up from $4000 in Summer, 2005). The principal relief sought in Small Claims Court is money, the recovery of specific personal property, or summary ejectment (eviction).

Online Access Note: The state AOC has public access for approved requesters on its Virtual Private Network. Charges are based on screens viewed rather than a specific fee per name. There is a question if the DOB will be taken off this system. A lesser valued product known as the Criminal Extract is available, but does not have the depth and quality of data as the Virtual Private Network. Call 919-716-5088 for details on these programs. For current civil and criminal calendars go to http://www1.aoc.state.nc.us/www/. Appellate and Supreme Court opinions can be found at www.aoc.state.nc.us/www/public/html/opinions.htm.

Cumberland County

Superior-District Court – Civil and Criminal Records
www.aoc.state.nc.us/district12/
Search civil court calendars at www1.aoc.state.nc.us/www/calendars.html.

County Level ... Recorders & Assessors

Recording Office Organization: 100 counties, 100 recording offices. The recording officers are the Register of Deeds and the Clerk of Superior Court (tax liens). The entire state is in the Eastern Time Zone (EST). Federal tax liens on personal property of businesses are filed with the Secretary of State. Other federal and all state tax liens are filed with the county Clerk of Superior Court, not with the Register of Deeds. (Oddly, even tax liens on real property are also filed with the Clerk of Superior Court, not with the Register of Deeds.) Refer to The Sourcebook of County Court Records for information about NC Superior Courts.

Online Access: A growing number of counties offer free access to assessor and real estate records via the web.

Alleghany County *Real Estate, Grantor/Grantee, Property, GIS Records*
www.alleghanycounty-nc.gov
Access to the Register of Deeds database is free atwww.allcorod.com/Opening.asp. Click on "View & Search records online." Records go back to 1/1/1993. Also, search for property information on a GIS mapping site at http://arcims.webgis.net/nc/Alleghany/default.asp. To name search click on Quick Search.

Anson County *Assessor, Real Estate, 911 Address Converter, Tax Collection Records*
www.co.anson.nc.us/services.php
Records on the county Online Tax Inquiry System are free at www.co.anson.nc.us/pubcgi/taxinq. There is a tax collections search at www.co.anson.nc.us/pubcgi/colinq/. Also, there is a 911 address converter at www.co.anson.nc.us/pubcgi/911addresslookup/

Ashe County *Assessor, Real Estate, Grantor/Grantee, Property Records*
www.ashencrod.org
Access to the register of deeds real estate data is free at www.ashencrod.org/Opening.asp. Full index goes back to 1/1995; images to 8/1940. Also, access to records on the county Tax Parcel Information System is free at http://ashegis.ashecountygov.com/webgis/.

Avery County *Recording, Grantor/Grantee, Property Records*
www.averyrod.com
Search the recorders database free at www.averyrod.com/view/disclaimer.html. Also, search for property info on the GIS site for free at http://arcims2.webgis.net/avery/default.asp. To name search click on Quick Search.

Bladen County *Real Estate, Grantor/Grantee, Deed Records*
www.bladeninfo.org
Access unofficial register of deeds site at www.withersravenel.com/deeds/; search comprehensive index or direct images.

Brunswick County *Recording, Deed Records*
http://rod.brunsco.net
Access to the recorder database is free at http://rod.brunsco.net. Free registration, logon and password are required. Records are updated on the 10th, 20th, and 30th of the month. Also, search the tax administration data for free at www.brunsconctax.org/.

Buncombe County *Assessor, Property Tax, Real Estate, Recording, Marriage, Death, Fictitious Name, Deed, Restaurants, Tax Sale Records*
www.buncombecounty.org
Access to county Register of Deeds records is free at http://registerofdeeds.buncombecounty.org/resolution/login.asp. Free registration is required; includes marriages, deaths, fictitious names, deeds. Also, county assessor tax records are free at www.buncombetax.org/lookup/default.html. Also GIS property search searching available at www.buncombecounty.org/governing/depts/GIS/disclaimer.htm. Also, search tax property sales free at www.buncombecounty.org/governing/citizens/prop4Sale.htm. Register to see restaurant grades free at http://buncombe.digitalhealthdepartment.com.

Burke County *Property, Assessor Records*
www.co.burke.nc.us
Access to the property information is free on the GIS mapping site at http://arcims.webgis.net/nc/Burke/default.asp. To name search click on Quick Search.

Cabarrus County
Assessor, Real Estate, Recorder, Deed, Lien, Grantor/Grantee, UCC, Tax Roll, Deliq Tax list Records
www.cabarruscounty.us
Access to the recorder records is free at http://166.82.128.235/welcome.asp by two methods: full system or image-only system. You can name search the former; book & page number required for the latter. Land records go back to 1983; images to 2001. Also, search tax assessor database free online at http://166.82.128.222/parcelinfo.html. Also, search tax bill scroll for free at http://onlineservices.cabarruscounty.us/Tax/TaxScroll/. Also, search tax appraisal cards by name free at http://onlineservices.cabarruscounty.us/Tax/TaxAppraisalCard/.

Caldwell County *Property, Assessor, Real Estate, Birth, Death, Marriage, Notary, Business Name Records*
www.co.caldwell.nc.us
Records on the county GIS map server site are free at http://maps.co.caldwell.nc.us. Click on "Start Spatial-data Explorer" then find query field at bottom of next page. Also, access to register of deeds recording data is for free at http://rod.co.caldwell.nc.us/resolution/. Choose advanced or simple search; online registration is required.

Carteret County *Property, Assessor Records*
www.co.carteret.nc.us
Search tax parcel cards free at http://tax.carteretcountygov.org.

Caswell County *Property, Map, Grantor/Grantee Records*
www.caswellrod.com
Access property data free at http://arcims.webgis.net/nc/caswell/. Also, to search for grantor/grantee (online documents) for free go to www.caswellrod.com/index.html

Catawba County *Assessor, Property, Grantor/Grantee, Real Estate, Deed Records*
www.catawbacountync.gov
Records on the Catawba County Geographic Information System database are free at www.gis.catawba.nc.us/. Click on "Online Mapping" then choose "Real Estate" then search using query fields. Also, access register of deeds information free at http://204.211.226.33/rod/index.html.

Chowan County *Real Estate, Recorder, Deed, Parcel Records*
www.chowancounty-nc.gov
Access county property data free at http://199.90.99.197/paas/. You may also build customized data downloads.

Clay County *Land, Property, Assessor, Recorder, Deed Records*
Access to property and deeds indexes and images is via a private company at www.titlesearcher.com. Fee/registration required.

Cleveland County *Real Estate, Assessor, Real Estate, Grantor/Grantee Records*
www.clevelandcounty.com
Access to property data free at http://arcims2.webgis.net/nc/Cleveland/default.asp. Also, access to register of deeds grantor/grantee index is free at http://cleveland.parker-lowe.net/view/softlic.html.

Columbus County *Real Estate, Recording, Deed, Lien, Assumed Name, Corporation, UCC Records*
Access to the Recorder's database is free at www.titlesearcher.com/columbus/search.php/.

Craven County *Real Estate, Recording, Deed, Tax Assessor, Boat, Mobile Home, Foreclosure, GIS Records*
www.co.craven.nc.us
Access to the county Public Inquiry System is free at www.co.craven.nc.us/depts/reg/regwwwdisclaimer.htm. Also, access to assessor and property data is free at http://gismaps2.cravencounty.com/maps/map.asp.

Cumberland County *Land, Deed, Recording, UCC, Property Tax, Assessor, GIS Records*
www.ccrod.org
Search two systems free at www.ccrodinternet.org. The land records index and images go back to 1978; images go back to 1/21/1972; UCCs are from 1995 to 6/29/2001. Also, the county tax assessor real estate search is free at http://mainfr.co.cumberland.nc.us/oasearch.htm. Also, search property data free on the GIS mapping site at http://152.31.99.8/. Click on Search on the Parcel Viewer.

Currituck County *Real Estate, Deed, Notaries Records*
www.co.currituck.nc.us/registerofdeeds/registerofdeeds.aspx

Access to land recorded documents and notaries is free at https://currituckeoc.com/resolution/. Also ,search property, sales, assessor data and more free at www.co.currituck.nc.us/tax/tax_department_real_estate_searches.aspx.

Dare County   *Assessor, Real Estate, Marriage, UCC Records*
www.co.dare.nc.us
Assessor records are at www.co.dare.nc.us/public/TaxInquiry.htm. Other records are free at www.co.dare.nc.us/public/index.htm. Real estate from 1976 forward, UCC from 1989 forward, and marriage from 1990 forward. Additionally, tax files can be downloaded from this site.

Davidson County   *Property, Assessor, Real Estate Records*
www.co.davidson.nc.us
Records on the county Tax Dept database are free at www.co.davidson.nc.us/Tax/1252.asp. Also, search for property info on the GIS mapping site for free at http://arcims2.webgis.net/davidson/default.asp. To name search click on Quick Search.

Davie County   *Real Estate, GIS-mapping Records*
www.co.davie.nc.us
Access to county property data on the GIS-mapping site is free at http://davienc.roktech.net/. Click on "Start Spatial Data Explorer" then search at bottom of page.

Duplin County   *Real Property, Deed, Mortgage, Marriage, Death, Notary, Military Discharge Records*
http://rod.duplincounty.org
Access to the Register's multiple databases is free at http://rod.duplincounty.org. Vital stats and discharges are index only.

Durham County
Real Estate, Deed, Judgment, Recording, Voter Registration, Feeod/Lodging, GIS, Inmate Records
www.co.durham.nc.us
Access to the Register of Deeds database is free at http://207.4.222.118 or http://rodweb.co.durham.nc.us/. Access to the tax assessor data is free at www.co.durham.nc.us/departments/txad/TaxDB/. Search property records from the GIS mapping site free at http://gisweb2.ci.durham.nc.us/sdx/. After the disclaimer, click on "Spatial Data Explorer" to search. Also, search voter registration free at www.co.durham.nc.us/departments/elec/votersearch/VoterRecSearch.cfm. Find all searchable record types at www.co.durham.nc.us/common/PublRecordsdB.cfm

Edgecombe County   *Deeds, Property, Assessor Records*
www.edgecombecountync.gov
Access to county property data is free at http://207.4.48.133/paas/default.htm.

Forsyth County   *Real Estate, Recording, Property, Deed, Lien, Lien List, Voter Registration Records*
www.forsyth.cc
Access to the county Geo-Data Explorer database is free online at www.co.forsyth.nc.us/Tax/geodata.aspx. Click on "Launch Geo-Data Explorer." Address and Parcel ID searching only. Includes Board of Adjustment and building permit records. Also, Register of Deed records are on CD-ROM. Also, search tax liens by name lists free at www.forsyth.cc/Tax/advertisement.aspx. Search voter registration records free at www.co.forsyth.nc.us/elections/voterLookup.aspx. Also, access to property and deeds indexes and images is via a private company at www.titlesearcher.com or support@TitleSearcher.com. Fee/registration required; monthly and per day access available.

Franklin County   *Real Property Records*
www.co.franklin.nc.us
Access to the county spatial data explorer database is free at www.co.franklin.nc.us/docs/frame_tax.htm. Search the GIS map or click on "text search" for name searching.

Gaston County   *Real Estate, Deed, Lien, Corporation, Assumed Name, UCC Records*
www.co.gaston.nc.us/registerofdeeds
Access to recorded documents is free at http://207.235.60.108/resolution/ - registration and username are required.

Granville County   *Assessor, Property Records*
Access to assessor property data is available for a one-time $250 fee, call Tax Assessor office a 919-693-4181 or visit www.granvillegis.org.

Guilford County *Recorder, Deed, Lien, Assessor, Property, UCC, Vital Statistic, Tax Collector, Plat, GIS-mapping, Restaurant Records*
www.guilforddeeds.com
Access to county e-gov databases is free at http://gcms0004.co.guilford.nc.us/services/index.php. Also, you may search Birth, Death, Marriage, and military records directly at http://gcms0004.co.guilford.nc.us/Novation/rodvrpub.html. Also, search for property data free on the GI-mapping site at http://gisweb.co.guilford.nc.us/sdx/viewer.htm.

Harnett County *Real Estate, Grantor/Grantee, Vital Statistic, Military Discharge, UCC Records*
http://rod.harnett.org
County real estate and property tax information is free online at http://rod.harnett.org. Search Births, Deaths, Marriages, military discharges, UCCs and official public records.

Haywood County *Real Estate, Deed, Property, GIS-mapping Records*
www.haywoodnc.net
Records on the Register of Deeds database are free at http://rodweb.gov.co.haywood.nc.us. Real estate records go back to 1986. Also, search for property data on the GIS-mapping site for free at www.undersys.com/cweb/haywood.html.

Henderson County *Real Estate, GIS-mapping Records*
Search property records at the GIS site free at www.hendersoncountync.org/gis/.

Hertford County *Real Estate. Deed Records*
www.hertfordrod.com
Access recorded land data free at www.hertfordrod.com/index.html; click on Documents & Indexes.

Hoke County *Real estate, Recorder, Deed, Lien Records*
www.hokencrod.org
Access recorder data for free at www.hokencrod.org/Opening.asp. Land records index goes back to 7/1992; images back to 12/1994.

Hyde County *Real Property, Grantor/Grantee Records*
www.hyderod.com
Access to the Register of Deeds real property records is free at www.hyderod.com/view/disclaimer.html.

Iredell County *Real Estate, Recorder, Vital Statistic, Property Appraisal, Pre-2001 UCC, Permit Records*
www.co.iredell.nc.us
Access recorder records at www.co.iredell.nc.us/resolution/. Registration required. Also, search property appraisal cards free at www.co.iredell.nc.us/apprcard/. Access county permits and inspection history records free at www.mspection.com/counties/iredell/search.asp. Also, search property data free on the GI-mapping site at www.co.iredell.nc.us/Gismaps.asp. Once on the map page, click on the binoculars to text search.

Johnston County *Real Estate, UCC, Deed Records*
www.johnstonnc.com
Access to Register's indexes is free at http://johnstonnc.com/deedsearch. Land records go back to 1972; UCCs back to 7/1997.

Jones County *Real Estate, Deed, Recorded Documents Records*
www.jonesrod.com
Access recorded documents index at www.jonesrod.com/view/disclaimer.html.

Lee County *Real Estate, Grantor/Grantee, Deed, Lien Records*
www.leencrod.org/Opening.asp
Access to the Register of Deeds index and images are free at www.leencrod.org/Opening.asp. Land record index goes back to 1985; images to 1908 and all plat images.

Lincoln County *Real Estate, Deed, Lien, Mapping, UCC, Property Tax Records*
www.co.lincoln.nc.us
Access tax and property information for free at www.lincolncounty.org/County/faq.htm. Enable browser for Java. Grantor/Grantee indices go back to 1993. Images go back to Book 186. Search either of the 2 databases. Also, access to the county GIS Land System is free at www.co.lincoln.nc.us/County/gisd.htm. At the website, under Data Tools, click on Search.

McDowell County   *Land, Deed Records*
Access to property and deeds indexes and images is via a private company at www.titlesearcher.com. Fee/registration required; see state introduction. Images go back to 1/1971.

Macon County   *Property, Deed Image Records*
Access to county property data is free at http://63.167.19.252/dbp/deed.asp.

Madison County   *Real Estate, Recorder, Grantor/Grantee Records*
www.madisonrod.com
Access real property records free at www.madisonrod.com/view/disclaimer.html,

Mecklenburg County   *Assessor, Real Estate, Grantor/Grantee, Judgment, Lien, Vital Statistic, Personal Property, Accident Report Records*
http://meckrod.hartic.com
Access to birth, death, marriage, recordings, judgments, liens, and grantor/grantee indices are free at http://meckrod.hartic.com/default.asp. There is also a real estate lookup at http://meckcama.co.mecklenburg.nc.us/relookup/. Also, online access to the assessors records for real estate, personal property, and tax bills are free at http://mcmf.co.mecklenburg.nc.us:3007/cics/txar/txar00i/. Search warrants at http://mcmf.co.mecklenburg.nc.us:3007/cjcr01w/cjjl/webnull Sheriff's inmate lookup is at www.charmeck.org/Departments/MCSO/Divisions/Inmate+Information/InmateLookup.htm. Accident reports are at http://accident.ci.charlotte.nc.us/index.htm.

Mitchell County   *Granter/Grantee Index Records*
www.mitchellrod.com
Search records at www.mitchellrod.com/view/disclaimer.html.

Montgomery County   *Real Estate, Grantor/Grantee, Deed, Lien Records*
www.montgomeryrod.com
Access to recorders real estate data is free at www.montgomeryrod.com/view/disclaimer.html.

Moore County   *Real Estate, Lien, Grantor/Grantee, Vital Statistic (no images), Property Tax, Land Record, Restaurant Grade Records*
http://rod.moorecountync.gov
Access to the public record databases at www.co.moore.nc.us/main/page.asp?rec=/pages/propertyinfo/propertyinfo.asp. Also, access Register of Deeds grantor/grantee index free at http://rod.co.moore.nc.us/.

Nash County   *Real Estate, Real Property, Fixture Filings Records*
www.deeds.co.nash.nc.us
No fee required but must have your own user ID and password for this site. www.deeds.co.nash.nc.us/resolution

New Hanover County
Real Estate, Assessor, Grantor/Grantee, Lien, UCC, Judgment, Marriage, Military Discharge Records
www.nhcgov.com
Access to the Register of Deeds database is free at http://srvrodweb.nhcgov.com. Also, online access to the real estate tax database is free at www.nhcgov.com/Oasinq/Oasinput.jsp. Also, you may search for property information on the GIS-mappings site at www.nhcgov.com/GIS/GISservices.asp.

Onslow County   *Real Estate, GIS, Assessor Records*
http://co.onslow.nc.us/register_of_deeds
Access is to property information is free at http://maps.onslowcountync.gov/. Enter the site and name search using the advanced search in the Parcel Query box.

Orange County   *Property Records*
www.co.orange.nc.us/deeds/
Access to property records on the GIS mapping site is free at http://gis.co.orange.nc.us/gisdisclaimer.htm

Pasquotank County   *Property, Assessor, Recording, Deed, Grantor/Grantee Records*
www.co.pasquotank.nc.us/departments/rod/default.htm

Access recorder data free at http://pasquotankrod.com/view/softlic.html. Click on "I Agree." Also, access to the county tax parcel database is free at http://207.4.214.118/departments/gis/taxsearch.cfm.

Pender County *Property, Assessor, Real Estate, Grantor/Grantee, Deed Records*
www.pender-county.com/Departments/rod/
Access recorder data free with registration at http://rod.pender-county.com/~testsite/. This is a test site; web address may change. Also, access to property data on the Oasis-Webview system is $49.00 per quarter at www.undersys.com/penderord.html.

Perquimans County *Real Estate, Deed, Lien, Property Tax, Assessor, GIS Records*
www.perquimansrod.com
Access to county real property records is free at www.perquimansrod.com/view/disclaimer.html. Also, assess property assessor and GIS data free at http://mapping.perquimanscountync.gov/perquimans.

Person County *Real Estate, Recording, Grantor/Grantee Records*
www.personrod.com
Access to county real estate records is free at www.personrod.com/view/disclaimer.html. Index goes back to 1/1/1995.

Randolph County *Real Property Records*
www.co.randolph.nc.us
Access to the county GIS database is free at www.co.randolph.nc.us/gis.htm. In the "Search functions" on the map page, click on "parcel owner." Real Estate records access at www.randrod.com.

Richmond County *Property Records*
Access to County property records is via a subscription service; registration and fees are required. For information, call 334-344-3333.

Robeson County *Real Estate, Recorder, Deed, Grantor/Grantee, Land, Property, Assessor Records*
http://rod.co.robeson.nc.us
Access to recorder data is free at http://rod.co.robeson.nc.us/search.php. Also, Assessor is planning to have property records available through a GIS-mapping site; check at www.co.robeson.nc.us/departments/tax/index.htm. Also, access to property and deeds indexes and images is via a private company at www.titlesearcher.com. Fee/registration required

Rockingham County *Land, Grantor/Grantee, Judgment, Tax Sale, Property, GIS Records*
www.rockinghamcorod.org
Access to Register of Deeds database is free at www.rockinghamcorod.org/Opening.asp. Land indexes 1996 to present; and record images 1984 to present; plats 1907 to present. Also, online access to real estate (1996 forward) and tax appraiser data is free at www.co.rockingham.nc.us/taxinfo2.html. Also, search property data free at the GIS site at http://arcims.webgis.net/nc/rockingham/default.asp. To name search, click on Quick Search. Also, online access to the tax sales property is at www.co.rockingham.nc.us/forecl.htm.

Rowan County *Real Estate, Recording, Property Records*
www.co.rowan.nc.us/rod
Access to the Register of Deeds land records database is free after registration at http://rod.co.rowan.nc.us. Records go back to 1975; financing statements back to 1993; images back to 2000 (eventually to go back to 1990). Also, access to the county GIS mapping site is free at http://arcims2.webgis.net/nc/Rowan/default.asp. To name search click on Quick Search.

Rutherford County *Property, Tax Map Records*
Access property data free at http://arcims.webgis.net/nc/rutherford/.

Sampson County *Real Estate, Recorder, Deed, Grantor/Grantee Records*
www.sampsonrod.org
Access to county Register of Deeds land data is free at www.sampsonrod.org/Opening.asp. Index goes back to 1988.

Stanly County *Real Estate, Grantor/Grantee, Deed, Restaurant Records*
www.co.stanly.nc.us
Access the Register of Deeds index back to 1/1985 at http://216.27.81.170/login.asp?password=stqn342&accountid=stanlyhome. Also, find property data on the GIS search free at www.stanlygis.net/website/quicksearch/quicksearch.aspx. Search deeds-plats by address or number free at www.stanlygis.net/website/public/DeedPlatSearch.htm. Search restaurant grades at www.co.stanly.nc.us/Departments/health/grades/index.htm.

Stokes County *Grantor/Grantee, Deed, UCC, Property Records*
www.stokescorod.org
Access to the Register of Deeds Remote Access site is free at www.stokescorod.org/Opening.asp. Land records go back to 1993, images to mid-1970; UCCs back to 1994. Also, access to property info on the GIS mapping site is free at http://arcims2.webgis.net/stokes/default.asp. To name search click on Quick Search.

Surry County *Property, Tax Map Records*
www.co.surry.nc.us
Access property data free at http://arcims.webgis.net/nc/surry/default.asp. Click on Quicksearch. Tax maps also located at this site.

Swain County *Real Estate, Recorder, Deed, Grantor/Grantee Records*
www.swaincounty.org/page5.html
Access to recorder land data is free at www.swaincorod.org. There is a full system and an image only system. Land Record Indexing data goes back to 1/1995; images back to 8/1979.

Transylvania County *Real Estate, Deed, Assessor, Property, GIS, Drug Arrest Records*
www.transylvaniacounty.org
Access real estate records at www.titlesearcher.com. Images are viewable back to 12/30/2003, indices back to 1/3/1973. Also, access full or partial property data free on the GIS site at http://arcims.webgis.net/nc/transylvania/default.asp. Also, search county drug arrests at www.transylvaniasheriff.org/drugs.htm

Tyrrell County *Real Estate, Grantor/Grantee, Deed Records*
www.tyrrellrod.com
Access to Register of Deeds real estate records is free at www.tyrrellrod.com/view/disclaimer.html. Index goes back to 1997; images are from Book 137 forward.

Union County *Real Estate, Deed, Grantor/Grantee Records*
www.co.union.nc.us/gov_offices/rod/rod.htm
Access to recorder land records is free at www.unionconcrod.org/welcome.asp; index go back to 6-15-2003; images to 6/3/2000.

Wake County *Real Estate, Assessor, Deed, Judgment, Lien, Voter Registration Records*
http://web.co.wake.nc.us/rdeeds/
Records from the County Department of Revenue are downloadable by township for free at http://web.co.wake.nc.us/revenue/wcmap.html. Also, a free real estate property search is at http://msweb01.co.wake.nc.us/realestate/search.asp. Also, online access to the Register of Deeds database is free at http://rodweb01.co.wake.nc.us/books/genext/genextsearch.asp. Records go back to 10/1953. Registered voters can be found at http://msweb03.co.wake.nc.us/bordelec/Waves/WavesOptions.asp. Also, access to Town of Cary property info is free http://arcims2.webgis.net/nc/cary/default.asp.

Washington County
Real Estate, Recorder, Grantor/Grantee, Deed, Lien, Corporation, Assessor, Property Tax Records
www.washconc.org/register_of_deeds/register_of_deeds.htm
Access to recorder land records is available free at www.washingtonrod.com/view/disclaimer.html. You may choose to search all books. Also, search assessor property record cards free at http://taxweb.washconc.org.

Watauga County *Grantor/Grantee, Deed, UCC, Assessor, Property Records*
www.wataugacounty.org/deeds/index.html
Access to register of deeds database is free at www.wataugacounty.org/deeds/disclaimer.shtml. Also, online access to county tax search data is free at www.wataugacounty.org/tax/search_tax.shtml. Also, search Town of Blowing Rock property info at http://arcims2.webgis.net/blowingrock/default.asp. To name search click on Quick Search.

Wayne County *Real Estate, Deed, Grantor/Grantee, Property Tax, Assessor Records*
www.waynegov.com
Access to the registers CRP, financing statement, and real estate (back to 1969) databases are free at www.waynegov.com/departments/rod/disclaimer.asp. Real Estate may only include 1969-1994; others are current. Also, access property records free at www.waynegov.com/departments/tax/taxinquiry.asp. Only available 8AM-5PM.

Wilkes County *Property, GIS-mapping Records*
Access to property data is free on the GIS-mapping site at www.undersys.com/wilkesweb/wilkes.html.

Wilson County *Assessor, Real Estate, Property, Deed Records*

www.wilson-co.com/rod.html

Records on the county Geo-link property tax database are free at www.wilson-co.com/intro.html. Also, access the Register of Deeds search site at www.wilson-co.com/wcjav_begin.html. If using property search function, username or password required; deeds section does not.

Federal Courts in North Carolina...

Standards for Federal Courts: The universal PACER sign-up number is 800-676-6856. Find PACER and the Party/Case Index on the Web at http://pacer.psc.uscourts.gov. PACER dial-up access is $.60 per minute. Also, courts offering internet access via PACER, Web-PACER or the new CM-ECF charge $.08 per page fee ($.07 per page if record is pre-2005 or unless noted as free).

US District Court -- Eastern District of North Carolina

www.nced.uscourts.gov

PACER: Toll-free access phone: 800-995-0313. Local access phone: 919-856-4768. Case records are available back to 1989. Records are purged as deemed necessary. New records are available online after 3 days. **PACER Online Access:** The old RACER and PACER systems have been replaced by the new CM/ECF system. **Electronic Filing:** Civil case openings are also available via CM/ECF website. CM/ECF data at https://ecf.nced.uscourts.gov.
Eastern Division counties: Beaufort, Carteret, Craven, Edgecombe, Greene, Halifax, Hyde, Jones, Lenoir, Martin, Pamlico, Pitt.
Northern Division counties: Bertie, Camden, Chowan, Currituck, Dare, Gates, Hertford, Northampton, Pasquotank, Perquimans, Tyrrell, Washington.
Southern Division counties: Bladen, Brunswick, Columbus, Duplin, New Hanover, Onslow, Pender, Robeson, Sampson.
Western Division counties: Cumberland, Franklin, Granville, Harnett, Johnston, Nash, Vance, Wake, Warren, Wayne, Wilson.

US Bankruptcy Court -- Eastern District of North Carolina

www.nceb.uscourts.gov

PACER: Sign-up number is . **PACER Online Access:** ECF replaces PACER. **Electronic Filing:** For information on their electronic noticing and filing system using courtwatch.com, visit www.nceb.uscourts.gov/efiling.htm. CM/ECF data at https://ecf.nceb.uscourts.gov. **Opinions:** Selected significant decisions back to 2000. View court opinions at http://207.41.17.205. **Other Online Access:** Old free RACER system no longer available. Search calendars free at www.nceb.uscourts.gov/calendars.php. **Phone access:** Voice Case Information System, call 888-847-9138, 919-856-4618
Raleigh Division counties: Franklin, Granville, Harnett, Johnston, Vance, Wake, Warren.
Wilson Division counties: Beaufort, Bertie, Bladen, Brunswick, Camden, Carteret, Chowan, Columbus, Craven, Cumberland, Currituck, Dare, Duplin, Edgecombe, Gates, Greene, Halifax, Hertford, Hyde, Jones, Lenoir, Martin, Nash, New Hanover, Northampton, Onslow, Pamlico, Pasquotank, Pender, Perquimans, Pitt, Robeson, Sampson, Tyrrell, Washington, Wayne, Wilson.

US District Court -- Middle District of North Carolina

www.ncmd.uscourts.gov

PACER: Case records are available back to 9/1991. Records are purged never. New records are available online after 1 day. **PACER Online Access:** ECF replaces PACER. Document images available. **Electronic Filing:** CM/ECF data at https://ecf.ncmd.uscourts.gov. **Opinions:** View court opinions at www.ncmd.uscourts.gov. **Other Online Access:** Access court calendars at www.ncmd.uscourts.gov.
Greensboro Division counties: Alamance, Cabarrus, Caswell, Chatham, Davidson, Davie, Durham, Forsyth, Guilford, Hoke, Lee, Montgomery, Moore, Orange, Person, Randolph, Richmond, Rockingham, Rowan, Scotland, Stanly, Stokes, Surry, Yadkin. All other district divisions abolished as of 7/1997.

US Bankruptcy Court -- Middle District of North Carolina

www.ncmb.uscourts.gov

PACER: Case records are available back to 1992. New records are available online after 1 day. **PACER Online Access:** ECF replaces PACER. **Electronic Filing:** ECF images go back to 1999. CM/ECF data at https://ecf.ncmb.uscourts.gov. **Opinions:** View court opinions at http://www1.ncmb.uscourts.gov/opinions/search/Main.cfm. **Other Online Access:** Current calendars free at http://www1.ncmb.uscourts.gov/calendar/pdf_cal.cfm. **Phone access:** Voice Case Information System, call 888-319-0455, 336-333-5532
Greensboro Division counties: Includes Durham Division records. Alamance, Caswell, Chatham, Durham, Guilford, Hoke, Lee, Montgomery, Moore, Orange, Person, Randolph, Richmond, Rockingham, Scotland.
Winston-Salem Division counties: Cabarrus, Davidson, Davie, Forsyth, Rowan, Stanly, Stokes, Surry, Yadkin.

US District Court -- Western District of North Carolina

www.ncwd.uscourts.gov

PACER: Case records are available back to 1991. New records are available online after immediately. **PACER Online Access:** WebPACER replaced by CM-ECF system. **Electronic Filing:** CM/ECF data at https://ecf.ncwd.uscourts.gov. **Other Online Access:** Calendars free online at https://ecf.ncwd.uscourts.gov/cgi-bin/NCWD_GetPublicCal.pl.

Asheville Division counties: Avery, Buncombe, Burke, Cleveland, Haywood, Henderson, Madison, McDowell, Mitchell, Polk, Rutherford, Transylvania, Yancey. This Division now houses records from Shelby Division, which is closed. Asheville Div. also holds records for Bryson City Div.

Bryson City Division counties: Cherokee, Clay, Graham, Jackson, Macon, Swain.

Charlotte Division counties: Anson, Gaston, Mecklenburg, Union.

Statesville Division counties: Alexander, Alleghany, Ashe, Caldwell, Catawba, Iredell, Lincoln, Watauga, Wilkes.

US Bankruptcy Court -- Western District of North Carolina

www.ncwb.uscourts.gov

PACER: Case records are available back to 1992. Records are purged every 2 years. New records are available online after 1 day. **PACER Online Access:** ECF replaces PACER. **Electronic Filing:** CM/ECF data at https://ecf.ncwb.uscourts.gov. **Opinions:** Select New Cases or Miscellaneous Cases. View court opinions at www.ncwb.uscourts.gov/opinions/opinions.html. **Other Online Access:** Calendars are free at www.ncwb.uscourts.gov. **Phone access:** Voice Case Information System, call 800-884-9868, 704-350-7505

Charlotte Division counties: Alexander, Alleghany, Anson, Ashe, Avery, Buncombe, Burke, Caldwell, Catawba, Cherokee, Clay, Cleveland, Gaston, Graham, Haywood, Henderson, Iredell, Jackson, Lincoln, Macon, Madison, McDowell, Mecklenburg, Mitchell, Polk, Rutherford, Swain, Transylvania, Union, Watauga, Wilkes, Yancey. There are five offices within this division; records for all may be searched here or at Asheville: 100 Otis St #112, Asheville, NC 28801, 828-771-7300.

North Dakota

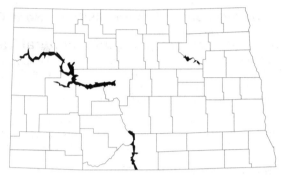

Capital: Bismarck
              Burleigh County
Time Zone: CST
Population: 634.366
# of Counties: 53

Quick Links

Website: www.nd.gov/
Governor: www.governor.state.nd.us
Attorney General: www.ag.state.nd.us
State Archives: www.state.nd.us/hist/sal.htm
State Statutes and Codes: www.legis.nd.gov/information/statutes/cent-code.html
Legislative Bill Search: www.legis.nd.gov/assembly/59-2005/leginfo/bill-inquiry/index.html
Unclaimed Funds: www.land.state.nd.us/abp/abphome.htm

State Level ... Major Agencies

Statewide Court Records

Court Administrator, North Dakota Supreme Court, 600 E Blvd Ave, Dept 180, Bismarck, ND 58505-0530; 701-328-4216, Fax-701-328-2092, 8AM-5PM.
www.ndcourts.com
Online search: You may search ND Supreme Court dockets and opinions at the website. Search by docket number, party name, or anything else that may appear in the text. Records are from 1982 forward. You may subscribe to receive e-mail notification when new Opinions are posted to the North Dakota Supreme Court website, and to be informed when Supreme Court Notices (of proposed or new rules, and the like) are posted.

Sexual Offender Registry

Bureau of Criminal Investigation, SOR Unit, PO Box 1054, Bismarck, ND 58502-1054 (Courier: 4205 N State St, Bismarck, ND 58501); 701-328-5500, Fax-701-328-5510, 8AM-5PM.
www.ndsexoffender.com
Online search: Access is available from the website. The online listings include offenders who are identified as lifetime registrants as defined by law, or have been designated as high-risk offenders by the Attorney General's Risk Level Committee.

Corporation, Limited Liability Company, Limited Partnership, Limited Liability Partnership, Trademarks/Servicemarks, Fictitious Name, Assumed Name

Secretary of State, Business Information/Registration, 600 E Boulevard Ave, Dept 108, Bismarck, ND 58505-0500; 701-328-4284, 800-352-0867, Fax-701-328-2992, 8AM-5PM.
www.nd.gov/sos/businessserv/
Online search: The Secretary of State's registered business database may be viewed at the Internet for no charge. Documents are not available online. Records include corporations, limited liability companies, limited partnerships, limited liability partnerships, limited liability limited partnerships, partnership fictitious names, trade names, trademarks, and real estate investment trusts. The database includes all active records and records inactivated within past twelve months. Access by the first few words of a business name, a

significant word in a business name, or by the record ID number assigned. If questions, email sosbir@state.nd.us. **Other options:** This agency provides a database purchase program. Cost is $35.00 per database and processing fees vary for type of media.

Uniform Commercial Code, Federal Tax Liens, State Tax Liens

UCC Division, Secretary of State, 600 E Boulevard Ave Dept 108, Bismarck, ND 58505-0500; 701-328-3662, Fax-701-328-4214, 8AM-5PM.
www.nd.gov/sos/businessserv/centralindex/index.html
Online search: There is a limited free public search and a commercial system for professionals. Sign-up for access to the Central Indexing System includes an annual subscription $150 fee and a one-time $50.00 registration fee. The UCC-11 fee (normally $7.00) applies, but documents will not be certified. Searches include UCC-11 information listing and farm product searches. **Other options:** The agency offers bulk access on IBM cartridge or paper copy. Call for details.

Sales Tax Registrations

Office of State Tax Commissioner, Sales & Special Taxes Division, State Capitol, 600 E Boulevard Ave, Bismarck, ND 58505-0599; 701-328-3470, Fax-701-328-0336, 8AM-5PM.
www.nd.gov/tax/salesanduse/
Online search: A permit number may be verified online at www.nd.gov/tax/salesanduse/permitinquiry/. System indicates valid permit registered to company name.

Birth, Death, Marriage Certificates

ND Department of Health, Vital Records, State Capitol, 600 E Blvd, Dept 301, Bismarck, ND 58505-0200; 701-328-2360, Fax-701-328-1850, 7:30AM-5PM.
http://ndhealth.gov/vital/
Online search: Records may be ordered online from the Internet site or from vitalchek.com. Records are not returned online.

Driver Records

Department of Transportation, Driver License & Traffic Safety Division, 608 E Boulevard Ave, Bismarck, ND 58505-0700; 701-328-2603, Fax-701-328-2435, 8AM-5PM.
www.state.nd.us/dot
Online search: The website offers record ordering at https://secure.apps.state.nd.us/dot/dlts/dlos/welcome.htm. Fee is $3.00 per record, record is returned by mail. If you are not ordering your own record, you must qualify per DPPA. Ongoing, approved commercial accounts may request records with personal information via a commercial system. There is a minimum of 100 requests per month. For more information, call 701-328-4790. **Other options:** Magnetic tape ordering is available for high volume users.

Vessel Ownership, Vessel Registration

North Dakota Game & Fish Department, Boat Registrations, 100 N Bismarck Expressway, Bismarck, ND 58501; 701-328-6335, Fax-701-328-6374, 8AM-5PM.
http://gf.nd.gov
Online search: There is a free public inquiry system at the web page. Click on "Register a Boat" then Find Watercraft Registration." One can also search lottery hunting permit applications and hunter safety listings. **Other options:** A printed list is available of all registered vessels.

GED Certificates

Department of Public Instruction, GED Testing - CKEN-11, 600 E Blvd Ave, Bismarck, ND 58505-0440; 701-328-2393, Fax-701-328-4770, 8AM-4:30PM.
www.dpi.state.nd.us/adulted/index.shtm
Online search: One may request records via email at JMarcell@state.nd.us. There is no fee, unless a transcript is ordered.

State Level ... Occupational Licensing

Alcoholic Beverage Control........................ www.ag.state.nd.us/Licensing/Beverage/Beverage.htm
Amusement Device, Coin-Operated .... www.ag.state.nd.us/Licensing/Amusement/Amusement.htm
Asbestos Landfill .... www.health.state.nd.us/wm/pdf/Asbestos_List.pdf
Attorney .... www.court.state.nd.us/court/lawyers/index/frameset.htm
Bank, Commercial .... www.state.nd.us/dfi/regulate/reg/regulated.asp
Charitable Solicitation .... www.nd.gov/sos/forms/pdf/charorg.pdf
Collection Agency .... www.state.nd.us/dfi/regulate/reg/regulated.asp
Consumer Finance Company .... www.state.nd.us/dfi/regulate/reg/regulated.asp
Contractor www.health.state.nd.us/AQ/IAQ/ASB/Asbestos%20Contractors.pdf
Contractor/General Contractor................... https://secure.apps.state.nd.us/sc/busnsrch/busnSearch.htm
Credit Union .... www.state.nd.us/dfi/regulate/reg/regulated.asp
Debt Collector... www.state.nd.us/dfi/regulate/reg/regulated.asp
Deferred Presentment Provider.................. www.state.nd.us/dfi/regulate/reg/regulated.asp
Drug Mfg./Wholesaler .... www.nodakpharmacy.com
Electrical Contractor .... www.ndseb.com/findcontractor.asp
Electrician... https://www.ndseb.com/secure-site/onlrenewallogin.asp
Electrician Apprentice .... https://www.ndseb.com/secure-site/onlrenewallogin.asp
Engineer.. www.ndpelsboard.org
Fireworks, Wholesale .... www.ag.state.nd.us/Licensing/Fireworks/Fireworks.htm
Gaming .... www.ag.state.nd.us/Gaming/listorg.PDF
Gaming Distributor .... www.ag.state.nd.us/Gaming/distlist.PDF
Gaming Manufacturer................................ www.ag.state.nd.us/Gaming/manlst.PDF
Grain Buyer .... www.psc.state.nd.us/jurisdiction/grain-entities.html
Grain Warehouse/Elevator......................... www.psc.state.nd.us/jurisdiction/grain-entities.html
Home Inspector... www.nd.gov/sos/forms/pdf/home-inspectors.pdf
Investment Advisor.................................... www.ndsecurities.com
Land Surveyor .... www.ndpelsboard.org
Livestock Agent... www.agdepartment.com/Programs/Livestock/Agents.html
Livestock Auction Market .... www.agdepartment.com/Programs/Livestock/markets.html
Livestock Dealer.. www.agdepartment.com/Programs/Livestock/Dealers.html
Lobbyist .... www.nd.gov/sos/lobbylegislate/lobbying/reg-mnu.html
Medical Doctor .... www.ndbomex.com/SearchPage.asp
Money Broker Firm .... www.state.nd.us/dfi/regulate/reg/regulated.asp
Nurse Assistant .... www.ndbon.org
Nurse-LPN, RN, Advanced Practice........... www.ndbon.org
Optometrist .... www.ndsbopt.org/directory.asp
Osteopathic Physician................................ www.ndbomex.com/SearchPage.asp
Pharmacist... www.nodakpharmacy.com
Pharmacy .... www.nodakpharmacy.com
Pharmacy Technician/Intern .... www.nodakpharmacy.com
Physician Assistant .... www.ndbomex.com/SearchPage.asp
Polygraph Examiner .... www.ag.state.nd.us/Licensing/Polygraph/Polygraph.htm
Private Investigation Agency .... www.nd.gov/pisb/holders.html
Private Investigator................................... www.nd.gov/pisb/holders.html
Public Accountant-CPA.............................. www.state.nd.us/ndsba/database/sbasearch.asp
Public Accounting Firm............................. www.state.nd.us/ndsba/database/sbasearch.asp
Racing... www.ndracingcommission.com/Forms.htm
Sale of Check... www.state.nd.us/dfi/regulate/reg/regulated.asp
Securities Agent/Dealer .... www.ndsecurities.com
Security Provider/Company....................... www.nd.gov/pisb/holders.html
Social Worker .... http://secure.ebigpicture.com/ndbswe/live/public.asp
Soil Classifier.. www.soilsci.ndsu.nodak.edu/soilclassifiers/pscand.htm
Speech-Language Pathologist/Audiologist . http://governor.state.nd.us/boards/bcpublicsearch.asp?searchtype=member

Tobacco, Retail/Wholesale .... www.ag.state.nd.us/Licensing/Tobacco/Tobacco.htm
Transient Merchant .... www.ag.state.nd.us/Licensing/Transient/TransientMerchant.htm
Trust Company .... www.state.nd.us/dfi/regulate/reg/regulated.asp
Water Well Driller .... www.health.state.nd.us/wq/gw/wells.htm
Water Well Pump & Pitless Unit .... www.health.state.nd.us/wq/gw/wells.htm
Well Contractor, Monitoring...................... www.health.state.nd.us/wq/gw/wells.htm

County Level ... Courts

Court Administration: State Court Administrator, North Dakota Judiciary, 600 E Blvd, 1st Floor Judicial Wing, Dept. 180, Bismarck, ND, 58505-0530; 701-328-4216; www.ndcourts.com or www.court.state.nd.us

Court Structure: In 1995, the County Courts merged with the District Courts statewide. County Court records are maintained by the 53 District Court Clerks in the seven judicial districts. It is recommended that you state "include all County Court cases" in search requests. There are 76 Municipal Courts that handle traffic cases.

Online Access Note: A statewide computer system for internal use only is in operation for most Nort Dakota counties. You may now search North Dakota Supreme Court dockets and opinions at www.ndcourts.com. Search by docket number, party name, or anything else that may appear in the text. Records are from 1982 forward. Email notification of new opinions is also available.

Cass County
East Central Judicial District Court – Probate Records
Search probate records online free at www.lib.ndsu.nodak.edu/ndirs/databases/probate.php.

County Level ... Recorders & Assessors

Recording Office Organization: 53 counties, 53 recording offices. The recording officer is the Register of Deeds. The entire state is in the Central Time Zone (CST). Federal tax liens on personal property of businesses are filed with the Secretary of State. Other federal and all state tax liens are filed with the county Register of Deeds. All counties will perform tax lien searches. Some counties automatically include business federal tax liens as part of a UCC search because they appear on the statewide database. (Be careful - federal tax liens on individuals may only be in the county lien books, not on the statewide system.) Separate searches are usually available at $5.00-7.00 per name. Copy fees vary. Copies may be faxed.

32 North Dakota Counties *Real Estate Records*
Subscription access the recorder's land records via NDRIN's central repository at www.ndrin.com. There is a $200 set-up fee and $50 monthly with $1.00 charge per image printed.
Counties Include-.Barnes, Benson, Billings, Burleigh, Cass, Cavalier, Dunn, Foster, Golden Valley, Griggs, Kidder, McHenry, McIntosh, McKenzie, McLean, Morton, Nelson, Pembina, Oierce, Ramsey, Ransom, Richland, Rolette, Sargent, Slope, Stark, Steele, Stutsman, Walsh, War, Wells, Williams,

Burleigh County *Real Estate, Treasurer/Auditor, Property Records*
Access to treasurer and auditor property data is free at www.co.burleigh.nd.us/property-information/. No name searching. Also, see setion introduction for real estate records.

Grand Forks County *Real Estate, Recording, Deed, Death, Judgment, Lien Records*
www.co.grand-forks.nd.us/homepage.htm
Access to county property information is free at www.co.grand-forks.nd.us/search.htm. Also, access to the recorder's database is free at www.co.grand-forks.nd.us/recorders%20search.htm. Also, see setion introduction for real estate records.

Ward County   *Real Estate, Property Tax Records*

Access to property tax data is free at www.co.ward.nd.us/ext/PropertyTax.htm. Also, see setion introduction for real estate records.

Williams County   *Property Tax, Treasurer, Real Estate Records*

www.williamsnd.com

Access to the county property tax data is free at www.williamsnd.com/taxes/search/default.asp. Also, see setion introduction for real estate records.

Federal Courts in North Dakota...

Standards for Federal Courts: The universal PACER sign-up number is 800-676-6856. Find PACER and the Party/Case Index on the Web at http://pacer.psc.uscourts.gov. PACER dial-up access is $.60 per minute. Also, courts offering internet access via PACER, Web-PACER or the new CM-ECF charge $.08 per page fee ($.07 per page if record is pre-2005 or unless noted as free).

US District Court -- District of North Dakota

www.ndd.uscourts.gov

PACER: Case records are available back to 10/1990. Records are purged never. New records are available online after 1 day. **PACER Online Access:** PACER online at http://pacer.ndd.uscourts.gov. **Electronic Filing:** CM/ECF data at (Currently in the process of implementing CM/ECF). **Opinions:** View court opinions at www.ndd.uscourts.gov/DNDOpinions/JudgesOpinions.htm. **Other Online Access:** Calendars free at www.ndd.uscourts.gov/CAL/CourtCal.htm.
Bismarck-Southwestern Division counties: Adams, Billings, Bowman, Burleigh, Dunn, Emmons, Golden Valley, Grant, Hettinger, Kidder, Logan, McIntosh, McLean, Mercer, Morton, Oliver, Sioux, Slope, Stark.
Fargo-Southeastern Division counties: Barnes, Cass, Dickey, Eddy, Foster, Griggs, La Moure, Ransom, Richland, Sargent, Steele, Stutsman. Rolette County cases prior to 1995 may be located here.
Grand Forks-Northeastern Division counties: Benson, Cavalier, Grand Forks, Nelson, Pembina, Ramsey, Towner, Traill, Walsh. Grand Forks office now unstaffed.
Minot-Northwestern Division counties: Bottineau, Burke, Divide, McHenry, McKenzie, Mountrail, Pierce, Renville, Rolette, Sheridan, Ward, Wells, Williams. Case records from Rolette County prior to 1995 may be located in Fargo-Southeastern Division.

US Bankruptcy Court -- District of North Dakota

www.ndb.uscourts.gov

PACER: Case records are available back to 1991. New records are available online after 1 day. **PACER Online Access:** PACER online at http://pacer.ndd.uscourts.gov. **Electronic Filing:** CM/ECF data at https://ecf.ndb.uscourts.gov. **Other Online Access:** RACER is no longer available, replaced by newer PACER system. **Phone access:** Voice Case Info System, call 701-297-7166.
Fargo Division counties: All counties in North Dakota.

> **Editor's Note:** The southwestern area of North Dakota (west and south of the Missouri River) is in Mountain Time Zone. The remainder of the state is in the Central Time Zone.

Ohio

Capital: Columbus
             Franklin County
Time Zone: EST
Population: 11,459,011
# of Counties: 88

Quick Links

Website: www.alabama.gov
Governor: http://governor.ohio.gov
Attorney General: www.ag.state.oh.us
State Archives: www.ohiohistory.org/ar_tools.html
State Statutes and Codes:
     http://onlinedocs.andersonpublishing.com/oh/lpExt.dll?f=templates&fn=main-
     h.htm&cp=PORC
Legislative Bill Search: www.legislature.state.oh.us/search.cfm
Unclaimed Funds: www.unclaimedfundstreasurehunt.ohio.gov

State Level ... Major Agencies

Criminal Records

Ohio Bureau of Investigation, Civilian Background Section, PO Box 365, London, OH 43140 (Courier: 1560 State Rte 56, London, OH 43140); 740-845-2000 (General Info), 740-845-2375 (Civilian Background Cks), Fax-740-845-2633, 8AM-4:45PM. www.webcheck.ag.state.oh.us
Online search: WebCheck is an Internet-based request program for civilian background checks for school districts, education associations, children's hospitals, and public institutions. Results are NOT returned via the Internet. Turnaround time is 2 days. Agencies can send fingerprint images and other data via the Internet using a single digit fingerprint scanner and a driver's license magnetic strip reader. Within two business days, the school or daycare center will receive their results of their background check requests.

Statewide Court Records

Administrative Director, Supreme Court of Ohio, 65 S Front Street, Columbus, OH 43215-3431; 614-387-9000, 800-826-9010, 614-387-9410 (Case Management), Fax-614-387-9419, 8AM-5PM.
www.sconet.state.oh.us
Online search: Appellate and Supreme Court opinions may be researched from the website. Go to www.sconet.state.oh.us/rod/newpdf/. At present, there is no statewide system for local court records, but many county level courts offer online access to their record index.

Sexual Offender Registry

Ohio Bureau of Investigation, Sexual Offender Registry, PO Box 365, London, OH 43140 (Courier: 1560 State Rte 56 SW, London, OH 43140); 740-845-2221, 740-845-2223, 866-406-4534, Fax-740-845-2633, 8AM-4:45PM.
www.esorn.ag.state.oh.us/Secured/p1.aspx
Online search: Search online eSORN at www.esorn.ag.state.oh.us/Secured/p1.aspx. Users can search by offender name, zip code, county and / or school district. The site is linked to all 88 of Ohio's sheriff's offices and all 32 Ohio correctional facility records offices

Incarceration Records

Ohio Department of Rehabilitation and Correction, Bureau of Records Management, 1050 Freeway Drive, N., Columbus, OH 43229; 614-752-1076, 614-752-1159 x3 (Inmate Records), Fax-614-752-1086, 8:30AM-5PM M-F.
www.drc.state.oh.us
Online search: From the website, in the Select a Destination box, select Offender Search. You can search by name or inmate number. The Offender Search includes all offenders currently incarcerated or under some type of Department supervision (parole, post-release control, or transitional control).

Corporation, Fictitious Name, Limited Partnership, Assumed Name, Trademarks/Servicemarks, Limited Liability Company

Secretary of State, Corporate Records Access, PO Box 130, Columbus, OH 43216 (Courier: 30 E Broad Street, 16th Fl, Columbus, OH 43215); 877-767-3453, 614-466-3910, Fax-614-466-3899, 8AM-5PM.
www.sos.state.oh.us/sos/businessservices/corp.aspx
Online search: The agency provides free Internet searching for business and corporation records at www.sos.state.oh.us/sos/businessservices/corp.aspx?Section=104. The site also includes UCC and campaign finance. Images are available, as well as Good Standings. **Other options:** This agency makes the database available for purchase, call for details.

Uniform Commercial Code

UCC Records, Secretary of State, PO Box 2795, Columbus, OH 43216 (Courier: 30 E Broad Street, Columbus, OH 43215); 877-767-3453, 614-466-3910, Fax-614-466-2892, 8AM-5PM.
www.sos.state.oh.us/sos/ucc/ucc.aspx
Online search: The Internet site offers free online access to records. Search by debtor, secured party, or financing statement number.
Other options: The complete database is available on electronic media with weekly updates. Call for current pricing.

Birth Certificates

Ohio Department of Health, Bureau of Vital Statistics, PO Box 15098, Columbus, OH 43215-0098 (Courier: 246 N High St, 1st Fl, Revenue Room, Columbus, OH 43215); 614-466-2531, 877-828-3101 (Vitalchek), Fax-877-553-2439, 7:45AM-4:30PM.
www.odh.ohio.gov
Online search: Records can be ordered from a state-designated vendor - www.vitalchek.com.

Death Records

Ohio Department of Health, Bureau of Vital Statistics, PO Box 15098, Columbus, OH 43215-0098 (Courier: 246 N High Street, 1st Fl, Revenue Room, Columbus, OH 43215); 614-466-2531, 877-828-3101, Fax-877-553-2439, 7:45AM-4:30PM.
www.odh.ohio.gov
Online search: The Ohio Historical Society Death Certificate Index Searchable Database at www.ohiohistory.org/dindex/ permits searching by name, county, index. Data is available from 1913 to 1937 only. Records can be ordered from a state-designated vendor - www.vitalchek.com.

Workers' Compensation Records

Bureau of Workers Compensation, Customer Contact Center - Records Mgr, 30 W Spring St, 10th, Columbus, OH 43215-2241; 800-644-6292, 614-728-3210 (Records), Fax-614-752-4732, 7:30AM-5:30PM.
www.ohiobwc.com
Online search: Injured workers, injured worker designees, representatives and managed care organizations (MCOs) can view a list of all claims associated with a given SSN, but are limited to viewing only the claims with which they are associated. Employers, their representatives or designees, and managed care organizations can view a list of all claims associated to their BWC policy number. Medical providers can view all claims associated with any given SSN. Access is through the website listed above. **Other options:** Bulk data is released to approved accounts; however, the legal department must approve requesters. The agency has general information available on a website.

Driver Records

Department of Public Safety, Bureau of Motor Vehicles, 1970 W Broad St, Columbus, OH 43223-1102; 614-752-7600, Fax-614-752-7987, 8AM-5:30PM M-T-W; 8AM-4:30PM TH-F.
www.ohiobmv.com
Online search: The Online Abstract System by FTP is suggested for requesters who order 100 or more motor vehicle reports per day in batch mode. The DL# or SSN and name are needed when ordering. Fee is $2.00 per record. For more information, call Fiscal Srvs at 614-752-2091. **Other options:** Overnight CD service is available for larger accounts.

Vehicle Ownership, Vehicle Identification

Bureau of Motor Vehicles, Motor Vehicle Title Records, 1970 W Broad St, Columbus, OH 43223-1102; 614-752-7671, Fax-614-752-8929, 7:30AM-4:45PM.
www.ohiobmv.com
Online search: Ohio offers online access through AAMVAnet. All requesters must comply with a contractual agreement prior to release of data, which complies with DPPA regulations. Fee is $2.00 per record. Call 614-752-7671 for more information. The website offers free access to title records for vehicles and watercraft. No personal information is release. Search by title number or ID. Also search at https://www.dps.state.oh.us/atps/. **Other options:** Bulk records are available for purchase, per DPPA guidelines.

Accident Reports

Department of Public Safety, OSHP Central Records, 1st Fl, PO Box 182074, Columbus, OH 43218-2074; 614-466-3536, Fax-614-644-9749, 8AM-4:45PM.
http://statepatrol.ohio.gov/crash.htm
Online search: Crash reports purchased online will be sent to your e-mail account the same day. Crash photographs purchased online will be sent in the mail. Online crash reports are available for crashes that occurred on or after August 5, 2001. Crash reports prior to August 5, 2001 are available by mail-in request. Reports must be purchased using a credit card.

State Level ... Occupational Licensing

Accounting Firm	http://acc.ohio.gov/lookup.html
Acupuncturist	https://license.ohio.gov/lookup/default.asp
Anesthesiologist Assistant	https://license.ohio.gov/lookup/default.asp
Architect	https://license.ohio.gov/lookup/
Athletic Trainer	https://license.ohio.gov/lookup/default.asp
Attorney (State)	www.sconet.state.oh.us/atty_reg/Public_AttorneyInformation.asp
Audiologist/Audiologist Aide	https://license.ohio.gov/lookup/default.asp
Backflow Prevention Assembly Insp.	www.com.state.oh.us/dic/plans/scripts/bkfloqy.htm
Backflow Tester	https://www.com.state.oh.us/dic/plans/scripts/bkfloqy.htm
Backflow Tester	www.com.state.oh.us/dic/plans/scripts/bkfloqy.htm
Bank	http://elicense2-lookup.com.ohio.gov/
Barber/Barber Instructor	https://license.ohio.gov/lookup/
Barber School	http://barber.ohio.gov/barbsch.htm
Barber Shop	https://license.ohio.gov/lookup/
Boiler Contractor	www.com.state.oh.us/dic/scripts/boilerctrqy.htm
Cemetery	https://www.com.state.oh.us/real/scripts/searchcriteria.htm
Check Cashing Service/Lending Service	http://elicense2-lookup.com.ohio.gov/
Child Care Type A or B House	www.odjfs.state.oh.us/cdc/query.asp
Child Day Care Facility	www.odjfs.state.oh.us/cdc/query.asp
Chiropractor	http://chirobd.ohio.gov/On-Line%20License%20Verification.htm
Clinical Nurse Specialist	www.nursing.ohio.gov/verification.stm
Coil Cleaner (Liquor/Beverage)	www.liquorcontrol.ohio.gov/coilalpha.txt
Consumer Finance Company	http://elicense2-lookup.com.ohio.gov/
Contractor	www.com.state.oh.us/dic/scripts/ociebqy.htm
Cosmetic Therapist	https://license.ohio.gov/lookup/default.asp
Cosmetologist/Managing Cosmetologist	https://license.ohio.gov/lookup/default.asp
Cosmetology Instructor	https://license.ohio.gov/lookup/default.asp
Counselor	http://cswmft.ohio.gov/query.asp
Day Camp, Children's	www.odjfs.state.oh.us/cdc/query.asp
Dental Assistant Radiologist	www.dental.ohio.gov/license/query.stm
Dental Hygienist	www.dental.ohio.gov/license/query.stm
Dentist	www.dental.ohio.gov/license/query.stm
Dialysis Technician	www.nursing.ohio.gov/verification.stm
Dietitian	www.dietetics.ohio.gov
Drug Wholesaler/Distributor	http://pharmacy.ohio.gov/license.htm

Electrical Safety Inspector .... www.com.state.oh.us/dic/default.htm
Electrician... www.com.state.oh.us/dic/scripts/ociebqy.htm
Emergency Medical Tech. Instr. .... https://www.dps.state.oh.us/ems/cert.asp
Emergency Medical Technician................... https://www.dps.state.oh.us/ems/cert.asp
Engineer... www.ohiopeps.org/files/license_lookup.html
Engineering/Surveying Company .... www.ohiopeps.org/files/license_lookup.html
Esthetician/Managing Esthetician.............. https://license.ohio.gov/lookup/default.asp
Fire Protection System Designer................ www.com.state.oh.us/dic/default.htm
Firefighter/Firefighter Instructor................ https://www.dps.state.oh.us/ems/cert.asp
Foreign Real Estate Property .... https://www.com.state.oh.us/real/scripts/searchcriteria.htm
Heating/Refrigeration (HVAC)................... www.com.state.oh.us/dic/scripts/ociebqy.htm
Hydronic-related Occupation...................... www.com.state.oh.us/dic/scripts/ociebqy.htm
Insurance Agent .... www.ohioinsurance.gov/ConsumServ/ocs/agentloc.asp
Landscape Architect..................................... https://license.ohio.gov/lookup/
Legislative Agent/Agent Employer............. www.jlec-olig.state.oh.us/olig2/search_form.aspx
Liquor Distributor .... www.liquorcontrol.ohio.gov/safekeep.txt
Liquor License/Liquor Store .... www.liquorcontrol.ohio.gov/phone.txt
Liquor License Cancellation .... www.liquorcontrol.ohio.gov/canceled.txt
Liquor Permit... www.liquorcontrol.ohio.gov/liquor5a.html
Lobbyist Lists .... www.jlec-olig.state.oh.us/AgentandEmployerLists.htm
Lobbyist/Lobbyist Employer .... www.jlec-olig.state.oh.us/olig2/search_form.aspx
Manicuring/Esthetician Instructor............... https://license.ohio.gov/lookup/default.asp
Manicurist/Managing Manicurist................ https://license.ohio.gov/lookup/default.asp
Marriage and Family Therapist................... http://cswmft.ohio.gov/query.asp
Massage Therapist .... https://license.ohio.gov/lookup/default.asp
Mechanotherapist... https://license.ohio.gov/lookup/default.asp
Medical Doctor .... https://license.ohio.gov/lookup/default.asp
Midwife Nurse .... www.nursing.ohio.gov/verification.stm
Mortgage Broker.. http://elicense2-lookup.com.ohio.gov/
Naprapath... https://license.ohio.gov/lookup/default.asp
Nurse Anesthetist... www.nursing.ohio.gov/verification.stm
Nurse-RN/LPN/Practitioner........................ www.nursing.ohio.gov/verification.stm
Occupational Therapist/Assistant................ https://license.ohio.gov/lookup/default.asp
Ocularist/Ocularist Apprentice .... https://license.ohio.gov/lookup/default.asp
Optical Dispenser... https://license.ohio.gov/lookup/default.asp
Optician/Optician Apprentice .... https://license.ohio.gov/lookup/default.asp
Optometrist .... www.optometry.ohio.gov/query.asp
Osteopathic Physician.................................. https://license.ohio.gov/lookup/default.asp
Pawnbroker.. http://elicense2-lookup.com.ohio.gov/
Pesticide Applicator/Operator/Business...... www.ohioagriculture.gov/pubs/divs/plnt/plnt-licensing.stm
Pesticide Dealer .... www.ohioagriculture.gov/pubs/divs/plnt/plnt-licensing.stm
Pharmacist.. http://pharmacy.ohio.gov/license.htm
Pharmacy/Pharmacy Dispensary................. http://pharmacy.ohio.gov/license.htm
Physical Therapist/Assistant .... https://license.ohio.gov/lookup/default.asp
Physician Assistant .... https://license.ohio.gov/lookup/default.asp
Plumber.. www.com.state.oh.us/dic/scripts/ociebqy.htm
Plumbing Inspector .... https://www.com.state.oh.us/dic/plans/scripts/plumbqy.htm
Podiatrist.. https://license.ohio.gov/lookup/default.asp
Precious Metals Dealer http://elicense2-lookup.com.ohio.gov/
Premium Finance Company........................ http://elicense2-lookup.com.ohio.gov/
Prescriptive Authority................................. www.nursing.ohio.gov/verification.stm
Private Investigator .... https://www.com.state.oh.us/real/scripts/searchcriteria.htm
Psychologist... https://license.ohio.gov/lookup/default.asp?division=83
Public Accountant-CPA.............................. http://acc.ohio.gov/lookup.html
Real Estate Agent/Sales/Broker .... https://www.com.state.oh.us/real/scripts/searchcriteria.htm
Real Estate Appraiser.................................. https://www.com.state.oh.us/real/scripts/searchcriteria.htm

Respiratory Therapist/Student...................... https://license.ohio.gov/lookup/default.asp
Savings Bank/Savings & Loan Association http://elicense2-lookup.com.ohio.gov/
School Psychologist..................................... https://license.ohio.gov/lookup/default.asp?division=83
Securities Filing... www.securities.state.oh.us/secu_apps/offering/disclaimer.aspx
Security Guard... https://www.com.state.oh.us/real/scripts/searchcriteria.htm
Social Worker.. http://cswmft.ohio.gov/query.asp
Speech Pathologist/Audiologist.................. https://license.ohio.gov/lookup/default.asp
Steam Engineer.. www.com.state.oh.us/dic/scripts/boilerctrqy.htm
Storage Tank Corrective Action.................. https://www.com.state.oh.us/sfm/bustr/CorrectiveActions.htm
Surveyor, Land .... www.ohiopeps.org/files/license_lookup.html
Teacher/Teacher's Aide https://www.ode.state.oh.us/Teaching-Profession/Teacher/Certification_Licensure/certifact.asp
Underground Storage Tank.......................... https://www.com.state.oh.us/sfm/bustr/PublicInquiry.htm
Underground Tank Inspector .... https://www.com.state.oh.us/sfm/bustr/PDFs/Data/WEBInspectorList
Underground Tank Installer......................... https://www.com.state.oh.us/sfm/bustr/PDFs/Data/WEBInstallerList
Underground Tank Instructor...................... https://www.com.state.oh.us/sfm/bustr/PDFs/TrainerApprovedlist.xls
Veterinarian/Veterinary Tech .... www.ovmlb.ohio.gov/

County Level ... Courts

Court Administration: Administrative Director, Supreme Court of Ohio, 65 S Front Street, Columbus, OH 43215-3431; 614-387-9000, Fax: 614-387-9419. www.sconet.state.oh.us

Court Structure: The Court of Common Pleas is the general jurisdiction court and County Courts have limited jurisdiction. Effective July 1, 1997, the dollar limits for civil cases in County and Municipal Courts were raised as follows: County Court - from $3,000 to $15,000; Municipal Court - from $10,000 to $15,000. In addition the small claims limit was raised from $2,000 to $3,000.

Effective in 2001, Ohio Common Pleas Courts may name their own civil action limits, though most of these courts elect not to make changes. In effect, these Common Pleas courts may take any civil cases. However, civil maximum limits for Ohio's County Courts and Municipal Courts remains the same – $15,000.

Online Access Note: There is no statewide computer system, but a number of Circuits and Municipal courts offer online access.

Allen County

Common Pleas Court – Civil and Criminal Records
www.co.allen.oh.us
Access is free at http://65.17.134.12/pa/pa.urd/pamw6500.display. Records go back to 12/1/1988.

Lima Municipal Court – Civil and Criminal Records
www.limamunicipalcourt.org
Search index information at www.limamunicipalcourt.org, click on Case Inquiry.

Ashland County

Common Pleas Court – Civil and Criminal Records
www.ashlandcounty.org/clerkofcourts
Access records at www.ashlandcountycpcourt.org. Computerized court records go back to 6/7/1995.

Ashtabula County

Common Pleas Court - County Courts – Civil and Criminal Records
Access to index is free at http://courts.co.ashtabula.oh.us/pa.htm.

Ashtabula Municipal Court – Civil and Criminal Records
www.ashtabulamunicipalcourt.com
Access to civil court cases are free at www.ashtabulamunicourt.com/searchcivildocket.asp?pageId=71.

Athens County

Common Pleas Court – Civil and Criminal Records
www.athenscountycpcourt.org
Access to the CP court records are free at www.athenscountycpcourt.org/genrlmnu.htm.

Athens Municipal Court – Civil and Criminal Records
Search by name or case number at http://docket.webxsol.com/athens/index.html. Records available from 1992.

Brown County

County Municipal Court – Civil and Criminal Records
www.browncountycourt.org
Access to records are free at www.browncountycourt.org/search.html.

Butler County

Common Pleas Court – Civil and Criminal Records
www.butlercountyclerk.org
Access to County Clerk of Courts records are free at www.butlercountyclerk.org/pa/pa.urd/pamw6500-display. Search by name, dates, or case number and type. Access to Probate Court records is free are http://66.117.197.22/index.cfm?page=courtRecords Search the Estate or Guardianship databases.

Hamilton Municipal Court – Civil and Criminal Records
www.hamiltonmunicipalcourt.org
Search records for free at www.hamiltonmunicipalcourt.org.

Clark County

Common Pleas Court – Civil and Criminal Records
www.clarkcountyohio.gov/courts/index.htm
Access to clerk's records is free at http://12.150.181.49/. The Sheriff's most wanted list is found at www.clarkcountysheriff.com.

Clark County Municipal Court – Civil and Criminal Records
www.clerkofcourts.municipal.co.clark.oh.us
Access to case information is free at www.clerkofcourts.municipal.co.clark.oh.us/web/welcome.nsf/HomePage?OpenForm. Images available back to 1/2003. Name searching on "New Cases;" other types require a case number. Records available since 03/90.

Clermont County

Common Pleas Court - Municipal Court– Civil and Criminal Records
Access to court records is free at www.clermontclerk.org/Case_Access.htm. Online records go back to 1/1987. Includes later Municipal Court records back to 5/1/1996. Includes Common Pleas court records.

Clinton County

Clinton County Municipal Court – Civil and Criminal Records
Search court records online at www.clintonmunicourt.org/search.html.

Columbiana County

Common Pleas Court - Municipal Court– Civil and Criminal Records
www.ccclerk.org
Access to all county court index and docket records is free at www.ccclerk.org/case_access.htm. Includes probate.

Coshocton County

Coshocton Municipal Court – Civil and Criminal Records
www.coshoctonmunicipalcourt.com
Access to civil records is at the website. Search by name, case number, attorney, date.

Crawford County

Common Pleas Court – Civil and Criminal Records
www.crawford-co.org/Clerk/default.html
Access to Common Pleas court records is free at www.crawford-co.org/Clerk/default.html and click on "Internet Inquiry."

Cuyahoga County

Common Pleas Court - General Division – Civil and Criminal Records
http://cp.cuyahogacounty.us/CCPCourt/index.aspx
Access to Common Please civil courts; click on Civil Case Dockets and Criminal at
http://cpdocket.cp.cuyahogacounty.us/cjisjs/servlet/cjis.urd/run/cmsw101. Access to Probate is at
http://probate.cuyahogacounty.us/pa/.

Bedford Municipal Court – Civil and Criminal Records
www.bedfordmuni.org
Access index to court records at www.bedfordmuni.org. Click on Case Information.

Berea Municipal Court – Civil and Criminal Records
www.bereamunicourt.org
Search docket information at www.bereamunicourt.org/info.asp?pageId=5.

Cleveland Heights Municipal Court – Civil and Criminal Records
www.clevelandheightscourt.com
Civil (to $15,000) or misdemeanor docket records for Municipal Court are on the website. Search by name or case number.

Garfield Heights Municipal Court – Civil and Criminal Records
www.ghmc.org
Access is limited to dockets; search by name, date or case number at http://docket.ghmc.org.

Lakewood Municipal Court – Civil and Criminal Records
www.lakewoodcourtoh.com
View weekly dockets only at www.lakewoodcourtoh.com/CourtDockets.htm.

Rocky River Municipal Court – Civil and Criminal Records
www.rrcourt.net
Public access to record index at https://rrcourt.net/pa/pa.urd/pamw6500.display.

Shaker Heights Municipal Court – Civil and Criminal Records
www.shakerheightscourt.org/home/
Search case records and dockets at www.shakerheightscourt.org/home/.

Delaware County

Common Pleas Court – Civil Records
www.delawarecountyclerk.org
Access to court records is free at www.delawarecountyclerk.org. Probate court index from 1852 to 1920 is free at
www.midohio.net/dchsdcgs/probate.html. Search the sheriff's county database of sex offenders, deadbeat parents, and most wanted list
for free at www.delawarecountysheriff.com.

Delaware Municipal Court – Civil and Criminal Records
www.municipalcourt.org
Municipal courts records are at www.municipalcourt.org:81/connection/court/lookup.xsp?in=cv. Misdemeanor and traffic case records
are free at www.municipalcourt.org:81/connection/court/lookup.xsp?in=ct. Also, search the court's DUI list at
www.municipalcourt.org/main_dui.asp.

Erie County

Vermilion Municipal Court – Civil and Criminal Records
www.vermilionmunicipalcourt.org
Access to municipal court records is at the website.

Fairfield County

Common Pleas Court – Civil and Criminal Records
www.fairfieldcountyclerk.com
Access to County Clerk's court records database is free at www.fairfieldcountyclerk.com/Search/.

Fairfield County Municipal Court – Civil and Criminal Records
www.fairfieldcountymunicipalcourt.org
Search cases online at www.fairfieldcountymunicipalcourt.org/connection/court/.

Fayette County

Common Pleas Court – Civil and Criminal Records
www.fayette-co-oh.com/Commplea/index.html
Search docket information free at http://appserv1.webxsol.com/fayettecp/case_dockets/Search.aspx.

Municipal Court – Civil and Criminal Records
www.wayneohio.org/public_access.html
Free search of record index at http://216.29.108.131/search.htm.

Franklin County

Common Pleas Court – Civil Records
www.franklincountyohio.gov/clerk/
Access records via the website. Java-enable web browser required.

Franklin County Municipal Court - Civil Division – Civil Records
www.fcmcclerk.com
Records from the Clerk of Court Courtview database free online at www.fcmcclerk.com/pa/pa.htm. Search by name or case number.

Franklin County Municipal Court - Criminal Division – Criminal Records
www.fcmcclerk.com
Criminal and traffic records from the Clerk of Court Courtview database free online at www.fcmcclerk.com/pa/pa.htm. Search by name, SSN, dates, ticket, DL or case numbers.

Geauga County

Common Pleas Court – Civil and Criminal Records
www.co.geauga.oh.us
Access is free from the Clerk of Courts at www.co.geauga.oh.us/departments/clerk_of_courts/Docket2/Courtintro.asp. Online records go back to 1990. Includes domestic cases.

Chardon Municipal Court – Civil and Criminal Records
www.co.geauga.oh.us/departments/muni_court.htm
Search court records free at www.auditor.co.geauga.oh.us/pa/.

Greene County

Common Pleas Court – Civil and Criminal Records
www.co.greene.oh.us/COC/clerk.htm
Access to clerk of court records is free at www.co.greene.oh.us/pa/pa.htm. Search by name or case number. Access to clerk of court criminal records is free at http://198.30.12.230/pa/pa.htm. Search by name or case number.

Fairborn Municipal Court – Civil and Criminal Records
http://ci.fairborn.oh.us/Court/municipal_court.htm
Website offers free access to civil, misdemeanor and traffic records.

Xenia Municipal Court – Civil and Criminal Records
http://xmcwa.ci.xenia.oh.us
Access to Municipal Court records is free through CourtView at http://xmcwa.ci.xenia.oh.us.

Guernsey County

Common Pleas Court – Civil and Criminal Records
www.guernseycountycpcourt.org
Access case index data online at www.guernseycountycpcourt.org.

Hamilton County

Common Pleas Court – Civil and Criminal Records
www.courtclerk.org
Records from the court clerk are free at the website or www.courtclerk.org/queries.aps. Online civil index goes back to 1991, criminal to 1986. Also, search probate records free at www.probatect.org/case_search/casesearch.asp.

Hamilton County Municipal Court – Civil and Criminal Records
www.courtclerk.org
Records from the court clerk are free at www.courtclerk.org/queries.aps.

Hancock County

Common Pleas Court – Civil and Criminal Records
www.co.hancock.oh.us/commonpleas
Search records online back to 1985 at website.

Findlay Municipal Court – Civil and Criminal Records
www.ci.findlay.oh.us/municourt/
Access from www.ci.findlay.oh.us/municourt/searchcivildocket.asp?pageId=71.

Highland County

Hillsboro County Municipal Court – Civil and Criminal Records
www.hillsboroohio.net
Access is free at http://24.123.13.34/.

Huron County

Common Pleas Court – Civil and Criminal Records
www.huroncountyclerk.com
Search court dockets and public records free at the website or http://64.186.204.42/search.shtml.

Jackson County

Jackson County Municipal Court – Civil and Criminal Records
www.jacksoncountymunicipalcourt.com/
Search the record index at www.jacksoncountymunicipalcourt.com/Search/.

Knox County

Common Pleas Court – Civil and Criminal Records
www.knoxcountyclerk.org
Search court index, dockets, calendars free online at www.knoxcountycpcourt.org. Search by name or case number.

Mount Vernon Municipal Court – Civil and Criminal Records
www.mountvernonmunicipalcourt.org
Access to the clerk's civil, criminal and traffic records are free at www.mountvernonmunicipalcourt.org/cmiflash/court/home.html.

Lake County

Common Pleas Court – Civil and Criminal Records
www.lakecountyohio.org
Access to court records, dockets, and quick index, including probate records, is free at http://phoenix.lakecountyohio.org/pa/.

Painesville Municipal Court – Civil and Criminal Records
www.pmcourt.com
Free access to records at www.pmcourt.com/search.html.

Lawrence County

Common Pleas Court – Civil and Criminal Records
www.lawrencecountyclkofcrt.org
Access to civil records is free at the website. Access to criminal records is free at www.lawrencecountyclkofcrt.org.

Lawrence County Municipal Court – Civil and Criminal Records
www.lawcomunicourt.com/
To search the record index, click on "Record Search" at the web page.

Licking County

Common Pleas Court – Civil and Criminal Records
www.lcounty.com/clerkofcourts/
The county clerk's office offers free Internet access to current records at www.lcounty.com/clerkofcourts/. Click on "Courtview 2000."

Licking County Municipal Court – Civil and Criminal Records
www.ci.newark.oh.us/city/municipalcourt/municourt.asp
Access to Municipal Court records is free at http://67.141.197.6/connection/court/.

Lorain County

Common Pleas Court – Civil and Criminal Records
www.loraincounty.com/clerk
Website offers free access to indices and dockets for civil and domestic relationship cases. Access probate records at www.loraincounty.com/probate/search.shtml.

Avon Lake Municipal Court – Civil and Criminal Records
www.avonlakecourt.com/
Search docket index by name at www.avonlakecourt.com/Search/.

Elyria Municipal Court – Civil and Criminal Records
www.elyriamunicourt.org
Search at the Internet site, also you can request information by email to civil@elyriamunicourt.org. Search misdemeanor and traffic records at the website, also send email requests to crtr@elyriamunicourt.org.

Lorain Municipal Court – Civil and Criminal Records
www.lorainmunicourt.org
Access municipal court records free at www.lorainmunicourt.org/search.shtml. Search by name, date, case number, driver license number or attorney.

Oberlin Municipal Court – Civil and Criminal Records
www.oberlinmunicipalcourt.org
Access case information free at www.oberlinmunicipalcourt.org/public.htm. Access criminal case information free at http://65.120.95.142/connection/court/index.xsp.

Vermilion Municipal Court – Civil and Criminal Records
www.vermilionmunicipalcourt.org
Access to municipal court records is at at www.vermilionmunicipalcourt.org/search.html.

Lucas County

Common Pleas Court – Civil and Criminal Records
www.co.lucas.oh.us/default.asp?RequestedAlias=clerk
Access to clerk of courts dockets is free at www.co.lucas.oh.us/ClerkDockets/Dockets.asp. Online records go back to 9/1997. Search probate records at www.lucas-co-probate-ct.org/. Search sex offenders at www.lucascountysheriff.org/sheriff/disclaimer.asp.

Maumee Municipal Court – Civil and Criminal Records
www.maumee.org/municipal/default.htm
Access to the web court system database is free at www.maumee.org/municipal/caseinfo.htm. Online includes civil, criminal, traffic.

Sylvania Municipal Court – Civil and Criminal Records
www.sylvaniacourt.com
Access to records is free at http://72.240.45.101/.

Toledo Municipal Court – Civil and Criminal Records
www.tmc-clerk.com
Daily dockets are online at www.tmc-clerk.com/case/default.asp. Direct email requests to clerk@tmc-clerk.com.

Madison County

Common Pleas Court – Probate Records
Search probate records but not civil records at www.madisonprobate.org/Search/.

Mahoning County

Common Pleas Court – Civil and Criminal Records
Access integrated justice system cases back to 1989 free at http://courts.mahoningcountyoh.gov/. Attorney searching also available.

County Courts – Civil and Criminal Records
http://courts.mahoningcountyoh.gov
Access integrated justice system cases back to 1989 free at http://courts.mahoningcountyoh.gov/. Attorney searching also available.

Medina County

Common Pleas Court – Civil and Criminal Records
www.medinacommonpleas.com
Search court documents, motion dockets, sexual predator judgments and court notices at the web page.

Medina Municipal Court – Civil and Criminal Records
www.medinamunicipalcourt.org
There are two systems; one is via the website and the other is a dial-up system. Both contain records from 1986 to present. Access to the dial-up system requires ProComm Plus. There are no fees. Search by name or case number. Access to traffic records is available. The computer access number is 330-723-4337. For more information, call Rich Armstrong at 330-723-3287 x230.

Miami County

Miami County Municipal Court – Civil and Criminal Records
www.co.miami.oh.us/muni/index.htm
Access to records is free at www.co.miami.oh.us/pa/index.htm.

Montgomery County

Common Pleas Court – Civil and Criminal Records
www.clerk.co.montgomery.oh.us
Access to the Courts countywide PRO system is free at www.clerk.co.montgomery.oh.us/legal/records.cfm. Access to criminal and traffic records is also available.

County Court - Area 1 and 2 – Civil and Criminal Records
www.clerk.co.montgomery.oh.us
Search countywide records online at www.clerk.co.montgomery.oh.us/areacourt/pro/.

Dayton Municipal Court – Civil and Criminal Records
www.daytonmunicipalcourt.org
Access to municipal court records is free at www.daytonmunicipalcourt.org/scripts/rgw.dll/Docket; includes traffic and criminal.

Vandalia Municipal Court – Civil and Criminal Records
www.vandaliacourt.com
Search records, including traffic, at http://64.108.110.4/cmiflash/court/.

Muskingum County

County Court – Civil and Criminal Records
www.muskingumcountycourt.org
Access to county court records is free at www.muskingumcountycourt.org/sear.html.

Zanesville Municipal Court – Civil and Criminal Records
www.coz.org/municipal_court.cfm
Access is free at http://216.29.90.62/connection/court/. Also includes traffic and civil.

Ottawa County

Ottawa County Municipal Court – Civil and Criminal Records
www.ottawacountymunicipalcourt.com
Search record index is at www.ottawacountymunicipalcourt.com/search.html. Includes small claims. Includes traffic.

Pickaway County

Common Pleas Court – Civil and Criminal Records
www.pickawaycountycpcourt.org
Search docket information at www.pickawaycountycpcourt.org.

Circleville Municipal Court – Civil and Criminal Records
www.circlevillecourt.com
Search online at www.circlevillecourt.com/AccessCourtRecords.asp.

Portage County

Common Pleas Court – Civil and Criminal Records
www.co.portage.oh.us/index.html
For records from 1992 forward, go to www.co.portage.oh.us/pa/pa.htm. Direct access questions to Pam Christy at 330-297-3646.

Portage County Municipal Court – Civil and Criminal Records
www.co.portage.oh.us
For records from 1992 forward, go to http://67.39.103.41/pa/pa.htm. Direct questions about online access to Matt W. at 330-296-4095.

Preble County

Eaton Municipal Court – Civil and Criminal Records
www.eatonmunicipalcourt.com
Search by name or case number at the website. Records go back to 1989. Computerized records begin in 1992 for civil, criminal and traffic cases.

Richland County

Common Pleas Court – Civil Records
www.richlandcountyoh.us/coc.htm
Access to court records is free at www.richlandcountyoh.us/courtv.htm.

Mansfield Municipal Court – Civil and Criminal Records
www.ci.mansfield.oh.us/
Access records free at http://docket.webxsol.com/mansfield/index.html for records from 1992 forward.

Ross County

Common Pleas Court – Civil and Criminal Records
www.co.ross.oh.us
Search records back to 11/89 at the website.

Chillicothe Municipal Court – Civil and Criminal Records
www.chillicothemunicipalcourt.org
Search docket information at http://216.201.21.130/Search/.

Scioto County

Common Pleas Court – Civil and Criminal Records
www.sciotocountycpcourt.org
Access to civil records is free at www.sciotocountycpcourt.org/search.htm. Search by court calendar, quick index, general index or docket sheet.

Portsmouth Municipal Court – Civil and Criminal Records
www.pmcourt.org
Access is free at www.pmcourt.org/Search/.

Seneca County

Common Pleas Court – Civil and Criminal Records
Search dockets online at www.senecaco.org/clerk/default.html. Click on Internet Inquiry.

Stark County

Common Pleas Court– Civil and Criminal Records
www.starkclerk.org
Access to the county online case docket database is free at www.starkcourt.org/docket/index.html. Search by name or case number.

Alliance Municipal Court – Civil and Criminal Records
www.starkcountycjis.org/alliance/
Search the Online Case Docket of the Alliance Court at www.starkcountycjis.org/alliance/docket/search_large_frame.html Includes traffic and misdemeanor records.

Canton Municipal Court – Civil and Criminal Records
www.cantoncourt.org
Search docket information at www.cantoncourt.org/docket.html. Includes traffic.

Massillon Municipal Court – Civil and Criminal Records
www.massilloncourt.org
Search the Online Case Docket of the Massillon Court at www.massilloncourt.org. Iincludes traffic and misdemeanor records.

Summit County

Common Pleas Court – Civil and Criminal Records
www.cpclerk.co.summit.oh.us

Access to county clerk of courts records is free at www.cpclerk.co.summit.oh.us. Click on "Case Search." Access to probate records at http://probatecourt.summitoh.net/CaseAccess.htm.

Akron Municipal Court – Civil and Criminal Records
http://courts.ci.akron.oh.us
Access to court records is free at http://courts.ci.akron.oh.us/disclaimer.htm.

Barberton Municipal Court – Civil and Criminal Records
www.cityofbarberton.com/clerkofcourts
Online records for Barberton, Green, Norton, Franklin, Clinton, Copley and Coventry are free at http://24.123.45.19/.

Cuyahoga Falls Municipal Court – Civil and Criminal Records
www.cfmunicourt.com
Court docket information is free at the website.

Trumbull County

Common Pleas Court – Civil and Criminal Records
www.clerk.co.trumbull.oh.us
Access to court records is free at www.clerk.co.trumbull.oh.us/search/search.htm. Records go back to May, 1996. Access to probate records is free at www.trumbullprobate.org/paccessfront.htm.

Newton Falls Municipal Court – Civil and Criminal Records
www.newtonfallscourt.com
Search record index free at www.newtonfallscourt.com/Search/.

Tuscarawas County

Common Pleas Court – Civil and Criminal Records
www.co.tuscarawas.oh.us
Search dockets online at www.co.tuscarawas.oh.us/ClerkofCourts/DocketSearch.htm.

County Court – Civil and Criminal Records
Search dockets only online at www.co.tuscarawas.oh.us/ClerkofCourts/DocketSearch.htm.

Union County

Common Pleas Court – Civil and Criminal Records
www.co.union.oh.us/Clerk_of_Courts/clerk_of_courts.html
Access to the court clerk's public record and index is free at http://www3.co.union.oh.us/clerkofcourts/. Records go back to 1/1990, older records added as accessed. Images go back to 1/2002.

Warren County

Common Pleas Court – Civil and Criminal Records
www.co.warren.oh.us/clerkofcourt/
Access to court records is free at www.co.warren.oh.us/clerkofcourt/search/index.htm. Index goes back to 1980.

Mason Municipal Court – Civil and Criminal Records
www.masonmunicipalcourt.org
Access to court records is free at http://courtconnect.masonmunicipalcourt.org/connection/court/.

Washington County

Marietta Municipal Court – Civil and Criminal Records
www.mariettacourt.com
Access to court dockets back to 1992 is free at www.mariettacourt.com.

Wayne County

Common Pleas Court – Civil and Criminal Records

Wayne County Municipal Court Clerk – Civil and Criminal Records
www.wayneohio.org/index.html
Access is free at www.wayneohio.org/public_access.html; probate index included. Your web browser must be Active-X enabled.

Wood County

Common Pleas Court – Civil Records
Search probate records online at www.probate-court.co.wood.oh.us.

Bowling Green Municipal Court – Civil and Criminal Records
www.bgcourt.org
Access is free to records at http://bgcourtweb.bgohio.org/connection/court/.

Perrysburg Municipal Court – Civil and Criminal Records
www.perrysburgcourt.com
Access to court records is free at www.perrysburgcourt.com/disc.html.

Wyandot County

Common Pleas Court – Civil and Criminal Records
www.co.wyandot.oh.us/clerk/index.html
Click on "Common Pleas Inquiry" form web page to view record index.

County Level ... Recorders & Assessors

Recording Office Organization: 88 counties, 88 recording offices. The recording officers are the County Recorder and Clerk of Common Pleas Court (state tax liens). The entire state is in the Eastern Time Zone (EST). All federal tax liens are filed with the County Recorder. All state tax liens are filed with the Clerk of Common Pleas Court. Refer to County Court section for information about Ohio courts. Federal tax liens are filed in the "Official Records" of each county. Most counties will not perform a federal lien search.

Online Access Note: A growing number of Ohio counties offer online access via the Internet to assessor and real estate data.

Adams County *Property Tax, Sex Offender Records*
Access to the treasurer and auditor property tax data is free at http://adamspropertymax.governmaxa.com/propertymax/rover30.asp.

Allen County *Property, Auditor, Property Sale, Cemetery, War Casualty, Death Records*
www.co.allen.oh.us/rec.php
Access to the auditor property data is free at www.allencountyauditorohio.com/Allen208/LandRover.asp Also, search cemetery, war, and death records free at www.delphos-ohio.com/history/cemeteri.htm.

Ashland County *Real Estate, Auditor, Property Sale, Sex Offender Records*
www.ashlandcounty.org/recorder/index.htm
Access property records on the Auditor's database free at www.ashlandcoauditor.org. Also, search the county sex offender list for free at www.ashlandcounty.org/sheriff/offenders.cfm.

Ashtabula County *Real Estate, Auditor, Property Sale Records*
www.co.ashtabula.oh.us
Property records on the county Auditor's database are free at www.ashtabulacountyauditor.org/propertymax/rover30.asp. Also, free search back to 01/84 at www.landaccess.com.

Athens County *Property, Deed, UCC, Inmate, Mapping Records*
www.athenscountygovernment.com
Access to county land and UCC records is free at www.landaccess.com. Records go back to 1/1981. Also, search the GIS mapping site by name at http://132.235.241.200/website/athens_v1/viewer.htm. Also, search the inmate list for free at http://xw.textdata.com:81/cgi/progcgi.exe?program=search.

Auglaize County *Property, Assessor, Recorder, Real Estate, Deed, Lien, UCC Records*
Access county property data for free at http://auglaizeauditor.ddti.net/. Also, search recorder data free at www.landaccess.com/sites/oh/disclaimer.php?county=auglaize. Records from 01/50 forward.

Belmont County   *Deed, Property Records*
www.belmontcountyohio.org
Access to recorder deed information is free at www.landaccess.com/sites/oh/disclaimer.php?county=belmont. Also, search auditor records at http://belmontpropertymax.governmaxa.com/propertymax/rover30.asp.

Brown County   *Property, Deed, UCC Records*
Access to recordings is free at www.landaccess.com/sites/oh/disclaimer.php?county=brown.

Butler County   *Property, Deed, UCC, Probate, Voter Registration, Tax Sale, Sex Offender Records*
http://66.117.197.5/recorder/
County voter records are at www.butlercountyelections.org/index.cfm?page=voterSearch. Search auditor records at http://propertysearch.butlercountyohio.org/butler/. Also, access county land and UCC records free at www.landaccess.com. Records go back to 1/1987. Also, http://66.117.197.5/recorder/index.cfm?page=regLand_search offers access to recorded documents free; must download software. Also, search county available property at www.butlercountyohio.org/edabc/availprop_index.cfm. The sheriff's tax sale and sex offender lists are at www.butlersheriff.org. Search vendors at www.butlercountyauditor.org/vl_search.cfm

Carroll County   *Auditor, Property Records*
Access to the Auditor's property data is free at http://carrollpropertymax.governmaxa.com/propertymax/rover30.asp. Also, free access to recorded documents back to 1/1990 at www.landaccess.com.

Champaign County   *Real Estate Records*
www.co.champaign.oh.us/auditor/
Auditor real estate data is free at http://champaignoh.ddti.net/.

Clark County   *Property, Deed, UCC, Sheriff Real Estate Sale, Tax Sale, Sex Offender Records*
www.co.clark.oh.us/
Access to county land and UCC records is free at www.landaccess.com. Records go back to 1/1988. Also, the sheriff's real estate sale, tax sale, sex offender and most wanted lists are at www.clarkcountysheriff.com. Also, search cemeteries for free at www.geocities.com/Heartland/Garden/3458/Cemeteries.htm. Search obituaries at http://guardian.ccpl.lib.oh.us/obits/.

Clermont County   *Property, Deed, UCC, Property Tax, Auditor, Sex Offender, Child Support Records*
http://recorder.co.clermont.oh.us
Records from the auditor's county property database are free at www.clermontauditorrealestate.org. Also, free access to the recorder's property, deed, and UCC records is at www.landaccess.com. Also, search county sex offenders database free at www.clermontsheriff.org/registered_sex_offenders.htm. Search child support wants at www.clermontsupportskids.org.

Clinton County   *Deed, Auditor, Property, Plat, Subdivision Records*
http://co.clinton.oh.us/recorder
Access deed references alphabetically by name at www.clintoncountyohgis.org/DeedReferences.htm. Also, access the Auditor's property database for free at http://clintonoh.ddti.net/auditor/iView/iView.asp. Also, beginning in 2006, search subdivision plats for free at www.clintoncountyohgis.org/subdivision_plats.htm.

Columbiana County
Real Estate, Recoder, Deed, Financing Statements, Auditor, Forfeited Land Sale Records
www.columbianacounty.org
Access the recorder index of official records back to 1993 and financing statements back to 3/1995 free at www.ccclerk.org/resolution/default.asp. Property records on the county Auditor's database are free at www.columbianacntyauditor.org/propertymax/rover30.asp. Both the Auditor and Sheriff's sales can be accessed here. www.ccclerk.org/resolution/default.asp

Coshocton County   *Property, Deed, UCC, Auditor, Property Tax, Sex Offender Records*
www.co.coshocton.oh.us
Access to county land and UCC records is free at www.landaccess.com. Records go back to 1/1980. Registration required. Also, search property tax records for free at www.coshcoauditor.org; click on "Property Search." The sex offender list can be searched at www.coshoctonsheriff.com/sexualpred.cfm.

Crawford County   *Auditor, Real Estate, Dog Tag Records*
Access to the auditor database is free at www.crawford-co.org/auditor/default.html.

Cuyahoga County
Auditor, Probate, Marriage, Real Estate, Tax Lien, Recording, Cemetery, Most Wanted, Sexual Predator Records
http://recorder.cuyahogacounty.us
Access the Recorders database free at http://recorder.cuyahogacounty.us. The Recorder's data includes land documents from 1925-2003. Search the auditor property tax database free at http://auditor.cuyahogacounty.us/repi/default.asp. Also, search 22 categories of Probate records including marriages free at http://probate.cuyahogacounty.us/pa/. Obits and death notices are at www.cleveland.com/obits/archives/. Also, sexual predators, most wanted lists, and foreclosure sales at www.cuyahogacounty.us/sheriff/default.htm. Cemetery: www.geocities.com/micheledanielle/cemetery.html. Vendors at https://auditor.cuyahogacounty.us/genservices/vendorList_report.asp.

Darke County   *Real Estate, Property Tax Records*
www.co.darke.oh.us
Property and property tax records on the Darke County database are free at http://darkepropertymax.governmax.com/propertymax/rover30.asp?.

Defiance County   *Auditor, Real Estate Records*
www.defiance-county.com/recorder.html
Assess to the auditor real estate data is at www.defiance-county.com/realestatesearch.html. Call 800-875-3953 or 419-784-3111 for necessary password.

Delaware County
Real Estate, Deed, UCC Auditor, Property Sale, Sheriff Sale, Most Wanted, Sex Offender, DUI Records
www.co.delaware.oh.us
Access to the Recorder's data plus UCCs is free at www.landaccess.com. Also, access to auditor's property and sales information is free at www.delawarecountyauditor.org/propertymax/rover30.asp?. Sheriff sales, Most Wanted, Sex Offender information is free at www.delawarecountysheriff.com. Search the municipal court DUI list at www.municipalcourt.org/main_dui.asp. Also, search cemeteries at http://delcohist.tripod.com/burials.htm.

Erie County   *Auditor, Property, Recording, Deed Records*
www.erie-county-ohio.net/officials.htm
Access the auditor property database for free at www.erie.iviewtaxmaps.com/iView/iView.asp. Access recorded documents at www.co-erie-oh-us-recorder.com.

Fairfield County   *Property, Deed, UCC, Auditor, Property Sale, Inmate, Sex Offender Records*
www.co.fairfield.oh.us
Access to county land and UCC records is free at www.landaccess.com. Records go back to 08/96. Also, online access to the Auditor's property and sales database is free at http://realestate.co.fairfield.oh.us/. Also, access to the sheriff's real estate sale list and sex offenders list is free at www.sheriff.fairfield.oh.us/. Search inmates list at http://xw.textdata.com:81/cgi/progcgi.exe?program=search3.

Fayette County   *Recorder, Deed, Lien, Auditor, Property, Sale, Sex Offender, Sheriff Sale Records*
www.fayette-co-oh.com
Search the auditor's database for property information at http://fayettepropertymax.governmax.com/propertymax/rover30.asp. Access to recorders index database is free at www.landaccess.com. Images go back to 5/20/02. Also, search the sheriff's lists for free at www.faycoso.com.

Franklin County   *Recorder, Property, Auditor, Unclaimed Funds, Marriage, Treasurer Refund, Most Wanted, Sheriff Sale, Sex Offender Records*
www.co.franklin.oh.us/recorder/
Access to the recorders data is free at www.co.franklin.oh.us/recorder/documents.html. Free registration required. Search marriage licenses back to 1995 at www.co.franklin.oh.us/recorder/. Search unclaimed funds at www.franklincountyohio.gov/clerk/unclaimedfunds.html. Search most wanted, sex offenders, sheriff sales lists at www.faycoso.com Also, auditor's property data is at http://franklin.governmaxa.com/propertymax/rover30.asp. Other county/municipal databases are free at www.co.franklin.oh.us.

Fulton County   *Property, Deed, Recorder, UCC, Auditor, Real Estate Records*
www.fultoncountyoh.com
Access to property, deed, and UCC records is to be free at www.landaccess.com/sites/oh/disclaimer.php?county=ohfulton. Also, search the auditor property data for free at http://fultonpropertymax.governmax.com/propertymax/rover30.asp.

Gallia County   *Property, Real Estate, Most Wanted, Sex Offender, Inmate Records*
www.gallianet.net/Gallia/recorder.htm
Property records on the county auditor real estate database are free at http://galliaauditor.ddti.net. Click on "attributes" for property information; click on "sales" to search by real estate attributes. Also, search the sheriff's database for inmates, sex offenders, ner'do'wells, etc at www.galliasheriff.org.

Geauga County   *Delinquent Property Tax, Tax Sale, Auditor, Property, Most Wanted, Sex Offender Records*
www.co.geauga.oh.us
Search the Auditor's property database at www.co.geauga.oh.us/departments/auditor/ag/. No name searching. Also, search the auditor's records at www.auditor.co.geauga.oh.us/ag/. Also, search the sheriff's tax sale, most wanted and sex offender lists for free at www.sheriff.geauga.oh.us.

Greene County
Real Estate, Auditor, Recording, Deed, Mortgage, Grantor/Grantee, Sheriff Sale, Sex Offender Records
www.co.greene.oh.us/recorder.htm
Access to the recorders data is free at www.co.greene.oh.us/recorder/documentSearch.asp. Also, records on the county Internet Map Server are free at www.co.greene.oh.us/gismapserver.htm. Click on "Click here to enter ... Server Site #1". Data includes owner, address, valuation, taxes, sales data, and parcel ID number. Also, search the sheriff's sales and sex offender list at www.co.greene.oh.us/sheriff/.

Guernsey County   *Sex Offender Records*
Search for sex offenders at www.guernseysheriff.com/sexoffenders.htm.

Hamilton County   *Real Estate, Lien, Deed, Mortgage, UCC, Auditor, Sex Offender, Most Wanted, Missing, Sheriff Sale, Marriage, Military Discharge, Partnership, Subdivision Records*
http://recordersoffice.hamilton-co.org
Access to recorder land records is free at http://recordersoffice.hamilton-co.org/hcro-pdi/index.jsp. Search the marriage license database at www.probatect.org/case_search/cs-scripts/ml_Input.asp. Also, online access to the auditor's tax records database is free at www.hamiltoncountyauditor.org./realestate/. Also, search probate records back to 1/2000 at www.probatect.org/case_search/cs-scripts/pimain.html. Also, search lists for most wanted, sex offender, deadbeat parents, missing persons, and sheriff's sale on the sheriff's site under "Public Services" at www.hcso.org.

Hancock County   *Property, Auditor, Sex Offender, Real estate, Recorder, Deed, UCC Records*
http://co.hancock.oh.us/recorder/recorder.htm
Search the auditor's property database free at http://hancock.iviewauditor.com. No name searching. Also, access to recorder records is free at www.landaccess.com. Index goes back to 1986; images to 12/19/2000. Also, search the sheriff's sex offender list at www.hancocksheriff.org/info/sexoffenders.htm.

Hardin County   *Auditor, Property, Sex Offender Records*
www.co.hardin.oh.us
Property records from the county database are at www.co.hardin.oh.us. Click on "Real Estate Internet Inquiry." Also, check a dog tag number for its owner's name here.

Henry County   *Land, Recording, Lien, Deed, Sheriff Sale, Sex Offender Records*
www.henrycountyohio.com
Access recorder data free at www.landaccess.com/sites/oh/disclaimer.php?county=ohhenry. Also, search county sex offender and sheriff sales lists for free at www.henrycountysheriff.com.

Highland County   *Property, Deed, UCC, Auditor, Property Sale, Sex Offender, Sheriff Sale Records*
Access to recorders database is free at www.landaccess.com/sites/oh/disclaimer.php?county=highland. Also, search the auditor's data for free at http://highlandpropertymax.governmaxa.com/propertymax/rover30.asp. The sheriff's sex offender and sales lists are free at www.highlandcoso.com/rso.htm.

Hocking County   *Property, Auditor, Sexual Offender, Inmate Records*
www.co.hocking.oh.us
Access to the auditor's real estate data (and dog tag ownership) is free at www.realestate.co.hocking.oh.us. Also, search the sheriff list of sexual offenders at www.hockingsheriff.org. Search the county list of inmates at http://xw.textdata.com:81/cgi/progcgi.exe?program=search3.

Holmes County *Property, Auditor, Sale Records*

Access to the auditor's property data is free at www.holmescountyauditor.org.

Huron County *Property, Auditor, Sale Records*

www.huroncountyrecorder.org
Access to the auditor data is free at www.huroncountyauditor.org.

Jackson County *Inmates, Sex Offender Records*

Access to the county inmate search is free at http://xw.textdata.com:81/cgi/progcgi.exe?program=search3.

Jefferson County *Property, Auditor Records*

Access to the county auditor property data is free at http://public.jeffersoncountyoh.com/tax/.

Knox County *Real Estate, Recorder, Deed, Financing Statement, Plat, Map Records*

www.recorder.co.knox.oh.us
Access index records free at www.recorder.co.knox.oh.us/Resolution/default.asp. Images have been temporarily removed.

Lake County *Recording, Lien, Deed, UCC, Land Bank Sale Records*

www.lakecountyrecorder.org/recorders/
Access to the Recorder's Document Index database is free at www.lakecountyrecorder.org/recorders/search/index.asp. Records go back to 1986. UCCs are index only. Access to the treasurer and auditor's real estate databases is free at www.lake.iviewauditor.com. Also, access Land Bank sales at www.lakecountyohio.org/auditor/index.htm and click on "Land Bank Sales".

Lawrence County *Auditor, Property, Real Estate, Deed, Lien, Recording Records*

http://64.193.97.62/
Access to the recorders database is free at http://64.193.97.62/record_search.htm. Deeds go back to 1982; mortgages to 1988; liens back to 1981. Also, the auditor's data is free at www.lawrencecountyauditor.org. Search county death index by years on a private site at www.lawrencecountyohio.com/deaths/index/.

Licking County *Real Estate, Tax Lien, Recording, Property Tax, Cemetery, Genealogy, Sex Offender Records*

www.lcounty.com/rec/
Access to the recorders database is free at www.lcounty.com/recordings/. Records with images go back to 1984. Also, online access to the Assessor's county property database is free at http://www2.lcounty.com/licking208/LandRover.asp?. Search the sheriff's sex offender lists for free at www.lcounty.com/sheriff/sex_offenders/. Also, search cemetery names free on private company site at www.rootsweb.com/~cemetery/ohio/licking.htm. Search the genealogy site for the county at www.rootsweb.com/~ohlickin/#data.

Logan County *Real Estate, Auditor, Recording, Deed, Lien, Jail Inmate, Sex Offender Records*

www.co.logan.oh.us/recorder/index.html
Records on the County Auditor's database are free at http://lcaweb.co.logan.oh.us/aweb/. Also, online access to the recorders database is free at http://www3.co.logan.oh.us/recordmax401/record40.asp. Click on "Document Search." Also, search the sheriff's inmate and sex offender lists at www.co.logan.oh.us/sheriff/.

Lorain County *Real Estate, Lien, Auditor, Property Sale, Sheriff Sale, Sex Offender Records*

http://loraincounty.com/recorder
Access to the county assessor database is free at www.loraincounty.com/recorder/register. Free registration is required. Also, access records on the County Auditor's database for free at http://oh-lorain-auditor.governmaxa.com/propertymax/rover30.asp. Search the sex offender and sheriff sales lists for free at www.loraincountysheriff.com.

Lucas County *Real Estate, Auditor, Sex Offender Records*

www.co.lucas.oh.us/
Property records on the County Auditor's Real Estate Information System (AREIS) database are free at www.co.lucas.oh.us/Areis/areismain.asp. This replaces the old system. Also, access to recorder real estate records is free with registration at www.co.lucas.oh.us/Recordings/. Search the sheriff's sex offender list at www.lucascountysheriff.org/sheriff/disclaimer.asp.

Madison County *Real Estate, Auditor, Deed, UCC, Recording, Sex Offender, Sheriff Sale Records*

www.co.madison.oh.us

Records on the County Auditor's database are free at www.co.madison.oh.us/auditor/iView/iView.asp. Also, online access to county land and UCC records is free at www.landaccess.com/sites/oh/disclaimer.php?county=madison. Records go back to 5/1994. Also, access to the sheriff's sale and sex offender lists are at www.madisonsheriff.org.

Mahoning County   *Real Estate, Auditor, Property Sale, Deed, UCC, Lien, Judgment, Recording Records*
www.mahoningcountyoh.gov/MahoningWeb
Access to recorder's property, deed, and UCC records is to be free at www.landaccess.com/sites/oh/mahoning/index.php. Records go back to 1985. Also, property tax records on the County Auditor's database are free at www.mahoningcountyauditor.org.

Marion County   *Real Estate, Auditor Records*
www.co.marion.oh.us
Access to the county auditor real estate database is free at www.co.marion.oh.us. Click on "Real Estate Inquiry."

Medina County   *Real Estate, Auditor, Property Transfer, Sex Offender, Records*
www.recorder.co.medina.oh.us
Access to indexes 1983 to present on the recorder database is free at www.recorder.co.medina.oh.us/fcquery.htm. Also, online access to property records on the Medina County Auditor database are free at www.medinacountyauditor.org/pptylook.htm. Also, search property transfers at www.medinacountyauditor.org/trbytd2.htm. Also, find a lost dog's owner at www.medinacountyauditor.org/finddog.htm. The sheriff's sex offender list is via www.medinasheriff.com; the county tax sale list is at www.medinacountyauditor.org/sheriff.htm#delinq.

Mercer County   *Real Estate, Auditor, Property Sale Records*
www.mercercountyohio.org
Access property records on County Auditor Real Estate database free at www.mercercountyohio.org/auditor/ParcelSearch/.

Miami County   *Property, Auditor Records*
www.co.miami.oh.us
Access auditor data free at www.miamicountyauditor.org.

Monroe County   *Real Estate Records*
www.monroecountyohio.net/
A commercial supscription program is available from the Auditor's office at http://monroecountyauditor.org/home.asp. Call 740-472-0873 for details.

Montgomery County   *Property, Real Estate, Lien, Recording, Auditor Records*
www.mcrecorder.org
Access to the recorders data is free at www.mcrecorder.org/search_selection.cfm. Also, property tax records on the county treasurer real estate tax information database are free at www.mctreas.org. also, search the sheriff's site for missing persons, property sales, and sex offenders at www.co.montgomery.oh.us/Sheriff/.

Morgan County   *Property, Auditor, Inmate, Tax Map Records*
Access to the auditor property data is free at http://morgancountyauditor.org. Use Quick search or Attribute Search. Also, search the county past inmate list for free at http://xw.textdata.com:81/cgi/progcgi.exe?program=search3. Also, search the Engineer website for tax map property data free at -www.morgancoengineer.com. Click on Tax Maps.

Morrow County   *Real Estate, Appraisal, Property Sale Records*
www.morrowcounty.info/morrowoff.htm
Access to the county auditor database is free at http://auditor.co.morrow.oh.us/iView/. Includes property sales data.

Muskingum County   *Real Estate, Assessor, Sheriff Sale, Sex Offender Records*
http://recorder.muskingumcounty.org/recorder1024.htm
Records on the county auditor database are free at www.muskingumcountyauditor.org/iView/iView.asp. Also, the sheriff's site provides sale lists and sex offender information at www.ohiomuskingumsheriff.org.

Ottawa County   *Property, Auditor, Cemetery, Sex Offender Records*
Access to the auditor's property database is free at www.ottawacountyauditor.org. Also, search cemetery registrations for free on private company website at www.rootsweb.com/~cemetery/ohio/ottawa.htm. Search the sheriff's sex offender list for free at www.ottawacountysheriff.org/sorn.html.

Paulding County *Real Estate, Recorder, Deed, Lien, UCC Records*

Access recorder data free at www.landaccess.com/sites/oh/disclaimer.php?county=paulding.

Perry County *Inmate Records*

Access to the county inmates search is free at http://xw.textdata.com:81/cgi/progcgi.exe?program=search3

Pickaway County *Property, Auditor, Real Estate, Recorder, Deed, UCC Records*

Access to the county auditor property data is free at http://pickaway.iviewauditor.com/iView/. Also, search the recorder database free at www.landaccess.com/sites/oh/disclaimer.php?county=pickaway.

Pike County *Recorder, Deed, Lien, UCC, Real Estate, Auditor, Inmate Records*

Access to the recorder's database is free at www.landaccess.com/sites/oh/disclaimer.php?county=pike. Also, access to the county auditor property tax data is free at http://207.90.76.229/pikeweb/browser/. Also, search the inmate list for free at http://xw.textdata.com:81/cgi/progcgi.exe?program=search3.

Portage County *Property, Auditor, Property Sale, Sheriff Sale, Sex Offender Records*

www.co.portage.oh.us
Access to the auditor's property records is free at http://portagepropertymax.governmaxa.com/propertymax/rover30.asp. Also, access to the sheriff's property sales and sex offender lists is free at www.co.portage.oh.us.

Preble County *Real Estate, Auditor Records*

Property records on the County Auditor's database are free at www.preblecountyauditor.org/iView.asp.

Putnam County *Property, Auditor, Property Sale Records*

Access to the county auditor property data is free at www.putnam.iviewauditor.com/iView.asp.

Richland County *Real Estate, Auditor, Deed, Property Sale, Sheriff Sale, Sex Offender Records*

www.richlandcountyauditor.org
Property records from the County Auditor database are free at www.richlandcountyauditor.org. Also, online access to county land records is free at www.landaccess.com. Records go back to 4/1989. Also, search the sheriff sales and sex offender lists for free at www.sheriffrichlandcounty.com.

Ross County *Property, Deed, UCC, Auditor, Recorder Records*

www.co.ross.oh.us
Access to county land, recording and UCC records is free at www.landaccess.com. Records go back to 1/1974. Also, access to the auditor's property and sales data is free at www.co.ross.oh.us/auditor/iView/iView.asp.

Sandusky County *Property, Auditor, Treasurer Records*

www.sandusky-county.org/County_Recorder.asp
Access to county auditor and treasurer property data is free at http://ohsanduskypropertymax.governmaxa.com/propertymax/rover30.asp. Click on "Property Search" and choose to search by name.

Scioto County *Property, Auditor Records*

www.sciotocountyohio.com
Access to the auditor's property data is free at www.sciotocountyauditor.org; click on Property Search.

Seneca County *Property, Most Wanted, Missing Person Records*

Access the sheriff's missing person and most wanted lists is free at www.bright.net/~senecaso/. Also, property data is accessible via www.landaccess.com.

Shelby County *Sheriff Sale, Sex Offender Records*

www.co.shelby.oh.us/Recorder/index.asp
Access to the sex offender and most wanted lists is free at shelbycountysheriff.com

Stark County *Real Estate, Deed, Recording, Auditor, Property, Sheriff Sale, Delinquent Taxpayer, Sex Offender, Unclaimed Funds Records*

www.co.stark.oh.us/internet/HOME.DisplayPage?v_page=recorder

Access to the recorder's database is free with registration at http://app.recorder.co.stark.oh.us/search.asp. Chose simple, advanced or instrument search. Also, search the auditor's property data for free at http://66.194.132.64/AccuGlobe/iView.asp. Also, a weekly delinquent taxpayers list is at www.starktaxes.com/list.cgi. Access to sheriff sales lists are at www.sheriff.co.stark.oh.us/RealEstate.htm. Sex offenders list at www.sheriff.co.stark.oh.us/OffenderLinks.htm. Louisville City library obituary list may be at http://louisvillelibrary.org/genealogy/.

Summit County
Real Estate, Auditor, Property Tax, Recording, Deed, Sex Offender, Most Wanted, Sheriff Sale, Dog Records
www.co.summit.oh.us/fiscaloffice
Access tax map information from the county fiscal officer for free at http://scids.summitoh.net/gis/default2.htm; choose Internet map server, then Parcel search. Also property appraisal, images and tax information are at above site. Access to full images requires registration, password. Call Data Ctr Help Desk at 330-643-2013 for info/sign-up. Also search property tax records at http://megatron.summitoh.net/summit/html/webintg.html. Recorder images are at www.co.summit.oh.us/fiscaloffice/defaultwebapps.htm. Also search sex offenders, most wanted, and sheriff tax sale lists for free at www.co.summit.oh.us/sheriff.

Trumbull County
Auditor, Property Tax, Recording, Deed, Mortgage, Lien, Unclaimed Funds, Warrant Records
www.tcrecorder.co.trumbull.oh.us
Access the recorder's database free at http://69.68.42.167:13131/recordings/default.asp. Dog registration is at www.dogtagsplus.com/Start.asp?CountyID=2. Also, search property data free at http://69.68.42.167:7036/propertysearch/ureca_asp/index.htm. Also, unclaimed funds list from probate court is at www.trumbullprobate.org/UnclaimedFunds.htm. The Sheriff's warrants list is at www.sheriff.co.trumbull.oh.us/warrants.htm.

Tuscarawas County *Real Estate, Delinquent Tax List Records*
www.co.tuscarawas.oh.us
County real estate records are free at www.co.tuscarawas.oh.us/tusca208/LandRover.asp. The auditor's delinquent tax list is updated in September.

Union County *Auditor, Property Tax, Real Estate, Recording, Delinquent Taxpayer Records*
www.co.union.oh.us/Recorder/recorder.html
Access to the Auditors tax assessment/property records database and the appraiser property information database is free at http://www3.co.union.oh.us/PropInfoGuide.htm. Also search for property information via the online GIS map. Search recorded documents at www.co.union.oh.us/Recorder/disclaimer.htm. Search the treasurers' list of delinquent taxpayers at www.co.union.oh.us/Treasurer/List_of_Delinquent_Taxpayers/list_of_delinquent_taxpayers.html.

Van Wert County *Property, Deed, UCC, Recording, Auditor Records*
Access to county land and UCC records is free at www.landaccess.com. Index go back to 1/1994, copies of document back to May, 1995; earlier records being added. Also, access to the auditor's property records is free at http://realestate.co.vanwert.oh.us.

Vinton County *Inmate Records*
Access to the county past inmate list is free at http://xw.textdata.com:81/cgi/progcgi.exe?program=search3.

Warren County *Property, Auditor, Mapping, Sex Offender Records*
www.co.warren.oh.us
Access to the county auditor database is free at www.co.warren.oh.us/auditor/property_search/index.htm. Also, search the sheriff's sex offender list at www.wcsooh.org/sheriff/criminal_investigation/offender.htm. Recorders Records access since 1979 found at www.co.warren.oh.us/recorder.

Washington County *Property, Auditor, Deed, UCC, Recorder, Real Estate Records*
Access to the county auditor's property search database is free at www.washingtoncountyauditor.org. Also, access to property, deed, and UCC records is free at www.landaccess.com/sites/oh/disclaimer.php?county=washington.

Wayne County *Property, Auditor, Sex Offender, Late Taxpayer Records*
www.co.wayne.oh.us
Access to the auditor's property data should be free at www.waynecountyauditor.org. The late taxpayer list should soon be appear at the treasurer's website, www.co.wayne.oh.us. Also, search the sheriff's sex offender list for free at www.waynecountysheriff.com/sexoffenders.htm

Williams County _Property, Auditor, Property Sale, Real Estate, Deed, Lien, UCC Records_
www.co.williams.oh.us
Access to the auditor's property data is free at www.co.williams.oh.us/realestate/LandRover.asp. Also, search recorder records free at www.landaccess.com/sites/oh/disclaimer.php?county=williams.

Wood County _Property, Auditor, Obituary, Treasurer Tax Records_
www.co.wood.oh.us/recorder
Access to the auditor's property data is free at http://auditor.co.wood.oh.us/. No name searching. Also, search the treasurer's tax data for free at http://woodtaxcollector.governmax.com/collectmax/collect30.asp? Also, search the library's obituaries from 1848 to present for free at http://wcdpl.lib.oh.us/databases/obitsearch.asp.

Wyandot County _Property, Auditor Records_
Access to the Auditor's real estate database is free at www.co.wyandot.oh.us/auditor/default.html. Click on "Real Estate Internet Inquiry." Also may search dog tags.

Federal Courts in Ohio...

Standards for Federal Courts: The universal PACER sign-up number is 800-676-6856. Find PACER and the Party/Case Index on the Web at http://pacer.psc.uscourts.gov. PACER dial-up access is $.60 per minute. Also, courts offering internet access via PACER, Web-PACER or the new CM-ECF charge $.08 per page fee ($.07 per page if record is pre-2005 or unless noted as free).

US District Court -- Northern District of Ohio
www.ohnd.uscourts.gov
PACER: Many cases prior to the indicated dates are also online. Case records are available back to 1/ 1990. Records are purged never. **PACER Online Access:** ECF replaces PACER. **Electronic Filing:** CM/ECF data at https://ecf.ohnd.uscourts.gov. **Other Online Access:** Make copy requests at www.ohnd.uscourts.gov/Clerk_s_Office/Copy_Request/copy_request.html. Read "Notable Cases at www.ohnd.uscourts.gov/Clerk_s_Office/Notable_Cases/index.html.
Akron Division counties: Carroll, Holmes, Portage, Stark, Summit, Tuscarawas, Wayne. Northern District is on a central draw- a case may be assigned here or at Cleveland or Youngstown. Cases filed prior to 1995 for counties in the Youngstown Division may be located here.
Cleveland Division counties: Ashland, Ashtabula, Crawford, Cuyahoga, Geauga, Lake, Lorain, Medina, Richland. Cases prior to 7/1995 for the counties of Ashland, Crawford, Medina and Richland are located in the Akron Division. Cases filed prior to 1995 from the counties in the Youngstown Division may be located here. Northern District is on a central draw- rarely a case may be located to Youngstown or Akron Divisions.
Toledo Division counties: Allen, Auglaize, Defiance, Erie, Fulton, Hancock, Hardin, Henry, Huron, Lucas, Marion, Mercer, Ottawa, Paulding, Putnam, Sandusky, Seneca, Van Wert, Williams, Wood, Wyandot. This is known as the Western Division of the Northern District.
Youngstown Division counties: Columbiana, Mahoning, Trumbull. This division was re-activated in the middle of 1995. Older cases will be found in Akron or Cleveland. Northern District is on a central draw- a case may be assigned here or at Cleveland or Akron.

US Bankruptcy Court -- Northern District of Ohio
www.ohnb.uscourts.gov
PACER: Case records are available back to 1/1985. New records are available online after 1 day. **PACER Online Access:** ECF replaces PACER. **Electronic Filing:** CM/ECF data at https://ecf.ohnb.uscourts.gov. **Opinions:** These judges' postings include calendars and opinions. View court opinions at www.ohnb.uscourts.gov. **Phone access:** Voice Case Information System, call 800-898-6899, 330-489-4731
Akron Division counties: Medina, Portage, Summit.
Canton Division counties: Ashland, Carroll, Crawford, Holmes, Richland, Stark, Tuscarawas, Wayne.
Cleveland Division counties: Cuyahoga, Geauga, Lake, Lorain.
Toledo Division counties: Allen, Auglaize, Defiance, Erie, Fulton, Hancock, Hardin, Henry, Huron, Lucas, Marion, Mercer, Ottawa, Paulding, Putnam, Sandusky, Seneca, Van Wert, Williams, Wood, Wyandot.
Youngstown Division counties: Ashtabula, Columbiana, Mahoning, Trumbull.

US District Court -- Southern District of Ohio

www.ohsd.uscourts.gov

PACER: Case records are available back to 1994. Records are purged never. New records are available online after 1 day. **PACER Online Access:** ECF replaces PACER. **Electronic Filing:** CM/ECF data at https://ecf.ohsd.uscourts.gov. **Opinions:** View court opinions at www.ohsd.uscourts.gov/opinions.htm.

Cincinnati Division counties: Adams, Brown, Butler, Clermont, Clinton, Hamilton, Highland, Lawrence, Scioto, Warren .

Columbus Division counties: Athens, Belmont, Coshocton, Delaware, Fairfield, Fayette, Franklin, Gallia, Guernsey, Harrison, Hocking, Jackson, Jefferson, Knox, Licking, Logan, Madison, Meigs, Monroe, Morgan, Morrow, Muskingum, Noble, Perry, Pickaway, Pike, Ross, Union, Vinton, Washington.

Dayton Division counties: Champaign, Clark, Darke, Greene, Miami, Montgomery, Preble, Shelby.

US Bankruptcy Court -- Southern District of Ohio

www.ohsb.uscourts.gov

PACER: Case records are available back to 1990. Records are purged every 6 months. New records are available online after 1 day. **PACER Online Access:** ECF replaces PACER. **Electronic Filing:** CM/ECF data at https://ecf.ohsb.uscourts.gov. **Opinions:** View court opinions at www.ohsb.uscourts.gov/OHSB/OpNet/search.aspx. **Other Online Access:** PDF lists pf judges' current schedules free at www.ohsb.uscourts.gov/OHSB/hsnet/hearingschedulejudges.aspx. **Phone access:** Voice Case Information System, call 800-726-1004, 937-225-2544

Cincinnati Division counties: Adams, Brown, Clermont, Hamilton, Highland, Lawrence, Scioto and part of Butler.

Columbus Division counties: Athens, Belmont, Coshocton, Delaware, Fairfield, Fayette, Franklin, Gallia, Guernsey, Harrison, Hocking, Jackson, Jefferson, Knox, Licking, Logan, Madison, Meigs, Monroe, Morgan, Morrow, Muskingum, Noble, Perry, Pickaway, Pike, Ross, Union, Vinton, Washington.

Dayton Division counties: Butler, Champaign, Clark, Clinton, Darke, Greene, Miami, Montgomery, Preble, Shelby, Warren; parts of Butler County are handled by Cincinnati Division.

Oklahoma

Capital:　Oklahoma City
　　　　　Oklahoma County
Time Zone: CST
Population: 3,523,553
# of Counties: 77

Quick Links

Website: www.state.ok.us/
Governor:　www.governor.state.ok.us
Attorney General:　www.oag.state.ok.us
State Archives:　www.odl.state.ok.us
State Statutes and Codes:　www.lsb.state.ok.us
Legislative Bill Search:　www.lsb.state.ok.us
Bill Monitoring:　www.gov.ok.gov/billtrack/
Unclaimed Funds:　www.ok.gov/unclaimed/

State Level ... Major Agencies

Statewide Court Records

Administrative Office of Courts, 1915 N Stiles, #305, Oklahoma City, OK 73105; 405-521-2450, Fax-405-521-6815, 8AM-5PM.
www.oscn.net
Online search: Free Internet access is available for District Courts in 12 populous counties and all Appellate courts at www.oscn.net.
Both civil and criminal docket information is available for the counties involved. Also, the Oklahoma District Court Records free
website at www.odcr.com offers searching from over 50 District Courts. More counties are being added as they are readied; they hope
to eventually feature all OK District Courts. Please note many of the county records in this system do not go back 7 years.

Sexual Offender Registry

Oklahoma Department of Corrections, Sex Offender Registry, 2901 N Classen Blvd, Ste 200, Oklahoma City, OK 73106; 405-962-
6104, 8AM-5PM.
www.doc.state.ok.us/DOCS/offender_info.htm
Online search: Searching is available from the website. The Sex Offender Lookup only lists lifetime (habitual and aggravated) sex
offenders, all others have not been put on the site yet. There are a number of search options. A parole status search is available at
http://gov.ok.gov/parole/parole_lookup.php.

Incarceration Records

Oklahoma Department of Corrections, Offender Records, PO Box 11400, Oklahoma City, OK 73136 (Courier: 3400 Martin Luther
King Avenue, Oklahoma City, OK 73136); 405-425-2500, Fax-405-425-2608, 8AM-4:30PM.
www.doc.state.ok.us
Online search: At the main website, click on Offender Information. The online system is shut down from 3AM until 3:30 AM.

Corporation, Limited Liability Company, Limited Partnership, Trademark, Limited Liability Partnership Records

Secretary of State, Business Records Department, 2300 N Lincoln Blvd, Rm 101, Oklahoma City, OK 73105-4897; 405-522-4582 (Records), 900-733-2428 (Records), Fax-405-521-3771, 8AM-5PM.
www.sos.state.ok.us
Online search: Visit SOONERAccess at https://www.sooneraccess.state.ok.us/home/home-default.asp for free searches on business entities, including registered agents and Trademarks. Customers may also order and receive status certificates as well as certified and plain copies.

Uniform Commercial Code

UCC Central Filing Office, Oklahoma County Clerk, 320 R.S. Kerr Ave, County Office Bldg, Rm 105, Oklahoma City, OK 73102; 405-713-1521, Fax-405-713-1810, 8AM-5PM.
www.oklahomacounty.org/countyclerk
Online search: Records of all UCC financing statements may be viewed free on the Internet at www.oklahomacounty.org/coclerk/default.htm. Neither certified searches nor record requests are accepted at the web. Search by debtor or secured party. **Other options:** The entire database is available on microfilm or computer tapes, prices start at $500.

Driver Records

MVR Desk, Records Management Division, PO Box 11415, Oklahoma City, OK 73136-0415 (Courier: 3600 Martin Luther King Blvd, Rm 206, Oklahoma City, OK 73111); 405-425-2262, 8AM-4:45PM.
www.dps.state.ok.us/dls/default.htm
Online search: Online access is available for qualified, approved users through www.ok.gov/. This is a batch mode process with plans for interactive service in the future. The $12.50 fee includes a $2.50 service fee. You will not find information about this program on the web, since it is not for the general public. For further information, call 800-955-3468.

Voter Registration

State Election Board, PO Box 53156, Oklahoma City, OK 73152 (Courier: State Capitol-Rm B6, Oklahoma City, OK 73105); 405-521-2391, Fax-405-521-6457, 8AM-5PM.
www.elections.state.ok.us
Online search: A searchable online database of registered voters is available at www.oklahomadata.com/Security/Login.asp. Requests may also be emailed to elections@oklaosf.state.ok.us. **Other options:** A statewide database can be purchased on CD for a fee of $150. Large counties are available on CD for $50-75. Smaller counties or precincts or district are available on disk for $10-35.

State Level ... Occupational Licensing

Accounting Firm .... www.ok.gov/oab/search.php
Alarm Company/Employee................... www.health.state.ok.us/program/ol/OklahomaLicensedAlarmCompanies.pdf
Architect .... www.ok.gov/architects/search.php?searchtype=0
Architect Firm...................................... www.ok.gov/architects/search.php?searchtype=2
Athletic Trainer/Apprentice
  www.okmedicalboard.org/display.php?content=md_search_advanced:md_search_advanced
Attorney .... www.oklahomafindalawyer.com/find
Audiologist www.obespa.state.ok.us/License%20Data.htm
Bank.. www.state.ok.us/~osbd/
Consumer Finance Company .... www.okdocc.state.ok.us/
Credit Services Organization .... www.okdocc.state.ok.us/
Credit Union .... www.state.ok.us/~osbd/
Dental Hygienist .... www.dentist.state.ok.us/lists/index.htm
Dental Laboratory .... www.dentist.state.ok.us/lists/index.htm
Dentist/Dental Assistant....................... www.dentist.state.ok.us/lists/index.htm
Dietitian/Provisional Dietitian
  www.okmedicalboard.org/display.php?content=md_search_advanced:md_search_advanced
Electrologist ... ...   www.okmedicalboard.org/display.php?content=md_search_advanced:md_search_advanced
Engineer.. www.pels.state.ok.us/roster/index.html

Funeral Home .... www.okfuneral.com/funeralhomedirectory/index.htm
Health Spa.. www.okdocc.state.ok.us/
Home Inspector.................................... www.health.state.ok.us/program/ol/homeinspectorlist.pdf
Investment Company .... www.securities.state.ok.us/_private/DB_Query/Corp_Fin_Search.htm
Landscape Architect............................ www.ok.gov/architects/search.php?searchtype=1
Lobbyist.. www.state.ok.us/~ethics/lobbyist.html
Medical Doctor ... ... www.okmedicalboard.org/display.php?content=md_search_advanced:md_search_advanced
Money Order Agent............................ www.state.ok.us/~osbd/
Mortgage Broker................................. www.okdocc.state.ok.us/
Notary Public .... https://www.sooneraccess.state.ok.us/notary/notary_search-menu.asp
Nurse Anesthetist, Certified Register'd . https://www.ok.gov/nursing/verify/index.php
Nurse Midwife Certified .... https://www.ok.gov/nursing/verify/index.php
Nurse-RN/LPN/Clinical/Specialist .... https://www.ok.gov/nursing/verify/index.php
Occupational Therapist/Assistant
  www.okmedicalboard.org/display.php?content=md_search_advanced:md_search_advanced
Optometrist .... www.arbo.org/index.php?action=findanoptometrist
Orthotist/Prosthetist ... www.okmedicalboard.org/display.php?content=md_search_advanced:md_search_advanced
Osteopathic Physician.......................... www.docboard.org/ok/df/oksearch.htm
Pawnbroker... www.okdocc.state.ok.us/
Payday Lender .... www.okdocc.state.ok.us/
Pedorthist ... ... www.okmedicalboard.org/display.php?content=md_search_advanced:md_search_advanced
Perfusionist ... ... www.okmedicalboard.org/display.php?content=md_search_advanced:md_search_advanced
Pesticide Applicator............................ http://kellysolutions.com/ok/
Pesticide Certification/Registration ...... http://kellysolutions.com/ok/
Pesticide Dealers................................. http://kellysolutions.com/ok/
Pharmacy Intern.................................. http://lv.pharmacy.state.ok.us/osbpinquire/
Pharmacy Technician........................... http://lv.pharmacy.state.ok.us/osbpinquire/
Physical Therapist/Assistant
  www.okmedicalboard.org/display.php?content=md_search_advanced:md_search_advanced
Physician Assistant ... www.okmedicalboard.org/display.php?content=md_search_advanced:md_search_advanced
Podiatrist ... ... www.okmedicalboard.org/display.php?content=md_search_advanced:md_search_advanced
Precious Metals & Gem Dealer .... www.okdocc.state.ok.us/
Private Investigator Individual/Agency www.opia.com/find_a_pi/default.asp
Prosthetist ... ... www.okmedicalboard.org/display.php?content=md_search_advanced:md_search_advanced
Public Accountant-CPA........................ www.ok.gov/oab/search.php
Real Estate Agent/Broker/Sales www.orec.state.ok.us/agents2.html
Real Estate Appraiser........................... www.asc.gov/content/category1/appr_by_state.asp
Real Estate Corp./Partnership www.orec.state.ok.us/agents2.html
Rent to Own Dealer .... www.okdocc.state.ok.us/
Respiratory Care Practitioner
  www.okmedicalboard.org/display.php?content=md_search_advanced:md_search_advanced
Savings & Loan Association................. www.state.ok.us/~osbd/
Social Worker .... www.osblsw.state.ok.us/licensee_search.php
Speech Pathologist.............................. www.obespa.state.ok.us/License%20Data.htm
Surveyor, Land .... www.pels.state.ok.us/roster/index.html
Trust Company .... www.state.ok.us/~osbd/

County Level ... Courts

Court Administration: Administrative Director of Courts, 1915 N Stiles #305, Oklahoma City, OK, 73105; 405-521-2450; www.oscn.net

Court Structure: There are 80 District Courts in 26 judicial districts. Cities with populations in excess of 200,000 (Oklahoma City and Tulsa) have municipal criminal courts of record. Cities with less than 200,000 do not have such courts.

Online Access Note: Free Internet access is available for District Courts in 12 counties and all Appellate courts at www.oscn.net. Both civil and criminal docket information is available for the counties invoved. Also, search the Oklahoma Supreme Court Network from the website.

Case information is available in bulk form for downloading to computer. For information, call the Administrative Director of Courts, 405-521-2450.

Also, the Oklahoma District Court Records free website at www.odcr.com offers searching for over 50 District Courts. More counties are being added as they are readied. The hope is to eventually feature all Oklahoma District Courts. Please note many of the county records in this system do not go back seven years.

Judicial District Court Civil and Criminal Records on the www.odcr.com system:

(Also see the pages at the end of this section for independent court record systems)

Atoka County
Free court records from 1/1998 to present online at www.odcr.com; updated monthly.

Beaver County
Free court records from 6/1/1997 to present online at www.odcr.com; updated monthly.

Beckham County
Free court records from 1/2000 to present online at www.odcr.com; updated daily.

Blaine County
Free court records from 8/1998 to present online at www.odcr.com; updated daily.

Bryan County
Free court records from 7/1/1994 to present online at www.odcr.com; updated daily.

Caddo County
Free court records from 1/1997 to present online at www.odcr.com; updated monthly.

Carter County
www.brightok.net/cartercounty/CarterCountyCourtClerk.html
Only current week dockets are online at clerk's website.
Free court records from 1/1997 to present online at www.odcr.com; updated monthly.

Cherokee County
Free court records from 1/1997 to present online at www.odcr.com; updated daily.

Cotton County
Free court records from 1/1997 to present online at www.odcr.com; updated daily.

Craig County
Free court records from 4/1/1997 to present online at www.odcr.com; updated daily.

Creek County
24th Judicial District Court - Sapulpa – Civil and Criminal Records
Free court records from 3/1998 to present online at www.odcr.com; updated daily.
Bristow – Civil and Criminal Records
Free court records from 10/25/1999 to present online at www.odcr.com; updated daily.
Drumright – Civil and Criminal Records
Free court records from 11/15/2004 to present online at www.odcr.com; updated daily.

Custer County
Free court records from 8/1/2001 to present online at www.odcr.com; updated daily.

Delaware County
Free court records from 6/1/1991 to present online at www.odcr.com; updated daily.

Garvin County
Access court records from 6/1/1995 to present free at www.odcr.com; updated daily.

Haskell County
Free court records from 11/1/1997 to present online at www.odcr.com; updated daily.

Hughes County
Free court records from 12/1998 to present online at www.odcr.com; updated daily.

Jefferson County
Free court records from 1/1998 to present online at www.odcr.com; updated monthly.

Kay County
www.courthouse.kay.ok.us/home.html
Free court records from 5/1/1995 to present online at www.odcr.com; updated daily.
Blackwell and Ponca City online goes back to 1/1997.

Kingfisher County
Free court records from 10/1/1997 to present online at www.odcr.com; updated daily.

Latimer County
Free court records from 11/1999 to present online at www.odcr.com; updated monthly.

Le Flore County
Free court records from 7/1/1997 to present online at www.odcr.com; updated daily.

Lincoln County
Free court records from 7/1/1994 to present online at www.odcr.com; updated daily.

Major County
Free court records from 1/1/1998 to present online at www.odcr.com; updated monthly.

Marshall County
Free court records from 1/1/1998 to present online at www.odcr.com; updated daily.

Mayes County
Free civil court records back to 7/1/1998 online at www.odcr.com; updated daily. Has criminal court records back to 1/1/1998.

McClain County
Free court records from 1/1997 to present online at www.odcr.com; updated daily.

McCurtain County
Free court records from 6/1/1998 to present online at www.odcr.com; updated monthly.

McIntosh County
Free court records from 5/1/1996 to present online at www.odcr.com; updated monthly.

Murray County
Free court records from 1/1/1998 to present online at www.odcr.com; updated monthly.

Muskogee County
Free court records from 1/3/2003 to present online at www.odcr.com; updated daily.

Noble County
Free court records from 1/1997 to present online at www.odcr.com; updated daily.

Nowata County
Free court records from 7/1/1998 to present online at www.odcr.com; updated monthly.

Okfuskee County
Free court records from 1/1997 to present online at www.odcr.com; updated monthly.

Okmulgee County
Free court records from 1/1998 to present online at www.odcr.com; updated monthly.

Osage County
10th Judicial District Court – Civil and Criminal Records
Free court records from 1/1996 to present online at www.odcr.com; updated daily.

Ottawa County
Free court records from 9/1/1997 to present online at www.odcr.com; updated daily.

Pawnee County
14th Judicial District Court – Civil and Criminal Records
Free court records from 1/1997 to present online at www.odcr.com; updated daily.

Pittsburg County
Free court records from 7/1/1997 to present online at www.odcr.com; updated monthly.

Pontotoc County
Free court records from 1/1997 to present online at www.odcr.com; updated monthly.

Pottawatomie County
Free court records from 7/1/1997 to present online at www.odcr.com; updated daily.

Seminole County
Free court records from 1/1995 to present online at www.odcr.com; updated daily.

Sequoyah County
Free court records from 7/1/1997 to present online at www.odcr.com; updated daily.

Stephens County
Free court records from 1/1996 to present online at www.odcr.com; updated monthly.

Texas County
Free court records from 1/15/1995 to present online at www.odcr.com; updated daily.

Wagoner County
Free court records from 1/1990 to present online at www.odcr.com; updated daily.

Washington County
Free court records from 1/1999 to present online at www.odcr.com; updated daily.

Washita County
Free court records from 10/1/1997 to present online at www.odcr.com; updated daily.

Woods County
Free court records from 7/2002 to present online at www.odcr.com; updated monthly.

* * *

Adair County
15th Judicial District Court – Civil and Criminal Records
Access to court dockets is free at www.oscn.net/applications/oscn/casesearch.asp.

Canadian County
26th Judicial District Court – Civil and Criminal Records
Access to court dockets is free at www.oscn.net/applications/oscn/casesearch.asp. Dockets go back to 3/1993.

Cleveland County
21st Judicial District Court– Civil and Criminal Records
Access to court dockets is free at www.oscn.net/applications/oscn/casesearch.asp. Dockets go back to 1/1989.

Comanche County
5th Judicial District Court – Civil and Criminal Records
Access to court dockets is free at www.oscn.net/applications/oscn/casesearch.asp. Dockets go back to 8/1988.

Ellis County
2nd Judicial District Court – Civil and Criminal Records
Access to court dockets is free at www.oscn.net/applications/oscn/casesearch.asp.

Garfield County
4th Judicial District Court – Civil and Criminal Records
Access to court dockets is free at www.oscn.net/applications/oscn/casesearch.asp. Dockets go back to 3/1989.

Logan County
9th Judicial District Court – Civil and Criminal Records
Search court dockets free at www.oscn.net/applications/oscn/casesearch.asp.

Oklahoma County
District Court – Civil and Criminal Records
Access to court dockets is free at www.oscn.net/applications/oscn/casesearch.asp. Civil dockets go back to 12/1984. Criminal dockets back to 9/1988. The sheriff's current inmates and warrants list is free at www.oklahomacounty.org/cosheriff/.

Payne County
9th Judicial District Court – Civil and Criminal Records
Access to court dockets is free at www.oscn.net/applications/oscn/casesearch.asp. Dockets go back to 1/1994.

Pushmataha County
17th Judicial District Court – Civil and Criminal Records
Access to court dockets is free at www.oscn.net/applications/oscn/casesearch.asp.

Roger Mills County
2nd Judicial District Court – Civil and Criminal Records
Access to court dockets is free at www.oscn.net/applications/oscn/casesearch.asp. No fee to view records.

Rogers County
12th Judicial District Court – Civil and Criminal Records
Access to court dockets is free at www.oscn.net/applications/oscn/casesearch.asp. Dockets go back to 7/1997.

Tulsa County
14th Judicial District Court – Civil and Criminal Records
Access to court dockets is free at www.oscn.net/applications/oscn/casesearch.asp. Civil dockets go back to 10/1984. Criminal dockets back to 1/1988.

County Level ... Recorders & Assessors

Recording Office Organization: 77 counties, 77 recording offices. The recording officer is the County Clerk. The entire state is in the Central Time Zone (CST). Federal tax liens on personal property of businesses are filed with the County Clerk of Oklahoma County, which is the central filing office for the state. Other federal and all state tax liens are filed with the County Clerk. Usually state and federal tax liens on personal property are filed in separate indexes. Some counties will perform tax lien searches. Search fees vary from county to county.

Online Access Note: Very little is available online from the counties directly. A private company - OKAssessors.com - provides subscription access to assessor indices and property images for all but 1 Oklahoma county; see www.okassessor.com or call 800-535-6467 or email tracy@okassessor.com for information. Generally, all records are within 90 days of current. Sub packages: $30 per county or 10 counties $150 or $250 for entire state, except for Osage County which is separate and not on the OKAssessors.com system. Data is also available on CD-rom. Plat Maps also available.

Adair County *Property, Assessor Records*
With registration you may search assessment data free temporarily at www.pvplus.com/freeaccess/free_login.aspx.

Beaver County *Assessor, Property Records*
Access to property data is available by subscription at http://oklahoma.usassessor.com.

Bryan County   *Real Estate Recording, Deed Records*
Access recording office land data at www.etitlesearch.com; registration required, fee based on usage.

Canadian County   *Land, Grantor/Grantee, Deed, Lien, Judgment Records*
www.canadiancounty.org
Access to recorders database is free http://landrecords.canadiancounty.org/coclerk/deeds/default.asp. Records go back to 1/2000.

Carter County   *Assessor, Unsolved Case Records*
www.brightok.net/chickasaw/ardmore/county/coclerk.html
Access the sheriff's unsolved mysteries page for free at www.brightok.net/cartercounty/UnsolvedMysteries.html. Search the county assessor database for free at www.cartercountyassessor.org/disclaim.htm.

Cleveland County   *Recording, Lien, Judgment, UCC, Fictitious Name, Military Discharge Records*
http://search.cogov.net/okclev/
Access to the Clerk Index is free at http://search.cogov.net/okclev/default.asp. For access to Tax Liens, Real Estate, UCC, Physician Liens and Mechanic Liens go to clevelandcountyclerk.net.

Creek County   *Property, Assessor Records*
Access to access property records is by subscription from Visual Lease Services- OK Assessors.com, 800-535-6467; weekly and monthly plans available. See note about OKassessors.com at beginning of section.

Delaware County   *Real Estate, Deed, Recorder Records*
www.delawareclerk.org
Access land records index free at www.okcountyrecords.com or http://okcountyrecords.com/search.php?County=021. Subscription required for images; $10.00 per month.

Dewey County   *Assessor, Property Records*
Access to assessor data may be available at www.pvplus.com/freeaccess/free_login.aspx. Registration required. Subscription and fees for full access.

Grady County   *Assessor, Property Records*
Access assessor property data free at www.gradycountyassessor.org/search.stm; for full data, registration and $25.00 monthly fee required.

Kay County   *Property, Assessor, Treasurer Records*
Access the treasurer tax lookup page free at www.kaycounty.org/Creek1.htm. Also, the assessor office has a subscription service with property data; fee is $10.00 per month with new information being added. A basic index search is to be available online later in 2006. Call 580-362-2565 for details and to request a signup form.

Le Flore County   *Real Estate, Deed, Recorder Records*
Access land records index free at www.okcountyrecords.com or http://okcountyrecords.com/search.php. Subscription required for images; $10.00 per month.

Logan County   *Real Estate, Recorder, Deed, Lien, Divorce Records*
Assess recorded data free at www.okcountyrecords.com/search.php. Subscription required for images; $10.00 per month.

McClain County   *Assessor, Property Records*
Access to access property records is by subscription from Visual Lease Services- OK Assessors.com, 800-535-6467; weekly and monthly plans available. See note about OKassessors.com at beginning of section.

Marshall County   *Property, Assessor Records*
Access to access property records is by subscription from Visual Lease Services- OK Assessors.com, 800-535-6467; weekly and monthly plans available. See note about OKassessors.com at beginning of section.

Murray County   *Assessor, Property Records*
With registration you may search assessment data free temporarily at www.pvplus.com/freeaccess/free_login.aspx.

Oklahoma County   *Real Estate, Assessor, Grantor/Grantee, UCC, Property Tax, Inmate, Sex Offender, Most Wanted Records*

www.oklahomacounty.org

Assessor and property information on the county assessor database are free at www.oklahomacounty.org/assessor/disclaim.htm. Real estate, UCC, grantor/grantee records on the county clerk database are free at www.oklahomacounty.org/coclerk. Also, search the treasurer's property info at www.oklahomacounty.org/treasurer/PublicAccessSearch.htm. Also, search the sheriff lists of inmates, wanted, and sex offenders at www.oklahomacounty.org/sheriff/default.htm.

Okmulgee County   *Property, Assessor Records*

Access is free for basic info from a private company at www.pvplus.com/freeaccess/register.aspx - free registration is required.

Ottawa County   *Property, Assessor Records*

Access to property data is through a subscription with a private company, visit www.pvplus.com. Fee is $10.00 per month per county.

Payne County   *Real Estate, Deed, Recorder Records*

www.okcountyrecords.com

Access land records index free at www.okcountyrecords.com or http://okcountyrecords.com/search.php. Subscription required for images; $10.00 per month.

Pontotoc County   *Recording, Land, UCC, Judgment, Lien, Military Records*

www.pontotoccountyclerk.org

Access to the recorders records is free on the website. To search, login as guest and password a21b23. Password is case sensitive.

Pottawatomie County   *Recorded Documents Records*

Acces an index of recorded dcouments at https://www.landaccess.com. No fees.

Rogers County   *Assessor, Property Tax, Treasurer, Tax Roll, Real Estate Recording Records*

www.rogerscounty.org

Access to the assessor database is free at www.rogerscounty.org/search.html. Also, you may search the treasurers tax roll database free at www.rogerscounty.org/treasurer/search.html. Also, access land records at http://etitlesearch.com; for registration and subscription, call 870-856-3055.

Stephens County   *Real Estate, Deed, Recorder Records*

Access land records index free at www.okcountyrecords.com or http://okcountyrecords.com/search.php. Subscription required for images; $10.00 per month.

Tulsa County   *Assessor, Treasurer, Recording, Deed, Property, Inmate Records*

www.tulsacounty.org

Access to Tulsa County's Land Records System requires an approved user agreement, username and password, see http://lrmis.tulsacounty.org. Monthly access fee is $60.00 and 1st trial month is free. Records go back to 1979. For more information or signup, contact Dorise at 918-596-5206 or LRMIShelp@tulsacounty.org. Also, search inmate info on private company website at www.vinelink.com/index.jsp.

Washington County   *Land, Deed, Mortgage, Lien, Sex Offender Records*

www.countycourthouse.org

Access to the recorders database is free at www.countycourthouse.org/countyclerk/disclaimer.htm. Also, access to the sex offenders registry is free at www.countycourthouse.org/registry/index.htm.

Washita County   *Property, Assessor Records*

Access to property data is by subscription from a private company, registration and login required, see http://washita.oklahoma.usassessor.com/Shared/base/Subscriber/Subscribe.php.

Federal Courts in Oklahoma...

Standards for Federal Courts: The universal PACER sign-up number is 800-676-6856. Find PACER and the Party/Case Index on the Web at http://pacer.psc.uscourts.gov. PACER dial-up access is $.60 per minute. Also, courts offering internet access via PACER, Web-PACER or the new CM-ECF charge $.08 per page fee ($.07 per page if record is pre-2005 or unless noted as free).

US District Court -- Eastern District of Oklahoma

www.oked.uscourts.gov

PACER: Toll-free access phone: 866-863-3767. Local access phone: 918-687-2166. Case records are available back to 1996. Records are purged never. New records are available online after 1 day. **PACER Online Access:** PACER online at http://pacer.oked.uscourts.gov. **Electronic Filing:** CM/ECF data at https://ecf.oked.uscourts.gov.

Muskogee Division counties: Adair, Atoka, Bryan, Carter, Cherokee, Choctaw, Coal, Haskell, Hughes, Johnston, Latimer, Le Flore, Love, McCurtain, McIntosh, Marshall, Murray, Muskogee, Okfuskee, Okmulgee, Pittsburg, Pontotoc, Pushmataha, Seminole, Sequoyah, Wagoner.

US Bankruptcy Court -- Eastern District of Oklahoma

www.okeb.uscourts.gov

PACER: Case records are available back to 1986. Records are purged every 6 months. New records are available online after 1 day. **PACER Online Access:** ECF replaces PACER. **Electronic Filing:** Document images available. CM/ECF data at https://ecf.okeb.uscourts.gov. **Other Online Access:** Calendars available free http://pacer.okeb.uscourts.gov/calendars.html **Phone access:** Voice Case Information System, call 877-377-1221, 918-756-8617

Okmulgee Division counties: Adair, Atoka, Bryan, Carter, Cherokee, Choctaw, Coal, Haskell, Hughes, Johnston, Latimer, Le Flore, Love, Marshall, McCurtain, McIntosh, Murray, Muskogee, Okfuskee, Okmulgee, Pittsburg, Pontotoc, Pushmataha, Seminole, Sequoyah, Wagoner.

US District Court -- Northern District of Oklahoma

www.oknd.uscourts.gov

PACER: Case records are available back to 1992. New records are available online after 1 day. **PACER Online Access:** PACER has been replaced by the new CM/ECF system. **Electronic Filing:** CM/ECF data at https://ecf.oknd.uscourts.gov. **Other Online Access:** With a case number you may search the archives for documents at www.oknd.uscourts.gov/officeoperations/archives.nsf?open.

Tulsa Division counties: Craig, Creek, Delaware, Mayes, Nowata, Osage, Ottawa, Pawnee, Rogers, Tulsa, Washington.

US Bankruptcy Court -- Northern District of Oklahoma

www.oknb.uscourts.gov

PACER: Case records are available back to 1990. Records are purged never. New records are available online after 1 day. **PACER Online Access:** ECF replaces PACER. **Electronic Filing:** Document images available 1998-present. CM/ECF data at https://ecf.oknb.uscourts.gov. **Other Online Access:** WebPACER at www.oknb.uscourts.gov/perl/bkplog.html. RACER data has a 24-hour lag time. Also search judgment book free at www.oknb.uscourts.gov/court_information/judgment/judgments.htm. Search opinions and calendars by judge name free at main website. **Phone access:** Voice Case Information System, call 888-501-6977, 918-699-4001

Tulsa Division counties: Craig, Creek, Delaware, Mayes, Nowata, Osage, Ottawa, Pawnee, Rogers, Tulsa, Washington.

Oklahoma City Division counties: Alfalfa, Beaver, Beckham, Blaine, Caddo, Canadian, Cimarron, Cleveland, Comanche, Cotton, Custer, Dewey, Ellis, Garfield, Garvin, Grady, Grant, Greer, Harmon, Harper, Jackson, Jefferson, Kay, Kingfisher, Kiowa, Lincoln, Logan, Major, McClain, Noble, Oklahoma, Payne, Pottawatomie, Roger Mills, Stephens, Texas, Tillman, Washita, Woods, Woodward.

Oregon

Capital: Salem
              Marion County
Time Zone: PST
Population: 3,594,586
# of Counties: 36

Quick Links

Website: www.oregon.gov
Governor: www.governor.state.or.us
Attorney General: www.doj.state.or.us
State Archives: http://arcweb.sos.state.or.us
State Statutes and Codes: www.leg.state.or.us/ors/home.htm
Legislative Bill Search: www.leg.state.or.us/bills_laws/
Unclaimed Funds: http://mscfprod2.iservices.state.or.us/dsl/unclaimed_property/search.cfm

State Level ... Major Agencies

Criminal Records

Oregon State Police, Unit 11, Identification Services Section, PO Box 4395, Portland, OR 97208-4395 (Courier: 3772 Portland Rd NE, Bldg C, Salem, OR 97303); 503-378-3070, Fax-503-378-2121, 8AM-5PM M-F.
http://egov.oregon.gov/OSP/ID/
Online search: A web based site is available for requesting and receiving criminal records. Website is ONLY for high-volume requesters who must be pre-approved. Results are posted as "No Record" or "In Process" ("In Process" means a record will be mailed in 14 days). Use the "open records" link to get into the proper site. Fee is $10.00 per record. Call 503-373-1808 x230 to receive the application, or visit the website.

Statewide Court Records

Court Administrator, Supreme Court Bldg, 1163 State St, Salem, OR 97301-2563; 503-986-5500, Fax-503-986-5503, 8AM-5PM.
www.ojd.state.or.us/osca
Online search: Appellate opinions are found at www.publications.ojd.state.or.us/. Online computer access is available through the Oregon Judicial Information Network (OJIN) which includes almost all cases filed in the Oregon state courts. There is a one-time setup fee of $295.00 plus usage fees of $10-13.00 per hour. The database contains criminal, civil, small claims, probate, and some but not all juvenile records. However, it does not contain any records from municipal nor county courts. For further information visit www.ojd.state.or.us/ojin, or call 800-858-9658 or 503-986-5588. **Other options:** Purchase of bulk record is available, call for details.

Incarceration Records

Oregon Department of Corrections, Offender Information & Sentence Computation, PO Box 5670, Wilsonville, OR 97070-5670 (Courier: 24499 SW Grahams Ferry Rd, Bldg Z, Wilsonville, OR 97070); 503-570-6900, Fax-503-570-6902, 8AM-4PM.
www.doc.state.or.us
Online search: No online offender searching is available from this agency; there is a "Corrections Most Wanted" list in the pull down menu box. A private company offers free web access at www.vinelink.com/index.jsp; includes state, DOC, and most county jails. Also, use imate.info@doc.state.or.us to request by email. **Other options:** Bulk sale of information is available. Contact ISSD.

Corporation, Limited Partnership, Trademarks/Servicemarks, Fictitious Name, Assumed Name, Limited Liability Company Records

Corporation Division, Public Service Building, 255 Capital St NE, #151, Salem, OR 97310-1327; 503-986-2317, Fax-503-378-4381, www.filinginoregon.com
Online search: There is free access at the website for business registry information. Search by name or business registry number. Displays active and inactive records. **Other options:** A subscription service for new business lists on email, diskettes and CDs of the database are available for $15.00 per month or $180.00 for an annual subscription. Call 503-986-2343 for more information.

Uniform Commercial Code, Federal Tax Liens, State Tax Liens

UCC Division, Attn: Records, 255 Capitol St NE, Suite 151, Salem, OR 97310-1327; 503-986-2200 x6, Fax-503-373-1166. www.filinginoregon.com/ucc/index.htm
Online search: UCC index information and filings can be obtained for free from the website. You can search by debtor name or by lien number. You can also download forms from here. **Other options:** Monthly UCC information is released via e-mail, FTP or CD. Prices start at $15.00 per month or $150.00 annually for new filings, or $200 per month for all active filings. For more information, call Program Services at 503-986-2212.

Birth, Marriage, Divorce Certificates

Department of Human Services, Vital Records, PO Box 14050, Portland, OR 97293-0050 (Courier: 800 NE Oregon St, #205, Portland, OR 97232); 503-731-4108, 503-731-4095 (Recorded Message), Fax-503-234-8417, 8AM-4:30PM. http://oregon.gov/DHS/ph/chs/order/index.shtml
Online search: Order records online at www.vitalchek.com, a state designated vendor. **Other options:** Many state libraries offer record indexes.

Death Records

Department of Human Services, Vital Records, PO Box 14050, Portland, OR 97293-0050 (Courier: 800 NE Oregon St, #205, Portland, OR 97232); 503-731-4108, 503-731-4095 (Recorded Message), Fax-503-234-8417, 8AM-4:30PM. http://oregon.gov/DHS/ph/chs/order/index.shtml
Online search: Records from 1903-1930 are available at www.heritagetrailpress.com/Death_Index/. You may order directly on VitalChek's web page at www.VitalChek.com. **Other options:** Indexes are available at many state libraries.

Workers' Compensation Records

Department of Consumer & Business Srvs, Workers Compensation Division, PO Box 14480, Salem, OR 97309-0405 (Courier: 350 Winter Street NE Rm 27, Salem, OR 97301-3879); 503-947-7818, 503-947-7993 (TTY), Fax-503-945-7630, 8AM-5PM M-F. www.oregonwcd.org
Online search: A search of employers that have coverage, and employers that have coverage ending soon is found at www.oregonwcd.org/compliance/ecu/empcoverage.html. **Other options:** State is allowed to deliver data in other forms to parties that qualify under ORS 192.502(19).

GED Certificates

Dept of Community Colleges/ Workforce Development, Oregon GED Program, 255 Capitol St NE, Salem, OR 97310; 503-378-8648 x369, Fax-503-378-8434, 8AM-5PM M-F. www.odccwd.state.or.us
Online search: For records from 2002 forward, online access is available with the access code provided by the testing center.

State Level ... Occupational Licensing

Acupuncturist	http://egov.oregon.gov/BME/liccred.shtml
Airport/Aircraft Landing Area	www.aviation.state.or.us/Aviation/municipal_airports.shtml
Animal Euthanasia Technician/Facility	http://ovmeb.oregonlookups.com
Animal Feed (Livestock)	http://oregon.gov/ODA/oda_licenses.shtml
Animal Food Processor	http://oregon.gov/ODA/oda_licenses.shtml
Animal Health Technician	http://ovmeb.oregonlookups.com
Architect	http://new.orbae.com/index.php?option=com_obae
Architectural Firm	http://new.orbae.com/index.php?option=com_obae
Athletic Trainer	https://elite.hlo.state.or.us/elitepublic/LPRBrowser.aspx

Attorney	www.osbar.org/members/start.asp
Audiologist	http://bspa.oregonlookups.com
Auditor, Municipal	http://boahost.com/egovlicsearch.lasso
Bakery	http://oregon.gov/ODA/oda_licenses.shtml
Barber	https://elite.hlo.state.or.us/elitepublic/LPRBrowser.aspx
Body Piercer	https://elite.hlo.state.or.us/elitepublic/LPRBrowser.aspx
Boiler Welder	www.oregonbcd.org/licensesearch.html
Boilermaker	www.oregonbcd.org/licensesearch.html
Brand (Livestock)/Brand Inspector	http://oregon.gov/ODA/oda_licenses.shtml
Building Official	www.oregonbcd.org/licensesearch.html
Building Service Mechanic	www.oregonbcd.org/licensesearch.html
Chiropractor/Chiropractic Assistant	http://obce.alcsoftware.com/liclookup.php
Christmas Tree Grower	http://oregon.gov/ODA/oda_licenses.shtml
Construction Contractor/Subcontractor	https://ccbed.ccb.state.or.us/ccb_frames/consumer_info/ccb_index.htm
Cosmetologist	https://elite.hlo.state.or.us/elitepublic/LPRBrowser.aspx
Counselor, Professional	www.oblpct.state.or.us/OBLPCT/type.shtml
Dairy Establishment	http://oregon.gov/ODA/oda_licenses.shtml
Dentist/Dental Hygienist	http://egov.oregon.gov/Dentistry/licensee_lookup.shtml
Denture Technologist	https://elite.hlo.state.or.us/elitepublic/LPRBrowser.aspx
Denturist	https://elite.hlo.state.or.us/elitepublic/LPRBrowser.aspx
Diagnostic Radiologic Technologist	www.obrt.state.or.us
Dietitian	http://bld.oregonlookups.com/
Dog Racing Occupation	http://licenseinfo.oregon.gov/
Egg Handler/Breaker	http://oregon.gov/ODA/oda_licenses.shtml
Electrician/Electrical Installation	www.oregonbcd.org/licensesearch.html
Electrician, Maintenance	www.oregonbcd.org/licensesearch.html
Electrologist	https://elite.hlo.state.or.us/elitepublic/LPRBrowser.aspx
Electrology Instructor/School	https://elite.hlo.state.or.us/elitepublic/LPRBrowser.aspx
Elevator Journeyman, Limited	www.oregonbcd.org/licensesearch.html
Energy Technician, Limited/Restricted	www.oregonbcd.org/licensesearch.html
Engineer	www.osbeels.org
Facial Technician/Technologist	https://elite.hlo.state.or.us/elitepublic/LPRBrowser.aspx
Fertilizer/Mineral/Lime Registrant	http://oregon.gov/ODA/oda_licenses.shtml
Florist	http://oregon.gov/ODA/oda_licenses.shtml
Food Establishment, Retail	http://oregon.gov/ODA/oda_licenses.shtml
Food Exporter/Facility/Producer/Distrib'r	http://oregon.gov/ODA/oda_licenses.shtml
Food Storage Facility	http://oregon.gov/ODA/oda_licenses.shtml
Frozen Desert-related Industry	http://oregon.gov/ODA/oda_licenses.shtml
Geologist	www.open.org/~osbge/registrants.htm
Geologist, Engineering	www.open.org/~osbge/registrants.htm
Greenhouse Grower of Herbaceous Plants	http://oregon.gov/ODA/oda_licenses.shtml
Hair Salon	https://elite.hlo.state.or.us/elitepublic/LPRBrowser.aspx
Hair Stylist	https://elite.hlo.state.or.us/elitepublic/LPRBrowser.aspx
Hairdresser	https://elite.hlo.state.or.us/elitepublic/LPRBrowser.aspx
Heliport	www.aviation.state.or.us/Aviation/municipal_airports.shtml
Horse Racing Occupation	http://licenseinfo.oregon.gov/
Inspector, Building Code	www.oregonbcd.org/licensesearch.html
Inspector, Structural/Mechanical	www.oregonbcd.org/licensesearch.html
Insurance Adjuster	http://www4.cbs.state.or.us/ex/ins/inslic/agent/
Insurance Agency	www.cbs.state.or.us/external/imd/database/inslic/agency_main.htm
Insurance Agent	http://www4.cbs.state.or.us/ex/ins/inslic/agent/
Insurance Company	www.cbs.state.or.us/external/imd/database/inslic/comp_main.htm
Insurance Consultant	http://www4.cbs.state.or.us/ex/ins/inslic/agent/
Landscape Business	https://orlsc.glsuite.us/renewal/glsweb/homeframe.aspx
Landscaper	http://oregon.gov/ODA/oda_licenses.shtml
Livestock-Related Business	http://oregon.gov/ODA/oda_licenses.shtml

Lobbyist	www.gspc.state.or.us/GSPC/public_records.shtml
Manicurist/Nail Technician	https://elite.hlo.state.or.us/elitepublic/LPRBrowser.aspx
Manufactured Housing Construction	www.oregonbcd.org/licensesearch.html
Marriage & Family Therapist	www.oblpct.state.or.us/OBLPCT/type.shtml
Massage Therapist	www.oregonmassage.org/liclookup.php
Measuring Devices	http://oda.state.or.us/dbs/search.lasso#msd
Medical Doctor/Surgeon	http://egov.oregon.gov/BME/liccred.shtml
Midwife	https://elite.hlo.state.or.us/elitepublic/LPRBrowser.aspx
Milk Hauler/Milk Stabilization/Handler	http://oregon.gov/ODA/oda_licenses.shtml
Motor Fuel Quality	http://oda.state.or.us/dbs/search.lasso#msd
Nail Technician	https://elite.hlo.state.or.us/elitepublic/LPRBrowser.aspx
Naturopathic Physician	www.obne.state.or.us/OBNE/FindADoctor.shtml
Non-Alcoholic Beverage Plant	http://oregon.gov/ODA/oda_licenses.shtml
Nurse	www.osbn.state.or.us/search/searchResults-submit.do
Nursery Dealer	http://oregon.gov/ODA/oda_licenses.shtml
Nursery Stock/Native Plants Collector	http://oregon.gov/ODA/oda_licenses.shtml
Nursing Assistant	www.osbn.state.or.us/search/searchResults-submit.do
Nursing Home Administrator	http://nhabd.oregonlookups.com
Occupational Therapist	http://otlb.oregonlookups.com
Occupational Therapy Assistant	http://otlb.oregonlookups.com
Oil Module	www.oregonbcd.org/licensesearch.html
Optometrist	www.oregonobo.org/doctorinfo.htm
Oral Pathology Endorsement	https://elite.hlo.state.or.us/elitepublic/LPRBrowser.aspx
Oregon Product	http://oregon.gov/ODA/oda_licenses.shtml
Osteopathic Physician/Surgeon	http://egov.oregon.gov/BME/liccred.shtml
Permanent Color Technician	https://elite.hlo.state.or.us/elitepublic/LPRBrowser.aspx
Pesticide Applicator/Trainee/Dealer	http://oregon.gov/ODA/oda_licenses.shtml
Pesticide Product	http://oregon.gov/ODA/oda_licenses.shtml
Physical Therapist/Assistant	www.ptboard.state.or.us
Physician	http://egov.oregon.gov/BME/liccred.shtml
Physician Assistant	http://egov.oregon.gov/BME/liccred.shtml
Plans Examiner	www.oregonbcd.org/licensesearch.html
Plitical Candidate Statement	www.gspc.state.or.us/GSPC/public_records.shtml
Plumber	www.oregonbcd.org/licensesearch.html
Podiatrist	http://egov.oregon.gov/BME/liccred.shtml
Pressure Vessel Installer	www.oregonbcd.org/licensesearch.html
Psychologist	http://mscfprod1.iservices.state.or.us/obpe/search/obpe_lookup.cfm
Psychologist Associate	http://mscfprod1.iservices.state.or.us/obpe/search/obpe_lookup.cfm
Public Accountant-CPA	http://boahost.com/egovlicsearch.lasso
Public Accounting Firm	http://boahost.com/egovlicsearch.lasso
Pump Installation Contr., Limited	www.cbs.state.or.us/external/imd/database/bcd/licensing/cont/index.html
Radiologic Technologist Ltd Permit	www.obrt.state.or.us
Radiologic Therapy Technologist	www.obrt.state.or.us
Real Estate Appraiser	http://oregonaclb.org/index.php?option=com_content&task=view&id=20&Itemid=112
Refrigerated Plant	http://oregon.gov/ODA/oda_licenses.shtml
Respiratory Care Practitioner/Therapist	https://elite.hlo.state.or.us/elitepublic/LPRBrowser.aspx
Sanitarian	https://elite.hlo.state.or.us/elitepublic/LPRBrowser.aspx
Shellfish-related Industry	http://oregon.gov/ODA/oda_licenses.shtml
Sign Contractor, Limited	www.cbs.state.or.us/external/imd/database/bcd/licensing/cont/index.html
Sign Journeyman, Electrical	www.oregonbcd.org/licensesearch.html
Slaughterhouse	http://oregon.gov/ODA/oda_licenses.shtml
Speech Language Pathologist	http://bspa.oregonlookups.com
Stage Journeyman, Electrical	www.oregonbcd.org/licensesearch.html
Steamfitter	www.oregonbcd.org/licensesearch.html
Surveyor, Land	www.osbeels.org
Tattoo Artist	https://elite.hlo.state.or.us/elitepublic/LPRBrowser.aspx

Teacher .... www.tspc.state.or.us/lookup_query.asp
Therapeutic Radiologic Technologist .... www.obrt.state.or.us
Transaction Verification .... http://oda.state.or.us/dbs/search.lasso#msd
Veterinarian .... http://ovmeb.oregonlookups.com
Veterinary Clinic/Product, Livestock.......... http://oregon.gov/ODA/oda_licenses.shtml
Veterinary Technician................................. http://ovmeb.oregonlookups.com
Waste Water System Operator.................... www.deq.state.or.us/wq/OpCert/opcert.htm
Water Heater Installer, Limited.................. www.oregonbcd.org/licensesearch.html
Water Rights Examiner............................... www.osbeels.org
Water Treatment Installer .... www.oregonbcd.org/licensesearch.html
Weighing Devices....................................... http://oda.state.or.us/dbs/search.lasso#msd

County Level ... Courts

Court Administration: Court Administrator, Supreme Court Building, 1163 State St, Salem, OR, 97301-2563; 503-986-5500; www.ojd.state.or.us

Court Structure: Effective January 15, 1998, the District and Circuit Courts were combined into "Circuit Courts." At the same time, three new judicial districts were created by splitting existing ones.

Online Access Note: Online computer access is available through the Oregon Judicial Information Network (OJIN). OJIN Online includes almost all cases filed in the Oregon state courts. Generally, the OJIN database contains criminal, civil, small claims, probate, and some but not all juvenile records. However, the system does not contain any records from Municipal Courts or County Courts. There is a one-time setup fee of $295.00, plus a monthly usage charge (minimum $10.00) based on transaction type, type of job, shift, and number of units/pages (which averages $10-13 per hour). For further information or a registration packet, write to: Oregon Judicial System, Information Systems Division, Attn: Technical Support, 1163 State Street, Salem OR 97310, or call 800-858-9658, or visit www.ojd.state.or.us/ojin

Appellate opinions are found at www.publications.ojd.state.or.us

Deschutes County
Deschutes County Courts – Civil and Criminal Records
Index remotely online on the statewide OJIN system, call 800-858-9658 for information. Has criminal records from 07/86 forward. Also, current calendars are free at www.ojd.state.or.us/des/calendar.nsf/.

Statewide Access
The www.ojd.state.or.us/ojin website offers commercial access to almost all cases filed in the Oregon state courts. See the state introduction for details.

County Level ... Recorders & Assessors

Recording Office Organization: 36 counties, 36 recording offices. The recording officer is the County Clerk. 35 counties are in the Pacific Time Zone (PST) and one is in the Mountain Time Zone (MST). All federal and state tax liens on personal property are filed with the Secretary of State. Other federal and state tax liens are filed with the County Clerk. Search fees vary widely.

Online Access Note: A number of counties offer Internet access, usually to assessor records. There is no statewide system available.

Baker County   *Property, Assessor Records*
www.bakercounty.org
Access to the assessor property database is free at www.bakercounty.org/Assessor/Assessor_Search.html. Also for daily inmate listing go to www.bakersheriff.org/jaillist.htm.

Benton County   *Assessor, Surveys, Inmate, 30-day Released Inmate Records*

www.co.benton.or.us

The County is developing a Geographic Info System Internet site for viewing property information at http://gis.co.benton.or.us/v09_10/source/container.htm. Search fee is $3.75 per record found. Also, assessment and taxation database download is free at www.co.benton.or.us/assessor/data_extract.html. Search the sheriff's inmate list and 30-day release list at www.co.benton.or.us/sheriff/index.html. Also, sheriff's wanted "absconders' list at www.co.benton.or.us/sheriff/corrections/bccc/Absconders/. Also, a law enforcement case system may soon offer open case data.

Clackamas County   *Real Property, Most Wanted Records*

www.co.clackamas.or.us/clerk

Records on the County Metromap database are free at http://topaz.metro-region.org/metromap/metromap.cfm. No name searching. Also, search the sheriff's most wanted list at www.co.clackamas.or.us/sheriff/news/mostwanted.htm.

Coos County   *Assessor, Property, Sale Records*

www.co.coos.or.us

Access to the assessor property and sales data is free at http://coos.gtrsoft.com.

Deschutes County   *Real Estate, Deed, Mortgage, Lien, Assessor, Property Tax Records*

http://recordings.co.deschutes.or.us

Access records on the county "Assessor Inquiry System" website at www.co.deschutes.or.us/dial.cfm. Access tax information, assessment, appraisal details, ownership, sales information, transaction histories, account histories, land use records, and lot numbers for no fee. Also, search real estate, deeds, mortgages, liens on the clerk's recording system web inquiry for free at http://recordings.co.deschutes.or.us. Free registration for username and password is required.

Douglas County   *Assessor, Property Records*

Access to the assessor property data is free at www.co.douglas.or.us/puboaa/cgi/oaasearch.pl.

Lane County   *Assessor, Real Estate, Property Records*

Property records on the County Tax Map site are free at www.co.lane.or.us/TaxStatement/Search.aspx. No name searching. Also, access to the Regional Land Information Database RLID is by subscription. Visit www.rlid.org or call Eric at 541-682-4338 for more information or signup. Initiation fee is $200; monthly access fee is $80.00.

Linn County   *Assessor, Real Estate, Property Sale Records*

www.co.linn.or.us

Real estate ownership reocrds are free at www.co.linn.or.us/assessor/NewPropSearch.asp. Tax assessor rolls may be viewed at www.co.linn.or.us/assessorshomep/assessor.htm.

Marion County   *Jail Inmate, Sex Offender Records*

http://clerk.co.marion.or.us/records

Access to the sheriff's database of inmates and sex offenders is free at http://sheriff.co.marion.or.us.

Multnomah County   *Real Property, Released Inmate, Restaurant Inspection Records*

www.co.multnomah.or.us/dss/at/index.html

Records on the County Metromap database are free at http://topaz.metro-region.org/metromap/metromap.cfm. No name searching. The GIS-mapping site is very similar at http://gis.co.multnomah.or.us/sail/. Also, search the sheriff's release inmate list at www.inmatereleases.org/search.cfm. Search the Health Dept. restaurant inspections at www.mchealthinspect.org/inspections/index.html.

Tillamook County   *Assessor, Property Tax, Recording, Deed, Lien, Judgment Records*

www.co.tillamook.or.us/gov/clerk/default.htm

Access to recorded document index free at www.co.tillamook.or.us/gov/clerk/recinq/Login.asp; use username "public" and password "inquiry." Viewing document images is not available online. Assessment and taxation records on the County Property database are free at www.co.tillamook.or.us/Documents/Search/query.asp. Search by property ID number or by name in the general query. Also, search for property info on the GIS-mapping service site at http://gisweb.co.tillamook.or.us.

Umatilla County   *Jail Records*

Access to the sheriff's current jail roster is free at www.co.umatilla.or.us/deptwebs/jail/inmates/ICURRENT.HTM.

Union County *Property Tax, Assessor Records*
www.union-county.org
Access property tax free at www.union-county.org/assessor_search.html.

Washington County *Real Estate Records*
www.co.washington.or.us/deptmts/at/recordng/record.htm
Records on County GIS Intermap database are free at http://washims.co.washington.or.us/gis/InterMap/index.cfm but no name searching. Also, map and land records are free online at www.co.washington.or.us/deptmts/lut/gis/intermap/map_land.htm.

Yamhill County *Assessor, Property, Mapping Records*
www.co.yamhill.or.us/clerk
Search assessor property data free at www.co.yamhill.or.us/taxinfo/PropSearch.aspx. No name searching. Also, limited property information from the county surveyor is free at www.co.yamhill.or.us/surveyor/; no name searching.

Federal Courts in Oregon...

Standards for Federal Courts: The universal PACER sign-up number is 800-676-6856. Find PACER and the Party/Case Index on the Web at http://pacer.psc.uscourts.gov. PACER dial-up access is $.60 per minute. Also, courts offering internet access via PACER, Web-PACER or the new CM-ECF charge $.08 per page fee ($.07 per page if record is pre-2005 or unless noted as free).

US District Court -- District of Oregon

www.ord.uscourts.gov
PACER: Case records are available back to 9/1988. Records are purged never. **PACER Online Access:** ECF replaces PACER. **Electronic Filing:** CM/ECF data at https://ecf.ord.uscourts.gov. **Opinions:** A few selected recent rulings only. View court opinions at www.uscourts.gov/rulings/rulings.html.
Eugene Division counties: Benton, Coos, Deschutes, Douglas, Lane, Lincoln, Linn, Marion.
Medford Division counties: Curry, Jackson, Josephine, Klamath, Lake. Court set up in 4/1994; Cases prior to that time were tried in Eugene.
Portland Division counties: Baker, Clackamas, Clatsop, Columbia, Crook, Gilliam, Grant, Harney, Hood River, Jefferson, Malheur, Morrow, Multnomah, Polk, Sherman, Tillamook, Umatilla, Union, Wallowa, Wasco, Washington, Wheeler, Yamhill.

US Bankruptcy Court -- District of Oregon

www.orb.uscourts.gov
PACER: Case records are available back to 1989. Records are purged every 6 months. New records are available online after 1 day. **PACER Online Access:** PACER online at http://pacer.orb.uscourts.gov. **Electronic Filing:** CM/ECF data at https://ecf.orb.uscourts.gov. **Opinions:** View court opinions at www.orb.uscourts.gov/opinion. **Other Online Access:** Access judges' calendars by judge name at www.orb.uscourts.gov/orb/cal.nsf/Judges'+Hearings+Calendars. **Phone access:** Voice Case Information System, call 800-726-2227, 503-326-2249
Eugene Division counties: Benton, Coos, Curry, Deschutes, Douglas, Jackson, Josephine, Klamath, Lake, Lane, Lincoln, Linn, Marion.
Portland Division counties: Baker, Clackamas, Clatsop, Columbia, Crook, Gilliam, Grant, Harney, Hood River, Jefferson, Malheur, Morrow, Multnomah, Polk, Sherman, Tillamook, Umatilla, Union, Wallowa, Wasco, Washington, Wheeler, Yamhill.

Editor's Tip: Just because records are maintained in a certain way in your state or county do not assume that any other county or state does things the same way that you are used to.

Pennsylvania

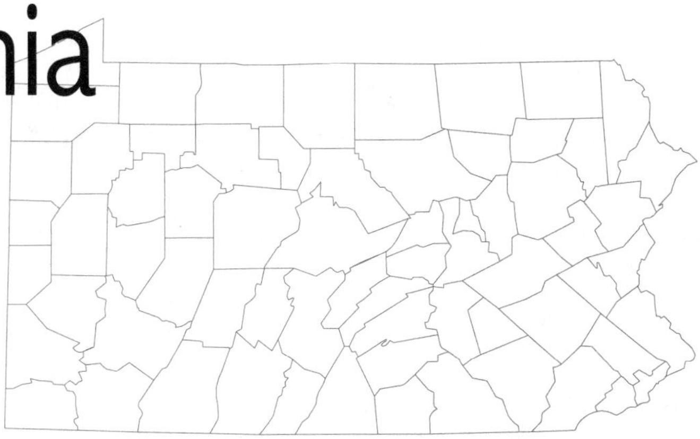

Capital: Harrisburg
　　　　Dauphin County
Time Zone: EST
Population: 12,406,292
# of Counties: 67

Quick Links

Website: www.state.pa.us
Governor: www.governor.state.pa.us
Attorney General: www.attorneygeneral.gov
State Archives: www.phmc.state.pa.us
State Statutes and Codes: http://members.aol.com/StatutesPA/Index.html
Legislative Bill Search: www.legis.state.pa.us/cfdocs/legis/home/session.cfm
Unclaimed Funds: www.patreasury.org/search.htm

State Level ... Major Agencies

Criminal Records

State Police, Central Repository -164, 1800 Elmerton Ave, Harrisburg, PA 17110-9758; 717-783-5494, 717-783-9973, Fax-717-772-3681, 8:15AM-4:15PM.
www.psp.state.pa.us/psp/site/default.asp
Online search: Record checks are available for approved agencies through the Internet on the Pennsylvania Access to Criminal Histories (PATCH). Ongoing requesters may become registered users. This is a commercial system, the same $10.00 fee per name applies. PATCH accepts Visa, Discover, MasterCard, AmEx cards. Go to https://epatch.state.pa.us/Home.jsp or call 717-705-1768 to register. Up to 10 records may be requested at one session.

Statewide Court Records

Administrative Office of PA Courts, PO Box 229, Mechanicsburg, PA 17055; 717-795-2097, 717-795-2062 (Communications), 717-255-1650 (Civil Appellate Cases), Fax-717-795-2013, 9AM-5PM.
www.courts.state.pa.us
Online search: The Web Portal offers access to a variety of the Judiciary's Electronic Services (E-Services) such as Web Docket Sheets, DA Link, Superior Court's Web Docketing Statements, etc. Web Docket provides public access to view and print Case Docket Sheets from Pennsylvania's three Appellate Courts and Criminal Cases only from Courts of Common Pleas. Search by docket number, name or organization. Go to http://ujsportal.pacourts.us for details.

Sexual Offender Registry

State Police Central Repository, Megan's Law Unit, 1800 Elmerton Ave, Harrisburg, PA 17110-9758; 717-783-4363, 866-771-7130, Fax-717-705-8839, 7AM-3PM.
www.pameganslaw.state.pa.us
Online search: Limited information on all registered sex offenders can be viewed online from the webpage. Complete address information is listed only for sexually violent predators. Search by name, alias, city, county or ZIP. To make a specific request for information on Sexually Violent Predators, please email to ra-pspsvp@state.pa.us.

Incarceration Records

Pennsylvania Department of Corrections, Bureau of Inmate Services, PO Box 598, Camp Hill, PA 17001-0598; 717-737-6538, 717-730-2721 (Records), Fax-717-731-7159, 8AM-4PM.
www.cor.state.pa.us

Online search: At the website, click on Inmate Locator for information about each inmate currently under the jurisdiction of the Department of Corrections. The site indicates where an inmate is housed, race, date of birth, marital status and other items. The Inmate Locator does not contain information on inmates not currently residing in a state correctional institution.

Corporation, Limited Partnership, Trademarks/Servicemarks, Fictitious Name, Assumed Name, Limited Liability Company, Limited Liability Partnerships

Corporation Bureau, Department of State, PO Box 8722, Harrisburg, PA 17105-8722 (Courier: 206 North Office Bldg, Harrisburg, PA 17120); 717-787-1057, Fax-717-783-2244, 8AM-5PM.
www.dos.state.pa.us/corps/site/default.asp
Online search: There is free general searching by entity name or number from the website. Searching by name provides a list of entities whose name starts with the search name entered. Users can click on any one entity in the list displayed to get more detailed information regarding that entity.

Uniform Commercial Code

UCC Division, Department of State, PO Box 8721, Harrisburg, PA 17105-8721 (Courier: North Office Bldg, Rm 206, Harrisburg, PA 17120); 717-787-1057 x3, Fax-717-783-2244, 8AM-5PM.
www.dos.state.pa.us/DOS/site/default.asp
Online search: The website allows a search of UCC-1 financing statements filed with the Corporation Bureau by debtor name or financing statement number; a list of financing statements is displayed. The site also allows a search of financing statement records filed with the Corporation Bureau by financing statement number. **Other options:** Daily computer tapes and copies of microfilm are available. Call the number above for details.

Birth, Death Certificates

PA Department of Health, Division of Vital Records, PO Box 1528, New Castle, PA 16101-1528 (Courier: 101 S Mercer St, Room 401, New Castle, PA 16101); 724-656-3100 (Message Phone), Fax-724-652-8951, 8AM-4PM.
www.dsf.health.state.pa.us/health/cwp/view.asp?a=168&q=229939
Online search: Expedited service is available at www.vitalchek.com, a state designated vendor. Access to this site is also linked from the home page above.

Driver Records

Department of Transportation, Driver Record Services, PO Box 68695, Harrisburg, PA 17106-8695 (Courier: 1101 S Front Street, 3rd Fl, Harrisburg, PA 17104); 717-391-6190, 800-932-4600 (In-state only), 7:30AM-4:30PM.
www.dmv.state.pa.us
Online search: The online system is available to high volume requesters for three or ten-year records. Fee is $5.00 per record. Call 717-787-7154 for more information. The resale of records by vendors to other vendors is strictly forbidden. Also, drivers may order their own record from the web page. **Other options:** Magnetic tape processing is available for batch requesters. There is a 500 record minimum order per day.

State Level ... Occupational Licensing

Acupuncturist	http://licensepa.state.pa.us/default.asp
Amphetamine Program	http://licensepa.state.pa.us/default.asp
Anesthesia Permit, Dental	www.licensepa.state.pa.us/default.asp
Animal Health Technician	http://licensepa.state.pa.us/default.asp
Appraiser, Residential/Broker	http://licensepa.state.pa.us/default.asp
Architect/Architectural Firm	http://licensepa.state.pa.us/default.asp
Athletic Agent	www.licensepa.state.pa.us/default.asp
Athletic Trainer	http://licensepa.state.pa.us/default.asp
Attorney	http://padisciplinaryboard.org/attsearchdc.php
Attorney, Disciplined	http://padisciplinaryboard.org/attsearchdcd.php
Auctioneer/Auction House/Company	http://licensepa.state.pa.us/default.asp
Audiologist	http://licensepa.state.pa.us/default.asp
Bank	www.banking.state.pa.us/Banking/Banking/InstListQuery.asp
Barber/Barber School/Teacher	http://licensepa.state.pa.us/default.asp

Barber Shop/Manager .... http://licensepa.state.pa.us/default.asp
Boxer .... www.dos.state.pa.us/sac/cwp/view.asp?a=1090&q=436810&sacNav=|
Builder/Owner, Real Estate......................... http://licensepa.state.pa.us/default.asp
Campground Membership Seller .... http://licensepa.state.pa.us/default.asp
Cemetery Broker/Seller/Regis. .... http://licensepa.state.pa.us/default.asp
Check Casher .... www.banking.state.pa.us/Banking/Banking/InstListQuery.asp
Chiropractor.. http://licensepa.state.pa.us/default.asp
Consumer Discount Company .... www.banking.state.pa.us/Banking/Banking/InstListQuery.asp
Continuing Education Provider, Financ'l.... www.banking.state.pa.us/Banking/Banking/InstListQuery.asp
Cosmetologist/ Cos. Teacher/School/Shop . http://licensepa.state.pa.us/default.asp
Counselor, Professional .... http://licensepa.state.pa.us/default.asp
Credit Services Loan Broker....................... www.banking.state.pa.us/Banking/Banking/InstListQuery.asp
Credit Union .... www.banking.state.pa.us/Banking/Banking/InstListQuery.asp
Debt Collector... www.banking.state.pa.us/Banking/Banking/InstListQuery.asp
Dental Assistant, Expanded Function .... www.licensepa.state.pa.us/default.asp
Dentist/Dental Hygienist............................ www.licensepa.state.pa.us/default.asp
Dietitian/Nutritionist LDN........................ http://licensepa.state.pa.us/default.asp
Engineer.. http://licensepa.state.pa.us/default.asp
Evaluator, Appraisal .... http://licensepa.state.pa.us/default.asp
Financial Holding Company .... www.banking.state.pa.us/Banking/Banking/InstListQuery.asp
Funeral Director/Supervisor/Establishment http://licensepa.state.pa.us/default.asp
Geologist... http://licensepa.state.pa.us/default.asp
Hearing Examiners .... http://licensepa.state.pa.us/default.asp
Installment Loan Seller.............................. www.banking.state.pa.us/Banking/Banking/InstListQuery.asp
Insurance Agent... http://164.156.71.30/producer/ilist1.asp
Landscape Architect................................... http://licensepa.state.pa.us/default.asp
Loan Correspondent................................... www.banking.state.pa.us/Banking/Banking/InstListQuery.asp
Lobbyist.. www.lobbyistnetwork.com/
Manicurist... http://licensepa.state.pa.us/default.asp
Marriage & Family Therapist .... http://licensepa.state.pa.us/default.asp
Medical Doctor .... http://licensepa.state.pa.us/default.asp
Midwife .... http://licensepa.state.pa.us/default.asp
Money Transmitter .... www.banking.state.pa.us/Banking/Banking/InstListQuery.asp
Mortgage Banker/Broker/Provider/Corres.. www.banking.state.pa.us/Banking/Banking/InstListQuery.asp
Nuclear Medicine Technologist .... http://licensepa.state.pa.us/default.asp
Nurse, Nurses Aide .... http://licensepa.state.pa.us/default.asp
Nursing Home.. http://app2.health.state.pa.us/commonpoc/nhLocatorie.asp
Nursing Home Administrator...................... http://licensepa.state.pa.us/default.asp
Occupational Therapist/Assistant................ http://licensepa.state.pa.us/default.asp
Optometrist .... http://licensepa.state.pa.us/default.asp
Osteopathic Acupuncturist.......................... http://licensepa.state.pa.us/default.asp
Osteopathic Physician/Surgeon/Assistant ... http://licensepa.state.pa.us/default.asp
Osteopathic Respiratory Care .... http://licensepa.state.pa.us/default.asp
Pawnbroker... www.banking.state.pa.us/Banking/Banking/InstListQuery.asp
Pharmacist/Pharmacy................................. http://licensepa.state.pa.us/default.asp
Physical Therapist/Assistant .... http://licensepa.state.pa.us/default.asp
Physician Assistant .... http://licensepa.state.pa.us/default.asp
Pilot, Navigational .... http://licensepa.state.pa.us/default.asp
Podiatrist.. http://licensepa.state.pa.us/default.asp
Psychologist.. http://licensepa.state.pa.us/default.asp
Public Accountant-CPA/Corp./Partner .... http://licensepa.state.pa.us/default.asp
Public Adjuster/ Solicitor........................... http://164.156.71.30/producer/ilist1.asp
Radiation Therapy Technician.................... http://licensepa.state.pa.us/default.asp
Radiologic Auxiliary, Chiropractic............. http://licensepa.state.pa.us/default.asp
Radiologic Technologist .... http://licensepa.state.pa.us/default.asp
Real Estate Agent/Broker/Sales/School...... http://licensepa.state.pa.us/default.asp

Real Estate Appraiser	http://licensepa.state.pa.us/default.asp
Rental Listing Referral Agent	http://licensepa.state.pa.us/default.asp
Repossessor	www.banking.state.pa.us/Banking/Banking/InstListQuery.asp
Respiratory Care Practitioner	http://licensepa.state.pa.us/default.asp
Sales Finance Company	www.banking.state.pa.us/Banking/Banking/InstListQuery.asp
Savings Association	www.banking.state.pa.us/Banking/Banking/InstListQuery.asp
Social Worker	http://licensepa.state.pa.us/default.asp
Speech-Language Pathologist	http://licensepa.state.pa.us/default.asp
Surplus Lines Broker	http://164.156.71.30/producer/ilist1.asp
Surveyor, Land	http://licensepa.state.pa.us/default.asp
Table Funder, Wholesale	www.banking.state.pa.us/Banking/Banking/InstListQuery.asp
Teacher	https://www.tcs.ed.state.pa.us/validchk.asp
Therapist, Drugless	http://licensepa.state.pa.us/default.asp
Thrift Holding Company	www.banking.state.pa.us/Banking/Banking/InstListQuery.asp
Timeshare Salesperson	http://licensepa.state.pa.us/default.asp
Trust Company	www.banking.state.pa.us/Banking/Banking/InstListQuery.asp
Used Vehicle Lot	http://licensepa.state.pa.us/
Vehicle Auction	http://licensepa.state.pa.us/
Vehicle Dealer/Manufacturer/Dist./Sales	http://licensepa.state.pa.us/
Veterinarian/Veterinary Technician	http://licensepa.state.pa.us/default.asp
Viatical Settlement Broker	http://164.156.71.30/producer/ilist1.asp

County Level ... Courts

Court Administration: Administrative Office of Pennsylvania Courts, PO Box 719, Mechanicsburg, PA, 17055; 717-795-2097; www.courts.state.pa.us

Court Structure: The Courts of Common Pleas are the general trial courts, with jurisdiction over both civil and criminal matters and appellate jurisdiction over matters disposed of by the special courts. The civil records clerk of the Court of Common Pleas is called the Prothonotary.

Small claims cases are, usually, handled by the District Justice Courts. These courts, which are designated as "special courts," also handle civil cases up to $8,000. However, all small claims and civil actions are recorded through the Prothonotary Section of the Court of Common Pleas, which then holds the records. It is not necessary to check each Magisterial District Court, but rather to check with the Prothonotary for the county.

Online Access Note: The state's 556 District Justice Courts are served by a statewide, automated case management system. Online access to the case management system is not available.

The web portal offers access to a variety of the Judiciary's Electronic Services (E-Services) such as Web Docket Sheets, DA Link, Superior Court's Web Docketing Statements, etc. Web Docket provides public access to view and print Case Docket Sheets from Pennsylvania's three Appellate Courts and Criminal Cases only from Courts of Common Pleas. Search by docket number, name or organization. Go to http://ujsportal.pacourts.us for details. Also, search Appellate Court dockets at http://pacmsdocketsheet.aopc.org.

The Infocon County Access System provides direct dial-up access to court record information for over 20 counties. Set up entails a $50.00 base set-up fee plus $25.00 per county. The monthly usage fee minimum is $25.00, plus time charges. For info, call Infocon at 814-472-6066 or visit www.infoconcountyaccess.com.

Adams County
Court of Common Pleas – Criminal Records
Search dockets online free at http://ujsportal.pacourts.us/WebDocketSheets/OtherCriteria.aspx.

Allegheny County
Court of Common Pleas – Civil Records
www.alleghenycourts.us   more…

Access to opinions at www.alleghenycourts.us/search/default.asp?source=opinions_civil. Also, search dockets free by name at http://ujsportal.pacourts.us/WebDocketSheets/OtherCriteria.aspx.

Court of Common Pleas – Criminal Records
www.alleghenycourts.us
Access to Common Pleas criminal records is free at https://www.alleghenycourts.us/cims/default.asp. Search by name, docket number or SSN. Search opinions at www.alleghenycourts.us/search/default.asp?source=opinions_criminal. Also, search dockets free by name at http://ujsportal.pacourts.us/WebDocketSheets/OtherCriteria.aspx.

Armstrong County

Court of Common Pleas – Civil Records
www.geocities.com/acprothonotary/
Access to Register of Wills and civil records is by subscription from private company-Infocon at www.infoconcountyaccess.com, 814-472-6066. See note at beginning of section.

Court of Common Pleas – Criminal Records
www.co.armstrong.pa.us/courtindex.htm
Search dockets online free at http://ujsportal.pacourts.us/WebDocketSheets/OtherCriteria.aspx. Also, see note at beginning of section.

Beaver County

Court of Common Pleas – Criminal Records
www.beavercountypa.gov/Courts/index.htm
Search dockets online free at http://ujsportal.pacourts.us/WebDocketSheets/OtherCriteria.aspx.

Bedford County

Court of Common Pleas – Civil and Criminal Records
Access to Register of Wills and civil records is by subscription from private company-Infocon at www.infoconcountyaccess.com, 814-472-6066. See note at beginning of section. Also, search dockets online free at http://ujsportal.pacourts.us/WebDocketSheets/OtherCriteria.aspx.

Berks County

Court of Common Pleas – Civil and Criminal Records
The Register of Wills has a free searchable website at www.berksregofwills.com/search_page.htm including marriage, estate, birth and death records for the county. The estate and marriage records are current. Also, the Prothonatary has a remote system to access dockets from 2002 forward. Fee is $300 per year. For information, call 610-478-6967. Also, search criminal dockets free at http://ujsportal.pacourts.us/WebDocketSheets/OtherCriteria.aspx.

Blair County

Court of Common Pleas – Civil and Criminal Records
Access to the REgister of Wills and Civil records is by subscription from private company-Infocon at www.infoconcountyaccess.com, 814-472-6066. See note at beginning of section. Also, search criminal dockets online free at http://ujsportal.pacourts.us/WebDocketSheets/OtherCriteria.aspx.

Bradford County

Court of Common Pleas – Criminal Records
As of 7/5/2005, search dockets online free at http://ujsportal.pacourts.us/WebDocketSheets/OtherCriteria.aspx.

Bucks County

Court of Common Pleas – Civil and Criminal Records
www.buckscounty.org/courts
For a limited time, access is free at http://4.43.65.248/autoform.asp?app=cvr. Register of Wills is also included. Domestic and family court dockets are free at http://4.43.65.248/autoform.asp?app=fcr. Also, access criminal court records free at http://4.43.65.248/autoform.asp?app=ccr. Also, search criminal dockets free at http://ujsportal.pacourts.us/WebDocketSheets/OtherCriteria.aspx.

Butler County

Court of Common Pleas – Civil and Criminal Records
Access to civil and Register of Wills records is by subscription from private company-Infocon at www.infoconcountyaccess.com, 814-472-6066. See note at beginning of section. Also, search criminal dockets free at http://ujsportal.pacourts.us/WebDocketSheets/OtherCriteria.aspx.

Cambria County

Court of Common Pleas – Criminal Records
Search dockets online free at http://ujsportal.pacourts.us/WebDocketSheets/OtherCriteria.aspx.

Cameron County

Court of Common Pleas – Criminal Records
Search dockets online free at http://ujsportal.pacourts.us/WebDocketSheets/OtherCriteria.aspx.

Carbon County

Court of Common Pleas – Civil Records
www.carboncourts.com
Access to Register of Will and the clerk of courts docket records is free at www.carboncourts.com/pubacc.htm. Registration required.

Court of Common Pleas – Criminal Records
www.carboncourts.com
Access to the clerk of courts docket records is free at www.carboncourts.com/pubacc.htm. Registration required. Also, search dockets free at http://ujsportal.pacourts.us/WebDocketSheets/OtherCriteria.aspx.

Centre County

Court of Common Pleas – Criminal Records
www.co.centre.pa.us/271.asp
Search dockets online free at http://ujsportal.pacourts.us/WebDocketSheets/OtherCriteria.aspx.

Chester County

Court of Common Pleas – Civil and Criminal Records
http://dsf.chesco.org
Internet access to county records including court records requires a sign-up and credit card payment. Application fee: $50. There is a $10.00 per month minimum (no charge for no activity); and $.10 each transaction beyond 100. Sign-up and/or logon at http://epin.chesco.org/. Also, a court case list is free at http://dsf.chesco.org/courts/site/default.asp; click on "Miscellaneous List." Also, search criminal dockets free at http://ujsportal.pacourts.us/WebDocketSheets/OtherCriteria.aspx.

Clarion County

Court of Common Pleas – Civil and Criminal Records
www.co.clarion.pa.us/
Access to Civil, Criminal and REgister of Wills records is by subscription from private company-Infocon at www.infoconcountyaccess.com, 814-472-6066. See note at beginning of section. Also, search criminal dockets online free at http://ujsportal.pacourts.us/WebDocketSheets/OtherCriteria.aspx.

Clearfield County

Court of Common Pleas – Criminal Records
www.clearfieldco.org
As of 11/7/2005, search dockets online free at http://ujsportal.pacourts.us/WebDocketSheets/OtherCriteria.aspx.

Clinton County

Court of Common Pleas – Civil and Criminal Records
www.clintoncountypa.com/courts.htm
Access to Register of Will and civil records is by subscription from private company-Infocon at www.infoconcountyaccess.com, 814-472-6066. See note at beginning of section. Also, as of 8/1/2005, search dockets online free at http://ujsportal.pacourts.us/WebDocketSheets/OtherCriteria.aspx.

Columbia County

Court of Common Pleas – Criminal Records
http://columbiapa.org/courts/index.html
As of 8/15/2005, search dockets online free at http://ujsportal.pacourts.us/WebDocketSheets/OtherCriteria.aspx.

Crawford County

Court of Common Pleas – Criminal Records
http://co.crawford.pa.us/clerk_of_courts/clerk_of_courts_home.htm
Search dockets online free at http://ujsportal.pacourts.us/WebDocketSheets/OtherCriteria.aspx.

Cumberland County

Court of Common Pleas – Criminal Records
www.ccpa.net/cumberland/site/default.asp
Search dockets online free at http://ujsportal.pacourts.us/WebDocketSheets/OtherCriteria.aspx.

Dauphin County

Court of Common Pleas – Criminal Records
http://dsf.pacounties.org/dauphin/site/default.asp
Search dockets online free at http://ujsportal.pacourts.us/WebDocketSheets/OtherCriteria.aspx.

Delaware County

Court of Common Pleas – Civil and Criminal Records
www.co.delaware.pa.us
Access to court civil records free (may begin charging at any time) at www2.co.delaware.pa.us/pa/default.htm. For more information, call 610-891-4675. Search by document type, document number, etc. Also, search dockets online free at http://ujsportal.pacourts.us/WebDocketSheets/OtherCriteria.aspx.

Elk County

Court of Common Pleas – Criminal Records
www.co.elk.pa.us/Courthouse.htm
Search dockets online free at http://ujsportal.pacourts.us/WebDocketSheets/OtherCriteria.aspx.

Erie County

Court of Common Pleas – Civil and Criminal Records
www.eriecountygov.org/
Access to Register of Wills and civil records is by subscription from private company-Infocon at www.infoconcountyaccess.com, 814-472-6066. See note at beginning of section. Also, search criminal dockets free at http://ujsportal.pacourts.us/WebDocketSheets/OtherCriteria.aspx.

Fayette County

Court of Common Pleas – Criminal Records
Search dockets online free at http://ujsportal.pacourts.us/WebDocketSheets/OtherCriteria.aspx.

Forest County

Court of Common Pleas – Criminal Records
Search dockets online free at http://ujsportal.pacourts.us/WebDocketSheets/OtherCriteria.aspx.

Franklin County

Court of Common Pleas – Civil and Criminal Records
Access to Register of Wills and civil records is by subscription from private company-Infocon at www.infoconcountyaccess.com, 814-472-6066. See note at beginning of section. Also, search criminal dockets online free at http://ujsportal.pacourts.us/WebDocketSheets/OtherCriteria.aspx.

Fulton County

Court of Common Pleas – Criminal Records
Search dockets online free at http://ujsportal.pacourts.us/WebDocketSheets/OtherCriteria.aspx.

Greene County

Court of Common Pleas – Criminal Records
Search dockets online free at http://ujsportal.pacourts.us/WebDocketSheets/OtherCriteria.aspx.

Huntingdon County

Court of Common Pleas – Civil and Criminal Records
Access is by subscription from private company-Infocon at www.infoconcountyaccess.com, 814-472-6066. Also, search criminal dockets free at http://ujsportal.pacourts.us/WebDocketSheets/OtherCriteria.aspx.

Indiana County

Court of Common Pleas – Criminal Records
Search dockets online free at http://ujsportal.pacourts.us/WebDocketSheets/OtherCriteria.aspx.

Jefferson County
Court of Common Pleas – Criminal Records
Search dockets online free at http://ujsportal.pacourts.us/WebDocketSheets/OtherCriteria.aspx.

Juniata County
Court of Common Pleas – Criminal Records
Search dockets online free at http://ujsportal.pacourts.us/WebDocketSheets/OtherCriteria.aspx.

Register of Wills – Civil Records
Access is by subscription from private company-Infocon at www.infoconcountyaccess.com, 814-472-6066. See beginning of section.

Lackawanna County
Court of Common Pleas – Criminal Records
Search dockets online free at http://ujsportal.pacourts.us/WebDocketSheets/OtherCriteria.aspx.

Lancaster County
Court of Common Pleas – Civil Records
www.co.lancaster.pa.us/courts/site/default.asp
Access to the Prothonotary's civil court records is free at www.co.lancaster.pa.us/scripts/bannerweb.dll. Also, historical court case schedules are free at www.co.lancaster.pa.us, click on "Court Schedules" Includes Register, Treasurer, and other courthouse record data. Search by name or case number. Call Kathy Harris at 717-299-8252 for more information.

Court of Common Pleas – Criminal Records
www.co.lancaster.pa.us/courts/site/default.asp
Search dockets online free at http://ujsportal.pacourts.us/WebDocketSheets/OtherCriteria.aspx.

Lawrence County
Court of Common Pleas – Civil and Criminal Records
www.co.lawrence.pa.us
Access is by subscription from private company-Infocon at www.infoconcountyaccess.com, 814-472-6066. See note at beginning of section. Also, search criminal dockets free at http://ujsportal.pacourts.us/WebDocketSheets/OtherCriteria.aspx.

Lebanon County
Court of Common Pleas – Criminal Records
Search dockets online free at http://ujsportal.pacourts.us/WebDocketSheets/OtherCriteria.aspx.

Lehigh County
Court of Common Pleas – Civil and Criminal Records
www.lccpa.org
Access to the county online system requires annual usage fee. Search by name or case number. Call Lehigh Cty Fiscal Office at 610-782-3112 for more information. Also, search criminal dockets free at http://ujsportal.pacourts.us/WebDocketSheets/OtherCriteria.aspx. Also, free criminal access is under development; currently calendars and bench warrants are online at www.lehighcountycourt.org under "Calendars & Schedules."

Luzerne County
Court of Common Pleas – Criminal Records
As of 12/5/2005, search dockets online free at http://ujsportal.pacourts.us/WebDocketSheets/OtherCriteria.aspx.

Lycoming County
Court of Common Pleas – Criminal Records
Search dockets online free at http://ujsportal.pacourts.us/WebDocketSheets/OtherCriteria.aspx.

McKean County
Court of Common Pleas – Criminal Records
Search dockets online free at http://ujsportal.pacourts.us/WebDocketSheets/OtherCriteria.aspx.

Mercer County
Court of Common Pleas – Civil and Criminal Records
Access is by subscription from private company-Infocon at www.infoconcountyaccess.com, 814-472-6066. See note at beginning of section. Also, search criminal dockets free at http://ujsportal.pacourts.us/WebDocketSheets/OtherCriteria.aspx.

Mifflin County

Court of Common Pleas – Civil and Criminal Records
www.co.mifflin.pa.us/mifflin/site/default.asp
The court calendar available at the website. Internet access to Register of Wills and civil records is by subscription from a private company-Infocon at www.ic-access.com, 814-472-6066. See note at beginning of section. The court calendar at the website. Internet access to court records is by subscription from a private company-Infocon at www.ic-access.com, 814-472-6066. See note at beginning of section. Also, search dockets online free at http://ujsportal.pacourts.us/WebDocketSheets/OtherCriteria.aspx.

Monroe County

Court of Common Pleas – Criminal Records
Search dockets online free at http://ujsportal.pacourts.us/WebDocketSheets/OtherCriteria.aspx.

Register of Wills – Civil Records
Access to wills is through a private company at www.landex.com/remote/. Fee is $.20 per minute and $.50 per fax page. Wills go back to 11/1836.

Montgomery County

Court of Common Pleas – Civil and Criminal Records
http://www2.montcopa.org
Court and other records are free online at www.montcopa.org/mway/index.html. This includes active and purged civil cases, also active probate cases.
Also, search criminal dockets free at http://ujsportal.pacourts.us/WebDocketSheets/OtherCriteria.aspx.

Montour County

Court of Common Pleas – Civil and Criminal Records
www.montourco.org/montour/site/default.asp
Access to Register of Wills and civil records is by subscription from private company-Infocon at www.infoconcountyaccess.com, 814-472-6066. See note at beginning of section. Internet access to court records is by subscription from a private company-Infocon at www.ic-access.com, 814-472-6066. See note at beginning of section. Also, as of 8/29/2005, search dockets online free at http://ujsportal.pacourts.us/WebDocketSheets/OtherCriteria.aspx.

Northampton County

Court of Common Pleas – Criminal Records
www.nccpa.org
Search calendars and schedules for free online at www.nccpa.org/schedule.html. Also, as of 10/17/2005, search dockets online free at http://ujsportal.pacourts.us/WebDocketSheets/OtherCriteria.aspx.

Northumberland County

Court of Common Pleas – Criminal Records
Search dockets online free at http://ujsportal.pacourts.us/WebDocketSheets/OtherCriteria.aspx.

Perry County

Court of Common Pleas – Criminal Records
Search dockets online free at http://ujsportal.pacourts.us/WebDocketSheets/OtherCriteria.aspx.

Philadelphia County

Court of Common Pleas – Civil Records
http://courts.phila.gov
Access to 1st Judicial District Civil Trial records is free at http://fjdwebserver.phila.gov. Search by name, judgment and docket information. There is also a civil docket access name search at http://courts.phila.gov.

Municipal Court - Civil – Civil Records
http://fjd.phila.gov
Access muni court dockets online free at http://claims.courtapps.com/phmuni/cms/search2.do.

Municipal Court - Misdemeanor – Criminal Records
http://courts.phila.gov./municipal/criminal
Access free to docket info at http://claims.courtapps.com/phmuni/publicLogin.jsp.

Pike County

Court of Common Pleas – Civil and Criminal Records

Access to Register of Wills and civil records is by subscription from private company-Infocon at www.infoconcountyaccess.com, 814-472-6066. See note at beginning of section. Internet access to court records is by subscription from a private company-Infocon at www.ic-access.com, 814-472-6066. See note at beginning of section. Also, search criminal dockets free at http://ujsportal.pacourts.us/WebDocketSheets/OtherCriteria.aspx.

Potter County

Court of Common Pleas – Civil and Criminal Records
Access to Register of Will and civil records is by subscription from private company-Infocon at www.infoconcountyaccess.com, 814-472-6066. See note at beginning of section. Also, search criminal dockets free at http://ujsportal.pacourts.us/WebDocketSheets/OtherCriteria.aspx.

Schuylkill County

Court of Common Pleas – Civil and Criminal Records
www.co.schuylkill.pa.us
Access civil court records and judgments free at www.co.schuylkill.pa.us/info/Civil/Inquiry/Search.csp. Search criminal dockets free at http://ujsportal.pacourts.us/WebDocketSheets/OtherCriteria.aspx.

Snyder County

Court of Common Pleas – Criminal Records
www.seda-cog.org/snyder/site/default.asp
Search dockets online free at http://ujsportal.pacourts.us/WebDocketSheets/OtherCriteria.aspx.

Somerset County

Court of Common Pleas – Criminal Records
www.co.somerset.pa.us
As of 9/6/2005, search dockets online free at http://ujsportal.pacourts.us/WebDocketSheets/OtherCriteria.aspx.

Sullivan County

Court of Common Pleas – Criminal Records
As of 5/23/2005, search dockets online free at http://ujsportal.pacourts.us/WebDocketSheets/OtherCriteria.aspx.

Susquehanna County

Court of Common Pleas – Civil and Criminal Records
Access is by subscription from private company-Infocon at www.infoconcountyaccess.com, 814-472-6066. See note at beginning of section. Also, search criminal dockets free at http://ujsportal.pacourts.us/WebDocketSheets/OtherCriteria.aspx.

Tioga County

Court of Common Pleas – Criminal Records
Search dockets online free at http://ujsportal.pacourts.us/WebDocketSheets/OtherCriteria.aspx.

Register of Wills – Civil Records
Access to wills is through a private company at www.landex.com/remote/. Fee is $.20 per minute and $.50 per fax page. Images and wills go back to 2/1999.

Union County

Court of Common Pleas – Criminal Records
www.unionco.org
Search dockets online free at http://ujsportal.pacourts.us/WebDocketSheets/OtherCriteria.aspx.

Register of Wills – Civil Records
Search wills online at www.courthouseonline.com/WillsSearch.asp?State=PA&County=Union&Abbrev=Un&Office=RW .

Venango County

Court of Common Pleas – Criminal Records
www.co.venango.pa.us
Search dockets online free at http://ujsportal.pacourts.us/WebDocketSheets/OtherCriteria.aspx.

Warren County

Court of Common Pleas – Criminal Records
Search dockets online free at http://ujsportal.pacourts.us/WebDocketSheets/OtherCriteria.aspx.

Washington County

Court of Common Pleas – Criminal Records
www.co.washington.pa.us
As of 6/20/2005, search dockets online free at http://ujsportal.pacourts.us/WebDocketSheets/OtherCriteria.aspx.

Wayne County

Court of Common Pleas – Criminal Records
Search criminal dockets free at http://ujsportal.pacourts.us/WebDocketSheets/OtherCriteria.aspx.

Westmoreland County

Court of Common Pleas – Civil Records
www.co.westmoreland.pa.us
Access civil court dockets back to 1985 free at http://westmorelandweb400.us:8088/EGSPublicAccess.htm. Also, search Register of
Wills and marriages free back to 1986. Access to full remote online system has $100 setup (no set-up if accessed via Internet) plus $20
monthly minimum. System includes civil, criminal, prothonotary indexes and recorder data. For info, call 724-830-3874, or click on
"e-services" at website.

Court of Common Pleas - Criminal – Criminal Records
www.co.westmoreland.pa.us
Access to the commercial setup plus monthly minimum fee. For info, call 724-830-3734 or click on "e-services" at
www.co.westmoreland.pa.us. Also, search dockets online free at http://ujsportal.pacourts.us/WebDocketSheets/OtherCriteria.aspx.

Wyoming County

Court of Common Pleas – Criminal Records
Search dockets online free at http://ujsportal.pacourts.us/WebDocketSheets/OtherCriteria.aspx.

York County

Court of Common Pleas – Civil and Criminal Records
www.york-county.org/departments/courts/crtf1.htm
Access to the remote online system is set-up through Information Services. For more information call 717-771-9235. Also, search
criminal dockets free at http://ujsportal.pacourts.us/WebDocketSheets/OtherCriteria.aspx.

Register of Wills – Civil Records
Access to wills is through a private company at www.landex.com/remote/. Fee is $.20 per minute and $.50 per fax page. Images and
wills go back to 2/1999.

County Level ... Recorders & Assessors

Recording Office Organization: 67 counties, 67 recording offices and 134 UCC filing offices. Each
county has two different recording offices: the Prothonotary - their term for "Clerk" - who accepted UCC and
tax lien filings until 07/01/2001, and the Recorder of Deeds who maintains real estate records. All federal and
state tax liens on personal property and on real property are filed with the Prothonotary. Usually, tax liens on
personal property are filed in the judgment index of the Prothonotary. Some Prothonotaries will perform tax
lien searches. Search fees are usually $5.00 per name.

Online Access Note: A number of counties provide web access to assessor data. Also, the Infocon County
Access System provides internet and direct dial-up access to recorded record information for over twenty
Pennsylvania counties; for information call Infocon at 814-472-6066 or visit www.infoconcountyaccess.com

Allegheny County Prothonotary *UCC, Tax Lien, Real Estate, Assessor Records*

http://prothonotary.county.allegheny.pa.us
Access to records is free at http://prothonotary.county.allegheny.pa.us/allegheny/welcome.htm. Registration is required. UCC records
are pre-7-1-2001. Online access to the certified values database is free at the website. Also, online access to Allegheny County real
estate database is free at http://www2.county.allegheny.pa.us/realestate/Search.asp.

Allegheny County Recorder *Recorder, Deed, Mortgage, Real Estate Records*

www.county.allegheny.pa.us

Access Allegheny Recorder's Index free at https://www.recorder.county.allegheny.pa.us/palr/pa003/index.jsp. Index goes back to 1986; images to 2002. Fee for doc is $1.00 per page, max fee 10 pages; Commercial draw down account copy fee is $.50 per page. Also, Land & A/R Inquiries found at www.county.allegheny.pa.us/dcs/dcsland.asp.

Armstrong County
Real Estate, Recording, Marriage, Prothonotary, Tax Lien, Judgment, Probate, Orphans Court Records
Access is through a private company. For info, call Infocon at 814-472-6066 or www.infoconcountyaccess.com. Includes Orphan Court, Recorder of Deeds, Register of Wills images.

Beaver County Recorder   *Real Estate, Deed, Mortgage, Assessor Records*
www.co.beaver.pa.us
Access to the Recorder's database is free at www.co.beaver.pa.us/Recorder/disclaimer.htm. Deed index back to 1957, images to 1957. Access the Assessment office at www.co.beaver.pa.us/AssessmentPublic/.

Bedford County   *Real Estate, Recorder, Assessor, Probate, Marriage, RE Assessor, Tax Claim, Prothonotary, Tax Lien, Judgment Records*
www.bedford.net/regrec/home.html
Access is via a private company; call Infocon at 814-472-6066 or www.infoconcountyaccess.com. Includes Recorder of Deeds and Register of Wills images.

Berks County Prothonotary   *Judgment, Lien, UCC, Civil Court Records*
www.co.berks.pa.us/berks/cwp/view.asp?a=1150&q=444559
Prothonotary offers internet access to above info back to 1/1996. Fee is $300. For info, call 610-478-6967.

Berks County Recorder   *Vital Statistic, Probate, DR Warrant Records*
www.berksrecofdeeds.com
Access to the Registry of Wills' databases are free at www.berksregofwills.com/search_page.htm including county marriage, estate, birth and death records. Estate and marriage records are current. Also, search the domestic relations warrants list at www.drs.berks.pa.us/dro_warrant_list.htm.

Blair County   *Real Estate, Recording, Assessor, Marriage, Probate, Orphans Court, Tax Claim, Prothonotary, Tax Lien, Judgment, Civil Records*
www.blairco.org
Access is via a private company; call Infocon at 814-472-6066 or www.infoconcountyaccess.com. Indexes from 1998.

Bradford County Recorder   *Real Estate, Deed, Mortgage, Will Records*
Access to Recorder of Deeds and Wills and Orphans Court is by subscription at www.landex.com/remote/. Fee is $.20 per minute, $.50 per fax page. Recorder data goes back to 1971. Images go back to 1985, also 1985-89. Wills and orphan court goes back to 1997.

Bucks County   *Assessor, Recorder, Real Estate, Prothonotary, Tax Lien, Probate, Court, Will, Voter Registration, Sheriff Sales, Probate, Vital Statistic Records*
www.buckscounty.org/courts/
Access prothonotary records free at http://4.43.65.248/menu.asp back to 1980. Includes lending agency, Register of Wills, liens, sheriff sales, voter registration, civil and criminal courts as well as assessor and recorder of deeds records. For info on the new fee system, contact Jack Morris 215-348-6579 or view details at website. Search civil cases directly at http://4.43.65.248/autoform.asp?app=cvr. Search family and domestic dockets free at http://4.43.65.248/autoform.asp?app=fcr. Access to Vital Records at www.vitalchek.com.

Butler County   *Marriage, Judgment, Prothonotary, Fed Lien, Divorce, Probate, Orphans Court, Guardianship, Commitment Records*
www.co.butler.pa.us
Access marriage, probate, and prothonotary records via a private company; call Infocon at 814-472-6066, www.infoconcountyaccess.com. Images available. Also access probate court estate and guardianship records free at http://66.117.197.22/index.cfm?page=home. At bottom of webpage, click on the type of "lookup" you want.

Cambria County   *Property, Assessor, Marriage, Probate, Tax Claim, Orphans Court, Tax Claim, Prothonotary, Lien, Civil, Judgment, Divorce Records Records*
www.co.cambria.pa.us/cambria

Access Cambria County records via a private company. Subscription required; images available. For info, call Infocon at 814-472-6066, www.infoconcountyaccess.com.

Carbon County Prothonotary *Tax Lien, Judgment, UCC, Probate, Will Records*

Access to county prothonotary, Register of Wills, and Clerk of Courts remote public access dial-up database is free; 570-325-3288; instructions/ registration at www.carboncourts.com/pubacc.htm.

Carbon County Recorder *Property, Assessor Records*

www.carboncounty.com/deeds.htm
Access assessor property data free at www.carboncounty.com/records.htm.

Centre County Prothonotary *Fed Lien, Judgment, Marriage, Personal Property Records*

www.co.centre.pa.us/223.htm
Access Prothonotary data and more at http://epin.chesco.org; registration and fees required.

Centre County Recorder

Real Estate, Recorder, Deed, Domestic Relations Warrant, Tax Assessment, Naturalization, Slave Records
www.co.centre.pa.us/133.htm
Access Recorder data by online subscription; fee is $250 set-up plus $.10 per click or other per click plan. This replaces the old dial-up system. See http://webia.co.centre.pa.us/login.asp. Also, access pre-1929 naturalization and slave records free at http://county.centreconnect.org/hrip/index.htm. Also, access to the county list of bench warrants for child support non-payment is free at http://county.centreconnect.org/drs/default.asp.

Chester County Recorder *Real Estate, Recording, Deed, Vital Statistic, Prothonotary, Property Tax, Warrant, Lien, Assessor, Genealogy, Archive Records*

http://dsf.chesco.org/recorder/site/default.asp
Searching countywide records including court records requires a sign-up and credit card payment. Application fee is $50. with $10.00 per month minimum -no charge for no activity; and $.10 each transaction beyond 100. Sign-up and/or logon at http://epin.chesco.org. Also purchase county data as reports, labels, magnetic tape, and diskette. Also, genealogical and older vital statistics are free at http://dsf.chesco.org/archives/site/default.asp. Also, search Recorder of Deeds records free at http://rod.chesco.org/icris/splash.jsp.

Clarion County Recorder *Real Estate, Recording, Assessor, OCC/PC, Marriage, Voter Registration, Orphans Court, Probate, Tax Claim, Prothonotary, Tax Lien, Judgment Records*

Access is through a private company. For info, call Infocon at 814-472-6066 or www.infoconcountyaccess.com. Includes images for Recorder, Register of Wills, and Orphans court.

Clearfield County Recorder *Real Estate, Deed, Mortgage, Probate, Orphans Court Records*

www.clearfieldco.org
Access to Recorder of Deeds and Wills and Orphans Court is by subscription at www.landex.com/remote/. Fee is $.20 per minute, $.50 per fax page. Recorder data goes back to 1986. Images go back to 1997. Wills and orphan court records go back to 1990. Also, assessors county tax sale list is updated weekly at www.clearfieldco.org/tax_sale_list.html.

Clinton County *Real Estate, Recorder, Assessor, Probate, Orphan Court, Property, Tax Claim, Prothonotary, Tax Lien, Judgment Records*

www.clintoncountypa.com/register_&_recorder.htm
Access to limited property data is free at www.clintoncountypa.com; click on "Parcel Query by Name." Site may be down. Also, access available via a private company. For info call Infocom at 814-472-6066 or www.infoconcountyaccess.com. Includes images for Recorder, Register of Wills, Orphans Court, Prothonotary.

Columbia County Recorder *Real Estate, Deed, Recording, UCC Records*

www.columbiapa.org/reg_rec/index.html
Access is via a private company at www.landex.com/remote/. Fee is $.20 per minute. Recorders index goes back to 1974; wills index back to 1995; UCCs to 1992; images go back to 1/1974; wills and UCCs to 10/1999.

Cumberland County Recorder *Property Tax, Assessor, Real Estate, Recording, Marriage, Orphans Court, Probate, Tax Claim, Prothonotary, Tax Lien, Judgment, Cemetery Records*

Access to the property assessment data is free at www.ccpa.net/cumberland/cwp/view.asp?A=1137&Q=479825. No name searching. Also, access available via a private company. For info call Infocom at 814-472-6066 or www.infoconcountyaccess.com. Includes images for Recorder of Deeds records. Also, search cemetery records free on a private company site at www.rootsweb.com/~usgenweb/pa/cumberland/cemet.htm.

Dauphin County Recorder *Property, Assessor, Property Sale Records*

Access to county property data is free at www.dauphinpropertyinfo.org/propertymax/rover30.asp. To search free, create a limited guest account. Full access fee is $50.00 per month. If you wish to include property sales data, there is an add'l fee of $20.00

Delaware County Recorder *Assessor, Deed, Real Estate, Judgment Records*

http://www2.co.delaware.pa.us/pa/default.htm
Access to the public access system is free - temporarily - at http://www2.co.delaware.pa.us/pa/publicaccess.asp. Records go back to 1982. No name searching.

Erie County Recorder *Real Estate, Sale, Recorder, Marriage, Probate, Orphan Court, Sale List Records*

www.eriecountygov.org
Recorder access is through a private company. Includes images, courts, and prothonotary; call Infocon at 814-472-6066 or www.infoconcountyaccess.com. Also, access property records data free at www.eriepa.us/Assessment/Property/Search.aspx, no name searching. Data for real estate professionals available by subscription at https://secure.eriepa.us/Login.aspx?ReturnUrl=%2fMembers%2fProfessional.aspx. Also, you may purchase judicial and/or sheriff sale property sale lists for $10.00 each, see https://secure.eriepa.us/Assessment/Property/PropertySales.aspx.

Fayette County

Property, Assessor, Marriage, Will, Probate, Prothonotary, Tax Lien, Judgment, Orphans Court Records
Access to property assessments is free at www.fayetteproperty.org/assessor. Also, search marriages, orphan court, and Register of Wills data from a private company; for info call Infocom at 814-472-6066 or www.infoconcountyaccess.com.

Franklin County *Real Estate, Recorder, Probate, Prothonotary, Tax Lien, Judgment Records*

http://co.franklin.pa.us
Access is via a private company; call Infocon at 814-472-6066 or www.infoconcountyaccess.com. Prothonotary record images not available online.

Greene County Recorder *Property, Assessor, Real Estate, Deed Records*

http://co.greene.pa.us
Access Assessor property records by web subscription, see www.co.greene.pa.us/secured/gc/depts/cc/asses/prop-records.htm or call Pam at 724-627-5428. Fee is $700 per year; includes Property Record Card System. Also, real estate deed records by subscription at http://216.27.81.170/login.asp. Contact Recorder office for sign-up details. Real estate deed records also available on microfilm. Microfilm images are also available.

Huntingdon County *Real Estate, Recorder, Marriage, Probate, Prothonotary, Tax Lien, Judgment, Orphans Court Records*

http://huntingdoncounty.net
Access is via a private company; call Infocon at 814-472-6066 or www.infoconcountyaccess.com.

Juniata County Recorder *Real Estate, Marriage, Probate, Orphans Court Records*

Access is via a private company; call Infocon at 814-472-6066 or www.infoconcountyaccess.com. Includes Recorder's record images.

Lackawanna County Recorder *Assessor, Property Records*

www.lackawannacounty.org
Access property data free at http://ao.lackawannacounty.org/agreed.php.

Lancaster County Recorder *Assessor, Real Estate, Recording, Tax Lien, UCC Records*

www.lancasterdeeds.com/lanco_rod/site/default.asp
Access to deeds, UCCs and other recordings is free at http://icris.lancasterdeeds.com/icris/splash.jsp. Also, access to property data is free on the GIS-mapping site at www.co.lancaster.pa.us/gis/site/default.asp?. Click on GIS-Property Search, then choose Query to search by owner name.

Lawrence County *Real Estate, Recording, Deed, Marriage, Probate, Prothonotary, Tax Lien, Judgment, Orphans Court, Assessor, Property Tax Records*

www.co.lawrence.pa.us

Access is via a private company; document images included; call Infocon at 814-472-6066 or www.infoconcountyaccess.com. Also, search assessments pdf pages by ward, borough or town at www.co.lawrence.pa.us/Preliminary_Assessment/Preliminary_Assessment.html

Lebanon County Recorder   *Real Estate, Deed, Lien, Judgment, Recording, Assessor Records*
www.lebcounty.org
Access to Recorder of Deeds official records is by subscription at www.landex.com/remote/. For info call OSS at 717-274-5890. Deed and mortgage index back to 1933; Misc index back to 1972; Deed images back to 1996; Mortgage images back to 2000; Miscellaneous images back to 2001. Also, access property data by subscription at www.courthouseonline.com/MyProperty.asp. Sub fee $9.95 3-days, up to $275 per year. View for free if you have control number and password from tax notice or are registered.

Lehigh County
Tax Lien, Judgment, Assessor, Property, Tax Sale, Delinquent Taxes, County Grants, Game License Records
County's full-access internet pay system initial cost is $318.00 a year but that fee is being reduced since the database is now smaller; a per minute usage fee may apply. For signup info, call the Fiscal Office at 610-782-3112 or County Computer Svcs Dept at 610-782-3286. Also, at www.lehighcounty.org, the County Grants database is searched free; free registration required. You may also search assessments at www.lehighcounty.org/Assessment/Puba.cfm but no name searching. Also, search tax sale data by community free at www.lehighcounty.org/Fiscal/taxsale.cfm.

Luzerne County Recorder   *Recorder, Deed, Land, Property Tax, Assessor Records*
www.luzernecounty.org
Access is through a private company at www.landex.com/remote/. Fee is $.20 per minute. Index goes back to 1/1993; images go back to 9/1993. Also, access county property assessment database at www.wbtimesleader.com/cgi-bin/authenticate.cgi. Also, access property data by subscription at www.courthouseonline.com/MyProperty.asp. Sub fee $9.95 3-days, up to $275 per year. A free view available if you have control number and password from tax notice or are registered.

Lycoming County Recorder   *Property, Assessor Records*
Access property data by subscription at www.courthouseonline.com/MyProperty.asp. Sub fee $9.95 3-days, up to $275 per year. A free view available if you have control number and password from tax notice or are registered.

Mercer County   *Property, Assessor, Occ/PC, Tax Claim, Prothonotary, Tax Lien, Judgment Records*
www.mcc.co.mercer.pa.us
Access to recorded records is available at http://141.151.130.246/resolution/. Also, access to index is via a private company. For info, call Infocon at 814-472-6066 or www.infoconcountyaccess.com.

Mifflin County Recorder   *Real Estate, Recorder, Assessor, Probate, GIS Mapping, Prothonotary, Tax Lien, Judgment, Orphans Court, Marriage, Tax Claim Records*
www.co.mifflin.pa.us/mifflin
Access is via a private company; call Infocon at 814-472-6066 or www.infoconcountyaccess.com; recorder back to 1993, probate, orphans and marriages back to 2000; images soon to be available for Recorder records, indexes for others. Also, property data is free at http://gis.co.mifflin.pa.us/website/mifflincounty/viewer.htm?. Use the new free Web Mapping Parcel Application to name search for property data.

Monroe County Prothonotary   *Tax Lien, Judgment, Marriage Records*
Access is via a private company; call Infocon at 814-472-6066 or www.infoconcountyaccess.com.

Monroe County Recorder   *Real Estate, Deed, Will, Mortgage Records*
Access is through a private company at www.landex.com/remote/. Fee is $.20 per minute and $.50 per fax page. Land Index goes back to 1/1979; wills go back to 11/1836; images go back to 8/1997.

Montgomery County Recorder   *Assessor, Real Estate, Recording, Deed, Tax Lien, Owner Name, Estate, Tax Claim Property Records*
www.montcopa.org
Register of Deeds records are free at www.montcopa.org/MWAY/index.html. There are several search options. Records on the County PIR database are free at www.montcopa.org/reassessment/boahome0.htm. Records date back to 1990. Lending agency and prothonotary information are on the system. Also, search estate names for free at www.montcopa.org/MWAY/estate.html. Search BOA owner names at www.montcopa.org/MWAY/owner.html Also, search tax claim properties list at www.montcopa.org/taxclaim/repoproperties.asp.

Montour County
Real Estate, Recorder, Deed, Probate, Marriage, Prothonotary, Tax Lien, Judgment, Orphans Court Records
www.montourco.org/montour
Access to Register of Deeds data is by subscription from a private company, visit www.infoconcountyaccess.com. Also includes Prothonotary, Clerk of Courts. Will index 1850 to present is free at www.montour.org, click on Register & Recorder, then Will Index, or try www.montourco.org/montour/cwp/view.asp?a=770&Q=417826&montourNav=|8473|.

Northampton County Recorder *Real Estate, Deed, Mortgage, Misc. Recording, Property, Assessor Records*
http://northamptoncounty.org
Two sources available. One is a private company at www.landex.com/remote/. Fee is $.20 per minute and $.50 per fax page. Deeds data goes back to 11/85; mortgages to 2/86; faxable images go back to 11/85. Also, online access to assessor's property records data is free at www.ncpub.org/Main/Home.aspx.

Northumberland County Recorder *Real Estate, Recorder, Deed, Probate, Orphans Court Records*
Access to Recorder of Deeds, Register of Wills and Orphans Court is by subscription at www.landex.com/remote/. Fee is $.20 per minute, $.50 per fax page. Land data and images go back to 1974; images to 1820; Wills back to 1999; Orphans to 1987.

Perry County Recorder *Real Estate, Deed, Assessor, Property Tax Records*
Access to Recorder of Deeds is by subscription at www.landex.com/remote/. Fee is $.20 per minute, $.50 per fax page. Recorder data goes back to 1973; images to 1820. Also, access property data by subscription at www.courthouseonline.com/MyProperty.asp. Sub fee $9.95 3-days, up to $275 per year. A free view available if you have control number and password from tax notice or are registered.

Philadelphia County Prothonotary *Judgment, Lien Records*
Assess to Prothonotary records is free at http://fjdweb2.phila.gov/fjd1/repl1/zk_fjd_public_qry_00.zp_main_idx.html. Also, includes judgments and liens on behalf of governmental entities. Also, search Board of Revision of Taxes records for free at http://brtweb.phila.gov/index.aspx. No name searching.

Philadelphia County Recorder *Property, Assessor, Death, Recording, Deed, UCC Records*
http://philadox.phila.gov
Search property assessment data for free at http://brtweb.phila.gov/index.aspx. No name searching. Also, name search recorder data for a fee at http://philadox.phila.gov/; registration required; fee is $125.00 per month or $15.00 per hour. Or, $750 per year or $60.00 per week. Images go back to 1976, index to 1957. Also, name searching is by subscription from a private company at http://currentstatus.com; call 800-477-8288 for info. Also, search Philadelphia area obituaries for free at www.legacy.com/philly/DeathNotices.asp.

Pike County Recorder
Property, Assessor, Probate, Marriage, Prothonotary, Tax Lien, Judgment, Orphans Court Records
www.pikepa.org/recorder.htm
Access property data free at www.pikegis.org/pike/viewer.htm. Also, access is through a private company. For info, call Infocon at 814-472-6066 or www.infoconcountyaccess.com.

Potter County Recorder *Real Estate, Assessor, Probate, Marriage, Prothonotary, Tax Lien, Judgment,*
Orphans Court, Tax Claim Records
Access is via a private company; call Infocon at 814-472-6066 or www.infoconcountyaccess.com.

Schuylkill County Prothonotary *Judgment, Marriage, Sheriff Sale Records*
www.co.schuylkill.pa.us
Search marriage dockets 1885-1969 and 1989-present free at www.co.schuylkill.pa.us/info/Offices/Archives/MarriageDockets.csp. Also, judgments on civil court files at www.co.schuylkill.pa.us/info/Civil/Inquiry/Search.csp.

Somerset County Prothonotary *Property, Assessor, Maps Records*
www.co.somerset.pa.us
Access property records by monthly subscription; $35.00 start-up fee plus $10.00 per month. For info or signup, call Cindy or John at 814-445-1536. Provide your email, company info and check. System will eventually provide images and comparable sales.

Somerset County Recorder *Real Estate, Deed, Lien, Judgment, Recording Records*
www.co.somerset.pa.us
Access is through a private company at www.landex.com/remote/. Fee is $.20 per minute and $.50 per fax page. Recorders index and images go back to 1/1985.

Susquehanna County Recorder   *Property, Assessor, Prothonotary, Tax Lien, Judgment Records*
www.susqco.com/subsites/gov/pages/govhome.htm
Access property data by subscription at www.courthouseonline.com/MyProperty.asp. Sub fee $9.95 3-days, up to $275 per year. A free view available if you have control number and password from tax notice or are registered.

Tioga County Recorder   *Real Estate, Deed, Will, Property, Assessor Records*
www.tiogacountypa.us
Access is through a private company at www.landex.com/remote/. Fee is $.20 per minute and $.50 per fax page. Recorders data goes back to 1977; images and wills go back to 2/1999. Also, access property data by subscription at www.courthouseonline.com/MyProperty.asp. Sub fee $9.95 3-days, up to $275 per year. A free view available if you have control number and password from tax notice or are registered.

Union County Recorder   *Property, Assessor Records*
www.unionco.org
Access property data by subscription at www.courthouseonline.com/MyProperty.asp. Sub fee $9.95 3-days, up to $275 per year. A free view available if you have control number and password from tax notice or are registered.

Venango County Recorder   *Property, Assessor Records*
www.co.venango.pa.us/Directory/index.htm
Access property data by subscription at www.courthouseonline.com/MyProperty.asp. Subscription fee $9.95 3-days, up to $275 per year. A free view available if you have control number and password from tax notice.

Washington County Recorder   *Real Estate Tax, Treasurer, Recorder, Deed, Records*
www.co.washington.pa.us
Access treasurer real estate tax data free at www.co.washington.pa.us:81/wcmtp/tri.asp Recorded documents and deeds are being prepared for internet access and may be available by subscription later in 2006.

Wayne County Recorder   *Assessor, Property, Arrest Warrants Records*
www.co.wayne.pa.us/?pageid=10
Search assessor property data free after registering at http://taxpub.co.wayne.pa.us/Main.asp. Also, search active arrest warrants at www.co.wayne.pa.us/?pageid=42.

Westmoreland County Recorder   *Real Estate, Tax Lien, Mortgage, UCC, Deed Records*
www.co.westmoreland.pa.us
The Register's fee-based system has been replaced by a free, searchable site at www.wcdeeds.us/dts/default.asp. Choose simple, advanced, or instrument search.

York County Recorder   *Assessor, Real Estate, Deed, Death, Naturalization Records*
www.york-county.org/departments/deeds/deeds.htm
Two sources available. Online access to the assessor database is free through the GIS data at http://207.140.67.68/york. Also, access is by subscription from Landex at www.landex.com/remote. Base fee is $.20 per minute, $.50 per fax page. Records go back to 1990; images to 1990. Search inmate list at www.york-county.org/departments/prison/prison.htm. View sheriff's most wanteds at http://ycwebserver.york-county.org/sheriff/MostWanted.htm Also, search parcel numbers at www.york-county.org/departments/assessment/tx_asmnt.htm. Search the death index prior to 1959 at www.york-county.org/cgi-bin/Affdeath.cgi; naturalizations at www.york-county.org/cgi-bin/natural.cgi.

Federal Courts in Pennsylvania...

Standards for Federal Courts: The universal PACER sign-up number is 800-676-6856. Find PACER and the Party/Case Index on the Web at http://pacer.psc.uscourts.gov. PACER dial-up access is $.60 per minute. Also, courts offering internet access via PACER, Web-PACER or the new CM-ECF charge $.08 per page fee ($.07 per page if record is pre-2005 or unless noted as free).

US District Court -- Eastern District of Pennsylvania

www.paed.uscourts.gov

PACER: Sign-up number is 215-597-5710. Case records are available back to 7/1990. Records are purged never. New records are available online after 1 day. **Electronic Filing:** Criminal cases go back to 7/1992. CM/ECF data at https://ecf.paed.uscourts.gov. **Opinions:** Opinions go back to 1997. View court opinions at www.paed.uscourts.gov/us03006.asp. **Other Online Access:** Online access is available free at www.paed.uscourts.gov/us04000.asp?19. No fee to search; select document type and enter name as search string.

Allentown/Reading Division counties: Berks, Lancaster, Lehigh, Northampton, Schuylkill.

Philadelphia Division counties: Bucks, Chester, Delaware, Montgomery, Philadelphia.

US Bankruptcy Court -- Eastern District of Pennsylvania

www.paeb.uscourts.gov

PACER: Case records are available back to 1988. Records are purged every 6 months. New records are available online after 1 day. **PACER Online Access:** PACER online at http://pacer.paeb.uscourts.gov. **Electronic Filing:** CM/ECF data at https://ecf.paeb.uscourts.gov. **Other Online Access:** Click on "Published Opinions" at main website. Limited calendars are also available. **Phone access:** Voice Case Information System, call 215-597-2244.

Philadelphia Division counties: Bucks, Chester, Delaware, Montgomery, Philadelphia.

Reading Division counties: Berks, Lancaster, Lehigh, Northampton.

US District Court -- Middle District of Pennsylvania

www.pamd.uscourts.gov

PACER: Case records are available back to 5/1989. Records are purged never. New records are available online after 1 day. **PACER Online Access:** ECF replaces PACER. **Electronic Filing:** Document images available. CM/ECF data at https://ecf.pamd.uscourts.gov. **Opinions:** View court opinions at www.pamd.uscourts.gov/opinions.htm.

Harrisburg Division counties: Adams, Cumberland, Dauphin, Franklin, Fulton, Huntingdon, Juniata, Lebanon, Mifflin, York.

Scranton Division counties: Bradford, Carbon, Lackawanna, Luzerne, Monroe, Pike, Susquehanna, Wayne, Wyoming.

Williamsport Division counties: Cameron, Centre, Clinton, Columbia, Lycoming, Montour, Northumberland, Perry, Potter, Snyder, Sullivan, Tioga, Union.

US Bankruptcy Court -- Middle District of Pennsylvania

www.pamb.uscourts.gov

PACER: Case records are available back to 8/1986. Records are purged never. New records are available online after 1 day. **PACER Online Access:** PACER online at http://pacer.pamb.uscourts.gov. Document images available. **Electronic Filing:** CM/ECF data at https://ecf.pamb.uscourts.gov. **Other Online Access:** Calendars free at www.pamb.uscourts.gov/calendars.htm. **Phone access:** Voice Case Information System, call 877-440-2699.

Harrisburg Division counties: Adams, Centre, Cumberland, Dauphin, Franklin, Fulton, Huntingdon, Juniata, Lebanon, Mifflin, Montour, Northumberland, Perry, Schuylkill, Snyder, Union, York.

Wilkes-Barre Division counties: Bradford, Cameron, Carbon, Clinton, Columbia, Lackawanna, Luzerne, Lycoming, Monroe, Pike, Potter, Schuylkill, Sullivan, Susquehanna, Tioga, Wayne, Wyoming.

US District Court -- Western District of Pennsylvania

www.pawd.uscourts.gov

PACER: Case records are available back to 1989. Records are purged never. New records are available online after 1 day. **Electronic Filing:** CM/ECF data at https://ecf.pawd.uscourts.gov. **Opinions:** Search opinions by judge name. View court opinions at www.pawd.uscourts.gov/Pages/opinions.htm. **Other Online Access:** Access daily court calendar at www.pawd.uscourts.gov.

Erie Division counties: Crawford, Elk, Erie, Forest, McKean, Venango, Warren.

Johnstown Division counties: Bedford, Blair, Cambria, Clearfield, Somerset.

Pittsburgh Division counties: Allegheny, Armstrong, Beaver, Butler, Clarion, Fayette, Greene, Indiana, Jefferson, Lawrence, Mercer, Washington, Westmoreland.

US Bankruptcy Court -- Western District of Pennsylvania

www.pawb.uscourts.gov

PACER: Case records are available back to 1991. Records are purged every 6 months. New records are available online after 1 day. **PACER Online Access:** ECF replaces PACER. **Electronic Filing:** CM/ECF data at https://ecf.pawb.uscourts.gov. **Opinions:** View court opinions at www.pawb.uscourts.gov/opinions.htm. **Other Online Access:** Search calendars by judge name free at www.pawb.uscourts.gov/calendar.htm. **Phone access:** Voice Case Information System, call 412-355-3210.

Erie Division counties: Clarion, Crawford, Elk, Erie, Forest, Jefferson, McKean, Mercer, Venango, Warren.

Pittsburgh Division counties: Allegheny, Armstrong, Beaver, Bedford, Blair, Butler, Cambria, Clearfield, Fayette, Greene, Indiana, Lawrence, Somerset, Washington, Westmoreland.

Rhode Island

Capital: Providence
              Providence County
Time Zone: EST
Population: 1,080,632
# of Counties: 5

Quick Links

Website: www.state.ri.us/
Governor: www.governor.state.ri.us
Attorney General: www.riag.ri.gov
State Archives: www.state.ri.us/archives
State Statutes and Codes: www.rilin.state.ri.us/Lawrevision/Genlaw2005/genlaws2005.htm
Legislative Bill Search: http://dirac.rilin.state.ri.us/BillStatus/webclass1.asp
Unclaimed Funds: www.treasury.ri.gov/moneylst.htm

State Level ... Major Agencies

Statewide Court Records

Court Administrator, Supreme Court, 250 Benefit St, Providence, RI 02903; 401-222-3266, Fax-401-222-4224, 8:30AM-4:30PM.
www.courts.state.ri.us
Online search: The Rhode Island Judiciary offers free Internet access to court criminal records statewide at
http://courtconnect.courts.state.ri.us. A word of caution, this website is provided as an informational service only and should not be
relied upon as an official record of the court. Supreme Court opinions are available from the website. **Other options:** Bulk data is
available, call for details.

Incarceration Records

Rhode Island Department of Corrections, Records, PO Box 8249, (Courier: 40 Howard Avenue, Cranston, RI 02920); 401-462-3900,
Fax-401-462-2630, 8AM-4:30PM.
www.doc.state.ri.us
Online search: There is no access to inmate records through the agency, however the agency refers requesters to a private company
offers free web access to DOC records at www.vinelink.com/index.jsp.

Corporation, Fictitious Name, Limited Partnerships, Limited Liability Companies, Limited Liability Partnerships, Not For Profit Entities

Secretary of State, Corporations Div., 100 N Main St, Providence, RI 02903-1335; 401-222-3040, Fax-401-222-1309, 8:30-4:30.
www.corps.state.ri.us/corporations.htm
Online search: At the web, search filings for active and inactive Rhode Island and foreign business corporations, non-profit
corporations, limited partnerships, limited liability companies, and limited liability partnerships. Weekly listings of new corporations
are also available. There is no fee. **Other options:** The corporation database may be purchased on CD.

Driver Records

Division of Motor Vehicles, Driving Record Clerk, Operator Control, 286 Main St, Pawtucket, RI 02860; 401-721-2650, 8:30\-4:30.
www.dmv.state.ri.us
Online search: Driving records are available online for permissible users from the state's web portal. The fee is $18.00 per record. All
users must be approved by the DMV's Administrator's Office. For details, please call Ms. Darlene Walsh at 401-588-3003.

State Level ... Occupational Licensing

Acupuncturist............................. http://health.ri.mylicense.com
Ambulatory Care Facility .... http://health.ri.mylicense.com
Asbestos Abatement Worker .... http://health.ri.mylicense.com
Assisted Living Facility .... http://health.ri.mylicense.com
Athletic Trainer............................ http://health.ri.mylicense.com
Audiologist .... http://health.ri.mylicense.com
Automobile Body Shop ... www.dbr.state.ri.us/pdf_forms/clr/Auto%20Body%20Shop%20-%20Licensee%20List.pdf
Automobile Glass Installer .... www.dbr.state.ri.us/pdf_forms/clr/Auto%20Glass%20-%20Licensee%20List.pdf
Automobile Wrecker   ...   www.dbr.state.ri.us/pdf_forms/clr/Auto%20Wrecking%20-%20Licensee%20List.pdf
Barber Shop .... http://health.ri.mylicense.com
Barber/Barber Instructor .... http://health.ri.mylicense.com
Birth Center .... http://health.ri.mylicense.com
Blood Test Screener...................... http://health.ri.mylicense.com
Cable Installer.............................. www.crb.state.ri.us/search.php
Charter School .... www.ridoe.net/charterschools/list.htm
Check Casher................................ www.dbr.state.ri.us/pdf_forms/bank/List%20of%20Licensees%2001-28-04.pdf
Chimney Sweep .... www.crb.state.ri.us/search.php
Chiropractor................................. http://health.ri.mylicense.com
Clinical Lab Scientist, Cytogenetichttp://health.ri.mylicense.com/
Clinical Lab Scientist/Technician . http://health.ri.mylicense.com/
Contractor, Resid'l Building.......... www.crb.state.ri.us/search.php
Contractor, Watch List.................. www.crb.state.ri.us/watchlist.php
Controlled Substance Wholesaler . http://health.ri.mylicense.com/
Cosmetologist/Cosmetology Instr. http://health.ri.mylicense.com
CPA .... www.dbr.state.ri.us/pdf_forms/ba/Licensed%20CPAs%20and%20PAs.pdf
Cytotechnologist .... http://health.ri.mylicense.com/
Debt Pooler .... www.dbr.state.ri.us/pdf_forms/bank/List%20of%20Licensees%2001-28-04.pdf
Dental Hygienist .... http://health.ri.mylicense.com
Dentist... http://health.ri.mylicense.com
Dietitian/Nutritionist.................... http://health.ri.mylicense.com
Electrologist................................. http://health.ri.mylicense.com
Electron Microsc'y, Lab Scientist. http://health.ri.mylicense.com/
Embalmer..................................... http://health.ri.mylicense.com
Emergency Care Facility............... http://health.ri.mylicense.com
Emergency Medical Tech/Svcs..... http://health.ri.mylicense.com
Esthetician................................... http://health.ri.mylicense.com
Financial Institution .... www.dbr.state.ri.us/pdf_forms/bank/List%20of%20Licensees%2001-28-04.pdf
Funeral Director........................... http://health.ri.mylicense.com
Group Home .... http://health.ri.mylicense.com
Hairdresser/Hairdresser Instructor http://health.ri.mylicense.com
Hazardous Waste Transporter....... www.dem.ri.gov/programs/benviron/waste/transpor/index.htm
Hearing Aid Dispenser.................. http://health.ri.mylicense.com
Histologic Technician, Clinical..... http://health.ri.mylicense.com/
Home Care Provider .... http://health.ri.mylicense.com
Home Nursing Care .... http://health.ri.mylicense.com
Hospice Provider.......................... http://health.ri.mylicense.com
Hospital....................................... http://health.ri.mylicense.com
Hypodermic Dispenser.................. http://health.ri.mylicense.com/
Insurance Broker/Producer/Agent. www.dbr.state.ri.us/lic_search.php
Interpreter for the Deaf .... http://health.ri.mylicense.com
Laboratory, Medical...................... http://health.ri.mylicense.com
Lender/Loan Broker...................... www.dbr.state.ri.us/pdf_forms/bank/List%20of%20Licensees%2001-28-04.pdf
Lobbyist .... www.corps.state.ri.us/lobby/default.asp

Manicurist/Manicurist Shop.......... http://health.ri.mylicense.com
Marriage & Family Therapist .... http://health.ri.mylicense.com
Massage Therapist .... http://health.ri.mylicense.com
Medical Doctor .... http://health.ri.mylicense.com
Medical Waste Transporter........... www.dem.ri.gov/programs/benviron/waste/transpor/index.htm
Mental Health Counselor .... http://health.ri.mylicense.com
Midwife .... http://health.ri.mylicense.com
Money Broker.............................. www.dbr.state.ri.us/pdf_forms/bank/List%20of%20Licensees%2001-28-04.pdf
Money Transferer .... www.dbr.state.ri.us/pdf_forms/bank/List%20of%20Licensees%2001-28-04.pdf
Mortgage Broker.......................... www.dbr.state.ri.us/pdf_forms/bank/List%20of%20Licensees%2001-28-04.pdf
Notary Public .... www.corps.state.ri.us/notaries/notaries.htm#data
Nuclear Medicine Technologist .... http://health.ri.mylicense.com
Nurse/Nursing Assistant .... http://health.ri.mylicense.com
Nursing Home Administrator........ http://health.ri.mylicense.com
Nursing Service .... http://health.ri.mylicense.com
Occupational Therapist .... http://health.ri.mylicense.com
Office Operatories (Medical)........ http://health.ri.mylicense.com
Optician .... http://health.ri.mylicense.com
Optometrist .... http://health.ri.mylicense.com
Osteopathic Physician.................. www.docboard.org/ri/df/search.htm
Outpatient Rehabilitation .... http://health.ri.mylicense.com
Pharmacist/Pharmacy Technician . http://health.ri.mylicense.com
Pharmacy .... http://health.ri.mylicense.com
Phlebotomy Station...................... http://health.ri.mylicense.com
Physical Therapist, Assistant .... http://health.ri.mylicense.com
Physician, Assistant .... http://health.ri.mylicense.com
Physicians Controlled Substance .. http://health.ri.mylicense.com
Podiatrist..................................... http://health.ri.mylicense.com
Prosthetist .... http://health.ri.mylicense.com
Psychologist................................ http://health.ri.mylicense.com
Public Accountant-CPA................ www.dbr.state.ri.us/pdf_forms/ba/Licensed%20CPAs%20and%20PAs.pdf
Public Accounting Firm................ www.dbr.state.ri.us/pdf_forms/ba/Licensed%20Public%20Accounting%20Firms.pdf
Radiation Therapist...................... http://health.ri.mylicense.com
Radiographer................................ http://health.ri.mylicense.com
Real Estate Agent/Sales .... www.dbr.state.ri.us/pdf_forms/RE-Real%20Estate%20Salespersons.pdf
Real Estate Appraiser.................... www.dbr.state.ri.us/pdf_forms/RE-Real%20Estate%20Appraisers.pdf
Real Estate Broker .... www.dbr.state.ri.us/pdf_forms/RE-Real%20Estate%20Brokers.pdf
Residential Care Facility............... http://health.ri.mylicense.com
Residential Facility .... www.dcyf.ri.gov
Respiratory Care Practitioner........ http://health.ri.mylicense.com
Roofer, Commercial...................... www.crb.state.ri.us/search.php
Salvage Yard................................ www.dbr.state.ri.us/pdf_forms/clr/Auto%20Salvage%20-%20Licensee%20List.pdf
Sanitarian .... http://health.ri.mylicense.com
Security Alarm Installer................ www.crb.state.ri.us/search.php
Septic Transporter........................ www.dem.ri.gov/programs/benviron/waste/transpor/index.htm
Social Worker .... http://health.ri.mylicense.com
Speech/Language Pathologist .... http://health.ri.mylicense.com
Surgery Center, Freestanding........ http://health.ri.mylicense.com
Tanning Facility........................... http://health.ri.mylicense.com
Tattoo Artist................................ http://health.ri.mylicense.com
Underground Sprinkler Installer ... www.crb.state.ri.us/search.php
Veterinarian .... http://health.ri.mylicense.com
X-ray Facility& Portable............... http://health.ri.mylicense.com

County Level ... Courts

Court Administration: Court Administrator, Supreme Court, 250 Benefit St, Providence, RI, 02903; 401-222-3266; www.courts.state.ri.us

Court Structure: Rhode Island has five counties but only four Superior/District Court Locations— 2nd-Newport, 3rd-Kent, 4th-Washington, and 6th-Providence/Bristol Districts). Bristol and Providence counties are completely merged at the Providence location. Civil claims between $5000 and $10,000 may be filed in either Superior Court or District Court at the discretion of the filer. For questions regarding the Superior Courts, telephone 401-222-2622. For questions regarding the District Courts, telephone 401-458-3156.

Online Access Note: The Rhode Island Judiciary offers free internet access to court criminal records statewide at http://courtconnect.courts.state.ri.us. A word of caution– this website is provided as an informational service only and should not be relied upon as an official record of the court. Superior Court (civil and family records) and Appellate Courts are online internally for court personnel only.

There are no known courts that independently offer access to their records.

County Level ... Recorders & Assessors

Recording Office Organization: 5 counties and 39 towns, 39 recording offices. The recording officer is the Town/City Clerk (Recorder of Deeds). The Town/City Clerk usually also serves as the Recorder of Deeds. There is no county administration in Rhode Island that handles recording. The entire state is in the Eastern Time Zone (EST). Be aware that the recordings in the counties of Bristol, Newport, and Providence can relate to property located in other cities/ towns even though each of these three cities bears the same name as the county.

Towns will not perform real estate searches. Copy fees are usually $1.50 per page. Certification usually costs $3.00 per document. All federal and state tax liens on personal property and on real property are filed with the Recorder of Deeds. Towns will not perform tax lien searches.

Online Access Note: A number of towns have property records available. A private vendor has placed on the Internet the assessor records from several towns. Visit http://data.visionappraisal.com.

Bristol County

Bristol Town   *Property Records*
Property information is listed on a private site at http://69.95.33.2/Newdatabases.html.

Warren Town   *Property Records*
Property information is listed on a private site at http://69.95.33.2/Newdatabases.html.

Kent County

Coventry Town   *Property, Assessor Records*
Property information is listed on a private site at http://69.95.33.2/Newdatabases.html. Also, 2005 Assessment and property data is available at www.town.coventry.ri.us/assess.htm.

East Greenwich Town   *Property Records*
www.eastgreenwichri.com
Property information is listed on a private site at http://69.95.33.2/Newdatabases.html.

Warwick City   *Tax Assessor Records*
www.warwickri.com
Access found at www.warwickri.gov.

West Warwick Town *Property Tax, Assessor Records*
www.westwarwickri.org
Access property data free at http://westwarwick.univers-clt.com no name searching.

Newport County
Jamestown Town *Property Records*
www.jamestownri.net
Property information is listed on a private site at http://69.95.33.2/Newdatabases.html.

Middletown Town *Assessor, Property Records*
www.middletownri.com
Records on the town assessor database are online at http://data.visionappraisal.com/MiddletownRI/. Free registration is required for full data.

Newport City *Assessor, Property Records*
www.cityofnewport.com
Access is via a private company at http://data.visionappraisal.com/NewportRI/. Free registration is required for full data.

Portsmouth Town *Assessor, Property Records*
www.portsmouthri.com/frames.htm
Search town assessor database at http://data.visionappraisal.com/PortsmouthRI/. Free registration for full data.

Providence County
Burrillville Town *Property, Tax Assessor Records*
www.burrillville.org
Access to property records is free at www.opaldata.com/crcdb/burrillville.htm.

Central Falls City *Property, Assessor Records*
www.centralfallsri.us
Access to city property data is free at http://data.visionappraisal.com/CentralFallsRI/. Does not require a username & password. Simply click on link.

Cranston City *Assessor, Property Records*
www.cranstonri.com/
Records on the city assessor database are online at http://data.visionappraisal.com/CranstonRI/. Free registration is required for full data.

Cumberland Town *Property, Assessor Records*
www.cumberlandri.org
Access to property data is free at www.opaldata.com/crcdb/cumberland.htm.

East Providence City *Assessor, Property Records*
www.eastprovidenceri.net/citygov/cityclerk.php
Assess to Town property data is free at http://data.visionappraisal.com/EastProvidenceRI/. Does not require a username & password. Simply click on link.

Johnston Town *Assessor, Property Records*
www.johnston-ri.com
Assess to Town property data is free at http://data.visionappraisal.com/JohnstonRI/. Free registration for full data.

Lincoln Town *Assessor Records*
www.lincolnri.org/

North Providence Town *Property Records*
Property information is listed on a private site at http://69.95.33.2/Newdatabases.html.

North Smithfield Town   *Assessor, Property Records*
www.northsmithfieldri.com
Access is via a private company at http://data.visionappraisal.com/NorthsmithfieldRI/. Free registration is required to view full data.

Pawtucket City   *Recording, Deed, Real Estate Records*
www.pawtucketri.com
Access real estate data free at http://209.113.149.21/alis/ww400r.pgm. Online indices go back to 1970. Also, search the assessors database free at http://pawtucket.univers-clt.com/index.php?orderby=sort_property_loc.

Scituate Town   *Property, Assessor Records*
www.scituateri.org/townhall.htm
Access to town property data is free at www.opaldata.com/crcdb/scituate.htm.

Smithfield Town   *Property, Assessor Records*
www.smithfieldri.com
Access to town property data is free at http://data.visionappraisal.com/SmithfieldRI/. Free registration for full data.

Woonsocket City   *Wanted Person Records*
www.ci.woonsocket.ri.us
Access wanted persons list free at www.woonsocketpolice.com/wanted.htm.

Washington County

Charlestown Town   *Assessor Records*
www.charlestownri.org
Search town assessor database at http://data.visionappraisal.com/CharlestownRI/. Does not require a username & password. Simply click on link.

Exeter Town   *Assessor, Property Records*
www.town.exeter.ri.us
Access may be available from a private company at www.opaldata.com/crcdb/exeter.htm.

Hopkinton Town   *Property, Assessor Records*
http://hopkintonritownhall.com/
Access to town property data is free at www.opaldata.com/crcdb/hopkinton.htm.

Narragansett Town   *Assessor, Property, Sex Offender Records*
www.narragansettri.com
Records on the town assessor database are online at http://data.visionappraisal.com/NarragansettRI/. Free registration is required for full data. Also search data free at http://69.95.33.2/Newdatabases.html. Also, sex offender site at www.paroleboard.ri.gov/L3_offenders/listings.htm

New Shoreham Town   *Assessor, Property Records*
Assess to Town property data is free at http://data.visionappraisal.com/NewShorehamRI/. Does not require username & password. Simply click on link.

North Kingstown Town   *Assessor, Property Records*
www.northkingstown.org
Access via a private company at http://data.visionappraisal.com/NorthkingstownRI/. Free registration required for full data.

Richmond Town   *Assessor Records*
www.richmondri.com
Search town assessor database at http://data.visionappraisal.com/RichmondRI/. Does not require a username & password. Simply click on link.

South Kingstown Town   *Real Estate, Assessor Records*
www.southkingstownri.com

Access to the property values database is free at www.southkingstownri.com/code/propvalues_search.cfm. Also, assess to Town property data is free at http://data.visionappraisal.com/SouthKingstownRI/. Does not require a username & password. Simply click on link.

Westerly Town *Property, Assessor Records*
http://westerly.govoffice.com
Access town property assessment data free at http://data.visionappraisal.com/WesterlyRI/search.asp.

Federal Courts in Rhode Island...

Standards for Federal Courts: The universal PACER sign-up number is 800-676-6856. Find PACER and the Party/Case Index on the Web at http://pacer.psc.uscourts.gov. PACER dial-up access is $.60 per minute. Also, courts offering internet access via PACER, Web-PACER or the new CM-ECF charge $.08 per page fee ($.07 per page if record is pre-2005 or unless noted as free).

US District Court -- District of Rhode Island
http://www.rid.uscourts.gov
PACER: Case records are available back to 12/1988. Records are purged never. New records are available online after 1 day.
PACER Online Access: ECF replaces PACER.. **Electronic Filing:** CM/ECF data at https://ecf.rid.uscourts.gov. **Opinions:** Court opinions are available online at http://www.rid.uscourts.gov/Judges%20Opinions.asp. **Other Online Access:** Court calendars can be found at www.rid.uscourts.gov/calendars.asp.
Providence Division counties: All counties in Rhode Island.

US Bankruptcy Court -- District of Rhode Island
www.rib.uscourts.gov
PACER: ECF replaces PACER. Case records are available back to 1990. Records are purged every three years. New records are available online after 1 day. **Electronic Filing:** CM-ECF is available online at https://ecf.rib.uscourts.gov. **Opinions:** http://www.rib.uscourts.gov/CourtResources/Opinions/opinions.htm
Providence Division counties: All counties in Rhode Island.

South Carolina

Capital: Columbia
                Richland County
Time Zone: EST
Population: 4,198,068
# of Counties: 46

Quick Links

Website: www.sc.gov
Governor: www.scgovernor.com
Attorney General: www.scattorneygeneral.org
State Archives: www.state.sc.us/scdah
State Statutes and Codes: www.scstatehouse.net/html-pages/research.html
Legislative Bill Search: www.scstatehouse.net/html-pages/legpage.html
Unclaimed Funds: http://webprod.cio.sc.gov/SCSTOWeb/mainFrame.do

State Level ... Major Agencies

Criminal Records

South Carolina Law Enforcement Division (SLED), Criminal Records Section, PO Box 21398, Columbia, SC 29221 (Courier: 4400 Broad River Rd, Columbia, SC 29210); 803-896-7043, Fax-803-896-7022, 8:30AM-5PM.
www.sled.state.sc.us
Online search: SLED offers commercial access to criminal record history from 1960 forward on the website. Fees are $25.00 per screening or $8.00 if for a charitable organization. Credit card ordering accepted. Visit the website or call 803-896-7219 for details.

Statewide Court Records

Court Administration, 1015 Sumter St, 2nd Floor, Columbia, SC 29201; 803-734-1800, Fax-803-734-1355, 8:30AM-5PM M-F.
www.sccourts.org
Online search: Appellate and Supreme Court opinions and calendars are available from www.sccourts.org/opinions/index.cfm. There is no online access to statewide trial court records.

Sexual Offender Registry

Sex Offender Registry, c/o SLED, PO Box 21398, Columbia, SC 29221 (Courier: 4400 Broad River Rd, Columbia, SC 29210); 803-896-7043, Fax-803-896-7022, 8:30AM-5PM.
www.sled.state.sc.us
Online search: Access is available from the website. Click on Sexual Offender Registry. Search by name or ZIP Code, county or city.

Incarceration Records

Department of Corrections, Inmate Records Branch, 4444 Broad River Rd, Columbia, SC 29221-1787; 803-896-8531, 877-846-3472 (Automated Information), Fax-803-896-1217, 8AM-5PM.
www.doc.sc.gov
Online search: The Inmate Search on the Internet is found at http://sword.doc.state.sc.us/incarceratedInmateSearch/index.jsp or click on Inmate search at the main website.

Corporation, Trademarks/Servicemarks, Limited Partnerships, Limited Liability Companies, Limited Liability Partnerships

Corporation Division, Capitol Complex, PO Box 11350, Columbia, SC 29211 (Courier: Edgar A. Brown Bldg, Room 525, 1205 Pendleton Street, Columbia, SC 29201); 803-734-2158, Fax-803-734-1614, 8:30PM-5PM.
www.scsos.com
Online search: This free web-based program is called the Online Business Filings, the search page is at www.scsos.com/corp_search.htm. The database provides access to basic filing information about any entity filed with the office. Registered agents' names and addresses, dates of business filings and types of filings are all available. The database is updated every 48 hours.

Uniform Commercial Code

UCC Division, Secretary of State, PO Box 11350, Columbia, SC 29211 (Courier: Edgar Brown Bldg, 1205 Pendelton St #525, Columbia, SC 29201); 803-734-1961, Fax-803-734-1610, 8:30AM-5PM.
www.scsos.com/Uniform_Commercial_Code.htm
Online search: Free access to index of records filed before 10/27/03 at www.scsos.com/uccsearch.htm. Search by debtor name or number. Information on filings after that date must be obtained by mail or email (SCUCC@INFOAVE.NET).

Birth, Death, Marriage, Divorce Certificates

South Carolina DHEC, Vital Records, 2600 Bull St, Columbia, SC 29201-1797; 803-898-3630, 803-898-3631 (Order Line), 877-284-1008 (Expedite), Fax-803-898-3761, 8:30AM-4:30PM.
www.scdhec.net/vr/index.htm
Online search: Order from state-designated vendor - www.vitalchek.com. Fee is $17.00 plus costs of shipping overnight.

Driver License Information, Driver Records

Department of Motor Vehicles, Driver Records Section, PO Box 1498, Blythewood, SC 29016-0028; 803-896-5000, Fax-803-737-1077, 8:30AM-5PM.
www.scdmvonline.com
Online search: Commercial records are available from the portal https://app.sc.gov/dmv/. Authorized businesses must establish an account through a formal approval and acceptance process. The fee is $7.25 per record and a $75.00 annual fee is required. Members have access to additional online services. For more information about setting up an account, call 803-737-2819 or email support@sc-egov.com. From www.scdmvonline.com/dmvpublic one may obtain a summary of a driving record. The summary includes points history and current status. There is no fee. SC drivers more purchase their o wn record after viewing; a certified copy is mailed for is $6.00.The DL, SSN and DOB are needed. **Other options:** Magnetic tape and cassette batch processing is available.

State Level...Occupational Licensing

Accounting Practitioner-AP	https://verify.llronline.com/LicLookup/
Acupuncturist	http://verify.llronline.com/LicLookup/Med/Med.aspx?div=16
Airport Contact	www.scaeronautics.com/directorySearch.asp
Animal Health Technician	https://verify.llronline.com/LicLookup/
Architect	https://verify.llronline.com/LicLookup/
Architectural Partners/Corp	https://verify.llronline.com/LicLookup/
Attorney	www.scbar.org/member/directory.asp
Auctioneer/Auction'r Apprentice/Firm	https://verify.llronline.com/LicLookup/
Audiologist	https://verify.llronline.com/LicLookup/
Aviation Facility	www.scaeronautics.com/AirportSearch.asp
Barber Instructor/School	https://verify.llronline.com/LicLookup/
Barber/Barber Apprentice	https://verify.llronline.com/LicLookup/
Bodywork Therapist	https://verify.llronline.com/LicLookup/
Building Inspector/Official	https://verify.llronline.com/LicLookup/
Burglar Alarm Contractor	https://verify.llronline.com/LicLookup/
Chiropractor	https://verify.llronline.com/LicLookup/
Contractor, General, Mechanical, Resid'l	https://verify.llronline.com/LicLookup/
Cosmetologist	https://verify.llronline.com/LicLookup/
Cosmetology Instructor/School	https://verify.llronline.com/LicLookup/

Counselor, Professional	https://verify.llronline.com/LicLookup/
Dentist/Dental Hygienist/Specialist/Tech	https://verify.llronline.com/LicLookup/
Embalmer	https://verify.llronline.com/LicLookup/
Emergency Medical Svc. Ambulance Co	www.scems.com/emsassn/members.html
Engineer	https://verify.llronline.com/LicLookup/
Esthetician	https://verify.llronline.com/LicLookup/
Ethics Debtors	www.state.sc.us/ethics/Debtors%20page%20Lead.htm
Forester	http://verify.llronline.com/LicLookup/Forestry/Foresters.asp?div=30
Funeral Director/Funeral Home	https://verify.llronline.com/LicLookup/
Geologist	https://verify.llronline.com/LicLookup/
Hair Care Master Specialist	https://verify.llronline.com/LicLookup/
Home Builder, Residential	https://verify.llronline.com/LicLookup/
Housing Inspector	https://verify.llronline.com/LicLookup/
Inspector, Mech./Elec./Plumb./Prov.	https://verify.llronline.com/LicLookup/
Insurance Agent/Agency/Company/Filing	https://www.doi.sc.gov/Eng/Public/Static/DBSearch.aspx
Landscape Architect	www.dnr.sc.gov/water/envaff/prolicense/prolicense.html
Lobbyist/Lobbyist Principal	www.scstatehouse.net/reports/ethrpt.htm
Manicurist/Manicure Assistant	https://verify.llronline.com/LicLookup/
Manufactured House Mfg/Dealer/Rep	https://verify.llronline.com/LicLookup/
Manufactured House Sales/Install/Repair	https://verify.llronline.com/LicLookup/
Marriage & Family Therapist	https://verify.llronline.com/LicLookup/
Massage Therapist	https://verify.llronline.com/LicLookup/
Medical Doctor	http://verify.llronline.com/LicLookup/Med/Med.aspx?div=16
Nail Technician	https://verify.llronline.com/LicLookup/
Nurses, RN / LPN	https://verify.llronline.com/LicLookup/
Nursing Home Administrator	https://verify.llronline.com/LicLookup/
Occupational Therapist/Assistant	https://verify.llronline.com/LicLookup/
Optometrist	https://verify.llronline.com/LicLookup/
Osteopathic Physician	http://verify.llronline.com/LicLookup/Med/Med.aspx?div=16
Percolation Test Technician	https://verify.llronline.com/LicLookup/
Pharmacist/Pharmacy Technician	https://verify.llronline.com/LicLookup/
Pharmacy/Drug Outlet	https://verify.llronline.com/LicLookup/
Physical Therapist/Therapist Asst	https://verify.llronline.com/LicLookup/
Physician Assistant	http://verify.llronline.com/LicLookup/Med/Med.aspx?div=16
Pilot	www.scaeronautics.com/AirportSearch.asp
Plans Examiner	https://verify.llronline.com/LicLookup/
Podiatrist	https://verify.llronline.com/LicLookup/
Produce Whlse Dealer	www.scda.state.sc.us/buyscproducts/wholesalers/wholesalers.htm
Psycho-Educational Specialist	https://verify.llronline.com/LicLookup/
Psychologist	https://verify.llronline.com/LicLookup/
Public Accountant-CPA	https://verify.llronline.com/LicLookup/
Real Estate Appraiser	http://verify.llronline.com/LicLookup/Rea/Rea.aspx?div=25
Residential Care, Community	https://verify.llronline.com/LicLookup/
Respiratory Care Practitioner	http://verify.llronline.com/LicLookup/Med/Med.aspx?div=16
Shampoo Assistant	https://verify.llronline.com/LicLookup/
Social Worker	https://verify.llronline.com/LicLookup/
Soil Classifier	www.dnr.sc.gov/water/envaff/prolicense/prolicense.html
Solid Waste Landfill	www.scdhec.net/lwm/html/min.html
Speech-Language Pathologist	https://verify.llronline.com/LicLookup/
Sprinkler Systems Contractor	https://verify.llronline.com/LicLookup/
Surveyor, Land	https://verify.llronline.com/LicLookup/
Swimming Pool/Spa Operator	https://verify.llronline.com/LicLookup/
Veterinarian	https://verify.llronline.com/LicLookup/
Waste Water Plant Operator	https://verify.llronline.com/LicLookup/
Well Driller	https://verify.llronline.com/LicLookup/
Wholesaler/Shipper (Food)	www.scda.state.sc.us/buyscproducts/shippers/shippers.htm

County Level ... Courts

Court Administration: Court Administration, 1015 Sumter St, 2nd Floor, Columbia, SC, 29201; 803-734-1800; www.sccourts.org

Court Structure:
The 46 SC counties are divided among sixteen judicial circuits. Circuit Courts are in operation at the county level and consist of a Court of General Sessions (criminal) and a Court of Common Pleas (civil). A Family Court is also in operation at the county level. The over 300 Magistrate and Municipal Courts (often referred to as "Summary Courts") only handle misdemeanor cases involving a $500.00 fine and/or thirty days or less jail time.

Online Access Note:
Appellate and Supreme Court opinions are available from the website. There is no access to statewide trial court records, but several counties offer online access.

Anderson County

Circuit Court – Civil and Criminal Records

Access to Circuit Court records is free at http://acpass.andersoncountysc.org/coc_main.htm. Includes Family Court records.

Charleston County

Circuit Court – Civil and Criminal Records

http://www3.charlestoncounty.org

Access to civil records 1988 forward, also judgments and lis pendens are free at http://www3.charlestoncounty.org/connect. Online document images go back to 1/1/1999. Access to criminal records from 04/92 forward free at http://www3.charlestoncounty.org/connect. Search by name or case number.

Charleston Magistrate Court – Civil and Criminal Records

www.charlestoncounty.org

Access civil records from 1998 forward at http://www3.charlestoncounty.org/connect. Access criminal and traffic records from 1993 forward free at http://www3.charlestoncounty.org/connect. Requests for background checks forwarded to Sheriff's Office, except if military personnel.

Charleston Count Maginstrate Courts - East Cooper - Edisto Island - James Island - Johns Island - McClellanville - North Charleston - North Charleston - Ravenel - West Ashley – Civil and Criminal Records

www.charlestoncounty.org

Civil records from 1998 forward can be access via http://www3.charlestoncounty.org/connect. Criminal and traffic records from 1993 forward can be access via http://www3.charlestoncounty.org/connect/LU_GROUP_1.

Florence County

Circuit Court – Civil and Criminal Records

www.florenceco.org

Search judgments, liens, deeds, recorded documents back to 1994 at http://web.florenceco.org/cgi-bin/coc/coc.cgi. Access criminal record from 1995 forward free at http://web.florenceco.org/cgi-bin/warrants/war.cgi.

Greenville County

Circuit Court – Civil and Criminal Records

www.greenvillecounty.org

Access court records free at www.upstatepublicindex.org. Click on Greenville. Records go back to 1983.

Pickens County

Circuit and Magistrate Courts – Civil and Criminal Records

www.co.pickens.sc.us

Access to court records is free at www.upstatepublicindex.org. Click on Pickens.

Richland County

Circuit Court – Civil and Criminal Records

Limited court rosters online at www.richlandonline.com/departments/clerkofcourt/courtroster.asp; search by date.

Sumter County

Circuit Court – Civil Records
www.sumtercountysc.org
Family court records are online at the website.

County Level ... Recorders & Assessors

Recording Office Organization: 46 counties, 46 recording offices. The recording officer is the Register of Mesne Conveyances or Clerk of Court (the title varies by county). The entire state is in the Eastern Time Zone (EST). All federal and state tax liens on personal property and on real property are filed with the Register of Mesne Conveyances (Clerk of Court). Some counties will perform tax lien searches. Search fees and copy fees vary.

Online Access Note: There is no statewide system, but a number of counties have placed free record data on their websites.

Aiken County *Land, Property, Assessor, Recorder, Deed Records*
Access to property and deeds indexes and images is via a private company at www.titlesearcher.com. Fee/registration required.

Anderson County
Real Estate, Property Tax, Sale, Assessor, Marriage, Estate, Guardianship, Vehicle, Permit, Court Records
www.andersoncountysc.org
Access to the county ACPASS super search site is free at http://acpass.andersoncountysc.org/courts.htm.

Beaufort County
Real Estate, Recording, Deed, Lien, Judgment, Assessor, Property Records
www.co.beaufort.sc.us
Access to the public records search database is free at http://rodweb.co.beaufort.sc.us/nvtest/or_sch_1.asp. Also, search assessor data at www.co.beaufort.sc.us/assessor/frameset.asp. A fuller records subscription service requiring registration, fees, and logon is under development.

Berkeley County
Property, Assessor, Personal Property, Vehicle Tax, Property Sale, Real Estate, Recording, UCC Records
www.co.berkeley.sc.us
Access real estate data is at www.co.berkeley.sc.us/e_services/index.php. Also, search the clerks document database for free at www.landaccess.com. Click on SC-Berkeley. Records go back to 1/2/1997.

Calhoun County *Land, Property, Assessor, Recorder, Deed Records*
Access to property and deeds indexes and images is via a private company at www.titlesearcher.com. Fee/registration required.

Charleston County *Real Estate, Deed, Mortgage, Property Tax, Judgment, Marriage, Will/Estate, Guardianship, Conservatorship Records*
www.charlestoncounty.org
Access to the county's GIS mapping database of property records is free at http://gisweb.charlestoncounty.org. Also, online access the auditor & treasurer's tax system database is free at http://taxweb.charlestoncounty.org. Also, search the court records for judgments at http://www3.charlestoncounty.org/connect?ref=MIE. Also, search all records including marriages, estates/wills, and guardianships at www.charlestoncounty.org/index2.asp?p=/publicrecords.htm.

Cherokee County *Most Wanted Records*
www.cherokeecountysc.com
Search the sheriff's lists online free at www.cherokeecountysheriff.net.

Darlington County *Property, Assessor, Tax Records Records*
www.darcosc.com
Access property records free at www.darcosc.com/assessor/search.asp. Lookup tax records at www.darcosc.com/OnlineTaxes/.

Fairfield County *Property, Assessor, GIS Records*
Search property/GIS data free at www.emapsplus.com/SCFairfield/maps/.

Florence County *Recorder, Grantor/Grantee, Deed, Lien, Judgment, Property, Assessor, Vehicle Records*
http://web.florenceco.org
Access recorder data free at http://web.florenceco.org/cgi-bin/coc/coc.cgi. Also, access property tax records free at http://web.florenceco.org/cgi-bin/ta/tax-inq.cgi. Access vehicle tax records free at http://web.florenceco.org/cgi-bin/ta/vehinq.cgi.

Georgetown County *Property, GIS, Recording, Real Estate, Deed, UCC Records*
www.georgetowncountysc.org
Access to property data on the GIS-mapping site is free at http://gismap.georgetowncountysc.org/viewer.htm. Click on the binoculars to get to the name search feature. Also, access the Register's database free at www.landaccess.com. Click on SC-Georgetown. Index goes back to 1/1977 for deeds, 7/1986 for mortgages, 1/1989 for UCC and 7/1989 for tax liens.

Greenville County *Real Property, Deed, Vehicle, Property Tax, Most Wanted, Missing Person Records*
www.greenvillecounty.org
Search the Register of Deeds database free online at www.greenvillecounty.org. Click on Register of Deeds Search. Also, search the property tax and vehicles data at www.greenvillecounty.org/voTaxQry/wcmain.asp. Also, search the real estate information data at www.greenvillecounty.org/vrealpr24/clrealprop.asp. No name searching. Also, search the sheriff's most wanted and missing persons lists at www.gcso.org.

Greenwood County *Assessor, Property Records*
www.co.greenwood.sc.us
Records on the County Parcel Search database are free at http://165.166.39.5/giswebsite/default.htm. Click on search and choose to search by owner name. An interactive map is included.

Horry County *Recorder, Deed, Lien, Real Property Records*
www.horrycounty.org
Access to the recorders database is free at www.horrycounty.org/gateway/disclaimer/idx_rod.html. Also, search the real property database at www.horrycounty.org/gateway/disclaimer/idx_real.html.

Lancaster County *Real Estate, Deed, Property, Assessor Records*
www.lancastercountysc.net
Access property data free at www.lancastercountysc.net/onlinetaxes/. Also, access to property and deeds indexes and images is via a private company at www.titlesearcher.com. Fee/registration required.

Lexington County *Assessor, Property, Real Property Records*
www.lex-co.com/Departments/RegisterOfDeeds/Index.html
Access to county Re-assessment Information is free at www.myscgov.com/cgi/hsrun/Distributed2/LCDAE/LCDAE.hjx;start=LCDAE.Hsmaster.run. Register of Deeds records are found at www.lex-co.com/Departments/RegisterOfDeeds/OnlineServices.html.

Newberry County *Assessor, Real Estate, Auditor, Property Tax, Treasurer Records*
Access to databases for the assessor is free at http://209.213.28.38/vpn/assessor2.htm. Access to property tax data is at www.newberrycounty.net/auditor/Index.html. Also, the treasurer database is free at http://209.213.28.38/vpn/treasurer.htm.

Oconee County *Land, Deed, Mortgage, Plat Records*
www.oconeesc.com
Access to county land records is free at www.oconeesc.com/resolution/default.asp.

Orangeburg County *Assessor, Property Records*
www.orangeburgscrod.org
Access to county property tax records is free at www.orangeburgcounty.org/Assessor/main.asp.

Pickens County *Property, Assessor, Most Wanted, Property Tax Records*
www.co.pickens.sc.us/regofdeeds/
Search property tax records at www.co.pickens.sc.us/onlinetaxes/. Also, search assessor property records free at http://67.32.48.35/assessor/disclaim.asp. View the sheriff's most wanted list at www.pickenscosheriff.org/most_wanted.htm.

Richland County *Assessor, Property, Register of Deeds, Real Estate, Marriage, Inmate, Lost Pet Records*

Access to county property information is free at www.richlandmaps.com. Click on "Property Info" however, there is no name searching. Also, search assessments at www.richlandonline.com/services/assessorsearch/assessorsearch.asp; no name searching. Also, search register of deeds free at www.richlandonline.com/services/rodsearch.asp; no name searching. Also, search marriages, inmates, and lost pet databases free at www.richlandonline.com/services/onlineservices.asp.

Sumter County *Real Estate, Recording, Deed, Property Tax Records*

www.sumtercountysc.org
Search county e-gov data free at www.sumtercountysc.org/disclaim.htm.

York County *Property, GIS, Recorder, Real Estate Records*

Access to the county GIS and property data is free at http://maps.yorkcountygov.com/gisonline/. Click on "GIS Online" and name search at the main map page.

Federal Courts in South Carolina...

Standards for Federal Courts: The universal PACER sign-up number is 800-676-6856. Find PACER and the Party/Case Index on the Web at http://pacer.psc.uscourts.gov. PACER dial-up access is $.60 per minute. Also, courts offering internet access via PACER, Web-PACER or the new CM-ECF charge $.08 per page fee ($.07 per page if record is pre-2005 or unless noted as free).

US District Court -- District of South Carolina

www.scd.uscourts.gov
PACER: ECF replaces PACER. Document images available. Case records are available back to January 1990. New records are available online after 1 day. **Electronic Filing:** CM/ECF data at https://ecf.scd.uscourts.gov. **Opinions:** Available on subscription WebPacer system..
Anderson Division counties: Anderson, Oconee, Pickens.
Beaufort Division counties: Beaufort, Hampton, Jasper.
Charleston Division counties: Berkeley, Charleston, Clarendon, Colleton, Dorchester, Georgetown.
Columbia Division counties: Kershaw, Lee, Lexington, Richland, Sumter.
Florence Division counties: Chesterfield, Darlington, Dillon, Florence, Horry, Marion, Marlboro, Williamsburg.
Greenville Division counties: Greenville, Laurens.
Greenwood Division counties: Abbeville, Aiken, Allendale, Bamberg, Barnwell, Calhoun, Edgefield, Fairfield, Greenwood, Lancaster, McCormick, Newberry, Orangeburg, Saluda.
Spartanburg Division counties: Cherokee, Chester, Spartanburg, Union, York.

US Bankruptcy Court -- District of South Carolina

http://www.scb.uscourts.gov
PACER: Case records are available back to 11/1988. Records are purged never. New records are available online after immediately. **PACER Online Access:** ECF replaces PACER. Document images and creditor lists available.. **Electronic Filing:** CM/ECF data at https://ecf.scb.uscourts.gov. **Opinions:**   Court opinions are available online at http://www.scb.uscourts.gov/opinions.html. **Other Online Access:** Calendars free at www.scb.uscourts.gov/calendars/calendars.htm.
Columbia Division counties: All counties in South Carolina.

South Dakota

Capital: Pierre
              Hughes County

Time Zone: CST

South Dakota s eighteen western-most counties are MST:
They are: Bennett, Butte, Corson, Custer, Dewey,
Fall River, Haakon, Harding, Jackson, Lawrence,
Meade, Mellette, Pennington, Perkins, Shannon, Stanley, Todd, and Ziebach

Population: 770,883

# of Counties: 66

Quick Links

Website: www.state.sd.us

Governor: www.state.sd.us/governor/

Attorney General: www.state.sd.us/attorney

State Archives: www.sdhistory.org

State Statutes and Codes: http://legis.state.sd.us/statutes/index.aspx

Legislative Bill Search: http://legis.state.sd.us/sessions/2006/index.aspx

Bill Monitoring: http://legis.state.sd.us/mylrc/index.cfm

Unclaimed Funds:
      www.sdtreasurer.com/default.asp?page=unclaimed_property_page&section=search_claim

State Level ... Major Agencies

Statewide Court Records

State Court Administrator, State Capitol Bldg, 500 E Capitol Ave, Pierre, SD 57501-5059; 605-773-3474, Fax-605-773-5627, 8AM-5PM.
www.sdjudicial.com
Online search: The Supreme Court calendar, opinions, and 2nd oral arguments may be searched from the website. All active judgments and inactive civil judgments from 04/19/2004 forward are available from a web subscription service offered by this agency. The access cost is $250 monthly or $2500 annually. The system permits bulk downloading of information. However, the agreement with the agency disallows any resell of the data. This subscription system does not include probate or criminal information. For more details contact Ms. Jill Gusso at 605-773-4874. **Other options:** Historical civil judgment data may be purchased, electronic format is provided. Contact Ms. Gusso.

Sexual Offender Registry

Division of Criminal Investigation, Identification Section - SOR Unit, 500 E Capitol, Pierre, SD 57501-5070 (Courier: 3444 East Highway 34, Pierre, SD 57501); 605-773-3331, 605-773-4614, Fax-605-773-2596, 8AM-5PM.
http://dci.sd.gov/administration/id/sexoffender/index.asp
Online search: Searching is available from the website. Note that there is no statewide search, all searches are done on a county basis.

Corporation, Limited Partnerships, Limited Liability Company, Trademarks/Servicemarks

Corporation Division, Secretary of State, 500 E Capitol Ave, Suite B-05, Pierre, SD 57501-5070; 605-773-4845, 605-773-3539 (Trademarks), Fax-605-773-4550, 8AM-5PM.
www.sdsos.gov/corporations/
Online search: Search the Secretary of State Corporations Div. Database free at www.state.sd.us/applications/st02corplo ok/corpfile.asp. Trademark searches may be requested via e-mail at anissa.grambihler@state.sd.us. **Other options:** The corporate database may be purchased on CD for $1,000 with $500 monthly updates.

Uniform Commercial Code, Federal Tax Liens

UCC Division, Secretary of State, 500 East Capitol, Pierre, SD 57501-5077; 605-773-4422, Fax-605-773-4550, 8AM-5PM.
www.sdsos.gov/ucc
Online search: Dakota Fast File is the filing and searching service available from the website. This is a commercial service that requires registration and a $120-360 fee per year. A certified search is available. **Other options:**FTP downloads available for purchase

Birth, Death, Marriage, Divorce Certificates

South Dakota Department of Health, Vital Records, 600 E Capitol, Pierre, SD 57501-2536; 605-773-4961, Fax-605-773-5683, 8-5PM.
www.state.sd.us/doh/VitalRec/index.htm
Online search: You can order recent (less than 100 years) vital records at the website, for a fee. You can search free at the website for birth records over 100 years old.

Driver Records

Dept of Public Safety, Office of Driver Licensing, 118 W Capitol, Pierre, SD 57501; 605-773-6883, Fax-605-773-3018, 8AM-5PM.
www.state.sd.us/dps/dl/
Online search: The system is open for batch requests 24 hours a day. There is a minimum of 250 requests daily. It generally takes 10 minutes to process a batch. The current fee is $4.00 per record and there are some start-up costs. For more information, call 605-773-6883. **Other options:** Lists are available to the insurance industry.

State Level ... Occupational Licensing

Abstractor Business	www.state.sd.us/drr2/reg/abstracters/roster.htm
Ambulance Service	www.state.sd.us/dps/ems/
Animal Remedy/Animal medicine/drug	www.state.sd.us/doa/das/hp-af-ar.htm
Architect	www.state.sd.us/dol/boards/engineer/Roster/roster.htm
Athletic Trainer	www.state.sd.us/doh/medical/
Auctioneer	www.state.sd.us/drr2/reg/realestate/roster_licensees/roster.htm
Audiologist	www.state.sd.us/doh/audiology/roster.htm
Bail Bond Agent	www.state.sd.us/drr2/reg/insurance/producers/bailbonds.xls
Bank	www.state.sd.us/drr2/reg/bank/licensee.htm
Barber	www.state.sd.us/dol/boards/barber/barbers.htm
Barber Shop	www.state.sd.us/dol/boards/barber/shops.htm
Beauty Shop/Salon	www.state.sd.us/applications/LD19Cosmet/license.asp
Cosmetologist	www.state.sd.us/applications/LD19Cosmet/license.asp
Cosmetology Instructor	www.state.sd.us/applications/LD19Cosmet/license.asp
Cosmetology Salon	www.state.sd.us/applications/LD19Cosmet/license.asp
Counselor	www.state.sd.us/dhs/boards/counselor/roster.htm
Crematory	www.state.sd.us/doh/funeral/roster.htm
Dietitian/Nutritionist	www.state.sd.us/doh/medical/
Driller, Oil and Gas	www.state.sd.us/denr/DES/Mining/Oil&Gas/NewPermit.htm
Embalmer	www.state.sd.us/doh/funeral/roster.htm
Engineer	www.state.sd.us/dol/boards/engineer/Roster/roster.htm

Engineer, Petroleum Environmen'l .... www.state.sd.us/dol/boards/engineer/Roster/roster.htm
Esthetician... www.state.sd.us/applications/LD19Cosmet/license.asp
Fertilizer.. www.state.sd.us/doa/das/hp-fert.htm
Funeral Dir/Embalmer/Establ't/Service ...... www.state.sd.us/doh/funeral/roster.htm
Gaming Manufacturer................................. www.state.sd.us/drr2/reg/gaming/manufac.htm
Health Insurer .... www.state.sd.us/drr2/reg/insurance/consumer/major_med_carriers.html
Hearing Aid Dispenser............................... www.state.sd.us/doh/audiology/roster.htm
Home Inspector.. www.state.sd.us/drr2/reg/realestate/roster_licensees/roster.htm
Insurance Company www.state.sd.us/drr2/reg/insurance/consumer/index.html
Insurer of Health .... www.state.sd.us/drr2/reg/insurance/consumer/major_med_carriers.html
Landscape Architect................................... www.state.sd.us/dol/boards/engineer/landsurveynumbers.htm
Lobbyist... www.sdsos.gov/lobbyist/
Manicurist/Nail Technician........................ www.state.sd.us/applications/LD19Cosmet/license.asp
Marriage & Family Therapist .... www.state.sd.us/dhs/boards/counselor/roster.htm
Medical Assistant....................................... www.state.sd.us/doh/medical/
Medical Doctor .... www.state.sd.us/doh/medical/
Money Lender.. www.state.sd.us/drr2/reg/bank/licensee.htm
Money Order Business................................ www.state.sd.us/drr2/reg/bank/licensee.htm
Mortgage Broker/Lender www.state.sd.us/drr2/reg/bank/licensee.htm
Nail Salon www.state.sd.us/applications/LD19Cosmet/license.asp
Notary Public... www.sdsos.gov/notaries/
Nursing Home Administrator...................... www.state.sd.us/doh/nursingfacility/roster.htm
Occupational Therapist/Assistant............... www.state.sd.us/doh/medical/
Oil & Gas Driller .... www.state.sd.us/denr/DES/Mining/Oil&Gas/NewPermit.htm
Optometrist .... www.arbo.org/index.php?action=findanoptometrist
Osteopathic Physician................................ www.state.sd.us/doh/medical/
Pesticide Applicator/Dealer .... www.state.sd.us/doa/das/
Pet Health Insurer .... www.state.sd.us/drr2/reg/insurance/consumer/pet_companies.pdf
Petrol. Release Assessor/Remediator.......... www.state.sd.us/dol/boards/engineer/Roster/roster.htm
Physical Therapist/Assistant .... www.state.sd.us/doh/medical/
Physician/Medical Assistant .... www.state.sd.us/doh/medical/
Podiatrist.. www.state.sd.us/doh/podiatry/podiatrist.pdf
Property Manager .... www.state.sd.us/drr2/reg/realestate/roster_licensees/roster.htm
Psychologist... www.state.sd.us/dhs/boards/psychologists/roster.htm
Public Accountant-CPA www.state.sd.us/dol/boards/accountancy/Annual%20Register%20-%20Jan05.pdf
Real Estate Agent/Sales .... www.state.sd.us/drr2/reg/realestate/roster_licensees/roster.htm
Real Estate Broker .... www.state.sd.us/drr2/reg/realestate/roster_licensees/roster.htm
Re-insurer, Accredited/Qualified www.state.sd.us/drr2/reg/insurance/Financial/AQReinsurers.pdf
Respiratory Care Practitioner..................... www.state.sd.us/doh/medical/
Social Worker .... www.state.sd.us/dhs/boards/socialwork/roster.htm
Surveyor, Land .... www.state.sd.us/dol/boards/engineer/Roster/roster.htm
Timeshare Real Estate................................ www.state.sd.us/drr2/reg/realestate/roster_licensees/roster.htm
Trust Company www.state.sd.us/drr2/reg/bank/licensee.htm
Waste Wate System Operator .... www.state.sd.us/denr/databases/operator/index.cfm
Waste Water Treatment Plant Operator ...... www.state.sd.us/denr/databases/operator/index.cfm
Water Distributor .... www.state.sd.us/denr/databases/operator/index.cfm
Water Treatment Operator .... www.state.sd.us/denr/databases/operator/index.cfm
Weapon, Concealed .... www.sdsos.gov/firearms/

County Level ... Courts

Court Administration: State Court Administrator, State Capitol Building, 500 E Capitol Av, Pierre, SD, 57501; 605-773-3474; www.sdjudicial.com

Court Structure:
South Dakota has a statewide criminal record search database, administered by the State Court Administrator's Office in Pierre. All criminal record information from July 1, 1989 forward, statewide, is contained in the database. Requesters with accounts may mail requests to one of the addresses listed below for statewide searching. Requesters may set up a commercial account by faxing a written request to Jill Gusso, Unified Court System at 605-773-4874 or email jill.gusso@ujs.state.sd.us. Accounts are billed monthly. The search fee is $15.00 per record. State-authorized commercial accounts may order and receive records by fax; there is an additional $5.00 fee unless a non-toll free line is used.

Online Access Note: There is no statewide online access computer system currently available for trial court records. The Supreme Court calendar, opinions, and second oral arguments may be searched from the website.

There are no known courts that independently offer online access to their records.

County Level ... Recorders & Assessors

Recording Office Organization: 66 counties, 66 recording offices. The recording officer is the Register of Deeds. 48 counties are in the Central Time Zone (CST) and 18 are in the Mountain Time Zone (MST). Federal and state tax liens on personal property of businesses are filed with the Secretary of State. Other federal and state tax liens are filed with the county Register of Deeds. Most counties will perform tax lien searches. Search fees and copy fees vary.

Online Access Note: Access to UCC records is available through the Secretary of State's Fast File Internet Access System at www.sdsos.gov/ucc/. Registration and annual fee is required. A certified search is also available. A new system named "Expa" is soon to be available for the occasional user.

9 South Dakota Countis   *Property, Assessor, GIS Records*
http://webgishome.promap.com/Default.aspx
Search assessor property data for a fee on the GIS system at http://webgishome.promap.com/Default.aspx. Registration and username required.
Counties include- Brown, Clay, Custer, Fall River, Harding, McCook(?), Meade, Moody, Union

Clark County   *Cemetery, Birth, Marriage, Death, Rebirth Records*
The county WebGen site provides access to older vital statistic records at www.rootsweb.com/~sdclark/index.htm.

Custer County   *Property, Assessor, GIS Records*
Search assessor property data for a fee on the GIS system at http://webgishome.promap.com/Default.aspx. Registration and username required.

McCook County   *Property, Assessor, GIS Records*
Access to assessor property data MAY be on the GIS system at http://webgishome.promap.com/Default.aspx.

Minnehaha County   *Property Tax Records*
www.minnehahacounty.org/depts/register_deeds/register_deeds.asp
Access the county property tax database free at www.minnehahacounty.org/property_tax/Index.asp. No name searching at this time.

Pennington County   *Property Tax, Assessor Records*
www.co.pennington.sd.us
Access to the county property tax database is free at www.co.pennington.sd.us/search/search.aspx.

Federal Courts in South Dakota...

Standards for Federal Courts: The universal PACER sign-up number is 800-676-6856. Find PACER and the Party/Case Index on the Web at http://pacer.psc.uscourts.gov. PACER dial-up access is $.60 per minute. Also, courts offering internet access via PACER, Web-PACER or the new CM-ECF charge $.08 per page fee ($.07 per page if record is pre-2005 or unless noted as free).

US District Court -- District of South Dakota

www.sdd.uscourts.gov

PACER: Case records are available back to 1991. Records are purged every 6 months. New records are available online after 1 day. **PACER Online Access:** ECF replaces PACER. **Electronic Filing:** CM/ECF data at https://ecf.sdd.uscourts.gov. **Other Online Access:** Access to very limited court calendar at www.sdd.uscourts.gov.
Aberdeen Division counties: Brown, Campbell, Clark, Codington, Corson, Day, Deuel, Edmunds, Grant, Hamlin, McPherson, Marshall, Roberts, Spink, Walworth. Judge Battey's closed case records are located at the Rapid City Division.
Pierre Division counties: Buffalo, Dewey, Faulk, Gregory, Haakon, Hand, Hughes, Hyde, Jackson, Jerauld, Jones, Lyman, Mellette, Potter, Stanley, Sully, Todd, Tripp, Ziebach.
Rapid City Division counties: Bennett, Butte, Custer, Fall River, Harding, Lawrence, Meade, Pennington, Perkins, Shannon. Judge Battey's closed cases are located here.
Sioux Falls Division counties: Aurora, Beadle, Bon Homme, Brookings, Brule, Charles Mix, Clay, Davison, Douglas, Hanson, Hutchinson, Kingsbury, Lake, Lincoln, McCook, Miner, Minnehaha, Moody, Sanborn, Turner, Union, Yankton.

US Bankruptcy Court -- District of South Dakota

www.sdb.uscourts.gov

PACER: Case records are available back to 10/1991. Records are purged never. **PACER Online Access:** ECF replaces PACER. Document images available. **Electronic Filing:** CM/ECF data at https://ecf.sdb.uscourts.gov. **Opinions:** View court opinions at www.sdb.uscourts.gov/Decisions.htm. **Phone access:** Voice Case Information System, call 800-768-6218, 605-330-4559
Sioux Falls Division counties: Aurora, Beadle, Bon Homme, Brookings, Brule, Charles Mix, Clay, Davison, Douglas, Hanson, Hutchinson, Kingsbury, Lake, Lincoln, McCook, Miner, Minnehaha, Moody, Sanborn, Turner, Union, Yankton.
Northeastern Division counties: Carter, Cocke, Greene, Hamblen, Hancock, Hawkins, Johnson, Sullivan, Unicoi, Washington.
Northern Division counties: Anderson, Blount, Campbell, Claiborne, Grainger, Jefferson, Knox, Loudon, Monroe, Morgan, Roane, Scott, Sevier, Sullivan, Unicoi, Union, Washington.
Southern Division counties: Bedford*, Bledsoe, Bradley, Coffee*, Franklin*, Grundy*, Hamilton, Lincoln*, Marion, McMinn, Meigs, Moore*, Polk, Rhea, Sequatchie, Van Buren*, Warren*. This court also holds records for the Winchester Division, which is not a staffed office. Winchester Division counties are marked with an asterisk (*).

Tennessee

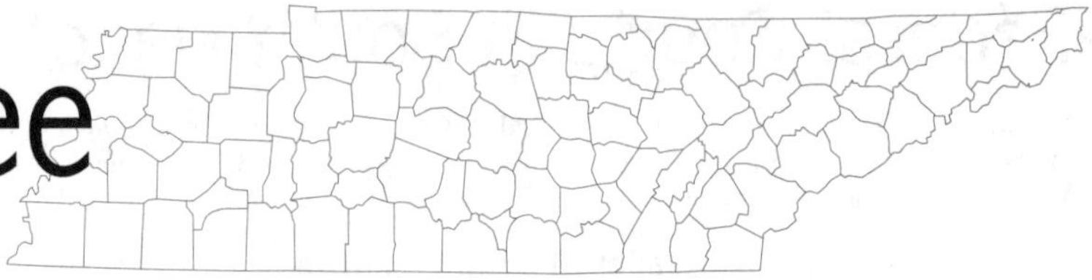

Capital: Nashville
           Davidson County

Time Zone: CST

Tennessee's twenty-nine eastern-most counties are EST.
They are: Anderson, Blount, Bradley, Campbell, Carter, Claiborne, Cocke, Grainger, Greene, Hamilton, Hancock, Hawkins, Jefferson, Johnson, Knox, Loudon, McMinn, Meigs, Monroe, Morgan, Polk, Rhea, Roane, Scott, Sevier, Sullivan, Unicoi, Union, Washington.

Population: 5,841,748

# of Counties: 95

Quick Links

Website: www.state.tn.us

Governor: www.tennesseeanytime.org/governor/Welcome.do

Attorney General: www.attorneygeneral.state.tn.us

State Archives: www.tennessee.gov/tsla/

State Statutes and Codes:
           http://198.187.128.12/tennessee/lpext.dll?f=templates&fn=fs-main.htm&2.0

Legislative Bill Search: www.legislature.state.tn.us

Unclaimed Funds: www.tennesseeanytime.org/unclp/

State Level ... Major Agencies

Statewide Court Records

Administrative Office of the Courts, Nashville City Center, 511 Union St, Suite 600, Nashville, TN 37219; 615-741-2687, Fax-615-741-6285, 8AM-4:30PM.
www.tncourts.gov
Online search: The Administrative Office of Courts provides access to Appellate Court opinions at www.tsc.state.tn.us/geninfo/Courts/AppellateCourts.htm. Several counties offer online access to court records, but there is no statewide access system.

Sexual Offender Registry

Tennessee Bureau of Investigation, Sexual Offender Registry, 901 R S Gass Blvd., Nashville, TN 37216; 888-837-4170 (SOR Hotline), Fax-615-744-4655 .
www.ticic.state.tn.us
Online search: Search sexual offenders at website by last name, city, county or ZIP Code. One may also search for missing children, and people placed on parole who reside in Tennessee.

Incarceration Records

Tennessee Department of Corrections, Rachel Jackson Building, Ground Fl, 320 6th Avenue, N., Nashville, TN 37243-0465; 615-741-1000, Fax-615-532-1497, 8AM-5PM.
www.state.tn.us/correction/
Online search: Extensive search capabilities are offered from the website. Click on FOIL - Inmate Search. **Other options:** A CD-Rom is available with only public information from current offender database; nominal fee; contact the Planning & Research Division.

Corporation, Limited Partnership, Fictitious Name, Assumed Name, Limited Liability Company Records

TN Sec of State: Corporations, William R Snodgrass Tower, 312 Eighth Ave. N, 6th Fl, Nashville, TN 37243; 615-741-2286, 615-741-6488 (Copies), Fax-615-741-7310, 8AM-4:30PM.
www.state.tn.us/sos/bus_svc/index.htm
Online search: There is a free online search at www.tennesseeanytime.org/sosname/ for name availability and at www.tennesseeanytime.org/soscorp/ for business records. This gives online access to over 4,000,000 records relating to corporations, limited liability companies, limited partnerships and limited liability partnerships formed or registered in Tennessee. **Other options:** Some data can be purchased in bulk or list format. Call 615-532-9007 for more details.

Trademarks/Servicemarks, Trade Names

Secretary of State, Trademarks/Tradenames Division, 312 8th Ave North, 6th Fl, Nashville, TN 37243-0306; 615-741-0531, Fax-615-741-7310, 8AM-4:30PM.
www.state.tn.us/sos/bus_svc/trademarks.htm
Online search: The Internet provides a record search of TN Trademarks, newest records are 3 days old. Go to www.ja.state.tn.us/sos/iets2/ietm/PgTrademarkSearch.jsp. **Other options:** The agency will provide a file update every three months for $1.00 per page. Requests must be in writing.

Uniform Commercial Code

TN Sec of State - UCC Records, William R Snodgrass Tower, 312 Eighth Ave N, 6th Fl, Nashville, TN 37243; 615-741-3276, Fax-615-741-7310, 8AM-4:30PM.
www.state.tn.us/sos
Online search: Free access to general information at www.ja.state.tn.us/sos/iets3/ieuc/PgUCCSearch.jsp. Search by debtor name or file number. Images are not available.

Birth, Marriage, Divorce Certificates

Tennessee Department of Health, Office of Vital Records, 421 5th Ave North, 1st floor, Nashville, TN 37247; 615-741-1763, 615-741-0778 (Credit card order), Fax-615-741-9860, 8AM-4PM.
www2.state.tn.us/health/vr/index.htm
Online search: Records may be ordered from the website, but are returned by mail. Go to https://health.state.tn.us/vrocs/vr.aspx. There is an additional $9.00 fee involved to use this service.

Death Records

Tennessee Department of Health, Office of Vital Records, 421 5th Ave North, 1st floor, Nashville, TN 37247; 615-741-1763, 615-741-0778 (Credit card order), Fax-615-741-9860, 8AM-4PM.
www2.state.tn.us/health/vr/index.htm
Online search: Records may be ordered online at the website, but are returned by mail. Go to https://health.state.tn.us/vrocs/vr.aspx. There is an additional $9.00 fee involved to use this service. The Cleveland (Tennessee) Public Library staff and volunteers have published the 1914-1925 death records of thirty-three counties at www.tennessee.gov/tsla/history/vital/death.htm. It should be noted that the records of children under two years of age have been omitted from this project.

Driver Records

Dept. of Safety, Financial Responsibility Section, Attn: Driving Records, 1150 Foster Ave, Nashville, TN 37210; 615-741-3954, Fax-615-253-2093, 8AM-4:30PM.
www.tennessee.gov/safety/
Online search: Driving records are available to subscribers, signup at www.tennesseeanytime.org. There is a $75 registration fee. Records are available 24 hours daily on an interactive basis. Records are $7.00 each. Suggested only for ongoing users. Companies retrieving more than 500 records per month can use a "batch" process in which multiple license numbers can be searched and the results are returned in one file. Call 1-866-886-3468 for more info. The agency also offers a DL or status check online. Fee is $1.25. **Other options:** Magnetic tape retrieval available for high volume users. Purchase of DL file is available for approved requesters.

Vehicle Ownership, Vehicle Identification

Title and Registration Division, Information Unit, 44 Vantage Way #160, Nashville, TN 37243-8050; 615-741-3101 (Titles), 888-871-3171, Fax-615-253-4259, 8AM-4:30PM.
www.tennessee.gov/safety/titleandregistration.htm
Online search: Online access is available for approved subscribers at www.tennesseeanytime.org/ivtr. This is the same subscription system used to pull driving records. $75.00 annual fee includes 10 users. IVTR allows subscribers to retrieve vehicle, title, and

registration information for vehicles registered in Tennessee. Search with license plate or VIN. The fee is $2.00 per search. All subscribers must be approved per DPPA.

State Level ... Occupational Licensing

Accounting Firm	www.state.tn.us/cgi-bin/commerce/roster3.pl
Alarm Contractor	www.state.tn.us/cgi-bin/commerce/roster3.pl
Animal Euthanasia Technician	http://www2.state.tn.us/health/licensure/index.htm
Architect	www.state.tn.us/cgi-bin/commerce/roster3.pl
Athletic Trainer	http://www2.state.tn.us/health/licensure/index.htm
Attorney	www.tbpr.org/Consumers/AttorneySearch/
Auction Company	www.state.tn.us/cgi-bin/commerce/roster3.pl
Auctioneer	www.state.tn.us/cgi-bin/commerce/roster3.pl
Audiologist	http://www2.state.tn.us/health/licensure/index.htm
Barber/Barber Tech/School/Barber Shop	www.state.tn.us/cgi-bin/commerce/roster3.pl
Boxing/Racing Personnel	www.state.tn.us/cgi-bin/commerce/roster3.pl
Chiropractor/Chiropractic Therapy Assist.	http://www2.state.tn.us/health/licensure/index.htm
Clinical Lab Technician/Personnel	http://www2.state.tn.us/health/licensure/index.htm
Collection Agent/Manager	www.state.tn.us/cgi-bin/commerce/roster3.pl
Contractor	www.state.tn.us/cgi-bin/commerce/roster3.pl
Cosmetologist/Cosmetology Shop/School	www.state.tn.us/cgi-bin/commerce/roster3.pl
Counselor, Alcohol & Drug Abuse	http://www2.state.tn.us/health/licensure/index.htm
Counselor, Associate/Professional	http://www2.state.tn.us/health/licensure/index.htm
Dental Hygienist	http://www2.state.tn.us/health/licensure/index.htm
Dentist/Dental Assistant	http://www2.state.tn.us/health/licensure/index.htm
Dietitian/Nutritionist	http://www2.state.tn.us/health/licensure/index.htm
Electrologist/Electrol. Instructor/School	http://www2.state.tn.us/health/licensure/index.htm
Embalmer	www.state.tn.us/cgi-bin/commerce/roster3.pl
Emergency Medical Personnel/Dispatcher	http://www2.state.tn.us/health/licensure/index.htm
Engineer	www.state.tn.us/cgi-bin/commerce/roster3.pl
First Responder EMS	http://www2.state.tn.us/health/licensure/index.htm
Funeral & Burial Director/Apprentice	www.state.tn.us/cgi-bin/commerce/roster3.pl
Funeral & Burial Est./Cemetery	www.state.tn.us/cgi-bin/commerce/roster3.pl
Geologist	www.state.tn.us/cgi-bin/commerce/roster3.pl
Hearing Aid Dispenser	http://www2.state.tn.us/health/licensure/index.htm
Home Improvement	www.state.tn.us/cgi-bin/commerce/roster3.pl
Insurance Agent/Insurance Firm	www.state.tn.us/cgi-bin/commerce/roster3.pl
Interior Designer	www.state.tn.us/cgi-bin/commerce/roster3.pl
Laboratory Personnel, Medical	http://www2.state.tn.us/health/licensure/index.htm
Landscape Architect/Architect Firm	www.state.tn.us/cgi-bin/commerce/roster3.pl
Lobbyist	www.state.tn.us/tref/lobbyists/lobbyists.htm
Manicurist	www.state.tn.us/cgi-bin/commerce/roster3.pl
Marriage & Family Therapist	http://www2.state.tn.us/health/licensure/index.htm
Massage Therapist/Establishment	http://www2.state.tn.us/health/licensure/index.htm
Medical Disciplinary Tracking	http://www2.state.tn.us/health/abuseregistry/index.html
Medical Doctor	http://www2.state.tn.us/health/licensure/index.htm
Midwife	http://www2.state.tn.us/health/licensure/index.htm
Motor Vehicle Auction	www.state.tn.us/cgi-bin/commerce/roster3.pl

Motor Vehicle Dealer/Salesperson www.state.tn.us/cgi-bin/commerce/roster3.pl
Notary Public www.ja.state.tn.us/sos/iets1/ieny/PgIenySearch.jsp
Nurse-RN/LPN, Nurse's Aide http://www2.state.tn.us/health/licensure/index.htm
Nursing Home Administrator http://www2.state.tn.us/health/licensure/index.htm
Occupational Therapist/Assistant http://www2.state.tn.us/health/licensure/index.htm
Optician, Dispensing http://www2.state.tn.us/health/licensure/index.htm
Optometrist http://www2.state.tn.us/health/licensure/index.htm
Orthopedic Physician Assistant http://www2.state.tn.us/health/licensure/index.htm
Osteopathic Physician http://www2.state.tn.us/health/licensure/index.htm
Pastoral Therapist, Clinical http://www2.state.tn.us/health/licensure/index.htm
Personnel Leasing www.state.tn.us/cgi-bin/commerce/roster3.pl
Pest Control Operator .... www.tennesseeanytime.org/agrso/
Pharmacist/Pharmacy/Pharm'cy Research'r www.state.tn.us/cgi-bin/commerce/roster3.pl
Physical Therapist/Assistant http://www2.state.tn.us/health/licensure/index.htm
Physician Assistant http://www2.state.tn.us/health/licensure/index.htm
Podiatrist http://www2.state.tn.us/health/licensure/index.htm
Polygraph Examiner www.state.tn.us/cgi-bin/commerce/roster3.pl
Private Investigative Company www.state.tn.us/cgi-bin/commerce/roster3.pl
Private Investigator/Security Guard www.state.tn.us/cgi-bin/commerce/roster3.pl
Psychological Examiner http://www2.state.tn.us/health/licensure/index.htm
Psychologist http://www2.state.tn.us/health/licensure/index.htm
Public Accountant-CPA www.state.tn.us/cgi-bin/commerce/roster3.pl
Racetrack www.state.tn.us/cgi-bin/commerce/roster3.pl
Radiologic Technologist http://www2.state.tn.us/health/licensure/index.htm
Real Estate Agent/Broker/Sales/Firm www.state.tn.us/cgi-bin/commerce/roster3.pl
Real Estate Appraiser www.state.tn.us/cgi-bin/commerce/roster3.pl
Respiratory Care Therapist/Tech./Assist. http://www2.state.tn.us/health/licensure/index.htm
School Administrator www.k-12.state.tn.us/tcertinf/Search.asp
School Counselor/Librarian/Psychologist ... www.k-12.state.tn.us/tcertinf/Search.asp
School Food Service Supervisor www.k-12.state.tn.us/tcertinf/Search.asp
School Reading Specialist www.k-12.state.tn.us/tcertinf/Search.asp
School Vocational Endorsement www.k-12.state.tn.us/tcertinf/Search.asp
Security Company/Security Guard/Trainer. www.state.tn.us/cgi-bin/commerce/roster3.pl
Shampoo Technician www.state.tn.us/cgi-bin/commerce/roster3.pl
Social Worker, Master/Clinical http://www2.state.tn.us/health/licensure/index.htm
Speech Pathologist http://www2.state.tn.us/health/licensure/index.htm
Surveyor, Land www.state.tn.us/cgi-bin/commerce/roster3.pl
Teacher www.k-12.state.tn.us/tcertinf/Search.asp
Timeshare Agent www.state.tn.us/cgi-bin/commerce/roster3.pl
Veterinarian http://www2.state.tn.us/health/licensure/index.htm
X-ray Operator http://www2.state.tn.us/health/licensure/index.htm
X-ray Technologist, Podiatry http://www2.state.tn.us/health/licensure/index.htm

County Level ... Courts

Court Administration: Administrative Office of the Courts, 511 Union St (Nashville City Center) #600, Nashville, TN, 37219; 615-741-2687; www.tsc.state.tn.us

Court Structure: Criminal cases are handled by the Circuit Courts and General Sessions Courts. Generally, misdemeanor cases are heard by General Sessions, but in Circuit Court if connected to a felony. All General Sessions Courts have raised the maximum civil case limit to $15,000 from $10,000. The Chancery Courts, in addition to handling probate, also hear certain types of equitable civil cases. Combining of Circuit Court and General Sessions Courts varies by county, and the counties of Davidson, Hamilton, Knox, and Shelby have separate Criminal Courts.

Online Access Note: The Administrative Office of Courts provides access to Appellate Court opinions at the website www.tsc.state.tn.us. Several counties offer online access to court records.

Davidson County

20th District Criminal Court – Criminal Records
www.nashville.gov/ccc/index.htm
Access Metropolitan Nashville and Davidson County Criminal Court database free at www.jis.nashville.org/ccc/CaseSearch.asp. Search by name, warrant, or case number.

Circuit Court and General Sessions – Civil Records
www.nashville.gov/circuit
Access filed cases online on CaseLink at www.nashville.gov/circuit/caselink/; $20.00 per month fee required plus username, password. Email Caselink@Nashville.Gov for signup or add'l info. Intended to be free searching, soon.

Hamilton County

11th District Civil Court and Chancery Court – Civil Records
www.hamiltontn.gov/courts
Access to current court dockets are free at www.hamiltontn.gov/Courts/Chancery/dockets/default.htm.

11th District Criminal Court – Criminal Records
www.hamiltontn.gov/courts
Access to current court dockets is free at www.hamiltontn.gov/Courts/CriminalClerk/dockets/default.htm.

Shelby County

Circuit Court and Chancery Court and General Sessions Civil – Civil Records
www.circuitcourt.co.shelby.tn.us
Search the clerk's circuit court records for free at the website or at
http://gs2.co.shelby.tn.us:7779/pls/crweb/ck_public_qry_main.cp_main_idx.

30th District Criminal Court and General Sessions Criminal – Criminal Records
http://co4.shelbycountytn.gov/court_clerks/criminal_court/index.html
Search the criminal court records for free at http://jssi.co.shelby.tn.us/.

Sullivan County

Bristol General Sessions Court – Civil and Criminal Records
www.bridgeweb.org/docketts.htm
Access to dockets and rules is free at www.bridgeweb.org/docketts.htm. Access to dockets and rules is free online at www.bridgeweb.org/docketts.htm.

County Level ... Recorders & Assessors

Recording Office Organization: 95 counties, 96 recording offices. The recording officer is the Register of Deeds. Sullivan County has two offices. 66 counties are in the Central Time Zone (CST) and 29 are in the Eastern Time Zone (EST). All federal tax liens are filed with the county Register of Deeds. State tax liens are filed with Sec. of State or the Register of Deeds. Counties will not perform tax lien searches.

Online Access Note: The State Comptroller of the Treasury Real Estate Assessment Database can be searched free at http://170.142.31.248/. Select a county then search by name for real property information. Counties not on this system are Davidson, Hamilton, Knox, Shelby, and Unicoi.

Online access to a number of county' property and deeds indexes and images is available via a private company at www.titlesearcher.com or email support@TitleSearcher.com. Registration, login, and monthly $35 fee per county required, plus a one-time $20.00 set up fee. A $5 per day plan is also available.

Also, online access to a large group of county property, deeds, judgment, liens, and UCCs is available via a private company at www.ustitlesearch.com or call 615-223-5420. Registration, login, and monthly $25 fee required, plus $50 set up fee. Use DEMO as your username to sample the system.

Also, www.tnrealestate.com offers free and fee services for real estate information from all Tennessee counties.

Anderson County *Land, Property Assessor, Recorder, Deed Records*

Bedford County *Land, Property Assessor, Recorder, Deed Records*
See state introduction and http://170.142.31.248/ and www.titlesearcher.com.

Benton County *Real Estate, Deed, Judgment, Lien, UCC, Property Assessor Records*
Access real estate records at http://tnassessment.ustitlesearch.net/SelectCounty.asp?map=true&SelectCounty=003 registration/fee required. Also see state introduction and http://170.142.31.248/.

Bledsoe County *Land, Property Assessor, Deed, Recording Records*
See state introduction and http://170.142.31.248/ and www.titlesearcher.com and www.ustitlesearch.net.

Blount County *Property Assessor Records*
See state introduction and http://170.142.31.248/.

Bradley County *Real Estate, Deed, Judgment, Lien, UCC, Property Assessor Records*

Campbell County *Real Estate, Deed, Judgment, Lien, UCC, Property Assessor Records*

Cannon County *Real Estate, Deed, Judgment, Lien, UCC, Property Assessor Records*

Carroll County *Real Estate, Deed, Judgment, Lien, UCC, Property Assessor Records*

Carter County *Real Estate, Deed, Judgment, Lien, UCC, Property Assessor Records*
www.carterdeeds.com
See state introduction and http://170.142.31.248/ and www.titlesearcher.com.

Cheatham County *Real Estate, Deed, Judgment, Lien, UCC, Property Assessor Records*

Chester County *Real Estate, Deed, Judgment, Lien, UCC, Property Assessor Records*

Claiborne County *Real Estate, Deed, Judgment, Lien, UCC, Property Assessor Records*

Clay County *Real Estate, Deed, Judgment, Lien, UCC, Property Assessor Records*

Cocke County *Real Estate, Deed, Judgment, Lien, UCC, Property Assessor Records*

Coffee County *Real Estate, Deed, Judgment, Lien, UCC, Property Assessor Records* See state introduction and http://170.142.31.248/ and www.titlesearcher.com.

Crockett County *Real Estate, Deed, Judgment, Lien, UCC, Property Assessor Records*
See state introduction and http://170.142.31.248/ and www.ustitlesearch.net

Cumberland County *Land, Property Assessor, Deed, Recording Records*
See state introduction and http://170.142.31.248/ and www.titlesearcher.com.

Davidson County *Property, Inmate, Recording, Deed, Judgment, Lien Records*
www.nashville.gov/ROD/
Property records on the Metro Planning Commission Nashville City database are free at www3.nashville.org/property/. Click on "text only search." Search county assessments free at http://hobsvtxie01.nashville.org/Default.asp?br=exp&vr=6. Also, Register of Deeds offers records access by subscription; monthly fees vary, a set-up fee is $25.00. For info, call 615-862-6790. Includes books A thru 3784. Also, a commercial online service allows subscribers to download data via an FTP site. To subscribe fill out application and send $25.00 check. Also, search inmate info on private company website at www.vinelink.com/pickplat.jsp?stateCode=TN.

Decatur County *Land, Property Assessor, Deed, Recording Records*
See state introduction and http://170.142.31.248/ and www.titlesearcher.com.

De Kalb County *Property Assessor Records*
See state introduction and http://170.142.31.248/.

Dickson County *Real Estate, Deed, Judgment, Lien, UCC, Property Assessor Records*
See state introduction and http://170.142.31.248/ and www.titlesearcher.com and www.ustitlesearch.net.

Dyer County *Real Estate, Deed, Judgment, Lien, UCC, Property Tax Records*
www.co.dyer.tn.us
See state introduction and http://170.142.31.248/ and www.ustitlesearch.net

Fayette County *Land, Property Assessor, Deed, Recording Records*
Fentress County *Land, Property Assessor, Deed, Recording Records*
Franklin County *Land, Property Assessor, Deed, Recorder Records*
See state introduction and http://170.142.31.248/ and www.titlesearcher.com.

Gibson County *Real Estate, Deed, Judgment, Lien, UCC, Property Assessor Records*
See state introduction and http://170.142.31.248/ and www.ustitlesearch.net

Giles County *Land, Property Assessor, Deed, Recording Records*
Grainger County *Land, Property Assessor, Deed, Recording Records*
Greene County *Land, Property Assessor, Deed, Recording Records*
See state introduction and http://170.142.31.248/ and www.titlesearcher.com.

Grundy County *Real Estate, Deed, Judgment, Lien, UCC, Property Assessor Records*
www.tngenweb.org/grundy/
See state introduction and http://170.142.31.248/ and www.titlesearcher.com.

Hamblen County *Land, Property Assessor, Deed, Recording Records*
See state introduction and http://170.142.31.248/ and www.titlesearcher.com

Hamilton County *Real Estate, Recording, Deed, Property Assessor, Delinquent Tax Records*
www.hamiltontn.gov/register
The County Register of Deeds subscription service is $50 per month and $1.00 per fax page. Search by name, address, or book & page. For info, call 423-209-6560; or visit www.hamiltontn.gov/Register/default.htm. Credit cards accepted. Also, property assessor and register of deeds records are free at www.hamiltontn.gov/DataServices/default.htm. Click on "Assessor of Property Inquiry." Also, search here for court records. Also back tax lists are at www.hamiltontn.gov/Trustee/delinquent%20taxes.htm. Also, search City of Chattanooga property tax database at http://propertytax.chattanooga.gov.

Hancock County *Real Estate, Deed, Judgment, Lien, UCC, Property Assessor Records*
See state introduction and http://170.142.31.248/ and www.ustitlesearch.net

Hardeman County   *Real Estate, Deed, Judgment, Lien, UCC, Property Assessor Records*
Hardin County   *Real Estate, Deed, Judgment, Lien, UCC, Property Assessor Records*
See state introduction and http://170.142.31.248/ and www.ustitlesearch.net

Hawkins County   *Land, Property Assessor, Deed, Recording Records*
See state introduction and http://170.142.31.248/ and www.titlesearcher.com.

Haywood County   *Property Assessor, Real Estate Records*
See state introduction and http://170.142.31.248/ and www.ustitlesearch.net.

Henderson County   *Real Estate, Deed, Judgment, Lien, UCC, Property Assessor Records*
Henry County   *Real Estate, Deed, Judgment, Lien, UCC, Property Assessor Records*
See state introduction and http://170.142.31.248/ and www.ustitlesearch.net

Hickman County   *Land, Property Assessor, Deed, Recording Records*
See state introduction and http://170.142.31.248/ and www.titlesearcher.com.

Houston County   *Real Estate, Deed, Judgment, Lien, UCC, Property Assessor Records*
See state introduction and http://170.142.31.248/ and www.ustitlesearch.net

Humphreys County   *Land, Property Assessor, Deed, Recording Records*
Jackson County   *Land, Property Assessor, Deed, Recording Records*
Jefferson County   *Land, Property Assessor, Deed, Recording Records*
Johnson County   *Land, Property Assessor, Deed, Recording Records*
See state introduction and http://170.142.31.248/ and www.titlesearcher.com

Knox County   *Real Estate, Assessor, Property Tax Records*
www.knoxcounty.org/register/
Search the property tax rolls for free at www.knoxcounty.org/trustee/taxsearch-site.php. Also, the GIS Dept offers a property map and details report at www.kgis.org/OnlineData/ParcelMapandDetailsReport/tabid/40/Default.aspx. Address searching only.

Lake County   *Real Estate, Deed, Judgment, Lien, UCC, Property Assessor Records*
See state introduction and http://170.142.31.248/ and www.ustitlesearch.net

Lauderdale County   *Real Estate, Deed, Judgment, Lien, UCC, Property Assessor Records*
See state introduction and http://170.142.31.248/ and www.ustitlesearch.net

Lawrence County   *Land, Property Assessor, Deed, Recording Records*
www.co.lawrence.tn.us
See state introduction and http://170.142.31.248/ and www.titlesearcher.com.

Lewis County   *Real Estate, Deed, Judgment, Lien, UCC, Property Assessor Records*
See state introduction and http://170.142.31.248/ and www.ustitlesearch.net

Lincoln County   *Land, Property Assessor, Deed, Recording, GIS Records*
Search property/GIS data free at www.emapsplus.com/TNLincoln/maps/. Also see state introduction and http://170.142.31.248/ and www.titlesearcher.com.

Loudon County   *Land, Property Assessor, Deed, Recording Records*
See state introduction and http://170.142.31.248/ and www.titlesearcher.com.

McMinn County   *Real Estate, Deed, Judgment, Lien, UCC, Property Assessor Records*
McNairy County   *Real Estate, Deed, Judgment, Lien, UCC, Property Assessor Records*
See state introduction and http://170.142.31.248/ and www.ustitlesearch.net

Macon County   *Land, Property Assessor, Deed, Recording Records*
www.maconcountytn.com/register_of_deeds.htm
Access to records must go through Business Information Systems (BIS) at 866-604-3673 who maintain their records. See state introduction and http://170.142.31.248/ and www.titlesearcher.com.

Madison County   *Land, Property Assessor, Deed, Recording Records*
Marion County   *Land, Property Assessor, Deed, Recording Records*
See state introduction and http://170.142.31.248/ and www.titlesearcher.com

Marshall County   *Real Estate, Deed, Judgment, Lien, UCC, Property Assessor Records*
See state introduction and http://170.142.31.248/ and www.titlesearcher.com and www.ustitlesearch.net

Maury County   *Land, Property Assessor, Deed, Recording, GIS, Sexual Offender Registry Records*
Search property/GIS data free at www.emapsplus.com/TNMaury/maps/. Also, Sexual offender registry found at www.ticic.state.tn.us/SEX_ofndr/search_short.asp. For more property data, see state introduction and http://170.142.31.248/ and www.titlesearcher.com.

Meigs County   *Land, Property Assessor, Deed, Recording Records*
Monroe County   *Land, Property Assessor, Deed, Recording Records*
Montgomery County   *Land, Property Assessor, Deed, Recording Records*
Moore County   *Land, Property Assessor, Deed, Recording Records*
See state introduction and http://170.142.31.248/ and www.titlesearcher.com.

Morgan County   *Real Estate, Deed, Judgment, Lien, UCC, Property Assessor Records*
See state introduction and http://170.142.31.248/ and www.ustitlesearch.net

Obion County   *Property Assessor Records*
See state introduction and http://170.142.31.248/

Overton County   *Property Assessor, Real Estate Records*
See state introduction and http://170.142.31.248/ and www.ustitlesearch.net

Perry County   *Land, Property Assessor, Deed, Recording Records*
See state introduction and http://170.142.31.248/ and www.titlesearcher.com.

Pickett County   *Property Assessor Records*
See state introduction and http://170.142.31.248/

Polk County   *Land, Property Assessor, Deed, Recording Records*
See state introduction and http://170.142.31.248/ and www.titlesearcher.com

Putnam County   *Real Estate, Deed, Judgment, Lien, UCC, Property Assessor, GIS Records*
Search property/GIS data free at www.emapsplus.com/TNputnam/maps/. See state introduction and http://170.142.31.248/ and www.titlesearcher.com.

Rhea County   *Land, Property Assessor Records*
Roane County   *Land, Property Assessor Records*
See state introduction and http://170.142.31.248/ and www.titlesearcher.com

Robertson County   *Real Estate, Deed, Judgment, Lien, UCC, Property Assessor Records*
See state introduction and http://170.142.31.248/ and www.ustitlesearch.net

Rutherford County   *Real Estate, Deed, Judgment, Lien, UCC, Property Assessor Records*
See state introduction and http://170.142.31.248/ and www.ustitlesearch.net

Scott County   *Property Assessor Records*
See state introduction and http://170.142.31.248/

Sequatchie County   *Land, Property Assessor, Deed, Recording Records*
Sevier County   *Land, Property Assessor, Deed, Recording Records*
See state introduction and http://170.142.31.248/ and www.titlesearcher.com.

Shelby County   *Real Estate, Lien, Recording, Judgment, Lien, Property Assessor Records*
http://register.shelby.tn.us
Access the register of deeds database free at http://register.shelby.tn.us/index.php. Partial indexes and images go back to 1986; full to 12/2001. Also, access property assessor data free at www.assessor.shelby.tn.us/content.aspx. Also, access property and deeds indexes/images at www.titlesearcher.com; fee/registration required.

Smith County   *Land, Property Assessor, Deed, Recording Records*
Stewart County   *Land, Property Assessor, Deed, Recording Records*
See state introduction and http://170.142.31.248/ and www.ustitlesearch.net

Sullivan County   *Property Assessor Records*
See state introduction and http://170.142.31.248/

Sumner County   *Real Estate, Recording, Deed, Property Tax, Assessor Records*
www.deeds.sumnercounty.org
Search property data free on the GIS site at http://tn.sumner.geopowered.com. At the map, click on "search for property" then name search. Also See state introduction and http://170.142.31.248/ and www.ustitlesearch.net.

Tipton County   *Real Estate, Deed, Judgment, Lien, UCC, Property Assessor Records*
Trousdale County   *Real Estate, Deed, Judgment, Lien, UCC, Property Assessor Records*
See state introduction and http://170.142.31.248/ and www.ustitlesearch.net

Unicoi County   *Land, Property Assessor, Deed, Recorder Records*
Union County   *Land, Property Assessor, Deed, Recorder Records*
Van Buren County   *Land, Property Assessor, Deed, Recorder Records*
See state introduction and http://170.142.31.248/ and www.titlesearcher.com

Warren County   *Real Estate, Deed, Judgment, Lien, UCC, Property Assessor Records*
See state introduction and http://170.142.31.248/ and www.ustitlesearch.net

Washington County   *Real Estate, Deed, Judgment, Lien, UCC, Property Assessor Records*
See state introduction and http://170.142.31.248/ and www.titlesearcher.com

Wayne County   *Land, Property Assessor, Deed, Recording Records*
See state introduction and http://170.142.31.248/ and www.titlesearcher.com and www.ustitlesearch.net

Weakley County   *Land, Property Assessor, Deed, Recording Records*
White County   *Land, Property Assessor, Deed, Recorder Records*
See state introduction and http://170.142.31.248/ and www.titlesearcher.com.

Williamson County   *Deed, Property, Tax Assessor, Recording Records*
Access to the Professional Access database by subscription is a $50 per month fee. Information and sign-up at http://williamson-tn.org/co_gov/profacc.htm. Also, see state introduction and http://170.142.31.248/ and www.titlesearcher.com .

Wilson County   *Real Estate, Lien, Recording, Property Assessor Records*
www.wilsondeeds.com
Access to the Register of Deeds database requires a $10 registration fee and $25.00 per month usage fee at www.wilsondeeds.com. Includes indices back to 1992; images back to 1996. Also, See state introduction and http://170.142.31.248/ and www.titlesearcher.com.

Federal Courts in Tennessee...

Standards for Federal Courts: The universal PACER sign-up number is 800-676-6856. Find PACER and the Party/Case Index on the Web at http://pacer.psc.uscourts.gov. PACER dial-up access is $.60 per minute. Also, courts offering internet access via PACER, Web-PACER or the new CM-ECF charge $.08 per page fee ($.07 per page if record is pre-2005 or unless noted as free).

US District Court -- Middle District of Tennessee

www.tnmd.uscourts.gov

PACER: Case records are available back 3 years. Records are purged yearly. New records are available online after 1 day. **PACER Online Access:** ECF replaces PACER. **Electronic Filing:** Opinions and dockets available on ECF; registration required. CM/ECF data at https://ecf.tnmd.uscourts.gov.
Columbia Division counties: Giles, Hickman, Lawrence, Lewis, Marshall, Maury, Wayne.
Cookeville Division counties: Clay, Cumberland, De Kalb, Fentress, Jackson, Macon, Overton, Pickett, Putnam, Smith, White.
Nashville Division counties: Cannon, Cheatham, Davidson, Dickson, Houston, Humphreys, Montgomery, Robertson, Rutherford, Stewart, Sumner, Trousdale, Williamson, Wilson.

US Bankruptcy Court -- Middle District of Tennessee

www.tnmb.uscourts.gov

PACER: Sign-up number is 615-736-5577. Case records are available back to 9/1989. Records are purged never. New records are available online after immediately. **PACER Online Access:** ECF replaces PACER. **Electronic Filing:** CM/ECF data at https://ecf.tnmb.uscourts.gov. **Other Online Access:** A court docket query is free at www.tnmb.uscourts.gov/courtdocket.html. Court now participate in the US party case index. **Phone access:** Voice Case Information System, call 615-736-5584 x0.
Nashville Division counties: Cannon, Cheatham, Clay, Cumberland, Davidson, De Kalb, Dickson, Fentress, Giles, Hickman, Houston, Humphreys, Jackson, Lawrence, Lewis, Macon, Marshall, Maury, Montgomery, Overton, Pickett, Putnam, Robertson, Rutherford, Smith, Stewart, Sumner, Trousdale, Wayne, White, Williamson, Wilson. Nashville holds records for the Columbia and Cookeville Divisions.

US District Court -- Western District of Tennessee

www.tnwd.uscourts.gov

PACER: Case records are available back to 1993. Records are purged as deemed necessary. New records are available online after 1 day. **PACER Online Access:** ECF replaces PACER. Document images available. **Electronic Filing:** CM/ECF data at https://ecf.tnwd.uscourts.gov.
Jackson Division counties: Benton, Carroll, Chester, Crockett, Decatur, Gibson, Hardeman, Hardin, Haywood, Henderson, Henry, Lake, McNairy, Madison, Obion, Perry, Weakley.
Memphis Division counties: Dyer, Fayette, Lauderdale, Shelby, Tipton.

US Bankruptcy Court -- Western District of Tennessee

www.tnwb.uscourts.gov

PACER: Case records are available back to 1989. Records are purged never. New records are available online after 1 day. **PACER Online Access:** PACER online at http://pacer.tnwb.uscourts.gov. **Electronic Filing:** CM/ECF data at https://ecf.tnwb.uscourts.gov. **Opinions:** View court opinions at www.tnwb.uscourts.gov/Opinions/search.asp. **Other Online Access:** Calendars at www.tnwb.uscourts.gov/vCal/Cal3.asp. Also, case closings located at www.tnwb.uscourts.gov/CaseInfo/CaseInfo.asp. **Phone access:** Voice Case Information System, call 888-381-4961, 901-328-3509
Eastern Division counties: Benton, Carroll, Chester, Crockett, Decatur, Gibson, Hardeman, Hardin, Haywood, Henderson, Henry, Lake, Madison, McNairy, Obion, Perry, Weakley.
Western Division counties: Dyer, Fayette, Lauderdale, Shelby, Tipton.

> **Editor's Tip:** Just because records are maintained in a certain way in your state or county do not assume that any other county or state does things the same way that you are used to.

Texas

Capital: Austin
           Travis County

Time Zone: CST
      Texas' two most western ounties are in MST:
      They are El paso and Hudspeth.

Population: 4,530,182
# of Counties: 254

Quick Links

Website: www.state.tx.us
Governor: www.governor.state.tx.us
Attorney General: www.oag.state.tx.us
State Archives: www.tsl.state.tx.us
State Statutes and Codes: www.capitol.state.tx.us/statutes/statutes.html
Legislative Bill Search: www.lrl.state.tx.us/legis/billChapter/lrlhome.cfm
Bill Monitoring: www.capitol.state.tx.us/tlo/legislation/login.htm
Unclaimed Funds: https://txcpa.cpa.state.tx.us/up/Search.jsp

State Level ... Major Agencies

Criminal Records

Dept of Public Safety, Correspondence Section, Crime Records Service, PO Box 15999, Austin, TX 78761-5999; 512-424-2474, Fax-512-424-5011, 8AM-5PM.
https://records.txdps.state.tx.us/dps_web/APP_PORTAL/index.aspx
Online search: Records can be pulled from the website. Requesters may use a credit card and establish an account to pre-purchase credits. The fee established by the Department (Sec. 411.135(b)) is $3.15 per request plus a $.57 handling fee. These checks are instantaneous and provide convictions and deferred adjudications only.

Statewide Court Records

Office of Court Administration, PO Box 12066, Austin, TX 78711-2066 (Courier: 205 W 14th St, Ste. 600, Austin, TX 78711); 512-463-1625, Fax-512-463-1648, 8AM-5PM.
www.courts.state.tx.us/oca
Online search: Case records of the Supreme Court can be searched at www.supreme.courts.state.tx.us. Court of Criminal Appeals opinions at www.cca.courts.state.tx.us. All Appellate Court case records at www.courts.state.tx.us/appcourt.asp.

Sexual Offender Registry

Dept of Public Safety, Sex Offender Registration, PO Box 4143, Austin, TX 78765-4143; 512-424-2800, Fax-512-424-5666, 8-5PM.
http://records.txdps.state.tx.us
Online search: Sex offender data is available online at https://records.txdps.state.tx.us/soSearch/default.cfm. There is no charge for a sex offender search. To see which organizations have purchased the sexual offender database, go to http://records.txdps.state.tx.us/forsale.cfm.

Incarceration Records

Texas Department of Criminal Justice, Bureau of Classification and Records, PO Box 99, Huntsville, TX 77342 (Courier: 861 IH 45 North, Huntsville, TX 77320); 936-295-6371 (Offender Locator), 800-535-0283 (In State Parole Status line), 8AM-5PM.
www.tdcj.state.tx.us
Online search: No online searching is available direct from this agency, but you may send an email search request to classify@tdcj.state.tx.us. Also, a private company offers free web access at www.vinelink.com/index.jsp.

Corporation, Fictitious Name, Limited Partnership, Limited Liability Company, Assumed Name, Trademarks/Servicemarks

Secretary of State, Corporation Section, PO Box 13697, Austin, TX 78711-3697 (Courier: J Earl Rudder Bldg, 1019 Brazos, B-13, Austin, TX 78701); 512-463-5555 (Information), 512-463-5578 (Copies), Fax-512-463-5709, 8AM-5PM.
www.sos.state.tx.us
Online search: There are several online methods available. Web access is available 24 hours daily. There is a $1.00 fee for each record searched. Filing procedures and forms are available from the website or from 900-263-0060 ($1.00 per minute). Also, Corporate and other TX Sec of State data is available via SOSDirect on the Web; visit www.sos.state.tx.us/corp/sosda/index.shtml. SOSDA accounts are converted to SOSDirect. Printing and certifying capabilities. Also, general corporation information is available at no fee at http://ecpa.cpa.state.tx.us/coa/Index.html from the State Comptroller office. **Other options:** The agency makes portions of its database available for purchase. Call 512-475-2755 for more information.

Uniform Commercial Code, Federal Tax Liens

UCC Section, Secretary of State, PO Box 13193, Austin, TX 78711-3193 (Courier: 1019 Brazos St, Rm B-13, Austin, TX 78701); 512-475-2703, Fax-512-463-1425, 8AM-5PM.
www.sos.state.tx.us/ucc/index.shtml
Online search: UCC and other Texas Secretary of State data is available via SOSDirect on the Web at www.sos.state.tx.us/corp/sosda/index.shtml. UCC records are $1.00 per search, with printing ($1.00 per page) and certifying ($10.00), also. General information and forms can also be found at the website. **Other options:** This agency offers the database for sale, contact the Information Services Dept at 512-463-5609 for further details.

Sales Tax Registrations

Comptroller of Public Accounts, Sales Tax Permits, PO Box 13528, Austin, TX 78711-3528 (Courier: LBJ Office Bldg, 111 E 17th St, Austin, TX 78774); 800-531-5441 x66013, 800-252-1386 (Other Business Searches), Fax-512-475-1610, 8AM-5PM.
www.window.state.tx.us/taxinfo/sales/
Online search: This office makes general corporation information available at http://ecpa.cpa.state.tx.us/vendor/tpsearch1.html. There is no fee. Go to http://aixtcp.cpa.state.tx.us/star/ to search 16,000+ documents by index or collection. Send email requests, send to open.records@cpa.state.tx.us. **Other options:** Sales tax registration lists are available to download as ftp files.

Death Records

Department of State Health Srvs, Bureau of Vital Statistics, PO Box 12040, Austin, TX 78711-2040 (Courier: 1100 W 49th St, Austin, TX 78756-3191); 512-758-7366, Fax-512-758-7711, 8AM-5PM.
www.dshs.state.tx.us/vs/default.shtm
Online search: Death records form 1964 thru 1998 may be viewed at http://vitals.rootsweb.com/tx/death/search.cgi. **Other options:** Death Indexes from 1964-1998 are available on CD-Rom and microfiche.

Marriage Certificates

Department of State Health Srvs, Bureau of Vital Statistics, PO Box 12040, Austin, TX 78711-2040 (Courier: 1100 W 49th St, Austin, TX 78756-3191); 512-758-7366, Fax-512-758-7711, 8AM-5PM.
www.dshs.state.tx.us/vs/default.shtm
Online search: Marriage records for 1966 to 2001 available through a private company at www.genlookups.com/texas_marriages/.

Divorce Records

Department of State Health Srvs, Bureau of Vital Statistics, PO Box 12040, Austin, TX 78711-2040 (Courier: 1100 W 49th St, Austin, TX 78756-3191); 512-758-7366, Fax-512-758-7711, 8AM-5PM.
www.dshs.state.tx.us/vs/default.shtm
Online search: Divorce indexes can be downloaded and searched by year at www.dshs.state.tx.us/vs/marriagedivorce/dindex.shtm. A second private company website at www.genlookups.com/texas_divorces/ offers records from 1968 to 2001.

Workers' Compensation Records

Texas Department of Insurance - Worker's Comp, 7551 Metro Center Dr, #100, MS-92B, Austin, TX 78744; 512-804-4200, 512-804-4325 (Records Dept), Fax-512-804-4993, 8AM-5PM.
www.tdi.state.tx.us/wc/indexwc.html
Online search: The website gives administrative decisions for cases back to 1991 and also permits searching for employers with coverage.

Driver Records

Department of Public Safety, Driver Records Section, PO Box 149246, Austin, TX 78714-9246 (Courier: 5805 N Lamar Blvd, Austin, TX 78752); 512-424-2032, 512-424-2600, Fax-512-424-7285, 8AM-5PM.
www.txdps.state.tx.us/administration/driver_licensing_control/dlindex.htm
Online search: Access is limited to only high volume users who have a permissible use and sign an agreement. The fee is $6.50 for a three-year Type 2 record and $7.50 for a complete Type 3 record. Both batch and interactive modes are available. Call 512-424-5457 to receive a copy of the license agreement. The state also offers access to TX license holders to request their own record, at the web page. Fees vary from $4.50 to $22.00, depending on type of record and if certified. **Other options:** Bulk data is available in electronic format for approved requesters. Weekly updates are available. The file does not include driver history data.

Vehicle Ownership, Vehicle Identification

Department of Transportation, Vehicle Titles and Registration Division,, Austin, TX 78779 (Courier: 4000 Jackson Ave, Austin, TX 78731); 512-465-7611, Fax-512-465-7736, 8AM-5PM.
www.dot.state.tx.us/vtr/vtrreginfo.htm
Online search: Online access is available for pre-approved accounts by contract. A $200 deposit is required, there is a $23.00 charge per month and $.12 fee per inquiry. Searching by name is not permitted. For more information, contact Production Data Control. **Other options:** The department offers tape cartridge retrieval for customized searches or based on the entire database, to eligible organizations under signed contract. Weekly updates and batch inquiries are available. Database contains about 28,000,000 records.

State Level ... Occupational Licensing

Acupuncturist	http://reg.tsbme.state.tx.us/onlineverif/phys_noticeverif.asp?
Air Conditioning/Refrigeration Contr.	www.license.state.tx.us/LicenseSearch/
Alarm Installer/Company/Sales	www.tcps.state.tx.us/individual/individual_search.aspx
Alarm/Security Instructor	www.tcps.state.tx.us/individual/individual_search.aspx
Alcoholic Bev. Dist./Mfg./Retailer	www.tabc.state.tx.us/pubinfo/rosters/default.htm
Alcoholic Beverage Permit	www.tabc.state.tx.us/pubinfo/rosters/default.htm
Architect	www.tbae.state.tx.us/PublicInfo/FindProfessional_Arch.shtml
Architectural Barrier	www.license.state.tx.us/LicenseSearch/
Athletic Trainer	www.dshs.state.tx.us/at/at_roster.shtm
Attorney	www.texasbar.com
Auctioneer	www.license.state.tx.us/LicenseSearch/
Audiologist/Audiology Assistant	www.dshs.state.tx.us/plc/default.shtm
Bank Agency, Foreign	www.banking.state.tx.us/asp/fba/lookup.asp
Bank, State Chartered	www.banking.state.tx.us/asp/bank/lookup.asp
Barber/Barber Shop/Barber Student	www.tsbbe.state.tx.us
Barber School	www.tsbbe.state.tx.us/barbers/barberschools.htm
Boiler Inspector/Installer	www.license.state.tx.us/LicenseSearch/
Boxing/Combative Sports Event	www.license.state.tx.us/LicenseSearch/
Career Counselor	www.license.state.tx.us/LicenseSearch/
Child Care Facility	www.dfps.state.tx.us/Child_Care/Search_Texas_Child_Care/ppFacilitySearchDayCare.asp
Child Care Facility Administrator	www.dfps.state.tx.us/Child_Care/Information_for_Child_Care_Professionals/directory_24hourAdministrators.asp
Child Care Operation	www.dfps.state.tx.us/Child_Care/Search_Texas_Child_Care/ppFacilitySearchResidential.asp
Child Support Agency, Private	www.banking.state.tx.us/pcsea/licensed.htm
Counselor, Professional	www.dshs.state.tx.us/counselor/lpc_rosters.shtm

Courier Company.. www.tcps.state.tx.us/individual/individual_search.aspx

CPA Individual/Firm/Sponsor .... www.tsbpa.state.tx.us/srcmain.htm

Currency Exchange.................................... www.banking.state.tx.us/asp/msb/lookup.asp

Day Care Center ... ... www.dfps.state.tx.us/Child_Care/Search_Texas_Child_Care/ppFacilitySearchDayCare.asp

Day Care, Residential ... www.dfps.state.tx.us/Child_Care/Search_Texas_Child_Care/ppFacilitySearchDayCare.asp

Deaf Service Provider................................ www.dars.state.tx.us/dhhs/list.shtml

Dentist/Dental Hygienist/Dental Lab.......... www.tsbde.state.tx.us/dbsearch/

Dietitian .... www.dshs.state.tx.us/plc/default.shtm

ECA .... http://dshsregn.dshs.state.tx.us/ems/certquery.htm

Elevator/Escalator...................................... www.license.state.tx.us/LicenseSearch/

Emergency Medical Technician.................. http://dshsregn.dshs.state.tx.us/ems/certquery.htm

Engineer.. www.tbpe.state.tx.us/downloads.htm

Engineering Firm .... www.tbpe.state.tx.us/downloads.htm

Family Home Day Care ... www.dfps.state.tx.us/Child_Care/Search_Texas_Child_Care/ppFacilitySearchDayCare.asp

Fire Alarm System Contr. .... www.tdi.state.tx.us/fire/fmli.html

Fire Extinguisher/Sprinkler Contractor....... www.tdi.state.tx.us/fire/fmli.html

Fire Inspector/Investigator .... www.tcfp.state.tx.us

Fire Suppression Specialist .... www.tcfp.state.tx.us

Firearm Instructor .... www.tcps.state.tx.us/individual/individual_search.aspx

Firefighter .... www.tcfp.state.tx.us

Fireworks Display....................................... www.tdi.state.tx.us/fire/fmli.html

Funeral Prepaid Permit Holder .... www.banking.state.tx.us/asp/pfc/lookup.asp

Guard Dog Company .... www.tcps.state.tx.us/individual/individual_search.aspx

Hearing Instrument Dispenser/Fitter........... www.dshs.state.tx.us/plc/default.shtm

Independent Instructor .... www.dshs.state.tx.us/massage/default.shtm

Industrialized Housing................................ www.license.state.tx.us/LicenseSearch/

Insurance Adjuster .... www.texasonline.state.tx.us/NASApp/tdi/TdiARManager

Insurance Agency/Agent/Company .... www.texasonline.state.tx.us/NASApp/tdi/TdiARManager

Interior Designer... www.tbae.state.tx.us/PublicInfo/FindProfessional_IntDes.shtml

Landscape Architect.................................... www.tbae.state.tx.us/PublicInfo/FindProfessional_LandArch.shtml

Lead Abatement Project Designer .... www.tdh.state.tx.us/beh/lead/default.htm

Lead Firm .... www.tdh.state.tx.us/beh/lead/default.htm

Lead Risk Assessor/Inspector .... www.tdh.state.tx.us/beh/lead/default.htm

Lead Training Program Provider .... www.tdh.state.tx.us/beh/lead/default.htm

Lobbyist.. www.ethics.state.tx.us/php/lobsearch.cfm

Manicurist/Manicurist Shop....................... www.tsbbe.state.tx.us

Marriage & Family Therapist .... www.dshs.state.tx.us/mft/mft_contact.shtm

Massage Therapist/Establishment.............. www.dshs.state.tx.us/massage/default.shtm

Massage Therapy School, Instructor.......... www.dshs.state.tx.us/massage/default.shtm

Medical Doctor/Physician........................... http://reg.tsbme.state.tx.us/onlineverif/phys_noticeverif.asp?

Medical Specialty (Doctor)........................ http://reg.tsbme.state.tx.us/onlineverif/phys_noticeverif.asp?

Money Service Business .... www.banking.state.tx.us/asp/msb/lookup.asp

Nurse, Advanced Practice........................... https://www.bne.state.tx.us/olv/apninq.htm

Nurse, Vocational .... https://www.bne.state.tx.us/olv/vninq.htm

Nurse/RN .... https://www.bne.state.tx.us/olv/rninq.htm

Occupational Therapist/Assistant............... www.ecptote.state.tx.us/license/otverif.php

Occupational/Physical Therapy Facility ..... www.ecptote.state.tx.us/license/ftverif.php

Optometrist www.tob.state.tx.us/tob%20verifications.htm

Orthotics & Prosthetics Facility................. www.dshs.state.tx.us/plc/default.shtm

Orthotist/Prosthetist .... www.dshs.state.tx.us/plc/default.shtm

Paramedic .... http://dshsregn.dshs.state.tx.us/ems/certquery.htm

Perfusionist .... www.dshs.state.tx.us/plc/default.shtm

Perpetual Care Cemetery .... www.banking.state.tx.us/asp/pcc/lookup.asp

Personal Employment Service .... www.license.state.tx.us/LicenseSearch/
Pharmacist, Intern/Pharmacy Technician.... www.tsbp.state.tx.us/dbsearch/Default.htm
Pharmacy .... www.tsbp.state.tx.us/dbsearch/Default.htm
Physical Therapist/Assistant .... www.ecptote.state.tx.us/license/ptverif.php
Physician Assistant .... http://reg.tsbme.state.tx.us/onlineverif/phys_noticeverif.asp?
Physicist, Medical .... www.dshs.state.tx.us/plc/default.shtm
Podiatrist.. www.foot.state.tx.us/verifications.htm
Political Action Committee List.................. www.ethics.state.tx.us/dfs/paclists.htm
Political Contributor .... www.ethics.state.tx.us/php/cesearch.html
Polygraph Examiner of Sex Offenders........ www.dshs.state.tx.us/plc/default.shtm
Private Business Letter of Auth. .... www.tcps.state.tx.us/individual/individual_search.aspx
Private Investigator .... www.tcps.state.tx.us/individual/individual_search.aspx
Property Tax Consultant .... www.license.state.tx.us/LicenseSearch/
Psychological Associate............................. www.tsbep.state.tx.us/
Psychologist... www.tsbep.state.tx.us/
Public Accountant-CPA, Firm .... www.tsbpa.state.tx.us/srcmain.htm
Public Account't-CPA Educator/Sponsor ... www.tsbpa.state.tx.us/srcmain.htm
Radiology Technician .... www.dshs.state.tx.us/mrt/mrt_roster.shtm
Real Estate Agent/Broker/Sales/Inspector .. www.trec.state.tx.us/licenseeLookup/search.aspx
Real Estate Appraiser................................. www.talcb.state.tx.us/appraisers/Appraiser_Search.asp
Representative Offices (Foreign Banks) ..... www.banking.state.tx.us/asp/rep/lookup.asp
Respiratory Care Practitioner..................... www.dshs.state.tx.us/respiratory/rc_roster.shtm
Sanitarian .... www.dshs.state.tx.us/plc/default.shtm
School Psychology Specialist .... www.tsbep.state.tx.us/
Security Agency, Private .... www.tcps.state.tx.us/individual/individual_search.aspx
Security Agent/Service/Sales...................... www.tcps.state.tx.us/individual/individual_search.aspx
Service Contract Provider .... www.license.state.tx.us/LicenseSearch/
Sex Offender Treatment Provider .... www.dshs.state.tx.us/plc/default.shtm
Social Worker .... www.dshs.state.tx.us/plc/default.shtm
Speech-Language Pathologist...................... www.dshs.state.tx.us/plc/default.shtm
Staff Leasing.. www.license.state.tx.us/LicenseSearch/
STAP Vendor... www.puc.state.tx.us/relay/stapc/vendors.cfm
Surveyor, Land http://txls.state.tx.us/sect03/rosters.html
Talent Agency.. www.license.state.tx.us/LicenseSearch/
Tax Appraisal Professional .... www.txbtpe.state.tx.us
Teacher .... https://secure.sbec.state.tx.us/SBECONLINE/virtcert.asp
Temporary Common Worker...................... www.license.state.tx.us/LicenseSearch/
Transportation Service Provider .... www.license.state.tx.us/LicenseSearch/
Trust Company .... www.banking.state.tx.us/asp/trustco/lookup.asp
Underground Storage Tank Installer........... www.tceq.state.tx.us/compliance/compliance_support/licensing/ust_lic.html
Vehicle Protection Provider .... www.license.state.tx.us/LicenseSearch/
Veterinarian .... www.tbvme.state.tx.us/verify.htm
Water Well & Pump Installer...................... www.license.state.tx.us/LicenseSearch/
Weather Modification Service .... www.license.state.tx.us/LicenseSearch/

County Level ... Courts

Court Administration: Office of Court Administration, PO Box 12066, Austin, TX, 78711; 512-463-1625; www.courts.state.tx.us

Court Structure: The legal court structure for Texas is explained extensively in the "Texas Judicial Annual Report." Generally, Texas District Courts have general civil jurisdiction and exclusive felony jurisdiction, along with typical variations such as contested probate and divorce. There can be several districts in one courthouse. As of January 15, 2004, four additional District Courts were implemented.

The County Court structure consists of two forms of courts - "Constitutional" and "At Law." The Constitutional upper claim limit is $100,000 while the At Law upper limit is $5,000. For civil matters up to $5000, we recommend searchers start at the Constitutional County Court as they, generally, offer a shorter waiting time for cases in urban areas. District Courts handle felonies. County Courts handle misdemeanors and general civil cases. In some counties the District Court or County Court handles evictions. In 69 counties, District Court and County Court are combined.

Often, a record search is automatically combined for two courts, for example a District Court with a County Court, or both County Courts.

Online Access Note: A number of local county courts offer online access to their records but there is no statewide system of local level court records. Appellate Court case information is searchable free at the website of each Appellate Court, reached online from www.courts.state.tx.us/appcourt.asp. Court of Criminal Appeals opinions are found at www.cca.courts.state.tx.us.

Angelina County

County Court – Civil and Criminal Records
www.angelinacounty.net
Access of dockets is through www.idocket.com; registration and password required. Civl cases from 11/30/96; probate from 1/31/95. Misdemeanor cases from 12/31/83.

Bailey County

District Court – Civil and Criminal Records
Access is through www.idocket.com; registration and password required. Records go back to 12/31/1995.

County Court – Civil and Criminal Records
Access is through www.idocket.com; registration and password required. Civil records go back to 12/31/1995 and 13/31/96 for probate. Crimiinal records goes back to 12/31/1996.

Bandera County

District Court – Civil and Criminal Records
www.banderacounty.org/departments/district_clerk.htm
Civil case information is free at www.idocket.com. Registration and password required. Free searching is limited. Records go back to 12/31/1990. Criminal records go back to 12/31/1990.

Bee County

District Court – Civil and Criminal Records
www.co.bee.tx.us/ips/cms/districtcourt/
Access is at www.idocket.com; registration and password required. This is a fee service, but free if only one name searched a day. Records may go back to 12/31/1987.

Bexar County

District Court and County Court - Central Records – Civil and Criminal Records
www.co.bexar.tx.us/dclerk
Access to the remote online system requires $100 setup fee, plus a $25 monthly fee, plus inquiry fees. Call Jennifer Mann at 210-335-0212 for more information. Also, free online access to records at www.co.bexar.tx.us/webapps/html/dklitinq01.asp.

Brazoria County

District Court – Civil and Criminal Records
www.brazoria-county.com/dclerk
Access civil record docket free at http://records.brazoria-county.com. Access criminal record docket free at http://records.brazoria-county.com; search of Sheriff bond and jail records also available.

County Court – Civil and Criminal Records
www.brazoria-county.com
Access civil record docket free at http://records.brazoria-county.com. Also, access at www.idocket.com; registration and password required. This is a fee service, but free if only one name searched a day. Records go back to 1/1/1986. Access criminal court and county inmate and bond records free at http://records.brazoria-county.com.

Brazos County

District Court – Civil and Criminal Records
www.co.brazos.tx.us/courts
Case index and hearing index available at http://justiceweb.co.brazos.tx.us/judicialsearch/.

Brooks County

District and County Court – Civil and Criminal Records
Civil case information is online at www.idocket.com. Free searching is limited. District court records go back to 12/31/1993. County court records go back to 12/31/94.

Burnet County

District Court – Civil and Criminal Records
http://dcourt.org
One may signup for email notifications of civil and criminal dockets at www.dcourt.org/_attys/dockets.htm.

Cameron County

District and County Court – Civil and Criminal Records
Access is at www.idocket.com; registration and password required. This is a fee service, but free if only one name search a day. District records may go back to 12/31/1988. County records go back to 12/01/93 including probate.

Cherokee County

County Court – Civil and Criminal Records
Access at www.idocket.com; registration and password required. This is a fee service, but free if only one name searched a day.

Cochran County

District & County Court – Civil and Criminal Records
Email address for search requests is cclerk@door.net.

Collin County

District Clerk – Civil and Criminal Records
www.co.collin.tx.us/district_courts/index.jsp
Name and case look up is at www.co.collin.tx.us/rsp-bin/pbkr125.pgm. Search case schedules for free at www.co.collin.tx.us/ShowScheduleSearchServlet. There is also a commercial system- see county courts. Call Lisa Zoski at 972-548-4503 for subscription info.

County Court At Law – Civil and Criminal Records
www.co.collin.tx.us/county_court_law/index.jsp
Access is free at www.co.collin.tx.us/ShowCaseLookupServlet?district_or_county_court=county.

Comal County

District and County Court – Civil and Criminal Records
www.co.comal.tx.us
Access to county judicial records is free at www.co.comal.tx.us/recordsearch.htm. Search civil by either party name. Search criminal by defendant name.

Crane County

District & County Court – Civil and Criminal Records

www.co.crane.tx.us/ips/cms/districtcourt/
Record index can be access online at www.edoctecinc.com. However, be advised the site demands cookie settings to be changed, the instructions have typos and are confusing.

Dallas County

District Court and County Court – Civil Records
www.dallascounty.org
Search civil judgment index at www.dallascounty.org/pars2/. There is no fee unless a record is viewed.

District Court and County Court - Felony and Misdemeanor – Criminal Records
www.dallascounty.org
Public Access System allows remote access at $1.00 per minute to this court and other court/public records. Dial-in access number is 900-263-INFO. ProComm Plus is recommended. Search by name or case number. Call the Public Access Administrator at 214-653-7717 for more info and order $2.00 set-up CD-rom. Also, name search at www.dallascounty.org/applications/english/record-search/intro.html; index includes DOB. $5.50 fee per search, use credit card. Also, search criminal record at www.dallascounty.org/pars2/. There is no fee unless a record is viewed.

Denton County

District Court – Civil and Criminal Records
http://dentoncounty.com/dept/main.asp?Dept=26
Search records free at http://justice.dentoncounty.com. Search by name or cause number. Criminal records go back to 1994 forward. Access also includes sheriff bond and jail records.

County Court – Civil and Criminal Records
http://dentoncounty.com/deptall.asp
Access to civil court records is free at http://justice.dentoncounty.com/CivilSearch/civfrmd.htm. Access to county criminal records is free at http://justice.dentoncounty.com/CrimSearch/crimfrmd.htm. Jail, bond, and parole records are also available at http://justice.dentoncounty.com. Search for registered sex offenders by ZIP Code at http://sheriff.dentoncounty.com/sex_offenders/default.htm.

El Paso County

District Court and County Court – Civil and Criminal Records
www.co.el-paso.tx.us/districtclerk
Access to civil court records is free at www.epcounty.com/search.htm. Also, access is at www.idocket.com; registration and password required; online civil records go back to 12/31/1986. Images available. Access to criminal court records is free at www.epcounty.com/search.htm. Also, online access is at www.idocket.com; registration and password required; online records go back to 12/31/1986. Images available.

Probate Court – Civil Records
Access probate records at through www.idocket.com; registration and password required. Records go back to 12/31/1986.

Fort Bend County

District Court – Civil and Criminal Records
www.co.fort-bend.tx.us
Search for free at http://courtcn.co.fort-bend.tx.us/. Records go back to 9/2000; no DOBs.

County Court – Civil and Criminal Records
www.co.fort-bend.tx.us
Access to the civil records index free at http://ccweb.co.fort-bend.tx.us/search.asp?cabinet=civil. Includes Probate records index online.

Galveston County

County Court – Civil and Criminal Records
www.co.galveston.tx.us/County_Courts
Access is at http://ccweb.co.galveston.tx.us. Index search if free; records go back to 1983 generally. Probate records go back to 1987. Access to the GCNET remote online service has been suspended.

Grayson County

County Court – Civil and Criminal Records
www.co.grayson.tx.us
Access to civil records free at www.co.grayson.tx.us:3004/judsrch.asp. Also includes sheriffs' bail, and sheriff's jail searching.

Gregg County

District Court and County Court – Civil and Criminal Records
www.co.gregg.tx.us/government/courts.asp
Access to county judicial records is free at www.co.gregg.tx.us/judsrch.htm. Search by name, cause number, status. Also includes jail and bond search.

Guadalupe County

District Court – Civil and Criminal Records
www.co.guadalupe.tx.us
Access is at www.idocket.com; one free search per day; subscription required for more. Online dockets go back to 12/31/1991.

Harris County

District Court – Civil and Criminal Records
www.hcdistrictclerk.com/Home/Home.aspx
First, an online case lookup service is free at legacy.hcdistrictclerk.com/CFTS/CaseLocationSearch.asp. Online records go back to 10/1989. Second, register for free-to-view e-docs service at https://e-docs.hcdistrictclerk.com/eDocs.Web/Login.aspx and pay $1 per page (credit cards accepted) for civil documents. The e-docs service does not offer access to criminal records. Also, access to records is to qualified JIMs subscribers at www.jims.hctx.net.

County Court – Civil Records
www.cclerk.hctx.net
Access is free at www.cclerk.hctx.net. System includes civil data search and county civil settings inquiry and other county clerk functions. For further information, visit the website or call 713-755-6421. Also, online access is at www.idocket.com; registration and password required. This is a fee service, unless only one name search a day. Records go back to 12/31/1997.

Probate Court – Civil Records
Probate dockets are through the Harris County online system. Call 713-755-7815 for information. Dockets are free at www.cclerk.hctx.net/coolice/default.asp?Category=ProbateCourt&Service=pc_inquiry. Records go back to 1837.

Hays County

District Court and County Court – Civil and Criminal Records
www.co.hays.tx.us
Access is through www.idocket.com; registration and password required. District records go back to 12/31/1986. County court civil records from 01/88. County court misdemeanor records go back to 12/31/1987.

Hidalgo County

District Court and County Court – Civil and Criminal Records
www.co.hidalgo.tx.us/dc/
Access is through www.idocket.com; registration and password required. Records go back to 12/31/1986. Misdemeanor records go back to 12/31/1991.

Hill County

District Court – Civil and Criminal Records
Access to court records is through www.idocket.com. One search a day is free; subscription required for more. Records go back to 12/31/1990.

Jefferson County

District Court – Civil and Criminal Records
www.co.jefferson.tx.us
Access to the civil records index at www.co.jefferson.tx.us/dclerk/civil_index/main.htm. Search by year by defendant or plaintiff by year 1985 to present. Also, you may name search at http://jeffersontxclerk.hartic.com/search.asp?cabinet=civil. Index goes back to 1995; images back to 12/1998. Access to the criminal records index is at www.co.jefferson.tx.us/dclerk/criminal_index/main.htm. Search by name by year 1981 to present. Also, felony records are free at http://jeffersontxclerk.hartic.com/search.asp?cabinet=criminal. Add'l criminal records are being added.

County Court – Civil and Criminal Records
http://jeffersontxclerk.hartintercivic.com
Search the county clerk's civil database free at http://jeffersontxclerk.hartintercivic.com/search.asp?cabinet=civil. Index goes back to 1995; images back to 12/1998. Access to Class A&B and C Misdemeanor that are appealed records back to 1982 are free at http://jeffersontxclerk.hartintercivic.com/search.asp?cabinet=criminal. Add'l criminal records are being added.

Johnson County

District Court and County Court – Civil and Criminal Records
www.johnsoncountytx.org
Access at www.idocket.com; registration and password required. This is a fee service, but free if only one name searched a day. Records go back to 11/10/1989. Images available. County Court civil records back to 12/31/85, probate to 12/31/88. County Court misdemeanor (no felony) records back to 12/31/88.

Kaufman County

County Court – Civil and Criminal Records
www.kaufmancountyclerk.com/
Search records online at http://12.14.175.23/. Search record index online at http://12.14.175.23/.

Kleberg County

District & County Court at Law – Civil and Criminal Records
Access is at www.idocket.com; registration and password required. There is a fee service, but free if only one name search is done a day. Civil records go back to 1992 for District; 1997 for County. District criminal records go back to 12/31/1995.

Lamar County

District Court – Civil and Criminal Records
www.co.lamar.tx.us
Access to county judicial records is free at www.co.lamar.tx.us/. Search by either party name. Access to county judicial records is free online at www.co.lamar.tx.us. Search by defendant name.

County Court – Civil and Criminal Records
www.co.lamar.tx.us
Access to county judicial records is free at http://68.89.102.225/. Search by either party name. Access to county judicial records is free online at www.co.lamar.tx.us. Search by defendant name.

Llano County

District Clerk – Civil Records
http://dcourt.org
One may signup for email notifications of civil and criminal dockets at www.dcourt.org/_attys/dockets.htm.

Maverick County

County Court – Civil and Criminal Records
Access at www.idocket.com; registration and password required. This is a fee service, but free if only one name searched a day.

McCulloch County

District and County Courts – Civil and Criminal Records
Civil case information is free at www.idocket.com. Free searching is limited. District court records go back to 12/31/1995. County Court records go back to 12/31/1996; includes probate records.

Midland County

District and County Courts – Civil and Criminal Records
www.co.midland.tx.us/DC/default.asp
Access to the district Clerk database is at www.co.midland.tx.us/DC/Database/search.asp. Registration and password required; contact the clerk for access.

Montgomery County

County Court – Criminal Records
www.co.montgomery.tx.us
Access at www.idocket.com; registration and password required. This is a fee service, but free if only one name searched a day. Records go back to 12/31/1989.

Nacogdoches County

District and County Courts – Civil and Criminal Records
Access is available by subscription at www.idocket.com including district court records back to 12/31/1986.

Navarro County

District Court – Civil and Criminal Records
www.co.navarro.tx.us/ips/cms/districtcourt/
Civil case information is online at www.idocket.com. Free searching is limited. Records go back to 12/31/1990.

Nueces County

District & County Court – Civil and Criminal Records
www.co.nueces.tx.us/districtclerk
Access to civil District & County Court records are free at www.co.nueces.tx.us/districtclerk/. Click on Civil/Criminal Case Search, register, then search by name, company, SID number, or cause number.

Parker County

District and County Courts – Civil and Criminal Records
www.parkercountytx.com
Access to court records is free at www.parkercountytx.com. Access to criminal records and sheriff inmates and bonds searching is free at www.parkercountytx.com. District court records go back to 7/88.

Parmer County

District Court – Civil and Criminal Records
Access is through www.idocket.com; registration and password required. Records go back to 12/31/1995.

Potter County

District Court – Civil and Criminal Records
www.co.potter.tx.us/districtclerk
Civil case information from 1988 forward is online at www.idocket.com. Free case searching is limited

Randall County

District and County Courts – Civil and Criminal Records
www.randallcounty.org
Civil case information is free at www.idocket.com. Free searching is limited. District records go back to 12/31/84. County Court civil records go back to 12/31/1999; probate back to 12/31/1969. Criminal records go back to 12/31/1991.

Refugio County

District and County Courts – Civil and Criminal Records
Access at www.idocket.com; registration and password required. This is a fee service, but free if only one name searched a day.

Rockwall County

District and County Courts – Civil and Criminal Records
www.rockwallcountytexas.com
Access is free at www.rockwallcountytexas.com/judicialsearch/. Search sheriff bond and jail lists too.

Starr County

District & County Court – Civil and Criminal Records
Access at www.idocket.com; registration and password required. This is a fee service, but free if only one name searched a day. Civil records go back to 1/01/99. Criminal records go back to 12/31/96.

Tarrant County

District and County Courts – Civil and Criminal Records
www.tarrantcounty.com/ecourts/site/default.asp
Access to the remote online system requires $50 setup that includes software and a monthly fee of $35 per month with add'l month prepaid; for 1 to 5 users; fees increase with more users. Call 817-884-1345 for info and signup. Index records are available for free at http://cc.co.tarrant.tx.us/CivilCourts/ccl/default.asp. Also, probate records are at http://cc.co.tarrant.tx.us/CivilCourts/Probate/default.asp?eprobatecourtsNav=|

Tom Green County

District and County Courts – Civil and Criminal Records
www.co.tom-green.tx.us/distclrk/

Access to civil case records back to 1994 is online at http://justice.co.tom-green.tx.us. Search by name, case number. Website also includes sheriff's jail and bond records.

Travis County

County Court – Civil Records
www.co.travis.tx.us
Access to probate court records only is free at http://deed.co.travis.tx.us/search.aspx?cabinet=probate.

Val Verde County

District Court – Civil and Criminal Records

Access at www.idocket.com; registration and password required. This is a fee service, but free if only one name searched a day. Civil records go back to 12/01/89. Criminal back to 12/31/93.

Victoria County

District and County Courts – Civil and Criminal Records

Access is through www.idocket.com; registration and password required. District court records go back to 12/31/1993. Images available. County court records go back to 12/31/1989.

Washington County

District and County Courts – Civil and Criminal Records

Access to court records is through www.idocket.com. District court dockets from 12/30/1988. One search a day is free; subscription required for more. Search County court civil records back to 12-31-85; probate to 12-31-68. County Court misdemeanor records back to 12/31/1985.

Webb County

District Court – Civil and Criminal Records
www.webbcountytx.gov
Access is through www.idocket.com; registration and password required. Records go back to 12/31/1988.

Williamson County

County Court – Civil and Criminal Records
Access to limited case records is free at http://judicialsearch.wilco.org. Criminal case records go back to 1983. Sheriff bond and inmate data is also available.

Wood County

District Court – Civil and Criminal Records
http://judicial.co.wood.tx.us
Search civil case index at http://judicial.co.wood.tx.us/CivilSearch/civfrmd.asp. Search criminal case index at http://judicial.co.wood.tx.us/CrimSearch/crimfrmd.asp.

Young County

District Court – Civil and Criminal Records
Access at www.idocket.com; registration and password required. This is a fee service, if only one name searched a day. Records go back to 3/1/1998.

County Level ... Recorders & Assessors

Recording Office Organization: 254 counties, 254 recording offices. The recording officer is the County Clerk. 252 counties are in the Central Time Zone (CST) and 2 are in the Mountain Time Zone (MST). Federal tax liens on personal property of businesses are filed with the Secretary of State. Other federal and all state tax liens are filed with the County Clerk. All counties will perform tax lien searches. Search fees and copy fees can vary, but records are usually provided as part of the UCC search.

Online Access Note: Numerous counties offer online access to assessor and recordered document data. A good place to link to county appraisal districts is www.texascad.com where you can click through to many county appraisers, many with free searching. Also, two private companies offer access to multiple counties' tax assessor data: www.taxnetusa.com and www.txcountydata.com. Many Texas counties may be accessed from multiple sites, some mentioned below. A search at the State Archives' TRAIL website at http://www2.tsl.state.tx.us/trail/ lets you locate information from over 180 Texas state agency web servers.

www.txcountydata.com - Assessor and property information records for many Texas counties on the TXCOUNTYDATA site are available for no fee. At this site click on "County Search" then use the pull down menu in the county field to select the county to search. The County Info page for each county lists the Appraiser, mailing address, phone, fax, website, email. Generally, you can search any county account, owner name, address, or property ID number. A search allows you to access owner address, property address, legal description, taxing entities, exemptions, deed, account number, abstract/subdivision, neighborhood, valuation info, and more.

www.taxnetusa.com - TaxNetUSA offers appraisal district and property information records for a large number of Texas counties. They offer a free search as well as online subscriptions services using a sliding fee scale, or you may purchase bulk data as downloads. Visit the website or call 877-652-2707 for more information. To search free at the TaxNetUSA site, click on the "Coverage Area" and select a county. Generally, but in varying degrees from county to county, the basic search allows you to access general property information: name, address, valuation, etc., and you may search by parcel number, owner name, or address. Depending on the county, more "detailed" information may be available.

www.titlex.com offers recording office records in county grantor/grantee indices - including real estate, deeds, liens, judgments records and more - free for many Texas counties.

www.texaslandrecords.com offers free land index searching at a group of 22 or more Texas counties, plus a deeper real estate subscription service for those counties which requires fees, registration, and password.

Anderson County   *Appraiser, Property Tax, Real Estate, Deed, Judgment, Lien, Grantor/Grantee Records*
Access recording records free at www.titlex.com; select Anderson county. Records range is 6/1972 to 12/2003. Also, property tax inquiries can be made at www.txcountydata.com/county.asp?County=001.

Angelina County   *Appraiser, Property Tax, Probate, Judgment Records*
www.angelinacounty.net
Access appraisal district data free at www.angelinacad.org/Appraisal/PublicAccess/. Also see note at beginning of section. Access assessment records at www.texaslandrecords.com and at www.txcountydata.com. Also, search probate records and judgment records at http://idocket.com/countycourt.htm.

Aransas County   *Appraiser, Property Tax Records*
www.aransascounty.org
Access to dated appraiser and property tax information is at www.aransascad.org/Appraisal/PublicAccess/. Also see note at beginning of section.

Archer County   *Appraiser, Property Tax Records*
Access property tax records free at http://216.61.193.135/archcad/main.jsp. Also, access property records free at www.taxnetusa.com.

Atascosa County   *Real Estate, Grantor/Grantee, Judgment, Deed, Lien, Appraiser, Property Tax Records*
Access recording records free at www.titlex.com; select Atascosa County. Also, see note at beginning of section.

Austin County *Appraiser, Property Tax, Real Estate, Deed, Judgment, Lien, Grantor/Grantee Records*

Access recording records free at www.titlex.com; select Austin county. Records range is 8/1997 to 8/2001. Also, search property tax records for free at www.austincad.org. Also, see note at beginning of section.

Bailey County *Property, Appraiser, Probate, Judgment Records*

Access to Appraisal District records is free at http://clientdb.trueautomation.com/clientdb/main.asp?id=3. Also, to search probate records and judgment records go to http://idocket.com/countycourt.htm

Bandera County *Property, Personal Property, Appraiser, Probate, Judgment Records*

www.banderacounty.org

Access to county property search is free at www.taxnetusa.com. Also, See note at beginning of section. Search Tax Collector data at https://tax.co.bexar.tx.us/. Also, to search probate records and judgment records go to http://idocket.com/countycourt.htm.

Bastrop County *Appraiser, Property Tax, Real Estate, Judgment, Lien, Grantor/Grantee Records*

Access recording records free at www.titlex.com; select Bastrop county. Record range is 3/2001 to 8/31/2001. Also, access to tax office records is free at www.bastroptac.com. Also, see note at beginning of section.

Bee County *Property Tax, Land Records*

Access property records free at www.beecad.org/beecad/main.jsp. Also, search land records online at www.texaslandrecords.com.

Bell County *Property, Appraiser Records*

www.bellcountytx.com/countyclerk/index.htm

Access to Appraisal District records is free at http://clientdb.trueautomation.com/clientdb/main.asp?id=21.

Bexar County *Real Estate, Grantor/Grantee, Marriage, UCC, Assumed Name, Recording, Property Tax, Appraiser, Probate Records*

www.countyclerk.bexar.landata.com

Access to the County Clerk database is free at www.countyclerk.bexar.landata.com. Includes land records, deeds, UCCs, assumed names and foreclosure notices. Probate is recently added. Images are to be added on a new subscription service. Also, access to the county Central Appraisal District database is free at www.bcad.org/clientdb/?cid=1.

Blanco County *Appraiser, Property Tax Records*

Access at ww.txcountydata.com, see note at beginning of section.

Bosque County *Appraisal, Property Records*

Access property records at www.txcountydata.com.

Bowie County *Property Tax, Appraiser Records*

Assess to Appraisal District's Appraisal Roll data is free at www.bowiecad.org/Search.htm.

Brazoria County

Appraiser, Property Tax, Real Estate, Grantor/Grantee, Deed, Lien, Judgment, Bond, Inmate Records

www.brazoria.tx.us.landata.com

Access to the county Central Appraisal District database is free at www.brazoriacad.org. Click on "appraisal roll." Access recording records free at www.titlex.com; select Brazoria county. Records range from 3/2001 to 1/2004. Also, see note at beginning of section. Also, access sheriff bond and inmate records free at http://records.brazoria-county.com.

Brazos County *Appraiser, Property Tax, Land Records*

Access to County Appraisal District data is free at www.brazoscad.org/Appraisal/PublicAccess/. Also, for land records search go to www.texaslandrecords.com. Also, see notes at beginning of section.

Brewster County *Property, Appraiser Records*

Access property data by download from a private company; fees apply; add'l data includes minerals, ofc exports, delinquents; visit www.ptax.org/tax_office_data.htm or phone 201-571-0425.

Brooks County *Real Estate Recording, Deed, Probate, Judgment Records*

Access recording office land data at www.etitlesearch.com; registration required, fee based on usage. Also, to search probate records and judgment records go to http://idocket.com/countycourt.htm

Brown County   *Appraiser, Property Tax Records*

Access to Appraisal District records is free at http://clientdb.trueautomation.com/clientdb/main.asp?id=30. Also, see note at beginning of section.

Burleson County   *Appraiser, Property Tax Records*

Access property tax records at www.txcountydata.com and click on Burleson. Also, see note at beginning of section.

Burnet County   *Real Estate, Grantor/Grantee, Deed, Lien, Judgment, Appraiser, Property Tax Records*

Access recording records free at www.titlex.com; select Burnett county. Records range from 1/1998 to 11/2001. Also, see note at beginning of section, www.txcountydata.com.

Caldwell County   *Appraiser, Property Tax, Personal Property Records*

Access the county Appraisal District database now free at www.txcountydata.com. Also, access Appraisal District records free at http://clientdb.trueautomation.com/clientdb/main.asp?id=37. Also, see notes at beginning of section.

Calhoun County   *Real Estate, Grantor/Grantee, Deed, Judgment, Lien, Property Tax, Appraiser Records*

Access recording records free at www.titlex.com; select Calhoun county. Records range up to 9/2003. Also, access Appraisal District records free at http://clientdb.trueautomation.com/clientdb/main.asp?id=24.

Callahan County   *Property Records*

Find property information at appraiser site at www.myswdata.com/wfFind.aspx. Name searching available.

Cameron County   *Appraiser, Property Tax, Probate, Judgment Records*

www.co.cameron.tx.us
Access appraisal district property records free at www.cameroncad.org/ClientDB/PropertySearch.aspx?cid=1. Access probate and judgment records free at http://idocket.com/countycourt.htm Also, see note at beginning of section.

Camp County   *Property Tax, Appraiser Records*

Access property tax records free at www.campcad.org/aspxsearchnew.aspx.

Cass County   *Property, Appraiser Records*

Access to property records is free at www.casscad.org. Click on search our data.

Chambers County   *Property Tax, Appraiser Records*

Search the appraiser property tax database for free at www.chamberscad.org. Also, see note at beginning of section.

Cherokee County

Real Estate, Grantor/Grantee, Deed, Judgment, Lien, Property Tax, Appraiser, Land, Probate Records
Access recording records free at www.titlex.com; select Cherokee county. Records range from 5/1973 to 2/2004. Also, see note at beginning of section. Also, search the Cherokee CAD database for free at http://clientdb.trueautomation.com/clientdb/main.asp?id=2. Also, for land records search go to www.texaslandrecords.com. Also, to search probate records and judgment records go to http://idocket.com/countycourt.htm

Clay County   *Property Tax, Appraiser Records*

Access property tax records free at www.claycad.org/claycad/main.jsp. Also, see note at beginning of section.

Coleman County   *Appraiser, Property Tax Records*

See note at beginning of section, www.txcountydata.com.

Collin County

Appraiser, Property Tax, Business Personal Property, Deed, Lien, Judgment, Vital Statistic, Mortgage Records
www.co.collin.tx.us
Access to the county clerk Deeds database is free at www.collincountytexas.gov/DeedSearch. Also, search the Appraiser's property tax and business property database for free at www.collincad.org/search.php. Also, search the tax assessor and collector look up free at www.co.collin.tx.us/tax_assessor/taxstmt_search.jsp. Also, see note at beginning of section.

Colorado County
Real Estate, Grantor/Grantee, Deed, Judgment, Lien, Cemetery, Property Tax, Appraiser Records
www.co.colorado.tx.us/ips/cms
Access recording records free at www.titlex.com; select Colorado county. Records range is 5/1997 to 9/2001. Also, vital statistics are free from an unofficial at www.rootsweb.com/~txcolora/vitalrecords.htm. Divorces go back to 1968; deaths back to 1964; marriages back to 1966. Also, access Appraisal District records free at http://clientdb.trueautomation.com/clientdb/main.asp?id=31. Also, see note at beginning of section. Also for property search go to www.coloradocad.org/ and click on property search.

Comal County   *Property, Appraiser Records*
www.co.comal.tx.us
Access Appraisal District records free at http://clientdb.trueautomation.com/clientdb/main.asp?id=35. Also search property free at www.comalcad.org.

Comanche County   *Appraiser, Property Tax Records*
Access Appraisal District records free at http://clientdb.trueautomation.com/clientdb/main.asp?id=12. Also, see note at beginning of section, www.txcountydata.com.

Cooke County   *Property, Appraiser Records*
Access to the Cooke CAD Live database is free at http://clientdb.trueautomation.com/clientdb/main.asp?id=10.

Coryell County   *Property, Appraiser Records*
www.co.coryell.tx.us
Access Appraisal District property records free at http://clientdb.trueautomation.com/clientdb/main.asp?id=45.

Crane County   *Real Estate, Deed, Official Records*
www.co.crane.tx.us
Search official records after choosing county at www.edoctecinc.com. If records are Unofficial, you search or copy them freely; if not Unofficial, a $1.00 per page fee applies. For details and signup, contact clerk or Jerry Anderson at 800-578-7746.

Dallas County
Property Tax, Personal Property, Voter Registration, Marriage, UCC, Assumed Name, Probate Records
www.dallascounty.org/applications/english/record-search/rec-search_intro.html
Name search indices of marriages, assumed names, UCCs, probate, court records and real estate back to 1977 on the search page at www.realestate.countyclerk.dallascounty.org. Indices include DOB. $6.00 fee to view and print documents; credit cards accepted. Purchase per item or subscribe for $75 annual fee. Also, access Central Appraisal District data free at www.dallascad.org/SearchOwner.aspx. Also, access County Voter Registration Records free at www.dalcoelections.org/voters.asp. Will show if registered and in what precinct. Online record searches found at www.dallascounty.org/pars2/

Deaf Smith County   *Property, Appraiser Records*
Search the appraisal tax rolls for free at www.txcountydata.com/county.asp?County=059.

Delta County   *Property, Appraiser Records*
Access Appraisal District records free at http://clientdb.trueautomation.com/clientdb/main.asp?id=39.

Denton County
Real Estate, Recording, Voter Registration, Most Wanted, Parolee, Sex Offender, Bond, Jail, Conviction Records
www.dentoncounty.com/dept/ccl.htm
Access county property database indices free for name/instrument searches; no fee for access, but to view and print images is $1.00 per page; see https://www.texaslandrecords.com/txlr/TxlrApp/index.jsp. With a full subscription, you can search full indices and download images. Also, search voter registration rolls free at http://elections.dentoncounty.com/VRSearch/default.asp. Search the "justice" database free at http://justice.dentoncounty.com. Includes parolees, sex offenders, most wanted lists, bond, jail, convictions and court records databases.

De Witt County   *Property Tax, Appraiser Records*
Access to property data is free at www.beecad.org/dewicad/main.jsp.

Dimmit County   *Property, Appraiser Records*
Access Appraisal District records free at http://clientdb.trueautomation.com/clientdb/main.asp?id=40.

Donley County *Property, Appraiser Records*
Access property data by download from a private company; fees apply; add'l data includes minerals, ofc exports, delinquents; visit www.ptax.org/tax_office_data.htm or phone 201-571-0425.

Eastland County *Vital Statistic Records*
Access to vital statistics from an unofficial source is free at http://ftp.rootsweb.com/pub/usgenweb/tx/eastland/vitals/. Births go back to 1926; deaths to 1964, Divorce to 1968, Marriages to 1966.

Ector County
Real Estate, Grantor/Grantee, Appraiser, Personal Property, Recording, Lien, UCC, Judgment Records
www.co.ector.tx.us
Search the county appraisal district property data and personal property for free at www.ectorcad.org. Also, search the recorder index free at www.texaslandrecords.com. Click on coutnies to locate Ector. Free search available, also a subscription service with search/payment options for full document viewing.

Ellis County *Appraiser, Property Tax Records*
Search the property appraiser database for free at www.elliscad.org. Also, see note at beginning of section.

El Paso County *Assumed Name, Property Tax, Real Estate, Vital Statistic, Probate, Judgment Records*
www.co.el-paso.tx.us/search.htm
Search vital statistics (birth, death, marriage), assumed names, and property records free at www.co.el-paso.tx.us/search.htm. Also, search property tax data free at www.elpasocad.org. Also, to search probate records and judgment records go to http://idocket.com/countycourt.htm Also, see note at beginning of section.

Erath County *Property Tax, Appraiser Records*
Find property information at appraiser site at www.myswdata.com/wfFind.aspx. Name searching available. Also, see note at beginning of section.

Falls County *Property Tax, Appraiser, Map Records*
Access to property data is free at www.fallscad.org. Click on Search Our Data. Maps may also be available.

Fannin County *Appraiser, Property Tax Records*
Access Appraisal District records free at http://clientdb.trueautomation.com/clientdb/main.asp?id=34. Also, see beginning of section.

Fayette County *Real Estate, Grantor/Grantee, Deed, Lien, Judgment Records*
www.co.fayette.tx.us
Access recording records free at www.titlex.com; select Fayette county.

Fort Bend County
Real Estate, Grantor/Grantee, Deed, Lien, Judgment, Appraiser, UCC, Marriage, Death, Birth, Probate Records
www.co.fort-bend.tx.us
Access to the county clerk database is free at www.co.fort-bend.tx.us/admin_of_justice/County_Clerk/index_info_research.htm. Search the property index by name, or the plat index. And, search county probate and court records. For information, contact Diane Shepard at 281-341-8664. UCCs records can be searched for free at http://ccweb.co.fort-bend.tx.us/search.asp?cabinet=ucc. Also, access recording records free at www.titlex.com; select Ft Bend county. Record range is 1/1974 to 11/2001. Also, see note at beginning of section for add'l fee service for tax records and recordings.

Franklin County *Property Tax, Appraiser Records*
www.co.franklin.tx.us
Access to property data is free at www.franklincad.com. Click on Search Our Data. Also, see note at beginning of section.

Freestone County *Property Tax, Appraiser Records*
Access to Appraiser's property data is free at www.freestonecad.org. Click on Search Our Data.

Gaines County *Property, Appraiser Records*
Access Appraisal District records free at http://clientdb.trueautomation.com/clientdb/main.asp?id=47.

Galveston County *Real Estate, Grantor/Grantee, Deed, Lien, Judgment, Appraiser, Property Tax, Personal Property, Sheriff Sale, Most Wanted, UCC, Vital Statistic, Court Records*
www.co.galveston.tx.us/County_Clerk/
Several sources exist. Access the county online official records index free at http://ccweb.co.galveston.tx.us/localization/menu.asp.
Recording index records dates back to 1965; courts back to mid-'80s generally. Still in development. No images as yet. For info, call
409-766-5115. Also, search recorder records free at www.titlex.com. Also, Central Appraisal Dist. database is free at
www.galvestoncad.org. Also, search county most wanted list at http://www2.galveston.tx.us/Sheriff/most_wanted.htm. Also,
sheriff sales data free at http://www2.co.galveston.tx.us/sheriff/sheriff_sale.pdf. Also, a Grantor/Grantee index is at www.titlex.com;
select Galveston County; records go back to 1/1965. Also, see note at beginning of section.

Gillespie County *Appraiser, Property Tax Records*
See note at beginning of section.

Goliad County *Real estate, Grantor/Grantee, Deed, Lien, Judgment Records*
www.goliadcogovt.org
Access recording records free at www.titlex.com; select Goliad county. Records range is 1/1950 to 12/2003. Also, see note at
beginning of section.

Grayson County *Real Estate, Grantor/Grantee, Lien, Judgment, Appraiser, Property Tax, Bad Check, Sheriff Sale, Sheriff Bond, Jail, Vital Statistic Records*
www.co.grayson.tx.us/main.htm
Search the Grayson CAD system for property, mortgage, and property data at
http://clientdb.trueautomation.com/clientdb/main.asp?id=15. Also search Appraiser property data for free at www.graysoncad.org.
Access recording records free at www.titlex.com; select Grayson county. Also, sheriff sales data is at
www.co.grayson.tx.us/Tax%20Office/ssale.pdf. Also, search the county attorney's hot check list at
www.co.grayson.tx.us/Attorney/HC%20List.PDF. Also, for land records search and vital records go to www.texaslandrecords.com.
Search the sheriff bond records and jail data at http://co.grayson.tx.us:3004/judsrch.asp. Also, see note at beginning of section.

Gregg County *Real Estate, Grantor/Grantee, Deed, Mortgage, Lien, Judgment, Assessor, Property Tax, Vital Statistic, UCC Records*
www.co.gregg.tx.us
Access to the County Clerk's Official Public Records database is free to view at www.co.gregg.tx.us/hartIAM/. Fee to copy
documents. Also, search property tax records for free at www.co.gregg.tx.us/tax/viking.asp. Also, access recording records free at
www.titlex.com; select Gregg county. Records range is 4/1977 to 5/2005. Also, see note at beginning of section.

Guadalupe County *Property, Appraiser, Probate, Judgment Records*
Access to Appraisal District records is free at http://clientdb.trueautomation.com/clientdb/main.asp?id=27. Also, to search probate
records and judgment records go to http://idocket.com/countycourt.htm

Hale County *Property, Appraiser Records*
Access to property data is free at http://clientdb.trueautomation.com/clientdb/main.asp?id=8.

Hansford County *Property, Appraiser, Personal Property Records*
Access to property data is free at www.ptax.org/offices/hansford/hansfordcad.htm. Also, access property data by download; fees
apply; add'l data includes minerals, ofc exports, delinquents; visit www.ptax.org/tax_office_data.htm or phone 201-571-0425.

Harris County *Real Estate, Grantor/Grantee, Lien, Judgment, Appraiser, Voter, UCC, Assumed Name, Vital Statistic, Personal Property, Delinquent Tax, Probate Records*
www.cclerk.hctx.net
Access to Assumed Name records, UCC filings, vital statistic, and Real Property are at
www.cclerk.hctx.net/coolice/default.asp?Category=RealProperty&Service=mastermenu. Appraiser records are at
www.hcad.org/Records. County Court Civil, marriage and informal marriage records also available. Also, search tax assessor data free
at www.tax.co.harris.tx.us/dbsearch/dbsearch.asp. Also, access recording records free at www.titlex.com; select Harris county. Also,
to search probate records and judgment records go to http://idocket.com/countycourt.htm

Harrison County *Property Tax Records*
Find property information at appraiser site at www.myswdata.com/wfFind.aspx. Name searching available.

Hartley County *Property, Appraiser Records*
Access property data free at www.ptax.org/offices/hartley/hartley01.html. Data also available by download; fees apply; visit www.ptax.org/tax_office_data.htm or phone 201-571-0425. Add'l data includes minerals, ofc exports, delinquents.

Hays County *Appraiser, Property Tax, Probate, Judgment Records*
www.co.hays.tx.us
Access probate and judgment records free at http://idocket.com/countycourt.htm Also, search land record index free at www.texaslandrecords.com. Also, see notes at beginning of section.

Hemphill County *Property Tax, Appraiser Records*
Access to county property data is free at www.hemphillcad.org. Site may be under construction.

Henderson County *Property, Appraiser Records*
Find property information at appraiser site at www.myswdata.com/wfFind.aspx. Name searching available. Also see note at beginning of section (overview).

Hidalgo County *Appraiser, Property Tax, Probate, Judgment Records*
www.hidalgo.tx.us.landata.com
Access probate and judgment records free at http://idocket.com/countycourt.htm Also, search land record index free at www.texaslandrecords.com. Also, see note at beginning of section.

Hill County *Property, Appraiser, Personal Property, Probate, Judgment Records*
Access to Appraisal district property records is free at www.hillcad.org/in/reportshome.php. Also, access Appraisal District records free at http://clientdb.trueautomation.com/clientdb/main.asp?id=23. Also, to search probate records and judgment records go to http://idocket.com/countycourt.htm Also, see note at beginning of section.

Hockley County *Appraiser, Property Records*
www.co.hockley.tx.us/coclerk.html
Access property records free at http://clientdb.trueautomation.com/clientdb/main.asp?id=50.

Hood County *Appraiser, Property Tax Records*
Find property information at appraiser site at www.myswdata.com/wfFind.aspx. Name searching available. Also, see note at beginning of section.

Hopkins County *Property Records*
www.hopkinscountytx.org
Find property information at appraiser site at www.myswdata.com/wfFind.aspx.

Houston County *Real Estate, Deed, Official, Property Tax, Assessor Records*
www.co.houston.tx.us
Search official records after choosing county at www.edoctecinc.com. If records are Unofficial, you search or copy them freely; if not Unofficial, a $1.00 per page fee applies. For details and signup, contact clerk or Jerry Anderson at 800-578-7746. Also, access to property tax records is free at www.houstoncad.org/houscad/main.jsp.

Hunt County *Appraiser, Property Tax, Sheriff Sale Records*
www.huntcounty.net
Access property tax data and sheriff sales data free at www.hctax.info. Also, see notes at beginning of section.

Hutchinson County *Property Tax, Appraiser Records*
Access to property tax data is free at www.hutchinsoncad.org/aspxSearchNew.aspx.

Jackson County *Real Estate, Grantor/Grantee, Deed, Lien, Judgment Records*
Access recording records free at www.titlex.com; select Jackson county. Records range is 1/1993 to 9/2004. Also, see note at beginning of section.

Jefferson County *Recording, Deed, Lien, Judgment, Property Tax, Marriage, UCC, Assumed Name Records*
www.co.jefferson.tx.us

Access the Jefferson recorder database free at http://jeffersontxclerk.hartintercivic.com. Recording index goes back to 1983; images to 1983. Marriages go back to 1995; UCCs to 7/2001. Also, access property tax records free at www.jcad.org/search/. Also, see note at beginning of section.

Jim Hogg County *Real Estate Recording, Deed Records*
Access recording office land data at www.etitlesearch.com; registration required, fee based on usage.

Jim Wells County *Real Estate Recording, Deed Records*
Access recording office land data at www.etitlesearch.com; registration required, fee based on usage.

Johnson County *Appraiser, Property Tax, Deed, Marriage, UCC, Probate, Judgment Records*
www.johnsoncountytx.org
Records from the County Appraiser are free at www.johnsoncountytaxoffice.org/accountSearch.asp or at www.johnsoncountytaxoffice.org/accountSearch.asp. Also, to search probate records and judgment records go to http://idocket.com/countycourt.htm. Also, see note at beginning of section.

Karnes County *Property, Appraiser Records*
Access property data by download from a private company; fees apply; add'l data includes minerals, ofc exports, delinquents; visit www.ptax.org/tax_office_data.htm or phone 201-571-0425.

Kaufman County *Real Estate, Grantor/Grantee, Deed, Lien, Judgment, Appraiser, Property Tax Records*
www.kaufmancounty.net
Access recording records free at www.titlex.com; select Kaufman county. Records range is 3/1/1969 to within a month of present. Also, see note at beginning of section. Also, search land records at www.texaslandrecords.com; a free search is allowed; later, signup or one-day pass is required. Also, search appraisal roll data free at www.kaufmancad.org and at http://clientdb.trueautomation.com/clientdb/main.asp?id=36

Kendall County *Real Estate, Grantor/Grantee, Deed, Lien, Judgment, Appraiser, Property Tax Records*
Access recording records free at www.titlex.com; select Kendall county. Also see note at beginning of section.

Kerr County *Appraiser, Property Tax, Real Estate, Recorder Records*
www.co.kerr.tx.us/
Access to recorder land data is to be available in 2005 at www.kerr.tx.us.landata.com. Search index after free registration; fee required for full benefits. Also, see note at beginning of section.

Kleberg County *Appraisal, Property, Property Tax, Probate, Judgment Records*
www.klebergcad.org
Access to county appraisal rolls and property data is free at www.klebergcad.org/search_appr.php. Also, to search probate records and judgment records go to http://idocket.com/countycourt.htm. Also, see note at beginning of section.

Knox County *Real Estate, Grantor/Grantee, Deed, Lien, Judgment Records*
Access recording records free at www.titlex.com; select Knox county.

Lamar County *Property, Appraiser, Inmate, Sheriff Bond, Death Records*
Access Appraisal District records free at http://clientdb.trueautomation.com/clientdb/main.asp?id=7. Also, access court records, sheriff bond,and inmate data free at http://68.89.102.225/. Also, cemetery records in Lamar County are free at http://userdb.rootsweb.com/cemeteries/TX/Lamar.

Lamb County *Appraiser, Property Tax Records*
Access Appraisal District records free at http://clientdb.trueautomation.com/clientdb/main.asp?id=44. Also see note at beginning of section.

La Salle County *Property, Appraiser, Real Estate Recording, Deed Records*
Access property data by download from a private company; fees apply; add'l data includes minerals, ofc exports, delinquents; visit www.ptax.org/tax_office_data.htm or phone 201-571-0425. Also, access recording office land data at www.etitlesearch.com; registration required, fee based on usage.

Lee County   *Property, Appraiser Records*
Access Appraisal District records free at http://clientdb.trueautomation.com/clientdb/main.asp?id=9.

Leon County   *Property, Appraiser Records*
Access property data by download from a private company; fees apply; add'l data includes minerals, ofc exports, delinquents; visit www.ptax.org/tax_office_data.htm or phone 201-571-0425.

Liberty County   *Appraiser, Property Tax Records*
Limestone County   *Appraiser, Property Tax Records*
See notes at beginning of section.

Lipscomb County   *Property, Appraiser Records*
Access property data by download from a private company; fees apply; add'l data includes minerals, ofc exports, delinquents; visit www.ptax.org/tax_office_data.htm or phone 201-571-0425.

Llano County   *Appraiser, Property Tax Records*
See note at beginning of section.

Lubbock County   *Election, Appraiser, Property Tax Records*
www.co.lubbock.tx.us
Access to the county clerks records is limited to election results at www.co.lubbock.tx.us/CClerk/county_clerk.htm. Also, search the property appraiser database for free at www.lubbockcad.org/Appraisal/PublicAccess/.

McCulloch County   *Criminal Record, Misdemeanor Record, Felony Record, Probate, Judgment Records*
Access criminal, misdemeanor and felony records at http://idocket.com/homepage2.htm. Also, to search probate records and judgment records go to http://idocket.com/countycourt.htm

McLennan County   *Real Estate, Grantor/Grantee, Deed, Lien, Judgment, Appraiser, Property Tax Records*
www.co.mclennan.tx.us/cclerk/index.html
Access recording records free at www.titlex.com; select McLennan county. Records range from 1/1996 to 12/2002. Also, see note at beginning of section. Also, real estate appraisal records are at www.mclennancad.org. Also, access land records at http://etitlesearch.com. You can do a name search; choose from $50.00 monthly subscription or per-click account. Also, see note at beginning of section.

Madison County   *Property Records*
For a land records search go to www.texaslandrecords.com.

Marion County   *Real Estate, Grantor/Grantee, Deed, Lien, Judgment, Property Tax, Appraiser Records*
Access recording records free at www.titlex.com; select Marion county. Also, access property tax records free at www.marioncad.org/aspxsearchnew.aspx.

Martin County   *Property Tax, Appraiser Records*
Access to property data is free at www.martincad.org/martcad/main.jsp.

Matagorda County   *Property, Appraiser Records*
www.co.matagorda.tx.us
Access to Appraisal District records is free at http://clientdb.trueautomation.com/clientdb/main.asp?id=25.

Maverick County   *Appraiser, Property Tax Records*
www.maverickcounty.org
Vsit www.maverickcad.org/searchaccounts.htm for the appraisal roll. Also, see note at beginning of section.

Midland County
Real Estate, Grantor/Grantee, Deed, Lien, Judgment, Appraiser, Property Tax, Voter Registration Records
www.co.midland.tx.us
Access the property tax database free at www.co.midland.tx.us/Tax/Property/Database/search.asp or at www.myswdata.com/wfFind.aspx. Also, search property data on the mapping page at www.midcad.org/Search/index.htm. Access recording records free at www.titlex.com; select Midland county. Also, access voter registration data free at

www.co.midland.tx.us/Elections/VoterDatabase/input.asp. Check names on warrant lists at www.co.midland.tx.us/Warrants/default.asp

Milam County *Real Estate, Grantor/Grantee, Deed, Lien, Judgment, Appriaser, Property Tax Records*

Access recording records free at www.titlex.com; select Milam county. Records range is 5/2000 to 8/2001. Also, see note at beginning of section. Also, appraisal district data at www.txcountydata.com. Also see note at beginning of section.

Mills County *Property Records*

Find property information at the appraiser site at www.myswdata.com/wfFind.aspx. Name searching available.

Mitchell County *Real Estate, Deed, Official Records*

Search official records after choosing county at www.edoctecinc.com. If records are Unofficial, you search or copy them freely; if not Unofficial, a $1.00 per page fee applies. For details and signup, contact clerk or Jerry Anderson at 800-578-7746.

Montgomery County *Real Estate, Grantor/Grantee, Deed, Lien, Judgment, Probate Records*

www.co.montgomery.tx.us

Access recording records free at www.titlex.com; select Montgomery county. Records go back to 1/1966. Similar index search may also be performed free at www.courthousedirect.com/IndexSearches.aspx. Registration and password required for full data. Also, to search probate records and judgment records go to http://idocket.com/countycourt.htm

Moore County *Property Tax, Appraiser Records*

Access to property data is free at www.moorecad.org/moorcad/main.jsp.

Nacogdoches County

Real Estate, Lien, Judgment, Deed, Vital Statistic, Property Tax, Appraiser, Probate Records

www.co.nacogdoches.tx.us

Access to view and search the county Real Property (recorder) index is free at https://www.texaslandrecords.com/txlr/TxlrApp/index.jsp. Monthly subscription is recommended, but there is a pay as you go plan for $1 per document. Also, access property tax data free at www.nacocad.org. Click on Search Our Data. Also, access to the county Appraisal Roll from TaxNetUSA MAY be at www.taxnetusa.com/texas/nacogdoches/ Access to civil, criminal or misdemeanor records at www.idocket.com. Fees involved.

Navarro County *Appraiser, Property Tax, Probate, Judgment Records*

Access probate and judgment records free at http://idocket.com/countycourt.htm Also, see note at beginning of section for "Advanced" fee service.

Newton County *Appraiser, Property Tax, Death Records*

For Appraiser/property tax: see note at beginning of section. Death records in this county may be accessed over the Internet at www.jas.net/jas.htm (site may be temporarily down).

Nueces County *Real Estate, Grantor/Grantee, Deed, Judgment, Lien, Appraiser, Property Tax Records*

www.co.nueces.tx.us

Access to county clerk recording records is free at www.co.nueces.tx.us/countyclerk/records/; access is also free at www.titlex.com; select Nueces county. Also, access County Appraiser records free at www.nuecescad.net/Appraisal/PublicAccess/. Also, see notes at beginning of section.

Ochiltree County *Property, Appraiser Records*

Access property data by download from a private company; fees apply; add'l data includes minerals, ofc export, delinquents; visit www.ptax.org/tax_office_data.htm or phone 201-571-0425.

Orange County *Property, Appraiser Records*

www.co.orange.tx.us

Access to the county appraisal district records is free at www.orangecad.org.

Palo Pinto County *Property Tax, Appraiser Records*

Access to property data is free at www.palopintocad.org. Click on Search Our Data.

Panola County   *Real Estate, Grantor/Grantee, Deed, Lien, Judgment Records*
Access recording records free at www.titlex.com; select Panola county.

Parker County   *Appraiser, Property Tax Records*
See note at beginning of section for "Advanced" fee service.

Parmer County   *Probate, Judgment Records*
Access probate and judgment records free at http://idocket.com/countycourt.htm.

Pecos County   *Property Tax, Appraiser Records*
Access to property data is free at www.pecoscad.org/aspxsearchnew.aspx.

Polk County   *Real Estate, Recording, Deed, Lien Records*
www.co.polk.tx.us
Access to County Clerk's data is by subscription at www.co.polk.tx.us/ips/cms/countyoffices/countyClerk.html. Username and password required.

Potter County   *Real Estate, Grantor/Grantee, Deed, Lien, Judgment, Appraiser, Property Tax, Probate Records*
www.prad.org
Records on the Potter-Randall Appraisal District database are free at www.prad.org. Records periodically updated; for current tax information call Potter-806-342-2600 or Randall- 806-665-6287. Also, access recording records free at www.titlex.com; select Potter county. Also, for land searches go to www.texaslandrecords.com. Also, to search probate records and judgment records go to http://idocket.com/countycourt.htm. Also, see note at beginning of section.

Randall County   *Appraiser, Property Tax, Business Personal Property, Sheriff Sale, Real Estate, Recorder, Lien, Deed, Marriage, Probate, Judgment Records*
www.randallcounty.org
Access Real Estate records from 2000 forward free at http://ccopr.randallcounty.org/, click on Official Public Records and then OPR search, or marriages, or Comm Court for Commissioner's Court data. Also, Criminal, Probate and Civil records found at www.idocket.com. Randall County appraisal, sheriff sales, and personal property records are combined online with Potter County; see Potter County for access information or www.prad.org. Also, see notes at beginning of section.

Red River County   *Appraiser Records*
Access to county appraisal district records is free at www.redrivercad.org.

Refugio County   *Property Tax, Appraisal, Marriage, Birth, Death, Divorce Records*
Access property data free at www.refugiocad.org. Click on Search Our Data. Also, access to 19th & 20th century marriage, birth (1951 forward) and death records is free at www.rootsweb.com/~txrefugi/Marriageshome.htm. Also, search individual years for births (1926-1995), deaths (1964-1999), marriages (1966-2001), divorces (1968-2001) for free at www.rootsweb.com/~usgenweb/tx/refugio/refugtoc.htm.

Robertson County   *Real Estate, Grantor/Grantee, Deed, Lien, Judgment Records*
Access recording records free at www.titlex.com; select Robertson county. Also, access to land records is free or by subscription at www.texaslandrecords.com

Rockwall County   *Real Estate, Deed, Appraiser, Property Tax Records*
Access real estate records free at www.texaslandrecords.com. Also, access appraisal district property records free at www.rockwallcad.com.

Rusk County   *Real Estate, Grantor/Grantee, Deed, Judgment, Lien, Property Tax, Appraiser Records*
Access recording records free at www.titlex.com; select Rusk county. Record range is 1/1979 to 11/2003. Also, see note at beginning of section. Also, access property data free at www.ruskcad.org. Click on Search Our Data. Also, access land records free at www.texaslandrecords.com. See www.taxnetusa.com for property tax records.

San Jacinto County   *Appraiser, Property Tax Records*
Access Appraisal District value records free at http://clientdb.trueautomation.com/clientdb/main.asp?id=46. Also, see note at beginning of section.

San Patricio County *Appraiser, Property Tax, Personal Property Records*

Access to county property data is free at www.sanpatriciogov.org. Click on Search Our Data. Also, search the Appraiser database for free at www.taxnetusa.com/texas/sanpatricio/.

Scurry County *Land Records*

For land records search go to www.texaslandrecords.com.

Smith County *Property, Appraiser Records*

Access to county appraisal district records is free at www.smithcad.org. Also, for land records search go to www.texaslandrecords.com. Also, see note at beginning of section.

Somervell County *Appraiser, Property Tax Records*

Access Appraisal District records free at http://clientdb.trueautomation.com/clientdb/main.asp?id=29 or via http://somervellcad.org. Also see note at beginning of section.

Starr County *Probate, Judgment Records*

Access probate and judgment records free at http://idocket.com/countycourt.htm

Swisher County *Appraiser, Property Tax Records*

Search the appraisal tax rolls for free at www.txcountydata.com/county.asp?County=219. Also see notes at beginning of section.

Tarrant County *Property Tax, Appraiser, Real Estate, Grantor/Grantee, Lien, Judgment, Deed, Assumed Name, Marriage, UCC, Traffic, Court Records*

www.tarrantcounty.com/eCountyClerk/site/default.asp
Access to the county Appraisal District Property data is free at www.tad.org/Datasearch/datasearch.htm. Also, search grantor/grantee index at http://ccanthem.co.tarrant.tx.us/search.aspx?cabinet=opr. Also, access a real estate and grantor/grantee index free at www.titlex.com where records range from 4/1997 to 11/2001 only; select Tarrant County. Also, search assumed names, marriages, courts, UCCs, Traffic at www.tarrantcounty.com/ecountyclerk/cwp/view.asp?A=735&Q=427570. Also see note at beginning of section.

Taylor County *Appraiser, Property Tax, Personal Property, Unclaimed Property Records*

Access to the county Central Appraisal District database is free at www.taxnetusa.com/texas/taylor/ or at www.taylorcad.org. Search is by name; other methods are at the first website listed. Search business personal property at www.taylorcad.org. Also, search the treasurer's database of unclaimed property free at www.taylorcountytexas.org/unclaime.html. Also, for land records search go to www.texaslandrecords.com. Real Property records at www.taylorcountytexas.org. Also, access Appraisal District records free at http://propaccess.trueautomation.com/clientdb/?cid=32. Also, see note at beginning of section.

Terrell County *Property, Appraiser Records*

Access to Appraisal District records is free at http://clientdb.trueautomation.com/clientdb/main.asp?id=16.

Titus County *Property, Appraiser Records*

Access property data by download from a private company; fees apply; add'l data includes minerals, ofc exports, delinquents; visit www.ptax.org/tax_office_data.htm or phone 201-571-0425.

Tom Green County *Real Estate, Grantor/Grantee, Deed, Lien, Judgment Records*

Access recording records free at www.titlex.com; select Tom Green county.

Travis County *Appraiser, Property Tax, Business Property, Voter Registration, Grantor/Grantee, Recording, UCC, Marriage, Probate Records*

www.traviscad.org
Access to recorders official records is free at http://deed.co.travis.tx.us/search.aspx?cabinet=opr. Access to the Central Appraisal District database is free at www.traviscad.org/search.htm. Also search business personal property. Also, you may search on the county tax payment system at www.texasonline.state.tx.us/NASApp/rap/BaseRap. Also, See note at beginning of section.

Tyler County *Property, Appraiser Records*

Access to the county appraisal district records is free at www.tylercad.org.

Upshur County *Real Estate, Grantor/Grantee, Deed, Lien, Judgment, Appraiser, Property Tax Records*

Access recording records free at www.titlex.com; select Upshur county. Records go back to 4/1978. Also, see note at beginning of section.

Uvalde County *Property, Appraiser Records*

Access to the county appraisal district tax information may be available through www.uvaldecounty.com; search page may be temporarily down.

Val Verde County *Property, Appraiser, Probate, Judgment Records*

Access Appraisal District records free at http://clientdb.trueautomation.com/clientdb/main.asp?id=42. Also, to search probate records and judgment records go to http://idocket.com/countycourt.htm

Van Zandt County *Real Estate, Grantor/Grantee, Deed, Judgment, Lien, Appraiser, Property Tax Records*

www.vanzandtcounty.org
Search the county appraisal rolls for free at www.vanzandtcad.org; includes plat maps online. Find property information at www.myswdata.com/wfFind.aspx. Name searching available. Also, access recording records free at www.titlex.com; select Van Zandt county. Record range is 1/1971 to 9/2003. Also, see note at beginning of section.

Victoria County
Real Estate, Grantor/Grantee, Deed, Judgment, Lien, Probate, Appraiser, Property Tax Records

http://victoriacountytx.org/departments/county_clerk/cclerk.htm
Access recording records free at www.titlex.com; select Victoria county. Records range is 1/1964 to 5/26/2005 only. Also, access to appraisal district records is free at www.victoriacad.org, and at http://clientdb.trueautomation.com/clientdb/main.asp?id=33. Also, to search probate records and judgment records go to http://idocket.com/countycourt.htm. Also, see note at beginning of section

Walker County *Property, Appraiser, Land Records*

www.co.walker.tx.us
Access to county appraisal district records is free at http://clientdb.trueautomation.com/clientdb/main.asp?id=4. Also, for land records search go to www.texaslandrecords.com. Indexes from 1960-forward; images of the records from 1/1/2003 to current.

Waller County *Appraiser, Property Tax Records*

See note at beginning of section.

Washington County
Real Estate, Grantor/Grantee, Deed, Judgment, Lien, Assessor, Property, Probate Records

www.co.washington.tx.us/cclerk/index.html
Access recording records free at www.titlex.com; select Washington county. Records go back to 1/1965. Also, to search probate records and judgment records go to http://idocket.com/countycourt.htm. Also, see note at beginning of section. Also, search official records after choosing county at www.edoctecinc.com. If records are Unofficial, you search or copy them free; if not Unofficial, a $1.00 per page fee applies. For details and signup, contact clerk or Jerry Anderson at 800-578-7746.

Webb County *Appraiser, Property Tax, Real Estate Recording, Deed, Probate, Judgment Records*

www.webbcounty.com
Search the county Central Appraisal District database at www.webbcad.org/Propertysearch/propertysearch.html and at http://clientdb.trueautomation.com/clientdb/main.asp?id=1. Also, access recording office land data at www.etitlesearch.com; registration required, fee based on usage. Also, to search probate records and judgment records go to http://idocket.com/countycourt.htm. Also, see note at beginning of section.

Wharton County *Real Estate, Grantor/Grantee, Deed, Lien, Judgment, Assessor, Property Tax Records*

Access recording records free at www.titlex.com; select Wharton county. Records go up to 11/2003. Also, see note at beginning of section.

Wichita County *Property, Appraisal, Land Records*

Access to county appraisal district records is free at http://clientdb.trueautomation.com/clientdb/main.asp?id=43. Also, for land records search go to www.texaslandrecords.com. Also, see note at beginning of section.

Wilbarger County   *Property Tax, Personal Property, Appraiser Records*

Access to property data is free at www.wilbargerappraisal.org/aspxsearchnew.aspx. Also, search the appraisal rolls for free at www.taxnetusa.com. Also see note at beginning of section.

Willacy County   *Real Estate, Grantor/Grantee, Deed, Judgment, Lien, Appraiser, Property Tax Records*

Access recording records free at www.titlex.com; select Willacy county. Record range is 8/1998 to 1/2004. Access Appraisal District records free at http://clientdb.trueautomation.com/clientdb/main.asp?id=14. Also, see note at beginning of section.

Williamson County

Real Estate, Appraiser, Property Tax, Tax Sale, Grantor/Grantee, Judgment, Lien, Jail, Sheriff Bond Records
www.wilco.org
Access recording records free at www.titlex.com; select Williamson county. Records go back to 5/1999. Also, access the appraiser database free at www.wcad.org. Also, see note at beginning of section. Also, access the monthly delinquent tax sale list at http://wcportals.wilco.org/tax%5Fassessor/.

Wilson County   *Property Tax, Appraiser Records*

Access to the county CAD records is free at http://clientdb.trueautomation.com/clientdb/main.asp?id=22. Also, see note at beginning of section.

Wise County   *Property, Appraiser, Land Records*

Find property information at www.myswdata.com/wfFind.aspx. Name searching available. Also, for land records search and vital records go to www.texaslandrecords.com.

Wood County   *Real Estate, Grantor/Grantee, Deed, Lien, Judgment Records*

www.co.wood.tx.us
Access recording records at www.titlex.com; select Wood county. Registration and login required; purchase tokens in order to search.

Young County   *Property Tax, Appraiser Records*

Access to property data is free at www.youngcad.org. Click on Search Our Data.

Zapata County   *Property, Appraiser, Real Estate Recording, Deed Records*

Access to appraisal district records is free at http://clientdb.trueautomation.com/clientdb/main.asp?id=28. Also, access recording office land data at www.etitlesearch.com; registration required, fee based on usage.

Federal Courts in Texas...

Standards for Federal Courts: The universal PACER sign-up number is 800-676-6856. Find PACER and the Party/Case Index on the Web at http://pacer.psc.uscourts.gov. PACER dial-up access is $.60 per minute. Also, courts offering internet access via PACER, Web-PACER or the new CM-ECF charge $.08 per page fee ($.07 per page if record is pre-2005 or unless noted as free).

US District Court -- Eastern District of Texas

www.txed.uscourts.gov
PACER: Case records are available back to 1992. Records are purged once yearly. New records are available online after 1 day. **PACER Online Access:** ECF replaces PACER. **Electronic Filing:** CM/ECF data at https://ecf.txed.uscourts.gov. **Other Online Access:** View Frequently Requested Cases free at www.txed.uscourts.gov.
Beaumont Division counties: Delta*, Fannin*, Hardin, Hopkins*, Jasper, Jefferson, Lamar*, Liberty, Newton, Orange, Red River. Counties marked with an asterisk are the old Paris Division, whose case records are maintained here. New records are at Sherman Div.
Lufkin Division counties: Angelina, Houston, Nacogdoches, Polk, Sabine, San Augustine, Shelby, Trinity, Tyler.
Marshall Division counties: Camp, Cass, Harrison, Marion, Morris, Upshur.
Sherman Division counties: Collin, Cooke, Delta*, Denton, Fannin*, Grayson, Hopkins*, Lamar*. Counties marked with an asterisk were part of the old Paris Division; these old records are at Beaumont. New records are at Sherman.
Texarkana Division counties: Bowie, Franklin, Titus.
Tyler Division counties: Anderson, Cherokee, Gregg, Henderson, Panola, Rains, Rusk, Smith, Van Zandt, Wood.

US Bankruptcy Court -- Eastern District of Texas

www.txeb.uscourts.gov

PACER: Case records are available back to 1989. Records are purged every 6 months. **PACER Online Access:** ECF replaces PACER. **Electronic Filing:** Document images available. CM/ECF data at https://ecf.txeb.uscourts.gov. **Opinions:** Click on Chapter 7 Asset Case Trustee's Final Reports. View court opinions at www.txeb.uscourts.gov/reports.asp. **Other Online Access:** Calendars at www.txeb.uscourts.gov/judges.asp. **Phone access:** Voice Case Information System, call 800-466-1694, 903-590-3251

Beaumont Division counties: Angelina, Hardin, Houston, Jasper, Jefferson, Liberty, Nacogdoches, Newton, Orange, Polk, Sabine, San Augustine, Shelby, Trinity, Tyler.

Marshall Division counties: Camp, Cass, Harrison, Marion, Morris, Upshur.

Plano Division counties: Collin, Cooke, Delta, Denton, Fannin, Grayson, Hopkins, Lamar, Red River.

Texarkana Division counties: Bowie, Franklin, Titus.

Tyler Division counties: Anderson, Cherokee, Gregg, Henderson, Panola, Rains, Rusk, Smith, Van Zandt, Wood.

US District Court -- Northern District of Texas

www.txnd.uscourts.gov

PACER: Case records are available back to 6/1991. Records are purged once yearly. New records are available online after 1 day. **PACER Online Access:** ECF replaces PACER. Document images available. **Electronic Filing:** CM/ECF data at https://ecf.txnd.uscourts.gov. **Opinions:** View court opinions at www.txnd.uscourts.gov/judges/.

Abilene Division counties: Callahan, Eastland, Fisher, Haskell, Howard, Jones, Mitchell, Nolan, Shackelford, Stephens, Stonewall, Taylor, Throckmorton.

Amarillo Division counties: Armstrong, Briscoe, Carson, Castro, Childress, Collingsworth, Dallam, Deaf Smith, Donley, Gray, Hall, Hansford, Hartley, Hemphill, Hutchinson, Lipscomb, Moore, Ochiltree, Oldham, Parmer, Potter, Randall, Roberts, Sherman, Swisher, Wheeler.

Dallas Division counties: Dallas, Ellis, Hunt, Johnson, Kaufman, Navarro, Rockwall.

Fort Worth Division counties: Comanche, Erath, Hood, Jack, Palo Pinto, Parker, Tarrant, Wise.

Lubbock Division counties: Bailey, Borden, Cochran, Crosby, Dawson, Dickens, Floyd, Gaines, Garza, Hale, Hockley, Kent, Lamb, Lubbock, Lynn, Motley, Scurry, Terry, Yoakum.

San Angelo Division counties: Brown, Coke, Coleman, Concho, Crockett, Glasscock, Irion, Menard, Mills, Reagan, Runnels, Schleicher, Sterling, Sutton, Tom Green.

Wichita Falls Division counties: Archer, Baylor, Clay, Cottle, Foard, Hardeman, King, Knox, Montague, Wichita, Wilbarger, Young.

US Bankruptcy Court -- Northern District of Texas

www.txnb.uscourts.gov

PACER: Case records are available back to 1994. Records are purged every 6 months. New records are available online after 1 day. **PACER Online Access:** ECF replaces PACER. **Electronic Filing:** Document images available back to 2/03. CM/ECF data at https://ecf.txnb.uscourts.gov. **Opinions:** View court opinions at www.txnb.uscourts.gov/opinions/. **Other Online Access:** Calendars free at www.txnb.uscourts.gov/judges/. **Phone access:** Voice Case Information System, call 800-886-9008, 214-753-2128

Amarillo Division counties: Armstrong, Briscoe, Carson, Castro, Childress, Collingsworth, Dallam, Deaf Smith, Donley, Gray, Hall, Hansford, Hartley, Hemphill, Hutchinson, Lipscomb, Moore, Ochiltree, Oldham, Parmer, Potter, Randall, Roberts, Sherman, Swisher, Wheeler.

Dallas Division counties: Dallas, Ellis, Hunt, Johnson, Kaufman, Navarro, Rockwall. This court maintains records for the Wichita Falls Division.

Fort Worth Division counties: Comanche, Erath, Hood, Jack, Palo Pinto, Parker, Tarrant, Wise.

Lubbock Division counties: Bailey, Borden, Brown, Callahan, Cochran, Cooke, Coleman, Concho, Crockett, Crosby, Dawson, Dickens, Eastland, Fisher, Floyd, Gaines, Garza, Glasscock, Hale, Haskell, Hockley, Howard, Irion, Jones, Kent, Lamb, Lubbock, Lynn, Menard, Mills, Mitchell, Motley, Nolan, Reagan, Runnels, Schleicher, Scurry, Shackelford, Stephens, Sterling, Stonewall, Sutton, Taylor, Terry, Throckmorton, Tom Green, Yoakum.

Wichita Falls Division counties: Archer, Baylor, Clay, Cottle, Foard, Hardeman, King, Knox, Montague, Wichita, Wilbarger, Young.

US District Court -- Southern District of Texas

www.txsd.uscourts.gov

PACER: Case records are available back to 6/1990. Records are purged every 6 months. New records are available online after 1 day. **PACER Online Access:** ECF replaces PACER. **Electronic Filing:** Document images available. CM/ECF data at https://ecf.txsd.uscourts.gov. **Opinions:** View court opinions at www.txsd.uscourts.gov/opinions/dcdisclaimer.htm.

Brownsville Division counties: Cameron, Willacy. Also holds bankruptcy court records here. You may search entire Southern District electronically at any of the seven courthouse locations.

Corpus Christi Division counties: Aransas, Bee, Brooks, Duval, Jim Wells, Kenedy, Kleberg, Live Oak, Nueces, San Patricio.

Galveston Division counties: Brazoria, Chambers, Galveston, Matagorda. Also holds bankruptcy court records here. You may search entire Southern District electronically at any of the seven courthouse locations.

Houston Division counties: Austin, Brazos, Colorado, Fayette, Fort Bend, Grimes, Harris, Madison, Montgomery, San Jacinto, Walker, Waller, Wharton.

Laredo Division counties: Jim Hogg, La Salle, McMullen, Webb, Zapata. Also holds bankruptcy court records here. You may search entire Southern District electronically at any of the seven courthouse locations.

McAllen Division counties: Hidalgo, Starr. Also holds bankruptcy court records here. You may search entire Southern District electronically at any of the seven courthouse locations.

Victoria Division counties: Calhoun, De Witt, Goliad, Jackson, Lavaca, Refugio, Victoria. Also holds bankruptcy court records here. You may search entire Southern District electronically at any of the seven courthouse locations.

US Bankruptcy Court -- Southern District of Texas

www.txsd.uscourts.gov

PACER: Case records are available back to 6/1991. New records are available online after 1 day. **PACER Online Access:** Document images available. **Electronic Filing:** CM/ECF data at https://ecf.txsb.uscourts.gov. **Opinions:** Search bankruptcy orders by year back to 2001 free. View court opinions at www.txsd.uscourts.gov/opinions/dcdisclaimer.htm. **Other Online Access:** Court calendars at www.txsd.uscourts.gov/judges/judgeban.htm. **Phone access:** Voice Case Information System, call 800-745-4459, 713-250-5049

Corpus Christi Division counties: Aransas, Bee, Brooks, Cameron*, Duval, Hidalgo**, Jim Wells, Kenedy, Kleberg, Live Oak, Nueces, San Patricio, Starr**, Willacy*. Files from Brownsville, Corpus Christi, and McAllen are maintained here. You may search entire Southern District electronically at any of the seven courthouse locations. Open case records for counties marked with a single asterisk (*) are at Galveston Division (see US Dist Court). Open case records for counties marked with a double asterisk (**) are at McAllen Division (see US Dist Court).

Houston Division counties: Austin, Brazoria**, Brazos, Calhoun***, Chambers**, Colorado, De Witt***, Fayette, Fort Bend, Galveston**, Goliad***, Grimes, Harris, Jackson***, Jim Hogg*, La Salle*, Lavaca***, Madison, Matagorda**, McMullen*, Montgomery, Refugio*** San Jacinto, Victoria***,Walker, Waller, Wharton, Webb* Zapata*. Open case records for counties with a single asterisk (*) are at Laredo Division (see US Dist Court). Open case records for counties with double asterisk (**) are at Galveston Div. (see US Dist Court). Open case records for counties with 3 asterisks (***) are at Victoria Div (see US Dist Court). Search entire Southern District electronically at any of the 7 courthouse locations.

US District Court -- Western District of Texas

www.txwd.uscourts.gov

PACER: Case records are available back to 1994. Records are purged every 6 months. New records are available online after 1 day. **PACER Online Access:** PACER online at http://pacer.txwd.uscourts.gov. **Electronic Filing:** ECF may still be under development. CM/ECF data at https://ecf.txwd.uscourts.gov. **Opinions:** View court opinions at www.nysd.uscourts.gov/courtweb/public.htm. **Other Online Access:** Access judges' calendars free at www.txwd.uscourts.gov/calendar/default.asp.

Austin Division counties: Bastrop, Blanco, Burleson, Burnet, Caldwell, Gillespie, Hays, Kimble, Lampasas, Lee, Llano, McCulloch, Mason, San Saba, Travis, Washington, Williamson.

Del Rio Division counties: Edwards, Kinney, Maverick, Terrell, Uvalde, Val Verde, Zavala.

El Paso Division counties: El Paso.

Midland Division counties: Andrews, Crane, Ector, Martin, Midland, Upton.

Pecos Division counties: Brewster, Culberson, Hudspeth, Jeff Davis, Loving, Pecos, Presidio, Reeves, Ward, Winkler.

San Antonio Division counties: Atascosa, Bandera, Bexar, Comal, Dimmit, Frio, Gonzales, Guadalupe, Karnes, Kendall, Kerr, Medina, Real, Wilson.

Waco Division counties: Bell, Bosque, Coryell, Falls, Freestone, Hamilton, Hill, Leon, Limestone, McLennan, Milam, Robertson, Somervell.

US Bankruptcy Court -- Western District of Texas

www.txwb.uscourts.gov

PACER: Case records are available back to 5/1987. Records are purged every 6-8 months. New records are available online after 1 day. **PACER Online Access:** ECF replaces PACER. **Electronic Filing:** CM/ECF data at https://ecf.txwb.uscourts.gov. **Opinions:** View court opinions at www.txwb.uscourts.gov/opinions/judges.php. **Other Online Access:** Calendars free at www.txwb.uscourts.gov/information/calendars/calendar_index.htm. **Phone access:** Voice Case Information System, call 888-436-7477, 210-472-4023

Austin Division counties: Bastrop, Blanco, Burleson, Burnet, Caldwell, Gillespie, Hays, Kimble, Lampasas, Lee, Llano, Mason, McCulloch, San Saba, Travis, Washington, Williamson.

El Paso Division counties: El Paso.

Midland/Odessa Division counties: Andrews, Brewster, Crane, Culberson, Ector, Hudspeth, Jeff Davis, Loving, Martin, Midland, Pecos, Presidio, Reeves, Upton, Ward, Winkler.

San Antonio Division counties: Atascosa, Bandera, Bexar, Comal, Dimmit, Edwards, Frio, Gonzales, Guadalupe, Karnes, Kendall, Kerr, Kinney, Maverick, Medina, Real, Terrell, Uvalde, Val Verde, Wilson, Zavala.

Waco Division counties: Bell, Bosque, Coryell, Falls, Freestone, Hamilton, Hill, Leon, Limestone, McLennan, Milam, Robertson, Somervell.

Utah

Capital: Salt Lake City
          Salt Lake County
Time Zone: MST
Population: 2,389,039
# of Counties: 29

Quick Links

Website: www.utah.gov
Governor: www.utah.gov/governor/
Attorney General: http://attorneygeneral.utah.gov
State Archives: www.archives.state.ut.us
State Statutes and Codes: http://le.utah.gov/Documents/code_const.htm
Legislative Bill Search: http://le.utah.gov/Documents/bills.htm
Bill Monitoring: http://le.utah.gov/asp/billtrack/track.asp
Unclaimed Funds: https://www.up.state.ut.us

State Level ... Major Agencies

Statewide Court Records

Court Administrator, PO Box 140241, Salt Lake City, UT 84114-0241 (Courier: 450 S State, Salt Lake City, UT 84114); 801-578-3800, 801-238-7832 (Search Request Info), Fax-801-578-3859, 8AM-5PM.
www.utcourts.gov
Online search: Case information from all Utah District Court locations is available through XChange. Fees include $25.00 registration and $30.00 per month which includes 200 searches. Each additional search is billed at $.20 per search. Information about XChange and the subscription agreement can be found at www.utcourts.gov/records. One can search for supreme or appellate opinions at the website.

Sexual Offender Registry

Sex Offenders Registration Program, 14717 S Minuteman Dr, Draper, UT 84020; 801-545-5908, Fax-801-545-5911, 8AM-5PM.
www.corrections.utah.gov
Online search: The Registry may be searched from the web page. Records are searchable by name, ZIP Code, or name and ZIP Code. The information released includes photos, descriptions, addresses, vehicles, offenses, and targets. Also, requests nay be emailed to registry@utah.gov

Corporation, Limited Liability Company, Fictitious Name, Limited Partnership, Assumed Name, Trademarks/Servicemarks

Commerce Department, Corporate Division, PO Box 146705, Salt Lake City, UT 84114-6705 (Courier: 160 E 300 S, 2nd fl, Salt Lake City, UT 84111); 801-530-4849 (Call Center), Fax-801-530-6111, 8AM-5PM.
www.commerce.utah.gov
Online search: A business entity/principle search service is available at www.utah.gov/services/business.html. Basic information (name, address, agent) is free. Detailed data is available for minimal fees, but registration is required. The website also offers an Unclaimed Property search page. **Other options:** State allows e-mail access for orders of Certification of Existence at orders@br.state.ut.us.

Uniform Commercial Code

Department of Commerce, UCC Division, Box 146705, Salt Lake City, UT 84114-6705 (Courier: 160 E 300 South, Heber M Wells Bldg, 2nd Floor, Salt Lake City, UT 84111); 801-530-4849, 877-526-3994 (In State), Fax-801-530-6438, 8AM-5PM.
http://corporations.utah.gov/uccpage.html
Online search: UCC uncertified records are available free online at https://secure.utah.gov/uccsearch/. Search by debtor individual name or organization, or by filing number. Certified searches may also be ordered for $12.00 per search. To receive certified searches, you must be a registered user. The website gives details. Note there is a $50 annual registration fee which includes 10 user logins. Email requests are accepted at orders@br.state.ut.us. **Other options:** Records are available on CD-ROM. Suggest writing or faxing, as the phone number above can give 30-60 minute waits.

Birth, Marriage, Divorce Certificates

Department of Health, Office of Vital Records & Statistics, Box 141012, Salt Lake City, UT 84114-1012 (Courier: 288 N 1460 W, Salt Lake City, UT 84114); 801-538-6105 (This Agency), 801-538-6380 (Vitalchek), Fax-801-538-9467, 9AM-5PM (walk-in counter closes at 4:30 PM).
http://health.utah.gov/vitalrecords/
Online search: Orders can be placed via a state designated vendor. Go to www.vitalchek.com. Extra fees are involved.

Death Records

Department of Health, Office of Vital Records & Statistics, Box 141012, Salt Lake City, UT 84114-1012 (Courier: 288 N 1460 W, Salt Lake City, UT 84114); 801-538-6105 (This Agency), 801-538-6380 (Vitalchek), Fax-801-538-9467, 9AM-5PM (walk-in counter closes at 4:30 PM).
http://health.utah.gov/vitalrecords/
Online search: Orders can be placed via a state designated vendor. Go to www.vitalchek.com. Extra fees are involved. **Other options:** Search the state Cemetery and Burials database for free at http://history.utah.gov/apps/burials/execute/searchburials.

Driver Records

Department of Public Safety, Driver License Division, Customer Service Section, PO Box 30560, Salt Lake City, UT 84130-0560 (Courier: 4501 South 2700 West, 3rd Floor South, Salt Lake City, UT 84119); 801-965-4437, Fax-801-965-4496, 8AM-5PM.
http://driverlicense.utah.gov
Online search: Driving records are available to eligible organizations through the eUtah. The system is available 24 hours daily. The fee per driving record is $7.25. There is an annual $60.00 subscription fee which includes access for 10 users. For more information, visit the website at www.utah.gov/registration/. Utah drivers may order their own record at https://secure.utah.gov/recordrequest/. The fee is $4.25 per record.

Vehicle & Vessel Ownership, Registration

State Tax Commission, Motor Vehicle Records Section, 210 North 1950 West, Salt Lake City, UT 84134; 801-297-3507, Fax-801-297-3578, 8AM-5PM.
http://dmv.utah.gov
Online search: Motor Vehicle Dept. titles, liens, and registration searches are available at www.utah.gov/registration/. Registration and a $60.00 annual subscription fee is required plus $2.00 per record access.

State Level ... Occupational Licensing

Accounting Firm	https://secure.utah.gov/llv/llv
Acupuncturist	https://secure.utah.gov/llv/llv
Alarm Company	https://secure.utah.gov/llv/llv
Alarm Company Agent/Response Runner	https://secure.utah.gov/llv/llv
Animal Euthanasia Agency	https://secure.utah.gov/llv/llv
Arbitrator, Alternate Dispute Resolution	https://secure.utah.gov/llv/llv
Architect	https://secure.utah.gov/llv/llv
Athletic Event Promoter	https://secure.utah.gov/llv/llv
Athletic Judge	https://secure.utah.gov/llv/llv
Athletic Manager	https://secure.utah.gov/llv/llv
Attorney	www.utahbar.org/html/find_a_lawyer.html
Bank	www.dfi.utah.gov/Banks.htm
Barber	https://secure.utah.gov/llv/llv

Barber School/Instructor .... https://secure.utah.gov/llv/llv
Bedding/Upholstery Mfg/Whlse/Dealer ..... http://ag.utah.gov/licenses/Cur_Lic.html
Beekeeper .... http://ag.utah.gov/licenses/Cur_Lic.html
Boxer .... https://secure.utah.gov/llv/llv
Brand Inspector... http://ag.utah.gov/licenses/Cur_Lic.html
Building Inspector/Trainee .... https://secure.utah.gov/llv/llv
Building Trades, General .... https://secure.utah.gov/llv/llv
Burglar Alarm Agent .... https://secure.utah.gov/llv/llv
Check Cashier/Payday Lender .... www.dfi.utah.gov/ckcash.htm
Chiropractor.. https://secure.utah.gov/llv/llv
Consumer Lender.. www.dfi.utah.gov/consumer.htm
Contractor .... https://secure.utah.gov/llv/llv
Controlled Substance Precursor Dist. .... https://secure.utah.gov/llv/llv
Cosmetologist .... https://secure.utah.gov/llv/llv
Cosmetology School/Instructor................... https://secure.utah.gov/llv/llv
Counselor Trainee, Professional .... https://secure.utah.gov/llv/llv
Counselor, Professional .... https://secure.utah.gov/llv/llv
Credit Union .... www.dfi.utah.gov/CreditUn.htm
Deception Detection Examiner/Intern......... https://secure.utah.gov/llv/llv
Dentist/Dental Hygienist............................. https://secure.utah.gov/llv/llv
Dental Hygienist/Local Anesthesia............. https://secure.utah.gov/llv/llv
Dietitian .... https://secure.utah.gov/llv/llv
Egg & Poultry Inspector .... http://ag.utah.gov/licenses/Cur_Lic.html
Electrician, Apprentice/Journey'n/Master .. https://secure.utah.gov/llv/llv
Electrologist.. https://secure.utah.gov/llv/llv
Employee Leasing Company .... https://secure.utah.gov/llv/llv
Employment Provider, Professional............ https://secure.utah.gov/llv/llv
Endowment Care/Cemetery .... https://secure.utah.gov/llv/llv
Engineer.. https://secure.utah.gov/llv/llv
Engineer, Structural Professional................ https://secure.utah.gov/llv/llv
Environmental Health Specialist................. https://secure.utah.gov/llv/llv
Escrow Agent.. www.dfi.utah.gov/escrow.htm
Feed Type, Food & Dairy Inspector .... http://ag.utah.gov/licenses/Cur_Lic.html
Funeral Service Dir./Apprentice/Establ't.... https://secure.utah.gov/llv/llv
Genetic Counselor....................................... https://secure.utah.gov/llv/llv
Geologist... https://secure.utah.gov/llv/llv
Grain & Seed .... http://ag.utah.gov/licenses/Cur_Lic.html
Health Care Assistant.................................. https://secure.utah.gov/llv/llv
Health Facility Administrator .... https://secure.utah.gov/llv/llv
Hearing Aid Specialist .... https://secure.utah.gov/llv/llv
Hearing Instrument Prof./Intern.................. https://secure.utah.gov/llv/llv
Holding Company.. www.dfi.utah.gov/HCSList.htm
Industrial Bank.. www.dfi.utah.gov/industbk.htm
Insurance Agent/Establishment................... www.insurance.state.ut.us/companies.html
Interpreter for the Deaf .... www.aslterps.utah.gov/UIP/terp_dir.php
Laboratory, Analytical .... https://secure.utah.gov/llv/llv
Landscape Architect.................................... https://secure.utah.gov/llv/llv
Lien Recovery Fund Member .... https://secure.utah.gov/llv/llv
Manufactured Housing Seller .... https://secure.utah.gov/llv/llv
Marriage & Family Therapist/Trainee .... https://secure.utah.gov/llv/llv
Massage Technician/Apprentice .... https://secure.utah.gov/llv/llv
Meat Inspector .... http://ag.utah.gov/licenses/Cur_Lic.html
Mediator, Alternate Dispute Resolution...... https://secure.utah.gov/llv/llv
Medical Doctor/Surgeon............................. https://secure.utah.gov/llv/llv
Midwife Nurse .... https://secure.utah.gov/llv/llv
Mortgage Broker, Residential .... http://realestate.utah.gov/database.html

Mortgage Loan Service .... www.dfi.utah.gov/mortgage.htm
Naturopath .... https://secure.utah.gov/llv/llv
Naturopathic Physician .... https://secure.utah.gov/llv/llv
Negotiator, Alternate Dispute Resolution ... https://secure.utah.gov/llv/llv
Nuclear Pharmacy .... https://secure.utah.gov/llv/llv
Nurse .... https://secure.utah.gov/llv/llv
Occupational Therapist/Assistant .... https://secure.utah.gov/llv/llv
Optometrist .... https://secure.utah.gov/llv/llv
Osteopathic Physician .... https://secure.utah.gov/llv/llv
Pesticide Dealer/Applicator .... http://ag.utah.gov/licenses/Cur_Lic.html
Pharmaceutical Admin. Facility .... https://secure.utah.gov/llv/llv
Pharmaceutical Dog Trainer .... https://secure.utah.gov/llv/llv
Pharmaceutical Researcher .... https://secure.utah.gov/llv/llv
Pharmaceutical Teaching Org. .... https://secure.utah.gov/llv/llv
Pharmaceutical Whse./Dist./Mfg. .... https://secure.utah.gov/llv/llv
Pharmacist/Pharmacist Intern/Technician ... https://secure.utah.gov/llv/llv
Pharmacy Retail/Branch .... https://secure.utah.gov/llv/llv
Pharmacy, Institutional/Hospital .... https://secure.utah.gov/llv/llv
Physical Therapist .... https://secure.utah.gov/llv/llv
Physician Assistant .... https://secure.utah.gov/llv/llv
Plumber Apprentice/Journeyman .... https://secure.utah.gov/llv/llv
Podiatrist .... https://secure.utah.gov/llv/llv
Polygraph Examiner .... https://secure.utah.gov/llv/llv
Pre-Need Provider/Sales Agent .... https://secure.utah.gov/llv/llv
Probation Provider, Private .... https://secure.utah.gov/llv/llv
Psychological Assistant .... https://secure.utah.gov/llv/llv
Psychologist .... https://secure.utah.gov/llv/llv
Public Accountant-CPA .... https://secure.utah.gov/llv/llv
Radiology Practical Technician/Tech. .... https://secure.utah.gov/llv/llv
Real Estate Agent/Broker/Company .... http://realestate.utah.gov/database.html
Real Estate Appraiser .... http://realestate.utah.gov/database.html
Real Estate Establishment .... https://secure.utah.gov/llv/llv
Recreational Therapist .... https://secure.utah.gov/llv/llv
Recreational Vehicle Dealer .... https://secure.utah.gov/llv/llv
Referee .... https://secure.utah.gov/llv/llv
Respiratory Care Practitioner .... https://secure.utah.gov/llv/llv
Sanitarian .... https://secure.utah.gov/llv/llv
Savings & Loan .... www.dfi.utah.gov/sls.htm
Securities Broker/Dealer .... https://secure.utah.gov/llv/llv
Security Company .... https://secure.utah.gov/llv/llv
Security Officer, Armed/Unarmed Private .. https://secure.utah.gov/llv/llv
Shorthand Reporter .... https://secure.utah.gov/llv/llv
Social Service Aide/Worker/Trainee .... https://secure.utah.gov/llv/llv
Social Worker .... https://secure.utah.gov/llv/llv
Speech Pathologist/Audiologist .... https://secure.utah.gov/llv/llv
Substance Abuse Counselor .... https://secure.utah.gov/llv/llv
Surveyor, Land .... https://secure.utah.gov/llv/llv
Third Party Payment Issuer .... www.dfi.utah.gov/montrans.htm
Title Lender .... www.dfi.utah.gov/titlelen.htm
Trade Instructor .... https://secure.utah.gov/llv/llv
Trust Company .... www.dfi.utah.gov/trslist.htm
Upholsterer/Upholstery Mfg/Whlse/Dealer http://ag.utah.gov/licenses/Cur_Lic.html
Veterinarian/Veterinary Intern .... https://secure.utah.gov/llv/llv
Veterinary Pharmaceutical Outlet .... https://secure.utah.gov/llv/llv
Weights & Measures .... http://ag.utah.gov/licenses/Cur_Lic.html
Wine Store .... www.alcbev.state.ut.us/Stores/wine_stores.html

County Level ... Courts

Court Administration: Court Administrator, 450 S State Street, Salt Lake City, UT, 84114; 801-578-3800; www.utcourts.gov

Court Structure: 41 District Courts are arranged in eight judicial districts. Branch courts in larger counties, such as Salt Lake, which were formerly Circuit Courts and now elevated to District Courts have full jurisdiction over felony as well as misdemeanor cases. Justice Courts are established by counties and municipalities and have the authority to deal with class B and C misdemeanors, violations of ordinances, small claims, and infractions committed within their territorial jurisdiction. The Justice Court shares jurisdiction with the Juvenile Court over minors 16 or 17 years old who are charged with certain traffic offenses. Those charges are handled through Juvenile Court.

Online Access Note: Case information from all Utah District Court locations is available online through XChange. Fees include $25.00 registration and $30.00 per month which includes 200 searches. Each additional search is billed at $.20 per name. Records go back to at least 1998 for all District Courts. Information about XChange and the subscription agreement is found at www.utcourts.gov/records/xchange One may search for Supreme Court or Appellate Courts opinions at the main website.

Salt Lake County
3rd District Court - Salt Lake Dept. – Civil and Criminal Records
Access through Xchange, see www.utcourts.gov/records/ see state introduction. An automated court information line allows phone access to court dates, fine balances, and judgment/divorce decrees (case or citation number required) at 801-238-7830.

Weber County
2nd District Court – Civil and Criminal Records
Access through Xchange, see www.utcourts.gov/records/ see state introduction. An automated court information line allows phone access to court dates, fine balances, and judgment/divorce decrees (case or citation number required) at 801-395-1111.

County Level ... Recorders & Assessors

Recording Office Organization: 29 counties 29 recording offices. The recording officers are the County Recorder and the Clerk of District Court (state tax liens). The entire state is in the Mountain Time Zone (MST). County Recorders will not perform real estate searches. All federal tax liens are filed with the County Recorder. All state tax liens are filed with Clerk of District Court, many of which have online access. Refer to the County Court section for information about Utah District Courts.

Online Access Note: A number of counties offer online access, some are fee-based.

Box Elder County   *Real Estate, Recorder, Deed Records*
www.boxeldercounty.org
Access County recorder data by subscription at www.opisweb.com. Monthly subscriptions and per doc payment plans available.

Cache County   *Recording, Grantor/Grantee, Lien, Property Records*
www.cachecounty.org/recorder/index.php
Access to recording records is via subscription at www.landlight.com. Choose from 3 subscription plans; short free trial is offered. Grantor/Grantee Index goes back to 10/1980; Abstracts to 7/1984; images to 12/1992. Call 435-787-9003 for more information regarding online access.

Davis County   *Real Estate, Lien Records*
www.co.davis.ut.us
Access to the county land records database requires written registration and $15.00 per month fee plus $.10 per transaction. Records go back to 1981. For information and sign-up, contact Janet at 801-451-3347.

Emery County   *Plat, Property Records*
www.emerycounty.com
Access plat map data by parcel ID number of location on county map free at www.emerycounty.com/recorder/needa_plat.htm

Salt Lake County *Assessor, Property Tax, Land Records*

www.co.slc.ut.us

Records on the county Truth-In-Tax Information website are free at www.slpropertyinfo.org.

Tooele County *Property Tax Records*

www.co.tooele.ut.us

Access to the property information database may be operational at www.co.tooele.ut.us/taxinfo.html.

Utah County *Recorder, Deed, Real Estate, Lien, Assessor, Delinquent Tax, Property Tax, Treasurer Records*

www.utahcountyonline.org

Access to the land records database and also map searching is free at
www.utahcountyonline.org/Dept/Record/LandRecordsandMaps/WebAccess.asp. Indexes go back to 1978; parcel indexes back to
1981. Document images go back to 1965. Building and GIS information is also online. Also, name search property data free at
http://pbw.co.utah.ut.us/scripts/pbcgi70.exe/uc/u_functions/uof_namesearch.

Wasatch County *Real Property, Grantor/Grantee, Marriage Records*

www.co.wasatch.ut.us/d/recorder.html

Access to a limited grantor/grantee index also maps and subdivisions are at www.co.wasatch.ut.us/web_access.htm. Only documents
from 10/15/1998 to present are accessible. Grantor/Grantee can only be searched for data since 5/20/2002. Use "Advanced Search."
Includes marriages. Also, the county GIS Dept. plans to have "metadata" property information free at its GIS mapping site at
www.co.wasatch.ut.us/d/dpgis.html.

Washington County *Property, Tax Roll, Treasurer Records*

www.washco.state.ut.us

Access to the tax roll database is free at www.washco.state.ut.us/index.php?page=taxes&sub=taxsearch. Also, access the treasurer's
property tax data free at www.washingtontreasurer.com/AccountQuery.cfm but no name searching.

Weber County *Real Estate, Deed Records*

www.co.weber.ut.us

Property records on the County Parcel Search site are free at www.co.weber.ut.us/gis/2002/psearch/. Also, access Abstract Title
Registrations for a monthly fee at http://otgweb.co.weber.ut.us/abstract/login.asp.

Federal Courts in Utah...

Standards for Federal Courts: The universal PACER sign-up number is 800-676-6856. Find PACER and the Party/Case Index on
the Web at http://pacer.psc.uscourts.gov. PACER dial-up access is $.60 per minute. Also, courts offering internet access via PACER,
Web-PACER or the new CM-ECF charge $.08 per page fee ($.07 per page if record is pre-2005 or unless noted as free).

US District Court -- District of Utah

www.utd.uscourts.gov

PACER: Case records are available back to 7/1989. Records are purged never. New records are available online after 1 day. **PACER
Online Access:** ECF replaces PACER. Document images available. **Electronic Filing:** CM/ECF data at https://ecf.utd.uscourts.gov.
Opinions: View court opinions at www.utd.uscourts.gov/opinions/opinions.html. **Other Online Access:** Calendars at
www.utd.uscourts.gov/reports/dt.pl.
Division counties: All counties in Utah. Though all cases are heard here, the district is divided into Northern and Central Divisions.
Northern Div. includes the counties of Box Elder, Cache, Rich, Davis, Morgan and Weber; Central Div. includes all other counties.

US Bankruptcy Court -- District of Utah

www.utb.uscourts.gov

PACER: Case records are available back to 1/1985. Records are purged after 12 months. **PACER Online Access:** ECF replaces
PACER. Document images available. **Electronic Filing:** Recent case filings reports are free. CM/ECF data at
https://ecf.utb.uscourts.gov. **Opinions:** View court opinions at www.utb.uscourts.gov/LocalOpinions/opinions.htm. **Other Online
Access:** Calendars free at www.utb.uscourts.gov/chamberaccess/chambers.htm. **Phone access:** Voice Case Information System, call
800-733-6740, 801-524-3107
Division counties: All counties in Utah. Although all cases are handled here, the court divides itself into 2 divisions. Northern
Division includes counties of Box Elder, Cache, Rich, Davis, Morgan and Weber, and the Central Division includes the remaining
counties. Court is held 3 times per month in Ogden for northern cases and once a month in St. George for southern.

Vermont

Capital: Montpelier
                   Washington County
Time Zone: EST
Population: 621,394
# of Counties: 14

Quick Links

Website: http://vermont.gov/
Governor: www.vermont.gov/governor/
Attorney General: www.atg.state.vt.us
State Archives: http://vermont-archives.org
State Statutes and Codes: www.leg.state.vt.us/statutes/statutes2.htm
Legislative Bill Search: www.leg.state.vt.us/database/database2.cfm
Unclaimed Funds: www.tre.state.vt.us/unclaimed/ownerSearch.asp

State Level ... Major Agencies

Statewide Court Records

Court Administrator, Administrative Office of Courts, 109 State St, Montpelier, VT 05609-0701; 802-828-3278, Fax-802-828-3457, 7:45AM-4:30PM.
www.vermontjudiciary.org/default.aspx
Online search: Vermont Courts Online provides access to cases 12 of the counties' District, Family, and Superior Courts. It provides court calendar information for each court and detailed case information for Superior Court. Not available for Chittenden and Franklin. Criminal records are not included. Go to https://secure.vermont.gov/vtcdas/user. Records are in real-time mode. There is a $10.00 registration fee plus a fee of $.50 per case for look-up. Supreme Court opinions are available from the main web site and are also maintained by the Vermont Department of Libraries at http://dol.state.vt.us.

Sexual Offender Registry

State Repository, Vermont Criminal Information Center, 103 S. Main St., Waterbury, VT 05671-2101; 802-244-8727, 802-241-5400, Fax-802-241-5552, 8AM-4:30PM.
www.dps.state.vt.us/cjs/s_registry.htm
Online search: The webpage gives access to the high-risk offenders only. Each requesters must register with his/her name and address. The requestor must also acknowledge a statement which specifies the conditions under which the registry information is being released.

Incarceration Records

Vermont Department of Corrections, Inmate Information Request, 103 S. Main Street, Waterbury, VT 05671-1001; 802-241-2276, Fax-802-241-2565, 8AM-4:30PM.
www.doc.state.vt.us
Online search: The website provides an Incarcerated Offender Locator to ascertain where an inmate is located. Click at the top of main page, or go directly to www.doc.state.vt.us/offender. The search results gives name, DOB, location and case worker. This is not designed to provide complete inmate records nor is it a database of all inmates past and present in the system.

Corporation, Limited Liability Company, Limited Liability Partnerships, Limited Partnerships, Trademarks/Servicemarks

Secretary of State, Corporation Div, 81 River St, Montpelier, VT 05609-1104; 802-828-2386, Fax-802-828-2853, 7:45AM-4:30PM. www.sec.state.vt.us

Online search: Information on Corporate and trademark records can be accessed from the Internet for no fee. For the Corporation Name Finder, go to www.sec.state.vt.us/seek/database.htm#2. Many records, included corporation, UCC, trademark, tradename, and name look-ups are available. The Trade Name Finder is at www.sec.state.vt.us/seek/TRADSEEK.HTM. **Other options:** There is an option on the Internet to download the entire corporation (and tradename) database.

Uniform Commercial Code

UCC Division, Secretary of State, 81 River St, Drawer 4, Montpelier, VT 05609; 802-828-2386, Fax-802-828-2853, 7:45-4:30PM. www.sec.state.vt.us/tutor/dobiz/ucc/ucchome.htm

Online search: Searches are available from the Internet site. You can search by debtor or business name, there is no fee.

Driver Records, Driver License Information

Department of Motor Vehicles, DI - Records Unit, 120 State St, Montpelier, VT 05603-0001; 802-828-2050, Fax-802-828-2098, 7:45AM-4:30PM. www.aot.state.vt.us/dmv/dmvhp.htm

Online search: Online access costs $8.00 per 3 year record. The system is called "GovNet." Two methods are offered-single inquiry and batch mode. The system is open 24 hours a day, 7 days a week (except for file maintenance periods). Only the license number is needed when ordering, but it is suggested to submit the name and DOB also. For more information, call Driver Improvement at 802-828-2053. **Other options:** This agency will sell its license file to approved requesters, but customization is not available.

State Level ... Occupational Licensing

Accounting Firm	www.vtprofessionals.org
Acupuncturist	www.vtprofessionals.org
Alcohol & Drug Abuse Counselor	www.vtcertificationboard.org/counselors2.htm
Anesthesiologist Assistant	http://healthvermont.gov/hc/med_board/docfinder.aspx
Architect	www.vtprofessionals.org
Armed Courier	www.vtprofessionals.org
Athletic Trainer	www.vtprofessionals.org
Auctioneer	www.vtprofessionals.org
Bank	www.bishca.state.vt.us/BankingDiv/banking_index.htm
Barber	www.vtprofessionals.org
Body Piercer	www.vtprofessionals.org
Boxing Manager/Promoter	www.vtprofessionals.org
Boxing Professional	www.vtprofessionals.org
Chemical Suppression TQP Cert	www.state.vt.us/labind/weblic/cstqpcert.htm
Chimney Sweep	www.state.vt.us/labind/weblic/cswtqpcert.htm
Chiropractor	www.vtprofessionals.org
Cosmetologist	www.vtprofessionals.org
Credit Union	www.bishca.state.vt.us/BankingDiv/banking_index.htm
Crematory	www.vtprofessionals.org
Dentist/Dental Assistant/Dental Hygienist	www.vtprofessionals.org
Dietitian	www.vtprofessionals.org
Electrician	www.state.vt.us/labind/weblic/elicenses.htm
Electrologist	www.vtprofessionals.org
Embalmer	www.vtprofessionals.org
Engineer	www.vtprofessionals.org

Esthetician... www.vtprofessionals.org
Fire Alarm System Installer/Dealer .... www.state.vt.us/labind/weblic/fatqpcert.htm
Fire Sprinkler System Designer/Installer .... www.state.vt.us/labind/weblic/slicenses.htm
Funeral Director.. www.vtprofessionals.org
Hearing Aid Dispenser................................. www.vtprofessionals.org
LPG/Propane Installer................................. www.state.vt.us/labind/weblic/gpicert.htm
Manicurist... www.vtprofessionals.org
Marriage & Family Therapist .... www.vtprofessionals.org
Medical Doctor/Surgeon............................. http://healthvermont.gov/hc/med_board/docfinder.aspx
Mental Health Counselor, Clinical.............. www.vtprofessionals.org
Midwife, Licensed .... www.vtprofessionals.org
Natural Gas System Installer....................... www.state.vt.us/labind/weblic/gnicert.htm
Naturopathic Physician .... www.vtprofessionals.org
Notary Public... www.vtprofessionals.org
Nurse/Nurse Practitioner/LNA .... www.vtprofessionals.org
Nursing Home Administrator....................... www.vtprofessionals.org
Occupational Therapist .... www.vtprofessionals.org
Oil Burning Equipment Installer................. www.state.vt.us/labind/weblic/oicert.htm
Optician .... www.vtprofessionals.org
Optometrist .... www.vtprofessionals.org
Osteopathic Physician................................. www.vtprofessionals.org
Pharmacist/Pharmacy.................................. www.vtprofessionals.org
Photographer, Itinerant .... www.vtprofessionals.org
Physical Therapist/Assistant .... www.vtprofessionals.org
Physician, Assistant .... http://healthvermont.gov/hc/med_board/docfinder.aspx
Plumber... www.state.vt.us/labind/weblic/plicenses.htm
Podiatrist.. http://healthvermont.gov/hc/med_board/docfinder.aspx
Private Investigator .... www.vtprofessionals.org
Psychoanalyst .... www.vtprofessionals.org
Psychologist/Psychotherapist...................... www.vtprofessionals.org
Public Accountant-CPA............................... www.vtprofessionals.org
Race Driver/Track Personnel .... www.vtprofessionals.org
Racing Promoter .... www.vtprofessionals.org
Radiologic Technologist .... www.vtprofessionals.org
Real Estate Agent/Broker/Sales .... www.vtprofessionals.org/
Real Estate Appraiser.................................. www.vtprofessionals.org/
Security Guard .... www.vtprofessionals.org
Social Worker, Clinical............................... www.vtprofessionals.org
Surveyor, Land .... www.vtprofessionals.org
Tattoo Artist... www.vtprofessionals.org
Vendor, Itinerant.. www.vtprofessionals.org
Veterinarian .... www.vtprofessionals.org
Waste Water Treatment Plant Operator ...... www.anr.state.vt.us/dec/ww/opcert.htm

County Level ... Courts

Court Administration: Administrative Office of Courts, Court Administrator, 109 State St, Montpelier, VT, 05609-0701; 802-828-3278; www.vermontjudiciary.org

Court Structure: As of September, 1996, all small claims came under the jurisdiction of Superior Court, the court of general jurisdiction. All counties have a diversion program in which first offenders go through a process that includes a letter of apology, community service, etc. and, after 2 years, the record is expunged. These records are never released.

The Vermont Judicial Bureau has jurisdiction over Traffic, Municipal Ordinance, and Fish and Game, Minors in Possession, and hazing.

Online Access Note: Vermont Courts Online provides access to cases 12 of the counties' District, Family, and Superior Courts at https://secure.vermont.gov/vtcdas/user. The website provides court calendar information for each court and detailed case information for Superior Court. Not available for Chittenden and Franklin counties. Criminal records are not included. Records are in real time mode. There is a $10.00 registration fee plus a fee of $.50 per case for look-up.

Supreme Court opinions are available from the main website and are also maintained by the Vermont Department of Libraries at http://dol.state.vt.us.

Chittenden County

Superior Court – Civil Records
www.chittendensuperiorcourt.com/index.htm
Website offers access to court case information on cases from 1998 forward. Current calendars for district court at
www.vermontjudiciary.org/courts/district/index.htm.

County Level ... Recorders & Assessors

Recording Office Organization: 14 counties and 246 towns/cities, 246 recording offices. The recording officer is the Town/City Clerk. There is no county administration in Vermont. Many towns are so small that their mailing addresses are in different towns. Four towns/cities have the same name as counties - Barre, Newport, Rutland, and St. Albans. The entire state is in the Eastern Time Zone (EST).

Many towns are now charging a $2.00 per hour vault time fee for in-person searchers. All federal and state tax liens on personal property and on real property are filed with the Town/City Clerk in the lien/attachment book and indexed in real estate records. Most towns/cities will not perform tax lien searches.

Online Access Note: There is limited online access to county recorded documents. State recorded UCC data is available online from the Vermont Secretary of State.

Bennington Town *Property, Assessor Records*
www.bennington.com/local.html
Access to the Grand List search program is free at www.bennington.com/government/grandlist/index.html. No name searching at this time; site is under construction and data is incomplete.

Burlington City *Property Tax, Assessor Records*
www.ci.burlington.vt.us
Access to city property tax data is free at http://ci.burlingtontelecom.com/assessor/search/.

Newport City *Assessor, Property Records*
Access to Newport City assessor data is free at http://data.visionappraisal.com/newportvt/.

Newport Town   *Assessor, Property Records*
Search assessor records at http://data.visionappraisal.com/newportvt/. There is no fee.

Federal Courts in Vermont...

Standards for Federal Courts: The universal PACER sign-up number is 800-676-6856. Find PACER and the Party/Case Index on the Web at http://pacer.psc.uscourts.gov. PACER dial-up access is $.60 per minute. Also, courts offering internet access via PACER, Web-PACER or the new CM-ECF charge $.08 per page fee ($.07 per page if record is pre-2005 or unless noted as free).

US District Court -- District of Vermont

www.vtd.uscourts.gov

PACER: Case records are available back to 1/1991. New records are available online after 1 day. **PACER Online Access:** Login to RACER at https://pacer.login.uscourts.gov/cgi-bin/login.pl?court_id=r_vtdc. **Electronic Filing:** CM/ECF data at https://ecf.vtd.uscourts.gov. **Opinions:** Filings of interest free at www.vtd.uscourts.gov/Decisions.html. View court opinions at http://nysd.uscourts.gov/cwrulings.fwx?mode=rptform&cascode=D02VTXC. **Other Online Access:** Search monthly court calendar at www.vtd.uscourts.gov/Calendars.htm.
Burlington Division counties: Caledonia, Chittenden, Essex, Franklin, Grand Isle, Lamoille, Orleans, Washington. However, cases from all Vermont counties are randomly assigned to either Burlington or Rutland. Brattleboro is a hearing location only, not listed in this database.
Rutland Division counties: Addison, Bennington, Orange, Rutland, Windsor, Windham. However, cases from all Vermont counties are randomly assigned to either Burlington or Rutland. Brattleboro is a hearing location only, not listed in this database.

US Bankruptcy Court -- District of Vermont

www.vtb.uscourts.gov

PACER: Case records are available back to 1992; limited information prior. Records are purged never. New records are available online after 1 day. **PACER Online Access:** ECF replaces PACER. Document images available. **Electronic Filing:** CM/ECF data at https://ecf.vtb.uscourts.gov. **Opinions:** View court opinions at www.vtb.uscourts.gov/opinions.html. **Other Online Access:** Calendars on main website. **Phone access:** Voice Case Information System, call 800-260-9956, 802-776-2007
Division counties: All counties in Vermont.

> **Editor's Tip:** Just because records are maintained in a certain way in your state or county do not assume that any other county or state does things the same way that you are used to.

Virginia

Capital:　Richmond
　　　　　　Richmond City County
Time Zone: EST
Population: 7,459.827
# of Counties: 95

> Plus there are 41 independent cities with recording offices.

Quick Links

Website: www.myvirginia.org/cmsportal/
Governor:　www.governor.virginia.gov
Attorney General:　www.oag.state.va.us
State Archives:　www.lva.lib.va.us
State Statutes and Codes:　http://leg1.state.va.us/000/src.htm
Legislative Bill Search:　http://leg1.state.va.us/051/bil.htm
Bill Monitoring:　http://legis.state.va.us/SiteInformation/SubscriptionServices.htm
Unclaimed Funds:　https://www.trs.virginia.gov/propertysearchdotnet/

State Level ... Major Agencies

Criminal Records

Virginia State Police, CCRE, PO Box C-85076, Richmond, VA 23261-5076 (Courier: 7700 Midlothian Turnpike, Richmond, VA 23235); 804-323-2277, Fax-804-323-0861, 8AM-5PM.
www.vsp.state.va.us
Online search: Certain entities, including screening companies, are can apply for online access via the NCJI System. The system is ONLY available to IN-STATE accounts and allows you to submit requests faster. Fees are same as manual submission-$15.00 per record or $20.00 SOR record search. Username and password required. There is a minimum usage requirement of 10 requests per month. Turnaround time is 24-72 hours.

Statewide Court Records

Executive Secretary, Administrative Office of Courts, 100 N 9th St, 3rd Floor, Richmond, VA 23219; 804-786-6455, Fax-804-786-4542, 8AM-5PM.
www.courts.state.va.us
Online search: There are 3 available systems. None are statewide; each county must be searched separately. Cases from 132 General District Courts may be searched free at www.courts.state.va.us/courts/gd.html. You can search records from over 120 Circuit courts at www.courts.state.va.us/courts/circuit.html. While these systems do not include DOBs, SSNs and addresses, another access system known as LOPAS does. There are no fees to use LOPAS, but access is granted on a request-by-request basis. Call 804-786-6455 for details. The main webpage above offers access to Supreme Court and Appellate opinions.

Sexual Offender Registry

Virginia State Police, Sex Offender and Crimes Against Minors Registry, PO Box 27472, Richmond, VA 23261-7472 (Courier: 7700 Midlothian Turnpike, Richmond, VA 23235); 804-323-2153, Fax-804-323-0862, 8AM-5PM.
http://sex-offender.vsp.state.va.us/cool-ICE/
Online search: Search by violent offenders from the website by name, city, county or ZIP Code.

Incarceration Records

Virginia Department of Corrections, Central Criminal Records Section, PO Box 26963, Richmond, VA 23261-6963 (Courier: 6900 Atmore Drive, Richmond, VA 23225); 804-674-3131, Fax-804-674-3598, 8AM-5PM.
www.vadoc.state.va.us
Online search: At www.vipnet.org/cgi-bin/vadoc/doc.cgi is an Incarcerated Offender Locator to ascertain where an inmate is located. This is not designed to provide complete inmate records nor is it a database of all inmates past and present in the system. Also, a private company at www.vinelink.com/index.jsp offers free web access at DOC records. Also, there is a DOC wanted/fugitives list at www.vadoc.state.va.us/offenders/wanted/fugitives.htm.

Corporation, Limited Liability Company, Fictitious Name, Limited Partnership, Business Trust Records

State Corporation Commission, Clerks Office, PO Box 1197, Richmond, VA 23218-1197 (Courier: Tyler Bldg, 1st Floor, 1300 E Main St, Richmond, VA 23219); 804-371-9733, Fax-804-371-9133, 8:15AM-5PM.
www.scc.virginia.gov/division/clk/index.htm
Online search: Their system is called Clerk's Information System and is available at www.scc.virginia.gov/division/clk/diracc.htm. There are no fees. A wealth of information is available on this system. **Other options:** Magnetic tape purchase is offered to those who wish the entire database.

Trademarks, Service Marks

State Corporation Commission, Virginia Securities Division, PO Box 1197 (1300 Main St, 9th Fl), Richmond, VA 23218 (Courier: 1300 Main St, 9th Fl, Richmond, VA 23219); 804-371-9187, Fax-804-371-9911, 8:15AM-5PM.
www.scc.virginia.gov/division.htm
Online search: Trademarks and Service Marks are available at http://securities.scc.virginia.gov/SERFIS/wbq_tmsm$.startup.

Uniform Commercial Code, Federal Tax Liens

UCC Division, State Corporation Commission, PO Box 1197, Richmond, VA 23218-1197 (Courier: 1300 E Main St, 1st Floor, Richmond, VA 23219); 804-371-9733, Fax-804-692-0681, 8:15AM-5PM.
www.scc.virginia.gov/division/clk/fee_ucc.htm
Online search: Their system is called Clerk's Information System and is available at www.scc.virginia.gov/division/clk/diracc.htm. There are no fees. A wealth of information is available on this system.

Driver Records

Motorist Records Services, Attn: Records Request Work Center, PO Box 27412, Richmond, VA 23269; 804-367-0538, 8:30AM-5:30PM M-F; 8:30AM-12:30PM S.
www.dmv.state.va.us
Online search: Online service is provided by the Virginia Interactive. Online reports are provided via the Internet on an interactive basis 24 hours daily. There is a $75 annual administrative fee and records are $7.00 each. Go to www.virginiainteractive.org/cmsportal for more information (search "online services") or call 804-786-4718. **Other options:** The agency offers several monitoring programs for employers. Call 804-497-7155 for details.

Vehicle Ownership, Vehicle Identification

Department of Motor Vehicles, Vehicle Records Work Center, PO Box 27412, Richmond, VA 23269; 804-367-0538, 8:30AM-5:30PM M-F; 8:30AM-12:30PM S.
www.dmv.state.va.us
Online search: The online system, managed by the Virginia Interactive, open 24 hours daily. There is an annual $75.00 administration fee and records are $7.00 each. All accounts must be approved by both the DMV and Virginia Interactive. Call 804-786-4718 to request an information use agreement application. The URL is www.virginiainteractive.org/cmsportal/. Also, a $12.00 vehicle verification search is for prospective vehicle buyers is available at https://www.dmv.virginia.gov/dmvnet/ppi/intro.asp. **Other options:** Bulk release of vehicle or ownership information is not available except for statistical and vehicle recall purposes.

Vessel Ownership, Vessel Registration

Game & Inland Fisheries Dept, Boat Registration Dept, 4010 W Broad St, Richmond, VA 23230; 804-367-6135, Fax-804-367-1064, 8:15AM-5PM.
www.dgif.virginia.gov
Online search: The VA boat registration database may be searched on the web at www.virginiainteractive.org/cmsportal/. here is both a free service and a more advanced pay service, but both require a subscription which is $75.00 a year. Other motor vehicle records are available.

> **Editor's Note:** Virginia Independent Cities are listed separately in the County Courts Section and in the County Recording Office Section

State Level ... Occupational Licensing

Acupuncturist	www.vipnet.org/dhp/cgi-bin/search_publicdb.cgi
Alcoholic Beverage Distributor	www.abc.state.va.us/proj/enft/enforcement/jsp/firstpage.jsp
Architect	www.dpor.state.va.us/regulantlookup/selection_input.cfm
Asbestos-related Occupation	www.dpor.state.va.us/regulantlookup/selection_input.cfm
Athletic Trainer	www.vipnet.org/dhp/cgi-bin/search_publicdb.cgi
Attorney/Attorney Associate	www.vsb.org/attorney/attSearch.asp?S=D
Auctioneer/Auction Company	www.dpor.state.va.us/regulantlookup/selection_input.cfm
Audiologist	www.vipnet.org/dhp/cgi-bin/search_publicdb.cgi
Barber/Barber School/Business	www.dpor.state.va.us/regulantlookup/selection_input.cfm
Boxer	www.dpor.state.va.us/regulantlookup/selection_input.cfm
Boxing/Wresting Occupation	www.dpor.state.va.us/regulantlookup/selection_input.cfm
Carpenter	www.dpor.state.va.us/regulantlookup/selection_input.cfm
Cemetery Company/Seller	www.dpor.state.va.us/regulantlookup/selection_input.cfm
Check Casher	www.scc.virginia.gov/division/banking/chk_cash.htm
Chiropractor	www.vipnet.org/dhp/cgi-bin/search_publicdb.cgi
Clinical Nurse Specialist	www.vipnet.org/dhp/cgi-bin/search_publicdb.cgi
Contractor	www.dpor.state.va.us/regulantlookup/selection_input.cfm
Cosmetic Procedure Certification	www.vipnet.org/dhp/cgi-bin/search_publicdb.cgi
Cosmetologist/Cosmo School/Business	www.dpor.state.va.us/regulantlookup/selection_input.cfm
Counselor, Professional	www.vipnet.org/dhp/cgi-bin/search_publicdb.cgi
Crematory	www.vipnet.org/dhp/cgi-bin/search_publicdb.cgi
Dentist/Dental Hygienist	www.vipnet.org/dhp/cgi-bin/search_publicdb.cgi
Embalmer	www.vipnet.org/dhp/cgi-bin/search_publicdb.cgi
Engineer	www.dpor.state.va.us/regulantlookup/selection_input.cfm
Fair Housing	www.dpor.state.va.us/regulantlookup/selection_input.cfm
Funeral Director/Establ./Trainee	www.vipnet.org/dhp/cgi-bin/search_publicdb.cgi
Funeral Service Provider	www.vipnet.org/dhp/cgi-bin/search_publicdb.cgi
Gas Fitter	www.dpor.state.va.us/regulantlookup/selection_input.cfm
Geologist	www.dpor.state.va.us/regulantlookup/selection_input.cfm
Hair Braider	www.dpor.state.va.us/regulantlookup/selection_input.cfm
Hearing Aid Specialist	www.dpor.state.va.us/regulantlookup/selection_input.cfm
Home Inspector	www.dpor.state.va.us/regulantlookup/selection_input.cfm
Humane Society	www.vipnet.org/dhp/cgi-bin/search_publicdb.cgi
Interior Designer	www.dpor.state.va.us/regulantlookup/selection_input.cfm
Investment Advisor/Advisor Agency	www.scc.virginia.gov/division/srf/webpages/databd.htm
Landscape Architect	www.dpor.state.va.us/regulantlookup/selection_input.cfm
Lead-Related Occupation	www.dpor.state.va.us/regulantlookup/selection_input.cfm
Lobbyist	http://secure01.virginiainteractive.org/lobbyist/cgi-bin/search_lobbyist.cgi
Marriage & Family Therapist	www.vipnet.org/dhp/cgi-bin/search_publicdb.cgi
Massage Therapist	www.vipnet.org/dhp/cgi-bin/search_publicdb.cgi
Medical Doctor	www.vipnet.org/dhp/cgi-bin/search_publicdb.cgi
Medical Equipment Supplier	www.vipnet.org/dhp/cgi-bin/search_publicdb.cgi
Medical Wholesaler/Mfg	www.vipnet.org/dhp/cgi-bin/search_publicdb.cgi
Money Transmitter	www.scc.virginia.gov/division/banking/moneytrans.htm
Mortgage Lender/Broker	www.scc.virginia.gov/division/banking/news/mort.pdf

Nail Technician.. www.dpor.state.va.us/regulantlookup/selection_input.cfm
Nurse/Nurse's Aide .... www.vipnet.org/dhp/cgi-bin/search_publicdb.cgi
Nursing Home Administ'r/Preceptor .... www.vipnet.org/dhp/cgi-bin/search_publicdb.cgi
Occupational Therapist .... www.vipnet.org/dhp/cgi-bin/search_publicdb.cgi
Optician .... www.dpor.state.va.us/regulantlookup/selection_input.cfm
Optometrist .... www.arbo.org/index.php?action=findanoptometrist
Oral/Maxillofacial Surgeon......................... www.vipnet.org/dhp/cgi-bin/search_publicdb.cgi
Osteopathic Physician................................. www.vipnet.org/dhp/cgi-bin/search_publicdb.cgi
Payday Lender .... www.scc.virginia.gov/division/banking/paydaylend.htm
Pharmacist/Pharmacy................................. www.vipnet.org/dhp/cgi-bin/search_publicdb.cgi
Physical Therapist...................................... www.vipnet.org/dhp/cgi-bin/search_publicdb.cgi
Physician.. www.vipnet.org/dhp/cgi-bin/search_publicdb.cgi
Physician Assistant .... www.vipnet.org/dhp/cgi-bin/search_publicdb.cgi
Pilot, Branch .... www.dpor.state.va.us/regulantlookup/selection_input.cfm
Podiatrist.. www.vipnet.org/dhp/cgi-bin/search_publicdb.cgi
Polygraph Examiner .... www.dpor.state.va.us/regulantlookup/selection_input.cfm
Prescriptive Authorization .... www.vipnet.org/dhp/cgi-bin/search_publicdb.cgi
Property Association................................... www.dpor.state.va.us/regulantlookup/selection_input.cfm
Psychologist at School .... www.vipnet.org/dhp/cgi-bin/search_publicdb.cgi
Psychologist, Clinical/Applied.................... www.vipnet.org/dhp/cgi-bin/search_publicdb.cgi
Psychology School...................................... www.vipnet.org/dhp/cgi-bin/search_publicdb.cgi
Radiologic Technologist-limited................. www.vipnet.org/dhp/cgi-bin/search_publicdb.cgi
Real Estate Agent/Business/School .... www.dpor.state.va.us/regulantlookup/selection_input.cfm
Real Estate Appraiser/Appraiser Business .. www.dpor.state.va.us/regulantlookup/selection_input.cfm
Rehabilitation Provider .... www.vipnet.org/dhp/cgi-bin/search_publicdb.cgi
Respiratory Care Practitioner...................... www.vipnet.org/dhp/cgi-bin/search_publicdb.cgi
School Guidance Counselor......................... https://eb01.vak12ed.edu/tinfo/
School Library Media Specialist................. https://eb01.vak12ed.edu/tinfo/
School Principal/Superintendent................. https://eb01.vak12ed.edu/tinfo/
Securities Broker/Dealer/Dealer Agent....... www.scc.virginia.gov/division/srf/webpages/databd.htm
Securities Brokerage .... http://securities.scc.virginia.gov/SERFIS/wbq_bdia$.startup
Social Worker, Clinical/Registered............. www.vipnet.org/dhp/cgi-bin/search_publicdb.cgi
Soil Scientist .... www.dpor.state.va.us/regulantlookup/selection_input.cfm
Speech Pathologist at School .... www.vipnet.org/dhp/cgi-bin/search_publicdb.cgi
Speech Pathologist/Audiologist .... www.vipnet.org/dhp/cgi-bin/search_publicdb.cgi
Substance Abuse Counselor........................ www.vipnet.org/dhp/cgi-bin/search_publicdb.cgi
Substance Abuse Treatment Practitioner .... www.vipnet.org/dhp/cgi-bin/search_publicdb.cgi
Surveyor, Land .... www.dpor.state.va.us/regulantlookup/selection_input.cfm
Tattoo Artist... www.dpor.state.va.us/regulantlookup/selection_input.cfm
Teacher https://eb01.vak12ed.edu/tinfo/
Tradesman... www.dpor.state.va.us/regulantlookup/selection_input.cfm
University Limited Medical License............ www.vipnet.org/dhp/cgi-bin/search_publicdb.cgi
Veterinarian/Veterinary Technician............. www.vipnet.org/dhp/cgi-bin/search_publicdb.cgi
Warehouser, Medical .... www.vipnet.org/dhp/cgi-bin/search_publicdb.cgi
Waste Management Facility Operator......... www.dpor.state.va.us/regulantlookup/selection_input.cfm
Waste Water Plant Operator .... www.dpor.state.va.us/regulantlookup/selection_input.cfm
Wax Technician .... www.dpor.state.va.us/regulantlookup/selection_input.cfm
Wetlands Delineator .... www.dpor.state.va.us/regulantlookup/selection_input.cfm
Wrestler .... www.dpor.state.va.us/regulantlookup/selection_input.cfm

County Level ... Courts

Court Administration: Executive Secretary, Administrative Office of Courts, 100 N 9th Street, 3rd Fl, Supreme Court Building, Richmond, Virginia, 23219; 804-786-6455, www.courts.state.va.us

Court Structure: The Circuit Courts in 31 districts are the courts of general jurisdiction. There are 132 District Courts of limited jurisdiction. Please note that a district can comprise a county or a city. Records of civil action from $3000 to $15,000 can be at either the Circuit Court or District Court as either can have jurisdiction. It is necessary to check both record locations as there is no concurrent database nor index.

Online Access Note: 3 systems available; none statewide. Each county must be searched separately.

132 General District Courts (many are combined courts) may be searched free at http://208.210.219.132/vadistrict/select.jsp. Here you can search both active and inactive cases.

Also, Virginia has the growing "Circuit Court Case Information Pilot Project" with free access to Circuit Court records. You may search records from over 90 courts at http://208.210.219.132/vacircuit/select.jsp

While these first 2 systems do not include DOBs, SSNs, and addresses, the dialup system known as LOPAS does have birth month and day. There are no fees to use LOPAS, but access is granted on a request-by-request basis. Anyone wishing to establish an account or receive information on LOPAS must contact the Supreme Court of Virginia, 100 N 9th St, Richmond, VA, 23219 or by phone at 804-786-6455 or fax at 804-786-4542. LOPAS is a difficult system to "get on" as it is an old dial-up system gradually being phased out.

The www.courts.state.va.us website offers access to Supreme Court and Appellate Courts opinions.

Virginia Counties (Virginia Independent Cities are listed following this County Section)

Accomack County

2nd Circuit Court – Civil and Criminal Records
www.courts.state.va.us/courts/circuit.html
Remote access to court case indexes is via LOPAS; call 804-786-5511 to apply.

2A General District Court – Civil and Criminal Records
Search at http://208.210.219.132/vadistrict/select.jsp. Also, access case indexes is via LOPAS; call 804-786-5511 to apply.

Albemarle County

16th Circuit & District Court – Civil and Criminal Records
www.courts.state.va.us/courts/circuit.html
Select and search Circuit Courts online at www.courts.state.va.us/caseinfo/circuit.html. Search District courts at http://208.210.219.132/vadistrict/select.jsp. Also search via LOPAS; call 804-786-5511 to apply.

Alleghany County

25th Circuit Court – Civil and Criminal Records
www.alleghanycountyclerk.com
Search free at www.courts.state.va.us/caseinfo/circuit.html.

25th General District Court – Civil and Criminal Records
Search free at http://208.210.219.132/vadistrict/select.jsp. Also search via LOPAS; call 804-786-5511 to apply.

Amelia County

11th Circuit Court – Civil and Criminal Records
Search free at www.courts.state.va.us/caseinfo/circuit.html. Also search via LOPAS; call 804-786-5511 to apply.

11th General District Court – Civil and Criminal Records
Search free at http://208.210.219.132/vadistrict/select.jsp. Also search via LOPAS; call 804-786-5511 to apply.

Amherst County

24th Circuit Court – Civil and Criminal Records
www.courts.state.va.us/courts/circuit.html

Remote access to court case indexes is via LOPAS; call 804-786-5511 to apply.

24th General District Court – Civil and Criminal Records
Search free at http://208.210.219.132/vadistrict/select.jsp. Also search via LOPAS; call 804-786-5511 to apply.

Appomattox County

10th Circuit Court – Civil and Criminal Records
www.courts.state.va.us/courts/circuit.html
Search free at www.courts.state.va.us/caseinfo/circuit.html. Also search via LOPAS; call 804-786-5511 to apply.

10th General District Court – Civil and Criminal Records
Search free at http://208.210.219.132/vadistrict/select.jsp. Also search via LOPAS; call 804-786-5511 to apply.

Arlington County

17th Circuit Court – Civil and Criminal Records
www.courts.state.va.us/courts/circuit.html
Access free at www.courts.state.va.us/caseinfo/circuit.html.

17th General District Court – Civil and Criminal Records
Search free at http://208.210.219.132/vadistrict/select.jsp. Also search via LOPAS; call 804-786-5511 to apply.

Augusta County

25th Circuit Court – Civil and Criminal Records
www.courts.state.va.us/courts/circuit.html
Access free at www.courts.state.va.us/caseinfo/circuit.html.

25th General District Court – Civil and Criminal Records
www.courts.state.va.us/courts/gd/Augusta/home.html
Search online free at http://208.210.219.132/vadistrict/select.jsp.

Bath County

25th Circuit Court – Civil and Criminal Records
www.courts.state.va.us/courts/circuit.html
Remote access to court case indexes is via LOPAS; call 804-786-5511 to apply.

25th General District Court – Civil and Criminal Records
Search free at http://208.210.219.132/vadistrict/select.jsp. Also search via LOPAS; call 804-786-5511 to apply.

Bedford County

County Circuit Court – Civil and Criminal Records
www.courts.state.va.us/courts/circuit.html
Access free at www.courts.state.va.us/caseinfo/circuit.html. Remote access to case indexes is via LOPAS; call 804-786-5511 to apply.

24th General District Court – Civil and Criminal Records
Search free at http://208.210.219.132/vadistrict/select.jsp. Also search via LOPAS; call 804-786-5511 to apply.

Bland County

27th Circuit Court – Civil and Criminal Records
www.courts.state.va.us/courts/circuit.html
Search free at www.courts.state.va.us/caseinfo/circuit.html. Also search via LOPAS; call 804-786-5511 to apply.

27th General District Court – Civil and Criminal Records
Search free at http://208.210.219.132/vadistrict/select.jsp. Also search via LOPAS; call 804-786-5511 to apply.

Botetourt County

25th Circuit Court – Civil and Criminal Records
www.courts.state.va.us/courts/circuit.html
Search free at www.courts.state.va.us/caseinfo/circuit.html. Also search via LOPAS; call 804-786-5511 to apply.

25th General District Court – Civil and Criminal Records
Search free at http://208.210.219.132/vadistrict/select.jsp. Also search via LOPAS; call 804-786-5511 to apply.

Brunswick County

6th Circuit Court – Civil and Criminal Records
www.courts.state.va.us/courts/circuit.html
Search free at www.courts.state.va.us/caseinfo/circuit.html. Also search via LOPAS; call 804-786-5511 to apply. Also access record images via http://208.210.219.102/cgi-bin/p/rms.cgi; registration and password required.

6th General District Court – Civil and Criminal Records
Search free at http://208.210.219.132/vadistrict/select.jsp. Also search via LOPAS; call 804-786-5511 to apply.

Buchanan County

29th Circuit Court – Civil and Criminal Records
www.courts.state.va.us/courts/circuit.html
Remote access to court case indexes is via LOPAS; call 804-786-5511 to apply.

29th Judicial District Court – Civil Records
Search free at http://208.210.219.132/vadistrict/select.jsp. Also search via LOPAS; call 804-786-5511 to apply.

Buckingham County

10th Circuit Court – Civil and Criminal Records
www.courts.state.va.us/courts/circuit.html
Remote access to court case indexes is via LOPAS; call 804-786-5511 to apply.

Buckingham General District Court – Civil and Criminal Records
Search free at http://208.210.219.132/vadistrict/select.jsp. Also search via LOPAS; call 804-786-5511 to apply.

Campbell County

24th Circuit Court – Civil and Criminal Records
www.courts.state.va.us/courts/circuit.html
Remote access to court case indexes is via LOPAS; call 804-786-5511 to apply.

24th General District Court – Civil and Criminal Records
Search free at http://208.210.219.132/vadistrict/select.jsp. Also search via LOPAS; call 804-786-5511 to apply.

Caroline County

15th Circuit Court – Civil and Criminal Records
www.courts.state.va.us/courts/circuit.html
Remote access to court case indexes is via LOPAS; call 804-786-5511 to apply.

15th General District Court – Civil and Criminal Records
Search free at http://208.210.219.132/vadistrict/select.jsp. Also search via LOPAS; call 804-786-5511 to apply.

Carroll County

27th Circuit Court – Civil and Criminal Records
www.courts.state.va.us/courts/circuit.html
Search free at www.courts.state.va.us/caseinfo/circuit.html. Also search via LOPAS; call 804-786-5511 to apply.

Carroll Combined District Court – Civil and Criminal Records
Search free at http://208.210.219.132/vadistrict/select.jsp. Also search via LOPAS; call 804-786-5511 to apply.

Charlotte County

10th Circuit Court – Civil Records
www.courts.state.va.us/courts/circuit.html
Remote access to court case indexes is via LOPAS; call 804-786-5511 to apply.

Charlotte General District Court – Civil and Criminal Records
Search free at http://208.210.219.132/vadistrict/select.jsp. Also search via LOPAS; call 804-786-5511 to apply.

1st General District Court – Civil and Criminal Records
Select and search District Courts at www.courts.state.va.us.

Chesterfield County

12th Circuit Court – Civil Records

www.co.chesterfield.va.us/JusticeAdministration/CircuitCourtClerk/clerhome.asp
Remote access to court case indexes is via LOPAS; call 804-786-5511 to apply.

12th General District Court – Civil and Criminal Records
www.courts.state.va.us/courts/gd/Chesterfield/home.html
Search free at http://208.210.219.132/vadistrict/select.jsp. Also search via LOPAS; call 804-786-5511 to apply.

Clarke County

26th Circuit Court – Civil and Criminal Records
www.courts.state.va.us/courts/circuit.html
Remote access to court case indexes is via LOPAS; call 804-786-5511 to apply.

General District Court – Civil and Criminal Records
www.co.clarke.va.us
Search free at http://208.210.219.132/vadistrict/select.jsp. Also search via LOPAS; call 804-786-5511 to apply.

Craig County

25th Circuit Court – Civil and Criminal Records
www.courts.state.va.us/courts/circuit.html
Remote access to court case indexes is via LOPAS; call 804-786-5511 to apply.

25th General District Court – Civil and Criminal Records
Search free at http://208.210.219.132/vadistrict/select.jsp. Also search via LOPAS; call 804-786-5511 to apply.

Culpeper County

16th Circuit Court – Civil and Criminal Records
www.courts.state.va.us/courts/circuit/Culpeper/home.html
Acces civil record index at www.courts.state.va.us/caseinfo/circuit.html. There are no DOBs, so system not so useful. Also, remote access to court case indexes is via LOPAS; call 804-786-5511 to apply. DOBs and criminal records included in LOPAS.

16th General District Court – Civil and Criminal Records
Search free at http://208.210.219.132/vadistrict/select.jsp. Also search via LOPAS; call 804-786-5511 to apply.

Cumberland County

10th Circuit Court – Civil and Criminal Records
www.courts.state.va.us/courts/circuit.html
Search free at www.courts.state.va.us/caseinfo/circuit.html. Also search via LOPAS; call 804-786-5511 to apply.

10th General District Court – Civil and Criminal Records
Select and search District Courts at http://208.210.219.132/vadistrict/select.jsp.

Dickenson County

29th Circuit Court – Civil and Criminal Records
www.courts.state.va.us/courts/circuit.html
Access free at www.courts.state.va.us/caseinfo/circuit.html.

29th General District Court – Civil and Criminal Records
Search free at http://208.210.219.132/vadistrict/select.jsp. Also search via LOPAS; call 804-786-5511 to apply.

Dinwiddie County

11th Circuit Court – Civil and Criminal Records
www.courts.state.va.us/courts/circuit.html
Select and search Circuit Courts online at www.courts.state.va.us/caseinfo/circuit.html.

11th General District Court – Civil and Criminal Records
Search free at http://208.210.219.132/vadistrict/select.jsp. Also search via LOPAS; call 804-786-5511 to apply.

Essex County

15th Circuit Court – Civil Records
www.courts.state.va.us/courts/circuit.html
Remote access to court case indexes is via LOPAS; call 804-786-5511 to apply.

15th General District Court – Civil and Criminal Records
Search free at http://208.210.219.132/vadistrict/select.jsp. Also search via LOPAS; call 804-786-5511 to apply.

Fairfax County

19th Circuit Court – Civil and Criminal Records
www.fairfaxcounty.gov/courts/circuit
Remote access to current court case indexes is via CPAN; call 703-246-2366 to apply. Fee is $25.00 per month per user.

19th General District Court – Civil and Criminal Records
www.fairfaxcounty.gov/courts/gendist
Access to civil records at http://208.210.219.132/vadistrict/select.jsp. Access to criminal & traffic records at http://208.210.219.132/vadistrict/select.jsp. For info about the statewide systems, see the state introduction.

Fauquier County

Circuit Court – Civil and Criminal Records
www.fauquiercounty.gov/government/departments/circuitcourt
Access free at www.courts.state.va.us/caseinfo/circuit.html.

20th General District Court – Civil and Criminal Records
Search free at http://208.210.219.132/vadistrict/select.jsp. Also search via LOPAS; call 804-786-5511 to apply.

Floyd County

27th Circuit Court – Civil and Criminal Records
www.courts.state.va.us/courts/circuit.html
Search free at www.courts.state.va.us/caseinfo/circuit.html. Also search via LOPAS; call 804-786-5511 to apply.

27th General District Court – Civil and Criminal Records
Select and search District Courts at http://208.210.219.132/vadistrict/select.jsp. Also, remote access to court case indexes is via LOPAS; call 804-786-5511 to apply.

Fluvanna County

16th Circuit Court – Civil and Criminal Records
www.courts.state.va.us/courts/circuit.html
Search free at www.courts.state.va.us/caseinfo/circuit.html. Also search via LOPAS; call 804-786-5511 to apply.

16th General District Court – Civil and Criminal Records
Search free at http://208.210.219.132/vadistrict/select.jsp. Also search via LOPAS; call 804-786-5511 to apply.

Franklin County

22nd Judicial Circuit Court – Civil and Criminal Records
www.courts.state.va.us/courts/circuit/Franklin/home.html
Select and search Circuit Courts online at www.courts.state.va.us/caseinfo/circuit.html.

22nd General District Court – Civil and Criminal Records
www.courts.state.va.us/courts/combined/Franklin_City/home.html
Search free at http://208.210.219.132/vadistrict/select.jsp. Also search via LOPAS; call 804-786-5511 to apply.

Frederick County

Circuit Court – Civil and Criminal Records
www.winfredclerk.com
Search free at www.courts.state.va.us/caseinfo/circuit.html. Also search via LOPAS; call 804-786-5511 to apply.

26th District Court – Civil and Criminal Records
Search free at http://208.210.219.132/vadistrict/select.jsp. Also search via LOPAS; call 804-786-5511 to apply.

Giles County

27th General District Court – Civil and Criminal Records
www.courts.state.va.us/courts/combined/Giles/home.html
Search free at http://208.210.219.132/vadistrict/select.jsp. Also search via LOPAS; call 804-786-5511 to apply.

Gloucester County

9th Circuit Court – Civil and Criminal Records
www.co.gloucester.va.us
Access free at www.courts.state.va.us/caseinfo/circuit.html.

9th General District Court – Civil and Criminal Records
Search free at http://208.210.219.132/vadistrict/select.jsp. Also search via LOPAS; call 804-786-5511 to apply.

Goochland County

16th Circuit Court – Civil and Criminal Records
www.courts.state.va.us/courts/circuit.html
Remote access to court case indexes is via LOPAS; call 804-786-5511 to apply. Also, may be free online at
http://208.210.219.132/vacircuit/select.jsp?court=.

General District Court – Civil and Criminal Records
Search free at http://208.210.219.132/vadistrict/select.jsp. Also search via LOPAS; call 804-786-5511 to apply.

Grayson County

27th Circuit Court – Civil and Criminal Records
www.courts.state.va.us/courts/circuit.html
Select and search Circuit Courts online at www.courts.state.va.us/caseinfo/circuit.html.

27th General District Court – Civil and Criminal Records
Search free at http://208.210.219.132/vadistrict/select.jsp. Also search via LOPAS; call 804-786-5511 to apply.

Greene County

16th Circuit Court – Civil Records
www.courts.state.va.us/courts/circuit.html
Remote access to court case indexes is via LOPAS; call 804-786-5511 to apply.

16th General District Court – Civil and Criminal Records
Search free at http://208.210.219.132/vadistrict/select.jsp. Also search via LOPAS; call 804-786-5511 to apply.

Greensville County

6th Circuit Court – Civil and Criminal Records
www.courts.state.va.us/courts/circuit.html
Search free at www.courts.state.va.us/caseinfo/circuit.html. Also search via LOPAS; call 804-786-5511 to apply.

Greenville/Emporia Combined Court – Civil and Criminal Records
Select and search District Courts at http://208.210.219.132/vadistrict/select.jsp.

Halifax County

10th Circuit Court – Civil and Criminal Records
www.courts.state.va.us/courts/circuit.html
Access free at www.courts.state.va.us/caseinfo/circuit.html. Criminal access is free at http://208.210.219.132/vacircuit/select.jsp. For information about the statewide online systems, see the state introduction.

10th General District Court – Civil and Criminal Records
Search free at http://208.210.219.132/vadistrict/select.jsp. Also search via LOPAS; call 804-786-5511 to apply.

Hanover County

15th Circuit Court – Civil and Criminal Records
www.co.hanover.va.us/circuitct/default.htm
Remote access to court case indexes is via LOPAS; call 804-786-5511 to apply.

15th General District Court – Civil and Criminal Records
Search free at http://208.210.219.132/vadistrict/select.jsp. Also search via LOPAS; call 804-786-5511 to apply.

Henrico County

14th Circuit Court – Civil and Criminal Records
www.co.henrico.va.us/clerk/
Remote access to court case indexes is via LOPAS; call 804-786-5511 to apply.

14th General District Court – Civil and Criminal Records
Search free at http://208.210.219.132/vadistrict/select.jsp. Also search via LOPAS; call 804-786-5511 to apply.

Henry County

21st Circuit Court – Civil and Criminal Records
www.courts.state.va.us/courts/circuit/Henry/home.html
Access free at www.courts.state.va.us/caseinfo/circuit.html.

21st General District Court – Civil and Criminal Records
www.courts.state.va.us/courts/gd/Henry/home.html
Search free at http://208.210.219.132/vadistrict/select.jsp. Also search via LOPAS; call 804-786-5511 to apply.

Highland County

25th Circuit Court – Civil and Criminal Records
www.courts.state.va.us/courts/circuit.html
Remote access to court case indexes is via LOPAS; call 804-786-5511 to apply.

25th General District Court – Civil and Criminal Records
Search free at http://208.210.219.132/vadistrict/select.jsp. Also search via LOPAS; call 804-786-5511 to apply.

Isle of Wight County

5th Circuit Court – Civil and Criminal Records
www.courts.state.va.us/courts/circuit.html
Access free at www.courts.state.va.us/caseinfo/circuit.html.

5th General District Court – Civil and Criminal Records
Search free at http://208.210.219.132/vadistrict/select.jsp. Also search via LOPAS; call 804-786-5511 to apply.

King and Queen County

9th Circuit Court – Civil and Criminal Records
www.courts.state.va.us/courts/circuit.html
Remote access to court case indexes is via LOPAS, call 804-786-5511 to apply.

King & Queen General District Court – Civil and Criminal Records
www.kingandqueenco.net/html/Govt/gendist.html
Search free at http://208.210.219.132/vadistrict/select.jsp. Also search via LOPAS; call 804-786-5511 to apply.

King George County

15th Circuit Court – Civil and Criminal Records
www.courts.state.va.us/courts/circuit.html
Access free at www.courts.state.va.us/caseinfo/circuit.html.

15th Judicial District King George Combined Court – Civil and Criminal Records
Access is at http://208.210.219.132/vadistrict/select.jsp.

King William County

9th Circuit Court – Civil and Criminal Records
www.courts.state.va.us/courts/circuit.html
Search free at www.courts.state.va.us/caseinfo/circuit.html. Also search via LOPAS; call 804-786-5511 to apply.

King William General District Court – Civil and Criminal Records
Search free at http://208.210.219.132/vadistrict/select.jsp. Also search via LOPAS; call 804-786-5511 to apply.

Lancaster County

15th Circuit Court – Civil and Criminal Records
www.courts.state.va.us/courts/circuit.html
Search free at www.courts.state.va.us/caseinfo/circuit.html. Also search via LOPAS; call 804-786-5511 to apply.

15th General District Court – Civil and Criminal Records
Search free at http://208.210.219.132/vadistrict/select.jsp. Also search via LOPAS; call 804-786-5511 to apply.

Lee County

30th Circuit Court – Civil and Criminal Records
www.courts.state.va.us/courts/circuit.html
Select and search Circuit Courts online at www.courts.state.va.us/caseinfo/circuit.html. Phone & fax access limited to short searches.

30th General District Court – Civil and Criminal Records
Search free at http://208.210.219.132/vadistrict/select.jsp. Also search via LOPAS; call 804-786-5511 to apply.

Loudoun County

20th Circuit Court – Civil and Criminal Records
www.loudoun.gov/clerk
Remote access to court case indexes is via LOPAS; call 804-786-5511 to apply. Also, docket lists are free at
http://inetdocs.loudoun.gov/clerk/docs/dockets_/index.htm.

20th General District Court – Civil and Criminal Records
Search free at http://208.210.219.132/vadistrict/select.jsp. Also search via LOPAS; call 804-786-5511 to apply.

Louisa County

16th Circuit Court – Civil and Criminal Records
www.courts.state.va.us/courts/circuit.html
Search free at www.courts.state.va.us/caseinfo/circuit.html. Also search via LOPAS; call 804-786-5511 to apply.

16th General District Court – Civil and Criminal Records
Search free at http://208.210.219.132/vadistrict/select.jsp. Also search via LOPAS; call 804-786-5511 to apply.

Lunenburg County

10th Circuit Court – Civil and Criminal Records
www.courts.state.va.us/courts/circuit.html
Search free at www.courts.state.va.us/caseinfo/circuit.html. Also search via LOPAS; call 804-786-5511 to apply.

10th General District Court – Civil and Criminal Records
Search free at http://208.210.219.132/vadistrict/select.jsp. Also search via LOPAS; call 804-786-5511 to apply.

Madison County

16th Circuit Court – Civil and Criminal Records
www.courts.state.va.us/courts/circuit.html
Select and search Combined Courts online at www.courts.state.va.us/caseinfo/circuit.html.

16th General District Court – Civil and Criminal Records
Search free at http://208.210.219.132/vadistrict/select.jsp. Also search via LOPAS; call 804-786-5511 to apply.

Mathews County

9th General District Court – Civil and Criminal Records
Search free at http://208.210.219.132/vadistrict/select.jsp. Also search via LOPAS; call 804-786-5511 to apply.

Mecklenburg County

10th Circuit Court – Civil and Criminal Records
www.courts.state.va.us/courts/circuit.html
Remote access to court case indexes is via LOPAS; call 804-786-5511 to apply.

10th General District Court – Civil and Criminal Records
Search free at http://208.210.219.132/vadistrict/select.jsp. Also search via LOPAS; call 804-786-5511 to apply.

Middlesex County

9th Circuit Court – Civil Records
www.courts.state.va.us/courts/circuit.html
Remote access to court case indexes is via LOPAS; call 804-786-5511 to apply.

9th General District Court – Civil and Criminal Records
Search free at http://208.210.219.132/vadistrict/select.jsp. Also search via LOPAS; call 804-786-5511 to apply.

Montgomery County

27th Circuit Court – Civil and Criminal Records
www.courts.state.va.us/courts/circuit.html
Access free at www.courts.state.va.us/caseinfo/circuit.html.

27th General District Court – Civil and Criminal Records
Search free at http://208.210.219.132/vadistrict/select.jsp. Also search via LOPAS; call 804-786-5511 to apply.

Nelson County

24th Circuit Court – Civil and Criminal Records
www.courts.state.va.us/courts/circuit.html
Access free at www.courts.state.va.us/caseinfo/circuit.html.

24th General District Court – Civil and Criminal Records
Search free at http://208.210.219.132/vadistrict/select.jsp. Also search via LOPAS; call 804-786-5511 to apply.

New Kent County

9th Circuit Court – Civil and Criminal Records
www.courts.state.va.us/courts/circuit.html
Access free at www.courts.state.va.us/caseinfo/circuit.html.

9th General District Court – Civil and Criminal Records
Search free at http://208.210.219.132/vadistrict/select.jsp. Also search via LOPAS; call 804-786-5511 to apply.

Northampton County

2nd Circuit Court – Civil and Criminal Records
www.courts.state.va.us/courts/circuit.html
Search free at www.courts.state.va.us/caseinfo/circuit.html. Also search via LOPAS; call 804-786-5511 to apply.

Northampton General District Court – Civil and Criminal Records
Search free at http://208.210.219.132/vadistrict/select.jsp. Also search via LOPAS; call 804-786-5511 to apply.

Northumberland County

15th Circuit Court – Civil and Criminal Records
www.courts.state.va.us/courts/circuit.html
Access free at www.courts.state.va.us/caseinfo/circuit.html.

15th General District Court – Civil and Criminal Records
Search free at http://208.210.219.132/vadistrict/select.jsp. Also search via LOPAS; call 804-786-5511 to apply.

Nottoway County

11th Circuit Court – Civil and Criminal Records
www.courts.state.va.us/courts/circuit.html
Search free at www.courts.state.va.us/caseinfo/circuit.html. Also search via LOPAS; call 804-786-5511 to apply.

11th General District Court – Civil and Criminal Records
Search free at http://208.210.219.132/vadistrict/select.jsp. Also search via LOPAS; call 804-786-5511 to apply.

Orange County

16th Circuit Court – Civil and Criminal Records
www.courts.state.va.us/courts/circuit.html
Search free at www.courts.state.va.us/caseinfo/circuit.html. Also search via LOPAS; call 804-786-5511 to apply.

16th General District Court – Civil and Criminal Records
Search free at http://208.210.219.132/vadistrict/select.jsp. Also search via LOPAS; call 804-786-5511 to apply.

Page County

26th Circuit Court – Civil and Criminal Records
www.courts.state.va.us/courts/circuit.html
Access free at www.courts.state.va.us/caseinfo/circuit.html.

26th General District Court – Civil and Criminal Records
Search free at http://208.210.219.132/vadistrict/select.jsp. Also search via LOPAS; call 804-786-5511 to apply.

Patrick County

21st Circuit Court – Civil and Criminal Records
www.courts.state.va.us/courts/circuit.html
Search free at www.courts.state.va.us/caseinfo/circuit.html. Also search via LOPAS; call 804-786-5511 to apply.

21st General District Court – Civil and Criminal Records
Search free at http://208.210.219.132/vadistrict/select.jsp. Also search via LOPAS; call 804-786-5511 to apply.

Pittsylvania County

22nd Circuit Court – Civil and Criminal Records
www.courts.state.va.us/courts/circuit.html
Access to civil is free at www.courts.state.va.us/caseinfo/circuit.html. If documents mailed, add $.50 per page if SASE not included. Access to Criminal is free at http://208.210.219.132/vacircuit/select.jsp. For information about the statewide online systems, see the state introduction.

22nd General District Court – Civil and Criminal Records
www.courts.state.va.us/courts/gd/Pittsylvania/home.html
Search free at http://208.210.219.132/vadistrict/select.jsp. Also search via LOPAS; call 804-786-5511 to apply.

Powhatan County

11th Circuit Court – Civil and Criminal Records
www.courts.state.va.us/courts/circuit.html
Remote access to court case indexes is via LOPAS; call 804-786-5511 to apply.

11th Judicial District Court – Civil and Criminal Records
Search free at http://208.210.219.132/vadistrict/select.jsp. Also search via LOPAS; call 804-786-5511 to apply.

Prince Edward County

Circuit Court – Civil and Criminal Records
www.courts.state.va.us/courts/circuit.html
Remote access to court case indexes is via LOPAS; call 804-786-5511 to apply.

General District Court – Civil and Criminal Records
Search free at http://208.210.219.132/vadistrict/select.jsp. Also search via LOPAS; call 804-786-5511 to apply.

Prince George County

Circuit Court – Civil and Criminal Records
www.courts.state.va.us/courts/circuit.html
Search free at www.courts.state.va.us/caseinfo/circuit.html. Also search via LOPAS; call 804-786-5511 to apply.

6th General District Court – Civil and Criminal Records
Search free at http://208.210.219.132/vadistrict/select.jsp. Also search via LOPAS; call 804-786-5511 to apply.

Prince William County

31st General District Court – Civil and Criminal Records
www.courts.state.va.us/courts/gd/Prince_William/home.html
Search free at http://208.210.219.132/vadistrict/select.jsp. Also search via LOPAS; call 804-786-5511 to apply.

Pulaski County

Circuit Court – Civil and Criminal Records
www.pulaskicircuitcourt.com
Access to civil court records is $300 annual fee http://records.pulaskicircuitcourt.com/icris/splash.jsp. Registration required; search by name, document type or number. Also, access to criminal is free at http://208.210.219.132/vacircuit/select.jsp.

27th General District Court – Civil and Criminal Records
Search free at http://208.210.219.132/vadistrict/select.jsp. Also search via LOPAS; call 804-786-5511 to apply.

Rappahannock County

20th Circuit Court – Civil and Criminal Records
www.courts.state.va.us/courts/circuit.html
Search free at www.courts.state.va.us/caseinfo/circuit.html. Also search via LOPAS; call 804-786-5511 to apply.

20th Combined District Court – Civil and Criminal Records
Search free at http://208.210.219.132/vadistrict/select.jsp. Also search via LOPAS; call 804-786-5511 to apply.

Richmond County

15th Circuit Court – Civil and Criminal Records
www.courts.state.va.us/courts/circuit.html
Search free at www.courts.state.va.us/caseinfo/circuit.html. Also search via LOPAS; call 804-786-5511 to apply.

15th Judicial District Court – Civil and Criminal Records
Search free at http://208.210.219.132/vadistrict/select.jsp. Also search via LOPAS; call 804-786-5511 to apply.

Roanoke County

23rd Circuit Court – Civil and Criminal Records
www.co.roanoke.va.us
Access free at www.courts.state.va.us/caseinfo/circuit.html.

23rd General District Court – Civil and Criminal Records
www.roanokecountyva.gov/
Search free at http://208.210.219.132/vadistrict/select.jsp. Also search via LOPAS; call 804-786-5511 to apply.

Rockbridge County

25th Circuit Court – Civil and Criminal Records
www.courts.state.va.us/courts/circuit.html
Search free at www.courts.state.va.us/caseinfo/circuit.html. Also search via LOPAS; call 804-786-5511 to apply.

District Court – Civil and Criminal Records
Search free at http://208.210.219.132/vadistrict/select.jsp. Also search via LOPAS; call 804-786-5511 to apply.

Rockingham County

26th Circuit Court – Civil and Criminal Records
www.courts.state.va.us/courts/circuit.html
Access free at www.courts.state.va.us/caseinfo/circuit.html.

26th General District Court – Civil and Criminal Records
Search free at http://208.210.219.132/vadistrict/select.jsp. Also search via LOPAS; call 804-786-5511 to apply.

Russell County

29th Circuit Court – Civil and Criminal Records
www.courts.state.va.us/courts/circuit.html
Search free at www.courts.state.va.us/caseinfo/circuit.html. Also search via LOPAS; call 804-786-5511 to apply.

29th General District Court – Civil and Criminal Records
Search free at http://208.210.219.132/vadistrict/select.jsp. Also search via LOPAS; call 804-786-5511 to apply.

Scott County

Circuit Court – Civil and Criminal Records
www.courts.state.va.us/courts/circuit.html
Search free at www.courts.state.va.us/caseinfo/circuit.html. Also search via LOPAS; call 804-786-5511 to apply.

30th General District Court – Civil and Criminal Records
Search free at http://208.210.219.132/vadistrict/select.jsp. Also search via LOPAS; call 804-786-5511 to apply.

Shenandoah County

26th Circuit Court – Civil and Criminal Records
www.courts.state.va.us/courts/circuit.html
Search free at www.courts.state.va.us/caseinfo/circuit.html. Also search via LOPAS; call 804-786-5511 to apply.

26th General District Court – Civil and Criminal Records
Search free at http://208.210.219.132/vadistrict/select.jsp. Also search via LOPAS; call 804-786-5511 to apply.

Smyth County

28th Circuit Court – Civil and Criminal Records
www.courts.state.va.us/courts/circuit.html
Search free at www.courts.state.va.us/caseinfo/circuit.html. Also search via LOPAS; call 804-786-5511 to apply.

28th General District Court – Civil and Criminal Records
Search free at http://208.210.219.132/vadistrict/select.jsp. Also search via LOPAS; call 804-786-5511 to apply.

Southampton County

5th Circuit Court – Civil and Criminal Records
www.courts.state.va.us/courts/circuit.html
Search free at www.courts.state.va.us/caseinfo/circuit.html. Also search via LOPAS; call 804-786-5511 to apply.

5th General District Court – Civil and Criminal Records
Search free at http://208.210.219.132/vadistrict/select.jsp. Also search via LOPAS; call 804-786-5511 to apply.

Spotsylvania County

15th Circuit Court – Civil and Criminal Records
www.courts.state.va.us/courts/circuit.html
Search free at www.courts.state.va.us/caseinfo/circuit.html. Also search via LOPAS; call 804-786-5511 to apply. Select and search
Circuit Courts online at http://208.210.219.132/vacircuit/select.jsp. For information about the statewide online systems, see state intro.

15th General District Court – Civil and Criminal Records
Search free at http://208.210.219.132/vadistrict/select.jsp. Also search via LOPAS; call 804-786-5511 to apply. For information about
the statewide online systems, see the state introduction.

Stafford County

15th Circuit Court – Civil and Criminal Records
www.co.stafford.va.us/Departments/Courts_&_Legal_Services/Index.shtml
Search free at www.courts.state.va.us/caseinfo/circuit.html. Also search via LOPAS; call 804-786-5511 to apply.

15th General District Court – Civil and Criminal Records
Search free at http://208.210.219.132/vadistrict/select.jsp. Also search via LOPAS; call 804-786-5511 to apply.

Surry County

6th Circuit Court – Civil and Criminal Records
www.courts.state.va.us/courts/circuit.html
Remote access to court case indexes is via LOPAS; call 804-786-5511 to apply.

6th General District Court – Civil and Criminal Records
Search free at http://208.210.219.132/vadistrict/select.jsp. Also search via LOPAS; call 804-786-5511 to apply.

Sussex County

6th Circuit Court – Civil and Criminal Records
www.courts.state.va.us/courts/circuit.html
Remote access to court case indexes is via LOPAS; call 804-786-5511 to apply.

6th Judicial District Court – Civil and Criminal Records
Search free at http://208.210.219.132/vadistrict/select.jsp. Also search via LOPAS; call 804-786-5511 to apply.

Tazewell County

29th Circuit Court – Civil and Criminal Records
www.courts.state.va.us/courts/circuit.html
Access free at www.courts.state.va.us/caseinfo/circuit.html.

29th General District Court – Civil and Criminal Records
Search free at http://208.210.219.132/vadistrict/select.jsp. Also search via LOPAS; call 804-786-5511 to apply.

Warren County

Circuit Court – Civil and Criminal Records
www.courts.state.va.us/courts/circuit/warren/home.html
Access free at www.courts.state.va.us/caseinfo/circuit.html.

26th General District Court – Civil and Criminal Records
Search free at http://208.210.219.132/vadistrict/select.jsp. Also search via LOPAS; call 804-786-5511 to apply.

Washington County

28th General District Court – Civil and Criminal Records
Search free at http://208.210.219.132/vadistrict/select.jsp. Also search via LOPAS; call 804-786-5511 to apply.

Westmoreland County

15th Circuit Court – Civil Records
www.courts.state.va.us/courts/circuit.html
Remote access to court case indexes is via LOPAS; call 804-786-5511 to apply.

15th General District Court – Civil and Criminal Records
Search free at http://208.210.219.132/vadistrict/select.jsp. Also search via LOPAS; call 804-786-5511 to apply.

Wise County

30th Circuit Court – Civil and Criminal Records
www.wisecircuitcourt.com
Access free at www.courts.state.va.us/caseinfo/circuit.html. Also, court indexes and images are at www.courtbar.org, registration and a fee is required. Records go back to June, 2000.

30th General District Court – Civil and Criminal Records
Search free at http://208.210.219.132/vadistrict/select.jsp. Also search via LOPAS; call 804-786-5511 to apply.

Wythe County

27th Circuit Court – Civil and Criminal Records
www.courts.state.va.us/courts/circuit.html
Remote access to court case indexes is via LOPAS; call 804-786-5511 to apply.

Wythe General District Court – Civil and Criminal Records
Search free at http://208.210.219.132/vadistrict/select.jsp. Also search via LOPAS; call 804-786-5511 to apply.

York County

9th Circuit Court – Civil and Criminal Records
www.yorkcounty.gov/circuitcourt/
Access free at www.courts.state.va.us/caseinfo/circuit.html.

9th Judicial District Court – Civil and Criminal Records
www.yorkcounty.gov/districtcourt/
Search free at http://208.210.219.132/vadistrict/select.jsp. Also search via LOPAS; call 804-786-5511 to apply.

Virginia Independent Cities -- Courts

Alexandria City

18th District Court – Civil and Criminal Records
Search free at http://208.210.219.132/vadistrict/select.jsp.

Bristol City

28th Circuit Court – Civil and Criminal Records
www.courts.state.va.us/courts/circuit.html
Search free at www.courts.state.va.us/caseinfo/circuit.html. Also search via LOPAS; call 804-786-5511 to apply.

28th General District Court – Civil and Criminal Records
Search free at http://208.210.219.132/vadistrict/select.jsp. Also search via LOPAS; call 804-786-5511 to apply.

Buena Vista City

25th Circuit & District Court – Civil and Criminal Records
www.courts.state.va.us/courts/circuit.html
Select and search Circuit Courts online at www.courts.state.va.us/caseinfo/circuit.html. Search District courts at http://208.210.219.132/vadistrict/select.jsp. Also search via LOPAS; call 804-786-5511 to apply.

Charles City

9th Circuit Court – Civil and Criminal Records
www.courts.state.va.us/courts/circuit.html
Search free at www.courts.state.va.us/caseinfo/circuit.html. Also search via LOPAS; call 804-786-5511 to apply.

9th General District Court – Civil and Criminal Records
Search free at http://208.210.219.132/vadistrict/select.jsp. Also search via LOPAS; call 804-786-5511 to apply.

Charlottesville City

Charlottesville Circuit Court – Civil and Criminal Records
Search search via LOPAS; call 804-786-5511 to apply.

Charlottesville General District Court – Civil and Criminal Records
Search free at http://208.210.219.132/vadistrict/select.jsp. Also search via LOPAS; call 804-786-5511 to apply.

Chesapeake City

1st Circuit Court – Civil and Criminal Records
www.courts.state.va.us/courts/circuit.html
Access free at www.courts.state.va.us/caseinfo/circuit.html.

Clifton Forge City

25th General District Court – Civil and Criminal Records
Search free at http://208.210.219.132/vadistrict/select.jsp. Also search via LOPAS; call 804-786-5511 to apply.

Colonial Heights City

12th General District Court – Civil and Criminal Records
Search free at http://208.210.219.132/vadistrict/select.jsp. Also search via LOPAS; call 804-786-5511 to apply.

Danville City

22nd Circuit Court – Civil and Criminal Records
www.danville-va.gov/home.asp
Access free at www.courts.state.va.us/caseinfo/circuit.html. Also, search daily docket from the web page.

22nd General District Court – Civil and Criminal Records
Select and search District Courts at http://208.210.219.132/vadistrict/select.jsp. For info about the statewide systems, see the state introduction.

Emporia City

6th General District Court – Civil and Criminal Records
Search free at http://208.210.219.132/vadistrict/select.jsp. Also search via LOPAS; call 804-786-5511 to apply.

Fairfax City

19th General District Court – Civil and Criminal Records
www.courts.state.va.us/courts/gd/Fairfax_City/home.html
Search free at http://208.210.219.132/vadistrict/select.jsp.

Falls Church City

17th District Courts Combined – Civil and Criminal Records
www.ci.falls-church.va.us
Search free at http://208.210.219.132/vadistrict/select.jsp. Also search via LOPAS; call 804-786-5511 to apply.

Franklin City

5th Judicial General District Combined – Civil and Criminal Records
www.courts.state.va.us/courts/combined/Franklin_City/home.html

Select and search Circuit Courts online at http://208.210.219.132/vadistrict/select.jsp. For info on the statewide online systems, see the state introduction.

Fredericksburg City

15th Circuit Court – Civil and Criminal Records
www.courts.state.va.us/courts/circuit.html
Access free at www.courts.state.va.us/.

15th General District Court – Civil and Criminal Records
Search free at http://208.210.219.132/vadistrict/select.jsp. Also search via LOPAS; call 804-786-5511 to apply.

Galax City

27th General District Court – Civil and Criminal Records
Search free at http://208.210.219.132/vadistrict/select.jsp. Also search via LOPAS; call 804-786-5511 to apply.

Hampton City

8th Circuit Court – Civil and Criminal Records
www.courts.state.va.us/courts/circuit.html
Access free at www.courts.state.va.us/caseinfo/circuit.html.

8th General District Court – Civil and Criminal Records
Search free at http://208.210.219.132/vadistrict/select.jsp. Also search via LOPAS; call 804-786-5511 to apply.

Hopewell City

6th Circuit Court – Civil and Criminal Records
www.courts.state.va.us/courts/circuit.html
Search free at www.courts.state.va.us/caseinfo/circuit.html. Also search via LOPAS; call 804-786-5511 to apply.

Hopewell District Court – Civil and Criminal Records
Search free at http://208.210.219.132/vadistrict/select.jsp. Also search via LOPAS; call 804-786-5511 to apply.

James City

Williamsburg-James City Circuit Court – Civil and Criminal Records
www.courts.state.va.us/courts/circuit.html
Access free at www.courts.state.va.us/caseinfo/circuit.html.

9th General District Court – Civil and Criminal Records
Search free at http://208.210.219.132/vadistrict/select.jsp. Also search via LOPAS; call 804-786-5511 to apply.

Lynchburg City

24th Circuit Court – Civil and Criminal Records
www.courts.state.va.us/courts/circuit.html
Search free at www.courts.state.va.us/caseinfo/circuit.html. Also search via LOPAS; call 804-786-5511 to apply.

24th General District Court - Civil Division – Civil Records
Search free at http://208.210.219.132/vadistrict/select.jsp. Also search via LOPAS; call 804-786-5511 to apply.

24th General District Court - Criminal Division – Criminal Records
Select and search General District Courts at http://208.210.219.132/vadistrict/select.jsp. For information about the statewide systems, see the state introduction.

Martinsville City

21st Circuit Court – Civil and Criminal Records
www.ci.martinsville.va.us/circuitclerk
Access free at www.courts.state.va.us/caseinfo/circuit.html. Also, with password, access judgments at
www.ci.martinsville.va.us/crms/.

21st General District Court – Civil and Criminal Records
www.courts.state.va.us/courts/gd/Martinsville/home.html
Search free at http://208.210.219.132/vadistrict/select.jsp. Also search via LOPAS; call 804-786-5511 to apply.

Newport News City

7th Circuit Court – Civil and Criminal Records
www.newport-news.va.us/court/index.htm
Access free at www.courts.state.va.us/caseinfo/circuit.html.

7th General District Court – Civil and Criminal Records
Search free at http://208.210.219.132/vadistrict/select.jsp. Also search via LOPAS; call 804-786-5511 to apply.

Norfolk City

4th Circuit Court – Civil and Criminal Records
www.courts.state.va.us/courts/circuit.html
Access to civil is free at www.courts.state.va.us/caseinfo/circuit.html. Also access record images via http://208.210.219.102/cgi-bin/p/rms.cgi; registration and password required. Also, the Clerk of Circuit court subscription online system contains judgment records, wills, marriages, recorded documents etc at www.norfolk.gov/Circuit_Court/remoteaccess.asp. Fee is $50 per month. Judgments, Wills, Marriages, etc back to 1993. Access to criminal dockets is free at http://208.210.219.132/vacircuit/select.jsp. Also access record images via http://208.210.219.102/cgi-bin/p/rms.cgi; registration and password required.

4th General District Court – Civil and Criminal Records
Search free at http://208.210.219.132/vadistrict/select.jsp. Also search via LOPAS; call 804-786-5511 to apply.

Petersburg City

11th Circuit Court – Civil and Criminal Records
www.courts.state.va.us/courts/circuit.html
Access free at www.courts.state.va.us/caseinfo/circuit.html.

11th Judicial District Court – Civil and Criminal Records
www.courts.state.va.us/courts/gd/Petersburg/home.html
Search free at http://208.210.219.132/vadistrict/select.jsp. Also search via LOPAS; call 804-786-5511 to apply.

Portsmouth City County

Circuit Court – Civil and Criminal Records
www.courts.state.va.us/courts/circuit.html
Access free at www.courts.state.va.us/caseinfo/circuit.html.
General District Court – Civil and Criminal Records
Search free at http://208.210.219.132/vadistrict/select.jsp. Also search via LOPAS; call 804-786-5511 to apply.

Radford City

27th Circuit Court – Civil and Criminal Records
www.courts.state.va.us/courts/circuit.html
Search free at www.courts.state.va.us/caseinfo/circuit.html. Also search via LOPAS; call 804-786-5511 to apply.

27th General District Court – Civil and Criminal Records
Search free at http://208.210.219.132/vadistrict/select.jsp. Also search via LOPAS; call 804-786-5511 to apply.

Richmond City

13th Circuit Court – Civil and Criminal Records
www.courts.state.va.us/courts/circuit/Richmond/home.html
Access free at www.courts.state.va.us/caseinfo/circuit.html.
13th General District Court - Civil Division – Civil Records
Search free at http://208.210.219.132/vadistrict/select.jsp. Also search via LOPAS; call 804-786-5511 to apply.

13th General District Court - Division II – Criminal Records
For information about the statewide online systems, see the state introduction. Select and search General District Courts at http://208.210.219.132/vadistrict/select.jsp.

Roanoke City

23rd Circuit Court – Civil and Criminal Records
www.roanokecountyva.gov/Departments/CircuitCourtClerksOffice
Access free at www.courts.state.va.us/caseinfo/circuit.html.
General District Court – Civil and Criminal Records
Select and search District Courts at www.courts.state.va.us/.

Salem City

23rd Circuit Court – Civil and Criminal Records
www.courts.state.va.us/courts/circuit.html
Search free at www.courts.state.va.us/caseinfo/circuit.html. Also search via LOPAS; call 804-786-5511 to apply.

23rd General District Court – Civil and Criminal Records
Search free at http://208.210.219.132/vadistrict/select.jsp. Also search via LOPAS; call 804-786-5511 to apply.

Staunton City

25th Circuit Court – Civil and Criminal Records
www.courts.state.va.us/courts/circuit.html
Search free at www.courts.state.va.us/caseinfo/circuit.html. Also search via LOPAS; call 804-786-5511 to apply.

Staunton General District Court – Civil and Criminal Records
Select and search District Courts at http://208.210.219.132/vadistrict/select.jsp.

Suffolk City

Suffolk Circuit Court – Civil and Criminal Records
www.courts.state.va.us/courts/circuit.html
Search free at www.courts.state.va.us/caseinfo/circuit.html. Also search via LOPAS; call 804-786-5511 to apply.

5th General District Court – Civil and Criminal Records
Search free at http://208.210.219.132/vadistrict/select.jsp. Also search via LOPAS; call 804-786-5511 to apply.

Virginia Beach City

2nd Circuit Court – Civil and Criminal Records
www.vbgov.com/courts
Access free at www.courts.state.va.us/caseinfo/circuit.html.

2nd General District Court – Civil and Criminal Records
www.vbgov.com/courts
Search free at http://208.210.219.132/vadistrict/select.jsp. Also search via LOPAS; call 804-786-5511 to apply.

Waynesboro City

25th Circuit Court – Civil and Criminal Records
www.courts.state.va.us/courts/circuit.html
Access free at www.courts.state.va.us/caseinfo/circuit.html.

25th General District Court - Waynesboro – Civil and Criminal Records
www.courts.state.va.us/courts/gd/Waynesboro/home.html
Search court records free at http://208.210.219.132/vadistrict/select.jsp.

Winchester City

26th Circuit Court – Civil and Criminal Records
www.winfredclerk.com
Access free at www.courts.state.va.us/caseinfo/circuit.html.

26th General District Court – Civil and Criminal Records
Search free at http://208.210.219.132/vadistrict/select.jsp. Also search via LOPAS; call 804-786-5511 to apply.

County Level ... Recorders & Assessors

Recording Office Organization: 95 counties and 41 independent cities, 123 recording offices. The recording officer is the Clerk of Circuit Court. Fifteen independent cities share the Clerk of Circuit Court with the county - Bedford, Covington (Alleghany County), Emporia (Greenville County), Fairfax, Falls Church (Arlington or Fairfax County), Franklin (Southhampton County), Galax (Carroll County), Harrisonburg (Rockingham County), Lexington (Rockbridge County), Manassas and Manassas Park (Prince William County), Norton (Wise County), Poquoson (York County), South Boston (Halifax County), and Williamsburg (James City County). Charles City and James City are counties, not cities. The City of Franklin is not in Franklin County, the City of Richmond is not in Richmond County, and the City of Roanoke is not in Roanoke County. The entire state is in the Eastern Time Zone (EST). Federal tax liens on personal property of businesses are filed with the State Corporation Commission. Other federal and all state tax liens are filed with the county Clerk of Circuit Court. They are usually filed in a "Judgment Lien Book."

Online Access Note: A growing number of Virginia counties and cities provide free access to real estate related information via the Internet. A limited but growing private company network named VamaNet provides free residential, commercial, and vacant property and tax records; visit www.vamanet.com/info/home.jsp.

Virginia Counties (Virginia Independent Cities are listed following this County Section)

Arlington County   *Real Estate, Assessor, Trade Name Records*
www.co.arlington.va.us
Property records on the County assessor database are free at
www.arlingtonva.us/Departments/RealEstate/RealEstateAssessmentsMain.aspx.

Augusta County   *Property, Appraisal Records*
Click on Augusta County to search property data for free at www.vamanet.com/cgi-bin/LOCS.

Bath County   *Property, Land Records*
Access property and land records for free at www.vamanet.com/cgi-bin/MAPSRCHPGM?LOCAL=BAT

Bedford County   *Property Tax Records*
Real estate records on the Bedford County GIS site are free at www.co.bedford.va.us/Res/GIS/index.htm; however, no name searching at this time. Records on the City of Bedford are free at www.bedfordva.gov/taxf.shtml. Search by name, address or tax map reference number. Also, access City of Bedford property info on the GIS site free at http://bedfordgis.bedfordva.gov/bedfordcity/search.asp?skipopen=1.

Campbell County   *Property Records*
www.co.campbell.va.us
Access county property data from Dept of Real Estate an Mapping free at
http://campbellvapropertymax.governmaxa.com/propertymax/rover30.asp?.

Caroline County   *Appraiser, Property Records*
Click on Caroline County to search property records for free at www.vamanet.com/cgi-bin/LOCS.

Carroll County   *Real Estate, Judgment, UCC, Plat Records*
www.chillsnet.org
Access to Carroll county property information is a $25 monthly fee. Username and password required; signup through Clerk of Circuit Court, 276-730-3090. Land index and images go back to 1985; plats to 2002. Access to Town of Hillsville property information is on the gis mapping site at http://arcims2.webgis.net/Hillsville/default.asp. Click on Quick Search to search by name.

Chesterfield County   *Assessor, Property Tax, Property Sale Records*
www.chesterfield.gov
Search the real estate assessment data for free at
www.co.chesterfield.va.us/ManagementServices/RealEstateAssessments/Rea_Search_Home.asp.

Clarke County *Property, Appraiser Records*
Click on Clarke County to search property data for free at www.vamanet.com/cgi-bin/LOCS.

Dickenson County *Real Estate, Property Tax Records*
www.dickensonctyva.com
Access to the Commissioner of Revenue real estate data is free at http://dcva.tinex.net/html/commissioner.html.

Essex County *Real Estate, Personal Property, Assessor, Property Card, Paid Taxes, Treasurer Records*
www.essex-virginia.org
Search the Real Estate and Personal Property Public Inquiries site free at http://county.essex-va.org/applications/trapps/REIindex.htm.
Access county property cards free at http://county.essex-va.org/applications/txapps/PropCardsIndex.htm. Also, access the paid taxes
index free at http://county.essex-va.org/applications/trapps/YREindex.htm.

Fairfax County *Real Estate, Property Tax, Tax Sale Records*
www.fairfaxcounty.gov/courts/circuit/land_records_info.htm
Records on the Dept. of Tax Administration Real Estate Assessment database are free at
http://icare.fairfaxcounty.gov/Search/GenericSearch.aspx?mode=ADDRESS. Also, the Automated Information System operates
Monday-Saturday 7AM-7PM at 703-222-6740. Hear about property descriptions, assessed values and sales prices. Fax-back service is
available. Also, the list of auction properties is free at www.fairfaxcounty.gov/dta/auction.htm. Search the City Assessment at for free
at www.fairfaxrealestate.org/fairfax208/LandRover.asp. No name searching.

Fluvanna County *Appraiser, Property Records*
Click on Fluvanna County to search property data for free at www.vamanet.com/cgi-bin/LOCS.

Franklin County *Property Records*
Access property data free at http://arcims2.webgis.net/va/franklin/.

Giles County *Appraiser, Property Records*
Click on Fluvanna County to search for property records for free at www.vamanet.com/cgi-bin/LOCS. Also, search property info on
the county GIS site for free at http://arcims2.webgis.net/giles/default.asp. To name search click on Quick Search.

Gloucester County *Judgment Records*
Access to Law and Chancery cases is free at www.courts.state.va.us/caseinfo/circuit.html.

Goochland County *Property, Assessor Records*
Access property records at www.vamanet.com. Choose Goochland as locality to search.

Grayson County *Property Records*
Access property data free at http://arcims2.webgis.net/va/grayson/.

Greensville County *Appraiser, Property Records*
Click on Greensville County to search property data for free at www.vamanet.com/cgi-bin/LOCS.

Halifax County *Property Records*
Access property data free at http://arcims2.webgis.net/halifax/.

Henry County *Property Records*
Access property data free at http://arcims2.webgis.net/henryco/. City of Martinsville property data also available online here.

James City County *Real Estate Records*
www.jccegov.com/resources/clerkofcircrt/index.html
Records on the James City County Property Information database are free at www.regis.state.va.us/jcc/public/disclaimer.htm. Also,
search the City of Williamsburg property assessor data for free at www.ci.williamsburg.va.us/dept/realestate/disclaimer.htm.

Lancaster County *Chancery, Law Records*
www.lancova.com
Access to court records is free at www.courts.state.va.us.

Loudoun County *Deed, Will, Estate, Judgment, Plat, UCC, Property, Assessor Records*
www.loudoun.gov/clerk
Access to recorders land records of deeds, wills, judgment, plats and UCCs is available by subscription, see Land Records in Quick Links at www.loudoun.gov/clerk/. Fee is $1500 per year; deeds go back to 1893, wills 1928, judgments 1985, UCCs 1996. Also, search the property assessor data for free at http://inter1.loudoun.gov/webpdbs/. No name searching; search by address, #, or ID only.

Montgomery County *Real Estate, Property Tax Records*
Access to the county Tax Parcel Information System database is free online at www.montva.com/departments/plan/igis.php. Records on Town of Blacksburg GIS site are free at http://arcims2.webgis.net/blacksburg/default.asp?. To name search, click on Quick Search.

New Kent County *Assessor, Property Records*
Access to New Kent county assessor records is free at http://data.visionappraisal.com/NewKentCountyVA/. Register free for full data.

Northumberland County *Property, Assessor Records*
www.co.northumberland.va.us
Access Land Book data free at www.co.northumberland.va.us/NH-land-book.htm.

Nottoway County *Property Records*
Access property data free at http://arcims2.webgis.net/va/nottoway/.

Patrick County *Property, Map Records*
Access property data free at http://arcims2.webgis.net/patrick/default.asp. Map searching only, no name searching.

Pittsylvania County *Real Estate, Assessor Records*
Access to county real estate data is free at www.pittgov.org/real%20search.htm. Most recent assessment data is for the previous year. See Danville City for Real Estate and Lien records online for Danville City.

Powhatan County *Appraiser, Property Records*
Click on Powhatan County to search property data for free at www.vamanet.com/cgi-bin/LOCS.

Prince William County *Land, Property Assessor Records*
www.pwcgov.org/default.aspx?topic=040017
Records on the county Property Information database are free at http://www4.pwcgov.org/realestate/LandRover.asp. Also, City of Manassas Commissioner of the Revenue's real estate assessment data is at http://data.visionappraisal.com/ManassasVA/. Free registration is required to access full data.

Pulaski County *Property, GIS Records*
Access to the county GIS mapping info is free at http://arcims2.webgis.net/pulaski/default.asp. No name searching.

Rockbridge County *Property, Appraiser Records*
Access county records on the GIS-property mapping site free at http://quicksearch.webgis.net/search.php?site=va_rockbridge. Also, access City of Lexington property data free at www.vamanet.com/cgi-bin/MAPSRCHPGM?LOCAL=LEX.

Rockingham County *Real Estate Records*
Access to real estate assessment records at http://rockingham.gisbrowser.com/home.cfm.

Southampton County *Appraiser, Property, GIS Tax Map Records*
Only the City of Franklin appraisal data is available free at www.vamanet.com/cgi-bin/MAPSRCHPGM?LOCAL=FRA. As far as can be determined, this does not include county appraisal records. GIS tax map data is free at www.onlinegis.net/VaSouthampton/asp/controlVersion.asp. No name searching.

Stafford County *Real Estate, Recorder Records*
Subscription access is scheduled to be available in July, 2006.

Sussex County *Land Tax, Marriage,Will Records*
http://sussexcounty.govoffice.com
A private search company website at http://genealogyresources.org/index.html offers access to ancient records including marriage, census, wills, deeds, land tax, guardian bonds and tithing lists, plus Civil and Revolutionary War records.

Warren County *Recording, Deed, Land, Lien, Court, Will, Marriage, UCC Records*
Access the Clerk's data on the web; username and password required. For username and password contact Jennifer Sims at 540-635-2435 or at jsims@courts.state.va.us. Images go back to 1994.

Washington County *Property, Land Records*
Access property and land records free at www.vamanet.com/cgi-bin/mapsrchpgm?local=was.

Westmoreland County *Real Estate Tax, Treasurer, Property Card, Utility Payment Records*
www.westmoreland-county.org
Access real estate tax payment database free at http://166.61.239.88/applications/trapps/REIindex.htm. Also, search property car records free at http://166.61.239.88/applications/txapps/PropCardsIndex.htm. Also, search utility payment records free at http://166.61.239.88/applications/trapps/UTIindex.htm.

Wise County *Assessor, Real Estate, Lien, Probate, Marriage, Property Tax, Appraisal Records*
www.courtbar.org
Includes City of Norton. For full access fee is $440 annually; see www.courtbar.org website. Free access is at http://arcims2.webgis.net/wise/default.asp; click on Quick Search. The fee service includes index and images, court orders, land documents from 1970 and links to RE tax assessments, 50-year RE, tax maps, plat maps, delinquent taxes, permit images, probate, marriage, judgment liens for 20 years, and more. UCC-1 indices for past 5 years. Also, property data is at http://egov.mixnet.com/wise/search.asp. Egov also offers a $440 per year subscription service.

York County *Property Records*
www.yorkcounty.gov/circuitcourt
Property records from the County GIS site are free at www.regis.state.va.us/york/pub/disclaimer.htm.

Virginia Independent Cities -- Recorder Offices

Alexandria City *Assessor, Property Records*
www.ci.alexandria.va.us
Access to city real estate assessments is free at www.ci.alexandria.va.us/city/reasearch/. No name searching.

Bristol City *Property, Land Records*
Access property and land records for free at www.vamanet.com/cgi-bin/MAPSRCHPGM?LOCAL=BRS

Buena Vista City *Appraiser, Property Records*
Access city appraisal data free at www.vamanet.com/cgi-bin/MAPSRCHPGM?LOCAL=BUE.

Chesapeake City *Property Appraiser, Inspection, Most Wanted Records*
http://cityofchesapeake.net
Access to property appraiser data is free at http://cityofchesapeake.net/rea/welcome.html. No name searching at this time Also, search city inspections for free at http://cityofchesapeake.net/Cdbidt2/IDT100A.do. Also, search the police most wanted list at http://cityofchesapeake.net/services/depart/police/police/wanted.shtml

Danville City *Property, Tax Assessor Records*
www.danville-va.gov/home.asp
Access to Danville City assessor online records is free at www.danvillevaassessor.org. Also, see note at beginning of section for statewide land record access.

Fredericksburg City *Appraiser, Property Records*
www.fredericksburgva.gov
Click on Fredericksburg City to search for property records for free at www.vamanet.com/cgi-bin/LOCS.

Hampton City
Land, Treasurer, Property Tax, Assessor, Judgment, Property Transfer, Daily Traffic Accident Records
www.hampton.gov
Access the City Real Estate Information site free at http://198.252.241.11/realinfo/. Also, search for limited judgment records on the state court website at www.courts.state.va.us. Also, search daily list of traffic accidents at www.hampton.gov/traffic/. Search property transfer pdf lists free at www.hampton.gov/assessor/ see bottom of page and click on Real Estate Property Transfers now online.

Hopewell City *Judgment, Court Appeals Granted, Chancery Records*
www.ci.hopewell.va.us
Access to court records is free at www.courts.state.va.us/caseinfo/circuit.html.

Martinsville City *Property, Deed, Judgment, Will, Marriage, Delinquent Tax Records*
www.ci.martinsville.va.us/Circuitclerk
Access to Circuit clerk records is at www.ci.martinsville.va.us/Circuitclerk. Fee is $30.00 per month, or you may search at a rate of $1 per doc. For info, call office of Ashby Pritchett at 276-656-5106 or visit website.

Newport News City *Assessor, Real Estate Records*
www.newport-news.va.us
Access to the City's "Real Estate on the Web" database is free at http://216.54.20.244/reisweb1. Search by address or parcel number; new "advanced search" may include name searching.

Norfolk City *Real Estate, Assessor, Sex Offender Registry, Marriage, Recording, Deed, Judgment, Will Records*
www.norfolk.gov/Circuit_Court/ccchome.asp
Access Clerk of Circuit Court recording data by $50 per month subscription at www.norfolk.gov/Circuit_Court/remoteaccess.asp. Deeds and land records go back to 1988. Judgments, Wills, Marriages, etc, back to 1993. Records on the City of Norfolk Real Estate Property Assessment database are free at www.norfolk.gov/NRealEstate/search.asp. Sex offender registry search for free found at http://sex-offender.vsp.state.va.us/Static/Search.htm.

Radford City *Property Records*
Access to City property info on the GIS mapping site is free at http://arcims2.webgis.net/radfordcity/default.asp. To name search click on Quick Search.

Richmond City *Property, Assessor Records*
Search the city's Property & Real Estate Assessment Information for free at www.ci.richmond.va.us/departments/gis/webmapper.aspx. If you click on Property Search, you cannot name search, but name searching available through the Webmapper. At the Webmapper page, click on "Advanced Search" then "Assessments" to name search.

Roanoke City *Property, GIS, Tax Appraisal Records*
www.ci.roanoke.va.us
Access to property data is free on the City GIS website at http://gis.roanokegov.com/text.htm.

Staunton City *Property, GIS, Tax Appraisal Records*
www.staunton.va.us
Online access to the property mapping system is free at http://gis.ci.staunton.va.us:8082/gis/mgdefault.asp. Name searching allowed.

Virginia Beach City
Real Estate, Property Tax, Assessor, Marriage, Judgment, UCC, Will, Business Name Records
www.vbgov.com/courts/circourt/cclerk/0,1506,8092,00.html
Online access Virginia Beach land records and recordings is free at http://vblandrecords.com/vabeach/index.aspx. But, there is a new fee for images, which is payable by credit card only. Also, notarized registration for images is required. For credit card account, call 866-793-6505. Direct general questions to Tracey Entwisle at 757-385-8819. Also, you may search the assessor database for free at www.vbgov.com/dept/realestate/. No name searching.

Waynesboro City *Property, Appraiser Records*
Access to city property appraiser data is free at www.vamanet.com/cgi-bin/LOCS.

Federal Courts in Virginia...

Standards for Federal Courts: The universal PACER sign-up number is 800-676-6856. Find PACER and the Party/Case Index on the Web at http://pacer.psc.uscourts.gov. PACER dial-up access is $.60 per minute. Also, courts offering internet access via PACER, Web-PACER or the new CM-ECF charge $.08 per page fee ($.07 per page if record is pre-2005 or unless noted as free).

US District Court -- Eastern District of Virginia www.vaed.uscourts.gov

PACER: Case records are available back to 6/1990. New records are available online after 1 day. **PACER Online Access:** ECF replaces PACER. **Electronic Filing:** CM/ECF data at https://ecf.vaed.uscourts.gov.

Newport News Division counties: Gloucester, James City, Mathews, York, City of Hampton, City of Newport News, City of Poquoson, City of Williamsburg. This division houses misdemeanor records only. Please direct civil and felony record requests to Norfolk Division.

Norfolk Division counties: Accomack, City of Chesapeake, City of Franklin, Isle of Wight, City of Norfolk, Northampton, City of Portsmouth, City of Suffolk, Southampton, City of Virginia Beach.

Richmond Division counties: Amelia, Brunswick, Caroline, Charles City, Chesterfield, Dinwiddie, Essex, Goochland, Greensville, Hanover, Henrico, King and Queen, King George, King William, Lancaster, Lunenburg, Mecklenburg, Middlesex, New Kent, Northumberland, Nottoway, City of Petersburg, Powhatan, Prince Edward, Prince George, Richmond, City of Richmond, Spotsylvania, Surry, Sussex, Westmoreland, City of Colonial Heights, City of Emporia, City of Fredericksburg, City of Hopewell.

US Bankruptcy Court -- Eastern District of Virginia www.vaeb.uscourts.gov

PACER: Case records are available back to mid 1989. Records are purged never. **PACER Online Access:** ECF replaces PACER. **Electronic Filing:** CM/ECF data at https://ecf.vaeb.uscourts.gov. **Opinions:** View court opinions at www.vaeb.uscourts.gov/dtsearch.html. **Other Online Access:** Court calendars at www.vaeb.uscourts.gov/cal/calroot/judges.htm. Court now participates in the U.S. party case index. **Phone access:** Voice Case Info System, call 800-326-5879, 804-771-2736

Alexandria Division counties: City of Alexandria, Arlington, Fairfax, City of Fairfax, City of Falls Church, Fauquier, Loudoun, City of Manassas, City of Manassas Park, Prince William, Stafford.

Newport News Division counties: Newport News City. Records are at the Norfolk Bankruptcy Court.

Norfolk Division counties: Accomack, City of Cape Charles, City of Chesapeake, City of Franklin, Gloucester, City of Hampton, Isle of Wight, James City, Matthews, City of Norfolk, Northampton, City of Poquoson, City of Portsmouth, Southampton, City of Suffolk, City of Virginia Beach, City of Williamsburg, York.

Richmond Division counties: Amelia, Brunswick, Caroline, Charles City, Chesterfield, City of Colonial Heights, Dinwiddie, City of Emporia, Essex, City of Fredericksburg, Goochland, Greensville, Hanover, Henrico, City of Hopewell, King and Queen, King George, King William, Lancaster, Lunenburg, Mecklenburg, Middlesex, New Kent, Northumberland, Nottoway, City of Petersburg, Powhatan, Prince Edward, Prince George, Richmond, City of Richmond, Spotsylvania, Surry, Sussex, Westmoreland.

US District Court -- Western District of Virginia www.vawd.uscourts.gov

PACER: Case records are available back to mid 1990. Records are purged never. **PACER Online Access:** ECF replaces PACER. **Electronic Filing:** CM/ECF data at https://ecf.vawd.uscourts.gov. **Opinions:** View court opinions at www.vawd.uscourts.gov/opinion.asp. **Other Online Access:** Judges' calendars free at www.vawd.uscourts.gov/judgescal/default.asp.

Abingdon Division counties: Buchanan, City of Bristol, Russell, Smyth, Tazewell, Washington.

Big Stone Gap Division counties: Dickenson, Lee, Scott, Wise, City of Norton.

Charlottesville Division counties: Albemarle, Culpeper, Fluvanna, Greene, Louisa, Madison, Nelson, Orange, Rappahannock, City of Charlottesville.

Danville Division counties: Charlotte, Halifax, Henry, Patrick, Pittsylvania, City of Danville, City of Martinsville, City of South Boston.

Harrisonburg Division counties: Augusta, Bath, Clarke, Frederick, Highland, Page, Rockingham, Shenandoah, Warren, City of Harrisonburg, City of Staunton, City of Waynesboro, City of Winchester.

Lynchburg Division counties: Amherst, Appomattox, Bedford, Buckingham, Campbell, Cumberland, Rockbridge, City of Bedford, City of Buena Vista, City of Lexington, City of Lynchburg.

Roanoke Division counties: Alleghany, Bland, Botetourt, Carroll, Craig, Floyd, Franklin, Giles, Grayson, Montgomery, Pulaski, Roanoke, Wythe, City of Covington, City of Clifton Forge, City of Galax, City of Radford, City of Roanoke, City of Salem.

US Bankruptcy Court -- Western District of Virginia www.vawb.uscourts.gov

PACER: Case records are available back to 3/1986. Records are purged never. **PACER Online Access:** ECF replaces PACER. **Electronic Filing:** CM/ECF data at https://ecf.vawb.uscourts.gov. **Opinions:** View court opinions at http://pacer.vawb.uscourts.gov/courtweb/enter1.html. **Other Online Access:** Calendars back to 1999 at http://pacer.vawb.uscourts.gov/Calendars/2005calendar.html. Court does not participate in the U.S. party case index.

Harrisonburg Division counties: Alleghany, Augusta, Bath, City of Buena Vista, Clarke, City of Clifton Forge, City of Covington, Frederick, City of Harrisonburg, Highland, City of Lexington, Page, Rappahannock, Rockbridge, Rockingham, Shenandoah, City of Staunton, Warren, City of Waynesboro, City of Winchester.

Lynchburg Division counties: Albemarle, Amherst, Appomattox, Bedford, City of Bedford, Buckingham, Campbell, Charlotte, City of Charlottesville, Culpeper, Cumberland, City of Danville, Fluvanna, Greene, Halifax, Henry, Louisa, Lynchburg City, Madison, Martinsville City, Nelson, Orange, Patrick, Pittsylvania, City of South Boston.

Roanoke Division counties: Bland, Botetourt, City of Bristol, Buchanan, Carroll, Craig, Dickenson, Floyd, Franklin, City of Galax, Giles, Grayson, Lee, Montgomery, City of Norton, Pulaski, City of Radford, Roanoke, City of Roanoke, Russell, City of Salem, Scott, Smyth, Tazewell, Washington, Wise, Wythe.

Washington

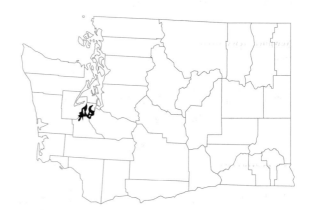

Capital: Olympia
                Thurston County
Time Zone: PST
Population: 6,203,788
# of Counties: 39

Quick Links

Website: http://access.wa.gov

Governor: www.governor.wa.gov

Attorney General: www.atg.wa.gov

State Archives: www.digitalarchives.wa.gov/default.aspx

State Statutes and Codes: www1.leg.wa.gov/LawsAndAgencyRules/

Legislative Bill Search: http://apps.leg.wa.gov/billinfo/

Bill Monitoring:
        https://leginfo.leg.wa.gov/user/login.aspx?ReturnUrl=%2fbilltracking%2fDefault.aspx

Unclaimed Funds: http://ucp.dor.wa.gov/

State Level ... Major Agencies

Criminal Records

Washington State Patrol, Identification and Criminal History Section, PO Box 42633, Olympia, WA 98504-2633 (Courier: 3000 Pacific Ave. SE #204, Olympia, WA 98501); 360-705-5100, Fax-360-570-5275, 8AM-5PM.
www.wsp.wa.gov
Online search: WSP offers access through a system called WATCH, which can be accessed from their website. The fee per search is $10.00. The exact DOB and exact spelling of the name are required. Credit cards are accepted online. To set up a WATCH account, call 360-705-5100 Ext 5 or email watch.help@wsp.wa.gov.

Statewide Court Records

Administrative Office of Courts, Temple of Justice, PO Box 41174, Olympia, WA 98504-1174 (Courier: 1206 Quince St SE, Olympia, WA 98504); 360-753-3365, Fax-360-586-8869, 8AM-5PM.
www.courts.wa.gov
Online search: The AOC provides facilities that allow one to access information in the Judicial Information System's (JIS) statewide computer. This program of services is called JIS-Link. JIS-Link provides access to all counties and court levels. Fees include a one-time $100.00 per site, a transaction fee of $.065 per record. Case records include criminal, civil, domestic, probate, and judgments. Call 360-357-3365 or visit www.courts.wa.gov/jislink. Supreme and Appellate opinions are at www.courts.wa.gov/appellate%5Ftrial%5Fcourts/. The page offers a notification service also. **Other options:** Indexes are available electronically and via microfiche for a fee. Call the JISLink Coordinator for details.

Sexual Offender Registry

Washington State Patrol, SOR, PO Box 42633, Olympia, WA 98504-2633 (Courier: 3000 Pacific Ave. SE #204, Olympia, WA 98501); 360-705-5100 x3, Fax-360-570-5275, 8AM-5PM.
www.wsp.wa.gov
Online search: In cooperation with the Washington Assoc. of Sheriffs and Police Chiefs, online access to Level II and Level III sexual offenders is available at http://ml.waspc.org/.

Incarceration Records

Washington Department of Corrections, Office of Correctional Operations, 410 W. 5th, MS-41118, Olympia, WA 98504-1118; 360-725-8852 (Public Disclosure), Fax-360-664-4056, 8AM-5PM M-F.
www.doc.wa.gov
Online search: No online searching provided; however, email requests can be directed to correspondence@doc1.wa.gov. **Other options:** Data is available by subscription for bulk users; for information, contact the Contracts Office at 360-725-8363.

Corporation, Trademarks/Servicemarks, Limited Partnerships, Limited Liability Company Records

Secretary of State, Corporations Division, PO Box 40234, Olympia, WA 98504-0234 (Courier: Dolliver Bldg, 801 Capitol Way South, Olympia, WA 98501); 360-753-7115, Fax-360-664-8781, 8AM-5PM.
www.secstate.wa.gov/corps/
Online search: Free searching of corporation registrations is at www.secstate.wa.gov/corps/search.aspx. Information is updated daily.

Uniform Commercial Code, Federal Tax Liens

Department of Licensing, UCC Records, PO Box 9660, Olympia, WA 98507-9660 (Courier: 405 Black Lake Blvd, Olympia, WA 98502); 360-664-1530, Fax-360-586-4414, 8AM-5PM.
www.dol.wa.gov/unfc/uccfront.htm
Online search: For online access, go to https://fortress.wa.gov/dol/ucc. There is a $15.00 search fee for a name search. Fee is $26.57 if copies included. Copies are mailed. **Other options:** The database may be purchased on microfilm or CD.

Sales Tax Registrations

Department of Revenue, Taxpayer Services, PO Box 47478, Olympia, WA 98504-7478; 360-705-6705, 800-647-7706, Fax-360-705-6655, 8AM-5PM.
http://dor.wa.gov/Default.aspx
Online search: The agency provides a state business records database with free access at http://dor.wa.gov/content/brd/default.aspx. Lookups are by owner names, DBAs, and tax reporting numbers. Results show a myriad of data.

Birth, Death, Marriage, Divorce Certificates

Department of Health, Center for Health Statistics, PO Box 9709, Olympia, WA 98507-9709 (Courier: 101 Israel Rd SE, Tumwater WA 98501); 360-236-4300 (Main Number), 360-236-4313 (Credit Card Ordering), Fax-360-352-2586, 9AM - 4PM.
www.doh.wa.gov
Online search: Records may requested from www.Vitalchek.com, a state-endorsed vendor. **Other options:** The Digital archives, launched in 2004, contains various periods for marriages, death, birth, military, naturalization, institution, and various historical records at www.digitalarchives.wa.gov/default.aspx.

Driver Records

Department of Licensing, Driver Record Section, PO Box 9048, Olympia, WA 98507-9030 (Courier: 1125 Washington Street SE, Olympia, WA 98504); 360-902-3913, 360-902-3900 (General Information), Fax-360-586-9044, 8AM-4:30PM.
www.dol.wa.gov
Online search: You may check the status of a driver license, permit or ID card online for free at https://fortress.wa.gov/dol/ddl/dsd/. **Other options:** FTP retrieval is offered for high volume requesters, minimum of 2,000 requests per week. Call 360-902-3839.

Vehicle & Vessel Ownership, Registration

Department of Licensing, Vehicle Records, PO Box 2957, Olympia, WA 98507-2957 (Courier: 1125 S Washington MS-48001, Olympia, WA 98504); 360-902-3780, Fax-360-902-3827, 8AM-5PM.
www.dol.wa.gov
Online search: This Internet Vehicle/Vessel Information Processing System is a commercial subscription service and all accounts must be pre-approved. A $25.00 deposit is required and there is a fee per hit. For more information, call 360-902-3760. **Other options:** Large bulk lists cannot be released for any commercial purposes. Lists are released to non-profit entities and for statistical purposes. For more information, call 360-902-3760.

State Level ... Occupational Licensing

Acupuncturist.. https://fortress.wa.gov/doh/hpqa1/Application/Credential_Search/profile.asp
Adult Family Home www.aasa.dshs.wa.gov/Lookup/AFHRequestv2.asp
Animal Technician................................ https://fortress.wa.gov/doh/hpqa1/Application/Credential_Search/profile.asp
Announcer, Athletic Event (Ring) .... https://fortress.wa.gov/dol/dolprod/profquery/
Applicator, Commercial........................ http://agr.wa.gov/PestFert/LicensingEd/ListPrivateApplicators.htm
Architect/Architect Corporation............ https://fortress.wa.gov/dol/dolprod/profquery/
Athlete, Professional/Inspector .... https://fortress.wa.gov/dol/dolprod/profquery/
Athletic Judge/Timekeeper/Physician... https://fortress.wa.gov/dol/dolprod/profquery/
Athletic Mgr/Promoter/Matchmaker..... https://fortress.wa.gov/dol/dolprod/profquery/
Attorney .... http://pro.wsba.org
Auction Company................................. www.dol.wa.gov/main/biglist.htm
Auctioneer... www.dol.wa.gov/main/biglist.htm
Audiologist .... https://fortress.wa.gov/doh/hpqa1/Application/Credential_Search/profile.asp
Bail Bond Agent/Agency .... https://fortress.wa.gov/dol/dolprod/profquery/
Bank.. www.dfi.wa.gov/banks/commercial_banks.htm
Barber/Barber Instructor/School .... https://fortress.wa.gov/dol/dolprod/profquery/
Barber Shop/Mobile/Booth .... https://fortress.wa.gov/dol/dolprod/profquery/
Beauty Shop/Salon/Mobile .... https://fortress.wa.gov/dol/dolprod/profquery/
Boarding Home..................................... www.aasa.dshs.wa.gov/Lookup/BHRequestv2.asp
Boiler Inspector.................................... www.lni.wa.gov/TradesLicensing/Boilers/Inspectors/default.asp
Boxer .... https://fortress.wa.gov/dol/dolprod/profquery/
Camping Resort .... www.dol.wa.gov/main/biglist.htm
Cemetery... https://fortress.wa.gov/dol/dolprod/profquery/
Charitable Gift Annuity .... www.insurance.wa.gov/cgi-bin/PubInfoApps/CharitableGA.exe
Check Casher/Seller.............................. https://fortress.wa.gov/dfi/licquery/dfi/licquery/default.aspx
Chiropractor.. https://fortress.wa.gov/doh/hpqa1/Application/Credential_Search/profile.asp
Collection Agency .... https://fortress.wa.gov/dol/dolprod/profquery/
Consumer Loan Company .... https://fortress.wa.gov/dfi/licquery/dfi/licquery/default.aspx
Contractor, Construction/General .... https://fortress.wa.gov/lni/bbip/
Cosmetologist .... https://fortress.wa.gov/dol/dolprod/profquery/
Cosmetology (Barber)........................... www.dol.wa.gov/main/biglist.htm
Cosmetology Instructor/School............. https://fortress.wa.gov/dol/dolprod/profquery/
Counselor.. https://fortress.wa.gov/doh/hpqa1/Application/Credential_Search/profile.asp
Court Reporter .... www.dol.wa.gov/main/biglist.htm
Crematory .... https://fortress.wa.gov/dol/dolprod/profquery/
Currency Exchange............................... https://fortress.wa.gov/dfi/licquery/dfi/licquery/default.aspx
Dealer, Fishing/Hunting License .... http://wdfw.wa.gov/lic/vendors/vendors.htm
Dentist/Dental Hygienist...................... https://fortress.wa.gov/doh/hpqa1/Application/Credential_Search/profile.asp
Dietitian .... https://fortress.wa.gov/doh/hpqa1/Application/Credential_Search/profile.asp
Domestic Insurance Carrier .... https://fortress.wa.gov/oic/laa/LAAMain.aspx
Electrical Contractor/Admin. .... https://fortress.wa.gov/lni/bbip/
Electrician .... https://fortress.wa.gov/lni/bbip/
Elevator Contr./Mechanic .... https://fortress.wa.gov/lni/bbip/
Embalmer.. https://fortress.wa.gov/dol/dolprod/profquery/
Emergency Medical Technician............ https://fortress.wa.gov/doh/hpqa1/Application/Credential_Search/profile.asp
Employment Agency/Directory Service https://fortress.wa.gov/dol/dolprod/profquery/
Escrow Company/Officers..................... https://fortress.wa.gov/dfi/licquery/dfi/licquery/default.aspx
Esthetician/Esthetician Instructor.......... https://fortress.wa.gov/dol/dolprod/profquery/
Esthetician/Salon/Booth/Mobile .... https://fortress.wa.gov/dol/dolprod/profquery/
Feedlot .... http://agr.wa.gov/FoodAnimal/Livestock/CertifiedFeedlots.htm
Franchise... https://fortress.wa.gov/dfi/licquery/dfi/licquery/default.aspx
Funeral Director/Establishment .... https://fortress.wa.gov/dol/dolprod/profquery/
Gaming Operation/Occupation .... www.wsgc.wa.gov/LicSearch.asp

Healthcare Service Company .... www.insurance.wa.gov/cgi-bin/PubInfoApps/CGIAuthComp.exe
Hearing Instrument Fitter/Dispenser ..... https://fortress.wa.gov/doh/hpqa1/Application/Credential_Search/profile.asp
HMO .... www.insurance.wa.gov/cgi-bin/PubInfoApps/CGIAuthComp.exe
Home Health Care Agency .... www.doh.wa.gov/Licensing.htm
Hospital .... www.doh.wa.gov/Licensing.htm
Hypnotherapist .... https://fortress.wa.gov/doh/hpqa1/Application/Credential_Search/profile.asp
Insurance Agent/Broker .... https://fortress.wa.gov/oic/laa/LAAMain.aspx
Insurance Company/Corporation .... www.insurance.wa.gov/cgi-bin/PubInfoApps/CGIAuthComp.exe
Investment Advisors .... https://fortress.wa.gov/dfi/licquery/dfi/licquery/default.aspx
Kickboxer .... https://fortress.wa.gov/dol/dolprod/profquery/
Landscape Architect .... https://fortress.wa.gov/dol/dolprod/profquery/
Liquor Store .... www.liq.wa.gov/services/storesearch.asp
Livestock Market .... http://agr.wa.gov/FoodAnimal/Livestock/PublicMarkets.htm
Manicure Salon/Mobile/Booth .... https://fortress.wa.gov/dol/dolprod/profquery/
Manicurist/Esthetician .... www.dol.wa.gov/main/biglist.htm
Manicurist/Manicurist Instructor .... https://fortress.wa.gov/dol/dolprod/profquery/
Marriage & Family Therapist .... https://fortress.wa.gov/doh/hpqa1/Application/Credential_Search/profile.asp
Massage Therapist .... https://fortress.wa.gov/doh/hpqa1/Application/Credential_Search/profile.asp
Medical Doctor .... https://fortress.wa.gov/doh/hpqa1/Application/Credential_Search/profile.asp
Medical Gas Plumber .... https://fortress.wa.gov/lni/bbip/
Mental Health Counselor .... https://fortress.wa.gov/doh/hpqa1/Application/Credential_Search/profile.asp
Midwife .... https://fortress.wa.gov/doh/hpqa1/Application/Credential_Search/profile.asp
Money Transmitter .... https://fortress.wa.gov/dfi/licquery/dfi/licquery/default.aspx
Mortgage Broker .... https://fortress.wa.gov/dfi/licquery/dfi/licquery/default.aspx
Naturopathic Physician .... https://fortress.wa.gov/doh/hpqa1/Application/Credential_Search/profile.asp
Notary Public .... https://fortress.wa.gov/dol/dolprod/profquery/
Nurse/Nursing Assistant .... https://fortress.wa.gov/doh/hpqa1/Application/Credential_Search/profile.asp
Nursing Home .... www.aasa.dshs.wa.gov/Professional/NFDir/directory.asp
Nursing Home Administrator .... https://fortress.wa.gov/doh/hpqa1/Application/Credential_Search/profile.asp
Occupational Therapist .... https://fortress.wa.gov/doh/hpqa1/Application/Credential_Search/profile.asp
Ocularist .... https://fortress.wa.gov/doh/hpqa1/Application/Credential_Search/profile.asp
Optician .... https://fortress.wa.gov/doh/hpqa1/Application/Credential_Search/profile.asp
Optometrist .... https://fortress.wa.gov/doh/hpqa1/Application/Credential_Search/profile.asp
Osteopathic Physician .... https://fortress.wa.gov/doh/hpqa1/Application/Credential_Search/profile.asp
Payday Lender .... https://fortress.wa.gov/dfi/licquery/dfi/licquery/default.aspx
Pharmacist/Pharmacy Technician .... https://fortress.wa.gov/doh/hpqa1/Application/Credential_Search/profile.asp
Physical Therapist .... https://fortress.wa.gov/doh/hpqa1/Application/Credential_Search/profile.asp
Physician Assistant .... https://fortress.wa.gov/doh/hpqa1/Application/Credential_Search/profile.asp
Plumber .... https://fortress.wa.gov/lni/bbip/
Podiatrist .... https://fortress.wa.gov/doh/hpqa1/Application/Credential_Search/profile.asp
Private Investigative Agency/Trainer .... https://fortress.wa.gov/dol/dolprod/profquery/
Private Investigator, Armed/Unarmed .. https://fortress.wa.gov/dol/dolprod/profquery/
Professional Athlete .... www.dol.wa.gov/main/biglist.htm
Psychologist .... https://fortress.wa.gov/doh/hpqa1/Application/Credential_Search/profile.asp
Public Accountant-CPA .... www.cpaboard.wa.gov/search/default.htm
Purchasing Group (Insurance) .... www.insurance.wa.gov/cgi-bin/PubInfoApps/CGIRiskPG.exe
Radiologic Technologist .... https://fortress.wa.gov/doh/hpqa1/Application/Credential_Search/profile.asp
Referee (Athletic) .... https://fortress.wa.gov/dol/dolprod/profquery/
Respiratory Therapist .... https://fortress.wa.gov/doh/hpqa1/Application/Credential_Search/profile.asp
Risk Retention Group .... www.insurance.wa.gov/cgi-bin/PubInfoApps/CGIRiskRG.exe
Salon .... www.dol.wa.gov/main/biglist.htm
Savings & Loan/Savings Bank .... www.dfi.wa.gov/banks/commercial_banks.htm
Securities Broker/Dealer/Seller .... https://fortress.wa.gov/dfi/licquery/dfi/licquery/default.aspx
Security Guard, Priv. Armed/Unarmed . https://fortress.wa.gov/dol/dolprod/profquery/
Security Guard/Agency .... https://fortress.wa.gov/dol/dolprod/profquery/
Service Contract Provider (Ins) .... www.insurance.wa.gov/cgi-bin/PubInfoApps/CGIServiceCP.exe

Sex Offender Treatment Provider .... https://fortress.wa.gov/doh/hpqa1/Application/Credential_Search/profile.asp
Social Worker .... https://fortress.wa.gov/doh/hpqa1/Application/Credential_Search/profile.asp
Speech-Language Pathologist............... https://fortress.wa.gov/doh/hpqa1/Application/Credential_Search/profile.asp
Structural Pest Inspector .... http://agr.wa.gov/PestFert/LicensingEd/ListStructuralPestInspectors.htm
Telephone Solicitor.............................. https://fortress.wa.gov/dol/dolprod/profquery/
Timeshare Seller/Company/Project ...... www.dol.wa.gov/main/biglist.htm
Travel Agency/Travel Seller................. www.dol.wa.gov/main/biglist.htm
Trust Company .... www.dfi.wa.gov/banks/trusts.htm
Vehicle for Hire .... https://fortress.wa.gov/dol/dolprod/profquery/
Vehicle Sales/Disposal......................... https://fortress.wa.gov/dol/dolprod/profquery/
Veterinarian/Vet Medical Clerk............ https://fortress.wa.gov/doh/hpqa1/Application/Credential_Search/profile.asp
Veterinarian, Livestock........................ http://agr.wa.gov/FoodAnimal/Livestock/CertifiedVeterinarians.htm
Viatical Settlement Provider................. www.insurance.wa.gov/cgi-bin/PubInfoApps/CGIViaticalSP.exe
Whitewater River Outfitter .... https://fortress.wa.gov/dol/dolprod/profquery/
Wrestler .... https://fortress.wa.gov/dol/dolprod/profquery/
X-ray Technician .... https://fortress.wa.gov/doh/hpqa1/Application/Credential_Search/profile.asp

County Level ... Courts

Court Administration: Court Administrator, Temple of Justice, PO Box 41174, Olympia, WA, 98504; 360-753-3365, Fax: 360-586-8869. www.courts.wa.gov

Court Structure: District Courts retain civil records for ten years from date of final disposition, then the records are destroyed. District Courts retain criminal records forever. Washington has a mandatory arbitration requirement for civil disputes for $35,000 or less. However, either party may request a trial in Superior Court if dissatisfied with the arbitrator's decision.

Online Access Note: The AOC provides facilities that allow one to access information in the Judicial Information System's (JIS) statewide computer. This program of services is called JIS-Link. JIS-Link provides access to all counties and court levels. Fees include a one-time $100.00 per site and a transaction fee of $.065 per record. Case records include criminal, civil, domestic, probate, and judgments. Call 360-357-3365 or visit www.courts.wa.gov/jislink. Indexes are available electronically and via microfiche for a fee; telephone the JISLink Coordinator for details.

At www.courts.wa.gov/appellate_trial_courts you will find Supreme Court and Appellate Courts opinions. The webpage offers a notification service also.

Benton County

Superior Court – Civil and Criminal Records
www.co.benton.wa.us/clerk
Index online from JIS-Link; see www.courts.wa.gov/jislink (also, see state introduction). Also, subscription access to court docs back to 3/2/1981 and indexes back to 4/1/1979 available at www.landlight.com. Demo subscription available.

Chelan County

Superior Court – Civil and Criminal Records
www.co.chelan.wa.us/scj/scj_main.htm
Civil records back to 1993 and probate back to 1975 and criminal back to 1992 are by subscription at web page. Subscribers may also file online. Also, search current dockets and cases are at www.courts.wa.gov/jis/jis_superior/. Index online from JIS-Link; see www.courts.wa.gov/jislink (also, see state introduction). Also, subscription access to indexes back to 4/30/1984 available at www.landlight.com. Demo subscription available.

Clark County

Superior and District Courts – Civil and Criminal Records
www.clark.wa.gov/courts/superior/index.html
Index online from JIS-Link; see www.courts.wa.gov/jislink (also, see state introduction). Also, daily dockets are at www.clark.wa.gov/courts/superior/docket.html.

Franklin County

Superior Court – Civil and Criminal Records
www.co.franklin.wa.us/clerk
Index online from JIS-Link; see www.courts.wa.gov/jislink. Also, search index at www.co.franklin.wa.us/clerk/search_frame.cfm.

Kitsap County

Superior Court – Civil and Criminal Records
www.kitsapgov.com/sc
Index online from JIS-Link; see www.courts.wa.gov/jislink. Also, subscription access to court docs back to 2/2/2000 and indexes back to 4/1/1978 available at www.landlight.com. Demo subscription available.

Pierce County

Superior Court – Civil and Criminal Records
www.co.pierce.wa.us/abtus/ourorg/supct/abtussup.htm
Statewide index is remotely online (see state introduction). Also, calendars, inmates, and Courts records are online at www.co.pierce.wa.us/cfapps/linx/search.cfm.

County Level ... Recorders & Assessors

Recording Office Organization: 39 counties, 39 recording offices. The recording officer is the County Auditor. County records are usually combined in a Grantor/Grantee index. The entire state is in the Pacific Time Zone (PST). All federal tax liens on personal property are filed with the Department of Licensing. Other federal and all state tax liens are filed with the County Auditor.

Online Access Note: A number of counties offer online access to assessor or real estate records.

Adams County *Property Tax, Sales, Inmates Records*
www.co.adams.wa.us
Access to county property tax and sales records, and inmate records is free at http://adamswa.taxsifter.com/taxsifter/disclaimer.asp.

Asotin County *Real Estate Recording, Deed Records*
www.co.asotin.wa.us
Access recording office land data at www.etitlesearch.com; registration required, fee based on usage.

Benton County
Real Estate, Grantor/Grantee, Recording, Deed, Assessor, Property, Parcel, Tax Roll, Court Records
Assess to Benton County assessor data is free at http://bentonpropertymax.governmaxa.com/propertymax/rover30.asp. Search by parcel ID#, address or map; no name searching. Also, subscription access to grantor/grantee index back to 1/2/1995, parcels back to 1/1997, recordings to 2/17/1985 and Superior court docs and tax rolls are available at www.landlight.com. Fees apply but you may get a Free Tax Roll Summary Report.

Chelan County *Recording, Real Estate, Grantor/Grantee, Property, Marriage, Parcel, Tax Roll, Court Records*
www.co.chelan.wa.us
Access to the Auditor's iCRIS database is free at http://64.146.227.74/icris/documentSearch.jsp. Images go back to 1974; marriage images to 1990. Also, subscription access to grantor/grantee index back to 8/26/90, parcels back to 1/1972, recordings to 4/6/1988 and Superior court docs and tax rolls are available at www.landlight.com. Fees apply but you may get a Free Tax Roll Summary Report.

Clallam County *Property, Assessor Records*
www.clallam.net
Access to assessor property data is free at www.clallam.net/RealEstate/html/land_parcel_search.htm; search by address or property number only. Auditor property maps are also downloadable at www.clallam.net/RealEstate/html/recorded_maps.htm. Auditor records will be online at a later date.

Clark County *Real Estate, Lien, Vital Statistic, Recording, Most Wanted, Sex Offender Records*
www.co.clark.wa.us/auditor/
Access to County Auditor's database is at http://auditor.co.clark.wa.us/auditor_new/index.cfm. Court documents are excluded from this index. Also, search maps online for property data at http://gis.clark.wa.gov/ccgis/mol/property.htm. No name searching.

Cowlitz County *Most Wanted, Missing Person Records*
www.co.cowlitz.wa.us/auditor/
Access to sheriff's most wanted, registered sex offender and missing persons lists is free at www.co.cowlitz.wa.us/sheriff/.

Douglas County *Assessor, Plat, Property Records*
www.douglascountywa.net
Access to the County Parcel Search is free at http://douglaswa.taxsifter.com/taxsifter/disclaimer.asp.

Ferry County *Assessor, Property Records*
www.ferry-county.com
Access property data on the taxsifter database free at http://ferrywa.taxsifter.com/taxsifter/disclaimer.asp.

Franklin County *Assessor, Property, Sex Offender Records*
Search for property information by address or parcel number at www.co.franklin.wa.us/assessor. Also, search for residential sales data. Also, search the level 2 sex offenders at www.co.franklin.wa.us/sheriff/?p=14&v=2. Level 3 sex offenders are at www.co.franklin.wa.us/sheriff/?p=14&v=3.

Grays Harbor County
Assessor, Treasurer, Property Tax, Docket Information, Registered Sex Offenders Records
www.co.grays-harbor.wa.us
Access to the county Parcel Database is free at http://bentonpropertymax.governmaxa.com/propertymax/rover30.asp. Search by parcel ID#, address, legal description, but no name searching. Also, Docket information access at www.co.grays-harbor.wa.us/info/clerk/docket/index.htm. Also, Registered Sex Offenders access at www.co.grays-harbor.wa.us/info/sheriff/Offenders/index.html

Island County *Parcel, Proeprty Tax, Sex Offender, Most Wanted Records*
www.islandcounty.net/auditor
Access county property tax data free at www.islandcounty.net/PublicInformation/Property/AccountSearch.aspx. No name searching. Also, search sexual offenders, kidnappers and most wanted lists free at www.islandcounty.net/sheriff/.

Jefferson County *Assessor, Real Estate, Recording, Vital Statistic, Grantor/Grantee, Lien, Deed, UCC, Permit, Restaurant, Inmate, Plat, Permit Records*
www.co.jefferson.wa.us/auditor/recording/Recording.asp
Access the "Recorded Document Search" database at www.co.jefferson.wa.us/_hidden/disclaimer.htm. Includes grantor/grantee index and records on the County Property (Tax Parcel) Database Tool, also plats and survey images. Also, search for building permits but no name searching.

King County *Real Estate, Lien, Marriage, Recorder, Deed, Judgment, Vital Statistic Records*
www.metrokc.gov
Access to the recorder's database is free at www.metrokc.gov/recelec/records or at http://146.129.54.93:8193/legalacceptance.asp?. Also, property records on Dept. of Developmental and Environmental Resources database are free at www.metrokc.gov/ddes/gis/parcel. After the disclaimer page, search by parcel number, address, street intersection, or map.

Kitsap County *Real Estate, Grantor/Grantee, Recording, Deed, Lien, Vital Statistic, Judgment, Auditor, Property Tax, Parcel, Court Records*
www.kitsapgov.com/aud/default.htm
Access to the auditor's recording database is free at http://kcwppub4.co.kitsap.wa.us/icris/splash.jsp. Fee to print official documents. Searches can also be performed for property and tax information on the land information system site at http://kcwppub3.co.kitsap.wa.us/website/assessor/search.asp. No name searching. Also, subscription access to grantor/grantee index back to 8/26/1990, parcels back to 1/1972, recordings to 4/6/1988 and Superior court docs and tax rolls are available at www.landlight.com. Fees apply but you may get a Free Tax Roll Summary Report.

Kittitas County *Property, Assessor Records*
www.co.kittitas.wa.us
Access property data free at www.co.kittitas.wa.us/taxsifterpublic/disclaimer.asp but no name searching.

Lewis County *Property, Assessor Records*
Access property data free on the PATS system at https://fortress.wa.gov/lewisco/home/ click on PATS. No name searching.

Mason County *Assessor, Property Records*
http://auditor.co.mason.wa.us
Access to Assessor data is free at www.co.mason.wa.us/disclaimer.php. Auditor records from 1985 to 2005 are free at
http://auditor.co.mason.wa.us.

Okanogan County *Assessor, Property Records*
www.okanogancounty.org
Access to county assessment data is free at www.okanogancounty.org/Assessor/map.htm. Taxsifter site may be temporarily down.

Pacific County *Property, Auditor, Foreclosure Records*
www.co.pacific.wa.us
Access County Auditor property data free on the TaxSifter system at http://pacificwa.taxsifter.com/taxsifter/T-Parcelsearch.asp.
Foreclosures are posted on the website in August.

Pierce County
Assessor, Real Estate, Recording, Deed, Lien, Vital Statistic, Judgment, Assumed Name, Inmate Records
www.piercecountywa.org/auditor
Search the auditor's recording database for free at http://hartweb.piercecountywa.org/search.asp?cabinet=opr. Also, property records
on County Assessor-Treasurer database are free at www.co.pierce.wa.us/CFApps/atr/epip/search.cfm. Also, the county sexual
offender/kidnappers list is at http://pso.co.pierce.wa.us. Marriage records at
http://hartweb.piercecountywa.org/search.asp?cabinet=oprmarriage. Also, search inmate info on private company website at
www.vinelink.com/index.jsp.

San Juan County *Assessor, Property Tax, Auditor, Real Estate, Deed, Lien Records*
www.co.san-juan.wa.us
Online access to assessor property records is free at www.co.san-juan.wa.us/assessor/rpsrch.asp?tp=N. No name searching. Also,
access to the auditor database of real estate recording records is free at http://sjc-imaging.rockisland.com/SJCdocSearch/?. Images go
back to 1997; index goes back to 1/1984.

Skagit County *Recording, Property Tax, Assessor, Treasurer, Deed, Lien, Vital Statistic, Auditor Records*
www.skagitcounty.net/Common/asp/default.asp?d=Home&c=General&P=main.htm
Assessor, Treasurer, Auditor's recorded documents as well as permits are all free at www.skagitcounty.net; click on Records Search.

Snohomish County *Real Estate, Assessor, Recording, Marriage, Jail, Offender, Jail Booking Records*
http://www1.co.snohomish.wa.us/Departments/Auditor/
Access to the Auditor's office database is free at http://198.238.192.100/localization/menu.asp. Search on the recorded documents or
marriage icons. Also, search the assessor property data for free at http://web5.co.snohomish.wa.us/propsys/asr-tr-propinq/ - no name
searching. Search county sheriff jail register at http://www1.co.snohomish.wa.us/Departments/Corrections/Services/default.htm.

Spokane County *Property Tax, Land Records*
www.spokanecounty.org/auditor
Search the County Parcel Locator database for free at www.spokanecounty.org/pubpadal/. No name searching.

Stevens County *Assessor, Property Records*
www.co.stevens.wa.us
Access assessor property data free at http://64.85.21.111/screalprop/; no name searching.

Thurston County *Assessor, Real Estate, Auditor, Recording Records*
www.co.thurston.wa.us/auditor
Assessor and property data on Thurston GeoData database is free at www.geodata.org/parcelsrch.asp. No name searching. Also,
access the Auditor Recording I-CRIS database, no images, at www.co.thurston.wa.us/auditor. Click on online records.

Wahkiakum County *Sheriff Warrant Records*
Search the sheriff's warrant list at www.sd.co.wahkiakum.wa.us.

Walla Walla County *Property Tax, Assessor, Residential Sale, Farm Sale Records*
www.co.walla-walla.wa.us
Access to the TaxSifter parcel search is free at http://wallawallawa.taxsifter.com/taxsifter/t-parcelsearch.asp.

Whatcom County *Assessor, Real Estate, Voter Registration Records*

www.co.whatcom.wa.us/auditor

Search the assessor parcel database information system free at

www.co.whatcom.wa.us/cgibin/db2www/assessor/search/RPSearch.ndt/disclaimer. Also, acquire voter registration lists for political purposes only; information and request information at www.co.whatcom.wa.us/auditor/election_division/labels_lists/index.jsp.

Yakima County *Assessor, Real Estate, Property Tax Records*

www.pan.co.yakima.wa.us

Assessor and property information on County Assessor database are free at www.co.yakima.wa.us/assessor/propinfo/asr_info.asp. No name searching. Also, access to the treasurer parcel database is free at www.co.yakima.wa.us/treasurer/database/taxes.asp. No name searching. Also, search the sheriff's sex offender list at www.pan.co.yakima.wa.us/Sheriff/soffenders.htm.

Federal Courts in Washington...

Standards for Federal Courts: The universal PACER sign-up number is 800-676-6856. Find PACER and the Party/Case Index on the Web at http://pacer.psc.uscourts.gov. PACER dial-up access is $.60 per minute. Also, courts offering internet access via PACER, Web-PACER or the new CM-ECF charge $.08 per page fee ($.07 per page if record is pre-2005 or unless noted as free).

US District Court -- Eastern District of Washington

www.waed.uscourts.gov

PACER: Case records are available back to 7/1989. Records are purged every 6 months. New records are available online after 1 day. **PACER Online Access:** ECF replaces PACER. **Electronic Filing:** CM/ECF data at https://ecf.waed.uscourts.gov. **Other Online Access:** Access weekly calendar at www.waed.uscourts.gov/calendar/default.htm.

Spokane Division counties: Adams, Asotin, Benton, Chelan, Columbia, Douglas, Ferry, Franklin, Garfield, Grant, Lincoln, Okanogan, Pend Oreille, Spokane, Stevens, Walla Walla, Whitman. Also, some cases from Kittitas, Klickitat and Yakima heard here.

Yakima Division counties: Kittitas, Klickitat, Yakima. Case hearings are held in Yakima. Direct mail to Spokane. Some cases from Kittitas, Klickitat and Yakima are heard in Spokane or Richland.

US Bankruptcy Court -- Eastern District of Washington

www.waeb.uscourts.gov

PACER: Pacer records go back to 1997. **PACER Online Access:** ECF replaces PACER. **Electronic Filing:** CM/ECF data at https://ecf.waeb.uscourts.gov. **Opinions:** View court opinions at www.waeb.uscourts.gov/JudicialOpinions/. **Phone access:** Voice Case Information System, call 509-353-2404.

Spokane Division counties: Adams, Asotin, Benton, Chelan, Columbia, Douglas, Ferry, Franklin, Garfield, Grant, Kittitas, Klickitat, Lincoln, Okanogan, Pend Oreille, Spokane, Stevens, Walla Walla, Whitman, Yakima.

US District Court -- Western District of Washington

www.wawd.uscourts.gov

PACER: Case records are available back to 1988. Records are purged never. New records are available online after 1 day. **PACER Online Access:** ECF replaces PACER. Document images available. **Electronic Filing:** CM/ECF data at https://ecf.wawd.uscourts.gov. **Other Online Access:** Calendars and court orders are at www.wawd.uscourts.gov/docs.

Seattle Division counties: Island, King, San Juan, Skagit, Snohomish, Whatcom.

Tacoma Division counties: Clallam, Clark, Cowlitz, Grays Harbor, Jefferson, Kitsap, Lewis, Mason, Pacific, Pierce, Skamania, Thurston, Wahkiakum.

US Bankruptcy Court -- Western District of Washington

www.wawb.uscourts.gov

PACER: Case records are available back to 1/1986. Records are purged never. New records are available online after 1 day. **PACER Online Access:** PACER online at http://pacer.wawb.uscourts.gov. **Electronic Filing:** CM/ECF data at https://ecf.wawb.uscourts.gov. **Opinions:** View court opinions at www.wawb.uscourts.gov/opinions.htm. **Other Online Access:** Calendars free at www.wawb.uscourts.gov. **Phone access:** Voice Case Information System, call 888-409-4662, 206-370-5285

Seattle Division counties: Clallam, Island, Jefferson, King, Kitsap, San Juan, Skagit, Snohomish, Whatcom.

Tacoma Division counties: Clark, Cowlitz, Grays Harbor, Lewis, Mason, Pacific, Pierce, Skamania, Thurston, Wahkiakum.

West Virginia

Capital: Charleston
                 Kanawha County
Time Zone: EST
Population: 1,815,354
# of Counties: 55

Quick Links

Website: www.wv.gov
Governor: www.wvgov.org
Attorney General: www.wvs.state.wv.us/wvag/
State Archives: www.wvculture.org/history/wvsamenu.html
State Statutes and Codes: www.legis.state.wv.us/WVCODE/masterfrm3Banner.cfm
Legislative Bill Search: www.legis.state.wv.us/bill_status/bstatmenux/bstatfrm.cfm
Bill Monitoring: www.legis.state.wv.us/billstatus_personalized/persbills_login.cfm
Unclaimed Funds: www.wvtreasury.com/sites/unclaimed/index.html

State Level ... Major Agencies

Statewide Court Records

Administrative Office, State Supreme Court of Appeals, 1900 Kanawha Blvd, Bldg 1, Rm E 100, Charleston, WV 25305-0830; 304-558-0145, Fax-304-558-1212, 9AM-5PM.
www.state.wv.us/wvsca
Online search: Supreme Court of Appeals Opinions/Calendar is available at the web page. 14 circuit courts have accessible records at www.swcg-inc.com/products/circuit_express.html. Fees are involved. Records are from 02/1997. Magistrate Court records are on also on this private system at www.swcg-inc.com/products/municipal_courts.html.

Sexual Offender Registry

State Police Headquarters, Sexual Offender Registry, 725 Jefferson Rd, South Charleston, WV 25309; 304-746-2133, Fax-304-746-2403, 8:30AM-4:30PM.
www.wvstatepolice.com/sexoff/
Online search: Online searching is available from website, search by county or name.

Incarceration Records

West Virginia Division of Corrections, Records Room, 112 California Ave, Bldg 4, Room 300, Charleston, WV 25305; 304-558-2037, Fax-304-558-5934, 8AM-5PM.
www.wvf.state.wv.us/wvdoc/
Online search: There is no online searching is available from this agency. However, a private company offers free web access at www.vinelink.com/index.jsp.

Corporation, Limited Liability Company, Limited Partnerships, Trademarks/Servicemarks, Limited Liability Partnerships

Secretary of State, Corporation Division, State Capitol Bldg, Room W151, Charleston, WV 25305-0776; 304-558-8000, Fax-304-558-5758, 8:30AM-5PM.

www.wvsos.com

Online search: Corporation and business types records on the Secretary of State Business Organization Information System are available free online at www.wvsos.com/wvcorporations/. Search by organization name. Certified copies may be ordered online or via email to business@wvsos.com.

Driver License Information, Driver Records

Division of Motor Vehicles, 1800 Kanawha Blvd, Building 3, Rm 124, State Capitol Complex, Charleston, WV 25317; 304-558-3915, 304-558-4444, 304-558-0238, Fax-304-558-0465, 8:30AM-5PM.

www.wvdot.com/6_motorists/dmv/6G_DMV.HTM

Online search: Online access is available 24 hours a day. Batch requesters receive return transmission about 3 AM. Users must access through AAMVAnet. A contract is required and accounts must pre-pay. Fee is $5.00 per record. For more information, call 304-558-3915. **Other options:** This agency will sell its DL file to commercial vendors, but records cannot be re-sold.

State Level ... Occupational Licensing

Aesthetician	www.wvdhhr.org/bph/wvbc/licensees.cfm
Architect	http://wvbrdarch.org/roster/lic/searchdb.asp
Asbestos Clearance Air Monitor	www.wvdhhr.org/rtia/allair.cfm
Asbestos Contractor	www.wvdhhr.org/rtia/allcon.cfm
Asbestos Inspector	www.wvdhhr.org/rtia/allinsp.cfm
Asbestos Laboratory	www.wvdhhr.org/rtia/licensing.asp
Asbestos Project Designer	www.wvdhhr.org/rtia/alldesign.cfm
Asbestos Supervisor	www.wvdhhr.org/rtia/allsup.cfm
Asbestos Worker	www.wvdhhr.org/rtia/allwork.cfm
Attorney	www.wvbar.org/barinfo/mdirectory/
Barber	www.wvdhhr.org/bph/wvbc/licensees.cfm
Barber/Beauty Culture School	www.wvdhhr.org/bph/wvbc/licensees.cfm
Contractor, General	www.labor.state.wv.us/search/default.asp
Cosmetologist	www.wvdhhr.org/bph/wvbc/licensees.cfm
Counselor LPC, Profession'l	www.wvbec.org/alps.htm
Electrician	www.wvfiremarshal.org/search.htm
EMS Agency	www.wvochs.org/shared/content/ems/pdfs/agencylist011906.pdf
Engineer	www.wvpebd.org
Insurance Agency	www.wvinsurance.gov/agency%5Fdetail/
Insurance Agent	www.wvinsurance.gov/agent%5Fdetail/
Insurance Company	www.wvinsurance.gov/company%5Fdetail/
Lobbyist	www.wvethicscommission.org
Manicurist	www.wvdhhr.org/bph/wvbc/licensees.cfm
Medical Corporation	www.wvdhhr.org/wvbom/Directory/2003/medcorps2003.pdf
Medical Doctor	www.wvdhhr.org/wvbom/Directory/2003/mds2003.pdf
Medical License, Special Volunteer	www.wvdhhr.org/wvbom/Directory/2003/specialvolunteer2003.pdf
Medical Professional LLC/Company	www.wvdhhr.org/wvbom/Directory/2003/pllcs2003.pdf
Nurse-LPN	www.lpnboard.state.wv.us/
Occupational Therapist/Assistant	www.wvbot.org
Optometrist	www.arbo.org/index.php?action=findanoptometrist
Pesticide Applicator	www.kellysolutions.com
Physician Assistant	www.wvdhhr.org/wvbom/Directory/2003/pas2003.pdf
Podiatrist	www.wvdhhr.org/wvbom/Directory/2003/podiatrists2003.pdf
Public Accountant-CPA	www.wvboacc.org/Verify_A_Licensee.htm
Radiologic Technologist	www.wvrtboard.org/
Real Estate Agent/Broker/Sales	www.arello.com/ArelloWeb/ShowPage?command=main

Real Estate Appraiser (Nat'l) .... www.asc.gov/content/category1/appr_by_state.asp
Real Estate Appraiser (WV list)................. www.wvappraiserboard.org/roster.pdf
Respiratory Care Practitioner...................... www.wvborc.org/licensees/default.asp
Veterinarian .... www.wvlicensingboards.com/vetmed/licensed.cfm

County Level ... Courts

Court Administration: Administrative Office, Supreme Court of Appeals, 1900 Kanawha Blvd, 1 E 100 State Capitol, Charleston, WV, 25305; 304-558-0145; www.state.wv.us/wvsca

Court Structure: The 55 Circuit Courts are the courts of general jurisdiction. Probate is handled by the Circuit Court. Records are held at the County Commissioner's Office. Family Courts were created by constitutional amendment and were formed as of January 1, 2002. Family Courts hear cases involving divorce, annulment, separate maintenance, family support, paternity, child custody, and visitation. Family Court judges also conduct final hearings in domestic violence cases.

Online Access Note: Supreme Court of Appeals Opinions and Calendar are available at the web page. There are plans for a statewide system to allow access to Circuit Court, Family Court, and Magistrate Court records, which may be available in 2006.

Magistrate Court records are available on a private system, see www.swcg-inc.com. Also available are Circuit Court civil and criminal records for counties of **Calhoun, Fayette, Grant, Hancock, Kanawha, Logan, Mason, McDowell, Mineral, Nicholas, Ohio, Putnam, Roane, and Wetzel** by subscription to Circuit Express. More counties to be added.

County Level ... Recorders & Assessors

Recording Office Organization: 55 counties, 55 recording offices. The recording officer is County Clerk. The entire state is in the Eastern Time Zone (EST). All federal and state tax liens are filed with the County Clerk.

Online Access Note: There is no state-operated system open to public although a private company offers subscription access to land book assessment information statewide at http://digitalcourthouse.com. Only one county – Monongalia – offers online access to its assessor records.

9 West Virginia Counties *Property Tax Records*
Access property tax data free at www.softwaresystems.com/ssi/taxinquiry/
Counties include- Berkeley, Boone, Cabell, Greenbriar, Jefferson, Kanawha, Monongalia, Nicholas.

- - -

Hardy County *Deed, Mortgage, Grantor/Grantee Records*
Access to Records is free at http://216.27.81.170/login.asp or at www.onlinecountyrecords.com. Username Id and Password is hardywv, all small letters. Index goes back to 1/1993.

Monongalia County *Assessor, Real Estate, Property Tax Records*
Access the County Parcel Search database free at www.assessor.org/parcelweb. Search by a wide variety of criteria including owner name and address. Also, access property tax data free at www.softwaresystems.com/ssi/taxinquiry/.

Summers County *Property Tax, Assessor Records*
www.summerscountywv.org
Access the tax inquiry database free at http://129.71.205.119/.

Wayne County *Real Estate, Recording, Deed, Lien, Marriage, Birth, Death, Will, UCC, Property Tax Records*
www.waynecountywv.us
Access recorded document index back to 4/1/1991 free at www.waynecountywv.us/WEBInquiry/. Also, access property tax data free at www.waynecountywv.us/WEBTax/.

Wood County *Recording, Deed, Will, Death, Birth, Marriage, Lien Records*
www.woodcountywv.com/countyclerk/index.html
Access is by dial-up modem; visit www.woodcountywv.com/countyclerk/modem.htm for instructions for free connection. Records go back to July 1, 1986. Click on document imaging to download.

Federal Courts in West Virginia...

Standards for Federal Courts: The universal PACER sign-up number is 800-676-6856. Find PACER and the Party/Case Index on the Web at http://pacer.psc.uscourts.gov. PACER dial-up access is $.60 per minute. Also, courts offering internet access via PACER, Web-PACER or the new CM-ECF charge $.08 per page fee ($.07 per page if record is pre-2005 or unless noted as free).

US District Court -- Northern District of West Virginia
www.wvnd.uscourts.gov
PACER: Case records are available back to 10/1994. Records are purged every 5 years. New records are available online after 1 day.
PACER Online Access: ECF replaces PACER. Document images available. **Electronic Filing:** CM/ECF data at https://ecf.wvnd.uscourts.gov. **Opinions:** Opinions go back to 1999. View court opinions at www.wvnd.uscourts.gov/opinions.htm.
Clarksburg Division counties: Braxton, Calhoun, Doddridge, Gilmer, Harrison, Lewis, Marion, Monongalia, Pleasants, Ritchie, Taylor, Tyler.
Elkins Division counties: Barbour, Grant, Hardy, Mineral, Pendleton, Pocahontas, Preston, Randolph, Tucker, Upshur, Webster.
Martinsburg Division counties: Berkeley, Hampshire, Jefferson, Morgan.
Wheeling Division counties: Brooke, Hancock, Marshall, Ohio, Wetzel.

US Bankruptcy Court -- Northern District of West Virginia
www.wvnb.uscourts.gov
PACER: Case records are available back to early 1990. Records are purged never. New records are available online after 1 day.
PACER Online Access: ECF replaces PACER. Document images available. **Electronic Filing:** CM/ECF data at https://ecf.wvnb.uscourts.gov. **Opinions:** View court opinions at www.wvnb.uscourts.gov/courtopinions.htm. **Phone access:** Voice Case Information System, call 800-809-3028, 304-233-7318
Wheeling Division counties: Barbour, Berkeley, Braxton, Brooke, Calhoun, Doddridge, Gilmer, Grant, Hampshire, Hancock, Hardy, Harrison, Jefferson, Lewis, Marion, Marshall, Mineral, Monongalia, Morgan, Ohio, Pendleton, Pleasants, Pocahontas, Preston, Randolph, Ritchie, Taylor, Tucker, Tyler, Upshur, Webster, Wetzel. Clarksburg location is 324 Main St, Clarksburg, 26302, phone-304-623-7866.

US District Court -- Southern District of West Virginia
www.wvsd.uscourts.gov
PACER: Case records are available back to 1991. Records are purged as deemed necessary. New records are available online after 1 day. **PACER Online Access:** ECF replaces PACER. Document images available. **Electronic Filing:** CM/ECF data at https://ecf.wvsd.uscourts.gov. **Opinions:** View court opinions at www.wvsd.uscourts.gov/district/opinions/. **Other Online Access:** Judges' calendars free at www.wvsd.uscourts.gov/judgetree/index.html.
Beckley Division counties: Fayette, Greenbrier, Raleigh, Sumners, Wyoming.
Bluefield Division counties: McDowell, Mercer, Monroe.
Charleston Division counties: Boone, Clay, Jackson, Kanawha, Lincoln, Logan, Mingo, Nicholas, Putnam, Roane.
Huntington Division counties: Cabell, Mason, Wayne.
Parkersburg Division counties: Wirt, Wood.

US Bankruptcy Court -- Southern District of West Virginia
www.wvsd.uscourts.gov/bankruptcy/index.htm
PACER: Case records are available back to 1988. New records are available online after 1 day. **PACER Online Access:** ECF replaces PACER. Document images available. **Electronic Filing:** CM/ECF data at https://ecf.wvsb.uscourts.gov. **Other Online Access:** Access limited hearing dockets by day free at www.wvsd.uscourts.gov/bankruptcy/dailydocket.htm. **Phone access:** Voice Case Information System, call 304-347-5337.
Charleston Division counties: Boone, Cabell, Clay, Fayette, Greenbrier, Jackson, Kanawha, Lincoln, Logan, Mason, McDowell, Mercer, Mingo, Monroe, Nicholas, Putnam, Raleigh, Roane, Summers, Wayne, Wirt, Wood, Wyoming.

Wisconsin

Capital: Madison
           Dane County
Time Zone: CST
Population: 5,509,026
# of Counties: 72

Quick Links

Website: www.wisconsin.gov
Governor: www.wisgov.state.wi.us
Attorney General: www.doj.state.wi.us/ag/
State Archives: www.wisconsinhistory.org/libraryarchives/
State Statutes and Codes: www.legis.state.wi.us/rsb/stats.html
Legislative Bill Search: www.legis.state.wi.us
Bill Monitoring: http://notify.legis.state.wi.us/(sqsdjq45dnqby045cvkinq45)/Home.aspx
Unclaimed Funds: www.ost.state.wi.us/home/unclaimed_property.htm

State Level...Major Agencies

Criminal Records

Wisconsin Department of Justice, Crime Information Bureau, Record Check Unit, PO Box 2688, Madison, WI 53701-2688 (Courier: 17 W Main St, Madison, WI 53703); 608-266-5764, 608-266-7780 (Online Questions), Fax-608-267-4558, 8AM-4:30PM. www.doj.state.wi.us
Online search: The agency offers Internet access at http://wi-recordcheck.org. An account with PIN is required or a credit card can be used. Records must be "picked up" at the website within 10 days. They are not returned by mail. Fee is $13 per request, $7.00 if a non-profit, and $10.00 if a government agency. Only daycare centers and other caregivers can receive immediate online response but pay an additional $2.50 per record.

Statewide Court Records

Director of State Courts, Supreme Court, PO Box 1688, Madison, WI 53701-1688; 608-266-6828, Fax-608-267-0980, 8AM-5PM. http://wicourts.gov
Online search: Wisconsin Circuit Court Access (WCCA) allows users to view circuit court case information at http://wcca.wicourts.gov/index.xsl. Data is available from all counties except Portage County offers only probate records online. WCCA provides detailed information about circuit cases and for civil cases on either a statewide or county basis. The system displays judgment and judgment party information and offers the ability to generate reports. Appellate and Supreme Courts opinions are available from the main web page. **Other options:** Bulk access to data may be arranged on contract, fees are involved. Contact the Office of Court Operations at 608-266-3121 for details.

Sexual Offender Registry

Department of Corrections, Sex Offender Registry Program, PO Box 7925, Madison, WI 53707-7925 (Courier: 3099 E Washington Avenue, Madison, WI 53704); 608-240-5830, Fax-608-240-3355, 7:45AM-4:30PM. http://offender.doc.state.wi.us/public/
Online search: Search for offenders by name or location at the website.

Incarceration Records

Wisconsin Department of Corrections, Bureau of Technology Management, PO Box 8980, Madison, WI 53708-8980 (Courier: 3099 E Washington Ave, Madison, WI 53708); 608-240-5741, Fax-608-240-3385, 7:30AM-4PM.
www.wi-doc.com
Online search: No online searching is available for the public from this agency, however a private company provides free web access at www.vinelink.com/index.jsp.

Corporation, Limited Partnership, Limited Liability Company, Limited Liability Partnerships

Division of Corporate & Consumer Services, Corporation Record Requests, PO Box 7846, Madison, WI 53707-7846 (Courier: 345 W Washington Ave, 3rd Floor, Madison, WI 53703); 608-261-7577, Fax-608-267-6813, 7:45AM-4:30PM.
www.wdfi.org
Online search: Selected elements of the database ("CRIS" Corporate Registration System) are available online on the department's website at www.wdfi.org/apps/cris/. **Other options:** Some data released in database format, available electronically via email or CD.

Uniform Commercial Code, Federal Tax Liens, State Tax Liens

Department of Financial Institutions, CCS/UCC, PO Box 7847, Madison, WI 53707-7847 (Courier: 345 W Washington Ave 3rd Fl, Madison, WI 53703); 608-261-9548, Fax-608-264-7965, 7:45AM-4:30PM.
www.wdfi.org
Online search: There is free Internet access for most records. Some records may require a $1.00 fee. You may do a free debtor name search at www.wdfi.org/ucc/search/. Instant filings are available immediately. **Other options:** Bulk Index data is available on CD. The initial subscription is $3,000, monthly updates are $250.00. Images are available on CD for $200 per month.

Birth, Death, Marriage, Divorce Certificates

Bureau of Health Information and Policy, Vital Records, PO Box 309, Madison, WI 53701-0309 (Courier: One W Wilson St, Room 158, Madison, WI 53702); 608-266-1373, 608-266-1371 (Recording), 608-267-7820 (Genealogy), Fax-608-255-2035, 8AM-4:15PM.
www.dhfs.wisconsin.gov/vitalrecords/
Online search: Records may be ordered online via www.vitalchek.com, a state approved vendor.

Driver Records

Division of Motor Vehicles, Records & Licensing Info. Section, PO Box 7995, Madison, WI 53707-7995 (Courier: 4802 Sheboygan Ave, Room 350, Madison, WI 53707); 608-266-2353, Fax-608-267-3636, 7:30AM-5:15PM.
www.dot.wisconsin.gov/drivers/index.htm
Online search: Commercial online access is available for high volume users only, fee is $5.00 per record. Call 608-266-2353 for more information. Approved accounts may email requests to driverrecords.dmv@dot.state.wi.us. The Employer Notification program provides an employee's MVR when an accident, suspension, revocation or out of service order occurs. Cost is $20.00 to sign up and $2.00 per employee. Call 608-266-5769 to set up the program. Check status of a DL at https://trust.dot.state.wi.us/occsin/occsinservlet?whoami=statusp1. Must submit SSN and DOB. There is no charge. **Other options:** The agency offers a magnetic tape retrieval system for high volume users. The agency will, also, sell its license file without histories to qualified entities. For more information, call 608-266-2353.

State Level...Occupational Licensing

Accounting Firm .... http://drl.wi.gov/lookupjump.htm
Acupuncturist.. http://drl.wi.gov/drl/drllookup/LicenseLookupServlet?page=lookup_health
Adjustment Service Company .... www.wdfi.org/fi/lfs/licensee_lists
Aesthetics Establ./Specialty School........... http://drl.wi.gov/lookupjump.htm
Aesthetics Instructor .... http://drl.wi.gov/lookupjump.htm
Ambulance Service Provider .... http://dhfs.wisconsin.gov/ems/Provider/WICounties.htm
Appraiser, General/Residential .... http://drl.wi.gov/lookupjump.htm
Architect .... http://drl.wi.gov/lookupjump.htm
Architectural Corporation .... http://drl.wi.gov/lookupjump.htm
Art Therapist... http://drl.wi.gov/drl/drllookup/LicenseLookupServlet?page=lookup_health
Attorney .... www.wisbar.org/AM/Template.cfm?Section=Lawyer_Directory

Auction Company .... http://drl.wi.gov/lookupjump.htm
Auctioneer.. http://drl.wi.gov/lookupjump.htm
Audiologist .... http://drl.wi.gov/drl/drllookup/LicenseLookupServlet?page=lookup_health
Bank... www.wdfi.org/fi/savings_institutions/licensee_lists/
Barber/Barber School................................. http://drl.wi.gov/lookupjump.htm
Barber/Apprentice/Instrct./Mgr................... http://drl.wi.gov/lookupjump.htm
Boiler Repairer.. http://apps.commerce.state.wi.us/SB_Credential/SB_CredentialApp
Boxer .... http://drl.wi.gov/lookupjump.htm
Boxing Club, Amateur or Prof. .... http://drl.wi.gov/lookupjump.htm
Boxing Show .... http://drl.wi.gov/lookupjump.htm
Building Inspector...................................... http://apps.commerce.state.wi.us/SB_Credential/SB_CredentialApp
Cemetery Authority/Warehouse .... http://drl.wi.gov/lookupjump.htm
Cemetery Pre-Need Seller/Salesperson....... http://drl.wi.gov/lookupjump.htm
Charitable Organization.............................. http://drl.wi.gov/lookupjump.htm
Check Seller... www.wdfi.org/fi/lfs/licensee_lists
Chiropractor... http://drl.wi.gov/drl/drllookup/LicenseLookupServlet?page=lookup_health
Collection Agency .... www.wdfi.org/fi/lfs/licensee_lists
Cosmetologist/Cosmetology School .... http://drl.wi.gov/lookupjump.htm
Cosmetology Instr./Mgr./Apprentice .... http://drl.wi.gov/lookupjump.htm
Counselor, Professional .... http://drl.wi.gov/drl/drllookup/LicenseLookupServlet?page=lookup_health
Credit Service Organization........................ www.wdfi.org/fi/cu/chartered_lists/default.asp
Credit Union .... www.wdfi.org/fi/cu/chartered_lists/default.asp
Currency Exchange..................................... www.wdfi.org/fi/lfs/licensee_lists
Dance Therapist.. http://drl.wi.gov/drl/drllookup/LicenseLookupServlet?page=lookup_health
Debt Collector.. www.wdfi.org/fi/lfs/licensee_lists
Dental Hygienist .... http://drl.wi.gov/drl/drllookup/LicenseLookupServlet?page=lookup_health
Dentist.. http://drl.wi.gov/drl/drllookup/LicenseLookupServlet?page=lookup_health
Designer of Engineering Systems .... http://drl.wi.gov/lookupjump.htm
Dietitian .... http://drl.wi.gov/drl/drllookup/LicenseLookupServlet?page=lookup_health
Drug Distributor/Mfg.................................. http://drl.wi.gov/lookupjump.htm
Electrical Inspector .... http://apps.commerce.state.wi.us/SB_Credential/SB_CredentialApp
Electrician.. http://apps.commerce.state.wi.us/SB_Credential/SB_CredentialApp
Electrologist/Electrology Instructor .... http://drl.wi.gov/lookupjump.htm
Electrology Establ./School.......................... http://drl.wi.gov/lookupjump.htm
Engineer/Engineer in Training.................... http://drl.wi.gov/lookupjump.htm
Engineering Corporation............................. http://drl.wi.gov/lookupjump.htm
Firearms Permit .... http://drl.wi.gov/lookupjump.htm
Fireworks Manufacturer.............................. http://apps.commerce.state.wi.us/SB_Credential/SB_CredentialApp
Fund Raiser, Professional .... http://drl.wi.gov/lookupjump.htm
Fund Raising Counsel................................. http://drl.wi.gov/lookupjump.htm
Funeral Director/Director Apprentice .... http://drl.wi.gov/lookupjump.htm
Funeral Establishment/Pre-Need Seller ...... http://drl.wi.gov/lookupjump.htm
Geologist.. http://drl.wi.gov/lookupjump.htm
Geology Firm... http://drl.wi.gov/lookupjump.htm
Hearing Instrument Specialist..................... http://drl.wi.gov/drl/drllookup/LicenseLookupServlet?page=lookup_health
Home Inspector.. http://drl.wi.gov/lookupjump.htm
HVAC Contractor....................................... http://apps.commerce.state.wi.us/SB_Credential/SB_CredentialApp
Hydrologist/Hydrology Firm .... http://drl.wi.gov/lookupjump.htm
Insurance Premium Financier .... www.wdfi.org/fi/lfs/licensee_lists
Interior Designer.. http://drl.wi.gov/lookupjump.htm
Investment Advisor/Advisor Rep................ www.wdfi.org/fi/securities/licensing/licensee_lists/default.asp
Land Surveyor .... http://drl.wi.gov/lookupjump.htm
Landscape Architect................................... http://drl.wi.gov/lookupjump.htm
Loan Company... www.wdfi.org/fi/lfs/licensee_lists
Loan Solicitor/Originator............................ www.wdfi.org/fi/lfs/licensee_lists/default.asp
Lobbying Organization, Principal............... http://ethics.state.wi.us/Scripts/2003Session/OELMenu.asp

Lobbyist http://ethics.state.wi.us/Scripts/2003Session/LobbyistsMenu.asp
Manicurist Establ./Specialty School .... http://drl.wi.gov/lookupjump.htm
Manicurist/Manicurist Instructor .... http://drl.wi.gov/lookupjump.htm
Marriage & Family Therapist .... http://drl.wi.gov/drl/drllookup/LicenseLookupServlet?page=lookup_health
Massage Therapist/Bodyworker.................. http://drl.wi.gov/drl/drllookup/LicenseLookupServlet?page=lookup_health
Medical Doctor/Surgeon .... http://drl.wi.gov/drl/drllookup/LicenseLookupServlet?page=lookup_health
Midwife Nurse .... http://drl.wi.gov/drl/drllookup/LicenseLookupServlet?page=lookup_health
Mobile Home & RV Dealer .... www.wdfi.org/fi/lfs/licensee_lists
Mortgage Banker/Broker .... www.wdfi.org/fi/lfs/licensee_lists/default.asp
Motorcycle Dealer .... www.wdfi.org/fi/lfs/licensee_lists
Music Therapist .... http://drl.wi.gov/drl/drllookup/LicenseLookupServlet?page=lookup_health
Nurse-RN/LPN .... http://drl.wi.gov/drl/drllookup/LicenseLookupServlet?page=lookup_health
Nursing Home Administrator...................... http://drl.wi.gov/lookupjump.htm
Occupational Therapist/Assistant............... http://drl.wi.gov/drl/drllookup/LicenseLookupServlet?page=lookup_health
Optometrist .... http://drl.wi.gov/drl/drllookup/LicenseLookupServlet?page=lookup_health
Osteopathic Physician............................... http://drl.wi.gov/drl/drllookup/LicenseLookupServlet?page=lookup_health
Payday Lender .... www.wdfi.org/fi/lfs/licensee_lists
Pesticide Applicator.................................. www.kellysolutions.com/WI/Applicators/index.asp
Pesticide Applicator Business.................... www.kellysolutions.com/WI/Business/searchbyCity.asp
Pesticide Dealer .... www.kellysolutions.com/WI/Dealers/searchbyCity.asp
Pharmacist/Pharmacy................................ http://drl.wi.gov/drl/drllookup/LicenseLookupServlet?page=lookup_health
Physical Therapist..................................... http://drl.wi.gov/drl/drllookup/LicenseLookupServlet?page=lookup_health
Physician Assistant .... http://drl.wi.gov/drl/drllookup/LicenseLookupServlet?page=lookup_health
Plumber.. http://apps.commerce.state.wi.us/SB_Credential/SB_CredentialApp
Podiatrist.. http://drl.wi.gov/drl/drllookup/LicenseLookupServlet?page=lookup_health
Private Detective/Detective Agency .... http://drl.wi.gov/lookupjump.htm
Psychologist... http://drl.wi.gov/drl/drllookup/LicenseLookupServlet?page=lookup_health
Public Accountant..................................... http://drl.wi.gov/lookupjump.htm
Real Estate Agent/Broker/Sales .... http://drl.wi.gov/lookupjump.htm
Real Estate Appraiser................................ http://drl.wi.gov/lookupjump.htm
Real Estate Business Entity........................ http://drl.wi.gov/lookupjump.htm
Respiratory Care Practitioner..................... http://drl.wi.gov/drl/drllookup/LicenseLookupServlet?page=lookup_health
Sales Finance/Loan Company..................... www.wdfi.org/fi/lfs/licensee_lists
Savings & Loan Financer........................... www.wdfi.org/fi/lfs/licensee_lists
Savings Institution .... www.wdfi.org/fi/savings_institutions/licensee_lists/
School Librarian/Media Specialist.............. https://www2.dpi.wi.gov/lic-tll/home.do
School Psychology Private Practice............ http://drl.wi.gov/drl/drllookup/LicenseLookupServlet?page=lookup_health
Securities Broker/Dealer/Agent .... www.wdfi.org/fi/securities/licensing/licensee_lists/default.asp
Security Guard .... http://drl.wi.gov/lookupjump.htm
Social Worker .... http://drl.wi.gov/drl/drllookup/LicenseLookupServlet?page=lookup_health
Soil Science Firm...................................... http://drl.wi.gov/lookupjump.htm
Soil Scientist.. http://drl.wi.gov/lookupjump.htm
Soil Tester.. http://apps.commerce.state.wi.us/SB_Credential/SB_CredentialApp
Speech Pathologist/Audiologist .... http://drl.wi.gov/drl/drllookup/LicenseLookupServlet?page=lookup_health
Teacher https://www2.dpi.wi.gov/lic-tll/home.do
Timeshare Salesperson.............................. http://drl.wi.gov/lookupjump.htm
Veterinarian/Veterinary Technician............ http://drl.wi.gov/drl/drllookup/LicenseLookupServlet?page=lookup_health
Welder .... http://apps.commerce.state.wi.us/SB_Credential/SB_CredentialApp

County Level ... Courts

Court Administration: Director of State Courts, Supreme Court, PO Box 1688, Madison, WI, 53701; 608-266-6828; http://wicourts.gov

Court Structure: The Circuit Court is the court of general jurisdiction. The Register in Probate maintains guardianship and mental health records, most of which are sealed but may be opened for cause with a court order. In some counties, the Register also maintains termination and adoption records; actual practices vary widely across the state.

Online Access Note: Wisconsin Circuit Court Access (WCCA) allows users to view Circuit Court case information on the Wisconsin court system website at http://wcca.wicourts.gov. Data is available from all counties (except only probate records are available from Portage). Searches can be conducted statewide or county-by-county. WCCA provides detailed information about circuit cases and for civil cases, the program displays judgment and judgment party information. WCCA also offers the ability to generate reports. Due to statutory requirements, WCCA users will not be able to view restricted cases. There are probate records for all counties. Appellate Courts and Supreme Court opinions are available from the main web page. Public access terminals are available at each court.

Probate records are available online at the http://wicourts.gov web page.

Milwaukee County

Circuit Court - Criminal Division – Criminal Records
www.county.milwaukee.gov/display/router.asp?docid=10507
Access criminal index free at http://wcca.wicourts.gov/index.xsl. Also, criminal case records on Milwaukee Municipal Court Case Information System database are free at www.court.ci.mil.wi.us/. Search by Case Number, by Citation Number, or by Name.

Ozaukee County

Circuit Court – Civil and Criminal Records
www.co.ozaukee.wi.us/ClerkCourts/default.htm
Civil court records free online at http://wcca.wicourts.gov/index.xsl. Access is also with the use of county "Remote Access". This data is for inquiries only and includes civil, family, and traffic courts. For info, contact the Technology Resources Dept. at 262-284-8309. Access criminal index free at http://wcca.wicourts.gov/index.xsl.

Portage County

Circuit Court (Branches 1, 2 & 3) – Civil and Criminal Records
www.co.portage.wi.us/
Internet access is upon approval. Request in writing to Data Processing Dept, 1462 Strong Ave, Stevens Point 54481. Explain purpose of record requests.

Statewide Access – Civil, Criminal and Probate

See the Online Access Note above for details.

County Level ... Recorders & Assessors

Recording Office Organization: 72 counties, 72 recording offices. The recording officers are the Register of Deeds and the Clerk of Court (state tax liens). The entire state is in the Central Time Zone (CST). Only federal tax liens on real estate are filed with the county Register of Deeds. State tax liens are filed with the Clerk of Court, and at the State Treasurer at the State Department of Revenue.

Online Note: A number of cities and a few counties offer online access to assessor and property records.

Ashland County   *Property, Assessor Records*
www.co.ashland.wi.us
Search property records free at www.ashlandcogiws.com/textsearch/index.htm.

Barron County   *Land, Assessor, Recorder, Real Estate, Deed, Lien Records*
www.co.barron.wi.us
Access to county land records is at www.gcssoftware.com/product/web_search.asp. Registration, $300.00 annual fee, username, password required; call Yvonne at the county treasurer's office, 715-537-6280. Also, recorder office data by subscription on either the Laredo system using subscription and fees or the Tapestry System using credit card, https://tapestry.fidlar.com/tapsearch.aspx; $3.99 search; $.50 per image.

Brown County   *Real Estate, Recording, Deed, Lien Records*
www.co.brown.wi.us/rod
Recorder office data by subscription on either the Laredo system using subscription and fees or the Tapestry System using credit card, https://tapestry.fidlar.com/tapsearch.aspx; $3.99 search; $.50 per image. Also, land records without name searching is at www.co.brown.wi.us/treasurer/landrecordssearch/entryform.asp. And land records can be downloaded from an ftp site; contact the Land Information office at 920-448-6295 to register and user information.

Buffalo County   *Land, Property Tax Records*
Access to county land records is free at www.gcssoftware.com/applications/search/index.asp?County=Buffalo.

Burnett County   *Property, Tax Assessor Records*
www.burnettcounty.com
Access to limited county property and assessment records is free at http://burnettims.homeip.net/. No name searching. For full data, an online subscription service is $100 per year.

Calumet County   *Assessor, Property Tax Records*
www.co.calumet.wi.us
Access to assessor property tax data is free at http://calum400.co.calumet.wi.us/nsccalo/nsclndrec.

Chippewa County   *Recording, Deed, Judgment, Real Estate Records*
www.co.chippewa.wi.us/Departments/RegisterDeeds
Search Register of Deeds data at https://landshark.co.chippewa.wi.us/eddie/, index search is free, but fees apply for images and copies.

Clark County   *Assessor, Property Records*
www.co.clark.wi.us
Search for assessor/property tax information on the county GIS-mapping site at www.co.clark.wi.us/Website/ClarkIMS/viewer.htm. Search by PIN or address.

Columbia County   *Property Tax, Land, Real Estate, Deed Records*
www.co.columbia.wi.us/ColumbiaCounty/
Access the county land records system free at http://lrs.co.columbia.wi.us/lrsweb/search.aspx. Also, search property info freely on the GIS- mapping site at http://lrs.co.columbia.wi.us/website/ColumbiaCo/ColumbiaCo.asp. Also, recorder office data by subscription on either the Laredo system using subscription and fees or the Tapestry System using credit card, https://tapestry.fidlar.com/tapsearch.aspx; $3.99 search; $.50 per image.

Crawford County *Recording, Deed, Judgment, Real Estate Records*
http://crawfordcounty-wi-us.org
Search Register of Deeds data at https://landshark.crawfordcounty-wi-us.org/eddie/, index search free, fees apply for images & copies.

Dane County *Assessor, Property Tax, Recording, Real Estate, Deed, Lien Records*
www.co.dane.wi.us/regdeeds/rdhome.htm
A fee-based system is at www.co.dane.wi.us/regdeeds/laredotapestry/accesstorealestate.htm. Also, access recording office land data at www.etitlesearch.com; registration required, fee based on usage. Also, City of Madison tax assessor data is at www.ci.madison.wi.us/assessor/property.html. Search Sun Prairie property at http://public.sun-prairie.com/proplisting/index.php. Also, search property info for Cross Plains, Mazomanie, Berry, Medina Towns at www.wendorffassessing.com/municipalities.htm. Also, Professional companies may register to use assessor/land record services at www.co.dane.wi.us and select "AccessDane" from the bottom of this home page.

Douglas County *Real Estate, Grantor/Grantee, Deed, Fed Lien, Plat Records*
www.douglascountywi.org
Access to the county Landshark system is at http://rdlandshark.douglascountywi.org/eddie/. Free registration is required.

Dunn County *Recording, Real Estate, Deed, Lien Records*
Recorder office data by subscription on either the Laredo system using subscription and fees or the Tapestry System using credit card, https://tapestry.fidlar.com/tapsearch.aspx; $3.99 search; $.50 per image.

Eau Claire County *Recording, Real Estate, Deed, Lien, Warrant, Most Wanted Records*
www.co.eau-claire.wi.us
Recorder office data by subscription on either the Laredo system using subscription and fees or the Tapestry System using credit card, https://tapestry.fidlar.com/tapsearch.aspx; $3.99 search; $.50 per image. Search the sheriff's most wanted list and warrants list at www.co.eau-claire.wi.us/sheriff/sheriff.asp.

Fond du Lac County *Property, Assessor, GIS Mapping Records*
www.co.fond-du-lac.wi.us
Access to parcel information is free through the GIS-mapping site at www.co.fond-du-lac.wi.us/Website/FondduLacIMS/viewer.htm. Click on search to search by address or parcel number. No name searching.

Forest County *Land, Assessor Records*
Access to county property and assessor data free is at www.gcssoftware.com/applications/search/index.asp?County=Forest

Grant County *Land, Assessor Records*
http://grantcounty.org
Access to county property and assessor data is at www.gcssoftware.com/product/web_search.asp. Registration, $200.00 annual fee, username, and password required; call John at the Tax Lister office, 608-723-2666.

Jefferson County *Grantor/Grantee, Treasurer, GIS-Mapping, Assessor Property Tax Records*
www.co.jefferson.wi.us
To order records oline using your credit card, click www.wrdaonline.org. Call 920-674-7254 for info and fee.

Kenosha County *Real Estate, Lien, Vital Statistic, Assessor Records*
www.kenosha.org
Access to recorder records requires a set-up fee is $500, plus $6.00 per hour usage fee. The system operates 24 hours daily; records date back to 5/1986. Federal tax liens and lending agency information is available. For further information, contact Joellyn Storz at 262-653-2511. Also, search the Kenosha City Assessor's property database for free at www.kenosha.org/departments/assessor/search.html. No name searching.

Kewaunee County *Grantor/Grantee, Deed, Tract & Image, GIS Mapping, Property Tax, Real Estate Records*
www.kewauneeco.org
Access to the Register of Deeds CherryLAN Indexing and Imaging System is available for a monthly subscription fee of $300. Escrow subscription with an initial $100 deposit are also available. Index begins 2/1992. Also, search property tax data free on the GIS mapping site at http://rmgis.ruekert-mielke.com/KewauneeCo/index.htm. Subscription required for full data. Search land/tax records free at www.gcssoftware.com/applications/search/index.asp?County=Kewaunee.

La Crosse County   *Land, Deed, Property Owner, Recording, Lien Records*
www.co.la-crosse.wi.us/Departments/departments.htm
Recorder office data by subscription on either the Laredo system using subscription and fees or the Tapestry System using credit card, https://tapestry.fidlar.com/tapsearch.aspx; $3.99 search; $.50 per image. Index back to 1992; images to 6/1992. Also, search for property owner and land information for free at www.co.la-crosse.wi.us/landrecordsportal/default.aspx.

Lafayette County   *Recording, Real Estate, Deed, Lien Records*
Recorder office data by subscription on either the Laredo system using subscription and fees or the Tapestry System using credit card, https://tapestry.fidlar.com/tapsearch.aspx; $3.99 search; $.50 per image.

Langlade County   *Property, GIS-mapping, Birth, Death Records*
http://co.langlade.wi.us
Access property data free at http://206.176.217.197/Website/PASystem/PA/viewer.htm no name searching. Access county birth index free at www.co.langlade.wi.us/Births/; search death index free at www.co.langlade.wi.us/Deaths/.

Lincoln County   *Land Records*
www.co.lincoln.wi.us
Access to county land records is free at www.lrs.co.lincoln.wi.us/apps/lrs/. No name searching.

Manitowoc County   *Assessor, Real Estate Records*
www.manitowoc-county.com
Records on the City of Manitowoc Assessor database are free at http://assessor.manitowoc.org/default.htm. No name searching. Access Two Rivers assessor data free at http://tworivers.patriotproperties.com/default.asp.

Marathon County   *Land Records*
www.co.marathon.wi.us
Access to county property records is free at www.co.marathon.wi.us/online/apps/lrs/index.asp. No name searching.

Marinette County   *Real Estate, Recording, Deed Records*
www.marinettecounty.com
Access to real estate index is free at http://landshark.marinettecounty.com/eddie/. Search index free but $2.00 fee to view document. Registration and escrow account required.

Milwaukee County   *Real Estate, Property Sale, Recorder, Deed, Lien Records*
www.milwaukee.gov
Property, assessment data & sales data on Milwaukee City (not county) Assessor database at www.city.milwaukee.gov/display/router.asp?docid=720. No name searching. Search Greendale, Brown Deer, Oak Creek at www.gcssoftware.com/product/web_search.asp. Also, search the City of Cudahy assessor property data for free at http://exch02.ci.cudahy.wi.us/Scripts/GVSWeb.dll/Search, and Wauwatosa property at www.wauwatosa.net/display/wspTosaAssessmentTemplate.asp. No name searching. Search Franklin assessor at www.ci.franklin.wi.us/dynamic/pagetemplate.cfm?template=assessmentSearch.cfm. Glendale assessor at http://ts.glendale-wi.org; West Allis at www.ci.west-allis.wi.us/assessor/property_search/address_search.aspx; no name search.

Oconto County   *Property, Assessor Records*
www.co.oconto.wi.us
Access to the county SOLO tax parcel search is free or by subscription at http://solo.co.oconto.wi.us/ocontoco/. The free service does not include name searching. Subscription fee for full data is $300 per calendar year. Phone 920-834-6800 for more information. Also, access to Registrar of Deeds available by subscription or escrow account at https://landshark.co.oconto.wi.us/eddie/. You may also purchase a document with a credit card.

Oneida County   *Property, Assessor, GIS Records*
www.co.oneida.wi.gov
Access to property tax data is available free at http://octax.co.oneida.wi.us/ONCTax/Taxrtr. Also, search land records by name on the GIS mapping site at http://ocgis.co.oneida.wi.us/oneida/index.htm.

Outagamie County
Real Estate, Recorder, Deed, Judgment, Assessor, Property Tax, GIS-Mapping Inmate, Offender Records
www.co.outagamie.wi.us
Access recorder records after registration and creation of escrow account at https://landshark.co.outagamie.wi.us/eddie/. Index searching is free but fee applies to print images- $2.00 1st page, $1.00 each add'l. Search assessor data free at www.co.outagamie.wi.us/applications/arcims/public/textsearch/index.htm no name searching. Sub required for full data. Search GIS-parcel data free at www.co.outagamie.wi.us/applications/arcims/public/html/default.htm, no name searching. Search inmate information free on private company website at www.vinelink.com/offender/searchNew.jsp?siteID=50002.

Ozaukee County
Recording, Real Estate, Grantor/Grantee, Vital Statistic, Property Tax, Tracts, Civil Court Records
www.co.ozaukee.wi.us
Access is by "Remote Access" requiring dial-up modem. This data is for inquiries only and includes civil, family, and traffic courts with Register of Deeds (back to 1960's) and Treasurer (back 11 years) property data. Software is supplied by the county. First month is free, then $50.00 per month subscription. For info, contact the Technology Resources Dept. at 262-284-8309. Also, recorder office data by subscription on either the Laredo system using subscription and fees or the Tapestry System using credit card, https://tapestry.fidlar.com/tapsearch.aspx; $3.99 search; $.50 per image.

Pepin County   *Land, Property Tax, Map Records*
www.co.pepin.wi.us
Access maps, land record/tax data at www.co.pepin.wi.us.

Pierce County   *Real Estate, Assessor, Property Tax, Recording, Deed, Lien Records*
www.co.pierce.wi.us
Access to county property data is free at www.co.pierce.wi.us/Disclaimer.htm. Click on Property Data Search. Also, recorder office data by subscription on either the Laredo system using subscription and fees or the Tapestry System using credit card, https://tapestry.fidlar.com/tapsearch.aspx; $3.99 search; $.50 per image. Visit www.co.pierce.wi.us/reg_of_deeds/Records.access.page.htm for more Tapestry info. Records go back to 1998.

Polk County   *Assessor, Land Records*
www.co.polk.wi.us
For assessor and land records free go to www.gcssoftware.com/applications/search/index.asp?County=Polk

Portage County   *Property Tax, Assessor, Recording, Land, Deed, Criminal Complaint Records*
www.co.portage.wi.us
Access to county records is free at www.co.portage.wi.us. Registration required; searching is free; fee for copies of images. Property tax data does not include Steven Point City.

Racine County   *Real Estate, Deed Records*
www.goracine.org
Real estate record access is via a dial-up system; email or call the Racine County Register of Deeds Office, 262-636-3208.

Richland County   *Property, Assessor, GIS Records*
Access property data free at www.rclrs.net.

Rock County   *Real Estate, Deed, Assessor, Property Tax Records*
www.co.rock.wi.us/Dept/RegisterDeeds/ROD.htm
Real estate record access is via a dial-up system; email or call the Rock County Register of Deeds Office, 608-757-5650. Records on the City of Janesville Assessor database are free at www.ci.janesville.wi.us/Scripts2/gvsweb.dll/search. No name searching. Also, search Evansville property assessor records for free at www.wendorffassessing.com/Evansville%20options.htm. No name searching.

Rusk County   *Property, Assessor Records*
www.ruskcounty.org/services/deeds.asp
Access assessor land data free at www.ruskcogiws.com/textsearch/index.htm.

St. Croix County   *Recording, Real Estate, Deed, Lien Records*
www.co.saint-croix.wi.us
Recorder office data by subscription on either the Laredo system using subscription and fees or the Tapestry System using credit card, https://tapestry.fidlar.com/tapsearch.aspx; $3.99 search; $.50 per image.

Sauk County *Property, Assessor Records*
www.co.sauk.wi.us/dept/regodeed/index.html
Access to recorder's land records is available free or by subscription for full-time access at http://landshark.co.sauk.wi.us/eddie/. Registration required; setup account thru Recorder office. Occasional users search free, but view documents for $2 first page, $1 each add'l. Search Village of Spring Green property data free at www.wendorffassessing.com/Spring%20Green%20options.htm. No name searching. Also, search Village of Plain property data at www.wendorffassessing.com/Plain%20options.htm.

Sawyer County *Recording, Real Estate, Deed, Lien Records*
http://sawyercountygov.org
Recorder office data by subscription on either the Laredo system using subscription and fees or the Tapestry System using credit card, https://tapestry.fidlar.com/tapsearch.aspx; $3.99 search; $.50 per image.

Sheboygan County *Recording, Deed, Real Estate, Tax Lien Records*
Recorder office data by subscription on either the Laredo system using subscription and fees or the Tapestry System using credit card, https://tapestry.fidlar.com/tapsearch.aspx; $3.99 search; $.50 per image. Index back to 1/1992; images to 5/1994.

Taylor County *Real Estate - 1995 forward Records*
www.co.taylor.wi.us/departments/registerofdeeds/rodmain.htm
Found at https://landshark.co.taylor.wi.us/eddie/login.jsp; username and password required. Records go back to 1998. Index search is free; images are $2.00 1st page, $1.00 each add'l.

Trempealeau County *Property, Assessor Records*
www.tremplocounty.com
Access to the county assessor's database is free at www.tremplocounty.com/Search/Search.asp.

Walworth County *Property Tax, Recording, Grantor/Grantee, Deed Records*
www.co.walworth.wi.us
Search the Register of Deeds index for free on the county e-government web page at www.co.walworth.wi.us. Click on "Public Records." Online records go as far back as 1976. Also, search the treasurer's tax roll list under "Tax Roll Documents" on the county e-government web page. Also search the Village of Walworth property data for free at www.wendorffassessing.com/Walworth%20options.htm.

Waukesha County *Property, Assessor, Recording, Deed, Lien, Marriage, UCC, Personal Property Records*
www.waukeshacounty.gov/cm/Business%20Units/Register%20of%20Deeds/
Access the recorder database free at http://dwprd.waukeshacounty.gov/applications/production/ROD_TRACT_DOCUMENTS/. Also, for property assessment go to www.wauwatosa.net/display/wspTosaAssessmentTemplate.asp. Also, search county tax listing at http://dwprd.waukeshacounty.gov/applications/production/ROD_TAX_LISTING/. No name searching at either of these sites. Also search assessor property data at www.ci.waukesha.wi.us/Parcel/DataInquiry1.jsp. No name search. Also, search City of Waukesha assessor property database or sales lists for free at www.ci.waukesha.wi.us/Assessor/propertySalesInformation.html. Search City personal property at www.ci.waukesha.wi.us/Assessor/Documents/ppAssessmentRoll.txt

Waupaca County *Register of Deed, Land, Property Records*
www.co.waupaca.wi.us
Access to the Register of Deeds data requires subscription, username and password. Annual fee is $125.00. For info, call 715-258-6235. Register of Deeds also has a second subscription access website for land records; visit https://public1.co.waupaca.wi.us/eddie/registration.jsp. Records go back to 1982; monthly or daily subscriptions are available. Also, access land information office data free at http://public1.co.waupaca.wi.us/gisaccess/access.asp?access=1. A fee and registration is required for name searching.

Waushara County *Property, Assessor Records*
www.co.waushara.wi.us
Search property data free on the county land information system at www.co.waushara.wi.us/Website/WausharaPA/viewer.htm.

Winnebago County *Assessor, Real Estate, Recording, Deed, Lien Records*
www.co.winnebago.wi.us
Recorder office data by subscription on either the Laredo system using subscription and fees or the Tapestry System using credit card, https://tapestry.fidlar.com/tapsearch.aspx; $3.99 search; $.50 per image. Also, property records on the City of Oshkosh assessor database are free at www.ci.oshkosh.wi.us/assessor/ProcessSearch.asp?cmd=NewSearch. Also, City of Neenah property data is at

www.ci.neenah.wi.us/PropInfo/PropertyAssessmentSearch.asp but no name searching. Also, records on the City of Menasha Tax Roll Information database are free at www.cityofmenasha-wi.gov/content/departments/finance/(3)tax_roll_information.php.

Wood County *Recording, Real Estate, Deed, Lien Records*

www.co.wood.wi.us

Recorder office data by subscription on either the Laredo system using subscription and fees or the Tapestry System using credit card, https://tapestry.fidlar.com/tapsearch.aspx; $3.99 search; $.50 per image.

Federal Courts in Wisconsin...

Standards for Federal Courts: The universal PACER sign-up number is 800-676-6856. Find PACER and the Party/Case Index on the Web at http://pacer.psc.uscourts.gov. PACER dial-up access is $.60 per minute. Also, courts offering internet access via PACER, Web-PACER or the new CM-ECF charge $.08 per page fee ($.07 per page if record is pre-2005 or unless noted as free).

US District Court -- Eastern District of Wisconsin

www.wied.uscourts.gov

PACER: Case records are available back to 1991. Records are purged never. New records are available online after 1 day. **PACER Online Access:** ECF replaces PACER. **Electronic Filing:** CM/ECF data at https://ecf.wied.uscourts.gov.
Milwaukee Division counties: Brown, Calumet, Dodge, Door, Florence, Fond du Lac, Forest, Green Lake, Kenosha, Kewaunee, Langlade, Manitowoc, Marinette, Marquette, Menominee, Milwaukee, Oconto, Outagamie, Ozaukee, Racine, Shawano, Sheboygan, Walworth, Washington, Waupaca, Waukesha, Waushara, Winnebago.

US Bankruptcy Court -- Eastern District of Wisconsin

www.wieb.uscourts.gov

PACER: Case records are available back to 1991. Records are purged after case is closed. New records are available online after 1 day. **PACER Online Access:** PACER online at http://pacer.wieb.uscourts.gov. **Electronic Filing:** CM/ECF data at https://ecf.wieb.uscourts.gov. **Opinions:** Limited opinions. View court opinions at www.wieb.uscourts.gov/JUDCAL4i/judpol4i_index.htm. **Other Online Access:** Calendars at www.wieb.uscourts.gov/judcal4i/judcal4i_calendars.htm. **Phone access:** Voice Case Information System, call 877-781-7277, 414-297-3582
Milwaukee Division counties: Brown, Calumet, Dodge, Door, Florence, Fond du Lac, Forest, Green Lake, Kenosha, Kewaunee, Langlade, Manitowoc, Marinette, Marquette, Menominee, Milwaukee, Oconto, Outagamie, Ozaukee, Racine, Shawano, Sheboygan, Walworth, Washington, Waukesha, Waupaca, Waushara, Winnebago.

US District Court -- Western District of Wisconsin

www.wiwd.uscourts.gov

PACER: Case records are available back to 1990. Records are purged never. New records are available online after 1 day. **PACER Online Access:** PACER online at http://pacer.wiwd.uscourts.gov. Document images available. **Electronic Filing:** CM/ECF data at (Currently in the process of implementing CM-ECF.). **Opinions:** View court opinions at www.wiwd.uscourts.gov/opinsearch/index.html. **Other Online Access:** Weekly court calendars free at www.wiwd.uscourts.gov/calendar/calfrm.html .
Madison Division counties: Adams, Ashland, Barron, Bayfield, Buffalo, Burnett, Chippewa, Clark, Columbia, Crawford, Dane, Douglas, Dunn, Eau Claire, Grant, Green, Iowa, Iron, Jackson, Jefferson, Juneau, La Crosse, Lafayette, Lincoln, Marathon, Monroe, Oneida, Pepin, Pierce, Polk, Portage, Price, Richland, Rock, Rusk, Sauk, Sawyer, St. Croix, Taylor, Trempealeau, Vernon, Vilas, Washburn, Wood.

US Bankruptcy Court -- Western District of Wisconsin

www.wiw.uscourts.gov/bankruptcy

PACER: Case records are available back to 4/1991. New records are available online after 1 day. **PACER Online Access:** ECF Replaces PACER. **Electronic Filing:** Document images available. CM/ECF data at https://ecf.wiwb.uscourts.gov. **Opinions:** View court opinions at www.wiw.uscourts.gov/bankruptcy/decision_home.htm. **Phone access:** Voice Case Information System, call 800-743-8247, 608-264-5035
Madison Division counties: Adams, Columbia, Crawford, Dane, Grant, Green, Iowa, Jefferson, Lafayette, Richland, Rock, Sauk.

Wyoming

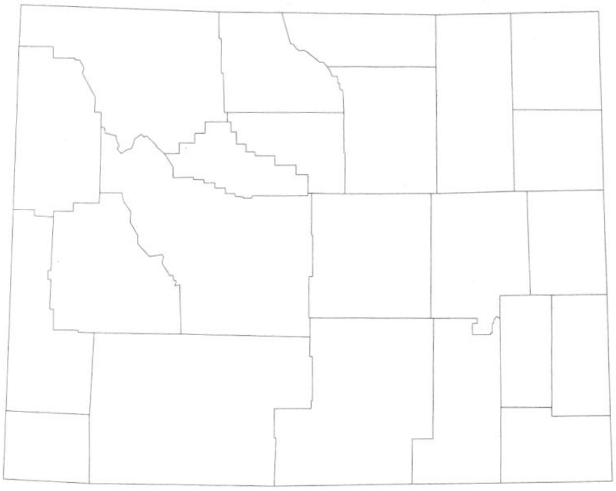

Capital: Cheyene
            Laramie County
Time Zone: MST
Population: 506,529
# of Counties: 23

Quick Links

Website: http://wyoming.gov/
Governor: http://wyoming.gov/governor/governor_home.asp
Attorney General: http://attorneygeneral.state.wy.us
State Archives: http://wyoarchives.state.wy.us/index.htm
State Statutes and Codes: http://legisweb.state.wy.us/statutes/statutes.htm
Legislative Bill Search: http://legisweb.state.wy.us/2005/billsInfo.htm
Unclaimed Funds: http://treasurer.state.wy.us/search.asp

State Level ... Major Agencies

Statewide Court Records

Court Administrator, Supreme Court Bldg, 2301 Capitol Ave, Cheyenne, WY 82002; 307-777-7583, Fax-307-777-3447, 8AM-5PM. www.courts.state.wy.us
Online search: Supreme Court opinions available at web, listed by date. Wyoming's statewide case management system is for internal use only. Planning is underway for a new case management system that will ultimately allow public access.

Sexual Offender Registry

Division of Criminal Investigation, ATTN: WSOR, 316 W 22nd St, Cheyenne, WY 82002-0001; 307-777-7809, Fax-307-777-7252. http://attorneygeneral.state.wy.us/dci/index.html
Online search: The Internet is the search method offered by this agency to the public. Search is by county. The website contains offenders found to have a high risk of re-offense. Data includes name, address, date and place of birth, date and place of conviction, crime for which convicted, photograph and physical description.

Incarceration Records

Wyoming Department of Corrections, 700 W. 21st Street,, Cheyenne, WY 82002; 307-777-7405, Fax-307-777-7479, 8AM-5PM. http://doc.state.wy.us/corrections.asp
Online search: No searching online direct from this agency; a private company provides access to DOC records at www.vinelink.com/index.jsp. However, one may send requests to this agency via email from the web page.

Corporation, Limited Liability Company, Limited Partnership, Fictitious Name, Trademarks/Servicemarks

Corporations Division, Attn: Records, 200 W 24th Street, Rm 110, Cheyenne, WY 82002; 307-777-7311, Fax-307-777-5339, 8-5PM. http://soswy.state.wy.us
Online search: Information is available through the Internet site listed above. You can search by corporate name or even download the whole file. Also, they have several pages of excellent searching tips.

Uniform Commercial Code, Federal Tax Liens

Secretary of State, UCC Division - Records, 200 W 24th St, #110, Cheyenne, WY 82002-0020; 307-777-5372, Fax-307-777-5988. http://soswy.state.wy.us/uniform/uniform.htm

Online search: The online filing system permits unlimited record searching. There is a $150 annual fee, with no additional fees charged for searches. Subscribers are entitled to do filings at a 50% discount. Visit the webpage. **Other options:** Lists of filings on CD or diskette are available for purchase. Download the database for $2,000 per year.

Driver License Information, Driver Records

Wyoming Department of Transportation, Driver Services, 5300 Bishop Blvd, Cheyenne, WY 82009-3340; 307-777-4800, Fax-307-777-4773, 8AM-5PM.   www.dot.state.wy.us

Online search: This method is available using FTP and RJE technology. Only approved vendors and permissible users are supported. Write or call Mark Briggs at the above address for details. **Other options:** Cartridge tape retrieval is available at $3.00 per record. The entire driver license file may be purchased for $2,500. Write or call 307-777-3864 for details.

State Level ... Occupational Licensing

Attorney	www.wyomingbar.org/directory/index.html
Bank	http://audit.state.wy.us/banking/banking/bankingregulatedentities.htm
Check Casher	http://audit.state.wy.us/banking/uccc/uccclicensees.htm
Collection Agency	http://audit.state.wy.us/banking/cab/cablicensees.htm
Engineer	www.wrds.uwyo.edu/wrds/borpe/roster/roster.html
Feed/Fertilizer	www.kellysolutions.com/wy/
Funeral Pre-Need Agent	http://insurance.state.wy.us/search/search.asp
Geologist	http://wbpgweb.uwyo.edu/roster_search.asp
Guide, Outdoor	http://outfitte.state.wy.us/directory.html
Insurance Claims Adjuster	http://insurance.state.wy.us/search/search.asp
Insurance Consultant/Producer/Svc Rep	http://insurance.state.wy.us/search/search.asp
Lender, Supervised	http://audit.state.wy.us/banking/uccc/uccclicensees.htm
Lobbyist	http://soswy.state.wy.us/election/lob-list.htm
Medical Doctor	http://wyomedboard.state.wy.us/roster.asp
Motor Club Agent	http://insurance.state.wy.us/search/search.asp
Optometrist	www.arbo.org/index.php?action=findanoptometrist
Outfitter	http://outfitte.state.wy.us/directory.html
Pawnbroker	http://audit.state.wy.us/banking/uccc/uccclicensees.htm
Pharmacist/Pharmacy Technician	http://pharmacyboard.state.wy.us/search.asp
Physical Therapist	Under construction; check http://plboards.state.wy.us/PTherapy/
Physician Assistant	http://wyomedboard.state.wy.us/PARoster.asp
Psychologist	http://plboards.state.wy.us/psychology/
Public Accountant-CPA, Individ'l/Firm	http://cpaboard.state.wy.us/database.aspx
Real Estate Appraiser	www.asc.gov/content/category1/appr_by_state.asp
Rent-to-own Company	http://audit.state.wy.us/banking/uccc/uccclicensees.htm
Sales Finance Company	http://audit.state.wy.us/banking/uccc/uccclicensees.htm
Savings & Loan Association	http://audit.state.wy.us/banking/banking/bankingregulatedentities.htm
Surplus Line Broker, Resident	http://insurance.state.wy.us/search/search.asp
Surveyor, Land	www.wrds.uwyo.edu/wrds/borpe/roster/roster.html
Trust Company	http://audit.state.wy.us/banking/banking/bankingregulatedentities.htm
Veterinarian	Under construction; check http://plboards.state.wy.us/VetBoard/

County Level ... Courts

Court Administration: Court Administrator, 2301 Capitol Av, Supreme Court Bldg, Cheyenne, WY, 82002; 307-777-7583; www.courts.state.wy.us

Court Structure: Each county has a District Court of "higher jurisdiction" and a Circuit Court. Prior to 2003, for their "lower jurisdiction" court some counties had Circuit Courts and others had Justice Courts. Effective January 1, 2003 all Justice Courts became Circuit Courts and follow Circuit Court rules.

Circuit Courts handle civil claims up to $7,000 while the former Justice Courts handle civil claims up to $3,000. The District Courts take cases over the applicable limit in each county. Three counties have two

Circuit Courts each: Fremont, Park, and Sweetwater. Cases may be filed in either of the two court offices in those counties, and records requests are referred between the two courts. Municipal courts operate in all incorporated cities and towns; their jurisdiction covers all ordinance violations and has no civil jurisdiction. The Municipal Court judge may assess penalties of up to $750 and/or six months in jail.

Probate is handled by the District Court.

County Courts Online Access Note: Wyoming's statewide case management system is for internal use only. Planning is underway for a new case management system that will ultimately allow public access. Supreme Court opinions are listed by date at www.courts.state.wy.us/slip_opinions.htm.

Teton County
9th Judicial District Court   *Civil and Criminal Records*
Email record search requests are accepted at clerk-of-district-court@tetonwyo.org.

County Level ... Recorders & Assessors

Recording Office Organization: 23 counties, 23 recording offices. The recording officer is the County Clerk. Montana is in the Mountain Time Zone (MST). Federal tax liens on personal property of businesses are filed with the Secretary of State. Other federal and all state tax liens are filed with the County Clerk.

Online Access Note: Only Teton County offers access to the Clerk's database of recorded documents.

Campbell County   *Assessor, Property Records*
http://ccg.co.campbell.wy.us
Search property records at http://ccg.co.campbell.wy.us/assessor/html/property_record_search.html.

Park County   *Warrants, Most Wanted, Sex Offender Records*
www.parkcounty.us/countyclerk.htm
Search the sheriff's lists free at www.cityofcody.com/cpd/.

Teton County   *Real Estate, Lien, Recording Records*
http://www2.tetonwyo.org/clerk/
Access to the Clerk's database of scanned images is free at http://www2.tetonwyo.org/clerk/query/. Search for complete documents back to 7/1996; partial documents back to 4/1991.

Federal Courts in Wyoming...

Standards for Federal Courts: The universal PACER sign-up number is 800-676-6856. Find PACER and the Party/Case Index on the Web at http://pacer.psc.uscourts.gov. PACER dial-up access is $.60 per minute. Also, courts offering internet access via PACER, Web-PACER or the new CM-ECF charge $.08 per page fee ($.07 per page if record is pre-2005 or unless noted as free).

US District Court -- District of Wyoming
http://www.ck10.uscourts.gov/wyoming/district/index.html
PACER: Case records are available back to 1988. Records are purged once yearly. New records are available online after 1 day.
PACER Online Access: ECF replaces PACER.. **Electronic Filing:** CM/ECF data at https://ecf.wyd.uscourts.gov.
Cheyenne Division counties: All counties in Wyoming. Some criminal records are held in Casper but all are available electronically at Cheyenne..

US Bankruptcy Court -- District of Wyoming
www.wyb.uscourts.gov
PACER: Case records are available back one year. Records are purged annually. New records are available online after 1 day.
PACER Internet Access: PACER is available online at http://pacer.wyb.uscourts.gov. Document images available.
Electronic Filing: Electronic filing information is available online at https://ecf.wyb.uscourts.gov.
Opinions Online: Court opinions are available online at http://opinions.wyb.uscourts.gov/.
Cheyenne Division counties: All counties in Wyoming. The Casper Bankruptcy Court records are located here

Guam

Sex Offenders Registry
www.sor.guamjustice.net

Vital Statistics
http://ns.gov.gu/genealogy/guam-a.htm

Federal Courts in Guam...

US District and Bankruptcy Court -- District of Guam

Home Page: www.gud.uscourts.gov
PACER: Case records are available back to 2002. Records are never purged. New records are available online after .
PACER Internet Access: PACER is available online at https://pacer.login.uscourts.gov/cgi-bin/login.pl?court_id=gudc.
Other Online Access: Does not participate in the US Party case index.
Division counties: Guam. Address Bankruptcy requests to the Guam Bankruptcy Division.

Puerto Rico

Corporations
www.estado.gobierno.pr/CorporacionesOnLine.asp

Overview of Online Services
www.serviciosenlinea.gobierno.pr/CitizenPortal/Introduccion.aspx

Tribunal Court Records
www.tribunalpr.org/tribunalespr/general/cons00alt.asp

Yellow Pages - Telephone Book
www.paginasamarillas.com/pagamanet/puertoRico/home.aspx

White Pages - Telephone Book
www.paginasamarillas.com/pagamanet/paginasblancas/home.aspx?pi=0&ps=*&es=*&cs=*

Federal Courts in Puerto Rico...

US District Court -- District of Puerto Rico

Home Page: www.prd.uscourts.gov
PACER: Toll-free access phone: 800-517-2441. Local access phone: 787-766-5774. Records are never purged. New records are available online after cinco days.   **PACER Internet Access:** PACER is available online at http://pacer.prd.uscourts.gov.
Other Online Access: Participates in the US Party Case Index.   **Division counties:** All counties.

US Bankruptcy Court -- District of Puerto Rico

Home Page: www.prb.uscourts.gov/
PACER: Toll-free access phone: 800-792-8338. Local access phone: 787-977-6140. New records are available online after cinco days.   **PACER Internet Access:** https://pacer.login.uscourts.gov/cgi-bin/login.pl?court_id=prbk. Also, document images are available on the WebPacer online system. **Division counties:** All counties.

Section III

Vendor Information Index

The Information Index is designed to direct you to a public record vendor specializing in an information category you need.

Why These Vendors Appear in the Book

Obviously, there are many more public record vendors than the 160+ firms appearing in this book. The reason these particular companies were chosen is because they provide either a **Proprietary Database** or offer a non-intervention **Gateway**. We call these vendors "**Distributor**s."

Distributors are automated public record firms who combine public sources of bulk data and/or online access to develop their own database product(s). **Primary Distributors** include companies that collect or buy public record information from its original source and reformat the information in some useful way. They tend to focus on one or a limited number of types of information, although a few firms have branched into multiple information categories.

Gateways are companies that either compile data from or provide an automated gateway to Primary Distributors. Gateways thus provide "one-stop shopping" for multiple geographic areas and/or categories of information. A gateway company serves as a middleman for data, allowing you to link directly to the information through them - as one electronic transaction.

Companies can be both Primary Distributors and Gateways. For example, a number of online database companies are both primary distributors of corporate information and also gateways to real estate information from other Primary Distributors.

There are plenty of excellent record vendors not listed in this book who most likely use these companies or government agencies as their primary source. We call these companies "**Search Firms**." For information about 1500 vendors of all categories, go to www.brbpub.com/pubrecsites_ven.asp.

Record Information Categories

This index consists of 23 Information Categories. The vendors are listed alphabetically within each category. Each listing includes geographic coverage area and the evndor's web address. Note that CD = Canada. Itl = International.

The information categories are listed below.

Addresses/Telephone Numbers	Litigation/Judgments/Tax Liens
Aviation	Military Svc
Bankruptcy	Patents
Corporate/Trade Name Data	Real Estate/Assessor
Credit Information	SEC/Other Financial
Criminal Information	Tenant History
Driver and/or Vehicle	Trademarks
Education/Employment	Uniform Commercial Code
Environmental	Vessels
Foreign Country Information	Vital Records
Genealogical Information	Voter Registration
Licenses/Registrations/Permits	Workers Compensation

Address/Telephone Numbers

Address/Phone Number Records Companies	Website	Region
555-1212.com	www.555-1212.com/mindex.jsp	US
Accurint	www.accurint.com	US
Alacra	www.alacra.com	US, FR, GB, CD, Itl
American Business Information	www.infousa.com	US
American City Business Leads	www.bizjournals.com	AL, AZ, CA, CO, DC, FL, GA, HI, KS, KY, MA, MD, MI, MN, NC, NM, NY, OH, OR, PA, TN, TX, WA, WI
Ameridex Information Systems	www.ameridex.com	US
ARISTOTLE International	www.aristotle.com/page.asp	US
Avantex Inc	www.avantext.com	US
Cambridge Statistical Research Associates	www.csrainc.com	US
ChoicePoint - Public Records Group	www.choicepointonline.com	US
ChoicePoint Inc	www.choicepointinc.com	US
Data-Trac.com, USCrimsearch.com	www.data-trac.com	US
DCS Information Systems	www.dcs-amerifind.com	US
Dun & Bradstreet	www.dnb.com/us	US
Equifax Credit Services	www.equifax.com	US
Experian Online	www.experian.com	US
First American Real Estate Solutions	www.firstamres.com/jsp/index.jsp	US
Hoovers Inc	www.hoovers.com/free/	US
InsightAmerica	www.insightamerica.com	US
Intelius Intelifinder	http://find.intelius.com/search-name.php	US
IQ Data Systems	www.iqdata.com	US
KnowX	www.knowx.com	US
Kompass USA Inc	www.kompass-intl.com	US, Itl
LocatePlus.com Inc	https://www.locateplus.com/welcome.asp	US
Merlin Information Services	www.merlindata.com	US
Motznik Information Services	www.motznik.com	AK
National Credit Information Network NCI	www.wdia.com/home-entrypage.htm	US
Navigator Research Group	https://www.irb-online.com	US
Northwest Location Services	www.nwlocation.com	WA
OPENonline	www.openonline.com	US
Pallorium Inc	www.pallorium.com	US, PR
Plat System Services Inc	www.platsystems.com	MN
Public Record Research System	www.brbpub.com	US
Querydata.com	www.querydata.com	FL
Residentialdatabase.com	www.residentialdatabase.com	FL
Search Company of North Dakota LLC	www.searchcompanynd.com	ND
Skipease	www.skipease.com	US
Superior Information Services LLC	www.soplus.com/application/publicrxwf	US
Tenstar Business Services Group	www.tenstarcorporation.com	LA, MS
U.S. Information Search	www.usinformationsearch.com	US
US SEARCH.com	www.ussearch.com/consumer/index.jsp	US
USADATA	www.usadata.com	US
Webstigate	www.webstigate.com	US
Westlaw Public Records	www.westlaw.com	US

Aviation

Aviation Public Records Companies	Website	Region
Accurint	www.accurint.com	US
Accu-Source Inc.	www.accu-source.com	US
Avantex Inc	www.avantext.com	US
IQ Data Systems	www.iqdata.com	US
KnowX	www.knowx.com	US
Landings.com	www.landings.com	US
LocatePlus.com Inc	https://www.locateplus.com/welcome.asp	US
Merlin Information Services	www.merlindata.com	US
Navigator Research Group	https://www.irb-online.com	US
OPENonline	www.openonline.com	US
Pallorium Inc	www.pallorium.com	US
Querydata.com	www.querydata.com	US
UCC Direct Services	www.uccdirectservices.com	US
US SEARCH.com	www.ussearch.com/consumer/index.jsp	US
Westlaw Public Records	www.westlaw.com	US

Bankruptcy

Bankruptcy Public RecordsCompanies	Website	Region
Accurint	www.accurint.com	US
Accu-Source Inc.	www.accu-source.com	AK, AR, AZ, CA, CO, FL, GA, HI, IA, ID, IL, IN, KS, KY, LA, MN, MO, NC, ND, NE, NM, NV, OK, OH, OR, SC, SD, TN, TX, UT,WA, WI,WY
American City Business Leads	www.bizjournals.com	AL,AZ,CA,CO,DC,FL,GA,HI, KS, KY, MA, MD, MI,MN,NC,NM,NY,OH,OR,PA,TN,TX,WA,WI
Banko	www.banko.com	US
CaseClerk.com	www.caseclerk.com/search/default.htm	TN, US
CCH Washington Service Bureau	www.wsb.com	US
ChoicePoint - Public Records Group	www.choicepointonline.com	US
Diligenz Inc	www.diligenz.com	US
Dun & Bradstreet	www.dnb.com/us	US
Equifax Credit Services	www.equifax.com	US
Experian Online	www.experian.com	US
InsightAmerica	www.insightamerica.com	US
IQ Data Systems	www.iqdata.com	US
KnowX	www.knowx.com	US
LEXISNEXIS CourtLink	www.lexisnexis.com/courtlink/online/	US
Merlin Information Services	www.merlindata.com	US
Motznik Information Services	www.motznik.com	AK
OPENonline	www.openonline.com	US
Querydata.com	www.querydata.com	US, FL
Record Information Services Inc	www.public-record.com	IL
Search Company of North Dakota LLC	www.searchcompanynd.com	ND
Superior Information Services LLC	www.soplus.com/application/publicrxwf	CT, DC, DE, MD, MA, ME, NC, NH, NJ, NY, PA, RI, VA, VT
Tenstar Business Services Group	www.tenstarcorporation.com	LA, MS
UCC Direct Services	www.uccdirectservices.com	US

Bankruptcy Public RecordsCompanies	Website	Region
US SEARCH.com	www.ussearch.com/consumer/index.jsp	US
Virtual Docket LLC	www.virtualdocket.com	DE
Westlaw Public Records	www.westlaw.com	US

Corporate/Trade Name Data

Corporate/Trade Name Public Records Companies	Website	Region
Accurint	www.accurint.com	US
Accutrend Data Corporation	www.accutrend.com	US
Alacra	www.alacra.com	US, FR, GB, CD, Itl
American City Business Leads	www.bizjournals.com	AL, AZ, CA, CO, DC, FL, GA, HI, KS, KY, MA, MD, MI, MN, NC, NM, NY, OH, OR, PA, TN, TX, WA, WI
Attorneys Title Insurance Fund	www.thefund.com/portal/	FL
Background Information Services	www.bisi.com	CO
Better Business Bureau	www.bbb.org	US
ChoicePoint Public Records Group	www.choicepointonline.com	US
Derwent Information	www.derwent.com	US
Dialog	www.dialog.com	US
Diligenz Inc	www.diligenz.com	US
Dun & Bradstreet	www.dnb.com/us	US
Experian Online	www.experian.com	US
GoverNet	www.governet.net/home/index.cfm	NV
GuideStar	www.guidestar.org	US
Hoovers Inc	www.hoovers.com/free/	US
Household Drivers Reports Inc	www.hdr.com	TX
Idealogic	www.idealogic.com	CD
InsightAmerica	www.insightamerica.com	US
IQ Data Systems	www.iqdata.com	AK,CO,CT,FL,IN,IA,ME,MD,MA,MI,MN,MS,MO,MT, NE,NH,NC,ND,OH,OK,SC,SD,TN,UT,VA,DC,WV,WI
KnowX	www.knowx.com	US
Kompass USA Inc	www.kompass-intl.com	US, Itl
LEXISNEXIS	www.lexisnexis.com	US
LocatePlus.com Inc	https://www.locateplus.com/welcome.asp	AL,AK,AZ,AR,CA,CO,CT,FL,GA,ID,IA,KS,KY,LA, ME,MD,MA,MI,MN,MS,MO,NE,NV,NM,NY,NC,ND, OH,OK,OR,PA,RI,SC,SD,TN,VT,VA,WA,WI,WY
MegaCriminal Database	www.megacriminal.com	CA
Merlin Information Services	www.merlindata.com	US
Motznik Information Services	www.motznik.com	AK
Navigator Research Group	https://www.irb-online.com	US
Northwest Location Services	www.nwlocation.com	CA
OPENonline	www.openonline.com	US
Oso Grande Technologies Inc	www.osogrande.com	NM
Pallorium Inc	www.pallorium.com	US, PR
Querydata.com	www.querydata.com	FL
Residentialdatabase.com	www.residentialdatabase.com	FL, US
SEAFAX Inc	www.seafax.com	US
Superior Information Services LLC	www.soplus.com/application/publicrxwf	NY, PA

Corporate/Trade Name Public Records Companies	Website	Region
Tenstar Business Services Group	www.tenstarcorporation.com	LA, MS
Thomson & Thomson	www.thomson-thomson.com/do/pid/1	US
UCC Direct Services	www.uccdirectservices.com	US
US Corporate Services	www.uscorpserv.com	MN
US SEARCH.com	www.ussearch.com/consumer/index.jsp	US
USADATA	www.usadata.com	US
West Group	http://west.thomson.com	US
Westlaw Public Records	www.westlaw.com	US

Credit Information

Credit Information Companies	Website	Region
American Business Information	www.infousa.com	US
Dun & Bradstreet	www.dnb.com/us	US
Equifax Credit Services	www.equifax.com	US
Experian Credit Services	www.experian.com	US
Fidelifacts	www.fidelifacts.com	US
Merchants Association - MAF	www.mafscreening.com	FL
National Credit Information Network NCI	www.wdia.com/home-entrypage.htm	US
Owens OnLine Inc	www.owens.com	Intl
Trans Union - Credit Services	www.transunion.com/index.jsp	US

Criminal Information

Criminal Information Companies	Website	Region
Alacourt.com	www.alacourt.com	AL
Appriss Inc/VineLink	www.appriss.com/VINE.html	AR, AZ, CA, FL, GA, ID, IL, KY, LA, MA, MD, MN, MO, MT, NC, NE, OR, RI, TX, VA, WI, WV
Background Information Services Inc	www.bisi.com	CO, OK
backgroundchecks.com	http://www1.backgroundchecks.com	AK,AL,AR,AZ,CO,CT,DC,DE,FL,GA,IA,ID,IL, IN,KS,KY,LA,MD,ME,MI,MN,MO,MS,MT,NC, ND,NE,NH,NJ,NM,NY,OH,OK,OR,PA,RI,SC, TN,TX,UT,VA,WA,WI,WV,WY
CaseClerk.com	www.caseclerk.com/search/default.htm	TN
ChoicePoint Inc	www.choicepointinc.com	US
Circuit Court Express	www.swcg-inc.com/products/circuit_express.html	WV
CoCourts.com	www.cocourts.com	CO
Confi-Chek	www.confi-chek.com	CA
Court PC of Connecticut	http://courtpcofct.com	CT
CourtSearch.com	www.courtsearch.com	NC
Criminal Information Services Inc	www.criminalinfo.com	AK,AL,AR,AZ,CO,CT,DC,DE,FL,GA,IA,ID,IL, IN,KS,KY,LA,MD,ME,MI,MN,MO,MS,MT,NC, ND,NE,NH,NJ,NM,NY,OH,OK,OR,PA,RI,SC, TN,TX,UT,VA,WA,WI,WV,WY
Data-Trac.com, USCrimsearch.com	www.data-trac.com	NY
DCS Information Systems	www.dcs-amerifind.com	US
Doxpop	www.doxpop.com/prod/welcome.jsp	IN
Household Drivers Reports Inc	www.hdr.com	TX

Criminal Information Companies	Website	Region
iDocket.com	www.idocket.com	TX
InsightAmerica	www.insightamerica.com	CO
IntelliCorp Records Inc	https://www.intellicorp.net/Default.aspx	IN, IL IA, MN, OH
IQ Data Systems	www.iqdata.com	AL,AK,AZ,CA,CO,CT,DC,DE,FL,GA,HI,IA,IN, IL,KS,KY,MD,MA,MI,MN,MO,MT,NV,NH,NJ, NM,NC,OH,OR,PA,PR,RI,SC,TN,TX,UT,VA, VT,WA,WV,WI
Judici	www.judici.com	IL
MegaCriminal Database	www.megacriminal.com	CA,AR,AZ,FL,IA,IL,IN,KS,KY,MI,NC,NE,NV,NY, OH,OK,PA,VT
Merchants Association - MAF	www.mafscreening.com	FL
Motznik Information Services	www.motznik.com	AK
National Background Data	www.nationalbackgrounddata.com	US
OPENonline	www.openonline.com	AZ, AR, CT, FL, GA, ID, IL, IN, KY, ME, MI, MN, MS, MO, NE, NJ, NY, NC, OH, OK, OR, SC, TN, TX, UT, WA
Oso Grande Technologies Inc	www.osogrande.com	NM
Querydata.com	www.querydata.com	FL
Rapidcourt.com - NC Recordsonline.com	www.rapidcourt.com	NC, CT, TN, TX
Rapsheets.com	https://www.rapsheets.com/Default.aspx	AL, AZ, AR, CO, CT, FL, GA, IL, IN, ID. KS, KY, MI, MN, MS, MO, NC, NV, NJ, NY, OH, OK, OR, SC, TN, TX, UT, VA, WA
Search Company of North Dakota LLC	www.searchcompanynd.com	ND
Tenstar Business Services Group	www.tenstarcorporation.com	LA, MS
Tracers Information Specialists Inc	www.tracersinfo.com	40 States
TransUnion Vantage Data	www.vantagedatasolutions.com	AL,AZ,CA,CO,CT,DC,DE,FL,GA,IA,ID,IL,IN,KS, KY,LA,MD,ME,MI,MN,MS,MT,NC,ND,NE,NH,N J,NM,NY,OK,SC,TN,TX,UT,VA,WA,WI,WV,WY
US SEARCH.com	www.ussearch.com/consumer/index.jsp	US
USIS Commercial Services	www.usis.com/commercialservices/	US
Virtual Docket LLC	www.virtualdocket.com	DE
XPOFACT	www.xpofact.com	MN

Driver and/or Vehicle

Driver and/or Vehicle Records	Website	Region
Accurint	www.accurint.com	FL
American Business Information	www.infousa.com	US
American Driving Records	www.mvrs.com	US
AutoDataDirect, Inc	www.add123.com	FL
CARFAX	www.carfaxonline.com	US
ChoicePoint Inc	www.choicepointinc.com	US
CourtSearch.com	www.courtsearch.com	NC
Datalink Services Inc	www.imvrs.com	CA
DCS Information Systems	www.dcs-amerifind.com	TX
Explore Information Services	www.exploredata.com/publish/default.htm	AL, AZ, CA, CO, CT, DE, FL, ID, IA, KS, KY, MA, MD, ME, MI, MN, MO, MT, NE, NH, NV, NY, OH, OR, SC, TN, TX, UT, WI, WV, WY
First InfoSource	https://secure.firstinfosource.com	MO
Household Driver Reports Inc (HDR)	www.hdr.com	TX

Driver and/or Vehicle Records	Website	Region
iiX (Insurance Information Exchange)	www.iix.com	US
InsightAmerica	www.insightamerica.com	40 States
LocatePlus.com Inc	https://www.locateplus.com/welcome.asp	AL,AR,NE,UT,MS,ME,NH,VT,MA,CT, OH,WV,MD, FL,TN,KY,IN,MI,WI,LA, MO,IA,MN,TX,CO, WY,ID,AZ,OR
Logan Registration Service Inc	www.loganreg.com	CA, US
MDR/Minnesota Driving Records	www.mdrecords.us	MN
Merlin Information Services	www.merlindata.com	US
Motznik Information Services	www.motznik.com	AK
Navigator Research Group	https://www.irb-online.com	FL
Northwest Location Services	www.nwlocation.com	OR,ID
OPENonline	www.openonline.com	US
Oso Grande Technologies Inc	www.osogrande.com	NM
Querydata.com	www.querydata.com	AL,CO,CT,DE,DC,FL,HI,ID,IL,IN,IA,KS, KY,LA,ME,MD, MI,MN,MS,MO,NE,NJ,NM,NY, NC,ND,OK,OR, RI,SC,SD,TN,TX,UT,VT,WI
Records Research Inc	www.recordsresearch.com	CA,US
Samba MVRSearch	www.samba.biz/mvrsearch.html	NM
Softech International Inc	www.softechinternational.com	US
USIS Commercial Services	www.usis.com/commercialservices	US

Education/Employment

Education/Employment Records Companies	Website	Region
Credentials Inc	www.degreechk.com	US
Equifax Credit Services	www.equifax.com	US
National Student Clearinghouse	www.studentclearinghouse.com	US
Tenstar Business Services Group	www.tenstarcorporation.com	LA, MS

Environmental

Environmental Records Companies	Website	Region
Environmental Data Resources, Inc. (EDR)	www.edrnet.com	US
OSHA DATA	www.oshadata.com	US
Public Data Corporation	www.pdcny.com	NY
West Group	http://west.thomson.com/store/default.asp	US

Foreign Country Information

Foreign Country Information Companies	Website	Region
Ancestry	http://ancestry.com	Itl
CountryWatch Inc.	www.countrywatch.com	Itl
Derwent Information	www.derwent.com	Itl
Dialog	www.dialog.com	Itl
Dun & Bradstreet	www.dnb.com/us	Itl
Global Securities Information, Inc	www.gsionline.com	Itl
Hoovers Inc	www.hoovers.com/free/	Itl

Foreign Country Information Companies	Website	Region
Kompass USA Inc	www.kompass-intl.com	Itl
Owens OnLine Inc	www.owens.com	Itl
Thomson & Thomson	www.thomson-thomson.com/do/pid/1	Itl
Vital Records Information	http://vitalrec.com	Itl

Genealogical Information

Genealogical Information Companies	Website	Region
Ancestry	Ancestry.com	US, Itl
Roots Web - www.rootsweb.net	(Genealogy portal resource site)	US
American Business Information	www.infousa.com	US
Vital Records Information	http://vitalrec.com	US
VitalChek	www.vitalchek.com	49 states
USCerts	www.uscerts.com	25 states

Licenses/Registrations/Permits

Licenses/Registrations/Permits	Website	Region
Accutrend Data Corporation	www.accutrend.com	US
American City Business Leads	www.bizjournals.com	AL, AZ, CA, CO, DC, FL, GA, HI, KS, KY, MA, MD, MI, MN, NC, NM, NY, OH, OR, PA, TN, TX, WA, WI
ChoicePoint Inc	www.choicepointinc.com	US
E-Merges.com	www.e-merges.com	AK,AR,CT,DE,FL,GA,KS,MS,MO,NV,NJ,NC,ND, OH,SC,UT,VA,WA
GoverNet	www.governet.net/home/index.cfm	NV
InsightAmerica	www.insightamerica.com	FL, ID, IA, LA, MN, MS, MO, NV, NC, OR, TX, UT, WI, WY
IQ Data Systems	www.iqdata.com	CA
KnowX	www.knowx.com	US
LEXISNEXIS	www.lexisnexis.com	CA, CT, FL, GE, IL, MA,MI,NE,NJ,NC,OG,PA,TX,VA,WI
MegaCriminal Database	www.megacriminal.com	CA
Merlin Information Services	www.merlindata.com	US
Motznik Information Services	www.motznik.com	AK
Northwest Location Services	www.nwlocation.com	WA
Querydata.com	www.querydata.com	AL,AK,AZ,AR,CA,CO,CT,DE,DC,FL,GA,ID,IL.IA, KS,KY,LA,MA,MD,MA,MN,MS,MO,NE,NV,NH,NJ, NM,NC,ND,OH,OK,OR,PA,RH,SC,SD,TN,TX,UT, VT,VA,WV,WI,WY
Record Information Services Inc	www.public-record.com	IL
Search Company of North Dakota	www.searchcompanynd.com	ND
Thomson & Thomson	www.thomson-thomson.com/do/pid/1	US
Westlaw Public Records	www.westlaw.com	AZ, CA, CO, CT, FL, GA, IL, IN, LA, MA, MD, MI, NJ, OH, PA, SC, TN, TX, VA, WI

Litigation/Judgments/Tax Liens

Litigation/Judgment/Tax Liens Records	Website	Region
Accurint	www.accurint.com	US
Alacourt.com	www.alacourt.com	AL
American City Business Leads	www.bizjournals.com	AL, AZ, CA, CO, DC, FL, GA, HI, KS, KY, MA, MD, MI, MN, NC, NM, NY, OH, OR, PA, TN, TX, WA, WI
Attorneys Title Insurance Fund	www.thefund.com/portal/	FL
Banko	www.banko.com	US
CaseClerk.com	www.caseclerk.com/search/default.htm	TN
ChoicePoint - Public Records Group	www.choicepointonline.com	US
ChoicePoint Inc	www.choicepointinc.com	US
Circuit Court Express	www.swcg-inc.com/products/circuit_express.html	WV
CoCourts.com	www.cocourts.com	CO
Court PC of Connecticut	http://courtpcofct.com	CT
CourthouseData	www.courthousedata.com	AR
CourthouseDirect.com	http://courthousedirect.com/courth/	AZ, CA, FL, HI, IL, NY, OK, PA, TX, UT, WA
CourtSearch.com	www.courtsearch.com	NC
Diligenz Inc	www.diligenz.com	US
Doxpop	www.doxpop.com/prod/welcome.jsp	IN
Dun & Bradstreet	www.dnb.com/us	US
Equifax Credit Services	www.equifax.com	US
GoverNet	www.governet.net/home/index.cfm	NV
iDocket.com	www.idocket.com	TX
Infocon Corporation	www.infoconcorporation.com	PA
InsightAmerica	www.insightamerica.com	CO
IQ Data Systems	www.iqdata.com	US
Judici	www.judici.com	IL
KnowX	www.knowx.com	US
LEXISNEXIS CourtLink	www.lexisnexis.com/courtlink/online/	US
LocatePlus.com Inc	https://www.locateplus.com	AK,AZ,AR,CA,CO,DC,FL,HI,ID,IL,IN,IA,KS, KY,LA,MN,MS,MO,NE,NV,NM,NC,ND,OH, OK,OR,SD,TN,TX,UT,VA,WA, WI,WY
Merchants Association - MAF	www.mafscreening.com	US, FL
Merlin Information Services	www.merlindata.com	US
Motznik Information Services	www.motznik.com	AK
MyFloridaCounty.com	www.myfloridacounty.com	FL
Northwest Location Services	www.nwlocation.com	WA
OPENonline	www.openonline.com	US
Oso Grande Technologies Inc	www.osogrande.com	NM
Property Data Center Inc	www.mypdc.com	CO
Public Data Corporation	www.pdcny.com	NY
Rapidcourt.com - NC Recordsonline.com	www.rapidcourt.com	NC
Rental Research Services Inc	www.rentalresearch.com	MN, ND, WI
Search Company of North Dakota LLC	www.searchcompanynd.com	ND
Querydata.com	www.querydata.com	AL,AK, CA,CT,DE,DC,FL,GA,HI,ID,IL, IN,IA,KS,KY,LA,ME,MD,MA,MI,MN,MS,MT, NE, NH,NJ,NM,NY,NC,ND,OH,OK, OR,PA, RI,SC,SD,TN,TX,UT,VT,VI,VA, WV,WY

Litigation/Judgment/Tax Liens Records	Website	Region
Superior Information Services LLC	www.soplus.com/application/publicrxwf	CT, DC, DE, MD, MA, ME, NC, NH, NJ, NY, PA, RI, VA, VT
Tenstar Business Services Group	www.tenstarcorporation.com	LA, MS
TitleSearcher.com	www.titlesearcher.com	TN
TransUnion Vantage Data	www.vantagedatasolutions.com	AK,AR,CA,CO,CT,DE,DC,FL,ID,IL,IN, IA,KS,KY LA,MA,MI,MD,MN,MS,MT,NE,NV,NJ,NMNC,ND NY,OH,OK,OP,PA,SD,TN,TX,UT,VA,WA,WI
UCC Direct Services	www.uccdirectservices.com	US
Virtual Docket LLC	www.virtualdocket.com	DE
Westlaw Public Records	www.westlaw.com	US

Military Service

Military Service Records Companies	Website	Region
Ameridex Information Systems	www.ameridex.com	US
KnowX	www.knowx.com	US
Military Information Enterprises Inc	www.militaryusa.com	US

Patents

Patent Information Provider Companies	Website	Region
Derwent Information	www.derwent.com	US
Dun & Bradstreet	www.dnb.com/us	US
MicroPatent USA	www.micropat.com/static/index.htm	US, Itl
Questel Orbit Inc	www.questel.orbit.com/index.htm	US, Itl
Thomson & Thomson	www.thomson-thomson.com/do/pid/1	US

Real Estate/Assessor

Real Estate/Assessor Record Companies	Website	Region
Accurint	www.accurint.com	US
ACS Inc, Landaccess.com	www.landaccess.com	IL, IA, MI, NJ, NY, OH, TX
American Business Information	www.infousa.com	US
American City Business Leads	www.bizjournals.com	AL, AZ, CA, CO, DC, FL, GA, HI, KS, KY, MA, MD, MI, MN, NC, NM, NY, OH, OR, PA, TN, TX, WA, WI
ARCountyData.com - Apprentice Information Systems	www.arcountydata.com	AR
Attorneys Title Insurance Fund	www.thefund.com/portal/	FL
ChoicePoint - Public Records Group	www.choicepointonline.com	US
Courthouse Retrieval System Inc	www.crsdata.net/home/	AL, NC, TN
CourthouseData	www.courthousedata.com	AR
CourthouseDirect.com	http://courthousedirect.com/courth/	AZ,CA,FL,HI, IL, NY,OK,PA, X,UT, WA
DataQuick	www.dataquick.com	US
DCS Information Systems	www.dcs-amerifind.com	TX,US
DigitalCourthouse	http://digitalcourthouse.com/search.asp	WV
Diversified Information Services Corp	www.discaz.com	AZ
eTitleSearch	www.etitlesearch.com	AR, IA, IL, MO, OK

Real Estate/Assessor Record Companies	Website	Region
Experian Online	www.experian.com	US
First American Real Estate Solutions	www.firstamres.com/jsp/index.jsp	US
Foreclosure Freesearch.com	www.foreclosurefreesearch.com	US, FL
GoverNet	www.governet.net/home/index.cfm	NV
IDM Corporation	www.idmcorp.com	US
Infocon Corporation	www.infoconcorporation.com	PA
InsightAmerica	www.insightamerica.com	US
IQ Data Systems	www.iqdata.com	US
KnowX	www.knowx.com	US
LEXISNEXIS	www.lexisnexis.com	US
LocatePlus.com Inc	https://www.locateplus.com	US
Merlin Information Services	www.merlindata.com	US
Metro Market Trends Inc	www.mmtinfo.com/MMT/index.html	FL, AL
Motznik Information Services	www.motznik.com	AK
MyFloridaCounty.com	www.myfloridacounty.com	FL
Navigator Research Group	https://www.irb-online.com	US
NETR Real Estate Research and Info	www.netronline.com	US
OPENonline	www.openonline.com	US
Pallorium Inc	www.pallorium.com	US
Plat System Services Inc	www.platsystems.com	MN
Property Data Center Inc	www.mypdc.com	CO
Property Info	www.propertyinfo.com	US
Public Data Corporation	www.pdcny.com	NY
Querydata.com	www.querydata.com	FL
Real-info.com	www.real-info.com	NY
Realty Data Corp	www.realtydata.com	US
Record Information Services Inc	www.public-record.com	IL
SKLD Information Services LLC	www.skld.com	CO
Superior Information Services LLC	www.soplus.com/application/publicrxwf	US
Tenstar Business Services Group	www.tenstarcorporation.com	LA, MS
TitleSearcher.com	www.titlesearcher.com	TN
TitleX.com	www.titlex.com	TX
tnrealestate.com	www.tnrealestate.com	TN
UCC Direct Services	www.uccdirectservices.com	US
US SEARCH.com	www.ussearch.com/consumer/index.jsp	US
US Title Search Network	www.ustitlesearch.net	TN - 32 Counties
USADATA	www.usadata.com	US
USPDR.com	www.uspdr.com	NY
Vision Appraisal Technology	www.visionappraisal.com	CT, ME, MA, NH, RI
Webstigate	www.webstigate.com	US
Westlaw Public Records	www.westlaw.com	US

SEC/Other Financial

SEC/Financial Records Companies	Website	Region
Alacra	www.alacra.com	US, CD, Itl
American Business Information	www.infousa.com	US
CCH Washington Service Bureau	www.wsb.com	US
CountryWatch Inc.	www.countrywatch.com	Itl (193)
Dialog	www.dialog.com	US
Dun & Bradstreet	www.dnb.com/us	US
Global Securities Information, Inc	www.gsionline.com	DC
Hoovers Inc	www.hoovers.com/free/	US
LEXISNEXIS	www.lexisnexis.com	US
West Group	http://west.thomson.com/store/default.asp	US

Tenant History

Tenant History Companies	Website	Region
Criminal Information Services Inc	www.criminalinfo.com	AZ,CA,ID,NV,OR,WA
Merchants Association - MAF	www.mafscreening.com	FL
National Credit Information Network NCI	www.wdia.com/home-entrypage.htm	IN, KY, OH
Navigator Research Group	https://www.irb-online.com	FL
Querydata.com	www.querydata.com	US, FL
Rental Research Inc	www.researchinc.net	WA
Rental Research Services Inc	www.rentalresearch.com	MN
U.D. Registry Inc	www.udregistry.com	CA, AZ, CO, WA, NV, NM

Trademarks

Trademark Records Companies	Website	Region
Dialog	www.dialog.com	US
Dun & Bradstreet	www.dnb.com/us	US
Idealogic	www.idealogic.com	CD
MicroPatent USA	www.micropat.com/static/index.htm	US, Itl

Uniform Commercial Code

UCC Records Companies	Website	Region
Accurint	www.accurint.com	US
ACS Inc, Landaccess.com	www.landaccess.com	IL, IA, MI, NJ, NY, OH, TX
Background Information Services Inc	www.bisi.com	CO
Capitol Lien Records & Research Inc	www.capitollien.com	US
ChoicePoint - Public Records Group	www.choicepointonline.com	US
CourthouseData	www.courthousedata.com	AR
Diligenz Inc	www.diligenz.com	US
Dun & Bradstreet	www.dnb.com/us	US
Ernst Publishing Co, LLC	www.ernstpublishing.com	US

UCC Records Companies	Website	Region
Experian Online	www.experian.com	US
GoverNet	www.governet.net/home/index.cfm	NV
IQ Data Systems	www.iqdata.com	CA
KnowX	www.knowx.com	US
LEXISNEXIS	www.lexisnexis.com	US
LocatePlus.com Inc	https://www.locateplus.com/welcome.asp	AK,AZ,CA,CO,CT,FL,GA,ID,IL,IA,KS, KY, MD,ME,MN,MS,MO,NE,NV,NM, ND,OH, OR,PA,SC,SD,TX,WA,WI
Merlin Information Services	www.merlindata.com	US
Motznik Information Services	www.motznik.com	AK
OPENonline	www.openonline.com	US
Public Data Corporation	www.pdcny.com	NY
Querydata.com	www.querydata.com	US, FL
Search Company of North Dakota LLC	www.searchcompanynd.com	ND
Search Network Ltd	www.searchnetworkltd.com/searchnetworkltd/	IA,KS
Superior Information Services LLC	www.soplus.com/application/publicrxwf	PA, NJ
Tenstar Business Services Group	www.tenstarcorporation.com	LA, MS
UCC Direct Services	www.uccdirectservices.com	US
US Corporate Services	www.uscorpserv.com	CO, DE, ID, IA, MI, MN, MS, MO, NV, NM, NY, NC, OH, TX, UT, WA, WI, WY
West Group	http://west.thomson.com/store/default.asp	US

Vessels

Vessel Records Companies	Website	Region
AutoDataDirect, Inc	www.add123.com	FL
E-Merges.com	www.e-merges.com	US
KnowX	www.knowx.com	US
LEXISNEXIS	www.lexisnexis.com	AL, AZ, AR, CO,CT,FL,GE,IA,ME,MD,MA, MS,MO,MN,MT,NE,NV,NH,NC,ND,OH, OR,SC,UT,VA,WV,WI
LocatePlus.com Inc	https://www.locateplus.com/welcome.asp	US
Merlin Information Services	www.merlindata.com	US
Motznik Information Services	www.motznik.com	AK
National Marine Fisheries Service	www.st.nmfs.gov/st1/commercial/index.html	US
Navigator Research Group	https://www.irb-online.com	FL, OR, TX
OPENonline	www.openonline.com	US
Pallorium Inc	www.pallorium.com	US
Querydata.com	www.querydata.com	US,AL,AK,AZ,AR,CO,CT,FL,GA,IL,IS,KS, KY,ME,MD,MA,MI,MN,MS,MO,MT,NE,NV, NY,NC,NC,OH,SC,TN,UT,VA,WV,WI,WY
US SEARCH.com	www.ussearch.com/consumer/index.jsp	US
Westlaw Public Records	www.westlaw.com	US

Vital Records

Vital Records Companies	Website	Region
Ameridex Information Systems	www.ameridex.com	US
Ancestry	http://ancestry.com	US
Cambridge Statistical Research Associates	www.csrainc.com	US
DCS Information Systems	www.dcs-amerifind.com	TX
Household Drivers Reports Inc (HDR Inc)	www.hdr.com	TX
Infocon Corporation	www.infoconcorporation.com	PA
InsightAmerica	www.insightamerica.com	US
IQ Data Systems	www.iqdata.com	CA,CO,FL,KY,ME,NV,TX
KnowX	www.knowx.com	US
Merlin Information Services	www.merlindata.com	CA, US
MyFloridaCounty.com	www.myfloridacounty.com	FL
US Certs	www.uscerts.com	25 states
Vital Records Information	http://vitalrec.com	US
VitalChek Network	www.vitalchek.com	US
Webstigate.com	www.webstigate.com	US

Voter Registration

Voter Registration Records Companies	Website	Region
Accu-Source Inc.	www.accu-source.com	TX
ARISTOTLE International	www.aristotle.com/page.asp	US
E-Merges.com	www.e-merges.com	US
InsightAmerica	www.insightamerica.com	AK, AR, CO, DE, GA, KS, MI, NV, OH, OK, TX, UT
Merlin Information Services	www.merlindata.com	US
Motznik Information Services	www.motznik.com	AK
National Credit Information Network NCI	www.wdia.com/home-entrypage.htm	US
Pallorium Inc	www.pallorium.com	US

Workers Compensation

Workers Compensation Records Companies	Website	Region
Industrial Foundation of America	www.ifa-america.com	TX, OK, LA, NM
Tenstar Business Services Group	www.tenstarcorporation.com	LA, MS

Appendix

The Appendix Includes—

Editor's Choices–15 Great Websites

*Trade Associations–*A list of trade associations connected to the public information industry and their websites.

Editors' Choices –
15 Great Websites

Acronym Finder –
A comprehensive database of acronyms, abbreviations, and initialisms.
>   www.acronymfinder.com/

BRB Publications Free Resource Center –
Comprehensive and easy to use collection...with educational articles
>   www.brbpub.com/pubrecsites.asp

Crimetime Publishing – Home of Robert Scott's *Investigator's Little Black Book*
>   www.crimetime.com

Domain Name Search – Great tool from VeriSign
>   www.networksolutions.com/whois/index.jsp

Ernst Publishing –
Click on "Other Resources" for great information on real estate and UCC filings
>   www.ernstpublishing.com

FindLaw – Great overall legal reference site
>   www.findlaw.com

Newspaper Links – You can even make your own newspaper
>   crayon.net/using/links.html

PI Magazine – **Jimmie Mesis has made this magazine an industry standard**
www.pimagazine.com

Professional Vendor Locator
www.brbpub.com/pubrecsites_ven.asp

Search Systems.net
A great site, but charges a fee if you don't want to be subject to 20 second delay with ads and the # of links are counted by overlapping categories, not URLs
www.searchsystems.net/index.php

Sexual Offender Links – **Includes excellent article on Megan's Law**
www.sexoffender.com/search.html

State & Local Government on the Net – **Many government agency home pages**
www.statelocalgov.net/index.cfm

Social Security Number Verification Search – **and it is free!**
www.usinfosearch.com/Free_ssn_search.htm

Translation Sites – **English to ? – or ? to English!**
http://babelfish.altavista.com

US Post Office – ZIP +4 Look-ups
http://zip4.usps.com/zip4/welcome.jsp

Trade Associations

There are many trade associations related to the public records industry. Below is a list of many of these associations. The companies profiled in our Private Database Vendors Section (beginning on page 510) are often members of one or more of these associations.

Acronym	Organization	Website	Members
AALL	American Assn of Law Librarians	www.aallnet.org/index.asp	4600
AAMVA	American Assn of Motor Vehicle Administrators	www.aamva.org	1500
AAPL	American Assn of Professional Landmen	www.landman.org	7000
ABA (2)	American Banking Assn	www.aba.com/default.htm	470
ABI	American Bankruptcy Institute	www.abiworld.org	6500
ABA	American Bar Assn	www.abanet.org/home.html	417000
ABFE	American Board of Forensic Examiners	www.cfenet.com/home.asp	12000
ABW	American Business Women	www.abwahq.org	80000
AIPLA	American Intellectual Property Law Assn	www.aipla.org	10000
ALTA	American Land Title Association	www.alta.org	2400
ALA	American Library Assn	www.ala.org	56800
AMA	American Management Assn	www.amanet.org/index.htm	70000
APA (2)	American Psychological Assn	www.apa.org	155000
ASIS	American Society for Industrial Security	www.asisonline.org	40000
ASLET	American Society of Law Enforcement Trainers	www.aslet.org	7000
ASSE	American Society of Safety Engineers	www.asse.org	35000
ATA	American Truckers Assn	www.trucking.org	4100
USFN	America's Mortgage Banking Attorneys	http://imis.usfn.org	
AICPA	Assn of Certified Public Accountants	www.aicpa.org/index.htm	330000
ACFE	Assn of Certified Fraud Examiners	www.cfenet.com/home.asp	20000
ACA	Assn of Collectors and Collection Professionals	www.collector.com	3500
AFIO	Assn of Former Intelligence Officers	www.afio.com	2500
AIIP	Assn of Independent Information Professionals	www.aiip.org	750

Acronym	Organization	Website	Members
APG	Assn of Professional Genealogists	www.apgen.org	1000
ATLA	Assn of Trial Lawyers of America	www.atlanet.org	56000
CDIA	Consumer Data Industry Association	www.cdiaonline.org	500
CII	Council of Intl Investigators	www.cii2.org	
DMA	Direct Marketing Assn	www.the-dma.org	4500
EMA	Employment Management Assn	www.shrm.org/EMA	4200
EAE	Environmental Assessment Assn	www.iami.org/eaa.cfm	3500
EPIC	Evidence Photographers Intl Council	www.epic-photo.org	1000
FBINAA	FBI Natl Academy Assn	www.fbinaa.org	17000
IIAA	Independent Insurance Agents of America	www.iiaa.org	300000
IREM	Institute of Real Estate Management	www.irem.org	8600
IAAI	Intl Assn of Arson Investigators	www.fire-investigators.org	9000
IAHSS	Intl Assn of Healthcare Security & Safety	www.iahss.org	
IALEIA	Intl Assn of Law Enforcement Intelligence Analysts	www.ialeia.org	1000
NASIR	Intl Assn of Security & Investgt Regulators	www.iasir.org	90
INA	Intl Nanny Assn	www.nanny.org	
INOA	Intl Narcotics Officers Assn	www.ineoa.org	
INTA	Intl Trademark Assn	www.inta.org	4200
ION	Investigative Open Network	www.ioninc.com	500
LES	Licensing Executive Society	www.usa-canada.les.org	4700
MBAA	Mortgage Bankers Assn of America	www.mbaa.org	2700
NALS	NALS...the Association of Legal Professionals	www.nals.org	6000
NICB	National Insurance Crime Bureau	www.nicb.org	1000
NAC	Natl Assn of Counselors	http://nac.lincoln-grad.org	500
NACM	Natl Assn of Credit Managers	www.nacm.org	35000
NAFE	Natl Assn of Female Executives	www.nafe.com	150000
NAFI	Natl Assn of Fire Investigators	www.nafi.org	5000
NAHB	Natl Assn of Home Builders	www.nahb.org	197000
NAHRO	Natl Assn of Housing & Redvlp Officials	www.nahro.org	8500
NAIS	Natl Assn of Investigative Specialists	www.pimall.com/nais/nais.j.html	3000
NALFM	Natl Assn of Law Firm Marketers	www.legalmarketing.org	1000
NALA	Natl Assn of Legal Assistants	www.nala.org	17000
NALI	Natl Assn of Legal Investigators	www.nalionline.org	800
NALSC	Natl Assn of Legal Search Consultants	www.nalsc.org	130

Acronym	Organization	Website	Members
NAMSS	Natl Assn of Medical Staff Svcs	www.namss.org	4000
NAPBS	Natl Assn of Professional Background Screeners	www.napbs.com	450
NAPPS	Natl Assn of Professional Process Servers	www.napps.org	1100
NAPIA	Natl Assn of Public Insurance Adjustors	www.napia.com	
NAREIT	Natl Assn of Real Estate Investment Trusts	www.nareit.org	1080
NAR	Natl Assn of Realtors	www.realtor.com	805000
NARPM	Natl Assn of Residential Property Managers	www.narpm.org	1400
NASA	Natl Assn of Screening Agencies	www.n-a-s-a.com	25
NAWBO	Natl Assn of Women Business Owners	www.nawbo.org	3000
NCISS	Natl Council of Investigation & Security Services	www.nciss.org	
NCRA	Natl Court Reporters Assn	www.verbatimreporters.com	23
NCRA	Natl Credit Reporting Association	www.ncrainc.org	
NDIA	Natl Defender Investigator Assn	www.ndia-inv.org	32000
NFIB	Natl Federation of Independent Businesses	www.nfib.org	650
NFPA	Natl Federation of Paralegal Assn	www.paralegals.org	
NFPA	Natl Federation of Paralegal Associations	www.paralegals.org/	15000
NFIP	Natl Flood Insurance Program	www.fema.gov/business/nfip/	600000
NGS	Natl Genealogical Society	www.ngsgenealogy.org	
NHEMA	Natl Home Equity Mortgage Assn	www.nhema.org	240
NHRA	Natl Human Resources Assn	www.humanresources.org	1500
NLG	Natl Lawyers Guild	www.nlg.org	6000
NPPRA	Natl Public Record Research Assn	www.nprra.org	450
NSA	Natl Sheriffs' Association	www.sheriffs.org	20000
PBUS	Professional Bail Agents of the United States	www.pbus.com	800
PIHRA	Professionals in Human Resources Assn	www.pihra.org	3500
PRRN	Public Record Retriever Network	www.brbpub.com	672
REIPA	Real Estate Information Providers Assn	www.reipa.org	
SCIP	Society of Competitive Intelligence Professionals	www.scip.org	6500
SFSA	Society of Former Special Agents of the FBI	www.socxfbi.org	7800
SHRM	Society of Human Resources Management	www.shrm.org	65000
SILA	Society of Insurance License Administrators	www.sila.org	
SIIA	Software & Information Industry Association	www.siia.net	1200
SLA	Special Libraries Assn	www.sla.org	14000
WAD	World Assn of Detectives	www.wad.net	

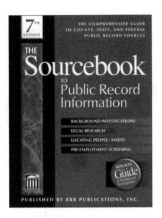